TA

MINNESOTA

TA

Mississippi

IOWA

River

AS

MISSOURI

AHOMA

ARKANSAS

ATLANTIC

OCEAN

LOUISIANA

W9-DGW-785

GULF OF

MEXICO

| 0 | 150 | 300 Miles |
| 0 | 150 | 300 Km. |

Encyclopedia

AMERICAN WEST

For Reference

Not to be taken from this room

Encyclopedia

OF THE

AMERICAN WEST

Charles Phillips
Alan Axelrod

Editors

VOLUME 2

Macmillan Reference USA
Simon & Schuster Macmillan
New York

SIMON & SCHUSTER AND PRENTICE HALL INTERNATIONAL
London • Mexico City • New Delhi • Singapore • Sydney • Toronto

Copyright © 1996 by Simon & Schuster

Produced by Zenda, Inc., Nashville, Tennessee
  Design: Gore Studios, Inc.
  Proofreading and Index of Professions: John Reiman
  General Index: Alexa Selph

Simon & Schuster Macmillan
1633 Broadway, New York, NY 10019

PRINTED IN THE UNITED STATES OF AMERICA

printing number
1 2 3 4 5 6 7 8 9 10

LIBRARY OF CONGRESS CATALOGING-IN-PUBLICATION DATA

Encyclopedia of the American West / Charles Phillips and Alan Axelrod, editors
        p   cm.
    Includes bibliographical references (p.   ) and index.
    ISBN 0-02-897495-6
    1. West (U.S.)—Encyclopedias.   I. Phillips, Charles, 1948–
    II. Axelrod, Alan, 1952–
    F591.E485   1996
    978—dc20   96-1685
                                                                   CIP

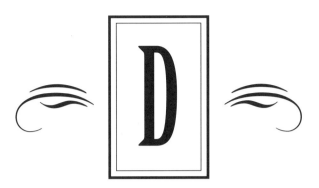

DAKOTA INDIANS

SEE: Native American Peoples: Peoples of the Great Plains

DAKOTA TERRITORY

SEE: North Dakota; South Dakota

DALLAS, TEXAS

Dallas, "Big D," as it is affectionately called, is a city with humble beginnings. Erected as a trading post in a dull setting, removed from commercial centers, and pounded at times by floods and inclement weather, Dallas has nonetheless become one of the more picturesque cities in the Southwest.

There are no records available to indicate how the city was named; the claim that it was dedicated to George Mifflin Dallas, a Philadelphia barrister who became the vice-president of the United States under JAMES K. POLK, remains unconfirmed.

The city was founded in 1841 by John Neely Bryan, a Tennessean who drifted from Arkansas to establish a trading post. After staking his claim near the three forks of the Trinity River, Bryan traveled back to Arkansas, sold what he owned there, and returned to TEXAS in November 1841. He invited settlers to join him. Initially just a rough shelter of cedar boughs, Dallas had become the county seat by 1846. Without a water-transportation system and with few natural resources, Dallas was a man-made city. It began to expand in earnest when Alexander Cockrell, a pioneer investor, purchased the last of the remaining lots and ferry rights from Bryan. Cockrell expanded the indus-

trial activities of the city by constructing a sawmill and a two-story brick building. After he died in 1858, his wife Sarah continued her husband's vision of Dallas by adding a steam-powered flour mill and the town's first hotel.

Dallas quickly attracted new residents and increased its commercial and agricultural activities. A considerable number of French, Swiss, and Belgian families settled nearby and formed a community known as "French Town," renamed "La Reunion" by its inhabitants. The colony was based on the principles of François Marie Charles Fourier: free development of human nature, the unrestrained indulgence of human passion, and societal reorganization based on cooperative communities. The organizers were so successful that thirty-four additional communities were founded on Fourierism.

In general, settlers from Tennessee, Arkansas, Louisiana, and Alabama populated Dallas. The most common occupation was farming. Before the Civil War, a merchant class rose to prominence among the settlers. Other occupations ranged from "catchers of wild horses" to domestic help. By the late 1860s, Dallas counted among its citizens doctors, lawyers, dentists, and clergymen.

Two developments—the expansion of the railway system and the agricultural successes of the 1870s—transformed the city into the largest cotton land market in the United States. After 1872, the movement of cattle also took on major importance. The Waco Tap Railroad, Houston and Texas Central, Texas and Pacific, and other rail lines helped supply the voracious demand for cattle and turned Dallas into a prosperous community.

In 1895, Dallas had fewer than seven hundred telephones. Twenty-five years later, Dallas had sixty-three thousand telephone subscribers. Dallas became known as the "Queen City" during this period, and many local businesses, such as the Queen City Drug Store and the Queen City Railway Company, adopted the name.

In the twentieth century, Dallas became a fast-growing international center and the tenth largest metropolitan and marketing area. In the late twentieth century, Dallas spanned more than three hundred square miles and had a population of approximately three million people. The Mexican and African American populations of Dallas grew considerably in the early part of the twentieth century; by the end of the century, they constituted important sectors of the metropolitan area. As the headquarters of the Eleventh District and Federal Reserve Bank, Dallas functions as a major banking center in the Southwest. In addition, the metropolitan area serves as the center for major industries—construction, insurance, fashion, marketing, wholesaling, and air transportation—and is home to major educational facilities, sports, and cultural activities.

—*Fred L. Koestler*

SUGGESTED READING:

Howard, James. *Big D is for Dallas: Chapters in the Twentieth-Century History of Dallas.* Austin, Tex., 1957.

Leslie, Warren. *Dallas, Public and Private: Aspects of an American City.* New York, 1964.

Rogers, John William. *The Lusty Texans of Dallas.* New York, 1960.

DALTON GANG

The Dalton Gang was a notorious band of outlaws who marauded the West during the early 1890s. The marriage of Lewis Dalton and Adeline Younger

The bodies of the Dalton Gang after the Coffeyville raid. *Courtesy Kansas State Historical Society.*

(through whom the family claimed kinship to the Younger outlaw band) produced fifteen children, ten of them boys. Six were law-abiding—Frank, Charles, Ben, Littleton, Henry, and Simon. Frank was a dedicated U.S. marshal who was killed in 1887 while arresting whiskey runners in the Indian Territory. He was succeeded by his brother Grattan (Grat, 1865–1892), who, in turn, named as assistant another brother, Robert (Bob, 1868–1892). Emmett (1871–1937) also became a deputy U.S. marshal, and all three served at times as policemen for the Osage and Cherokee nations. Unlike Frank, however, Grat, Emmett, and Bob worked both sides of the law. After stealing horses in Oklahoma and selling them in Kansas, they lost their badges in June 1890. Bob then organized the original Dalton Gang, which included his brother Emmett, George ("Bitter Creek") Newcomb, "Blackfaced Charley" Bryant, and Bill McElhanie. Grattan was in California visiting another brother, William (Bill, 1866–1894), when the gang was formed.

The gang's first robbery was of a crooked faro game in Silver City, New Mexico. Afterwards, Emmett returned to Oklahoma while Bob went to California. On February 6, 1891, Bob, Grat, and Bill were accused, probably falsely, of robbing a Southern Pacific train. Bob fled to Oklahoma, Bill was acquitted, and Grat was convicted. On May 9, 1891, Bob and Emmett Dalton, along with Newcomb and Bryant, robbed a Santa Fe train at Wharton (later Perry, Oklahoma). Four months later, the gang, which then included WILLIAM (BILL) DOOLIN, Bill Powers, Dick Broadwell, and Charlie Pierce, robbed a train of ten thousand dollars at Lelietta in the Indian Territory. Grat, who had escaped custody in California, joined the gang for its next robbery—a Santa Fe train at Red Rock in the Indian Territory on June 1, 1892. The gang robbed another train at Adair in the Indian Territory on July 13, 1892. Bob's lover, variously known as Florence Quick, Eugenia Moore, Mrs. Mundy, and (in masculine disguise) Tom King, supplied intelligence for the robberies, as did Bill Dalton, who had moved back from California.

Their final job, one of the more chronicled robberies in the West, was the failed attempt to rob two banks simultaneously. On October 5, 1892, Bob, Emmett, and Grat Dalton, along with Powers and Broadwell, rode into Coffeyville, Kansas, where they had lived as boys and where Frank Dalton was buried. Bob and Emmett took twenty-one thousand dollars from the First National Bank, but the other three gang members were foiled in their attempt to leave the Condon Bank with four thousand dollars. In the ensuing battle, aroused citizens killed all the gang except Emmett, who survived some twenty bullet wounds.

In the aftermath of the Coffeyville robbery, Bill Dalton, his political and business hopes ruined, joined with Doolin, Pierce, Newcomb, and others to form the Doolin-Dalton Gang, which operated until March 1894. Bill then formed another gang and robbed a Texas bank in May 1894. On June 8 of that year, he was killed by a posse near present-day Ardmore, Oklahoma.

The Daltons consciously modeled their exploits along their own romanticized view of the James-Younger Gang. They did not rob train passengers; they cultivated the sympathy of homesteaders; and they would fight to the finish rather than surrender. In later years, after his pardon from a life sentence at the Kansas State Penitentiary, Emmett Dalton moved to Hollywood where he helped shape the popular image of the daring Western outlaw by promoting books and movies, including *Beyond the Law,* a film about the Coffeyville raid in which he played himself.

—*James F. Hoy*

SEE ALSO: Social Banditry

SUGGESTED READING:
Preece, Harold. *The Dalton Gang: End of an Outlaw Era.* New York, 1963.
Shirley, Glenn. *Six-Gun and Silver Star.* Albuquerque, N. Mex., 1955.
Wellman, Paul I. *A Dynasty of Western Outlaws.* New York, 1961.

DALY, MARCUS

Montana mining magnate Marcus Daly (1841–1900) was born in County Cavan, Ireland. With WILLIAM ANDREWS CLARK and FREDERICK AUGUSTUS HEINZE, Daly became one of Montana's legendary "Copper Kings."

Daly arrived in the United States in 1856, at the age of fifteen. He worked from 1861 to 1865 in California as a miner and showed an unusual aptitude for mine engineering. In 1865, he located in Nevada and Utah, where the Walker Brothers recognized his abilities and detailed him to Butte in the Montana Territory in 1876 to purchase a silver mine. Daly quickly saw the potential for copper in "the Butte Hill" and secured funding from GEORGE HEARST and his associates. The partners purchased much of "the Hill" and began to produce copper for a burgeoning world market.

Daly encouraged the Northern Pacific Railroad's HENRY VILLARD to route the railroad's main line through Butte. He also purchased coal mines for his smelters, huge forest tracts to supply timber and fuel, and land on which to construct his own Anaconda smelter and community. He established banks, built hydroelectric-power plants, constructed irrigation systems, and created newspapers to handle his public relations. In 1884, Daly constructed the Butte, Anaconda and Pacific Railway to carry copper ore from the Butte mines to his smelter in nearby Anaconda.

With CHARLES ARTHUR BROADWATER, SAMUEL THOMAS HAUSER, and William Andrews Clark, Daly composed the Democratic party's "Big Four" in Montana. Through the 1880s, the behind-the-scenes quartet dominated Montana politics. Daly served as a member of the 1884 constitutional convention. In 1888, he squared off against Clark, and the War of the Copper Kings ran through Daly's death in 1900. The vicious, no-holds-barred contest included miners' underground battles, state and federal political chicanery, economic duplicity, and an expensive battle over the location of the state capital.

Daly developed a fine racehorse ranch in the Bitterroot Valley, where he experimented with fruit growing and large-scale irrigation. In 1900, just prior to his death, Daly sold his empire to the Standard Oil Company. He was perhaps the most important Montana capitalist in an era of unbounded entrepreneurial speculation.

—*David A. Walter*

SEE ALSO: Anaconda Mining Company; Butte, Montana; Copper Kings, War of the; Copper Mining

SUGGESTED READING:
Daly, H. *A Biography of Marcus Daly.* Butte, Mont., 1934.
"Hon. Marcus Daly." In *Progressive Men of the State of Montana.* Chicago, ca. 1902.
Marcosson, Isaac F. *Anaconda.* New York, 1957.
West, Carroll Van. "Historical Landscapes—Marcus Daly and Montana: One Man's Imprint on the Land." *Montana: The Magazine of Western History* 37:1 (Winter 1987): 60–62.

DAME SHIRLEY

When Louise Amelia Knappe Smith Clappe (1819–1906) published letters describing scenes from the California mining town of Rich Bar, her writings appeared under the name of "Dame Shirley." Born in New Jersey, Clappe became interested in writing in her twenties. By 1849, she had married Dr. Fayette Clappe, and the two had moved to San Francisco. In 1851, they settled in Rich Bar, a year after gold was discovered.

In 1851 and 1852, Clappe wrote twenty-three letters to her sister Molly in New England. The correspondence provided vivid descriptions of life in a gold-rush town, its rowdy miners, its one street lined with tents, hovels, and one grand hotel, and its four women. Beginning in 1854, the letters appeared in *The Pioneer: or California Monthly Magazine* as a series, "Letters from the California Mines."

When the gold played out in Rich Bar in 1852, the Clappes returned to San Francisco. Louise became a teacher and divorced her husband in 1857. Twenty years later, she moved to New York. She died in a New Jersey rest home.

—*Patricia Hogan*

SUGGESTED READING:
Clappe, Louise. *The Shirley Letters from the California Mines, 1851–1852.* Edited by Carl I. Wheat. New York, 1970.

DANA, RICHARD HENRY, JR.

Author and lawyer Richard Henry Dana, Jr. (1815–1882), was born in Cambridge, Massachusetts, the son of a literary family. He attended Harvard University but left school because of eye trouble. In 1834, he shipped out as an ordinary seaman on the commercial brig *Pilgrim.* He sailed around the Horn to the California coast and returned to Boston on the *Alert* in 1836.

His eye problems improved, he reenrolled and graduated from Harvard, finished law school, and was admitted to the bar in 1840. For the remainder of his life, he practiced law, specializing in maritime questions. President Ulysses S. Grant appointed him minister to England in 1876.

Dana's significance to the American West and to American literature lies in his account of his voyage to California, which he published in 1840 as *Two Years before the Mast.* His intent in writing was to be "a voice from the forecastle," to present the life of a merchant seaman, "the light and the dark together."

Historians have been even more interested in Dana's account of the Mexican province of California in the 1830s, its economy and the life style of its people. His ship was engaged in the hide and tallow trade, and his description of sailors tossing packs of hides over the cliffs to waiting ships has become a staple of California lore.

—*Robert V. Hine*

SUGGESTED READING:
Kemble, John. "Introduction." In *Two Years before the Mast.* By Richard Henry Dana. Los Angeles, 1964.

DANITES

A small renegade band of MORMONS under the leadership of Sampson Avard and formed briefly in 1838 in Missouri, the Danites protected Mormons against mob violence and at one point retaliated for anti-Mormon attacks that killed some church members and destroyed property. The group came to be known pejoratively as the "Destroying Angels."

No Danite organization existed in Utah. The renegades, who functioned for no more than four months in 1838, were said to have been secretive, militaristic, and extralegal. The brief existence of the group is well known, but Mormon historians deny that its vengeful, secretive, lawless outrages had official approval or support. Unquestionably, the Mormons in Missouri and later in Illinois and in pioneer Utah were a covenant community, organized after Biblical fashion into tens, fifties, and hundreds to build houses, care for the sick, and assist refugees from anti-Mormon mobs. The goal was the formation of an integrated community with each person contributing to the benefit of the whole.

One constructive result of the brief Danite affair was that it defined more clearly for the whole community the religious ethic of forbearance that later guided the Mormon response to the murder of JOSEPH SMITH, JR., in 1844, the forced exodus from Illinois in 1846, Indian harassment in the Utah Territory, and the UTAH EXPEDITION, or Utah War, of 1857.

Many writers built up a legend of the Danites and developed story lines of murder, pillage, and conspiracy against American and British citizens. At least fifty-six published novels used these themes. Arthur Conan Doyle in *A Study in Scarlet* (1886) created Sherlock Holmes to solve a murder committed by Danites. ZANE GREY in *Riders of the Purple Sage* (1912) found the image of the evil Danites useful in describing the struggles of self-reliant, brawny heroes loyal to the fancied ethics of the West and chivalrous toward weakly, naive heroines. Perhaps the height of the literary portrayal of Danites was *First Fam'lies of the Sierra* (1876), later published as *Danites in the High Sierra* (1881), by JOAQUIN MILLER. The book was later adapted to the stage.

—*Leonard J. Arrington*

SUGGESTED READING:
Arrington, Leonard J., and Jon Haupt. "Intolerable Zion: The Image of Mormonism in Nineteenth-Century Ameri-

can Literature." *Western Humanities Review* 22 (1968): 243–260.

Arrington, Leonard J., and Davis Bitton. *The Mormon Experience: A History of the Latter-day Saints.* New York, 1979.

Gentry, Leland H. "The Danite Band of 1838." *Brigham Young University Studies* 14 (1974): 421–450.

DARLEY, FELIX OCTAVIUS

SEE: Art: Book and Magazine Illustration

DAWES, HENRY LAURENS

Henry Laurens Dawes (1816–1903) served in the U.S. House of Representatives and the Senate, where he wrote major legislation dealing with Native Americans. Born in Cummington, Massachusetts, Dawes graduated from Yale University in 1839. He worked as a teacher for a short time and then became editor of the Greenfield *Gazette*. In 1842, he was admitted to the Massachusetts bar and began his law practice in North Adams, where he also published the *Transcript*. He served in the state senate from 1848 to 1850. Three years later, he was a delegate to the state constitutional convention. He then became attorney for the western district of Massachusetts until his election to the U.S. Congress on the Republican ticket in 1857. As a congressman, he supported antislavery legislation and served on the War Contracts Committee and on the Committee of Five, which was established to investigate Northern fears of Confederate plans to capture Washington, D.C., prior to Lincoln's inauguration.

Dawes chaired several important congressional committees—Elections, Ways and Means, and Appropriations. He sponsored bills on issuing national weather bulletins, creating YELLOWSTONE NATIONAL PARK, and establishing a Fish Commission. He also oversaw the completion of the Washington Monument and assisted in drafting a wool and woolen tariff act of 1868. From 1869 to 1875, he was the Republican leader of the House, a position for which he was well suited due to his diligence and expertise in parliamentary procedure.

Elected to the U.S. Senate as the successor of Charles Sumner in 1875 and reelected in 1881 and 1887, Dawes served as chairman of the Committee on Indian Affairs and as a spokesperson for the Indian rights and reform movement, which proposed assimilation into mainstream culture as a solution to the problem of Indian-white relations. Dawes's interest in assimilation began while he was serving in the House of Representatives. In 1870, he introduced a bill calling for an end to the treaty system; the bill passed as a rider to the Indian appropriations bill in 1871. Continuing to work on legislation dealing with Native Americans after his election to the Senate, he strongly opposed Secretary of the Interior CARL SCHURZ's stand in 1880 on the forced relocation of the Poncas from their reservation at the confluence of the Niobrara and Missouri rivers to the Indian Territory. While Schurz conceded that the United States had dealt unjustly with the Poncas when the government mistakenly ceded their entire reserve to the Sioux in the Fort Laramie Treaty of 1868, he maintained that the solution was not the return of the Ponca tribe to its northern reservation. Dawes thought differently and drafted a report that detailed the hardships of the Poncas and supported Chief Standing Bear's desire to return the tribe to its ancestral lands. In the end, Dawes's view of justice for the Poncas prevailed.

In 1887, Congress passed the General Allotment Act (DAWES ACT), designed to satisfy the land hunger of whites while making Indians self-supporting farmers or stock-raisers. Dawes also wrote the Sioux bill, which opened surplus land in the Great Sioux Reservation to white settlement, while providing the Lakotas with an annual income that would, in theory, further their education, civilization, and general self-support. Known for his strong efforts to assimilate Native Americans, Dawes was responsible for a bill, passed in 1885, that brought under federal jurisdiction Indians who committed major crimes against other Indians on reservations. He also wrote a bill providing for a system of Indian education.

Following his retirement from the Senate in 1893, Dawes became chairman of the Dawes Commission, whose mission was to allot the reservations of the Five Civilized Tribes in Oklahoma in compliance with the provisions of the General Allotment Act.

—*Henry E. Fritz and Marie L. Fritz*

SEE ALSO: United States Indian Policy: Civilization Programs, Indian Treaties, Reform Movement, Reservations

SUGGESTED READING:

Fritz, Henry E. *The Movement for Indian Assimilation, 1860–1890.* Philadelphia, 1963.

Mardock, Robert W. *The Reformers and the American Indian.* Columbia, Mo., 1971.

Nicklason, Fred H. *The Early Career of Henry L. Dawes, 1816–1871.* Ph.D. diss., Yale University, 1967.

Prucha, Francis Paul. *American Indian Policy in Crisis: Christian Reformers and the Indian, 1865–1900.* Norman, Okla., 1976.

DAWES ACT

The Dawes Act, also known as the General Allotment or Dawes Severalty Act, was the cornerstone of federal Indian policy from its passage on February 8, 1887, until the New Deal. Backed by a coalition of Eastern reformers and Western economic interests, the law established a pathway for bringing American Indians into "mainstream" American society. It called for the dissolution of tribal lands and the granting of plots or "allotments" to individual Indians. Tribal members became U.S. citizens when they received allotments. Indians who had separated from their tribes and were living in white communities became citizens immediately.

Passage of the Dawes Act reflected white reformers' naive view that Native Americans could become self-supporting U.S. citizens in a single generation. The U.S. government originally established reservations as isolated laboratories where missionaries and federal agents could teach American Indians to embrace Christianity and "civilized" ways. But by the early 1880s, Euro-American settlers were encroaching on reservations and clamoring for more land. Meanwhile, Indians maintained and adapted their own customs and seemed no closer to self-sufficiency than ever. Many white reformers concluded that, far from helping Indians assimilate, the reservations were actually hindering their progress. Thus, reformers decided to pursue a new strategy: total assimilation. Central to this strategy was private ownership of land. Well-intentioned but ethnocentric white reformers concluded that only by breaking up the tribes' communal landholdings—and restructuring Indian societies around male-headed nuclear families—could American Indians be oriented to "civilized" Euro-American values. "Total assimilation" also entailed the establishment of a universal school system among Indians and the extension of federal law over all tribes under the Major Crimes Act of 1885.

Dissolving tribal lands and allotting farms to individual Indians was not a new idea: Congress had divided the lands of Wisconsin's Brotherton tribe as early as 1839. But the Dawes Act systematized the approach by allowing the president to designate tribes ready for allotment. Under the act, each adult family head was to receive 160 acres of land; other tribal members received smaller allotments. To prevent the Indians from immediately selling their land, title to the property was to be held in trust by the U.S. government for twenty-five years.

Although the Dawes Act was the handiwork of Eastern reformers, it also pleased land-hungry white Westerners. The act called for the sale of "surplus" tribal lands—reformers reasoned that the Indians had far more than they could efficiently use—to settlers, cattlemen, railroads, and miners. Proceeds from the sales would be used by the government to "educate" the tribes.

Most Indians saw allotment as a threat to their cultures, and some tribes opposed it so strongly they were excluded from the Dawes Act. (The Five Civilized Tribes and the Osages of the Indian Territory were exempted from the 1887 law but subjected to allotment anyway under the Curtis Act of 1898.) However, some Indians—particularly mixed-bloods who often spoke English and had more ties to whites—saw allotment and citizenship as steps towards full integration into American society. White proponents of the policy were able to point to members of Nebraska's Omaha tribe, who, in 1881, had asked Congress to allot their land.

Embedded in the Dawes Act were powerful assumptions about the roles of women and family in a civilized society. Most middle-class white reformers linked "civilization" to male-headed nuclear families in which the man farmed, the woman kept house, and the couple remained together until death. However, in many Indian societies, women farmed, couples lived with the wife's family, and names and property were passed down through the mother's side. In many tribes, separation and "remarriage" were far easier and more common than in white society.

Through the Dawes Act and related rulings, white reformers and policy-makers tried to change long-standing cultural patterns, which they considered "savage." The Office of Indian Affairs urged reservation agents to "have children and wives known by the names of their husbands and fathers" in order to prevent "needless confusion." Agents also enforced inheritance laws that favored the male line, and sometimes prosecuted Indians who took new spouses without divorcing their old ones in state courts. Finally, the federal government sent middle-class white FIELD MATRONS to reservations to teach Indian women their proper domestic roles.

Such actions sparked Indian resistance. In 1894, 123 Hopi leaders sent a petition to the "Washington Chiefs" protesting allotment. The Hopis noted that, in their culture, women owned the fields and dwelling houses, and property passed through the mother's clan. On the Round Valley reservation in Northern California, Indians from several tribes quietly ignored field matrons' lessons about "civilized" cooking and home decoration. They also flouted white marital laws. Their actions prompted an escalating conflict with white agents, a conflict that culminated in a sweeping reservation revolt.

The Dawes Act proved a dismal failure. Much of the land allotted to American Indians was arid, wet, or rocky, and on some smaller reservations, allottees received far less than the 160 acres stipulated by the law. Many Indians could not afford farming implements, and Plains tribes often resisted farming for cultural reasons. Poverty also hindered efforts to transform Indian women into Victorian housewives. The Indian women of Round Valley, for instance, washed laundry and picked crops to support their families and had neither money nor time to invest in curtains and other niceties that the field matrons promoted.

American Indians lost much of their remaining land as a result of amendments to the Dawes Act. A series of laws passed between 1891 and 1908, including the BURKE ACT, gradually eroded the original restrictions on the sale and leasing of allotted land. Many impoverished Indians sold or leased their land for cash, often at prices far below market value. In 1887, when the Dawes Act was passed, American Indians owned about 138 million acres. By 1931, this figure had shrunk to 48 million acres, with nearly one-third of the acres leased to non-Indians. In 1934, the federal government finally admitted that the "total assimilation" policy had been a serious blunder. Congress passed the Indian Reorganization Act the same year to stop allotments under the Dawes Act and to permit unsold surplus lands to return to tribal ownership.

—*Wendy L. Wall*

SEE ALSO: United States Indian Policy

SUGGESTED READING:

Fritz, Henry E. "An American Dilemma: Administration of the Indian Estate under the Dawes Act and Amendments." *Journal of the Southwest* 37:1 (Spring 1995): 123–130.

———. "The Board of Indian Commissioners and Ethnocentric Reform, 1878–1893." In *Indian-White Relations: A Persistent Paradox*. Edited by Jane F. Smith and Robert M. Kvasnicka. Washington, D.C., 1976.

Hoxie, Frederick E. *A Final Promise: The Campaign to Assimilate the Indians, 1880–1920*. Lincoln, Nebr., 1984.

McDonnell, Janet. *The Dispossession of the American Indian*. Bloomington, Ind., 1991.

Olson, James S., and Raymond Wilson. *Native Americans in the Twentieth Century*. Urbana, Ill., 1984.

Prucha, Francis Paul, ed. *Americanizing the American Indians: Writings by the "Friends of the Indian," 1880–1900*. Cambridge, Mass., 1973.

Washburn, Wilcomb. *The Assault on Indian Tribalism: The General Allotment Law (Dawes Act) of 1887*. Melbourne, Fla., 1985.

DAWS, S. O.

Farmers' Alliance organizer S. O. Daws (1846–1916) was born in Kemper County, Mississippi, the son of poor farmers. At the age of twenty, he purchased a farm in Wise County, Texas, just a few miles from Springtown.

As a local, state, and national lecturer and organizer, Daws crafted the rapid expansion of the Farmers' Alliance from a regional Texas group to a national phenomenon in the 1880s. He was a major organizer and the state lecturer from 1880 to 1886; national organizer and lecturer from 1887 to 1888; secretary and treasurer from 1889 to 1890; and state lecturer from 1891 to 1892. He also encouraged alliance members to organize cooperatives and engineered a compromise between feuding factions in early 1886. Daws's compromise reaffirmed the nonpartisan nature of the alliance and temporarily focused it on education and cooperation, yet he also encouraged local organizations to form Anti-Monopoly Leagues to endorse candidates who supported alliance positions. This "Daws's formula" enabled the Farmers' Alliance to become a major political force in the AGRARIANISM of the late 1880s.

Daws was chairman of the State Executive Committee of the Farmers' Alliance when he moved to Oklahoma in the early 1900s and settled near Cordell. He was elected president of the Indiahoma State Farmers' Union, an organization composed of farmers in Oklahoma and the Indian Territory. He continued lecturing, first for the Farmers' Union and later independently, and served as Oklahoma's state librarian from 1908 to 1915. After he resigned, he founded the Farmers' Education and Cooperative Association.

—*Thomas A. Woods*

SUGGESTED READING:

Dunning, N. A., ed. *The Farmers' Alliance History and Agricultural Digest*. Washington, D.C., 1891. Reprinted in McCurry, Dan C., and Richard E. Rubenstein, eds. *American Farmers and the Rise of Agribusiness: Seeds of Struggle*. New York, 1975.

McMath, Robert C., Jr. *Populist Vanguard: A History of the Southern Farmers' Alliance*. Chapel Hill, N.C., 1975.

DEADWOOD, SOUTH DAKOTA

SEE: Mining: Mining Camps and Towns

DEADY, MATTHEW PAUL

Territorial judge from 1853 to 1859 and United States district judge for Oregon from 1859 until his death, Matthew Paul Deady (1824–1893) made an indelible mark on the laws of the state. Admitted to the Ohio bar in 1847, Deady moved to Oregon in 1849. He served in the territorial legislature in 1850 and as an associate justice on the territorial supreme court. After becoming district judge, Deady drafted the first volume of territorial laws and later codified all state laws. In 1862, he wrote a landmark law for corporations and, two years, later drafted the charter for the city of PORTLAND, OREGON, a charter that became a model for other cities.

—*Candace Floyd*

SUGGESTED READING:
Carey, Charles Henry. *History of Oregon.* Chicago, Ill., and Portland, Oreg., 1922.
Dodds, Gordon B. *Oregon: A Bicentennial History.* Nashville, Tenn., and New York, 1977.

DEAS, CHARLES

A painter best known for his idealized and often dramatic depiction of Native American subjects, Charles Deas (1818–1867) was born in Philadelphia and spent his youth there and in upstate New York. After failing to secure an appointment to the U.S. Military Academy at West Point in 1836, he turned to painting. He studied briefly in New York City at the National Academy of Design, where he exhibited his paintings in 1838 and 1839. He was elected an associate of the academy in 1839. A painting entitled *Turkey Shoot* was reproduced at that time as a lithographic print, which was widely sold; the artist gained a measure of popular national recognition.

Seeing an exhibition of paintings by GEORGE CATLIN in Philadelphia in 1837 or 1838 may have inspired Deas to venture westward himself in 1840 to visit a brother who was then stationed at Fort Crawford near Prairie du Chien, Wisconsin. During his stay there, Deas accompanied an expedition from the fort into the surrounding country and attended a council of the Sac (Sauk) and Fox (Mesquakie) Indians presided over by Chief KEOKUK. Deas later visited Fort Winnebago and Fort Snelling, Minnesota, where he made studies among the Dakotas or Eastern Sioux before traveling down the Mississippi in 1841 to St. Louis. Over the next six years, Deas accompanied several military or government-sponsored expeditions from St. Louis into the trans-Mississippi West. In 1844, he traveled as far as the upper Platte River in present-day Nebraska to visit a group of Pawnee encampments.

Throughout this period, Deas's work was exhibited at the National Academy of Design, the American Art Union, the Pennsylvania Academy of Fine Arts,

and the Boston Athenaeum. Soon after returning from St. Louis to New York City in 1847, however, he suffered a mental breakdown and spent the last fourteen years of his life confined to an asylum.

Deas's Western paintings were quite popular during his lifetime and are still prized by collectors of that genre, although relatively few of his works can be positively identified today. The principal collections attributable to Deas are found at Yale University, the Brooklyn Museum, and the THOMAS GILCREASE INSTITUTE.

—*David C. Hunt*

SEE ALSO: Art: Popular Prints and Commercial Art, Surveys and Expeditions, Western Art

SUGGESTED READING:
DeVoto, Bernard. *Across the Wide Missouri.* Boston, 1947.
Rathbone, Perry T. *Mississippi Panorama.* St. Louis, Mo., 1950.
Tyler, Ron, et al. *American Frontier Life.* Introduction by Peter H. Hassrick. Dallas, Tex., and New York, 1987.

DEATH VALLEY

Death Valley is a desert basin in Inyo County in southeastern CALIFORNIA. The valley, 140 miles long and varying in width from 5 to 15 miles, is a depression located between the Panamint Mountains to the west and the Amargosa Range to the east. Its colorful name suggests its emotional and near-mythic import. The hottest and driest portion of North America, it is also the lowest area in the Western Hemisphere, at 282 feet below sea level. For the gold-seekers of the 1849 gold rush, it was a terrible obstacle, and it was they who named it.

Death Valley is part of the Basin and Range geological province of the Western United States—an area made up primarily of a series of fault-block mountains and intervening basins. The valley began to sink during the Miocene Epoch, some twenty-five million years ago. While air temperatures have been recorded as high as 134° F (in 1913), ground temperatures sometimes exceed 175° F. Because the Panamint Mountains block the incursion of moist air, the valley receives an average annual rainfall of less than two inches. Although Furnace Creek and the Amargosa River sometimes carry mountain rains into the valley, they are often dry.

It is in the lowest areas that Death Valley most approximates the implication of its name. In these areas, prehistoric lakes have left salt flats, a soil in which nothing grows. Higher up, the valley floor consists of sand mixed with salt grains, and these areas support "survivor" vegetation such as coarse grass, mesquite, cacti, and poppies. Animal life in the area includes COY-OTES, kangaroo rats, horned toads, bighorn sheep, wild BURROS, and ravens.

Prospectors have braved the elements in Death Valley to mine gold, silver, lead, and copper. By far the most important mineral extracted from the region was borax, which was discovered in 1873 and used primarily for soap and detergent. The "twenty-mule teams" that hauled the ore out of the valley were transformed into something of a popular-culture icon by their depiction on the trademark tins of the Boraxo powdered-soap company. By the early twentieth century, the borax deposits petered out, and mining operations moved elsewhere, leaving a handful of forlorn and well-preserved GHOST TOWNS, which now help make Death Valley and the surrounding MOJAVE DESERT tourist attractions.

Tourism was also greatly stimulated by the establishment in 1933 of Death Valley National Monument, which extends partly into Nevada. Its area is 1,981 square miles, of which 550 square miles are below sea level.

—*Alan Axelrod*

SUGGESTED READING:

Adams, Ansel, and Nancy Newhall. *Death Valley*. 4th ed. Boston, 1954.

Kirk, R. *Exploring Death Valley*. Rev. ed. Stanford, Calif., 1981.

Lingenfelter, R. *Death Valley and the Amargosa*. Berkeley, Calif., 1986.

DEBO, ANGIE

A premier historian of Native Americans, Angie Debo (1890–1988) pioneered the field of ethnohistory. Born in Beattie, Kansas, Debo moved at the age of five with her parents from Kansas to Marshall in the Oklahoma Territory. Living in a region with few schools, she did not complete high school until she was twenty-three. She learned about frontier history when she went to study with Edward Everett Dale at the University of Oklahoma in 1915, shortly after he had returned from studying with famed frontier historian FREDERICK JACK-SON TURNER at Harvard. Alternating work as a high-school teacher with her own studies, she obtained a B.A. from the University of Oklahoma in 1918, a master's degree from the University of Chicago in 1924, and a doctorate from the University of Oklahoma in 1933.

In her dissertation on the Choctaws, Debo found her life's subject. Published as *The Rise and Fall of the*

Choctaw Republic in 1934, the book won the prestigious John H. Dunning Prize of the American Historical Association. Debo went on to write eight more books, most dealing with the situation of Indians in Oklahoma. She loved her adopted state, but with a critical eye. Her books clearly documented the injustice that had been visited upon native peoples by whites. They also brought to life the culture of the Five Civilized Tribes and of the Apaches, so that these peoples did not seem to be mere passive victims.

Because of widespread discrimination against women in academia, Debo never held a regular appointment in a department of history. She supported herself by a variety of means: teaching school, working with the Federal Writers' Project, and serving as maps librarian at Oklahoma A & M University in her later years. In April 1985, her portrait was installed in the state capitol in recognition of her role as Oklahoma's leading historian. A few weeks before her death, she received the American Historical Association's Award for Scholarly Distinction in honor of her great service to the discipline of history, an award personally delivered to her home by the governor of Oklahoma.

—*Glenna Matthews*

SUGGESTED READING:

Debo, Angie. *And Still the Waters Run*. Princeton, N.J., 1940.

———. *The Rise and Fall of the Choctaw Republic*. Norman, Okla., 1934.

DEER

SEE: White-tailed Deer

DEGOLYER LIBRARY

Located at Southern Methodist University in Dallas, Texas, the DeGolyer Library reflects changes in the history and scholarship of the trans-Mississippi West. Its interdisciplinary collections cover the evolution of the history, architecture, art, anthropology, archaeology, and literature of the West, among other subjects. A related strength is the library's collection of transportation resources, with a major emphasis on railroad books, manuscripts, and photographs. The library also houses the Center for Notable Women and the SMU archives.

The collections focus mainly on the Southwest, especially the borderlands region of what are now the United States and Mexico. The majority of the material deals with the nineteenth-century period of expansion, but the collections also include material on pre-Columbian life and culture and European exploration in North America. The library collects material on topics important in NEW WESTERN HISTORY—the twentieth century and the roles of women, minority cultures, and other previously neglected participants in the development of the region. Manuscript and photographic collections of note include the Baldwin Locomotive Works Collection, the Everett Lee DeGolyer, Jr. Collection of Railroad Photographs, the Sally Zaiser Collection of Paul Horgan, the Horton Foote Archive, and the Stanley Marcus Archive.

Everette Lee DeGolyer, Sr., a geologist and book collector, started buying books after World War I. He began with purchases of first editions of American and English literature and expanded to include the history of science and the trans-Mississippi West. Part of his Western Americana collection was housed at SMU during the 1960s, and the entire collection was donated to the university in 1974. The library opened in its present location in 1977. At DeGolyer's death in 1956, the collection numbered some 15,000 volumes. It has since grown to approximately 90,000 books, 250 periodical subscriptions, 3,000 linear feet of manuscripts, and 300,000 photographs.

—*Kristin Jacobsen*

SUGGESTED READING:

LaSalle, Patricia, and Pamela S. Lange. "From Classics to Cowboys: Special Collections of Books, Artifacts, Films, Letters, and More Strengthen the Resources of University Libraries." *SMU Magazine* 38 (1988): 20–27.

Rosenblatt, Jean. "From Ranching to Railroads: Documenting America's Westward Expansion." *The Chronicle of Higher Education* (December 5, 1990): B5.

Tinkle, Lon. *Mr. De: A Biography of Everette Lee DeGolyer.* Boston, 1970.

different ethnicities, Del Rio always took pride in her Mexican heritage.

After divorcing Jaime del Rio in 1928, she married Cedric Gibbons, head art director for MGM studios. Her beauty and elite background helped her secure roles in exotic and expensive movies. *The Girl of the Rio* (1932), *Bird of Paradise* (1932), and *Flying Down to Rio* (1933) are the best-known films of her career. By the mid-1930s, her career began to decline. She divorced Cedric Gibbons in 1941.

After the RKO film, *Journey into Fear* (1943), Del Rio returned to Mexico. Choosing her own directors, scripts, and camera crews, she began a new generation of film making in Mexico. Her films, during this period, included *Flor Silvestre* (1943), *María Candelaria* (1944), *La Malquerida* (1949), and *La Cucaracha* (1960).

In 1957, Del Rio returned to Hollywood to make *The Fugitive* (1957) with Henry Fonda and John Ford. She also played Elvis Presley's Native American mother in *Flaming Star* (1960). Del Rio married producer-documentary maker Lewis A. Riley in 1959. She continued to act in movies and television programs and on the stage in Mexico and other countries until 1978.

—*Alicia I. Rodríquez Estrada*

SEE ALSO: Film: Minority Images in Westerns; Stereotypes

SUGGESTED READING:

Bodeen, De Witt. "Dolores Del Rio Was the First Mexican of Family to Act in Hollywood." *Films in Review* 18 (March 1967): 266–283.

———. *From Hollywood: The Careers of 15 Great American Stars.* New York, 1976.

Hadley-Garcia, George. *Hispanic Hollywood: The Latins in Motion Pictures.* New York, 1990.

DEL RIO, DOLORES

The first Mexican movie actress in Hollywood, Dolores Del Rio (1905–1983) was born Lolita Dolores Asúnsolo y Lopez Negrete in Durango, Mexico. Growing up in an upper-class Mexican family, she married, at the age of fifteen, Jaime Martinez del Rio, the son of a wealthy Castillian family. In 1925, the director Edwin Carewe met the del Rios, and he inquired if Dolores would like to become a Hollywood star.

The silent film *What Price Glory?* (1926) made Del Rio a celebrity. She then starred in *Resurrection* (1927), *The Loves of Carmen* (1927), *Ramona* (1928), and *Evangeline* (1929). Although she portrayed women of

DEMERS, MODESTE P.

Canadian missionary and Catholic bishop Modeste P. Demers (1809–1871) was born in Quebec and attended seminary there. Ordained in 1836, he volunteered for missionary work in the Oregon Country. Demers made his westward journey under the auspices of the HUDSON'S BAY COMPANY. At the time, the company had established a network of forts, to which the Canadian priests and their later reinforcements attached their missions at such locations as Fort Vancouver, Walla Walla, Colville, Cowlitz, and Nisqually. Demers studied the Chinook language and translated church ceremony and prayers for native peoples.

At the time, Canadian trappers and Catholic priests were not the only ones with designs on Northwest lands. Americans, having discovered the fertile lands and bountiful natural resources of the Columbia River valley, feared that Britain and Rome conspired to wrest the lands from the United States. Protestant sects from the United States increased the number of missionaries that they sent to Oregon to strengthen the American claim to the region. In a numbers game, the Catholic missionaries won more converts among the native peoples than their frequently more evangelical Protestant rivals.

Catholic converts and churches multiplied, and Father Demers remained in the West to minister to them. He became the bishop of Vancouver in 1846, and held the office until his death.

—*Patricia Hogan*

SEE ALSO: Catholics; Missions: Nineteenth-Century Missions to the Indians

DENIG, EDWIN THOMPSON

Western ethnologist Edwin Thompson Denig (1812–1858) was a preeminent upper Missouri fur trader and author of voluminous writings on the Plains Indian tribes and the history of the upper Missouri country.

Born in Pennsylvania, the son of a doctor, Denig was lured to the fur business in 1833 by friend and successful trader Alexander Culbertson. In the service of the AMERICAN FUR COMPANY, Denig worked, first, at Fort Pierre Chouteau and, from 1837 on, at FORT UNION. His skill at business was evident quickly, and by his second year, he had been named superintendent of a wintering house near Fort Pierre. He subsequently rose through Fort Union's senior echelon from bookkeeper, to chief clerk, to bourgeois. Denig's tenure with the American Fur Company spanned twenty-three years.

Adventurers, artists, scientists, and others, such as JOHN JAMES AUDUBON, Thaddeus Culbertson, and PIERRE-JEAN DE SMET, visited Fort Union—known as a sanctuary in Plains Indian country—and stimulated Denig's scientific and ethnological curiosity. He penned for Audubon the first description of the construction and uses of Fort Union: the "principal and handsomest trading post on the Missouri River." For Audubon and Culbertson, Denig prepared major specimen collections of Upper Missouri birds and mammals and sent one assembly to the fledgling Smithsonian Institution. And particularly with De Smet's encouragement, Denig wrote exhaustively on the Upper Missouri Indian tribes and produced hundreds, perhaps thousands, of manuscript pages on the history, manners, and customs of the Assiniboin, Arikara, Cree, Crow, and Sioux peoples. Through his day-to-day contact with Indians at Fort Union, Denig came to view them as individuals, not as stereotypical savages.

Denig was not careful to guard his manuscripts, and many of his compositions were appropriated by others, often without attribution. In the mid-twentieth century, John C. Ewers of the Smithsonian Institution examined Denig's extant manuscripts. In a lively introduction to an expanded edition of the trader's most important work, *Indian Tribes of the Upper Missouri* (1930), Ewers described Denig as one of the most prolific and knowledgeable eyewitness writers on the tribes of that region.

Denig's fascination with Fort Union and the Upper Missouri region waned in the mid-1850s, perhaps as he sought a proper education for his mixed-blood children. In the summer of 1856, he quit the American Fur Company and moved with his Assiniboin wife, Deer Little Woman, and family to the Red River Settlement of Canada, where he continued to write and worked as a private trader. He died at the age of forty-six, stricken by an appendicitis attack.

—*Paul L. Hedren*

SUGGESTED READING:
Denig, Edwin Thompson. *Five Indian Tribes of the Upper Missouri.* Edited and with an introduction by John C. Ewers. Norman, Okla., 1961.

DENVER, COLORADO

Denver, the capital of COLORADO, was founded on November 22, 1858, after a gold discovery near the confluence of Cherry Creek and the South Platte River. Town founder William H. Larimer, Jr., named the city for James W. Denver, governor of the Kansas Territory, of which eastern Colorado was then a part. Numerous other gold discoveries sparked a mass migration of some 50,000 people to the area in 1859 and 1860, and the federal government established the Colorado Territory in 1861. Denver, known as the "Mile High City," was incorporated that year and became the permanent capital in 1867. The native Arapahos and Southern Cheyennes, who had initially welcomed Euro-Americans, were quickly dispossessed.

Denver's aggressive leadership, spearheaded by WILLIAM NEWTON BYERS, founding editor of the *Rocky Mountain News,* and Territorial Governor JOHN EVANS, built the Denver Pacific Railway (1870) to Cheyenne, Wyoming, and the Union Pacific main line. These transportation connections enabled Denver to emerge as

Denver, Colorado, in 1895. *Courtesy Denver Public Library, Western History Department.*

the trading center of the Rocky Mountain West. Denver became the banking, minting, supply, and processing center not only for Colorado but for neighboring states by constructing a spiderweb of rail lines. The largest and longest-lived of these local lines was the narrow-gauge DENVER AND RIO GRANDE RAILWAY COMPANY.

Between 1870 and 1890, with a population growth from 4,759 to 106,713, Denver became the second most populous metropolis in the West, behind only San Francisco. Mining fueled this growth; Colorado led the country in silver production during the 1880s and in gold during the 1890s. Denver's railroads carried many of the hinterland's ores to Denver's smelters, the city's largest nineteenth-century industry.

Denver's first boom was highly dependent on silver. When Congress repealed the SHERMAN SILVER PURCHASE ACT OF 1890 during the depression of 1893, the boom abruptly ended. Civic leaders began promoting economic diversity—farming of wheat and sugar beets, ranching and the Denver Livestock Exchange, manufacturing, tourism, and service industries. Denver began growing again after 1900 but at a slower rate.

Stockyards, brickyards, canneries, flour mills, tanneries, and rubber-goods manufacturers nourished the city during the early 1900s. Of many breweries, Coors

emerged as one of the three national giants. Regional or national headquarters of many oil and gas firms fueled much of Denver's post–World War II growth.

Located on high plains at the eastern base of the Rocky Mountains, Denver has a semiarid climate with an average of thirteen inches of precipitation a year. Once a drab, brown city, it was transformed into a city of parks, parkways, tree-lined streets, and handsome public buildings during the administration of Mayor ROBERT WALTER SPEER, who served from 1904 to 1912 and from 1916 to 1918. Speer, like thousands of others, came to Denver seeking the sunny, dry climate as a cure for tuberculosis. He hired America's leading experts in CITY PLANNING to create "a city beautiful." As Denver's most powerful—and ruthless—mayor, Speer implemented plans for a parklike Civic Center at the heart of the city. Parkways led to large neighborhood parks, designed as mini-civic centers and surrounded by schools, libraries, and other activity hubs. Creation of not only city parks but also municipal mountain parks, including the Winter Park ski area and the Red Rocks outdoor amphitheater, helped make tourism a major industry.

After World War II, the population of the city and county of Denver became relatively static, while the surrounding suburban counties mushroomed. Denver

County, however, remained the political, financial, and cultural hub. Notable institutions include the Denver Museum of Natural History, the Western History Department of Denver Public Library, the Colorado History Museum, the Denver Art Museum, and the Denver Center for the Performing Arts, as well as the region's only mint and major league baseball, basketball, and football teams. Denver's Auraria Higher Education Center (1977) is the state's largest campus with some 34,000 students attending the campus shared by the University of Colorado at Denver, Metropolitan State College, and the Denver Community College. The city's major private schools are the University of Denver (1864) and Regis University (1877).

Metro Denver is home to the state's largest Native American population—about 9,000 primarily Lakota-Sioux, Cheyennes, Utes, and Navajos. Germans were the largest foreign-born group in Denver until World War I, followed by Irish, English, Italians, Slavs, Canadians, and Scandinavians. Hispanic people had settled in southern Colorado before the 1858 and 1859 gold rush; after 1930, Mexicans became the largest and fastest growing foreign-born group. Roughly 12 percent of the population is Spanish-surnamed, and 5 percent is African American. In recent years, Denver has elected as mayor both a Hispanic (Federico Peña) and an African American (Wellington Webb). Asians—primarily Chinese, Japanese, Korean, and Vietnamese—compose about 3 percent of the city's population.

In the last decade of the twentieth century, the city's economic base included electronics, computers, aviation, and the nation's largest telecommunications center. As the single regional center of the federal government in a vast mountain and plain hinterland, Denver boasted more federal employees than any city besides Washington, D.C. Most were civilian employees, although Lowry Air Force Base and Fitzsimons Army Hospital were mainstays of the economy in Aurora, the second largest city in the metropolis with some 225,000 residents.

Denver had a 1990 population of 438,420 for the core city and county of Denver; its metropolitan area (Adams, Arapahoe, Boulder, Denver, Douglas, and Jefferson counties) had a population of 1.9 million. Because of its white-collar orientation and the stabilizing of many inner-city neighborhoods with protective local historic district designations, Denver remained more stable and prosperous than other large U.S. cities. With a light rail system (1994) and a fifty-five-square-mile Denver International Airport (1995), Denver continued to use transportation networks to make it the undisputed metropolis of the High Plains and the Rockies.

—*Thomas J. Noel*

SUGGESTED READING:
Leonard, Stephen J., and Thomas J. Noel. *Denver: Mining Camp to Metropolis.* Niwot, Colo., 1990.

DENVER AND RIO GRANDE RAILWAY COMPANY

WILLIAM JACKSON PALMER founded the Denver and Rio Grande Railway Company on October 27, 1870, as a narrow-gauge line to run south of Denver to Mexico City. From the outset, the road encountered public-relations difficulties with communities along its tracks, hard times instigated by the panic of 1873, and competition from other roads. Nevertheless, building continued into southern Colorado and the San Luis Valley.

After a clash with the ATCHISON, TOPEKA, AND SANTA FE RAILROAD over routes both lines desired, a series of lawsuits permitted the Rio Grande to enter Leadville in 1880 but stopped it from building south of a point seventy-five miles south of Conejos. The line passed into the possession of JAY GOULD. It then became the main railroad serving Colorado's Western Slope, much of it over standard-gauge track. In 1908, George Gould merged the Denver and Rio Grande with the Rio Grande Western to form the Denver and Rio Grande Western. Income from the new company helped pay for his newly formed WESTERN PACIFIC RAILROAD. The failure of the Western Pacific forced the Denver and

A Denver and Rio Grande train, requiring the power of two engines, makes its way through the Rocky Mountains. *Courtesy Denver Public Library, Western History Department.*

Rio Grande Western into receivership and ultimately sale in 1924 to the Western Pacific and the Missouri Pacific.

Although the Rio Grande declared bankruptcy during the Depression in 1935, a revival took place during World War II. Following reorganization in 1947, the line operated profitably for three decades. In 1984, Philip Anschutz acquired the Denver and Rio Grande Western, but in May 1992, the subsequent merger with the Southern Pacific retired the name from lists of active lines.

—*Liston E. Leyendecker*

SUGGESTED READING:

Athearn, Robert. *The Denver and Rio Grande Western Railroad: Rebel of the Rockies.* Lincoln, Nebr., 1977.

DEPOSIT ACT OF 1836

In 1836, the United States government had a surplus of nearly $40 million from tariff revenues and the sale of public lands. Congress authorized the U.S. Treasury to distribute the surplus, above a $5 million reserve, to banks in each of the states. The Deposit Act of 1836 divided the surplus funds among the states in proportion to their populations and distributed the payments in quarterly installments. The first installment was to be doled out on January 1, 1837.

In making funds available to several state banks, the Deposit Act had an impact on the country's fiscal well-being. It avoided the concentration of federal funds under the influence of a small number of financiers, as had been the case before President ANDREW JACKSON destroyed the Second Bank of the United States. It discouraged the sale of public lands in Western regions at low prices. (Some historians suggest that the opposite was true. The act encouraged wild speculation in land prices.) And it favored the older states with their established populations over the new states in the West.

The Deposit Act had its proponents and its detractors. JOHN C. CALHOUN and a reluctant President Jackson numbered among the former. But its popularity hardly mattered. Before the first year's allotments had been distributed, the panic of 1837 wiped out the federal government's surplus, and the nation slumped into a depression that lasted until the mid-1840s.

—*Patricia Hogan*

SEE ALSO: Banking; Financial Panics

SUGGESTED READING:

Gates, Paul W. *History of Public Land Law Development.* Washington, D.C., 1978.

DERBY, GEORGE HORATIO

Military topographer and comic author George Horatio Derby (1823–1861) was born in Dedham, Massachusetts. He first displayed a genius for puns and jokes at West Point, where he designed, for example, a cannon whose cannonballs could sail around corners and circle to hit the gunner's backside. After serving in the United States–Mexican War, Derby went to the West as chief topographer on General Bennet Riley's staff to survey the San Joaquin and Sacramento valleys and map the land that soon would be overrun in the CALIFORNIA GOLD RUSH. Following further surveys in northern California, he was sent to explore the COLORADO RIVER, which he found navigable in any season as a supply route for the newly constructed Fort Yuma. Derby also supervised flood-control efforts in San Diego and surveyed military roads through Oregon. Reassigned back East in October 1857, he spent his remaining years building lighthouses along the Florida and Alabama coasts and serving in office assignments in Boston. Derby was hospitalized for a mysterious degenerative disease that first blinded him and then killed him at the age of thirty-eight.

Derby wrote columns for San Francisco newspapers and a new magazine, *The Pioneer,* from the fall of 1850 until the spring of 1853. He wrote under the name "Squibob," formed from the word *squib* (a witty literary effort), until imitators began to use that name. He then decided to kill off that writer with great ceremony. Thereafter writing as "John Phoenix," he supplied the San Francisco press with a running commentary on mores and manners of sophisticated Easterners who tried to impose high culture on the lowly gold rushers. Typically, Derby would place Phoenix in the role of the sophisticated wit who thinks he is pulling a hoax over common folk, when in reality, he is the one being fooled.

That self-mockery set a pattern for the type of HUMOR that critics called "Californian." When Derby's columns were published as *Phoenixiana* (1855), the book was hailed as "the first work of any pretensions to literary merit written by a Californian." Although it became a best-selling work in America and overseas, Derby never earned a penny from its sales. Instead, he enjoyed celebrity from coast to coast and in his lifetime received praise from the press and saw legions of columnists imitate his style. Back East, he contributed to prestigious newspapers and even *The Knickerbocker,* the sophisticated forerunner of today's *New Yorker.* But away from the West, he became more self-absorbed, and his essays were more serious. Still, he directly influenced a generation of humorists including MARK

TWAIN, who perfected Derby's style to such a degree that the public forgot "John Phoenix."

—*P. M. Zall*

SUGGESTED READING:
Reynolds, Richard D., ed. *Squibob, An Early California Humorist*. San Francisco, 1990.
Stewart, George R. *John Phoenix, Esq*. New York, 1937.

DERN, GEORGE HENRY

George Henry Dern (1872–1936) was a state senator and governor of Utah. In 1894, he moved from his native state of Nebraska to Utah, where he found work as a bookkeeper for the Mercur Gold Mining and Milling Company. He soon rose to the position of treasurer and then general manager of the company. In 1902, he became general manager of the Consolidated Mercur Gold Mines Company. In 1915, he moved to the Tintic Milling Company as general manager. During this time, he invested in ranches and served as a director of the Mutual Dairy Company and on the boards of other companies and banks. Dern entered the state senate in 1914 as a Democrat from Salt Lake County. During his two terms, he chaired the committee on war materiel and was a member of the United States Fuel Administration for Utah. In 1924 and 1928, he was elected governor of the state. He campaigned for tax reform, secured the development of the COLORADO RIVER, and increased the government's support of public schools. Having met Franklin D. Roosevelt at governor's conferences in 1929 and 1930, he was named secretary of war when Roosevelt became president in 1932.

—*Candace Floyd*

SUGGESTED READING:
Poll, Richard D., ed. *Utah's History*. Provo, Utah, 1978.

DESERET, STATE OF

Mormon leaders established the state of Deseret in 1849 to provide a government while waiting for the U.S. Congress to enact territorial legislation. The name came from a BOOK OF MORMON word for the honeybee, symbolizing both industry and cooperative communalism. Deseret's constitution set up a bicameral legislature and executive and judicial branches of government. It affirmed religious freedom and separation of church and state, although church leaders were the sole candidates for office and were elected with nearly no dissent.

The boundaries of the state of Deseret enclosed some 490,000 square miles, from the Colorado Rockies to the Sierra Nevada and from the Oregon Country to the Gila River, with a southern strip of land stretching west to include the Pacific Coast from Los Angeles to San Diego. It was the sole functioning civil government in the region from July 2, 1849, until February 5, 1851, when BRIGHAM YOUNG took the oath of office as governor of a much diminished but still vast Utah Territory that included all of present-day Nevada and substantial parts of western Colorado and southern Wyoming. Utahans petitioned for statehood under the name of Deseret in 1849, 1862, 1867, and 1872. During the Civil War, they maintained a "ghost" government of Deseret to reenact and sanction laws passed by the territorial legislature.

Petitions for statehood in 1882, 1887, and 1895 contained the name Utah, suggesting a strategic retreat from the social values inherent in the Deseret concept. While the dream of founding a state of Deseret was realized in part when Utah became a state in 1896, the territory it covered, like the concept itself, was much shorn and altered by the realities of late nineteenth-century American political life.

—*Dean L. May*

SUGGESTED READING:
Campbell, Eugene E. *Establishing Zion: The Mormon Church in the American West, 1847–1869*. Salt Lake City, 1988.
Larson, Gustive O. *The "Americanization" of Utah for Utah for Statehood*. San Marino, Calif., 1971.
Lyman, Edward Leo. *Political Deliverance: The Mormon Quest for Utah Statehood*. Urbana, Ill., 1986.
Morgan, Dale L. *The State of Deseret*. Logan, Utah, 1987.

DESERT LAND ACT OF 1877

The Desert Land Act of 1877 sought to encourage irrigated farming in the arid West. The act continued the LAND POLICY, first set forward in the HOMESTEAD ACT OF 1862, of transferring public land into private hands. However, unlike the Homestead Act, preemption laws, and other land policies designed to promote rapid settlement in the humid East, the Desert Land Act intended to dispose of arid land in eleven states and territories west of the one-hundredth meridian. Only Colorado was excluded. The law offered claimants large land allotments of 640 acres (an entire section) for only $1.25 an acre, with the understanding that land would be irrigated within three years. The law required payment of $.25 per acre at the time a claim was filed and an additional $1 an acre upon proof of IRRIGATION.

The Desert Land Act was modeled after an 1875 law aimed at encouraging irrigated farming in Lassen County, California. When introduced in the House of Representatives in December 1876, the bill met with little opposition. It moved quickly through Congress and aroused only minor debate in the Senate Committee on Public Lands. President Rutherford B. Hayes signed the bill into law on March 3, 1877.

The Desert Land Act proved significant largely because of its weaknesses. Since "desert land" had an imprecise meaning at that time, no one knew exactly how much there was or whether it was accessible to water. The act failed to specify the amount of water needed for irrigation and the number of acres per section that needed to be irrigated in order to comply with the law. Claimants often obtained title to 640 acres without making the effort to irrigate the land. Furthermore, cattlemen and ditch companies frequently used fraudulent methods to acquire multiple adjoining sections. Flaws in the law actually inhibited settlement and often allowed speculators to gain monopoly control over water. Greatly understaffed, the GENERAL LAND OFFICE was ill equipped to ensure compliance with the law. Ultimately, the act stimulated the formation of private water companies and encouraged irrigation in some regions of the West. Recognizing its flaws, the General Land Office periodically called for repeal of the act. Congress significantly amended the law in the Desert Land Act of 1891.

—*Gail E. H. Evans*

SUGGESTED READING:

Gates, Paul. *History of Public Land Law Development.* Washington, D.C., 1968.

Hibbard, Benjamin Horace. *A History of the Public Land Policies.* Madison, Wis., 1965.

U.S. Statutes at Large. Vol. 19: 377.

DESERT LAND ACT OF 1891

The Desert Land Act of 1891, signed into law on March 3, 1891, amended the Desert Land Act of 1877. Part of an omnibus land-reform law, the 1891 law sought to remove serious weaknesses in the 1877 law. The new act restricted land claims to 320 acres, as opposed to the 640 acres allowed under the earlier law. The 1891 act required every claimant to present a formal IRRIGATION plan to the GENERAL LAND OFFICE at the time an entry was made. It stipulated that water must be available for the entire 320 acres and that at least one-eighth of the total should be cultivated within three years. The law required payment of $1 per acre every year for three years. The 1891 act limited claims to United States citizens, required claimants to reside in the state or territory of their claims, and insisted that all claimants file for themselves rather than through absentee parties. Finally, the amended act applied to Colorado, which had been excluded in the earlier law. Congress passed the 1891 bill with little debate.

Despite these changes, problems remained. The new law continued to encourage speculative schemes since it did not require claimants to reside on their lands. It still permitted a single claimant to obtain multiple adjoining parcels, and, thus, for those with thousands of acres near rivers or creeks, the act allowed monopoly control over water. The law failed to address questions about the cost and supervision of irrigation projects. Dissatisfied with the 1891 act, congressmen from some states, particularly Idaho, Nebraska, and Wyoming, initiated a movement calling for the cession of all desert lands to the states for the purpose of developing irrigation. Beginning in 1891, controversies over unresolved desert LAND POLICY prompted a series of IRRIGATION congresses, where participants also urged the cession of arid lands to states. Partly in response to these pressures, Congress passed the CAREY ACT OF 1894 to address problems of irrigation on desert lands.

—*Gail E. H. Evans*

SUGGESTED READING:

Hibbard, Benjamin Horace. *A History of the Public Land Policies.* Madison, Wis., 1965.

Robbins, Roy M. *Our Landed Heritage: The Public Domain, 1776–1936.* Princeton, N.J., 1942.

U.S. Statutes at Large. Vol. 26: 1096–1097.

DE SMET, PIERRE-JEAN

Jesuit missionary and frequent mediator between Euro-Americans and Native Americans, Pierre-Jean De Smet (1801–1873) received his religious training in his native Belgium. Recruited for American missionary work, he sailed for the United States in 1821 and joined the Jesuit order. Two years later, he headed west to establish a Jesuit novitiate near St. Louis. Ordained in 1827, De Smet spent his first decade in the priesthood engaged in routine duties, interrupted by trips to Europe to solicit recruits and support for Jesuit missionary work.

De Smet's career as a missionary among Native Americans of the Northwest and the Plains was brief, but his impact was immense and long lasting. In 1838, he established a mission among the Potawatomi Indians at present-day Council Bluffs. Then, in a matter of about six years, he aided the mission established in the Willamette Valley by Canadian priests Fathers Francis Norbert Blanchet and MODESTE P. DEMERS; he founded

Pierre-Jean De Smet. *Courtesy Library of Congress.*

St. Mary's Mission among the Flathead Indians in 1841; for the Kalispels, he established the Mission of St. Ignatius; and he started the Sacred Heart Mission among the Coeur d'Alene Indians.

De Smet's mission building ended in 1846, but he continued to influence the Native Americans and the Euro-Americans of the West. In addition to the native peoples for whom he established missions, De Smet touched nearly all the tribes of the Columbia Valley as well as the Sioux, Blackfoot, and other tribes east of the Rockies. A tireless man, short and stocky, muscular and resilient, friendly and inspiring trust, he won the confidence and admiration of the tribes he met. Known as "Blackrobe" to the West's natives, he intervened to settle differences among warring tribes and often served as mediator to Indians and Euro-Americans. He attended the great Sioux council near Fort Laramie in 1851 and calmed the Indians about white incursions on their territories. He also mediated in the Yakima War of 1858 and 1859. In 1868, he headed to SITTING BULL's camp in the Bighorn Valley and urged the Sioux to discuss peace with federal officials.

In his life as a missionary and diplomat, De Smet logged some one hundred thousand miles and often traveled in uncharted lands and among Native Americans who were clearly hostile to other whites. Black-robe's efforts to bring peace to Euro-Americans and

Native Americans proved especially costly for the Indians. Nevertheless, these efforts—more than his missions—are his legacy to the West.

—*Patricia Hogan*

SEE ALSO: Catholics; Missions: Nineteenth-Century Missions to the Indians

SUGGESTED READING:
Carriker, Robert. *Father Peter-John de Smet: Jesuit in the West.* Norman, Okla., 1995.

DEVOTO, BERNARD

Writer, critic, and historian Bernard DeVoto (1897–1955) defies definition. A novelist who excelled at historical writing, he was both an ardent defender of the West and its bitter critic. A conservationist who characterized the West as "the plundered province," he idealized the mountain men and pioneers who began the plundering. A literary critic of considerable power, he held the critics of his day in contempt and made bitter enemies among them.

Bernard DeVoto was born in Ogden, Utah, a community he later criticized sharply for its cultural backwardness and narrow-mindedness. He attended the University of Utah for a year and later taught high-school history in Ogden. He then enrolled in and graduated from Harvard University and turned his back on Utah, except as it figured in his writing, for the rest of his life. He taught at Northwestern University, Harvard, and the Breadloaf summer writers' conferences in Vermont, but it was as a writer that he made his reputation, primarily through "The Easy Chair" column in *Harper's,* several books on MARK TWAIN, and his Western novels and histories.

The five "serious" novels he wrote under his own name (he wrote several mysteries under the pen name "John August") portray the West as a demanding, democratic environment that fosters robust living and healthy values, in contrast to the artificiality of Eastern life. As fiction, they are heavily burdened with lengthy philosophical passages that make them less significant as literature than as avenues to understanding DeVoto's mind. While still worth reading, they have not attained the first rank among Western novels.

His histories, by contrast, while highly controversial, are deeply researched, original in method and interpretation, colorfully written, and fundamentally important in Western historiography. The brilliant introduction and notes to his skillful one-volume abridgment of *The Journals of Lewis and Clark,* for example, are the standard introduction for nonspecialists to the work of these great explorers. *Across the Wide Mis-*

souri, which began as notes for an exhibit of Western paintings, became a full-blown history of mountain men and the fur trade. His most ambitious work, *The Course of Empire,* is a history of the Euro-American discovery and exploration of the New World from the Spanish explorers to Lewis and Clark. Perhaps DeVoto's most original and interesting book—and the most controversial one—is *The Year of Decision: 1846,* in which he creatively employs the literary device of "synechdoche," whereby he uses the events of the year 1846 to typify the entire westward movement.

In addition to his lively prose and his vividly drawn portraits, the most conspicuous characteristic of DeVoto's histories is his opinionated interpretations, which are at once the delight and the frustration of historians. DeVoto paints in primary colors, with little complexity either to his heroes (the mountain men JAMES CLYMAN and JAMES (JIM) BRIDGER, for example) or his villains (explorer JOHN CHARLES FRÉMONT and entrepreneur LANSFORD WARREN HASTINGS). In spite of their controversial nature, DeVoto's books are perhaps the most enjoyable and stimulating introductions available to the history of the westward movement.

—*Gary Topping*

SEE ALSO: Historiography, Western

SUGGESTED READING:
DeVoto, Bernard. *Across the Wide Missouri.* Boston, 1947.
———. *The Course of Empire.* Boston, 1952.
———. *The Journals of Lewis and Clark.* Boston, 1953.
———. *The Year of Decision: 1846.* Boston, 1943.
Stegner, Wallace. *The Uneasy Chair: A Biography of Bernard DeVoto.* Garden City, N.Y., 1974.

DIAMOND HOAX

SEE: Great Diamond Hoax

DIEGUEÑO INDIANS

SEE: Native American Peoples: Peoples of California

DIEHL, CHARLES SANFORD

Journalist Charles Sanford Diehl (1854–1946) led a remarkable life as a war correspondent. Born in Mary-

land and raised in Ottawa and Wenona, Illinois, he began working for newspapers at the age of fourteen. Working for the *Chicago Times* from 1873 to 1883, he reported on the actions of Brigadier General ALFRED HOWE TERRY following the Battle of Little Bighorn. He attended the peace negotiations between Terry and SITTING BULL in Canada in 1877 after the Sioux leader sought refuge there following the Little Bighorn battle. Diehl also reported on the surrender of CHIEF JOSEPH. In an attack against the Sioux at the Poplar River Agency in Montana on January 2, 1881, Diehl fought with Major Guido Ilges's troops. Diehl worked as general manager of the Associated Press between 1883 and 1911 and organized the news bureau's coverage of the Spanish-American War. In 1911, he became a co-owner of the *San Antonio Light.*

—*Candace Floyd*

SUGGESTED READING:
Knight, Oliver. *Following the Indian Wars.* Norman, Okla., 1960.

DIGGS, ANNIE LA PORTE

A major figure in American POPULISM, Annie La Porte Diggs (1853–1916) was born in Canada, raised in New Jersey, and worked as a journalist in Washington, D.C., before moving to Lawrence, KANSAS, and taking a job in a music store in 1873. Soon married with children, she did not become active in reform movements until the early 1880s, when she joined the WOMAN'S CHRISTIAN TEMPERANCE UNION, the Unitarian church, and the Social Science Club of Kansas and western Missouri. As her interest in reform grew, she launched a column in the Lawrence newspaper in support of the Farmers' Alliance. The column landed her a job as associate editor and Washington correspondent for Topeka's Populist weekly, the *Advocate,* a platform from which she waged the fight for reform between 1890 and 1900. This decade opened with the birth of the Populist party and closed with Populism's utter absorption within the Democratic party, a process called by its proponents "fusion" and about which Diggs had much to say. Never the crowd pleaser that the better known, more tempestuous, and erratic MARY ELIZABETH LEASE was, Diggs became, other than Lease, the most prominent woman reformer in the Populist movement. Not only did she hold her own against Lease intellectually, but her charm often served to diffuse the charges about wild-eyed radicalism often leveled at Populists leaders.

—*Charles Phillips*

DILLON, SIDNEY

Best known as the man who headed the construction of the Union Pacific transcontinental line, Sidney Dillon (1812–1892) began his railroad career as a seven-year-old water boy during construction of the Mohawk and Hudson line in his native upstate New York. From water boy, he advanced to overseer and foreman, working on the construction of several lines in New York and New England. Before he was thirty, he struck out on his own, winning a contract to build a portion of the Boston and Albany Railroad. Completing this job in 1840, he went on, in the next twenty years, to build thousands of miles of rail lines in all parts of the country. He amassed a considerable fortune by taking partial payment for his contracts in stocks in the railroads he built. When OAKES AMES approached him about investing in the UNION PACIFIC RAILROAD in 1865, Dillon did so and took on the job of chief contractor for the Union Pacific's transcontinental line. He took part in the 1869 ceremony at PROMONTORY SUMMIT, marking the completion of the railroad line to California.

Dillon sat on the board of directors for the Union Pacific from 1864 to 1892 and served as its president from 1874 to 1884 in the difficult years following the scandal surrounding the CRÉDIT MOBILIER OF AMERICA and again from 1890 to 1892. By 1870, Dillon ended his career in railroad construction and became more of a financier and a close business associate of JAY GOULD. He died in 1892, before his Union Pacific went into receivership.

—*Patricia Hogan*

SEE ALSO: Railroads

SUGGESTED READING:
Athearn, Robert G. *Union Pacific Country.* Lincoln, Nebr., 1971.

DIME NOVELS

SEE: Literature: Dime Novels

DIMOND, ANTHONY J. (TONY)

Alaska politician Anthony J. (Tony) Dimond (1881–1953) was born in New York and moved to Alaska in 1905. His political career began when he served on the Valdez city council from 1917 to 1932 and as mayor nine times. Dimond, a Democrat, was also elected in 1922 and in 1928 to the territorial senate. In 1932, he defeated Republican JAMES WICKERSHAM and spent the next ten years working in Washington, D.C., as Alaska's delegate to Congress. He supported economic development for Alaska and equal rights for all citizens. He retired from Congress in 1944 and was appointed a federal district court judge, a position he held until his death.

—*William R. Johnson, Jr.*

SUGGESTED READING:
Mangusso, Mary Childers. "Anthony J. Dimond: A Political Biography." Ph.D. diss., Texas Tech University, 1978.

DISCIPLES OF CHRIST

SEE: Campbellites

DISEASE

The trans-Mississippi West was plagued by the same diseases that struck the rest of the United States—smallpox, influenza, tuberculosis, and cholera. Smallpox, especially, had a long history in the region. Indians in the Pacific Northwest, in California, on the Great Plains, and in the Southwest had all suffered devastating losses to the disease after Columbus first introduced the virus that caused smallpox into the Western Hemisphere. In 1798, Edward Jenner, an English doctor, had discovered something known to milkmaids and in country folklore for ages: infection from cowpox, a mild disorder acquired from cattle, protected one from smallpox. The vaccination Jenner developed remained controversial for decades, but it was accepted early in Spain and its colonies. When the first outbreaks of smallpox struck the settlements and pueblos of New Mexico in the eighteenth century, the Spanish government sent a flotilla to vaccinate the local population in 1803. The cowpox virus was kept alive during the Atlantic passage by a human chain of orphan boys; every two weeks the Spanish infected a new pair of orphans from a previous pair suffering from the disease. The procedure was continued from Mexico City to Chihuahua to Santa Fe and the pueblos, where there was some resistance from the Zunis, Lagunas, and Acomas. By 1805, however, several thousand settlers and Indians had been vaccinated.

Given the resistance to vaccination, the lack of understanding about how diseases were transmitted, and the absence of any true public-health system, smallpox continued to ravage the West periodically throughout the nineteenth and on into the twentieth centuries.

those with whom he or she had come into contact were quarantined into a single wagon. Their clothes were disinfected, and they were left alone to await their fates. Fear crippled Western communities during small-pox epidemics, and travelers were often afraid to enter new communities lest they be regarded by townspeople as the source of the infection.

Smallpox was by no means the only, the most deadly, or even the most feared of the plagues in the American West. The most common was probably malaria; the most deadly, perhaps tuberculosis (TB); the most dreaded, almost certainly cholera. In the middle of the nineteenth century, the Mississippi River valley was a dangerous place, rife with disease, especially malaria. Called more frequently at the time both the "fever" and the "ague," malaria was endemic to the river valley. Especially in the summers, when overflowing rivers receded and left behind pools of stagnant water, the Mississippi bottomlands became perfect breeding grounds for the mosquitoes that spread the disease. Not understanding how the sickness occurred, Midwesterners every year from July to October braced themselves for the coming of the fever and the ague. Another disease common to the Midwest was called "milk sickness" or "puking fever," which, like malaria, was spread by a host—the milk cow. Cows grazed on snakeroot plants (*Eupatorium ageratoides*), which made their milk poisonous to those who drank it. Although settlers understood that they were falling seriously ill because they drank milk, they had no idea why sometimes it was so dangerous and at other times it was perfectly safe. Long before gold was discovered in California, Midwesterners were heading to the West Coast and the Pacific Northwest to escape the malarial swamps of the middle border; the Far West had the reputation of being disease-free. MARK TWAIN, born on the Mississippi, summed up the mistaken ideas about the West Coast when he quipped that California was so healthy you had to leave the place to die.

Quiet and insidious, tuberculosis was one of the great killer diseases of the nineteenth century. Sometimes called "white plague" (because the body's im-

Top: This nineteenth-century engraving, entitled *Death Scene on the Plains,* offers a melodramatic depiction of a frequent occurrence. *Courtesy Bancroft Library.*

Bottom: Miners, inhaling dust day in and day out, were plagued by miner's consumption. *Courtesy National Cowboy Hall of Fame and Western Heritage Center.*

In 1829, it struck Bent's Fort, which was still under construction, when a party of infected Mexican workers arrived. By the time it had spread to William Bent and CHRISTOPHER HOUSTON ("KIT") CARSON, the Americans were warning the Indians to stay away until the disease had run its course. On wagon trains traveling the overland trails, the outbreak of smallpox created the same response as it did aboard ships. As soon as smallpox was diagnosed, the infected person and all

mune system, fighting off the invading airborne TB bacteria, not only destroyed pulmonary tissue, but also left behind a white residue), it was better known as "consumption" because TB victims seemed to waste and wither away. Those struck by the disease were euphemistically referred to as "invalids." Mid-nineteenth-century physicians, having no idea how to treat the disease, praised Colorado's mountain climate not merely for its effect on health in general but for its especially positive impact on tuberculosis. So many invalids went to Colorado that, for many years, one out of three Coloradans had active TB and one out of every four Coloradans who died did so from the disease. As did California and Oregon, Colorado turned its reputation for healthfulness to commercial advantage. By 1887, Colorado was dotted with sanitariums for the wealthy and was known as much for the white plague as for its mountains and mines. Later, Arizona would also become a major destination for consumptives, principally because of its dry air. Many popular Western histories have pointed out that the murderous, consumptive JOHN HENRY ("DOC") HOLLIDAY was in Tombstone mainly for health reasons when he joined in the gunfight at O.K. Corral.

Any claims the American West had to better health than the other sections of the country were laid to rest by the fearsome cholera epidemics of 1850, 1851, and 1852. Asiatic cholera, or cholera morbus, was caused by food-borne and water-borne bacteria. Striking terror everywhere it cropped up, cholera affected large numbers over vast areas, spread extraordinarily rapidly, caused many deaths accompanied by horrific suffering, and baffled doctors, who could do little but watch suffering patients die. A man healthy one morning might suddenly be struck with intense spasmodic abdominal pains and plagued by watery diarrhea. Dehydrated and prostrate by nighttime, he soon died, only to be tossed in a ditch with all the others victims of the disease. Cholera infantum, a diarrhetic disease that killed scores of infants each summer in Eastern slums, could be found as well on mountain trails and the Great Plains. In fact, diarrhea, associated with any number of diseases, was probably the most common symptom of illness in the West.

But the West did not need a disease like cholera, which roamed the earth, to puncture inflated claims about its healthful environment; it certainly had its own problems. Scurvy, for example, was a common ailment in the West. Traditionally associated with sailors, the disease plagued any population whose diet was devoid of fruit, vegetables, and—though they did not know it in the nineteenth century—vitamin C. The men of STEPHEN HARRIMAN LONG's expedition, surviving on "wild meats and about three ounces of hard bread per day," suffered from scurvy, although the mountain men and the Indians knew enough to protect themselves by eating wild onions and berries and by drinking cactus juice. The American soldier, however, with his regulation diet of bacon, salted beef, biscuits, beans, grease, and coffee, was a prime candidate for scurvy. Early on, the army depended on potash and citric acid to protect against scurvy, but they were not effective. By the mid-nineteenth century, army headquarters provided frontier troops with dried vegetables and urged post commanders to plant gardens.

Miners, too, had their health problems. Doctors, being as greedy as the next person for fast money and the easy life, were no strangers to the gold fields. At first, the doctors participating in the gold rushes found miners an interesting paradox—they lived in unhealthy conditions but seemed quite robust people. Soon, however, physicians noticed that the "hard and laborious" life of miners was taking its toll. Constantly exposed to extremes of heat and cold, eating a monotonous fare of flour-and-water pancakes, a strip or two of fried bacon, and a cup of tea or coffee, and soaking themselves in cold water as they panned for gold, miners came down with rheumatic illnesses and pneumonia, the latter perhaps the most dreaded disease of the mining camps. In addition, there was the mysterious Rocky Mountain fever. No one was ever quite sure whether it was one disease or several, but it may well have been typhoid. Typhoid certainly became one of the banes of the mining camps and towns, where a miner's wages went for a bunk, some grub, lots of whiskey and tobacco, and occasionally paid female companionship and a mine owner's profits went into great mansions, new investments, and bank vaults in distant cities. Neither cared much about pure drinking water, adequate sewers, or bathtubs. Animal carcasses rotted in the streets and alleys; when it rained, the streets turned to mud; on dry days, the air filled with dust. In short, the camps and towns were unhealthy—the streets unsafe, the food contaminated, the air polluted. And not only were miners subject to rheumatism, pneumonia, and typhoid outside the mines, inside the mine shafts, their lungs filled with dust, scarring their tissue, turning them hard as rocks. Known today as "silicosis" (after silica dust), at the time it was called "miner's consumption."

And Westerners were not merely subject to viral, bacteriological, and industrial diseases, but also to social diseases. So much drinking and carousing went on in the mining camps and cow towns of the West that alcoholism became rampant. In the Chinatowns of the Far West and the Chinese railroad camps, lonely and overworked laborers retired to opium dens and brief oblivion, and from there, opium use spread especially among prostitutes. Gamblers, cowboys, and hard-rock miners also used morphine and heroin, both opium derivatives, the first used as a painkiller in the Civil War, the second as a sedative for children. Over-the-counter laudanum, an opium-laced concoction, and cocaine also became common means of escape from an often brutal existence. And in the red-light districts of the booms towns, venereal disease was ubiquitous.

The rudimentary nature of Western medicine, the laissez-faire attitude of Western business, and the deplorably unhealthy working conditions and personal habits of many Westerners in general added to the already normally high toll claimed by disease in nineteenth-century America.

—*Charles Phillips*

SEE ALSO: Bent Brothers; Doctors; Medicine; Native American Cultures: Disease; Nursing

SUGGESTED READING:

Crossen, F. *Mining Camp Doctor and Other Stories.* Boulder, Colo., 1966.
Hopkins, D. R. *Princes and Peasants: Smallpox in History.* Chicago, 1983.
Jones, Billy M. *Health Seekers in the Southwest, 1817–1900.* Norman, Okla., 1967.
Rosenberg, Charles. *The Cholera Years: The United States in 1832, 1849, 1866.* Chicago, 1987.
Shikes, Robert H. *Rocky Mountain Medicine.* Boulder, Colo., 1986.

DIVORCE

Around the middle of the eighteenth century, as romantic love rather than patriarchal duty became the core of the ideal relationship, marriage in America began to take on a new meaning for people. The change may well have had to do with, among other things, a growing industrialization and a gradual shift toward urban life. Just as in Europe, where the romantic movement was a reaction to industrial ugliness, Americans responded to the threat urban life, which frequently split home from work, posed to conjugal unity by conceiving of marriage as more a matter of companionship and less an affair of dynastic continuity. One result was the appearance of what some historians refer to as the ideology (or cult) of domesticity and others call the CULT OF TRUE WOMANHOOD. As husbands, separated from their families during the day, grew to depend more on their mates' management of the households, women's status rose not so much by a repudiation of their traditional tasks as by the politicizing of their "sphere" and the expansion within it of female responsibilities. Household duties became infused with high moral purpose, and women charged with the moral

well-being of their families were transformed from the more lustful and carnal gender they had once been considered to be to the "passionless" sex. Certainly by the middle of the nineteenth century, women were believed to be by nature more moral than men, and marriage had become a partnership between mutually attracted individuals.

The cult of domesticity and the new companionate marriage took root easily in the American West, where a rapidly industrializing economy threatened to overwhelm family values on the one hand, and where, on the other, the notion of COMMUNITY PROPERTY had long held sway. Imported by the Spanish, community property treated marriage much like a business partnership as opposed to English common law, which subordinated a woman's legal rights of ownership to her husband's rights after marriage. Community property comported better with the companionate marriage and—once the increased expectations for marriage began to fall short of the ideal—more easily accommodated divorce. Guardians of a Victorian civilization that emphasized social respectability, strict personal morality, duty, hard work, sobriety, and moral autonomy, frontier women struggled against the rampant prostitution and drinking of a region previously inhabited mostly by males. Women also built schools, enforced the observance of the Sabbath, and, in general, tried to build a new civilization in the West, all under the auspices of the domestic ideal. According to Robert Griswold, marriages that did not reflect these values increasingly broke up as the century progressed. In the West, where the laws were kinder, the number of eligible men much higher, and the ability to go out and find work for themselves greater, women considered divorce less a threat to their status and their future. By the late 1870s, in some areas of the West, divorce seemed an epidemic. In 1876, in the hard-rock mining country of Lewis and Clark County, Montana, for example, one out of every three marriages ended in divorce, and a middle-class wife in nearby Helena remarked the next year, "Divorces are common here and it is a common remark that a man in the mountains cannot keep his wife."

It was in California in 1851 that new divorce laws first established that a man or women could sue for divorce after cohabitating for six months on any of the following grounds: impotency, adultery, extreme cruelty, willful desertion or neglect, habitual intemperance, fraud, and conviction of a felony. Although it might seem that those seeking legal dissolution would be mostly people who could afford divorces—those middle-class and wealthy families with high enough expectations about marriage to suffer sufficient disappointment to take what was still, at the time, drastic measures—instead, the majority filing for divorces in California following the law's passage were blue collar, perhaps, Griswold speculates, indicating that heightened marital demands affected people from all classes. In Montana, where divorce laws were based on those in California and Colorado, allegations of cruelty soon outnumbered those of adultery in divorce cases. At first, the courts held that cruelty, if used as grounds for divorce, needed to be life-threatening, not merely a single blow, not even one or two severe beatings, but repeated attacks numbering at least three, with the final abuses more deadly than those previous. But even in the early days in California, judges ruled that a woman's finer sensibilities deserved respect and that accusations of sexual misconduct—adultery was the primary reason men sued for divorce—constituted great cruelty to a lady of feeling, purity of thought, and refined sensibility. By century's end, mental cruelty, too, became grounds for divorce, and wives—who were the ones usually suing for divorce on the grounds of cruelty—complained to the courts about cold and aloof husbands as well as about drunken, loutish, lazy, and abusive mates. Although increasingly willing to grant women divorces, Western courts on the other hand rarely awarded alimony and hardly ruled on child custody; instead, they relied on traditional assumptions that the children would remain with their mothers except in cases of manifest unfitness.

Women's rising sense of personal autonomy and the emergence of sexually segregated and sharply defined spheres during the last two centuries had combined to reshape decisively personal relations within the family and had changed the meaning of manhood, womanliness, and the sanctity of marriage. The high rate of divorce, particularly in the West, provided clear evidence of the change. From 1870 to 1880, the population in the United States increased by slightly more than 30 percent, but the divorce rate grew by almost 80 percent. In California during the same period, the population doubled, but the divorce rate soared by 130 percent. Not surprisingly, in the late 1880s, many Americans—not just those in the West—were already talking about a "divorce crisis." In the 1990s, with the overall divorce rate in America hovering around 50 percent for all marriages, the West—with its Hollywoods, its Renos, and its Las Vegases—maintained its traditional reputation as a region for frequent and quick divorces.

—*Charles Phillips and Patricia Hogan*

SUGGESTED READING:

Blake, Nelson. *The Road to Reno: A History of Divorce in the United States.* New York, 1962.

Faragher, John Mack. *Men and Women on the Oregon Trail.* New Haven, Conn., 1979.

Griswold, Robert L. *Family and Divorce in California, 1850–1890.* Albany, N.Y., 1982.

Petrik, Paula. "If She Be Content: The Development of Montana Divorce Law, 1865–1907." *Western Historical Quarterly* 18:3 (July 1987): 261–291.

DOCTORS

The first Euro-America doctors in the trans-Mississippi West were probably military surgeons. Army surgeons, some of them civilian doctors under contract, not only ministered to the expeditions and treated their garrisons, they frequently tended to the surrounding ranches and settlements. A number of them remained in the West to open their own practices when their army duties ended, and many of the army's better-known surgeons—William Gorgas, George Sternberg, and Walter Reed—put in their time on the frontier. Civilian doctors accompanied early Western expeditions. For ZEBULON MONTGOMERY PIKE's 1806 reconnaissance of the Southwest, General JAMES P. WILKINSON recruited Dr. John H. Robinson, who soon became friendly with Pike and something of his right-hand man. Given Wilkinson's penchant for conspiracy, it should have been no surprise when Robinson at one point left the expedition for a mysterious trip to Santa Fe. By the time Spanish authorities caught up to Pike in present-day Colorado and arrested him, Robinson was already languishing in jail, and there the two were reunited. Doctors accompanied many expeditions not merely because of their medical skills, but also because they were more likely to be trained in other scientific fields. This certainly was the case with Dr. EDWIN JAMES, who traveled with Major STEPHEN HARRIMAN LONG on his explorations in 1820. A geologist and botanist, James's scientific credentials were far more impressive than his medical studies, which he had undertaken as an apprentice to his physician brother. Long had been ordered to vaccinate any Indians he met along the way against smallpox, but as Dr. James—who doubled as the expedition's chronicler—reported, the vaccine had been ruined when a keelboat overturned on the Missouri River.

Civilian doctors in the West frequently not only practiced medicine but took up other work as well. They doubled as preachers, opened drug stores, bought mineral claims, became miners, wrote for newspapers, and played prominent roles in the civic and economic affairs of state, territorial, and local governments. CHARLES ROBINSON and J. P. Root, for example, actively participated in the territorial councils leading to statehood for Kansas. Robinson became the state's first governor; Root, his lieutenant-governor. Many doctors turned to additional fields of endeavor because their patients were frequently slow and reluctant to pay them. A number of nineteenth-century doctors complained quite publicly that if only they could collect their fees, their money worries would be over. Instead, cash-strapped pioneers sent them fruit, vegetables, and meat or offered their own services in return, such as painting houses, repairing roofs, or chopping firewood. Since many stretches of the West suffered from a dearth of physicians, particularly before Western medical schools began graduating them after the 1830s, doctors saw patients infrequently and often contracted with them for yearly services. Frequent illnesses or accidents cost nothing extra beyond these contracts, under which physicians treated the entire family and provided the necessary medicines as well. Not a few doctors joined frontier lawyers and preachers in circuit riding, traveling for a week or fortnight at a time and living with their patients en route. They gathered herbs along the road, carried their often ineffective medicines and their rude medical equipment in their saddlebags, and worked in unhealthy and unsanitary conditions in the open or in cheerless sod homes and adobe dwellings. Ultimately, a number of nineteenth-century physicians penned self-help medi-

The first doctors in the West likely were surgeons accompanying military expeditions. Valentine T. McGillycuddy, surgeon and topographer, accompanied General George Crook's 1876 expedition to the Black Hills of South Dakota. *Courtesy National Archives.*

cal books as guides to domestic medicine, the best-known being perhaps *Gunn's Domestic Medicine, or Poor Man's Friend* by John C. Gunn.

Not all those practicing medicine in the West were as qualified as they said they were. By the mid-nineteenth century, most states had done away with licensing laws, and pretty much anyone who called himself a doctor and looked, acted, and talked like a doctor could be a doctor. Not until medicine became more scientific in the late nineteenth century and doctors formed professional associations that regulated their own members could patients be sure that the man, and occasionally the woman, who held their lives and limbs in hand knew much more than they did about what he or she was doing. Even after major advances in medical knowledge began to transform health-care practices, many doctors stuck to the old ways—blood-letting and leeching people with fevers, stuffing them with emetics and strong purgatives, and feeding them poisons like mercury chloride, better known as calomel. Since early doctors' offices were often nothing more than hastily set up tents, rude cabins, or huts, they did not necessarily inspire confidence. Many Westerners were leery of physicians whose black bags contained little more than instruments of torture, such as lancets and a set of cups, along with the awful tasting and, in some cases, actually sickening medicines, including calomel, jalap, quinine, laudanum, various smelly salves, and a few of the doctors' personal favorites, often alcohol-based. Sometimes they carried cocaine for topi-cal anesthesia, carbolic acid for antisepsis, bromides, belladonna, ergot, and perhaps a little morphine to kill the pain they caused. Bandages, dressings, and splints were improvised on the spot. Not surprisingly, in many Western homes, doctors were called in only as a last resort, even among those who could afford to pay for them.

The nature of their work dictated that doctors keep horses, either in a barn of their own or at stables in town. As trails became roads in the West, the horse and buggy became known as "the doctor's best friend," and doctors were often as knowledgeable about horses, saddles, and harnesses as they were about medicine, in some cases more so. When automobiles began to appear in the late 1890s, doctors were among the first to adopt this new mode of transportation, although dirt roads, deeply rutted, rocky, frequently muddy, often icy and snow-packed, led the more thoughtful to continue stabling horses. By then, doctors in general were becoming more respected in the West. Almost all of them were married; divorce was rare; and small families numbering two children were common.

Doctors' wives not only put up with unpredictable hours and late nights but had to keep themselves at

Doctors in the West often treated man-made afflictions. A horse-drawn stretcher carries a soldier wounded in the Battle of Slim Buttes, South Dakota, in 1876. *Courtesy National Archives.*

was quite similar to that of the urban East, outside of, perhaps, the wild and woolly mining camps and towns and the cow towns, where accidents, brawls, and gunfights added to the usual deadly toll of nineteenth-century diseases and epidemics. In other words, the differences, such as they were, lay not in the doctors themselves, nor in their rudimentary profession, but in the environmental and economic realities of a quickly industrialized, booming region of the country.

—*Charles Phillips*

SEE ALSO: Disease; Medicine; Native American Cultures: Disease, Spiritual Life

SUGGESTED READING:

Flexner, James T. *Doctors on Horseback: Pioneers of American Medicine.* New York, 1937. Reprint. 1969.

Shikes, Robert H. *Rocky Mountain Medicine: Doctors, Drugs, and Disease in Early Colorado.* Boulder, Colo., 1986.

Starr, Paul. *The Social Transformation of American Medicine: The Rise of a Sovereign Profession and the Making of a Vast Industry.* New York, 1982.

DODGE, GRENVILLE MELLEN

the peak of health; friends, as well as patients, expected a doctor's wife to avoid illness and, if she did get sick, to recover promptly and fully under her husband's care. A few doctors were themselves women, although like BETHENIA ANGELINA OWENS-ADAIR, who received her M.D. in 1881, they were shunned by many male physicians, excluded from hospitals and medical societies, and referred to derisively as "doctoresses" or as "Mrs. Doctor So-and-So." It was difficult for women to gain admission to medical schools, and when they graduated, they often found their practices limited to women and children. Still, by 1901 in Colorado, for example, 106 women had been licensed to practice medicine, women were being admitted to the medical schools, and gradually they were making a few inroads into hospitals and governmental institutions and agencies dealing with medicine.

In general, doctors and their medical practice throughout the nineteenth century varied little from that of doctors in other regions of the country, except for, perhaps, the more rugged conditions they had to contend with in the arid lands of the Southwest and the windswept Rocky Mountains. City practice, too,

Born in Danvers, Massachusetts, civil engineer Grenville Mellen Dodge (1831–1916) was responsible for much of the railroad construction in the West in the decades after the Civil War. Educated at Durham Academy in New Hampshire and Norwich University in Vermont, Dodge graduated from the latter institution as a military and civil engineer in 1851. He developed his skills as a railroad engineer during the 1850s and moved to Illinois and then to Council Bluffs, Iowa, in 1853. Commissioned a colonel at the beginning of the Civil War, he rose to the rank of major general of volunteers. He fought battles in the West and was wounded at Atlanta, but his most important work in the war was building railroads and bridges for the advancing Union army. At the Chattahoochee River, he supervised the construction, in three days, of a bridge 14 feet high and 710 feet long.

In 1866, Dodge became chief engineer of the UNION PACIFIC RAILROAD and supervised construction of the segment of the transcontinental line from the East to Utah until its completion in 1869. At the same time, he served one term in Congress as a Republican from 1867 to 1869. Although he refused to run for other offices, Dodge played an important role in Iowa Republican politics.

After completing the Union Pacific, Dodge served as chief engineer for the Texas and Pacific until its failure in 1873. In the next decade, he supervised construction of more than nine thousand miles of track for the Denver, Texas and Fort Worth and the Denver, Texas and Gulf railroads. Rather than retire, he built railroads in Cuba between 1898 and 1903. He also surveyed more than sixty thousand miles of railroad line in the Midwest, West, and Cuba.

At the end of his career, he lectured on the Civil War, Western expansion, and Western heroes. In Council Bluffs, his fourteen-room home is now a national landmark.

—*Patrick H. Butler, III*

SEE ALSO: Railroads; Transcontinental Railroad Surveys

SUGGESTED READING:

Dodge, Grenville M. *How We Built the Union Pacific Railway.* New York, 1910.
Hirshorn, Stanley P. *Grenville M. Dodge: Soldier, Politician, Railroad Pioneer.* New York, 1967.

DODGE, HENRY

Born in Vincennes, Indiana, Henry Dodge (1782–1867) was a businessman, militia leader, army officer, and Wisconsin politician.

As a lead miner and distiller in Missouri, Dodge became sheriff of the St. Genevieve district in 1805, the federal marshal in Missouri, and a militia general. In 1827, he moved to Wisconsin. There he led militiamen in the Winnebago scare of 1827 and in the 1832 BLACK HAWK'S WAR.

After serving as an army officer, Dodge became territorial governor of Wisconsin in 1836. From 1841 to 1845, he served as a territorial delegate to Congress and then as governor again. In 1848, he became a U.S. senator serving until his retirement in 1857.

—*Roger L. Nichols*

SUGGESTED READING:
Nichols, Roger L. *General Henry Atkinson: A Western Military Career.* Norman, Okla., 1965.

DODGE CITY, KANSAS

The worldwide symbol of Western violence, Dodge City, KANSAS, is the most famous of the frontier CATTLE TOWNS. Motivated by the approach of the ATCHISON, TOPEKA AND SANTA FE tracks in 1872, itinerant merchants joined officers from nearby Fort Dodge in townsite speculation at the railroad's southernmost dip, an ideal point for off-loading merchandise bound for the Texas Panhandle and New Mexico. Platted in 1873, the village served as a temporary center for collecting and shipping buffalo hides. Recognizing that the lucrative traffic in Texas cattle would be closed off by settlement beyond Wichita, railroad officials shifted the cattle trade down the line from Wichita to Dodge. For ten years beginning in 1876, thousands of "through" Texas cattle arrived via the western extension of the Chisholm Trail, the more direct Western Trail, and eventually shorter routes from the Panhandle. At Dodge City, cattle dealers and ranchers purchased beef for shipment to Eastern packing houses or, more frequently, for trailing to ranges to the north for fattening.

Unlike Wichita, frontier Dodge City never became more than a village. In 1880, it contained 1,275 citizens; in 1885 only 1,402. The railroad dominated its economy, which featured, in addition to the cattle trade, a division terminus with a work force somewhat more "working class" than in other cattle towns: in 1880, 26 percent of its employed were laborers.

Banks as well as the railroad reaped institutional profits through discounting the large volume of paper passing over their counters and through interest on large short-term loans to cattlemen who owed money both to their employees and to the ranchers from whom they had bought their herds. Drovers also required cash for current expenses. Groceries outclassed any other single item of merchandise in sale value, and they remained a staple of the largest "general" businesses in town: the York-Parker-Draper Mercantile Company and Wright, Beverley and Company.

The estimated fifteen hundred transients crowding Dodge City's streets each summer gave its small businesses life. The Dodge House and other hotels served the more affluent, but seasoned commercial veterans such as Henry M. Beverley, a clothier and former Texas cattleman, and John Mueller, manufacturer of fancy boots, sought profits from both drovers and cowboys, as did restaurants, barber shops, and saloons. In 1878, there were eight taverns in Dodge City; in 1879, fourteen; and in 1882, thirteen. Here congregated the town's professional gamblers, their prospects closely linked to the velocity of cattle sales. One "dance house" (a combination saloon, casino, dance hall, and brothel) was established before 1876, and for a time, Dodge City contained three. But normally there were two dance houses—one staffed by white women for the exclusive patronage of white males; the other staffed by African American women and patronized by whites and blacks alike. Local reformers attacked such "immoral" entrepreneurship with increasing ferocity in the 1880s and were aided, at one point, by railroad officials concerned about their line's corporate image.

Lawlessness had, in fact, characterized Dodge City's pre–cattle-trade career. Perhaps fifteen men died violently there in 1872 and 1873, before troops from Fort Dodge finally rescued the town from a band of vigilantes-turned-terrorists. Anticipating the cattle trade, citizens organized Dodge City as a municipality in 1875 and enacted violence-suppression measures including gun control. In at least one season, a prominent sign warned: "The Carrying of Fire Arms Strictly Prohibited." Dodge's several lawmen—carefully ranked as marshal, assistant marshal, and policemen—enforced these social controls. Since drinking, gambling, and whoring conspired with illegal weaponry to cause violence, a covert monthly tax on saloonkeepers, gamblers, and prostitutes helped finance the police, whose salaries composed nearly half the municipal budget.

Dodge City's actual homicide rate was low during its years as a cattle town from 1876 to 1885—15 victims in all, an average of only 1.5 per year. None died in the stylized street duel of Hollywood convention. One, indeed, was a woman. In two cattle-trading seasons and possibly a third, no homicides at all occurred in Dodge City, and only in 1878 did the number rise to as many as 5. The famous gunfighters JOHN HENRY ("DOC") HOLLIDAY and BARTHOLOMEW (BAT) MASTERSON lived in Dodge City without killing anyone. In his only lethal encounter during his career in Dodge City, policeman (never marshal) Wyatt Earp helped slay a celebrating cowboy.

In 1884, Kansas's governor quarantined the state against Texas cattle, the carriers of splenic fever, also known as TEXAS FEVER. That year and the next, agricultural settlers overran Dodge City's outlying cattle ranges, thus ending the traditional drives from Texas and Dodge City's life as a cattle town.

—*Robert R. Dykstra*

SUGGESTED READING:
Dykstra, Robert R. *The Cattle Towns.* New York, 1968.

DODGE CITY WAR

In 1883, the growing family-oriented population of cattle town Dodge City, Kansas, elected Larry E. Deger mayor. Promising to "clean up" the town, Deger arrested female "singers" at LUKE SHORT'S Long Branch saloon; other female saloon entertainers were not ar-

"Dodge City Peace Commission," 1890. *Courtesy National Archives.*

rested. Angered by the attack on his business, Short met Officer L. S. Hartman on the street and began firing. When Hartman tripped, Short thought he had killed the lawman. Barricading himself in a saloon, Short eventually surrendered to a posse, which ushered him out of town. He sought Governor George W. Glick's aid in returning to Dodge City, and when help from the governor was not forthcoming, he called on friends BARTHOLOMEW (BAT) MASTERSON and Wyatt Earp. Several gunfighters returned, strutted menacingly around town, and had their picture taken. Later, the picture with superimposition was facetiously labeled "The Dodge City Peace Commission" with the bogus claim that the gunmen had "tamed the town." Reports of violence carried the "war" beyond Dodge City. The furor and exaggerated newspaper reports caused Atchison, Topeka and Santa Fe officials to threaten to move the railroad facilities if a better moral climate were not established. The prospect of financial loss forced reforms. This bloodless war was the beginning of the downfall of the old cattle-town leadership and the triumph of antisaloon and other reformers.

—*C. Robert Haywood*

SEE ALSO: Cattle Towns; Earp Brothers

SUGGESTED READING:
Haywood, C. Robert. *Victorian West: Class and Culture in Kansas Cattle Towns.* Lawrence, Kans., 1991.

DOHENY, EDWARD LAURENCE

An oil baron implicated in the TEAPOT DOME scandal, Edward Laurence Doheny (1856–1935) was born near Fond du Lac, Wisconsin, the son of Patrick Doheny, an Irish immigrant, and Eleanor Elizabeth Quigley of Newfoundland. Leaving school at the age of sixteen, Doheny drove mules for the geological survey of the Arizona–New Mexico boundary, considered surveying, but turned to gold prospecting over the next twenty years. In 1892, while walking in Los Angeles, he saw a wagonload of brown earth, called "brea" or "pitch," which was used for fuel. After learning that the brea came from a field near Westlake Park, he leased a vacant lot, with Charles A. Canfield, and began digging, first by hand and then with a drill, for oil. Bringing in a field at a depth of 225 feet, Doheny launched an oil boom in Los Angeles.

In 1900, at the suggestion of A. A. Robinson, president of the Mexican Central Railway, Doheny explored for oil near Tampico, slated for use by the railway. By the time he struck oil, the management of the railway had changed, so Doheny used the oil for asphalt to pave the roads of Mexico City and other large urban areas. Encouraged by the increase in demand for oil following the appearance of the automobile, he organized the Mexican Petroleum Company of California and developed Tampico and Tuxpan fields. He maintained good relations with Mexican President Porfirio Díaz, but his fortunes were uncertain following the Mexican Revolution. Stock in his companies fluctuated.

In 1922, Doheny's company, the Pan-American Petroleum Company, undertook a contract from the U.S. government to build a naval fuel station at Pearl Harbor and received drilling rights to oil reserves at Elk Hills, California. When it became known that he had given Secretary of the Interior ALBERT B. FALL one hundred thousand dollars in an unsecured, interest-free loan, an investigation followed, which led to the cancellation of his contracts, restitution of profits, and trials for bribery and conspiracy. In 1926, both Doheny and Fall were acquitted of conspiracy. In 1930, however, Fall was convicted of receiving a bribe, although Doheny was not convicted of giving one.

During this period, Doheny's only son was killed by a servant. As a memorial to his son, Doheny built a library at the University of Southern California. He died at Beverly Hills, California, after a three-year illness.

—*Patrick H. Butler, III*

SEE ALSO: Oil and Gas Industry

SUGGESTED READING:
La Botz, Dan. *Edward L. Doheny: Petroleum, Power, and Politics in the United States and Mexico.* New York, 1991.

DOLAN, JAMES

SEE: Lincoln County War

DOLE, SANFORD B.

President of the Republic of HAWAII and first governor of the Territory of Hawaii, Sanford B. Dole (1844–1926) was born in Honolulu, the son of the Reverend Daniel Dole and his wife Emily, New England missionaries, who had arrived on the island in 1841. Dole spent his early years in Hawaii until he went to Williams College in Massachusetts in 1866. After graduating, he studied law in Boston and returned to Honolulu in 1868 to practice law. He wrote for various newspapers on political topics and was elected to the Hawaii legislature in 1884 and 1886. As a member of the Reform party, Dole criticized King David Kalakaua for his expenditures and the choice of his advisers, particularly Walter Murray Gibson and CLAUS SPRECKELS. He joined the Hawaiian League, an opposition group that forced Kalakaua to accept the Constitution of 1887 (the Bayonet Constitution) limiting royal powers. As one of the concessions to the reformers, Kalakaua appointed Dole to the Hawaii Supreme Court in 1887.

As a supreme court justice, Dole favored reform, rather than overthrow, of the monarchy and did not participate with the committee of safety that planned the Hawaiian Revolution. Once the revolution took place and Queen LILIOUKALANI was dethroned in January 1893, the committee asked Dole to become head of the provisional government set up to replace the monarchy, supposedly because of his rapport with both haoles (Caucasians) and Hawaiians.

As head of the provisional government, Dole refused to accept the request of U.S. President Grover Cleveland to restore Lilioukalani to power. Dole claimed the United States had no right to interfere with Hawaii's internal affairs. When it became clear that annexation to the United States would not be achieved under Cleveland, Dole helped create the Republic of Hawaii in 1894. He served as its only president (1894 to 1898) and defeated a royalist counterrevolution in 1895. After annexation was secured in 1898, Dole was a member of the commission that restructured the republic as a U.S. territory. He served as the first territorial governor (1900 to 1903) and then as a federal judge (1903 to 1915).

—*John S. Whitehead*

SUGGESTED READING:

Allen, Helena G. *Sanford Ballard Dole: Hawaii's Only President, 1844–1926.* Glendale, Calif., 1988.

Dole, Sanford Ballard. *Memoirs of the Hawaiian Revolution.* Honolulu, 1936.

DOLE, WILLIAM P.

Commissioner of Indian Affairs from 1861 to 1865, William P. Dole (1811–1889) was born in Danville, Vermont. He rejected the family occupation of farming and opted instead for a political career. In 1838, as a candidate of the Whig party, he was elected to the Indiana legislature and then to the state senate in 1844.

On March 12, 1861, as a reward for his successful efforts at the Republican National Convention to swing the votes of the Indiana and Pennsylvania delegations to Abraham Lincoln, he was appointed commissioner of Indian affairs. He soon encountered difficulties in this job.

Dole opposed military control of Indian affairs and had advocated that Native Americans be pressed to adopt the customs of white civilization and become self-reliant and self-supporting through the allotment of land in severalty and the practice of farming and stock raising. During his four years in office, Dole tried to bring all Western tribes into a treaty relationship with the government with a guarantee of rights to unceded lands. The Senate, however, insisted that Indian treaties not include any legal recognition of the Native Americans' title to land.

Dole also advocated the concentration of tribes on a few large reservations and their isolation from whites while being educated for assimilation into mainstream culture. In response to the Chivington Massacre, or the SAND CREEK MASSACRE, of the Cheyennes and Arapahos in November 1864 in Colorado, Congress demanded that all people responsible be removed from office. Dole was forced to resign on July 6, 1865. The Doolittle Committee, formed to investigate the government's dealings with Native Americans, unfairly blackened his reputation by charging him with inefficiency and corruption. Dole remained in Washington,

where he offered legal counsel to both Indians and whites in their claims against the United States government, until his death.

—*Henry E. Fritz and Marie L. Fritz*

SEE ALSO: United States Indian Policy: Reform Movement, Reservations

SUGGESTED READING:

Danziger, Edmund J., Jr. *Indians and Bureaucrats.* Urbana, Ill., 1974.

Kvasnicka, Robert M., and Herman J. Viola, eds. *The Commissioners of Indian Affairs, 1824–1877.* Lincoln, Nebr., 1979.

Nichols, David A. *Lincoln and the Indians.* Columbia, Mo., 1978.

Prucha, Francis Paul. *American Indian Policy in Crisis: Christian Reformers and the Indian, 1865–1900.* Norman, Okla., 1976.

DOLORES, NEW MEXICO

SEE: Ghost Towns

DOMESTIC SERVICE

Historical background

Colonial American housewives, apart from the wealthy slave-owning families in the South, employed neighborhood girls as domestic apprentices to help with the endless housework—cooking, spinning yarn, sewing clothes, and making bread, butter, and cheese—in return for room and board. As the United States began to industrialize at the end of the eighteenth and the beginning of the nineteenth centuries, large numbers of well-to-do urban housewives bought many of the products they might have made for themselves a century before. These housewives also managed the work of live-in servants, who cooked, cleaned, did laundry, served meals, and cared for the families' children. Sometimes, the young female servant fought off sexual assaults from the male head of the house or entered into an illicit, and usually her first, sexual relationship with him. Those making the transition from "help" to "service" were usually rural women or, as the century wore on, immigrants seeking wages in the city.

A majority of America's first-generation of female Irish teenagers worked as live-in domestics after 1840. Along with their male counterparts who took jobs as cooks, footmen, coachmen, and valets, they dwarfed the numbers of free African Americans in the North.

Because Irish women seeking work as domestics were so numerous, black women less frequently found domestic employment (except for heavy spring cleaning or hard tasks, such as laundry), and black men were often unemployed. Irish women became so identified with domestic service in the years before the Civil War that, in some Northeastern cities, domestics were generally called "Bridgets" or "Biddys" even as late as the 1920s.

Domestic service was itself a result of the initial impact of industrialization and urbanization on women laborers. Such work functioned for many of them as a transitional occupation in the shift from unpaid work in the home to wage work outside it and incorporated features of both family labor and employment. Domestic service involved no capital investment, required little division of labor, and reflected a low level of technology. Domestic servants were paid for their time and energy, not for any commodities they produced. And the work itself took place within the women's "sphere," meaning that relations between employer and employee were paternalistic and that work arrangements were casual and unregulated.

Domestic service comes into its own during a phase of rapid industrialization, when a growing urban middle class seeks household help to maintain its life style and when neither commercial services nor household technology are advanced enough to substitute for household labor. The number of people employed in domestic service declines later when a more fully developed economy offers new jobs in manufacturing, sales, and clerical and commercial services.

The post–Civil War United States was a rapidly industrializing nation, especially in the West where an expanding market economy developed from a number of booms in the extractive industries. Around the middle of the nineteenth century, millions of women became part of a vast migrant stream responding to the U.S. economy's call for cheap labor by leaving their homes in Europe, Latin America, and Asia. Some of them came alone, but many of the others were the wives and daughters of immigrating families. The fathers and husbands in these more traditional families, precisely because they had been recruited as "cheap hands," found it difficult to earn a living wage for the entire family, especially since they frequently had destitute kin back home to support as well. Not surprisingly, paid labor for immigrant women became essential for survival.

Already accustomed to the hard toil required in their own poor households, the female immigrants continued their traditional duties to produce domestic goods, raise children, keep house, and transmit their culture—work that was made all the more difficult by harsh conditions in urban slums, BARRIOS, CHINATOWNS, and Little Tokyos. Adding to the difficulty of maintaining their own households was their need to find wage work outside the home. At a time when the middle-class CULT OF TRUE WOMANHOOD demanded that women stay home and cultivate domestic virtues, migrant wives and daughters were forced to take up the double workday. Hampered by language, burdened by housework, unskilled at industrial jobs, facing racial prejudices and gender biases, they were confined to the lowest-paid, least-valued wage work. Although some became field hands and some found work in sweatshops and factories, most went into domestic service.

Domestic service in the United States reached a high-water mark in the second half of the nineteenth century. Even before the Civil War, the availability of land and other economic opportunities contributed to what had become a chronic shortage of labor for domestic service. By 1870, 85 percent of domestics were women, and almost two-thirds of women wage earners not working on farms were live-in servants, laundresses, or domestic day workers. Half the employed female immigrants not working on farms were domestics. This vast tribe of domestic workers began to decline in proportion by the turn of the century, dropping to one-third by 1900, one-fifth by 1930, and one-twentieth by 1970. The sheer numbers employed in service, however, actually doubled between 1870 and 1910 from slightly fewer than one million to around two million. The difference was in who was doing the work. Native white women turned to other work, including factory jobs and teaching. As a result, servants increasingly came from the lowest ranks, those most marginal to the urban economy—recent immigrants, migrants, and the racially ostracized.

Domestic service in the American West

In the North and Midwest, domestics were mostly Irish, German, and Scandinavian immigrants; perhaps a majority of these European-born women worked as servants before they got married, and some scholars claim it was a nearly universal experience for immigrant girls, especially the Irish. In the South, blacks remained the traditional servant caste. In the Southwest, Anglos, who had become a ruling elite since the United States–Mexican War, recruited their domestics from the ranks of the Mexican American women, both those born in America and those who migrated from below the border. Next to agriculture, domestic service became the largest form of employment for Chicanas, and it remained so from the 1880s to at least World War II. But in the Far West, the situation was different from that of the rest of the country.

Like the rest of the West after the Civil War, the California coast and the Pacific Northwest underwent rapid economic development, which created a chronic shortage of labor. Native-born workers, both men and women, could easily find work other than domestic service. If anything, female labor was even more scarce than in other sections of the country because men had migrated westward in far greater numbers than women. Asian men—Chinese—not only worked for low pay as manual laborers and farm hands but also took up jobs traditionally held by white native-born wives and female domestics. Chinese laundrymen and cooks replaced the unpaid labor of housewives, and Chinese house boys and cooks held positions as domestics that elsewhere would have gone to women. Far from the ports of disembarkation for European immigrants and on the wrong side of the country to serve as a destination for the growing emigration of African Americans from the rural South, California and Washington became the only two states where a majority of the domestics were men, and the Chinese made up perhaps a quarter of all domestics.

West Coast domestic wages were the highest in the nation by far, and when the only steady source of domestic labor was cut off abruptly by the Chinese Exclusion Act of 1882, native white women—who had been traveling to the West in ever greater numbers—filled in. By then, not only were there more women in the West, but the heavily extractive nature of Western industrialization—requiring backbreaking work—left fewer options in the work place for women than industrialization in the East had. By 1880, there were more Western women in domestic service than out of it. And, unlike the rest of the country, the number of servants in relation to the number of houses was increasing in California rather than falling. Despite these trends, Chinese house boys—long symbols of upper-class status in San Francisco—remained highly prized as servants; they worked for a third of what the rich paid white domestics, bought their own food, and appeared content to sleep on the kitchen floor or in a shed behind the house rather than demanding their own quarters.

As Chinese house boys began to die out or retire in the first two decades of the twentieth century and the denizens of Nob Hill reflected nostalgically on the "old-time Chinamen," Japanese men succeeded the Chinese in domestic service, just as they had in the building of the railroads and in the tilling of Western plantations. In the 1880s, Japanese schoolboys paid for their tuition and board at Reid's Boarding School in Belmont, California, by doing chores around the house and kitchen work. The term stuck. Any Japanese live-in domestic, regardless of whether he was seeking an education or not and no matter what his age, was called a "schoolboy." But as domestics, the Japanese did learn English and grow familiar with American customs. By 1905, there were enough Japanese men seeking day work as domestics to support employment agencies in San Francisco, Oakland, and Alameda, California. Receiving token wages of around two dollars a week (when trained servants earned anywhere between fifteen dollars and forty dollars a month) at the apex of Japanese immigration between 1904 and 1907, some four thousand were employed as schoolboys in San Francisco. Two years later, the number had dropped by half. A few of the schoolboys "graduated" to become professional servants, butlers, or cooks, but most moved on to other work or opened their own businesses. After 1909, Japanese women, many arriving as PICTURE BRIDES, began to take their place in domestic work.

As Evelyn Nakano Glenn points out, in Europe and Latin America, domestic work was a "bridging" occupation. Live-in jobs cut domestics off from family ties and provided them with an opportunity to observe—and mimic—middle-class ways. Domestic service fostered acculturation and became a means to upward social mobility. In the United States, too, some intergenerational mobility occurred, but it varied depending on race and ethnicity. Young, single European immigrants found live-in work a starting point; they worked after leaving school until they married, and thus their time spent as domestics was limited from early adolescence until their early or mid-twenties. Even if European women remained in domestic service, their daughters shunned such work and looked for jobs as secretaries or sales clerks. But if the daughters of European immigrants moved up and were absorbed into the more developed economy, people of color, routinely barred from skilled crafts, sales, clerical work, and even "light" manufacture, stayed in domestic service or in laundry work, often the only options outside farming for black women in the North, Chicanas in the Southwest, and Japanese American women in northern California. For them, American domestic service was not a bridging but a "ghettoizing" occupation.

Black domestics, South and North, were mostly married women working to support families, and they preferred to live outside the homes where they cleaned, washed, and cooked. For Mexican American women in the ethnically segmented labor markets of the Southwest, domestic service was a similar occupational ghetto. Regardless of where they were born, regardless of whether they were second-generation descendants of the Mexican-born or scions of the earliest Mexican settlers in California or New Mexico, Chicanas had little chance for upward mobility. For

Japanese women, too, domestic work was long an occupational ghetto. Socially segregated from the mainstream culture and entering a racially segmented occupation, Japanese women were isolated and made dependent upon ethnic networks for information about jobs and for connections to get them. Over time, however, says Glenn, Japanese American women, unlike African Americans and Chicanas, managed to break out of the domestic-service ghetto, rarely in the first or even the second generation, as the Euro-Americans had, but at least by the third generation.

Their success, however, did not change the nature of domestic service itself, which in California and the Southwest remains work for society's lowest status women, the very young and the very old, newcomers and racial minorities, the impoverished residents of ghettos and barrios and the increasingly vilified illegal aliens.

—*Patricia Hogan and Charles Phillips*

SEE ALSO: Irish Americans; Japanese Americans; Women in Wage Work; Working-Class Women

SUGGESTED READING:
Glenn, Evelyn Nakano. "The Dialectics of Wage Work: Japanese American Women and Domestic Service, 1905–1940." In *Unequal Sisters: A Multicultural Reader in U.S. Women's History.* Edited by Ellen Carol DuBois and Vicki L. Ruiz. New York, 1990.
———. *Issei, Nisei, War Bride: Three Generations of Japanese American Women in Domestic Service.* Philadelphia, 1986.
Katzman, David. *Seven Days a Week: Women and Domestic Service in Industrializing America.* New York, 1978.
Palmer, Phyllis. *Domesticity and Dirt: Housewives and Domestic Servants in the United States, 1920–1945.* Philadelphia, 1989.
Romero, Mary. *Maid in America.* New York, 1992.

DONALDSON, THOMAS CORWIN

U.S. land officer, land reformer, and key member of the PUBLIC LANDS COMMISSION OF 1879, Thomas Corwin Donaldson (1843–1898) was the author of *The Public Domain* (1880), an original and indispensable compendium and codification of the nearly three thousand congressional acts relating to the federal land system.

Born in Columbus, Ohio, Donaldson graduated from Capital University (Columbus) in 1862, served in the Union Army during the Civil War, studied law, and was admitted to the bar in 1867. Two years after Donaldson passed the bar, President Ulysses S. Grant

appointed him register of the Boise (Idaho Territory) Land Office. Six years later, he joined the first Public Land Commission, formed in Washington, D.C., by Colorado River geologist JOHN WESLEY POWELL. In 1879, President Rutherford B. Hayes named Donaldson to a special five-person commission to codify the land laws, classify the public domain, and recommend future land disposal. As the workhorse of the commission, Donaldson traveled throughout the West for three months and took public testimony from land officers, real-estate agents, lumbermen, miners, farmers, stock-raisers, and land reformers. The commission issued a massive five-volume report in 1880.

This project became the basis for Donaldson's *Public Domain,* which remains the seminal history of the land system. In an expanded and definitive 1884 edition, Donaldson included numerous land-office regulations and instructions and listed all land officers, Indian agents and reservations, and denominational mission stations. The tabular data on land sales compiled by Land Office staff members and the famous—and often reprinted—map of all railroad land grants contain invaluable information. Modern scholars have found occasional errors and discrepancies, but the meticulous Donaldson can usually be trusted.

The Public Domain was a clarion call for land reform. Donaldson criticized Congress for its laxity in land management, castigated speculators of every stripe, and demanded that the remaining public lands be safeguarded. His polemical tone and radical solutions, especially his call to abolish the 160-acre homesteads and preemptions authorized by Congress, aroused special-interest groups. His declaration in 1884 of the closing of the frontier was premature—two hundred thousand homestead claimants took title in the 1880s. Yet Congress, in 1891, ended the sale of public lands. Donaldson had a major hand in the fundamental reform of the land system, which had been based on the Land Ordinance of 1785.

Donaldson was a man of many talents. He published a book of reminiscences of his close friend, the poet Walt Whitman. He recovered the paintings of GEORGE CATLIN and, as an officer of the Smithsonian Institution, prepared the "George Catlin Indian Gallery" in the U.S. National Museum. In 1890, he served as a specialist on Indian cultures for the Census Bureau and wrote reports on the Iroquois nations, Eastern Cherokees, and Pueblo tribes. On the darker side, Donaldson shared the widespread resentment against southern European immigrants who took public lands at the expense of northern Europeans.

—*Robert P. Swierenga*

SEE ALSO: Land Policy

Suggested reading:

Donaldson, Thomas. *The Public Domain: Its History with Statistics*. 3d ed. Washington, D.C., 1884.

Gates, Paul W. *History of Public Land Law Development*. Washington, D.C., 1968.

Robbins, Roy M. *Our Landed Heritage: The Public Domain, 1776–1936*. Lincoln, Nebr., 1962.

DONIPHAN, ALEXANDER WILLIAM

A lawyer and soldier who made his reputation during the United States–Mexican War, Alexander William Doniphan (1808–1887) was born in Mason County, Kentucky. Graduating from Augusta College, the big red-headed Doniphan moved to Missouri to practice law in 1830. There, he served in the militia and was brevetted brigadier general. During the civil discord surrounding Missouri's Mormon colony, Doniphan successfully negotiated with Joseph Smith, Jr., to disarm and remove the Latter-day Saints to Nauvoo, Illinois. With the outbreak of the war with Mexico in 1846, the colorful lawyer was elected colonel of the First Missouri Volunteers, a not atypical group of irregulars, bloodthirsty but determined, who called themselves the "Ring-tailed Roarers."

Under the command of General Stephen Watts Kearny, Doniphan led his volunteers overland to Santa Fe—a route Missourians knew well—and occupied New Mexico, where Kearny put fellow Missourian Charles Bent in the governor's office. Doniphan, with others, drafted the Kearny Code, which became the basic law in the seized territory. Splitting from Kearny, Doniphan first headed west to Bear Springs near today's Arizona state line, where he signed a treaty with fourteen Navajo chiefs, among them Ganado Mucho. Then Doniphan turned south on December 14, accompanied by five hundred men and a 315-wagon caravan of Santa Fe traders seeking to sell their wares, war or no war. At Brazito, thirty miles north of El Paso, his ragtag army defeated twelve hundred spit-and-polish Mexican regulars. Doniphan's triumph was brief; learning that a rebellion in Taos had cut off his supplies, he headed south again, toward Cuidad Chihuahua, this time with around one thousand men. Driving headlong without quartermaster, postmaster, commissary, uniforms, tents, or formal discipline, the Ring-tailed Roarers reached Chihuahua on February 27, 1847. There, Doniphan defeated twenty-seven hundred Mexican regulars and an additional one thousand rancheros.

During the battle of Sacramento, the Mexicans' powder failed them—a common occurrence—and Doniphan's volunteers simply dodged slow-moving cannonballs while they returned fire with devastating chain shot. Doniphan seemed to many to epitomize the dry, drawling Anglo-American Westerner when he directed the battle from his horse. Whittling all the while as the cannonballs rolled in, he paused to remark, "Well, they're giving us hell now, boys." Although he had lost only one man killed and five wounded, Doniphan was, nevertheless, deep behind the enemy lines. He went on the march again, traveling one thousand more miles across completely unfamiliar country to rendezvous with General Zachary Taylor's main force at Saltillo and then, discovering that Taylor had already moved on, trooped to the Gulf Coast and on to New Orleans. There, "Doniphan's Thousand," as they came to be called, were discharged from service. In a single year, they had marched six thousand miles and defeated two armies, an amazing military feat made all the more extraordinary by the fact that Doniphan was so easy-going an officer, disinclined to give orders and caring little for army discipline.

After the war, Doniphan—who had already served two terms in the Missouri legislature in 1836 and 1840—again held office in 1854. The very victories that made his reputation helped edge the country toward civil war over whether to settle the vast new Western territories won from Mexico as slave states or free. Among those traveling officially to Washington in 1861 to seek an alternative to civil war, Doniphan served briefly as a Union major general in the Missouri State Guard after the war broke out. Continuing to practice law in Missouri, Doniphan died in 1887 in Richmond, Missouri.

—*Charles Phillips*

Suggested reading:

Eisenhower, John S. D. *The U.S. War with Mexico, 1846–1848*. New York, 1989.

Hughes, John T. *Doniphan's Expedition, Containing an Account of the Conquest of New Mexico*. New York, 1973.

DONNELLY, IGNATIUS

Ignatius Donnelly (1831–1901) became one of the West's more colorful political thinkers and writers. Born in Philadelphia and educated as a lawyer, Donnelly moved west to central Minnesota in 1856. Aligning himself with the new Republican party, Donnelly became lieutenant-governor and, in 1861 during the mobilization for the Civil War, acting governor. From 1863 to 1869, he served in Congress, where he was considered to be a leading Radical Republican. Losing a party fight in 1868, he left the Republican party and claimed that the great battle of the future would be "between humanity and property, between men and money."

Choosing to serve humanity, Donnelly became an independent and fought against the protective tariff. He briefly returned to the Republican party in 1872 as a supporter of Horace Greeley's presidential campaign. By 1873, Donnelly had left the party again to become active in the Grange and the Anti-Monopoly party, which elected him to the state senate. The decline of the Anti-Monopoly movement saw him lose power, but he returned to active politics as a leader of the Greenback movement and was reelected to the state legislature in 1878. After a failed bid for Congress, an election his opponent may have won by fraudulent tactics, he returned to Nininger, where he began writing.

In 1882, Donnelly's first book, *Atlantis,* an effort to prove the lost continent had existed in the Atlantic, was published to great success. His next book, *Ragnorak,* dealt with the origins of the earth. The success of these two works led to the start of his career as a lecturer. He returned to politics in an unsuccessful campaign for Congress in 1884. Two years later, he was elected to the Minnesota legislature, in part, through the efforts of the Farmers' Alliance. In 1888, Donnelly received a setback during a complicated set of political maneuvers: he ran for governor on the Farmer Labor ticket, withdrew from the race to support the Republicans a few weeks before the election, and then ran as a Democrat for a seat in the state legislature while hoping the legislature would select him as a United States senator.

Donnelly continued to write, and among his new work was an attempt to prove that Francis Bacon was the author of William Shakespeare's works. In 1889, Donnelly published *Caesar's Column,* a utopian novel predicting that in 1988 there would be television, radio, and poison gas and that the United States would be ruled by a ruthless financial oligopoly that dominated the working class.

Donnelly became allied with the growing Populist movement. He wrote the preamble to its Omaha platform, a severe indictment of American society. By the time of his death, his name had become synonymous with reform. While known today as a speculative writer, he had a tremendous impact on the reform movements in the upper Midwest during the last half of the nineteenth century and evolved into a severe critic of the laissez-faire traditions in American society.

—*Patrick H. Butler, III*

See also: Agrarianism; Greenback Party; Populism

Suggested reading:
Ridge, Martin. *Ignatius Donnelly: The Portrait of a Politician.* New York, 1962.

DONNER PARTY

During the winter of 1845, James Frazier Reed and Jacob and George Donner decided to leave their homes in Illinois and move to California after reading *The Emigrants' Guide to Oregon and California* by Lansford Warren Hastings. The book touted California as a place "where perennial spring and never failing autumn stand side by side" and recommended a route to California beginning in Independence, Missouri. The author suggested travelers proceed northwestward to the Kansas-Nebraska region, move on to the North Fork of the Platte River to Fort Laramie, cross the Continental Divide, and then proceed southwestward to Fort Bridger. From there, the author suggested a route that would cut two or three hundred miles from the journey: southwest to the Salt Lake Desert, west to the Humboldt River, and down to San Francisco Bay.

On April 15, 1846, emigrants gathered at Springfield, Illinois, to begin their trek across the country. Among the travelers were George and Tamsen Donner and five children from his previous marriages; Jacob and Elizabeth Donner and their seven children; and James and Margaret Reed, their three children, and James Reed's mother, known as Grandma Keyes. Other families included the Eddys, Breens, Murphys, Pikeses, Kesebergs, Wolfingers, Graves, and McCutchens.

Seventy-two wagons started from Springfield. By the time the caravan reached Independence, it included almost three hundred wagons. Once the group crossed the Sandy River and arrived at Fort Laramie, George Donner was elected captain of a caravan of about forty wagons.

The group traveled on to Fort Bridger, where the travelers discussed the shortcut proposed by Hastings's book—the so-called Hastings Cutoff. While some of the group opted for the trail to Fort Hall, George and Jacob Donner, the Reeds, and others decided to proceed to the shortcut. The Donner and Reed group found the trail through the Wasatch Mountains to be nearly impassable, and the trek across the Salt Lake Desert was grueling. The shortcut turned out to be a trail of horror and despair. As they headed for the Humboldt River, the eighty-nine emigrants began quarreling; one man was murdered, and his killer was banished from the group. Indians preyed on their livestock. On October 23, they prepared to enter the Sierra

Nevada. Toward the end of October, the advance party reached Truckee Lake (now called Donner Lake), while the remainder stayed behind at Prosser Creek to repair a broken wagon. Then a storm blew in, dumping six inches of snow on the ground and drifts three to five feet deep on the passes. The emigrants pressed ahead but were driven back by sleet. After another storm blew in that night, the emigrants knew they were trapped in the mountains. At both Donner Lake and Prosser Creek, they built shelters and huddled in them as the snows continued to fall and their food supplies dwindled. They could neither continue forward nor return. Most of the cattle had to be killed.

Fifteen individuals, later known as the "Forlorn Hope," set out to try to reach California by foot. With barely enough rations to last six days, they left the others on December 16. By Christmas Day, the Forlorn Hope travelers had been without food for four days, and they knew that if any of them were to reach civilization, one of them must die. They drew lots but then could not carry through the plan to kill one of their members. Two days later, after another snow storm had blanketed them, they found that four of their members had died. The survivors then stripped, roasted, and ate the flesh of the dead and tried to regain their strength. As they pressed on, their stores of flesh were exhausted; when the two Indian guides with them collapsed on the trail—they had refused to eat the human meat—the survivors shot and ate them. On January 10, 1847, the seven remaining members of Forlorn Hope at last reached an Indian village.

The first relief party reached the group camped at Donner Lake on February 19. There, survivors had eaten boiled hides and bones, and they too had resorted to cannibalism.

Of the eighty-nine members of the Donner Party, only forty-five survived. Jacob Donner died. George and Tamsen Donner's children were rescued. Although capable of saving herself, Tamsen Donner chose to remain with her dying husband. She was told that it would be impossible to carry him to safety. When the second rescue party arrived, both Tamsen and George Donner were dead. At the campsite, several pieces of bodies were strewn about—a grim reminder of the horrifying journey to paradise.

—*Fred L. Koestler*

SEE ALSO: California Overland Trails

SUGGESTED READING:
Billington, Ray Allen. *The Far Western Frontier, 1830–1860.* New York, 1956.
Stewart, George Rippey. *Ordeal by Hunger: The Story of the Donner Party.* New York, 1936.

DOOLIN, WILLIAM (BILL)

Bank and train robber William (Bill) Doolin (1858–1896) was born and raised in Arkansas and worked as a cowboy in the Indian Territory. In 1892, he joined the DALTON GANG. Following the gang's disastrous raid on Coffeyville, Kansas, Doolin formed a new outlaw band and embarked on a spectacular spree of bank and train robberies. He quickly became one of the more notorious outlaws in the Southwest. In 1893, his band killed three lawmen in a shootout at Ingalls in the Oklahoma Territory. Captured in Arkansas in 1896 by Deputy U.S. Marshal WILLIAM MATTHEW TILGHMAN, JR., he soon broke out of jail. He was shot to death by Deputy HENRY ANDREW ("HECK") THOMAS in Lawson, Oklahoma.

—*John Boessenecker*

SEE ALSO: Social Banditry

SUGGESTED READING:
Hanes, Bailey C. *Bill Doolin, Outlaw O. T.* Norman, Okla., 1968.
Shirley, Glenn. *West of Hell's Fringe.* Norman, Okla., 1978.

DORION, MARIE

The name of Marie Dorion (?–1850) is associated with some of the most dramatic events in the history of the FUR TRADE and the Pacific Northwest. An Iowa Indian and wife of trader Pierre Dorion, Jr., she first appeared in the historical record in mid-March 1811. WILSON PRICE HUNT, chief field agent for the JOHN JACOB ASTOR'S Pacific Fur Company, was busy preparing the second American overland expedition to the Pacific. Hunt asked Pierre Dorion, Jr., to serve as a guide, and Dorion accepted on condition that his wife Marie and their two children would be allowed to accompany him. Hunt agreed, and Marie became a member of the overland expedition to ASTORIA.

Despite Pierre Dorion's desire to be close to his family, all was not well with the couple. No sooner had the Astorians started up the Missouri from St. Louis than Pierre started beating his wife in a drunken rage. Marie also faced all the dangers and hardships of a transcontinental journey. She and her children suffered along with the other Astorians as the expedition made its way through the present-day states of Wyoming, Idaho, and Oregon. Near the end of the journey, Marie gave birth to a child; nine days after its birth, the child died. Two years after her overland journey, Marie accompanied her husband and other Astorians on a trading expedition. That trip ended in disaster when all the men, including Pierre, were killed by Indians. With great skill, Marie was able to save herself and her children. In later years, she remarried twice and spent her last years living in the Willamette Valley.

—*James P. Ronda*

SUGGESTED READING:
Ronda, James P. *Astoria and Empire.* Lincoln, Nebr., 1990.

DOUGLAS, STEPHEN A.

Politician and Democratic leader, Stephen A. Douglas (1813–1861) was born in Vermont, studied law in upstate New York, and moved to Illinois in 1833. Becoming involved in politics in his adopted state, he fashioned his ideals as a Jacksonian Democrat and captured a number of state offices before running for the U.S. Congress in 1837. He lost his first congressional race by thirty-five votes. Douglas was elected to Congress in 1843 and served two terms before winning a seat in the U.S. Senate in 1847. He served in the Senate until his death in 1861.

From Douglas's position as chair of committees on U.S. territories, he developed a strong interest in the American West. Believing in America's MANIFEST DESTINY, he proposed a number of measures to aid in the settlement of Western lands. His first proposals included a plan for territorial expansion and the rapid establishment of territorial governments, a homesteading law, and the construction of a transcontinental railroad. He supported the annexation of Texas, labored for the acquisition of Oregon, and favored the war with Mexico in 1846.

Douglas's vision of a united, expanding America was marred throughout the 1850s by the sectional differences embodied in the political battles over slavery and its expansion into new American territories. Much of his political energies in the decade were devoted to minimizing the struggle between Northern and Southern factions. His solution was popular sovereignty, allowing the citizens of a territory or state to decide for themselves if slavery would be permitted within their borders. He led the fight in Congress for HENRY CLAY'S COMPROMISE OF 1850, which allowed the Utah and New Mexico territories to decide the issue of slavery by a popular vote. Four years later, he incorporated the doctrine again in the KANSAS-NEBRASKA ACT, which repealed the MISSOURI COMPROMISE of 1820. Rather than being a Union-saving formula as Douglas had hoped, popular sovereignty sparked bitter opposition in the North and led to the formation of the Republican party.

Douglas's popularity vanished as the party system collapsed over slavery, and although he was twice put forward as a presidential candidate, he did not actually win the nomination until 1860 when the Union was already doomed. Douglas pledged his support to the man who had defeated him for president when Abraham Lincoln declared the Southern states to be in rebellion in April 1861. A month later, Douglas—his body exhausted, his spirit broken—died after touring the Northeast to rally Democrats to the Union cause.

—*Patricia Hogan*

SUGGESTED READING:
Johannsen, Robert W. *Stephen A. Douglas.* New York, 1973.

DOUGLAS FAMILY

For seventy years, from roughly 1880 to 1950, three generations of the Douglas family distinguished themselves in the American West. What they achieved in business, politics, and philanthropy had an impact not only on the United States, but also on Canada and Mexico.

The family's original interest in the West stemmed from the work of James Douglas (1837–1918). Born in Quebec, he grew up under comfortable circumstances and obtained an exceptional education in Canada and Europe. The first half of his life was characterized by limited success. Living in Phoenixville, Pennsylvania, and struggling to rescue his company, the Chemical Copper Company, from imminent demise, he began buying high-grade Western ores and developed a consulting business. That led him to the firm of Phelps Dodge and Company, a prominent export-import house in New York specializing in copper, other metals, and metal products. The partners of Phelps Dodge hired Douglas to investigate various mining properties in Montana and Arizona.

In 1881, Douglas traveled to Arizona, where he became intrigued with developments at both Clifton-Morenci and Bisbee. On his recommendation, Phelps Dodge purchased an interest in the Detroit Copper Company at Morenci and a Bisbee claim known as the Atlanta. While development of the mine was at first slow, finally, in 1885, the company struck a rich body of ore deep underground. Phelps Dodge then bought the nearby Copper Queen Company, merged its operations with the Atlanta, and created a new entity, the Copper Queen Consolidated Mining Company. Douglas obtained a huge loan from the company to buy a substantial, though minority, share in the enterprise. With Douglas at the helm of the Copper Queen, Phelps Dodge emerged as one of the great copper producers in the United States. Eventually, Douglas became the first president of the Phelps Dodge Corporation, formed to consolidate all of Phelps Dodge's mining properties.

Douglas's two sons followed him into the copper industry. Walter Douglas (1870–1946) was born in Quebec and grew up largely in Pennsylvania and New York. In 1890, he began his mining career with a Phelps Dodge subsidiary in Prescott, Arizona. In 1917, he succeeded his father as president of Phelps Dodge and continued as president until 1930.

James Douglas's eldest son, James S. ("Rawhide Jim") Douglas (1868–1949) went to work for Phelps Dodge as an assayer at the Copper Queen Mine. He continued his career as superintendent of various Phelps Dodge properties in Arizona and Sonora, Mexico. He also founded several banks in Bisbee, Douglas, and Jerome, Arizona. He made his reputation in mining at Jerome. Shortly after 1910, he and others obtained control of the Little Daisy Mine near the famous United Verde of WILLIAM ANDREWS CLARK. Other miners had drilled the Little Daisy without success. Douglas and his partners, however, struck a bonanza ore body in 1914, and over the next twenty-five years, the property, renamed the United Verde Extension, or UVX, produced more than $150 million in gold, silver, and copper.

Lewis Williams Douglas (1894–1974) was the son of Rawhide Jim. After graduating from college and compiling a distinguished record in World War I, he embarked on a career in politics that took him from the Arizona legislature to the U.S. Congress to the position of director of the budget for President Franklin D. Roosevelt in 1933. He broke with Roosevelt over the issue of government spending and a balanced budget and moved to Canada to become president of McGill University in Montreal. In 1940, he left the school to serve as head of the Mutual of New York Life Insurance Company. In 1947, President Harry S Truman named him ambassador to the Court of St. James.

The Douglas family and Arizona copper are inseparably linked. Through skill and determination—and good luck—James Douglas developed the great mineral empire than made both Arizona and the Phelps Dodge Corporation synonymous with the red metal; his sons Walter and James S. continued that tradition.
                                                        —*James E. Fell, Jr.*

SEE ALSO: Copper Mining

SUGGESTED READING:
Browder, Robert Paul, and Thomas G. Smith. *Independent: A Biography of Lewis W. Douglas.* New York, 1986.

Langton, H. H. *James Douglas: A Memoir.* Toronto, Ont., 1940.

DRED SCOTT DECISION

In 1857, at the height of the bloodletting in Kansas occasioned by the KANSAS-NEBRASKA ACT, the U.S. Supreme Court entered the controversy by choosing to hear the *Dred Scott* v. *Sandford* case, in which the question at issue became congressional power over slavery in the Western territories. Dred Scott, a St. Louis slave, had been trying to win his freedom through the courts. Scott had belonged to a U.S. Army surgeon named John Emerson, who was stationed first in Illinois, then in the Wisconsin Territory, and ultimately in Missouri. Scott accompanied Emerson to each new station until the surgeon's death in 1846. Seeking his freedom, Scott sued John Sanford, who, as the brother of Emerson's widow, managed her affairs. (Sanford's name was misspelled in the record.) Scott argued that, once taken north by his former owner into regions closed to slavery by both the NORTHWEST ORDINANCE (Illinois) and the MISSOURI COMPROMISE (Wisconsin), he was, under law, no longer a slave but a citizen of Missouri. The Missouri courts disagreed; Scott and his lawyers appealed to the Supreme Court.

Sentiment among the judges was almost evenly split. The antislavery jurists, led by John McLean of Ohio and Benjamin R. Curtis of Massachusetts, believed that Scott should indeed be freed because of the Missouri Compromise, which stipulated that slavery could not exist north of the $36°30'$ latitude, except in Missouri itself. Proslavery Southerners on the court followed Chief Justice Roger B. Taney, who ruled for the majority that neither free blacks nor enslaved blacks were citizens and thus could not sue in the federal courts. The majority also held that the Northwest Ordinance banning slavery in Illinois had no force over Scott and his owners after he returned to Missouri, where slavery was legal. The Missouri Compromise outlawing slavery in the Wisconsin Territory also had no force over Scott, the court ruled, because it was unconstitutional. The majority based its decision on the Fifth Amendment, which prohibits the government from depriving an individual of property and liberty without the due process of law. Taney argued that Congress was powerless to exercise restrictions on property, and since the court considered slaves to be property, the *Dred Scott* decision implied that slavery was safe—and, according to the South's reading of the decision, should be protected—everywhere in the nation.

Politically, the *Dred Scott* decision had an immediate impact. Republicans, struggling to get their new party on sound footing, viewed the decision as an attempt by Southern justices to destroy them. Northern and Western Democrats saw the ruling as an attack on popular sovereignty. Northern abolitionists—utterly astonished that the court had invoked the Bill of Rights to deny a man his freedom—saw the findings as a bid to extend slavery. And Southern slave owners began to call for strict enforcement of fugitive slave laws, which at last seemed to have the full force of law even in the Northern states and the free territories to the west. In short, the decision changed the terms of the national debate on slavery and made civil war inevitable. An argument about how the American West should be settled became a battle over the nature of property itself.

—*Charles Phillips*

SEE ALSO: National Expansion: Slavery and National Expansion

SUGGESTED READING:

Hopkins, Vincent C. *Dred Scott's Case.* New York, 1951.
Kutler, Stanley I. *The Dred Scott Decision: Law or Politics?* Boston, 1967.

DRYLAND FARMING

SEE: Farming: Dryland Farming

DUBUQUE, JULIEN

Fur trader and miner Julien Dubuque (1762–1810) was the first permanent white settler in Iowa. Born in a Quebec village, Dubuque headed west as a young man to seek his fortune as a trapper and settled in 1785 around present-day Prairie du Chien, Wisconsin. Quickly befriending the local Fox (Mesquakie) Indians, Dubuque became aware of the extensive lead deposits in their jealously guarded hunting grounds. The Fox Indians—who, along with the closely related Sacs (Sauks), had long mined lead in the region—granted him exclusive rights to develop lead mines on the Iowa side of the Mississippi River. Dubuque built a smelting furnace and opened new mines. He established a trading post near the site of the city that now bears his name and built up a thriving fur trade with the Indians. Twice annually, Dubuque floated downriver to St. Louis to exchange furs for manufactured goods. Spain governed Louisiana at the time, and Dubuque named his operation the "Mines of Spain" in hopes of garnering a legal title to his holdings as a complement to the grant awarded him by the Fox Indians. The Span-

ish obliged him. The Indians called Dubuque "Little Cloud," and when he died, the Sac and Fox Indians buried him with great ceremony.

—*Charles Phillips*

DUDE RANCHING

Dude ranching, the practice by Western ranchers of accepting paying guests, was a significant but little-known factor in the development of the trans-Mississippi West. In the last three decades of the nineteenth century and the early years of the twentieth, a few ranches in the Dakotas, Wyoming, Montana, and Colorado began accepting paying guests. These visitors were attracted to the Western ranches by big-game hunting, trout fishing, and beautiful scenery; they also wanted to see Indians and to visit historical sites. Since there were few accommodations for them in the West, they stayed at cattle or horse ranches, which became known as "dude ranches." Nothing derogatory was intended by the ranchers in the use of the word *dude*. It meant a visitor to the region who paid for food, lodging, and the use of a horse. The ranches were the homes of the owners, and the paying visitors were either friends of the family or considered as their guests.

Besides the attractions of the West and the availability of ranches, there were three other threads that led to the development of dude ranching. One was simply pioneer hospitality; Western ranchers welcomed visitors just as earlier pioneers had. Another factor was the appearance of "remittance men," generally the sons of wealthy Eastern or European families, young men who were sent West because of excessive drinking or some other failing or who traveled to the West to seek their own fortune or adventure. Receiving regular remittances and demanding better living conditions and food than was generally available at the few hotels in the region, they brought needed money into the West. A final factor was economic necessity. Ranchers suffered periodic economic reversals brought on by poor markets and foul weather. Eventually, all these threads came together, and a new industry was formed.

Howard Eaton is generally considered to be the first dude rancher; his operation set the pattern for many ranches that followed. He and his brothers, Willis and Alden, operated the Custer Trail Ranch near Medora in the Dakota Territory. Their first recorded paying guest came in 1882, and by 1891, the Eatons had a regular dude business. When their guests wanted a more scenic locale, the Eatons moved, in 1904, to the Bighorn Mountains in northern Wyoming. Eaton's Ranch has remained there, under family ownership,

Dude ranches were popular tourist attractions in the West and economic boons to ranch owners. *Courtesy National Cowboy Hall of Fame and Western Heritage Center.*

into the late twentieth century. Another important Wyoming dude rancher was I. H. (Larry) Larom. He and Winthrop Brooks bought a small homestead east of Yellowstone National Park, and Larom turned the property into the large and successful Valley Ranch, which he operated until 1969. Larom also became the first president of the Dude Ranchers' Association (DRA), formed by ranchers and officials of the Northern Pacific Railroad in 1926. Larom remained president of the DRA until 1945.

The man known as the "father" of Montana dude ranching was James (Dick) Randall. A cowboy who had to search for a new job after severe winter weather from 1886 to 1887 devastated the big cattle outfits, Randall eventually became a successful guide for big-game hunters. That business led him to start the OTO Ranch, which he and his wife, Dora, operated in southern Montana until 1934.

In Colorado, numerous ranches were developed, some as early as the 1870s. One of the more long lasting was Holzwarth's Neversummer Ranch near Grand Lake, just a few miles from Rocky Mountain National Park. John and Sophia Holzwarth moved there in 1918 and tried to make a living by ranching. They found that catering to guests, especially fisher-

men, was almost a necessity for survival. Their son, Johnnie, eventually developed a very successful ranch. It was one of the premier horseback-riding ranches in the West until it was sold in 1974 and incorporated into the national park.

The Union Pacific Railroad imitated the actions of the Northern Pacific by helping to organize the Colorado Dude and Guest Ranch Association (CD&GRA) in the early 1930s. The DRA and CD&GRA have remained the principal organizations for dude ranchers into the 1990s.

Significant numbers of dude ranches, usually called "guest ranches," were developed in Arizona and New Mexico, but none of the organizations that were formed there remained strong or active for long. Smaller numbers of dude ranches were operated in other Western states and in Canada.

While many dude ranches still thrived in the late twentieth century, their greatest impact came in their early years. One influence of dude ranches was the image they presented to visitors to the West. Most ranches that accepted paying guests were working ranches and the homes of their owners. People who visited them learned to appreciate the beauties of the Western landscape; they also often learned about the people, history, land, plants, and animals of the West. And, through active participation in ranch work, they learned something of the hardships of the West.

Dude ranchers were also very active conservationists. In addition to the men previously mentioned, Charles C. Moore and Billy Howell were well known in game-management and preservation programs. The Dude Ranchers' Association was also an active participant in conservation programs.

Dude ranches introduced thousands of people to the Rocky Mountain West and helped popularize its attractions. Along with railroads and national parks, dude ranches were a major factor in developing TOURISM, especially in Wyoming, Montana, and Colorado.

—*Lawrence R. Borne*

SUGGESTED READING:
Bernstein, Joel H. *Families That Take in Friends*. Stevensville, Mont., 1982.
Borne, Lawrence R. *Dude Ranching: A Complete History*. Albuquerque, N. Mex., 1983.
King, Bucky. *The Dude Connection*. Laramie, Wyo., 1983.
Rodnitzky, Jerome L. "Recapturing the West: The Dude Ranch in American Life." *Arizona and the West* 10 (Summer 1968): 111–126.
Roundy, Charles G. "The Origins and Early Development of Dude Ranching in Wyoming." *Annals of Wyoming* 45 (Spring 1973): 5–25.

DULL KNIFE

SEE: Morning Star

DUNDY, ELMER SCIPIO

Nebraska jurist and politician Elmer Scipio Dundy (1830–1896) was born in Trumbull County, Ohio, and migrated to the Nebraska Territory in 1857. He quickly became involved in turbulent local politics and was a strong advocate for the southeastern counties. Elected in 1858 as a Democrat to the thirteen-member Territorial Council, he subsequently served four years in the upper house of the legislature before being appointed federal judge for the Nebraska Territory in 1863. As a Republican convert, Dundy was appointed United States district judge five years later. In an 1879 landmark decision, he ruled that the government had no right to arrest Ponca Chief Standing Bear and his people for leaving their Indian Territory reservation and that Indians were guaranteed equal protection under the law. During the early 1870s, he rendered several decisions favorable to railroad tax deferments,

and amid the 1888 Burlington Railroad strike, he issued an injunction against strike activities.

—*Michael L. Tate*

SUGGESTED READING:
Price, David H. "The Public Life of Elmer S. Dundy 1857–1896." M.A. thesis, University of Nebraska at Omaha, 1971.

DUNIWAY, ABIGAIL SCOTT

The undisputed leader of the WOMEN'S SUFFRAGE movement in Oregon, Abigail Scott Duniway (1834–1915) fought for women's right to vote with, as she said, "jawbone and pen" for more than four decades. Called by historian Eleanor Flexnor "the hardest and most tireless suffrage worker the western states produced," Duniway established the state's first suffrage association, founded and edited its first suffrage newspaper, and spearheaded six statewide campaigns to amend Oregon's constitution to include the female franchise.

Born on a farm south of Peoria, Illinois, Abigail Jane Scott traveled the Oregon Trail with her family in 1852 and, less than a year later, married Ben C. Duniway, a Clackamas County farmer. During the next ten years, her feminist sensibilities were awakened as she bore four children, washed, scrubbed, cooked hundreds of free meals for bachelor farmers, churned thousands of pounds of butter, and, in her words, became "a servant without wages" and "a general pioneer drudge."

In the early 1860s, her husband lost their farm and soon thereafter became permanently disabled. Duniway became the family's sole financial supporter. She taught school briefly and operated a millinery and notions shop before moving the family to Portland, where, at age thirty-six, she began her life's work for suffrage.

In 1870, Duniway and two other Oregon women founded the Oregon State Equal Suffrage Association. Several months later, she began the first suffrage newspaper in the Pacific Northwest, *The New Northwest* (published from 1871 to 1887), a weekly she single-handedly edited and wrote for the next sixteen years. At the same time, she took to the lecture circuit and traveled thousands of miles by horseback, stagecoach, river boat, and railroad throughout the Northwest to speak on equal rights. Broadening her efforts, she lobbied the state legislature to place before Oregon voters a constitutional amendment to enfranchise women.

In 1884, the legislature finally placed the amendment on the ballot, but it was easily defeated. Duniway, however, was not. She continued the fight and led the state movement for most of the next three decades.

But Oregon voters defeated the equal suffrage amendment in 1900, 1906, 1908, and 1910. In 1912, when the amendment finally passed, Duniway, still the movement's titular leader at the age of seventy-eight, was confined to a wheelchair with rheumatism. A year later, she became Oregon's first registered female voter.

—*Lauren Kessler*

Suggested reading:

Duniway, Abigail Scott. *Pathbreaking: An Autobiographical History of the Equal Suffrage Movement in the Pacific Coast States*. Portland, Oreg., 1914.

Flexnor, Eleanor. *Century of Struggle: The Woman's Rights Movement in the United States*. New York, 1973.

Kessler, Lauren. "A Siege of the Citadels: Abigail Scott Duniway and the Fight for Oregon Suffrage." Ph.D. diss., University of Washington, 1980.

Moynihan, Ruth Barnes. *Rebel for Rights, Abigail Scott Duniway*. New Haven, Conn., 1982.

DURANT, THOMAS CLARK

Born in Lee, Massachusetts, the son of Thomas and Sybil Durant, Thomas Clark Durant (1820–1885) graduated from the Albany Medical College in 1840 but entered the business world in his uncle's flour- and grain-export firm. A successful speculator in stocks, he became interested in the West and in railroad development. In 1851, he joined Henry Farnam in constructing the Michigan Southern Railroad, followed by the Chicago and Rock Island and the Mississippi and Missouri.

Interested in a transcontinental railroad, Durant sent three exploration parties west in 1863 and played a part in influencing President Abraham Lincoln to choose Omaha as the beginning of the proposed Union Pacific Railroad. Chartered by Congress under the Pacific Railway Act of 1862, the Union Pacific encountered delays in amassing capital. Durant was elected vice-president of the new company on October 30, 1863, and remained the chief manager of the railroad until it was completed. He supported the amendment of the Railway Act in 1864 and used a "suspense" account for lobbying expenditures to support passage of the act, although bribery was never proved.

Attempting to push the road west in 1863 and 1864, he took over the construction contract when the first contractor failed. Unable to gain support from New York capitalists, he and major stockholders, including Oakes Ames, U.S. congressman from Massachusetts, formed Crédit Mobilier of America, a company that would build the railroad for Union Pacific. For the next three years, New York and Boston fac-

Thomas Clark Durant. *Courtesy University of Iowa, Special Collections.*

tions vied for control of the Union Pacific, and beginning in 1867, Ames sold or gave shares in Crédit Mobilier to congressmen, who, in turn, approved additional federal subsidies for the line. Durant drove construction at a rapid pace despite cost or difficulty, lived on the line for weeks at a time, and often did not change clothes for a week. On May 10, 1869, he joined Amasa Leland Stanford of the Central Pacific Railroad in driving in the last spike of the transcontinental line at Promontory Summit in Utah.

Two weeks later, Durant was removed from the directorate of the Union Pacific. Broken in health, he retired to the Adirondacks, where he engaged in the area's development. During the investigation of the Crédit Mobilier scandal, Ames was censured by Congress, but Durant was not found at fault. His vision of the transcontinental railroad did much to shape the growth of the West.

—*Patrick H. Butler, III*

Suggested reading:

Klein, Maury. *Union Pacific*. 2 vols. Garden City, N.Y., 1987. Reprint, 1989.

DUST BOWL

Filling the sky in the mid-1930s, dust blew off the dry Southern Plains, reached Washington, D.C., and sent a message of ecological disaster across the nation. Resulting from a combination of farming practices that had been practiced since the early twentieth century and a drought that began in 1931, the Dust Bowl reshaped life on the Southern Plains. It also substantially altered the role of government even as it was being redefined under the auspices of the New Deal in the mid- and late 1930s.

The Southern Plains had been a grazing area, first for buffaloes and then for the cattle and sheep of settlers. In the 1880s and 1890s, speculators purchased large tracts of land on which they established ranches until they could divide it into smaller parcels for sale to farmers. The great XIT Ranch, covering more than three million acres along the Texas–New Mexico border, exemplified this practice. Because rainfall was relatively frequent in the first two decades of the century, farming practices that ripped off the cover of grass to allow grain to be planted did not immediately affect the land, but as more land was put under cultivation, particularly during World War I, the land became more vulnerable to the effects of drought and wind. After World War I, in the agricultural depression of the 1920s, much of the land was allowed to go fallow. But the thick prairie grasses that held the soil did not return, and the stage was set for the disaster of the 1930s.

Beginning in 1931, drought powdered the soil of the Southern Plains and made it light and dry, thereby allowing the constant winds to pick up the dust and spread it across the country. Over the next five years, local dust storms combined, becoming vast regional storms that blackened the sky and turned day into night. Although soil loss was predominantly in the Southern Plains, the dust spread across the East, particularly in 1934 and 1935.

The natural disaster quickly became a human disaster. Cattle died, farms were wiped out, and about 60 percent of the population was driven off the land in the affected areas. The dispossessed became a generation of "Okies," whose lives were portrayed by John Steinbeck in *The Grapes of Wrath* and in other popular writing and film.

The federal government, attempting to deal with the effects of the Great Depression, reacted strongly to the Dust Bowl disaster. In 1934 and 1935, the Drought Relief Service purchased more than eight million cattle, thus cutting down on grazing, which had contributed to the problem by denuding the soil. In the process, the service saved the CATTLE INDUSTRY on the Plains. The TAYLOR GRAZING ACT of 1934 brought stock raising on public lands under federal management. At the same time, the New Deal government officials worked to return the region to grassland. Just as cattle grazing was reduced through federal price supports, the United States Department of Agriculture (USDA) attempted to take land out of production through payments for not growing crops. While this program proved to be a failure in the end, the USDA also established a program to change farming practices, including contour plowing and terracing. Temporarily successful, such programs required massive technical support supplied by the government.

The programs created the image of government waste through payment for not raising crops. In addition, those who were paid the most for taking land out of production were the large landowners. Small farmers were gradually forced off the land, as were renters and tenant farmers. During the 1940s, with the return of rain, many of the reforms were abandoned, and the land went back into production. In the 1950s, as disaster threatened again, Congress intervened with payments for restoring farm land to grass. Another result of the Dust Bowl was increased use of IRRIGATION practices. However, because much of the water used, particularly on the Southern Plains, was taken from the OGALLALA AQUIFER, which cannot be replenished, dryland-farming practices again returned to the Southern Plains.

—Patrick H. Butler, III

SEE ALSO: Farming: Dryland Farming; XIT Ranch, Texas

SUGGESTED READING:

Gregory, James. *American Exodus: The Dust Bowl Migration and Okie Culture in California.* New York, 1989.

Reisner, Marc. *Cadillac Desert: The American West and Its Disappearing Water.* New York, 1986.

Worster, Donald. *Dust Bowl: The Southern Plains in the 1930s.* New York, 1979.

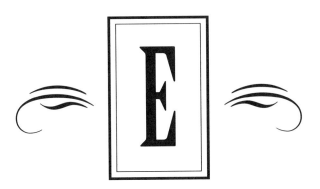

EARP BROTHERS

(Virgil Walter, 1843–1905; Wyatt Berry Stapp, 1848–1929; Morgan S., 1851–1882), Western lawmen. Virgil Walter Earp was born in Hartford, Kentucky. A Civil War veteran, he was elected constable of Prescott in Yavapai County, Arizona, on November 5, 1878. A year later, he was appointed deputy U.S. marshal for Yavapai County. From December 1, 1879, to December 29, 1881, he was deputy U.S. marshal for Pima County (later Cochise). Living in Tombstone, he served for five months as city marshal and chief of police, and as city marshal, he faced the Clanton Gang at the O. K. Corral on October 26, 1881. In 1887, despite his permanently crippled left arm, Virgil was elected the first city marshal of Colton, California. In 1900, he moved back to Prescott, where he was nominated sheriff of Yavapai County. Health problems forced him to drop out of the race. Virgil Earp died of pneumonia in 1905 in Goldfield, Esmeralda County, Nevada. At the time of his death, he was deputy sheriff of Esmeralda County.

Wyatt Berry Stapp Earp was born in Monmouth, Illinois. His first experience as a lawman was as constable of Lamar, Missouri, for four months in 1870. In April 1875, he was appointed to the Wichita, Kansas, police force. He was dismissed for insubordination on April 2, 1876. He then moved to Dodge City, Kansas, where he served as a policeman during three separate terms: May 17 to September 9, 1876; July 6 to late November 1877; and May 12, 1878, to September 8, 1879. Moving to Tombstone, Arizona, on December 1, 1879, he again took up law enforcement. During the twenty-eight months he lived there, his record as a lawman was a checkered one: he rode shotgun for WELLS, FARGO AND COMPANY for eight months; he was a deputy sheriff for Pima County from July 29 to November 9, 1880; and he was a Wells Fargo detective for an indeterminate period of service. At the O. K.

Corral gunfight, he was a stand-in deputy city marshal, appointed by his brother Virgil. When Virgil was ambushed and badly wounded on December 28, 1881, Wyatt was appointed deputy United States marshal, a position he held until late April 1882, when he left Arizona. Wyatt Earp died in Los Angeles.

Morgan S. Earp was born in Pella, Iowa. Other than his participation in the O. K. Corral gunfight, he had a negligible record in law enforcement. He rode shotgun for Wells Fargo in the Tombstone area, where

Wyatt Earp. *Courtesy Arizona Historical Society.*

Left, Virgil Earp. *Courtesy Arizona Historical Society.*
Right, Morgan Earp. *Courtesy Arizona Historical Society.*

he was deputized from time to time by his brother
Virgil. Morgan was a special policeman at the time of
the O. K. Corral gunfight. On the night of March 18,
1882, he was shot in the back and killed as he played
billiards in Hatches' Parlor on Allen Street in Tombstone. The killers escaped in the dark.

The shooting and maiming of Virgil Earp and the
killing of Morgan were acts of revenge for the shootout in the vacant lot known as the O. K. Corral. In just
seconds of gunfire, the three Earp brothers and JOHN
HENRY ("DOC") HOLLIDAY killed suspected rustlers Tom
and Frank McLaury and William (Billy) Clanton. Virgil
and Morgan suffered leg and shoulder wounds.

After the killing of Morgan, Deputy U.S. Marshal
Wyatt Earp issued warrants for the arrest of suspects
Frank Stilwell, Florentino Cruz, Peter Spenser, Jacob (?)
Fries, and Hank Swilling. Warrants were not issued
for rustler chiefs JOHN PETER RINGO and "CURLY" BILL
BROCIUS, although Wyatt suspected both men. In less
than a week, Wyatt and his posse killed Stilwell, Cruz,
and gang member Johnny Barnes. Ringo committed
suicide in July 1882. Wyatt claimed to have killed
Brocius as well, but others who knew him said that he
had left Arizona months before the alleged killing took
place.

Wyatt Earp had taken the law into his own hands.
He was charged with murder, and a warrant was issued for his arrest. A fugitive himself, he then rode to
Colorado and into myth and legend. His personal ven-
detta can hardly be called a contribution to law enforcement, but the disappearance of Brocius and the
isolation of Ringo broke the back of organized
outlawry in southeastern Arizona.

—*Jack Burrows*

SEE ALSO: O. K. Corral, Gunfight at

SUGGESTED READING:
Boyer, Glenn G. *I Married Wyatt Earp: The Recollections of
    Josephine Sara Marcus Earp.* Tucson, Ariz., 1976.
Burns, Walter Noble. *Tombstone.* New York, 1927.
Burrows, Jack. *John Ringo: The Gunfighter Who Never Was.*
    Tucson, Ariz., 1987.
Lake, Stuart N. *Wyatt Earp: Frontier Marshal.* Boston, 1931.
Marks, Paula Mitchell. *And Die in the West: The Story of
    the O. K. Corral Gunfight.* New York, 1989.
Waters, Frank. *The Earp Brothers of Tombstone: The Story
    of Mrs. Virgil Earp.* New York, 1960.

EARTHQUAKES

SEE: New Madrid Earthquake of 1811; San Andreas
Fault; San Francisco Earthquake of 1906

EAST INDIANS

Men from India's Punjab province came to work in
the American West and Canada in the early twentieth
century, and many stayed on to settle. India was still
under British colonial rule, and many farming families
sent one or more sons to work in the British army or
police service. Those serving in Hong Kong and Shang-
hai were probably the first to hear about the good
money to be earned in lumber, railroad building, and
farm work in America, and shiploads of migrants came
until new laws prejudicial to Asian immigration (the
1917 "Barred Zone" Act and the 1924 National Origins Quota Act) effectively stopped them. While some
called the immigrants from Punjab "Punjabis," others
called them "Hindus," meaning that they were from
Hindustan or India. They actually came from all three
major religious groups in their part of India—Sikhs,
Muslims, and Hindus. Most of the Punjabi men were
Sikhs from farming backgrounds, and once in America,
they went into farm work. They began as agricultural
laborers, traveling on the migratory laborer circuit together, living in "Hindu" camps, and contracting
through their "bossmen" for seasonal work. These
hard-working and ambitious farmers soon began to
acquire land and settle down, with the largest concentrations in California's Imperial, San Joaquin, and Sacramento valleys.

The Punjabi pioneer men were linked to each other
by their common language, Punjabi, and by the harsh
treatment accorded them by American laws. Federal
legislation restricted further Asian immigration and
prevented them from bringing their wives and children

from India. While a few early applicants became citizens, federal law barred "nonwhites" from American citizenship, and in 1923, the U.S. Supreme Court decided (*In Re Bhagat Singh Thind*) that South Asians were not "white." California and Arizona state laws restricted their rights to lease and own agricultural lands. These laws, stemming from California's initial formulation of 1913, were aimed against Japanese farmers but applied to all Asians as "aliens ineligible to citizenship." Antimiscegenation laws also prevented the Punjabi men from marrying across "racial" lines.

Various discriminatory laws were in effect by the mid-1920s, most importantly the ALIEN LAND LAWS following the 1923 U.S. Supreme Court decision regarding the *Thind* case. However, most of the Punjabi men remained in farming with the help of friendly neighbors, bankers, and lawyers. There were no women from India living in the Imperial Valley and fewer than ten living in all the rural areas of the West. For wives, the men had to choose women perceived by others to be of their "race," and most often they chose women of Mexican or Mexican American background. These marriages began in 1916, and there were at least five hundred such marriages by the 1940s. Most of the Punjabi Mexican couples lived in California's Imperial Valley along the Mexican border, but others were scattered across Texas, Arizona, New Mexico, Utah, and central and northern California. Catholicism became the dominant religion of the second generation, and most children spoke both Spanish and English, but very little Punjabi. The children's names (Maria Jesusita Singh and José Akbar Khan, for example) represented the community as well. Partly because of the biethnic nature of the Punjabi community, the Punjabi pioneers and their Mexican or Mexican American wives and children moved rapidly to become "American."

The Punjabi men were intensely political. They organized a militant nationalist group, the Ghadar party, in California to work for India's independence from Great Britain, and they formed several organizations to fight for U.S. citizenship. After the Punjabis lobbied for years, Congress passed the Luce-Celler Bill of 1946, a law that permitted South Asians to become naturalized United States citizens. Most of the old-timers then became citizens, and one of their number, Dalip Singh Saund, was elected to the House of Representatives from the Imperial Valley in 1956. As U.S. citizens, the men could own land in their own names, and many were quite successful in farming. Another important political turning point came in 1947, when British India became two free and independent nations, India and Pakistan. Those developments meant that the Punjabi immigrants could be proud of their old and new countries and establish meaningful connections with their South Asian relatives again.

After 1965, when liberalized immigration laws redressed the historical discrimination against Asians, many new immigrants came from South Asia. They revitalized the one religious institution the pioneers had established (a Sikh *gurdwara,* or "temple," in Stockton, California) and added many new religious and cultural institutions to the American landscape. The newcomers contrasted greatly with the old-timers, since they came from all over South Asia and were primarily highly educated, urban people migrating as family units. In the early decades of the twentieth century, the men from India numbered only a few thousand and settled in rural areas; in the 1990s, the South Asian immigrants in the American West numbered more than one hundred thousand and lived primarily in urban areas. Although their numbers were relatively small, the Punjabi pioneers and their descendants, claiming to be "Hindu," Mexican, and American, provided striking testimony to the flexibility of ethnic identity.

—*Karen Leonard*

SEE ALSO: *Bhagat Singh Thind, In Re;* Immigration Law; Intermarriage: Antimiscegenation Laws, Marriages between Asian Americans and Mexicans

SUGGESTED READING:

Jensen, Joan M. *Passage from India: Asian Indian Immigrants in North America.* New Haven, Conn., 1988.

La Brack, Bruce. *The Sikhs of Northern California, 1904–1975: A Socio-Historical Study.* New York, 1988.

Leonard, Karen. *Making Ethnic Choices: California's Punjabi Mexican Americans.* Philadelphia, 1992.

EASTMAN, CHARLES ALEXANDER (SIOUX)

Charles Alexander Eastman (1858–1939), whose Indian name was Ohiyesa, was recognized in 1900 as the most educated Indian living in the United States. He devoted his career to helping Indian people through his writings, lectures, and criticism of federal Indian policies.

Born near Redwood Falls, Minnesota, Ohiyesa was raised in the traditional ways of a Santee Sioux hunter and warrior. At the age of fifteen, he reluctantly abandoned that life and agreed to his recently Christianized father's request that he attend a white school. Over the next seventeen years, Eastman attended a number of schools. He earned a B.S. degree from Dartmouth in 1887 and a medical degree from Boston University School of Medicine in 1890.

Eastman held several government appointments. As government physician at the Pine Ridge Reservation in South Dakota from 1890 to 1893, he witnessed the Wounded Knee tragedy in 1890. He later held positions at the Carlisle Indian School in Pennsylvania in 1899 and the Crow Creek Reservation in South Dakota from 1900 to 1903. From 1903 to 1909, he was head of the revision of the Sioux allotment rolls. Then from 1923 to 1925, he was Indian inspector of reservations.

His nongovernment employment included a brief medical practice in St. Paul, Minnesota, in 1893, Indian secretary of the International Committee of the YMCA from 1894 to 1898, and a representative of a Santee Sioux claims case in Washington, D.C., for a number of years.

Eastman was a prolific writer. With the aid of his non-Indian wife, Elaine Goodale Eastman, he published numerous books and articles. Two of his books were autobiographies: *Indian Boyhood* (1902) and *From the Deep Woods to Civilization* (1916). Others, such as *The Soul of the Indian* (1911) and *The Indian Today* (1915), dealt with Indian-white relations and Indian culture and society. He even wrote a guidebook entitled *Indian Scout Talks* (1914) for Boy Scouts and Camp Fire Girls. He presented lectures throughout the United States and in England.

As an Indian reformer, Eastman helped organize and later served as president of the Society of American Indians, a pan-Indian organization established in 1911. He lobbied for Indian citizenship, condemned deplorable reservation conditions, and opposed the use of peyote by Indians. In 1933, he received the first Indian Council Fire's annual award in recognition of his work to help Indian and non-Indian people understand each other.

Eastman supported an acculturation policy in which Indians selected which non-Indian ways to adopt instead of an assimilation policy that often forced Indians to abandon their culture. He believed Indians could remain Indians and still operate successfully in the dominant culture.

—*Raymond Wilson*

SEE ALSO: Indian Schools; United States Indian Policy; Wounded Knee Massacre

SUGGESTED READING:

Eastman, Charles Alexander (Ohiyesa). *From the Deep Woods to Civilization: Chapters in the Autobiography of an Indian.* Boston, 1916.

———. *Indian Boyhood.* Boston, 1902.
———. *The Indian Today: The Past and Future of the First American.* Garden City, N.Y., 1915.
———. *The Soul of the Indian: An Interpretation.* Boston, 1911.
Wilson, Raymond. *Ohiyesa: Charles Eastman, Santee Sioux.* Urbana, Ill., 1983.

EASTMAN, ELAINE GOODALE

Teacher, author, and Indian school superintendent Elaine Goodale Eastman (1863–1952) was born near Mount Washington, Massachusetts. At the age of fifteen, she earned critical acclaim for *Apple Blossoms: Verses of Two Children*, a book she wrote with her sister Dora. She continued to receive favorable notice for her literary efforts, but she was increasingly drawn to teaching and reform work.

She first became a teacher in 1883 in the Indian Department at the Hampton Institute in Virginia. After a tour of the Greater Sioux Reservation in the Dakota Territory in 1885, she taught at one of the reservation's day schools and quickly became fluent in the Dakota dialect. In 1890, she was appointed the first superintendent of INDIAN SCHOOLS for the new states of North and South Dakota, despite opposition from politicians who did not want the post to be filled by a woman. During her first year as superintendent, she actively promoted reform in the Dakota schools; she also wrote numerous magazine and newspaper articles decrying the United States Army's massacre of Indians at Wounded Knee.

In 1891, she married Charles Alexander Eastman, a Sioux physician and reformer who had been educated at Dartmouth College and Boston University. After her marriage, she gave up her position as school superintendent but continued to write poetry and nonfiction and collaborated with her husband on numerous books.

Eastman wanted to be known as a friend of the Indian. She assumed a stance toward Native Americans that was patronizing rather than hostile. She believed that there was much to admire and cherish in Indian culture but argued that Indians had no choice but to give up most of their "primitive" traditions in favor of the more "advanced" Anglo-American culture. The Indian Wars of the 1870s left Indians with few resources and little autonomy; according to Eastman, their only hope for survival was integration into white society. As an educator and writer, Eastman promoted Indian assimilation and resisted the arguments of both racial segregationists and cultural pluralists. She died in Northampton, Massachusetts.

—*Ruth M. Alexander*

SEE ALSO: United States Indian Policy; Wounded Knee Massacre

SUGGESTED READING:

Graber, Kay, ed. *Sister to the Sioux: The Memoirs of Elaine Goodale Eastman, 1885–1891.* Lincoln, Nebr., 1978.
Wilson, Raymond. *Ohiyesa: Charles Eastman, Santee Sioux.* Urbana, Ill., 1983.

EASTMAN, SETH

Artist and soldier Seth Eastman (1808–1875) was born in Brunswick, Maine. His father nourished his interest in science and art. Upon graduating from West Point in 1829, Eastman began a military career that allowed him to portray with pencil, water colors, and oils both the landscapes of the West and the life of the Indians of the regions in which he was stationed. His first military assignments were at Fort Crawford, Wisconsin, and Fort Snelling, Minnesota. After additional duty in New Orleans, he returned to the U.S. Military Academy in 1833 to become an assistant teacher of drawing. This was a significant period in his artistic development, for he now had the opportunity to study privately with C. R. Leslie and Robert W. Weir. In 1840, Eastman served in the First Infantry during the Seminole War in Florida. From 1842 to 1848, he was stationed once more at Fort Snelling, and from 1848 to 1849, he rejoined the First Infantry in Texas. To devote more energy to the development of his artistic career, he sought and received a position in the Office of Indian Affairs to prepare drawings and illustrations for HENRY ROWE SCHOOLCRAFT's six-volume work entitled *History and Statistical Information Respecting the History, Condition, and Prospects of the Indian Tribes of the United States . . .* (1851–1857). Included in this work were more than three hundred of Eastman's drawings and illustrations of weapons, costumes, tools, and maps. After completing his work on Schoolcraft's books, Eastman returned to active military

Seth Eastman recorded scenes from the daily lives of the Native Americans he observed while stationed at Western posts in the U.S. Army. *Courtesy Library of Congress.*

service. He was always captivated by the experiences of Native Americans and prepared detailed sketches of almost every nuance of their lives. Although he participated in combat against Indians on several occasions, he seldom portrayed scenes of such conflicts. His empathy with the Indians and their future encouraged him to portray, as had GEORGE CATLIN and KARL (CARL) BODMER, scenes and customs of daily life.

Realizing that his artistic career could be advanced more in Washington than at a Western post, Eastman sought assignments in the nation's capital whenever possible. He found the Indians who served as models for the monumental sculptures for the Capitol. While attached to the secretary of the interior, he painted nine works for the House Committee on Indian Affairs and seventeen paintings for the House Committee on Military Affairs. He worked on congressional commissions until his death in 1875. In the context of the difficulties that Catlin and other artists who painted Western themes had in receiving government support, Eastman's achievements in this area were a signal accomplishment.

Less painterly and romantic than the works of George Catlin, Karl Bodmer, and ALFRED JACOB MILLER, Eastman's works reveal his training as a topographical artist and skills as a draftsman. His genre paintings often focus on the activities of Indian women confronting the daily dilemmas of traditional life, men at play in lacrosse games, and scenes of hunting and fishing. His work demonstrates sensitive observation, attention to detail, and meticulous execution.

—*Phillip Drennon Thomas*

SEE ALSO: Art: Western Art

SUGGESTED READING:

Axelrod, Alan. *Art of the Golden West.* New York, 1990.
Bushnell, David. *Seth Eastman: The Master Painter of the North American Indian.* Smithsonian Miscellaneous Collections. Vol. 87, no. 3. Washington, D.C., 1932.
McDermott, John Francis. *Seth Eastman, Pictorial Historian of the Indian.* Norman, Okla., 1961.

ECHO PARK

A small glen of trees flanked by sheer rock walls at the confluence of the Green and Yampa rivers in Dinosaur National Monument, Echo Park is located just east of the border of Utah and Colorado. In the 1950s, the site was at the center of a hard-fought conservation battle that proved vital to the American wilderness movement.

Encouraged by rapid economic and population growth during World War II, the BUREAU OF RECLAMATION proposed a dam on the Green River just below Echo Park. The dam was to be part of a series of dams, the COLORADO RIVER STORAGE PROJECT, on the upper COLORADO RIVER and several of its tributaries. The project was designed to store WATER in large quantities in Utah, Wyoming, Colorado, and New Mexico—a necessary step to allow those states to use their share of the river for IRRIGATION and hydroelectric power and to regulate its flow to supply water to downstream states. The Bureau of Reclamation considered the Echo Park Dam a critical component of the project.

The proposed dam sparked strident opposition from a host of conservation groups. While conservationists did not wish to thwart the West's use of Colorado River water, they argued that the Echo Park Dam and reservoir would severely intrude into Dinosaur National Monument and harm its scenic beauty. The dam would also establish a precedent for other invasions into protected areas in the national park system. Mounting a national campaign against the dam, the National Parks Association, Izaak Walton League, Wilderness Society, SIERRA CLUB, and dozens of other groups argued that the nation's commitment to the national park system and wilderness preservation was at stake.

The battle over Echo Park began in 1950 and lasted for more than six years. Both Oscar Chapman and Douglas McKay, secretaries of the interior in the Harry S Truman and Dwight D. Eisenhower administrations respectively, approved the dam and strengthened the hand of its supporters in Congress.

In order to pressure Congress to reconsider building the dam, conservationists published articles and photographs of the threatened national monument in journals such as *Living Wilderness* and the *Sierra Club Bulletin;* produced and strategically distributed films, fliers, and handbills; and employed lobbyists through such groups as the Trustees for Conservation and the Council of Conservationists. Publisher Alfred A. Knopf, a supporter of the national parks, contributed to the effort with a book entitled *This Is Dinosaur.* Edited by WALLACE STEGNER, the book contained a series of essays that described the beauty that would be lost if the dam and reservoir were constructed. Under the additional leadership of David Brower of the Sierra Club, BERNARD DEVOTO of *Harper's Magazine,* Howard Zahniser of the Wilderness Society, and Joe Penfold of the Izaak Walton League, conservationists forced Western senators to abandon the proposed dam late in 1955.

The bill approved by Congress the following year authorized the Colorado River Storage Project but prohibited dams in any portion of the national park system along the Colorado River. The defeat of the Echo Park Dam proved to be a milestone in national park history. It signified a heightened public interest in protecting parks and monuments for future generations, while it encouraged the establishment of legally designated wilderness on a variety of public lands.

—*Mark W. T. Harvey*

SEE ALSO: National Park Service

SUGGESTED READING:

Cohen, Michael P. *The History of the Sierra Club, 1892–1970.* San Francisco, 1988.

Harvey, Mark W. T. *A Symbol of Wilderness: Echo Park and the American Conservation Movement.* Albuquerque, N. Mex., 1994.

Nash, Roderick. *Wilderness and the American Mind.* 3d ed. New Haven, Conn., 1982.

EDGE, ROSALIE BARROW

Born to a prominent New York family, Rosalie Barrow Edge (1877–1962) possessed the twin advantages of social position and independent means throughout her long and turbulent career as a conservationist. Although an ardent suffragist before World War I and a supporter of conservation causes in the 1920s, she did not become actively involved in conservation efforts until 1929, when her personal passion for ornithology drew her into a bitter campaign to reinvigorate the entrenched leadership of the Audubon Society. Severely denounced and opposed at every turn, Edge and a small band of like-minded reformers, including Willard Van Name and Irving Brant, nonetheless persisted in their efforts to prod the Audubon Society into taking sterner measures on behalf of wildlife conservation.

Forceful, eloquent, and tenacious, Edge demonstrated that she could be neither ignored nor derailed from her purposes. Gathering her allies together under the banner of the Emergency Conservation Committee (ECC), she pursued a series of conservation crusades over the next thirty years with unrelenting vigor. While pressing ahead with her campaign to reform the Audubon Society, she also directed the ECC's participation in many other battles, such as the creation of Hawk Mountain Sanctuary in Pennsylvania and Olympic National Park in Washington.

Although scoring her greatest triumphs during the proconservation era of the New Deal, Edge remained a powerful advocate for conservation measures until her death in 1962. Freed by her financial security from the need to earn a living or to raise funds for her campaigns, she wielded the ECC as a personal weapon on behalf of causes that engaged her sympathy. A passionate amateur in the tradition of JOHN MUIR and the Sierra Club, she also reflected the growing influence exerted by upper- and middle-class women in the American conservation movement during the twentieth century.

—*Peter J. Blodgett*

SUGGESTED READING:

Axelrod, Alan, and Charles Phillips. *The Environmentalists: A Biographical Dictionary from the 17th Century to the Present.* New York, 1993.

Fox, Stephen. *John Muir and His Legacy: The American Conservation Movement.* Boston, 1981.

Taylor, Robert Lewis. "Oh, Hawk of Mercy!" *The New Yorker* 24 (April 17, 1948): 31–37, 40–43.

EDMUNDS ACT OF 1882

The Edmunds Act of 1882 was sponsored by Senator George Edmunds of Vermont as a corrective to the ineffective Morrill Anti-Bigamy Act of 1862, which had been passed to outlaw the Mormon practice of plural marriage, or the marrying of more than one wife at a time.

In 1852, the CHURCH OF JESUS CHRIST OF LATTER-DAY SAINTS announced publicly that its members (known as MORMONS) practiced plural marriage. In 1862, the antibigamy act had declared bigamy to be illegal and punishable by fines and prison time. When the lack of Mormon marriage documents made it difficult for the government to prosecute and convict polygamists, the Edmunds Bill, which circumvented the problem of proof of an illegal marriage by creating the crime of "unlawful cohabitation," was proposed.

In the Edmunds Act, "unlawful cohabitation" was defined as a married person living or cohabiting with someone other than his or her legal spouse. The bill disfranchised people convicted of unlawful cohabitation and barred them from serving on juries and holding public office. In addition, the bill declared vacant all offices connected with registration and election duties in the territory of Utah and appointed a five-man commission to perform such duties.

Building on widespread anti-Mormon sentiment, Congress passed the Edmunds bill, which became a law on March 22, 1882, by a wide margin. Its effect on Mormons' lives was dramatic. Men with plural wives were forced into hiding in order to avoid arrest and imprisonment. Households were upset as women and children had to fend for themselves, and children quickly learned not to trust strangers who asked personal questions about the identities of their parents.

About 830 Mormon men, nicknamed the "cohabs," eventually served time in the territorial penitentiary after their convictions under the Edmunds Act.

—*Craig L. Foster*

SEE ALSO: Polygamy: Polygamy among Mormons

SUGGESTED READING:

Allen, James B., and Glen M. Leonard. *The Story of the Latter-day Saints*. Salt Lake City, 1976.

Bradley, Martha Sonntag. "'Hide and Seek': Children on the Underground." *Utah Historical Quarterly* 51 (Spring 1985): 133–153.

Driggs, Ken. "The Prosecutions Begin: Defining Cohabitation in 1885." *Dialogue: A Journal of Mormon Thought* 21 (1988): 109–125.

Hardy, B. Carmon. *Solemn Covenant: The Mormon Polygamous Passage*. Urbana, Ill., 1992.

Van Wagoner, Richard S. *Mormon Polygamy: A History*. Salt Lake City, 1986.

EDMUNDS-TUCKER ACT OF 1887

The second of two major acts designed to stop the Mormon practice of plural marriage, the Edmunds-Tucker Act of 1887 went far beyond its predecessor, the Edmunds Act of 1882. Although members of the CHURCH OF JESUS CHRIST OF LATTER-DAY SAINTS (known as MORMONS) had been adversely affected by the first Edmunds Act and many men had been sentenced to the territorial penitentiary, members of the Mormon church still defiantly practiced plural marriage.

In response to repeated violations of antipolygamy legislation, Congressman J. Randolph Tucker, chairman of the House Judiciary Committee, drafted an amendment to the Edmunds Act. What eventually became the Edmunds-Tucker Act of 1887 punished not only violators of the antipolygamy laws but also the church, which taught the sanctity of the plurality of wives.

The 1887 law stated that witnesses could be compelled to attend trials and legal (or first) wives could testify against their husbands. The law also officially dissolved the LDS church as a legal corporation and forfeited all property in excess of fifty thousand dollars to the United States government. The PERPETUAL EMIGRATING FUND (which had provided inexpensive travel to Utah for thousands of Mormon converts) was dissolved, and its property escheated. The act also disbanded the Nauvoo Legion or territorial militia.

The law provided for a test oath: anyone who did not pledge support and obedience to the antipolygamy laws could not vote, serve on a jury, or hold public office. In addition, it repealed women's suffrage in Utah. All children born to polygamous families one year after the passage of the act were declared illegitimate in the eyes of the law and were disinherited. More than any other law, the Edmunds-Tucker Act of 1887 broke the back of the Mormon church.

—*Craig L. Foster*

SEE ALSO: Polygamy: Polygamy among Mormons

SUGGESTED READING:

Allen, James B., and Glen M. Leonard. *The Story of the Latter-day Saints*. Salt Lake City, 1976.

Hardy, B. Carmon. *Solemn Covenant: The Mormon Polygamous Passage*. Urbana, Ill., 1992.

Van Wagoner, Richard S. *Mormon Polygamy: A History*. Salt Lake City, 1986.

EDSON, KATHERINE PHILIPS

Suffragist, social reformer, and government official Katherine Philips Edson (1870–1933) pioneered in the development of California protective labor legislation. Born in Kenton, Ohio, she was the daughter of Dr. William Hunter Philips and Harriet J. Carlin. She married Charles Farwell Edson in 1890; the couple had three children and then divorced in 1925.

In 1899, Edson moved to Los Angeles. She quickly became involved in reform activities that made her part of the California women's movement and Progressive movement. She contributed much to the WOMEN'S SUFFRAGE victory in California in 1911 by serving as liaison between the two movements. In May 1907, for example, she helped persuade male Progressives in the Lincoln-Roosevelt League to endorse women's suffrage. In 1910, she campaigned for the Progressive gubernatorial candidate, HIRAM WARREN JOHNSON, and after his victory, helped pressure the state legislature to place in a referendum a constitutional amendment granting women's suffrage.

After the suffrage victory, Edson helped create the California Legislative Council of Women, an umbrella organization of women's groups that lobbied the state legislature regarding women's issues. She also was appointed by Governor Johnson to serve as a special agent to the Bureau of Labor Statistics. Edson and the Legislative Council successfully lobbied the 1913 legislature to pass numerous bills, including a minimum-wage act that Edson wrote. The law created an Industrial Welfare Commission, which had the power to establish minimum wages, maximum hours of work, and standard working conditions for women and children. Governor Johnson appointed Edson to the commission in 1913. She quickly became its most influential member, remained in that position for eighteen years, and became well known as a national leader in the field of protective labor legislation.

Edson held a variety of positions in the California Progressive party and, later, in the state and national Republican party. President Warren G. Harding appointed her to the Advisory Delegation to the Washington Disarmament Conference of 1921 to 1922. But in 1924, angry at the Republican party's treatment of Progressives and women, Edson turned down a party appointment.

Edson formed the Southern California League of Women Voters in 1919 and was serving as director of the Far West Region for the national league when she died in Pasadena.

—Gayle Gullett

SUGGESTED READING:
Braitman, Jacqueline R. "A California Stateswoman: The Public Career of Katherine Philips Edson." *California History* 65 (1986): 82–95, 151–152.
Hundley, Norris C., Jr. "Katherine Philips Edson and the Fight for the California Minimum Wage, 1912–1923." *Pacific Historical Review* 29 (1960): 271–285.

EDUCATION

SEE: Americanization Programs; Cherokee Male and Female Seminaries; Colleges and Universities; Compulsory School Law, Oregon (1922); Field Matrons; Houchen Settlement House; Indian Schools; Language Schools; Morrill Act of 1862; Parochial Schools; Presbyterian Woman's Board of Home Missions; Protestant Home Missionary Programs; Public Schools; School Life on the Frontier; Segregation: Segregation in Education; *Tape* v. *Hurley;* Teachers on the Frontier; United States Indian Policy: Civilization Programs; Woman's Home Missionary Society (Methodist Episcopal)

ELK

The most widespread of all North American ungulates, the American elk (*Cervus elaphus canadensis),* or *wapiti,* once ranged from southern Canada to Mexico and from the Carolinas to California. With the exception of the moose, the elk is the largest member of the deer family, *Cervidae.* Covering almost three-fourths of the United States, its historical range was almost congruent with that of the buffalo. As grazers and browsers, elks lived in a number of Western habitats. MERIWETHER LEWIS and WILLIAM CLARK, as they made their way westward in 1804 and 1805, frequently commented on the numbers of elks they encountered. By the time of the Civil War, however, settlers and market hunters had severely limited their populations, and they were then found almost exclusively west of the Mississippi River. While they were once hunted in more than thirty states, only three states still had elk seasons by 1927. Of the five extant subspecies, only the Rocky Mountain elk survives in substantial numbers.

A mature bull of the species may reach nine feet in length, stand five feet at the shoulders, and weigh up to one thousand pounds. A bull's antlers, which are shed annually, may weigh up to sixty pounds and spread forty-eight inches. Elks' antlers are much desired as a medicine and aphrodisiac in the Orient, and elks are often killed illegally while their antlers are in velvet.

Elks were important natural resources for the inhabitants of Western lands. They provided meat, hides, bones, and antlers, which could be used for a variety of purposes. The male elk's canine teeth were much desired for decoration by both Native Americans and Euro-Americans.

The expansion of Euro-American settlement in the West led to substantial habitat alteration, and with the sustained HUNTING pressures of the latter half of the nineteenth century, elk populations declined dramatically. The development of farms, ranches, and miles of fenced lands prevented elks from reaching their former winter ranges. After thousands of elks starved to death each winter in the Yellowstone and Teton region, attempts were made to feed them in the Jackson Hole, Wyoming, area. In 1912, the National Elk Refuge was created north of Jackson. From 1892 to 1939, more than ten thousand elks were transplanted from the refuge to more than thirty-six states. By the 1990s, there were more than nine hundred thousand elks in the United States.

—Phillip Drennon Thomas

SEE ALSO: Wildlife

SUGGESTED READING:
Bauer, Erwin A. *Horned and Antlered Game.* New York, 1986.
Murie, Olaus J. *The Elk of North America.* Harrisburg, Pa., 1951.

ELKINS, STEPHEN BENTON

Stephen Benton Elkins (1841–1911), lawyer, politician, and land speculator in New Mexico, was born in Ohio.

At the age of three, he moved with his family to Westport, Missouri. Soon after graduating from the University of Missouri in 1860, he joined the United States Army. Elkins was held as a prisoner of war by the Confederate Army, but his life was spared by the intervention of Thomas C. "Cole" Younger. When the outlaw Younger was later committed to life imprisonment for various crimes, Elkins helped obtain his pardon in 1891.

Moving to southern New Mexico Territory in 1863, Elkins soon mastered law and the Spanish language and advanced through the offices of district attorney in Mesilla, territorial attorney general, and U.S. attorney in Santa Fe. From 1873 to 1877, he was the territorial delegate to the U.S. House of Representatives. After his friend Thomas Benton Catron settled in Santa Fe, the two men were highly successful, individually and jointly, especially in the public-lands business. In keeping with common American practices of the period, they used their knowledge of law and languages to their own profit against native New Mexicans and others. In connection with the MAXWELL LAND GRANT COMPANY and other promotions, they were charged with (but rarely brought to court for) bribing surveyors, judges, sheriffs, and other officials, and even for violence. Their land-grant ring—the SANTA FE RING—flourished in the 1870s and 1880s. Elkins retained a residence in New Mexico until 1888. He maintained interests there until his death, but after 1877, his political officeholding was strictly in the East.

In 1875, he married Halli Davis, whose father, West Virginia Senator Henry G. Davis, was a close associate. In 1880, 1884, and 1888, Elkins was prominent in the presidential campaigns of James G. Blaine and Benjamin Harrison. He served in the latter's cabinet as secretary of war from 1891 to 1893. By then in command of West Virginia's Republican party, he served in the U.S. Senate from 1895 until his death.

The Elkins Act of 1903 and the Mann-Elkins Act of 1910 reflect several of his interests as chairman of the Senate Committee on Interstate Commerce—perhaps the apogee of his political achievements. Elkins's greatest claim to philanthropic fame—Davis and Elkins College, established in Elkins, West Virginia, in 1904—was made possible by the great wealth he acquired as a promoter, speculator, lobbyist, attorney, and business manager during the Gilded Age.

—*John Porter Bloom*

SEE ALSO: Younger Brothers

SUGGESTED READING:
Lambert, Oscar D. *Stephen Benton Elkins, American Foursquare*. Pittsburgh, Pa., 1955.

Westphall, Victor. *Thomas Benton Catron and His Era*. Tucson, Ariz., 1973.

ELLWOOD, ISAAC

SEE: Barbed Wire

EL PASO SALT WAR

In 1877, the Rio Grande region around El Paso erupted in the bloodiest civil disorder in the area's history. Mob violence, rape, looting, and murder accompanied the El Paso Salt War, a vicious border dispute centered around the county's largest settlement at the time, San Elizario, and characterized by personal rivalries and racial hostilities that pitted political faction against political faction, Anglo-Americans against Mexican Americans, and the United States against Mexico.

Lying one hundred miles east of El Paso, the Guadalupe salt beds had traditionally provided Mexicans and Mexican Americans living in the lower Rio Grande valley free salt for family use. In 1869, during Reconstruction, a group of moderate Republican businessmen had attempted to take control of the beds and charge a fee for extracted salt, but they were thwarted by a Radical Republican governor of Texas who—mostly to exploit the issue politically—voided their title to the beds by claiming they wanted to appropriate what rightfully belonged to Mexican Americans.

The next attempt to control the salt beds came in 1877, when Charles Howard, an Anglo judge, announced that the salt beds east of El Paso belonged to him and that he planned to charge a fee for extracting salt. Luis Cardis, an Italian American member of the state legislature, saw an opportunity to increase his political fortunes by championing the rights of the Mexican American voters who had elected him. Joining him in his protests against Howard's actions was the Reverend Antonio Borrajo, who as parish priest could ensure the support of San Elizario's ethnic Mexicans. Howard and Cardis engaged in several fist fights before Howard, armed with a shotgun, found Cardis in a general store on El Paso's San Francisco Street on October 10, 1877, and shot him dead. Howard was arrested and set free on bail. As news of the killing spread, a mob of Mexicans from both sides of the river tracked Howard down and executed him by firing squad. Killing two bondsmen in the process, the mob pillaged the homes of Howard's political supporters.

With El Paso's Fort Bliss closed for lack of funds in the U.S. government's post–Civil War military retrenchment, a group of raw, untrained TEXAS RANGERS was called on to quell the violence. Two rangers were killed, the rest were forced to surrender, and all semblance of order broke down. Talk of war between the United States and Mexico ranged both sides of the border, especially after a posse of thirty vigilantes from Silver City, New Mexico, ravaged the lower valley towns, killed people, and destroyed property at will. After peace was finally restored, the U.S. Congress began an investigation in 1878. Congress collected evidence, but no one was ever arrested, although Fort Bliss was reestablished in El Paso, where it has remained ever since. Perhaps because of the disturbance, when the railroad came to El Paso three years later, it bypassed San Elizario. And from the salt beds themselves, the Mexican families of the lower valley were allowed once again to haul out salt free of charge, only now under the watchful eyes of a Texas Ranger.

—*Charles Phillips*

Suggested reading:
Sonnichsen, C. L. *The El Paso Salt War of 1877.* El Paso, Tex., 1961.

EL PASO, TEXAS

At the far western tip of Texas, near the point where New Mexico and the Mexican state of Chihuahua meet, lies El Paso, Texas, the epitome of the Southwest borderland community. With a population in excess of one-half million, El Paso exists as part of a larger, international metropolitan complex that includes the Mexican city of Juárez. Together they compose the largest urban community along the United States–Mexican border, separated by the Rio Grande and national politics but economically, historically, and culturally interdependent. Although El Paso is home to some sixty-five ethnic groups, it is primarily bicultural: Anglo-American and Mexican American. More than 60 percent of the city's population is Mexican American, and Mexican Americans have been in the majority in El Paso since the 1890s. Much of its charm, many of its problems, and its uneasy symbiosis with Cuidad Juárez grow from its dual historical identity as a Spanish Mexican frontier town and as a booming city in the American West.

Spanish El Paso

For centuries, various Indian tribes inhabited the area the Spanish would come to call El Paso del Norte (the Pass of the North) where a great river cuts a deep chasm between two mountain ranges. Probably the first Spaniards to see the northern pass were stragglers from

an ill-fated 1528 expedition to Florida: Álvar Núñez Cabeza de Vaca and three companions had escaped Indian captivity in 1534 to wander the Southwest. Around 1535, they apparently stumbled across the Rio Grande at a spot where "the river . . . ran between some ridges" as they made their way toward Mexico City. The first expedition on record to arrive in the El Paso area from the south consisted of three Franciscans and an armed guard on their way to establish missions in New Mexico. In 1581, the friars heard from the local Indians tales of four Christians they had encountered years before (most historians assume this was a reference to Cabeza de Vaca and his men). In a ceremony near present-day San Elizario in 1598, Juan de Oñate and his troop of colonizers claimed formal possession of the territory drained by the Rio Grande. According to tradition, the first mission—Nuestra Señora de Guadalupe—was founded in 1659, and it still stands in downtown Juárez as the area's oldest historic landmark. Near the mission in the early 1680s, Spanish refugees and Tigua Indians fleeing the Pueblo Revolt in New Mexico established the village of El Paso del Norte (the future Juárez) and three additional missions—San Lorenzo, Senecú, and Sorroco—all in a row along the south bank of the Rio Grande.

By the eighteenth century, Spanish El Paso was a bustling commercial center on El Camino Real. Beginning as a supply route for the Spanish missions, its wagon trains and caravans initially controlled by friars, the Royal Highway ran from Mexico City to Santa Fe and Taos, New Mexico, and, for two centuries, served as the life line of Spain's northern frontier. After the founding of Chihuahua in the early eighteenth century, merchant concerns took precedence over religious interests, and El Paso grew into more than a way station, supplying products of its own to markets both in Santa Fe and in Chihuahua. El Paso's agriculture also flourished, especially its vineyards, which produced wine and brandy that contemporaries ranked among the best in the empire. By century's end, more than five thousand people lived in the area, the largest concentration of population on the frontier. Marauding Apaches, attracted in part by the relative prosperity of the area, had become a major worry, and in 1789, Spain established the presidio of San Elizario to protect its settlers.

An imperial power long in decline, Spain reached its nadir with Napoleon Bonaparte's 1808 invasion of the Iberian peninsula, an invasion that sparked a vast revolutionary movement within the empire and led to the establishment of independent republics throughout Spanish America. One of the last possessions to break from Spain was Mexico in 1821. Mexico incorporated the El Paso settlements into the state of Chi-

A view of El Paso, Texas, in 1883. *Courtesy Aultman Collection, El Paso Public Library.*

huahua. Hardly had the new nation been established, however, before it found its northern regions drawn into the expanding markets of the economically aggressive United States.

American El Paso

For decades, Spanish officials, hostile to American trappers and traders who pursued their callings into Spanish North America, tossed U.S. interlopers in jail.

Stormsville, an early twentieth-century Mexican enclave in the northern foothills of El Paso, was condemned in 1928 as a health hazard. Later, developers turned it into Rim Road, a residential showplace of El Paso's fine homes. *Courtesy Aultman Collection, El Paso Public Library.*

The American explorer ZEBULON MONTGOMERY PIKE, captured above Santa Fe in 1807 and brought to Chihuahua for questioning, found El Paso both friendly and prosperous and described the hospitality of San Elizario as unmatched. His arrival in El Paso might be considered the start of the Anglo-American "advance" into the area, which was only hastened when Mexico, upon independence, immediately invited Missouri traders to begin trafficking with Santa Fe. By the 1830s, many Mexicans were having second thoughts about the Americans, but El Paso was fully caught up in the Santa Fe–Missouri trade, which had extended naturally along El Camino Real to Chihuahua. In fact, Chihuahua—with twice the population of Santa Fe, with extensive and growing mining operations in gold, silver, and lead, and with a mint that issued annually more than one-half million pesos in coin—may well have hoped eventually to replace Santa Fe as "the principal emporium of the overland trade." Thus, El Paso, once a crossroads of the North-South trade along El Camino Real, became a crossroads of the East-West traffic along the SANTA FE AND CHIHUAHUA TRAIL. In addition, Apache raiding, which had begun in the middle of the previous century, continued to plague the El Paso area, and its citizens hoped that they would benefit from American protection of U.S. trade routes from Indian attacks.

By the 1840s, some fifty Americans were engaged in mining or merchandising, half in the capital city of

Chihuahua, a dozen or so more in Corralitos, and the rest in El Paso del Norte. Many of them married Mexican women from prominent and influential families, who provided them with social contacts and business opportunities. Not a few became Mexican citizens, if for no other reason than that doing so allowed them to escape the maze of Mexican regulations regarding "foreign" traders. Some even held office in state and local governments, and officeholding required citizenship, which put them in a good position to protect their personal interests. A number of them, especially among those arriving before 1840, made fortunes, men such as JAMES WILEY MAGOFFIN and Hugh Stephenson who took their place beside the Mexican rancheros, such as Juan Maria Ponce de León. None of these wealthy entrepreneurs wanted war, which would have disrupted trade, destroyed profits, and devastated their home life, but the same cannot be said for Americans arriving in El Paso after 1840.

Mostly men in their twenties who remained both American citizens and single, the new arrivals suffered from the expansionist fever gripping the United States, a fever that led them to believe Providence had declared it their MANIFEST DESTINY to extend the American nation to the Pacific. The Mexicans responded with a virulent anti-American rhetoric of their own, and the conflict flared into war in May 1846. By December, Colonel ALEXANDER WILLIAM DONIPHAN had led his Missouri volunteers to victory at Brazito (Little Arm), thirty miles north of El Paso del Norte, which itself fell to Doniphan the following February at the Battle of Sacramento. The Americans took possession of Chihuahua in March of 1847 and Mexico City in September. Following the Treaty of Guadalupe Hidalgo (which ended the UNITED STATES–MEXICAN WAR and fixed the border at the Rio Grande west to the Pacific) and the MEXICAN CESSION (a vast territory that was north of the treaty line and which composed half of the Mexican nation), the Anglo-Americans founded five new settlements along the left bank of the Rio Grande. One of those, Franklin, would be incorporated in 1873 as El Paso, Texas, with a population of eight hundred. Across the river, now an international boundary, lay the border town of El Paso del Norte, which would not be renamed Cuidad Juárez until more than a decade later in 1888.

El Paso, Texas, remained a little adobe village until the arrival of the railroad in 1881 transformed it into a thriving "frontier" town. Close to the mines of northern Mexico, New Mexico, and Arizona, El Paso became a mining and transportation center in large part because, as a gateway to Mexico, it had access to cheap labor. Serving as a terminal for arriving Mexican immigrants, El Paso tapped the labor pool to build its railroads, work on its ranches, clean its homes, clerk in its stores, and toil in the El Paso Smelter.

Considering themselves Mexicans, El Paso's immigrants were deeply involved in the Mexican Revolution of 1910, and they, in part, dragged the city into the conflict along with them. The El Paso–Cuidad Juárez area proved one of the more strategic locations for revolutionary activities. There in 1909, Mexican dictator Porfirio Díaz, hoping to revive his popularity, met with U.S. President William H. Taft. When the revolution broke out the following year, El Paso—with its large and sympathetic Mexican community and its ready access to American arms—became a natural haven for political exiles. After revolutionary forces under Francisco Madero seized Juárez in 1911, arms sales boomed, Mexican exiles sought safe haven and a base of operation in El Paso, and racial tensions soared along the border, especially during the U.S. occupation of Veracruz in 1914 and after FRANCISCO ("PANCHO") VILLA's raid on Columbus, New Mexico, in 1916. The Mexican Revolution was a cataclysmic upheaval: one million people lost their lives; property losses ran more than $1 billion; most of the major revolutionary leaders died violent deaths; treachery and betrayal were endemic. The revolution also revealed clearly the special relationship of El Paso, the border town, with Mexico in general and with Cuidad Juárez in particular.

The American army beefed up its presence at Fort Bliss; the expanded ranks enhanced El Paso's reputation as a military town and formed the historical nucleus of a defense industry that would become essential to the city's economy for the rest of the century. When Mexican immigrants poured into El Paso via the Central Mexico Railroad, the border town became a focal point of international commerce, in which the elite Mexican exiles played a role. In addition to being a smelter center and a major cattle town, El Paso developed local enterprises such as the wholesale and retail trade, manufacturing, tourism, and construction. While the "Chihuahuahita" barrio swelled into one of the worst slums in the country, Anglo leaders developed plans to exploit El Paso's mild climate, ample natural resources, and vast labor pool to the fullest. As early as 1906, for example, the city announced the construction of the Elephant Butte Dam, which landed it in a political war with New Mexico over water rights, a dispute that has yet to be resolved. By 1942, as another example, under the United States–Mexican *bracero* program, Anglos were bringing Mexicans into the country at the rate of two thousand per month to work in El Paso's cotton fields. Politicians as well as businessmen were aware of the potential offered by the concentration of Mexicans in El Paso. In the early decades of the twentieth century, the Democratic machine, called the "Ring," sought to dominate the immigrant vote through the use of Mexican American politicos, a vast patronage, and, if all else failed, outright purchase. Many immigrants—caring little about American politics one way or the other because they considered themselves Mexicans, lived close to their homeland, and hoped eventually to return—saw no reason not to accept a much needed job or cash in return for a vote.

Courtesy of the dam and Anglo development, white El Paso came to live in green valleys and to enjoy a solid economic base, an impressive downtown, and attractive residential areas, with many buildings designed by their favorite architect, Henry C. Trost. The vast immigrant labor pool ensured that BARRIOS became a permanent feature of border life, and residential segregation restricted economic mobility. In the twentieth century, Juárez became more El Paso's dark shadow than "sister" city. Juárez had long seemed to Anglos a wide-open border town of gambling dens, saloons, and houses of prostitution. The coming of Prohibition stimulated new industries—smuggling, bootlegging, and entertainment. Not only was Juárez in many respects "de-Mexicanized," it became, according to W. H. Timmons, something of an economic tributary of El Paso, the latter's red-light district and labor reserve, although it was certainly a major metropolitan area as well. In the late twentieth century, as U.S. companies struggled with rising labor costs at home, they turned increasingly to Mexico. El Paso and Juárez went through an economic revolution stimulated by the mixed blessings of the *maquila* industry, or "twin-plant program," by which U.S. raw materials were converted into component parts in El Paso and assembled into finished products in Juárez by such companies as General Electric, General Motors, Sylvania, and RCA, to name a few.

By the middle of the twentieth century, with El Paso's one-half million and Juárez's eight hundred thousand "joined"—as one historian put it—"at the cash register," ethnic tensions between Anglos and Mexican Americans seemed often to lay just beneath the surface. The poorest lived in slums west of Juárez or inhabited the *colonias* on the edge of the city, where tens of thousands made do in cardboard, cinder-block, and adobe shacks. In 1957, when El Paso elected Raymond Telles its first Hispanic mayor, a prominent El Paso businessman lamented, "How can we hold our heads up in the State of Texas when we have a Mexican mayor?" As the century drew to a close, the decline in the American defense industry and the backlash against immigrant labor posed great challenges for the borderland community of El Paso, whose international metropolitan population was approaching two million and whose

symbiosis with Juárez was not only a "problem" but had also been the traditional source of the area's dynamic growth.

—*Charles Phillips*

SEE ALSO: Mexican Settlement; Spanish-Mexican Towns

SUGGESTED READING:
Garcia, Mario T. *Desert Immigrants: The Mexicans of El Paso, 1880–1920.* New Haven, Conn., 1981.
Sonnichsen, C. L. *Pass of the North.* 2 vols. El Paso, Tex., 1968. Reprint. 1980.
Timmons, W. H. *El Paso: A Borderlands History.* El Paso, Tex., 1990.

EMIGRANT GUIDEBOOKS

The tradition of the emigrant guidebook in American literature begins, quite literally, with the publications of John Smith and his peers concerning conditions in seventeenth-century Virginia, complete with instructions for settlers. In the nineteenth century, as the United States faced the new West, settlers began to follow explorers to Texas, California, and Oregon, as well as to

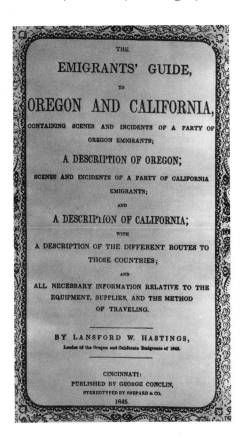

Title page from Lansford Warren Hastings's 1845 *The Emigrants' Guide to Oregon and California. Courtesy Library of Congress.*

the country between the Mississippi and the Pacific Coast. Among the earliest chroniclers of the way west was a relative of STEPHEN FULLER AUSTIN named Mary Austin Holley, who traveled to Texas in the early 1830s and published two guides (one in 1831 and one in 1836) that provided information for those planning to move to Texas.

The routes to California and Oregon gained importance during the 1840s with the discovery of gold in 1848 and the agricultural opportunities in the new Oregon Territory. The federal government provided support for the emigrants in a series of publications illustrated with maps and images produced by the exploratory expeditions. Government reports were first published in 1838. Noteworthy publications included the reports by JOHN CHARLES FRÉMONT on his expeditions to the West Coast and the TRANSCONTINENTAL RAILROAD SURVEYS of the 1850s.

The popular press supplemented government publications with a series of works that were based on the experiences of early explorers and settlers. Many newspapers published letters from those who had gone to the West—letters that served as guides for the settlers to follow. In the 1840s, private publications appeared, including JOHN BIDWELL's 1842 *A Journey to California*. The first real guidebook to the Pacific Coast was *The Emigrants' Guide to Oregon and California*, published in 1845 by LANSFORD WARREN HASTINGS; it was better for the Oregon Trail than for California trails. This guide was followed by books by Joel Palmer, who took advantage of interest in Oregon generated by the settlement of the Oregon border. In 1848, Edward Bryant provided the first guide to the California Trail, and William Clayton offered a guide, entitled *The Latter Day Saint's Emigrant Guide,* for travelers heading to Utah. Most popular was Joseph E. Ware's *The Emigrants Guide to California*. Ware had used reports of the trail but had never been to California.

All of the guides were full of inaccuracies, if not dangerous advice—the Hastings volume, used by the DONNER PARTY, suggested a precarious shortcut and contributed to the disaster suffered by that group. Many used the guides, including both newspaper accounts and the books, but most were careful not to rely solely on them. Even so, they were important in making the trails to the West accessible to people who wished to travel routes that, before the 1840s, had been traveled only by explorers and military men.

—*Patrick H. Butler, III*

SUGGESTED READING:

Goetzmann, William H. *Exploration and Empire: The Explorer and the Scientist in the Winning of the American West*. New York, 1966.

Holley, Mary Austin. *Texas*. Austin. Tex., 1985.

Tyler, Ron. *Prints of the West: Prints from the Library of Congress*. Golden, Colo., 1994.

Unruh, John D., Jr. *The Plains Across: The Overland Emigrants and the Trans-Mississippi West, 1840–1860*. Urbana, Ill., 1979.

EMMA MINE

The Emma Mine is remembered more for the financial machinations surrounding its development than for the quality or quantity of the ore it yielded. In 1868, two prospectors working the Little Cottonwood Canyon, near Alta, Utah, discovered a silver deposit. Too poor to exploit the find on their own, they were forced to give up a third of the future profits from the mine to New York investor James E. Lyon in exchange for cash to work their claim. The prospectors also offered a San Francisco mine promoter the option to buy the mine for $1.5 million if he could pay off Lyon's share. Instead, the promoter found two Eastern investors willing to buy a half interest in the venture for $375,000, and together the new investors and the promoter organized the Emma Silver Mining Company with the intention of selling the property to English backers. Lyon hired Nevada's U.S. Senator William M. Stewart to represent him in the affair, with the understanding that Lyon's part of the proceeds from the sale would not exceed $500,000, which represented his one-third share of the $1.5 million the two prospectors had been asking for originally.

Because the Emma Mine's ore was so rich, it quickly became well known in England, in part because the Americans had secretly hired Baron Albert Grant, a London financier whose reputation was dubious but whose promotional skills were unparalleled. By the time Grant was finished, a well-regarded Yale professor had reported favorably on the mine and its ore (for a $25,000 fee); a distinguished board of directors had been assembled (including, among others, three members of Parliament, the U.S. minister to the Court of St. James, the former president of the New York Central Railroad, and the senator from Nevada, William Stewart); Lyon had been bought out for a trifling £50,000 (half of what he expected); shares that began selling at £20 were going for £50; and shareholders had sunk more than £500,000 into the venture (many times more than what the American "vendors" had paid for the mine). Then a rival company pointed out that the Emma claim had been incorrectly recorded and that the company was working its mine simply in order to pay initial dividends with no hope of future profits. Next came news of a cave-in at the mine, and the bubble burst. By 1872, the directors admitted that the mine's ore was exhausted, and the public began to shout fraud.

Congress investigated the role of the U.S. minister to England in the affair and forced him to resign. When investors discovered that one of the board members also held shares in the rival company that had disclosed the Emma Mine's shortcomings, lawsuits followed. In the long run, the American vendors won, and the London shareholders were forced to sell at a fraction of their investment. In 1882, the Americans reorganized, establishing the first in a series of new Emma silver-mining companies, none of which succeeded. The mine shut down for good when the price of silver collapsed in 1893. By then, the Emma Mine had become the classic example of fraudulent investments in Western silver and gold mines, and Utah's mining community had such a reputation for chicanery and legerdemain that legitimate investors avoided the entire region for more than a generation after the 1870s.

—*Kurt Edward Kemper*

SEE ALSO: Silver Mining

SUGGESTED READING:
Spence, Clark. *British Investments and the American Mining Frontier, 1860–1901*. Ithaca, N.Y., 1958.

EMORY, WILLIAM HEMSLEY

An officer in the CORPS OF TOPOGRAPHICAL ENGINEERS, William Hemsley Emory (1811–1887) was an artillery officer in the Civil War and commander of the Washington Territory and the Department of the Gulf. He retired from the army with the rank of brigadier general in 1876.

"Bold Emory," as he was known to his friends, was born in Queen Anne's County, Maryland, to a family of wealthy landowners. He received his appointment to West Point from JOHN CALDWELL CALHOUN. He graduated in 1831, served for five years as an artillery officer, and then resigned; two years later, in 1838, he accepted the commission of first lieutenant in the Corps of Topographical Engineers. The appointment was to his liking, for Emory was intensely interested in science and was a leading member of scientific circles in Washington, D.C. He was also an excellent surveyor.

At the beginning of the UNITED STATES–MEXICAN WAR, Emory was assigned to accompany General STEPHEN WATTS KEARNY's army as it advanced from Fort Leavenworth by way of Bent's Fort and Santa Fe to San Diego. Although his primary role was as chief engineer, he was involved in several battles and was brevetted major. His report of the expedition, *Notes of a Military Reconnaissance from Ft. Leavenworth, in Missouri, to San Diego, in California,* revealed his superior capacities as a keen observer, scientist, and military leader.

From 1848 until 1853, Emory was engaged in the surveying the new United States–Mexican border. The boundary commission responsible for running the line according to terms of the Treaty of Guadalupe Hidalgo was poorly managed by a civilian, JOHN RUSSELL BARTLETT. The commission owed much of its success to the hard work of Emory and fellow topographical engineer, Lieutenant Amiel Weeks Whipple.

On August 16, 1854, Emory was appointed commissioner and chief astronomer for the survey of the GADSDEN PURCHASE. He handled the Apaches sternly but fairly, got along well with his Mexican counterparts, and prevented dissension in his own ranks. Work proceeded smoothly. By January 1857, the field records were closed, and Emory's *Report on the United States and Mexican Boundary Survey* was published. It included scientific and geographic articles; Emory's principal contribution was cartographic.

After the Gadsden Purchase survey, Emory transferred to the cavalry and served in the Utah Territory and the Indian Territory. At the outbreak of the Civil War, he reinforced Fort Leavenworth, Kansas. In March 1862, he was assigned major general of volunteers. He participated in the Peninsular and Red River campaigns and served under PHILIP H. SHERIDAN in the Shenandoah Valley.

Praised for his leadership and soldierly qualities, Emory enhanced nineteenth-century exploration of the American West by the emphasis he placed on the scientific and geographical study of the new land.

—*Richard A. Bartlett*

SEE ALSO: Exploration and Science

SUGGESTED READING:
Goetzmann, William H. *Army Exploration in the American West: 1803–1864*. New Haven, Conn., 1959. Reprint. Austin, Tex., 1991.
Wallace, Edward S. *The Great Reconnaissance*. New York, 1955.

EMPRESARIOS

Empresarios were land agents appointed by the Mexican government to promote settlement of Anglo-American families in the Southwest.

From the end of the eighteenth century to the beginning of the nineteenth, TEXAS lingered as an outpost of a disintegrating Spanish empire in America. Although various cities, missions, and trading posts dotted the region as centers of economic, religious, cultural, and military activities, most of Texas remained uninhabited, subject to continuing Indian raids and vulnerable to boundary disputes with the government of the United States.

In January 1821, MOSES AUSTIN applied for a grant to settle three hundred Anglo-American families in Texas. The Spanish government welcomed the opportunity to legitimize its territorial claim by awarding a grant of approximately two hundred thousand acres to Austin. While preparations for sectioning the land were being made, Austin died, and Mexico achieved independence from Spain. The new provisional Mexican government refused to recognize the Moses Austin grant, and his son, STEPHEN FULLER AUSTIN, was forced to reapply. In October 1821, he was granted a new empresario license to operate in Texas, and the era of the empresario in Texas began.

Throughout the 1820s, the licensing of American empresarios was very popular in Texas particularly after the Mexican government enacted a new Mexican Colonization Law in 1824. The law legitimized the role of the land agent and provided for his compensation: after settling a minimum of two hundred families, the empresario would receive roughly 66,778 acres of land.

The presidency of Mexico changed several times in the 1820s, but the terms of the original Stephen Fuller Austin grant remained essentially the same. Many entrepreneurs came to Texas to try their hand at land promotion. Some of the most renowned empresarios were Sterling C. Robertson, who received a grant to settle eight hundred families in the Brazos River basin; Samuel May Williams, private secretary and later a partner of Stephen Fuller Austin, who received, along with Austin, several grants to settle seventeen hundred families; and Green C. DeWitt, who received a grant to settle four hundred families in an area surrounded by the Guadalupe, San Marcos, and Lavaca rivers. Other empresarios who contributed to settling the region were General JAMES WILKINSON, Robert Leftwich, Martin DeLeon, Haden Edwards, James Power, James Hewetson, John McMullen, James McGloin, and Arthur G. Wavel. None was as successful in dealing with the Mexican authorities as Austin, however.

The empresarios in Texas provided favorable opportunities for the entry of thousands of Anglo-American families. Because they were so successful, the Mexican government gradually grew to distrust the land agents and their settlers, thus leading to political instability and eventually to the TEXAS REVOLUTION.

—*Fred L. Koestler*

SEE ALSO: National Expansion: Texas and National Expansion

SUGGESTED READING:
Todd, William N. *Guide to Spanish and Mexican Land Grants in South Texas.* Austin, Tex., 1988.

ENCOMIENDA SYSTEM

SEE: Slavery and Indenture in the Spanish Southwest

ENGRAVING

See: Art: Popular Prints and Commercial Art

ENLARGED HOMESTEAD ACT OF 1909

The Enlarged Homestead Act, also known as the Dry Farm Homestead Act, was a dry-farming homestead measure that provided for 320-acre grants of nonirrigable, nonmineral lands having no marketable timber. The first states covered by the law were Colorado, Montana, Nevada, Oregon, Utah, Washington, and Wyoming; the law also applied to the territories of Arizona and New Mexico. Idaho and California were included in 1910, North Dakota in 1912, and South Dakota in 1915. Initially, the law required homesteaders to live continuously for five years on the land before they were eligible to receive title to it, but that requirement was amended to three years in 1912.

The act was preceded by significant scientific advancements in dryland farming, particularly by agricultural experiment stations, and by the writings of such advocates as Hardy Webster Campbell and John A. Widtsoe. Endorsements by the Transmissouri Dry Farming Congress and President THEODORE ROOSEVELT further boosted the proposal's popularity. The latter viewed it as a conservation measure that promised to transform marginal lands into a productive agricultural resource.

The bill was championed by Representative Frank W. Mondell of Wyoming and Senator REED SMOOT of Utah. Support for it was generally strong in the West but also significant enough in other geographical regions to pass easily. It was signed into law by Roosevelt in February 1909.

Specialized studies have revealed that only spotty successes were achieved under the Enlarged Homestead Act. It has been criticized by public-land historians and other specialists for offering homesteads of insufficient size to be economically feasible in the semiarid West, for hastening the breakup of the public domain, and for contributing to the rise in farm tenancy.

—*Stanford J. Layton*

SEE ALSO: Farming: Dryland Farming; Homestead Act of 1862; Homesteading; Land Policy

SUGGESTED READING:

Gates, Paul W. *History of Public Land Law Development.* Washington, D.C., 1968.

Peffer, E. Louise. *The Closing of the Public Domain: Disposal and Reservation Policies, 1900–50.* Stanford, Calif., 1951.

EROSION

Erosion is a natural process, the wearing down and remolding by wind, running water, and various kinds of weather of all the landforms on the earth's surface. A removal of surface material from the earth's crust, primarily soil and rock debris, and the transportation of eroded materials from their point of removal, erosion can be greatly retarded or increased by human intervention. In the trans-Mississippi West of the late nineteenth century, as people became aware of the effects of agriculture and industry on a semiarid environment, erosion—especially soil erosion—became an economic and political issue that played a role in conflicts lasting well into the late twentieth century between cattlemen and sheep ranchers, agricultural interests and the FEDERAL GOVERNMENT, and environmentalists and entrepreneurs.

Not until the post–Civil War era would Americans in large numbers move onto the semiarid Great Plains or settle in the huge arid region that comprises a broad belt of mountains, valleys, and deserts between the western limit of the plains and the crests of the Sierra Nevada and Cascade Mountains. In these areas, where many of the mining, livestock, and agricultural booms of the late nineteenth and early twentieth centuries took place, the soils vary widely in texture, structure, and parent material. Reading like a map of Western place names—Sumas, Sunray, Dalhart, Richfield, Kim, Wiley, Ulysses, Sherm, Dallam, Baca—each of the soils respond differently to the sun, the rain, and the wind.

The sandier soils of the Great Plains and Southwest more readily absorb water than the clay soils of the region. Sandy soils have larger particles with fewer sides than clay to hold moisture and thus make more moisture available to plants, which means that plants take root in them more easily than in clay. Sandy soils dry out quicker and start blowing sooner than clay soils. In dry weather, clay cracks, opening "mouths" to the sky to trap rain, but puddles on the lips of the cracks frequently close the soil before it "drinks" deeply, resulting—especially in dry years—in a loss by drainage. Hard rains, quite common on the High Plains, pack clay soils tightly, limiting severely the speed with which the soil absorbs moisture and making it impossible to trap water. Within a small area, the soils change often and quickly, which becomes important because plains weather patterns are cyclical, periods of wet weather alternating with a series of dry years.

During the wet cycles, those grasses requiring more moisture spread from their havens into dangerous soils, only to die quickly during a dry spell and leave stretches of soil exposed to the winds. In some years, 40 percent of the native grass might fall victim to dry weather, and during extended droughts, all of it might vanish. The kinds of grass indigenous to the West also aid natural erosion. After a rain, buffalo grass shoots out stolons to reclaim barren soil, but the tender new blades—especially in open land removed from the home "colony"—fall prey to the dust hurled by Western winds. Animals, like plants, both adjust to the conditions of the soil in order to survive and aid in its erosion. In dry years, without ice, snow, and rain, more insect eggs—grasshopper, grass worm, and others—hatch, and hordes of insects denude the plains of plant life and expose huge swaths of soil. Populations of rabbits and other rodents also increase during dry cycles and eat more of the scant vegetation. When all else fails, there is FIRE, wild fires and man-made conflagrations, both occasionally producing grass fires that consume more than one million acres.

Land use and erosion

To some extent, Native American peoples disrupted the natural cycles of the Western ecosystem. Indians burned brush and prairie grass not only to scare up game but also to clear the soil so that the first light rain or dew would produce shoots on which the game—especially the buffalo—fed. When the buffalo herds began to thin dramatically after the arrival of Europeans, Native peoples continued to hunt as always, despite efforts by Spanish padres, Protestant missionaries, and U.S. government agencies to turn them to agriculture. The Indians saw themselves, however, not as conquerors of nature, but as part of it. As the Pawnees explained to Quaker agents in the 1870s, the hunts had to continue, for without them, there could be no true agriculture. Central to Pawnee ceremonies, buffalo meat ensured the continuance of the natural cycles that allowed human life to exist; hunting buffalo and growing corn were part of nature's cycle of annual renewal.

It was really the Europeans who, coming to America, set in motion the profound ecological transformations that utterly changed the scale of erosion in the delicate soils of the semiarid West. The plants and animals, not to mention the diseases, that the Spanish introduced to the New World took hold in North America faster than the Spaniards themselves. Cattle and horses spread across the Southern Plains and coastal California ahead of permanent Spanish settlement. Spanish mustangs galloped into the Great Basin and onto the Northern Plains where few Spaniards ever traveled. Sheep, more vulnerable to hot weather and natural predators, did not proliferate until the Spanish arrived, when they, too, flourished around the San Antonio missions, the higher reaches of New Mexico, and the California coast.

As they grew ever more numerous, the Spanish grazing animals rearranged the very nature of the arid and ecologically fragile Southwest. The Old World animals brought Old World grasses, "Kentucky" bluegrass, Mediterranean forage plants and weeds, wild oats, and soft cress. While these grasses provided excellent forage, they could hardly stand up to heavy grazing and were quickly replaced by less palatable forbs and TUMBLEWEED. Gathering in large numbers to graze and water, the animals trampled local grasses to the roots, compacted soils in the process, and broke down their structures. Water followed the migrating beasts along well-worn trails; the higher the hills they traveled, the more rapidly run-off from rain and snow eroded the denuded soil, eventually carving deep gullies—the Spanish called them *arroyos*—that swirled with water in heavy rains but lay parched and cracked in drier weather. Such gullying washed water away and lowered water tables rather than allowing it to soak into the soil. Tree-dotted, lush grasslands supporting an abundance of wildlife began to shrink in size, and in places, they turned to desert. The European livestock also altered the capacity of streams and rivers to support human life. Once lined with luxuriant vegetation, the lower reaches of the Gila, Zuni, and Pureco fed groves of cottonwood and provided the Indians with fish and water for their crops of maize and beans. But the alien herds ate the vegetation, and the Spanish chopped down the cottonwoods to make way for pastures and farms and to feed the fires of their mines. In the late nineteenth century, new settlers found the banks washed away, the stream beds widened, the water grown sluggish, the rivers mere gashes trundling through a barren land.

On the Great Plains, similar transformations began with the near extinction of the buffalo. Hunted relentlessly by Americans pouring onto the Great Plains after the Civil War, the buffalo was already in decline from a combination of drought, habitat destruction,

competition with herds of Indian horses and wild mustangs for food and water, and exotic cattle-borne diseases such as tuberculosis and brucellosis. The disappearance of the buffalo created an ecological vacuum on the Great Plains, a vacuum the Americans filled with cattle. First to feed the frontier army after the Civil War, then—with the coming of the railroads—to meet the needs of a nation hungry for beef, cattlemen drove their ever-larger herds onto the plains and overstocked the ranges. Pasture lands of buffalo grass and gamma grass declined as woody plants and forbs increased. When drought coincided with overgrazing, violent rains cut arroyos. The resulting lowering of water tables further weakened vegetation already stressed by constant grazing and drought. When the soil could no longer support cattle, sheep-raisers moved their livestock in, and the grazing sheep destroyed even the forbs the cattle would not eat. The cattle-sheep-erosion cycle was repeated on the sagebrush grasslands of the Great Basin where Russian thistle, the common Western tumbleweed, replaced sagebrush.

After the Civil War, homesteaders too moved onto the Great Plains. Although not enough rain fell beyond the one hundredth meridian to grow either corn or wheat by the methods then practiced in the East, farmers were buoyed by a theory prevailing in Europe (and preached by Professor Cyrus Thomas, who accompanied the UNITED STATES GEOLOGICAL SURVEY of the Territories) that "rain followed the plow." The idea was that by tilling and planting arid regions, farmers could draw more rain from the sky. When the rains did not come, farmers realized that the climate would not change simply because they plowed the plains, and they turned to the kind of dryland farming promoted by Hardy Webster Campbell. Farmers were urged to abandon corn growing and to plant drought-resistant grains like Turkey Red, a hard winter wheat, and sorghums. They plowed deeply in the fall and packed the subsoil, and in the summer, they plowed repeatedly to produce a dust mulch and left part of their fields fallow to trap moisture. As technology improved and mechanization came to farming, ever more acres on the Great Plains were plowed under on larger and larger farms. When World War I created a boom in wheat prices, farmers went crazy for profits and applied the large-scale factory methods of Henry Ford to the mass production of wheat. They practiced "suitcase farming," in which owners did not live on the farms but merely arrived at critical times to oversee planting and harvesting. During the "Great Plow-Up" of the 1920s, huge tracts of the Great Plains were plowed under and stripped of gamma brush and buffalo grass. When the bottom fell out of the market, which it did in 1931, farmers plowed more acres to make up their losses. By the time the long droughts of the early 1930s started, thirty-three million acres lay naked, denuded of grass, and open to the winds. The plowing went on up to the time giant dust storms began to roll across the plains.

Politics and erosion

In the late 1880s, when the cattle industry collapsed on the Southern Plains, it was clear enough that certain enterprises could so increase erosion in the fragile Western ecosystem as to court disaster. And since at least 1878, when JOHN WESLEY POWELL—the explorer who became America's foremost spokesman about the West—published his classic REPORT ON THE LANDS OF ARID REGIONS, many were aware that the key to the whole region was river drainage and erosion. But Westerners had always fought the notion that the government should regulate economic practices and land and water policy in order to prevent unnecessary and potentially devastating erosion. The DUST BOWL of the 1930s changed the dynamics. In a government report entitled *The Future of the Great Plains* (1936), New Dealers argued that the Dust Bowl was not merely the result of natural forces, imperfect farming techniques, or inadequate knowledge; instead, the Dust Bowl was a crisis brought on by socially destructive forces in American culture, by "attitudes of mind" inherent in a capitalist economy—in short, by a hunger for profits. The government planned to develop comprehensive land-use and soil-conservation plans that would ensure the Dust Bowl could never again occur.

Conservation efforts born in the New Deal became an accepted function of the federal government, although not one without critics. In 1935, the government incorrectly decided that the Navajos, who had been sheep-raisers since the Spanish arrived in the Southwest, were overgrazing their reservation lands and that the subsequent erosion was causing silt to build up in the COLORADO RIVER behind the newly constructed Boulder Dam. As a result, the New Dealers unnecessarily slaughtered more than half of the Navajo herds in what they called the NAVAJO STOCK-REDUCTION PROGRAM. By the mid-1940s, when rain had returned to the plains, it was evident that the environmental damage of the Dust Bowl and man-made erosion had not been permanent. Increasingly in recent decades, Western farmers have protested the federal government's excessive concern with conservation of all kinds. At the same time, high crop prices and the expectation of great profits produced new booms during which grasslands were destroyed in order to plant more crops, and in the aftermath came additional dust storms. While some argue that government reforms have hedged the big agribusinesses' power and influence sufficiently, others argue that only a series of serious and prolonged droughts could truly test the adequacy of current government regulation for soil conservation.

—*Charles Phillips*

SEE ALSO: Climate; Soil Conservation Service

SUGGESTED READING:
Bonnifield, Paul. *The Dust Bowl: Men, Dirt, and Depression.* Albuquerque, N. Mex., 1979.
Cooke, Ronald U., and R. W. Reeves. *Arroyos and Environmental Change in the American Southwest.* New York, 1976.
Crosby, Alfred W., Jr. *Ecological Imperialism: The Biological Expansion of Europe, 900–1900.* Cambridge, England, 1986.
Flores, Dan. "Bison Ecology and Bison Diplomacy: The Southern Plains from 1825 to 1850." *Journal of American History* (September 1991): 265–485.
Paul, Rodman W. *The Far West and the Great Plains in Transition, 1859–1900.* New York, 1988.
Paylore, Patricia, and Richard A. Haney, Jr. *Desertification: Process, Problems, and Perspectives.* Tucson, Ariz., 1976.
Worster, Donald. "Grassland Follies: Agricultural Capitalism on the Plains." In *Under Western Skies.* New York, 1992.

ESKIMINZIN (APACHE)

Aravaipa Apache Chief Eskiminzin (ca. 1828–1895) was blamed for many Indian depredations but never proven guilty. He was the son-in-law of Chief Santos, and when Santos died, he assumed leadership himself.

In 1871, Eskiminzin and his band settled in the southern part of present-day Arizona. Their village was adjacent to Camp Grant, commanded by Lieutenant Royal E. Whitman, who was cordial to the Apaches. In retaliation for supposed depredations, a mixed band of whites, Mexicans, and Papago Indians attacked the Apache village, and in the ensuing battle, known as the Camp Grant Massacre, about one hundred Apaches, mostly women and children, were slain. Eskiminzin was absent at the time.

In 1874, the new San Carlos agent, JOHN PHILIP CLUM, found Eskiminzin helpful in the management of the reservation for three turbulent years. The two formed a lasting friendship, and in 1876, Eskiminzin visited Washington, D.C., with Clum.

Eskiminzin became a prosperous small rancher, but his relationship by marriage to the APACHE KID raised suspicions that he was aiding that elusive outlaw. Although Eskiminzin denied the charges, he was arrested in 1891, and he and his band were exiled to Alabama. At the urging of Lieutenant Hugh Scott, who investigated the matter, the chief and his band were returned to San Carlos on November 23, 1894.

—*Dan L. Thrapp*

SUGGESTED READING:

Clum, Woodworth. *Apache Agent: The Story of John P. Clum.* Boston and New York, 1936.

Dockstader, Frederick J. *Great North American Indians: Profiles in Life and Leadership.* New York, 1977.

Schellie, Don. *Vast Domain of Blood: The Story of the Camp Grant Massacre.* Los Angeles, 1968.

ESKIMO INDIANS

SEE: Native American Peoples: Peoples of Alaska

ETHNIC GROUPS

SEE: African Americans; Barrios; Chinatowns; Chinese Americans; East Asians; German Americans; Irish Americans; Italian Americans; Japanese Americans; Jewish Americans; Métis People; Mexican Immigration, 1900–1935; Mexican Settlement; Native American Peoples; Segregation; Spanish Settlement; Stereotypes

EVANGELISTS

Methodists, Baptists, and Disciples of Christ had become famous for their frontier evangelism in the trans-Appalachian West, and the Anglo-American Protestant tradition continued in the trans-Mississippi West. Methodist William Taylor brought the populist tradition of Peter Cartwright to San Francisco and the gold-mining region between 1849 and 1856. Presbyterian SHELDON JACKSON single-handedly took on the missionary superintendency of the Rocky Mountains and Great Plains areas in 1869. By the time of his death, he had added Alaska to the territory in which he worked, and he had reputedly founded more than 150 churches.

Home missionaries faced an even more vast territory and more sparse population in much of the trans-Mississippi West than had been the case in the trans-Appalachian frontier. Travel was thus a common problem for evangelists. When railroad travel became available, missionaries readily took advantage of it. By the 1890s, Baptist Sunday School workers and colporteurs—peddlers of devotional literature—used specially designed Pullman railroad cars to reach remote or transient populations in the West. Eventually, automobiles and airplanes dramatically scaled back the missionaries' difficulties in transportation.

The trans-Mississippi West offered another distinctive challenge in addition to that of travel: groups with whom U.S. missionaries had little or no experience—Mormons, Chinese immigrants, and Southwestern Hispanics. CATHOLICS worked especially among Hispanics, although not without tension over Hispanic Catholic culture versus Romanizing trends in the church, as Archbishop JEAN BAPTISTE LAMY found in New Mexico. Some PROTESTANTS, most notably Presbyterians, worked not only with Spanish-speaking Americans but also with Chinese Americans and Mormons. For example, Presbyterian William Speer organized the first Protestant Chinese congregation outside of China in 1853 in San Francisco.

Women were integral to the home MISSIONS of Catholics and Protestants in the West. Among Catholics in Los Angeles, for example, Sister Mary Scholastica Logsdon led the educational and medical work of the Daughters of Charity of St. Vincent de Paul between 1856 and 1884. Among Protestants, Presbyterian DONALDINA MACKENZIE CAMERON stands out as a female evangelist to Chinese American women in turn-of-the-century San Francisco. The mission work among what were termed "exceptional populations" was, by and large, ethnocentric in its conduct and rationale, and for Protestants, it was not remarkable in winning converts, but it was remarkable for its persistence.

English-language Protestant groups sponsored mass evangelism in the urban West when the resources for sponsorship were available and an evangelist was willing to undertake the job. Provincial San Francisco, for example, witnessed two major evangelism campaigns by D. L. Moody from 1880 to 1881 and from 1888 to 1889. In the booming Spokane region from 1908 to 1909, Protestant leaders were worried enough about the growing working class in their young city to sponsor a revival campaign by Moody's most famous immediate successor, Billy Sunday.

Catholics had their own version of mass evangelism—the parish mission. Jesuit James Chysostom Bouchard, a Delaware Indian, was the most famous parish-mission preacher and Catholic lecturer in the nineteenth-century West. Based in San Francisco, he toured much of the Far West between 1861 and 1889 and drew crowds with his defense of Catholicism and attacks on Protestantism.

The Protestant Episcopal church did not have a Bouchard, but in DANIEL SYLVESTER TUTTLE they did have a missionary bishop of Montana, Utah, and Idaho from 1867 to 1886. Tuttle was indefatigable in touring his diocese and winsome in presenting the gospel in Episcopal form to Mormons and other townspeople, farmers, miners, and loggers in the region.

Other frontier evangelists who became at least local or denominational legends could be mentioned: William Wesley Van Orsdel, or "Brother Van," a Methodist circuit rider in Montana beginning in 1872; Methodist "Father" John L. Dyer, who made the Colorado mining camps his mission territory beginning in 1861; Texas Baptists George W. Slaughter and L. R. Millican; JASON LEE and A. J. McNamee, Methodists in Oregon; John Powell, a Disciples evangelist in Oregon; Bert Foster, a circuit-riding Episcopalian in the mining regions of Idaho, Utah, and Wyoming; and George D. Peacock, Jr., a convert from Mormonism who became an indefatigable Presbyterian Sunday School missionary and colporteur in the northern Rockies. By 1930, however, the maturation of the urban West was far enough along to overshadow the remaining home-mission efforts in parts of the rural West. While evangelism did not end, the frontier evangelist as a symbolic religious pioneer was already becoming a staple of nostalgia about the West.

—Douglas Firth Anderson

SUGGESTED READING:

Anderson, Douglas Firth. "San Francisco Evangelicalism, Regional Religious Identity, and the Revivalism of D. L. Moody." *Fides et Historia* 15 (Spring-Summer 1983): 44–66.

Cochran, Alice Cowan. *Miners, Merchants, and Missionaries: The Roles of Missionaries and Pioneer Churches in the Colorado Gold Rush and Its Aftermath, 1858–1870.* Metuchen, N.J., 1980.

Engh, Michael. *Frontier Faiths: Church, Temple, and Synagogue in Los Angeles, 1846–1888.* Albuquerque, N. Mex., 1992.

Loewenberg, Robert J. *Equality on the Oregon Frontier: Jason Lee and the Methodist Mission, 1834–43.* Seattle, Wash., 1976.

Maffly-Kipp, Laurie F. *Religion and Society in Frontier California.* New Haven, Conn., 1994.

Soden, Dale E. "Billy Sunday in Spokane: Revivalism and Social Control." *Pacific Northwest Quarterly* 79 (January 1988): 10–17.

Szasz, Ferenc Morton. *The Protestant Clergy in the Great Plains and Mountain West, 1865–1915.* Albuquerque, N. Mex., 1988.

Woo, Wesley S. "Presbyterian Mission: Christianizing and Civilizing the Chinese in Nineteenth-Century California." *American Presbyterians* 68 (1990): 167–178.

EVANS, DALE

SEE: Rogers, Roy, and Dale Evans

EVANS, JOHN

John Evans (1814–1897), the second territorial governor of Colorado and businessman, was born in Ohio,

John Evans. *Courtesy Western History Department, Denver Public Library.*

where he attended the Cincinnati College of Medicine. After receiving his degree in 1838, Evans hung out his shingle first in Ohio and then in Indiana before he moved to Chicago. There, he continued his medical practice, served on the faculty at Rush Medical College, and operated the *North-Western Medical and Surgical Journal*. Good investments in real estate made him wealthy by the time he reached his thirties. He entered politics, served on the city council, and made a bid for a congressional seat in 1854. Although he lost the race, he came to the attention of the Midwestern politicians who founded the Republican party.

In 1862, President Abraham Lincoln appointed Evans territorial governor of Colorado. He assumed the executive's seat three years after the discovery of gold swelled the number of white settlers on the Colorado plains. As the whites moved in, the Cheyenne and Arapaho Indians found their pasture lands and hunting grounds disappearing. Some Indians retaliated with raids on white settlements, but the raids were far fewer than those imagined by a territory of fearful settlers.

In August 1864, Evans authorized JOHN M. CHIVINGTON to raise the Third Colorado Cavalry, composed of one-hundred-day volunteers, to stand against the Indian threat. To avoid war, Cheyenne Chief BLACK KETTLE followed Evans's instructions and led his people to Sand Creek, near Fort Lyon. There Black Kettle, believing his people were under the protection of the military, made camp. On November 29, 1864, Chivington launched a brutal surprise attack on the Indians.

Evans's role in the SAND CREEK MASSACRE became the subject of bitter public debate and of intense federal investigation. The governor was forced out of office in 1865. As a private citizen, he worked to develop the Denver Pacific Railroad, connecting the city to the Union Pacific's transcontinental line, and established a seminary, which later became the University of Denver. He remained in his adopted state until his death.

—*Patricia Hogan*

In 1879, African Americans boarded a river boat in Nashville in preparation for their move to Kansas. *Courtesy Kansas State Historical Society.*

SUGGESTED READING:
Kelsey, Harry E., Jr. *Frontier Capitalist: The Life of John Evans.* Boulder, Colo., 1969.

EXODUSTERS

The promise of free land and a chance to work their own farms out West drew many AFRICAN AMERICANS, discontented with their lives in the post–Civil War South, to Kansas in the 1870s. Likening their migration to the Israelites' search for the Promised Land, the Exodusters sought a liberation from the South's repressive laws and economic practices that made them hardly better off than slaves, even though emancipation had freed them a decade before.

"Kansas Fever" occurred at a time of intense African-American mobility. Many Southern families moved only to the next county or to the next state west in search of better tenant contracts. Other black Americans, in organizations such as the National Colored Colonization Society, planned elaborate migrations to lands as far away as Cyprus and Liberia. The migrations of short distances changed only the location, but not the nature, of a black tenant's life. The schemes to establish settlements in foreign lands were expensive, and thus impractical, for a group of people too many of whom were trapped in debt by their tenant contracts. But out West was Kansas, not so far away as a foreign country and free of the restrictive laws and social customs prevalent in the South. Rumors of free transportation and free supplies circulated among blacks in Southern states. Although the rumors

were not true, it hardly mattered. African Americans began their trek with or without funds.

The movement had several leaders, including Henry Adams of Louisiana and BENJAMIN ("PAP") SINGLETON of Tennessee. Singleton promoted the exodus with a missionary's conviction and zeal. Traveling to Kansas himself in the mid-1870s, he returned to Nashville to report that settlers in Kansas were prospering and organized groups of migrants to colonies his Edgefield Real Estate and Homestead Association had established. Not all emigrants traveled under the auspices of the "exodus" promoters. Thousands migrated almost spontaneously.

African Americans with enough money to purchase workhorses, seed, and farming tools journeyed to Exoduster colonies such as Nicodemus in Graham County or the Singleton Colony at Dunlap. Nicodemus, the most successful of the African American colonies, was first settled in 1877 and 1878 by blacks from Lexington, Kentucky. By 1880, the settlement's population totaled about seven hundred, and the community continued to prosper into the mid-1880s.

The less fortunate Exodusters stopped in eastern Kansas and found work as farm or railroad laborers and scrubwomen or domestic servants. Some eventually saved enough money to begin farming; others remained in towns and cities and settled in sections such as Topeka's Tennessee Town. The large numbers of African Americans migrating to Kansas in 1879 alarmed a number of white Kansans. Reactions ranged from efforts to curtail further black settlement to compassionate appeals for relief for the most destitute of the Exodusters.

Estimates of the numbers of African Americans journeying to Kansas in the 1870s vary; the black population in Kansas during the decade increased by about twenty-six thousand, although not all of the increase was a result of migration.

—*Patricia Hogan*

SUGGESTED READING:

Painter, Nell. *Exodusters: Black Migration to Kansas after Reconstruction.* Lawrence, Kans., 1986.

Savage, W. Sherman. *Blacks in the West.* Westport, Conn., 1976.

EXPLORATION

Covered here are the North American explorations of various nations. For exploration in Alaska, see also ALASKAN EXPLORATION.

English Expeditions
Charles Phillips

French Expeditions
James P. Ronda

Russian Expeditions
James P. Ronda

Spanish Expeditions
James P. Ronda

United States Expeditions
Charles Phillips

ENGLISH EXPEDITIONS

After John Cabot, a Genoese sailor hired by Henry VII, made landfall in June 1497 along the southern shore of Newfoundland and laid claim to North America for the English Crown, England ignored the continent for nearly eighty years. Not until the Elizabethan period, when England entered wholeheartedly the competition with Spain for overseas empire, did English sea dogs take up exploring again. Sir Francis Drake sailed the *Golden Hind* up the California coast in 1578; Sir Humphrey Gilbert tried to establish a colony in Newfoundland in 1583; after Sir Walter Raleigh's colony at Roanoke foundered, Jamestown, in Virginia, was established in 1609. American colonials, men like Conrad Weisner, Christopher Gist, and George Croghan, historical archetypes of Western "frontiersmen," explored the North American interior from the compact Atlantic Coast settlements. Driven by land speculation and the FUR TRADE, they traipsed the Ohio River valley as far west as the Mississippi.

Launched on two centuries of imperial struggle with France and with an increasingly ailing Spain, caught up in the commercial scramble for overseas trade routes and commodities, and making a claim for its place in the Enlightenment's great scientific enterprise, England by the eighteenth century was fully engaged in worldwide exploration. Captain JAMES COOK's three voyages from 1768 to 1780, during which he "discovered" Hawaii and cruised the Northwest Coast from Puget Sound to Alaska, became the model of commercial and "scientific" exploration. In 1792, Captain George Vancouver mapped the coast from San Diego to Alaska. Both men were interested in the fur trade, which spawned explorations throughout both the Canadian Northwest and the trans-Mississippi West.

British exploration of the North American interior was spurred by the rivalry between the two giants of the American fur trade, the HUDSON'S BAY COMPANY and the North West Company. Profit-minded business ventures, both struggled fiercely to control the Northwest fur trade and concerned themselves with imperial policies or scientific investigations only as they affected their purses. By 1691, a Hudson's Bay Company factor named Henry Kelsey, working southwest from York on Hudson's Bay, had explored the vast Canadian plains. Captain James Knight founded a fort at Churchill in 1717. In 1755, Anthony Henday broached Blackfoot Indian country along the foothills of the Northern Rockies. But by far the most important of the early Hudson's Bay explorations was Samuel Hearne's expedition up the Coppermine River to the Arctic Sea in 1771. That difficult trek ended in the massacre of some Arctic Indians and should have laid to rest the legend of a short NORTHWEST PASSAGE flowing out of Hudson's Bay and connecting East and West.

All of these were company-sponsored expeditions, and with its chartered monopoly, the Hudson's Bay Company attempted to control all exploration into the interior. But free-lancers, many of them French, operating out of Montreal and traveling west by lakes and portages beyond the Rocky Mountains, continued to trap and explore, and a virtual war began. When American trappers entered the trade in 1783 after the American Revolution, the Canadian free-lancers founded the North West Company. Caught between the Americans to the south and Hudson's Bay posts to the north, the North West Company proved the more daring. By necessity, it adopted a policy of competing by expanding production, and that led to wandering the Canadian and American wilderness in search of routes to the Pacific.

"Northwesters," as members of the company were called, sometimes mingled with American free-lancers. One of the more important explorations grew out of just such connections. By 1778, an American from Connecticut named PETER POND, who together with another American trader and explorer, Henry Alexander, had allied himself with the company, established a trading post near Lake Athabaska. Fascinated by the possibility of a Northwest Passage, Pond and Alexander petitioned the British Royal Society in 1781 to finance an expedition to the newly discovered Cook Inlet on the Alaskan coast. Although they were turned town, Pond continued to believe in the passage and inspired the twenty-five-year-old Alexander Mackenzie, a full partner in the new North West Company, to launch an expedition in 1789. Crossing one thousand miles of tundra, Mackenzie followed a river that today bears his named and that led him not to the Pacific, but to the Arctic Ocean. He named the river "Disappointment" and sailed back to England to equip and train a second expedition. Setting out from Lake Athabaska in the spring of 1793, Mackenzie traveled west along the Peace River into the Canadian Rockies and discovered the Fraser River, which he believed to be the Columbia. Then, on July 9, he saw "a narrow arm of the Sea." Mackenzie and his men had reached the Pacific and had become the first white men to cross the entire North American continent.

In general, most Northwester expeditions were more modest, and the North West Company truly picked up where the old French explorers left off. As early as 1738, the French *coureur de bois* Vérendrye family had made contact with the Mandans on the Missouri. From there, the North West Company stretched west into the land of the Souris and Assiniboine rivers and the country around the Upper Missouri. Agent Antoine Larocque explored the Yellowstone River in 1805, and North West Company traders wintered each year with the Upper Missouri tribes—the Mandans and others. By then, Alexander Mackenzie had published his monumental *Voyage from Montreal through the Continent of North America to the Frozen and Pacific Oceans* based on the 1789 and 1793 journeys. The book became the bible of exploration for the company's new governor, Duncan McGillvary, who launched a series of trips into the Canadian Rockies and beyond during the opening decade of the nineteenth century.

McGillvary himself crossed the Rockies in 1801, and in 1805, he sent Simon Fraser on to the Pacific. But the greatest of all the North West Company's voyagers was without doubt DAVID THOMPSON, who had the soul of an explorer and a love for map making. Before signing on with the North West Company in 1797, he had traveled some nine thousand miles for the Hudson's Bay Company and mapped its entire domain. The monopoly forwarded his maps on to England's best-known cartographer, Aaron Arrow-

smith. It was Arrowsmith's maps that inspired THOMAS JEFFERSON to dream of the Pacific Northwest and to plan a major exploration of Louisiana. In turn, news of the LEWIS AND CLARK EXPEDITION drove Thompson to take a large party, including his wife and children, over the Canadian Rockies through the Saskatchewan Pass and down the Columbia River to Lake Windermere, where he planted the first trading post west of the mountains. From there, egged on by the threat of competition from arch-rival Hudson's Bay, Thompson threw up trading posts at every strategic spot west of the Rockies as far south as modern-day Montana and secured the cooperation of Native Americans along the way, except for the Blackfoot Indians, who, although they traded with the Canadians, would not let anyone near their hunting grounds.

The fur trade was virtually suspended during the War of 1812, and decay and dissolution set in upon the North West Company. David Thompson, needed elsewhere, was called back to eastern Canada for good, and his replacements were conservative, and, according to one company official, ridiculously inept. Profits fell, the Indians grew disenchanted with all white traders, and for three years, hardly a brigade departed for the interior without running into hostility. In 1821, the two British companies were merged, and the Hudson's Bay Company became an instrument of British foreign policy as well as a commercial enterprise. Company Governor George Simpson, operating on instructions from London, established FORT VANCOUVER inland on the Columbia, which became the center of its explorations.

PETER SKENE OGDEN led five explorations into the Western interior. He traveled south into California via the Willamette Valley and opened a new route to Spanish territory, discovered the Humboldt River flowing across northern Nevada, explored the northern shores of the Great Salt Lake, traversed the Great Basin from north to south, and trekked from the Humboldt Sinks in Nevada down the Colorado River through Needles, California, to the mouth of the river in the California gulf. Knowing more about the West than anyone except perhaps the American mountain man JEDEDIAH STRONG SMITH, Ogden—like Thompson—provided to Aaron Arrowsmith and the Paris map-maker A. H. Brué details so accurate that their maps became the maps of choice for American fur trappers. The Far Western trade of the Americans, in turn, sped the demise of the British influence in the Northwest and brought British exploration to an end.

—*Charles Phillips*

SEE ALSO: Cartography; Exploration and Science; Exploration Narratives

SUGGESTED READING:

Beaglehole, J. C. *Exploration of the Pacific.* Stanford, Calif., 1966.

Cline, Gloria G. *Peter Skene Ogden and the Hudson's Bay Company.* Norman, Okla., 1974

Goetzmann, William H. *Exploration and Empire: The Explorer and the Scientist in the Winning of the American West.* New York, 1966.

———. *New Lands, New Men: America and the Second Great Age of Discovery.* New York, 1986.

Karamanski, Theodore. *Fur Trade and Exploration: Opening the Far Northwest, 1821–1852.* Norman, Okla., 1983.

FRENCH EXPEDITIONS

For nearly two and a half centuries, from the 1530s to the 1760s, French explorers traveled much of North America. These journeys ranged from the St. Lawrence River valley to the Gulf of Mexico by way of the Great Lakes and the Mississippi River. French explorers pressed west beyond Lake Winnipeg and probed the mysteries of eastern Colorado and the northern Great Plains. Even after the defeat of the French empire in Canada in 1760, individual French travelers continued to explore the West. They worked for fur companies and served as scouts and guides for settlers bound for the Pacific. Like other European explorations in North America, the French efforts were driven by several interconnected motives. Capitalist energy—the desire to transform nature into profit—drew fur traders deep into the interior. French fur-trade exploration was prompted not only by the search for more beaver but also for routes that might eventually lead to the great markets of Asia. Fur and the fabled NORTHWEST PASSAGE were constants for several generations of French explorers. An equally powerful motive was the quest for souls to convert to Christianity. Missionary travelers, especially the Jesuits, not only explored territories new to Europeans but also prepared detailed reports. At the beginning of the eighteenth century, as France and Great Britain entered an era of intense competition over the control of eastern North America, exploration became part of imperial military policy. French soldiers spread the influence of the crown, and royal engineers mapped an expanding New France.

From the time of the earliest French voyages of discovery in the 1530s, French explorers were part of a war for America. In that conflict, the French enjoyed many advantages—advantages that put them far ahead of their English and Spanish rivals. The Great Lakes and the Mississippi River system offered the French unparalleled access to nearly half the continent. Using that water-highway network, French explorers moved quickly both east to west and north to south. The technology of birch-bark canoes, borrowed from native people, gave the French the means to use water transportation routes. The very nature of their empire in America compelled the French to study and cooperate with native people. The fur business demanded Indian partners; the missionary quest sought new souls to save; the empire required native allies. Like Spain, France made exploration an integral part of territorial expansion.

While Basque and Breton fishing vessels came to the Gulf of St. Lawrence long before the 1530s, the first official French voyage of discovery sailed those waters in 1534. Led by master mariner Jacques Cartier, the expedition aimed at finding a passage through North America to China. The Northwest Passage was not just a geographical fantasy. Its discovery promised not only economic gain but imperial advantage as well. Cartier's brief reconnaissance convinced him that the St. Lawrence River held the secret to the China passage, and two Indians, taken back to France, seemed to confirm that belief. Cartier's confident report led to a second and larger venture. This voyage, from 1535 to 1536, took him up the St. Lawrence as far as present-day Montreal. While the Lachine rapids blocked his way higher up the river, Cartier was now convinced that another river, the Ottawa, was the route to China. When Cartier returned to France in 1536, he was eager to launch a third venture. French officials did not share his enthusiasm, and it was not until 1541 that a third expedition headed toward the St. Lawrence. Led by Cartier and Jean François de la Rocque, seigneur de Roberval, the large-scale expedition was designed to establish French imperial power in what is now eastern Canada. That massive effort failed when bad weather, bad luck, and arguments between Cartier and Roberval disrupted the entire venture.

The three Cartier voyages did not establish a permanent French presence along the St. Lawrence, but they did emphasize the commercial benefits from such ventures. French explorers did not find gold or diamonds, but they did locate vast stocks of fur and fish. And it was fur and fish that kept French sailors coming back to the St. Lawrence each summer. By the end of the sixteenth century, there was a regular trading fair at Tadoussac, where French and Indian traders exchanged pelts for European iron and textile goods.

The French exploration of eastern Canada changed dramatically in the first years of the seventeenth century as private entrepreneurs and imperial strategists began to formulate colonization plans. No one was more central to that enterprise than Samuel de Champlain. Already an experienced traveler in the West Indies, Champlain came to New France in May 1603. Beginning that year, he undertook a remarkable series of exploration voyages up the Saguenay River and along the coast of northern New England. In 1608,

Champlain established a fur-trading post at Quebec, which he made a base for trading journeys to Lake Champlain and Lake Huron.

While Champlain's fur traders were busy finding new routes and new Indian business partners, a second group of French explorers reached New France with different goals in mind. Missionary priests, first Recollets and then Jesuits, came to Canada in search of souls to save. That spiritual quest took them far afield. By the 1640s, using Indian information, the Jesuits had a remarkably clear picture of the Great Lakes. The Jesuit map of the Great Lakes (1672) not only indicated the general shape of the lakes with considerable accuracy but also pointed to expedition beyond Lake Superior. The year after the Great Lakes map was drafted, French explorers Louis Joliet and Father Jacques Marquette headed down the Mississippi. That journey, aimed at finding a passage to the Pacific, expanded the reach of New France and the missionary spiritual empire.

In the eighteenth century, French explorers traveled well beyond the Great Lakes. War, trade, and missionary zeal all drove the French enterprise west from Lake Superior and south down the Mississippi. The epic journeys of Sieur de La Salle, the Mallet brothers, and the father-and-sons team of the Vérendryes extended the French empire over the center section of the continent. The conquest of Canada by the English in 1760 did not suddenly end the influence of French explorers. In maps and printed accounts and by word of mouth, what the French learned was passed to the next generation of European explorers.

—*James P. Ronda*

See also: Fur Trade

Suggested reading:
Cumming, William P., R. A. Skelton, and David B. Quinn. *The Discovery of North America.* New York, 1972.
Cumming, William P., Susan Hillier, David B. Quinn, and Glyndwr Williams. *The Exploration of North America, 1630–1776.* New York, 1974.
Eccles, William J. *The Canadian Frontier, 1534–1760.* New York, 1969.

RUSSIAN EXPEDITIONS

The Russian exploration of the Pacific coast and the Alaskan interior was part of a three-century process of expansion across Siberia and into the North Pacific. Like exploration enterprises pursued by England, France, Spain, and the United States, Russian strategies joined the fur trade, nation-state imperialism, and the scientific pursuit of knowledge.

On one of many eighteenth-century explorations of the California coast, a Russian artist recorded a tribal dance of Indians located at the San Jose mission. *Courtesy Library of Congress.*

It was largely due to the efforts of Peter the Great that Russian exploration moved beyond Siberia to North America. In the late 1690s, Peter learned from a Dutch geographer that Siberia and America were joined by a land bridge. In 1719, the Russian ruler decided to send two explorers to locate the land bridge. Ivan Evreinov and Fedor Luzhin spent 1720 and 1721 in a fruitless search. Their negative report did not dampen Peter's enthusiasm. In 1725, he prepared sailing directions for Vitus Bering. Peter's motives for creating what is sometimes referred to as the First Kamchatka Expedition remain uncertain. Some historians have argued that Bering was sent to find the fabled land bridge. More recent research has shown that Bering was directed to find land (that is, America) to the east. Peter's intentions were probably centered on the hope of revenue from gold, silver, and fur.

Bering's two voyages (1728 and 1741 to 1742) had dramatic consequences. One of the members of the Second Kamchatka Expedition was naturalist Georg Steller. His report on the fur-bearing animals of the Gulf of Alaska, especially the fur seal and sea otter, set off a fur rush in 1743. The fur trade had been a central factor in Russian expansion across Siberia, and fur now attracted entrepreneurs and hunters to Alaskan waters. Between 1743 and 1799, more than forty private companies made hunting and trading voyages into the North Pacific. Russian *promyshlenniki* (fur hunters) and their native partners reaped a bumper harvest of skins and pelts. By the 1780s, competition in the maritime fur trade was intense. English and American vessels made successful voyages along the coast of what is now British Columbia. In 1797, two of the most powerful Russian companies, the American Company and the Irkutsk Company, merged to form the United American Company. The guiding force for that merger and for future expansion was Gregory Shelikhov, whose vision of Russian America mixed commerce and nationalism.

That expansionist vision came to life between 1799 and 1819. Sometimes known as the Baranov period, the era was named for Governor ALEKSANDR BARANOV, field manager for the newly chartered RUSSIAN-AMERICAN COMPANY. Baranov represented both the Russian state and an influential fur-trade monopoly. He knew that the fortunes of Russian America depended on expansion. New hunting grounds had to be scouted, and reliable sources for foodstuffs had to be secured. During his years as governor, Baranov launched several expeditions, all aimed at solving the provision problem. From 1805 to 1806, Nikolai Rezanov took the ship *Juno* on an inspection trip down the Pacific Coast to the Spanish settlements. Two years later, Baranov planned a more extensive expedition, using two vessels. That venture failed when the schooner *Nikolai* wrecked off the coast of present-day Washington.

The expansionist energies of the Baranov years produced valuable geographic information but little that could immediately fill the company's treasury. In 1819, the company underwent a thorough reorganization. Corporate strategy now emphasized the exploitation of hunting territories in the Alaskan interior. That decision prompted a series of important land expeditions, including the Northern Land Expedition (1829 to 1830), which was led by Ivan Vasilyev and explored the Kuskokwim River. When Arvid Adolf Etholen became governor in 1840, the pace of inland exploration quickened. Etholen never matched Baranov as a patron of expeditions, but his support of the important Lawrence Zakoskin Expedition (1842 to 1844) to the Yukon-Kuskokwim basin was proof of continuing Russian interest in exploration. Despite Etholen's commitment, company officials moved away from such ventures in the 1850s. Changes in the global fur market, competition from the HUDSON'S BAY COMPANY, and moves toward the sale of Alaska to the United States spelled the end of Russian exploration.

—*James P. Ronda*

SUGGESTED READING:

Dmytryshyn, Basil, E. A. P. Crownhart-Vaughan, and Thomas Vaughan, eds. *To Siberia and Russian America: Three Centuries of Russian Eastward Expansion 1558–1867.* 3 vols. Portland, Oreg., 1985–1989.

Gibson, James R. *Imperial Russia in Frontier America.* New York, 1976.

Owens, Kenneth, and Alton S. Donnelly, eds. *The Wreck of the* Sv. Nikolai: *Two Narratives of the First Russian Expedition to the Oregon Country 1808–1810.* Portland, Oreg., 1985.

Smith, Barbara S., and Redmond J. Barnett, eds. *Russian America: The Forgotten Frontier.* Tacoma, Wash., 1990.

SPANISH EXPEDITIONS

No European nation made a greater effort to explore so large a part of North America as did Spain. Spanish explorers—missionaries, soldiers, traders, and bureaucrats—traced the continent from Florida and the Carolinas to the coast of British Columbia by way of Kansas, Texas, Arizona, and New Mexico. That impressive exploration enterprise spanned more than three centuries, from 1513 to 1819, and was driven by a complex set of motives. One adventurer summed up those motives by writing that he and his companions came to America "to serve God and his Majesty, to give light to those who were in darkness, and to grow rich as all men desire to do." For both missionaries and lay folk, the commitment to spread the Christian faith required evangelists to travel to the most remote places. Missionary journeys of exploration, like those undertaken by Father EUSEBIO KINO from 1687 to 1702 and the Franciscans Silvestre Escalante and Francisco Domínguez in 1776, expanded geographical knowledge and enhanced Spanish imperial power. Service to the king prompted the expansion and consolidation of Spain's vast American empire. José de Galvéz, inspector general in New Spain from 1765 to 1771, used exploration to establish Spanish influence in California. By the eighteenth century, service to the empire also involved scientific inquiry. Like their English contemporary Captain JAMES COOK, Spanish explorer-scientists Alejandro Malaspina and Dionisio Alacalá Galiano broadened both imperial and intellectual boundaries. "To grow rich" was a powerful source of energy at the heart of many Spanish voyages of discovery. Acquiring wealth—whether measured in gold, land, or labor—was not only a means to status and influence but also an end in itself.

Spanish exploration in North America focused on three distinct regions. After successful conquests in Cuba, Peru, and Mexico, some Spanish officials and private entrepreneurs looked to present-day Florida and the Southeast. Between 1521 and 1528, Spanish explorers made three unsuccessful efforts to probe the Southeast. Despite what could only be called disasters, the region still held the promise of great wealth. No one succumbed more fully to that illusory promise than Hernando de Soto. Fresh from service in the conquest of Peru, de Soto was eager to make his own fortune in America. Backed by a large armed force, de Soto landed around present-day Tampa Bay in May 1539 and began what would eventually be a four-year march. That journey took the expedition through the present-day states of Florida, Georgia, South Carolina, Alabama, Mississippi, Arkansas, and Texas. De Soto's grand cavalcade has sometimes been described as a colorful, romantic epic, but the journey's consequences were anything but that for the native peoples of the Southeast. The Spanish presence meant not only armed invasion and political confusion but also the spread of new diseases and the disruption of food sources. Students of Southeastern native cultures now recognize that the de Soto expedition was the beginning of profound and deadly transformations in the life of the region.

The Spanish exploration of the Southwest was linked to the de Soto venture by the remarkable overland journey of ÁLVAR NÚÑEZ CABEZA DE VACA and his sometime companions Andrés Dorantes, Alanso Maldonado, and the black slave Esteban. Survivors of the failed PÁNFILO DE NARVÁEZ expedition to Florida in 1528, the travelers had made their way through the Gulf Coast area by measures of cleverness and good luck. Once back in Mexico City, Cabeza de Vaca gave Viceroy Antonio de Mendoza a reasonably accurate report of the journey. That report quickly mixed with the more fantastic speculations propounded by FRAY MARCOS DE NIZA, a missionary priest bent on spreading the Christian faith. Fray Marcos insisted that there were great cities to the north. Those cities promised wealth, power, and souls eager for salvation. Worried that his political rival, Hernán Cortés, might conquer such centers first, Mendoza authorized Fray Marcos and Esteban to make a preliminary reconnaissance in March 1539. That journey cost Esteban his life at the hands of the Zunis. Fray Marcos never saw the Pueblo country, but his report to Mendoza was filled with fantasy about the Seven Cities of Cíbola.

Convinced that Cíbola would be another Mexico or Peru, the viceroy moved quickly to select a leader for what would be Spain's first great thrust into the Southwest. Mendoza's choice was FRANCISCO VÁSQUEZ DE CORONADO, a well-connected politician with no experience as a soldier or explorer. Despite his limitations, Coronado did organize an impressive expedition with a well-prepared set of plans. By April 1540, Coronado was ready to lead an advance guard to Cíbola. The Cíbola promised by Fray Marcos proved to be the Zuni pueblo of Hawikuh, whose wealth was counted not in gold but in corn, turkeys, cotton, and salt. Profoundly disappointed by what he found, Coronado looked beyond the pueblos for another land of promise. His new Eden carried the name Quivira and, as described by an Indian captive, was even grander than Cíbola. In the spring of 1541, Coronado and a small party went in search of Quivira. That quest took the explorers through present-day Texas and Oklahoma and onto the plains of central Kansas. Somewhere near present-day Wichita, the expedition halted when the explorers realized that Quivira was a dream just beyond reach.

While the de Soto and Coronado expeditions failed to attain their immediate goals, the journeys did lay the foundations for Spain's empire in North America. Exploration journeys by soldiers, missionaries, and traders filled in the outlines sketched by de Soto and Coronado. In the eighteenth century, Spanish exploration in North America changed in two important ways. First, exploration became part of a larger Enlightenment scheme for the scientific study of the natural world. Second, Spanish exploration increasingly reflected an imperial policy that was essentially defensive. On the northern reaches of the Pacific Coast, challenges came from the Russians and the English. Beginning in 1774, the Spanish sent out a number of maritime expeditions aimed at turning back those imperial rivals.

Journeys of exploration gave Spain an unprecedented store of information about vast portions of North America. That information was kept in journals, letters, maps, and drawings. Since Spain viewed virtually all such material as secret, many important observations and discoveries went unnoticed.

—*James P. Ronda*

SEE ALSO: Cíbola, Seven Cities of; Cartography

SUGGESTED READING:

Engstrand, Iris. *Spanish Scientists in the New World: The Eighteenth-Century Expeditions.* Seattle, Wash., 1981.

Goetzmann, William H., and Glyndwr Williams. *The Atlas of North American Exploration.* New York, 1992.

Milanich, Jerald, and Susan Milbrath, eds. *First Encounters: Spanish Explorations in the Caribbean and the United States, 1492–1570.* Gainesville, Fla., 1989.

Weber, David J. *The Spanish Frontier in North America.* New Haven, Conn., 1992.

UNITED STATES EXPEDITIONS

American exploration of the trans-Mississippi West, most of which took place in the nineteenth century, was not simply a matter of government-sponsored expeditions in search of new lands, new trade, and new knowledge, but also one of nation building, of individuals engaged in local commerce and settlement. By the time THOMAS JEFFERSON launched the LEWIS AND CLARK EXPEDITION in 1804 for all the proper official reasons—to explore and document the LOUISIANA PURCHASE, to befriend the Indians with an eye toward expanding trade, and to conduct a reconnaissance of vaguely defined boundaries—Yankee traders had long been plying the bays and inlets of the California and

Oregon coasts; backwoods hunters were trafficking with the native peoples along the Missouri; and Natchez and New Orleans merchants were trading deep into the Spanish-held Southwest. Jefferson's plans for an expedition, concocted before the Louisiana Purchase, were based in part on Captain Robert Gray's 1792 discovery of a river in the Pacific Northwest, which he named after his ship, the *Columbia*, a discovery, Jefferson argued, that gave the United States some title to the land between the Mississippi and the Pacific. But he would have mounted explorations in any case, without Gray and without the Louisiana Purchase, since, intellectually at least, he resembled that part of his constituency already dedicated to "westering."

Those engaged in the FUR TRADE were not only some of the first explorers of the trans-Mississippi West, but also the most intrepid. JOHN COLTER traveled west with MERIWETHER LEWIS and WILLIAM CLARK, but he left them upon meeting two Kentucky long hunters to take up trapping beaver and afterward went to work for MANUEL LISA'S MISSOURI FUR COMPANY. In the course of some incredible wanderings, he became the first white to behold, and report on, the wonders of the Yellowstone region. JOHN JACOB ASTOR, whose retail operations had made him the richest man in America, went into the production end of the fur trade, at Jefferson's urging, by establishing ASTORIA on the Pacific Coast. In order to do so, he sent WILSON PRICE HUNT overland to build a fort in Oregon, and Hunt—forewarned by Lewis and Clark that the Blackfoot Indians were hostile—took a more southerly route through new country. When company man Robert Stuart led a party of Astorians back east, he crossed the Continental Divide just south of the Wind River Mountains, thereby blazing the trail through the South Pass that would become the grand highway of westward migration to Oregon.

The heyday of the fur trade's rugged MOUNTAIN MEN came after the slump in the industry created by the War of 1812. Between 1820 and 1840, those who answered the call of two St. Louis fur traders—ANDREW HENRY and WILLIAM HENRY ASHLEY—for "enterprising young men" explored and trapped beaver along the Missouri and into the Rocky Mountains and beyond, and many of them became famous in the process. Without question, mountain man JEDEDIAH STRONG SMITH was one of the greater explorers America ever produced. In the late 1820s, he traversed every part of the trans-Mississippi West from the upper Missouri to the deserts of the far Southwest. He knew well the Rocky Mountains, the Great Plains, California and Oregon, the Columbia River region and the Great Basin, which he was the first to cross. He pioneered the central route across the Rockies through the South Pass, and he per-

sonally informed the United States government of the grand possibilities of settlement in Oregon and California in a keen geopolitical letter that gained national attention when it was published by Congress in 1830.

Smith, however, was by no means the only mountain-man explorer. In the early 1820s, hard on the heels of Mexico's declaration of independence from Spain, WILLIAM BECKNELL had journeyed south to Santa Fe from Missouri and set up trading along the Santa Fe Trail. By 1827, James Ohio Pattie and his father, Sylvester Pattie, had worked their way from Santa Fe west to southern California. They were followed in 1839 by EWING YOUNG and William Wolfskill, who forged the Old Spanish Trail to Los Angeles. In 1833, JOSEPH REDDEFORD WALKER had crossed the Sierra Nevada into California and, on his way back, located a major gateway through the mountains that immigrants would know as Walker's Pass. Walker's knowledge of the West was probably more comprehensive than that of any other save Jedediah Smith and possibly British fur trader PETER SKENE OGDEN. Many other mountain men—JAMES (JIM) BRIDGER, THOMAS FITZPATRICK, Milton Sublette to name three—made discoveries, although few mountain men recorded what they found. A second generation of explorers, not really mountain men but more adventurers or wayfarers, swept into the Rockies as the fur trade began to decline—the future army scout CHRISTOPHER HOUSTON ("KIT") CARSON, NATHANIEL JARVIS WYETH, and Captain BENJAMIN LOUIS EULALIE DE BONNEVILLE, who claimed to be on leave, but whose 1833 expedition may well have been as much a military reconnaissance as the fur-trading venture he said it was.

Spying and exploration sometimes went hand-in-hand. Most likely Lieutenant ZEBULON MONTGOMERY PIKE was spying on his 1806 expedition into the Southwest along the upper Rio Grande, where he was captured and interrogated by Spanish authorities. The advancement of scientific knowledge became the express mission for a growing number of government-sponsored Western expeditions, although that too may have sometimes served as a cover for espionage. In the wake of Lewis and Clark's explorations, Thomas Jefferson sent William Dunbar and John Hunter to explore the Ouchita River and Thomas Freeman to scout the Red River in addition to putting his stamp of approval on Pike's expedition, the brainchild of Missouri's territorial governor and intriguer JAMES WILKINSON.

When James Monroe became president, Major STEPHEN HARRIMAN LONG persuaded him to allow Long to explore the upper Missouri by steamboat, and Long launched the disaster-plagued expedition in 1820. After the formation of the U.S. CORPS OF TOPOGRAPHICAL

ENGINEERS in 1838, official American explorations were concentrated within that bureau. From 1838 to 1842, Lieutenant CHARLES WILKES of the U.S. Navy, led an expedition to Antarctica, the South Seas, Hawaii, and the coast of Oregon. Wilkes fell into disputes with his subordinates, who thought the autocratic and sometimes brutal Wilkes "more . . . a monster than a man." The expedition ended in recriminations that dragged on for years in a nearly endless series of courts-martial. JOHN CHARLES FRÉMONT made three official expeditions west for the corps, and his reports—edited, if not written, by his wife, JESSIE ANN BENTON FRÉMONT, daughter of Missouri's U.S. Senator THOMAS HART BENTON—were widely read by a public eager for land in Oregon and California, which much pleased Frémont's expansion-minded father-in-law. The TRANS-CONTINENTAL RAILROAD SURVEYS conducted by the corps also produced a wealth of knowledge about the West, much of it purely scientific.

After the Civil War, exploration became a matter of scientific investigation and mapping, with surveys being conducted by FERDINAND VANDEVEER HAYDEN, CLARENCE KING, JOHN WESLEY POWELL, George M. Wheeler, and Walter Jenny. All of Western exploration was ultimately concentrated in the United States Geological Survey, established in 1879.

—*Charles Phillips*

SEE ALSO: Alaskan Exploration; Art: Surveys and Expeditions; Cartography; Exploration and Science; Santa Fe and Chihuahua Trail; Sublette Brothers

SUGGESTED READING:

Billington, Ray Allen, and Martin Ridge. *Westward Expansion: A History of the American Frontier.* 5th ed. New York, 1982.

DeVoto, Bernard. *Across the Wide Missouri.* Boston, 1948.

———. *The Course of Empire.* Boston, 1952.

Goetzmann, William H. *Exploration and Empire: The Explorer and the Scientist in the Winning of the American West.* New York, 1966.

———. *Exploring the American West.* Washington, D.C., 1982.

Ronda, James P. *Astoria and Empire.* Lincoln, Nebr., 1990.

———. *Lewis and Clark among the Indians.* Lincoln, Nebr., 1984.

EXPLORATION NARRATIVES

Some twenty years after taking part in FRANCISCO VÁSQUEZ DE CORONADO's expedition from 1540 to 1542 into the American Southwest, Pedro de Castañeda wrote that "it is a worthy ambition for great men to desire to know and wish to preserve for posterity correct information concerning the things that have happened in distant parts, about which little is known." Even the quickest review of exploration narratives reveals that Castañeda touched on key elements in the genre. Explorers were driven by the "desire to know," and their narratives reflected the "wish to preserve for posterity correct information." And there was always the lure of events "in distant parts." Nearly every European explorer tramping across North America or probing its coasts made and brought back some record of the experience. From the fifteenth century to the twentieth, to explore was to record. No explorer expected to find an empty continent. All knew that North America was what Atlantic Coast Algonquians called their country—Tsenacommacah, "the densely inhabited place." Exploration narratives were written like journey reports. The narratives re-created pilgrimage paths filled with moments of encounter and discovery.

Whether written by fur traders, missionaries, or government explorers, exploration narratives fall into two large categories—written narratives and graphic representations.

Most European explorers who came to North America kept some sort of daily record. That record might have taken the form of a personal diary reflecting individual experiences or feelings. More often, as in the case of the government explorers MERIWETHER LEWIS and WILLIAM CLARK, the daily record was the official journal. Such journals took note of important diplomatic and scientific concerns as well as the route of travel. In nearly every case, daily records were not intended for publication. Explorer-authors expected that such records would be substantially rewritten before gaining wide public circulation.

The journal and diary narrative was an account composed close to the actual journey. A second form of exploration narrative, however, was written immediately after completion of the journey. Long and often highly detailed letters to distant company headquarters, national capitals, or religious centers reported on the results of a particular expedition. The annual *Relations* of the Jesuits in Canada represent that sort of narrative-letter approach.

Explorers' patrons expected formal reports. As printing and literacy expanded in Europe, these reports became a pamphlet literature eagerly read both for their information and as adventure stories. In the nineteenth century, exploration reports, like those written by JOHN CHARLES FRÉMONT and his wife JESSIE ANN BENTON FRÉMONT, were printed by the FEDERAL GOVERNMENT and avidly read by a wide audience.

Explorers generally drafted journals, letters, and reports when the events of their journeys were still reasonably fresh and vivid in their minds. But some explorers decided to write memoirs, often composed many years after their journeys. Near the end of his life, the Canadian explorer DAVID THOMPSON wrote his *Narrative*, a literate and compelling recollection of his extensive Western travels.

Not all exploration narratives were expressed in written language. Significant portions of a journey might be recorded and explained in maps and other graphic representations. Exploration CARTOGRAPHY always provided information on more than simply the shape of the terrain. Maps recorded important information about native peoples and cultures, languages, village locations, and tribal boundaries. Paintings and drawings, whether included in published reports or exhibited to the public, were an equally central part of the expanded narrative.

Exploration narratives proved to be more influential than the explorers themselves imagined. The narratives played important economic and diplomatic roles as merchants, entrepreneurs, and national leaders used information in them to formulate private plans and public policy. But on an even grander scale, the narratives were part of the invention of the American West. The West was not only a collection of real places rooted in time and terrain but also a galaxy of imaginary places and fantastic countries. This was a fabulous West, an invented landscape of salt mountains, herds of llamas, and Great Plains volcanoes. For all the effort to be factual and objective, exploration narratives always contained elements of wonder and fantasy. These narratives were the literature of Western invention, the words and representations of a world more in the mind than on the ground.

—*James P. Ronda*

SUGGESTED READING:
Stafford, Barbara M. *Voyage into Substance: Art, Science, Nature and the Illustrated Travel Account, 1760–1840.* Cambridge, Mass., 1984

EXPLORATION AND SCIENCE

In the Age of Discovery, Renaissance mariners began, around the middle of the fifteenth century, to explore the world in search of new trade routes to the Indies at first, then—after Columbus accidentally discovered America—gold and precious metals to swell their princes' mercantile treasuries and Native American

souls to convert to their Holy Roman Church. From the beginning, explorers were also part of a developing scientific enterprise conceived in the early Renaissance and born during the scientific revolution of the seventeenth century. By the early eighteenth century, science had emerged as a culture of its own, with its peculiar language, institutions, and symbols, its recognized practitioners, and especially its secular tests for truth. Along with the ever-growing belief in science came the idea of linear development, and men grew passionately committed to a systematic examination of all parts of the globe in the hope of promoting universal progress rather than simply catering to crude commercial concerns or feeding ancient national and religious rivalries.

Men still sailed the seas in search of gold and glory and new worlds to discover, explore, and frequently conquer; they did so, however, no longer exclusively in the name of the crown, but also at the behest of learned societies such as the British Royal Society and the French Academie des Sciences. Perhaps scientific discovery was merely a new, more subtle excuse for adventure and imperial conquest in the eighteenth and nineteenth centuries, but in countless instances, scientific institutions linked with exploration received acclaim and support from a public dazzled by the natural wonders scientific explorers brought back from the ends of the earth. Inevitably, the innovative methodologies of science took on a romantic cast, and the naturalists and artists who accompanied the explorers described a teeming and variegated world and reproduced it in brilliantly colored illustrations for the scientific tomes and reports that had become all the rage. But they also sought, no less diligently, the essential unity behind that variety. Under the twin objectives—science and progress—of what came to be known as the Enlightenment, exploration assumed a new dimension, the search for pure knowledge aimed to benefit mankind in general. North America, along with the rest of the New World, became a pristine collecting ground for scientifically curious Europeans and Anglo-Americans.

The influence of James Cook

Both the English explorer and map-maker Captain JAMES COOK and the Prussian aristocrat Alexander von Humboldt are central to understanding nineteenth-century scientific exploration and study of the trans-Mississippi West. Cook took with him on his three voyages to the Pacific a corps of scientists who collected data and specimens that caught the imagination of the public and the learned alike. Two men in particular, Joseph Banks and Dr. Daniel Solander, who accompanied Cook's initial expedition sponsored by

Top: An illustration from an 1829 textbook, *Interesting Events in the History of the United States*, depicts members of the Lewis and Clark Expedition arriving at the Pacific Coast. *Courtesy Library of Congress.*

Middle: Samuel Seymour, a British artist, accompanied Stephen Harriman Long's expedition of 1820 and painted *Distant View of the Rockies. Courtesy Library of Congress.*

Bottom: The U.S. government sponsored Western scientific expeditions. The government scientists were among the first Americans to explore the Grand Canyon. *Courtesy National Archives.*

the Royal Society, helped create a vogue for natural history that profoundly influenced American exploration. Banks was a protégé of Canadian explorer-artist Thomas Pennant; Solander a student of Carolus Linnaeus (who was the inventor of the Linnean system of classification for natural history and who, by the middle of the eighteenth century, had collectors and agents working all over the world). When Cook landed on the east coast of Australia on April 19, 1770, after visiting both Tahiti and New Zealand, it was Banks and Solander—in awe of the entirely new ecological system—who dubbed the barren spot "Botany Bay." And it was Banks and Solander who became the toast of London in 1771 for the remarkable natural-history specimens and drawings they brought back, a collection hailed by none other than Linnaeus himself as perhaps the greatest natural-history collection in the world.

Americans had their own reasons for being interested in CARTOGRAPHY, ethnology, and botany. For men hunting and living in the wilderness, accurate maps, a true understanding of Native American territories and customs, and knowledge of the animal world and plant life were not matters of mere curiosity but of survival. These practical concerns mingled with the naturalist tradition that had long been growing in England and among the Jesuits of New France to make Americans especially receptive to the new discoveries of natural history. By the late eighteenth century, the United States had developed its own network of naturalists, who emulated the European scientists and scientific institutions. Many of them were members of the American Philosophical Society for the Promotion of Useful Knowledge, founded in Philadelphia in 1743 at the behest of Benjamin Franklin and modeled after the British Royal Society. The Philosophical Society became a power in American science and the focal point for the exploration of the trans-Mississippi West, its geography, its flora, its fauna, its Indian lore. In 1801, THOMAS JEFFERSON was not only president of the United States, he was also president of the American Philosophical Society, and the latter may well have meant more to him. It was under his leadership that members of the society undertook the intensive scientific training of MERIWETHER LEWIS in preparation for his expedition into the LOUISIANA PURCHASE territory with WILLIAM CLARK.

James Cook's scientific expeditions had a much greater impact on science and exploration than on natural history. Indeed, it was Cook's world-renowned three voyages to the Pacific that first inspired the romantic young Alexander von Humboldt to dream of exploring himself. During the course of his independently financed expeditions to the New World and Central Asia in the late eighteenth and early nineteenth centuries, and his subsequent labors in Paris, where he wrote the majority of his books, Humboldt managed to create the science of modern geography. Because Humboldt's was a synthesizing discipline, it became the key to the scientific activity of the period and provided a model and a method for organizing data that poured into Europe from the ever-growing number of expeditions all over the world.

Humboldt was an admirer of Thomas Jefferson for his thorough, highly organized, yet romantically picturesque *Notes on Virginia,* which Jefferson published in Paris in 1784 and whose style Humboldt was to emulate in his own writings. As Humboldt came to the close of his Central American exploration in 1804, he headed for Philadelphia to meet Jefferson and to lecture at the American Philosophical Society, where he astounded America's leading amateur scientists. He did not, however, arrive in time to brief Meriwether Lewis, who was just then somewhere out in the Rocky Mountains.

American scientific exploration

Natural history and Humboldt's geography were the backdrops against which most of the scientific exploration of the trans-Mississippi West took place. Humboldt's dramatic explorations inspired European romantic adventurers, while government-sponsored American explorers set their goals to meet Humboldtian expectations of unity and comprehensiveness with a Linnaean precision of classification. George Catlin's travels, during which he attempted to capture on canvas the entire world of those he considered vanishing Native Americans, and the 1833 trip up the Missouri that Maximilian, Prince of Wied Neuwied, made with artist Karl (Carl) Bodmer, were two of many attempts to emulate Humboldt. And every official expedition—the Lewis and Clark Expedition; Zebulon Montgomery Pike's trip into the Southwest in 1806; Major Stephen Harriman Long's steamboat expedition to the upper Missouri in 1820; John Charles Frémont's explorations for the U.S. Corps of Topographical Engineers after 1838; U.S. Navy Lieutenant Charles Wilkes's expedition to the Antarctic, Oregon, and the Pacific from 1838 to 1842; even the transcontinental railroad surveys of the 1850s and 1860s—had an express scientific purpose.

Sometimes the science was an excuse for funding or a cover for espionage. In asking Congress for money for the Lewis and Clark Expedition, Jefferson emphasized the commercial and reconnaissance benefits of the trip; in talking to the Spanish envoy, he described it as a nonpolitical, scientific mission. Almost certainly, Pike was spying on the Spanish, and there were military reconnaissance aspects to Long's expedition and all the U.S. Army engineering surveys. The science itself was sometimes bad, as when Pike first described the Southwest as a desert. Long repeated the mistake, labeling the region the "Great American Desert," a "scientific" conclusion that led officials and settlers alike to consider the region uninhabitable until the conclusion was challenged, twenty years later, by Frémont. The very fact, however, that science was occasionally used as a cover demonstrates the cachet scientific investigation had acquired by the mid-nineteenth century.

Between 1840 and 1860, the U.S. government subsidized some sixty Western ventures and fifteen naval expeditions. Congress published the results of these explorations, many in elaborately printed series filled with esoteric reports by the scientists who accompanied the trips. The books were lavishly illustrated with lithographs of unfamiliar Western landscapes and their aboriginal inhabitants. Charles Wilkes's expedition alone resulted in a massive five-volume *Narrative of the United States Exploring Edition* (1844) and twenty volumes of scientific reports, which Wilkes edited from 1844 to 1874 (he wrote the volumes on meteorology and hydrography himself). But the scientific apogee of the military explorations was the thirteen-volume set generated by the Pacific Railroad Surveys. Representing "an encyclopedia of western experience," their publication alone cost in excess of $1 million, twice as much as the surveys themselves had cost.

The subsidies and publications were critical to the professionalization of science in America. Increasingly in the second half of the nineteenth century, expeditions were sponsored and supervised by large national organizations and federal bureaus, with the advancement of scientific knowledge their explicit goal and the emphasis placed on geology and archaeology rather than on botany, ethnology, and geography. Science was becoming a team discipline, employing groups of specialists, and that fact was reflected in the shifting focus of Western exploration. Photographers such as William Henry Jackson replaced the artists of an earlier era, while scientists such as Ferdinand Vandeveer Hayden, Clarence King, John Wesley Powell, and Lieutenant George M. Wheeler continued to explore the West even as they fought turf wars over various federal surveys. In 1879, Congress consolidated all exploration under the UNITED STATES GEOLOGICAL SURVEY. That agency defined the scope of the earth sciences in America well into the twentieth century, when science-oriented universities began to assume some of the burden. American geology—its successes stemming largely from explorations, surveys, and discoveries in the trans-Mississippi West—had by the end of the century come to command worldwide respect and to represent the country's scientific coming of age.

—*Charles Phillips*

SEE ALSO: Art: Surveys and Expeditions; Exploration: United States

SUGGESTED READING:
Boorstein, Daniel J. *The Lost World of Thomas Jefferson.* Boston, 1948.
Bosse, Jacques. *Great Voyages of Discovery: Circumnavigators and Scientists, 1764–1843.* Preface by Ferdinand Braudel. Translated by Stanley Hochman. New York, 1983.
Botting, Douglas. *Humboldt and the Cosmos.* New York, 1973.
Goetzmann, William H. *Army Exploration in the American West.* New Haven, Conn., 1959.
———. *New Lands, New Men: America and the Second Age of Discovery.* New York, 1986.

EXTINCTION OF SPECIES

One of the most striking features of the New World was its abundance of WILDLIFE. Rarely did written accounts of the first Euro-American explorers fail to marvel at the number and variety of animals. As Euro-Americans first hunted and trapped in the West during the late eighteenth and early nineteenth centuries, many retained the belief that wildlife populations were inexhaustible. The abundance of wildlife aided settlement in the West; animals provided meat as well as valuable furs and hides. Yet overuse of wild creatures began almost at the outset of white exploration and occupation. By the 1830s, for instance, fur traders had seriously depleted populations of otters and BEAVERS.

In the late nineteenth century, much of the damage to wildlife was caused by loss of habitat through such activities as farming, logging, and mining. The introduction of exotic animals also crowded out native species. Systematic killing or HUNTING, however, caused much of the wildlife destruction. One dramatic example was the large-scale slaughter of BUFFALOES, or bisons which once roamed the West in astonishing numbers. Hunters used transcontinental rail lines to gain access to the animals, and the railroads carried the meat and hides back to Eastern markets. By the 1880s, buffaloes had been hunted almost to extinction.

The problem was not killing for sport but killing for profit. Late nineteenth-century America provided favorable conditions for professional hunting: a large Eastern market and a relatively open West where game thrived. Because there were few restrictions, market hunters supplied urban Americans with a variety of birds and mammals that would seem inconceivable in the late twentieth century. During the nineteenth century, wild game figured prominently in the diets of even city dwellers. Game available for purchase in Eastern public markets included bisons, ELKS, CARIBOU, antelope, bighorn sheep, mountain goats, BLACK BEARS, wild cats, hares, and squirrels.

Although the effect of market hunting on most wildlife populations was difficult to determine, some nineteenth-century observers began crusades to halt the destruction of wildlife. The BOONE AND CROCKETT CLUB, an organization for sportsmen, pointed to the near-extinction of buffaloes to promote wildlife protection at the federal level. Club members lobbied to save buffaloes in YELLOWSTONE NATIONAL PARK from poaching, and in 1900, they helped persuade Congress to pass the LACEY ACT, which prohibited the smuggling of protected game.

In the twentieth century, degradation of wildlife habitat became a major concern of conservation and environmental groups. In 1973, they lobbied for the passage of the Endangered Species Act, which requires government agencies to take steps to recover dwindling wildlife populations. Government actions include both the suspension of activities that harm ecosystems and the reintroduction of species. By the late twentieth century, prominent Western animals listed as endangered or threatened included California CONDORS, northern spotted owls, northern gray WOLVES, and GRIZZLY BEARS.

—*Lisa Mighetto*

SUGGESTED READING:
Dunlap, Thomas R. *Saving America's Wildlife.* Princeton, N.J., 1988.
Grinnell, George Bird. *The Passing of the Great West: Selected Papers of George Bird Grinnell.* Edited by John F. Reiger. New York, 1972.
Matthiessen, Peter. *Wildlife in America.* New York, 1959.
Mighetto, Lisa. *Wild Animals and American Environmental Ethics.* Tucson, Ariz., 1991.

EYAK INDIANS

SEE: Native American Peoples: Peoples of Alaska

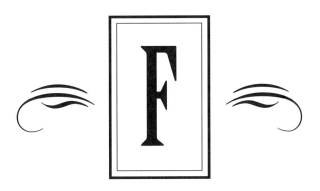

FAIR, JAMES GRAHAM

After joining the California gold rush at the age of eighteen, James Graham Fair (1831–1894) formed a partnership with JOHN W. MACKAY, James C. Flood, and William S. O'Brien in 1868. Five years later, the "Irish Four" discovered a huge deposit of silver and gold in Nevada. Named the "Big Bonanza" and part of the COMSTOCK LODE, the mines were the largest single ore deposit ever found. The mines produced $105 million between 1873 and 1882. After the mine's yields began to decrease, Fair ran in Nevada for a seat in the U.S. Senate and won, in part by spending approximately $350,000 on the campaign. After his election, his wife sued him for divorce on grounds of "habitual adultery" and won a $5 million settlement. Fair, however, recouped his losses. At the time of his death, his estate was valued at $45 million.

—*Candace Floyd*

SUGGESTED READING:

Lewis, Oscar. *Silver Kings: The Lives and Times of Mackay, Fair, Flood, and O'Brien, Lords of the Nevada Comstock Lode.* New York, 1947.

FALL, ALBERT B.

Secretary of the Interior from 1921 to 1923, Albert B. Fall (1861–1944) was convicted of accepting a bribe in the TEAPOT DOME scandal. Born in Frankfort, Kentucky, Fall grew up in Kentucky and Tennessee where he often lived with his grandparents. The Civil War largely destroyed the family's resources, and as a result, Fall received only a limited education. He went to work in a cotton factory when he was scarcely twelve years old and later studied under his father, who had become a teacher after the war. Eventually, Fall himself taught school and read law at night.

As he came into manhood, Fall began moving south and west. He worked as a cattle drover and cook in Texas, engaged in the real-estate business, and, finally, began to practice law in Clarksville, Texas. In 1883, he married Emma Morgan, the daughter of a railroad man. The couple had four children.

Ultimately, it was both the law and business that led Fall to New Mexico. He worked in the mines at Kingston (the source of a lifelong interest in hard-rock mining) and then settled in Las Cruces, where he practiced law and made his way into politics. At the outset, Fall was a Democrat. He served in both houses of the territorial legislature, was appointed by President Grover Cleveland to the New Mexico Supreme Court, and served twice as the territory's attorney general. Gradually, he switched to the Republican party, and in 1912, when New Mexico achieved statehood, he became one of its first U.S. senators. Fall was an inveterate poker player, and while in the Senate, he developed a close friendship with another good poker player, Senator Warren G. Harding of Ohio.

Fall is best remembered today not for his considerable achievements but for his notoriety. In 1921, after Harding took office as president, he appointed Fall secretary of the interior. In that position, Fall leased federal oil lands to two business leaders—the Teapot Dome Naval Oil Reserve in Wyoming to Harry F. Sinclair and the Elk Hills Reserve in California to EDWARD LAURENCE DOHENY, an old friend from Fall's mining days in Kingston.

About the time that Harding died suddenly in 1923, rumors were afloat of corruption in many quarters of the administration. In 1923 and 1924, Thomas J. Walsh, senator from Montana, began to investigate. By 1928, the investigation had revealed that Fall had received some $404,000 from Doheny and Sinclair in what had become known as the Teapot Dome scandal. Although Fall steadfastly maintained his innocence, he was convicted of accepting a $100,000 bribe, and in 1931, in failing health, he was taken by ambulance to begin serving time in a Santa Fe prison. He was the first cabinet officer ever convicted and imprisoned for committing a felony during his term of office. Doheny was acquitted of giving the bribe that Fall was convicted of receiving; both Sinclair and Doheny went free. After Fall's release from prison, he lived in near poverty.

Fall was a self-made man who rose from the devastated South, had little schooling or formal education, and yet earned a substantial fortune and rose to high office. He was an individual with a sometimes vitriolic temper, which belied his soft drawl. While he achieved high office during a time of growing interest in conservation, he did not hold to those views. He believed that the nation's natural resources should be developed to the fullest extent, particularly by private capital. And that belief contributed to his participation in the Teapot Dome scandal.

—*James E. Fell, Jr.*

Suggested reading:

Noggle, Burl. *Teapot Dome.* Baton Rouge, La., 1962.
Stratton, David H. "Albert B. Fall and the Teapot Dome Affair." Ph.D. diss., University of Colorado, 1955.

FAMILY LAW

See: Community Property; Divorce; Spanish Law

FANNIN, JAMES WALKER, JR.

Born January 1, 1804, the son of Dr. Isham Fannin in Georgia, James Walker Fannin, Jr., was adopted by his maternal grandfather and raised near Marion, Georgia. On July 1, 1819, he entered West Point but withdrew from school in November 1821 and returned to Georgia, where, several years later, he married Minerva Fort. In 1834, Fannin, his wife, and their two daughters moved to Texas and settled at Velasco, where he was a planter and slave trader.

Fannin agitated for the separation of Texas from Mexico and, on August 20, 1835, began to use his influence to call for the Consultation and seek military and financial aid for Texas from the United States. By September, he had joined the army and was captain of the Brazos Guards at the battle of Gonzales. He urged STEPHEN FULLER AUSTIN to support Gonzales which led to the advance on Bexar, for which Fannin and JAMES (JIM) BOWIE scouted. On October 28, Fannin led Texas forces in the battle of Concepcion. In November, he

was offered the position of inspector general of the army but instead chose to be discharged to campaign for a larger regular army. Although a volunteer force was established, Fannin was commissioned as a colonel of the regular army on December 7. He assembled supplies to support the attack on San Antonio de Bexar, but the city had fallen and the supplies were used in 1836.

On January 9, 1836, Fannin began to recruit forces for an expedition against Matamoros and was elected commander-in-chief of the expedition at Goliad on February 7. He served as commander of the army, but upon learning of General José Urrea's occupation of Matamoros, he withdrew to Goliad. As Urrea's advance destroyed other Texas forces on the lower Gulf Coast, Fannin waited at Goliad. Although first ordered to relieve the ALAMO in early March, he was then ordered by SAM HOUSTON to withdraw to Victoria. He waited, however, for part of his command to return from Refugio until he learned of their capture. He retreated on March 19 but was surrounded and forced to surrender by Urrea at the battle of Coleto from March 19 to 20. Fannin and his command were imprisoned at Goliad, and on March 27, at the order of ANTONIO LÓPEZ DE SANTA ANNA, the command was massacred by the Mexican forces. Fannin, who was in the hospital recovering from his wounds, was shot separately. The command became martyrs to the TEXAS REVOLUTION, and the phrase "Remember Goliad" was a part of the cry of the victors at San Jacinto on April 21.

—*Patrick H. Butler, III*

Suggested reading:

Long, Jeff. *Duel of Eagles: The Mexican and U.S. Fight for the Alamo.* New York, 1990.
Roell, Craig H. *Remember Goliad!* Austin, Tex., 1994.

FARGO, WILLIAM GEORGE

Businessman and express-company owner William George Fargo (1818–1881) was born in Pompey, Onondaga County, New York. At the age of thirteen, he became a mail carrier and rode on horseback over a thirty-mile route twice a week. In Syracuse, he worked for several years in a village inn and as a grocer's clerk. Later, he and his brother ran their own store, but it was a financial failure.

Finding the transportation business more profitable, Fargo became a fast-freight agent in Auburn on the newly completed Auburn and Syracuse Railroad. He soon turned his attention to the express business and became a messenger and later an agent for Livingston, Wells, and Pomeroy. In 1844, he became

William George Fargo. *Courtesy Wells Fargo Bank.*

one of three partners with HENRY WELLS and Daniel Dunning in Wells and Company, the first express firm operating west of Buffalo, and again served as a messenger. In 1850, Wells and Company joined two competing firms operating between Albany and Buffalo to form the American Express Company. Wells served as president, and Fargo as secretary. The express service had already been extended to Chicago, Cincinnati, Milwaukee, St. Louis, Galena, and Dubuque.

At the beginning of the California gold rush, the need for improved communication and transportation between the East Coast and the Pacific Slope as well as within California became clear. In response to that need, WELLS, FARGO AND COMPANY was organized in 1852. The company soon dominated the transportation business in California and carried gold dust, mail, packages, and passengers while conducting banking business for the state. Wells and Fargo were highly successful as a team, with the former concentrating on the financial aspects of the business and the latter serving as supervisor of field operations.

During the Civil War, the express businesses boomed, and various new companies entered the field. In the postwar period, several companies made profitable mergers. In the East, the Merchants Union Express Company, one of the new organizations, became so powerful that in 1868, the American Express Company was compelled to incorporate with it on equal terms to form the American Merchants' Union Express Company. At that time, Fargo became president, a

position he held until his death. The company name was later shortened to become again the American Express Company. Fargo was also president of Wells, Fargo and Company from 1870 to 1872.

Throughout his life, Fargo was identified with the economic development and political activity of Buffalo, New York. He was a Democratic mayor for two terms (from 1862 to 1866) but was unsuccessful in his bid for a seat in the state senate in 1871. His family ties were strong, and six of his brothers and one brother-in-law were associated with him in the express business for many years. While his partner, Henry Wells, was apparently shy, retiring, and sensitive, Fargo was a man of commanding presence, a dynamic personality, gregarious and popular. He had a reputation for being genuinely interested in his employees, and they, in turn, were devoted to him.

—*W. Turrentine Jackson*

SUGGESTED READING:
Harlow, Alvin. *Old Waybills: The Romance of the Express Companies.* New York, 1934.
Hungerford, Edward. *Wells Fargo: Advancing the American Frontier.* New York, 1949.
Stimson, A. L. *History of the Express Business.* New York, 1881.

FARMING

Dryland Farming
   Gilbert C. Fite

Farming on the Great Plains
   Garry L. Nall

Farming in the Imperial Valley and Salton Sea Region
   Richard H. Dillon

Tools and Machinery
   Gilbert C. Fite

DRYLAND FARMING

Dryland farming is a system or method of crop production in areas of scarce rainfall, such as the American Great Plains. As settlers pushed into western Texas, eastern New Mexico, eastern Colorado, Montana, and the western Dakotas in the late nineteenth and early twentieth centuries, they entered a region where rainfall averaged only ten to twenty inches a year. The dry environment was not conducive to the agricultural practices that were familiar to farmers who had migrated from more humid areas. For a time, farmers in the semiarid regions optimistically believed that rainfall would increase as settlement advanced, but frequent severe droughts exploded that theory.

A homesteader in Sun River, Montana, uses a team of horses and a plow to turn the sod in 1908. Photograph by Lubkin. *Courtesy National Archives.*

Could farmers adjust to a climate where moisture was scarce and evaporation high because of the strong hot winds? For some farmers and scientists, dryland-farming techniques were the answer. These techniques included cultivating the soil in a way that would conserve moisture and selecting crops that could resist dry conditions.

Hardy Webster Campbell was a strong advocate of dryland-farming techniques at the turn of the century. An Easterner who settled on a homestead in Brown County in the Dakota Territory in 1879, Campbell later managed farms in the region for several railroad companies. By the 1890s, he had become an avid publicist for specific methods of soil preparation for dryland farming. He promoted deep plowing in the early fall to open the ground to receive fall and winter moisture. Then he recommended using a machine that consisted of wheels with *V*-shaped rims to pack the subsoil but leave the top soil loose. The idea was to conserve as much of the scarce moisture as possible. Campbell did not initially pay much attention to the matter of planting drought-resistant crops or to the practice of summer fallowing.

Scientists in the United States Department of Agriculture contended that Campbell's methods were not supported by adequate research. In 1905, an Office of Dryland Agriculture was organized in the department to study the best farming practices for dryland areas of the West. Between 1906 and 1915, the department increased its spending on dryland-farming research from $15,000 to $160,000.

While the best methods of soil preparation for dryland farming were being studied, farmers on the southern Great Plains began using listers to plant their crops.

The lister dropped seed into a furrow six to ten inches deep, placing seed where there was a maximum amount of moisture. Farmers then used cultivators to push the soil from the ridges into the furrows as the plants grew, thus providing a deep root system for any row crop.

By the 1920s, summer fallowing had become an important aspect of dryland farming. That practice called for leaving part of the land fallow every other year. The fallow, or unplanted portion, was cultivated in a manner that would destroy weeds and stir the topsoil so it would absorb more moisture. The fallow part of the field would be planted the next year. The idea was that a crop would do better on land that absorbed two years of moisture for one crop. Summer fallowing became increasingly popular in the semiarid parts of the West, and by 1950, there were 25.6 million acres of cultivated summer fallow. Crop rotation was also an important dryland practice. In eastern Washington, farmers alternated wheat and peas, a technique that proved successful.

While the means of cultivation were important, drought-resistant crops were essential for dryland farming. Scientists searched for plant species that would do best in the semiarid regions. Sorghum grains proved adaptable to the dry plains where corn did not do well. By the 1890s, kafir corn, an import from Africa and India, had proven successful on the southern Great Plains. There were 600,000 acres of this crop in western Kansas alone by 1900. Milo maize, a grain crop similar to kafir, was also well adapted to western Kansas, Oklahoma, and western Texas. In the early 1900s, scientists traveled throughout the world to find other suitable drought-resistant crops, especially for the Great Plains. They introduced Durum wheat and later Marquis wheat, which did fairly well. By the 1920s, Ceres wheat had become popular on the High Plains in North Dakota and eastern Montana. Drought-resistant varieties of barley and flax were also introduced. Species of alfalfa that could better withstand drought, as well as Sudan grass, were imported, providing feed crops crucial to the livestock operations of dryland farmers and ranchers on the Great Plains.

By the 1930s and 1940s, farmers were using larger and more powerful machines to deal with dryland conditions. They used large disc plows and chisel plows to cut deeply into the soil and leave the ground rough with crop residue near the surface. With that type of cultivation, the land caught the winter snows and held run-off from spring rains. Some dryland farmers plowed furrows through their fields in a crosswind direction in order to slow EROSION by the high winds on the Great Plains.

There was a widespread belief that farmers on the Great Plains and in other parts of the West needed larger tracts of land than the 160 acres provided under the original HOMESTEAD ACT OF 1862. As part of the dryland-farming movement, Congress passed the ENLARGED HOMESTEAD ACT OF 1909, which permitted homesteads of 320 acres in nine Western states. The law was later extended to six more states.

It took nearly a half century to develop the best methods of soil management and cultivation and to find crops best suited for dryland farming. By 1950, when combined with IRRIGATION, farming in the semiarid parts of the West had become reasonably successful.

—*Gilbert C. Fite*

SUGGESTED READING:
Hargreaves, Mary Wilma M. *Dry Farming in the Northern Great Plains, 1900–1925.* Cambridge, Mass., 1957.
———. *Dry Farming in the Northern Great Plains: Years of Readjustment, 1920–1990.* Lawrence, Kans., 1993.
Kraenzel, Carl Frederick. *The Great Plains in Transition.* Norman, Okla., 1955.

FARMING ON THE GREAT PLAINS

Environmental conditions on the Great Plains have challenged farmers since the initial Euro-American settlement of the region in the 1870s. The flat, treeless area located between the ninety-eighth meridian on the east and the Rocky Mountains on the west and ranging from West Texas northward to the Canadian border is one of climatic extremes where temperatures range from summer highs in excess of 100° F to winter lows below zero and with growing seasons varying from one hundred days in the north to two hundred days in the south. However, the semiarid conditions— the average annual rainfall is approximately twenty inches or less and falls between April and June—have been the primary limiting factors influencing agricultural operations.

Among the first lessons learned by farmers of the Great Plains was the importance of selecting crops that could be planted early, would grow and mature quickly, and would be ready for harvest before the wilting heat of summer. While corn was usually the initial commodity planted on the Plains, its moisture requirements often forced farmers to look to other crops such as flax, oats, rye, alfalfa, castorbeans, millet, emmert, and, in Texas, cotton. Eventually, wheat and sorghum proved to be the most reliable. Although spring varieties of wheat were sowed along the Canadian border where the growing season was limited, winter wheat varieties—especially the hard red types of Russian origins—emerged as the leading cash crop. For livestock feed, the drought-resistant sorghums—especially kafir and milo—were particularly dependable.

Photographer W. A. Raymond recorded thirty horses pulling a harvester combine on an Oregon wheat field in 1880. *Courtesy The Bettmann Archive.*

To be successful, farmers also had to adapt their cultivation and organizational techniques. By the early twentieth century, dryland-farming proponents promoted various tillage practices, such as summer fallowing and subsoil packing. Among the valuable implements was the lister, a double plow that left untilled ridges to provide protection from the wind. Usually emphasizing diversification programs, agricul-

A steam plow and roller work the fields of a large South Dakota farm in 1908. *Courtesy The Bettmann Archive.*

tural advisors called for farmers to include in their operations "the cow, the sow, and the hen" to provide some income protection in the unpredictable CLIMATE.

Increasing demands for food during World War I marked the beginning of the transition to the modern agricultural system on the Great Plains. Farmers with tractors no longer needed as much pasture for draft animals, so they plowed up that land to increase crop acreage. The new tractors were capable of pulling large tillage implements, especially one-way disk plows and the newly developed combine. Yet the Great Depression, which brought low market prices, and the DUST BOWL conditions, caused by drought, wind EROSION, and land misuse, forced dramatic shifts in farming practices.

After World War II, scientific and technological inventions as well as improved managerial practices reshaped farming operations on the Great Plains. Although the number of farm units had declined by approximately 60 percent by 1990, the average size of these units increased from approximately nine hundred acres to sixteen hundred acres in the forty-five years after 1945. Increased tractor power allowed fewer operators to oversee farms. In addition, the application of chemicals—ranging from fertilizers to improve yields, HERBICIDES to control weeds, and PESTICIDES to limit insect and disease damage—alleviated several perennial problems. New wheat varieties and hybrids of grain sorghum and corn stimulated production to the extent that several auxiliary industries, including cattle feeding, were generating extensive wealth by the 1960s. The growth of crop IRRIGATION from both surface and underground sources such as the OGALLALA AQUIFER, which extends from Nebraska to the Texas High Plains further enhanced production. Furthermore, soil-conserving techniques such as strip-cropping, terracing, and the implementation of minimum or stubble-mulch tillage practices became common. Yet reports of the depletion of WATER resources or the sight of blowing soil force Great Plains farmers to remain cognizant of the hazards of their environment.

—*Garry L. Nall*

SUGGESTED READING:

Fite, Gilbert C. *American Farmers: The New Minority.* Bloomington, Ind., 1981.

———. *The Farmers' Frontier, 1865–1900.* New York, 1966.

Green, Donald E. *Lands of the Underground Rain: Irrigation on the Texas High Plains, 1910–1970.* Austin, Tex., 1973.

Haystead, Ladd, and Gilbert C. Fite. *The Agricultural Regions of the United States.* Norman, Okla., 1955.

Hurt, R. Douglas. *The Dust Bowl: An Agricultural and Social History.* Chicago, 1981.

Worster, Donald. *Dust Bowl: The Southern Plains in the 1930s.* New York, 1979.

FARMING IN THE IMPERIAL VALLEY AND SALTON SEA REGION

The eight-thousand-square mile Imperial Valley is the low-lying and arid, but now reclaimed, southeastern portion of California. The valley was, earlier, California's Colorado Desert, whose heart was the Cahuilla Basin or Salton Sink, almost three hundred feet below sea level. In the geological past, the valley was part of the Gulf of California, which extended through Imperial Valley's satellite of the Coachella Valley to Palm Springs and San Gorgonio Pass. But the COLORADO RIVER, in building a delta, walled off the depression from tidewater by depositing sediment.

Over the years, incursions of Colorado River floodwaters, some as late as 1861 and 1891, created lakes like ancient Lake Cahuilla. All eventually receded and dried up. The lakes left "bathtub rings," marking ancient shorelines on mountain slopes, and millions of fossilized freshwater clamshells (*coachella* is a bastardization of *conchilla*, or "little shell" in Spanish). The dried-up lakes also left rich deposits of alluvial soil up to one thousand feet deep.

The Imperial Valley is considered to be a triumph of land RECLAMATION via IRRIGATION. Engineers George Chaffey and Charles R. Rockwood led the California Development Company and its subsidiary, the Imperial Land Company, in transforming a desert waste into a great garden, a natural hothouse, and an agricultural empire. In 1901, using economical gravity-fed, uncemented ditches that needed no pumps, Chaffey improved Rockwood's original 60-mile canal route from a head gate on the Colorado near Pilot Knob. As early as 1904, ten thousand colonists raised wheat, oats, barley, sorghum, melons, grapes, and truck vegetables on 150,000 acres of land, irrigated by 780 miles of canals and ditches. Dairying alone yielded one hundred thousand dollars annually.

California Development Company holds its first auction of lands on April 12, 1904. *Courtesy National Archives.*

"City of Imperial, from ice plant water tank, July 9, 1904." *Courtesy National Archives.*

But the irrigation works (today replaced by the 80-mile long, 200-foot wide, All-American Canal and its branch, the Coachella Canal) were partly in Mexico. And, in dry years, the ditches failed to provide adequate water. Rockwood ousted his partner and "improved" Chaffey's canal by by-passing its head gate with a new intake. The Colorado broke through its natural levee at this point and inundated the trough of the Salton Sink, converting 480 square miles of farmland into California's largest lake, the 45-mile long Salton Sea. After much evaporation, which has increased its salinity, the lake is 30 miles long and 8 to 14 miles across.

EDWIN HENRY HARRIMAN led the Southern Pacific Railroad in taking over the bankrupt California Development Company in 1905. It took a half-dozen attempts, but a year after the founding of El Centro in 1906, the Southern Pacific retamed the Colorado with high dikes. In 1907, El Centro became the seat of government of the newly created Imperial County.

By the mid-1990s, the 500,000 arable acres of the valley had a population of almost 117,000, including many Mexican and Mexican American farm workers. The valley was the state's most productive agricultural region, and farmers there grew asparagus, broccoli, carrots, lettuce, honeydew melons, onions, dates, and cotton, as well as such old standby crops as wheat, alfalfa (for seed and hay), and sugar beets. Livestock was still important, too: cattle and calves, sheep (for lamb, mutton, and wool), and bees (for honey). The growing season was at least ten months long, and frequently, more than one crop could be harvested annually from a given acreage.

—*Richard H. Dillon*

SUGGESTED READING:

Starr, Kevin. *Material Dreams: Southern California through the 1920s.* New York, 1990.

TOOLS AND MACHINERY

Farmers in the West were leaders in the adoption and use of agricultural tools and machinery. Except in the irrigated areas, farms were larger in the West than in other parts of the country, and farmers bought the latest machines to work their large acreages and reduce the cost of labor. By 1900, California, Nevada, North Dakota, and Montana were the states that had the highest value of machinery per farm.

Improved machines to prepare the soil, plant crops, harvest and thresh grain, or cut, haul, and stack hay were the order of the day on Western farms after 1860. Most Western farmers used horse-drawn one- and two-bottom plows. Each plowshare turned a furrow fourteen to sixteen inches wide. By the 1880s, however, steam tractors had been developed and proved to be successful on large farms. Bonanza farmers in North Dakota and California hitched plows with as many as fourteen plowshares to huge steam-driven tractors and plowed hundreds of acres in a few days at much less labor cost. The steam tractor was confined almost exclusively to field operations in North Dakota and California before it was replaced by the gasoline tractor in the 1920s.

For planting wheat, the region's main crop, Western farmers used broadcast seeders that fastened to the end of a horse-drawn wagon. In the 1880s, most farmers shifted to improved drills to plant grain. Those machines were ten to twelve feet wide and dropped seed into small furrows created by the metal drill shoes. Two- and four-horse teams pulled the drills, which were common on Western farms by the 1890s.

Row crops, such as corn (important in eastern South Dakota, Nebraska, and Kansas) and cotton (in Oklahoma and Texas), were planted with two-row, horse-drawn planters. The machines made two shallow furrows into which seed was automatically dropped. Some Great Plains farmers adopted a lister planter, which placed seed in the bottom of a furrow six to ten inches deep. By planting in deep furrows, more of the scarce moisture was used, and the young plants were protected from hot winds. Farmers used listers to plant much of the milo or maize raised on the southern Great Plains in the late nineteenth century. Cultivation of row crops was also mechanized. Two-

A plow—pulled from one end by a beast of burden and pushed from the other end by a farmer—busted much of the sod of the trans-Mississippi West. *Courtesy The Bettmann Archive.*

row, horse-drawn cultivators that loosened the soil and destroyed weeds were common on Western farms by the 1880s. Machines for soil preparation and planting and cultivating greatly reduced the amount of labor needed on Western farms by 1900.

Except in California, most Western farmers used the same kind of harvesting and threshing machines as those used by Midwestern farmers. By the 1880s, most grain growers used the improved self-rake reaper, which cut grain with a reciprocating sickle and tied it into sheaves or bundles. The grain was then shocked by hand and was dried before being threshed.

Distinctive to Western farms were the header and the combine, machines for harvesting wheat and other small grains. The header was first developed in the 1840s, but it was not popular in California until two decades later. It usually had a twelve-foot cutting bar, which cut off the heads of grain and elevated them by conveyor belt into a hayrack or wagon. If the grain was sufficiently ripe when cut, the heads were hauled directly to a threshing machine. In other cases, the harvested grain was stacked and threshed later. Although headers were widely used in California in the 1860s, they were replaced by the combine in the 1880s. Many farmers on the Central Plains of Kansas, Nebraska, and the Dakotas also harvested with headers in the late nineteenth and early twentieth centuries.

The combine was the most advanced harvester available to large Western grain growers. After the grain was dead ripe, the combine cut and threshed it in a single operation. By the 1870s and 1880s, after years of experimentation, the combine was perfected to the point that many of the large California wheat ranchers had adopted it. In the early twentieth century, combines were also adopted in the Palouse country of east-

ern Washington and Oregon. The combine was powered by sixteen to twenty-four horses or mules; in some cases, a steam tractor replaced horses for propelling power. A combine with a thirty-foot cutter bar could harvest as much as one hundred acres of wheat a day. Studies of Nebraska farms in the 1920s showed that a combine could harvest wheat for only three to nine cents a bushel compared to thirty-one cents with separate harvesting and threshing machines. By 1940, the much more efficient self-propelled combine operated by one person was being used on a few farms. Twenty percent of the combines were of this type by 1960, and the number continued to grow.

Since Western farmers raised a great deal of livestock, haying equipment was important in their operations. Horse-drawn mowing machines with cutting bars of five to six feet were common on Western farms by the 1880s. They also had horse-drawn rakes that gathered the mown hay and dumped it into windrows. Although much hay was loaded and unloaded on hayracks by hand with pitchforks, mechanical hay stackers came into general use by the 1880s and 1890s. Many Western farmers and ranchers used hay balers and field-forage harvesters by the 1930s and 1940s.

The introduction of the general-purpose gasoline tractor in the 1920s did more than anything else to promote the mechanical revolution on American farms. The tractor provided more power and speed than horses, thus permitting farmers to plow, plant, and harvest much more efficiently. In the 1920s and 1930s, Western farmers shifted quickly from horse to tractor power. By 1940, more than 50 percent of the farmers in the Dakotas, Kansas, and Nebraska had tractors; 96 percent of the larger commercial farmers in these states used tractor power by 1950. In Montana and California, the percentages were 82 and 89 percent, respectively. By 1950, it was common for a large wheat farmer on the Great Plains to have two or three tractors, a truck, a self-propelled combine, and a long list of plows, harrows, discs, drills, and other machines. In some areas of the West, especially in the Palouse wheat country, some farmers used the crawler-type tractor.

Since IRRIGATION was so important in much of the West, technology to provide and distribute WATER efficiently was highly important. By the late nineteenth century, it was widely known that huge quantities of subsurface water existed on the Great Plains and elsewhere in the West. To tap that water supply, improved well-drilling equipment, large pumps, and power for pumps were needed. As early as 1907, some California farmers drilled deep wells and pumped irrigation water using gasoline-powered engines. By 1914, a few farmers in western Texas drilled deep wells with rotary rigs and installed centrifugal pumps powered by oil-burning engines; later they used both gasoline and electricity to power the engines. Rotary rigs and pumps opened the way for rapid expansion of deep-well irrigation on the Great Plains, in California, in Arizona, and elsewhere in the West. Deep-well water was also distributed by large-scale sprinklers, increasingly common by the 1940s. Over the next ten years, thousands of acres in the West were put under sprinkler irrigation. Other equipment important to irrigated farming were the huge machines to level and grade land to get proper flow of water and lightweight aluminum or plastic pipe. WINDMILLS, common on the Great Plains after 1880, were important sources of power to provide water for household use and livestock, as well as for irrigating small gardens.

The mechanical cotton picker also became highly important in the West. The first widespread use of the machine was in western Texas in the 1920s. Known as a cotton sled, this *V*-shaped tool was pulled over the cotton row to strip bolls from the stalk. A spindle-type cotton picker was developed in the 1940s and was soon in wide use in western Texas, Arizona, and California, where cotton was a major field crop. By 1953, California cotton growers had about three thousand spindle-type pickers in use.

Growers of fruits, nuts, and vegetables in the West resisted mechanization until well after World War II. Some of the machines that had come into general use by 1960 included hydraulic shakers used to jostle nuts onto an apron for easy pick up, machines for digging and loading potatoes and sugar beets, and equipment to harvest celery, cabbage, and lettuce with a minimum of hand labor. The tomato harvester was perfected in California in the 1960s. Finally, spraying crops from airplanes, which began in the 1920s, became the standard practice over Western wheat fields and orchards by the 1940s and 1950s.

Farmers throughout the West were in the forefront of agriculture in mechanizing their operations. The large size of farms and the desire to reduce labor costs and increase efficiency were the driving forces behind the adoption of the latest tools and machinery.

—*Gilbert C. Fite*

SUGGESTED READING:
Danhof, Clarence H. "The Tools and Implements of Agriculture." *Agricultural History* 46 (1972): 81–90.
Holbrook, Stewart H. *Machines of Plenty*. New York, 1955.
Hurt, R. Douglas. *American Farm Tools: From Hand-Power to Steam-Power*. Manhattan, Kans., 1982.
Rasmussen, Wayne D. "The Mechanization of American Agriculture." In *Agricultural Literature: Proud Heritage— Future Promise*. Edited by Alan Fusonie and Leila Moran. Washington, D.C., 1977.
Rogin, Leo. *The Introduction of Farm Machinery in Its Relation to the Productivity of Labor in the Agriculture of the United States during the Nineteenth Century*. Berkeley, Calif., 1931.

FARM MOVEMENTS

SEE: Agrarianism

FARNHAM, ELIZA WOOD BURHANS

Writer, lecturer, and reformer Eliza Wood Burhans Farnham (1815–1864) was born in New York. Her mother died when Eliza Burhans was six years old, and she moved to the home of an abusive uncle and aunt. She was forbidden to attend school and was ridiculed when she read on her own. At the age of sixteen, she left to live with another uncle and attended school for a time. In 1835, she moved to Illinois, where she married Thomas Jefferson Farnham the following year. In 1841, the couple moved to New York, where Eliza became active in arguments about political rights for women. She claimed that women did not need political rights but should strive to elevate society as mothers and homemakers.

In 1844, Farnham was appointed matron of the female department of the state prison at Sing Sing. Arguing that kindness went farther than harshness in rehabilitating wayward women, she developed reform programs, which met with a measure of success but caused enough friction with other administrators that she was forced to resign in 1848.

Inspired by her husband's stories of the West, Farnham, by then a widow, attempted to organize a party of unmarried women to move with her to California in 1849 in hopes of bringing some civility to the gold-mining camps. Her efforts were endorsed by a number of prominent New Yorkers, including Horace Greeley and Henry Ward Beecher. Because of illness, she was unable to gather more than a few women to accompany her on the trip. After arriving in California in late 1849, she bought a farm in Santa Cruz County. Her Western experience became the basis of her book entitled *California, Indoors and Out*, published in 1856.

When Farnham returned to New York in 1856, she began her most significant work, *Woman and Her Era*. In 1859, she returned to the West to lecture as well as to make another attempt to persuade single and destitute women to migrate to California. Upon her return to the East in 1861, she petitioned Congress to abolish slavery and served as a nurse at Gettysburg in July 1863, where she possibly contracted a sickness that hastened her death on December 15, 1864.

—*Kurt Edward Kemper*

FARNY, HENRY F.

Accurately portraying on canvas the life of the Plains Indians in the last decades of the nineteenth century, the paintings of Henry F. Farny (1847–1916) are characterized by a strong narrative theme realistically presented. Born in Ribeauville, Alsace, France, Farny moved with his family to western Pennsylvania in 1853. After an apprenticeship to a lithographer in Cincinnati, Ohio, Farny studied art in Europe from 1866 to 1870. In the last years of the 1870s, he was an illustrator for McGuffey's readers and *Harper's* and a painter of circus posters. In the fall of 1881, he traveled to the Sioux Agency at Standing Rock and began to acquire Indian artifacts and to make sketches, photographs, and notes of the Native Americans he encountered. After the trip, Indians and their way of life became his principal artistic focus. Working at his easel in Cincinnati, he prepared a series of Indian portraits.

His growing skills as an artist and his reputation as a painter sympathetic to the status of Native Americans led to his becoming one of the two illustrators for FRANK HAMILTON CUSHING's memoir, which appeared in *The Century Magazine*. After 1890, Farny devoted most of his energy to capturing the essence of Indian life on the Great Plains in his paintings and consequently prepared fewer illustrations for popular publications. Frequent trips to the West gave him a familiarity with the topography and a lasting insight into his subjects' vanishing way of life. Praised for his accuracy and skills as a painter by Presidents Ulysses S. Grant and THEODORE ROOSEVELT, Farny is among the more neglected of late nineteenth- and early twentieth-century Western artists.

—*Phillip Drennon Thomas*

SEE ALSO: Art: Book and Magazine Illustration, Western Art

SUGGESTED READING:
Carter, Denny. *Henry Farny.* New York, 1978.
Taft, Robert. *Artists and Illustrators of the Old West, 1850–1900.* New York, 1953.

FAUST, FREDERICK SCHILLER

SEE: Brand, Max

FEDERAL GOVERNMENT

In the United States and abroad, the popular image of the American West is of a wilderness conquered and settled by rugged individuals: Westerners may have been quick to reach for a gun, but they were self-reliant and beholden to no one. Richard White, among other scholars, has pointed out that this image is skewed in at least two ways. First, the West was a wilderness only to the Anglo-Americans who defined it so, and, second, the American West has always been something of a federal-government project.

In many ways, the federal government guided and molded the Anglo-American settlement of the trans-Mississippi West. The government purchased much of the region, and its armies conquered the rest. Federal troops protected the West's settlers from Native Americans. Government agents explored the area on federally funded expeditions. Federal officials administered Western territories. Government bureaucrats—in land offices, agricultural and interior departments, and RECLAMATION and engineering bureaus—supervised, if even at a distance, the division and development of Western resources. Federal programs underwrote the development of the West's infrastructure, and the federal government subsidized the growth of its industries. As White noted: "Except during the Civil War, most nineteenth-century Americans had little direct experience of the federal influence over their daily lives. Westerners were the great exception. . . . More than any other region, the West has been historically a dependency of the federal government." Early on, the region's territorial experience accustomed Westerners to asking for federal subsidies, as Patricia Nelson Limerick has pointed out, and the tendency to turn to Washington for economic aid—directly in the form of cash, when necessary; indirectly in federally mandated access to land, water, grass, and timber as a matter of course—was one Western habit that would live on long into the next century.

Not that those who came to consider themselves true Westerners ever admitted the central role the federal government played in their often precarious existence. The occupation by Anglo-Americans of the trans-Mississippi region during the first half of the nineteenth century was accompanied by a growing and almost evangelical belief in their MANIFEST DESTINY to

Top left: The federal government sponsored many expeditions into the West in advance of settlement. Photographer Timothy H. O'Sullivan and his portable darkroom accompanied one such expedition led by Clarence King through the sand dunes of Carson Desert, Nevada, 1867. *Courtesy National Archives.*

Bottom left: Aside from free land, what Westerners wanted most from the federal government was protection from hostile Native Americans. A correspondent of the *San Francisco Bulletin* takes notes on the battlefield during the U.S. Army's war with the Modoc Indians from 1872 to 1873. *Courtesy National Archives.*

inherit what they increasingly pictured as a social Eden. Men such as THOMAS HART BENTON, Missouri's U.S. senator and perhaps the West's foremost spokesman for NATIONAL EXPANSION in his day, propagated the idea that such expansion "was not an act of government leading people and protecting them." Instead, he argued, pioneers went forward without aid from or the official sanction of their government and then forced the government to follow "with its shield and spread it over them."

Certainly in the South—Georgia, Alabama, Mississippi—and in the Ohio Valley and parts of the

Land grants and easy credit from the federal government enabled railroad companies to build railways throughout the West. In this photograph, dormitory cars for the construction crews of the St. Paul, Minneapolis and Manitoba Railway approach the railhead of the line from Minot to Great Falls and Helena in 1887. The government sent U.S. Army troops to protect workers from hostile Indians. *Courtesy Burlington Northern Railroad Archives.*

Old Northwest, squatter encroachments on Indian lands led the federal government to adopt policies—wide-scale purchase under ill-defined treaties and, ultimately, Indian removal—to accommodate such "pioneering." But the United States negotiated the LOUISIANA PURCHASE long before American pioneers poured into the trans-Mississippi lands, and the government conducted a general reconnaissance of those lands with an eye toward eventual settlement far in advance of such settlement. While filibusters in Texas and Forty-niners in California pushed their territories toward statehood before the government was ready to act—and came close to destroying the government itself for precisely that reason—more typically the lands west of the Mississippi became, at some stage of their history, a colony of the United States. In each such colony, the federal government controlled the government of a territory whose residents did not hold the full rights and privileges enjoyed by other American citizens. Rather than following pioneers west, the federal government more often led them there, especially after the Civil War, when leaders in government and business began developing new markets in the West.

The Civil War itself was, in part, responsible for the kind of control the federal government would come to exercise over the trans-Mississippi West. During the conflict, the federal government, of necessity, expanded and exercised new and unprecedented powers over its citizens, often in collusion with the industrialists and financiers whose help allowed the Union ultimately to prevail over the rebel Confederacy. A great smasher of barriers, the war gave rein to industrial fortune-builders and created new expectations from the general public. During the war, bankers, bookkeepers, and manufacturers became accustomed to nationwide operations, large-scale enterprises, mass markets, and industrial production, while the government grew ever more comfortable with openhanded and even recklessly generous business policies that gave private enterprise access—and some control—of public funds and public resources.

While the wartime HOMESTEAD ACT OF 1862 and the postwar Indian policy of rounding up native peoples and confining them to reservations, from this point of view, can been seen as federal steps toward opening the West to expanded markets, they were actually enhanced versions of two key "frontier" activities that Westerners had come to expect of the government: control of the Indians and distribution of land. Although both policies, at times, involved considerable expense, it was really the federal subsidies to transportation—to overland freight, to RAILROADS, to harbors and highways—that characterized the post–Civil War federal investment in the West. Often touted as the prototypical laissez-faire government, the United States, in the late nineteenth century, kept its hand out of colonial enterprises in the sense that it failed to restrain or regulate access to public grazing lands, mineral deposits, or the vast federal stands of timber, but even that was a form of federal subsidy: it allowed lumber barons, cattle kings, and captains of industry unlimited use of natural resources. Without the massive public-land grants awarded the railroads, the transcontinental lines could never have been built, since private investors were initially quite leery of such enterprises, even when federal authority turned a blind eye to the illegal shenanigans of no-lose investment schemes like CRÉDIT MOBILIER OF AMERICA.

In the Western territories carved out of the "internal" colonial empire the United States had bought from France and taken from Mexico, federal money could have a dramatic impact. Federal officeholding was a major form of patronage. Many local newspaper publishers (with the proper political pedigree) depended on official government printing to make a go of their presses. Federal contracts—in the construction of public buildings, for example—boosted local economies. The UNITED STATES ARMY, brought in to pacify and control the Indians, became a major source of income for cattle-raisers and for volunteers who got federal pay. Indian reservations became captive markets for grain and beef suppliers. In the Dakotas, as Howard Lamar has noted, where the large Native American presence delayed the development of farming and mining, the federal government became "not only a paternalistic provider of land" but also a "subsidizing agency which furnished needed development funds" by offering these kinds of business opportunities and produced an "old Dakota attitude that government itself was an important paying business."

High profits from federal contracts, supply orders, and patronage positions plus the factionalism and boosterism of territorial politics spawned corrupt combinations of business owners and politicians whose very reason for being was to turn public expenditures into private income. In some cases, these combinations might involve a single industry, even one large company, as in Montana where politics and the fortunes of copper ran on parallel tracks and the ANACONDA MINING COMPANY, by 1915, clearly dominated the state's economy and political order. In others, groups of lawyers, bankers, businessmen, and federal officials formed territorial rings, as in New Mexico, where the SANTA FE RING long prospered from the territory's abundance of land; in the Dakotas the combination was known as the "Indian Ring." At first, rings frequently enjoyed popular support because early settlers considered them vehicles for funneling federal cash into their own pock-

Supplying beef and other necessities to the United States government's military outposts was a lucrative business for some Westerners. Members of Company B of the Tenth Infantry are shown crossing the Gila River in buckboards in the Arizona Territory in 1885. *Courtesy National Archives.*

ets. Federal officials freely took up membership in these rings during their territorial tours of duty, and the rings bound them together with local elites in the common cause of making money. On the other hand, rings also sparked growing resentments as the territorial periods, supposed to be temporary, stretched out and expanded the power of the federal government frequently to the financial benefit of an elite few. Washington State spent more than thirty years as a territory, Utah nearly half a century, and Arizona and New Mexico—which did not become states until 1912—more than sixty years. In Alaska and Hawaii, the territorial era, with its federal control, political corruption, and economic dependency, survived well into the second half of twentieth century.

In part because of the long territorial interlude, the expanded role of the federal government (which, in theory, should have been no greater in Wyoming than in Rhode Island) was one of the characteristics that set the West apart from other regions of the country. For in the West, the government itself changed and became a qualitatively different kind of state. Out West, federal power took on its modern guise. In effect, in the West, the federal government learned to be the federal government. Institutions that were locally based and controlled back East became federalized out West. While militias had represented the armed power of the states in the East, federal troops took on that role in the West, and, for the most part, the U.S. Army was a Western army. Although the East had its U.S. post offices and custom houses, the basic nineteenth-century federal bureaucracies—the BUREAU OF INDIAN AFFAIRS, the GENERAL LAND OFFICE, the UNITED STATES GEOLOGICAL SURVEY, the other various Interior Department agencies for land and resource management—were, in large measure, Western departments, and it was in these agencies that professionalism and centralized administration first began to replace patronage. By the twentieth century, the Western bureaucracies, joined by the new BUREAU OF RECLAMATION and the UNITED STATES FOREST SERVICE and enhanced by the growing power of the UNITED STATES ARMY CORPS OF ENGINEERS, had indeed taken on their modern form in what Richard White calls the "bureaucratic revolution." Staffed by salaried professionals, centrally controlled by certified administrators, the Western bureaucracies were frequently more powerful than local political interests. As a result of the expanding administrative power of the federal government in the West, the region's territorial period in many ways produced not a group of states that resembled those they would join in the East, but a national government whose spreading influence made the East (and South) come more to resemble the private-federal political order of the West.

The extended territorial period also affected Western attitudes toward the federal government. Shaping the political realities of the West, federal territorial administration meant that local political power, even when strong, always needed a stamp of approval from the outside. Given the territorial rings, many Westerners also came to associate public office with incompetence at best, but more often with corruption, and they resented both the government's power and its refusal to use that power against the rings. Sounding like all oppressed colonials, Dakotans declared in an 1877 newspaper: "We are so heartily disgusted with our dependent condition, with being snubbed at every turn in life, with having all our interests subjected to the whims and corrupt acts of persons in power that we feel very much as the thirteen colonies felt." Sustained by a fortune-hunter's code and myths of individual entrepreneurship, Westerners imagined themselves, as did colonials the world over, free of the cultural and social conditions that had made life in the homeland (the East) so constricting, even as the extractive fortunes typical of all colonies depended on the life line thrown them by the home government. Simultaneously denouncing federal tyranny while crying for increased federal spending in the region became a Western habit, an ambivalence toward the federal government that continues to characterize Western politics.

For the federal role in the West did not vanish with end of TERRITORIAL GOVERNMENT, nor did its participation in the Western economy diminish as that economy matured beyond the initial extractive-industry stage. Instead, it expanded as bureaucratic power expanded, helping to create what Donald Worster has called the West's "hydraulic civilization," one highly centralized, carefully administered, and, in large part, federally funded. The NEWLANDS RECLAMATION ACT OF 1902 placed the government at the center of the development and control of the arid West's key natural resource, WATER. The IRRIGATION and reclamation projects it spawned over the next half century not only underwrote the massive growth in Western agriculture, but made the West the most urban region in the country by creating the possibility of growth in such water-starved communities as Los Angeles, San Diego, Phoenix, and Tucson. Also early in the century, President THEODORE ROOSEVELT and GIFFORD PINCHOT pushed for professional management of national forests, which resulted in long-range and centralized plans for the industrial and recreational use of national forests. The TAYLOR GRAZING ACT of 1934 at last centralized federal control of GRAZING on the public domain. Especially after the country was hit by the Great Depression of the 1930s, the Progressive centralization of government that had occurred during the first two decades of the twentieth century proved a boon to the West, which was used to federal largess and where the policy mechanisms had long been in place for dispensing that largess.

There seems little doubt that the West benefited disproportionately from New Deal programs. The Civilian Conservation Corps did much of its work, and much of its best work, in the West. Various farm-credit programs saved some farmers and cattlemen from economic collapse. The SOIL CONSERVATION SERVICE worked to keep the West, hard hit by drought and devastated by the DUST BOWL created in part by regional agricultural practices, from further ecological disaster. The Farm Security Administration built camps to house California's and the Southwest's hard-pressed migrant workers, whose cheap labor was a key to the region's big-farm economy. The Indian New Deal, which aimed at reversing past mistreatments, had its major impact in the West, where most of the Native American tribes by then lived. According to Leonard Arrington, the New Deal "benefited the West more than other sections of the nation. Indeed, when one lists the states in order of the per capita expenditure of the federal economic agencies, the top fourteen states in benefits received were all in the West." Sixty percent more per capita went to the West, for example, than the poor regions of the South. From 1933 to 1939, Montana received $710 per capita in federal relief, while North Carolina got $143. Wyoming received three times more per capita than the United States as a whole, while paying a quarter of the U.S. average per capita in internal revenue collected; Colorado received twice as much from the federal government as it sent back to Washington.

The Western states responded to such federal aid with increased resentment. In part, this was because increased aid meant increased federal say in local affairs. Sometimes such control was indeed onerous; in the 1930s, the government insisted that the Navajos were overgrazing their lands and causing federal reclamation projects to silt up. In response, New Dealers introduced the NAVAJO STOCK-REDUCTION PROGRAM, which needlessly slaughtered half the sheep owned by the tribe. More often, however, federal meddling was much less egregious, and the response of Westerners to it was far out of proportion. Wyoming, whose cattle-raisers had long enjoyed the boon of federal land policies, considered federal relief to the poor a government intrusion; it took pride in being the one state to have yet requested federal aid until June of 1933, when continuing hard times forced the state to change its tune and accept its first welfare check. Colorado, says T. A. Larson, similarly considered the federal government "meddlesome and constitutionally threatening" even as so many of its citizens went on the federal dole. When the Drought Relief Service began buying cattle in 1934, it asked for future production-control plans in return for the $525 million it spent, according to John Schlebecker "to save the cattlemen from ruin and starvation. For this salvation, many cattlemen never forgave the government." In general, Westerners took the money and then complained about the spread of bureaucracy and federal giveaways.

The New Deal was the occasion for a much more substantial penetration into the Western economy, however, than federal relief programs and the modest regulations they proposed. It was during this period that imaginative financiers such as AMADEO PETER GIANNINI and innovative industrialists such as the energetic HENRY J. KAISER changed the dynamics of federal investment in the West. To them, the West appeared an economic colony because of the control Eastern investors exercised over the region, and rather than spurning the federal government, they sought its aid in breaking free of that control. After 1919, Giannini led a group of progressive Western bankers and businessmen in a revolution against such economic colonialism. Giannini, who had backed Kaiser as he built a construction empire in the West, urged President Franklin D. Roosevelt, in 1941, to entrust Kaiser with new manufacturing responsibilities that Giannini would underwrite, which helped Kaiser launch his massive shipbuilding operations in the Pacific Northwest. A New Deal favorite for his consistent support of Roosevelt's policies, Giannini—with his huge Bank of America—consciously sought to calm the typical distrust of smaller Western banks toward the government. The West, in turn, was well served by the New Deal's willingness to pour federal investment as well as federal relief into the region.

When the Bureau of Reclamation let bids for the construction of the massive Boulder Dam (now HOOVER DAM) as part of the federal foray into public works, Giannini and Kaiser regarded the dam's construction both as a key to large-scale industrial development in the West and as a chance to declare independence from the East. Kaiser persuaded Western contractors to pool their resources and take on what, at that time, was the world's largest construction venture. He argued that by eschewing the competitive course Western business

considered natural, the region would garner lucrative federal contracts in the future. The consortium of companies Kaiser organized in 1931 won the biggest labor contract yet awarded by the federal government, and true to his predictions, the construction of Boulder Dam was but the first step for the so-called Six Companies on a path to becoming multinational giants. Working almost exclusively with the Bureau of Reclamation, Kaiser's consortium laid the groundwork for the basic infrastructure of the modern American West.

Giannini and Kaiser promoted what Kaiser called the "higher industrialization"—the use of the federal government to spur Western development. But the higher industrialization was more a change in scale and directness of federal investment than a break with Western traditions. Kaiser and the government bureaucrats who worked with him redefined the basic relationship of government and business in the American West rather than the relationship between region and government. Government now directly put up the capital for creating an industry, while Kaiser and other corporate leaders provided the organization and the management that made the new corporations work. Kaiser took the West's territorial experience in relying on federal contracts and made it into a model for wide-scale industrial development; government, not private investors, now took the risks. The special pressures of World War II made the kind of New Deal government–private industry partnerships pioneered by Giannini and Kaiser standard operating procedure.

The West, which had always boasted a healthy army presence, became a region flush with government defense installations. The Manhattan Project, which produced the world's first atomic bombs in 1945, justified as a means to win the war, also became a huge research and development project for Western business, one that spawned a major postwar industry in nuclear power. Under wartime defense contracts, not only did Kaiser's shipbuilding—and later aluminum production—flourish, but so did such infant industries as mainframe aircraft production. By the time World War II was over, the basic shape of the federal role in the American West had become clear. As with New Deal programs, the West especially benefited from massive federal investment in defense, aerospace, electronics, and all those industries boosted or even created by a combination of Cold War fears and a scientific community swelled by wartime research. By the late 1950s, the West's share of federal spending actually topped World War II levels; and the modern West had become as addicted to federal spending on defense, "big science," and aerospace as the prewar West had been on New Deal reclamation projects and federally subsidized water and the old West had been on U.S. Army beef contracts.

In the modern West, scientists, businessmen, and military leaders worked under government contracts that funded research and development, frequently in the form of federal grants at the West's federally funded public universities. Western agriculture bloomed with help from government-financed university programs. Research, in turn, gave birth to modern industries nursed by federal protection into major enterprises. The AIRCRAFT INDUSTRY, for example, became aerospace, and the space program's needs for rapid, accurate, and miniaturized calculating machines ultimately helped give rise to a huge new high-tech industry in business and personal computing. Even the postwar Interstate Highway System, which would be justified as a national-defense measure necessary for the rapid deployment of forces and weapons and the mass evacuation of populations during nuclear war, was especially welcome in the West, where the car culture and the sprawling suburbs of Los Angeles were becoming models for cities throughout the Southwest. The white-collar managers and skilled engineers employed by the defense and high-tech industries, in turn, launched a suburban building boom made possible by federally subsidized water projects and federally funded highway programs, while the region's army of migrant workers and its working poor were maintained, in large part, by federally subsidized and mandated welfare and health-care programs.

And still Westerners refused to embrace their federal benefactor. Even as the giant freeway projects, the huge defense installations, and the massive reclamation programs of the twentieth century took center stage from the railroad, mining, and lumber industries of the last half of the nineteenth century, Western businessmen continued to expect the government to help them build their fortunes while keeping its hands out of their private affairs. Late in the century, it was not only post–Cold War retrenchments in defense spending, government programs, and federal research projects that threatened the peculiar federal-private partnership underlying the region's basic economy, but also tax revolts, nativist backlashes against the West's immigrant labor force, and attacks on the public sector that all had their roots in the West's traditional resentment against the region's historical dependence on the federal government.

—*Charles Phillips*

SEE ALSO: Banking; Booms; Burke Act; Central Valley Project; Colleges and Universities; Colorado River Compact; Colorado River Storage Project; Currency and Silver as Western Political Issues; Dawes Act; Deposit Act of 1836; Desert Land Act of 1877; Desert Land Act of 1891; Echo Park; Edmunds Act of 1882; Edmunds-Tucker Act of 1887; Enlarged Homestead Act of 1909; Exploration: United States Expeditions; Exploration and Science; Forest Management Act of 1897; Forest Reserve Act of 1891; Forestry; Financial Panics; Forts; Gadsden Purchase; Glen Canyon Dam; Glenn-Fowler Expedition; Grand Canyon and Grand Canyon National Park; Grant's Peace Policy; Harriman Expedition; Hetch Hetchy Controversy; Homesteading; Immigration Law; Interstate Commerce Act of 1887; Japanese Internment; Lacey Act of 1900; Land Policy; Legal System; Lewis and Clark Expedition; Mineral Lands Leasing Act of 1920; Mining Law of 1872; Morrill Act of 1862; Multiple-Use Doctrine; National Park Service; Native American Cultures: Acculturation; Native American Peoples: Peoples Removed from the East; Naturalization Law of 1790; Northwest Ordinance; Oklahoma Land Rush; Preemption Act of 1841; Public Lands Commission of 1879; Railroad Land Grants; *Report on the Lands of Arid Regions;* Roads and Highways; Sherman Anti-Trust Act; Sherman Silver Purchase Act of 1890; Stock Raising Homestead Act of 1916; Sustained Yield; Tariff Policy; Teapot Dome; Temperance and Prohibition; Territorial Law and Courts; Timber and Stone Act of 1878; Timber Culture Act of 1873; Trail of Tears; United States Indian Policy; Water; Women's Suffrage; Wright Irrigation Act of 1887; Yellowstone National Park; Yosemite Act of 1864; Yosemite National Park

SUGGESTED READING:

Arrington, Leonard. "The Sagebrush Resurrection: New Deal Expenditures in the Western States, 1933–39." *Pacific Historical Review* 52 (February 1983): 1–16.

Athearn, Robert. *The Mythic West in Twentieth Century America.* Lawrence, Kans., 1986.

Lamar, Howard R. *Dakota Territory, 1861–1889: A Study of Frontier Politics.* New Haven, Conn., 1956.

———. *The Far Southwest, 1846–1912: A Territorial History.* New York, 1970.

Limerick, Patricia Nelson. *The Legacy of Conquest: The Unbroken Past of the American West.* New York, 1987.

Lowitt, Richard. *The New Deal and the West.* Bloomington, Ind., 1984.

Malone, Michael, and Richard W. Etulain. *The American West: A Twentieth Century History.* Lincoln, Nebr., 1989.

Nash, Gerald. *World War II and the West: Reshaping the Economy.* Lincoln, Nebr., 1990.

———. *The American West Transformed: Impact of the Second World War.* Bloomington, Ind., 1985.

Pomeroy, Earl S. *The Territories of the United States: 1861–90.* Philadelphia, 1947.

Schlebecker, John. *Cattle Raising on the Plains, 1900–1961.* Lincoln, Nebr., 1963.

White, Richard. *"It's Your Misfortune and None of My Own": A New History of the American West.* Norman, Okla., 1991.

Wiley, Peter, and Robert Gottlieb. *Empires in the Sun: The Rise of the New American West*. Tucson, Ariz., 1985.

FEDERAL MARSHALS AND DEPUTIES

The law—and its lawmen—trailed behind the explorers and settlers who went, in John Steinbeck's phrase, "westering." When Congress passed the enabling legislation carving a new territory out of the West, the law usually included a provision to establish the office of United States marshal and deputy United States marshal. In the territories, marshals performed both police and administrative functions, much as their colleagues did in the states. However, at least initially, the police authority of the territorial marshals was considerably broader than that of the marshals in the states.

In the unorganized territories, the federal courts sat as district or circuit courts hearing all manner of cases, and marshals were the only lawmen. They essentially introduced law to the territory. Their jurisdiction extended over all types of crimes and all manner of criminals; they chased murderers, thieves, and brigands; rapists, robbers, and embezzlers. In the Indian Territory alone, U.S. marshals hauled hundreds of outlaws before "Hanging Judge" ISAAC CHARLES PARKER, who sentenced 160 of them to death. The marshals actually hanged 79.

Once a territory was organized, the federal courts acted in a dual capacity. Continuing to hear federal issues, with the rap of the judge's gavel, they transformed themselves into territorial courts hearing cases on appeal. The marshals supported the federal courts and, at the call of the territorial legislature, could also act as officers of the territorial courts. Each territory, however, could also establish its own offices of sheriff for each county and town marshals for each town. Most legislatures chose the latter course. As the individual territory verged on statehood, the marshals first surrendered their authority to territorial lawmen and then usually concerned themselves solely with the federal courts and federal laws.

Western officers frequently secured concurrent commissions as territorial lawmen and federal lawmen. That practice confused the distinction between local and national officers. Many sheriffs and town marshals also served as federal deputy marshals. The double office gave the lawmen considerable authority, as well as the opportunity to earn extra fees. In October 1882, Virgil Earp was the town marshal of Tombstone, Arizona, and a deputy U.S. marshal of the Arizona Territory. When he, his brothers, and JOHN HENRY ("DOC") HOLLIDAY gunned down the Clantons and McLaurys

"Black Jack" Ketchum was convicted of train robbery in the New Mexico Territory, where train robbery was a capital offense. He was hanged at Clayton in 1901. *Courtesy National Archives.*

just down the street from the O. K. Corral, they were exercising Virgil's authority as town marshal. Their excuse was their opponents' violation of Tombstone's gun laws; their intent was murder.

The lines of authority between territorial and federal lawmen were lax. If they did not always hold joint commissions, Western lawmen just as frequently moved from one office to the other with disconcerting frequency. JAMES BUTLER ("WILD BILL") HICKOK worked sometimes as town marshal, sometimes as a deputy U.S. marshal, depending on who would hire him. PATRICK FLOYD JARVIS (PAT) GARRETT moved from deputy U.S. marshal of the New Mexico Territory to sheriff of Lincoln County and back again, forever clouding by what authority he killed "BILLY THE KID." BARTHOLOMEW (BAT) MASTERSON was a sheriff in Kansas when he caught outlaw Dave Rudabaugh; he later served as a deputy U.S. marshal in New York City. Wyatt Earp was a policeman in Dodge City, Kansas, before moving to Arizona where he ran for election as sheriff of Cochise County. After Virgil Earp was wounded in ambush, Wyatt replaced him briefly as deputy U.S. marshal and used his commission to avenge those who had shot his brothers.

Almost as frequently, lawmen in the West worked both sides of the law. The Dalton brothers worked as deputy U.S. marshals in the Indian Territory until Frank Dalton was killed in the line of duty. His brothers then decided that they could, for the same risk, enjoy greater profits as outlaws than as lawmen. Even "Billy the Kid," notoriously disrespectful of the law, rode in a deputy marshal's posse early in the Lincoln County War.

In addition to their duties as territorial lawmen, the marshals also provided the federal government with a loose administrative structure for the territories. The marshals promulgated the laws, took the federal census, maintained the federal registers, rented rooms for the courts, handled the court's money, and issued proclamations of the president. During the great Oklahoma land rush of 1889, Deputy U.S. Marshal Ransome Payne officially signaled high noon and the start of the race for land claims. In the Alaska Territory, the marshals occasionally distributed medicines to the native population dying of white men's epidemics.

Despite their two-hundred-year history and their important, intimate role in most of the major domestic events in American history, from the Whiskey Rebellion of 1794 to the civil rights movements of the 1960s and the war on drugs in the 1990s, the marshals are best known for their role in the Western territories during the quarter of a century after the Civil War. Indeed, most people today fail to realize that the marshals still exist and that their law enforcement authority is the broadest of any federal agency. Dime novels, radio shows, movies, and television programs have portrayed the Western marshals as often the only law and just as often acting alone against gangs of desperadoes and outlaws. Wyatt Earp, Bat Masterson, and "Wild Bill" Hickok have entered American myth as saintly Western marshals—their goodness pitted against the evil of outlaws and murderers.

The myth, of course, is a quite profound exaggeration of the historical reality. In the great westward migration, the law always trailed as the last step to settlement. U.S. marshals and their deputies eased the transition from territory to state. They introduced law enforcement to the unorganized territories and helped establish an administrative structure for the government. As the population grew and local governments were formed, the marshals stepped back to allow the development of local jurisdiction and local law enforcement. At that point enforcing only federal law, the marshals let the locals take on the train robbers, horse thieves, and other desperadoes.

—*Frederick S. Calhoun*

See also: Dalton Gang; Earp Brothers; Law and Order; O. K. Corral, Gunfight at; Social Banditry; Territorial Law and Courts

Suggested reading:
Calhoun, Frederick S. *The Lawmen: U.S. Marshals and Their Deputies, 1789–1989*. Washington, D.C., 1990.

FERBER, EDNA

A popular novelist, whose Midwestern and Western fiction combines social satire with a sense of the sweep and diversity of American life, Edna Ferber (1887–1968) was born in Kalamazoo, Michigan, and grew up in Appleton, Wisconsin.

After graduating from high school in Appleton, Ferber became a newspaper reporter. Her first major novel, *So Big* (1924), grew out of her journalism and was set in a Midwestern farming community. A tremendous popular success, it was awarded the Pulitzer Prize. Her next novel, *Showboat* (1926), set along the Mississippi River, was adapted by Jerome Kern and

Edna Ferber, in 1930 aboard the *S.S. Ile de France*. *Courtesy The Bettmann Archive.*

Oscar Hammerstein, II, as a breakthrough Broadway musical and, later, film. Many of Ferber's Western novels—including *Cimarron* (1930), *Saratoga Trunk* (1941), *Giant* (1952), and *Ice Palace* (1959)—were made into highly successful films.

Although some critics scorned Ferber's works as relentlessly middlebrow and undistinguished in style, she was one of very few novelists who successfully combined a sweeping, even epic, vision with a sharp sense of social satire and social criticism. Contemporary readers often saw her works as attacks on the thoughtless vulgarity and heedless aggression of the Western character. Yet most of her fiction pivots on an Eastern "dude" who goes West, revealing not merely the crudity of Westerners, but, more importantly, the effete shortcomings that typify "refined" Eastern culture. Thus, if anything, Ferber portrayed the West satirically in order to satirize American culture, East *and* West.

In addition to her regional novels, Ferber collaborated with George S. Kaufman on a number of popular stage comedies, including *The Royal Family* (1927), *Dinner at Eight* (1932), and *Stage Door* (1936), all of which became films.

—*Alan Axelrod*

SUGGESTED READING:
Ferber, Edna. *A Peculiar Treasure* (autobiography). New York, 1939.

FERRIS, WARREN ANGUS

Born in Glen Falls, New York, Warren Angus Ferris (1810–1873) was a mountain man and surveyor. He spent much of his childhood and adolescence in Buffalo, where he learned land surveying. By 1830, he had moved to Missouri where he worked for approximately five years as an employee of the AMERICAN FUR COMPANY in St. Louis and participated in several expeditions of Western exploration. In cooperation with his brother Charles, he wrote a journal entitled *Life in the Rocky Mountains,* which dealt with his experiences on these expeditions. Widely read in the 1840s, his journal became a well-known, popular description of the region. Ferris moved to Texas in 1836 and participated in the TEXAS REVOLUTION. He became a county surveyor in 1837 and served in that position until 1841. During that time, he surveyed the original town plat for the city of DALLAS and led several expeditions that explored the rivers of northern Texas. He settled near Dallas in 1847, oversaw farming operations on his lands, and wrote columns for the *Dallas Herald.*

—*Light Townsend Cummins*

SUGGESTED READING:
Ferris, Warren Angus. *Life in the Rocky Mountains.* Rev. ed. Edited by LeRoy R. Hafen. Denver, 1984.
McCausland, Walter. "Warren Angus Ferris." In *The Handbook of Texas.* Vol. 1. Edited by Walter Prescott Webb. Austin, Tex., 1952.

FERTILITY

Fertility on the Frontier
Patricia Hogan

Fertility among Native Americans
Nancy Shoemaker

FERTILITY ON THE FRONTIER

Most demographers studying Euro-American fertility on the frontier acknowledge an initial increase in family sizes during a region's pioneering period followed by a decline in fertility rates as a region became more settled. This pattern occurred in each frontier region as Euro-Americans advanced from the Eastern regions of the country to the West Coast.

The dynamics of this phenomenon, according to most scholars, had to do with pioneering parents' desire to provide for each of their children. Parents hoped to supply their offspring with at least the same amount of land or capital that they had when they began life as adults. Thus, the explanation goes, the number of children parents could "afford" depended on their outlook for increasing their own wealth and dividing it in substantial chunks among their grown children. In a frontier region, land was initially cheap, and parents felt comfortable in having large families. But as a region became more settled and more populated, land prices rose, and parents were less confident that they could give their children a proper start in life.

It is difficult to generalize about family size on successive frontiers, but according to one historian, ten children in an average frontier family is a conservative estimate. After the initial pioneering stage in a settlement, family size more steadily approached the norm of about four children per family.

In the nineteenth and early twentieth centuries when much of the trans-Mississippi West was settled, birth-control technology was known to American families and practiced by husbands and wives. Pioneering couples, to a large extent, possessed the means to control the sizes of their families. Available literature recommended spermicidal douches, vaginal sponges, condoms, and coitus interruptus. After 1864, a vaginal diaphragm was available. The 1870s produced several publications on the rhythm method of birth control. In the middle decades of the nineteenth century, abortion, seldom recorded in diaries or likely discussed at the time, was an option if sometimes a difficult undertaking.

Some women on the frontier had other incentives to limit the sizes of their families. The addition of another infant increased the amount of work a wife had to do each day, and women, recent studies confirm, labored long at common household tasks, made more difficult by frontier conditions, and undertook additional "men's" chores that the survival of the family farm required. In addition, for many women, childbirth had lasting, detrimental effects on their health, effects that made the completion of necessary chores all the more difficult. One wife wrote to her husband: "I know no doom that would horrify me so much as to know or believe that 12 years to come, could add five more children to my number."

Although the same concern about launching children on their way likely motivated African American families on the frontier, their numbers were so small and their frontier experiences so different because of the legal and social restrictions they suffered at the hands of the dominant white culture that generalizing about of their fertility patterns is difficult. Likewise, Chinese immigrants in frontier regions were few, and exclusionary laws hampered family formation of any size until well into the twentieth century. It was an experience Chinese Americans shared generally with Japanese American families in America, although the arrival of Japanese PICTURE BRIDES in the early 1900s and the subsequent increase in native-born offspring alarmed many Anglo racists.

Fertility among Mormon women in community settlements was high. One study revealed that Mormon women of monogamous marriages averaged 7.83 children; women of polygamous marriages produced an average of 7.45 children.

Among Mexican American families of southwestern California in the second half of the nineteenth century, fertility rates appeared to have risen and then fallen after the United States annexed the region. Although the trend parallels Anglo fertility patterns, historian Richard Griswold del Castillo attributes the steady decline in fertility to the effects of racial discrimination and economic disenfranchisement.

In general, fertility patterns on the frontier of the American West follow the downward trend demographers have observed in most cultures that change from agrarian to industrial economies.

—*Patricia Hogan*

SEE ALSO: Child Rearing; Homesteading; Women on the Spanish-Mexican Frontier

SUGGESTED READING:

Bean, Lee L., Geraldine P. Mineau, and Douglas L. Anderton. *Fertility Change on the American Frontier: Adaptation and Innovation.* Berkeley and Los Angeles, 1990.

Chan, Sucheng. *Entry Denied: Exclusion in the Chinese Community in America, 1882–1943.* Philadelphia, 1991.

Griswold del Castillo, Richard. *La Familia: The Mexican-American Family in the Urban Southwest.* Notre Dame, Ind., 1984.

Jeffrey, Julie Roy. *Frontier Women: The Trans-Mississippi West, 1840–1880.* New York, 1979.

FERTILITY AMONG NATIVE AMERICANS

Scholars know little about the fertility of Native Americans before European contact or even before the twentieth century. Archaeological research provides information on mortality but tells us almost nothing about fertility, and the poor quality of data on Indians before 1900 makes reliable estimates of Indian fertility rates impossible. In the seventeenth through the nineteenth centuries, Euro-Americans who lived near Indian communities often remarked that the size of Indian families was either the same size as typical white families or smaller. More conclusive data from around 1900 confirms these observations. Depending on the tribe or cultural group, an average Indian woman probably had from five to seven children if she lived to the end of her child-bearing years. Demographers consider a fertility rate of five to seven children slightly lower than the fertility levels that usually prevail in nonindustrial societies.

There are several explanations for the relatively low Indian fertility. Indian women did have knowledge of some birth-control methods. Abortion appears to have been widely practiced through the use of abortion-inducing plants or aggressive body massage. Some women carried contraceptive charms, a form of birth control that modern medicine would not acknowledge as effective. Occasionally, infanticide served as a form of birth control, but the scant evidence available on infanticide suggests it was practiced only in times of stress and when other lives were at stake. Everyone, male and female, expected women to have children and fulfill the important and prestigious role of mother, so women probably used birth-control methods primarily to regulate the timing of births and to prevent pregnancies after they felt they had had enough children.

Other biological and cultural factors that were not deliberate attempts to control fertility affected Indian fertility rates. Venereal disease and tuberculosis, endemic among Indians in the late nineteenth century, reduced the chances of conception and affected a woman's ability to bear children. Breast feeding also inhibits conception, if combined with malnutrition or if couples abstained from sexual intercourse while the woman nurses a child, as was common among some Indian groups. Since Indian women nursed their children for a long time, usually three to four years, the biological and cultural side effects of breast feeding probably did lower fertility.

Under normal conditions, Indian births appear to have outnumbered deaths and allowed for population growth. However, European contact and the spread of Old World diseases led to devastating declines in the Indian population. Demographers have observed that fertility rates often rise immediately after an epidemic, but that does not seem to have happened among Indians exposed to new diseases. The morbidity, mortality, and stress caused by epidemic disease also had a negative impact on fertility. Still, fertility outpaced mortality, except during epidemics and other crises, so most Indian tribes made rapid recoveries from population decline.

In other ways, European contact seems to have boosted Indian fertility levels. Studies of fur-trade society, data from the 1900 census, and a 1910 U.S. census publication on Indians have all shown that Indian women who married white men had considerably more children than other Indian women. Evidently, INTER-MARRIAGE eliminated some of the constraints on fertility, perhaps because intermarriage into another culture restricted Indian women's access to traditional forms of birth control. The relationship between high fertility and intermarriage no longer exists. Since World War II, Indian and white intermarriages have resulted in lower fertility than that for Indian-Indian couples.

In the twentieth century, Indian fertility has experienced a rapid decline, especially since 1960. In 1910, there were about 850 children between the ages of 0 and 4 for every 1,000 women between the ages of 15 and 44. By 1980, this child-to-woman ratio had plummeted to about 450. While the fertility of whites and blacks in the United States reached an all-time low during the Great Depression, the decline in Indian fertility began slowly in the early twentieth century only to be interrupted by the postwar baby boom. In the midst of the transition to "modern" fertility levels, Indian fertility after World War II soared to nearly 1,000 children between the ages 0 and 4 for every 1,000 women between the ages of 15 and 44. For most of the twentieth century, Indians have had nearly twice as many children as whites and blacks, but the rapid drop in Indian fertility since 1960 has led to Indian fertility levels only slightly higher than those for other Americans.

—*Nancy Shoemaker*

SUGGESTED READING:
Shoemaker, Nancy. "The American Indian Recovery: Demography and the Family, 1900–1980." Ph.D. diss., University of Minnesota, 1993.
Thornton, Russell. *American Indian Holocaust and Survival: A Population History since 1492.* Norman, Okla., 1987.

FETTERMAN MASSACRE

Largely because of public fascination with the personality of "General" GEORGE ARMSTRONG CUSTER, his famed "massacre" in 1876 at the Battle of Little Bighorn all but obliterated memory of a similar defeat of the U.S. Army by Plains Indians ten years earlier. On December 21, 1866, at the foot of the Bighorn Mountains near present-day Story, Wyoming, more than fifteen hundred Sioux, Cheyenne, and Arapaho warriors decoyed seventy-nine soldiers and two civilians under the command of Captain William Judd Fetterman into an ambush that none survived. The Fetterman Massacre, remembered by Indians as the battle of "100 in the Hand," was the high point of RED CLOUD's War, a campaign by Sioux groups and their allies to protect shrinking hunting grounds from destruction by grow-

William Judd Fetterman. *Courtesy Denver Public Library, Western History Department.*

ing numbers of wagon trains traveling over the BOZEMAN TRAIL through present-day Wyoming to Virginia City, Montana, where gold had been discovered in 1862. Red Cloud, an extraordinary Oglala Sioux leader, joined with others to organize sustained resistance.

In the spring of 1866, the U.S. Army ordered units of the Eighteenth Infantry Regiment to secure the trail by maintaining Fort Reno on the Powder River and establishing two additional posts at intervals to the northwest. Political connections brought command of the expedition to Colonel Henry Beebe Carrington, a lawyer who had organized the regiment in Ohio at the outset of the Civil War, but who had remained behind to continue with recruiting and administrative work while the regiment fought through Tennessee and Georgia. Reaching the Powder River country, Carrington divided his troops among the fort sites on the trail and personally and meticulously directed construction of an elaborate central stockade called Fort Phil Kearny. The Indians continued their traditional hit-and-run attacks against soldiers and travelers alike, while Carrington complained that he had neither adequate manpower nor weapons to do more than fend them off.

Historians today debate Carrington's conduct as did the battle-seasoned officers under his command at the time. None of them felt more frustrated than Captain Fetterman, who had been commended for gallantry in the Civil War. Urging Carrington to take the offen-

sive, Fetterman allegedly boasted that "with eighty men I could ride through the Sioux nation." Given command of a unit assigned to drive Indians away from a wood-hauling detachment, Fetterman apparently disobeyed orders not to pursue them. He died with all his men in an ambush long planned by the Indians.

In a celebrated ride of 236 miles through snow, John "Portugee" Phillips brought word from the fort of the "massacre," which generated a national outcry. Official investigators recorded criticism of Carrington but did not blame him for the disaster.

Wagon travel and Indian attacks resumed while the United States, recognizing that railroads would likely make the trail obsolete, sought new treaties with the Indians. But Red Cloud accepted no peace terms until the United States in 1868 closed traffic on the Bozeman Trail, abandoned the forts, and agreed to recognize the Powder River country as "unceded Indian territory," completing the Indians' victory.

—*Gerald George*

SEE ALSO: Little Bighorn, Battle of; Sioux Wars

SUGGESTED READING:

Brown, Dee. *The Fetterman Massacre.* Lincoln, Nebr., and London, 1971. Originally published as *Fort Phil Kearny: An American Saga.* New York, 1962.

Carrington, Margaret. *AB-SA-RA-KA, Home of the Crows.* Philadelphia, 1868. Reprint. Lincoln, Nebr., 1983.

Charles Marion Russell's 1922 pen-and-ink drawing of *The Fetterman Fight. Courtesy Buffalo Bill Historical Center.*

George, Gerald. "An Open Letter to the Bozeman Trail Association." In *Visiting History: Arguments over Museums and Historic Sites.* Washington, D.C., 1990.

McDermott, John D. "Price of Arrogance: The Short and Controversial Life of William Judd Fetterman." *Annals of Wyoming* 63 (Spring 1991): 42–53.

Murray, Robert A. "Chapter 5. Operations in the Powder River Country from the Close of the Connor Campaign to the Abandonment of the Early Posts." In *Military Posts in the Powder River Country of Wyoming, 1865–1894.* Buffalo, Wyo., 1968.

Olson, James C. *Red Cloud and the Sioux Problem.* Lincoln, Nebr., and London, 1965.

FEWKES, JESSE WALTER

Zoologist and ethnologist Jesse Walter Fewkes (1850–1930) was born in Newton, Massachusetts, the son of a craftsman. He studied natural history at Harvard under Louis Agassiz and graduated in 1875. He received an M.A. and Ph.D., also from Harvard, in 1877. After further zoological study in Europe, he served as an assistant at Harvard's Museum of Comparative Zoology from 1880 to 1889 and published extensively on marine invertebrates.

On a journey to California in 1887, Fewkes became fascinated with the Pueblo Indians of New Mexico and Arizona. Having lost his position at the museum, he conducted ethnological investigations among the Zuni Indians from 1889 to 1890. The following year, he succeeded FRANK HAMILTON CUSHING as director of the Hemenway Southwestern Archeological and Ethnological Expedition. At first, he continued Cushing's investigations of the Zuni Indians, especially Zuni ceremonies. He is credited with being the first to make phonographic recordings of Zuni songs.

Fewkes next focused on the customs, art, and ceremonies of the Hopi Indians, who admitted him to their Antelope and Flute priesthoods. In 1895, he accepted a position with the Bureau of American Ethnology, and from that point on, his work was increasingly archaeological in nature. He made excavations and repairs at several sites including Casa Grande, Arizona; Navajo National Monument, New Mexico; and Mesa Verde National Park, Colorado. In addition to his many scholarly publications, he gave informal lectures to tourists and wrote for popular journals.

From 1918 until his resignation in 1928, Fewkes was chief of the Bureau of American Ethnology. He was an officer of several scientific societies and the recipient of many international honors. Although criticized for bringing a detached, natural history approach to his investigations, much of his work remains important.

—*Michael J. Brodhead*

Jesse Walter Fewkes examining pottery shards atop a shell mound near St. Petersburg, Florida, in 1923. *Courtesy The Bettman Archive.*

SUGGESTED READING:

Hinsley, Curtis. "Ethnographic Charisma and Scientific Routine: Cushing and Fewkes in the Southwest, 1879–1893." In *Observers Observed: Essays on Ethnographic Fieldwork.* Edited by George W. Stocking, Jr. Madison, Wis., 1983.

Hough, Walter. "Jesse Walter Fewkes, 1850–1930." *National Academy of Sciences Biographical Memoirs* 15 (1934): 261–283.

Swanton, John R., and F. H. H. Roberts, Jr. "Jesse Walter Fewkes." *Annual Report of the Smithsonian Institution* (1930): 609–616.

FICKLIN, BENJAMIN F.

Road builder and transportation manager Benjamin F. Ficklin (1827–1871) was a member of the field party that located Fort Kearney, South Pass, and Honey Lake Road in 1857 as part of the Pacific Wagon Road program of the U.S. government. When the work was abandoned, he served for a time as deputy U.S. marshal in the Utah Territory. Shortly thereafter, he became a rider for Albert S. Johnson, in command of the Army of Utah; that work entailed traveling into Flathead Indian country to procure beef and mules in midwinter and delivering dispatches to the East.

Ficklin supervised the construction of way stations and stocked the route from San Francisco to El Paso for the OVERLAND MAIL COMPANY. In 1859, he was employed by the Leavenworth and Pike's Peak Express Company, and when that firm expanded to become the Central Overland California and Pike's Peak Express Company, he became a road superintendent. Known for vigorous and dynamic leadership, Ficklin has been credited with proposing the idea for the PONY EXPRESS. He urged WILLIAM HEPBURN RUSSELL, who announced the establishment of the Pony Express, to double the service from once a week to twice a week, but Russell considered the proposal financially excessive and unsound. A quarrel and feud between the two men resulted in Ficklin's resignation despite the support he had from ALEXANDER MAJORS and WILLIAM BRADFORD WADDELL, Russell's partners. Ficklin then turned his attention to a government-subsidized overland TELEGRAPH with a pony-express run between the wires to be strung from East to West. He was one of the incorporators of the Pacific Telegraph Company in 1861.

When the Civil War broke out, Ficklin returned to Virginia and was commissioned a major in the quartermaster department of the Confederate Army. After the war, he returned to the Southwest where he continued working in the stagecoach business.

—*W. Turrentine Jackson*

SEE ALSO: Pike's Peak Express Company

SUGGESTED READING:

Austerman, Wayne R. *Sharps Rifles and Spanish Mules: San Antonio–El Paso Mail, 1851–1881.* College Station, Tex., 1985.

Jackson, W. Turrentine. *Wagon Roads West.* Berkeley, Calif., 1952.

Settle, Raymond W., and Mary L. Settle. *Saddles and Spurs: The Pony Express Saga.* Harrisburg, Pa., 1955.

FIDDLE

SEE: Music, Western

FIELD, SARA BARD

Suffragist and poet Sara Bard Field (1882–1974) came from a Cincinnati, Ohio, family. Her very stern Baptist father refused to support her quest for a college education because he feared it would weaken her faith, and the young Sara Field married a Baptist minister, Albert Ehrott, a man twice her age.

Shortly after her marriage, in 1900, Field spent two years in Asia, where her husband served with the Eurasian Baptist Church in Rangoon, Burma. En route to their assignment, they traveled through India where the disparity between the starving natives and their indifferent British overlords appalled Field. The experience was a turning point for her.

Upon returning to the United States in 1902, the couple and their son settled in New Haven, Connecticut, where Field audited courses in poetry at Yale University and began writing poems of her own. Ehrott's assignment to a poor church in Cleveland, Ohio, in 1903 gave Field the opportunity to advance her own notions of "a practical application of Christianity" through the kindergarten and soup kitchen she established. In Cleveland, Field embraced socialism, continued with her writing, and incurred the ire of her husband by making her first forays into politics and social reform.

The family moved to Portland, Oregon, in 1910, and a short time later, Field joined the Oregon College Equal Suffrage League and became an organizer in the 1912 campaign that secured the vote for women in the state. She continued the cause in Nevada in 1913 and 1914. Increasing differences with her husband led to a divorce in 1914. After her husband gained custody of the couple's son and daughter and moved to Berkeley, Field relocated in San Francisco to be near her children.

In California, Field promoted WOMEN'S SUFFRAGE for the Congressional Union. In 1915 and 1917, she traveled across the country to deliver messages to President Woodrow Wilson and the U.S. Congress urging national suffrage. An eloquent speaker with a youthful appearance, Field's presentations at the organizing convention of the National Woman's Party and at venues throughout the West won the party many advocates. Her activities were interrupted in 1918 by the death of her son and the breakdown she suffered following the accident.

Recovering from her loss, Field began a thirty-four-year union with Charles Erskine Scott Wood, a West Point graduate and wealthy corporate lawyer, who, by the age of fifty-eight, had become a writer and armchair anarchist. Although Wood's wife would not give him a divorce, Wood and Field lived together after 1918.

Field devoted herself to her poetry, much of which was published in journals and magazines. A collection of her works, *A Pale Woman*, was published in 1927. Field and Wood became the center of a bohemian literary circle in the Bay Area, encouraging other artists and writers and sponsoring in 1924 the School of the Arts of the Theatre in San Francisco. Her political activities continued as well: she and Wood supported a birth-control clinic, agitated for a pardon for labor radical THOMAS JOSEPH MOONEY, and entertained some of the day's prominent social critics.

Field and Wood retreated to a home in Los Gatos, south of the city. There she wrote her award-winning narrative poem *Barabbas* (1932), a work that tempered scripture with her radical politics. Another collection of her poems, *Darkling Plain*, followed in 1936. Two years later, after the death of Wood's wife, she married Wood. The marriage ended with Wood's death in 1944, after which Field devoted herself, for thirty years, to organizing and editing his works. She died in Berkeley on June 15, 1974.

—Patricia Hogan

SUGGESTED READING:

Fry, Amelia. "Along the Suffrage Trail: From West to East for Freedom Now!" *American West* 6 (January 1969): 16–17.

Myres, Sandra L. *Westering Women and the Frontier Experience, 1800–1915*. Albuquerque, N. Mex., 1982.

FIELD, STEPHEN J.

Stephen J. Field (1816–1899), a California lawyer, was appointed by President Abraham Lincoln to the United States Supreme Court. Born in Haddam, Connecticut, Field grew up in Stockbridge, Massachusetts, the son of a distinguished clergyman. He graduated from Williams College in 1837 at the head of his class. After reading law in New York, he was admitted to the bar in 1841 and practiced law with his brother until 1848.

After the discovery of gold in California, Field set out for the Feather River region to make his fortune as a miner. Once in California, however, he determined that practicing law would make him more money than mining gold. He arrived at Yubaville (later renamed Marysville) and was immediately elected alcalde of the town.

Field's office was abolished under the 1849 state constitution. After William R. Turner became the new district judge, the two men clashed over a minor point of court etiquette, and the resulting feud severely damaged Field's reputation. Turner had him disbarred and worked to block his election to the state legislature in 1850. Field won the election, however, and pushed the legislature to redistrict the state circuits to reduce Turner's judicial power.

While the feud with Turner occupied much of Field's time, he was active in the legislature on matters with lasting consequences for the state. He adapted the civil and criminal codes developed by his brother in New York to the special needs of California and included in his revisions several provisions liberal to debtors.

In 1857, Field was elected to the state supreme court. During his time on the bench, three issues were of major importance: mineral rights, property titles in San Francisco, and Indian lands. In *Biddle Boggs* v. *Merced Mining Co.* (1859), Field ruled in favor of individual rights over those of the state and federal government by barring governmental entities from authorizing mining on private property. In *Moore* v. *Smaw* (1861), he again favored the individual in his ruling that minerals in the earth belonged to the owner of the land—not to the state or federal government.

In March 1863, the Senate confirmed Field's nomination to the U.S. Supreme Court. He served on the court from 1863 to 1897—at the time, the longest tenure of any justice in the court's history. Meanwhile, his rulings as chief justice of the tenth circuit of the United States did much to allay discrimination against Asians who had immigrated to California. Those unpopular rulings and others that gave California railroads favorable tax advantages ended his hopes of becoming the Democratic nominee for president in 1880 and 1884. His rulings on the disputed will of U.S. Senator William Sharon of Nevada resulted in a courtroom brawls. Field ruled against the interests of Althea Hill, Sharon's widow, whose lawyer (and new husband) David Terry was arrested during the incident. When Terry threatened the judge's life, Field hired a bodyguard. On a trip to Los Angeles in the spring of 1889, Terry drew a knife on Field, whose bodyguard shot the assailant. Although charges against Field and his guard were dropped, the dissatisfactions of Californians over many of Field's rulings lingered.

—Candace Floyd

SUGGESTED READING:

McCloskey, Robert G. *American Conservatism in the Age of Enterprise: A Study of William Graham Sumner, Stephen J. Field, and Andrew Carnegie*. Cambridge, Mass., 1951.

Mendelson, Wallace. *Capitalism, Democracy, and the Supreme Court*. New York, 1960.

FIELD MATRONS

Created in 1890, the field-matron program, part of the attack of the BUREAU OF INDIAN AFFAIRS on American Indian tribalism, was designed to focus exclusively on Indian women. The program was intended to assist native women in redefining themselves and their roles according to Euro-American cultural standards. The BIA's "de-Indianization" campaign grew out of the belief that lessons in Euro-American concepts of gender ideology and domestic skills would expedite assimilation among tribal women, whom the agency regarded as potential catalysts of cultural change. To bring Euro-American ideas and practices directly to Native American women, the BIA employed field matrons to live and work in tribal communities and reservations across the trans-Mississippi West. Between 1890 and 1938, more than 250 field matrons functioned as emissaries of Euro-American culture by teaching American Indian women to accept and adopt "the ways of white women."

In 1890, domestic education and Euro-American concepts of gender roles defined the parameters of the field-matron program; by 1938, other factors had reshaped it. American Indian women proved themselves to be highly discriminating students of Euro-American domesticity and cultural values. Quilting, cooking, and dressmaking lessons proved very popular among tribal women; etiquette lessons that stressed the limits of "women's sphere" were not. The field matrons learned through experience that meeting the needs of American Indians was the only way to encourage assimilation. Because most tribal communities suffered from a host of poverty-related health problems and lacked adequate medical care, field matrons gradually took on greater responsibilities as providers of medical care. Over time, the BIA came to rely heavily on their expertise and developed public-health programs around them. Field matrons served as the principal medical practitioners from 1908 to 1917 in campaigns to prevent trachoma and tuberculosis and in the "Save the Babies" infant- and child-care campaign. After World War I, health care replaced domesticity as the centerpiece of the field-matron program.

Changes in the program's focus mirrored changes in its personnel between 1890 and 1938. The BIA drew the first field matrons from an elite pool of single, affluent Euro-American women who had dedicated their lives to activism in the cause of Indian assimilation. Between 1895 and 1917, expansion of the program led to the employment of women who saw the BIA and the field-matron corps as an opportunity for professional and economic advancement rather than for social or political activism. During this period, the BIA also conducted a short-lived program that employed assimilated Native American women as field matrons. After World War I, Euro-American women with professional credentials in health care began to enter the program. By 1938, these women and the professional BIA employees dominated the field-matron corps. That year, the BIA abolished the field-matron program and initiated a separate field-nurse program to address public-health needs of American Indians. The field-matron program, an experiment in assimilation through Euro-American domesticity, had outlived its usefulness.

—*Lisa E. Emmerich*

SEE ALSO: United States Indian Policy: Civilization Programs, Reservations

SUGGESTED READING:
Emmerich, Lisa E. "'Civilization' and Transculturation: The Field Matron Program and Cross-Cultural Contact." *American Indian Culture and Research Journal* 15 (1991): 34–48.
———. "'Right in the Midst of My Own People': Native American Women and the Field Matron Program." *American Indian Quarterly* (1991): 201–216.

FIGUEROA, JOSÉ

Mexican governor of Alta California from 1833 to 1835, José Figueroa was born in Jonacatepec, Morelos. Very little is known about his early career until his participation in 1821 in the Mexican independence movement as personal secretary for General Vicente Guerrero. In the first years of the Mexican republic, Figueroa assumed various military and political positions including, in 1824, *comandante general* of Sinaloa and Sonora, where he suppressed regional Indian revolts.

In 1832, the central government appointed Figueroa *comandante general* and *jefe político* (governor) of Alta California. His assignments included enfranchising and educating mission neophytes; dividing Indian lands; encouraging domestic commerce and colonization, particularly of skilled workmen and artisans; and investigating trade with the Russians and American whalers.

Figueroa was responsible for enforcing the 1833 order of the Mexican Congress to secularize the California missions. He also prevented José María Padrés, a friend of Mexico's acting president, and José María Híjar, who had been appointed Figueroa's replacement, from carrying out a scheme to establish colonies on mission lands. When President ANTONIO LÓPEZ DE SANTA ANNA resumed office, he directed Figueroa to continue as governor of Alta California. Figueroa then ordered the Padrés-Híjar colony of 250 skilled émigrés to settle on the northern frontier of Sonoma, Solano, and Petaluma to create a buffer against the Russians or to settle as individuals in other communities. Conflict with Padrés and Híjar persisted and led to their deportation by Figueroa, who, in 1835, defended his actions toward them in a position paper entitled *Manifesto a la republica Mexicana.*

After ousting Padrés and Híjar, Figueroa resumed his efforts to establish a garrison and town in the Sonoma area, but ill health prevented him from completing the work. He died on September 29, 1835, in Monterey, a week after his resignation as governor, and was buried in Santa Barbara.

—*Gloria E. Miranda*

SUGGESTED READING:
Figueroa, José. *The Manifesto to the Mexican Republic.* Oakland, Calif., 1952.
Hutchinson, C. Alan. *Frontier Settlement in Mexican California.* New Haven, Conn., 1969.

FILM

The Western
  Charles Phillips

Minority Images in Westerns
  Carlos E. Cortés

THE WESTERN

The movie western and movie narrative were born in the same film. In 1903, Edwin S. Porter created *The Great Train Robbery,* a "flicker" (so called because of the flickering quality of the light from early cameras projecting through celluloid film) based on the chases and gunfights first made popular in turn-of-the-century WILD WEST SHOWS. Porter's creation revolutionized the making of motion pictures through the use of "cuts" to show parallel and overlapping action leading up to a climax, and it turned a vaudeville oddity into a popular new art form.

Before the immense success of *The Great Train Robbery,* movies had been considered primarily curiosities, one-minute shorts produced and used as fillers in theaters between vaudeville acts or occasionally shown in bunches at crude movie houses, set up in the backs of stores or warehouses and called "nickelodeons" because customers were charged a nickel to watch them. A few nickelodeon owners had begun to produce their own flickers or pay for others that ran for about eight minutes, taking up approximately the same amount of time as a vaudeville "turn," or act. Porter's film established these eight-to-ten-minute one-reelers, as they came to be known, as the standard length for American movies. It also set the fashion and the pattern for the long-lived American "western" and encouraged others—such as the creative genius D. W.

Griffith, who in 1903 started directing one-reel westerns in New York for Biograph—to follow Porter's lead in exploring the implications of disjunctive editing, which took liberties with time and space.

Soon nickelodeons sprang up in almost every neighborhood in major American cities. Outright purchase of short flickers gave way to rentals. New "exchanges"—middlemen buying prints from studios and renting them to exhibitors—served some eight thousand nickelodeons by 1908, and the little theaters, immediately and immensely profitable, attracted more than twenty-five million viewers a week. The audience was mostly urban working-class people who watched the "flickers" and enjoyed them no matter what language they spoke, what country they came from, which tenement they lived in. The movies became the poor man's theater. Developed as mass entertainments for poor urban audiences, the movies quickly became formulaic melodramas that offered a means of escape from daily life through fantasy, displayed a certain populist aesthetic, and aimed at both justifying the dominant culture and assimilating their audiences to it. It was for movie audiences that the myth of the Wild West, first formulated in dimes novels and western genre novels, was perfected.

Richard Slotkin has pointed out that the movies—like the dime novels and such literary productions as OWEN WISTER's *Virginian*—promoted the frontier myth of regeneration through violence. In that myth, Americans corrupted by urban "civilization" are purified through the violent reclamation of a wilderness from savages in order to create a social Eden; hence the gunman hero tames the Wild West by banishing Indians, dangerous minorities, rogue villains, and occasionally evil capitalists (big ranchers, ringleaders, landlords) so that the common folk can build a decent town. Henry Nash Smith, who traced the origin of the genre back to the *Leather-Stocking Tales* of JAMES FENIMORE COOPER through its debasement in dime novels, and John G. Cawelti, who followed the genre's adaptation in novels and film, also have argued that the western involves a deep formula in which the hero mediates between civilization and savagery—or culture and nature or order and chaos. For them, and for Slotkin, the hero is transitional, employing frontier violence to establish peaceful values. Helping place this formula in context, Patricia Nelson Limerick has suggested that movie westerns were part of a foundation myth underscoring the claim to innocence that Americans in general made in their occupation of Western land; hence the codelike purity of the movie Western hero and the fragile vulnerability of their damsels in distress, as well as the demonizing of movie Indians, minorities, and individualistic villains. In the same vein, Richard White

Actor John Wayne treats a Native American woman none too kindly in the 1956 John Ford classic *The Searchers. Courtesy The Bettmann Archive.*

film-makers, at least, used the western "myths" for purposes other than the propagandizing of conservative social values; in fact, they used the myths in some cases to attack the dominant power structure, which, in Peckinpah's case, was represented by corporate Hollywood's control over his artistic production. John G. Cawelti and John Lenihan suggested that the formula itself, while imposing a strict narrative structure, also reflected different national forces, patterns, and concerns in each generation of western films. Christine Bold, Michael Denning, and Cynthia S. Hamilton have more directly claimed that the genre developed from dime novels could be subversive as well as assimilative, allowing—to paraphrase Denning—not only for "escapist adventure" but also for "social conflicts" through the figures of bank and train robbers, aggrieved cowboys, and range wars. The social outlaws, who first appeared in Western folklore and then in dime novels, rode onto the silver screen as the Jesse Jameses and Billy the Kids and Zorros of the flickers.

Richard M. Brown has argued that popular westerns in both print and film often reflected a "cognitive split in the mythology of the Western hero" in the face of the social violence accompanying the rapid industrialization of the trans-Mississippi West after the Civil War, which he calls the "Western Civil War of Incorporation." On the one hand, the industrial ruling class won the war, and from their control was bred the socially conservative myth of the civilizing gunslinging hero—Owen Wister's Virginian and the film versions of the real-life JAMES BUTLER ("WILD BILL") HICKOK and Wyatt Earp, for example. On the other hand, those resisting incorporation generated a dissident social-bandit myth whose heroes were frequently real-life outlaws such as Jesse James, "BILLY THE KID," JOAQUIN MURIETA (OR MURRIETA), and GREGORIO CORTEZ, and whose spirit also found its way into movies, more covertly in the early decades, more openly in the antiheroes of the "adult" westerns that began appearing in the late 1960s. "Both the conservative mythic hero," noted Brown, "and the insurgent social bandit have had wide

has argued that the concentration on individual violence, which lies at the heart of the Wild West myth presented in the movies, was a way for Americans to avoid the broader social violence inherent in the "settling" of the West. Neal Gabler has described how the immigrants, many of them Jewish, who came to own the studios and control the production of movies were both decidedly secular and assimilationist, and it was they who hired the Anglo directors who produced mainstream western fantasies in which white heroes fought evil threats to the social order and ensured that justice triumphed in the end.

Since at least the late 1960s, when movie westerns first seemed to being dying off as a popular genre, few scholars have been impressed with the aesthetic quality of formula westerns, and many have been offended by the movies' stereotyping of Mexicans and women and their outright calumny against Native Americans. A growing scholarly consensus has held that in the western—novels as well as movies—the hero always reflects deeply conservative social values and is aligned with the dominant law-and-order political culture against the threat of anarchy.

More recently, however, some scholars have been taking the western more seriously. In the 1980s, Paul Seydor—who went on to become a film editor—produced a study of the films of Sam Peckinpah and the use of genre as a narrative convenience that suggested some

appeal because Americans are deeply ambivalent about established power and dissident protests."

Roots of the cowboy movie

Certainly the central role that cowboys came to play in early films is passing strange. It happened almost immediately with the birth of the medium. If *The Great Train Robbery* established a basic plot of crime, pursuit, and retribution, it also introduced audiences to an actor, G. M. Anderson, who played four roles in Porter's film and who would, after going into film production himself, become the first cowboy personality of the flickers. With the purchase from Peter B. Kyne of the screen rights to his fictional character "Broncho Billy" (later known as "Bronco Billy"), Anderson launched the cowboy movie with its identifiable star and its regular release on an annual schedule. The virtuous, self-sacrificing "BRONCO BILLY" ANDERSON appeared in some 375 short films between 1908 and 1914. His innovation, which influenced western film production for decades, was to use his "personal" name on screen and off, giving birth to the idea that movie cowboys and the actors who played them were one and the same and that they were as impossibly pure as the one-dimensional characters they often brought to the screen. The purity itself, however, was an odd historical phenomenon, since in real life cowboys were poorly paid hired hands, mostly young men who drifted into the work, gambled away their wages, and drank and caroused during their off hours, and many of them were African American or Hispanic in contrast to their lily-white movie counterparts.

In fact, as Richard Slotkin has noted, cowboys were not heroes in the early dime novels precisely because their workingman status made them ineligible for marriage to upper-class heroines. Then, in the late nineteenth century, the cowboy's job itself went through a kind of urban mythologizing process, and his way of life captured the American imagination. The cowboy seemed a bit like the baseball hero who played (worked) an urban game (job) for a Gilded Age monopoly but somehow came to embody the mostly rural virtues of a pure craftsmanship just then being crushed by American industrial life. In a country increasingly made up of wage-earners trapped in urban slums and company towns, the cowboy was a worker of the wide-open spaces, a man who, like the wage-earners, made his living with his hands, but unlike them seemed free to roam. Although the hired hand of a ranching capitalist, the cowboy punching cows on the open range came to represent the essence of individual liberty in a workingman's America.

One of the agents of that changed perception was WILLIAM F. ("BUFFALO BILL") CODY, who some scholars credit with creating the Wild West. In the 1880s, Cody began publicizing his Wild West show as "America's National Entertainment," an emblematic telling of the entire course of American history. Its series of spectacles and "historical" reenactments were meant to unfurl for the spectator the different "epochs" of American history. In between, there were episodes called "Cowboy Fun," in which trick riding by cowboys and fancy shooting by the likes of ANNIE OAKLEY, called "Little Sure Shot," and Cody himself were the order of the day. Cody was responsible for reversing the negative image many held of cowboys.

Before his show, those who knew cowboys, including their employers, thought of them as an unsavory lot, distinguished only by their bad habits and rude behavior. Then Buffalo Bill in 1884 introduced William Levi Taylor, a young ranch hand, to his audiences as Buck Taylor, "king of the cowboys." Cody and his publicists fashioned a noble, patriotic biography of Taylor and told parents that the tall Texan was gentle with children. Taylor's popularity grew each year, and by 1887, he was the putative hero of a series of dime novels written by long-time Cody associate Prentiss Ingraham. It was during the Cowboy Fun, too, that Cody first introduced the "Rough Riders." Throughout the 1880s, dime novels had frequently applied the term to Western horsemen, and Cody adopted its use during a European tour to characterize his white American riders. THEODORE ROOSEVELT used the name for the band of adventurers—some of them Westerners—he took with him to Cuba during the Spanish-American War, and "cowboys" had become true national heroes.

By the time Owen Wister wrote *The Virginian*, then, the cowboy was more than worthy of being a romantic hero. In that novel, the Virginian—a cowboy with a blighted past who comes West to begin over—becomes a managerial hero who elevates himself to the upper class by marrying the boss's daughter after proving himself worthy by defeating the villain, Trampas (also a cowboy, but one in league with the dark forces of anarchy in a range war) in what became the classic Western shootout. Dustin Farnum, who played the Virginian on the stage in New York, also took the lead in Cecil B. DeMille's film version from Paramount in 1914, which along with DeMille's *Squaw Man* (also from Paramount in 1914) established the feature-length western that came to dominate film production in the teens. The formula and the hero were complete, and the tradition of violent acts married to pure motives embodied in a rugged hero became standard movie fare as the industry itself moved to southern California and ex-cowhands, old roustabouts, and rodeo stars drifted into Hollywood seeking work as extras, stunt men, and occasionally matinee idols.

Again, not unlike baseball players, cowboy heroes became celebrities in the new cult of personality being spawned by the early twentieth century's marriage of new media entertainments to a national audience. That no human could be as good or pure as the movie cowboys brought many of the early performers to personal ruin, just as it did sports stars, but American viewers continued to believe in movie cowboys almost as much as they believed in themselves. Among the movie cowboy heroes, WILLIAM S. HART created many of the traditions common to westerns. He went to Hollywood in the teens under contract to producer and director Thomas H. Ince, who had joined D. W. Griffith as a major director of Hollywood westerns. The first to emphasize realistic settings and action in his westerns, Hart became the writer, director, and star of a series of westerns that stressed melodrama, sentimentality, and a nearly morbid self-righteousness in his heroes, who were more often than not reformed badmen. His most famous film was also one of his earliest, *Hell's Hinges* (1915). A morality play with a strong temperance message, the film appeared in segments, or "chapters," that soon led to a tradition of serial movies and Saturday matinees.

There were other matinee cowboys in the teens and early twenties besides Anderson and Hart—most of them Hart imitators such as Jack Holt, Harry Carey, Hoot Gibson, Ken Maynard, Tim McCoy, Jack Huxie, Buck Jones. Hart's only serious rival during the silent era was TOM MIX. Mix's cowboy persona was a clean-living and virtuous man who had encounters with clearly evil outlaws, and his popularity marked a return to the simple virtues and morality rejected by Hart. A veteran of the Wild West shows, Mix brought to the screen a glamour missing from Hart's and even Anderson's austere vehicles. Bedecked in elaborate outfits astride a white horse, Mix became the model for low-budget movie cowboys with flashy personalities and lighthearted styles. Such matinee cowboys as Bob Steele, Hopalong Cassidy (a.k.a. William Boyd), and Johnny Mack Brown may have been shy in the presence of the heroine, but they were more than a match for anyone when it came to riding, roping, shooting, and fighting. And after sound was introduced, they could out-sing any man as well. The singing cowboys— GENE AUTRY, Roy Rogers, Tex Ritter, Fred Scott, Monte Hale, Rex Allen, and a dozen others—may seem a bit far-fetched today as authentic Western heroes, but they do emphasize just how close cowboy movies remained to the Wild West fantasy entertainments that they, in many ways, replaced.

Movie westerns

Had it not been for the surprise box-office success in 1924 of James Cruze's *Covered Wagon*, the Hollywood western might well have remained a secondary genre and B-movie phenomenon (B-movie for "budget movie," which is Hollywood lingo for low-budget genre productions, as opposed to A-movies, adequately financed features with some pretensions to art). This first of the big-budget western epics had roots in the early "story" westerns of Griffith and Ince. Griffith's best, *The Battle at Elderbush Gulch* (1914), centered around settlers who, besieged by Indians, are rescued at the last moment by the U.S. Cavalry, while one of Ince's more stirring stories—*The Invaders* (1912), starring Francis Ford, director John Ford's older brother— portrayed the Native Americans as victims of national expansion. *The Covered Wagon* chronicled the hazardous journey West by a group of early pioneers. John Ford repeated its success the next year with a better film, *The Iron Horse*, which traced the building of the transcontinental railroad. The box-office impact of these two films provided the incentive for further Hollywood westerns, and even given their crude notions about westward expansion, they established the genre's aesthetic respectability. Tapping into the growing American fascination with the "frontier" and the obsession for stark confrontations between good and evil, the movie western became a vehicle for expressing the mythic oppositions of American culture: civilization versus savagery; nature versus society; individualism versus conformity; wilderness versus Eden. They developed an iconography that included landscapes, stock characters, costumes, animals, and even weapons, all of which operated as symbols and often spoke to audiences on a level far more complex than the simple narratives they culled from the works of ZANE GREY and MAX BRAND.

In the late 1920s and early 1930s, Hollywood produced a group of western spectaculars that made the western a mainstay of the motion picture industry. Raoul Walsh's *In Old Arizona* (1929), the first all-talking western, won an Academy Award for William Baxter's portrayal of the "Cisco Kid," and Walsh's *Big Trail* (1930), although a box-office flop, offered JOHN WAYNE his first major role. In a long career, Walsh did his best to romanticize the West in movies featuring gritty, if simple-minded, action-adventure heroes: *The Dark Command* (1940), also with Wayne; *They Died with Their Boots On* (1941), with Errol Flynn playing a glorified GEORGE ARMSTRONG CUSTER; *Pursued* (1947); *The Tall Men* (1955); *A Distant Trumpet* (1964). Accompanying Walsh in his turn to the western was King Vidor, a major Hollywood director, whose 1930 fantasy *Billy the Kid* starred Johnny Mack Brown and was, in the language of Hollywood promotion, a "smash" hit. Edward Cahn's *Law and Order* (1932) was an important western that followed on the heels of Esley Ruggle's *Cimarron,* which won the 1931 Academy Award for best picture. The early 1930s also produced the first comedy western, George Marshall's *Destry Rides Again* (1932), starring Tom Mix. Despite these aesthetic and commercial triumphs, the Hollywood western of the 1930s became the province of the singing cowboys and the Saturday matinee serials. Partly because sound made them possible, partly because the Depression made them attractive, Gene Autry (and his horse Champion) and Roy Rogers (and his horse Trigger) captured the imagination of small-town adolescents nationwide. Some serials were not dominated by yodeling cowpokes: Harry Sherman's "Hopalong Cassidy" series, starring William Boyd and based on the works of Clarence E. Mulford, William Colt MacDonald's "Three Mesquiter" series, and the long-lived Zane Grey serials all boasted B-movie heroes better with guns than with guitars. Even they, however, along with such major features as John Ford's *Stagecoach* (1939), had to bow occasionally to the prevailing tastes and feature a song here, a musical interlude there. Although Hollywood—particularly the John Wayne–dominated Republic Films—would continue to produce B-westerns into the 1940s and 1950s, their budgets grew ever thinner, their reliance on stock footage ever greater, their hasty story lines ever less memorable. The best of them, *Hopalong Cassidy* and the *Lone Ranger,* for example, would be revived or continued on television, but even the shoddiest found their way onto the new medium in its early days and there found a new following not only for former matinee idols but for many of the actors who played the villains as well.

The 1940s witnessed the triumphant return of the big-budget western. In such movies as John Ford's *Stagecoach,* Henry King's *Jesse James,* and William Wyler's *Westerner,* all produced in 1939, all playing in 1940, many film critics have found the "classical period" of the genre. The 1940s, they argue, saw films whose purity and simplicity in dealing with the code of the Old West have never been equaled. New Western historians, on the other hand, attack the very same films for their convenient, self-congratulatory, reassuring fantasies of winning the West—fantasies that ignore the costs of the conquest to Native Americans, animal species, and the environment. A pivotal figure in this battle of the scholars is director John Ford. For Ford's champions, such as Andre Bazin, the director's *Stagecoach* and *My Darling Clementine* (1948) are astonishingly rich and intensely personal expressions. His "Cavalry Trilogy"— *Fort Apache* (1948), *She Wore a Yellow Ribbon* (1949), and *Rio Grande* (1950)—is a major examination of the meaning of American history that marks Ford's rehabilitation of the Native American. Many see *Fort Apache* as the first antiwestern, the first true attack on prevailing American myths about the building of the West. These scholars think of *The Searchers* (1856) as Ford's masterpiece, a moody meditation on the relativity of the environment, both Indian and white. They sympathize with the Ford who, in *The Man Who Shot Liberty Valence* (1962), deplored the decline of the freedom, even the anarchy, of the West and its sense of fair play and justice, and with the pessimist of *Cheyenne Autumn* (1964), who, they say, called for a return to the "savage wilderness" that existed before the arrival of the white man.

Director John Ford on the set of *My Darling* Clementine, one version of the gunfight at the O. K. Corral. *Courtesy The Bettmann Archive.*

Ford's critics, on the other hand, see him as a man who tried to raise the stature of the western from fantasy to myth without ever succeeding in doing so. *My Darling Clementine,* they point out, was based on Stuart N. Lake's specious biography of Wyatt Earp and continued the trend of making the vicious EARP BROTHERS and JOHN HENRY ("DOC") HOLLIDAY mythic heroes in highly dramatized and inaccurate accounts of the gunfight at the O. K. Corral. They say that, contrary to rehabilitating the Indian, Ford knew nothing about Native Americans and was basically contemptuous of them; he hired Navajos to play all his Indians so he could use their reservation for his locations, and he segregated his location shoots, down to the outhouses, between whites and nonwhites, including Indians, Hispanics, and African Americans. They call his *Wagonmaster* (1950) a formula western rife with melodrama. To these critics, *The Searchers* is Ford's most vicious anti-Indian film, whose idea of humor is to show a squaw being kicked out of bed and whose notion of the Comanches' character is that it is so savage as to drive white captives hopelessly insane. Similarly, in *Two Rode Together* (1961), hero James Stewart describes Comanches' life style as brutish and mocks their speech as "grunts Comanche." Ford's sympathy for the Indian, they argue, is, in fact, racism couched behind a facade of paternalism, a habit—says Jon Tuska—that John Wayne began to imitate. Most will admit that *Stagecoach* and other films are classics of a kind, but they argue that Ford's masterful use of outdoor locations, splendid images, memorable composition, and *mise en scene* are all too frequently marred by his penchant for sentimentality, low comedy, stereotypes, brawling male characters, and worship of military men.

Post–World War II westerns

Most film scholars recognize that during and immediately after World War II, Hollywood westerns took a decisive turn toward increased verisimilitude and more subdued heroics, becoming both more violent in some ways and more realistic, even as they expanded the genre to handle new themes reflecting the changed social environment in the United States. There was the clear liberalism, for example, of William Wellman's antilynching *The Ox-Bow Incident* (1943). And there was also Howard Hawks, who talked about making adult westerns for mature people rather than silly stories about mediocre cowboys. In many of Hawk's westerns, *Red River* (1948), *Rio Bravo* (1959), *El Dorado* (1967) and *Rio Lobo* (1970), he explored the nature of friendship, as Ford did also to an extent, and helped to launch a kind of Hollywood subgenre, the "buddy" movie. Sex also at last found its way into the western with Howard Hughes's *Outlaw* (1943) and King

Vidor's *Duel in the Sun* (1946). Several directors attempted to follow in Ford's footsteps or not, depending on your view, of supporting the Indians' cause, among them Delmar Daves in *Broken Arrow* (1950), Samuel Fuller in *Run of the Arrow* (1956), Don Segal in *Flaming Star* (1960) (which featured a surprisingly effective Elvis Presley), and Robert Aldrich in *Ulzana's Raid,* all introducing a theme that proved long-lived, appearing in such varied films as Arthur Penn's *Little Big Man* (1970), which attempted, somewhat perversely, to depict Custer as a glory-hungry lunatic, and Kevin Costner's elegiac *Dances with Wolves* (1990), which won the Academy Award for best picture. In between, there were Anthony Mann's series of revenge stories, depicting protagonists driven by Ahab-like emotions that destroy their reason and their humanity, such as *The Naked Spur* (1952) and *Man of the West* (1958). After the war, too, appeared the "psychological" westerns, the first being Walsh's *Pursued,* followed by a memorable portrait of an aging gunfighter played by Gregory Peck in King Vidor's *Gunfighter* (1950), reaching perhaps its apotheosis in Arthur Penn's fine *Left-Handed Gun* (1958). Something of the political despair of the 1950s also made its way into westerns, most notably in Fred Zimmerman's anti-McCarthy allegory *High Noon* (1952). There was also the arrival of a new constellation of western "stars," led by John Wayne, but also including Joel McCrea, Randolph Scott, Gary Cooper, James Stewart, and Clint Eastwood.

Beginning with George Steven's *Shane* (1952), the nature of the West itself—or at least the West as it had traditionally been depicted in films—increasingly became a theme of Hollywood westerns, which centered on the decline of the frontier, the growing "obsolescence" of the Western hero, the passing of a period of history into myth and legend. Sam Peckinpah was the master of this kind of demystifying mystification in such films as *Ride the High Country* (1962), *The Wild Bunch* (1969), *The Ballad of Cable Hogue* (1970), and *Pat Garrett and Billy the Kid* (1973), although any number of directors took up the themes: George Roy Hill in *Butch Cassidy and the Sundance Kid* (1969) and Robert Altman in *McCabe and Mrs. Miller* (1971) to name two fine examples. Some directors even more directly raised questions about Western values and America's touted manifest destiny in such films as Martin Ritt's *Hombre* (1967), Tom Gries's *Will Penny* (1969), Ralph Nelson's *Soldier Blue* (1970), Eichard Winner's *Lawman* (1971), Peter Fonda's *Hired Hand* (1971), and Cliff Robertson's *J. W. Coop* (1972). Social criticism, and a truly compassionate treatment for blacks and Indians, became not uncommon in Hollywood westerns such as Sidney Portier's *Buck and the*

Preacher (1972) and Altman's *Buffalo Bill and the Indians* (1976). And Milton Lott even managed to deal intelligently with the waste of the buffalo in *The Last Hunt* (1956), while his *Professionals* (1966) and *Bite the Bullet* (1975) centered around characters shaped by the land they lived on rather than mythic frontiers and manifest destinies. Sergei Leone pushed the self-conscious use of the West's mythical potential to absurd lengths in his string of "spaghetti" westerns, including *A Fist Full of Dollars* (1966) and *Once upon a Time in the West* (1969).

In the late twentieth century, independent Chicano producers, such as Moctezuma Esparza and Richard "Cheech" Marín, began making films. Some—playwright Luis Valdez's *La Bamba* (1987) and *Zoot Suit* (1981); writer-director Marín's *Born in East L.A.* (1987); Gregory Nava's *El Norte* (1983)—were set in the "modern" West and had contemporary story lines and themes at odds with the traditional western. Others—such as Esparza's *Ballad of Gregorio Cortez* (1982), an excellent account of the social bandit and folk hero from Texas, and even his *Milagro Beanfield War* (1988; directed by Robert Redford), about small-town New Mexican life and the struggle to preserve the old ways against modern (Anglo) intrusion—were true westerns, although they brought fresh perspectives to the genre. Robert Rodriguez's *El Mariachi* (1993) and his big-budget remake, *Desperado* (1995), spoofed both spaghetti westerns and Mexican action films.

In general, so self-conscious had the western become in the second half of the twentieth century that many began to talk about its death as a genre, only to have perhaps the most antiwestern, most politically correct western in the genre's history, Clint Eastwood's *Unforgiven*, win the Academy Award for best picture in 1992. *Unforgiven* was a dark and disturbing film that attempted to deflate the myths, stereotypes, and violence it depicted. The success of Eastwood's motion picture was not likely to cool the debate about the western among those who love the genre, perhaps because of its mythic celebrations of the American past, and those who despise it, precisely because it chose to ignore the ignominies of the past that popular westerns historically did so much to obscure.

—*Charles Phillips*

See also: James Brothers; Literature: Dime Novels, The Western Novel; Motion-Picture Industry; Rogers, Roy, and Dale Evans; Social Banditry; Violence: Myths about Violence in the West

Suggested reading:

Bold, Christine. *Selling the Wild West: Popular Western Fiction, 1860 to 1960.* Bloomington, Ind., 1987.

Cawelti, John G. *The Six-Gun Mystique.* Bowling Green, Ohio, 1984.

Denning, Michael. *Mechanic Accents: Dime Novels and Working-Class Culture in America.* London, 1987.

Etulain, Richard W. *Western Films: A Brief History.* Manhattan, Kans., 1983.

Gabler, Neal. *An Empire of Their Own: How the Jews Invented Hollywood.* New York, 1988.

Hamilton, Cynthia S. *Western and Hard-boiled Detective Fiction in America: From High Noon to Midnight.* Iowa City, Iowa, 1987.

Hutton, Paul Andrew. "Celluloid Lawmen." *American West: Its Land and Its People* 20 (May-June 1983): 58–65.

Lenihan, John H. *Showdown: Confronting Modern America in the Western Film.* Urbana, Ill., 1980.

Slotkin, Richard. *Gunfighter Nation: The Myth of the Frontier in Twentieth-Century America.* New York, 1992.

———. *Regeneration through Violence: The Mythology of the American Frontier, 1600–1860.* Middleton, Conn., 1973.

Smith, Henry Nash. *Virgin Land: The American West as Myth and Symbol.* Cambridge, Mass., 1950.

Steckmesser, Kent Ladd. *The Western Hero in History and Legend.* Norman, Okla., 1965.

Thoene, Bodie, and Rona Stuck. "Navajo Nation Meets Hollywood." *American West: Its Lands and Its People* 20 (September-October 1983): 38–44.

Tompkins, Jane. *West of Everything: The Inner Life of the Western.* New York, 1992.

MINORITY IMAGES IN WESTERNS

Minorities have generally played five basic roles in westerns: as antiwhite antagonists (usually villainous); as sexual threats and conveniences; as noble savages; as victims (often passive) of prejudice and discrimination; and as stalwart (sometimes antiracist) heroes.

The roots of the film treatment of minorities stretch back into premovie history. Indian captivity narratives, Wild West shows that celebrated the U.S. Army's victories over Indians, and Western "dime novels" in which Mexican Americans and Indians repeatedly served as evil threats or antagonists to white Americans established an Indian and Mexican American presence in premovie Western lore. The inchoate movie industry often drew from these popular traditions and manipulated the resulting audience predispositions.

In early westerns, two tendencies emerged in the treatment of minorities. First, Latinos (specifically Mexican Americans) and American Indians appeared frequently as antagonists to white settlers in the formula western. Taking advantage of premovie traditions, film-makers used Indians and Mexicans as common, easily identifiable, quickly established personifications of evil. Film titles such as *Too Much Injun* (1911), *The Half-Breed's Treachery* (1912), *The Greaser's Revenge*

Richard Dix and Lois Wilson in *The Vanishing American*, filmed in 1925. *Courtesy the Bettmann Archive.*

(1914), and *The Girl and the Greaser* (1915) typified Hollywood's stance toward these two minority groups.

Second, a gender gap soon developed. In contrast to their ethnic brethren who served mainly as threats—including sexual threats to white women—Mexican American and Indian women in movies often became sexual conveniences for white men, who generally loved them and left them and turned to white women for marriage. Demonstrating a preference for white men, minority women sometimes sacrificed themselves to save their white lovers' lives, as in *The Squaw's Sacrifice* (1909), *Carmenita the Faithful* (1911), *His Mexican Sweetheart* (1912), and *The Heart of an Indian* (1913).

Before World War II, only rarely did movies temper the convention of the gender gap by reversing the relationship. Moreover, when doing so, movies usually elevated minorities into their third category of western screen roles: the noble savage. For example, the acclaimed 1925 film, *The Vanishing American*, featured a love story between a stalwart Navajo man and a white reservation teacher, although he is killed—a typical, convenient Hollywood resolution to an interracial relationship.

In the 1920s, Latin American nations became concerned about Hollywood's depiction not only of Mexican Americans, but also of Latin Americans in general. That concern led to protests by individual governments, reciprocal treaties among Latin American nations, and threats to ban films from studios that perpetuated derogatory screen images of Latinos. Due to Hollywood's fear of losing its lucrative Latin American market, these strategies succeeded in reducing, although not eradicating, negative treatment. Lacking such international box-office leverage, Native Americans continued as screen savages, occasionally noble, but usually otherwise.

World War II brought further changes in the treatment of minorities in movies, including westerns. Following the war, many American movie-makers turned their attention from the external evils of Nazism and fascism to such internal evils as racism. From 1945 until the early 1970s, although westerns repeated traditional themes and presented time-honed minority images, they sometimes provided new twists. As part of this trend, westerns often treated Indians and Mexican Americans as human beings and even as victims of prejudice and discrimination, their fourth screen category.

Indians on the screen continued to slaughter (*The Battle of Apache Pass*, 1952, and *Arrowhead*, 1953) and abduct women (*The Searchers*, 1956). However, film-makers sometimes portrayed Indian actions as having been prompted by the manipulation (*Oh, Susanna!* 1951) or deception of white men, usually traders (*The Battles of Chief Pontiac*, 1952). Indians in movies were transformed from merciless savages into pitiable victims of white transgressions. Sometimes, this victimization of noble savages came in the form of massacres by an out-of-control army (*Soldier Blue,* 1970, and *Little Big Man,* 1970). At other times, Indians became activists, fighting for their freedom (*Apache,* 1954), for their land (*Cheyenne Autumn,* 1964), or against other Indians (*A Man Called Horse,* 1970).

The gender gap continued, but film-makers increasingly used white-Indian and Anglo-Mexican relationships to address larger societal issues. Films used intermarriages between white men and Indian women (usually Indian princesses) as metaphors for improving interracial relations (*The Big Sky*, 1952; *The Indian Fighter*, 1955; and *The Last Hunt*, 1956) or as vehicles to condemn white bigotry (*Broken Arrow*, 1950, and *Broken Lance*, 1954). Sometimes movies doubled the ethnic ante, with the white man having a relationship with a woman of mixed ethnic descent, such as Pearl Chavez in *Duel in the Sun* (1946), who is referred to by one racist character as both a "papoose" and a "hot tamale."

Mexican and Mexican American women continued in their traditional role as sexual conveniences, but they became more complex screen characters. For example, in *High Noon* (1952), strong, intelligent small-town entrepreneur Helen Ramirez cohabits with (but does not marry) a series of Anglos. However, in classic Hollywood interethnic fashion, she is dropped by the Anglo marshal in favor of a blonde Anglo wife.

In contrast to Indians, Mexican Americans generally remained in the background of traditional nineteenth-century westerns, although they surfaced occasionally as stereotypical bandits (*Ride, Vaquero*, 1953). More often, they appeared in modern westerns, films that operated according to traditional western movie tenets but were set in the modern American West. As did Indians in postwar traditional westerns, Mexican Americans in modern westerns often appeared as victims of discrimination (*Giant*, 1956) and exploitation (*Border Incident*, 1949; *Lawless*, 1950; and *The Big Carnival*, 1951).

In the 1960s, the civil rights movement spurred another new thrust in movies, including westerns. Minorities increasingly served as heroes, their fifth western screen category. A common theme involved minority heroes proving their mettle by outwitting and out-fighting white racists.

Almost completely absent from westerns during the first half-century of movie-making, African Americans began to appear on the frontier scene. At first, they showed up as sidekicks of Anglo heroes (*The Man Who Shot Liberty Valance*, 1962) or as victims of white injustice (*Sergeant Rutledge*, 1960). However, occasionally they became lead heroes, as in *Duel at Diablo* (1966), which depicts a black retired soldier helping an army detachment survive an Indian attack and successfully confronting a white racist. Other minority figures now whipped villainous white antagonists. In *Valdez Is Coming* (1971), a stalwart Mexican American sheriff outwits and defeats a sadistic Anglo rancher. In *Chato's Land* (1972), a lone Apache wipes out an entire Anglo posse.

American minorities now even helped defeat Mexican villains (as contrasted with Mexican Americans) in Mexi-westerns, set in Mexico (usually northern Mexico) rather than in the U.S. Southwest. Two Mexican Americans serve among the seven American gunmen who save a poor Mexican village from terrorism by bandits in *The Magnificent Seven* (1960). An African American munitions expert joins three white American comrades to rescue a Mexican woman, supposedly kidnapped by a Mexican revolutionary leader, in *The Professionals* (1966). An African American helps Mexican Indian rebels defeat the Mexican army in *100 Rifles* (1969).

Even Asian Americans gained a slightly expanded western film presence. Asian Americans had served as little more than occasional backdrops or victims in early westerns (*That Chink at Golden Gulch*, 1910). However, *Walk Like a Dragon* (1960) broke the mold by featuring a Chinese American who becomes skilled with a gun and confronts Anglo antagonists. While this film served more as an interesting aberration than as a trendsetter, Asian Americans appeared more frequently in westerns, although usually as background, mainly as opium-smokers (*McCabe and Mrs. Miller*, 1971) or as sexual liaisons for white men (*Young Guns*, 1988).

However, the entrance of minority heroes into the Hollywood western occurred as the genre began heading into the last sunset, as least temporarily. Since the early 1970s, movie westerns have been relatively rare. But where they do surface, they always include a significant minority presence.

In *Barbarosa* (1982), an Anglo cowboy and a Mexican American landowner wage an ongoing feud, but both characters are complex figures, neither traditional villains nor traditional heroes. In *Silverado* (1985), an African American rifleman joins three white cowboys to defeat an evil rancher. In *Young Guns* (1988) and *Young Guns II* (1990), one comrade of "BILLY THE KID" is a resourceful half-Navajo, half Mexican American named Chavez y Chavez. By 1993, African American cowboys took center stage in *Posse*.

A similar minority presence of Native Americans can be found in recent modern westerns. The heroic *Billy Jack* (1971), who fights against social and environmental injustices, is half-Indian. In *War Party* (1989), a group of brave young Indians die fighting rather than surrender to a pursuing national guard unit.

An endangered species in the 1970s and 1980s, westerns experienced a mini-renaissance in the early 1990s. Westerns with significant minority presence won Academy Awards for best motion picture in 1990 and 1992. *Dances with Wolves* (1990) continued the recent film tradition of extolling noble savages (in this case, the Lakotas) and portraying the army as racist and predatory. In *Unforgiven* (1992), the lead white professional gunman has a wise, sensitive African American partner, who also happens to have an Indian wife. It is premature, however, to assess whether or not these two films signal a true western renaissance, with an ongoing minority presence, or merely provide a blip on the contemporary movie spectrum.

—*Carlos E. Cortés*

SEE ALSO: Literature: Indian Captivity Narratives; Stereotypes: Stereotypes in Popular Westerns, Stereotypes of Asian Americans, Stereotypes of Mexicans, Stereotypes of Native Americans

SUGGESTED READING:

Bogle, Donald. *Toms, Coons, Mulattoes, Mammies and Bucks: An Interpretive History of Blacks in American Films.* 2d ed. rev. New York, 1989.

Friar, Ralph E., and Natasha A. Friar. *The Only Good Indian . . . the Hollywood Gospel.* New York, 1972.

Leab, Daniel J. *From Sambo to Superspade: The Black Experience in Motion Pictures.* Boston, 1975.

Noriega, Chon, ed. *Chicanos and Film: Essays on Chicano Representation and Resistance.* New York, 1992.

O'Connor, John E. *The Hollywood Indian: Stereotypes of the Native American in Films.* Trenton, N.J., 1980.

Pettit, Arthur G. *Images of the Mexican American in Fiction and Film.* College Station, Tex., 1980.

Woll, Allen L. *The Latin Image in American Film.* Rev. ed. Los Angeles, 1980.

Wong, Eugene Franklin. *On Visual Media Racism: Asians in the American Motion Picture.* New York, 1978.

FINANCIAL PANICS

As the United States began to develop a market economy beginning in the late eighteenth century, it was increasingly drawn into the boom-and-bust business cycles that characterized classic capitalism. This process was greatly accelerated by the rapid industrialization of the American West. Starting around the middle of the nineteenth century, industrialization reached a fever pitch after the Civil War with the construction of the transcontinental RAILROADS and the linking of Eastern financial markets with Western production. The advancement of an Anglo-American frontier was less a steady and metaphysical process than the growth of a capitalist economy constantly seeking to open new markets. Capital investment more surely than pioneers inexorably traveled west, but it did so in spurts, in stops and starts, drawn here by the discovery of gold and other minerals, there to the availability of vast timber stands and stretches of farm or grazing lands. In boom cycles, developing markets attracted those seeking to make a new living beyond the Appalachians into the Ohio Valley, the Old Northwest,

the Southern territories, and ultimately into the trans-Mississippi West. When BOOMS collapsed, as they inevitably did, the economic hard times often encouraged settled individuals to pull up stakes and seek their fortunes elsewhere.

Before the Civil War, economic downturns and the financial panics that usually preceded them were most often connected with the plantation production of cotton, and the social dislocations they created led both to some political unrest and to increased internal migration. After the Civil War, these economic troubles were more frequently associated with the spasms of railroad construction, which, for decades, came close to being the preoccupation if not the sole business of Wall Street. Waves of optimistic investment led eventually to fears about overbuilding that, in turn, produced panics and economic contractions until the economy had recovered enough to attract capital once again for investment in expanding markets. These waves of expansion created renewed needs for iron, steel, and timber for rails, ties, locomotives, cars, and passenger furniture, and workers to produce them, as well as calls for thousands of additional construction workers. Expansion also encouraged settlement along the railway lines on the cheap government-grant lands the railroads offered emigrants to promote the markets they were built to serve. As the upswings passed, however, these new Westerners were often caught in the downward spiral, and miners, loggers, suppliers, and workers had to find new markets for their labor and take up different jobs. Since the health of the West's export business in beef and farm goods depended on railroad shipping rather than local consumption, economic contractions also spelled disaster for cowboys and small farmers and even occasionally for cattlemen and bonanza capitalists. While the postwar recessions and depressions also created some internal migration farther west, they more significantly began to shape the society and politics of the West as a region.

1819

In the panic of 1819, America experienced for the first time one of the principal hazards of a commercial-industrial economy: the business cycle, that rhythmic rotation of booms, panics, and depressions that characterize modern life. Americans were so shaken by the panic of 1819 that they turned to the supernatural for an explanation—an angry God, many thought, brought hard times to punish the Americans for their extravagance, their speculation, their greed. In truth, it was Europe, especially England, who visited hard times upon them. The English demand for American agricultural products, particularly cotton, fell, and with its fall, the market for textiles shrank. Then, in early in 1819, the Bank of the United States, under new and more conservative management, began to call in its loans and to put pressure on the state banks to redeem their notes. The bank's belated attempt to save itself from the folly of making too many bad loans, many of them to the politicians who regulated the bank, was the immediate cause for the panic. In the depression that followed, the bottom fell out of both the cotton-export market and the real-estate market. Thousands of farmers saw their lands sold at public auction to satisfy the claims of their creditors—and so did the proud, aristocratic Charleston planters who had made fortunes from the cultivation of rice and cotton. In the cities of the East, one-half million workers lost their jobs as factories closed or trimmed their operations.

The nation ultimately weathered the panic of 1819, but the crisis brought about a lasting resentment against the Bank of the United States in the West. The panic sent planters into the Old Southwest where they carved major new cotton producing states—Alabama, Mississippi, and Louisiana—out of Indian territories. The appropriation of Indian lands and the expansion of plantation slavery in the South and the settlement of new lands in the Ohio Valley by small farmers dislocated by the panic increased the pressure for the removal of Indians west of the Mississippi. At the same time, Westerners and Southerners, embittered by national BANKING policy, began to look for someone who could teach the bankers a lesson. In ANDREW JACKSON, one of their own, they found their man: he hated the bank, he knew how to deal with the Indians, and he was a vocal promoter of growth and westward expansion.

1837

The United States experienced a period of prosperity and unprecedented expansion within its borders after the mid-1820s. The panic of 1819 had actually stimulated the growth of the fur trade in the trans-Mississippi West as entrepreneurs and trappers willing to take risks poured into the region from the East. Between 1831 and 1836, cotton exports tripled because of rising prices and extended production as planters with their slaves rushed into the states of the Old Southwest to open up vast new cotton lands after the Jackson administration cleared them of Indians. In the Old Northwest, farmers found ever better markets among Southern planters for the food they grew. The trans-Appalachian West's cities, undergoing phenomenal growth, developed commercial enterprises and factories of their own to serve their expanding local markets. Speculation again became an American ma-

nia; government land sales increased fivefold between 1834 and 1836, and land prices exploded.

The money came from England and from the wildcat financing of new state banks. British capitalists invested in private and state securities as the states and the wealthier private investors in the North undertook their ambitious canal building and early railroad construction. But the state banks would lend to anybody. In the decade before the panic of 1837, not only did state banks double their number, but they also vastly expanded the paper notes they issued and liberalized their loan policies. America was an "underdeveloped country" with a rapidly growing population and an overheated economy, and Andrew Jackson made matters worse with his heavy-handed approach to fiscal policy—closing the national bank, placing federal deposits in state banks and returning the federal surplus produced by a decade of prosperity—some $35 million of the $40 million in federal coffers—to the states directly to use for internal improvements. The result was an even more overheated economy.

The panic of 1837 and the long depression that followed—puncturing the swelled bubble of the Cotton Kingdom, dousing the explosive growth in manufactures, truncating the rapidly expanding transportation network, in short, cooling down all the developments that fired the American economy—also sent more Americans and American capital west, the former in search of a new living, the later in search of new markets. Some of them, mostly from the South, went to Texas. The financial panic that gripped the United States was a stroke of luck for newly independent Texas, which offered newcomers free homesteads and cheap additional land. Thousands of debt-ridden Americans fled to Texas as a haven of opportunity. In 1836, the population of Republic of Texas was 30,000; ten years later, it stood at 146,000. In the meantime, other pioneers headed for Oregon and American businessmen seeking new markets established infant trade relations with California and the territories of the American Southwest belonging to Mexico.

Back East, the depression not only kept alive the wrangling over fiscal policy and public lands, it created unusual tensions between capital and labor, farm and city. Traditionally, American factory owners, whose business seemed always to be expanding, had been frustrated by their sparsely settled country's shortage of manpower and by the relatively high cost of labor. Suddenly, in the early 1840s, they were operating at depression levels that could not absorb the continuous stream of new immigrants from Europe. As the Germans and the Irish poured into Eastern cities, the United States was asking itself for the first time how it was going to handle all these foreigners. Expansion west presented itself as an option, and an expansionist lobby within the Democratic party began to talk about officially annexing Texas—and by implication, taking over the entire trans-Mississippi West—as a "racial" safety valve.

Democrats constructed a platform that combined a demand for the annexation of Texas with a demand for the acquisition of Oregon, intentionally linking their Texas SAFETY-VALVE THEORY with arguments for economic growth. In both the North and the South, expansionists argued that the United States needed foreign markets to absorb the large agricultural surpluses American farmers could produce. Without these markets, politicians maintained, the economy would shrivel, which, they said, was precisely what happened in 1837. In the depression of the 1840s, politicians saw the struggle for markets in apocalyptic terms. Agrarian-minded imperialists insisted that Oregon was a key to the entire trade of the Far East. Out of the political pressures and fears created by the panic of 1837 and the depression that followed came the stirrings of a MANIFEST DESTINY.

1857

In 1857, the United States experienced the first of the railroad-inspired panics, which was followed by a brief but severe economic depression. When investors realized that the new railroad network had been built too fast and too far into thinly settled regions that offered little hope for immediate profits, they began to withdraw their money. The collapse of railroad financing, in turn, deflated the land boom that had been spreading across the trans-Mississippi states of today's Midwest and the Pacific Northwest. As land prices fell, owners defaulted on their mortgages, thereby placing a strain on the country's flimsy banking structure. To make matters worse, the Crimean War dried up markets in Europe, and Western farmers and cattle producers found themselves pressed to dispose of bumper crops of wheat and beef. While the South, where the cotton market continued to expand, weathered the depression without much trouble, the North—whose network of financial, manufacturing, and transportation interests was tied to the Western railroads—was, like the West, hit hard by the panic. Strapped settlers and busted land speculators in the Mississippi Valley rushed west to Colorado when gold was discovered around Pikes Peak. Blaming the hard times on the low tariff of 1857, both Northerners and Westerners flocked to the new Republican party and demanded a protective tariff, which in turn exacerbated the regional struggle over slavery. But the short downturn had none of the explosive impact on the region that the post–Civil War panics would have.

1873

In 1873, wild speculation among railroad investors led to a catastrophic bank panic that brought a thirty-year cycle of overall American expansion to a halt and kicked off not only the most serious and prolonged depression so far in American history but presaged some twenty years of chronic economic difficulty. Until then, the underlying strength of the economy, despite the brief panic of 1857, had been such that even the Armageddon of the Civil War had barely touched its growth curve, although the war had certainly ruined the South for the next several generations. The economic growth had coincided with the dramatic geographic expansion of the American West, as the West's colonial economy fed greatly enlarged markets and massive capital accumulations, much of it by Eastern investors. In the West, bonanza profits in extractive industries by large capital concerns had come to dominate the economic landscape just as they had before the 1850s in cotton and fur and just as they would in the future in cattle, wheat, timber, copper, and oil.

In the wake of the 1873 stock-market panic, many railroads—already ripe for disaster from intense competition and shaky financing—sold out to Civil War profiteer J. P. Morgan. As Morgan gobbled up the nation's transportation system, he set off of a series of rate wars, wrecking more railroads, then buying them up, too. In the carnage of America's railroads during the depression of 1873, Western towns, counties, and states that had bought bonds to finance railroad construction found those bonds worthless. There was little they could do as Morgan took control of the roads, and the West's colonial economy imploded. Morgan soon owned half the railroad tracks in America, and his friends owned the rest; they set exorbitant rates across the entire country, rates that hurt no one so much as Western farmers. But American workers everywhere reeled under the crushing blows of the economic crisis. The distress of the industrial workingman in particular grew immensely in the four long years of depression as the corporations tried to make up their losses by shoddy operating practices and wage cut after wage cut. The workers went on strikes, only to have their actions characterized as "riots." The strikes were broken by hired toughs from the PINKERTON NATIONAL DETECTIVE AGENCY, which since the Civil War had grown into a privately funded, anti-immigrant, antiworking-class, nationwide police force.

At the same time, a showdown over federal land policy was underway in the American West. The huge accumulation of Western lands by the railroads and by Eastern capitalists at a time when the federal government opened up acreage for homesteaders seemed to be depleting the nation's vast land reserve. The failure of the federal government to police Western territories for the railroads and to prevent continued resistance by Native Americans appeared to be creating a crisis of confidence in the country's political leadership. Clearly, the attempts at concentration that had begun in the 1850s were not working. President Ulysses S. Grant's Peace Policy, touted as the ultimate solution, was in deep trouble as sweetheart deals and pressures from big business corrupted the Bureau of Indian Affairs. In addition, the depression from 1873 to 1877 hit the economically volatile West especially hard and took its toll not only on Western farmers, but also on the overextended CATTLE INDUSTRY. CHARLES GOODNIGHT spoke for any number of cattle barons when he later observed, "[the depression] wiped me off the face of the earth."

As Richard Slotkin has pointed out, the owners, editors, and writers of the country's increasingly influential urban newspapers and journals believed that the financial panic and the failure of U.S. Indian policy were intimately, even organically, related to a third "national" crisis—the collapse of Reconstruction in the South. In each case, they argued, a "lower form of human being"—the Indian, the African American, the immigrant worker—had come into conflict with those who owned and ran American society and its new industrial system. The workers, the Indians, the freed slaves were demanding their "rights": control over their lives, a say in the terms of their labor, the freedom to use their land as they saw fit. Such demands in the context of massive economic failure were beginning to expose the gap between what America's corporate owners and money managers wanted and what its citizens thought they were getting from expansion, growth, and prosperity. For many, it was becoming clear that corporate America, the ruling elite, desired meek and submissive workers who subordinated private ambition to business needs. Indeed, it would appear that the real beneficiaries of the American dream—instant wealth, cheap land, a better future—were not the honest farmers and hopeful homesteaders nor the independent workers and small businessmen, but the tycoons who financed it. Precisely as America's manifest destiny was close to being realized, it seemed to many that the American dream was collapsing under the weight of corporate greed.

In this atmosphere, the series of wage cuts and abortive strikes, which had begun with the Tompkins Square "riot" of 1874, resulted in a wave of social insurrection that rocked America from coast to coast. On July 17, 1877, railroad workers in Martinsburg, West Virginia, went out on strike against the Baltimore and Ohio Railroad, which had cut their wages for the second time in one year. This strike touched off a series of sympathy strikes and work stoppages that would become known as the Great Strike of 1877. The first great industrial conflict in America caught the new president, Rutherford B. Hayes, without a set labor policy. Urged on by four state governors, Hayes took the fateful step and sent in federal troops. The nationwide struggle seemed to pit all workers against all employers, certainly the kind of prerevolutionary condition over which the journals of opinion fretted. The federal troops rushed from city to city, crushing strike after strike, and within a few weeks, the Great Strike of 1877 was over. In its wake, many states passed conspiracy laws, beefed up their militias, and built National Guard armories in their major cities. In the following years, state and territorial governors—particularly in the West—turned, almost as a matter of course, to federal troops for aid against striking workers. By the end of 1877, the depression was over, and the national "crisis" had passed, but the bitterness the depression created shaped the politics of the next two decades, which, in the West, witnessed a growing class conflict between mine workers and magnates, cattle kings and small ranchers, and railroad barons and farmers.

1893

The panic of 1893 started, as had the last panic twenty years earlier, with the railroads. In 1893, the Philadelphia and Reading Railroad went bankrupt, shaking the New York Stock Exchange into the biggest selling spree on record. Decades of wild industrial growth, financial manipulation, uncontrolled speculation, and profiteering brought the whole system crashing down. The nation's gold reserves had dwindled alarmingly by April, falling below the $100 million level most economists then considered necessary for maintaining the gold standard. Banks called in their loans. Credit dried up. Thanks in no small measure to the machinations of J. P. Morgan after the last panic—which had tied the fates of many roads to a few investors—the Erie, the Northern Pacific, the Union Pacific, and the Santa Fe all failed. Mills, factories, furnaces, and mines everywhere shut down. By the time it was over, 642 banks and sixteen thousand major firms had closed. Three million in a labor force of fifteen million were unemployed. Not a single state government voted relief, but mass demonstrations all over the country forced cities to set up soup kitchens and give folks public work on streets and in parks. In Chicago alone, two hundred thousand were without work, and the floors of City Hall and police stations were packed every night with homeless men trying to sleep. What had once seemed like wild rhetoric suddenly appeared more reasonable, and the outlandish Populist demands of the past twenty years—from an income tax to the franchise for women—seemed, if not entirely acceptable, at least thinkable.

The 1893 depression saw Emma Goldman addressing a huge crowd of the unemployed in New York's Union Square, where she urged those with children needing food simply to go into the stores and take it; it saw a radicalized young Eugene V. Debs, a former Railroad Brotherhood billing clerk, form the American Railway Union in an attempt to organize railroad workers nationwide. Whereas authorities might toss Emma Goldman in jail for two years for "inciting to riot," there were not prisons enough in America to hold all the railway workers. In 1894, GEORGE MORTIMER PULLMAN fired one-third of his workers and cut the wages of those who remained by 30 percent. But he would not cut prices for the homes or the cost of food in Pullman, the company town near Chicago he had built to house his employees. Debs ordered a strike after Pullman refused to negotiate with the union. The owners and managers of other lines sided with Pullman and provided scabs as Debs organized his rank and file. President Grover Cleveland, backing Pullman, insisted that strike-related violence and boycotts interrupted U.S. mail service. When, on July 2, 1894, Debs defied a federal injunction to return to work, the president of the United States had the president of railway union arrested. Over the objections of Illinois's prolabor governor, Cleveland sent in federal troops, among them the Seventh Cavalry called from posts in the Southwest, who ruthlessly put down the strike.

With the depression of 1893, the ideological front of the class war heated up, and over the next two decades, America's rulers would develop a domestic and Progressive political program that sought to undermine middle-class support for labor by cleaning up the worst abuses of the industrialists and by instituting a plan of "moral uplift" for the "depraved" masses. In many ways, the severe depression that began in 1893 merely fired a fever already growing in the elite political and financial circles of American society. In addition to a better managed government and a better behaved financial community, U.S. leaders began to seek larger overseas markets for American goods—markets that might relieve the problem of underconsumption at home—and overseas sources of raw materials—sources that might weaken the position of an increasingly hostile labor force. In short, economic colonies overseas might prevent the kind of economic crisis that, in the 1890s, threatened to bring class war to America. As one prominent editor, Henry Watterson, pointed out, America could "escape the menace and peril of socialism and agrarianism" at home by means of "a policy of colonization and conquest" abroad. Perhaps it was no accident that 1893 was the year FREDERICK JACKSON TURNER advanced his frontier thesis; for if the investment frontier had not actually closed in the West, as Jackson claimed for his hypothetical historical frontier, it had certainly begun to move beyond American shores.

1901

In 1901, a battle for the stock of the Northern Pacific Railroad set off a panic on Wall Street. In order to quiet the market, the antagonists in the speculative stock war made peace by creating the Northern Securities Company, a giant holding company for the Northern Pacific, the Great Northern, and the Chicago, Burlington and Quincy railroads. The financial titans who created Northern Securities hoped it would allow them ultimately to monopolize the transportation network of the rapidly growing Pacific Northwest. Instead, in the wake of the panic they had initially created with their ruthless speculation, which probably hurt stock brokers more than anyone else, the formation of such a colossus only cast a brighter light on its investors: J. P. Morgan and Company, the John D. Rockefeller interests, JAMES J. HILL, and EDWARD HENRY HARRIMAN. The long shadow they cast over the region enhanced the fears of ever-suspicious farmers, who fully expected freight rates to soar as they had in the past when such men monopolized transportation in the West. Whether fairly or not, their names had become synonymous with unbridled power, and several Western states quickly brought legal actions against the holding company.

Meanwhile, President THEODORE ROOSEVELT, new in office, was quietly planning, among the American elite, the managerial revolution that, for a decade, he had been calling PROGRESSIVISM. Viewed by the capitalist old guard as a wild-eyed cowboy whom a perverse fate had put in charge, Roosevelt ordered Attorney General Philander A. Knox to begin preparing in secret a government suit against Northern Securities for violating the SHERMAN ANTI-TRUST ACT. When the federal government announced the suit, a stunned Wall Street placed all its hope in Morgan, who, with typical arrogance, sent his lawyers to settle the matter with the attorney general in person and behind closed doors. Instead, the case went to trial, a federal court in 1903 ordered Northern Securities dissolved, and the following year, the U.S. Supreme Court upheld the decision. It was the first of Roosevelt's successful trust-busting suits, and it made him even more of a hero in the American West than he already was. Soon, he would take on the "beef trust" so despised by Western farmers, and ultimately, he would even square off against Standard Oil. Rather than signifying a victory for the common people, however, Roosevelt's trust-busting more truthfully signaled a transfer of elite power from lower Manhattan to Washington, a change that, in the long run, Western businessmen would learn to exploit fully. But more immediately they had their own problems with Teddy Roosevelt.

1907

An ardent conservationist who loved the natural landscapes of the trans-Mississippi West, Roosevelt had championed the passage of the NEWLANDS RECLAMATION ACT OF 1902. The act set aside some money from the sale of public lands to be used in building dams and launching reclamation projects. Urged on by his friend GIFFORD PINCHOT, Roosevelt had withdrawn from private use public lands valuable for their coal, mineral, and oil reserves or for their water, which Roosevelt and Pinchot hoped to develop as water-power sites. What was more, Roosevelt moved with dispatch against cattlemen and lumber barons who poached grass and timber on public lands. All of these actions put the president afoul of the West's big businessmen, who had grown rich off the nation's natural resources. They had their representatives in Congress attach a rider to the 1907 appropriations bill for the Department of Agriculture that barred Roosevelt from creating new forest reserves in six Western states unless he first sought consent from Congress, whose members were unlikely to grant it. Roosevelt had little choice but to sign the measure if he wanted the department funded; however, he struck back at the Westerners by adding some seventeen million acres to the nation's forests before he signed the bill. He also vetoed all subsequent bills that granted water rights to private businesses but failed also to provide for federal supervision of water development in general in the West.

Angry Western barons joined Eastern financial moguls in blaming the panic of 1907 and the short depression that followed on Roosevelt for destabilizing the Western economy by his public-policy tinkerings with federal land and water use. The root of the country's economic woes, however, lay in more traditional financial shortcomings associated with the West: production had slightly outrun consumption, and the problem was exacerbated by unregulated banks, a rigid monetary system, and excessive financial speculation. Depositors panicked when they learned that big New York trusts had attempted to corner the copper market through the ANACONDA MINING COMPANY and failed. The run on the city's big trusts spread to other, sound banks, which closed their doors and called in their loans. J. P. Morgan again showed his muscle by organizing a pool of funds to keep the Manhattan institutions afloat, and this time, he had help from Washington.

The U.S. Treasury came to the rescue of some banks, while Morgan schemed up the series of complex financial moves by which he created his reserve—moves involving, among others, the purchase of major coal and iron stocks through his United States Steel Corporation. Before he could act at all, however, Morgan needed and sought reassurance from Roosevelt that he would not slap the financial mogul with an antitrust suit. Giving "no binding promises," Roosevelt told Morgan to go ahead.

Most economic historians credit Morgan with averting general financial disaster, and the panic did indeed quickly subside. But the very fact that the country was forced to turn to Morgan—or any private banker—gave Roosevelt the ammunition he needed to make a case for monetary and banking reform. Congress, backed by both Roosevelt and his detractors, established a Monetary Commission headed by Nelson Aldrich, and the House launched a committee investigation of the panic. Chaired by Arsène Pujo, the committee concluded that those Western farmers who had long accused bankers of conspiring together were right after all and that financial power was indeed concentrated in the hands of a few powerful private bankers in the East. Louis Brandeis called them the "money trust" in his popular book, *Other People's Money* (1914), which summarized the committee's findings. The Pujo investigation and the report of Aldrich's Monetary Commission managed to turn the panic of 1907, which had underscored the nation's inflexible currency and inelastic credit, into a reason for Progressive reform. The result was the passage, under Woodrow Wilson in December 1913, of the Federal Reserve Act, which established the Federal Reserve Board and—most economists agree—allowed America to adjust to the financial strains of World War I without, however, providing sufficient controls to avoid the overheating of the economy afterward and its ultimate collapse in the Great Depression of the 1930s.

—*Charles Phillips*

SEE ALSO: Agrarianism; Dust Bowl; National Expansion; Labor Movement; Populism; Tariff Policy

SUGGESTED READING:

Adreano, Ralph L., ed. *The Economic Impact of the American Civil War.* Cambridge, Mass., 1962.

Brown, Richard D. *Modernization: The Transformation of American Life, 1600–1865.* New York, 1976.

Bruchey, Stuart. *Roots of American Economic Growth, 1607–1861.* New York, 1965.

Cochran, Thomas C. *Business in American Life: A History.* New York, 1962.

Dubofsky, Melvyn. *Industrialism and the American Worker, 1865–1920.* New York, 1975.

Fishlow, Albert. *American Railroads and the Transformation of the Antebellum Economy.* Cambridge, Mass., 1965.

Fogel, Robert W. *Railroads and Economic Growth: Essays in Economic History.* Baltimore, 1964.

Foner, Philip S. *The Great Labor Uprising of 1877.* New York, 1971.

Greenleaf, William, ed. *American Economic Development since 1860.* New York, 1968.

Grodinsky, Julius. *Transcontinental Railway Strategy, 1869–1893: A Study of Businessmen.* Philadelphia, 1962.

Gutman, Herbet G. *Work, Culture, and Society in Industrializing America: Essays in American Working Class and Social History.* New York, 1976.

Hobsbawm, Eric J. *The Age of Capital, 1848–1875.* New York, 1975.

Hofstader, Richard. *The Age of Reform.* New York, 1955.

Josephson, Mathew. *The Robber Barons: The Great American Capitalists, 1861–1901.* New York, 1962.

Kolko, Gabriel. *The Triumph of Conservatism: A Reinterpretation of American History, 1900–1916.* New York, 1963.

Porter, Glenn. *The Rise of Big Business, 1860–1910.* Arlington Heights, Ill., 1973.

Slotkin, Richard. *The Fatal Environment: The Myth of the Frontier in the Age of Industrialism, 1800–1890.* New York, 1985.

Trachtenberg, Alan. *The Incorporation of America: Culture and Society in the Gilded Age.* New York, 1982.

FINK, MIKE

SEE: Rivermen

FIRE

Wildfire is an ancient natural phenomenon, one that has occurred in nearly every age and on nearly every spot on earth. Yet natural fires account for a very low percentage of the conflagrations associated with the destruction of cities, homes, businesses, crops, or wilderness. Much about fire is culturally determined, and different regions and different historical periods have tended to produce different and characteristic fire regimes. Simple farming societies, with the slash-and-burn land-clearing techniques that anthropologists call "swidden" agriculture, produce kinds of fires different from complex industrial societies that use fire to fuel, among other things, internal-combustion machines. While historians, for example, tend to consider the fire that destroyed Chicago in 1871 a discreet event, perhaps initiated by Mrs. O'Leary's cow, specialists in the field have come to consider the GREAT CHICAGO FIRE but one bubble in a vast flaming cauldron that stretched that year from the Ohio Valley to the Great Lake states and the High Plains, one phase of a fire complex that consumed farms in Indiana, villages in Wisconsin and Iowa, and towns throughout the Dakotas. Most historical fires, they contend, were, in reality, such fire complexes, and those complexes were more often a result of a mix of weather conditions and the typical habits of a given culture than they were of an isolated and unfortunate accident.

Looked at in that way, the history of fire in the American West consists of a series of culturally determined, overlapping, and conflicting fire regimes. The fire from Asia, as Stephan J. Pyne has called it, was part of a Native American fire regime that, over the course of several millennia, swept eastward across the North American continent and created a vast stretch of savanna and thin-undergrowth forests that favored the Indians' hunting, gathering, and gardening culture. Different Native American tribes viewed fire differently, of course, and the uses to which they put such fire were as varied as their separate tribal cultures. For all Indians, however, fire was both something sacred, on the one hand, and the major tool for modifying their environment, on the other.

It is difficult to convey the degree to which Indian society apparently depended on fire. Indians used fire for cooking, light, and warmth as have most cultures. They made fires to bake clay and cast ceramics and metal for aesthetic objects, utensils, tools, and weapons. They used fire to shape canoes and to produce smoke for communicating at a distance. Fire and smoke played roles in Indian spiritual and ceremonial life. With fire, Indians cultivated natural grasses, such as sunflowers, and berries, such as the blueberry, and nuts, such as the acorn or mesquite bean. Indians set fires to kill off mosquitoes and flies and to rid their fields of vermin and diseases. They burned broad expanses of forests so they could harvest firewood and caramelized pine cones from them. They set broadcast fires to encourage the skies to produce rain. They flamed brush and woods to flush the animals they hunted or to trap enemies or as a defense when they were under attack. With fire, they thinned forests of underbrush so they could easily travel through them and could better see the game that lived in them. They burned off mistletoe when it invaded their mesquite and oak. Because they lacked chemical fertilizers or manure from domestic animals, they used fire to replace lost nutrients in the soil. And since they had few domestic animals to use for meat, they burned the edges of forests to cause the spread of grasslands that would, in turn, extend the range of the game they desired. In fact, except as fertilizer and some shade for their swidden agriculture, Indians had little use for closed forests.

Frank Leslie's Illustrated Weekly, in an October 1882 issue, depicted Texas herders driving their sheep to safety from a prairie fire. *Courtesy Patrick H. Butler, III.*

Indian fire not only served as a tactic for harvesting, hunting, and fighting but also sustained and extended the habitat on which these activities depended. Indian fire practices—although they were not uniform and although the fire seasons of the regions in which they set them varied greatly—produced widespread and cumulative results through a multiplication of local effects. As a result of repeated, controlled surface fires in cycles of one to three years, of occasional holocausts when fires raged out of control, and of periodic conflagrations created by droughts in regions made favorable to the spread of fire by Indian practices, these Asian immigrants modified the American continent so extensively that grassland or open savanna was probably the dominant type of vegetation when the Europeans first arrived in the New World. As a result, for example, the buffalo, naturally a creature of the plains, crossed the Mississippi during the first millennium A.D., entered the present-day South during the sixteenth century and, by the seventeenth century, roamed present-day Pennsylvania and Massachusetts.

The fire regime of the Native Americans was overlapped and ultimately replaced by the fire from Europe in a frontier fire regime that both adopted some aspects of the Native American regime and introduced others alien to the continent but ultimately intended to reclaim the grasslands for extended cultivation. At first, European pioneers adopted many Indian fire practices. Following native examples, they used fire for hunting, for slash-and-burn agriculture, to create pasturage for wild game and domestic stock, and as protective burning against other fires. In the long run, however, European settlers suppressed Indian fire practices. They were not, as a whole, seminomads but settled agriculturalists, and they looked to fire not as a means for the cyclic control of land to many uses but as a means to bring under control ever more land for a single use. When that use was no longer possible, they abandoned the land entirely. On the one hand, the draining of lowlands and swamps by European agriculturalists opened new fields of fire unavailable to the Indians; on the other, their neglect of Indian grasslands not under cultivation and their abandonment of marginal fields led to a rapid reforestation. The "Great American Forest," according to Pyne, was more a product of settlement than its victim. If it was the replacement of a hunting and gathering society by one devoted to agricultural settlement that turned grasslands back

Although a natural process, fire on the prairie was a threat to farmers and settlers. In this nineteenth-century print, a farmer makes a firebreak to keep the approaching flames from destroying his crops. *Courtesy Library of Congress.*

into woods, the transformation was initiated by a change in the use of fire.

Finally, the frontier fire regime itself came into conflict and was replaced by what Pyne calls the "counter-reclamation" of an industrial fire regime whose ultimate aim was to control and banish fire entirely from the lands it defined as "wildlands" in favor of its own internally generated combustions used to turn forests and landscapes into renewable industrial and marketable resources. Based on capital, accumulated wealth, machines, factories, and raw materials, industrial society found little use for broadcast fire practices; in fact, fire was a threat to its office buildings, warehouses, working-class and middle-class urban homes, and parks and wildlife preserves. The early controversies surrounding the UNITED STATES FOREST SERVICE's dedication to total fire prevention in the national forests were actually a conflict between these two regimes, with the frontier regime's agriculturalists and loggers considering fire an ally, and the Forest Service considering it an enemy.

In short, the European explorers and early settlers encountered no virgin forests in North America during the sixteenth and seventeenth century outside bogs and swamps the Indians could not burn. Instead, they found a large Indian grassland reserve for hunting, gathering, and gardening, maintained, on the whole, by fire. They often unintentionally, occasionally consciously, reforested this savanna as they made their way willy-nilly across the continent. America's virgin forest was an invention of the late eighteenth and early nineteenth centuries, later settlers, and European tour-

ists, who, unaware that the Indians had denuded the "natural" landscape with fire, romantically defined the regrowths created by a different fire regime as the forest primeval, home of the noble savage. Then, in the late nineteenth and early twentieth centuries, as more marginal farm lands were abandoned to woods, as conservationists began to worry about vanishing timber and water, as historians and popular writers bemoaned a closing frontier, as new industrial uses were found for wood, and as new fuels replaced wood, a "veritable fever for forests swept the country." Industrial America enshrined the growing wildlands it produced as a vanishing virgin land to be saved and savored as part of the America heritage, a compensation, in many ways, for the country's lack of a long history that could offer castles and cathedrals as a means of celebrating a common past.

Fire had no place in this holy country, and the federal agencies entrusted with protecting it dedicated themselves to fire prevention and dismissed the practices of the old frontier fire regime as based on folk wisdom and "Paiute forestry." The irony, as many have pointed out, was that by rejecting controlled burning—called at the time "light burning"—these agencies only ensured greater lightning-borne conflagrations, especially in the West, where the dry, arid climate was conducive to wildfires and where the underbrush and thick forest growth created by a refusal to "thin" national reserves served as so much tinder. Although in more recent times, federal agencies have abandoned their total-fire-prevention policies, that too has also occasioned controversy, especially when huge portions of national parks are allowed to burn simply because the fire began "naturally" rather than by "accident."

—*Charles Phillips*

SUGGESTED READING:

Jordan, Terry G., and Matti Kaups. *The American Backwoods Frontier: An Ethnic and Ecological Interpretation.* Baltimore, 1989.

Maclean, Norman. *Young Men and Fire.* Chicago, 1992.

Pyne, Stephan J. *Fire in America: A Cultural History of Wildland and Rural Fire.* Princeton, N.J., 1982.

FIREARMS

From colonial times, firearms played an integral role in American frontier life. Historians have cited the ax, the plow, and the Kentucky rifle as tools crucial in settling the Eastern frontier. As Americans moved into the trans-Mississippi West, other significant technologies aided settlement—among them, BARBED WIRE, WINDMILLS, and Colt revolvers.

Colt Model 1873 S. S. A. Revolver. *Courtesy Buffalo Bill Historical Center.*

In the West, firearms conveniently carried on horseback, powerful enough for large game, and of repeating design proved essential. Developments in arms design and technology provided the appropriate tools for settlement. Indeed, the West was a "proving ground" for Eastern gun-makers, and their products helped advance Western settlement.

The muzzle-loading "Kentucky" rifle was the first significant longarm carried into the trans-Mississippi West, but on the Great Plains it proved inadequate. Its caliber was too small for hunting buffaloes and grizzly bears, and it was too long to be carried handily on horseback. Another distinctly American arm then evolved—the muzzle-loading Plains rifle. Often called the "Mountain Man's Choice," it was shorter, heavier, and of larger caliber than the Kentucky rifle. Popular from the 1830s through the 1860s, the best Plains rifles were made by the Hawken brothers of St. Louis, Missouri.

The adoption of percussion ignition (using small detonating caps rather than flint and steel) to discharge the weapon, coupled with mass-production techniques in arms manufacture, led to the development of breech-loading and repeating arms during the 1830s and 1840s. This development was important to Westerners, as increased firepower often was crucial to survival.

The first repeating arm widely used in the West was the percussion pepperbox pistol, which had a rotating cluster of barrels discharged by a single hammer. While difficult to shoot accurately, pepperbox pistols were popular among overland emigrants and California gold-seekers in the 1840s and 1850s.

SAMUEL COLT's 1836 patent for revolving cylinder pistols and rifles introduced the practical percussion repeater. The first model widely adopted was the Colt 1851 Navy revolver. Although other Eastern manufacturers, like Remington and Whitney, competed for the Western market, the Navy Colt dominated in the region until 1870.

With the development of metallic cartridges in the late 1850s and early 1860s, repeating longarms became truly practical. Among the first was the Spencer lever-action design with a tubular magazine in the buttstock. The most popular lever-action repeaters had tubular magazines beneath the barrel and were made by the Winchester Repeating Arms Company. Available in rifle and carbine variations, they were so prevalent that the famed Model 1873 became known as the "Gun That Won the West."

For frontiersmen demanding long-range accuracy and high power—such as professional buffalo hunters—the single-shot, breech-loading rifle was preferred. Among the best, the Remington Rolling Block and the Model 1874 Sharps rifles incorporated strong actions for high-powered cartridges and came in a variety of calibers, weights, and styles.

The U.S. Army also favored single-shot, breech-loading longarms. Production of the famed Springfield Trapdoor rifle and carbine began in 1873 and continued into the 1890s. The military also adopted the Colt Model 1873 Single Action Army revolver as the standard sidearm during the period.

Top: Percussion Hawkins Plains Rifle. *Courtesy Buffalo Bill Historical Center.*

Middle: A percussion rifle, muzzle-loading, made about 1855 by J. P. Gemmer of St. Louis, Missouri. *Courtesy Buffalo Bill Historical Center.*

Bottom: Winchester Model 1873, made about 1877 by the Winchester Repeating Arms Company of New Haven, Connecticut. *Courtesy Buffalo Bill Historical Center.*

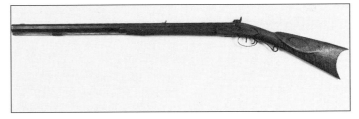

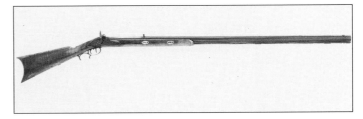

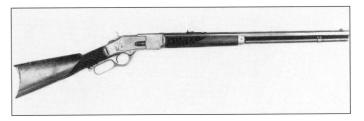

Available in various barrel lengths and calibers, the Colt Single Action Army revolver was also the most popular civilian handgun in the West from 1875 to 1900. Known as the "Peacemaker," it was chambered for the popular Winchester .44/40 cartridge in 1878; Westerners could then carry one standard cartridge for both sidearms and longarms. Other revolvers popular in the post–Civil War West included the Model 1875 Remington, the Smith and Wesson American, and the Merwin-Hulbert Army models.

The West provided a testing arena for Eastern arms manufacturers who improved their products to increase performance and sales. Colt developed the Lightning and Frontier double-action revolvers, while Winchester introduced the Model 1886 rifle, the first repeater using high-powered cartridges.

As the frontier era closed in the mid-1890s, the firearms industry developed new semiautomatic and automatic arms firing smokeless powder cartridges. But at no other time had the civilian- and industrial-arms segments of American society been as interdependent as during the era of trans-Mississippi settlement. And from that dramatic period, a mythic West emerged in which guns like the Colt Single Action revolver and the Winchester '73 rifle became significant icons of a romanticized frontier legacy.

—*Richard C. Rattenbury*

SEE ALSO: United States Army: Arms and Equipment

SUGGESTED READING:
Garavaglia, Louis A., and Charles G. Worman. *Firearms of the American West, 1803–1865*. Albuquerque, N. Mex., 1984.
———. *Firearms of the American West, 1866–1894*. Albuquerque, N. Mex., 1985.
Webb, Walter Prescott. *The Great Plains*. Boston, 1931.
Wilson, R. L. *The Peacemakers: Arms and Adventure in the American West*. New York, 1992.

FISHER, JOHN KING

Born in Upshur County, Texas, John King Fisher (1854–1884) eventually settled with his family in the South Texas community of Goliad. There, the handsome and popular youth developed an early antipathy for law and order. He was convicted of burglary at the age of sixteen and served four months of a two-year sentence in Huntsville Penitentiary before receiving a pardon.

In 1871, Fisher moved to Dimmit County, where he established a ranch. With the help of a group of unsavory companions, Fisher, a skilled gunman, flamboyant dresser, and charismatic leader, controlled the

John King Fisher, photographed when he was deputy sheriff of Uvalde County, Texas. *Courtesy Western History Collections, University of Oklahoma Library.*

remote and lawless border region around Eagle Pass. He developed a colorful reputation as a brigand and killer. In 1879, for example, he admitted to a least seven slayings, "not counting Mexicans." Many of his exploits, however, were wildly exaggerated.

In 1876, TEXAS RANGERS under LEANDER H. MCNELLY raided Fisher's ranch and arrested him and several of his associates on rustling and murder charges. Although such indictments dogged him for years, Fisher avoided conviction.

He married his childhood sweetheart in 1876 and fathered four daughters. A reformed King Fisher was named deputy sheriff of Uvalde County during the early 1880s and ran unopposed for sheriff in 1884. Before the election, however, he was murdered along with BENJAMIN F. THOMPSON at the Turner Hall Opera House in San Antonio.

—*B. Byron Price*

SUGGESTED READING:
Fisher, O. C., and J. C. Dykes. *King Fisher: His Life and Times*. Norman, Okla., 1966.
Jennings, N. A. *A Texas Ranger*. New York, 1899.
Webb, Walter Prescott. *The Texas Rangers*. New York, 1935.

FISHING INDUSTRY

Just as the Indians of the Great Plains could hardly have survived without the buffalo, the peoples of the Pacific Northwest relied on fish, and especially salmon, to sustain their existence. Salmon was the chief diet staple for the native peoples of coastal British Columbia, the Columbia River basin, and the coastal rivers south of the Columbia. Some have estimated the annual catch at around eighteen million pounds. Certainly, the fishing was of sufficient bounty to allow the various Indian tribes to thrive along the fast-flowing streams of the Pacific Coast. In Alaska, salmon proved even more abundant. There, some seventy-five thousand Native Americans lived off nearly thirty-four million pounds of salmon each year.

For catching salmon, a number of tribes used dip nets constructed of nettle or kelp, and occasionally of hemp. Where the salmon gathered over smooth bottomed spots in the Columbia and the Snake rivers, they dropped seine nets—constructed of wild hemp or silk grass, which grew east of the Cascades—some of them eight feet wide and three hundred feet long. The Clatsop and Chinook Indians used bone hooks, gigs, and lines to fish for salmon, while the Bella Coola tribes stretched large weirs across streams where the salmon ran. At waterfalls and river rapids, Indians hung over the rushing waters from rocks and platforms, stretched five-foot-wide hoops with dangling mesh webs out over the current, and scooped up leaping salmon.

Some Indians used dip nets, woven baskets really, to catch herring as well, while others trapped them with drag nets and herring rakes made of thin laths set with sharp bone spokes. In British Columbia, the local tribes fished the Pacific waters for herring, halibut, and cod by using forked branches with wooden hooks or two pieces of wood tied together at an acute angle, one piece held by a line of bark or seaweed, the other fitted with a bone or stone barb. In the area's freshwater fisheries, they used hand lines, spears, and seine nets and, in fast running water, dip nets to catch trout. Along the upper tributaries of Pacific Coast streams, they

frequently captured fish in weirs made of willow barricades stretched around stakes they drove into the stream beds. Some of their weirs contained baskets into which fish might swim.

Once they had made the catch, the Indians split open the salmon and hung it on a scaffold in the sun to dry. Sometimes, they then pounded the carcass to a powder between two rocks and tossed it in a grass basket lined with dried and stretched salmon skin. They pressed down the powder in the basket, covered it with skin, and tied the baskets together. The result—pemmican—stayed sweet and edible for years. At other times, they buried the dried salmon in straw-lined holes and covered them with dirt. The Pacific Coast Indians also sometimes smoked salmon to dry and preserve it. Halibut, on the other hand, was first dried, then cut into thin strips, which the Indians used both for food and for bartering.

When the first Europeans began arriving in the Pacific Northwest, they traded with the Indians for fish or took up Indian-style fishing themselves, using hand lines, nets, and—when they were adventurous—spears. By 1829, the Indians were exchanging one salmon for three leaves of tobacco on the Columbia or goods worth about one penny along the Fraser. Some commercial traffic in salmon also developed, enough, at least, to indicate there were markets for the fish, and by 1855, British Columbia had established an export trade in salmon second only to furs. Before the American Civil War, canneries began to spring up in both Oregon and Canada, and salmon fishing had be-

In 1888 or so, photographer Charles H. Townsend recorded the process of "Husking shrimp—treading out dried shrimps" on San Francisco Bay. *Courtesy National Archives.*

Top: Fishermen near San Francisco set out a gill net to dry, 1891. *Courtesy National Archives.*

Bottom: The crew of the schooner *Oscar and Hattie* pose with the first cargo shipment of halibut caught in Puget Sound, September 20, 1888. Photograph by N. B. Miller. *Courtesy National Archives.*

come an infant industry in the region. By 1878, two salmon canneries had been established in Alaska, and as commerce in canned Alaska salmon grew, Seattle and San Francisco became its financial centers, as well as its major market and its points of storage and transshipment to other markets. Neither in Alaska nor the Pacific Northwest, however, did commercial fisheries for halibut appear before 1880, although halibut and other kinds of fish—herring, sturgeon, shellfish, eulachon—were sold for local consumption in coastal ports. In 1880, commercial fishing, mostly for sturgeon, began on the Columbia River, and in 1892, the industry spread to the Fraser.

By the early twentieth century, the fishing industry off the Pacific Coast had emerged as a major commercial enterprise of an importance in the Far West to rival that of the cattle industry on the Great Plains. Just as the opening of Eastern markets for beef had created a boom in cattle, the growing population of the trans-

Mississippi West created new markets for fish that caused the West Coast fisheries to flourish. Not only New England Yankees, once the mainstay of the industry, but also Portuguese, Greeks, and Italians in California and Chinese and Japanese up and down the coast from Alaska to Baja California labored mightily to bring in a catch as varied as any on the globe. Alaska and the Pacific Northwest became especially well known for their salmon and halibut; California, for its tuna.

Between 1898 and 1914, San Francisco, Seattle, Los Angeles, and Anchorage began to dominate the Pacific's increasingly mechanized fishing industry the way Boston, Salem, and New York had once dominated the Atlantic's. Salmon, as always, remained the mainstay of Pacific Coast fishing. The main waters for harvesting commercial salmon lay off Alaska, the coasts of British Columbia and Washington, and the Puget Sound. Not only the ocean, but also the Columbia and Fraser river delta waters yielded a wide variety of salmon. Although some of the catch was still sold fresh in West Coast cities or was smoked, salted, or frozen and shipped on boats or inland by rail, most of it was canned. By 1914, Alaska was the leading producer of salmon worldwide, with Washington second, and Oregon third, and the number of canneries was growing at an extraordinary rate all along the coast.

Long considered one of the better tasting fish in the world, halibut too assumed a larger role in the Western fishing industry. The first real boost to the commercial harvesting of halibut came when a group of New England fisherman set up shop in 1888 north of Cape Flattery in Washington. Around that time, the completion of the transcontinental railroad put Eastern markets within reach of the West Coast fishermen. Trade was skimpy at first, mainly because Bostonians and other Easterners refused to eat Pacific halibut, which they typically considered inferior to the Atlantic variety. After 1900, however, they had little choice but to give the Western catch a try because Atlantic halibut fisheries were fast becoming exhausted. Urban growth in the East, where cities were swelling with new immigrants, also spurred demand. Finally, fisheries in the West, having developed later than those on the Atlantic Coast, were much more highly mechanized and, therefore, more efficient and competitive than their Eastern rivals. By 1914, cheap Pacific halibut had broken into Eastern markets, and the industry's annual catch topped fifty million pounds. Seattle became the major center of the industry, now the largest in the world, but smaller towns as well in the Northwest, in Prince Rupert, in British Columbia, even in Alaska, began sprouting halibut processing plants.

In California, the fishing industry centered on tuna. California also supported commercial salmon fishing

on the Sacramento River, but it declined rapidly in the first decade of the twentieth century. Tuna fishing, on the other hand, offered opportunities for small operators during this period, and Japanese American and Portuguese American fisherman in southern California aggressively expanded the industry. Taking to the sea in small, three-man motor boats and staying within fifty miles of landfall, the enterprising fishermen, by 1910, had made tuna California's major catch. By 1914, the tuna grounds stretched from Port Conception, two hundred miles north of Los Angeles, south to the Mexican border. The annual catch exceeded two hundred million pounds; the annual income from the tuna industry topped twenty-five million dollars.

In less than two decades, Pacific fishing had developed from a minor and usually supplemental economic pastime into one of the American West's major industries, but the two decades following 1914 were to prove as trying and troublesome for Western fisheries as the previous two had proved heady and rewarding. It was not that the industry ceased to grow; indeed, often the opposite was true. During the late teens and the 1920s, West Coast fishermen doubled their catch. Between 1914 and 1929, California developed the largest sardine industry in the world in addition to its tuna enterprises, with an annual sardine catch exceeding three hundred million pounds. To support this growth in production, the industry purchased larger boats and new equipment and became even more highly mechanized. By 1919, Western fishermen were ranging even farther afield, combing the waters off the coast from Alaska to South America and not infrequently sailing two thousand miles out onto the Pacific Ocean.

Almost in direct proportion to the industry's increased production, however, the price of fish fell. The markets for canned sardines never grew large enough to absorb the industry's massive overproduction, and much of the sardine catch was increasingly diverted to other uses—as fertilizer, fish oil, and a host of by-products. Tuna fishermen continued to bring in large catches into the 1920s, but as prices there also steadily declined, the tuna operations fell into a sharp slump. By 1919, California salmon fishermen had greatly depleted the once mammoth salmon schools, and the entire industry shrank into insignificance. Although commercial salmon and halibut fishing in the Pacific Northwest continued to grow modestly, at no point before 1929 did demand ever reach the levels salmon markets had enjoyed during World War I. Adding to industry woes, Japanese, Canadian, and Russian commercial operations began to offer the Pacific Coast a stiff competition.

The industry's financial troubles exacerbated the poor working conditions and labor problems it was experiencing in its canneries. In Alaska, because of the remoteness of different fishing grounds from each other and because of the state's immense coastline, fishing companies often placed their salmon canneries in isolated areas far from Alaska's relatively few cities, towns, and villages. In the long winters, these cannery complexes became industrial ghost towns, home only to a few watchmen. But during the short harvest season— June, July, and August—they became booming Western outposts, bustling with life. Also because of Alaska's remoteness and its small labor pool, company owners each year had to import from Seattle and San Francisco supplies and cannery workers as well as fishermen. In the early days, canning labor consisted mostly of Chinese Americans, but in later years Filipino Americans would take their place in the big tender vessels chugging up the coast. Housed at the canneries, which were, in effect, small communities, paid seasonally, and then transported back to Seattle or San Francisco, these workers suffered from blighted working conditions and

Top: In this photograph taken in about 1908, workers in Monterey, California, have spread out sardines to dry in the sun. *Courtesy National Archives.*

Bottom: Fishermen haul seine from the water's edge in Barid, California, in 1908. *Courtesy National Archives.*

rank labor policies. Conditions in Washington, Oregon, and California were hardly better. Employing a migrant labor force, much of it Hispanic, much of it female, the continental canneries became infamous for their bad working environments, long hours, and poor wages. Overproduction increased competition, and exhausted fishing grounds exacerbated the growing labor problems, as the slump in the industry continued into the Great Depression. The cannery workers began organizing and grew increasingly militant. Cannery operators responded in kind.

Even before World War I, commercial operations had begun to consider conservation measures to preserve a rapidly dwindling supply of fish. Halibut fishermen had to face the problem early. Although they would not significantly increase their production, the take had already grown so large that the American-Canadian Fisheries Conference was formed in 1918 to address conservation worries. In the 1920s, as California sardine operations continued to respond to falling prices with larger and larger catches that vastly exceeded demand, they fell afoul of California's Fish and Game Commission whose conservation policies the sardine companies flaunted. Despite attempts by the commission to limit the sardine take over the course of the decade, little changed, since enforcement proved quite difficult. In the salmon industry, too, Canada and the United States reached an agreement in 1924 that established an International Fisheries Commission, which was to recommend policies for conservation. But the commission had little real power, and salmon depletion became such a problem by 1930 that the United States and Canada were forced to negotiate the Sockeye Salmon Convention, creating an International Pacific Salmon Fisheries Commission to regulate fishing seasons and the total numbers of the annual salmon catch.

Increasingly, the industry's rapid exploitation of the Pacific Coast's fish resources brought it into conflict with American conservationists, both within government and outside. With the coming of the New Deal and its penchant for regulation and managed economies, the industry fell subject to further restriction by such long established Western resource-management bureaucracies as the UNITED STATES FOREST SERVICE and the BUREAU OF LAND MANAGEMENT. The limited number of fish in the sea and in streams and rivers inland, the growing problems of pollution and fish kills created by others such as the oil and gas industry and the huge California and Columbia rivers hydroelectric projects, and the intense interest of other nations in the stocks exploited by American commercial fishing, all gave rise to a modern fishing industry in the post-Depression West that was highly regulated, economi-cally volatile, politically divisive, and subject to world-wide disputatiousness.

—*Charles Phillips*

SEE ALSO: Whaling Industry

SUGGESTED READING:
McEcoy, Arthur F. *The Fisherman's Problem: Ecology and Law in the California Fisheries: 1850–1980.* Cambridge, Eng., 1986.
Nash, Gerald D. *The American West in the Twentieth Century: A Short History of an Urban Oasis.* Englewood Cliffs, N.J. 1973.
Netboy, Anthony. *The Columbia River Salmon and Steelhead Trout: Their Fight for Survival.* Seattle, Wash., 1980.
Ruiz, Vicki L. *Cannery Women, Cannery Lives: Mexican Women, Unionization, and the California Food Processing Industry, 1939–1950.* Albuquerque, N. Mex., 1987.

FITZPATRICK, THOMAS

Born in County Caven in Ulster, Northern Ireland, Thomas Fitzpatrick (1799–1854) was a fur trapper, partner in the ROCKY MOUNTAIN FUR COMPANY, guide, scout, and Indian agent. After immigrating to America, he answered WILLIAM HENRY ASHLEY's call for "enterprising young men" and became a trapper in Ashley's and ANDREW HENRY's company. An "Ashley man" in the fullest sense, he fought in the Arikara disaster, when the Arikaras unexpectedly attacked Ashley's men following an amicable trade for horses; discovered South Pass in the company of JEDEDIAH STRONG SMITH; and acted as a guide for the first RENDEZVOUS caravan. In 1830, Fitzpatrick and four other trappers bought out the Smith, Jackson, and Sublette fur-trading partnership (originally the Henry-Ashley outfit) and created the Rocky Mountain Fur Company. During the four-year partnership, Fitzpatrick led supply caravans to rendezvous, guided trapping brigades, and led a number of mountain men against the Blackfoot Indians at the Battle of Pierre's Hole in 1832. In 1834, he formed a partnership with Lucien Fontenelle and purchased Fort William (later to become FORT LARAMIE) from William Sublette.

Called "Broken Hand," "Bad Hand," or "Three Fingers" by the Indians, because of a shooting accident that crippled one hand, Fitzpatrick worked as a guide for Oregon- and California-bound emigrants. In 1836, he reluctantly escorted the Whitman-Spalding missionary group west as far as the Green River rendezvous. The following year, he met artist ALFRED JACOB MILLER and Sir William Drummond Stewart on one of

Stewart's grand Western tours. Fitzpatrick scouted for JOHN CHARLES FRÉMONT's second expedition through the Rockies to the Pacific Northwest and California in 1834, and over the following three years, he guided other military expeditions. In 1846, Fitzpatrick was appointed Indian agent for the Upper Platte and Arkansas region; his efforts to secure peace culminated with the 1851 Fort Laramie Treaty. Both whites and Indians admired him for his integrity as an agent.

—*S. Matthew Despain and Fred R. Gowans*

SUGGESTED READING:

Hafen, LeRoy R. *Broken Hand: The Life of Thomas Fitzpatrick: Mountain Man, Guide, and Indian Agent.* Denver, 1973.

Hafen, LeRoy R., and Ann W. Hafen. "Thomas Fitzpatrick." In *The Mountain Men and the Fur Trade of the Far West.* Vol. 7. Glendale, Calif., 1969.

FIVE CIVILIZED TRIBES

SEE: Native American Peoples: Peoples Removed from the East

FLAKE, WILLIAM J.

Mormon pioneer and Arizona cattleman William J. Flake (1839–1932) was born in Almanace, North Carolina. He moved with his parents to NAUVOO, ILLINOIS, in the mid-1840s and to Utah in 1848. He participated in the Mormon colonization of San Bernardino, California and, after 1858, ran cattle in Beaver, Utah. He moved to northern Arizona's Little Colorado Valley in 1877 and bought a ranch at Snowflake, which was named for him and for Mormon Apostle Erastus Snow. Instrumental in the Mormon move to Arizona, Flake negotiated major purchases for the Mormons at St. Johns and Showlow. His own range lay between Snowflake and Holbrook.

—*Charles S. Peterson*

SEE ALSO: Mormons: Far West Settlements

SUGGESTED READING:

Flake, Osmar D. *William J. Flake: Pioneer—Colonizer.* N.p., n.d.

Flake, S. Eugene. *James Madison Flake . . . Pioneer, Leader, Missionary.* Bountiful, Utah, 1970.

Peterson, Charles S. *Take up Your Mission: Mormon Colonizing along the Little Colorado River 1870–1900.* Tucson, Ariz., 1973.

FLATHEAD INDIANS

SEE: Native American Peoples: Peoples of the Pacific Northwest

FLETCHER, ALICE CUNNINGHAM

Anthropologist and influential advocate of reform for United States Indian policy, Alice Cunningham Fletcher (1838–1923) was born in Havana, Cuba, while her parents were on vacation. In the 1870s, she studied archaeology and ethnology at the Peabody Museum of Harvard University. In 1881, she moved to Nebraska to live with the Omaha tribe, where she studied all aspects of tribal life. In her time with the Omaha people, she developed both a passionate concern for their well-being and decidedly paternalistic ideas about improving the conditions under which reservation Indians lived.

In 1882, she journeyed to Washington, D.C., drafted a bill apportioning Omaha tribal lands into individual holdings, and shepherded the bill through the U.S. Congress. President Chester A. Arthur appointed her to implement the program, which was completed in 1884. Two years later, she went to Alaska and the Aleutian Islands to study the educational needs of the native peoples. She continued to agitate for better treatment of the Indians from the federal government. Her efforts were rewarded in 1887 by the passage of the DAWES ACT. This law directed that tribal lands be disbursed as the Omaha lands had been. Although reformers of the day considered the Dawes Act a major victory for Indian welfare, it fostered white exploitation and the dispossession of Indian lands.

Fletcher supervised the application of the Dawes Act provisions to the lands of the Winnebago and Nez Percé Indians. Later in her life, she wrote *Indian Story and Song from North America* (1900), *The Hako: A Pawnee Ceremony* (1904), and her major anthropological study, *The Omaha Tribe* (1911). The latter she produced with Francis LaFlesche, son of an Omaha chief, whom she treated as her adopted son. Fletcher died in Washington, D.C., at the age of eighty-five.

—*Kurt Edward Kemper*

SUGGESTED READING:

Mark, John T. *A Stranger in Her Native Land: Alice Fletcher and the American Indians.* Lincoln, Nebr., 1988.

FLOODS

Flooding was a primary nemesis of Westerners as the resources of the American West were put to use in the last half of the nineteenth century. As Anglo-Americans came to the West in larger numbers and began to fashion an economy, their activities changed the physical environment of many places. One result was seasonal, repeated flooding.

There had always been flooding in the West, but the new floods resulted as much from patterns of human use as from the erratic nature of rainfall. Widespread timber cutting, particularly in fragile arid and semiarid areas, created the context in which terrible floods could occur. Timber cutting at high elevations reduced the cover in snowy areas, thus accelerating the rate of melting and often causing floods downstream as Western rivers filled each spring.

Flooding became a common experience throughout the agricultural West. Since much of the region was not particularly good for agriculture, WATER was even more of a magnet than usual for farmers. The temptation to settle in extended flood plains was great. Rivers such as the Platte, with its inordinately wide plain, and those in arid areas, such as the Colorado, were attractive. Growing concentrations of people within the range of cascading water resulted, making flooding a fact of Western life.

Nearly every Western state experienced flooding. As the Mormons expanded in Utah, flooding became a consistent feature. The Imperial Valley in California flooded regularly, impeding its growth as an agricultural area. Floods along the Arkansas River in Colorado and Kansas damaged infrastructure and property. No place where there were humans was immune.

Even cities flooded. The first California flood on record took place along the Los Angeles River in 1770, and this flood was by no means the last. In one later example, flood waters destroyed a nascent water system in the 1860s. Phoenix survived disastrous floods in the early 1890s. Albuquerque flooded well into the twentieth century, with the floods of 1941 and 1942 among the most disastrous. Salt Lake City faced a devastating flood as late as 1983, and each year, as the snows melt, the prospect of flooding again looms large across the West.

The remedy for late nineteenth- and early twentieth-century flooding was legislative. The original act that created forest reserves, now national forests, in 1891, used watershed protection as its chief justification. Timber was protected because it slowed water run-off. Only after the passage of the NEWLANDS RECLAMATION ACT OF 1902 did the construction of dams, for the combined purpose of flood control and IRRIGATION, become reality.

In the modern era, the flow of nearly every Western river is controlled by a series of dams. Flooding remains a feared eventuality that many expect, but the vast majority of people who live in the West depend, for better or worse, on the chain of dams that regulate each river like a faucet. When floods come, they are even more frightening because water has been made to yield to technology and seemingly should not threaten humanity. The sheer power of floodwaters is testimony to the ambivalent controls humans have established over the West.

—*Hal Rothman*

SUGGESTED READING:
Hundley, Norris J. *The Great Thirst: Californians and Water, 1770s–1990s.* Berkeley, Calif., 1992.
Pisani, Donald J. *To Reclaim a Divided West: Water, Law, and Public Policy.* Albuquerque, N. Mex., 1992.

FLYNN, ELIZABETH GURLEY

Feminist and radical labor organizer Elizabeth Gurley Flynn (1890–1964) was born in Concord, New Hampshire. By the age of sixteen, Flynn was a Socialist, and by 1907, at the age of seventeen, she had begun speaking under the auspices of the Socialist party, the Socialist Labor party, and the INTERNATIONAL WORKERS OF THE WORLD (IWW). A force within the LABOR MOVEMENT of the American West, she acted as a liaison between the IWW and striking mine-workers' unions in 1909; she campaigned for free speech in Missoula, Montana, and Spokane, Washington; and she exposed poor jail conditions in Spokane.

Flynn was one of the key organizers of the Workers' Liberty Defense Union in December 1918 and was chairman of the International Labor Defense from 1926 to 1930. In 1936, she abandoned SOCIALISM for membership in the Communist party and became a columnist for the *Daily Worker.* In 1953, during the height of the McCarthy era, Flynn was convicted of violating the Smith Act by advocating the violent overthrow of the United States government. She served three years in federal prison. In 1961, she was named the first female chairman of the Communist Party U.S.A. Flynn died in 1964 during a visit to the Soviet Union and was buried with full state honors in Moscow.

—*Alan Axelrod*

SUGGESTED READING:

Camp, Helen C. *Iron in Her Soul: Elizabeth Gurley Flynn and the American Left.* Pullman, Wash., 1995.

Flynn, Elizabeth Gurley. *Words on Fire: The Life and Writings of Elizabeth Gurley Flynn.* New Brunswick, N.J., 1987.

FOLK ARCHITECTURE

SEE: Architecture: Folk (Ethnic)

FOLK ART

SEE: Art: Folk (Ethnic)

FOLK MEDICINE

SEE: Medicine

FOLK MUSIC

Folk music in the West, both vocal song and instrumental music, came from many different sources. Pioneers and settlers of different backgrounds and nationalities—British, Irish, Scots, Germans, Easterners, Southerners (particularly after the Civil War), African Americans, and smaller numbers of other ethnic groups—brought with them their own traditional music and songs, which remained important in their community, church, and family life in the West. Each ethnic or regional group made particular contributions to the new musical milieu. For example, the Germans introduced the accordion (later adopted by Mexican musicians); people from the British Isles brought their ballads, and Southerners—both black and white—brought the fiddle and banjo.

The immigrants found thriving musical traditions among the Native Americans and other ethnic groups already living in the West. American Indian music differed so drastically from the European traditions that there was not much musical interaction. The music of the Spanish and the Mexicans, however, mingled easily with incoming styles. The Hispanic communities' instrumental music and CORRIDOS, *decimas,* and other folk-song forms mixed with other ethnic traditions and eventually yielded such regional forms as *nortena* and Tex-Mex. Hispanic influence is also heard in COWBOY SONGS, Western swing, and popular music.

The time-honored tradition of composing songs and ballads about important events and experiences gave rise to several groups of Western topical songs. The exploits of the mountain men, scouts, and buffalo hunters who preceded the great westward migrations produced songs such as "Buffalo Skinners," which described the rigors of hunting buffalo on the open plains, and "California Joe," composed by Captain Jack Crawford, known as "The Poet Scout." Likewise, encounters with Indians gave rise to songs like "Sioux Indians," "The Dying Rangers," and "Custer's Last Stand." Also popular were songs and ballads about outlaws and badmen, such as "Cole Younger," "Sam Bass," "Jesse James," and "Billy the Kid."

The overland journey of the pioneers and settlers yielded a considerable body of songs reflecting their experiences, such as "Sweet Betsey from Pike" and "Crossing the Plains." The Mormon pioneers who settled in Utah and other areas of the West were particularly musical. It has been said that a history of the Mormons could be compiled from their songs alone, of which there were hundreds, including "The Desert Route," "The Way We Crossed the Plains," "The Seagulls and the Crickets," and "Don't You Marry the Mormon Boys."

Perhaps the most significant kind of folk song to spring directly from Western experience was the occupational song. Forced to live and work together in relative isolation, men employed in all-male occupations relied on themselves for entertainment. Cowboys, loggers, miners, sailors, railroad workers, and others produced large bodies of songs related to their specific lines of work.

Cowboy songs may be the best-known type of Western occupational folk song. The songs were mostly composed by working cowboys about their lives and experiences on the trail and at the ranch. They told of working with cattle ("The Old Chisholm Trail" and "Git along Little Dogies"), the dangers of the work ("Little Joe the Wrangler," composed by cowboy and song collector N. Howard Thorp), and day-to-day life ("A Cowboy's Life"). A number of cowboy songs, and other occupational songs as well, were parodies or reworked versions of older traditional or popular songs, such as "The Streets of Laredo," which was derived from an old Irish street ballad, "The Unfortunate Rake."

Logging, too, yielded many songs, but most logging songs found in the West were imported from the logging industry in the East. Some songs, however, seem to be Western compositions: "The Frozen Logger" refers to cutting Douglas fir in Oregon and Washington; "Them Days Is Gone Forever" is also an Oregon song. Many of the songs sung in the Northwest logging industry were union songs, such as "Fifty Thousand Lumberjacks," written by professional songwriters working for labor unions like the INDUSTRIAL WORKERS OF THE WORLD.

Mining songs fall into three groups: songs of the early prospectors, songs of the hard-rock miners, and union songs. Songs such as "When I Went to Prospect" were typical of the rush to find gold, whether it was in California, Idaho, Oregon, or South Dakota. Hard-rock miners, who dug for silver, copper, lead, and other valuable minerals underground, sang "When I Was a Hard Rock Miner." During the union-organizing days, songs such as "Stand by Your Union" came from supporters of the WESTERN FEDERATION OF MINERS.

Many sailors' songs were work songs; that is, they were actually sung while weighing anchor or hoisting or lowering sails, rather than for pure entertainment. Sea shanties such as "Haul on the Bowline" helped coordinate the work of the group of men performing the task. Other songs, however, like the gold-rush shanty "Sacramento," described the trip around Cape Horn to California and directly reflected part of the Western experience.

Like sailors, railroad workers sang many true work songs—hammer songs and tie-tamping songs. However, most railroad songs from the West were thematic or narrative in character—"Bishop Zack," "The Mormon Engineer," "Jerry Go and Ile That Car," and "The Railroad Cars are Coming."

Instrumental music has been as important as song in the folk cultures of the West, primarily for dancing and entertainment. Every ethnic group (with the exception of religious groups that prohibited music) had traditional dances and traditional dance music. Probably the most common instrument during the settlement period was the fiddle, known and played by many groups, from Southerners from the Appalachian Mountains to the Irish and the Ukrainians. At many pioneer-era dances, the only instrument would be a solo fiddle. Later, instruments such as the banjo, accordion, and mandolin were brought to the West as well. Obviously, the "Spanish" guitar was known to the Spanish and Mexicans of the Southwest. Occasional pianos and organs could be found in churches and schoolhouses.

All these forms of folk music enriched the lives of the Westerners who sang and played them. More than a form of entertainment or a creative outlet, folk music documented the Western experience, expressed ethnic and occupational group identity, and provided impor-tant traditional links with the cultures and diverse backgrounds of those who made their homes in the American West.

—*Charlie Seemann*

SEE ALSO: Music: Western

SUGGESTED READING:

Cheney, Thomas E. *Mormon Songs from the Rocky Mountains.* Austin, Tex., 1968.

Fife, Austin A., and Alta S. Fife. *Cowboys and Western Songs.* New York, 1969.

Lingenfelter, Richard E., and Richard A. Dwyer. *Songs of the American West.* Berkeley and Los Angeles, 1968.

Nettl, Bruno. *An Introduction to Folk Music in the United States.* Detroit, Mich., 1965.

Robb, Donald John. *Hispanic Folk Music of New Mexico and the Southwest.* Norman, Okla., 1980.

FOOTE, MARY HALLOCK

Western writer and illustrator Mary Hallock Foote (1847–1938) was a transplanted New Yorker who followed her mining engineer-husband to Colorado, Idaho, and California. She wrote more than a dozen novels, two collections of stories, and a posthumously published autobiography. In her work, she interpreted her Eastern reaction to the West and the importance of the West in molding human character. Perhaps not the least of her accomplishments was to inspire, through her letters and autobiography, Wallace Stegner's Pulitzer Prize-winning novel entitled *Angle of Repose* (1971).

Most of Foote's fiction contained autobiographical elements. Rough-edged frontier society and her husband's business conflicts, which led to his excessive drinking and marital stress, were severe tests to a genteel Eastern woman; she coped with them by pouring her feelings into her fiction and her letters back home to her school friend Helena Gilder.

Typical of the characters in Foote's early novels were an Eastern man and woman who came to recognize their need for each other's support in facing trying Western conditions. Their Western experiences proved to be only a temporary adventure, however, and they returned to the East to marry and resume a normal life. The early books are not Foote's best work; they contain a good deal of sentimentalism, which no doubt expressed her escapist hopes during her trying years in Colorado and Idaho. After 1895, though, when she and her husband moved to Grass Valley, California, his professional satisfaction and their marital stability led her to accept life in the West. A greater realism appeared in her writing, and her best work appeared between then and the end of World War I. Unfortunately, by then most of the readers of her earlier books had died, and the works of her literary maturity went largely unnoticed and unappreciated. After the war, she produced several manuscript versions of an auto-biography, which, although it was her greatest literary achievement, remained unpublished until 1972.

Foote's searching letters to Helena Gilder are yet unpublished, but they and her autobiography are the basis of one of the great monuments of Western litera-ture, Wallace Stegner's *Angle of Repose*. In Stegner's character of Susan Burling Ward, Foote's Western ex-periences and longings for the East come memorably alive in ways that even Foote herself could not achieve.

—*Gary Topping*

SEE ALSO: Women Artists; Women Writers

SUGGESTED READING:
Foote, Mary Hallock. *Edith Bonham*. Boston, 1917.
———. *The Ground-Swell*. Boston, 1919.
———. *A Victorian Gentlewoman in the Far West: The Reminiscences of Mary Hallock Foote*. Edited by Rod-man Paul. San Marino, Calif., 1972.
Maguire, James H. "Mary Hallock Foote." In *Fifty Western Writers*. Edited by Fred Erisman and Richard W. Etulain. Westport, Conn., 1982.

FORBES, JOHN MURRAY

China trader and Western railroad investor John Murray Forbes (1813-1898) was born in Bordeaux, France. He spent five years at Round Hill Middle School in Northampton, Massachusetts, following his father's death in 1824. He accepted an overseas ap-prenticeship in 1830 with Russell and Company, a Boston importing firm. Armed with the manage-ment skills and financial security that had eluded his father, Forbes returned to the United States in 1837 and applied his investment expertise to Western RAIL-ROADS.

In 1846, his Boston company acquired the Michi-gan Central. Attracted to expanding agricultural mar-kets in Iowa and Illinois, Forbes constructed the Chicago, Burlington and Quincy line in 1856. For the next thirty years, he directed this railroad and established his for-tune and his reputation. Forbes's aggressive invest-ments, personal management style, and keen sense of responsibility to stockholders typified those nineteenth-century entrepreneurs who made railroads the nation's first big business even as their individual empires yielded to more complex corporate management systems.

—*Mark Y. Hanley*

SEE ALSO: China Trade; Burlington Northern Railroad

SUGGESTED READING:
Larson, John Lauritz. *Bonds of Enterprise: John Murray Forbes and Western Development in America's Railway Age*. Cambridge, Mass., 1984.

FORD, JOHN

SEE: Film: The Western

FOREIGN MINERS' TAX OF 1850

In 1850, California leveled its first tax against foreign miners. The law ostensibly covered all "foreigners," but in truth, it was aimed at Californios, lifelong in-habitants of California from whom Anglos had taken the West Coast region in the United States–Mexican War only two years before. Foreigners working the gold fields were required to pay a tax for the privi-lege—sixteen dollars per month. The tax was obvi-ously intended to give Anglo-American newcomers an advantage in the quest for gold.

In the following decades, other state legislatures enacted their own taxes against foreign miners; in most instances, these laws were intended to discourage Chi-nese immigrants from taking up mining. The sponsor of one such bill proposed in the Idaho Territory com-mented with more honesty than most Anglos had: "The contemplated law was intended entirely for the ben-efit of the natives of the Flowery Kingdom."

The tax against foreign miners had a secondary impact: from the time the California law was reinstated in 1852 through the 1860s, the tax accounted for as much as one-quarter of the state's revenues.

—*Patricia Hogan*

SEE ALSO: California Gold Rush; Colorado Gold and Silver Rushes; Mining

SUGGESTED READING:
Takaki, Ronald. *A Different Mirror: A History of Multi-cultural America*. Boston, 1993.

FOREST MANAGEMENT ACT OF 1897

On June 4, 1897, President William McKinley signed an appropriations measure that included a statement of the purpose for forest reserves. That amendment, passed as part of the UNITED STATES GEOLOGICAL SURVEY allocation, is known variously as the Forest Management Act of 1897, the Organic Act of 1897, and sometimes the Pettigrew Amendment after the South Dakota senator who chaired the key public-lands committee.

Six years earlier, Congress had authorized the president to withdraw forest reserves from the public domain, but it failed to specify in statute the purposes for the reserves. Congressman Thomas C. McRae quickly became the chief advocate for remedial legislation. His bill stated initially that the reserves were needed to protect WATER supplies; eventually the protection of timber was added. McRae pushed hard to give states the exclusive authority over water generated on federal land, but the final language included the FEDERAL GOVERNMENT as a partner. The rights and needs of those living on or near a reserve were clearly stated in McRae's bill; they would have right of egress and regulated access to needed resources. Various resources, such as timber, minerals, and forage, were available for commercial use but never in such a way as to threaten future timber and water supplies. Finally, those directly affected by a proposed reserve, and their representatives in Congress, would be consulted in advance. In sum, the secretary of agriculture would regulate occupancy and use of the forest reserves.

Opponents saw the reserves as potential obstacles to local commercial interests, such as mining, and they delayed passage for six years. Proponents eventually persuaded Congress that the economy would be enhanced.

For three-quarters of a century, the 1897 law was viewed by the UNITED STATES FOREST SERVICE, the agency that has managed the national forests since 1905, as its organic act. While the 1960 Multiple Use–Sustained Yield Act lists uses for the forests, it states that the new measure was "supplemental to, but not in derogation of" the earlier law. Litigation in the early 1970s found the Forest Service to be in violation of 1897 timber sale stipulations; corrective legislation appeared as the National Forest Management Act of 1976.

As measured by its longevity, the amendment to the 1897 appropriations bill for the Geological Survey served well as legal authority for the Forest Service to manage the national forests. The much more prescriptive forestry and environmental legislation of the 1970s and later reflects a general rethinking of the proper role of the federal government in conservation and a shift of the public's priorities.

—*Harold K. Steen*

SEE ALSO: Forestry; Land Policy; Multiple-Use Doctrine; Sustained Yield

SUGGESTED READING

Dana, Samuel T. *Forest and Range Policy: Its Development in the United States*. New York, 1956.

Steen, Harold K. *The Beginning of the National Forest System*. Washington, D.C., 1991.

FOREST RESERVE ACT OF 1891

On March 3, 1891, Congress authorized the president to withdraw from the public domain certain forested lands. The first such reserve was established adjacent to YELLOWSTONE NATIONAL PARK on March 30. By 1897, more than 40 million acres had been set aside, and over the next decade, another 110 million acres were added to the reserves. In 1907, however, Congress essentially stripped the president of that authority, renamed the reserves as national forests, and reserved for itself the right to set aside forested acreage. In 1976, national forests proclaimed by earlier presidents were made permanent by statute.

During the two decades before 1891, Congress wrestled with the problem of managing America's forests. WATER was the primary issue; in the newly settled arid West, Congress sought to protect forested watersheds. Most bills died quickly; some moved through many of the parliamentary steps only to be defeated or abandoned. By 1888, a bill including presidential authority to proclaim forest reserves had scored yet another near miss, but the language survived and resurfaced in 1891. Opponents were largely concerned about issues of states' rights and delegation of power to the president.

In the meantime, Congress was deliberating over omnibus legislation to codify an immense body of statutes concerning the sale and disposition of the public domain. An 1880 study had revealed the existence of more than three thousand land laws; overlap, duplication, and even fraud were the result. From 1890 to 1891, Congress was in the final stages of a bill to "Repeal the Timber Culture Act and for Other Purposes." With twenty-three sections, the bill was referred to a conference committee and emerged with a Section 24 added by committee members. Because Congress was rushing to adjourn, it did not have the opportunity to examine the new section carefully. The bill squeaked by and was quickly signed by President Benjamin Harrison. Section 24, an amendment to a public-lands housekeeping measure, gave the president the authority to proclaim forest reserves. The section is generally called the Forest Reserve Act of 1891.

Although it is possible to question the means by which Section 24 became law, there is little question that its substance and intent were well understood. The language had passed the House in 1888 only to die in the Senate Public Lands Committee. Subsequently, the American Forestry Association, the American Association for the Advancement of Science, and congressional committee members continued to press for a forest-reserve measure. President Harrison promised to sign such a measure if it reached his desk. He did on March 3, 1891.

—*Harold K. Steen*

S<small>EE ALSO</small>: Federal Government; Land Policy; Timber Culture Act of 1873

S<small>UGGESTED READING</small>:

Dana, Samuel T. *Forest and Range Policy: Its Development in the United States.* New York, 1956.

Steen, Harold K. *The Beginning of the National Forest System.* Washington, D.C., 1991.

FORESTRY

Forestry, the science, art, and practice of wisely and efficiently managing for human benefit the natural resources associated with forest lands, was foreign to the early Western settlers, who with axes and FIRE converted forest land to farms. In 1864, G<small>EORGE</small> P<small>ERKINS</small> M<small>ARSH</small> offered a "woodman, spare that tree" response to the resulting environmental devastation of overcutting, and professional forestry arose in the United States in the late nineteenth century to prevent the adoption of Marsh's prescription to preserve valuable forest resources forever.

From 1886 to 1910, Bernhard Fernow and G<small>IFFORD</small> P<small>INCHOT</small>, foresters trained in Europe, headed the federal Division of Forestry, renamed the U<small>NITED</small> S<small>TATES</small> F<small>OREST</small> S<small>ERVICE</small> in 1905. Pinchot and Fernow shared a vision of forests as timber factories that could yield benefits forever through harvesting and subsequent reforestation. Neither felt the nation's forests should be locked up in parks or wilderness areas. Their views guided professional forestry throughout the twentieth century.

With few exceptions, federal foresters criticized private forest exploitation, and from 1900 to 1940, they sought regulatory authority over the states and private owners, who together owned two-thirds of the nation's forest land. Federal foresters attempted to persuade states and private owners to adopt reforestation and sustained-yield practices, but the states fought federal intrusion on the basis of separation of powers and states' rights; private owners had more complex reasons for resisting federal directives.

In the mid-nineteenth century, George Perkins Marsh cautioned the woodman to "spare that tree." *Editors' collection.*

To make money in the timber industry, one must sell logs at a high enough price to more than cover the original cost of timber, plus the cost of harvest and transportation to the mills. Existing timber stands obtained through RAILROAD LAND GRANTS, for example, could be harvested profitably and the land either sold for its residual value as a farm or abandoned. But if forced to practice sustained-yield forestry (that is, to plant trees on bare land or reforest after harvest), private owners faced severe obstacles that made the timber business unprofitable.

Planting trees for future harvest is profitable only if the value of the trees increases as fast as the value of interest that could be earned on some other equal investment. In the South, favorable soils and climate meant the time from planting to harvest was only thirty to fifty years, a period of time short enough to make reforestation profitable. But forests in the West took more than one hundred years to mature. Therefore, Western forest lands were simply stripped bare of their timber and then sold or abandoned. Professional foresters addressed the issue by conducting research on improved growing stock, pruning, thinning, and fertilization to increase the growth rate. Research in the

Top: U.S. Forest Service bureaucrats worked to preserve wooded lands, such as the forests surrounding Mount Ranier in Washington State, against the lumber industry's need for product. *Courtesy The Bettmann Archive.*

Bottom: This 1903 photograph depicts a manner of transporting harvested logs from the forest. *Courtesy National Cowboy Hall of Fame and Western Heritage Center.*

use of wood proved it was feasible to make some products from younger trees, thereby reducing the amount of time money was locked up in growing forests.

Professional foresters also addressed the problem of forest taxation. Timberland owners had an incentive to harvest the timber as soon as possible to cover annual property-tax burdens. Both public and private foresters promoted laws that reduced property taxes and rewarded reforestation.

Fire, forest pests, insects, and disease could completely destroy reforestation investments before the trees were mature enough for harvesting. Foresters organized fire protection and suppression, insect control, and research on forest diseases as a cooperative effort among the states, the private owners, and the Forest Service.

Finally, private owners always faced the threat of falling timber prices. During World War I, high demand raised market prices, but when demand fell after the war, prices began a downward trend, which lasted throughout the 1920s and 1930s. The timber industry feared a timber glut and a collapse of the market for wood products and rejected reforestation and SUSTAINED YIELD. After all, who would plant trees in a falling market? Industry leaders did, however, encourage the Forest Service to limit the harvest of timber on public lands. Sustained yield was advocated by private owners and the timber industry not because it would provide a steady flow of timber harvests in the long run but because it would limit competition in the short run.

After World War II, demand for wood products increased, and public and private foresters entered into a mutually supportive and symbiotic relationship. In exchange for private owners' practicing scientific forestry and reforestation on their lands, the Forest Service held public timber off the market. That arrangement lasted until late in the 1960s when private forests in the West were essentially depleted. Plans called for substituting timber from national forests for timber on private lands until the private forests were regrown. The plans backfired in the 1970s and 1980s, however, when recreationists and environmentalists complained that the harvesting levels on national forests were unwarranted and unsustainable. Moreover, the Forest Service had adopted clear-cutting, a practice in which all trees in harvested areas are removed. The general public refused to accept the professional foresters' attempts to justify clear-cutting as scientific forestry and called for a drastic reduction in timber harvests from public lands.

By the early 1990s, the controversy had become so heated that the integrity of the forestry profession came into question. The *Journal of Forestry,* the official voice of the Society of American Foresters founded by Gifford Pinchot in 1900, became an intellectual and philosophical war zone. Traditional foresters failed to recognize that rising prosperity brought a change in public goals for forest management. A highly vocal segment of the public refused to accept the view that forests were primarily factories to produce timber or other multiple-use benefits. A substantial minority of professional foresters allied themselves with environmental activists and social, ecological, and resource scientists who, in the spirit of George Perkins Marsh, called for ecosystem-based forestry. The integrity and health of forest ecosystems took priority over timber harvests, cattle grazing, recreation, and other commercial uses of the forests. Even the matter of public regulation of private forest management again appeared on the scene.

The decade of the 1990s was certain to challenge professional forestry.

—*Richard M. Alston*

SEE ALSO: Multiple-Use Doctrine

SUGGESTED READING:
Behan, Richard W. "Forestry and the End of Innocence." *American Forests* 81 (May 1975): 16–19, 38–49.
Cox, Thomas. *Mills and Market: A History of the Pacific Coast Lumber Industry to 1900.* Seattle, Wash., 1974.
Fernow, Bernhard. *Economics of Forestry.* New York, 1902.
Fricken, Robert E. *Lumber and Politics: The Career of Mark E. Reed.* Seattle, 1979.
Robbins, William G. *Lumberjacks and Legislators: Political Economy of the U.S. Lumber Industry, 1890–1941.* College Station, Tex., 1982.
Sharpe, G. W., C. W. Hendee, and W. F. Sharpe. *Introduction to Forestry.* 5th ed. New York, 1986.

FOREST SERVICE

SEE: United States Forest Service

FORT BENTON

Fort Benton was the last in a series of fur-trading posts constructed near the Great Falls of Montana, the head of steamboat navigation on the MISSOURI RIVER. Founded in 1847 by the Pierre Chouteau, Jr., and Company, the small adobe-walled fort was the site of an extensive trade with the Blackfoot Indians.

With the discovery of gold in western Montana in the early 1860s, a small freighting and warehousing community grew adjacent to the fort. In the 1860s and 1870s, the town prospered as goods arrived by Missouri River steamer and were then shipped to the gold fields or to Washington via the Mullan Road. Fort Benton was also a principal transfer site for Canadian-bound freight headed north on the Whoop-Up Trail.

The U.S. Army leased the adobe fort in 1864 and bought it five years later. The garrison stationed there was rarely larger than a company or two, and its principal duty was to guard the freighters and occasionally pursue whiskey traders. The army abandoned the post in 1881, but freighting activities continued for a few more years until the Northern Pacific and Great Northern railroads virtually eliminated the steamboat trade. The river levee and many vestiges of the freighting era survive in today's Fort Benton, as does an original adobe bastion used in the fur trade in the 1840s.

—*Paul L. Hedren*

SEE ALSO: Chouteau Family; Montana Gold Rush

SUGGESTED READING:
Overholser, Joel. *Fort Benton, World's Innermost Port.* Fort Benton, Mont., 1987.

FORT BRIDGER

Built on the Black Fork of the Green River by mountain man JAMES (JIM) BRIDGER and his partner LOUIS PIERRE VASQUEZ in 1843, Fort Bridger served as a supply post for emigrants along the Oregon-California trail. During the 1850's UTAH EXPEDITION during which the U.S. Army went to Utah to seat a newly appointed territorial governor to succeed BRIGHAM YOUNG, the post came under the control of the Mormons; Bridger disputed the Mormons' claim that he had sold them the fort, however. In 1858, Fort Bridger became a military post. The Fort Bridger Treaty, signed at the post in 1868, created the Wind River Indian Reservation for the Shoshone tribe. The army abandoned the fort in 1890; it is currently a Wyoming state historic site.

—*Phil Roberts*

SEE ALSO: California Overland Trails; Oregon Trail

SUGGESTED READING:
Ellison, Robert S. *Fort Bridger: A Brief History.* Cheyenne, Wyo., 1931. Rev. ed. 1981.

In about 1873, men, women, and children gathered on the grounds of Fort Bridger for an afternoon of croquet. *Courtesy National Archives.*

FORT HALL

After the ROCKY MOUNTAIN FUR COMPANY reneged on a contract with NATHANIEL JARVIS WYETH to supply the 1834 fur-trade RENDEZVOUS, Wyeth disposed of his goods by establishing a post, called Fort Hall, west of the rendezvous site near the SNAKE RIVER. At that time the only U.S. outpost in the Oregon Country, Fort Hall became a major supply station on the OREGON TRAIL.

Competition with HUDSON'S BAY COMPANY led Wyeth to negotiate the sale of the fort in 1838 to the company, which—following its usual practice—began farming operations around the fort. As the FUR TRADE declined and after emigrant traffic appeared in significant numbers in 1843, supplying those travelers on the Oregon and California trails and the Mormons headed for the Salt Lake Valley became the fort's major task. Emigrant traffic along the original overland route past Fort Hall declined after 1849, and Indian troubles in the mid-1850s resulted in the fort's closure in 1856. The name was applied to a U.S. military post and remains on an Indian reservation in the same area.

—*Judith Austin*

SEE ALSO: California Overland Trails; Overland Travel

SUGGESTED READING:

Austin, Judith. "Joseph Thing." In *The Mountain Men and the Fur Trade of the Far West.* Vol. 9. Edited by LeRoy R. Hafen. Glendale, Calif., 1972.

FORT LARAMIE

From 1834 to 1890, Fort Laramie, Wyoming, lay at a crossroads in the American West and witnessed a parade of settlement—the boisterous era of the fur traders, the cavalcade of overland travelers, the signing of significant Indian treaties and their resultant wars, and the coming of cattlemen and homesteaders. Founded in the summer of 1834 as a fur-trading post and initially named Fort William, the modest cottonwood stockade was also called Fort Laramie, after a Frenchman killed on the Laramie River a decade earlier. The fort was founded to serve the Rocky Mountain FUR TRADE, but it also quickly captured trade with the Oglala and Brulé Sioux Indians as well.

Pierre Chouteau, Jr., and Company acquired the fort in 1836 and rebuilt it five years later. The company named the enlarged adobe-walled post Fort John, although it remained better known as Fort Laramie. Fur trading along the Laramie River was steady, but it never equaled the much larger harvests in the Upper Missouri country or on the southern Great Plains.

The passing of a few Oregon-bound missionaries in the 1830s presaged an emigrant cavalcade traveling dirt trails in the 1840s and 1850s. The numbers were unparalleled, swelling from one thousand people through Fort Laramie in 1843, to three thousand in 1845, and eight thousand in 1847. In 1852, nearly sixty thousand individuals headed West, most lusting for California gold. To one and all, Fort Laramie was

Fort Laramie as illustrated in *A Report of the Exploring Expeditions of 1842 and 1843–44. Courtesy Library of Congress.*

a haven offering touches of civilization and opportunities to refit before continuing the arduous road ahead.

Emigrants soon cried out for protection, which the politicians willingly provided. In the summer of 1851, the Regiment of Mounted Riflemen arrived at the fort with an offer to buy Fort John for four thousand dollars. The acquisition was approved, and the post was rechristened Fort Laramie.

In 1851 and again in 1868, Fort Laramie hosted extraordinary delegations from the Sioux, Cheyenne, Arapaho, Crow, and other tribes of the Great Plains, first to negotiate unfettered emigrant passage on the trails and then to transform the Indians from nomadic hunters into Christianized farmers. In 1851, as many as ten thousand Indians attended the Fort Laramie or Horse Creek Treaty negotiations, during which the Indians agreed to allow traffic to pass unmolested through their country in return for annual payments of fifty thousand dollars.

Seventeen years later, the Fort Laramie Treaty of 1868 represented an honest attempt to end hostilities on the central and northern Great Plains—hostilities that had boiled continuously since 1854 when John L. Grattan's command was killed near the fort. By the 1860s, the Sioux and their allies fiercely contested white traffic on the overland road and the newer BOZEMAN TRAIL to the Montana gold fields. Peace overtures, however, included demands that the Sioux move to a permanent reservation and give up long-held traditions. Neither the 1851 treaty nor the 1868 treaty brought about intended results.

The decades of the 1860s and 1870s were particularly chaotic at Fort Laramie, as its enlarged garrisons protected the PONY EXPRESS, the overland TELEGRAPH, and trail traffic and engaged in repeated campaigns against the Indian tribes. These were heady times for the warriors of both races, and events like the Great Sioux War of 1876 to 1877 brought unparalleled excitement and intensity to the work at Fort Laramie.

With the end of the war, however, much larger posts were constructed to guard the Great Sioux Reservation in South Dakota, and the coming of the transcontinental railroads ended emigrant travel by foot and wagon. Cattlemen and homesteaders spread across Indian country in the 1880s making the old treaties and war fort obsolete. The army abandoned Fort Laramie in the spring of 1890. Today, Fort Laramie's considerable remains are preserved as a unit of the National Park Service.

—*Paul L. Hedren*

SEE ALSO: California Overland Trails; Chouteau Family; Grattan Massacre; Montana Gold Rush; Oregon Trail; Overland Travel; Sioux Wars

SUGGESTED READING:

Hafen, LeRoy R., and Francis M. Young. *Fort Laramie and the Pageant of the West, 1834–1890.* Glendale, Calif., 1938.

Hedren, Paul L. *Fort Laramie in 1876: Chronicle of a Frontier Post at War.* Lincoln, Nebr., and London, 1988.

FORT MANUEL

Fort Manuel was one of many fur-trading outposts erected along the Missouri River and its tributaries by the energetic St. Louis trader, MANUEL LISA. In his journal entry for October 19, 1812, Missouri Fur Company clerk John Luttig noted that the crew had finished construction, "hung the great Door of the Entrance of the fort . . . and Baptized the name MANUEL." Located a dozen miles above the Arikara villages near the mouth of Hunkpapa Creek, the fort was the only post to bear the first name of its owner. It also may have been the most short lived. Built by Lisa and his MISSOURI FUR COMPANY colleagues, Fort Manuel was destined to be a vain attempt to maintain trade on the Missouri in the face of the growing hostility that preceded the WAR OF 1812. The machinations of the British and the great Shawnee leader TECUMSEH had set tribe against tribe and native against white. Trade proved too poor and pressure too great, and the fort was abandoned in March 1813. The traders moved downstream to relative safety. The closing of Fort Manuel was another step in the dissolution of Lisa's Missouri Fur Company, which went out of business not long thereafter.

—*Richard E. Oglesby*

SEE ALSO: Fur Trade

SUGGESTED READING:

Oglesby, Richard E. *Manuel Lisa and the Opening of the Missouri Fur Trade.* Norman, Okla., 1963. Reprint. 1984.

FORT ROSS

The RUSSIAN-AMERICAN COMPANY, headquartered in Sitka, Unalaska (later Alaska), founded Fort Ross in 1812. The initial impetus came from Nicholas Petrovich Rezanov, a high company official, who visited San Francisco Bay in 1806. Cordially received by the Spanish authorities, Rezanov conceived the idea of a permanent Russian settlement on the northern coast of California to facilitate the hunting of sea otters, seals, and sea lions, as well as the production of agricultural crops and livestock. Such an outpost would help the company exploit the maritime FUR TRADE and provide a reliable source of foodstuff often in short supply for the company's Alaskan operations. Acting on Rezanov's suggestion, ALEKSANDR BARANOV, director general of the company in Sitka, dispatched Ivan A. Kustov in 1808 and then in 1811 to reconnoiter the coast north of the Spanish settlements. Finally, in the spring of 1812, Kustov entered Bodega Bay to establish a permanent settlement. He selected a site eighteen miles north of the bay. Work began on March 15 with the construction of a rectangular stockade. The post was dedicated on September 11 and named Fort Ross (*Rossiya* is the poetical name for Russia).

The complex was completed in 1814. Buildings within the stockade included a house for the commandant (Kustov held the post for nine years), barracks for soldiers and officers, warehouses, a kitchen, and a jail. Outside the stockade walls were shops for a blacksmith, baker, carpenter, cooper, and tanner; a boathouse; a flour and grain mill and threshing floors; a diary, stable, corral, and pens for livestock; and—for the employees and their families—baths, kitchens, and houses. The original colony numbered ninety-five Russians and eighty Aleut hunters brought from Unalaska. Eventually the fort mounted forty-one cannons. Land in the immediate vicinity was fenced and put into cultivation. Crops included a variety of cereal grains and staple vegetables, melons, flax, hemp, poppy, and tobacco. Later fruit trees and vineyards were planted, and satellite farms sprang up in the general vicinity. To augment the food supply, a small party of men was stationed on the nearby Farallone Islands to gather bird eggs, birds, seals, and sea lions. In addition, fish and wild game were also supplied to the company's Unalaskan outposts.

The essential contributions Fort Ross made to the Russian-American Company were as a reliable source of foodstuffs and as a secure base to carry on the maritime fur trade along the California coast. The latter provoked recurring confrontations with Spanish, and later Mexican, authorities in Alta California. Those officials refused to let the company hunt freely and repudiated its seizure of land at Bodega Bay and Fort Ross. But the Spanish officials were impotent. Later, with Mexican independence in 1821, Mexico lacked the resources to challenge the Russians.

By 1839, the Russian-American Company had become aware that the maritime fur trade had ceased to be profitable and that the agricultural returns from Fort Ross would never reach full expectation. The company decided to abandon the fort on April 15, 1839, and sold the property to JOHN AUGUST SUTTER, a Swiss-born resident on December 12, 1841, for thirty thousand dollars. Sutter failed to render full payment, and

the purchase availed him little; his claim was later rejected by the U.S. Land Commission.

In 1906, the *San Francisco Examiner* bought the site and presented it to the state of California. The stockade and major buildings, long destroyed by pillage, fire, and earthquake, were faithfully restored by the Department of Parks, Beaches and Recreation. Today Fort Ross is a state historical monument, a testament to the Russian presence in pre-American California.

—*Doyce B. Nunis, Jr.*

SEE ALSO: Exploration: Russian Expeditions

SUGGESTED READING:

Essig, E. O., Adele Ogden, and Clarence John DuFour. *Fort Ross: California Outpost of Russian Alaska, 1812–1841.* Edited by Richard A. Pierce. Kingston, Ont., and Fairbanks, Alaska, 1991.

Mathes, W. Michael, comp. and ed. *La frontera Ruso-Mexicana. Documentos mexicanos para la historia del establecimiento ruso en California, 1808–1841.* Mexico, D.F., 1990.

FORTS

As Euro-Americans spread across the trans-Mississippi West, a variety of presidios, cantonments, depots, and forts were constructed to safeguard trails, commercial enterprises, and settlements. The form and function of these outposts varied, yet each played a role in transforming Indian lands into a secured frontier.

In the American Southwest in the seventeenth and eighteenth centuries, small Spanish military garrisons protected scattered colonial missions and trading posts. The principal Spanish post was a presidio. Santa Fe, Tucson, San Diego, Monterey, and San Francisco are among American cities that were founded as Spanish garrisons. The French and Mexicans also maintained troops in the West, but they abandoned their colonial outposts as Americans acquired their land holdings.

Following the principle of MANIFEST DESTINY, America's self-professed right to conquer and transform the land, the U.S. Army established military posts to buffer settlers from the Indian tribes. A rough north-south string of fortifications, including Forts Snelling, Atkinson, and Smith and the Jefferson Barracks, generally defined the western boundary of settlement in the first quarter of the nineteenth century. As settlement advanced westward, the army constructed new posts and abandoned the older, interior forts.

Concurrent with the initial movements across the Mississippi River, fur-trading companies built forts on the plains. JOHN JACOB ASTOR'S AMERICAN FUR COMPANY made a calculated ascent of the MISSOURI RIVER in the late 1820s and established Forts Clark, Union, McKenzie, and others for the purposes of trading with the Indian tribes of the Great Plains. The physical appearance of the traders' forts typically mirrored their military counterparts of the era with stout log or stone palisades and bastions for defense and an array of interior quarters, warehouses, and other utilitarian structures. These posts were small—Fort Union at the confluence of the Yellowstone and Missouri rivers measured merely 220 by 240 feet—but each was fully adequate for its complement of traders or troops.

With the dramatic tide of Western migration after the United States–Mexican War, the army established garrisons to protect settlers in Texas, New Mexico, California, and Oregon. New forts spanned the OREGON TRAIL, for instance, from Phil Kearny and Laramie east of the Rocky Mountains to Cantonment Loring and Vancouver Barracks in the Far West.

Invariably, the army located its Western forts where water, construction material, fuel, and forage were available. Inevitably, too, the posts reflected their local environments. If stone was plentiful, the post's structures were built of that material. In the Southwest, adobe buildings predominated, and where timber was abundant, fort structures featured logs or planks.

From the mid-nineteenth century onward, most Western forts reflected an architectural sameness. All buildings faced a central, rectangular parade ground surmounted by an immense flagstaff and an American

Top: Troops of the Sixth Cavalry at Fort Bayard, New Mexico, training horses in about 1885. *Courtesy National Archives.*

Bottom: In 1890, the crude accommodations of Fort Keogh in Montana were still under construction. *Courtesy National Archives.*

Fort Thomas of the Arizona Territory. *Courtesy Arizona Historical Society.*

flag. Officers' quarters faced the parade ground along one long side, while barracks for enlisted men faced the officers' row from the other side. Other structures included hospitals, guardhouses, stables, and warehouses. Noticeably lacking at most of the West's military posts in the mid- and late-nineteenth century was a palisade. Construction material was typically costly, and the army fully appreciated that disciplined troops under arms made a wall unnecessary.

Daily bugle calls regulated the ebb and flow of movement within military forts, from "first call for reveille" at dawn to "tattoo" and "taps" after sunset. During the day, military life included well-regulated periods for drill, fatigues, guard mounting, inspections, and meals. The soldiers built and maintained their posts, and their lives were unusually dreary; one army wife labeled her life in a military fort "glittering misery."

During the peak of the Indian Wars from the 1860s through the 1880s, military posts were established and then abandoned as the army responded to the unending displacement of Indian tribes. Across the Northern Plains in the years preceding the Great Sioux War of 1876 to 1877, for instance, a loose network of small forts protected transportation routes and scattered settlements. The rush to the Black Hills gold fields in 1875 and 1876, however, triggered the final removal of the Sioux and their Indian allies from the Black Hills and adjacent buffalo country.

During the Great Sioux War, the army established numerous small cantonments and depots to facilitate operations. Some temporary stations, like the palisaded camps on the Sage Creek and Cheyenne River, protected gold-rush traffic to and from the Black Hills, while outposts, like the Powder River Depot and Glendive Cantonment, served as points of supply for the field troops. As the Sioux were finally subjugated, the army positioned new or enlarged forts like Robinson, Yates, Niobrara, and Meade around the Sioux reservation. Other forts, like Assiniboine, Custer, and McKinney, dotted the Sioux's former hunting range to ensure the Indians' complete compliance and domination.

During the mid-1890s, the army rapidly abandoned the innumerable small Western posts and consolidated their garrisons into large central bases on well-established rail lines. A few interior posts—Snelling, Leavenworth, D. A. Russell, and Bliss—became major installations serving training and garrisoning purposes. But for most of the forts, the frontier and its challenges had ended.

—*Paul L. Hedren*

SEE ALSO: Bent's Fort; Black Hills Gold Rush; Fort Benton; Fort Bridger; Fort Hall; Fort Laramie; Fort Manuel; Fort Ross; Fort Union; Fort Vancouver; National Expansion; Sioux Wars; Spanish-Mexican Towns; Spanish Settlement; United States Army: Military Life on the Frontier; Sioux Wars

SUGGESTED READING:
Frazer, Robert W. *Forts of the West: Military Forts and Presidios and Posts Commonly Called Forts West of the Mississippi River to 1898.* Norman, Okla., 1965.
Prucha, Francis P. *A Guide to the Military Posts of the United States, 1789–1895.* Madison, Wis., 1964.

FORT UNION

Established in 1828 by JOHN JACOB ASTOR's AMERICAN FUR COMPANY, Fort Union prospered as a fur-trading bastion at the confluence of the Yellowstone and Missouri rivers for nearly four decades. Assiniboin, Blackfoot, Crow, Cree, and Sioux Indians delivered bison robes and other furs to trade for an enticing array of weaponry, dry goods, tinware, and baubles procured from throughout the industrialized world.

Pierre Chouteau, Jr., of St. Louis succeeded Astor in 1834 and redoubled the traditions of hospitality for which the American Fur Company was renowned. GEORGE CATLIN, Prince Maximilian of Wied Neuwied, KARL (OR CARL) BODMER, JOHN JAMES AUDUBON, PIERRE-JEAN DE SMET, John Paliser, and WILLIAM DE LA MONTAGNE CARY were among many who experienced—and chronicled—Fort Union's gracious style.

Architecturally, Fort Union was distinctive for its extensive use of stone; its massive, square-sawn, and whitewashed palisade timbers set on a full foundation; its ostentatious Bourgeois House; and its colorful decorative trimmings. The coming of soldiers and settlers in the 1860s doomed the traders, however, and the U.S. Army bought and dismantled the fort in 1867. In the mid-1980s, the National Park Service preserved and reconstructed much of Fort Union as a national historic site.

—*Paul L. Hedren*

SEE ALSO: Chouteau Family; Fur Trade

SUGGESTED READING:
Thompson, Erwin N. *Fort Union Trading Post: Fur Trade Empire on the Upper Missouri.* Williston, N. Dak., 1994.

FORT VANCOUVER

In 1824 and 1825, the HUDSON'S BAY COMPANY established FORT VANCOUVER on the north bank of the Columbia River, some one hundred miles from its mouth. The British company constructed a walled fort on high ground but added newer buildings nearer the river. The post soon became the company's headquarters for the vast Columbia Department, stretching from the Russian settlements in Alaska south to the California border and from the Rockies to the Pacific. The fort was the major settlement in Oregon until the 1840s when Americans founded towns in the Willamette Valley. George Simpson, who headed the company's operations in Canada, assigned Chief Factor JOHN MCLOUGHLIN to Fort Vancouver. A pivotal figure in Oregon, McLoughlin supervised 450 men at twenty-two fur-trading posts, kept peace with the Indians, harvested furs (he used the brigade system in the Snake River country), produced foodstuffs and lumber for local and international markets, attempted to keep the lands north and west of the Columbia River under English control, and supplied needy Americans. The fort received supplies from company ships arriving from England and returned beaver and other furs. Visitors commented on the fort's vast and fruitful farms, diverse population, and McLoughlin's comfortable home. Following the Oregon Treaty of 1846, the Hudson's Bay Company moved its headquarters to Vancouver Island. Under American control in the 1850s, Fort Vancouver served as the army's district headquarters, dispatching troops against interior tribes. In 1947, the army abandoned the post; in 1961, it became the Fort Vancouver National Historic Site.

—*G. Thomas Edwards*

SEE ALSO: Fur Trade; Missions: Nineteenth-Century Missions to the Indians; Willamette River

SUGGESTED READING:

Gibson, James R. *Farming the Frontier: The Agricultural Opening of the Oregon Country, 1786–1846.* Seattle, Wash., 1985.

Johansen, Dorothy O., and Charles M. Gates. *Empire of the Columbia: A History of the Pacific Northwest.* New York, 1967.

FORTY-NINERS

SEE: California Gold Rush

FOUNTAIN, ALBERT JENNINGS

Attorney, publisher, and political leader Albert Jennings Fountain (1838–1896) was born on Staten Island, New York. He studied law in California and, in August 1861, joined the California Column, a Union force occupying Arizona, New Mexico, and West Texas. Fountain married Marianna Pérez de Ovante and became a Texas state senator. During the EL PASO SALT WAR, he killed a man in downtown El Paso.

In 1875, Fountain and his family moved to Mesilla, New Mexico, where he became a successful attorney, militia captain, Republican member of the New Mexico legislature, Speaker of the House, and publisher of the *Mesilla Independent.* In 1881, he unsuccessfully defended the outlaw "BILLY THE KID" on murder charges. Fountain waged a huge legal struggle against a rising New Mexico Democrat, ALBERT B. FALL. On February 1, 1896, Fountain and his eight-year-old son, Henry, disappeared near today's White Sands Missile Range in southern New Mexico. Their deaths remain one of New Mexico's greatest mysteries.

—*Leon C. Metz*

SUGGESTED READING:

Gibson, A. M. *The Life and Death of Colonel Albert Jennings Fountain.* Norman, Okla., 1965.

Keleher, William A. *The Fabulous Frontier: Twelve New Mexico Items.* Albuquerque, N. Mex., 1962.

Metz, Leon C. *Pat Garrett: The Story of a Western Lawman.* Norman, Okla., 1974.

Rhodes, May D. "Frontier Mystery." *New Mexico Magazine* (May 1947): 17, 35, 37.

FOUR HORNS (SIOUX)

A Hunkpapa Lakota military leader and medicine man, Four Horns (1814–1887) was an important holy man. He appeared during a Lakota council in 1851 to prepare for defense against non-Indian intrusion. Four Horns was SITTING BULL's "uncle" and a person with vision about how the resistance should be organized. He first emerged as one of four leading "shirt wearers," who served as liaisons among other leaders in the tribe. Four Horns was most respected and influential among them and evidently the one largely responsible for inspiring similar organizations in other Lakota as well as in Yanktonai (Ihanktuwala) tribal groups.

Into the 1860s, Four Horns was the most persuasive leader among Hunkpapas. Judiciously he deferred to Sitting Bull, however, and relinquished the leadership role. As a relative who evidently put Sitting Bull up on the hill to fast, guided his emergence as a medicine man, and supported his rise as the principal leader in defense of Lakota and Yanktonai land and culture, Four Horns was Sitting Bull's most trusted adviser and friend.

At the Killdeer battle against a superior force under U.S. Army General ALFRED SULLY, Four Horns was wounded by a bullet in his back—a bullet he carried throughout his life. Thereafter, he and Sitting Bull shunned negotiations pertaining to the 1868 Fort Laramie Treaty and committed themselves to defend against further encroachment on the Great Sioux Reservation.

After the Battle of Little Bighorn, Sitting Bull and BLACK MOON counseled their people to take exile in Canada as an alternative to bloody resistance or surrender. In Canada, Four Horns was the only major Lakota leader to stay with Sitting Bull until his surrender in 1881.

Thereafter, Four Horns advised peaceful negotiation and accommodation. His disposition was important, for within Standing Rock Agency jurisdiction, only Four Horns and Running Antelope remained as original shirt wearers, although aging and perhaps the pain of combat wounds reduced his influence among traditionalists. U.S. Agent JAMES MCLAUGHLIN included Four Horns's name among those of "chiefs" overseeing a Grand River district identified in federal records as "Hunkpapa," separate from the one that included Sitting Bull. Four Horns did not stand out as a leading adversary in debates about the surrender of Lakota land to the United States, and he died before the time of decision regarding the Agreement of March 2, 1889, which reduced Sioux lands by nine million acres.

—*Herbert T. Hoover*

SEE ALSO: Little Bighorn, Battle of; Sioux Wars

SUGGESTED READING:
National Archives. Record Group 75, Standing Rock Agency.

FRAEB, HENRY

Mountain man Henry Fraeb (?–1841) was a founder of the ROCKY MOUNTAIN FUR COMPANY. Details of his birth and early life are unknown. As a mountain man, he was referred to as a German, and his name was often pronounced "Frapp." By 1829, he was an accomplished trapper. After the rendezvous that year, Fraeb, Milton Sublette, and Jean Baptiste Gervais led a trapping party down the Bighorn River. At the 1830 rendezvous, he and THOMAS FITZPATRICK, JAMES (JIM) BRIDGER, Milton Sublette, and Jean Baptiste Gervais bought out JEDEDIAH STRONG SMITH, David Jackson, and William Sublette to found the Rocky Mountain Fur Company.

The new company trapped on the Snake River and wintered in Cache Valley, Utah. The men were at the rendezvous of 1832 and took part in the Indian battle there. At the rendezvous two years later, the company was dissolved, and Fraeb spent the winter of 1835 to 1836 in St. Louis.

Early in 1837, Fraeb entered in partnership with Peter A. Sarpy to build Fort Jackson on the South Platte River. Competition from two other forts in the area— Fort Lupton and Fort St. Vrain—led them to sell most of their stock in 1839 to Bent, St. Vrain and Company.

Fraeb went to St. Louis and formed a partnership with Jim Bridger. The two men brought goods to the last rendezvous in 1840 and then established a fort on the Green River to capitalize on the emigrant trade. During the summer of 1841 on a hunt for game to be used in winter, the men were attacked by a group of Sioux, Cheyenne, and Arapaho Indians, and Fraeb was killed by an arrow. The administrator of his estate, John B. Sarpy, reported to the court that he knew of no heirs to Fraeb and no list of his assets was available, but that "he died largely indebted to Pierre Chouteau Jr. & Co."

—*Charles E. Hanson, Jr.*

SEE ALSO: Fur Trade; Mountain Men; Sublette Brothers; Trappers

SUGGESTED READING:
Hafen, LeRoy R. "Henry Fraeb." In *The Mountain Men and the Fur Trade of the Far West.* Vol. 3. Edited by LeRoy R. Hafen. Glendale, Calif., 1966.
Morgan, Dale L., and Eleanor Towles Harris. "Henry Fraeb." In *The Rocky Mountain Journals of William Marshall Anderson.* Edited by Dale L. Morgan and Eleanor Towles Harris. San Marino, Calif., 1967.

FRANCHÈRE, GABRIEL

Gabriel Franchère (1786–1863) was a clerk in JOHN JACOB ASTOR's Pacific Fur Company, the first American commercial enterprise in the Pacific Northwest. Born in Montreal, Franchère was the son of a city merchant. As a young man, he had a modest formal education and worked in his father's shop. Ambition and the lure of adventure in the West prompted him to join the Pacific Fur Company in the summer of 1810. He traveled to New York with a group of Canadian and Scots company employees and embarked on the ship *Tonquin* bound for the Northwest Coast. After a hazardous voyage, made even more so by the erratic behavior of the ship's captain Jonathan Thorn, Franchère and the maritime Astorians reached the mouth of the Columbia River in March 1811. There they built Fort ASTORIA (present-day Astoria, Oregon), the fur-trade entrepôt for Astor's commercial empire. At Fort Astoria, Franchère served in many capacities—clerk, Indian diplomat, and provisioning agent. In early April 1814, after Astoria was sold to the North West Company, Franchère joined a canoe convoy bound for Montreal. He spent the rest of his life as an agent for various fur companies. His importance rests not so much in his own activities but in the detailed journal he kept between 1810 and 1814. The journal recorded not only major events in the FUR TRADE and Western history but also important details about Native American life and natural history. The journal was first published in French in 1820, with an inadequate English translation in 1854. Franchère's work finally got a reliable English and French printing in 1969.

—*James P. Ronda*

SUGGESTED READING:
Lamb, W. Kaye, ed. *Journal of a Voyage on the North West Coast of North America during the Years 1811, 1812, 1813, and 1814 by Gabriel Franchère*. Toronto, Ont., 1969.

FRANCISCAN MISSIONS

SEE: Missions: Early Franciscan and Jesuit Missions

FREDONIA REBELLION

Settlers in the Nacogdoches area of eastern Texas revolted against the Mexican government in late 1826 and early 1827 when the land grant on which they had settled was revoked. After proclaiming the region to be an independent republic named Fredonia, the rebels fled the region in the face of the advance of Mexican troops.

Haden (or Hayden) Edwards, a Virginian, had obtained the empresario (land grant) license in 1825 from the Mexican government. The grant allowed him to settle Anglo-Americans in eastern Texas and provided Edwards with a large tract of land around the Nacogdoches area partially bordering on the Neutral Ground zone, an area whose ownership was disputed by the United States and Mexico. Within the grant were squatters, descendants of colonists who had settled in the region in 1779, members of various Indian tribes, and others.

Edwards ordered all residents to produce proof of ownership or pay him for the value of the land claimed. Aware of the sensitive issue at hand, STEPHEN FULLER

AUSTIN wrote Edwards on several occasions to warn him to proceed with caution.

Edwards ignored that advice, and soon his adversaries petitioned the Mexican government for protection. In May 1826, he left his brother Benjamin in charge of his affairs and went to Louisiana to recruit more settlers. The following month, when relations with the empresario deteriorated, the Mexican government revoked the grant and expelled Haden Edwards from Texas.

Later, in December 1826, Benjamin Edwards and a band of thirty volunteers occupied the Old Stone Fort, raised a flag with the words "Independence, Liberty, and Justice," and declared the area to be the Republic of Fredonia. Six weeks later, in January 1827, the rebellion ended. As the Mexican troops approached Nacogdoches, Benjamin Edwards and his followers fled to Louisiana.

—*Fred L. Koestler*

SEE ALSO: Empresarios; National Expansion; Texas Revolution

SUGGESTED READING:
Pattie, James D. *The Personal Narrative of James O. Pattie*. Edited by Timothy Flint. New York, 1976.

FREE SILVER

SEE: Currency and Silver as Western Political Issues

FRÉMONT, JESSIE ANN BENTON

Writer Jessie Ann Benton Frémont (1824–1902), the daughter of THOMAS HART BENTON and the wife of JOHN CHARLES FRÉMONT, seemed destined for a life dominated by politics. Born near Lexington, Virginia, at the ancestral home of her mother's highly political family—also active in politics—Jessie Benton came into the world the same year her father began his first of five terms as Missouri's representative in the U.S. Senate.

Jessie Benton's schooling included the French and Spanish languages and literature, English classics, and piano. Her most important lessons, however, came from her father, for whom she often served as confidante and secretary, and from the politicians, military officers, journalists, and Missouri pioneers who were frequent house guests. Because her mother was a semi-invalid, Jessie Benton became hostess to her father and his associates. One of these was a young officer of the CORPS OF TOPOGRAPHICAL ENGINEERS, John Charles Frémont, whom Jessie Benton married in 1841.

Jessie Frémont brought to her marriage uncommon intelligence, fierce pride, and a willful spirit. She also shared with her husband and her father a vision of westward expansion, and after her husband undertook a series of Western expeditions in the 1840s for the U.S. Army, Jessie Frémont's collaborations on his reports infused the works with the enthusiasm and drama that won them wide attention. When John Charles Frémont ran afoul of his military superiors in the 1846 Bear Flag Revolt, Jessie Frémont's loyalty to him was unswerving, and the twenty- three-year-old wife pleaded Frémont's case to no less an audience than President JAMES K. POLK himself. Her support, no less than her father's, sustained Colonel Frémont during his 1847 court-martial.

The explorer's military career seemingly at an end, the Frémonts looked to Las Mariposas, the estate THOMAS O. LARKIN had acquired for them and determined to live in the West. While John Charles Frémont undertook a fourth westward expedition, seeking railroad routes, Jessie Frémont and her daughter traveled to the West by way of the Isthmus of Panama, a grueling experience she wrote of and sold to *Harper's* magazine. In 1849, the Frémonts lived for a time in Monterey and then on their frontier estate. But Jessie Frémont headed east with her husband when he was elected to a term as California's senator in 1850, and from there, they proceeded to Europe, where they sought investors to develop the gold mines on their Western property. Returning to the United States, they were settled in New York City when John Charles Frémont received the 1856 presidential nomination of the new Republican party. Jessie Frémont's official role in the campaign was limited by convention, but her popularity accounted for much of her husband's good showing.

After John Charles Frémont's defeat, the couple returned to California and remained there until the Civil War erupted and he was called to head the Union's Department of the West. Jessie Frémont defended her husband's controversial policies during his short command and again pleaded his case before the president, this time, Abraham Lincoln. But once again, Jessie Frémont's intervention did not save her husband's military career.

Following the war, the Frémonts fell on hard times financially. Jessie Frémont's writings—magazine articles about her travels and her acquaintances with prominent Americans and short stories for children—supported the family through the lean times. The best of the works she collected into four books: *A Year of American Travel* (1878), *Souvenirs of My Time* (1887); *Far-West Sketches* (1890); and *The Will and the Way*

Stories (1891). John Charles Frémont's *Memoirs of My Life* (1887) was largely the work of his wife.

John Charles Frémont's appointment as governor of the Arizona Territory in 1878 sent the family back to the West. Settling in Los Angeles in 1887, Jessie Frémont remained after her husband died in 1890 and moved into a house provided to her by the women of the city upon his death. She continued to write until a fall in 1900 incapacitated her. She died two years later.

—*Patricia Hogan*

SUGGESTED READING:

Herr, Pamela. *Jessie Benton Frémont: A Biography*. New York, 1987.

———, and Mary Lee Spence, eds. *The Letters of Jessie Benton Frémont*. Urbana, Ill., 1993.

FRÉMONT, JOHN CHARLES

Sometimes called "the Pathfinder" or "the West's Greatest Adventurer," John Charles Frémont (1813–1890) traversed more of the American West than any other explorer including MERIWETHER LEWIS and WILLIAM CLARK. Frémont was also a political leader and entrepreneur. Illegitimately born in Savannah, Georgia, to a French Canadian wanderer and a Southern woman of upper-class origins, Frémont entered the College of Charleston where he attracted the attention of Joel Poinsett, ultimately secretary of war. Poinsett secured an appointment for the handsome lad as a teacher of mathematics aboard a navy vessel sailing to South America. Poinsett then secured yet another promotion for Frémont: he became a lieutenant in the CORPS OF TOPOGRAPHICAL ENGINEERS. In 1838, he worked as an assistant engineer on a railroad survey from Charleston, South Carolina, to Cincinnati, Ohio. For the next three years, he assisted the noted French explorer Jean Nicholas Nicolet in the upper Mississippi and Missouri river valleys.

In 1841, Frémont headed an expedition of his own to survey the Des Moines River. On the journey, he showed the first signs of an impetuous nature; he endangered his party and its scientific instruments by insisting on crossing the swollen Platte River in a rubber raft, which capsized. On October 19, 1841, upon his return to St. Louis, he married Jessie Benton, daughter of Senator THOMAS HART BENTON of Missouri. Both men yearned to open up America's western expanses.

In 1842, when migration to Oregon became important nationally, Poinsett sent Frémont on a second venture to survey trails as far west as South Pass in Wyoming. On that occasion, he ascended the highest point in the Wind River Range (13,730 feet), since then

John Charles Frémont. *Courtesy Library of Congress.*

known as Frémont Peak. In 1843, he attempted another survey as far as the mouth of the Columbia River on the Pacific Coast. On that foray, Frémont suddenly decided to go over the Sierra crest from east to west in mid-winter. There were few passes in the snow-covered peaks soaring to 14,000 feet and no maps. Before beginning the ascent, he discarded a heavy howitzer, which he had actually been forbidden to take along. His men suffered terribly in the blinding snow, and when they finally emerged at Sutter's Fort in California, they resembled a band of skeletons. Because several of Frémont's men had disappeared mysteriously, rumors of cannibalism began to circulate.

On another expedition, in 1845, the explorer stood off several hundred Mexican troops on top of Gavilan Peak near Monterey—against the advice of the American consul. On the eve of the UNITED STATES–MEXICAN WAR, Frémont hardly acted as though he were in California, a foreign territory, as the head of a scientific group. His expedition became merged with the Bear Flag Revolt. Once war broke out, he argued with his superior officers over who was the actual conqueror of the province. General STEPHEN WATTS KEARNY ultimately arrested Frémont and marched him to Fort Leavenworth, Kansas. Following a court-martial trial in Washington, D.C., Frémont was discharged from the army. Although President JAMES K. POLK offered him reinstatement, he refused clemency.

In 1848, Frémont headed a fourth expedition, privately financed. Against the advice of local guides, he plunged into the Sangre de Cristo range of southern Colorado and northern New Mexico, again in the middle of winter. This time, he lost a third of his men, and charges of cannibalism again surfaced. Yet, fortune smiled on Frémont. In California, gold was discovered on his Las Mariposas property, and he became an instant millionaire. The Californian legislature also selected him to be the state's first U.S. senator.

In 1853, a fifth and final expedition, which traversed some of the same territory as the fourth one, encountered severe winter weather; it was, therefore, unsuccessful. Three years later, Frémont became the first presidential nominee of the Republican party but was defeated. When the CIVIL WAR broke out, President Abraham Lincoln appointed Frémont one of the four highest ranking generals of the Union Army. As military commander of the Western sector of the war, he again became involved in controversies, one of which centered on his issuing an emancipation proclamation of his own. He was dismissed from command after only a hundred days. Lincoln next posted him to Virginia's Shenandoah Valley command, where he unsuccessfully faced Stonewall Jackson.

Frémont's last years were far less spectacular. Having lost his fortune on speculative railroad and mining ventures, he served as governor of the Arizona Territory from 1878 to 1881. The "Pathfinder" died in near poverty in a New York boarding house, far removed from his wife, Jessie, and their daughter who had settled in Los Angeles.

—*Andrew Rolle*

SEE ALSO: Frémont, Jessie Ann Benton

SUGGESTED READING:

Egan, Ferol. *Frémont, Explorer for a Restless Nation.* New York, 1977.

Goodwin, Cardinal. *John Charles Frémont: An Explanation of His Career.* Palo Alto, Calif., 1930.

Nevins, Allan. *Frémont, Pathmarker of the West.* New York, 1939.

Rolle, Andrew. *John Charles Frémont: Character as Destiny.* Norman, Okla., 1991.

FRENCH, PETER

Oregon cattleman Peter French (1849–1897) was born in Calloway County, Missouri. In 1872, he moved to the Harney River basin of southeastern Oregon. At first, he worked as the manager for the ranch of Californian HUGH JAMES GLENN, and later he became

Glenn's partner. French developed the P Ranch into a model enterprise through the introduction of irrigation and fencing. He became embroiled in disputes over land titles with neighboring homesteaders and was murdered by one of them. French's career shows the influence of California on the livestock-raising industry in Oregon: his capital, his cowboys, and his cattle drives were all imports from California.

—*Gordon B. Dodds*

SEE ALSO: Cattle Industry

SUGGESTED READING:
French, Giles. *Cattle Country of Peter French*. Portland, Oreg., 1972.

FRENCH-MÉTIS PEOPLE

SEE: Métis People

FRONTIER

Frontier Thesis
David M. Wrobel

Comparative Frontier: Canada
Paul Voisey

Comparative Frontier: South Africa
Richard A. Van Orman

FRONTIER THESIS

In the summer of 1893, at the Chicago World's Fair, a young historian from the University of Wisconsin, FREDERICK JACKSON TURNER, delivered a paper that would help change the face of American history. Up to that time, American historians viewed the development of American social and political institutions as a direct outgrowth of European influences. American democracy had evolved from European (more specifically, medieval Teutonic German) "germs" transplanted and literally carried to the "New World." Indeed, Herbert Baxter Adams, one of Turner's teachers at Johns Hopkins University, was one of the chief proponents of the germ theory. According to this theory, there was nothing intrinsically original about American society. Turner's paper, "The Significance of the Frontier in American History," a reaction against the germ theory, was an effort to demonstrate the uniqueness of American development. The essay provided Americans with a distinct history, one that emphasized the Western interior of the continent, not European influences.

In Europe, the word *frontier* was traditionally used to describe a stationary boundary (often a geographic barrier, such as a mountain range) between countries. But in the United States, the term suggested a meeting place between white settlers and native cultures. So, as white Americans moved westward, the frontier also moved; it was a transient process, not a stationary place. Turner viewed the frontier in this way, as a process. He stated in his 1893 essay that "The existence of an area of free land, its continuous recession, and the advance of American settlement westward, explain American development." He saw the frontier as the source of American democracy, individualism, and nationalism. The frontier provided to the American people certain advantages that no longer existed in Europe, where land was expensive and population was high. "So long as free land exists," he declared, "the opportunity for competency exists. . . ." But how exactly did the frontier process work? How did the frontier make Americans more democratic, individualistic, and nationalistic than other people in other countries?

Turner explained that, as white American civilization moved westward, the process of social evolution occurred over and over again as each new frontier was reached. As Americans came into contact with a dangerous frontier wilderness they were transformed by that environment and its inhabitants. Turner noted in one of the more famous passages of his essay: "The wilderness masters the colonist. It finds him a European in dress, industries, tools, modes of travel, and thought. It takes him from the railroad car and puts him in the birch canoe. It strips off the garments of civilization and arrays him in the hunting shirt and the moccasin." Then, as the colonist (or "frontiersman") adjusted to the new environment and transformed it, he became a different person, more rugged, independent, self-reliant, and individualistic.

Furthermore, in that sparsely populated frontier environment, as communities began to form, settlers were directly involved in establishing their governmental structures. This direct involvement in local politics fostered democracy. Also, on the frontier, social ancestry counted for little. People were judged on their individual merits, and not according to their family background, and this helped produce a unique brand of rugged frontier democracy. As for nationalism: those colonists who ventured out onto the frontier were at the forefront of the nation-building process, extending the boundaries of their country, and thus were likely to be more nationalistic than Americans on the East Coast. Indeed, Turner suggested that the frontier—the farthest removed point of white civilization from the

East Coast with all its European influences—was the most American part of America.

On the frontier, Turner added, as waves of new settlers came into contact with the rugged wilderness, they became, quite literally, a new breed of men (Turner said little about women pioneers). The frontier was the place where European immigrants were Americanized and assimilated. It was also the source of distinctly American character traits such as strength, inquisitiveness, practicality, inventiveness, and restlessness. As the frontier moved west and the country became settled, the frontier influences would continue to have a positive effect on the nation as a whole, although Turner was not sure for how long.

These were the benefits of the frontier process according to Turner. The frontier accounted for every benign aspect of the American character and every positive feature of American political institutions. But Turner did also point to certain negative frontier influences. For example, frontier individualism could be selfish, "intolerant of administrative experience and education." Too much individualism hindered the development of a civic spirit, which in turn could lead to political corruption. But Turner's biggest concern was not the negative impact of the frontier (on the whole he viewed it as a tremendously positive force) but its disappearance.

Turner began his essay with a quotation from the census of 1890: "Up to and including 1880 the country had a frontier of settlement, but at present the unsettled area has been so broken into by isolated bodies of settlement that there can hardly be said to be a frontier line." He concluded the essay by declaring that "the frontier has gone, and with its going has closed the first period of American history." So the frontier thesis, while it provided a positive account of America's unique democratic heritage, actually began and ended on a pessimistic note. Now, if the frontier had been the wellspring of so many positive features of American life, then it followed that, in its absence, America would lose those benefits. If the frontier had been the chief force for assimilating immigrants, then how would immigrants be Americanized without it? If the frontier had been the foundation stone of American nationalism, then would the national spirit and national unity crumble once that foundation was removed? If the frontier had sustained and fortified American democracy, then would democracy disappear as the frontier closed? The frontier had quite literally been an antidote to social disease and decay, but now that it was used up, the nation's immune system would deteriorate. Thus Turner's frontier thesis, while in part a glorification of the nation's frontier past, was also an ominous portent of the country's frontierless future.

For generations American thinkers would ponder the dilemma of a frontierless America. In fact, the issue of how a frontier nation could survive without its frontier had been around for quite some time before Turner delivered his famous paper.

Turner's frontier thesis gave academic legitimacy to a set of assumptions that had been present in American thinking for a century. Back in the 1780s, statesmen such as THOMAS JEFFERSON and Benjamin Franklin had pointed to the West as the most American part of America. They believed that the presence of available land guaranteed the nation's democratic future and shielded the "New World" from the social problems that accompanied overpopulation in the "Old World"—Europe. America was a country with few people and a great deal of land; in Europe, the equation was reversed.

In the next century, numerous commentators, such as French observer Alexis De Toqueville, E. L. Godkin, editor of *The Nation,* evangelical missionary Josiah Strong, Social Darwinist William Graham Sumner, Italian economist Achille Loria, and the English Lord James Bryce, pointed to the influence of the frontier of Western lands on American life and character. Indeed, the argument that free or cheap lands helped preserve democracy and economic opportunity was a staple of American thought. By the 1880s, many American thinkers were expressing concern that the supply of Western lands was running out. With the imminent disappearance of the frontier, many wondered whether America could retain its democratic system, Americanize new immigrants, or avoid the class conflict that afflicted Europe. In the crisis-ridden 1890s—a decade marked by economic depression, urban-industrial problems, and rural discontent—some writers suggested that the effects of the frontier's closing were already being felt in America. It was in this climate of concern that Turner formulated his frontier thesis.

Turner drew on the ideas of numerous earlier commentators on the frontier's significance and synthesized them into a full-blown thesis explaining American development. While the frontier thesis was very much a product of its time, it was a radically new approach among American historians. Turner, as one scholar noted, "revolutionized the study of American history." But, contrary to popular assumption, the frontier thesis did not immediately win the attention and approval of historians. However, in a series of subsequent essays appearing in widely distributed magazines such as the *Atlantic Monthly,* in the late 1890s and early 1900s, Turner popularized his ideas. Meanwhile, he was training large numbers of University of Wisconsin graduate students, who would also popularize the frontier thesis. Certainly by the end of the first decade of the twentieth century, Turner's frontier thesis was widely known in academic circles. By that time, he had became president of the American Historical Association (1910) and joined the Harvard University faculty (1910). With the publication of his collection of essays, *The Frontier in American History* (1920), the frontier thesis came to be accepted as the most logical explanation of American development.

In the 1920s, the influence of the frontier thesis could be seen in the publication of works on American literature such as Ralph Rusk's *Literature of the Middle Western Frontier* (1925) and Lucy L. Hazard's *Frontier in American Literature* (1927). Many other books, including Frederick Logan Paxson's *History of the American Frontier, 1763–1893* (1924) and Archer Butler Hulbert's *Frontiers: The Genius of American Nationality* (1929), further popularized the frontier thesis. However, by this time, some of the early criticisms of the frontier thesis were also beginning to appear. Some historians stressed the influence of other factors—such as the city, industrialization, and immigration—on America's institutions and character, rather than the frontier. Around the same time that these early criticisms of the frontier thesis appeared, some writers were reassessing the frontier's influence. Social critics such as Waldo Frank, Van Wyck Brooks, John Dewey, and Lewis Mumford argued (as Turner had, though to a much lesser degree, in his 1893 essay) that the frontier was an antisocial force, that unrestrained frontier individualism was dangerous, and that America had failed to develop artistic and literary genius comparable to Europe's because the frontier was an anti-intellectual force.

By the time of Turner's death in 1932, the thesis was being used to justify government efforts to provide relief from the Great Depression. New Deal spokesmen, including President Franklin D. Roosevelt, argued that America's physical frontier had once acted as a safety valve for the poor and discontented. According to the SAFETY-VALVE THEORY (which, incidentally, Turner did not place much emphasis on in the 1893 essay), Eastern laborers could make a fresh start as farmers on Western lands and leave their economic troubles behind them. Arguing that the safety valve of opportunity had shut down when the frontier closed, New Dealers proposed that the government would have to replace it with direct assistance to the needy. In short, the government would have to provide a safety net because there was no longer a safety valve. Critics of the New Deal claimed that there was still a great deal of opportunity left in America, that new frontiers of business enterprise were always open to those who had the necessary individualistic pioneer spirit. However, former president HERBERT HOOVER declared, the government was killing that self-reliant frontier spirit by providing assistance to people who ought to be taking care of themselves.

While the frontier theme became an important part of the debates over government policy in the 1930s, scholars mounted a strong assault on the validity of Turner's frontier thesis. Turner's essay, which stressed agrarianism and rugged individualism, seemed for scholars to have less relevance for explaining an urban-industrial society in the midst of economic catastrophe and in desperate need of cooperation to survive.

Criticisms were many and varied. Some scholars pointed to Turner's loose definition of *frontier*. In "The Significance of the Frontier in American History," Turner described the frontier variously as "the hither edge of free land," "the meeting point between savagery and civilization," and "the margin of that settlement which has a density of two or more to the square mile." Critics wondered how a thesis could be convincing when its key element was not clearly defined.

Other historians and social scientists questioned the validity of the thesis itself. How, they asked, did the frontier create democracy if settlers on the frontier established political systems based on those in the East? How did the frontier nurture individualism when settlers moved in groups for the purpose of building communities and better defending themselves? How could the frontier have promoted nationalism when there was no real evidence that Westerners were any more nationalistic than their Eastern counterparts. Others argued that a single geographic factor such as the frontier was insufficient for explaining the complexities of American development. Still others reacted negatively to the frontier thesis because it stressed American uniqueness, or exceptionalism, when what the world needed (in light of the rise of fascism in Germany and in Italy) was an emphasis on the essential unity among peoples, not their national differences.

Ironically, perhaps, one of the largest piles of scholarship on the frontier thesis centered on the notion of the frontier as a safety valve for urban discontent—a factor that Turner had not heavily emphasized in his 1893 essay, but one that his students defended vigorously. Critics argued that poor Eastern laborers could not have afforded to fund the cost of a move to the frontier to take up Western lands. Defenders of the thesis argued that even if the frontier had not acted as a direct safety valve, it did work in a more indirect way by providing opportunities for Eastern farmers and immigrants who might have moved to the cities, swelling the labor supply and reducing wages.

While Turner's fortunes and those of the frontier thesis have periodically risen and fallen in the last half century, since the mid-1960s scholars have been particularly critical of the thesis. This criticism centers as much on what the thesis failed to include as it does on the actual content of the thesis. While in many ways an academic innovator, Turner was also very much a product of his time. His thesis chronicled the triumphant march of white European men across the continent. Turner paid little attention to the role of women in settling the frontier. Furthermore, he presented Native Americans as merely an impediment to the advance of the white frontier and as a foil for frontiersmen, who would adopt the useful aspects of native cultures and ignore, discard, or destroy the rest. When Turner spoke of the frontier as the "meeting point between savagery and civilization," there was no mistaking who he thought to be the savages. Turner's explanation for American development fit the mood of an expanding nation that rarely questioned the absolute superiority of white Anglo-Saxons. But such an account was less acceptable in the increasingly liberal and socially concerned climate of the 1960s. And since the 1960s, as scholars have devoted more attention to the history of women, Native Americans, other peoples of color, and the environment, the frontier thesis has increasingly come to be seen as old-fashioned, and Euro-centric.

In the 1980s and 1990s, Turner's essay became the target of particularly spirited attacks from a new generation of Western historians who view it as a narrow, Euro-centric justification for the conquest of peoples of color and the despoliation of the environment. Leading the most recent charge of the new Western historians against the frontier thesis are Donald Worster, Patricia Nelson Limerick, and Richard White. In *Rivers of Empire* (1985), Donald Worster argues that Turner's thesis, while it may have applied to the old Northwest, is not helpful for explaining conditions in the trans-Mississippi West. Worster contends that the key feature of the Far West is aridity, the result of a comparative lack of rainfall. This aridity (or better semi-aridity), which affects much of the West, means that control of the inadequate water supply is tremendously important. For Worster, it is the struggle for control of Western water resources, not the mythic frontier of Turner, that explains the development of the West.

Perhaps the most influential of the recent attacks on the frontier thesis is Limerick's *Legacy of Conquest: The Unbroken Past of the American West* (1987). Limerick argues that Turner's colorful, romantic thesis has obscured the darker realities of the settlement of the West—the exploitation of labor, women, peoples of color, and the environment. Limerick warns that Turner's emphasis on the closing of the frontier in 1890 brings Western history to a close before the twentieth century even began. She emphasizes the West as a distinct geographically bounded region—a place—not a frontier process, and focuses attention on the twentieth-century history of that region.

Richard White's recent textbook, *"It's Your Misfortune and None of My Own": A New History of the American West* (1991), deemphasizes Turner and the frontier thesis by not mentioning either. By ignoring both author and essay, White, like Limerick and Worster, emphasizes the West as a place on the map, not a moving frontier line. White's book serves as a counterpoint to the late RAY ALLEN BILLINGTON's famous text, *Westward Expansion: A History of the American Frontier* (first published in 1949, and most recently in 1982). Billington's text was the most important and influential of the many books inspired by the frontier thesis. In fact, Billington was Turner's most vocal defender in the 1960s and 1970s. Consequently, recent critics of the frontier thesis have been as critical of Billington as they have of Turner. They view *Westward Expansion* as a shamelessly romanticized and triumphal version of a shamefully tragic story.

The NEW WESTERN HISTORY is clearly in the ascendancy a century after Turner first delivered his paper. Turner's frontier thesis has few defenders and no longer serves as the theoretical framework for studies of the West. Still, praised or damned, defended of attacked, the thesis seems to have a hold on the imaginations of many Americans. While the frontier concept has become something of a cliché, its symbolic power is still strong. The term *new frontiers* is used to promote new products, new technologies, and new ways of thinking and has become common parlance in the United States. Turner's theory may no longer be convincing, but some Western historians still find it necessary to attack Turner's thesis—as the worst kind of late nineteenth-century, Euro-centric, "male-centric," anti-environmental, anti-Indian propaganda—before launching into their un-Turnerian accounts of the Western past. The frontier thesis still serves as a guidepost of sorts, marking the path that Western historians now generally avoid traveling down. Turner's ghost still haunts the field of Western history and national history, where textbook coverage of the West still often ends at 1890 (with the supposed closing of the frontier). In retrospect, Turner's short essay (roughly thirty pages) has had a remarkable history.

—David Wrobel

SUGGESTED READING:

Billington, Ray Allen. *America's Frontier Heritage.* New York, 1966.

———. *The Frontier Thesis: Valid Interpretation of American History?* New York, 1966.

———. *Westward Expansion: A History of the American Frontier,* 1st ed. New York, 1949. Later editions, 1960,

1967, 1974, with James Blaine Hedges, and 1982, with Martin Ridge.

Carpenter, Ronald H. *The Eloquence of Frederick Jackson Turner.* San Marino, Calif., 1983.

Cronon, William. "Revisiting the Vanishing Frontier: The Legacy of Frederick Jackson Turner." *Western Historical Quarterly* 18 (1987): 157–176.

Faragher, John Mack, ed. *Rereading Frederick Jackson Turner: "The Significance of the Frontier in American History" and Other Essays.* New York, 1994.

Grossman, James R., ed. *The Frontier in American Culture: Essays by Richard White and Patricia Nelson Limerick.* Berkeley, Calif., 1994.

Jacobs, Wilbur. *On Turner's Trail: 100 Years of Writing Western History.* Lawrence, Kans., 1994.

Jones, Mary Ellen, ed. *The American Frontier: Opposing Viewpoints.* San Diego, Calif., 1994.

Limerick, Patricia Nelson. "Turnerians All: The Dream of Helpful History in an Intelligible World." *American Historical Review* 100 (1995): 697–716.

Nash, Gerald. *Creating the West: Historical Interpretations, 1890–1990.* Albuquerque, N. Mex., 1991.

Ridge, Martin, ed. *History, Frontier, and Section: Three Essays by Frederick Jackson Turner.* Albuquerque, N. Mex., 1993.

Smith, Henry Nash. *Virgin Land: The American West as Symbol and Myth.* Cambridge Mass., 1950. Reprint. 1978.

Taylor, George Rogers, ed. *The Turner Thesis: Concerning the Role of the Frontier in American History.* 3d ed. Lexington, Mass., 1972.

Turner, Frederick Jackson. *The Frontier in American History.* New York, 1920.

Wrobel, David M. *The End of American Exceptionalism: Frontier Anxiety from the Old West to the New Deal.* Lawrence, Kans., 1993.

COMPARATIVE FRONTIER: CANADA

FREDERICK JACKSON TURNER's famous frontier thesis has never enjoyed much scholarly or popular acceptance in Canada. Indeed, the thesis has rarely received serious debate. In the nineteenth century, educated Canadians believed that cultural heritage shaped new societies in the North American wilderness. This view offered a ready explanation for differences between English Canada and French Canada at a time when cultural conflict preoccupied the nation. By emphasizing English Canada's British character, the cultural heritage thesis also provided English Canadians with a powerful sense of identity that distinguished them from the disloyal republicans to the south. The frontier thesis, therefore, received nearly no comment regarding its applicability to Canada in the quarter-century following its appearance.

Difficulties with Britain regarding Canada's autonomy during and after World War I led some schol-

ars to become disillusioned with the British connection, and wartime cooperation between Canada and United States encouraged a continental interpretation of the nation's history. Some prominent historians flirted with the frontier thesis to explain North American similarities and to mark off differences between Canada and the Old World. A. L. Burt, for example, argued that New France had became less feudal in character and more egalitarian and socially mobile as a result of the frontier experience. Critics, however, pointed out that in spite of tremendous exposure to the wilderness, New France failed to develop a democratic society; its government and other institutions clearly resembled those of prerevolutionary France. Arthur Lower speculated that the frontier might encourage greater democracy, but only if the founding culture already possessed democratic tendencies. Thus even among those willing to consider frontierism, cultural heritage still played a commanding role.

Other historians argued that the wilderness experience of Canada and the United States differed significantly. Most importantly, Canada lacked an extensive agricultural frontier. The population of the rocky Atlantic region remained on the coastline and looked to the sea for its livelihood. Elsewhere—in the glacial-scared Laurentian Shield, the frozen North, and the mountainous West—the fur trade assumed overwhelming importance. In contrast to the United States, where agrarian frontiersmen relentlessly pushed inland and battled Indians for control of the land, Canadian frontiersmen entered into a cooperative partnership with native peoples. By the late nineteenth century, when other resources in the vast, infertile regions of Canada commanded attention, corporate interests brought company towns and class divisions to the new mines, forest industries, and hydro-electrical sites—a far different frontier experience from the one Turner described.

In all of Canada, only two regions offered significant blocks of arable land that attracted large-scale agricultural settlement: southern Ontario and the Prairie West. Although both regions offered abundant parallels with adjacent American frontiers, historians rarely described their development in terms of the frontier thesis. In most accounts, the key to understanding early Ontario lay in its Loyalist origins and the stable, conservative society it produced. The stubborn defense against American invaders in the War of 1812 bolstered the British connection, as did massive immigration from Britain in the decades after the war. Accounts of the Prairie West stressed the orderly character of agrarian settlement by a peaceful, law-abiding people quite unlike those who populated America's "Wild West." In these regional histories, scholars overlooked many similarities with adjacent American frontiers and exaggerated differences.

Even so, the frontier thesis served one critical purpose; it became a useful ally in the ongoing quest for a national identity. Canadian historians often conceded that the theory had validity for the United States. Indeed, long after the Turner thesis came under attack in the United States, Canadian scholars found it convenient to believe that it remained acceptable and applicable to Americans. Thus, cultural tradition shaped one nation; the frontier, the other.

Environmental interpretations of Canadian development did arise between the world wars but not in the context of the frontier thesis. Instead of focusing on the confrontation of pioneers with empty wilderness, some scholars concentrated on the specific geographical features that continued to shape regional societies long after the pioneering era had passed. These environmental interpretations explained the basis for regional identities and the regional protest movements that erupted in the period between the wars. But an environmental interpretation could also serve historians of nation building. Harold Innis and Donald Creighton noted that water routes tended to run west and east, linking the various physical regions of Canada and providing the basis for a separate economic and national existence from the United States. Such could be seen in the emergence of fur-trading empires in northern Canada, while in more recent times, the building of trans-Canada railways provided modern substitutes for these east-west waterways.

This variant of environmentalism provided Canada with an alternative explanation for national development: metropolitanism. J. M. S. Careless, who refined the concept in the 1950s, described it as the ability of a city of outstanding size to influence not only its own immediate countryside but other cities and their countrysides as well. Instead of an egalitarian frontier revitalizing and reshaping the east, the metropolis devised elaborate economic and political networks that extended into the frontier and exerted control over it. Thus the mercantile and colonial policies emanating from Paris, and then London, explained the development of early Atlantic and Central Canada. During the nineteenth century, Canadian metropolitan centers, led first by Montreal, and later joined by upstart Toronto, shaped much of the nation's internal development. In developing the Prairie West, for example, the metropolitan centers' corporate and political interests made provisions for the acquisition of territory, for land policy, for railway development, for government, and for law and order, long in advance of actual settlement. Agrarian protests that first arose in early Ontario and again during the settlement of the Prairie West were not seen as the democratic impulses of egalitarian frontiersmen, but rather as revolts against Eastern metropolitan power—revolts fostered as much by emerging regional metropolitan centers as by farmers. Ironically, however, by using metropolitanism to discredit the frontier thesis, historians also conceded the importance of the frontier as a field for metropolitan exploitation.

As metropolitanism became increasingly fashionable after World War II, historians exerted less energy attacking the frontier thesis. Instead, they simply ignored it. The postwar scholar most influenced by Turner, S. D. Clark, was a sociologist by training, and historians criticized his work as much for disciplinary and methodological reasons as for his infatuation with frontierism. During and after the late 1960s, Canadian historians grew less interested in questions about the nature of new societies generally. Attention focused almost wholly on postsettlement society, and class, ethnicity, and gender became the focal points for analysis.

—*Paul Voisey*

SUGGESTED READING:

Berger, Carl. *The Writing of Canadian History: Aspects of English-Canadian Historical Writing, 1900 to 1970.* Toronto, Ont., 1976.

Careless, J. M. S. "Frontierism, Metropolitanism, and Canadian History." *Canadian Historical Review* 35 (1954): 1–21.

Cross, Michael S., ed. *The Frontier Thesis and the Canadas: The Debate on the Impact of the Canadian Environment.* Toronto, Ont., 1970

Voisey, Paul. *Vulcan: The Making of a Prairie Community.* Toronto, Ont., 1988.

COMPARATIVE FRONTIER: SOUTH AFRICA

Although the South African frontier was a unique experience, there are several comparisons that may be made to the American frontier. The frontier period in South Africa lasted from 1652 to 1898. Those 250 years can be summed up as European expansion concluding with native African defeat and retreat.

This tragic story can be divided into four periods. The first began with the arrival of the Dutch at the Cape of Good Hope in the 1650s and ends in the 1720s as the settlers moved farther inland. Wars with Africans over land and cattle led to Dutch victories and the disintegration of African society.

The second phase began in the early 1700s and continued for a century. During those years, the *trekboers* advanced to the north and east. The European military gained many successes at the expense of the native Africans—successes created by superior firepower, native disunity, and smallpox. By 1806, the

British became involved in the South African frontier by taking the Cape of Good Hope from the Dutch.

The third stage of South African frontier was initiated by the Great Trek of the 1830s and lasted into the 1860s, when mineral discoveries changed the face of South Africa. The rise of the Zulus under Shaka led to wars and tribal dislocations, known as *Mfecane,* among the Africans. Taking advantage of that upheaval, thousands of *voortrekkers* migrated into Natal and used commando units to defeat ten thousand Zulus at Blood River in 1838.

The final phase of the South African frontier began with the discoveries of diamonds and gold and closed at the turn of the century with the last wars. As South Africa began to modernize, British forces defeated the Zulus and Xhosas and, finally, in 1898, the Vendas.

The frontiers of South Africa and America were similar in several ways. Both began within a few decades of each other—South Africa's in the 1650s and America's at Jamestown and Plymouth Colony, in 1607 and 1620. The closing of the frontiers in South Africa and America occurred at about the same time: 1898 in South Africa, and 1890 in America.

Deserts, mountains, and the lack of rainfall often impeded settlement on the South African and American frontiers. Both countries were rich in animal life and experienced important mining booms. Both frontier experiences are considered critical in creating myths and legends that help define their nations.

Contrasts between the frontiers should also be noted. In the United States, the defeat of the native population led to the exclusion of Native Americans from society as a whole. In South Africa, the natives were incorporated into the nation's economic life as a cheap and plentiful labor force.

Another contrast was the great effect that disease had on the native populations. Native Americans suffered tremendous losses due to disease, and by 1900, many tribes had been totally annihilated. In Africa, except for a few tribes, disease played a less disastrous role.

When the first settlers arrived, there were roughly the same number of native inhabitants in both nations—about four million. By 1900, there was a huge disparity. The Native American population was less than 250,000—less that 1 percent of the total U.S. population. In South Africa, the native Africans numbered close to six million in 1900, or 80 percent of the total population.

Finally, as the frontiers closed, there was another important distinction. Although both frontiers had been started and fueled by the expansion of European capitalism, South Africa had not really merged into the world market. The United States had not only merged but would soon be the center of the global market.

—*Richard A. Van Orman*

Suggested reading:

Lamar, Howard, and Leonard Thompson, eds. *The Frontier in History: North America and Southern Africa Compared.* New Haven, Conn., 1981.

Thompson, Leonard. *A History of South Africa.* New Haven, Conn., 1990.

Walker, Eric A. *The Frontier Tradition in South Africa.* London, 1930.

FRUIT AND VEGETABLE GROWING

In the late nineteenth century, California's entrance in large-scale commercial fruit and vegetable farming was predicated on the establishment of a national market and on the development of refrigerated railroad cars. The two factors, of course, were related. The bountiful yields of California's orchards and fields were more than a local market could consume. Thus the rapid transportation of oranges, apples, pears, and other perishable fruits and vegetables to Midwestern and Eastern dining tables enabled California growers to reach consumers beyond their local fruit stands and grocers. Although California took an early lead and soon dominated the production of fruits and vegetables, other states in the West contributed substantially to the nation's food supply. All told, the Southwest, barely significant in national fruit and vegetable markets in 1900, was responsible for 40 percent of the country's output by 1929.

The native peoples of the West and especially of California had found an abundance of wild fruits, berries, and nuts, which gave variety to their diets. In the eighteenth century, Spanish missionaries introduced some Mediterranean fruits to the region and developed healthy orchards of citrus fruits. These orchards satisfied local markets throughout the nineteenth century.

When IRRIGATION improved the productive yield of California lands, it seemed that the state had at least some acreage combining climate and topography suitable for growing every edible product imaginable. On the coast, in the inland valleys, and atop the foothills, fruits of all kinds flourished: apples, pears, cherries, plums, apricots, prunes, olives, walnuts, almonds, peaches, raisins, figs, melons, dates, and, of course, grapes for the wine cask and for the dining table.

Vegetable growing in California owes its commercial success in part to the Chinese and Japanese immigrants of the late nineteenth and early twentieth centuries. These immigrants specialized in truck farming on small family plots and catered, at first, to urban markets in San Francisco and northern California. By the 1920s, California produced a large share of the nations' supplies of celery, beans, artichokes, lettuce, carrots, asparagus, cauliflower, tomatoes, potatoes, spinach, cucumbers, pumpkins, cabbage, peppers, and eggplants. By 1937, the dollar value of its field crops was greater than that of any other state in the nation.

California's immense farms required a huge labor force, and, migrant laborers, many of whom were Mexicans and Mexican Americans, toiled in the fields and orchards and worked long hours in intense desert heat for scant wages, decent living conditions, or job security. Even as California's "factories in the fields" thrived, the workers on whom they depended became resentful of their working conditions. Strikes in the 1920s and 1930s, and more successful labor activities in the 1960s under the leadership of Cesar Chávez, stirred the public conscience and improved, to some extent, the working conditions of farm laborers.

—*Patricia Hogan*

SUGGESTED READING:

McWilliams, Carey. *Factories in the Field: The Story of Migratory Farm Labor in California.* Boston, 1939.

Pisani, Donald J. *From the Family Farm to Agribusiness: The Irrigation Crusade in California and the West, 1850–1931.* Berkeley and Los Angeles, 1984.

Reisler, Mark. *By the Sweat of Their Brow: Mexican Immigrant Labor in the United States, 1900–1940.* Westport, Conn., 1976.

Starr, Kevin. *Inventing the Dream: California through the Progressive Era.* New York, 1985.

FUNG CHING

Shoe manufacturer and San Francisco merchant Fung Ching (1863–1997) lived a short and shady life among the Chinese citizens of San Francisco. Arriving in the city as a teenager, Fung Ching succeeded as the head of the F. C. Peters and Company, a concern that made shoes. The position earned him the sobriquet "Little Pete." As a leading merchant of the city's Chinatown, he garnered influence among its residents and in relation to the Anglos of the city as well. Friendly with city bosses, he was also at ease in the underworld. A five-year prison term when Fung Ching was twenty-four for attempting to corrupt officials investigating a murder barely interrupted his influence in Chinatown.

He died at the hands of assassins five years after being released from prison.

—*Patricia Hogan*

SEE ALSO: Chinatowns; Chinese Americans

FUR TRADE

In early July 1534, sailors from Jacques Cartier's expedition were busy exploring Chaleur Bay in what is now the Canadian province of New Brunswick. These probes were suddenly interrupted when a large number of Indians arrived by canoe, shouted at the sailors, and held up furs on sticks. Cartier later reported that the Indians "bartered all they had to such an extent that they went back naked without anything on them; and they made signs to us that they would return on the morrow with more furs." This first recorded account of the North American fur trade tells us much about what became a powerful force for cultural change and environmental transformation.

Placing value on animals skins and hides and then exchanging these items for other desired objects were habits long before the first European voyages to the New World. Both Native Americans and Europeans prized fur for its functional uses and its ornamental decoration. As European stocks of fur dwindled during the sixteenth century, the desire for fur exceeded the supply.

The Indians at Chaleur Bay made it plain that this was not the first time they had handed over pelts for European goods. For several decades, Breton and Basque fishermen were regulars in those waters. Native people near the Gulf of St. Lawrence knew long before Cartier's arrival that the bearded strangers had a passion for fur, a passion that could provide Indians with the valued products of industrial Europe.

Jacques Cartier's three voyages of discovery to the St. Lawrence (1534, 1535 to 1536, and 1541) did not establish a permanent fur-trade relationship with native people, but his reports did alert fishing captains to what was already maritime wisdom. A summer spent catching cod and whales could involve trading for fur as well. The days of trading at Chaleur Bay revealed how eager native people were to join their European partners in a commercial enterprise. Both parties left the trading ground convinced that they had made the best bargain. Cartier's sailors exchanged what they saw as inexpensive and easily replaced iron and textile goods for valuable furs. Native trappers and traders handed over skins and got in return objects that seemed both exotic and useful. By the end of the sixteenth century,

The fur trade in the West had its share of legendary figures, one of whom was James Pierson Beckwourth (left), and another, Jedediah Strong Smith (right). *Beckwourth image, courtesy Colorado Historical Society. Smith image, Kansas State Historical Society.*

the WHALING base at Tadoussac (where the Saguenay River runs into the St. Lawrence) had become the site for a seasonal fur-trade fair.

The Tadoussac fair set a pattern in the fur trade that persisted for most of the history of the business. Native people were the fur hunters and processors. They brought skins to a fixed site or post and exchanged them for European goods. What had begun in the early 1500s as an enterprise for cod and whale now branched out to include fur. The trading bond was made. It would endure for more than three and a half centuries and, in the process, shape much of the history of North America.

The coastal and seasonal fur trade of the St. Lawrence expanded dramatically in the first years of the seventeenth century with the arrival of Samuel de Champlain. Already an experienced maritime explorer in the West Indies, Champlain came to eastern Canada in 1603 with several goals in mind: colonization, fishing, and the fur trade. In 1608, he established a modest fur-trading station at what is now Quebec. He evidently hoped that its location higher up the river would make it more attractive than Tadoussac. He expected fleets

of canoes to bring stacks of pelts to Quebec at his command, but when those fleets did not arrive, he made two decisions that greatly extended the reach of the French-Indian trading system. First, he traveled out of Quebec directly to native villages. Between 1609 and 1615, Champlain made several such journeys, culminating in an expedition to the Huron villages. The trips expanded Champlain's commercial horizons, but they also embroiled him and future French traders in intense band and tribal rivalries, especially those between the Iroquois and the Hurons. Champlain's second decision was another acknowledgment that his native partners possessed great power and influence. Among the Hurons and their neighbors, trading routes and relationships were held within family kinship units. Outsiders, whether native or European, simply had no secure place in the trade. Beginning in 1610, Champlain sent young French men to live in Indian villages. Traders like Étienne Brûlé and Nicolas Vignau made the required personal alliances and became successful merchants. But the presence of these French traders in native villages had more than economic significance. Their marriages became the biological and cultural foundation for the MÉTIS PEOPLE, whose ways of life blended Native American and French values and habits.

Despite some interruptions, the trade arrangements fashioned by Champlain and his Indian partners flourished into the 1640s. Champlain understood that the Hurons were the most influential of his partners. Trouble in Huronia could only mean disruption in the entire fur business. In the 1640s, large-scale Iroquois raiding parties burned villages and destroyed both the Huron agricultural economy and the fur-trade system. The raids wiped out Huronia and threatened the very survival of New France. They were also a reminder that the fur trade had become a matter of imperial rivalry as Huron, French, Dutch, and Iroquois traders all sought to monopolize nature for profit.

The fall of Huronia forced French traders to extend their operations into the Great Lakes. The French enjoyed several advantages denied to their Dutch and English rivals—advantages that eventually made possible a vast French trading empire. Entering North America via the St. Lawrence, the French had access to much of the continent by means of interconnected lakes and rivers, which took French traders to the edge of the Rockies and down the Mississippi to the Gulf of Mexico. Birch-bark canoes, the product of inspired Indian technology, gave the French the means to travel these waterways and to carry trade goods and furs over long distances. Finally, New France had a resident population of experienced traders and canoemen. The voyageurs were especially important as the trade moved into and beyond the Great Lakes.

From the 1660s to the 1760s, French traders spread the commercial and imperial power of New France across the middle third of the continent. In the 1670s and 1680s, LOUIS JOLIET, Father JACQUES MARQUETTE, and SIEUR DE LASALLE carried French influence down the Mississippi and into the Gulf of Mexico. At the same time, other trader-explorers established a ring of posts around Lake Superior. Each of these posts drew more native people into the French commercial sphere. French policy-makers supported the fur trade even when it lost money, because as conflicts with the English colonies in America intensified, the fur trade was an effective strategy to acquire and secure native allies.

By the beginning of the eighteenth century, French traders moved beyond Lake Superior to the western country, the land called the *pays d'en haut*. Shut out from Hudson Bay by the Treaty of Utrecht (1713), French traders looked for routes and potential Indian partners west toward Lake Winnipeg. A key figure in that expansion was the commandant of the *postes du nord*, Pierre Gaultier de Varennes, Sieur de La Vérendrye. In the early 1730s, Vérendrye and his sons

established important trading centers at the Lake of the Woods, on the Red River of the North, and at Fort La Reine on the Assiniboine River. Vérendrye led an expedition into present-day North Dakota in 1738. His sons Louis-Joseph and François made an even more ambitious reconnaissance in 1742 and 1743, swinging west into present-day Wyoming.

By the 1750s, the French fur-trade empire had a geographic and commercial reach almost beyond any rival. In 1760, however, France's empire in Canada collapsed with the English conquest of Quebec. The fur trade had played a relatively minor role in the pre-1760 English colonial empire. Farming, not fur, was the economic mainstay. Before the fall of New France, sustained English fur-trade activity was limited to the western frontiers and Hudson Bay.

The creation of the HUDSON'S BAY COMPANY proved to have enduring consequences not only for the fur trade but for the political destiny of all North America. In 1659 and 1660, a century before the conquest of New France, two French traders (Pierre Radisson and Medart Chouart, Sieur de Groseilliers) made a trading journey into present-day Minnesota. After seeing the bundles of fur carried by Cree traders heading for the Great Lakes, Radisson and Groseilliers realized that a route using Hudson Bay would be swifter and more economical. When French officials showed little interest, the traders sold their idea to a group of English investors. In 1668, Groseilliers and the ship *Nonsuch* wintered over at James Bay (at the southern edge of Hudson Bay) and traded for a large store of fur. This successful voyage launched the Hudson's Bay Company, chartered in 1670.

Over the span of nearly two hundred years, the Hudson's Bay Company became the dominant force in the northern fur trade. Its trading strategy, at least in its first century, was essentially the time-tested French approach. The company built a series of trading posts or factories from James Bay around the western edge of Hudson Bay. The posts were supplied each season by company-owned ships from England. Indian trappers brought furs to the posts and exchanged them for a wide variety of European goods. While the company was committed to its fixed-post strategy before 1800, trading journeys to Indians not yet part of the exchange system were not ruled out.

As the Hudson's Bay Company expanded west and south in the 1770s, it was challenged by a new group of remarkably aggressive traders. After 1760 and the fall of New France, dozens of independent traders moved into the Great Lakes to take the places once held by the French. Alexander Henry the Elder, PETER POND, and Thomas and Joseph Frobisher all quickly established themselves in the business. These "peddlers from Quebec," as they were sometimes called, used both fixed posts and long trading journeys. Excluded from any Hudson Bay supply routes, the peddlers established a major post at Grand Portage on the western end of Lake Superior. Peter Pond, perhaps the most daring of these traders, pushed into the fur-rich Athabasca country in 1778 and 1779. The loose financial ties between these traders and their Montreal and London suppliers were formalized as the North West Company in 1779. Until it merged with the Hudson's Bay Company in 1821, the North West Company was Canada's most expansionist-minded fur enterprise.

At the same time that Canadians were pushing the fur trade into the Northwest, a group of St. Louis entrepreneurs and adventurers put all their efforts on expeditions up the Missouri River. After its founding in 1764, St. Louis became the center for a local fur trade. Powerful merchant families, such as the Chouteaus, carried on an extensive trade with the Osage Indians and other nearby tribes. In 1792, a trading party ventured up the Missouri beyond the Platte to the Mandan villages. Jacques d'Eglise made the first recorded trade connection between St. Louis and the northern Great Plains. The following year, entrepreneur Jacques Clamorgan founded the Missouri Fur Company. Clamorgan fashioned a compelling trade strategy—one that envisioned the Missouri River as part of the NORTHWEST PASSAGE to the Pacific.

The fur business was already part of life in much of the American West before THOMAS JEFFERSON wrote EXPLORATION instructions for MERIWETHER LEWIS in June 1803. But the LEWIS AND CLARK EXPEDITION did change the trade and move it in new directions. When Jefferson directed Lewis and Clark to find a passage for "commerce" between Atlantic and Pacific waters, he had in mind both the fur trade and agriculture. The president knew that redirecting the fur trade away from Canadian posts and into American hands was an essential part of an expanding federal empire in the West. Lewis and Clark were not traders, but they did pay special attention to trading possibilities. They noted which Indian tribes might be good customers; they surveyed sites for future posts; and they carefully recorded the presence and location of fur-bearing animals.

Lewis and Clark returned to St. Louis in 1806 with vital information—something more valuable than stacks of pelts. The first to act on that new geographic and economic knowledge was MANUEL LISA, St. Louis's most competitive fur entrepreneur. After failing to gain a place in the Santa Fe trade, Lisa aimed at the upper Missouri and beyond. Joined by a number of influential St. Louis citizens including WILLIAM CLARK, Pierre Chouteau, Sr., and Sylvestre Labbadie, Lisa founded

the St. Louis MISSOURI FUR COMPANY in 1809. Company employees included Lewis and Clark veterans George Drouillard, John Potts, and JOHN COLTER. Lisa's trade strategy used both fixed posts and trapping journeys, but his ambitious plans were disrupted by the WAR OF 1812.

Lisa was not the only fur promoter inspired by recent explorations. JOHN JACOB ASTOR, a New York fur broker with grand ambitions, drew on information from Lewis and Clark as well as from Canadian travelers to fashion an impressive transcontinental commercial enterprise. As early as 1808, Astor was thinking about a trade empire that would stretch from the Great Lakes up the Missouri to the Pacific. His plan eventually involved China and Russian Alaska. He understood that the fur business was always more than simple economics; it involved territorial expansion, the creation of national empires. Astor's Pacific Fur Company, founded in 1810, acted not only as a trading concern but also as an agent for American expansion in the Far West.

Astor's plan called for the development of a complex set of transportation routes, some by sea around South America and others across the continent. Between 1810 and 1812, his employees made important journeys of trade and exploration. WILSON PRICE HUNT, Astor's chief field agent, led the second American crossing of the continent in 1810 and 1811. Employees from Astor's ship, the *Tonquin,* completed work on Fort ASTORIA at the mouth of the Columbia in the spring of 1811. While Astor could be a daring imperial strategist, his fur-trading tactics were wholly conventional. Astor's men were traders, not trappers. No matter how carefully prepared, Astor's plans were susceptible to forces and events beyond his control. The loss of several of his ships by storm and Indian attack revealed the dangers of long transportation and communication lines. But it was the War of 1812 that eventually defeated the Pacific Fur Company. Threatened by an attack from British naval forces, Astor's partners at Astoria sold the company to the North West Company in October 1813.

The War of 1812, disruptions in European markets and Atlantic shipping, and the financial chaos produced by the panic of 1819 all deadened the American fur trade. Lisa's death in 1820 robbed the business of an energetic promoter. And Astor showed no interest in the Western section of the trade. In Canada, the Hudson's Bay Company and the North West Company were locked in the final years of bloody and exhausting competition. By the mid-1820s, the trade on the upper Missouri and the northern Great Plains began to revive. The Hudson's Bay Company, now merged with its defeated rival, was stronger than ever.

On the American side of the border, three new companies all sought beaver and Indian trading partners: the French Fur Company, led by St. Louis merchants Pierre Chouteau, Jr., Bartholomew Berthold, and Bernard Pratte, Sr.; the Columbia Fur Company, directed by Canadians KENNETH MCKENZIE and Joseph Renville; and the Henry-Ashley Fur Company, led by ANDREW HENRY, Lisa's former field manager, and WILLIAM HENRY ASHLEY, a St. Louis merchant and would-be politician.

What some scholars call the "Rocky Mountain trapping system" grew out of Ashley's Arikara fiasco. When his traders were ambushed and cut to pieces by the Arikaras in June 1823, Ashley was forced to improvise. Moving away from the Missouri, Ashley sent two hunting and trading parties west. Andrew Henry took one group into the Yellowstone River country, while JEDEDIAH STRONG SMITH led a second expedition into the central Rockies. Driven by necessity, Ashley created a new trading culture. It was a culture in which Indians played, at best, a secondary role. Ashley's trappers were Europeans and Euro-Americans, not Native Americans. His system eventually employed three distinct kinds of trappers—company employees who worked for a salary; skin trappers, a group who worked on a credit basis; and free trappers, self-employed men who sold pelts and bought supplies at each annual RENDEZVOUS. Ashley understood that his trading system required a new kind of supply arrangement, one quite unlike the fixed-post strategy. While trade fairs had been part of the fur business for centuries, Ashley used the idea in a new way. Beginning in 1824, Ashley and his successors organized annual supply caravans bound for rendezvous sites in present-day western Wyoming, eastern Idaho, and northeastern Utah. By 1826, Ashley had made a fortune in the Rocky Mountain fur and supply business. Increasingly interested in politics and knowing that the beaver resource base was sure to decline, Ashley sold out to Jedediah Smith, David Jackson, and William Sublette.

In a fur-boom atmosphere, Smith, Jackson, and Sublette expanded their trapping ranges. Hiring anywhere from 80 to 180 TRAPPERS in a given year, the new partners worked throughout the central Rockies and made moves toward California and the Pacific Northwest. They were not alone in this rapid hunting expansion. Trappers from Taos led by ETIENNE PROVOST and the Hudson's Bay Company SNAKE RIVER brigades commanded by PETER SKENE OGDEN intensified the competition. By 1830, Smith, Jackson, and Sublette knew that time was running out for the Rocky Mountain system. Beaver populations were falling, the prices for trade goods were rising, and silk had become the preferred material for men's hats. That year, the partners sold out to a group calling itself the ROCKY MOUNTAIN FUR COMPANY. The men who made up the company—THOMAS FITZPATRICK, JAMES (JIM) BRIDGER, Milton Sublette, HENRY FRAEB, and Jean Baptiste Gervais—did not lack trapping experience. But the year they formed their company, Astor's AMERICAN FUR COMPANY decided to enter the Rocky Mountain trade. From 1830 to 1834, the Rocky Mountain Fur Company and the American Fur Company waged a trade war that was both commercial and personal. In many ways, it was an unequal contest. Astor's company had all the long-term advantages—substantial financial resources, reliable banking and market connections, and a sound transportation system. The Rocky Mountain Fur Company simply could not survive in such a competitive world. At the 1834 rendezvous, the partners sold out to Astor. From 1834 to 1840, the rendezvous system struggled on toward its final doom. The status of the MOUNTAIN MEN fell with the price of beaver. As fur-trade entrepreneur NATHANIEL JARVIS WYETH put it, the trapper had become "a mere slave to catch Beaver for others."

The North American fur trade did not suddenly end in the late 1830s. The American Fur Company continued in the trade until mid-century, doing more business in bison robes than beaver pelts. To the north, the Hudson's Bay Company remained a potent economic force. But by the 1860s, the fur trade was no longer a human institution capable of shaping the environment of North America as it had in previous centuries.

The consequences of the fur trade far outweighed its economic significance. Along with fish, precious metals, and the quest for the Northwest Passage, fur was one of the central attractions for Europeans coming to North America, and the promise of profit in fur carried Europeans deep into the American interior. For most of its history, the fur trade was an Indian trade. The fur business was one of the principal arenas for encounter between native people and Europeans. That contact had profound and enduring consequences for Native Americans. The fur trade introduced Indians to new objects, the products of industrial Europe. In many cases, items like iron pots, textiles, and firearms replaced traditional goods. While some of these new objects made life more convenient, they also increased dependency on non-Indian suppliers. Because the trade was a feature of global capitalism, Indians became part of a worldwide exchange system. It was a system over which native people had relatively little control. The system brought some material rewards, but it also drew Indians into wars waged by European nations.

Over some three centuries, the fur business became a global enterprise, touching the lives of countless Native Americans, Europeans, and Asians. Unlike farming, mining, or ranching, the fur trade fashioned a complex and often violent set of relationships between three congregations of living beings—Europeans, Native Americans, and fur-bearing animals.

Some of these relationships and consequences were biological. The fur trade was an assault on animals, an assault that served the needs of fashion in clothing and hats. Populations of beaver, muskrat, bison, lynx, marten, and sea otter all declined under the pressure of hunting by both native and European trappers. As animals populations diminished, the numbers of native people also decreased in some areas. The fur trade spread European diseases, not by intention but by contagion. The 1837 Missouri River smallpox epidemic was carried upriver by an American Fur Company steamboat and eventually decimated the Mandan and Hidatsa peoples. But the biological consequences of the fur business were not always so destructive. Personal relationships between male European traders and Native American women—relationships sought by both parties to mutual advantage—created a new people, the Métis.

The fur trade was an encounter of cultures, a human intersection that rearranged many lives. That rearranging can be seen in the wide variety of trade goods suddenly available to native people. The fur business changed travel routes and altered seasonal work for both men and women. In many bands and villages, the fur business commercialized life and changed relationships between men and women. What seemed at first a simple exchange of one part of nature for something made by humans proved in the end a vastly powerful force for change in North America.

—*James P. Ronda*

SEE ALSO: Alaskan Exploration; Beavers; Buffaloes; Chouteau Family; Intermarriage: Marriages between Euro-Americans and Native Americans; Native American Cultures: Disease; Sublette Brothers

SUGGESTED READING:

Gilman, Carolyn. *Where Two Worlds Meet: The Great Lakes Fur Trade.* St. Paul, Minn., 1982.

Innis, Harold A. *The Fur Trade of Canada.* Toronto, Ont., 1956.

Phillips, Paul C. *The Fur Trade.* 2 vols. Norman, Okla., 1961.

Ray, Arthur J. *Indians in the Fur Trade.* Toronto, Ont., 1974.

Rich, E. E. *The Fur Trade and the Northwest to 1857.* Toronto, Ont., 1967.

Swagerty, William R. "Indian Trade in the Trans-Mississippi West to 1870." In *History of Indian-White Relations.* Edited by Wilcomb E. Washburn. Washington, D.C., 1988.

Van Kirk, Sylvia. *Many Tender Ties: Women in Fur-Trade Society, 1670–1870.* Norman, Okla., 1980.

Weber, David J. *The Taos Trappers: The Fur Trade in the Far Southwest, 1540–1846.* Norman, Okla., 1970.

Wishart, David J. *The Fur Trade of the American West, 1807–1840.* Lincoln, Nebr., 1979.

GADSDEN PURCHASE

The Gadsden Purchase, a treaty between Mexico and the United States, ceded to the United States 29,142,400 acres of land within the modern states of Arizona and New Mexico in return for $10 million. A revision of the border agreement following the UNITED STATES–MEXICAN WAR of 1846 to 1848, the Gadsden Purchase provided for the acquisition of Mexican territory south of the Gila River to enable the construction of a railroad line that would connect the East and South to

Gadsden Purchase, 1854.

California. The treaty was one of the relatively few diplomatic successes of President Franklin Pierce's administration.

In the early 1850s, Southerners sought a means to improve communication between the Southern states and the newly acquired Western territories, particularly California. With support from Jefferson Davis, secretary of war, surveyors had determined that the land south of the Gila River would be the best route for a transcontinental railroad. James Gadsden, a native of South Carolina and U.S. ambassador to Mexico, was given the task of negotiating with Mexico to acquire the land.

Taking advantage of the unstable finances of the Mexican government, again under the leadership of ANTONIO LÓPEZ DE SANTA ANNA, Gadsden offered to buy territory. Signed by delegations from the United States and Mexico on December 30, 1853, the treaty faced trouble in the United States because of partisan strife surrounding the KANSAS-NEBRASKA ACT, which terminated the MISSOURI COMPROMISE and allowed residents of each new territory to vote on whether slavery would be allowed within its borders. A slightly revised version of the treaty was approved by the U.S. Senate on April 25, 1854, and President Pierce signed it on June 29, 1854. With the exception of the purchase of Alaska, the Gadsden Purchase was the last major land acquisition by the United States on the North American continent.

—*Patrick H. Butler, III*

SEE ALSO: National Expansion; Transcontinental Railroad Surveys

SUGGESTED READING:

Garber, Paul N. *The Gadsden Treaty*. Philadelphia, 1923.
Horsman, Reginald. *Race and Manifest Destiny*. Cambridge, Mass., 1981.

GALL (SIOUX)

The Hunkpapa Lakota Gall (1840–1895)—also known as Wokoyake Luta Mani, or "Walks in Red Clothing"—took as his principal name Pizi, meaning the "gall of an animal." Born near the Moreau River, Gall stands out among Hunkpapas as a military leader in defense of Lakota land and as a diplomat seeking accommodation to life under federal jurisdiction.

Gall grew up the son of a widowed mother and rose in rank as a military leader. At some 250 pounds, the gregarious, diplomatic Gall was powerful but graceful.

Gall, Hunkpapa Lakota Sioux. Photo by David F. Barry. *Courtesy State Historical Society of North Dakota.*

Among Gall's childhood companions was SITTING BULL. As young adults, both were members of the elite Strong Heart Society of tribal soldiers *(akicita).*

Gall appeared in federal records first for acting in concert with RED CLOUD near Fort Phil Kearny at the FETTERMAN MASSACRE, where CRAZY HORSE was in charge of military operations. In 1856, Gall led an assault on Fort Buford where he was wounded and, for a time, was assumed to be dead. He then joined Red Cloud in resisting the Fort Laramie Treaty of 1868 until all of the U.S. Army FORTS and posts were abandoned on land protected by the previous Fort Laramie Treaty of 1851. While Gall eventually approved the 1868 document, he assumed that non-Indians would withdraw from their stations along the upper Missouri River as well as along the BOZEMAN TRAIL.

Thereafter, he appeared at the Grand River Agency with his band to draw annuity rations and occasionally talked to non-Indian spokesmen. He sternly opposed the sale of the Black Hills and appeared on June 17, 1876, at the Battle of the Rosebud against General GEORGE CROOK, who considered Gall the equal of Crazy Horse as a war leader. Subsequently, during the Little Bighorn battle, Gall was assigned to accompany BLACK MOON in the pursuit of Major Marcus Reno, but Gall either decided to let Reno go or handed off his responsibility to Inkpaduta. After Black Moon was injured, Gall joined Crazy Horse in the attack on GEORGE ARMSTRONG CUSTER. Gall lost two wives and three children during the fight. Most observers perceived Gall as the leader who maintained discipline among Indian forces under fire—through the force of his own example and personality—and who even enjoyed deference from Crow King and Crazy Horse.

In the wake of military victory, Gall led attacks on Colonel Elwell Otis and General NELSON APPLETON MILES during September 1876 before he guided his band into exile in Canada with Sitting Bull.

Early in 1881, Gall and Sitting Bull parted to find their separate ways back to the United States. Gall engaged General Miles on the Poplar River in Montana before he surrendered, moved to Fort Buford, and then settled near the Standing Rock Agency. From then on, he promised to remain at peace with the United States.

At the Standing Rock Agency, JAMES MCLAUGHLIN found in Gall as well as in JOHN GRASS and Crow King his strongest symbols of adjustment to reservation life. Gall engaged in physical labor on a land assignment, hoed potatoes, and put up hay. He became a judge on the Court of Indian Offenses and U.S. (district) farmer. Although, according to McLaughlin, Gall "held to the Indian code" on religion, he also earned a reputation as a "counselor for peace."

With persuasive oration, Gall opposed the sale of additional land on the Great Sioux Reservation in 1888 yet encouraged dialogue with federal spokesmen. He counseled suspicion about the GHOST DANCE as a strategy of resistance and, in the end, accepted the Sioux Agreement of March 2, 1889, which reduced tribal lands from 21.7 million acres to 12.7 million acres, without visible opposition. While he had earned respect as a successful field commander of Lakota and Yanktonai military forces, he later gained recognition among federal officials for his diplomatic leadership and peaceful accommodation to reservation life. Most observers acknowledged that Gall did not possess oratorical ability comparable to that of SPOTTED TAIL, Red Cloud, Sitting Bull, JOHN GRASS, or several other leaders, but under agency jurisdiction, he was as influential as any of them and a favorite among tribal members and non-Indians alike for his courtesy, dignity, and integrity.

—*Herbert T. Hoover*

SEE ALSO: Little Bighorn, Battle of; Native American Peoples: Peoples of the Great Plains

SUGGESTED READING:

Barry, David F. *David F. Barry's Indian Notes on "The Custer Battle."* Edited by Usher L. Burdick. Baltimore, 1937.

Dykshorn, Jan M. "Leaders of the Sioux Indian Nation." *Dakota Highlights* 3 (1975): 1–8.

Fielder, Mildred. *Sioux Indian Leaders.* Seattle, Wash., 1975.

National Archives. Record Group 75, Standing Rock Agency.

Pfaller, Louis L., O.S.B. *James McLaughlin: The Man with an Indian Heart.* New York, 1978.

GALLEGOS, JOSÉ MANUEL

A Catholic priest and the second Hispanic to serve in the United States Congress, José Manuel Gallegos (1815–1875) was born in Abiquiu, New Mexico. He attended the private school of Father ANTONIO JOSÉ MARTÍNEZ in Taos, New Mexico, for a time, and then studied theology at the College of Durango, Mexico. He graduated in 1835 and returned to New Mexico where he entered the priesthood. Stationed initially at the San Juan Pueblo, he was later transferred to Albuquerque.

As his mentor and colleague Martínez had done, Gallegos violated the church's rules on celibacy when he married in 1867. He was subsequently suspended from his priestly duties by Archbishop JEAN BAPTISTE LAMY. Nevertheless, Gallegos remained popular with the Hispanic people. Again, as Martínez had done, Gallegos pursued an active political career while carrying out his duties as a priest. He served in the New Mexico Departmental Assembly from 1843 to 1846, and when New Mexico became part of the United States in 1850, he served in the first New Mexico Territorial Council.

In 1852, Gallegos was elected the New Mexico Territory's delegate to the U.S. Congress, and he served from March 1853 to March 1855. Gallegos thus became the second Hispanic to serve in the U.S. Congress; the first was Joseph Marion Hernandez, the Florida Territory's delegate to Congress in 1822. Although unable to speak English, Gallegos secured a $127,000 appropriation for New Mexico. He was reelected in 1854, but that election was contested by his opponent, MIGUEL ANTONIO OTERO, SR., who had questioned Gallegos's loyalty to the United States in a speech before the House of Representatives. Otero was subsequently seated as New Mexico's delegate.

In 1860 and 1861, Gallegos served as Speaker of the New Mexico House of Representatives. In 1862, he ran again for Congress but was defeated. He ran a third time, in 1870, and was successful. Gallegos was a Hispanic political pathfinder whose trail led to the steps of the U.S. Congress.

—*Maurilio E. Vigil*

Suggested reading:

Chavez, Fray Angelico. *Tres Macho—He Said, Padre Gallegos of Albuquerque, New Mexico's First Congressman.* Santa Fe, N. Mex., 1985.

Vigil, Maurilio E. "Jose Manuel Gallegos." In *Los Patrones: Profiles of Hispanic Political Leaders in New Mexico History.* Edited by Maurilio E. Vigil. Washington, D.C., 1980.

GALVESTON, TEXAS

The island of Galveston was first explored by Europeans as early as 1528. Spanish explorer Álvar Núñez Cabeza de Vaca was washed ashore after a storm wrecked boats of the Pánfilo de Narváez expedition off the coast of the island named, by the Spanish, Malhado, or "Island of Doom." The island first appeared on maps in 1721 when Benard de La Harpe mapped it as a part of an abortive French settlement attempt. In 1785, the bay behind Galveston Island was mapped by José de Evia and named for Count Bernardo de Galvéz, viceroy of Mexico. Stephen Fuller Austin named the island San Luis in 1822, but the name was changed to Galveston by 1833.

A sand barrier on the Gulf Coast of Texas, the island is separated from the mainland by a series of bays on its west side. Settlement by Europeans began in 1816 when Jean Laffitte, fleeing from the United States government and commissioned with a letter of marque by the Mexican rebels, established a base at the site of the future city. Occupation of the island by pirates, French émigrés, and Mexican rebels and their supporters from the United States was sporadic over the next decade.

A fort and refuge for the Texas government during the Texas Revolution, Galveston caught the eye of developers led by Michel Menard and Samuel May Williams, who organized the Galveston City Company and purchased the site of the city at the northeast end of the island from the Texas government in 1838. The site was already a port of entry with more than three thousand inhabitants. The city became a major entrepôt for Texas and quickly developed the civic, cultural, and social institutions of an important center. In 1853, the Buffalo Bayou, Brazos and Colorado Railroad connected the city to the Texas mainland. Mercantile and cotton-trading firms, including those operated by the Ball, Sealy, and Hutchings families, dominated the economic life of the city.

During the Civil War, the city was the site of fighting between Union and Confederate forces in the fall and winter of 1862 and 1863. After the war, the city recovered quickly as new families, particularly the Moodys and Kempners, became active in the cotton-trading, banking, and shipping activities that made the community a center of Texas finance. In 1900, Galveston was probably the wealthiest city in the state.

On September 8, 1900, Galveston was struck by a major hurricane, which tore away parts of the island, flooded the city to a depth of ten feet, and killed more than six thousand people. The storm reshaped Galveston. To protect the city in the future, Galvestonians and the United States Army Corps of Engineers built a massive sea wall, eventually extending nearly ten and a half miles or one-third the length of the island, and raised the grade of land behind it. The impact of the storm on Galveston was lasting. Already facing competition from Houston, which was improving Buffalo Bayou to permit ocean-going ships to by-pass Galveston, the city invested its money in recovery rather than in the new oil fields of East Texas. Houston and Dallas quickly passed Galveston as centers of finance, and the city became a stable community dominated by a few wealthy families. It was a center of gambling and entertainment for the first half of the twentieth century, but eventually, historical tourism became a mainstay of the economy along with the University of Texas Medical Branch and the Port of Galveston.

—*Patrick H. Butler, III*

Galveston, a port of entry for Texas, as it appeared in a nineteenth-century magazine. *Courtesy Patrick H. Butler, III.*

SUGGESTED READING:
McComb, David. *Galveston: A History.* Austin, Tex., 1986.

GAMBLING

Gambling, conjuring fanciful images of river-boat dandies and JAMES BUTLER ("WILD BILL") HICKOK's notorious "Dead Man's Hand," played a major role in popular portrayals of the American "Wild West." Nineteenth-century writers—writers of the caliber of MARK TWAIN and BRET HARTE as well as dime novelists and romanticizers—considered gambling an inextricable part of the Western character. Gambling's deep cultural affinities with the bust-and-boom cycles of an expanding market economy and with the capitalists' psychology of risk and quick profit—a marked trait of America's post–Civil War westward expansion—seem clear; gambling fever followed gold fever just as surely as the professional gamblers followed the Forty-niners. By the twentieth century, Western businessmen, despite a reliance on heavy federal investment in the region, typically prided themselves on their willingness to take chances,

In a 1900 photograph by C. S. Fly, several men engage in a game of faro at the Orient Saloon in Bisbee, Arizona. *Courtesy National Archives.*

on their entrepreneurial spirit; risk-takers in any profession were called "cowboys"; and the West, with its Renos and Las Vegases, was the gambling center of America.

Native Americans were inveterate gamblers. They wagered on a variety of games, some of whose outcomes were matters of skill, stamina, or dexterity, others

Gambling required little in the way of equipment or ambiance. In about 1887, F. A. Ames captured a "poker party" in progress at John Doyle's ranch in Arizona. *Courtesy National Archives.*

that produced winners and losers by chance. Since pre-historic times, they had been throwing dice, two-sided objects with each side painted, carved, or decorated with chips of colored shells. They shook the dice in a basket or bowl, tossed them in the air, and let them fall on blankets or hides. Another virtually universal game resembled button-who's-got-the-button, a hand game in which the opponent guessed the hand holding a small wood button or a shell chip. Indians wagered wildly on the outcome of physical contests, some of them violent enough to resemble battles. Various ball games, archery matches, and foot races—short dashes or miles-long relays—were all highly popular betting events. Bow-and-arrow-shooting contests were less matters of marksmanship than of speed: shooting the arrows straight upward, the winner was he who got the greatest number of arrows in the air at once. With the coming of the Spanish, betting on horse racing and tests of horsemanship became favorite forms of gambling for many tribes.

The Spanish Southwest, like most frontier regions, with their loneliness and boredom, was a haven for gambling. The region's favorite card game was monte, a Mexican invention. In monte, a player tries his luck in matching cards against a dealer. In New Mexico of the 1830s, Santa Fe boasted the area's best-known gambling den, run by Doña Tules Gertrudes Barceló, the high-born mistress of New Mexico's governor and the sharpest card dealer in the province. The Spanish and Mexicans also played *chuza,* a game of chance resembling roulette. In Alta California, fiestas were frequently enlivened by horse races and displays of ranching skills and marksmanship, as well as bullfights and bear baiting, all of which allowed ample opportunities for wagering. Throughout Hispanic America, the poor man's game of choice was the cockfight, which the Spanish turned into a contest of deadly seriousness by introducing spurs to enhance the killing power of the fighting roosters' claws.

In the young republic of the United States, gambling was at first associated most strongly with the plantation South. President ANDREW JACKSON's addiction to horse racing was only the most famous example of the region's obsession with games of chance, perhaps not unrelated to the high-risk economy of the cotton kingdom. Southern gentlemen prided themselves on their ability to lose enormous stakes without flinching, and the heyday of Mississippi River gambling rested on the fat pockets of steamboat-traveling cotton planters. When inflated cotton prices crashed, as they did frequently in the early nineteenth century, more and more Southerners headed west, taking with them their predilection for gambling. New Orleans was the wellspring of Anglo-American gambling, which spread first up the Mississippi, then on into the West. There card games, horse racing, shooting matches, and gambling dens—with their attendant whiskey drinking, hair-trigger violence, and prostitution—grew so ubiquitous that moralists despaired, saying "God will never cross the Mississippi." The California gold rush, cotton's post–Civil War decline, and the rise of the cattle kingdom lured Mississippi Valley gamblers to the West where they hoped to find easy pickings among the miners and cowboys.

Frontier gambling was often as much a confidence game as it was a matter of chance. It was not merely that casino dealers and professional gamblers cheated, which they did to a man and, not infrequently, to a woman; some forms of gambling were hardly games at all, but sleight-of-hand tricks. Three-card monte, developed from the Mexico card game, asked the question: "Which of the three face-down cards is the queen?" The answer was most often none of them, since the dealer palmed the winning card, only to replace it after the player had made the wrong choice. And monte was only one variation of the old shell game, which in the West was sometimes called "soap" or "thimberling." By any name, the shell games allowed con men to bilk drunken and rowdy gamblers of their wages. The legitimate games of chance most frequently associated with Western gambling were faro, poker, blackjack (or twenty-one), and roulette. Faro was a favorite for the speed of its betting; now quite rare, it involved players betting against a dealer about the order in which cards might be dealt. Since American card manufacturers typically printed tigers on the backs of their playing cards, faro was often referred to as "the tiger," and those who played the game were said to be "bucking the tiger." Westerners preferred five-card draw in poker, and at the time, four-kings-and-an-ace was the highest possible hand, not a straight-flush. Shooting craps, a fast-paced dice game based on the French game called "hazard" and played by slaves and black workmen below decks on the Mississippi, also became popular in the West. But Westerners would bet on anything—impromptu horse races, boxing contests, arm-wrestling matches—except, perhaps, whether the sun would rise tomorrow.

During the California gold rush, San Francisco became a gambling center, a rousing town filled with a few prostitutes and fifty thousand mostly young men, virtually all of them heavily armed, hard-drinking, hopeless gamblers. They filled the city's more than five hundred bars and one thousand gambling dens and betting parlors, houses such as the El Dorado where a daily turnover in excess of one hundred thousand dollars was not at all unusual. In San Francisco, Ed Moses placed the largest single faro bet ever made in

America—eighty thousand dollars—in a marathon eight-hour session that left him poorer by some two hundred thousand dollars. Gambling in San Francisco spread well beyond the games mounted by full-time professionals. The town's leading banker, WILLIAM CHAPMAN RALSTON, frequented the gaming tables where he always played for high stakes. Some claim that Nevada's U.S. Senator William Sharon dropped more than $1 million at the Pacific Club during fifteen years of frequent visits.

California's Chinese were also dedicated gamblers. In San Francisco's Chinatown and in those communities scattered throughout the northern California mine fields, they played interminable games of dice and proved extremely fond of dominoes. Chinese casinos offered *pak kop piu*, or "white pigeon ticket," and *fan tan*, a game that seemed so complicated to Anglo-Americans they disparaged the Chinese for playing it. In *fan tan*, the dealer *(tan kun*, or "ruler of spreading out")* grabbed a random number of Chinese brass coins from a large bowl, clapped them down on a table, then quickly covered them with a metal lid. Players tried to guess the remainder of coins, if any, after the rest had been divided into groups of four. White pigeon ticket was named for the bits of paper, five inches square, on which were printed the graphic symbols, or characters, for the first eighty Chinese words in the *Ts'intsz'man*, the *Thousand Character Classic*, a book containing exactly one thousand characters, none the same. Players purchased an eighty-character ticket, checked off ten characters at random, turned the ticket over to an agent, and awaited drawings held twice each day. Thousands of Anglos in San Francisco, as well as the Chinese, daily played the "Chinese lottery." Chinese pool halls, and later Japanese pool halls, seemed almost as ubiquitous as the gambling dens in the city's Asian communities.

San Francisco was not the only town in the West dedicated to gambling, of course. Following the Civil War, gambling towns became legion from the Missouri River to the Pacific Ocean as the railroad spread across the continent and booming CATTLE TOWNS sprang up. And with each new discovery of gold or silver, a mining town dominated by saloons and gambling houses appeared, its principal purpose apparently to fleece free-spending miners. Cowboys and cattle kings gambled in Dodge City, miners and magnates in Denver, and gamblers and prostitutes flocked to them all—Deadwood, Tombstone, Virginia City. When the mines played out or the railheads moved farther west, the customers and the professionals moved on as well, frequently leaving behind a ghost town. By the twentieth century, gambling had become so associated with the American West in the popular imagination that it only seemed natural for Nevada to become the first, and for many years the only, state to legalize gambling (in 1931) after a spate of reform had chased the casinos—and the saloons—south of the border into such cities as Juárez and Tijuana. RENO, NEVADA, was the legal gambling mecca of the modern West before mobster Bugsy Segal began dreaming of transforming a desert G.I. stopover named Las Vegas into a gambler's notion of heaven. After World War II, luxury casinos sprouted along the strip in Las Vegas, and gambling in Nevada blossomed into a billion-dollar industry.

Some historians attribute the important role gambling played in the history of the West to the frontier, to a kind of life in which men of necessity staked their existence on speculative ventures and second chances; others point to the American capitalists' exploitative "creed" in the West—get in, get rich, get out. Certainly many of those traveling to the West, from Spanish conquistador FRANCISCO VÁSQUEZ DE CORONADO to young parking-lot attendants in Hollywood, have dreamed of instant wealth and fame, which has always been primarily a gambler's dream.

—*Charles Phillips*

SEE ALSO: Ghost Towns; Las Vegas, Nevada; Mining: Mining Camps and Towns

SUGGESTED READING:

Chafetz, Henry. *Play the Devil: A History of Gambling in the United States from 1492 to 1955.* New York, 1960.

Culin, Stewart. *The Gambling Games of the Chinese in America.* New York, 1972.

———. *Games of North American Indians.* New York, 1975.

DeArment, Robert K. *Knights of the Green Cloth: The Saga of Frontier Gamblers.* Norman, Okla., 1982.

Findlay, John. *People of Chance: Gambling in American Society from Jamestown to Las Vegas.* New York, 1986.

Marks, Paula Mitchell. *Precious Dust: The American Gold Rush Era, 1848–1900.* New York, 1994.

GANADO MUCHO (NAVAJO)

A Navajo-Hopi tribal leader, Ganado Mucho (1809–1893) was an advocate of peace throughout much of the conflict between the Navajos and the United States from 1846 to the end of the Civil War. Accused of theft because of the size of his herds when the Americans took control of New Mexico, he successfully defended himself. Joining a group of peaceful Navajo leaders in 1858, he signed an agreement aimed at ending the traditional hostility between Navajos and Hispanic New Mexicans. When the failure of the agreement led to Colonel EDWARD RICHARD SPRING CANBY'S effective 1860 campaign against the Navajos, Ganado Mucho was again among those signing the peace accords in 1861. In the Navajo War that broke out during the American Civil War, Ganado Mucho lost two daughters and a son in raids by Utes and New Mexicans. Surrendering after Colonel CHRISTOPHER HOUSTON ("KIT") CARSON's campaign from 1863 to 1866 against the Navajos, Ganado Mucho led his band on the brutal "long march" to Bosque Redondo in New Mexico. Two years later, he and others signed a peace treaty that allowed the Navajos to leave the reservation and return to a Navajo reservation in their traditional homelands. There Ganado Mucho lived until his death at the age of eighty-four.

—*Patricia Hogan*

SEE ALSO: Native American Peoples: Peoples of the Southwest; Navajo Wars

GARLAND, AUGUSTUS HILL

United States Attorney General Augustus Hill Garland (1832–1899) was born in Tipton County, Tennessee, and grew up in Washington, Hempstead County, Arkansas. After private schooling, he graduated from St. Joseph's College in Bardstown, Kentucky. He studied law with his stepfather, Judge Thomas Hubbard, and practiced in Little Rock until elected to the secession convention in 1861. Joining the Confederate Congress in the same year, he became a senator in 1864.

Immediately after the Civil War, Garland was denied the right to practice law, despite a presidential pardon. Arkansans elected him U.S. senator in 1867, but the Senate refused to seat him because Arkansas was an "un-Reconstructed" former Confederate state. He resumed his law practice until elected governor in 1874. He was again elected to the Senate in 1877, was seated, and served until 1885. He became attorney general in the Cleveland administration. When it was discovered that he was financially connected with the Pan-Electric Telephone Company, which was challenging Alexander Graham Bell's telephone patents, the conflict of interest kept him from attaining a seat on the Supreme Court. He died while arguing a case before the court.

—*Michael B. Dougan*

SUGGESTED READING:
Ashmore, Harry S. *Arkansas: A History.* New York, 1984.
Newberry, Farrar. *A Life of Mr. Garland of Arkansas.* N.p., 1908.

GARLAND, HAMLIN

An American writer credited with destroying the myth of rural life as a pastoral utopia, Hamlin Garland (1860–1940) is remembered today primarily for his association with the movement of literary realism in the late nineteenth and early twentieth centuries and for his stories of the grinding lives of farmers and their families on the prairies of the northern Midwest. He called his brand of realism "veritism."

Born on a farm near West Salem, Wisconsin, Garland grew up on farms in Iowa and South Dakota. His career fell into three distinct parts: a writer of realistic stories about small farms in the upper Midwest and crusader for literary realism; a writer of popular Western romances set in the Rocky Mountains; and finally an autobiographer. Today his most important work is generally thought to have taken place during his early years when he wrote *Main-Travelled Roads* (1891), a collection of stories often considered to be one of the most important works of the late nineteenth century, and *Prairie Folks* (1893). During the 1890s, Garland was closely associated with William Dean Howells in the battle over literary realism; Garland's "veritism" was a more personal and impressionistic form of Howell's "objective" realism. Garland also achieved a reputation as a reform journalist during this period.

After 1895, Garland wrote a number of popular romances set in the Rocky Mountains and then, in his later years, turned to autobiography. The best of his autobiographical writings is *A Son of the Middle Border* (1917)—a volume of significant historical value that covers Garland's first thirty-four years. The sequel to that book, *A Daughter of the Middle Border* (1921), ostensibly tells the stories of his wife and mother but is actually the continuation of Garland's autobiography to about 1919. Garland won the Pulitzer Prize for biography with the latter book in 1922.

—*Larry Hartsfield*

SUGGESTED READING:
Garland, Hamlin. *Crumbling Idols: Twelve Essays on Art Dealing Chiefly with Literature, Painting and the Drama.* Chicago, 1894.
———. *A Daughter of the Middle Border.* New York, 1921.
———. *Main-Travelled Roads.* Boston, 1891.
———. *Prairie Folks.* Chicago, 1893.
———. *Rose of Dutcher's Coolly.* Chicago, 1895.
———. *A Son of the Middle Border.* New York, 1917.

GARNER, JOHN NANCE

Democratic politician, Speaker of the House, and U.S. Vice-president John Nance Garner (1868–1967) was born in Red River County, Texas. He served as county judge in Uvalde, as a state legislator for two terms, as a member of the U.S. House of Representatives from 1903 to 1933, and as vice-president of the United States from 1933 to 1941. While in Congress, he served as party whip and, in 1931, was elected Speaker of the House.

Garner joined the Populist wing of the Democratic party and advocated a graduated income tax and an idea that would later be embodied in the Federal Deposit Insurance Act. During his first term as vice-president, he supported Franklin Roosevelt's programs, but he later disagreed with the president over reorganization of the Supreme Court and recognition of Russia. He also believed that Roosevelt should not have sought a third term. In 1941, he returned to Uvalde where he remained active in the Democratic party.

—*Patrick H. Butler, III*

SUGGESTED READING:
Timmons, Bascom N. *Garner of Texas: A Personal History.* New York, 1948.

GARRETT, PATRICK FLOYD JARVIS (PAT)

Patrick Floyd Jarvis Garrett (1850–1908), Western sheriff and a U.S. collector of customs in El Paso, Texas, was born in Chambers County, Alabama. He was the son of John Lumpkin Garrett and Elizabeth Ann Jarvis Garrett. He left home at the age of seventeen to become a buffalo hunter on the Texas plains. In 1876, he killed hunter Joe Briscoe during an argument. Garrett then settled in Fort Sumner, New Mexico, and married Apolinaria Gutiérrez on January 14, 1880. They had nine children.

Garrett was elected sheriff of Lincoln County, New Mexico, on November 2, 1880, and began the manhunt for "BILLY THE KID." Garrett and his posse killed outlaws Tom O'Folliard on December 19 and Charlie Bowdre on December 23. The sheriff then shot and killed "Billy the Kid" at Fort Sumner on July 14, 1881. Afterwards, Garrett, with ghost writer Ash Upson, wrote *The Authentic Life of Billy the Kid.*

After the labor disputes that culminated in the cowboy strike of 1883, Garrett commanded a group of private Texas Rangers in 1884 at Tascosa, Texas. He then invested in an irrigation project at Roswell, New

Mexico; when the venture failed, he drifted to Uvalde, Texas, and raced horses with John Nance Garner, later vice-president of the United States. In 1896, Garrett became sheriff of Dona Ana County, New Mexico, and sought the slayers of Colonel ALBERT JENNINGS FOUNTAIN and his son Henry. Three suspects were acquitted.

President THEODORE ROOSEVELT named Garrett collector of customs at El Paso in 1901. His administration, however, was controversial, and in 1906,

Patrick Floyd Jarvis (Pat) Garrett. *Courtesy Denver Public Library.*

Roosevelt refused to reappoint Garrett. He drifted back to his ranch in the San Andres Mountains near Las Cruces, New Mexico. He was murdered by Wayne Brazel, a local cowboy, on February 29, 1908, and is buried in Las Cruces.

—*Leon C. Metz*

SUGGESTED READING:
DeMattos, Jack. *Garrett and Roosevelt.* College Station, Tex., 1988.
Garrett, Pat. F. *The Authentic Life of Billy the Kid.* Norman, Okla., 1965.
Metz, Leon C. *Pat Garrett: Story of a Western Lawman.* Norman, Okla., 1974.
Nolan, Frederick. *The Lincoln County War: A Documentary.* Norman, Okla., 1992.
Rickards, Colin. *How Pat Garrett Died.* Santa Fe, N. Mex., 1970.

GATES, SUSA AMELIA YOUNG

Mormon writer, educator, and women's rights advocate Susa Amelia Young Gates (1856–1933) was born in Salt Lake City, Utah, the forty-first child of polygamous Mormon leader BRIGHAM YOUNG. Having received her early education at home, she entered the University of Deseret (later renamed the University of Utah) at the age of thirteen. She became coeditor of the school newspaper, the *College Lantern.* In 1872, at the age of sixteen, she married Alma Bailey Dunford, with whom she had two children. The marriage ended in divorce in 1877, due largely to Dunford's alcoholism. The following year, she enrolled at Brigham Young

Academy in Provo. There, while still a student, she established the school's department of music. In 1880, she met and married Jacob F. Gates. The couple had eleven children, four of whom survived to adulthood.

Gates pursued her talents as a writer and editor. She wrote two biographies, including one about her father, and several works of fiction. She wrote articles for various Mormon church publications, specifically the *Deseret News, Juvenile Instructor,* and *Woman's Exponent.* She also founded and edited the *Young Woman's Journal* and the *Relief Society Magazine.*

Gates was a strong advocate for women's rights. Promoting suffrage for women, she served as an officer of the National Woman's Suffrage Association and was active in the International Congress of Women.

She was also interested in the history of early Mormon settlers and was an officer in the Daughters of the Utah Pioneers. Acclaimed as the "founder of modern Mormon genealogical research," she worked as head of the Research Department and Library of the Genealogical Society of Utah beginning in 1923.

—*Newell G. Bringhurst*

SUGGESTED READING:

Cornwall, Rebecca Foster. "Susa Young Gates: The Thirteenth Apostle." In *Sister Saints.* Edited by Vicky Burgess-Olson. Provo, Utah, 1978.

Person, Carolyn W. D. "Susa Young Gates." In *Mormon Sisters.* Edited by Claudia Bushman. Cambridge, Mass., 1976.

Van Wagoner, Richard S., and Stephen C. Walker. "Susa Young Gates." In *A Book of Mormons.* Salt Lake City, 1982.

GEARY, JOHN WHITE

John White Geary (1819–1873), first mayor of San Francisco, governor of "Bleeding" Kansas, and later governor of Pennsylvania, attended Jefferson College in Canonsburg, Pennsylvania. Before he could graduate, his father died, leaving him with substantial debts to pay. After finding work in Kentucky, Geary became successful in land speculation and paid off his father's creditors. With the outbreak of the United States–Mexican War, he served as lieutenant colonel in the Pennsylvania infantry. After the war, Geary, a well-known Democrat, was appointed by President JAMES K. POLK to be postmaster for San Francisco and the Pacific Coast. In 1850, he was elected San Francisco's first mayor and was instrumental in securing the admission of California as a free state.

In July 1856, President Franklin Pierce appointed Geary governor of the Kansas Territory. Pierce charged Geary with bringing order to the territory, which was in a state of civil insurrection over the question of slavery. Geary promptly disbanded the proslavery militia and used federal troops to intercept twenty-five hundred invading Missourians intent on attacking the abolitionist stronghold of Lawrence. However, the proslavery legislature, which was openly hostile to Geary, either overrode his vetoes or simply ignored them. Frustrated by continual harassment and the lack of further federal support, Geary resigned in March 1857.

During the Civil War, Geary resumed his military career, rose to the rank of brigadier general, and served as military governor of Georgia. After the war, he was elected to two terms as governor of Pennsylvania, where he supported deficit reduction, the eight-hour workday, and the Fifteenth Amendment. Three weeks after he left office, he died of a heart attack on February 8, 1873.

—*Kurt Edward Kemper*

SUGGESTED READING:

Tinkcom, Harry M. *John White Geary: Citizen of the World.* Philadelphia, 1940.

GEARY ACT OF 1892

Sponsored by California Democrat Thomas Geary, the Geary Act of 1892 extended the Chinese Exclusion Law of 1882 another ten years and added provisions designed to rout out illegal Chinese immigrants. The act required Chinese laborers who were lawful residents of the United States to obtain certificates of residence from the government within one year. After that date, Chinese laborers found without certificates were subject to deportation and might also be sentenced to one year of hard labor in prison before their deportation. The Chinese community in the United States vehemently opposed the law, but the Supreme Court upheld its constitutionality in *Fong Yue Ting* v. *United States* (1893). The court did, however, invalidate the provision for punishment at hard labor in *Wong Wing* v. *United States* (1896).

—*Lucy E. Salyer*

SEE ALSO: Chinese Americans; Chinese Exclusion; Immigration Law

SUGGESTED READING:

Act of May 5, 1892 (27 Stat. 25).

McClain, Charles J. *In Search of Equality: The Chinese Struggle against Discrimination in Nineteenth-Century America.* Berkeley, Calif., 1994.

Salyer, Lucy E. *Laws Harsh as Tigers: Chinese Immigrants and the Shaping of Modern Immigration Law.* Chapel Hill, N.C., 1995.

GENE AUTRY WESTERN HERITAGE MUSEUM

SEE: Autry Museum of Western Heritage

GENERAL ALLOTMENT ACT

SEE: Dawes Act

GENERAL LAND OFFICE

Founded in 1812, the General Land Office was created to relieve the secretary of the treasury from the obligation of overseeing local land offices. In 1849, it was incorporated into the newly created Department of the Interior, where it became the primary vehicle through which the FEDERAL GOVERNMENT administered and disposed of the public domain. Among the office's responsibilities were the sale of public land; the administration of the HOMESTEAD ACT OF 1862, which gave land to settlers for improvement and a filing fee; and the final disposition of any piece of land that defied easy categorization. In 1946, along with the Grazing Service, the General Land Office became part of the new BUREAU OF LAND MANAGEMENT.

Although the General Land Office earned a reputation as the most corrupt bureau in the federal government, its problems also stemmed from its broad range of responsibilities and a lack of funds, adequate staff, and a clear mandate for implementing decisions. Despite being oblivious to fraud and, in some cases, clearly corrupt, General Land Office officials and their representatives negotiated the legalities of westward expansion in a consistent if idiosyncratic manner. General Land Office agents viewed natural and cultural features; surveyed lands and commented on their economic potential; reserved large sections of natural, historic, and prehistoric features from private claims; and generally did a reasonable job of sorting out the conflicting demands, needs, and values of a society in transition. The General Land Office stood in the forefront of efforts to give land to people who lacked it; its measure of accomplishment can be derived from the combination of its successes and failures.

—*Hal Rothman*

SEE ALSO: Land Policy

SUGGESTED READING:
Clawson, Marion. *Federal Lands Revisited.* Baltimore, 1983.
Conover, Milton. *The General Land Office: Its History, Activities, and Organization.* Baltimore, 1923.

GENTLEMEN'S AGREEMENT

In a series of diplomatic notes between the United States and Japan, the Japanese government agreed to limit, after 1908, the number of visas it issued to its citizens wishing to emigrate.

Euro-Americans living on the West Coast at the beginning of the twentieth century noted with alarm a steady increase in the number of Japanese immigrants inhabiting Western towns and working Western jobs. Initially, Japanese laborers were welcomed, at least by the farmers, railroad managers, and miners who employed them in backbreaking work for low wages. Californians, however, saw the arrival of Japanese immigrants—as they had seen the arrival of Chinese immigrants decades before—as part of the "yellow peril." Believing in white supremacy, Americans viewed the arrival of Asians as a threat to their racial purity and to their dominance of U.S. society. Little did it matter that the number of Japanese living on the North American mainland in 1902 totaled only about seventy-two thousand.

On October 11, 1906, the board of San Francisco's public-school system instructed its principals to segregate all Chinese, Korean, and Japanese students in an Asian school on the excuse that Asians—all ninety-three of them—were crowding out white students.

Japan objected to the insult against the Japanese people. President THEODORE ROOSEVELT realized that he might soon have an international crisis. Although he had no jurisdiction over schools in San Francisco, he tried to bully the city into rescinding its order. When that tactic failed, Roosevelt called members of the school board to Washington, D.C., to discuss the matter. The school board capitulated after Roosevelt agreed to limit the number of Japanese immigrants permitted into the United States. The board, like many Americans on the West Coast, from the start had wanted Japanese immigration to stop; its segregation order was in many ways no more than a ruse to get the president's attention.

In diplomatic exchanges in 1907 and 1908, the United States and Japan reached an understanding.

The Gentlemen's Agreement was implemented to keep Japanese laborers, such as these railroad workers, from immigrating into the United States. *Courtesy Denver Public Library, Western History Department.*

Through the Gentlemen's Agreement, Japan voluntarily consented to issue no more passports to Japanese laborers for passage to the United States.

Immigration did not end, but the number of immigrants dwindled substantially. Students and travelers were given passports, and the agreement allowed Japanese people currently residing in the United States to remain. It also allowed relatives of Japanese settlers to enter the country. Many Japanese men, who had been single since their arrival and who had viewed their stay in America as temporary, returned to their homeland to marry and brought their wives back to the United States. Other Japanese men took PICTURE BRIDES—strangers, really—in marriages arranged by Japanese parents and characterized by the exchange of pictures between the future husband and wife.

Although the Gentlemen's Agreement allowed Japanese immigrants to settle in communities and raise families, later laws restricted Japanese farmers from owning land or leasing it for longer than three years. Barred from jobs in industry and trades and treated with hostility by labor unions, Japanese settlers faced the unrelenting animosity of white Americans for decades.

—*Patricia Hogan*

SEE ALSO: Japanese Americans; Japanese Internment

SUGGESTED READINGS:
Ichioka, Yuji. *The Issei: The World of the First Generation Japanese Immigrants, 1885–1924.* New York, 1988.
Takaki, Ronald. *Strangers from a Different Shore: A History of Asian Americans.* New York, 1989.

GEOLOGICAL SURVEY

SEE: United States Geological Survey

GEORGE, HENRY

Economist, printer, and philosophical reformer Henry George (1839–1897) was born in Philadelphia to a publisher of religious books and a schoolteacher. An avid reader all his life, he left school, however, before turning fourteen and went to sea as a foremast boy. Traveling in India and other countries, he was introduced to the theme that would haunt him his entire life: the contrast between enormous wealth and abject poverty.

Returning to Philadelphia, he worked as an apprentice printer. He heard of better job opportunities on the Pacific Coast and sailed as a ship's steward for San Francisco in 1857. At first he was unable to find work, and he toyed with the ideas of mining or returning to sea, but in time, he found a job as a typesetter. Before long, he was part owner of a small daily newspaper.

In 1861, George married Annie Fox, a convent-schooled Irish woman. His work, however, did not go well. The paper failed, and he sank into real poverty. When his second child was born and the doctor told him that his wife and baby were suffering from malnutrition, he walked a San Francisco street and vowed that if the next man he accosted failed to give him five dollars, he would strike him and take it. (Fortunately, the stranger he met was generous.)

After 1865, matters improved for George, although poverty remained vividly in his memory. By 1868, he was in New York City as an agent for the *San Francisco Herald,* and there he experienced another epiphany over the tragedy between "monstrous wealth and debasing want."

Since 1865, George had been reading extensively and writing articles for local journals. The most important of these appeared in the October 1868 issue of the *Overland Monthly:* "What the Railroad Will Bring Us." In the article, he concluded that the transcontinental railroad would result in greater wealth for a few but increasing want for the many. Further thought on this theme led to his publication of a pamphlet entitled *Our Land and Land Policy* (1871), in which he described how social progress, like the building of a railroad, adds an unearned increment to the value of land. George argued that this increased value robs the laborer of his natural right to the fruits of his labor. If taxes were levied only on the unearned increment, the community would be taking back what it alone had created, and the tax burden on both labor and industry would be eased. The thesis was fleshed out in his book entitled *Progress and Poverty* (1879). The taxation on the unearned increment that society adds to the value of land became widely known as the "single tax" and was claimed by George as not only a solution to the unequal distribution of wealth but also the answer to corporate monopoly and business depression.

Shortly after the publication of *Progress and Poverty,* George moved to New York and began his career as a lecturer and writer. He entered politics on a platform of social reform and came close to winning the election for mayor of New York City in 1886. In spite of declining health, he ran again for mayor in 1897

and drove himself to the point of a second stroke. He died in a New York hotel. His funeral was attended by an estimated one hundred thousand people. His influence continued for several years after his death, and many politicians continued to call for the single tax.

—*Robert V. Hine*

SUGGESTED READING:

Barker, Charles A. *Henry George.* New York, 1955.

Cord, Steven B. *Henry George: Dreamer or Realist?* Philadelphia, 1965.

Rose, Edward. *Henry George.* New York, 1968.

GERMAN AMERICANS

Before 1820, those Germans setting out for America resembled earlier Old World émigrés. Poor people dispossessed by war or flagging economies, they were looking for a new start in a land where possibilities abounded for those willing to work with their hands. After the mid-1820s, however, a new kind of German immigrant joined the masses pouring into New York, Philadelphia, Baltimore, and New Orleans. Generally from Southwest Germany and along the Rhine, the new immigrants were strongly influenced by political and romantic notions of German nationalism. Educated men and women, people of some means, they looked to America as the land of liberty (while their less-well-off compatriots perhaps thought of it more as the land of opportunity), and they came with more or less definite ideas of establishing German states in America, of occupying unsettled and unorganized territory "in order that a German republic, a rejuvenated Germany may arise in North America."

In the fifteen years before 1847, 600,000 Germans landed in the United States. Following the settlement patterns of earlier German immigrants, those fleeing economic hard times took up farming on the cheap lands of the American West, in the territories just west of the Mississippi—Iowa, Wisconsin, and Missouri. Younger Germans, many of whom had hired on as factory workers in the East, eventually joined the American army. Along with the Irish, they would make up 42 percent of the U.S. regulars by the United States–Mexican War in 1846. Better-off Germans set up shop in Western towns and cities; they established breweries in St. Louis, Missouri; they opened general stores along emigrant trails and catered to a westering crowd. In the long run, a number of Germans would go into BANKING in the trans-Mississippi West. Not a few of the politically minded newcomers headed for Texas.

Germans in Texas

In 1836, Texas was a newly established republic, seeking to build itself into a nation of sorts even as it tried to persuade a reluctant United States, racked by sectional disputes, to annex its territory. In need of settlers, the Texas legislature primed the pump of immigration by offering pioneers an unbeatable deal: huge tracts of free land for all newcomers, at first 1,280 acres—or two square miles—of public domain for every family willing to take up residence and 640 acres for each unmarried male settler. Although the grants were gradually reduced, even after 1844—when immigrants regardless of marital status received only 320 acres—a Texas land grant was twice that of the average homestead elsewhere in the American West. In the years between independence and annexation in 1845, Texas became the focus of much interest in Europe. Henry Castro, a veteran of Napoleon's army, published a number of pamphlets on the Lone Star Republic in Paris during those years, translations of which became well known throughout France, Switzerland, and Germany and encouraged many to imagine a future in Texas.

Ninety percent of the immigrants to Texas before 1848 were Americans, mostly from the slave-holding South, not a few of them adventurers and debtors a jump ahead of their home-town sheriffs. The Americans, generally too poor to pay for boat transportation, came overland. But the relatively well-heeled European immigrants typically came by ship from New York and disembarked at Galveston. Most of the Europeans were Germans. Some Germans, having come West with the EMPRESARIOS, lived in Texas when it was still part of Mexico, and a number fought in the TEXAS REVOLUTION, but it was after independence that Germans moved to the area in such numbers as to make West Texas something of a German colony.

In New York in 1839, a group of 130 men and women from all classes of German society organized the Germania Gesellschaft, a society dedicated to forming a German state in Texas and pledging to work land in common for three years. Sailing in November on the *North*, a brig owned by the society, the colonists reached Houston without misadventure. Once there, however, perhaps recognizing for the first time the magnitude of their undertaking in a harsh new land, the society's president and those who had any money returned to New York, leaving the others to flounder. Such, too, was the fate of the short-lived Teutonic Order, formed in Texas in 1841.

The most serious attempt yet to found an enduring German settlement in the new republic came in 1844, when Prince Karl of Solms-Braunfels paved the way for the first contingent of settlers sponsored by the Society for the Protection of German Immigrants in Texas. Founded by Karl and twenty-four other German nobles, the society planned to channel German immigration to Texas into a cohesive colony. The aristocrats, having each contributed toward some eighty thousand dollars in working capital, hoped to provide homes for deserving workers, open markets for German products, and develop trade between their homeland and Mexico. They also hoped, said some, to establish a feudal kingdom that would recapture the class arrangements of their life in Germany, increasingly under threat by German revolutionaries.

In June 1844, Texan Henry Fritz traveled to Germany holding a colonization contract from the republic's legislature. Prince Karl's society bought from him a 4-million-acre grant between Texas's Colorado and Llano rivers. After arriving in the West later that year, Karl discovered that the land was not so ideal as Fritz had described. Two hundred fifty miles inland, the grant was far too isolated for trade with Mexico and not all that accessible to the 439 original company pioneers, who had paid $240 each in return for 329 acres, transportation to the colony, a house, farm tools, and free food until the first harvest. Worse, they were set to arrive in December. A haughty aristocrat, Karl made no friends among Texas's democratic politicians, and when the immigrants sailed into Matagorda Bay, he had yet to solve the company's problems. Leaving the new arrivals in port, he made arrangements to have the pioneers fed fresh meat daily and given unlimited credit against society funds. Meanwhile, Karl went looking for land between the coast and the original grant that could serve as a way station to the colony. By the time he returned in March 1845, after purchasing 9,000 acres thirty miles north of San Antonio, company coffers had been drained.

By April, Karl had ensconced the colonists at New Braunfels, as he called the site (after his German estate), and was making plans to return to Germany. The colony's finances did not improve, however, especially when the immigrants, thinking it too late to plant crops, insisted that the company live up to its promise to feed them until the first harvest a year later. Arriving home on June 4, Karl asked the society to install as head of the Texas venture John O. Meusebach, who had reached News Braunfels shortly before the prince left. A capable man, Meusebach was shocked to find the company's capital already exhausted, especially with another 4,000 settlers scheduled to arrive by wintertime. The society responded to Meusebach's staggering estimates of the costs of maintaining the colony through 1845 by sending him less than half the amount he requested. Somehow, he managed, settling not only the first 4,000 but an additional 3,000 arrivals over the next two years. He founded Fredericksburg, eighty miles northwest of New Braunfels, in 1845 and Castell on the original grant fifty miles farther north in 1847. That year the Society for the Protection of German Immigrants in Texas declared bankruptcy.

The Germans made no further attempts to found colonies in Texas, but those already established made lasting peace with the Comanches, persuaded the Texas legislature to create a German university, launched German-language newspapers of high quality, and generally laid the ground for a round of new immigration. By the mid-1850s, 35,000 Germans had moved to the area. Second in number only to the Anglo-Americans, they were a force in West Texas. Meusebach would live out his life among them as a farmer and their elected representative.

After 1848

Germany's harsh suppression of its 1848 liberal revolution led millions of Germans to emigrate during the next decade. As Otto von Bismark came to power in Prussia and introduced universal conscription into the brutal Prussian army, the revolutionaries were joined by young German draft dodgers and those from a number of religious sects whose beliefs forbade military service. For forty years, until about 1890, millions of Germans scattered over the New World, not to mention other European countries and nations adjacent to Europe. In the American West, their number was increased in the 1870s by more than 150,000 German Russians, nearly half of them Mennonites, after Czar Alexander II withdrew the special privileges that Catherine the Great had used to entice German peasants to Russia a century before.

Most of the new German immigrants debarked at Northern ports. Those who arrived in New Orleans tended to take steamboats up the Mississippi to free states. The immigrants were drawn north by their preference for colder climates, by their unwillingness to compete with slave labor, and in many cases—especially among the freethinkers and the revolutionaries—by their outright opposition to slavery. The exception was West Texas, with its already established German colonies. Before the Civil War, German freethinkers swept into the German settlement areas of Texas and set up communities almost as rigid in their beliefs as those of the German religious sects. They took over the editorships of or founded their own German-language newspapers, some two dozen of them in the area's villages. Most Texas Germans, not just the freethinkers, were markedly different from their Anglo-American neighbors. Very few of them owned slaves, and those who did often had settled in Texas before it became independent of Mexico. Industrious and fru-

gal, many Germans complained of the Texans' lazy habits and their dishonesty in business matters. The Germans located in village communities rather than spreading out over the landscape as American farmers did. They built their churches in Gothic style, not the A-frame constructions of the Anglos. Although the majority of the Germans were Protestants, they leaned toward a Lutheranism decidedly less evangelical than the Texas Methodists and Baptists, and even their sects were more pious than emotional. A large minority of the Germans were Catholic. In general, with traditions stretching back to the end of the near genocidal Thirty Years' War, the Texas Germans were tolerant of the beliefs of others.

These differences proved very trying to the Southern-spawned Texans once they discovered that many German-language newspaper editors were spouting abolitionist sentiments. As the anti-immigrant Know-Nothings grew in influence in the decades before the Civil War, the Americans grew more threatening; they publicly declared the many German social organizations—singing societies, literary clubs, debate groups, and especially ethnic political clubs—subversive to the "Southern" way of life and its peculiar institution, slavery. Prudent Germans responded by denouncing the freethinkers, and some even tried to remove the more vociferous editors from their posts. Accused of plotting to break from Texas as a free state, the German colonies went out of their way to remain neutral as the crisis of secession loomed. Some Germans took up the Confederate cause after 1861, but many more slipped over into Mexico and enlisted in the U.S. Army, following the huge numbers of Germans in the North and Midwest who fought for union and an end to slavery. The Germans of Texas joined the Republican party after the Civil War in large numbers and played a prominent role in the Reconstruction government.

Meanwhile, those Forty-eighters who had migrated to the urban areas of the American West, particularly to St. Louis and San Francisco, infused their proud socialist traditions into the political life of the trans-Mississippi West. Politics in the region, throughout the rest of the nineteenth and on into the twentieth centuries, witnessed the growth of progressive causes, radical parties, and ever more vigorous and militant labor unions. Much of the labor unrest and violence in the West of the late 1900s had its root in radical and anarchist German traditions born earlier in the century and transplanted by immigrants. A nativist backlash against European, and especially German, radicals culminated in the "red scare" of the 1920s when the Western-born INDUSTRIAL WORKERS OF THE WORLD was dismantled by Woodrow Wilson's administration. But the German American working class was not the only group to suffer from nativist sentiment and racist backlash. As German businessmen and bankers assumed a prominent role in Western finance and "frontier" society, resentment also grew among Anglo-Americans against the "foreign" element among the Western elite.

First- and second-generation German American farmers moved onto the Great Plains after the Civil War in the towns and communities given birth by the coming of the railroad. Many of these ethnic Germans had first settled in Illinois, Iowa, Missouri, and Wisconsin before moving farther to the west. And they were joined by a growing number of German Russians, who worked hard, lived frugally, clung to ethnic traditions and the German language, married early, and raised large, patriarchal families. Although the German Russians did not adapt as readily as other Germans to "American" farming, by the late 1880s, they, too, were raising cash crops, including corn, mostly for market. After a generation or so, many German American farmers, especially the German Russians, reverted to a more diversified agriculture resembling that practiced by their ancestors in the homeland, in a process ethnic historians call "cultural rebound."

Despite cultural rebounds, German Americans were the most likely of all American ethnic groups to assimilate to the American mainstream. Especially outside rural areas, Germans frequently intermarried with established Anglo-American populations, entered enthusiastically into American politics, and, in general, shed all but the most superficial aspects of their older ethnic identities.

—*Charles Phillips*

Geronimo, Apache leader and shaman. *Courtesy National Archives.*

SUGGESTED READING:

Baltensperger, Bradley H. "Agricultural Change among Nebraska Immigrants." In *Ethnicity of the Great Plains.* Edited by Frederick C. Luebke. Lincoln, Nebr., 1980.

Benjamin, Gilbert C. *The Germans in Texas.* New York, 1910. Reprint. Austin, Tex., 1974.

Biesele, Rudolph L. *The History of the German Settlements in Texas, 1831–1861.* Austin, Tex., 1930.

Jordan, Terry G. *German Seed in Texas Soil: Immigrant Farmers in Nineteenth-Century Texas.* Austin, Tex., 1966.

———. "A Religious Geography of the Hill Country Germans of Texas." In *Ethnicity of the Great Plains.* Edited by Frederick C. Luebke. Lincoln, Nebr., 1980.

Sowell, Thomas. *Ethnic America: A History.* New York, 1981.

GERONIMO (APACHE)

Chiricahua war leader and shaman Geronimo (or Goyahkla, "He Who Yawns," ca. 1823–1909) was born on the upper Gila River in present-day Arizona or New Mexico. During much of his life, he followed and deferred to Chief JUH of the Southern Chiricahuas, and later he accompanied and deferred to Chief NAICHE, the last chief of the Chiricahuas.

Geronimo was married seven or nine times and lived with several Chiricahua bands, depending on which was that of his current wife. Moving from band to band, he never acquired a large following, and his moves may have prevented him from becoming a chief. Due to his guerrilla activity, however, he was probably the most famous Apache among whites during his active years.

With Chief MANGAS COLORADAS, Geronimo and his family moved to Mexico and settled temporarily near Janos in Chihuahua. There, on March 5, 1851, a surprise attack by Sonoran troops killed twenty-one Apaches, including Geronimo's mother, wife, and three children. That incident, according to Geronimo, engendered his lifelong hatred of Mexicans, a hatred that was reflected in his many depredations against them.

General GEORGE CROOK, in command in Arizona, considered Geronimo to be a consummate liar. With a following of 134 men and women, Geronimo left the San Carlos reservation in May 1865 and remained a fugitive, hunted by Lieutenant Charles Gatewood, for sixteen months. Gatewood at last caught up with Geronimo and persuaded him to surrender to General NELSON APPLETON MILES in September 1886. His surrender marked the end of the APACHE WARS. Miles sent Geronimo and all the Chiricahuas to the East as prisoners of war.

Held in detention in Florida and then in Alabama and Oklahoma, Geronimo became well known to Euro-Americans. His name came to have more meaning in legend than he ever earned by his guerrilla exploits.

During his confinement in Oklahoma, he became a monumental public attraction. He appeared in President THEODORE ROOSEVELT's 1905 inaugural parade along with five other Indian leaders. Geronimo had learned to write his name, and at his public appearances, including the St. Louis World's Fair of 1904, he sold autographed pictures of himself and bows and arrows he had made to eager white buyers. He died near Fort Sill, Oklahoma, of pneumonia.

—Dan L. Thrapp

SUGGESTED READING:

Debo, Angie. *Geronimo: The Man, His Time, His Place.* Norman, Okla., 1976.

Thrapp, Dan L. *Encyclopedia of Frontier Biography.* Glendale, Calif., and Spokane, Wash., 1988 and 1989.

GHOST DANCE

The Ghost Dance was a religious movement of Western tribes intended to bring about the restoration of the Native American way of life before contact with white culture. WOVOKA (or Jack Wilson), a Northern Paiute prophet-messiah from the Mason and Smith valleys in western Nevada, founded the movement, which swept through a large part of the Western United States from 1889 to 1891. Wovoka was influenced by an earlier Ghost Dance movement that originated around 1870, also in western Nevada, and by Christianity and the Protestant work ethic. He experienced a deathlike coma on New Year's Day in 1889. He reportedly died and went to heaven where the Creator instructed him to carry the following message to the Indian tribes: they must be honest and hard working and must not commit warfare against themselves or whites. The Great One then told Wovoka that after the Indians performed round dances over a prescribed

period, their earlier native world, including former vegetation, animal life, and deceased Indians, would be restored. If the natives carried out the dances and songs, the renewed world would come about in early 1891.

Wovoka's restoration message appealed to many tribes of the Far West for several reasons. They had experienced sizable population loss due to European diseases and to the numerous Indian-white military conflicts. The FEDERAL GOVERNMENT's reservation policy had reduced their land base substantially in the second half of the nineteenth century. The allotment of reservations under the DAWES ACT of 1887 decreased Indian land even further. Expansion by whites into the West had considerably depleted the tribes' principal food sources, including the all-important buffalo for the Great Plains natives. White expansion had also disrupted the native cultures, and the government's assimilation policies of the late nineteenth century suppressed native practices.

In 1889 and 1890, various self-appointed Indian emissaries—including SHORT BULL and KICKING BEAR, both Lakotas (Sioux) from South Dakota, and Porcupine, a Northern Cheyenne from Montana—traveled to western Nevada to hear Wovoka's teachings. Having received his words and rituals, the delegations spread the message across the intermountain West and into the Great Plains where they modified and added to Wovoka's teachings.

The Lakotas provide an excellent example of the impact of Wovoka's teachings on tribal religion. Along with the other Great Plains tribes, the Lakotas called the teachings the "Ghost Dance," a term the general public used to label the entire movement. The Lakotas took sweat baths (cleansing) before dancing, placed a pole or tree in the middle of the dance circle, danced and sang, and induced vision-producing trances. Those rituals were meant to bring back deceased Indians and the vast buffalo herds and to make the whites disappear. Because of their own warrior tradition and their history of battles against the white intruders, the Lakotas wore shirts they believed to be bulletproof. They had modified Wovoka's teachings, for his restoration movement did not involve sweats, poles in the dance circle, or Ghost Dance shirts.

Assuming that the Lakotas were preparing for war, the federal government took measures to suppress the new religion. Reservation police on the Standing Rock Sioux Reservation attempted to arrest SITTING BULL, the influential Lakota medicine man and a supposed Ghost Dance sympathizer. When Sitting Bull's supporters came to his aid, shots were fired and Sitting Bull was killed. The military tracked down BIG FOOT and his Lakota followers who had traveled southward to the Pine Ridge Reservation, and on December 29, 1890,

The Ghost Dance religion spread rapidly among reservation tribes in the late nineteenth century. Here, Arapaho Indians participate in the ceremonial dance. *Courtesy National Archives.*

the Seventh Cavalry shot down more than 150 of his band at Wounded Knee, a tragic incident in Native American history.

The Ghost Dance movement faded away after the WOUNDED KNEE MASSACRE and after the predicted renewal of the native world did not occur in early 1891. The religion did not completely disappear, however. The Kiowas revived the Ghost Dances from 1894 to 1916 to induce vision-producing trances for communicating with the deceased, including children, who had died of sickness and disease. The Kiowas connected their dances with annual Fourth of July celebrations, a move that made it difficult for the federal agents to stamp them out. While the federal harassment eventually ended the Kiowa Ghost Dance in the early twentieth century, the movement, during the times it flourished, helped some tribes reestablish their own waning tribal practices.

—*Steven J. Crum*

SEE ALSO: Native American Cultures: Spiritual Life; Native American Peoples: Peoples of the Great Plains; United States Indian Policy

SUGGESTED READING:
Hittman, Michael. "The 1890 Ghost Dance in Nevada." *American Indian Culture and Research Journal* 16 (1992): 123–166.
———. *Wovoka and the Ghost Dance.* Carson City, Nev., 1990.
Kracht, Benjamin R. "The Kiowa Ghost Dance, 1894–1916: An Unheralded Revitalization Movement." *Ethnohistory* 39 (1992): 452–477.
Moody, James. *The Ghost-Dance Religion and the Sioux Outbreak of 1890.* Westport, Conn., 1991.
Osterreich, Shelley Anne. *The American Indian Ghost Dance, 1870 and 1890.* 1896. Reprint. Chicago, 1966.
Thornton, Russell. *We Shall Live Again: The 1870 and 1890 Ghost Dance Movements as Demographic Revitalization.* Cambridge, Mass., 1986.
Utley, Robert M. *The Last Days of the Sioux Nation.* New Haven, Conn., 1963.

GHOST TOWNS

The boom-and-bust economy of the nineteenth-century West produced entire settlements rapidly founded in remote locations to exploit a single resource—usually gold, silver, or other minerals. These settlements vanished just as quickly as they were founded when the resource was exhausted. Distant from established communities and major transport routes, such towns became empty shells and forlorn ghosts when abandoned by their inhabitants. While a great many settlements failed to take root and disappeared, relatively few well-preserved ghost towns exist, since the decamping residents customarily dismantled buildings to salvage precious construction materials. Most ghost towns are little more than vague archaeological sites or collections of stray artifacts and, perhaps, structural foundations.

A handful of ghost towns retained a core population of enterprising residents who recognized that their communities held an irresistible appeal for Western tourists. Americans frequently bemoaned their nation's dearth of romantic historical ruins, such as the decaying castles, disused monasteries, and crumbling cathedrals of Europe. As monuments to lost glory and gaudy dreams now vanished and as the former homes to a cast of Western characters made legendary by popular fiction and film, ghost towns attracted casual sightseers as well as amateur and professional artists and photographers. In places such as Virginia City, Nevada; Central City, Colorado; Tombstone, Arizona; and Calico and Nevada City, California, residents and outside entrepreneurs restored saloons, shops, and hotels expressly to attract visitors. These towns may now more properly be referred to as centers of amusement—and, perhaps edification—rather than ghost towns.

A great variety of ghost towns exists in Arizona, California, Colorado, Montana, Nevada, New Mexico, and Utah.

Arizona

Gila City, located on the Gila River east of its junction with the Colorado, was built in 1858 at the site of the first placer gold rush in Arizona. By 1864, the placer deposits were exhausted, and the settlement's twelve hundred residents abandoned the town for La Paz, where gold had been discovered in 1862.

Silver King grew up around the great Silver King Mine in Pinal County. From 1875, when silver was first discovered there, until 1888, when production finally flagged, the town boomed. Silver King struggled on into the early twentieth century but was finally abandoned and exists today as a collection of a few deserted structures.

Tombstone is undoubtedly Arizona's most famous ghost town, largely because it had been the home of such figures as "CURLY" BILL BROCIUS, JOHN HENRY ("DOC") HOLLIDAY, NASHVILLE FRANKLIN (FRANK) LESLIE, JOHN PETER RINGO, LUKE SHORT, and the EARP BROTHERS. On October 26, 1881, it was the scene of the gunfight at the O. K. Corral, the culmination of a feud between the Earps and the so-called Clanton clan.

Located seventy miles southeast of Tucson, Tombstone came into being in 1877 when rich silver deposits were discovered in the area. By the year of the O. K. Corral shootout, the town had about ten thousand residents and was so notoriously lawless that President Chester A. Arthur threatened to impose martial law in 1882. Largely through the crusading efforts of civic leaders such as JOHN HORTON SLAUGHTER and the crusading journalists of the *Tombstone Epitaph,* a degree of law and order was introduced. The town, however, declined by the 1890s as silver production slowed; by 1911, mining operations ended completely. In 1929, Tombstone ceased to be the seat of Cochise County, and the town seemed destined to die until residents and others began to restore Tombstone as a tourist attraction in the early 1970s.

California

Auburn, in Placer County, is unique because it exists in three distinct levels. The lowest, which consists of a few building foundations, was established in May 1848, when the gold was first discovered there. The next level, known as Old Town, dates from the 1850s and features well-preserved buildings from the community's economic heyday. The top level of Auburn is not a ghost town at all, but the active center of a large fruit-growing region.

Bodie, on the eastern slope of the Sierra Nevada, was a very well-preserved mining ghost town until a fire destroyed two-thirds of its buildings in 1932. Established in 1859, when placer gold was discovered there, it earned a reputation as the most lawless of the generally lawless mining camps of California. It hit a second boom in the late 1870s, when a substantial lode was discovered, but by the end of the century, it was a ghost town—despite the sporadic mining that continued in the region.

Coloma is the site of James Marshall's discovery of gold in the mill race of JOHN AUGUST SUTTER's sawmill on the American River in January 1848. Coloma boomed with the subsequent gold rush of 1849 and is preserved as a state historical site.

Columbia, a gold-mining town in the Sierra Nevada foothills, was established in March 1850 and was christened the "gem of the southern mines." It flourished for thirty years, until all of the region's gold had been extracted. Today, its business district is maintained as a state park.

Old Shasta, six miles west of Redding, boomed during the gold rush of 1849 and lasted into the 1880s, when the gold ran out and major transportation routes by-passed the town. Old Shasta is one of the West's best-preserved ghost towns.

Panamint City was among California's shortest-lived settlements. It boomed with the discovery of copper and silver in 1872 and was rapidly diminishing in 1876, when a flash flood destroyed it. It is a true ghost town, existing in isolation and ruin.

Weaverville, a gold-mining settlement on the Weaver Creek, is especially interesting for its Chinese Joss House, built in 1864 as a place of worship for the thousands of Chinese laborers who worked the mines in the 1860s.

Colorado

Central City was built on the site of the first major gold discovery in Colorado in 1859 and quickly grew to a major town of between ten and fifteen thousand by the early 1860s. The exhaustion of the placer deposits threatened to cut short the town's boom by the mid-1860s, but improved mining techniques revitalized extractive operations, and the town prospered into the 1870s and 1880s. It boasted an opera house that

An 1875 issue of *Harper's Weekly* depicts the ruins of a Colorado mining camp one year after the gold played out. *Courtesy Library of Congress.*

hosted such entertainers as Sarah Bernhardt, Edwin Booth, and Otis Skinner. The opera house, restored in 1932, continued to be used for performances during summer festivals.

Silver Plume, about fifty miles west of Denver, was founded in 1870 following the discovery of silver and lead in the region. In 1884, the business district was ravaged by fire, and in 1899, a catastrophic avalanche killed twenty people and did heavy damage to property.

Montana

Bannack, the site of Montana's first great gold strike, was established on the Grasshopper Creek in 1862. Its most notorious citizen was WILLIAM HENRY PLUMMER, mastermind of a murderous gang of "road agents" and the town's marshal. Bannack was briefly the territorial capital of Montana, an honor it soon yielded to Virginia City, which was itself a boom town and, ultimately, a ghost town—now a popular tourist attraction and very well preserved.

Nevada

Aurora—City of the Golden Dawn—came into existence in 1860, not with the discovery of gold (as its name would imply) but silver. By the end of the decade, the silver had played out, and the town was moribund. Significant traces of the original brick structures remain, but they are traces only.

Rhyolite was founded late for a ghost town—in 1905 on the heels of gold strikes in the region—and climbed to a population of sixteen thousand by 1906. By 1911, it was well on its way to death, as the gold deposits quickly petered out. Its remains included structures of stone and brick, as well as a house built entirely of bottles.

Virginia City is the best known of the Nevada ghost towns, having sprung up in 1859 with the discovery of the COMSTOCK LODE. Propelled by the rich ore, Virginia City mushroomed to a metropolis of thirty thousand people. The census of 1960 reported 515 inhabitants. It is now a tourist attraction.

New Mexico

Dolores, a short distance south of Santa Fe, has the distinction of being the site of the first gold strike in the trans-Mississippi West. Gold was discovered there in 1832. Scarcity of water doomed the town to an early death. Thomas Edison literally attempted to shock the forlorn settlement to life again in 1900, when he experimented—unsuccessfully—with a process of extracting placer gold from gravel by means of static electricity. While historically significant, very little remains of the town.

Elizabethtown sits starkly against the Sangre de Cristo Mountains in the northern part of the state. The first incorporated municipality in the New Mexico Territory, it was established with a gold strike in 1866 and faded, with the gold, by 1875. In 1901, dredges were brought in, and the town briefly revived only to succumb to a disastrous fire.

Golden grew up with Dolores but survived long after it, thanks to the discovery of a series of mineral deposits, including gold, silver, copper, turquoise, coal, and zinc. Yet, like Dolores, it was dogged by a lack of water and became a ghost town early in the twentieth century.

Mogollon, in Catron County, boomed in the 1920s, reached its zenith in 1926, and then slowly lapsed into a ghostly existence.

Utah

Ophir was founded by soldiers stationed in the area after they learned that Indians were mining gold, silver, and lead. The ore veins there proved extremely rich. The town prospered well into the twentieth century but became a ghost town in the late 1940s and early 1950s.

Silver Reef, in southwestern Utah, is desolate. Its stark remains include a Wells, Fargo and Company bank. It existed for about ten years, roughly between 1870 and 1880.

—Alan Axelrod

SEE ALSO: Booms; California Gold Rush; Colorado Gold and Silver Rushes; Mining: Mining Camps and Towns; Montana Gold Rush; O. K. Corral, Gunfight at

SUGGESTED READING:
Silverberg, Robert. *Ghost Towns of the American West.* Athens, Ohio, 1994.

GIANNINI, AMADEO PETER

Raised on a fruit orchard outside San Jose, California, Amadeo Peter Giannini (1870–1949) developed a career as a successful San Francisco fruit merchant before he devoted himself to the BANKING industry, where he would make his most notable contributions to Western history. After his father-in-law's death in 1904, Giannini took the older man's seat on the board of the Columbus Savings and Loan Society but quickly clashed with the conservative banking policies of the "Banco Columbo." When he resigned from the board later in the year and founded his own Bank of Italy in San Francisco, he was—unlike most of the city's other savings and loans, which provided loans at high interest rates to the area's wealthier ranchers, miners, and lumbermen—in a position to encourage all San Franciscans to make small deposits and offer modest loans to the town's citizens at reasonable rates.

Depending, at first, on friends and family in North Beach, at the time San Francisco's Italian American business quarter, Giannini became well known locally when he whisked the bank's deposits to safety outside the city during the 1906 earthquake and fire. In 1912, he opened two of what would become an ever-growing number of branch banks, which he called "money stores" and in which local managers and personnel provided easy access to money for farmers and businessmen. Sneered at by his financial peers because he advertised for customers and even launched a corps of aggressive salesmen to drum up business, Giannini realized what most other bankers would not grasp for another generation. In an industrialized mass-market economy, capital could be accumulated from millions of small depositors just as well as from syndicates of wealthy individuals and corporations. To reach those multitudes of depositors, Giannini reasoned, bankers could no longer remain centralized in formidable downtown splendor. They had to go where the people were, and they had to tell the people they were there.

By 1920, Giannini had opened twenty-four new branches and made the Bank of Italy the largest in California. Initially frustrated by state and federal regulations that blocked his attempts to establish branch banking nationwide, Giannini eventually won a bitter political battle with California banking superintendents; in the 1920s, he secured permission to create 150 new branches, which he then consolidated into one comprehensive system. Supplying much of the credit that Westerners—not only in California, but also in neighboring states—needed to fuel the region's economic growth, he had, on the eve of the Great Depression in 1929, built the largest bank in the West and controlled 40 percent of California's banking capital. By the time he renamed his operation the Bank of America, National Trust and Savings Association in 1930, it was the third largest bank in the United States. In 1945, the Bank of America was the largest commercial and savings institution in the world.

An imaginative investor, Giannini—who had loaned money to San Francisco's first nickelodeon in 1909—financed the nascent film industry when its early pioneers moved to California in the late teens and early twenties. Giannini also backed the dynamic industrialist HENRY J. KAISER from Oakland, California; it was Giannini who urged President Franklin D. Roosevelt, in 1941, to entrust Kaiser with new manufacturing responsibilities that Giannini would underwrite, thus launching Kaiser's massive shipbuilding operations in the Pacific Northwest. Giannini was a New Deal favorite for his consistent support of Roosevelt's policies. Giannini—and the West—benefited, in turn, by such New Deal legislation as the Banking Act of 1933, which finally eased restrictions on the establishment of branches by national banks. Both the 1933 act and the Banking Act of 1935 reduced the number of bank failures and bolstered the stability of Western banks. In fact, the West Giannini helped to build received a disproportionate amount of federal spending, three times the national average, and was transformed by the big New Deal programs.

Until 1914, the West had been dependent on Eastern and foreign capital, but after 1919, Giannini led a group of imaginative Western bankers in a revolution against such economic colonialism. By the time Giannini died in 1949, not only had his Bank of America freed much of the West from "outside" financing, but also its operations were widely imitated. All over America, bankers adopted the flexible, Western notion of branch banking.

—*Charles Phillips*

SEE ALSO: Federal Government

SUGGESTED READING:

James, Marquis, and Bessie R. James. *Biography of a Bank: The Story of the Bank of America.* New York, 1954.

Nash, Gerald D. *The American West in the Twentieth Century: A Short History of an Urban Oasis.* Englewood Cliffs, N.J., 1973. Reprint. Albuquerque, N. Mex., 1977.

———. *A. P. Giannini and the Bank of America.* Norman, Okla., 1992.

GIBBON, JOHN OLIVER

John Oliver Gibbon (1827–1896) was most closely associated with two major campaigns of the Indian Wars, the Sioux campaign of 1876 and the Nez Percé campaign of 1877. Born near Harrisburg, Pennsylvania, Gibbon was educated at the U.S. Army Military Academy at West Point and graduated in 1847, barely in time to participate in the closing actions of the United States–Mexican War. After a brief stint in Virginia, he was next posted to Fort Brooke, Florida, where he worked to keep the Seminole Indians in check. From 1850 to 1852, he was assigned to the Texas frontier, and then after a leave of absence, he returned to Florida to assist in the removal of the Seminoles to the Indian Territory. In 1854, he served as assistant instructor at West Point, where he specialized in artillery. In 1859, he published *The Artillerist's Manual,* which was officially adopted by the War Department.

On November 2, 1859, Gibbon was promoted to captain and assigned to an artillery battery at Camp Floyd in the Utah Territory. At the outbreak of the Civil War, he signed an oath of allegiance to the United States, even though his family, who had settled in North Carolina, sympathized with the Confederate cause. Gibbon was jumped in rank to commander of volunteers. During the Civil War, Brigadier General Gibbon was wounded at Fredericksburg on December 13, 1862, and again at Gettysburg on July 3, 1863. He also served in the Richmond campaign, where he led troops at the battles of the Wilderness, Spotsylvania, North Anna, Totopotomoy, Cold Harbor, and Petersburg. Promoted the major general of volunteers, he participated in the pursuit of the Army of Northern Virginia to Appomattox Courthouse and was chosen by General Ulysses S. Grant as one of three commissioners to arrange the details of the surrender of Robert E. Lee's army.

Briefly reverting to the rank of captain at the end of the war, Gibbon was then promoted to colonel and, on December 1, 1866, was ordered to command Fort Kearney, Nebraska. Except for a brief assignment to the recruiting service in New York City in 1873, Gibbon spent the rest of his military career in the West—at posts in Nebraska, the Dakota Territory, Utah, the Montana Territory, Minnesota, and the Wyoming Territory. In 1884, he was given command of the Department of the Platte. The following year promoted to brigadier general in the regular army, he was given command of the Division of the Pacific, a post he held until his retirement in 1891.

In the Western phase of his career, Gibbon is best remembered for his service against the Sioux in 1876 and the Nez Percé in 1877. He was in command of the Montana column that rescued the survivors of the Battle of Little Bighorn, and it was his men who buried GEORGE ARMSTRONG CUSTER and the Seventh Cavalry troopers killed in that engagement. During the Nez Percé War, Gibbon attacked CHIEF JOSEPH's band at Big Hole in the Montana Territory on August 9, 1877. Badly outnumbered, Gibbon suffered a tactical defeat yet inflicted heavy casualties on the Indians.

Gibbon's Civil War service is recounted in his *Personal Recollections of the Civil War,* which was published posthumously in 1928. His various writings on his service in the West are collected in *Adventures on the Western Frontier* (1994).

—*Alan Axelrod*

SEE ALSO: Little Bighorn, Battle of; Pacific Northwest Indian Wars; Sioux Wars

SUGGESTED READING:

Gaff, Alan, and Maureen Gaff, eds. *Adventures of the Western Frontier by Major General John Gibbon.* Bloomington and Indianapolis, Ind., 1994.

GIBSON, PARIS

Paris Gibson (1830–1920), agriculturalist, the founder of Great Falls, Montana, and a U.S. senator, represents a coterie of Progressive Montana capitalists who combined public service with financial success.

Gibson grew up in Maine and graduated from Bowdoin College in 1851. He moved to St. Anthony's Falls (Minneapolis), Minnesota, in 1858, built the town's first flour mill, and founded the North Star Woolen Mills. He arrived in Montana in 1879 and engaged in sheep raising. In 1883, he founded the city of Great Falls, based on its hydroelectric potential. When JAMES J. HILL built his St. Paul, Minneapolis and Manitoba Railroad (Great Northern Railway) mainline to Great Falls in 1887, the community's success was secure.

Gibson had served in the Maine House of Representatives at the age of twenty-four and remained an active Democrat after his move to Montana. He served in the 1889 Constitutional Convention and represented Cascade County in the state senate for one term (from 1891 to 1895). When WILLIAM ANDREWS CLARK resigned his U.S. Senate seat in 1901, Gibson completed the term.

Gibson's business interests were diverse—banking, irrigation, coal mining, livestock raising, and hydroelectric generation. As the "father of Great Falls," he exerted considerable influence over the community's growth and prosperity.

—*David A. Walter*

SUGGESTED READING:

Gibson, Paris. *The Founding of Great Falls, and Some of Its Early Records.* Great Falls, Mont., 1914.

Roeder, Richard B. "A Settlement on the Plains: Paris Gibson and the Building of Great Falls." *Montana: The Magazine of Western History* 42:4 (Autumn 1992): 4–19.

White, W. Thomas. "Paris Gibson, James J. Hill, and the 'New Minneapolis': The Great Falls Water Power and Townsite Company, 1882–1908." *Montana: The Magazine of Western History* 33:3 (Summer 1983): 60–69.

GILA CITY, ARIZONA

SEE: Ghost Towns

GILCREASE INSTITUTE

SEE: Thomas Gilcrease Institute

GILLESPIE, ARCHIBALD H.

Archibald H. Gillespie (1812–1873) served as a secret governmental courier during the months preceding the outbreak of the UNITED STATES–MEXICAN WAR. A lieutenant of marines, he took an active role in the fighting in southern California in 1846 and 1847.

A native of Philadelphia, Gillespie arrived on the West Coast in April 1846 disguised as an American businessman. Under orders from President JAMES K. POLK, he brought to American consul THOMAS OLIVER LARKIN and Captain JOHN CHARLES FRÉMONT dispatches that warned of the possibility of war between the United States and Mexico. Finding that Frémont had retreated north following an acrimonious exchange with Mexican officials, Gillespie pursued him and caught up with him in southern Oregon. Gillespie's information encouraged Frémont to return to the California settlements, where rumors of an impending Mexican attack against American pioneers sparked the Bear Flag Rebellion. Frémont and Gillespie soon joined the rebel forces.

Upon ROBERT F. STOCKTON's assumption of command in California, Gillespie and Frémont placed their men under the commodore's direction. During the late summer and early fall, Gillespie commanded the garrison at Los Angeles. Later, his harsh policies sparked a revolt by local residents, and he and his soldiers had to abandon the community. In the battles at San Pasqual in December 1846 and at San Gabriel in January 1847, Gillespie suffered serious wounds. He continued his service with the Marine Corps after the war and held the post of secretary to Governor John B. Weller. He was later employed in a secretarial position for the American legation in Mexico.

—*Gerald Thompson*

SUGGESTED READING:
Marti, Werner H. *Messenger of Destiny: The California Adventures, 1846–1847, of Archibald H. Gillespie, U.S. Marine Corps.* San Francisco, 1960.

GILMAN, CHARLOTTE PERKINS

A turn-of-the-century author, lecturer, and theorist, Charlotte Perkins Gilman (1860–1935) was a critic of history and society. She created a cohesive world view to explain human behavior, past and present, and to project the outlines of her vision for the future. Gender was at the core of her analysis; she believed that people had the power to create a humane social order in which men and women would be freed from the prison of worn-out beliefs and limiting conventions.

Born in New England, Gilman found that the West provided a nourishing environment for both her fiction and her own life. Gilman's is an urban, not a male-dominated "frontier," West. In her view, Western cities served as a place for the new, the untried; rules there were stretchable. Men far outnumbered women, so women could select their mates from competing males—a selection process that Gilman believed to be the way in nature. Her West was a great leveler; its cities were powerful sources of community and civilization. Thus the West was an idea, a process, a metaphor, and a place, not just for Horace Greeley's young men, but for Gilman's fictional young, middle-aged, and elderly women—in fact, for anyone struggling to escape confining conventions. For example, in Gilman's novel, *What Diantha Did,* Diantha flees her smothering New England community and heads west to create a new life; she starts a high-powered business and finds a loving, open-minded husband who supports her endeavors.

Gilman herself visited California to regain her emotional strength after her first marriage ended and returned in the last months of her life. The move not only provided Gilman a place of safety and healing but also offered bustling reform activity and intellectual and social ferment, with which she immediately identified and from which she found her life's work as an activist and intellectual in behalf of her humanist-socialist perspective.

—*Ann J. Lane*

SUGGESTED READING:
Hill, Mary Armfield. *Charlotte Perkins Gilman: The Making of a Radical Feminist, 1860–96.* Philadelphia, 1980.
Lane, Ann J. *To "Herland" and Beyond: The Life and Work of Charlotte Perkins Gilman.* New York, 1990.
Scharnhorst, Gary. *Charlotte Perkins Gilman: A Bibliography.* Metuchen, N.J., 1985.

GILPIN, WILLIAM

Explorer, politician, editor, lawyer, soldier, and promoter William Gilpin (1813–1894) was born into a wealthy family in Brandywine, Pennsylvania. He achieved greatness in no field and notoriety in many. In his prime, a handsome six-footer with a bushy beard and piercing hazel eyes, he commanded respect—just the right quality for a prophet of urban destiny.

Educated in England and at the University of Pennsylvania, from which he graduated in 1834, he briefly attended West Point. He received a direct commission and served in the Seminole War. After resigning from the army in 1838, he became editor of the pro-Jacksonian Democrat *Missouri Arqus* in St. Louis. For a short time, he was chief clerk of the Missouri General Assembly. In 1841, he moved to Independence, Missouri, his nominal home for the next twenty years. He practiced law, ran a newspaper, fought Indians, participated in the United States–Mexican War, sold real estate, and made frequent trips to the West. He joined the Republican party over the slavery issue and was a member of president-elect Abraham Lincoln's security detail. Appointed the first territorial governor of Colorado, Gilpin took quick action to save New Mexico and Colorado for the Union. He was removed as territorial governor for unorthodox financial practices—he issued territorial scrip—but he remained in Colorado where he reportedly made a fortune in real estate.

His historical importance stems from his lectures and articles, all incorporated into three books, *The Central Gold Region* (1860), *Mission of the North American People* (1873), and *The Cosmopolitan Railway* (1890). Touching on every conceivable aspect of the westward movement, he always returned to a central theme—that natural scientific laws ensured the development of great cities in the West. He drew on the theories of German geopolitician Alexander von Humboldt, who argued that a wide climatic belt, called the "Isothermal Zodiac," encircled the globe in the northern latitudes. Within the belt, an "Axis of Intensity," which passed through the Western Hemisphere at roughly the thirty-ninth parallel, dictated the location of future great metropolitan centers. Even more fortuitous was a city's "gravitational" attributes. Pirating a mathematically based "concentric circle" theory of urban gravitation from S. H. Goodin, an obscure Cincinnati promoter, Gilpin claimed that, in circle-fashion, large cities grew at a distance of five hundred to seven hundred leagues. At the center of a great circle would be the largest place in the world, the "Centropolis" of fifty million people.

Gilpin unfolded his vision in the *Central Gold Region*. He first concluded that Kansas City would become the Centropolis, but after moving to Denver, he said he had made an error. In *Mission of the North American People*, he fixed the Colorado city as the true Centropolis. In *The Cosmopolitan Railway*, he envisioned Denver as the terminal of a vast worldwide railroad system that would ensure international peace and harmony through trade and communications among different nations. Despite flawed logic, Gilpin

successfully predicted that the last half of the nineteenth century would see the building of great cities in the West.

—*Lawrence H. Larsen*

SUGGESTED READING:

Glaab, Charles N. "Visions of Metropolis: William Gilpin and Theories of City Growth in the American West." *Wisconsin Magazine of History* 45 (Autumn 1961): 21–31.

Karnes, Thomas. *William Gilpin: Western Nationalist.* Austin, Tex., 1970.

GLASS, HUGH

Fur trapper Hugh Glass (c. 1790–1833), known as "Old Glass" to his comrades, is remembered largely for one event that took place in the course of an otherwise obscure life. Almost nothing reliable is known about him.

In the early 1820s, he turned up in St. Louis, Missouri. In 1823, he traveled up the Missouri River in WILLIAM HENRY ASHLEY's party of fur trappers, a party that sustained a number of casualties in a fight with the Arikaras. Glass himself was wounded in the leg.

In September 1823, he joined a fur-trapping party led by Ashley's partner ANDREW HENRY. The group set out from Fort Kiowa, a trading post on the upper Missouri, and headed west across present-day South Dakota. Henry sent a party of hunters ahead, and the strong-willed, independent Glass went with them. While out ahead of the hunting party, Glass was suddenly attacked by a grizzly bear and was badly mauled. When Henry and the main party arrived on the scene, it appeared that Glass would soon die. Henry decided to pay two men, John S. Fitzgerald and JAMES (JIM) BRIDGER, to remain with Glass until he died, while the main party pressed on. Henry then led his men to their destination; they were soon joined by Fitzgerald and Bridger, who reported that Glass was dead. They had buried the remains, they said, and had brought along his gun, knife, and other equipment.

Fitzgerald and Bridger were wrong. Glass was far from dead; he had apparently only fallen asleep or slipped into a coma, from which he awoke to find that he was alone in hostile Indian country with nothing more than his clothes and a razor blade. His chances of survival were bleak. To regain some measure of strength, he ate wild berries and stayed ten days at the spring where he had been abandoned. Then he decided that his only chance was to scrape his way back to Fort Kiowa. Living on dead buffalo, wild berries, and roots, he crawled and stumbled perhaps two hundred miles. In the final stages of his odyssey, he may have been helped by a band of Sioux Indians. Glass survived, and his story became a legend.

Ultimately, Glass confronted Fitzgerald and Bridger, recovered his rifle and some other property, and then resumed his career as a trapper and trader. He went to New Mexico, trapped in the southern Rockies, had an arrowhead cut out of his back, and then returned to the northern Rockies where he worked near Fort Union. While trapping on the Yellowstone during the winter of 1832 and 1833, Glass and his companion EDWARD ROSE were killed by Arikaras.

—*James E. Fell, Jr.*

SEE ALSO: Fur Trade; Mountain Men; Trappers

SUGGESTED READING:
Hafen, LeRoy R., ed. *The Mountain Men and Fur Trade of the Far West.* Glendale, Calif., 1965.
Morgan, Dale L. *Jedediah Smith and the Opening of the West.* Lincoln, Nebr., 1964.

GLENN, HUGH JAMES

Born in Virginia and educated as a doctor, Hugh James Glenn (1824–1883) became a leading California rancher and businessman. Lured to California in the gold-rush years, Glenn made a success of driving cattle, sheep, and horses to West Coast settlers. In 1867, he established a ranch and wheat farm along the Sacramento River in Colusa County. In 1879, he produced one million bushels of wheat. Responding to pressure from farmers who objected to his open-range ranching, Glenn entered into a partnership in 1872 with his foreman PETER FRENCH, who moved the cattle to Harney

County in southeastern Oregon and operated the P Ranch. The operation expanded, eventually including 132,000 acres, and supported thirty thousand cattle under the name of the French-Glenn Livestock Company. Glenn was murdered by a former employee—a bookkeeper he had recently fired—in 1883.

—*Patricia Hogan*

SUGGESTED READING:
French, Giles. *Cattle Country of Peter French.* Portland, Oreg., 1964.

GLENN-FOWLER EXPEDITION

The Glenn-Fowler Expedition from 1821 to 1822 was one of several groups that traveled across the Sangre de Cristo Range to reopen American trade with New Mexico following Mexico's independence from Spain. Led by Hugh Glenn of Cincinnati, Ohio, and Jacob Fowler of Covington, Kentucky, the expedition of twenty men set out for a hunting and trapping trip into the Rocky Mountains in September 1821. They traveled up the Verdigris River in eastern Oklahoma in present-day Kansas and reached the Arkansas River near the present-day site of Wichita. From there, they followed the Arkansas River west into Colorado and spent the winter with the Kiowa and Arapaho tribes.

On December 20, 1821, the explorers met a party of sixty Mexican traders, who encouraged them to travel across the Sangre de Cristo Range to Taos. Glenn and four of his men accompanied the Mexicans to Taos and sent word back to the band of explorers that the

The expedition of Hugh Glenn and Jacob Fowler paved the way for trade between Americans and Mexicans in Santa Fe. An image from Josiah Gregg's *Commerce of the Prairies* depicts a well-guarded wagon train of trade goods at camp. *Courtesy Library of Congress.*

New Mexican authorities had granted them permission to hunt and trap in the region.

Fowler then led the rest of the band across the mountains, and for the remainder of the winter, they trapped and hunted in the mountains north of Taos. Glenn continued on to Santa Fe in April 1822. With the end of the trapping season that year, the expedition returned to St. Louis, having opened what Fowler called the "old Taos trail" and others called the "Santa Fe Trail" into New Mexico.

Others who arrived at Santa Fe at about the same time included WILLIAM BECKNELL, Thomas James, and JOSEPH REDDEFORD WALKER. The trail these men and the Glenn-Fowler Expedition opened would become the most used route to Santa Fe over the next two decades. For the fur-trading companies in the East, the newly opened Mexican territories provided a bountiful source of new profits.

—*Candace Floyd*

SEE ALSO: Fur Trade; Santa Fe and Chihuahua Trail

SUGGESTED READING:

Chalfant, William Y. *Dangerous Passage: The Santa Fe Trail and the Mexican War.* Norman, Okla., 1994.

Fowler, Jacob. *The Journal of Jacob Fowler.* Edited, with notes, by Elliott Coues. Lincoln, Nebr., 1970.

GLIDDEN, JOSEPH

SEE: Barbed Wire

GODBE, WILLIAM S.

A leading Mormon dissident and schismatic leader, William S. Godbe (1833–1902) was born in Middlesex, England. He converted to Mormonism (the CHURCH OF JESUS CHRIST OF LATTER-DAY SAINTS) during the 1840s. In 1849, he migrated to the United States and joined a Mormon emigrant company in Council Bluffs, Iowa. He moved to Salt Lake City in 1851 and established a mercantile and importing business. Eventually, he was one of the wealthiest men in the Utah Territory.

Initially, Godbe was strongly devoted to the Mormon faith. He served as bishop's counselor and was a member of the Salt Lake School of the Prophets. After marrying Annie Thompson in 1855, he embraced polygamy and took on a total of three wives.

By 1868, he disagreed with Mormon leader BRIGHAM YOUNG and his policies. Godbe insisted that the MORMONS should take the lead in developing Utah's mineral resources and should integrate itself into the larger American economy. These goals ran counter to Young's quest for Mormon economic self-sufficiency.

Joining Godbe were other disaffected Mormon businessmen and intellectuals—E. L. T. Harrison, Edward Tullidge, and T. B. H. and Fanny Stenhouse. As leaders of a schismatic group dubbed the "Godbeite" movement, they criticized Young's church doctrine and his economic policies. Godbeites embraced spiritualism—claiming the ability to communicate with the dead—objected to the authoritarian leadership of Young, and called for greater individual economic freedom.

The Mormon church formally excommunicated Godbe for "apostasy" in 1869. With his fellow dissidents, he formed the schismatic Church of Zion with former Mormon apostle Amasa Lyman as its spiritual leader. The movement was short lived, however. Of greater significance was Godbe's establishment of a periodical, the *Utah Magazine.* The publication evolved into a newspaper, the *Salt Lake Tribune,* which was the largest daily newspaper in Utah in the 1990s. Godbe died at his home in Brighton, Utah.

—*Newell G. Bringhurst*

SUGGESTED READING:

Bitton, Davis. "Mormonism's Encounter with Spiritualism." *Journal of Mormon History* 1 (1974): 51–72.

Walker, Ronald W. "The Commencement of the Godbeite Protest: Another View." *Utah Historical Quarterly* 42 (Summer 1974): 216–244.

GOLD MINING

Although the discovery of gold in Georgia brought a large and cosmopolitan group of miners to the state between 1828 and 1830, the large-scale search for gold and the massive movement of population in connection with that pursuit began in California in 1848. From there, the search spread across the American West and into Alaska over the next half century.

John W. Marshall's discovery of gold on JOHN AUGUST SUTTER's estate in January 1848 launched what became known as the CALIFORNIA GOLD RUSH, and in response to the discovery and rapid mining successes, three hundred thousand Americans and others from around the world descended on the California Sierra Nevada over the next dozen years. As the placer diggings played out and were replaced by large corporate enterprises, other gold discoveries in the West drew a restless population intent on recreating the heady returns of the original Forty-niners.

In July 1859, discoveries of gold in the foothills of the Rockies near present-day Denver triggered a rush to Pikes Peak by men known as the Fifty-niners. Rich strikes in Gilpin County soon required smelters, indicative of the changing nature of gold mining, but the movement of people to Colorado laid the basis for an expanding population and made news across the nation.

Similar discoveries in Nevada led to the opening of the great silver mines known as the COMSTOCK LODE. Other mining strikes in Idaho in 1860 and in Montana in 1862 prompted the first large-scale movement of Euro-Americans into those areas. By the 1870s, miners in search of gold were busy panning and crushing at sites across the American West, from Washington and Oregon to Arizona and New Mexico. The discovery of gold in the Black Hills of South Dakota led to a mining rush in 1876 and 1877, and the huge HOMESTAKE MINE established there became the largest gold producer in the nation.

The gradual shift from placer mining by individuals and small groups to corporate mining—with large-scale

John W. Marshall poses before Sutter's Mill where his discovery of gold started the California gold rush. *Courtesy Wells Fargo Bank.*

In 1851, in an area not far from Sutter's Mill, miners use a sluice to separate gold from dirt. The mounds of dirt surrounding the workers suggest that the ground has been well worked over. *Courtesy Wells Fargo Bank.*

investment, the latest in technology, and a mining force hired by the day—changed the landscape of the American West in the last decades of the nineteenth century. The discovery of gold and its extraction in CRIPPLE CREEK, COLORADO, in 1892 represented this rapid transition. Then, with the discovery of gold on the Klondike River in Canada, the search by individuals for new mining opportunities revived and spread into Alaska. The Klondike rush and the strikes on the American side of the Yukon Valley represented one final chapter in the search by individuals for gold. Another took place at Goldfield, Nevada, the site of a prosperous mining operation after the turn of the century.

Gold mining had the potential to generate enormous riches within a short time, and as such, it transformed American views about wealth, which up to the middle of the nineteenth century had been based on agriculture and land ownership. The aggregate numbers were astonishing: almost $400 million worth of gold was mined in California between 1848 and 1856, $500 million by the Homestake Mine since 1875, and $150 million in Goldfield, Nevada, most of it between 1900 and 1909.

While the largest portion of the wealth went to a score of individuals, the influence of the gold rushes and gold mining was long lasting. At the onset, the large-scale movements of people infringed on the rights of Indians, and innumerable confrontations between them and miners occurred from the foothills of California to the Black Hills of South Dakota. Gold strikes brought a diverse population that included merchants, freighters, boarding-house owners, gamblers, saloonkeepers, prostitutes, and skilled craftsmen in the building trades. The prospect of wealth also attracted many professionals—doctors, lawyers, and, soon, engineers. While many of the mining camps failed, elements of the population often stayed on to establish towns based on other economic enterprises. The possibility of instant wealth also led to the establishment of gold-mining stock exchanges. Such speculative activities allowed absentee investors across the Western world to invest in remote mines in the American West, and they did so in astonishing numbers, most of them losing their money. The transition from placer mining by individuals to corporate mining also meant the appearance of a work force of professional miners, and this work force soon led to unions and, in due course, to violence over wages and conditions of employment.

—*Malcolm J. Rohrbough*

SEE ALSO: Alaska Gold Rush; Black Hills Gold Rush; Colorado Gold and Silver Rushes; Ghost Towns; Klondike Gold Rush; Montana Gold Rush; Mining; Silver Mining

SUGGESTED READING:

Greever, William S. *Bonanza West: The Story of Western Mining Rushes.* Norman, Okla., 1963.

Marks, Paula Mitchell. *Precious Dust: The American Gold Rush Era, 1848–1900.* New York, 1994.

Paul, Rodman W. *California Gold: The Beginning of Mining in the Far West.* Cambridge, Mass., 1947.

Zanjani, Sally. *Goldfield: The Last Gold Rush on the Western Frontier.* Athens, Ohio, 1992.

GOLDEN, NEW MEXICO

SEE: Ghost Towns

GOLDWATER FAMILY

Senator Barry Goldwater has long been honored as Arizona's most illustrious citizen, but the Goldwater name was well known in the Arizona Territory for nearly a half-century before his birth in 1909.

Polish-born Michel Goldwater (1821) immigrated to California with his younger brother Joseph in 1852. Michel operated a saloon in Sonora, California, and when the business failed, he engaged in other unsuc-

Michel Goldwater. *Courtesy Arizona Historical Society.*

cessful ventures. In 1860, he moved to what would soon become the Arizona Territory, where he sold merchandise from a wagon to gold miners in Gila City, east of Yuma. In 1862, he opened his first general store in La Paz, across the Colorado River from present-day Blythe, California. Goldwater stores were prominent in Arizona history for 120 years thereafter.

Michel and his eldest son, Morris, had moderate success in a general store in Ehrenberg, Arizona, and in 1872, they opened another store in the new town of Phoenix. It failed, but their next venture, in Prescott in 1876, prospered for many decades.

In 1896, after Michel's retirement, Morris sent his youngest brother, Baron, to try the Phoenix market again. Baron proved to be a mercantile genius. His Phoenix department store, catering especially to women, became nationally known and made him a wealthy man.

In 1907, Baron married Josephine Williams, a nurse who had come to Arizona from Nebraska to seek relief from tuberculosis. At her death in 1966 at the age of ninety-one, she was honored as one of the outstanding women of early Arizona.

Upon Baron's death in 1929, his son Barry became president of Goldwater's. When Barry entered politics in 1952, his younger brother, Robert, succeeded him and, over the years, established Goldwater's department stores throughout Arizona and in New Mexico and Nevada.

Several Goldwaters earned prominent places in Arizona history. Michel (known as "Big Mike") was not only a pioneer merchant but also a builder of wagon roads across the wilderness and a founder of several towns. His brother Joseph, severely wounded in an Indian ambush near Prescott in 1872, later established six stores in southeastern Arizona.

Morris, born in 1850, was a giant among territorial pioneers. He was a founder of the Arizona Democratic party, the patriarch of Arizona Freemasonry for a half-century, vice-president of the 1910 Arizona Constitutional Convention, and mayor of Prescott for twenty years. He was the early political mentor of his nephew Barry, whose middle name is Morris.

Barry Goldwater, in his first try for national political office, was elected to the U.S. Senate in 1952. He led the fight to revitalize conservative political philosophy in America and was the Republican presidential candidate in 1964.

—*Dean Smith*

SEE ALSO: Jewish Americans

SUGGESTED READING:
Smith, Dean. *The Goldwaters of Arizona*. Flagstaff, Ariz., 1986.

Charles Goodnight. *Courtesy Panhandle-Plains Museum.*

GOODNIGHT, CHARLES

A native of Macoupin County, Illinois, Charles Goodnight (1836–1929) went to Texas with his family in 1846 and settled near Waco. As a youth, he farmed, split rails, and worked as a teamster before taking charge of a herd of cattle in 1856 with a cousin named Wes Sheek for a share of the profits.

In 1857, Goodnight and Sheek moved westward into Palo Pinto County. There, Goodnight was soon involved in the hostilities surrounding the nearby Brazos River Indian reservations. He scouted for various military and civilian expeditions mounted against the Comanche and Kiowa tribes during the late 1850s and participated in the Pease River fight in 1860.

During the Civil War, Goodnight served as a scout and guide for the Frontier Regiment. Mustered out in 1864, he began to rebuild his herds and, by the fall of 1865, had gathered about two thousand head. Indian raiders, however, drove them off before he could find a market.

The following spring, Goodnight and OLIVER LOVING, a merchant and experienced trail driver, delivered the first of several profitable herds to government buyers at Fort Sumner, New Mexico. After Loving's death at the hands of Indians while on a drive in 1867, Goodnight continued as a drover for several years. He moved between eight thousand and twelve thousand head to market annually.

In 1869, Goodnight established a ranch near Pueblo, Colorado, married two years later, and acquired interests in an irrigation and milling operation, a slaughterhouse, a bank, city lots, and an opera house. Goodnight prospered until nearly bankrupted in the panic of 1873.

Seeking a fresh start, three years later, he moved a small herd from Colorado into the Texas Panhandle. The next summer, he entered into a partnership with Irish financier John G. Adair to establish the JA Ranch. With Adair's financial backing and Goodnight's ranching expertise, the enterprise thrived for nearly a decade. In 1887, about one hundred thousand JA cattle grazed on more than one million West Texas acres. With Adair's death and the cattle industry depressed in the mid-1880s, the partnership faltered, and the ranch was partitioned. Goodnight acquired the Quitaque division, which he operated in partnership with L. R. Moore for several years before selling out and establishing the Goodnight-Thayer Cattle Company. He disposed of that interest about 1900 and retreated in semiretirement to a modest ranch near the town of Goodnight, Texas, where he built Goodnight College in 1898.

Goodnight remained politically active throughout his career. He took special interest in state and local issues related to land policy and law enforcement. In 1880, he helped found the Pan Handle Stock Association to protect and promote the livestock interests of the region. A year later, he organized the "Winchester Quarantine," an extralegal measure designed to protect his herd from tick-infested cattle being driven from South Texas through his region.

Considered one of the premier cattle breeders in the West, Goodnight continually improved his herds through the infusion of blooded stock. He also conducted widely heralded experiments to breed buffalo to Polled Angus cattle to create the "cattalo."

At his wife Mary's behest, Goodnight had rescued four buffalo calves in 1878, thereby helping save the buffalo from extinction on the Southern Plains. By 1916, the two hundred animals in his herd represented one-tenth of the total number of buffalo in the United States.

That year, he invited a party of Kiowa Indians to hold an old-fashioned buffalo hunt at his ranch. A few months later, he staged another chase as part of the motion picture entitled *Old Texas,* produced by the old rancher himself and loosely based on his frontier experiences.

After the death of his first wife in 1926, Goodnight married Corrine Goodnight, a distant relative, in 1927. He died at his winter home in Tucson two years later.

—*B. Byron Price*

SEE ALSO: Cattle Breeds and Breeding; Cattle Industry; Cattle Trails and Trail Diving; JA Ranch, Texas

SUGGESTED READING:

Burton, Harley T. *A History of the JA Ranch.* Austin, Tex., 1928.

Haley, J. Evetts. *Charles Goodnight: Cowman and Plainsman.* Boston, 1936. Reprint. Norman, Okla., 1949.

GOODNIGHT-LOVING TRAIL

Named for Charles Goodnight (1836–1929) and OLIVER LOVING (1812?–1867), who drove cattle herds in 1866 and 1867 from West Texas to markets in the Western territories, the Goodnight-Loving Trail was used by drovers, emigrants, and stage lines until the early 1880s.

The establishment of the trail was primarily a response to beef markets that developed during the Civil War in New Mexico and Colorado. The major market was the Bosque Redondo Reservation on the Pecos River in New Mexico, where the army collected more than eight thousand Navajos in 1862 and built Fort Sumner nearby. Farther north, booming mining districts around Denver promised a steady outlet for beef. As early as 1864, contractors sent agents into West Texas to purchase cattle, and Texans began using the trail regularly the following year.

Goodnight and Loving were experienced frontiersmen. Loving had taken a herd to Chicago in 1858 and one to Denver via the Arkansas River in 1859; Goodnight had served as a scout during the Civil War. In the summer of 1866, they gathered a herd of two thousand cattle near Fort Belknap in Texas, and with heavily armed herders, they followed the old Butterfield mail road across the prairies north of present-day San Angelo to the Middle Concho and west to the Horsehead Crossing of the Pecos. They turned north up the east bank, shifted to the west bank at Pope's Crossing on the New Mexico line, then back east near Carlsbad, and eventually reached Fort Sumner. Loving took the stock cows, which the contractors refused to accept, north through Raton Pass, skirted the Rockies, and sold them in Denver. The partners drove a second herd that fall. During a third trip in the spring of 1867, Loving, ranging ahead on the Pecos, was attacked by Indians and died from his wounds.

In 1868, the Bosque Redondo market vanished when the government returned the Navajos to their homelands, but the cattle traffic continued on the trail. Goodnight arranged with JOHN SIMPSON CHISUM to deliver herds to him regularly at Bosque Grande, below

Fort Sumner, for sale in Colorado and Wyoming. Goodnight established a ranch near Pueblo but left Colorado in 1876 to resume ranching in Texas.

Texas cattlemen began seeking pastures along the trail. Chisum claimed 150 miles along the Pecos for his expanding herds. Violence flared as Indian raiders swarmed onto his holdings to steal cattle, horses, and mules. The LINCOLN COUNTY WAR in 1877 and 1878 was fought along parts of the old highway. Branches soon ran east into the Texas Panhandle and west toward Arizona. When the railroads arrived in New Mexico in the early 1880s, it was estimated that three hundred thousand head of cattle had passed over the Goodnight-Loving Trail, the third most used cattle route in the nation.

A lonely desert pathway, the trail provided Texans early access to cattle markets, then served as a highway to one of the last pockets of free-grass ranching in the nation.

—*Harwood P. Hinton*

SEE ALSO: Cattle Industry; Cattle Trails and Trail Driving

SUGGESTED READING:
Flanagan, Sue. *Trailing the Longhorns.* Austin, Tex., 1974.
Haley, J. Evetts. *Charles Goodnight: Cowman and Plainsman.* Boston, 1936. Reprint. Norman, Okla., 1949.

GORRAS BLANCAS, LAS

Las Gorras Blancas (the White Caps) were New Mexico rural night-riders who resisted Anglo encroachments on a half-million-acre communal land tract known as the Las Vegas Community Grant. Pulling white caps over their heads to avoid detection, Las Gorras Blancas rode through the countryside in the late nineteenth century, cut barbed wire fences erected by Anglos, and burned the homes, barns, and haystacks of some of the intruders in order to drive them off the land. Their efforts were supported by Hispanic farmers and sheepherders who shared the pasture and woodlands of the 1821 Mexican land grant.

The grant had remained secure until 1879, when the Atchison, Topeka and Santa Fe Railroad brought a number of land-hungry Anglo farmers and cattlemen to the plains of northeastern New Mexico. The resistance of Las Gorras Blancas proved quite successful. After 1890, the number of fence cuttings declined significantly because most of the hated fences had been destroyed. A victory of sorts was achieved in 1903 when the federal Court of Private Land Claims granted a patent to the town of Las Vegas—a patent that gave the community ownership and control over the land.

Las Gorras Blancas was part of a widespread protest movement, originating in Indiana in 1888 and manifesting itself in various states and territories, including Georgia, Mississippi, Texas, and New Mexico. It was a moral regulation movement. In Indiana, members of the movement kept poor whites of questionable probity in line. The movement bridged the gap between the first KU KLUX KLAN of the post–Civil War era and the second Ku Klux Klan of the 1920s. Although the first Klan probably influenced the dress and methods of punishment used by Las Gorras Blancas, there is no conclusive evidence of any tie between the two groups.

The key personality in Las Gorras Blancas was Juan José Herrera, a native New Mexican who had come into contact with the sometimes militant Knights of Labor while living outside the territory. Upon his return to New Mexico in the late 1880s, he became a district organizer for the union. He also became involved with Las Gorras Blancas when he angrily stuffed into a rain barrel an Anglo neighbor who had fenced off so much grazing land that there was no room for others. Following that incident, he and his two brothers, Pablo and Nincanor, went on to become the leaders of Las Gorras Blancas, which by 1890 had grown to about seven hundred members.

Las Gorras Blancas infiltrated the Knights of Labor. Juan José Herrera introduced some tough tactics to the union; he and his followers destroyed the railroad ties of teamsters who did not charge the Santa Fe railroad enough for their work. Members of Las Gorras Blancas also joined a political party that became part of the national Populist movement. In 1890, the Populist slate of candidates won all the seats in the territorial legislature for San Miguel County where Las Vegas was located. Pablo Herrera was elected to the territorial legislature that year, and Juan José Herrera became a probate judge two years later. Populists were sympathetic to the threatened grantees but were not strong enough to do much for them. By the end of the century, Las Gorras Blancas, the Knights of Labor, and the Populists ceased to be significant in the affairs of New Mexico.

—*Robert W. Larson*

SEE ALSO: Labor Movement; Populism; Violence

SUGGESTED READING:
Brown, Richard M. "Historical Patterns of Violence in America." In *Violence in America: Historical and Comparative Perspectives—A Report to the National Commission on the Causes and Prevention of Violence.* Edited by Hugh Graham and Ted Robert Gurr. Washington, D.C., 1969.
Larson, Robert W. *New Mexico Populism: A Study of Radical Protest in a Western Territory.* Boulder, Colo., 1974.

———. "The White Caps of New Mexico: A Study of Ethnic Militancy in the Southwest." *Pacific Historical Review* 44 (1975): 171–185.

Rosenbaum, Robert J. *Mexicano Resistance in the Southwest: "The Sacred Right of Self-Preservation."* Austin, Tex., 1981.

Schlesinger, Andrew Bancroft. "Las Gorras Blancas, 1889–1891." *Journal of Mexican American History* 1 (1971): 87–143.

GOULD, JAY

By the age of forty-five, railroad magnate Jay (born Jason) Gould (1836–1892) had amassed a fortune of more than $100 million, a record for that day. Through a series of astute and sometimes shady financial dealings, Gould, called "the Great Manipulator," left a trail of gigantic fortunes, gutted companies, and ruined entrepreneurs, some of them his former friends.

Born in Roxbury, New York, Gould grew up on his father's farm and learned at an early age that agricultural labor was not for him. He mastered surveying, tried inventing and banking, and turned his leather business into the nation's largest tannery. He amassed his fortune not in these enterprises, however, but in transportation.

After the Civil War, Gould borrowed money from his father-in-law for his first rail investment—the Rutland and Washington—and quickly sold the line at a profit of $130,000. Over the next several years, he refined his technique of buying while the price was low and selling while the price was high and purchased small, vulnerable lines. He also "invested" in legislators, judges, and other influential people who helped him become a director of Daniel Drew's Erie Railroad.

What Gould lacked in scruples, he made up in audacity and acumen. With Drew and speculator James Fisk, he precipitated the Erie "rate war" against rival Cornelius Vanderbilt, at that time the richest man in the country. Gould and Fisk won, partly by printing reams of suspect stock and forcing Drew out of his own line. Vanderbilt dubbed Gould "the smartest man in America." Drew, later driven into poverty, was not so charitable. He said of Gould: "His touch is death."

Gould and Fisk tried to buy enough gold to corner the market and send prices up. When Gould learned the U.S. Treasury Department was about to open its gold reserves, he abandoned Fisk and sold out. Prices plummeted, triggering the gold panic called "Black Friday" on September 24, 1869.

Gould then focused on several struggling RAILROADS in the West. He scooped up the troubled Union Pacific, and in turn, the Kansas Pacific, Denver Pacific, Central Pacific, and much of the Texas and Pacific. He said candidly, "I don't build railroads. I buy them."

Gould kept the Missouri and Pacific and added the Texas and Pacific and other lines to form "The Gould System," which controlled more than eight thousand miles of track, more than half of all the lines in the Southwest.

Gould was no more a "robber baron" than other great railroad magnates, but his methods became models for a generation of younger, faster imitators. The financial panic of 1884 cost him $20 million and his health. He had run out of influential friends, ready investors, and potential victims. He spent his last years dreaming of the coast-to-coast rail network he could not complete before he died of tuberculosis at the age of fifty-seven.

—*Carol M. Martel*

SEE ALSO: Financial Panics

SUGGESTED READING:

Grodinsky, Julius. *Jay Gould: His Business Career, 1867–1892.* Philadelphia, 1957.

Klein, Maury. *The Life and Legend of Jay Gould.* Baltimore, 1986.

GRAHAM-TEWKSBURY FEUD

Also known as the Pleasant Valley War or the Tonto Basin War, the Graham-Tewksbury feud has sometimes been described as a classic conflict between cattle ranchers and sheep ranchers. Although such a dispute may have sparked the outbreak of violence between the two families, in the conflict that spread throughout Arizona's Pleasant Valley from 1886 to 1892 and resulted in the death of more than twenty—and perhaps as many as fifty—men, the hatreds and prejudices that kept the war raging were far more complicated. Indeed, the feud might best be viewed as a case study in the character of Western VIOLENCE.

Located in a corner of the remote Tonto Basin, which in the 1870s had been Apache country, Pleasant Valley spread out for fifty miles beneath the seven-thousand-foot-high Mogollon Rim, a good two-day ride from the nearest town, the mining camp of Globe, Arizona, and one hundred miles from the territorial capital at Prescott. As the Apaches became less a threat in the late 1870s, the valley's lush, well-watered meadows began to attract small ranchers. Men such as John D. Tewksbury and Thomas Graham were typical of those of modest means settling their families in the area.

Three Tewksbury brothers and three Graham brothers worked as cowhands for neighboring ranch-

Cowboys working for the Aztec Land and Cattle Company, one of the powerful Arizona ranching operations backing the Graham brothers in the Graham-Tewksbury feud. *Courtesy National Archives.*

ers, tended their own herds, and remained friends until 1884. The falling out, when it came, was apparently over cattle. Some claimed that the Grahams and the Tewksburys were rustling neighboring herds, others that they were "mavericking," or rounding up unclaimed calves and branding them as their own (a fine distinction from rustling made most frequently by the outfit, large or small, rounding up the mavericks). One source suggested that John Tewksbury, upon learning about the cattle theft, insisted that his sons disassociate themselves from the Grahams, and this order led to the bad blood between them. Another held that when the Graham operation began to grow more profitable, the Graham brothers registered the brand they were using as their own, cutting out the Tewksburys.

Relations between the two families were already strained when Mart Blevins and his five sons arrived from Texas early in 1884 and set up a small cattle ranch next to the Grahams. One of the sons introduced the Grahams to some fellow toughs working as cowboys for the powerful Aztec Land and Cattle Company, situated north of the valley and known locally as the Hash Knife outfit after the shape of its brand. The Blevins

and the Hash Knife boys helped the Grahams expand their small maverick operation into one of the more extensive and lucrative rustling rings in the entire Southwest. The operation spread beyond Pleasant Valley throughout Arizona to Utah and Colorado, and even into Mexico. A frequent target, evidently, was the Tewksburys' fine horse herd.

The Tewksburys and the Grahams became fierce enemies. A local rancher charged the Grahams with rustling; the case was dismissed because prosecution witnesses, perhaps worried about reprisals, failed to appear in court. In response, the foreman of a prominent local rancher and a Graham partisan picked a quarrel with the Tewksburys over "misbranded" cattle, and Edward Tewksbury shot him. The Grahams filed charges, but when Ed was hauled into court in January 1886, the judge ruled that Tewksbury had shot in self-defense. By then, it was already clear the feud was expanding beyond the merely personal. The Grahams, however they had acquired their herd, were allied with the area's larger ranchers, while the Tewksburys, increasingly excluded from the affairs of the valley they had pioneered, were the champions of the smaller ranchers and settlers. And a racial dimension had crept into the conflict as the Grahams called the mixed-blood Tewksburys "Injuns" and "blacks" and vowed to "run the damn blacks out of the country."

Then, the Tewksburys violated the strongest of Pleasant Valley's taboos. Everyone knew the Tonto Basin was cattle country; everyone knew the ranchers had specifically forbidden sheep from grazing the valley pastures. The Tewksburys, looking for a way to strike back at the Grahams, could find no better means of revenge than the deal they made in the fall of 1886 with some prominent Flagstaff sheepmen, the Daggs brothers, who owned the largest sheep operation in northern Arizona. For years, Hash Knife raiders had been harassing the Daggses's sheep, ultimately driving them from their traditional range along the Mogollon Rim. Desperate for winter grazing land, the Daggses snapped up the Tewksburys' offer to range their sheep in Pleasant Valley. Woolly animals by the thousands poured into the area with—according to some accounts—Tewksbury partisans riding guard for the Navajo sheepherders. The cattlemen ambushed the herd, slaughtered the sheep, and—despite injunctions from Tom Graham to limit the killing to animals—brutally murdered and beheaded a Navajo sheepherder. By the summer of 1887, the sheep were gone, but the feud dragged on.

Over the next two years, the Tewksburys, the Grahams, the Blevinses, hired guns from the Aztec Land and Cattle Company in league with the Grahams, and local lawmen, mostly in sympathy with the Tewksburys, ambushed each other with alarming frequency. The new sheriff of Apache County, COMMODORE PERRY OWENS, and the sheriff of Yavapai County, William Mulvenson, were brought into the fight and between them killed most of the Grahams, who resisted arrest, and arrested the remaining Tewksburys, who did not. But the atmosphere of hate and fear in the county was such that neither could witnesses be found to testify nor juries impaneled to convict the Tewksburys. A vicious VIGILANTISM raged, mostly on the side of the Tewksburys, and even men who had not participated in the fighting—and some who may have been outright strangers to the valley—were lynched. By the end of 1888, only Ed Tewksbury and Tom Graham were still alive from the two originally feuding families, and they seemed willing to let the feud die. Graham married and left the valley. Then in September 1891, one of Ed Tewksbury's friends disappeared, never to be heard from again, and in August 1892, after returning briefly in June to clear up business affairs in the valley, Tom Graham was assassinated near Tempe, Arizona. Witnesses identified one of the killers as Ed Tewksbury, who stood trial for murder in 1893 and was convicted.

Granted a new trial on a technicality, Tewksbury went free when the trial ended in a hung jury. All charges were dropped in 1896, and not long afterward, Tewksbury became a lawman in Globe, where he died in 1904 of tuberculosis.

The stuff of "Wild West" legend, the feud formed the basis of ZANE GREY's novel *To the Last Man*. Although sometimes hailed as a tragedy in which basically honest men were trapped by violent frontier conditions into conflicts with other basically honest men, the Graham-Tewksbury feud perhaps points more toward the West's legacy of quick-tempered personal violence, exploitative lawlessness, racial prejudice, and politically motivated vigilante justice than to the working out of problems under a code of the West endorsed by strong and silent, rugged individuals.

—*Charles Phillips*

SUGGESTED READING:
Dedera, Don. *A Little War of Our Own*. Flagstaff, Ariz., 1988.
Forrest, Earle. *Arizona's Dark and Bloody Ground*. Caldwell, Idaho, 1953.
Woody, Clara T., and Milton L. Scwartz. *Globe, Arizona*. Tucson, Ariz., 1977.

GRAND CANYON AND GRAND CANYON NATIONAL PARK

In all its physical dimensions, the Grand Canyon constitutes one of the most remarkable geologic features of the North American continent. Extending for a distance of 277 miles across northern Arizona along the main course of the COLORADO RIVER from Lee's Ferry to the Grand Wash Cliffs, the great chasm reaches a depth of nearly one mile at its heart and averages ten miles in width. North of the canyon lies the Kaibab Plateau, eight thousand to nine thousand feet above sea level, with its forests of aspen and evergreen inhabited by herds of Kaibab deer and a climate marked by temperate summers and harsh winters; to the canyon's south is the Coconino Plateau, nearly one thousand feet lower and with a correspondingly warmer and dryer weather cycle that fosters the growth of piñon and juniper. Over a period of ten million years, the steady erosive flow of the COLORADO RIVER and its tributary streams has carved through numerous layers of limestone, sandstone, and shale to expose a level of metamorphic rock that may have been created two billion years ago.

In contrast with the vast periods over which that evolution has unfolded, the human presence at the

Grand Canyon has been confined to a mere instant in time. Current archaeological evidence suggests that American Indians began to establish themselves in the region between three thousand and five thousand years ago. Settling on the plateau country surrounding the canyon, they developed an increasingly sophisticated agriculture to supplement their earlier reliance on hunting and gathering. In their adaptation to the generally arid climate of the region, some native peoples, such as the Anasazi culture, even developed IRRIGATION techniques to maximize their use of scarce water. By the fifteenth century A.D., various communities of Pueblo peoples had settled in the vicinity of the canyon while members of one tribal grouping, the Havasupai, had established themselves in some of the subsidiary gorges.

Unlike the Indians, who had become deeply entrenched on the Colorado Plateau by the mid-sixteenth century, initial European and Euro-American contacts with the Grand Canyon proved fleeting, although their cumulative impact on the canyon's history would be considerable. During the three centuries after FRANCISCO VÁSQUEZ DE CORONADO's lieutenant García López de Cárdenas reached the canyon in September 1540, the sparse Euro-American population of the Colorado Basin ensured that no more than a handful of wandering missionaries or trappers would come across the canyon. Only in the wake of northern Mexico's absorption by the United States in 1848 following the United States–Mexican War did the Southwest receive systematic attention from American explorers and scientists. Even then, not until Civil War veteran and amateur naturalist JOHN WESLEY POWELL ran the Colorado through the Grand Canyon in 1869 would anyone examine the canyon at close range.

Published accounts of Powell's harrowing 1869 voyage and his second journey in 1872 aroused public interest about this great wonder, an interest further stimulated by the works of the artist THOMAS MORAN and of photographers such as TIMOTHY H. O'SULLIVAN. Public awareness of the canyon's existence increased during the 1880s and 1890s, and visitors were attracted to the site in small but growing numbers. Eventually, by the early twentieth century, the tourist trade overshadowed all other efforts to exploit the canyon.

Popular fascination with and delight in the canyon also fueled efforts to ensure its protection against destructive exploitation. President THEODORE ROOSEVELT designated the Grand Canyon National Monument on January 11, 1908. The canyon received a new status by act of Congress as Grand Canyon National *Park,* on February 26, 1919. Subsequent measures, culminating with the passage of the Grand Canyon National Park Enlargement Act signed by President Gerald R.

The Grand Canyon's Inner Gorge. Photo by George A. Grant. *Courtesy U.S. Department of the Interior, National Park Service.*

Ford on January 3, 1975, incorporated 1,892 square-miles into the park and absorbed all of the canyon's 277-mile length under the federal government's management.

Even before the national park era began, continued improvements in access to the canyon, first by rail and then by road, allowed annual visitation to rise at a sometimes startling rate, especially after World War II. Between 1919 and 1937, for example, the annual visitation rose from forty-four thousand to more than three hundred thousand, while from 1956 to 1976, the figures leapt from more than one million to more than three million. By the late 1980s, the total had regularly surpassed four million. The inexorable pressure of these skyrocketing numbers on the limited space and facilities of the park engendered one of the more difficult challenges the canyon's natural environment had faced since the arrival of humans in the region. Deteriorating trails, contaminated campsites, and enormous traffic jams forced the NATIONAL PARK SERVICE, in the 1970s, to impose increasingly stringent regulations, such as limitations on the use of private vehicles in peak season and rigorous garbage removal by river-running parties from their campsites in the canyon.

Perhaps the greatest changes of all in the canyon's environment, however, have come from relatively recent efforts to harness the Colorado River as a whole for irrigation and power generation. Conservationists and an aroused public led by the SIERRA CLUB defeated two potential intrusions into the canyon when plans for constructing the Marble and Bridge Canyon dams were derailed in the 1960s. Other projects, however, such as HOOVER DAM in 1935 and especially Glen Canyon Dam in 1956, have substantially altered the character of the Colorado River and, by extension, the Grand Canyon. Erected upstream from the canyon to produce hydroelectric power for the COLORADO RIVER STORAGE PROJECT, Glen Canyon Dam routinely traps most of the reddish silt that inspired the river's Spanish name and creates high- and low-water periods based on the water releases used to sustain the power-generating turbines. The resulting changes in the erosion of the river's banks and the canyon's walls have created a new ecosystem that has eradicated some animal and vegetative species and encouraged others, both native and exotic, to flourish in and along the river.

Human activities in the Grand Canyon country since the middle of the twentieth century thus have transformed much of the region in unexpected and unpredictable ways. Continued human intervention will be required in the twenty-first century to strike an appropriate balance among conflicting human uses of the river and the canyon in order to preserve it as a unique scientific and scenic marvel.

—*Peter J. Blodgett*

SEE ALSO: Tourism

SUGGESTED READING:

Babbitt, Bruce, comp. *Grand Canyon: An Anthology.* Flagstaff, Ariz., 1978.

Brown, Bryan T., and Steven W. Carothers. *The Colorado River through Grand Canyon Natural History and Human Change.* Tucson, Ariz., 1991.

Hughes, J. Donald. *In the House of Stone and Light: A Human History of the Grand Canyon.* Grand Canyon, Ariz., 1978.

GRAND TETON NATIONAL PARK

Lying a few miles south of the YELLOWSTONE NATIONAL PARK, Grand Teton National Park includes the Grand Teton Mountains, which shoot up suddenly from the flat lands around Jackson Hole, Wyoming. Unsurpassed for the beauty of its forests, the park is home to abundant wildlife, which feeds along the lakes formed in glacier-carved valleys and along the Snake River. Mountain man JOHN COLTER was the first white to discover the Grand Tetons and the Jackson Hole Valley on one of his extended trapping explorations for MANUAL LISA's MISSOURI FUR COMPANY. Although Indians and trappers roamed the region for years, the first Euro-American settlers did not arrive until 1887, after which the region became home to cattle ranches and, later, dude ranches.

The NATIONAL PARK SERVICE's STEPHEN TYNG MATHER and HORACE MARDEN ALBRIGHT long desired to make the Grand Tetons part of Yellowstone National Park, but when they took steps toward that end in 1916, strong opposition to federal ownership developed among cattlemen, dude ranchers, and big-game hunters. By 1919, Albright found himself at the center of an intense political battle, one in which the UNITED STATES FOREST SERVICE (under whose jurisdiction fell the Teton National Forest) sided with Albright's enemies, in order to keep the region from being "carved up."

In 1929, the year Albright became head of the National Park Service, Congress compromised and declared part of the mountains and a narrow strip at their base the Grand Teton National Park. After Albright introduced John D. Rockefeller, Jr., to the Jackson Hole region, the latter began buying up land in the area with the intention of donating it to the government as soon as someone assured him it would come under the jurisdiction of the Park Service. By 1933, when Albright retired, Rockefeller's Snake River Land Company had bought more than thirty-three thousand acres north of Jackson Hole, and the Park Service opponents had grown more vociferous about keeping Jackson Hole from becoming part of the Grand Teton park. As they complained of "monied interests" back East "locking up" the wilderness, Grand Teton's fate became an issue in Wyoming politics. In 1943, President Franklin D. Roosevelt declared the area the Jackson Hole National Monument, but the fight went on in the U.S. Congress and in the courts to "save" the spot from the national park system. As the economic benefits of the tourist trade became more evident, however, the political opposition dwindled. In 1949, Rockefeller turned his holdings over to the government, and the U.S. Congress passed an act authorizing the consolidation of the monument lands and Rockefeller gift, and in September 1950, they too became part of the Grand Teton National Park.

—*Charles Phillips*

SUGGESTED READING:

Axelrod, Alan, and Charles Phillips. *The Environmentalists: A Biographical Dictionary from the 17th Century to the Present.* New York, 1993.

Righter, Robert. *Crucible for Conservation: The Creation of Grand Teton National Park.* Niwot, Colo., 1982.

Runte, Alfred. *National Parks: The American Experience.* 2d ed. Lincoln, Nebr., 1987.

GRANGERS

SEE: Agrarianism; Greenback Party; Populism

GRANT, HEBER J.

President of the CHURCH OF JESUS CHRIST OF LATTER-DAY SAINTS and Utah community leader Heber J. Grant (1856–1945) was the son of Jedediah M. Grant, a member of the First Presidency of the LDS church and counselor to BRIGHAM YOUNG. Shortly after Heber's birth, his father died. His mother scrimped to provide an education for her son, and he enjoyed the patronage of prominent authorities. Revealing an early talent in business, he founded and headed numerous enterprises. At the age of twenty-five, he was called to the Quorum of Twelve Apostles, the second governing body after the first presidency in the LDS church. From 1882 to 1901, he spent most of his time in business enterprises while filling assignments in the church. He helped the church meet its debts during the depression of the 1890s through business contacts outside the LDS community.

Between 1901 and 1907, Grant presided over LDS missions in Japan and Europe. After returning to the United States, he promoted health reform and served as a director of the Utah Health League. He worked to improve health conditions in order to conquer tuberculosis and improve the quality of milk supplies. He also worked diligently in a campaign that eventually brought prohibition to Utah in 1917. During World War I, he used his considerable promotional skills as chairman of Utah's Liberty Bond Drive.

In 1918, with the death of LDS President JOSEPH FIELDING SMITH, Grant became president of the church. He traveled widely, renewing old acquaintances among non-MORMONS and building ties with nationally prominent politicians and business leaders. At the same time, he promoted increased spirituality among members through his service and sermons.

Strongly opposed to big government, unionism, the welfare state, and alcohol, Grant was committed to private charity, honor, and hard work. Although he had been a lifelong Democrat, he broke with the party during the 1930s because of his opposition to many New Deal initiatives. He supported the church's own welfare program to provide assistance to needy members—a program begun in the 1930s.

—Thomas G. Alexander

SUGGESTED READING:

Gibbons, Francis M. *Heber J. Grant: Man of Steel, Prophet of God.* Salt Lake City, 1979.

Walker, Ronald W. "Heber J. Grant." In *Presidents of the Church.* Edited by Leonard J. Arrington. Salt Lake City, 1986.

GRANT'S PEACE POLICY

Grant's Peace Policy was designed to solve a crisis on the Great Plains caused by the rapid advance of white settlement after the Civil War and, at the same time, to begin assimilating young Native Americans into mainstream American society. The policy, devised by President Ulysses S. Grant, was aimed at both warring Native Americans and those who were more docile. One of its goals was the pacification of those tribes that resisted the power of the United States government by attacking railroad survey crews, mail and stage stations, ranches, and other isolated settlements or westward-bound settlers. The intent of the policy was to make the Great Plains safe for both travel and settlement. But the policy was also intended to make it possible for the military, whose personnel were greatly reduced after 1865, to cope with hostile tribesmen. As General WILLIAM TECUMSEH SHERMAN commented in 1867, "Fifty hostile Indians will checkmate three thousand soldiers." The term *peace policy* is a misnomer; the policy did not achieve peace with warlike tribes until they had been overwhelmed by military force.

The peace-policy strategy could accurately be described as "divide and conquer." Its proponents believed that the number of Native Americans with which the military must cope could be reduced by creating havens of refuge and sustenance for those Indians who did not want to engage in war. The havens were reservations where peaceably inclined tribespeople gathered to be fed, clothed, and sheltered under the watchful eye of church-appointed agents. The generals observed that it was cheaper to feed the Indians than fight them. In 1872, Commissioner of Indian Affairs Francis A. Walker wrote, "By the reservation system and the feeding system combined, the occasions for collision are so reduced by lessening the points of contact, and the number of Indians available for hostile expeditions involving exposure, hardship, and danger is so diminished through the appeal made to their indolence and self-indulgence, that the Army in its present force is able to deal effectively with the few marauding bands which refuse to accept the terms of the Government." Thus the FEDERAL GOVERNMENT approached the Native Americans of the mountains and plains with a carbine in one hand and a Bible in the other. Those who chose to resist federal authority would either perish at the hands of the military or be driven to a reservation where they would come under the supervision and influence of church-appointed agents. An important aspect of the peace policy was that Christian teachers would persuade Native Americans that it was in their best interest to become assimilated into mainstream American culture.

This approach to dealing with the crisis on the Great Plains can be understood in the context of the ethnocentric values of mainstream Americans in the late nineteenth century. They believed that their culture was superior to all others and that minorities of other cultures in their midst would be greatly improved by adopting the ways and beliefs associated with Anglo-American culture. Minorities would not be allowed to decide for themselves whether or not to adopt white culture; if persuasion failed, force would be administered. Thus the peace policy was a harbinger of the policy of forced assimilation, made effective through legislation and administrative fiat in the 1880s and 1890s.

The peace policy also resulted from a compromise between the generals who wanted jurisdiction over Indian affairs transferred to the War Department and Protestant reformers who thought that peace and assimilation could be achieved through persuasion and without the use of military force. Under the policy, the army was given control over Native Americans who refused to come to reservations, while the churches assumed authority over those who elected to locate on the reservations. Before making this arrangement, Grant, who favored military control, conducted an experiment in the Northern and Central superintendencies—Nebraska, Kansas and the Indian Territory—by assigning the agencies there to the Society of Friends. When Congress voted in 1870 to exclude military officers from holding civilian posts, the president invited nearly all Christian denominations to participate in his peace policy, and the newly formed Board of Indian Commissioners took charge of assigning agencies to the churches.

Rivalry among the denominations over assignments raised the issue of whether it was proper to have such an association of church and state. The government, however, had subsidized missionary activities among Native Americans since 1819. By the 1880s, the Catholic church, through its Catholic Board of Indian Missions, had secured the lion's share of government contracts for schools among the Native Americans. Protestant reformers fought against the practice of awarding contracts to religious denominations and succeeded in eliminating contracts by 1900.

The peace policy was in decline by 1878, and church appointment of agents was ended by 1883. As a policy that pacified warlike tribes, it was very successful. Only the Apaches of the Southwest continued to resist the military by the late 1870s. The policy also eliminated much of the corruption and fraud associated with Indian administration. The peace policy was not effective, however, as a program to promote the assimilation of young Native Americans.

—Henry E. Fritz

SEE ALSO: Indian Schools; Missions: Nineteenth-Century Missions to the Indians; United States Indian Policy

SUGGESTED READING:

Fritz, Henry E. *The Movement for Indian Assimilation, 1860–1890*. Philadelphia, 1963.

Keller, Robert H., Jr. *American Protestantism and United States Indian Policy, 1869–92*. Lincoln, Nebr., 1983.

Mardock, Robert W. *The Reformers and the American Indian*. Columbia, Mo., 1971.

Prucha, Francis Paul. *American Indian Policy in Crisis: Christian Reformers and the Indian, 1865–1900*. Norman, Okla., 1976.

GRASS, JOHN (CHARGING BEAR) (SIOUX)

John Grass (ca. 1839–1918), also known as Mato Natan, or "Charging Bear," was born near the Grande River in the Lakota country, the son of a Blackfoot Lakota father and a Two Kettle (Oohe Numpa) mother. Grass was a Blackfoot Lakota civilian leader who laid no claim to military accomplishment as a young adult and who stood aloof during the Battle of Little Bighorn in the summer of 1876.

John Grass, Blackfoot Lakota Sioux. *Courtesy Denver Public Library.*

When Standing Rock Agent JAMES MCLAUGHLIN selected "chiefs" and "headmen" to manage clusters of families during the 1880s, Grass was a logical choice. He had refrained from military resistance, and it seemed that his Blackfoot Lakota tribal group at Standing Rock had been the least involved in the Great Sioux War.

The recognition of Grass with RAIN-IN-THE-FACE and two others as the heads of clusters of families in a Blackfoot-Hunkpapa district demonstrated the ingenuity of McLaughlin and his Mdewakanton Dakota wife, Marie. While the agent elevated GALL in one discrete Hunkpapa district to counteract the influence of SITTING BULL, he elevated Grass with Rain-in-the-Face to control other Hunkpapas in the Blackfoot-Hunkpapa district. Both Gall and Grass served as judges in the Standing Rock Court of Indian Offenses and opposed the relinquishment of additional Great Sioux Reservation land during negotiations in 1888. Gall and Grass signed the Agreement of March 2, 1889, however, which brought about a reduction from 21.7 million acres to 12.7 million acres and the concentration of Lakota and Yanktonai populations mainly on six reservations.

Thereafter, Grass served as an influential orator among Blackfoot and Hunkpapa Lakotas and Yanktonais in favor of accommodation while he supported the work of Catholic missionaries.

—*Herbert T. Hoover*

SUGGESTED READING:

Dykshorn, Jan M. "Leaders of the Sioux Indian Nation." *Dakota Highlights* 3 (1975): 1–8.

National Archives. Record Group 75, Standing Rock Agency.

Pfaller, Louis L., O.S.B. *James McLaughlin: The Man with an Indian Heart.* New York, 1978.

GRATTAN MASSACRE

On August 19, 1854, Brevet Second Lieutenant John L. Grattan and twenty-nine men of the Sixth U.S. Infantry, plus their interpreter, were killed by Brulé Sioux warriors along the North Platte River, seven miles east of Fort Laramie, Wyoming. Subsequently labeled the "Grattan Massacre," the episode foreshadowed a generation of bloodletting on the Northern Plains.

The 1851 Fort Laramie Treaty obliged the Plains tribes to assemble each autumn to receive food and trade goods in payment for their allowing travelers to pass through their territory unmolested. These annual gatherings typically occasioned trouble. As Indians collected near Fort Laramie in 1854, a passing emigrant's cow strayed into a Brulé village and was slaughtered by a visiting Minneconjou Sioux. Upon reaching the fort, the emigrant demanded restitution. Brulé leader Conquering Bear offered amends, but his offer was refused.

John Grattan, recently graduated from West Point, asserted that he should command a sortie to the Indian camp to arrest the Minneconjou. Post commander Hugh B. Fleming relented. Ignoring Fleming's warning to exercise discretion and avoid an engagement, Grattan loaded a small contingent into wagons and embarked for the Indian village. On the trail, Grattan's interpreter, Auguste Lucien, became thoroughly intoxicated, and at Conquering Bear's camp, he hurled abuses at the Sioux. As excitement intensified, Grattan ordered his command to fire. Retaliation was swift and sure. Grattan and Lucien were among the first to die. So was Conquering Bear, who had tried to forestall the confrontation. By nightfall, all the whites except Private John Cuddy lay dead. Cuddy, rescued from the field, never regained consciousness before he died on August 21. Conquering Bear was the lone Sioux casualty.

Although many in the United States were shocked and outraged, not all officials called for revenge. Indian agents quickly adopted the view that the army had blundered, but the War Department disagreed. When Sioux warriors, buoyed by the victory over Grattan, began raiding along major emigrant routes, Secretary of War Jefferson Davis concluded that the "massacre" had been deliberate and that retaliation was needed. He recalled Colonel WILLIAM SELBY HARNEY from Paris to direct operations against the Indians. These operations, in turn, led to a major confrontation between the Sioux and the U.S. Army at Blue Water Creek in early September 1855.

—*Paul L. Hedren*

SEE ALSO: Sioux Wars

SUGGESTED READING:

Lazarus, Edward. *Black Hills, White Justice: The Sioux Nation versus the United States, 1775 to the Present.* New York, 1991.

McCann, Lloyd E. "The Grattan Massacre." *Nebraska History* 37 (1956): 1–26.

GRAY, ROBERT

Robert Gray (1755–1806), explorer of the COLUMBIA RIVER and the Northwest Coast, was born in Tiverton, Rhode Island, and grew up in a world of sailing ships and maritime exploration. While there is no reliable evidence to support stories of his service in the American navy during the Revolution, Gray did gain a reputation as a skilled mariner. In 1787, this reputation brought him to the attention of Boston merchant Joseph Barrell. Having recently read accounts of Captain JAMES COOK's voyage to the Northwest Coast (1778) and the rise of the sea-otter trade with China, Barrell and five other merchants were eager to have a share of the profits. The Boston investors purchased and outfitted two ships, the *Columbia* and the *Washington*, and hired Gray to command the *Washington*. His first voyage to the Northwest Coast from 1787 to 1790 was not a commercial success. Undaunted by this failure, Barrell and his partners persuaded Gray to take the *Columbia* on a second trading voyage. This journey had far-reaching political and diplomatic consequences. Long before Gray set sail, there had been intense speculation about a great "River of the West," a water highway that might form part of the NORTHWEST PASSAGE through North America. Other maritime explorers had caught a glimpse of the mouth of the Columbia River, but none had crossed its dangerous bar to explore the river. In May 1792, Gray and the *Columbia* crossed the bar and mapped the river estuary. This action not only gave the river its European name but also provided the basis for future American claims to the Northwest. Gray spent the rest of his sailing career trading along the Atlantic Coast and died in obscurity in 1806.

—*James P. Ronda*

SEE ALSO: Exploration: United States Expeditions

SUGGESTED READING:

Howay, Frederic, ed. *Voyages of the "Columbia" to the Northwest Coast 1787–1790 and 1790–1793*. Boston, 1941.

GRAZING

Grazing lands were one of the earlier natural resources used in the American West. When human hunters arrived from Asia some fifteen thousand to thirty thousand years ago, they found a variety of native herbivores (grazing animals), including large ancient bison, but a great dying off of those animals followed because of either overhunting or natural catastrophe. On the Great Plains, a dramatic transformation then occurred; a smaller variety of bison (also popularly called the American buffalo) with great capacity to reproduce multiplied in an ongoing coevolutionary process with the vegetation of the plains. Later, large numbers of domestic livestock introduced by Europeans displaced native animals. European animals, especially cattle, altered the environment by destroying the habitat for smaller animals and birds and by consuming the forage on which native grazers depended. Sometimes a crop-farming economy succeeded grazing, but because of distance from markets, poor soil, and aridity, grazing became a permanent fixture in many regions. In addition to cattle, Europeans also introduced HORSES, pigs, sheep, and goats, which also displaced

native animals. Horses escaped their domesticity and ran wild in the environment, thus placing additional pressure on public ranges.

Cattle ultimately became the greatest consumers of the grazing resources of the West. The Spanish first brought their domestic cattle to Mexico sometime around 1525. The English, while bringing their milk-cattle domestic stock to New England, also developed a cattle culture in the Carolinas. As cattle raisers moved their herds north from Mexico into Texas, a Hispanic grazing system took effect and later blended with the westward moving cattle culture from the Carolinas. In 1769, the Spanish colonized northward into California and established the beginnings of what would be an extensive cattle-grazing economy based on the exportation of hides and tallow. The Spanish also grazed sheep for the missions and produced mules for the lucrative Santa Fe trade that opened after Mexico won its independence from Spain in 1821. California animals populated the grazing lands around the fur-trading posts of Hudson's Bay Company in Oregon by the 1840s, and in the same decade, Mormons obtained California cattle to blend with those they had brought from the East. The California gold rush in 1849 created great demands for cattle and sheep. The large numbers of animals accelerated the destruction of California's native grasses. Severe drought in the state from 1862 to 1865 cut the number of cattle in California in half by 1870, and wheat farming replaced grazing in the Central Valley.

Meanwhile on the Great Plains, the Texas system of free- and open-range ranching established itself as far north as MONTANA. A cattle kingdom prevailed on the Great Plains until the mid-1880s and extended into the Great Basin. At the same time, heavy hunting of the great buffalo herds by hide hunters and Indians and the ravages of disease brought about a near extermination of BUFFALOES and opened the way for livestock herds. But a severe winter from 1885 to 1886 decimated cattle on the Southern Plains, and the following winter reduced herds on the Northern Plains by as much as 90 percent. Already, however, the ranges had suffered from overgrazing, and less nutritious annuals had replaced native perennial grasses. On the northern Great Plains in the "White Winter" of 1889 to 1890, livestock had no forage, and the Texas system of open-range ranching failed in part because herders did not grow hay crops during the summer for winter feeding.

Because cattle grazers did not consolidate their control of the public grazing domain, sheepherders entered the lands, and a range war between herders of the two animals resulted. Sheep and cattle competed relentlessly for the remaining resources. With the establishment of forest reserves, authorized by Congress

A herd of Texas cattle grazes, rests, and waters under the attentive of eyes of cowboys in an 1874 illustration from *Harper's Weekly. Courtesy Patrick H. Butler, III.*

in 1891, some order to selected lands was restored; the UNITED STATES FOREST SERVICE devised a permit system in 1906 that designated the number of head to be grazed, the land to be used, and the months of grazing. Those who owned base ranches near the forest reserves or who traditionally ran stock on Forest Service lands received priority for grazing privileges. That system of priorities often excluded landless itinerant sheepherders. Sheep continued to graze freely, as did cattle, however, on the public domain not under the control of the Forest Service.

The crisis of the Great Depression and drought in the 1930s demanded a solution to the question of grazing on public lands in the West. Congress passed the TAYLOR GRAZING ACT of 1934 to organize grazing districts under the direction of locally elected boards. These boards issued permits that stipulated the number of head to be grazed, the time allowed on the range, and the location of the range to be used. The Grazing Service imposed a small fee to help cover administrative costs. When the agency was abolished in appropriations disputes, Congress replaced it with the BUREAU OF LAND MANAGEMENT (BLM) in 1946.

After World War II, both the U.S. Forest Service and the BLM worked to improve range lands in order to meet increased demands for grazing privileges. The improvements, financed largely by the public treasury, included water facilities, reseeded lands, and new stock trails—all to allow for larger numbers of stock to graze on public lands. Many private ranchers depended on access to public grazing lands, and the permits they received from the Forest Service or the BLM added to the sale value or loan-collateral value of their ranches. Since permit fees were below market price for comparable private grazing land, some viewed the grazing permits as windfalls or subsidies from the government to ranchers. With the overstocking of the public ranges and resulting damage to waterways and wildlife, environmentalists became critical of grazing on public lands and called for either the removal of all cattle or at least a fair market price for the resources used.

—*William D. Rowley*

SEE ALSO: Burros; Cattle Breeds and Breeding; Cattle Industry; Erosion; Mules and Mule Trade; Mustangs and Mustang Trade; Sheep and Sheep Ranching

SUGGESTED READING:

Jordan, Terry G. *North American Cattle-Ranching Frontiers.* Albuquerque, N. Mex., 1993.

Rowley, William D. *U.S. Forest Service Grazing and Rangelands.* College Station, Tex., 1985.

Schlebecker, John T. *Cattle Raising on the Plains, 1890–1961.* Lincoln, Nebr., 1963.

Wentworth, Edward N. *America's Sheep Trails.* Ames, Iowa, 1948.

Young, James A. *Cattle in the Cold Desert.* Logan, Utah, 1985.

GREAT AMERICAN DESERT

The *Great American Desert* is an emotionally charged, culturally freighted term for an area that extends from the Rio Grande at the United States–Mexican border to the Mackenzie River delta along the Arctic Ocean coastline and from the escarpments that end in the Central Lowlands and the Canadian Shield to the Rocky Mountains. In the United States, parts of ten states are encompassed by the region, now usually called the "Great Plains." Generally, the vast area is semiarid.

In 1806, Zebulon Montgomery Pike, comparing the region to the Sahara, called the area the "Great Sandy Desert." In 1820, Stephen Harriman Long dubbed it the "Great American Desert." Both explorers identified it as a vast barrier to westward expansion, a wasteland unfit for civilization, and for that very reason, territory admirably suited to domicile the Indians once they were evicted from the East.

In fact, the "Great American Desert" was one of American history's great misnomers. Most of the area receives an average annual rainfall of forty inches— about twice the amount that would be expected in a genuine desert. While true that vegetation in much of the region is sparse and that it is mainly unforested, the area readily supports livestock. That fact was discovered by John Charles Frémont during his explorations in 1838 and from 1843 to 1844, and he challenged the "desert" appellation. Nevertheless, it was not until after the Civil War, when railroad builders and land speculators were eager to bring settlement to the region, that the popular image of the territory was rehabilitated. Through the early 1870s, a concerted public-relations campaign was mounted under the banner of "Rains Follow the Plow." Congress passed the Timber Culture Act of 1873, which gave homesteaders an incentive to plant trees and was based on the mistaken belief that planting trees would increase moisture and thereby alter the CLIMATE of the region.

Coincidentally with the influx of farmers and ranchers, however, rainfalls during the 1870s and early 1880s were exceptionally heavy, and the region underwent a popular transformation from the "Great American Desert" to something like the "Great American Garden." Unfortunately, that transformation also proved

to be an illusion, as John Wesley Powell observed in his landmark 1878 *Report on the Lands of Arid Regions.* Powell believed that the proliferation of 160-acre homesteads in the region would ultimately destroy the semiarid lands. His dire prediction was soon borne out by the droughts of late 1880s, which were accompanied by blizzards, dust storms, and grasshopper plagues. It was not until the introduction of dryland-farming techniques, scientific IRRIGATION, and the widespread development of drought-resistant crops beginning in the early twentieth century that the region recovered agriculturally. The Dust Bowl of the 1930s and the protracted droughts of the 1950s revived for a time the "Great American Desert" image.

—*Alan Axelrod*

See also: Erosion; Exploration: United States Expeditions; Farming: Dryland Farming

Suggested reading:

Hollon, W. Eugene. *The Great American Desert, Then and Now.* New York, 1966.

GREAT CHICAGO FIRE

The 1871 fire in Chicago, which resulted in property damage as high as $196 million and killed an estimated three hundred people, was one of the great nineteenth-century urban disasters.

The fire broke out in a barn in the West Side of Chicago on October 8, 1871, at about 8:45 A.M. A few minutes after 9:00, a watchman at the courthouse saw the flames but thought they were insignificant. Thirty minutes after the blaze started, the watchman realized his error and sounded an alarm. Fire-fighters arrived at the scene on DeKoven Street at about 9:45 A.M., but a mild wind thwarted their initial efforts to put out the fire and sent sparks flying through the air. Some landed on the roof of St. Paul's Church, five blocks north of the barn, and soon the fire spread to the building next door—a furniture-finishing factory. Paints, varnishes, and other highly combustible materials in the factory caught fire, and the blaze was out of control.

The fire raged through the city all day and night, spreading into the South Side at about midnight. By the morning of October 9, it had spread to the city's North Side, By about 11:00 P.M. that evening, a light rain began to fall, and the winds abated; the fire had consumed an area five miles long and one mile wide.

Chicagoans began to rebuild their city quickly. A year after the fire, residents and other investors had spent some $40 million on the construction of new buildings. The fire had shown the fragility of nineteenth-century cities, and through the subsequent rebuilding of the city, Chicago became a model of urban planning.

—*Candace Floyd*

SEE ALSO: Chicago, Illinois

SUGGESTED READING:

Chicago Historical Society. *The Great Chicago Fire*. Chicago, Ill., 1971.
Floyd, Candace. *America's Great Disasters*. New York, 1990.

GREAT DIAMOND HOAX

One of the most impressive swindles in the history of the American West, the Great Diamond Hoax was the work of two Kentuckians, Philip Arnold and his cousin John Slack. Early in 1872, posing as legitimate, if naive, prospectors, they took a bag of uncut diamonds to the Bank of California and attempted to deposit them. Bank director WILLIAM CHAPMAN RALSTON and other California financiers quickly learned of the two rubes and determined to gain control of what was apparently a Western diamond field.

Arnold and Slack escorted a blindfolded representative of Ralston and the other potential investors on a circuitous journey to a remote location in northwestern Colorado. After the blindfold was removed, the representative was shown a "natural" deposit of diamonds and rubies. Always prudent, the San Franciscans had samples examined by Tiffany and Company, which certified their authenticity and value. The San Francisco tycoons then formed the San Francisco and New York Mining and Commercial Company, capitalized it at $10 million, and paid Arnold and Slack some $600,000—surely a bargain.

Word of the enterprise soon spread, touching off an avalanche of rumor and speculation. Guides purporting to know the location of the diamond fields sold their services to all comers, and no fewer than twenty-five mining companies were formed, representing $200 million in capital, all determined to extract precious gems from the Western soil.

During this period, CLARENCE KING was leading the United States Geological Exploration of the Fortieth Parallel. Intrigued by the rumors of diamonds, he identified the site of the field and, being a geologist, proved that the site had been "salted"—deliberately strewn with the gems. The San Francisco and New York Mining and Commercial Company acknowledged that it had been taken, and Ralston and the other syndicate organizers eventually repaid their stockholders' losses.

Arnold and Slack escaped prosecution. Arnold returned to Kentucky, where he spent his share of the $600,000 lavishly—although he did make a $150,000 settlement with his victims. Slack sank into increasing obscurity, ultimately becoming a coffin-maker in the town of White Oaks, New Mexico.

The public—at least the noninvesting portion of it—was hardly outraged by the Great Diamond Hoax. If anything, Easterners and Westerners alike took pleasure in contemplating the tweaked noses of big-monied San Francisco tycoons.

—*Alan Axelrod*

SUGGESTED READING:

Woodward, Bruce A. *Diamonds in the Salt*. Boulder, Colo., 1967.

GREAT NORTHERN RAILROAD

SEE: Burlington Northern Railroad

GREEN, JOSHUA

Joshua Green (1869–1975) was a Seattle shipping magnate and banker. Born in Jackson, Mississippi, Green moved to the Washington Territory in 1883. He later acquired a one-hundred-foot sternwheeler and laid the foundation for his Puget Sound Navigation Company, which would become dominant in the Northwest maritime trade. At the age of 57, the wealthy Green purchased a struggling Seattle bank and developed it into the People's National Bank, which became one of the region's largest with branch offices throughout the state. Active in civic organizations and an avid outdoorsman, Green was a Seattle legend when he died at the age of 105.

—*Charles P. LeWarne*

SUGGESTED READING:

Newell, Gordon. *The Green Years: The Development of Transportation, Trade and Finance in the Puget Sound Region from 1886 to 1969 as Recalled by Joshua Green*. Seattle, 1969.

GREENBACK PARTY

Growing out of the agrarian unrest in the West and South during the 1870s, the Greenback party was a focal point of resistance to the tight monetary policies of the Republican administrations of the period. During the Civil War, the United States government had issued $432 million in paper money, termed "greenbacks," to help finance the war. This currency fluctuated in value and was popular with debtor classes, particularly farmers. Creditors and businessmen wanted a stable currency, and in 1866, legislation was passed to provide for the gradual retirement of $100 million over the next two years. The tight-money policy was hard on farmers and others who had gone into debt to expand production. Accompanied by a drop in demand for crops after the Civil War, the tight-money policies contributed to the economic problems of the late 1860s and the panic of 1873.

In 1874, as a reaction to these policies, farmers and others organized the Greenback party, growing out of the Granger movement, to campaign for the issuance of additional greenbacks and the unlimited coinage of silver. The primary support for the party came from the Midwest and West, although it always drew substantial support from the East. The Specie Payment Act of 1875—which continued the program of withdrawing greenbacks, put greenbacks on a par with gold, and required the payment of specie in exchange for greenbacks by 1878—was a victory for the "hard-money" interests. In reaction to the law, the Greenback party grew markedly more popular.

The first presidential candidate of the party, New York philanthropist and inventor Peter Cooper, drew fewer than one hundred thousand votes in 1876, but the party continued to grow and, as the Greenback-Labor party, got more than one million votes in the congressional elections of 1878 and elected fourteen members of Congress. That success led to the BLAND-ALLISON ACT of 1878 and other legislation to block the retirement of greenbacks, but the party also wanted a more fundamental revision of the currency system. In 1880, JAMES B. WEAVER of Iowa ran as the party's presidential candidate and received more than three hundred thousand votes, primarily from the West. In 1884, as the party was in decline, it joined the Antimonopoly party in nominating Benjamin F. Butler for president.

Although the party slipped from the scene in the 1880s, its impact on politics was important for the remainder of the century as others, particularly the Populists and the Democrats who would find a leader in WILLIAM JENNINGS BRYAN, continued to support its issues including the graduated income tax, the postal savings system, a federal labor bureau, equal pay for equal work by men and women, an interstate-commerce commission and equal suffrage for men and women, among others. In the end, most of the propos-als of the party would be adopted into law, and it would have a far-reaching influence on reform movements of both parties in the late nineteenth and early twentieth centuries.

—*Patrick H. Butler, III*

SEE ALSO: Agrarianism; Banking; Currency and Silver as Western Political Issues; Financial Panics; Populism

SUGGESTED READING:

Unger, Irwin. *The Greenback Era: A Social and Political History of American Finance*. New York, 1964.

GREENWOOD, CALEB

By his own calculation, mountain man Caleb Greenwood (ca. 1763–1850) was born in Virginia. Nothing is known of his early life, and precious little more about the rest of it, yet "Old Greenwood" cast a long shadow in the West and is a firm part of both its myth and its reality. The first verifiable trace of him is in employment records of JOHN JACOB ASTOR's fur company from 1810 to 1811, but his tenure there was brief; in 1812, he turned up in the employ of MANUEL LISA. Three years later, Greenwood was spotted by Jules DeMun on the Arkansas River, and Greenwood's name appeared in the company books of WILLIAM HENRY ASHLEY in 1824.

Greenwood may have spent some time with the Crow Indians and, probably in 1827, married Batchicka Youngcault, a half-French, half-Crow woman. The next record of Greenwood placed him in Independence, Missouri, in May 1844, hired to guide the Elisha Stevens party to FORT HALL. He continued on with Stevens to California and was credited with ascertaining from Chief Truckee the route through what later became known as Donner Pass. Thus, at the age of eighty-one, Caleb Greenwood had found a new career as a guide. In 1845, he went east to Fort Hall to earn some cash by guiding people to California. Taking a large group through, he pioneered the easiest path over Donner Summit, by way of Dog Valley. He repeated the performance in 1846, perhaps going as far east as the cutoff north of Fort Bridger, a route that came to bear his name. He participated in one of the relief efforts to aid the DONNER PARTY in 1847 and went to Coloma after the discovery of gold. Thereafter, he moved to the valley that bears his name in El Dorado County, California, where, still sleeping under the stars and defying anyone who tried to put him in a house, he died in the early months of 1850.

—*Richard E. Oglesby*

See also: Mountain Men; Trappers

Suggested reading:
Kelly, Charles, and Dale L. Morgan. *Old Greenwood: The Story of Caleb Greenwood, Trapper, Pathfinder, and Early Pioneer.* Georgetown, Calif., 1965.

Suggested reading:
Gregg, Josiah. *Commerce of the Prairies* (with a biographical sketch by Max L. Moorhead). Norman, Okla., 1954.
Horgan, Paul. *Josiah Gregg and his Vision of the Early West.* New York, 1941.

GREGG, JOSIAH

Author of *Commerce of the Prairies,* a pivotal study of the Santa Fe Trail, Josiah Gregg (1806–1850) was engaged in trade in New Mexico from 1831 to 1840. Born and raised in Missouri, he received a scanty formal education but read widely in a variety of fields, including mathematics, surveying, medicine, and law. When his health deteriorated during his mid-twenties, his doctor sent him to the West in hopes that his condition would improve. At the beginning of the trip, Gregg was confined to a wagon bed, but along the trail, he regained his strength and was soon able to ride a horse. During the trip he studied Spanish, and when the wagon train reached Santa Fe, he began his trading enterprise with the New Mexicans in their own language.

Gregg collected natural history and frontier lore and recorded his observations in little pocket notebooks. He made eight trips to Santa Fe between 1831 and 1840. From the observations he had recorded, he wrote a two-volume story of the Santa Fe Trail. Published in 1844, *Commerce of the Prairies* describes prairie culture, Mexican society, and caravans and mule trains. It provides a vivid taste of prairie travel along the eight-hundred-mile trek from Missouri to Santa Fe. Over the next ten years, the book was reprinted five times.

Gregg served with the Arkansas Volunteers in the United States–Mexican War and wrote several accounts of the Battle of Buena Vista for American newspapers. Having earned a medical degree while living in Kentucky in the mid-1840s, he practiced medicine in Saltillo, Mexico. He then joined an expedition to find an overland trail to northern California. After reaching Humboldt Bay in December 1849, he and his band of explorers started their return from northern California. The group had little ammunition and food, and Gregg grew weak on a diet of herbs and acorns. In February 1850, he fell from his horse and died at the age of forty-four.

—*Candace Floyd*

See also: California Overland Trails; Santa Fe and Chihuahua Trail; Overland Travel

GREY, ZANE

Zane Grey (1872–1939) invented the popular western novel. Although there were popular writers of western novels before he began his career and important innovators after him, it was Grey who fully defined and developed the genre.

Pearl Zane Gray (he dropped the first name and changed the spelling of the last when he began his literary career) was born in Zanesville, Ohio, to a pioneer family who had fallen upon financially hard times. Young Grey pulled himself up by his bootstraps, however, with a baseball scholarship to the University of Pennsylvania. He graduated with a dentistry degree in 1896. Unfulfilled by his dental profession, he began writing novels based on exploits of his frontier ancestors, but three books on that theme failed to sell.

An important turning point occurred in 1907 when Grey met the old frontiersman Charles J. ("Buffalo") Jones and spent a few weeks on Jones's ranch near the Grand Canyon. There, Grey met some Mormon cowboys whose way of life, set in the spectacular northern Arizona scenery, provided material for his literary success. Although his first two books based on that experience met only modest sales, the third, *Riders of the Purple Sage* (1912), became the most famous popular western ever written. Grey's output from then until his death averaged at least two novels per year (though his publisher released only one annually), plus short stories and magazine articles.

The classic westerns Grey produced during the 1920s often featured a physical and moral weakling from the East who developed both strength and fortitude through contact with cowboys or other wholesome characters in the West. Grey condemned modern urban, industrial civilization as physically unhealthy and morally corrupt and pointed to the robust Darwinian social conditions of the frontier as a much more humane environment.

Although most of Grey's approximately ninety books are westerns, many are much more than just cowboy stories, for he included a wide variety of character types. Indians, sheepherders, prospectors, railroad workers, traders, and others appear in primary roles. Although Grey's dialogue is often stilted and his later stories lack originality, his descriptive abilities, action scenes, and vision of the West's redemptive role in American civilization have won for him a memorable place in literary history.

—*Gary Topping*

SEE ALSO: Literature: the Western Novel

SUGGESTED READING:
Grey, Zane. *The Call of the Canyon.* New York, 1924.
————. *The Heritage of the Desert.* New York, 1910.
————. *The Man of the Forest.* New York, 1920.
————. *Riders of the Purple Sage.* New York, 1912.
Gruber, Frank. *Zane Grey: A Biography.* New York, 1970.
Kant, Candace C. *Zane Grey's Arizona.* Flagstaff, Ariz., 1984.

GREY BEARD (CHEYENNE)

Grey Beard (?–1875)—also known as Grey Head—surfaced in federal records with Tall Bull, Bull Bear, Roman Nose, and WHITE HORSE as one of several Southern Cheyenne tribal leaders determined to defend a province on the southern Great Plains for hunting, gathering, and casual farming. Grey Beard was prominent as a leader of the Dog Soldiers in the "war faction," which faced General PHILIP H. SHERIDAN at war.

When Southern Cheyennes gathered around Brinton Darlington's agency in 1871, the agent regarded Grey Beard as the most volatile among the leaders and one of considerable influence because of the presence of eighty-two lodges in his camp. In 1874, Grey Beard and Medicine Water mounted a cooperative effort with Kiowas and Comanches to remove or kill the buffalo hunters at Adobe Walls. Grey Beard stood out as a leader of the intertribal force during the ensuing unsuccessful attack.

U.S. Agent John D. Miles soon thereafter reported the continued resistance of Southern Cheyennes under Grey Beard. He was the primary leader of the retreat onto land surrounding the rivers that drained the Texas Panhandle to avoid capture. Grey Beard remained recalcitrant and was a primary target for capture at the end of the Red River War. Among the thirty-two selected for incarceration at Fort Marion in Florida, Grey Beard was shot and killed while attempting to escape from a railroad car that was to carry him into exile.

Other Southern Cheyenne leaders laid blame for Cheyenne resistance on Grey Beard and Lean Bear—perhaps in hopes of sparing themselves further punishment. Grey Beard posthumously recovered respect for his determination to defend traditional life among peoples of the south-

ern Great Plains and for the loss of his life during an escape from ignominious incarceration.

—*Herbert T. Hoover*

SEE ALSO: Native American Peoples: Peoples of the Great Plains; Texas Frontier Indian Wars

SUGGESTED READING:
Berthrong, Donald J. *The Southern Cheyennes.* Norman, Okla., 1963.
National Archives. Record Group 75, Cheyenne-Arapaho Agency.

GRIERSON, BENJAMIN HENRY

Soldier and colonel in the Tenth Cavalry composed of BUFFALO SOLDIERS, Benjamin Henry Grierson (1826–1911) was born in Pittsburgh, Pennsylvania, grew up in Youngstown, Ohio, and, in his mid-twenties, moved to Jacksonville, Illinois. A former band leader, musician, and merchant, he gained national prominence as the leader of a spectacular U.S. cavalry raid from La Grange, Tennessee, to Baton Rouge, Louisiana, from

Benjamin Henry Grierson. *Courtesy National Archives.*

April 17 to May 2, 1863. He rose to the rank of major general of volunteers. Appointed colonel of the Tenth Cavalry, one of the post–Civil War army's two mounted regiments composed of white officers and black enlisted men, Grierson was an outspoken defender of the rights of blacks and Indians. A builder more than a fighter, he supervised the construction of Fort Sill in present-day Oklahoma and expanded the facilities at Forts Concho and Davis, Texas. As commander of the District of the Pecos from 1878 to 1881, he defeated VICTORIO's warriors at Tinaja de las Palmas and at Rattlesnake Springs, thereby ending the Apache threat in West Texas. Troops under his command explored and mapped thousands of miles of territory, strung telegraph wires, escorted railroad construction crews, guarded freight and the mails, and opened the West to settlement. Grierson served in Arizona from 1885 to 1886 and commanded the District of New Mexico from 1886 to 1888 and the Department of Arizona from 1888 until his retirement, as a brigadier general, on July 8, 1890.

—*Bruce J. Dinges*

SUGGESTED READING:

Dinges, Bruce J. "Benjamin H. Grierson." In *Soldiers West: Biographies from the Military Frontier*. Edited by Paul A. Hutton. Lincoln, Nebr., 1987.

Leckie, William H., and Shirley A. Leckie. *Unlikely Warriors: General Benjamin H. Grierson and His Family*. Norman, Okla., 1984.

GRIMES, JAMES WILSON

Governor of Iowa and Republican Senator James Wilson Grimes (1816–1872) was born in Deering, New Hampshire. He studied at Dartmouth College, read law, and moved to Burlington, Iowa, in 1836. He served as city solicitor and was elected to the territorial assembly, the state legislature, and the governorship as a Whig. He also served two terms in the U.S. Senate as a Republican. He was editor of *Iowa Farmer and Horticulturist* and a benefactor of Grinnell College and Dartmouth College. In the Senate, he was one of only seven Republicans to vote for President Andrew Johnson's acquittal during his impeachment trial.

—*Loren N. Horton*

SUGGESTED READING:

Christoferson, Eli C. "The Life of James W. Grimes." Ph.D. diss., State University of Iowa, 1924.

Haefner, Marie. "A Man of Character." *The Palimpsest* 22:6 (June 1941): 184-192.

Lewellen, Fred B. "Political Ideas of James W. Grimes." *Iowa Journal of History and Politics*. 42:4 (October 1944): 339-404.

Salter, William. *The Life of James W. Grimes*. New York, 1876.

GRINNELL, GEORGE BIRD

An advocate on behalf of the Plains Indians and a founder of the North American conservation movement, George Bird Grinnell (1849–1938) was born in Brooklyn, New York. He was introduced to nature and the outdoors by his neighbor and tutor Lucy Audubon, widow of JOHN JAMES AUDUBON, and her son Jack. Grinnell attended Yale and, in 1870 at the end of his senior year, volunteered to join paleontologist Othniel C. Marsh's Western expedition.

During repeated summer visits to the West, he hunted buffalo with the Pawnees, joined GEORGE ARMSTRONG CUSTER's Black Hills expedition, participated in William Ludlow's survey of Yellowstone, and hunted with WILLIAM F. ("BUFFALO BILL") CODY. Meanwhile, Grinnell studied for a doctorate in paleontology under Marsh. Overwhelmed with academic work in 1876, he fortunately declined Custer's invitation to travel with him on what became the fatal expedition to the Little Bighorn. Grinnell became a rancher and explored regions of Wyoming and Montana. He discovered Montana's Grinnell Glacier in 1885. Despite his passion for the West, he continued to make his home in New York.

Grinnell's writings record the West and the Plains Indians just before and while they underwent radical change. Much of his work was devoted to preserving what he could before it disappeared. During his Western trips, he studied the Plains Indians and eventually published many books and journal articles about the life and folklore of the Pawnee, Blackfoot, and especially the Cheyenne Indians. His major work was *The Cheyenne Indians, Their History and Ways of Life* (two volumes, 1923). Other books included *Pawnee Hero Stories and Folk Tales, With Notes on the Origins, Customs and Character of the Pawnee People* (1889) and *The Fighting Cheyennes* (1915). Although he did not make major contributions to anthropology, his descriptive studies of Plains Indians continue to be consulted.

Some of Grinnell's most important achievements were in the field of conservation. In 1876, he became natural-history editor of *Forest and Stream*. When he purchased the sporting magazine in 1880, he became editor, a post he held for thirty-one years. The magazine was a leader in efforts to rally sportsmen to support hunting regulations and the conservation of

George Bird Grinnell. *Editors' collection.*

America's vanishing wildlife. His other campaigns included establishing proper management of Yellowstone National Park, creating Glacier National Park, and bringing European forestry methods to the United States. Grinnell influenced THEODORE ROOSEVELT's views on conservation through his magazine and their friendship, which began in 1885. In 1887, he joined Roosevelt in founding the BOONE AND CROCKETT CLUB, a group of hunters dedicated to promoting wildlife conservation.

In 1886, he created the Audubon Society for the Protection of Birds as an extension of his magazine. People joined by signing a pledge to protect birds. As membership grew to fifty thousand, supporting the society became too burdensome for the magazine, and the program was discontinued in 1889. However, his work was the forerunner of a movement that resulted in the establishment of the Massachusetts Audubon Society in 1896 and the rapid appearance of other state Audubon societies. Grinnell served on the National Audubon Society board of directors for twenty-six years.
—*Ralph H. Lutts*

SUGGESTED READING:
Reiger, John F. *American Sportsmen and the Origins of Conservation.* Rev. ed. Norman, Okla., 1986.

————. "A Dedication to the Memory of George Bird Grinnell, 1849–1938." *Arizona and the West* 21 (Spring 1979): 1–4.
————. *The Passing of the Great West: Selected Papers of George Bird Grinnell.* New York, 1976.

GRIZZLY BEARS

The grizzly bear, *Ursus arctos horribilis*—standing three to three and a half feet high at the shoulders, reaching a length of six to seven feet, and weighing up to 1,000 pounds—is the largest carnivore found in Canada and the continental United States. Females are smaller than males and seldom exceed 450 pounds in weight. Only its near relative, the Alaska brown bear *(Ursus arctos middendorffi),* or Kodiak bear, and the polar bear *(Thalarctos maritimus)* are larger than the grizzly bear. Declared an endangered species in 1966, the grizzly bear was once present in all states west of the Mississippi River including Alaska, throughout the western one-third of Canada, and in the northern half of Mexico. Reproducing more slowly than any other large animal found in North America, the grizzly bear does not begin bearing young until the female is four and a half years old. There is often a two- to seven-year interval between litters. Grizzly bears may live to be as old as twenty-five years.

The grizzly bear's color varies from a light, straw color to brown to black. White-tipped hairs give it a grizzled effect, thus providing both its name "grizzly" and its nickname "silver tip." Remarkably agile, a grizzly can sprint up to thirty miles an hour and is an adept swimmer. Unlike the black bear, a mature grizzly generally does not climb trees. It is easily recognized by the prominent hump on its shoulders, its large, dish-shaped (concave) face, grizzled coat, and prominent front claws, which may reach up to four inches in length.

Grizzlies are omnivores and consume more herbaceous vegetation than carrion or fresh animal material. In the absence of livestock and in habitats rich in vegetation, more than 90 percent of their diet comes from vegetable materials. They also consume insects, rodents, and larger game, but they are not effective predators of deer and ELKS. Their home ranges often exceed 180 square miles.

Native Americans and Euro-American settlers in the West feared grizzly bears more than any other animal. Although rare, their attacks on humans led to more deaths than those produced by any other wild animal in the West.

Native American cultures often incorporated the bear into their medical, mythological, and military traditions. The supernatural power of bears was an important aspect of the belief systems of those cultures. As the paintings of GEORGE CATLIN and KARL (OR CARL) BODMER and the artifacts and accounts of rituals collected by early explorers so aptly illustrate, bear claws, teeth, skins, and paws were often worn by medicine men, clans, and warrior societies. Native Americans respected bears for their strength, intelligence, and habits. Like humans, bears can walk upright, and their footprint is dissimilar to that of most other animals. The musculature and gross anatomy of a skinned bear was thought to be similar to that of a human. The somewhat unpredictable nature of a bear also suggested a relationship to humans. Because of these assumed anthropomorphic similarities, the killing of a bear entitled one to join a scalp or warrior society. While some tribes had taboos against the hunting of bears, most pursued them as game and preferred their meat to that of deer and elk. The fat of the grizzly also provided bear oil, which had many applications in Indian society as a cooking oil, medicine, and liniment. A mature grizzly could provide more than fifteen gallons of this important resource. Bears played a significant role in the medical practices and curing rites of many tribes. Among the Pueblo tribes, where illness was thought to be caused by witches, the bear gave strength to the medicine man who was in conflict with those forces. Since bears were often seen digging for roots and plants believed to have curative powers, bears were considered to be powerful agents for healing. Medicine men called on the bear and wore its relics in their healing rituals.

The increasing pace of white settlement and the development of sheep and cattle raising after the Civil War doomed the grizzly bear. The HOMESTEAD ACT OF 1862, the TIMBER CULTURE ACT OF 1873, and the STOCK RAISING HOMESTEAD ACT OF 1916 encouraged settlement in the grizzly's habitat. As sheep and cattle began to be raised in larger numbers, grizzlies preyed on livestock, and farmers and ranchers demanded their eradication. Bounty hunting, trapping, and strychnine poisoning reduced their numbers. By 1910, grizzlies were under pressure throughout the West. The creation of the Predatory Animal and Rodent Control (PARC) as a branch of the Biological Survey of the U.S. Department of Agriculture in 1914 ensured that grizzlies would be pursued ruthlessly wherever it was claimed that they endangered livestock. By 1928, the U.S. Forest Service estimated that there were fewer than thirty grizzlies in the national forests of the Southwest. By the 1950s, with the exception of populations found in and near national parks in Wyoming and Montana, grizzlies were absent from most Western states. In Colorado, only a small, remnant population existed; and

by 1980, it was impossible to document the existence of this relic population. In the late twentieth century, grizzlies were found primarily in Alaska and in national parks and wilderness areas in Montana, Wyoming, and Idaho. With a population of approximately one thousand in 1994 in the contiguous United States, grizzlies existed on approximately 2 percent of their former range. They were abundant only in northwestern Canada and Alaska, where there were populations of twenty-five thousand and forty thousand grizzlies, respectively.

—*Phillip Drennon Thomas*

SEE ALSO: Black Bears; Extinction of Species; Wildlife

SUGGESTED READING:

Brown, David E. *The Grizzly in the Southwest*. Norman, Okla., 1985.
Craighead, F. C., Jr. *Track of the Grizzly*. San Francisco, 1979.
Haynes, B. D., and E. Haynes. *The Grizzly Bear: Portraits from Life*. Norman, Okla., 1966.

GRUENING, ERNEST

Ernest Gruening (1887–1974), publicist, newspaper editor, author, territorial governor of Alaska, and U.S. senator, was born in New York City, the son of Phebe and Emil Gruening. After attending private schools, Gruening entered Harvard College in the fall of 1903 and graduated with a bachelor of arts in science in 1907. He earned a medical degree from Harvard in 1912, but having taken a liking to the challenge and excitement of journalism, he never practiced medicine. Between 1912 and 1933, he worked at various newspapers in Boston and New York.

In 1921, he accepted the job of managing editor of *The Nation*, a liberal weekly magazine in New York. During his stewardship, he recruited a number of the nation's foremost writers—including H. L. Mencken, Sherwood Anderson, Dorothy Canfield, Sinclair Lewis, and Theodore Dreiser—as contributors. In 1924, Gruening became director of publicity for Senator Robert M. LaFollete's 1924 presidential campaign.

While still at *The Nation*, Gruening had become interested in Latin America. He traveled to Mexico to study its people and institutions. His book *Mexico and Its Heritage* (1928) was considered then, and still is today, a standard work on that country.

In 1927, Gruening and his family moved to Portland, Maine, where he took charge of a new newspaper, *The Portland Evening News*. From the beginning, the paper took very liberal and vigorous positions on important matters facing the state. In 1932, he returned to New York and became one of four editors of *The Nation*. He participated actively in public affairs and, in 1933, was named advisor to the United States delegation to the seventh Pan-American Conference, held in Montevideo, Uruguay.

In 1934, President Franklin D. Roosevelt appointed Gruening director of the newly established Office of Territories and Island Possessions and a year later named him administrator of the Puerto Rican Reconstruction Administration (PRRA). Gruening resigned that post in June 1937. The president appointed him territorial governor of ALASKA in 1939.

Gruening was a vocal and highly effective critic of Alaska's inadequate governmental structure and truncated powers. Having long before decided that only statehood could cure Alaska's ills, he tirelessly advocated Alaska's admission to the Union. After he left office in 1953, he wrote *The State of Alaska* (1954), an effective polemic and convincing argument for Alaska statehood. In 1956, Alaskans elected him territorial delegate to Congress. Gruening spent the next two years lobbying for Alaska statehood in the nation's capital. Congress passed the Alaska statehood bill in 1958, and Alaska joined the Union as the forty-ninth state on January 3, 1959.

Alaskans elected Gruening U.S. senator in 1959 and in 1962. He was a crusading liberal in the forefront of every major issue of the age, ranging from birth control to civil rights. He was one of the first and most eloquent opponents of the war in Vietnam. He lost his bid for reelection in 1968 to Anchorage real-estate developer Mike Gravel.

—*Claus-M. Naske*

SUGGESTED READING:
Gruening, Ernest, ed. *An Alaskan Reader.* New York, 1967.
———. *The Battle for Alaska Statehood.* College, Alaska, 1967.
———. *Many Battles.* New York, 1973.
———. *Mexico and Its Heritage.* New York and London, 1928.
———. *The Public Pays.* New York, 1931.
———. *The State of Alaska.* New York, 1954.
———, ed. *These United States.* New York, 1923.
———, with Herbert Beaser. *Vietnam Folly.* Washington, D.C., 1968.

GUADALUPE HIDALGO, TREATY OF

SEE: United States–Mexican War

GUERIN, ELSA JANE

Cross-dresser, cabin boy, railroad brakeman, freighter, rancher, fur trader, miner, and saloonkeeper Elsa Jane Forest Guerin (1834–?), also known as "Mountain Charley," donned the clothing and manners of a man in order to earn enough money to raise her children and secure the freedom of movement needed to avenge the murder of her husband. Aside from her autobiography, sources on her life are scarce, and there may have been more than one female cross-dresser calling herself "Mountain Charley." Her story—perhaps occasionally apocryphal—fascinated nineteenth-century readers.

Born the illegitimate child of a unmarried Louisiana planter, Guerin lived on her father's plantation until she was sent to boarding school at the age of twelve. That same year, she ran off with a river-boat pilot named Forest. She and Forest married, and for four years, Guerin lived a conventional life in St. Louis as a wife and young mother of two children. In 1850, her husband was killed in a fight with a man named Jamieson, a member of his crew.

A widow at the age of sixteen, Guerin had limited employment options. She had no trade, and she despaired of earning enough money to support her family. Her solution was to dress as a man and seek employment in a man's world. Leaving her children with the Sisters of Charity in St. Louis, she found work as a cabin boy on a Mississippi steamer. She remained on the river for four years and then worked briefly as a brakeman for the Illinois Central Railroad until she overheard a conductor reveal his suspicions that she was in disguise. Each month, she would trade her man's clothing for a dress to visit her children.

Guerin discovered that she enjoyed the freedom her disguise afforded. "I could go where I chose," she wrote in her autobiography, "[and] do many things which while innocent in themselves, were debarred by propriety from association with the female sex. The change from cumbersome, unhealthy attire of woman to the more convenient, healthful habiliments of man, was in itself almost sufficient to compensate for its unwomanly character." She spent many evenings in man's clothing wandering saloons, theaters, steamboat decks, and other male haunts. On one of her nocturnal sojourns, she spied her husband's murderer, and although she wounded him with her revolver, he escaped.

In 1855, Guerin was bitten with gold fever and joined an expedition to California. The rigors of prospecting were too strenuous for her, but she found work cleaning a saloon for one hundred dollars a month. Living frugally, she bought into the business after six months. After selling her interest in the saloon, she began trading in pack mules, built a thriving business in freighting, and established a small ranch in California's Shasta Valley. When she sold her Western enterprises, she returned to St. Louis richer by thirty thousand dollars and determined to live the conventional life of woman and mother.

Her determination, however, did not last very long. Bored with her life in St. Louis, she again donned her male disguise and worked as a fur trader for the American Fur Company, then wandered to Colorado where, as "Mountain Charley," she operated the Mountain Boy's Saloon in Denver.

A second encounter with Jamieson near Denver signaled the end of her masquerade. Meeting him on a deserted road, she emptied her six shooter, but only one bullet struck him. Jamieson survived and, before leaving Denver, revealed all he knew about Guerin's past. She became famous, gave up her life as a man, and married H. L. Guerin, the bartender from her saloon.

—*Patricia Hogan*

SEE ALSO: Passing Women

SUGGESTED READING:
Guerin, Mrs. E. *Mountain Charley*. Norman, Okla., 1968.

GUERRILLAS

Guerrillas, also known as partisans and bushwhackers, are members of small, irregular armed forces whose mobility allows them to engage in small-scale, hit-and-run actions against regular military forces. Their name, "guerrilla," derives from the phrase *little war* in Spanish. Usually part of a larger political and military strategy, guerrilla tactics include deception and surprise, terrorism, ambush, and the taking of hostages. The success of guerrilla bands lies in their unpredictability, lightning-swiftness, knowledge of the terrain, popular support, and elaborate intelligence networks.

In America, guerrilla warfare developed from Indian-style fighting. Used by early settlers in Virginia and the New England colonies, it was espoused by the Swiss mercenary Henry Bouguet in the French and Indian War. Francis ("Swamp Fox") Marion and his band of South Carolina partisans used Indian-style fighting against the British forces during the American Revolution. British generals, fighting in the New World, never quite understood decentralized tactical formations. A similar blindness afflicted Union commanders during the Civil War and afterwards during the Indian wars in the West.

Throughout the Civil War, bands of Confederate guerrillas harassed the Union forces, especially in Virginia, West Virginia, the Shenandoah Valley, Missouri, and Kansas. Only two partisan units were officially sanctioned by the Confederate Congress: John Singleton Mosby's Partisan Rangers and John Hanson McNeill's Rangers. Other guerrilla bands—WILLIAM CLARKE QUANTRILL's Raiders, for example—operated in the twilight zone between Confederate sympathies and personal interest. Little coordination existed among Confederate guerrilla bands; their effectiveness diminished considerably during the last year of the war.

Mosby's rough-riders terrorized Union troops and raided federal pickets and supply lines throughout northern Virginia and Maryland ("Mosby's Confederacy"). McNeill's band operated in West Virginia and the Shenandoah Valley. Unlike Mosby and McNeill, Quantrill and his deputies—including WILLIAM "BLOODY BILL" ANDERSON and George Todd—operated hundreds of miles from Confederate lines. They showed little restraint in executing guerrilla tactics against Union troops. Wherever they raided, their methods were the same: terrorism, mayhem, and murder. Quantrill devastated Lawrence, Kansas, and burned nearby Olathe on August 21, 1863. Until the end of the war, he continued to harass Union forces with raids on unguarded towns sympathetic to the Union. Among Anderson's exploits was the rape and pillage of Centralia, Missouri, on September 27, 1864. Years later, Frank James would compare this raid to the battles of Thermopylae and the Alamo.

In order to staunch the hemorrhage caused by Confederate guerrillas, Union authorities sanctioned counterinsurgency groups, such as Jim Lane's JAYHAWKERS in Kansas and Missouri, Captain Edwin Terrill's band of so-called federal guerrillas in Kentucky, JOHN M. CHIVINGTON's Third Colorado Cavalry, and General Richard Blazer's Scouts in Virginia. These and other pro-Union guerrillas proved either counterproductive or reverted to sheer banditry.

After the war, the guerrillas disbanded and took advantage of the general amnesty. Missouri guerrillas, however, were denied amnesty and returned home as outlaws. Frank James was paroled in Kentucky. His brother, Jesse, who had also served with Quantrill and Anderson, tried to turn himself in but was seriously wounded by Union troops near Lexington, Missouri. He escaped to his mother's farm in Kearney, Missouri, where he recovered. Together with fellow aggrieved guerrilla veterans, including Cole and Bob Younger, the JAMES BROTHERS rode out to commit daring bank and railroad robberies in the Midwest throughout the 1870s.

Federal troops, who had fought against Confederate guerrillas during the war, now found themselves attached to the Department of the West. Their new

Confederate guerrillas, led by William Clarke Quantrill, attacked the pro-Union town of Lawrence, Kansas, in 1863. *Courtesy New-York Historical Society.*

mission was to pacify the Indian nations of the Great Plains. Civil War personalities, such as Union commanders PHILIP H. SHERIDAN, GEORGE Crook, Winfield Scott Hancock, RANALD SLIDELL MACKENZIE, and GEORGE ARMSTRONG CUSTER, faced a different kind of guerrilla warfare waged by entire nations to protect their threatened homelands. Following Custer's defeat at the Battle of Little Bighorn on June 25, 1876, Indian resistance to the reservation system gave rise to a new breed of guerrilla represented by such leaders as MANUELITO (Navajo), DULL KNIFE (Northern Cheyenne), JUH (Nednihi Apache), VICTORIO (Mescalero Apache), CHOCHISE (Chiricahua Apache), NANA (Mimbres Apache), and GERONIMO (Chiricahua Apache). With the capture of Geronimo by General NELSON APPLETON MILES in 1894, organized guerrilla activities on the American frontier ended.

—*Maurice Law Costello*

SEE ALSO: Social Banditry; Younger Brothers

SUGGESTED READING:

Alexander, Jeffry D. *Mosby's Rangers.* New York, 1990.

Alexander, John H. *Mosby's Men.* New York, 1907.

Asprey, Robert B. *War in the Shadows: The Guerrilla in History.* Vol. 1. Garden City, N.Y., 1975.

Brownlee, Richard M. *The Gray Ghosts of the Confederacy.* Baton Rouge, 1958.

Garrett, Richard. *The Raiders: The Elite Strike Forces that Altered the Course of War and History.* New York, 1980.

Jones, Virgil Carrington. *Gray Ghosts and Rebel Raiders.* New York, 1956.

Wert, John H. *Mosby's Men.* New York, 1907.

GUNFIGHT AT O. K. CORRAL

SEE: O. K. Corral, Gunfight at

GUNFIGHTERS

The word *gunfighter* can be traced back to 1874, perhaps earlier, but it was not in general use until the turn of the twentieth century. BARTHOLOMEW (BAT) MASTERSON wrote a series of articles for *Human Life* in 1907 on "Famous Gun Fighters of the Western Frontier" and used the term instead of an earlier used and more explicit term *man-killers*. Similarly, the word *shootist* appeared occasionally in the contemporary press to denote a gunfighter, but the word was primarily used when describing target shots rather than those who had "got their man."

The so-called gunfighter owes his origin to the birth of Colt's revolver, since it was this weapon that gave him life and purpose. Once the "Revolving Pistol" (as SAMUEL COLT himself described his invention) became commonplace, its value as a weapon was much appreciated, especially by TEXAS RANGERS who used it with great effect against Comanche Indians in the 1840s and later during the UNITED STATES–MEXICAN WAR from 1846 to 1848. In the hands of civilians, however, the revolver aroused much controversy. In the wake of the California gold rush (from 1848 to 1851) and during the mid-1850s (when the pro- and antislavery factions fought over control of the Kansas Territory), even the most cowardly of individuals when armed with a Colt pistol was the equal of stronger and braver opponents—provided, of course, he was able to get the "drop" or advantage over his foe.

There were many who regretted the revolver's very existence. By the end of the Civil War, the gun was the favorite of cavalrymen and guerrillas on both sides. It was thus a natural progression to the plains when "pistol-packing" COWBOYS rode the cattle trails up from Texas to the Kansas cow towns to be met by similarly armed police who, for the most part, were more adept with such weapons than were the cowboys.

The era of the gunfighter is generally regarded as the period between 1850 and 1900. This period witnessed mass migration to the West, the coming of the railroads, cattle and mining boom towns, and the Indian Wars. But to understand the gunfighter's significance both historically and as a figure in folklore, one must appreciate the social conditions that spawned him. Those who ventured west in the early years and established settlements found themselves in the wilderness. LAW AND ORDER, such as it was, was slow to keep up with migration. For many people in the more remote areas, it was a case of settling problems themselves. What law enforcement existed in a state or a territory might be days or weeks away, so individuals fought their own battles. And even when the railroads brought more people and communities held elections, the qual-

ity of law and order depended a great deal on the people enforcing it. So it was not unusual for some of the more notorious places (such as Abilene, Dodge City, Ellsworth, and various mining boom towns) to hire tough characters to keep the peace. Some proved remarkably efficient, while others were no better than those they sought to control. And it was during this period that the gunfighter came into his own. His exploits became the stuff of legend.

The real-life gunfighter-cum-lawman proved to be an asset during some of the more wild and lawless periods of Western history; yet his presence did little to change it. He was a necessary and expensive temporary means of keeping the mob at bay. Only in fiction did he become a "town tamer" or "civilizer," single-handedly shooting or driving out innumerable badmen to make the town a fit place for women and children. Thus in legend, the two-gun paragon became a judge, jury, and executioner in the fight against evil.

The reality was different. Men elected or appointed to police towns or counties were expected to obey city, state, and federal laws and to uphold them to the best of their ability. If they used a pistol and became involved in a shootout in the course of their duties, they had to explain their actions to coroners or the courts.

The image of a gunfighter as a two-gun walking arsenal (such as JAMES BUTLER ["WILD BILL"] HICKOK) is misleading. Criticism of Hickok and others for carrying two pistols when only one would seem necessary fails to take into account that ammunition during the period was unreliable. Hickok, for example, used a pair of Colt .36 caliber percussion Navy revolvers loaded with paper or foil cartridges or loose powder and ball. The ammunition often got damp or the per-

The Western gunfighter, outlaw or lawman, is one of the region's most legendary archetypes. Here, outlaw Clay Allison guns down Chunk Colbert in this romanticized depiction entitled *A Duel at Dinner. Courtesy Denver Public Library, Western History Department.*

cussion caps failed to detonate, so a second or reserve pistol was needed.

But it was the gunfighter's skill with his pistols that inspired myth. Some were excellent shots. Hickok, regarded by many as the epitome of the Western gunfighter, was also credited with being a "dead shot." Tales are told of his skill with his revolvers and his success in shooting at seemingly impossible targets. The truth is that he may well have been an excellent shot and gifted with reflexes that got him out of trouble many times, but his strength lay in his ability to assess and to react to a situation. The same went for most of his contemporaries. Only in later years, when legends grew up around the better-known gunfighters, was skill with a pistol regarded as a prerequisite of law enforcement.

The gunfighter's role in the West has been greatly magnified, but in fiction his contribution toward the "winning of the West" is unsurpassed. One reason for this may be the public's need for heroes; even if it means the adulation of an individual who kills to preserve law and order. Whatever the reason, the image of the old-time gunfighter remains a potent force.

—*Joseph G. Rosa*

SEE ALSO: Cattle Towns; Film; Firearms; Literature: The Western Novel; Mining: Mining Camps and Towns; Social Banditry; Violence: Historical Overview, Myths about Violence in the West

SUGGESTED READING:

Miller, Nyle H., and Joseph W. Snell. *Why the West Was Wild.* Topeka, Kans., 1963.

Rosa, Joseph G. *The Gunfighter: Man or Myth?* Norman, Okla., 1969.

———. *Age of the Gunfighter.* London and New York, 1993.

GUNS

SEE: Firearms

GWIN, WILLIAM

California politician William McKendree Gwin (1805–1885) was born in Sumner County, Tennessee, and received his medical degree from Transylvania University in Kentucky. He practiced medicine in Clinton, Mississippi, between 1828 and 1833 and then accepted an appointment as U.S. marshal from his father's friend President ANDREW JACKSON. In 1840, Gwin served one term in the U.S. Congress and then spent several years in New Orleans.

Gwin moved to California in 1849, quickly immersed himself in the politics of the territory, and participated in the leadership of California's constitutional convention. His main goal was to secure statehood for California and a seat in the U.S. Senate for himself, and, in fact, he served as a senator from 1849 to 1861. His sympathy with the Southern cause and his control of federal patronage—and thus, the Democratic party—in California led to conflict with DAVID C. BRODERICK, California's other senator and a free-soil advocate. During the Civil War, Gwin was arrested for his support of the Confederacy. By the end of the war, Gwin had lost his influence in California politics, and when he died in New York, he had long since passed from public notice.

—*Kurt Edward Kemper*

SUGGESTED READING:

Quinn, Arthur. *The Rivals: William Gwin, David Broderick, and the Birth of California.* New York, 1994.

Thomas, Lately. *Between Two Empires: The Life Story of California's First Senator, William McKendree Gwin.* Boston, 1969.

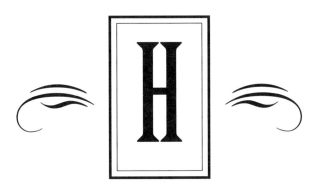

HAIDA INDIANS

SEE: Native American Peoples: Peoples of Alaska

HALCHIDOMA INDIANS

SEE: Native American Peoples: Peoples of California

HALE (SMITH), EMMA

Wife of Mormon leader JOSEPH SMITH, JR., and first president of the Female Relief Society, Emma Hale (1804–1879) was born in Harmony, Pennsylvania, into a Methodist family of eleven children. In 1827, she eloped with Smith against her parents' wishes. In the Mormon settlement of NAUVOO, ILLINOIS, Smith named his wife first president of the Female Relief Society, (later called the Relief Society) in 1842. The group proselytized the Mormon faith and provided aid to the sick and poor. Within two years' time, Hale presided over an organization of twelve hundred members.

Hale opposed her husband's doctrine of plural marriage and attempted to use her position in the Relief Society to undermine the practice of polygamy. The Relief Society was dissolved in 1844. When BRIGHAM YOUNG became the leader of the MORMONS upon the death of Smith and moved his followers west to Utah, Hale remained in Nauvoo and married a non-Mormon. With her husband, Hale operated a tavern until her death in 1879. Hale had four children. Her eldest, Joseph Smith, III, became the leader of the Reorganized Church of Jesus Christ of Latter-Day Saints.

—*Barbara Harper*

SEE ALSO: Church of Jesus Christ of Latter-day Saints; Church of Jesus Christ of Latter-Day Saints, Reorganized; Polygamy: Polygamy among Mormons; Relief Society (LDS)

SUGGESTED READING:
Derr, Jill Mulvay, Janath Russell Cannon, and Maureen Ursenbach Beecher. *Women of the Convenant: The Story of Relief Society.* Salt Lake City, 1992.

HALL, FRANK

Colorado politician and newspaper editor Frank Hall (1835–1917) was born in Poughkeepsie, New York, and moved in 1860 to Colorado, where he prospected for gold. After serving as territorial secretary from 1866 to 1874, he entered the newspaper field, published the *Mining Journal* in Black Hawk, and later bought and edited the *Daily Central City Register.* During his years in Black Hawk, he was elected to the territorial legislature. In 1877, he moved to Denver where he edited the *Daily Evening Times.* From 1879 to 1880, he served as Colorado adjutant general. His four-volume *History of the State of Colorado* was published between 1889 and 1895. He worked as mining editor for the *Denver Post* from 1895 until his death.

—*Candace Floyd*

SUGGESTED READING:
Abbott, Carl. *Colorado: A History of the Centennial State.* Boulder, Colo., 1976.

HALL, JAMES

A prolific writer of fiction and nonfiction about the American West, James Hall (1793–1868) was coauthor (with Thomas L. McKenney) of the extremely influential *History of the Indian Tribes of North America* (published from 1836 to 1844). Born in Philadelphia, Hall was educated at home and served with the military during the War of 1812 and afterward. After resigning his commission in 1818, he practiced law in Illinois. In 1820, he was appointed prosecuting attorney and then elected circuit judge. Hall served as state treasurer from 1828 to 1833 and then moved to Cincinnati.

Hall edited the *Western Monthly Magazine* from 1833 to 1835 and produced a number of books. His most important works of nonfiction include *Letters from the West* (1828), *Sketches of History, Life, and Manners in the West* (1834 to 1835), *Statistics of the West* (1836; subsequent editions were titled *Notes on the Western States)*, and his coauthored *History of the Indian Tribes.* Hall's novels and short fiction are less successful than his nonfiction, mainly because their weak and cliché-afflicted plots are smothered in long, digressive factual accounts of (to borrow from the title of his 1834–1835 volume) "history, life, and manners in the West." His fiction includes *Legends of the West* (1832), *The Soldier's Bride and Other Tales* (1833), *The Harpe's Head* (1833), and *The Romance of Western History* (1857).

—*Alan Axelrod*

HALLETT, MOSES

Colorado's most respected nineteenth-century jurist, Moses Hallett (1834–1913) was born in Galena, Illinois. He attended Rock River Seminary and Beloit College and then read law in Chicago. Admitted to the Illinois bar in 1858, he practiced in Chicago until the spring of 1860 when he joined Colorado's gold rush. That fall, he moved to Denver and was admitted to the Colorado bar in July 1861. Hallett was briefly a partner of Hiram P. Bennet, who became a territorial delegate to Congress in 1862. Hallett served in the Council of the Territorial Assembly from 1863 to 1865. He became an extremely prominent mining attorney before serving as chief justice of the territorial supreme court from 1866 to 1876. From 1877 to 1906, he was a U.S. district court judge. Rarely reversed on appeal, his decisions contributed significantly to American mining and water law.

—*John D. W. Guice*

SUGGESTED READING:
Guice, John D. W. *The Rocky Mountain Bench: The Territorial Supreme Courts of Colorado, Montana, and Wyoming, 1861–1890.* New Haven, Conn., 1972.

HANCOCK'S CAMPAIGN

In 1867, as the United States War Department and the BUREAU OF INDIAN AFFAIRS battled over Indian policy in the trans-Mississippi West, the Cheyennes, Sioux, and Arapahos of the Southern and Central Plains were nei-

ther unambiguously hostile nor especially friendly toward American settlements in the area. They tended to be fragmented, the older leaders favoring peace, the younger warriors spoiling for a fight. Menacing words and minor raids were common, and General WILLIAM TECUMSEH SHERMAN, not untypically, responded with an absolutist reading of the ambiguity of the situation. "If not a state of war," he said of conditions on the Southern and Central Plains, "it is the next thing to it, and will result in war."

On April 7, 1867, responding to rumors that the Cheyennes planned to attack Kansas settlements and transportation routes, Major General Winfield Scott Hancock—an impressive Civil War commander new to Indian fighting—led about fourteen hundred troopers of the Seventh Cavalry, the Thirty-Seventh Infantry, and the Fourth Artillery to Fort Larned, Kansas. He summoned a body of Cheyenne chiefs to the fort for a conference in hopes that they would see for themselves the might of the United States Army. Bad weather delayed the meeting and resulted in a small turnout on April 12 of only two chiefs and twelve warriors. Hancock decided to march a column of soldiers the next day to a combined Cheyenne and Sioux village in order to deliver his stern message to a wider audience.

Given the U.S. Army's actions during the recent SAND CREEK MASSACRE, the women and children of the village scattered for the hills as they saw the soldiers approaching. Despite Hancock's order to his principal field officer, Lieutenant Colonel GEORGE ARMSTRONG CUSTER, to take the Seventh Cavalry he commanded, surround the village, and prevent the Indian men from escaping as well, the village lodges were deserted by morning. At twenty-three years of age, Custer had attained the rank of major general in the Civil War. Earning a reputation as a brilliant, if erratic and egotistical, commander, the flamboyant, yellow-haired "boy general" was, like many other officers, reduced in rank at the conclusion of the war. He was determined to recover his former glory by fighting Indians. Acting on Hancock's orders, Custer led his Seventh Cavalry in pursuit of the fleeing Cheyennes and Sioux. When Hancock learned that the Indians had burned a stagecoach station on the Smoky Hill Route, he remarked, "This looks like the commencement of war," and burned the village and marched back to Fort Larned.

From mid-April through July, Custer and his men followed the chase vainly as the Indians terrorized Kansas. What began as an offensive campaign became a series of desperate, if futile, attempts at defense, not the least because four thousand officers and men spread over fifteen hundred miles of trails could hardly be expected to patrol the region effectively. At one point, Custer's cavalry was immobilized when it reached Fort

Hays only to discover that forage supposedly stored there for him had never arrived. Taking the field under Sherman, Custer's Seventh roamed Kansas and Nebraska and engaged in several skirmishes, none the decisive battle Custer sought. Exhausted, Custer and the Seventh withdrew when the lieutenant colonel went to Fort Riley, Kansas, ostensibly to obtain supplies but actually to see his wife. Court-martialed for taking unofficial leave and for abusing his men and animals, he was suspended from rank and pay for a year.

The Indian agent traveling with Hancock, E. W. Wynkoop, publicly attacked the general's handling of the campaign, and many—within the army and out, locally and in Washington—blamed both Hancock and Custer for the Indian raids that spread across the plains during the summer of 1867. Hancock's war seemed yet another costly failure for the U.S. Army, and it prompted renewed calls for peace at a time when peace commissioners were already negotiating with the Cheyennes and Sioux around Wyoming's Powder River. Two sets of treaties resulted, one at Medicine Lodge Creek, Kansas, in 1867, the other at Fort Laramie, Wyoming, the following year.

—*Alan Axelrod*

SEE ALSO: Central Plains Indian Wars; Medicine Lodge Treaty of 1867

SUGGESTED READING:

Axelrod, Alan. *Chronicle of the Indian Wars: From Colonial Times to Wounded Knee.* New York, 1993.

Utley, Robert. *Cavalier in Buckskin: George Armstrong Custer and the Western Military Frontier.* Norman, Okla., 1988.

———. *Frontier Regulars: The United States Army and the Indian, 1866–1890.* Lincoln, Nebr., 1984.

HANDCART COMPANIES

Handcart companies were used by some three thousand Mormon pioneers to migrate from Iowa to Utah between 1856 and 1860. Mormon leader BRIGHAM YOUNG initiated this experiment in overland travel because he wanted to find a more efficient, economical means of bringing poor European members of the CHURCH OF JESUS CHRIST OF LATTER-DAY SAINTS to the Great Basin in the wake of reduced church tithing receipts. The small two-wheeled carts were similar in size and appearance to those used by fruit peddlers in Eastern cities and to those used by California gold rushers. Each cart carried the essential items of four or five people; heavier provisions and food were transported in conventional wagons.

Young felt that handcarts would work since most emigrants in conventional wagon companies actually walked most of the distance and used wagons for carrying their possessions and supplies. Handcarts would be both less expensive and more efficient than ox-drawn wagons. Moreover, handcarts would require no time-consuming harnessing or concern for the maintenance of livestock.

When news of the proposed experiment in handcart travel reached Europe in early 1856, applications from a backlog of poor MORMONS flooded the church's Liverpool, England, headquarters. The handcart emigrants traveled from Europe to the railroad terminus in Iowa City where they picked up their handcarts—already built by Mormon carpenters and blacksmiths.

Initially, all went smoothly. The first three handcart companies left Iowa in early June 1856 and arrived in Salt Lake City with minimal difficulty in late September. But two other companies migrating much later that year ran into unforeseen difficulties. Already burdened by a late start, the emigrants found that their handcarts were not well constructed. The lumber was green, which made the carts heavier and harder to push. The green lumber, moreover, caused the boards to shrink and the iron rims to fall off the wheels. Hampered by delays along the trail, the two companies ran out of supplies. Worse still, winter storms hit early in the season—just as the hard-pressed emigrants reached the rugged Wyoming mountains. When Young received word that the handcart companies were stranded, he immediately dispatched teamsters with relief supplies. Despite this help, some two hundred of the nine hundred pioneers in the ill-fated companies perished.

Negative publicity surrounding the tragedy dealt a mortal blow to the whole handcart experiment. Nevertheless, Young developed elaborate plans to construct a chain of way stations all along the MORMON TRAIL to make handcart travel safer. The plans were never implemented due to the UTAH EXPEDITION of 1857, which brought a temporary halt to all Mormon westward migration. Ultimately, however, several more handcart companies—two in 1857, one in 1859, and two in 1860—brought emigrants to Utah with little difficulty and in relative safety. Handcart travel was discontinued after 1860 in favor of church-organized wagon teams, which became the primary means of transporting poor Mormon pioneers to the Great Basin.

—*Newell G. Bringhurst*

SUGGESTED READING:

Arrington, Leonard J., and Rebecca Cornwall. *Rescue of the 1856 Handcart Companies.* Midvale, Utah, 1984.

Hafen, LeRoy. "Handcarts to Utah, 1856–1860." *Utah Historical Quarterly* 24 (October 1956): 309–317.

———, and Ann W. Hafen. *Handcarts to Zion: The Story of a Unique Western Migration 1856–1860.* Glendale, Calif., 1960.

Jensen, Richard L. "By Handcart to Utah: The Account of C. C. A. Christensen." *Nebraska History* 64 (Winter 1985): 333–348.

"HANGING JUDGE"

SEE: Parker, Isaac Charles

HANNIBAL AND ST. JOSEPH RAILROAD

SEE: Burlington Northern Railroad

HARDIN, JOHN WESLEY

Schoolteacher, murderer, gunfighter, farmer, outlaw, convict, and attorney, John Wesley Hardin (1853–

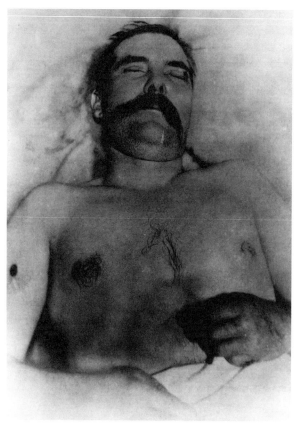

John Wesley Hardin, after he was killed in El Paso, Texas, August 19, 1895. *Courtesy Western History Collections, University of Oklahoma Library.*

1895) was named for the founder of Methodism. Born in Bonham, Texas, he was the son of Methodist preacher James G. Hardin and his wife Elizabeth. Hardin was the only Western gunman to write his autobiography, and although he killed only thirty men—not the fabled forty—he was the greatest gunfighter who ever lived.

Hardin grew up in Reconstruction-era Texas. His first victim was a black freedman. This killing led to the slaying of soldiers, cowboys, gamblers, state policemen, and Charles Webb, Brown County deputy sheriff. Hardin then married Jane Bowen and fled to Florida in 1874 where he took the name J. H. Swain. In 1877, the TEXAS RANGERS brought him back to the state to stand trial. He was sentenced to twenty-five years in the penitentiary. His wife died while he was incarcerated.

Hardin studied law in prison and was pardoned after fifteen years. Upon his release, he went to Junction, Texas, and then moved to El Paso. Working as an attorney, Hardin represented "Killin Jim" Miller, a hired assassin. He then accepted the case of Martin Mroz, a New Mexico cattle rustler hiding in Juárez, Chihuahua. Hardin had an affair with Mroz's wife, Beulah, and reportedly had his client assassinated by law officers who lured Mroz across the Rio Grande into El Paso.

Soon after starting work on his autobiography, Hardin was killed in El Paso's Acme Saloon by Constable JOHN HENRY SELMAN. The newspapers said that except for being dead, he was in fine shape. Hardin was buried in El Paso's Concordia Cemetery.

—*Leon C. Metz*

SUGGESTED READING:

Hardin, John Wesley. *The Life of John Wesley Hardin, as Written by Himself.* Norman, Okla., 1961.

Nordyke, Lewis. *John Wesley Hardin: Texas Gunman.* New York, 1957.

Parsons, Chuck. *The Capture of John Wesley Hardin.* College Station, Tex., 1978.

———, and Marjorie Parsons. *Bowen and Hardin.* College Station, Tex., 1991.

HARE, WILLIAM HOBART

Known as the "Apostle to the Sioux," William Hobart Hare (1838–1909) was the first Episcopal bishop of South Dakota. He was born in Princeton, New Jersey. Withdrawing from the University of Pennsylvania before he graduated, Hare set upon a life in ministry. He received his orders in 1859, was ordained three years later, and then journeyed to Michigan and Minnesota where he had his first contact with Indians. In 1871, he served as secretary to the Board of Missions, and his zeal soon earned him a bishopric. Although he was initially considered for a post in Africa, Hare was eventually chosen to work with the Sioux Indians in present-day South Dakota. He won some trust from Indians by mediating as best he could with white influences but largely concerned himself with establishing schools and chapels. In 1883, his duties were expanded to include the white population, and he founded his episcopate at Sioux Falls, the first in the area. Hare opened the All Saints School for Girls and cemented the Episcopal influence in the area.

—*Kurt Edward Kemper*

SUGGESTED READING:
Addison, James Thayer. *The Episcopal Church in the United States, 1789–1931.* Hamden, Conn., 1969.

HARNEY, WILLIAM SELBY

Soldier and Indian fighter William Selby Harney (1800–1889) was born in Haysborough, Tennessee, and received an education at home and advanced schooling at Cumberland College. He began his military career in 1818 at Baton Rouge Barracks after receiving his commission as a second lieutenant. In 1825, he traveled with General HENRY ATKINSON and Indian agent Benjamin O'Fallon to the upper Missouri River to sign treaties with the Indian tribes. Declaring that the Sac (Sauk) and Fox (Mesquakie) tribes had broken the treaty and should be punished, he fought in the Battle of Bad Axe against Black Hawk in 1832. Five years later, he fought in the Second Seminole War in Florida as the second ranking officer of the recently organized Second Dragoons. There, his boldness and impulsiveness came to light; these traits enhanced his reputation as an Indian fighter and brought him honors for gallant and meritorious service.

During the UNITED STATES–MEXICAN WAR, Harney was a colonel and ranking officer of the Second Dragoons, and he served with distinction on the U.S. Army's march to Mexico City. When his unit captured Cerro Gordo, a hill overlooking the road to Mexico City, he turned the enemy's guns on the retreating Mexican soldiers. After the war, Harney returned to Texas to protect communities from attack by Indian tribes. He was then assigned commander of the 1855 Sioux Expedition, whose objective was to punish the Upper Brulé for committing depredations against Anglo-Americans. In September 1855, his soldiers routed Little Wound's Brulé village at the Battle of Blue Water in western Nebraska. After the battle, he marched to the

William Selby Harney. *Courtesy National Archives.*

upper Missouri River region. At Fort Pierce, he recommended the deployment of mounted units instead of the use of troops at permanent posts to fight Plains tribes.

Harney was promoted to brigadier general in 1858 and became commander of the Department of Oregon. He caused an international incident when he ordered troops on San Juan Island to protect American citizens from both Indian tribes and British forces. Acting without higher authority, he recklessly violated the nation's joint-occupation agreement with Great Britain and pushed the country toward war. Harney was reassigned to a new duty station to prevent further embarrassment.

The diplomacy and finesse associated with careful leadership eluded Harney at the next major command he assumed. In May 1861, he took command of the Department of the West and returned to St. Louis where Secessionists and Unionists were scrambling to control Missouri. In order to preserve the peace, Harney concluded an agreement with General STERLING PRICE, the states' rights leader. Harney pledged not to attack state forces if they in turn agreed not to attack Union forces. Once again, Harney was removed from his command due to the unsound agreement. He never received another command; Union officials distrusted him be-

cause of his Southern loyalty. The Indian fighter retired in 1863 and in 1865 received the rank of brevet
major general.

Harney returned to the Great Plains when President Andrew Johnson appointed him to the 1865 peace
commission. He also served with the peace commission of 1867. The Indian-fighter-turned-diplomat negotiated peace between the United States and the Plains
tribes. He returned to temporary duty when he established three agencies for the Western Sioux on the
Missouri River in 1868.

Harney provided effective leadership under combat conditions where quick, sound decisions were im-
perative. The San Juan affair and the Missouri disaster
illustrated his inability to consider the far-reaching rami-
fications of his hasty decisions. This shortcoming, however, did not diminish the value of Harney's career as
a Western soldier during the era of expansion.

—*Richmond L. Clow*

See also: Black Hawk's War; Sioux Wars

Suggested reading:
Clow, Richmond L. "William S. Harney." In *Soldiers West:
Biographies from the Military Frontier.* Edited by Paul
Hutton. Lincoln, Nebr., 1987.
———. "General William Harney on the Northern Plains."
South *Dakota History* 16 (1986): 229–248.
Lecheminant, William Hull. "A Crisis Averted? General
Harney and the Charge of the Utah Expedition." *Utah
Historical Quarterly* 51 (1983): 30–45.

HARRIMAN, EDWARD HENRY

A major figure at the Illinois Central Railroad, Edward Henry Harriman (1848–1909) became the leader
of the reorganization and rebuilding of the Union Pacific Railroad after 1897. Under his guidance, the
Union Pacific took over the Southern Pacific Railroad in 1901.

Born in the Episcopal rectory at Hempstead, Long
Island, Harriman entered Wall Street as an office boy
in 1861, advanced to messenger clerk working the street
market, and by 1869, became the managing clerk for
the D. C. Hayes Company. In 1870, he bought a seat
on the New York Stock Exchange. A dominant figure
on Wall Street, he operated E. H. Harriman and Company until 1885.

In 1880, Harriman became a director of his father-
in-law's railroad, the Ogdensburg and Lake Champlain
Railroad Company. In the fall of 1881, Harriman and
his partners bought control of the Lake Ontario South-

Edward Henry Harriman. *Courtesy The Bettmann
Archive.*

ern. In October 1883, Harriman became the sole owner.
He then sold his interests to the Pennsylvania in 1884.

In 1883, Harriman was elected a director of the
Illinois Central. He worked with Stuyvesant Fish in
management of the railroad. His major business achievement, however, was the reorganization and rebuilding
of the Union Pacific Railroad. The Union Pacific increased its productivity, and its operational success
produced a handsome return on investment.

Harriman and his associates acquired the Chicago
and Alton in 1899. Improvements he made to the line
increased its profitability and raised its productivity
above the national average.

James J. Hill and J. P. Morgan interests obtained
the Burlington in 1899, when Harriman wanted it for
the Union Pacific. Harriman mounted an effort to buy
a half-interest in the Northern Pacific to gain control
of the Burlington. Hill's compromise produced the
Northern Securities Company. In 1904, Supreme Court
found that company guilty of monopoly and required
divestiture of the Great Northern and Northern Pacific Stock.

In 1901, the Union Pacific acquired control of the
Southern Pacific and rebuilt the line to increase its
profitability and productivity. The government won a
Supreme Court judgment in 1913 forcing the Union
Pacific to sell its Southern Pacific stock.

Because of an interest in an around-the-world
transportation line, Harriman visited Japan in 1905.
His plan failed because of Japanese opposition.

When the Colorado River flooded in 1905 and created a large new lake in the Salton Sink in California in 1905, the job of battling the flood fell to the Southern Pacific under Harriman's leadership. In 1906, Harriman raced to San Francisco after the great earthquake to assist in recovery.

Harriman married Mary Williamson Averell on September 10, 1879. They had three sons and three daughters. In 1885, Harriman bought the Parrott estate in the Ramapo Highlands, ten miles west of the Hudson River. Construction of the Harriman mansion at Arden began in 1905. In the summer of 1899, Harriman took his family, scientists, photographers, and artists to Alaska on an expedition that produced many scientific achievements. During the summer of 1909, Harriman went to Europe, seriously ill. He returned to Arden where he died the day before his thirtieth wedding anniversary probably from cancer of the stomach.

—*Lloyd J. Mercer*

SEE ALSO: Financial Panics; Harriman Expedition

SUGGESTED READING:

Eckenrode, H. J., and Pocohontas Wight Edmuds. *E. H. Harriman: The Little Giant of Wall Street.* New York, 1933.

Hughes, Jonathan, "E. H. Harriman, the Financier and the Railroads." In *The Vital Few.* Boston, 1966.

Kahn, Otto H. *Edward Henry Harriman.* New York, 1911.

Kennan, George. *Edward Henry Harriman: A Biography.* Boston, 1922.

HARRIMAN, JOB

Lawyer, socialist politician, and communitarian Job Harriman (1861–1925) was born on a farm in Indiana. He studied for the ministry at Northwestern College (later Butler College) in Indianapolis, attended Colorado College in Colorado Springs, and then turned to the law. He was admitted to the bar in Indiana and in 1886 moved to California.

Harriman was a tall, angular man with a thin nose and a remarkable speaking voice. He married Theodosia Gray in 1893, and the couple had one surviving son, Gray. In San Francisco, Harriman became involved in politics, read Edward Bellamy's *Looking Backward,* joined the Nationalist Club, and devoted much of his attention to labor unions. He helped form the local branch of the Socialist Labor Party. For a time, he was associated with a short-lived communi-tarian experiment in CHRISTIAN SOCIALISM, the Altrurian Colony near Cloverdale, north of San Francisco.

Sometime earlier, he had contracted tuberculosis, and, for his health, he moved his family to Los Angeles in 1895. He continued to practice law with a strong emphasis on labor and unions and gained national political notice in 1900 when he ran for vice-president on the Socialist party ticket that included Eugene Debs as the presidential candidate. He was the Socialist party's candidate for mayor of Los Angeles in 1911 and came within a few hundred votes of winning the office in the primaries. Meanwhile, however, the *Los Angeles Times,* the organ of the antilabor spokesman HARRISON GRAY OTIS, had been bombed and twenty men had been killed. Just before the final elections, two unionists, the McNamara brothers, who had been charged with the bombing and had been defended by Harriman, admitted their guilt. The city's consequent revulsion dashed Harriman's chances for political office.

Turning to a direct experiment in communitarian SOCIALISM, Harriman then founded the LLANO DEL RIO Colony in Antelope Valley in 1914. At times during the next four years, the colony was home to more than eight hundred people. Because of problems with water rights and other issues, the colony moved to Newllano, Louisiana, where it lasted well into the Great Depression. Because of his health, Harriman returned to California where he died in 1925.

—*Robert V. Hine*

SUGGESTED READING:

Greenstein, Paul, Nigey Lennon, and Lionel Rolfe. *Bread and Hyacinths.* Los Angeles, 1992.

Hine, Robert V. *California's Utopian Colonies.* Berkeley, Calif., 1983.

Mellon, Knox. "Job Harriman: The Early and Middle Years, 1861-1912." Ph.D. diss., Claremont Graduate School, 1972.

HARRIMAN EXPEDITION

In 1899, with the aid of the Smithsonian Institution, railroad magnate EDWARD HENRY HARRIMAN organized and sponsored a grand recreational and scientific reconnaissance of the Alaskan coast. Aboard his "floating university," the steamship *George W. Elder,* was one of the most distinguished faculties of the arts and sciences in America.

The scientists included C. Hart Merriam, zoologist and chief of the U.S. Biological Survey; Henry Gannett, geographer of the United States; William Healey Dall, the senior Alaskan expert in several scientific specialties; Bernard Fernow, forester; and G. K.

Gilbert, a geologist who wrote a valuable study of glaciers from observations made during the journey. Among the artists and writers were JOHN MUIR and JOHN BURROUGHS, both well-known nature writers; GEORGE BIRD GRINNELL, ethnologist and editor of *Forest and Stream;* EDWARD SHERIFF CURTIS, later a respected photographer of Native Americans; and Louis Agassiz Fuertes, who has been called the "John James Audubon of the twentieth century." Harriman brought his family. He hoped to shoot a Kodiak bear, survey the economic potential of Alaska, and scout the feasibility of an intercontinental railroad.

The *Elder* steamed from Seattle northward through the southeastern Alaska archipelago, to Yakutat, Prince William Sound, Cook Inlet, and through the Aleutian Islands to the Seal Islands, Seward Peninsula, and Siberia. The ship traveled nine thousand miles and made fifty stops during the two-month trip. Along the way, in addition to engaging in scientific and artistic work, the experts lectured on the flora, fauna, and history of the country. Everyone marveled at the awesome beauty of Alaska's scenery, but many aboard feared its desecration by the gold-seekers then overrunning the territory.

Thousands of biological and geological specimens were collected and analyzed in a dozen handsome volumes that contributed to several scientific disciplines. No new lands were discovered, but the expedition may be viewed as the culmination of more than a century of great scientific maritime explorations exemplified by those of Captain JAMES COOK, who had investigated the same waters in 1778.

—*Morgan Sherwood*

SEE ALSO: Alaskan Exploration; Exploration: United States Expeditions

SUGGESTED READING:

Burroughs, John. "Narrative of the Expedition." In *Harriman Alaska Series, Volume 1: Narrative, Glaciers, Natives.* Washington, D.C., 1910.

Goetzmann, William H., and Kay Sloan. *Looking Far North: The Harriman Expedition to Alaska, 1899.* New York, 1982.

Sherwood, Morgan. *Exploration of Alaska, 1865–1900.* New Haven, Conn., 1965. Reprint. Fairbanks, Alaska, 1992.

HART, WILLIAM S.

Actor and director William S. Hart (1864?–1946), known as "Two Gun Bill," was born in Newburgh, New York. During his boyhood, he traveled through-

William S. Hart. *Courtesy The Bettmann Archive.*

out the Midwest with his family. The pioneer atmosphere Hart experienced then, along with encounters with Indians, ranchers, and cowboys, impressed him enormously. Years later, Hart used those experiences in directing motion pictures in which he starred.

Hart took up acting as a teen-ager in New York, and for thirty-five years, he worked the theatrical circuit. His roles were varied: Shakespeare, other classics, and new plays. His first western was a 1905 stage production of *The Squaw Man,* followed by numerous others including the title role in a fabulously successful production of *The Virginian.*

Hart was over fifty years old when he moved to California to make western films. In his 1929 autobiography, *My Life East and West,* he wrote that he felt extraordinarily well suited to the task; his enormous popularity in more than sixty films over an eleven-year period proved him correct. Hart introduced a fresh approach to westerns that has been revived in the 1990s: he insisted on and provided authentic props and costumes, and he personified the prototypical Western hero.

Tumbleweeds, made in 1925, was Hart's final and best FILM. The Oklahoma land rush was reenacted on a scale that challenged cinema technology. Sadly, because of a disagreement between Hart and the film's distributors over marketing the epic, Hart withdrew from the increasingly studio-dominated industry. Not unlike the individualistic Westerner he often portrayed, Hart preferred to maintain control over his own endeavors.

Hart spent the next two decades in active retirement at the ranch he built in Newhall, about forty miles north of Los Angeles. He wrote more than a dozen books and entertained scores of motion-picture and other celebrities at the Horseshoe Ranch. Hart solidified his legacy by bequeathing his ranch, collections of Western art and Native American artifacts, and authentic film props to the county of Los Angeles.

—*Janet R. Fireman*

SEE ALSO: Motion-Picture Industry

SUGGESTED READING:

William S. Hart Papers. Seaver Center for Western History Research, Natural History Museum of Los Angeles County.

William S. Hart. *My Life East and West*. Boston, 1929.

HARTE, BRET

Although Bret Harte (1836–1902) wrote a considerable body of fiction, his literary reputation as a Western "local-color" writer rests primarily on a single volume of short stories, *The Luck of Roaring Camp and Other Stories* (1870), which includes his two most popular tales, the title story (1868) and "The Outcasts of Poker Flat" (1869). Born in Albany, New York, Francis Brett Harte was the son of an impecunious schoolmaster, who died when Harte was nine years old. Harte delighted in his father's sole legacy: a good personal library, which included the works of Charles Dickens, the literary example that would most influence him. In 1853, Harte's mother moved from the family's last Eastern home, Brooklyn, and settled in California. Harte followed in 1854 and earned his living by various odd jobs until 1860, when he moved to San Francisco and became a typesetter and writer for *The Golden Era*, a local newspaper. The following year, he went to work at the surveyor-general's office; he became a clerk in the San Francisco mint in 1863.

During this period, Harte was gaining a local reputation as a literary man, publishing occasional poetry and stories. His first book, *Outcroppings*, a collection of California verse, was published in 1865. *The Lost Galleon and Other Tales*, another poetry collection, appeared in 1867, as did *Condensed Novels and Other Papers*. The latter reveals Harte's flair for literary parody, and his "Muck-a-Muck," a send-up of JAMES

FENIMORE COOPER's *Leather-Stocking Tales*, remains especially amusing.

In 1868, Harte became editor of the *Overland Monthly* and published in it his own short story "The Luck of Roaring Camp," a romantically colored yet authentic tale of life in a California mining camp. It was widely read, not only locally but back East, and immediately made the writer's reputation. Other stories followed, most notably "The Outcasts of Poker Flat" in 1869, and Harte published a collection, *The Luck of Roaring Camp and Other Stories* in 1870, which was enormously successful. It took very little persuasion to lure the young writer to the East the following year to write for *Atlantic Monthly*. The one-year contract was lucrative—ten thousand dollars—but Harte's new stories were mediocre, and perhaps even worse, his dandified appearance and effete manners disappointed a public expecting a grizzled prospector.

Atlantic Monthly did not renew his contract, although Harte recovered somewhat with a new collection of California fiction, the *Tales of the Argonauts* (1875); a novel, *Gabriel Conroy* (1876); and two plays, *Two Men of Sandy Bar* (1876) and *Ah Sin* (1877)—the latter written in collaboration with another young "Western" writer, MARK TWAIN. While these works did

Bret Harte. *Courtesy The Bettmann Archive.*

not produce the sensation of *The Luck of Roaring Camp,* they generated decent revenues, which nevertheless failed to make a dent in the Hartes' mounting debt. Mrs. Harte had lavish tastes, and her husband was a spendthrift. When the greater security of a government appointment beckoned, Harte took the post of U.S. consul in Rhenish Prussia in 1878. Two years later, he moved to the consulate in Glasgow, but the election of President Grover Cleveland in 1884 resulted in the loss of his appointment in 1885.

Harte did not return to the United States. He settled in London, where he resumed his writing career. Although he never regained his initial popularity and struggled with debt until the end of his life, he enjoyed a solid literary reputation, particularly in England. Although later generations of readers have had little patience with the sentimental Dickensian veneer of even his best stories—"Miggles," "Tennessee's Partner," "The Iliad of Sandy Bar," "The Luck of Roaring Camp," and "The Outcasts of Poker Flat"—all but the harshest modern critics acknowledge Harte's skill in portraying action and in creating comic scenes that suggest a genuine feel for traditions of Western folk HUMOR.

—Alan Axelrod

SEE ALSO: Literature; Magazines and Newspapers; Women Writers

SUGGESTED READING:

O'Connor, Richard. *Bret Harte: A Biography.* Boston, 1966.

Stewart, George R. *Bret Harte, Argonaut and Exile.* Boston, 1931.

HARVEY, FORD FERGUSON

Ford Ferguson Harvey (1866–1928) built a major chain of HOTELS and RESTAURANTS throughout the West from 1901 until his death. His empire continued after him, however, until travel by airplane and automobile supplanted TOURISM by passenger train following World War II.

Born in Leavenworth, Kansas, Harvey attended college briefly before starting work in a restaurant that belonged to his father, Fred Harvey. The elder Harvey had opened a chain of restaurants—the Fred Harvey Houses—along the route of the ATCHISON, TOPEKA AND SANTA FE RAILROAD. At the death of his father in 1901, Ford Ferguson Harvey expanded the business to include HOTELS and dining rooms. In addition, he managed the dining-car service for the railway.

His company, Fred Harvey's, named in honor of his father, was headquartered in Kansas City, Missouri.

In addition to the independent chain, he gained the rights to run concessions at the Grand Canyon National Park. His hotels included the Bisonte in Hutchinson, Kansas; the La Fonda in Santa Fe, New Mexico; the Castañeda in Las Vegas, New Mexico; and the El Tovar in the Grand Canyon National Park. With a boom in tourism after the depression of the 1890s and with a growing interest in America's new national parks, Ford Ferguson Harvey's empire was secure.

In 1902, Harvey established the Fred Harvey Indian Department, which bought and sold traditional Native American arts and crafts and gained a reputation for treating the artists and craftspeople fairly.

—Candace Floyd

SUGGESTED READING:

Henderson. James David. *Meals by Fred Harvey: A Phenomenon of the American West.* Fort Worth, Tex., 1969.

Poling-Kempes, Lesley. *The Harvey Girls: Women Who Opened the West.* New York, 1989.

HARVEY GIRLS

"Harvey Girls" was the name given to the women who, in 1883, began staffing the numerous first-class lunch counters, restaurants, and hotel dining rooms that Fred Harvey was establishing along the ATCHISON, TOPEKA AND SANTA FE RAILROAD. Strengthened by agreements with railroad companies, the "Harvey system" eventually stretched from the Great Lakes into the Southwest and across to the Pacific and from the Kansas prairies to the Gulf of Mexico. The system included

Fred Harvey, founder of the Harvey House restaurant chain. *Courtesy Kansas State Historical Society.*

dining rooms in the fine tourist hotels: El Tovar at the Grand Canyon, the Montezuma and Castañeda in Las Vegas in northern New Mexico, the Alvarado in Albuquerque, and La Fonda in Santa Fe.

A news story of 1929 reported that in "normal times" the Harvey Company employed fourteen hundred waitresses; in 1961, a personnel officer estimated that there had been around one hundred thousand Harvey Girls to that date. Fred Harvey

Harvey Girls and customers in the dining room of the Bisonte Hotel, Hutchinson, Kansas, 1926. *Courtesy Kansas State Historical Society.*

demanded a high standard of performance and sought young women, preferably unmarried and inexperienced, who were strong, healthy, independent, and unafraid of hard work. A Harvey Girl started out with a week of training in the smaller units and then transferred step-by-step to more important dining rooms and restaurants. Hired for a minimum of six months, she was furnished transportation and food from the Santa Fe railroad station nearest her home to her first assignment. After six months, she was entitled to a month's vacation without pay and a railroad pass to her original point of departure.

The girls lived in housing adjacent to the restaurants or in the upper rooms of the hotels where they worked and were supposedly watched over by matrons who enforced curfew and other rules. In addition to room, board, tips (usually a dime), and free railroad passes, they received wages. In the early years, wages were $17.50 a month, but by 1929, the job paid $35 a month with a $5 increase after the first six months until the maximum of $50 a month was reached. No Harvey girls seem to have belonged to waitresses' unions, although they lived and worked close to unionized railroad workers. Uniforms changed somewhat over the years, but basically they were black dresses with white aprons (with or without bibs) and black shoes and stockings. Ethnically, most of the waitresses were Anglo-Saxons born in the East, Midwest, Europe, and Canada.

As automobile travel became popular, the Harvey Company located its RESTAURANTS with little reference to rail lines, but even so, many houses, large and small, were closed during the Great Depression. Soon, faster, more luxurious trains came to feature dining-car service, all with male waiters. The demands of World War II eroded the Harvey "standard," and afterwards air travel and the changing nature of TOURISM ended the system.

The Harvey Girls hold the distinction of having been the first group of women working in the West for a common employer. They left behind a romantic image of sweet youth, virtue, and good moral character, and undoubtedly they raised the general stature of the waitress in the eyes of the public. EDNA FERBER fictionalized the Harvey Girl in a short story entitled "Our Very Best People," and Samuel Hopkins Adams's novel *The Harvey Girls* became the basis for Metro-Goldwyn-Mayer's film starring Judy Garland.

—*Mary Lee Spence*

SEE ALSO: Harvey, Ford Ferguson

SUGGESTED READING:
Poling-Kempes, Lesley. *The Harvey Girls: Women Who Opened the West.* New York, 1989.
Spence, Mary Lee. "Waitresses in the Trans-Mississippi West." In *The Women's West.* Edited by Susan Armitage and Elizabeth Jameson. Norman, Okla., 1987.

HASKELL, CHARLES NATHANIEL

First governor of Oklahoma, Charles Nathaniel Haskell (1860–1933) was born in Leipsic, Ohio. He read law and was admitted to the bar in 1880. As a lawyer, his chief interest involved railroad promotions. He relocated in 1901 to promote railroads and other enterprises in Muskogee in the Indian Territory.

Haskell entered politics as the Democratic floor leader at Oklahoma's constitutional convention. Elected the state's first governor, he served from 1907 to 1911. While governor, he was indicted on federal charges of fraud involving his Muskogee promotions, but the charges were dismissed on a technicality.

After 1917, Haskell promoted oil and other ventures on Wall Street.

—*Danney Goble*

SUGGESTED READING:
Fowler, Oscar Presley. *The Haskell Regime: The Intimate Life of Charles Nathaniel Haskell.* Oklahoma City, 1933.

HASTINGS, LANSFORD WARREN

Lawyer, Western promoter, and author Lansford Warren Hastings (1818?–1868) was a native of Ohio. With Elijah White, Hastings led the first expedition of American emigrants to Oregon in 1842 and practiced law for a winter in the Willamette Valley. Disappointed with Oregon, however, the following year he journeyed to California, where he believed he saw boundless opportunities for Americans willing to make the journey West.

To aid migrants traveling westward and to people his own town site just south of Sutter's Fort, Hastings penned *The Emigrants' Guide to Oregon and California* (1845). The 152-page book offered advice on equipment and supplies, and methods of travel and suggested routes, including what became known as the Hastings Cutoff, a route the author imagined but had not traveled. It was the misfortune of the DONNER PARTY to attempt Hastings's route in the fall of 1846.

Earlier that summer, Hastings led his own party of migrants across the Rocky Mountains and, upon arriving in California, the Ohioan joined JOHN CHARLES FRÉMONT's forces in the war against Mexico. Hastings served as a delegate to the constitutional convention that preceded California's admission to the Union, and in the early 1850s, he practiced law near the California gold fields.

Hastings sided with the Confederacy during the Civil War and made for Brazil after the South's defeat. He published a emigrant book in 1867, hoping to establish a colony of defeated Southerners on the Amazon River. He died during a recruiting mission to Alabama.

—*Patricia Hogan*

SEE ALSO: California Overland Trails; Emigrant Guidebooks; Overland Travel

HAUSER, SAMUEL THOMAS

Among Montana's early entrepreneurs, Samuel Thomas Hauser (1833–1914) was remarkable for his diverse investments and for his vision of economic development. Born in Falmouth, Kentucky, he was educated as a civil engineer. In 1854, he moved from Kentucky to Missouri, where he supervised railroad construction. He arrived in Montana in 1862, joined the Bannack gold rush and, in 1863, became a member of James Stuart's Yellowstone Prospecting Expedition.

Hauser began building his financial empire in 1865, when he and Nathaniel P. Langford organized a Virginia City bank. At the same time, he founded several mining companies and built the first silver mill in the Montana Territory in Argenta. Ultimately, he controlled banks in Virginia City, Helena, Butte, Fort Benton, and Missoula; financed the construction of numerous short-line railroads; owned and operated several smelters; invested in significant real-estate and irrigation projects; and became a partner with A. J. Davis and GRANVILLE STUART in the DHS cattle operation. Hauser backed scores of gold-, silver-, copper-, and coal-mining projects across Montana and became the state's preeminent mining promoter.

With MARCUS DALY, WILLIAM ANDREWS CLARK, and CHARLES ARTHUR BROADWATER, Hauser composed the Democratic party's "Big Four" in Montana. The men wielded great political influence in the territory through the 1880s. In 1885, President Grover Cleveland appointed Hauser the territory's first resident governor.

Hauser's economic fortunes suffered in the panic of 1893, and his hydroelectric dam on the Missouri River collapsed in 1908. Nevertheless, the significant political, social, and financial influence of this competitive capitalist survived beyond his death.

—*David A. Walter*

SUGGESTED READING:

Addresses on the Occasion of a Dinner Given to Honor Samuel T. Hauser at the Montana Club, by His Neighbors and Friends on the Evening of August 22, 1908. Helena, Mont., 1908.

Robbins, William G. "The Deconstruction of a Capitalist Patriarch." *Montana: The Magazine of Western History* 42:4 (Autumn 1992): 20–33.

"Samuel T. Hauser." In *A History of Montana.* Vol. 2. Edited by Helen Fitzgerald Sanders. Chicago, 1913.

HAWAII

Lying in the central Pacific Ocean just below the Tropic of Cancer, 2,397 miles west of San Francisco, Hawaii consists of a group of volcanic islands, 8 of them major islands, 124 of them islets, forming a 1,500-mile crescent from Kure Island in the west to "the big island" of Hawaii in the east, with a combined land mass of 6,471 square miles. Called variously "the Paradise of the Pacific" or "the Crossroads of the Pacific," Hawaii, in 1990, was home to 1,115,274 people, most of whom—80 percent—lived on Oahu in and around Hawaii's capital city of Honolulu, the only incorporated town or city in the entire state.

Although a building boom in the 1950s and 1960s changed more traditional patterns of settlement, especially on Oahu, where thirty-story skyscrapers and commuter-spawned suburbs replaced a once sprawling and low Honolulu and Pearl Harbor, much of Hawaii remains dominated by small fishing and farming villages far from major highways, isolated clusters of small houses in obscure valleys, scattered and solitary farm and ranch houses, and a number of large coastal and upland plantations and ranch towns. Tourism, Hawaii's major industry, has transformed urban life—once a matter of single-family dwellings, small shops, and comfortable old hotels—into a crush of

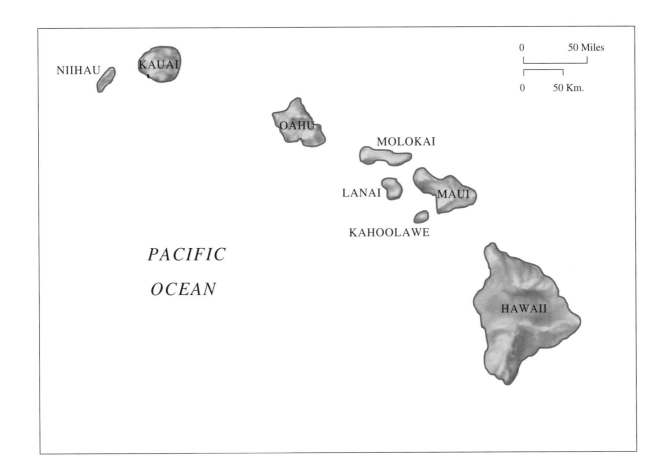

high-rise apartments, luxury hotels, and shopping malls. In the villages of rural Hawaii, older homes housing single families in frame structures under corrugated iron roofs predominate. All but the smallest of the towns have a school, local markets, a post office, a fire station, and a church or two. There life follows the sun, beginning with dawn, winding down at dusk, and many of Hawaii's distinctive ethnic groups retain more of their traditional speech patterns and customs. On Oahu, cosmopolitan Hawaii's polyglot population of Caucasians, Japanese, Chinese, Koreans, Filipinos, native Hawaiians, and others, speaking forty languages and dialects, live and work together in what some scholars have considered, for the most part, a model multiethnic society.

In Hawaii, the only state whose majority is of Asian rather than European origin, everyone, in effect, belongs to an ethnic minority: Caucasians and Japanese each make up about 25 percent of the population, Filipinos around a 10 percent, the Chinese about 6 percent, and native Hawaiians, depending on which source one reads, who is doing the counting, and how inclusively one uses the term *native*, between 8 and nearly 20 percent. A large number of Hawaiians are descended from foreign-born laborers brought to the islands during the nineteenth century to work on sugar and pineapple plantations—first the Chinese, then the Japanese, Portuguese, Puerto Ricans, Koreans, Spanish, and Filipinos. While the Asians were initially considered foreigners by the native Hawaiians and early Anglos,

The Iolani Palace, built originally as the residence of the Hawaiian royal family, about 1887. *Courtesy Hawaii State Archives.*

whom the native islanders called *haoles,* the weight of Asian numbers, increased by later immigrations, ensured the need to accommodate them. Haloes continued to dominate Hawaii, however, certainly up until World War II, although less dramatically so since. The Japanese, treated harshly after Pearl Harbor, rebounded to play a prominent role in governing the state. The Chinese, their numbers high among professionals, bankers, insurance-company owners, and real-estate dealers, are perhaps the wealthiest of the ethnic groups. Many Filipinos, the last large group of outsiders brought in to work the plantations, still labor in the fields, although younger Filipinos have moved in large numbers to the city where, since the 1960s, they have been joined in menial jobs by Samoans. Filipino and Samoan neighborhoods remain the last identifiable ethnic enclaves in a city once filled with them. African Americans, many of them servicemen and their families, do not live in ghettos as on the mainland but in the same communities as others in Honolulu and its outlying areas.

With a climate many consider nearly perfect and a tradition and reputation for hospitality, Hawaii continues to strike the outside world as an island paradise despite the fact that rampant tourist development and a spirit of crass commercialism have threatened to mar the islands' natural beauty and, combined with a strain of racial exploitation that runs through modern Hawaiian history, have fired the resentments of Hawaii's native people. In the 1970s, native Hawaiians began to demand a greater share of the state's wealth and power. Some of the more militant called for a return to Hawaiian independence, and although that is unlikely, Hawaii has made some efforts to control the excesses of commercial development and to preserve native traditions and cultures, while at the same time opening up its political process in a way that has made the state something of progressive model for innovative programs in education, social welfare, business development, and health care.

Natural Hawaii

The eight major islands in the Hawaiian chain from east to west are Niihau (a privately owned island and a refuge for the practitioners of traditional native Hawaiian life), Kauai, Oahu, Molokai, Lanai, Kahoolawe, Maui, and Hawaii. Created by VOLCANOES and expanded by coral deposits, the islands are the peaks of very large mountains that rest on the ocean floor, some as far down as 15,000 feet. The original volcanoes have fallen silent, except Mauna Loa and Kilauea on the eastern edge of Hawaii, where now and again spectacular eruptions are followed by immense and dangerous lava flows that threaten life and home. Mauna

Kea and Mauna Loa are Hawaii's tallest mountains, 13,796 feet and 13,677 feet above sea level, respectively. The extinct Diamond Head, overlooking Waikiki Beach on Oahu, is only one of a number of mountains on the islands. Geologically younger areas appear domelike in their terrain, with clearly defined volcanic craters. Older regions have mountains shaped by erosion; their craggy shapes include sharp, grooved cliffs pocked with caves, deep valleys, and collapsed craters called *calderas*. Coastal plains stretch to broad beaches where the Pacific surf pounds lava shorelines and coral reefs and reduces the coral and large shells to sand.

Humid by mainland standards, Hawaii's weather is conditioned by the Northwest trade winds, which blow most of the year for many miles over the open ocean and bring sea-level temperatures averaging 75° F and varying little from month to month. Rainfall varies: on Mount Waialeale—often called the wettest spot on earth—the average rainfall for the past sixty years has been 444 inches; in places on Hawaii, the average rainfall is only 8.2 inches, and much of the island resembles the deserts of Arizona. In general, however, warm rains—sometimes brought by spring storms borne on southerly winds called *kona*—nourish Hawaii's lush vegetation, which grows in a soil made of volcanic ash, gravel, rotted vegetation, crumbling lava, and wind-blown sand and dust. Iron oxidizes in the dampness and creates the ubiquitous bright red dirt and rocks. There is not enough iron for commercial exploitation, however, nor coal, nor oil deposits. Heavy rains seep through porous mountains and collect in underground chambers and layers, thus creating artesian water, which the Hawaiians frequently tap for irrigation and drinking.

Plant life comes to the island from seeds dropped by birds, or blown in by the wind, or tossed up by the sea. Since the first Polynesians arrived, a tremendous number of food plants and showcase flora have been introduced, including sugar cane, pineapples, papayas, bananas, mangoes, nuts, limes, passion fruit, taros, and tamarinds, plus garden-variety vegetables, all of them growing year round. Some birds, isolated for eons, have developed characteristics peculiar to Hawaii, such as the Hawaiian goose and the Hawaiian stilt. Seabirds nest on the islands, and others—brought in by various travelers—proliferate: mynas, sparrows, cardinals, doves. Each fall, tiny golden plovers arrive in Hawaii after having flown nonstop from Alaska, some 3,000 miles away. They are joined for the winter by ducks from North America. Mongooses, rats, frogs, toads, and, in more remote regions, deer, sheep, pigs, and goats live on the islands. There are no snakes, which give Hawaiians yet another reason for believing they live in paradise.

Native peoples

Polynesian ancestors of the native Hawaiians migrated probably from Indonesia east into the South Pacific sometime in the first millennium B.C. Around 400 A.D., a group of their descendants traveled northwest from the Marquesas Islands to Hawaii. A second round of Polynesian migration northward from Tahiti occurred in the ninth or tenth century A.D. In an odyssey rarely matched in human history, the Tahitians moved 2,700 miles over open ocean in huge double, outrigger canoes. Upon reaching the islands, the Hawaiians soon found little need for resupply from their homeland, and they underwent centuries of isolation. Although the Hawaiians and their culture changed in the process, there remained a remarkable similarity—linguistically, physically, and culturally—between them and their Polynesian relatives in the South Seas.

The culture of the Hawaiians was oral and rich in both myth and legend, on the one hand, and practical knowledge, especially of plant and animal life and navigation, on the other. Lacking metal, pottery, and beasts of burden, they learned to use woods, shells, stones, and bones with great skill and produced among other items the technological marvels in which they had first traveled to the islands. Highly proficient at fishing and farming, they honed their strength and warrior reflexes in athletic contests. They raised pigs and cultivated a starchy root, taro, from which they made poi, a paste flush with nutrients. Worshipping and fearing a group of gods some have compared in character and power to the ancient Greek deities of Mount Olympus, they developed an elaborate calendar and a rigid, strict system of laws, or taboos, called *kapus* in Hawaiian. Ruled by frankly despotic chiefs, who were supported most of the time by a powerful and vigilant priesthood, the Hawaiians lived off nature's bounty in grass houses similar to those of their overlords.

The Hawaiians most likely made their first contact with people from a different culture on January 18, 1778. That was the day British naval captain and explorer JAMES COOK, having run across the islands by accident during a voyage from Tahiti to the Pacific Northwest, sailed into view. Cook's arrival corresponded with some priestly predictions and Hawaiian stories, and the natives not only welcomed Cook warmly but hailed him as a god. A year later, when Cook returned to the islands, the situation had changed. According to historian Gavan Daws, Cook probably walked into the middle of a power struggle among various chiefs and the priesthood; after a tense face down between Europeans and Hawaiians on February 19, 1779, Cook was killed in the ensuing brawl. Cook's discovery, however, sparked four decades of growing European and American influence over the

Hawaiians as explorers, adventurers, trappers, and whalers stopped over for fresh supplies at what Cook had named the Sandwich Islands.

Missionary and territorial period

Eventually missionaries and colonizers came to the Sandwich Islands and touched off a stage in the Hawaiian history that—despite the absence of major armed conflict between native Hawaiians and Euro-Americans—resembles stages in the rest of the trans-Mississippi West, including the devastation of indigenous populations by exotic diseases, concerted attempts to Christianize and Americanize the Hawaiians, the introduction of homesteading legislation as an enticement from the feudal-like system of land ownership practiced by the natives, and even the establishment of a reservation system for "pure-blooded" Hawaiians.

In 1796, King Kamehameha I—with European backing—unified the Hawaiian islands by conquest. Meanwhile, the previously virtually disease-free Hawaiians had already begun to experience the effects of diseases from both West and East because of their lack of natural immunities. Cook's sailors had introduced venereal disease to the islands, and as Europeans brought items that Hawaiians came particularly to value, such as livestock (horses, cattle, goats) and trees and fruits (eucalyptus and guava, for example), they

also brought cholera, smallpox, measles, bubonic plague, and leprosy. By 1819, a population estimated at 300,000 before Cook's arrival had fallen to around 135,000.

Then came the missionaries. The Protestants arrived from the United States in 1820, and soon they dominated the island. Enthused by the new secular or reform Calvinism, men such as the Reverend Hiram Bingham and missionary and physician Gerrit P. Judd preached the gospel, founded schools, and promoted agriculture. They produced a spiritual revolution as members of the royal family, their basic beliefs in the Hawaiian religion undermined, tossed out the once powerful priests and abolished the *kapu* system in a series of deviant acts that shook the stability of the Hawaiian people and accelerated their decline. Their loss of faith in the old gods, their intense curiosity about the ways of Americans and Europeans, their lust for learning to read and write, and something like a need to identify spiritually with those coming to control the islands led the Hawaiians to adopt the new religion quickly. By 1840, Bingham was dictator of Hawaii in all but name, and the islands were largely a Christian kingdom. That year, Bingham returned to America, and two years later, Judd succeeded him as prime minister. As the native population declined, settlers seized the best Hawaiian lands for large-scale commercial farming. For a decade, Judd defended Hawaii from

Japanese women laborers of Hawaii's plantations. *Courtesy Hawaii State Archives.*

the imperialist designs of the British and the French and protected the WHALING and ranching industries, which were then Hawaii's main sources of wealth. By the 1850s, young Hawaiians, called locally *kanakas*, who had shipped out on whaling crews, began to show up in San Francisco and San Diego. In 1853, the last year Judd was in office, the Hawaiian native population had dwindled to 70,036.

After 1854, missionary influence over Hawaii dissipated as the islands' economy shifted toward plantation sugar and pineapple production. Foreigners, first from China and later from Japan, were shipped in to harvest the crops in the face of native resistance and decline, and King Kamehameha III's successors lost sympathy for the preachers. Under the growing power of big plantation owners, Hawaiian politics quickly grew corrupt, especially during Kalakaua's reign from 1874 to 1891 and his successor's, the willful and conservative Queen LILIOUKALANI, from 1891 to 1893. The last Hawaiian king and last Hawaiian monarch respectively, neither could match the power of the big planters, who, in 1875, wrangled a Reciprocity Treaty with the United States that protected their profits in sugar, which quickly became Hawaii's major source of income. Hawaii's native population continued to die off at an alarming rate, dropping to around 40,000 by 1890, and the sugar kings imported ever more foreign labor, now from Portugal and Spain as well as Japan. In 1893, the Americans overthrew the autocratic Lilioukalani and formed, in 1894, the Republic of Hawaii under a new kind of autocrat, controversial judge and then president STANFORD B. DOLE. Four years of sporadic and maddeningly complicated negotiations led to annexation by the United States in 1898 in the spasm of national expansion that produced, among other things, the Spanish-American War. Hawaii became an American territory on June 14, 1900.

Beset by a mixture of racial and ethnic groups, saddled with an unstable government, and in the throes of a rapidly expanding plantation economy, the Hawaii Territory had its problems. Like all territories, it was afforded only limited self-government, and with an economy already essentially exploitative, Hawaii—like much of the trans-Mississippi West after the Civil War—had clearly been relegated to colonial status. Not unlike the copper kings in MONTANA or the railroad barons in CALIFORNIA, Hawaii's sugar kings took advantage of the disfranchised mixture of ethnic groups to monopolize the economy. In 1903, President Dole's cousin James Drummond Dole launched a pineapple plantation, and thirty years later, exported canned pineapples would be Hawaii's second most valuable cash crop. Meanwhile, five firms—American Factors, Brewer and Company, Alexander and Baldwin, Castle

By the first decades of the twentieth century, sugar accounted for 90 percent of Hawaii's income. *Courtesy Hawaii State Archives.*

and Cooke, and Davis and Company, Ltd.—had come to control Hawaii's plantations and, with them, Hawaii itself.

Managed and held by thirty or forty families who frequently intermarried, the "Big Five" established a virtual hereditary succession of board chairmen and company presidents, and—through direct ownership or interlocking boards—controlled the islands' banks, public utilities, insurance firms, and hotels. Well into the twentieth century, these companies ran the island as they saw fit. In 1960, the year after Hawaii became the nation's fiftieth state, the state government owned somewhat less than 40 percent of the land in Hawaii, the federal government almost 10 percent, small landowners under 5 percent, and the rest—47 percent—lay in the hands of seventy-two big landowners, many of them haole shareholders in the Big Five companies.

Twentieth-century Hawaii

For four decades, Hawaii's oligopoly enjoyed the benefits of a colonial economy in which they ruled something like patricians of old did, supported in part by federal subsidies in the form of protective tariffs and a growing number of military bases. These bases formed a strategically important center of operations for the U.S. Navy, which since the 1890s had been the foundation of American military power worldwide and its security at home. Then came December 7, 1941, and the surprise attack by Japan on Pearl Harbor, which precipitated the United States's entry into World War II. In Hawaii, the U.S. reaction was draconian. Responding to rumors of sabotage by resident Japanese—

rumors which later proved false—the federal government imposed severe martial laws, some clearly unconstitutional. Dismissing Japanese Americans from Hawaii's National Guard and interning others in camps, the federal government, for much of the war, ignored entreaties from Hawaiians of Japanese ancestry that they be allowed to enlist and fight. When they ultimately prevailed, Hawaii's Japanese citizens fought with distinction in Italy and France, where they suffered disproportionate losses. Not only did the war prove that the Japanese in Hawaii were loyal, it also revealed that the United States considered Hawaii as much a part of its nation as any spot on the homeland, and thus paved the way for statehood.

After the war, a Montana-born policeman opened the local Democratic party to the Japanese, formed ethnically balanced tickets, and smashed the ancient Republican regime founded by the haole elite connected with Hawaii's Big Five companies, all on his way to winning for his adopted state its long-sought acceptance into the union. JOHN A. BURNS, three times Hawaii's governor, plain spoken, direct, intensely loyal, dogged, a Roman Catholic and a Democrat, realized that racial equality was the way to win the ethnic votes needed to beat Republicans at election time and that TOURISM was the way to undercut the control those backing the Republicans exercised over the Hawaiian economy.

Before 1941, tourism—a matter of long steamship rides across a daunting ocean—had been slow to catch on; that year, only 32,000 visitors came to the Hawaiian Islands. Burns's promotion of tourism eventually made the industry the largest in the islands, followed by federal employment, then big agriculture. But tourism also helped open the islands to mainlanders, who began to emigrate in large numbers after 1950. Over the next twenty years, Hawaii's population increased by 50 percent, its gross state product rose fivefold from $830 million to $4 billion, and the number of tourists soured from 46,000 to 1.4 million each year. With more and more people pouring into the islands, it became increasingly difficult for the U.S. Congress to continue to deny Hawaii statehood in a debate moving into its third decade and based on specious anti-Communist arguments that were actually a mask for racist sentiment. Southerners in Congress feared that two Hawaii senators would destroy their ability to continue to kill civil-rights legislation, which, since the war, had been introduced almost annually. Hawaii's—and Burns's—argument for statehood was simple: it was unfair to continue to levy federal taxes on the islands without representation in Congress.

It was no accident that the erosion of the Big Five's control over Hawaii's economy and life accompanied the successful drive toward statehood. Immediately after the war, the International Longshoreman's and Warehouseman's Union (ILWU), led by radical firebrand Jack Hall, staged and won a series of strikes to organize sugar and pineapple workers. Since most of the workers were members of Hawaii's numerous ethnic groups, and since the Democratic party became the party of choice for labor, they flocked to Burns's standard and swelled the ranks of those agitating for statehood. When the great tourist explosion, with its demands for the building of huge hotels and resorts, hit in the early 1950s, the Big Five, lacking the know-how, flinched; capital poured in from outside the state, and contractors such as the liberal HENRY J. KAISER moved in to do the building and diluted the clubby patterns of local control. Although Hall "took the fifth" before the House Un-American Activities Committee in 1953 and was convicted under the Smith Act as a Communist conspiring to overthrow the government by violence and force, his conviction was overturned along with those of six other Hawaiians. The ILWU's bid to control the Hawaiian Democratic party floundered, however, and the union settled into playing a more relaxed role. By 1959, the oligopoly was in retreat, Hawaii had gone Democratic, and on March 13, 1959, the United States accepted its petition for statehood.

The new state born of that decades-long struggle may well be one of the more progressive in the nation. The constitution that went into effect with statehood provides for perhaps the most centralized government in all fifty states. The only statewide officials who run for election are the governor and lieutenant-governor (who, by law, must be on the same ticket) and the members of the state board of education. Taxing and spending rests with the state, which spends 80 percent of all funds. The counties spend the other 20 percent; there are no city governments. Hawaiians, in general, demand a lot from their government, and they pay handsomely for it. Heavy and steeply graduated income taxes and a general sales tax on everything, including food and hotels, add to the naturally high cost of living in an island society that must import most of its goods, much of its building materials, and a good deal of its energy, all of whose costs are passed on to the consumer. On the other hand, in the closing decades of the twentieth century, Hawaii's unemployed were well cared for (so much so that residency laws were required to prevent a "hippy" takeover), its children were well educated in state schools, its museums and cultural institutions—including the Bishop Museum of the Pacific and the Honolulu Academy of Arts—were well funded, its elderly citizens were provided for, and its universal health-care system was both a success statewide and a challenge to reformers on the mainland.

Although not without problems, Hawaii was a multiethnic society whose minorities had learned, for the most part, to cooperate. English may have been the official language most frequently spoken, but Hawaiian, too, had been made official. The Center for Cultural and Technical Interchange between East and West, a unique educational institution, published daily newspapers in Japanese and Chinese as well as in English. Hawaii regularly sent members of its various ethnic groups to Congress, and did so long before redistricting in other states created "ethnic seats." By the 1990s, citizens groups had managed to check the worst excesses of overdevelopment, while the state's world-class resorts had become destinations in themselves. Little wonder that Hawaii, exotic, friendly, and interesting, remained, according to surveys, the most satisfying destination for tourists in the world; and its residents, who invented surfing, enjoyed the place as well.

—*Charles Phillips*

SEE ALSO: American Board of Commissioners for Foreign Missions; Bingham, Hiram and Sybil; Missions: Missions in Hawaii; National Expansion: The Imperial Impulse; Native American Peoples: Peoples of Hawaii

SUGGESTED READING:

Daws, Gavan. *Shoal of Time: A History of the Hawaiian Islands*. Honolulu, Hawaii, 1968.

Tabrah, Ruth M. *Hawaii: A Bicentennial History*. States and the Nations. New York and Nashville, Tenn., 1984.

trol. Pitting one ethnic group against another, planters instituted a hierarchy of occupations and corresponding wages according to race: whites held skilled and supervisory positions; Asian workers—Chinese, Japanese, Filipino, and Korean—were locked into a pool of unskilled field hands. Even among field workers, pay scales differed according to nationality. Among member plantations, pay scales were the same. A laborer quitting one plantation because of low wages would be offered no more pay at the next. The HSPA also used long-term contracts and a bonus system in which pay was withheld until workers completed their years of employment. Workers who left the plantation before fulfilling the terms of the contract forfeited their wages and bonuses.

As plantation workers began to organize for better working conditions in the twentieth century, the HSPA employed a network of spies and agitators to discourage the formation of unions and had labor leaders arrested, often on the slimmest of charges. The HSPA hegemony, however, could not exploit its workers forever. Strikes occurred in 1909, 1920, and 1924, and the planters were forced to increase wages and improve living conditions.

—*Patricia Hogan*

SUGGESTED READING:

Beechert, Edward D. *Working in Hawaii: A Labor History*. Honolulu, Hawaii, 1985.

Takaki, Ronald. *Pau Hana: Plantation Life and Labor in Hawaii, 1835–1920*. Honolulu, Hawaii, 1983.

HAWAIIAN SUGAR PLANTERS' ASSOCIATION

Founded in 1894, the Hawaiian Sugar Planters' Association (HSPA) reflected the common interests of sugar-plantations owners throughout the islands.

From 1875 to 1910, sugar production in Hawaii increased from 12,000 acres of cultivated plantation lands to 214,000 acres. By the early twentieth century, sugar produced 90 percent of Hawaii's income. Work in the sugar-cane fields was labor-intensive and backbreaking. Laborers lived on isolated plantations in company shacks and worked long hours in the hot sun for low wages. Planters were always short of workers, and the HSPA used a number of tactics to ensure an adequate labor supply. Prior to Hawaii's annexation to the United States, laborers from China and Japan were brought to the islands under a contract system hardly better than slavery. When contract labor ended in 1900, the association found other methods of worker con-

Workers on a sugar plantation on the island of Kauai gather cut cane from the field. *Courtesy Hawaii State Archives.*

HAWAII LABORER'S ASSOCIATION

An unusual example of cross-ethnic labor solidarity, the Hawaii Laborer's Association (HLA) had its roots in the Japanese Federation of Labor (JFL), formed on December 1, 1919, and in a strike called by Filipino sugar-plantation workers in January 1920.

Working and living conditions on Hawaiian sugar plantations had always been abysmal, and workers had organized before to effect improvements. But after World War I ruined the cost of living, workers found little relief and, in fact, encountered opposition from plantation owners, whose HAWAIIAN SUGAR PLANTERS' ASSOCIATION (HSPA) resisted worker demands. In a move of uncommon solidarity for a common cause, members of the JFL met with the recently formed Filipino Labor Union (FLU), and the two organizations presented their demands to the HSPA: an increase in daily wages from $.77 to $1.25 for male workers and from $.58 to $.95 for women; an eight-hour workday, overtime pay for Sundays and holidays, improved medical care and recreational facilities, and eight weeks paid maternity leave for women workers.

When the union of Filipino workers decided to strike the sugar plantations in January 1920, the JFL joined and raised some six hundred thousand dollars to support the eight thousand strikers—77 percent of the entire work force on Oahu.

When work on the plantations came to a halt, the HSPA reacted with brutality. The planters issued forty-eight-hour eviction notices to workers in the midst of an influenza epidemic, attempted to bribe labor leaders, and fomented distrust between Japanese and Filipino workers by accusing Japanese union leaders of being puppets of Japan's imperial ambitions. And planters attempted to replace workers with Hawaiian, Portuguese, and Korean laborers, who received two to three times the wages union members were seeking.

In the midst of the strike, the JFL and the FLU joined forces to become the HLA, and the workers held out until support funds ran dry around July 1920. The planters claimed a complete victory but quietly increased wages by 50 percent three months later and made improvements in worker housing. It was a case, however, of too little too late. Japanese workers left the plantations in search of employment elsewhere. Never again did Japanese workers constitute a majority of the plantation work force.

—*Patricia Hogan*

SUGGESTED READING:
Beechert, Edward D. *Working in Hawaii: A Labor History.* Honolulu, Hawaii, 1985.

Takaki, Ronald. *Pau Haua: Plantation Life and Labor in Hawaii, 1835-1928.* Honolulu, Hawaii, 1983.

HAWLEY, JAMES HENRY

Lawyer and politician James Henry Hawley (1847–1929) was born in Dubuque, Iowa. After mining in California and Idaho from 1861 to 1864, he read law in San Francisco and then returned to Idaho in 1868.

Hawley, a Democrat, was a legislator, district and U.S. attorney, mayor of Boise from 1902 to 1904, and governor of Idaho from 1911 to 1913. Although he represented the miners' unions, whose members formed the WESTERN FEDERATION OF MINERS, he also served as a prosecutor in the trial of WILLIAM D. ("BIG BILL") HAYWOOD, who was accused of conspiracy in the murder of FRANK STEUNENBERG in 1905. Hawley was an outstanding criminal lawyer and also specialized in irrigation law.

—*Judith Austin*

SUGGESTED READING:
MacLane, John F. *A Sagebrush Lawyer.* New York, 1953.

HAYDEN, CARL T.

A Democratic representative and senator from Arizona and champion of federal RECLAMATION in the American West, Carl T. Hayden (1877–1972) was a native of Arizona. He was one of the principal architects of the federal policies on reclamation, policies that entailed IRRIGATION, WATER use, and dams. Known as the "silent senator" for his avoidance of speeches on the floor of Congress, the Arizona Democrat had served longer in the House and Senate—from 1912 to 1969—than any other person in American history when he retired.

While Hayden developed expertise in the field of reclamation, he also worked to aid the growth and development of Western states. He promoted legislation for federal highways and coauthored the landmark Hayden-Cartwright Act of 1934, which established the formula for distributing federal aid for highways to the states on the basis of area rather than population. He introduced several measures that advanced mining operations throughout the country. He worked tirelessly for social-security legislation and, in 1950, proposed an amendment to the act to include American Indians within its framework. He was also active in developing federal legislation on forest conservation, national parks, public lands, agriculture, and veterans affairs. Significantly, most of these issues were crucial to the growth and development, as well as to the conservation and preservation, of the American West.

Hayden's overriding concern, however, was the use and distribution of water. During his first term in the House of Representatives, he obtained authorization for an investigation that led to the construction of Coolidge Dam on the Gila River and the San Carlos Irrigation Project. He helped shape federal reclamation policy in its early years by writing and securing passage of the provision that allowed local water-user associations to take over the care, maintenance, and operation of federal reclamation projects. Finally, Hayden played a prominent role in securing passage of the Colorado River Basin Project Act of 1968, a law that mandated, among other things, the construction of the Central Arizona Project. This legislation represented the capstone of Hayden's political career.

—*Jack L. August, Jr.*

SUGGESTED READING:
Mann, Dean. *The Politics of Water in Arizona.* Tucson, Ariz., 1963.

HAYDEN, FERDINAND VANDEVEER

A nineteenth-century American geologist and explorer for the federal government, Ferdinand Vandeveer Hayden (1829–1887) was director of the United States Geological and Geographical Survey of the Territories. He supervised production of an *Atlas of Colorado* and led the first government-sponsored scientific expeditions into the Yellowstone region.

Hayden was born in Westfield, Massachusetts. He graduated from Oberlin College in 1850 and received a degree in medicine from Albany Medical School. His greatest interest lay in geology, however, and when his landlord, the paleontologist James Hall, suggested that he travel to the White River Badlands of present-day South Dakota for a summer expedition, Hayden jumped at the chance.

Thus began Hayden's career as a geologist. Year after year, he traveled to Kansas, the Dakota Badlands, and the territories of Wyoming and Colorado. Collecting fossils and geological data, he wrote about his discoveries for scientific journals. By the outbreak of the Civil War, he was well known in scientific circles.

After the Civil War, Hayden returned to his favorite vocation. In 1867, using funds left over when the territorial legislature of Nebraska was disbanded, he made a natural-history survey of the new state, a survey in which he emphasized the practical uses of the

Hunters accompanied Ferdinand Vandeveer Hayden's 1872 expedition to the Yellowstone. Photograph by William Henry Jackson. *Courtesy National Archives.*

land. From that beginning came the United States Geological and Geographical Survey of the Territories, popularly known as the Hayden Survey. Because he needed annual appropriations from Congress, Hayden worked to make his survey widely known to the American people. He employed the pioneer photographer WILLIAM HENRY JACKSON to supply photographs and stereopticon slides, welcomed on his survey the landscape artist THOMAS MORAN, and gave jobs to journalists. In 1871 and 1872, the survey explored Yellowstone and the Grand Tetons. Jackson's photographs were especially helpful in persuading Congress to create YELLOWSTONE NATIONAL PARK.

In 1873, partly because of troubles with Native Americans in Wyoming and partly due to encouragement from entrepreneurs, Hayden moved his survey activities to Colorado. Over the next several years, survey parties explored the state and conducted extensive geological and natural history investigations. The data collected were published in Hayden's extensive *Annual Reports* and in hundreds of scientific journals. The *Atlas of Colorado* that the survey members produced was useful to entrepreneurs.

In 1879 Hayden's survey was consolidated with three other geological and geographical surveys of the West—those of CLARENCE KING, JOHN WESLEY POWELL, and Lieutenant George M. Wheeler—into the UNITED STATES GEOLOGICAL SURVEY.

—*Richard A. Bartlett*

SEE ALSO: Exploration: United States Expeditions

SUGGESTED READING:
Bartlett, Richard A. *Great Surveys of the American West.* Norman, Okla., 1962.

Goetzmann, William H. *Exploration and Empire.: The Explorer and the Scientist in the Winning of the American West*. New York, 1966.

HAYS, JOHN COFFEE (JACK)

Often considered the archetypal Texas Ranger, John Coffee (Jack) Hays (1817–1883) settled in San Antonio while in his early twenties. A native of Little Cedar Lick, Tennessee, he joined the TEXAS RANGERS around 1838 and served under Deaf Smith and Henry Kearnes in conflicts against Indians and Mexicans. After two years, Hays was made captain and placed in charge of protecting San Antonio. Shortly after his promotion, he challenged Comanche Indians at Plum Creek and in several other engagements, including Enchanted Rock in 1841 and Bandera Pass in 1842.

Disciplined, stern, direct, and skilled in tactical and strategic planning, Hayes promoted the mystique of the Texas Rangers as an efficient and effective law-enforcement agency. An able leader and a good judge of character, he recruited the trackers, soldiers, and rugged men who advanced the image of the rangers as a powerful force in Texas.

In the late 1840s, Hays left Texas for California where he became sheriff of San Francisco County in 1850. In 1853, President Franklin Pierce appointed him surveyor-general of California, but by 1860, he had moved on to Nevada. There, he became involved in the so-called Pyramid Lake War against the Paiutes. It was his last brush with combat. Hays retired from law enforcement and took up a successful career in California land speculation until his death at Piedmont in 1883.

—*Patricia Hogan*

SEE ALSO: Texas Frontier Indian Wars

SUGGESTED READING:
Webb, Walter Prescott. *The Texas Rangers: A Century of Frontier Defense*. Austin, Tex., 1965.

HAYWOOD, WILLIAM D. ("BIG BILL")

From rude beginnings in Salt Lake City, Utah, a fatherless Bill Haywood (1869–1928) went to work in the underground mines out West at the age of fifteen. Joining the WESTERN FEDERATION OF MINERS (WFM) in 1898, he worked his way up through the ranks of the union to become the era's preeminent radical labor-union leader. "Big Bill" was with the WFM in Colorado between 1903 and 1905, when the union's conflict with

Big Bill Haywood as photographed in Moscow in 1924. *Courtesy The Bettmann Archive.*

mining and smelting corporations flared into open class warfare that pitted miners against state militia in one of the more bitter and violent labor disputes in the country's history. Convinced by his Colorado experience that American workers needed to organize into "one big union," Haywood, in 1905, joined Socialist party leader Eugene V. Debs, Socialist ideologue Daniel de Leon, and the aging United Mine Workers organizer MARY HARRIS ("MOTHER") JONES, in the founding convention of the INDUSTRIAL WORKERS OF THE WORLD (IWW), perhaps the most militant labor union in American history. Calling this Chicago meeting the "continental congress" of the working class, Haywood endeared himself to the rank and file, mostly migrant, mostly Western, mostly radical IWW "Wobblies," by virtue of his "genuine power and genuine simplicity."

In 1906, Idaho threw Haywood in jail for complicity in the murder of the state's former governor, FRANK STEUNENBERG. Acquitted after a sensational trial, Haywood became a leader in the Socialist Party of America, but he continued to preach the Wobbly gospel of sabotage and violence despite party disaffection with the radical Westerners. Haywood helped the Socialists purge the IWW of the relatively conservative WFM; then he helped the even more radical migrants of the West purge the IWW of the Socialists. More

that the political agenda of the Socialist party, the IWW's taste for direct action suited his temperament. Assuming the union's highest office, Haywood nursed the organization's massive growth among migrant workers on Western farms, at Western logging camps, and in Western mines during World War I. Caught up in the espionage indictments of 1918, Haywood was tried and convicted in Chicago along with one hundred or so other IWW leaders. Alcoholic now and racked by diabetes, Haywood jumped bail when his appeal was rejected by the Supreme Court and after he had made arrangement for the bail to be paid out of union coffers. Fleeing to Russia, Haywood died in Moscow, alone and alien. Some scholars have come to consider Haywood to be what many of the rank and file at the time almost instinctively felt he was: an exemplar of the native-born American working class whose career illustrated the viciousness with which the rulers of liberal democracy in the Gilded Age responded to truly militant domestic adversaries.

—*Charles Phillips*

SEE ALSO: Labor Movement

SUGGESTED READING:
Carlson, Peter. *Roughneck: The Life and Times of Big Bill Haywood.* New York, 1983.
Dubofskey, Melvyn. *"Big Bill" Haywood.* Manchester, Eng., 1987.

HEALTH CARE

SEE: Disease; Doctors; Medicine

HEARST, GEORGE

Enjoying a colorful and spectacular career as a Western mining promoter, publisher, philanthropist, and then United States senator from California, George Hearst (1800–1895) amassed one "pile" in the Nevada silver mines only to buy into the most productive property of the BLACK HILLS GOLD RUSH—the Homestake lode at Lead near Deadwood—to make another. The son of a Missouri farmer, Hearst had first arrived in California in 1850. Failing to make a fortune as a placer miner, Hearst set up as a storekeeper before returning to mining after he had located two promising quartz claims. Upon hearing about the incredible gold and silver lode named after Henry T. P. Comstock in the Washoe Indians region of the Sierra Nevada, Hearst headed across the mountains in 1859 and, with borrowed money, acquired one-sixth interest in the Ophir

Mine for three thousand dollars that returned some ninety thousand dollars in profit. The COMSTOCK LODE was the basis of his ultimately immense fortune. After rich placer deposits were discovered in the Black Hills during the late 1870s, the fifty-seven-year-old Hearst arrived in the mining camp of Lead in 1877, where, amid charges of fraud and threats on his life, the California tycoon secured an interest in the HOMESTAKE MINE. The industrial colossus he built ultimately took hundreds of millions of dollars out of the Black Hills. Hearst was also one of the principal early investors in the ANACONDA MINING COMPANY in Butte, Montana. From 1886 to 1893, Hearst served as California's Republican senator in the U.S. Congress, and he was instrumental in launching the newspaper career of his son, WILLIAM RANDOLPH HEARST. Having acquired 240,000 acres of old rancho land in San Luis Obispo and Monterey counties and having married socially active and philanthropically minded Phoebe Apperson Hearst, George Hearst died one of the grand figures from California's "frontier" period.

—*Charles Phillips*

HEARST, PHOEBE APPERSON

Philanthropist Phoebe Apperson Hearst (1842–1919) was born in Franklin County, Missouri, the eldest child born to Randolph Walker Apperson of Virginia and Drucilla Whitmore Apperson of South Carolina. At the age of seventeen, she became a village schoolteacher.

Three years later, she married George Hearst, a miner recently returned from California and Nevada. She accompanied her husband to San Francisco where their only child, William Randolph Hearst, was born in 1863. Her attentive involvement in her son's education and career continued throughout her lifetime.

Hearst was a noted hostess and patron of the intellectual community. She devoted herself to the study of the arts and relished in her collections of *objets d'art*, which became the initial holdings of the museum established in the Palace of Fine Arts.

With her husband's increasing financial and political successes, she expanded her good will to scholars, libraries, schools, and, particularly, the Golden State Kindergarten Association. When George Hearst became a member of the U.S. Senate, Phoebe shifted her philanthropy to Washington, D.C., where she joined in the organization of the Columbian Kindergarten Association in 1893, contributed to the restoration of Mount Vernon and the construction of the National Cathedral, endowed the National Cathedral School for

Girls, and organized the forerunner of the National Congress of Parents and Teachers in 1897.

Influenced by the establishment of Stanford University by AMASA LELAND STANFORD and JANE ELIZA LATHROP STANFORD, Hearst took on the fledgling University of California across the East Bay from San Francisco in the 1890s. She offered to finance an international architectural competition for a master plan of Berkeley's campus. She gave funds for a mining building, an outdoor theater, a women's gymnasium, and a social center. Her largesse funded a university museum and the anthropology department and its expeditions to Italy, Mexico, Russia, and Egypt. Hearst's interest in the school did much to turn Berkeley into a first-rate university.

—*Gloria Ricci Lothrop*

SUGGESTED READING:
Black, Winifred. *The Life and Personality of Phoebe Apperson Hearst.* Privately printed, 1928.

HEARST, WILLIAM RANDOLPH

Noted Western newspaperman William Randolph Hearst (1863–1951) was born in San Francisco, the son of George and Phoebe Apperson Hearst. Beginning in 1873, he toured Europe for twenty-one months. On the trip he became well versed in art and antiquities and developed a lifelong passion for collecting. In 1879, he enrolled at St. Paul's preparatory school in New Hampshire, but, after two years, he was asked to leave. After another European trip in 1881, he entered Harvard University; his lack of discipline precipitated his expulsion in the spring of 1885.

In 1887, Hearst persuaded his father to make him proprietor and editor of the *San Francisco Examiner.* Hearst thus began a fabled career as a newspaperman. He immediately revolutionized West Coast journalism by adopting techniques successfully employed by Joseph Pulitzer in New York City. In 1894 and 1895, he bought two New York newspapers, which he named the *Morning* and *Evening Journal.* In competition with Pulitzer's *World,* Hearst pushed sensationalism to its limits by playing to the lowest tastes of his readership and exploiting acts of human weakness. He also provided entertainment through serial novels, political cartoons, advice to the lovelorn, and the first comic-strip character, the "Yellow Kid." (From that comic strip character's name comes the term *yellow journalism.)* The rivalry between Hearst and Pulitzer helped bring about the Spanish-American War; in fact, Hearst be-

lieved that he was the major contributor in forcing the government's hand in the conflict. Another result of the rivalry and sensationalism was that the *Journal* had the largest circulation of any newspaper in the world; more than 1.25 million copies were sold daily beginning in 1898.

Hearst was not nearly as successful in politics as he was in the newspaper business. In the presidential campaigns of 1896 and 1900, he wholeheartedly supported Democratic nominee WILLIAM JENNINGS BRYAN. In 1902, he ran for, and won, a congressional seat for Manhattan. He then tried, unsuccessfully, to become the Democratic presidential nominee in 1904. The following year, he and Judge Samuel Seabury helped create a Municipal Ownership League in a third-party effort to win the mayor's seat in New York City. He became the league's nominee but lost narrowly to incumbent George B. McClellan. In 1906, he was defeated in a race for governor of New York by Republican Charles Evans Hughes. By 1908, somewhat disenchanted with the major political parties, he launched a third party named the Independence League. The following year, he ran somewhat reluctantly for mayor of New York City and finished third in the race. He was never again a threat as a political candidate.

In the meantime, Hearst began amassing a communications empire. He acquired eighteen newspapers

William Randolph Hearst. *Courtesy The Bettmann Archive.*

in twelve cities including Boston, Baltimore, Chicago, Detroit, Los Angeles, Milwaukee, New York, and San Francisco. He supplied news and features through King Features Syndicate, International News Service, and International News Photos. He owned nine magazines, including *Cosmopolitan, Good Housekeeping, Harper's Bazaar, House Beautiful,* and *Town and Country.*

After 1910, Hearst increasingly moved to the political right. Often a critic of President Woodrow Wilson, he so strongly opposed the administration's pro-Allied leanings that the British and French barred his news empire from using their cables and mails after October 1916; Canada likewise banned all Hearst newspapers. Although softening his stance with America's entry into World War I, Hearst bitterly denounced the League of Nations and the World Court. In the 1920s, he ardently endorsed President Calvin Coolidge and Secretary of the Treasury Andrew Mellon. While flirting briefly with the Democratic party by supporting Speaker of the House JOHN NANCE GARNER from Texas for president in 1932 and at first approving of Franklin D. Roosevelt's handling of the Great Depression, Hearst soon instructed his editors to call the New Deal the "Raw Deal."

By 1937, Hearst's empire was financially hard pressed. Because of his personal extravagance, he was forced to surrender control of his properties to legal adviser Clarence Shearn, who promptly began to retrench economically by closing or selling Hearst newspapers, magazines, radio stations, and supplementary news wires. Shearn also liquidated real-estate holdings, auctioned off many valuable art objects, and halted construction on the Hearst castle at San Simeon, a 275,000-acre estate north of Los Angeles. Despite these measures, the Hearst empire did not begin to stabilize until after World War II. And although Hearst resumed control over the largest publishing conglomerate in the United States, his power was somewhat diminished.

Hearst led a social life that was quite bizarre, if not scandalous, to most Americans. As a young man, he kept a mistress until his mother disrupted the arrangement. He was especially fascinated by women in show business. In New York City during 1897, he escorted Broadway dancers, the Willson sisters, about town; on April 28, 1903, he married the younger sister Millicent. Fourteen years and five sons later, he met Marion Davies, a Ziegfeld Follies showgirl thirty years his junior. After his wife refused to divorce him, he lived with Davies, mainly at San Simeon, while his wife resided in New York.

In 1947, Hearst suffered a heart attack that partially incapacitated him. He moved from San Simeon to Davies's villa in Beverly Hills. He died at the age of eighty-eight.

—*Ben Procter*

SEE ALSO: Hearst, George; Hearst

SUGGESTED READING:
Swanberg, W. A. *Citizen Hearst.* New York, 1961.
Winkler, John K. *William Randolph Hearst: A New Appraisal.* New York, 1955.

HEARST SAN SIMEON STATE HISTORICAL MONUMENT

Better known as Hearst Castle, the Hearst San Simeon State Historical Monument is a historic house museum that was given to the state of California in 1957 by the Hearst Corporation, in memory of media magnate William Randolph Hearst and his mother PHOEBE APPERSON HEARST.

Built in California's Santa Lucia Mountains overlooking the Pacific Ocean, the castle boasts a Mediterranean-revival architectural style, which complements its Spanish and Italian art collections from the sixteenth and seventeenth centuries. The main building looks like a Spanish cathedral, while the guest houses, gardens, and pools arranged around it create the impression of a hilltop village.

Construction at San Simeon began in 1919, and while 165 rooms, two pools, a zoo, tennis courts, and more than one hundred acres of gardens and terraces were completed, the estate was far from finished when Hearst was forced by ill health and financial reversals to stop construction in 1947.

—*John Blades*

SUGGESTED READING:
Moss, Roger W. *The American Country House.* New York, 1991.
Pavlik, Robert C. "'Something a Little Different': La Cuesta Encantada's Architectural Precedents and Cultural Prototypes." *California History* (Winter 1992–1993): 462-477.

HEINZE, FREDERICK AUGUSTUS

Frederick Augustus Heinze (1869–1914) was one of the major participants in the War of the Copper Kings that shaped MONTANA politics and economic development during the late nineteenth and early twentieth centuries. He attended the Brooklyn Polytechnic Institute and the Columbia School of Mines before moving to Butte in 1889. While working intermittently as a mining engineer with the Boston and Montana Copper Company, he acquired some of the richest mines in Butte and Trail, British Columbia. He formed the Montana Ore Purchasing Company in the spring of 1892 and began constructing a smelter the following year. His company was sued by the Boston and Montana Mining Company to keep it from mining the Rarus ore deposit, which Heinze had purchased in 1895. Heinze had based his right to mine the deposit on the apex theory, which held that the company that owned the spot where a mineral vein surfaced could mine all along the vein, even if it led onto the lands of competitors. Adding to his unpopularity among mine owners was his introduction of labor reforms. He sold his mining interests in Butte in 1906 and returned to New York.

—*Candace Floyd*

SEE ALSO: Copper Kings, War of the; Mining Law of 1872

SUGGESTED READING:
McNelis, Sarah. *Copper King at War.* Missoula, Mont., 1968.

HELL ON WHEELS

As the UNION PACIFIC RAILROAD and CENTRAL PACIFIC RAILROAD began building through the unsettled West toward their meeting at PROMONTORY SUMMIT, Utah, in the late 1860s, they provided their work crews with temporary camps built of tents and small wooden shacks and known as "Hell on Wheels." Every time the head of track reached a point sixty miles beyond the camp, workers packed up the camp, took everything to the end of the line, and reassembled it in a matter of hours. Often, these camps had three thousand residents.

At the center of a "Hell on Wheels" stood a large tent, one hundred by forty feet, which held a bar, dance floor and gambling equipment. Outside the tent were smaller tents and crude shacks serving as saloons, dance halls, brothels, and living quarters for the workers, who left camp each morning on trains taking them to the end of the line.

Although both railroads used temporary camps, the Union Pacific camps between Omaha and Utah were usually the ones identified as "Hell on Wheels" because the Irish workers who built that road lived more boisterously in the camps than the Chinese laborers of the Central Pacific.

Although temporary in nature, some of these sites became permanent towns, even though the railhead had moved farther west. Often these sites became junc-

tions and division headquarters that served the railroad and the settlers following behind the tracks.

Cheyenne, Wyoming, begun in late 1867 when the Union Pacific stopped construction to await spring, grew so fast that it was nicknamed the "magic city." It lived on after the camp moved to Laramie. Cheyenne prospered as a shipping point for freight sent to nearby gold fields and to a growing Denver City. Laramie, the next "Hell on Wheels" site, survived because its location in a fertile valley attracted settlers. The growth of the two towns prompted efforts to organize the Wyoming Territory, created on July 25, 1868.

Ogden, Utah, near Promontory Summit, the point where the railroads were to meet, was a "Hell on Wheels" site even before the railroad arrived when it became the center of a gold rush along the Wyoming-Idaho border. The miners and the railroad crews changed the sleepy little Mormon town forever. The last Union Pacific "Hell on Wheels" town was Corinne, Utah Territory, which did not survive.

Although the Central Pacific camps did not have the rough reputation of those on the Union Pacific, towns including Reno, Nevada, Wadsworth, Lovelock, Winnemucca, Argenta, Carlin, and Elko were established along the line in the trail of the camps.

Without the railroad, it is unlikely that these towns would have been founded. Because the railroad provided settlers a link to the world, trading points grew up to serve the growing West. Former "Hell on Wheels" sites calmed down, organized civic authority, and developed into permanent homes for the settlers who followed the rail lines.

—*Patrick H. Butler, III*

SUGGESTED READING:
Aikman, Duncan, ed. *The Taming of the Frontier.* New York, 1925.
Ames, Charles E. *Pioneering the Union Pacific.* New York, 1969.
Dary, David. *Entrepreneurs of the Old West.* Lincoln, Nebr., 1986.

HENEY, FRANCIS JOSEPH

A special prosecutor for the attorney general of the United States, Francis Joseph Heney (1859–1937) tried Oregon land-fraud cases and political corruption cases in San Francisco in the early 1900s, most famously perhaps the case that brought down political boss ABRAHAM (ABE) RUEF. Born in New York, Heney moved with his family to San Francisco when he was still an infant. There he attended public school before dropping out to work in his father's furniture store. Attending school at night, then taking up a job teaching math at a local grammar school, Heney eventually saved enough money to enroll at the University of California and take up full-time studies. Within a year he was expelled for fighting. Teaching, which he again tried, had lost its appeal, and Heney headed for Idaho, where he went to work in the mines. Under the loose conditions prevailing in mining camps and towns, Heney undertook the defense of a local man charged with murder, and—despite his lack of legal experience—won acquittal for his client. He moved back to San Francisco, enrolled in Hastings Law School, and passed the California bar in 1884. After law school, Heney moved to Tucson, Arizona, and became the attorney general of the Arizona Territory by 1893. That year, he again moved back to San Francisco, this time setting up in private practice.

Hired by United States Attorney General Philander Knox, Heney was assigned the prosecution of an Oregon land-fraud case in 1903. Fighting the state's entrenched political machine, Heney made a case of conspiracy against a U.S. attorney, a U.S. senator, and countless local politicians, and he made the charges stick. Success in Oregon landed him the job of assistant U.S. district attorney in San Francisco, where, with the encouragement of President THEODORE ROOSEVELT, he took on the city's powerful and corrupt political machine run by the UNION LABOR PARTY's cynical Abe Ruef. Backed by the best-known detective in the country, WILLIAM J. BURNS, early head of the Bureau of Investigation (later the Federal Bureau of Investigation), Heney conducted a four-year investigation that brought down hundreds of city officials, including San Francisco's mayor, its police chief, and "Boss" Ruef himself in 1906.

When Heney announced that he intended to pursue relentlessly all those who had offered him bribes in the course of his investigations, public opinion swung loudly and overwhelmingly in his favor. Amid visions of a political future, Heney did as he promised. But among those he indicted were prominent businessmen and their companies, and when the economic fallout of the prosecution began to hit home among the city's opinion-makers, Heney himself increasingly came under public attack in the local press. The 1908 trials following the indictments were nothing short of high drama. Defendants hired Los Angeles attorney Earl Rogers, and the battle between Heney and Rogers quickly grew personal. Rogers called Heney a coward; Heney accused Rogers of being a drunk. Everybody hired private detectives to follow everybody else and their private detectives, and Heney received a number of death threats. On Friday 13, 1908, a man stood up in court and shot Heney in the neck.

Heney's solidly Progressive stance against all parties to graft in the hearings cost him his political dreams. Twice he ran for governor of California; twice he was defeated. After he made a bid for a U.S. Senate seat and was denied that opportunity to serve as well, Heney retired into private practice.

—Charles Phillips

SUGGESTED READING:
Axelrod, Alan, and Charles Phillips. *Cops, Crooks, and Criminologists: An International Biographical Dictionary of Law Enforcement.* New York, 1996.

HENRY, ANDREW

Fur trapper and partner in the Ashley-Henry Fur Company, Andrew Henry (1775?–1833) was born in York County, Pennsylvania. He left home at the age of eighteen and in 1803 settled in Ste. Genevieve, Missouri, where, as a respected member of the community, he served in various civic capacities.

In 1806, Henry and his close friend WILLIAM HENRY ASHLEY became co-owners of a mining operation. By 1809, Henry also became involved in the fledgling St. Louis MISSOURI FUR COMPANY. Spending the next three years in the mountains, he became an able field captain. During the fall of 1810, Henry and his party established Fort Henry, the first American fort west of the Continental Divide. After an extremely difficult winter in the mountains, he returned to Missouri.

Following the War of 1812, in which Henry served as major in a volunteer militia, he returned to farming and mining. In 1822, he and his old friend Ashley established the Henry-Ashley Fur Company. Their partnership was an ideal blending of abilities; Henry took charge of field operations while Ashley handled finances and supplies. Through their company, the partners introduced several new concepts into the FUR TRADE: they emphasized trapping, not trading; they had no permanent trading posts; and they hired independent trappers.

From 1822 to 1824, Henry and his men trapped and explored the upper Missouri, Bighorn, and Yellowstone rivers. Due largely to difficulties with various Native Americans, particularly the Blackfoot and Arikara tribes, the trappers had limited success. In the summer of 1824, Henry retired from the fur trade, just one year before the company achieved financial success. He returned to St. Louis where he mined and took to drinking heavily. He died in Harmony, Missouri.

Henry was liked and respected for his honesty, intelligence, and enterprise. He once told an associate that "honor and self-respect were more to be prized than anything else." He was an exceptional mountain man whose leadership and innovative ideas helped revolutionize the fur trade.

—*Linda White and Fred R. Gowans*

SEE ALSO: Mountain Men; Trappers

SUGGESTED READING:

Clements, Harvey L. "Andrew Henry." *The Mountain Men and the Fur Trade of the Far West.* Vol. 6. Edited by LeRoy R. Hafen. Glendale, Calif., 1968.

Clokey, Richard M. *William H. Ashley: Enterprise and Politics in the Trans-Mississippi West.* Norman, Okla., 1989.

Morgan, Dale L., ed. *The West of William H. Ashley.* Denver, 1964.

White, Linda, and Fred R. Gowans. "Traders to Trappers: Andrew Henry and the Rocky Mountain Fur Trade." *Montana: The Magazine of Western History* 43 (Winter 1993): 58–65 (Summer 1993): 54–63.

HENSLEY, JOSEPHINE ("CHICAGO JOE")

Businesswoman and madame Josephine Hensley (1844–1899) established a "hurdy-gurdy" or dance hall in the raw gold-mining town of Helena, Montana, in 1867. At her place, a modest log cabin, miners enjoyed liquor for fifty cents a drink and a dance with one of the "girls" for twenty-five cents. Her dance-hall girls earned a portion of the money collected from liquor sold and dances danced, and they could make arrangements with miners for other favors as well. Given the nickname "Chicago Joe" in honor of her origins, Hensley made a spectacular success of her establishment, moved into larger quarters in 1874, invested her earnings in Helena real estate, and made friends among the city's important businessmen and politicians.

Hensley enjoyed her prosperity and her novelty as an independent businesswoman for nearly twenty years. Then, in 1885, the territorial legislature banned hurdy-gurdy houses, and Hensley was arrested. At her trial, her lawyer countered the charges that hers was a typical hurdy-gurdy by pointing out that no such barrel organ could be found in her place of business. The music for dancing came from a three-piece ensemble of a piano, violin, and cornet. Hensley was acquitted.

After the trial, Hensley added a theater area to her establishment and provided stage entertainment to better disguise the curtained cribs where her prostitutes continued to supply entertainments of a different nature. When Hensley died in 1899, some of Helena's most prominent citizens attended her funeral.

—*Patricia Hogan*

Josephine Hensley, "Chicago Joe." *Courtesy Montana Historical Society.*

SEE ALSO: Prostitution; Women in Wage Work

SUGGESTED READING:

Petrik. Paul. *No Step Backward: Women and Family on the Rocky Mountain Mining Frontier, Helena, Montana, 1865–1900.* Helena, Mont., 1987.

HERBICIDES

Farmers have long sought ways to control weeds and brush; however, it was not until the late nineteenth century that artificial means were used. In the West, some experimentation occurred on a small scale with chemical by-products or the selective use of various oils, but these products provided only minimal advantage. None of these methods was selective enough to kill off the undesired weeds while leaving the crop intact.

Other industries were suffering for want of weed control as well. The vast rail lines of the West needed to be kept weeded so as not to impede the track, and the telegraph and, later, telephone poles that were the lifeblood of communication could be overcome by unchecked weeds. The use of herbicides remained rather dormant until 1945, when chemical research flooded the market with products that were billed as "miracle weed killers."

Chemists and botanists doing research on plant hormones developed an artificial growth hormone in 1935 as a synthetic compound. After the United States's entry into World War II, much of that research was applied to the effects and feasibility of crop-directed chemical warfare. In April 1942, scientists from the University of Chicago developed a compound known as 2,4-D that had ideal use as a growth regulator. Having to wait until the end of the war for approval from the army, the product was finally marketed in 1945. It was quickly hailed as the miracle weed killer, promising to eradicate the problem of weeds for good. In the first year of commercial production, sales went sky high.

However, within ten years, alarmists began to note changes in the environment near large agricultural areas. Many felt these changes were due to 2,4-D and its successor 2,4,5-T. In 1962, Rachel Carson published *Silent Spring*, a book about the effects of chemicals like 2,4-D and 2,4,5-T and their insecticide counterpart, DDT, on birds and fish and other forms of wildlife. What animals the chemicals did not kill off developed immunities to the chemicals, and by the late 1960s, scientists estimated that almost four hundred different species of weeds and insects were immune to the effects of 2,4-D, 2,4,5-T, and DDT. Worse still, these chemicals had a much longer half-life than expected, staying in the soils, seeping into water tables, and eventually working their way up the food chain. Prolonged exposure has been known to cause cancer and birth defects. In the large agricultural states such as California and Texas, these chemicals had a debilitating effect on local ecologies as well as on migrant farm workers who were exposed to the chemicals for extended periods of time. By the late 1960s and early 1970s, 2,4-D, 2,4,5-D, and DDT had been banned by the federal government.

—*Kurt Edward Kemper*

SEE ALSO: Agriculture; Carson, Rachel, and *Silent Spring*; Pesticides

SUGGESTED READING:

Schlebecker, John T. *Whereby We Thrive: A History of American Agriculture, 1607–1972.* Ames, Iowa, 1975.
Trost, Cathy. *Elements of Risk: The Chemical Industry and Its Threat to America.* New York, 1984.

HETCH HETCHY CONTROVERSY

The Hetch Hetchy Valley, lying within YOSEMITE NATIONAL PARK, was an uncommonly beautiful valley located along the Tolumne River. The valley became the object of a critical early battle in the American environmental movement. In 1901, the city of San Francisco, which needed a new source of domestic WATER, set out to build a dam that would flood the valley to create a reservoir. On October 16 of that year, the city applied for use of the valley. Three times, the federal government, which administered Yosemite National Park, rejected the application (January 20, 1903, December 22, 1903, and February 20, 1905), but a revised application, filed on December 27, 1905, was approved on June 11, 1908. Against the planned Hetch Hetchy Dam and reservoir, the naturalist JOHN MUIR— through the organization he had founded, the SIERRA CLUB— mounted a massive campaign.

Muir and his organization faced formidable odds. The November 11, 1908, city election in San Francisco revealed public opinion running six-to-one in favor of the Hetch Hetchy Dam project, and even some Sierra Club members believed that Muir and the organization should back down. Nevertheless, the Sierra Club appealed to the courts and to Congress but ultimately failed to stop the project. On December 19, 1913, President Woodrow Wilson signed the Raker Act into law, authorizing construction of the O'Shaughnessy Dam and the Hetch Hetchy Reservoir. Despite the ultimate failure of the Sierra Club's efforts, the Hetch Hetchy controversy taught conservationists the value of organized action on well-defined environmental issues. In particular, Hetch Hetchy made the Sierra Club a significant force in the growing environmental movement.

—*Alan Axelrod*

SUGGESTED READING:

Fox, Stephen. *John Muir and His Legacy: The American Conservation Movement.* Boston, 1981.

HEWETT, EDGAR L.

Edgar L. Hewett (1865–1946), known as "El Toro"— the bull (but only behind his back)—was a Western educator, archaeologist, and entrepreneur responsible for the revival of SANTA FE, NEW MEXICO. Born and raised on a farm in western Illinois, Hewett attended Tarkio College in Missouri. After graduating, he taught there and at the Colorado Normal School in Greeley before becoming president of New Mexico Normal School in Las Vegas, New Mexico, in 1898. Even before Hewett's arrival in New Mexico, the romantic grandeur of the prehistoric Southwest captured his imagination. Archaeologist, cultural entrepreneur, and tireless promoter of his causes, Hewett wrote the ANTIQUITIES ACT OF 1906, the most important preservation legislation passed before 1966. He also persuaded officials of the Archaeological Institute of America to locate a research center, now known as the School of American Research, in Santa Fe. In addition, he was the primary excavator of the Pajarito Plateau region of New Mexico and developed most of the important cultural institutions in Santa Fe. The MUSEUM OF NEW MEXICO, the Museum of Fine Arts, and the revival of both the Fiesta and the Indian Market were results of his work. Hewett also sat on the commission that wrote Santa Fe's restrictive building codes.

Hewett was a difficult person, a wily adversary who manipulated reality to suit his purposes. Although he was one of the first to undertake the training of students in archaeology and earned a Ph.D. in the field from the University of Geneva in 1908, he was tied to the romantic cosmology of the late nineteenth century. As a result, when ideas such as stratigraphy and dendrochronology became analytical tools, Hewett's former students—such as Alfred V. Kidder, who undertook excavations at Pecos, New Mexico—surpassed him. Swaggeringly self-confident, Hewett resented changes in the field.

As a turn-of-the-century institution builder, Hewett ranks in the top echelon. His actions saved Santa Fe from the fate of communities by-passed by railroads and created the climate in which artists and writers have felt comfortable ever since. When he died, he was buried in one of the interior walls of the Museum of Fine Arts in Santa Fe, testimony to both the power he wielded and his commitment to the creation of a cultural heritage.

—*Hal Rothman*

SUGGESTED READING:
Chauveret, Beatrice. *Hewett and Friends: A Biography of Santa Fe's Vibrant Era.* Santa Fe, N. Mex., 1983.
Rothman, Hal. *On Rims and Ridges: The Los Alamos Area since 1880.* Lincoln, Nebr., 1992.

HICKOK, JAMES BUTLER ("WILD BILL")

Legendary U.S. Marshal James Butler ("Wild Bill") Hickok (1837–1876) was born in Illinois and moved

James Butler ("Wild Bill") Hickok, about 1875. *Courtesy Buffalo Bill Historical Center.*

to the Kansas Territory in 1856. There he served as a village constable in 1858 and worked as a teamster on the Santa Fe Trail. During the Civil War, he was a Union Army wagonmaster, detective, scout, and spy in Missouri (where he was first called "Wild Bill"). In the Indian Wars of 1867 to 1869, he was a scout and courier for the Seventh and Tenth Cavalry regiments. He also served as a deputy U.S. marshal from 1867 to 1870; acting sheriff in 1869; and marshal of Abilene, Kansas, in 1871.

During his career Hickok killed fewer than ten men (in personal combat and in the line of duty), but when he was featured in Harper's *New Monthly Magazine* in February 1867, it was claimed that he single-handedly had killed ten of the so-called McCanles Gang in Nebraska. The account inspired later reports that, in his role as a town marshal or "civilizer," he had killed more than one hundred badmen. Hickok himself hated his man-killer reputation. Those who were acquainted with him (among them GEORGE ARMSTRONG CUSTER and his wife) found that his soft-spoken, courteous, and gentlemanly manner belied his violent reputation. But Custer did state that Hickok could control others by his strength of character. That was particularly evident in Hays City and Abilene where drunken teamsters or Texas cowboys thought twice about tackling "Wild Bill" when he set out to preserve law and order.

In 1872 at Niagara Falls, Ontario, Hickok appeared in a "Grand Buffalo Hunt" that presaged WILLIAM F. ("BUFFALO BILL") CODY's "Wild West" show of 1883. In 1873, Cody persuaded Hickok to join his theatrical company that presented Western melodramas to Eastern audiences. After eight months, Hickok quit and returned to the West. In March 1876, he married Agnes Lake Thatcher, a former circus owner and performer. While she remained in Ohio, he went to Deadwood in the Dakota Territory to search for gold. On August 2, Hickok was shot from behind as he sat playing poker in a saloon. His murderer, John (alias "Jack") McCall was later tried, found guilty, and hanged on March 1, 1877. The cards Hickok held—aces and eights—are now known as "The Dead Man's Hand."

The real James Butler Hickok has passed into history. But the legendary "Wild Bill Hickok" epitomizes the gunfighting hero of Western books and films and is now firmly established as an American folk hero.

—*Joseph G. Rosa*

SEE ALSO: Gunfighters; Violence: Historical Overview, Myths about Violence

SUGGESTED READING:

Custer, Gen. G. A. *My Life on the Plains, or Personal Experiences with Indians.* New York, 1874.

Miller, Nyle H., and Joseph W. Snell. *Why the West Was Wild.* Topeka, Kans., 1963.

Rosa, Joseph G. *They Called Him Wild Bill: The Life and Adventures of James Butler Hickok.* Norman, Okla., 1964. Reprint. 1974.

HIDATSA INDIANS

SEE: Native American Peoples: Peoples of the Great Plains

HIGHWAYS

SEE: Roads and Highways

HILL, JAMES J.

One of the West's great railroad men, James J. Hill (1838–1916) did much to promote the development of the Northwest through his Great Northern Railway. Born near Rockwood, Ontario, Hill settled in St. Paul, Minnesota, at the age of eighteen and quickly built a reputation as an innovative and highly competent manager of railroad and steamboat operations. In 1878, he and three Canadian partners—Donald

Alexander Smith (later the first Baron Strathcona and Mount Royal), Sir George Stephen, and Norman Rittson—purchased the ailing St. Paul and Pacific Railroad. Hill became president of the company in 1882. Through astute and aggressive management, building, and acquisition, he used the railroad as the core around which he organized a much larger system. In 1890, his holdings were united as the Great Northern Railway Company, and three years later, the line extended to Seattle. He served as its president from 1893 to 1907, became chairman of the board of directors in 1907, and served in that capacity until 1912.

Hill allied himself with financier J. Pierpont Morgan against EDWARD HENRY HARRIMAN in a struggle for control of the Chicago, Burlington, and Quincy Railroad, which ignited a major national financial panic in 1901. Ultimately, the Northern Pacific Railroad and the CB&Q came under Hill's control. When he added banking to his portfolio by becoming president of the Northern Securities Company, he was challenged by the federal government. In 1904, however, the company was dissolved when the Supreme Court declared it to be in violation of the SHERMAN ANTI-TRUST ACT. This setback notwithstanding, Hill took control of the First and Second National banks of St. Paul in 1912 and merged them into a formidable financial institution.

James J. Hill, on the left, with his son Louis W. Hill in 1911. *Courtesy Burlington Northern Railroad Archives.*

The "empire builder," as Hill was popularly called, had an abiding interest in nature conservation and saw the railroad as helping promote the nation's fledgling environmental movement. He presented his conservationist views in his 1910 book entitled *Highways of Progress*.

—*Alan Axelrod*

SEE ALSO: Financial Panics; Railroads

SUGGESTED READING:
Holbrook, Stewart H. *James J. Hill*. New York, 1955.
Pyle, Joseph Gilpin. *The Life of James J. Hill*. 2 vols. New York, 1917.

HILL, JOE

SEE: Industrial Workers of the World

HILL, THOMAS

Frequently called the "artist of the Yosemite," Thomas Hill (1829–1908) was born in Birmingham, England. He immigrated to the United States in 1840 and was raised in Taunton, Massachusetts. Apprenticed to a coach painter until he was fifteen years old, Hill moved to Boston to work as an ornamental painter. Fine art beckoned, however, and he went to Philadelphia to study at the Pennsylvania Academy of the Fine Arts. He soon earned a reputation as a painter of portraits and historical canvases. In 1853, he won a prize from the Maryland Institute in Baltimore for one of his allegorical works.

Ill health prompted him to move to the West, and in 1861, he settled in San Francisco, where he worked as a portrait painter. In 1866, he traveled to Paris to study with Paul Meyerheim and then returned to Boston in 1867. At this time, he abandoned portraiture for landscape painting and traveled extensively through the West. He was particularly attracted to the Yosemite region. His *Yosemite Valley* of 1876 (Kahn Collection of the Oakland Museum) was widely hailed. Henceforth specializing in Yosemite landscapes, Hill spent the summers from 1871 to 1888 there before establishing a permanent studio in the area. Also typical of his work is the spectacular *Early Morning, Yosemite Valley* (1884; Chrysler Museum, Norfolk, Virginia).

Perhaps his single best-known canvas is his depiction of the driving of the "Golden Spike" at PROMON-TORY SUMMIT, Utah, on May 10, 1869—an event that marked the completion of the transcontinental railroad. *The Last Spike* (California State Railroad Museum), a monumental canvas of ten by thirteen feet, was executed between 1887 and 1891. It includes some four hundred carefully delineated figures, among them the "Big Four" of the transcontinental railroad project—AMASA LELAND STANFORD, COLLIS P. HUNTINGTON, MARK HOPKINS, and CHARLES CROCKER—even though only Stanford had actually been present at the ceremony. Also depicted is THEODORE DEHONE JUDAH, the engineering mastermind behind the railroad, who had died half a dozen years before the golden spike was driven home.

—*Alan Axelrod*

SUGGESTED READING:
Axelrod, Alan. *The Art of the Golden West*. New York, 1990.

HISTORIOGRAPHY, WESTERN

One might assume that Western history can be easily divided into two broad, opposing categories—the frontier "process" approach of FREDERICK JACKSON TURNER and his followers, and the West-as-region, or place, approach, espoused by new Western historians. But this easy division, while it does provide a framework for examining Western historiography, is too simplistic. Western historians cannot be split into two diametrically opposed groups—Turner and his followers (including Frederick Logan Paxson and RAY ALLEN BILLINGTON) and the new Western historians (Patricia Nelson Limerick, Richard White, Donald Worster, and others). Such a division obscures the complexity and variety of historical scholarship on the West during the last century or so. In fact, Western historians have been employing both organizing themes—the West as frontier and the West as geographically defined region—for more than a century.

Americans had started to write about the West a century before Turner. In the late eighteenth century, leading statesmen, including THOMAS JEFFERSON and Benjamin Franklin, and the French expatriate Hector St. John de Crévecoeur, all commented on the wonderful advantages that Western lands offered to the new American nation. A few decades later, at the beginning of the nineteenth century, MERIWETHER LEWIS and WILLIAM CLARK made their mark as the most important of the early Anglo explorers and chroniclers of the West. During the rest of the nineteenth century, a good deal of writing about the West—much of it more stirring than scholarly (and less reliable than Lewis and Clark's journals)—fueled the public's desire to learn more.

By the time Frederick Jackson Turner delivered his essay "The Significance of the Frontier in American History" (1893), FRANCIS PARKMAN's famous account of frontier life, *The Oregon Trail* (1849), had been published, and dime novels about Wild West legends such as JAMES BUTLER ("WILD BILL") HICKOK, CALAMITY JANE, and WILLIAM F. ("BUFFALO BILL") CODY had popularized a mythic West. By the early 1880s, Buffalo Bill's Wild West show was wooing crowds across the country, and the writings of THEODORE ROOSEVELT and OWEN WISTER and the sketches of FREDERIC REMINGTON were further romanticizing the cowboy. The first part of Roosevelt's four volume study, *The Winning of the West* (1889–1896), appeared before the decade was over.

Still, while much had been written about the West before Turner's famous frontier thesis, it was nonetheless his essay and his tireless work as a teacher, first at the University of Wisconsin and then at Harvard University, that really gave birth to the field of Western history and ensured its growth. Turner argued that the frontier had been the most important influence on the development of American institutions. The process of settling the frontier of Western lands, he explained, had molded a uniquely American brand of democracy, had made Americans intensely individualistic and nationalistic, and had nurtured a unique American character that was highly inventive and practical and decidedly unphilosophical.

While Turner's essay was a stirring piece, high on literary power and narrative structure, it was also, and more importantly, an essay about the development of social, political, and economic institutions. It was a departure from the grand, colorful, romantic narratives of Parkman and Roosevelt, and it gave the field of Western history academic legitimacy.

By the beginning of the twentieth century, the frontier thesis, which Turner had elaborated on in a number of magazine articles, had become quite widely known. In 1910, Turner assumed the presidency of the American Historical Association and moved to Harvard University. A decade later, his essay collection entitled *The Frontier in American History* (1920) was published and further helped popularize the frontier thesis. Indeed, by this time, the settlement of the frontier had come to be viewed as the key to the nation's growth and development. The story of the frontier had become America's story. Moreover, Western history and national history had become intertwined. Popular books, such as Frederick Logan Paxson's Pulitzer Prize–winning *History of the American Frontier, 1763–1893* (1924) and Robert E. Riegel's *America Moves West*

(1930) followed the Turnerian model, making the history of the West and the history of the frontier one and the same—when the frontier process ended (when the Western lands were "settled" and "tamed"), the history of the West came to an end, too. According to the Turnerian process-centered model, *frontier, West,* and *nation* became almost interchangeable terms in the story of American development.

After Turner, Paxson was the most important historian of the frontier process in the first half of the twentieth century and his *History of the American Frontier* was the most widely used text in the field. Then, in 1949, Ray Allen Billington's influential textbook *Westward Expansion* appeared. Billington inherited the Turnerian legacy and became Turner's staunchest defender as criticisms of the frontier thesis, which had begun in the 1930s and 1940s, mounted in the post–World War II years. *Westward Expansion* was republished in numerous additions (most recently in 1982) and became the leading text in the field.

In the 1980s and early 1990s, Martin Ridge, Billington's successor at the Huntington Library (where Turner spent his last years and where his papers are housed), wrote a number of essays in defense of the process-centered Turnerian model. Ridge emphasized that Turner was a far more complex and modern-minded historian than his critics had suggested. In *On Turner's Trail: 100 Years of Writing Western History* (1994), Wilbur Jacobs, while often critical of Turner, also sought to demonstrate the richness of his legacy and the extent of his influence on Western historians, even his most recent critics. In the 1980s and 1990s, Michael Steiner also produced several essays that showed, ironically, that Turner—so often criticized by Western regionalists—was himself an important regionalist thinker. It is also interesting that one of the most influential of recent Western revisionists, William Cronon, is also an advocate of process-centered analyses of Western history. In an important essay entitled "Revisiting Turner's Vanishing Frontier" (1987), Cronon, while certainly not uncritical of Turner's essay, found much in the Turnerian legacy that was still useful for Western historians.

The frontier model was not the only one employed in the late nineteenth century for studying the West. Before Turner outlined the positive effects of the frontier process, and before Roosevelt had begun to publish his account of *The Winning of the West*, the philosopher JOSIAH ROYCE had published his history of the early settlement of California (1886), which stressed the immorality of the conquest of that region and the failure of the conquerors to assume any moral responsibility in the immediate aftermath of their action. While Royce concluded on a positive note, pointing to the development of a dynamic community in California, his history emphasized the cruel and intolerant treatment of foreigners there.

Also before Turner had delivered his frontier paper in 1893, HUBERT HOWE BANCROFT, writing in a grand narrative style more reminiscent of Parkman and Roosevelt than Turner, had produced more than fifty volumes of American Western history, including *The Native Races of the Pacific States of North America* (five volumes, 1874–1876), *The Works of Hubert Howe Bancroft* (thirty-nine volumes, 1882–1890), and *The Chronicles of the Builders of the Commonwealth* (seven volumes, 1891–1892). And, unlike Turner, whose most precious frontier was the Midwest, the center of Bancroft's historical universe was California. Bancroft viewed California as a land of immense possibility, the culmination of the frontier process, and the center of a region that stretched from the Pacific Coast to the Great Divide. Bancroft, like Royce, was a regionalist, more interested in the story of a place than in the frontier process that had resulted in the settlement of that place. Bancroft's faith in MANIFEST DESTINY and his Darwinist notions of racial superiority and inferiority (ideas that were common at the time he wrote) distinguish his work from the writings of modern-day Western regionalists. However, it is important to note that regionalist approaches have a long and rich tradition in American Western history.

While Turner's ideas on the frontier were gaining widespread popularity in the first decades of the twentieth century, Turner's own student HERBERT EUGENE BOLTON was becoming a renowned historian of the Spanish borderlands. Interestingly, in 1911, Bolton moved from the University of Texas to the University of California at Berkeley, drawn in part to the massive collection of materials on Mexico and the West that had been assembled by Hubert Howe Bancroft and acquired by Berkeley (Bolton later became director of the famous Bancroft Collection). In addition to compiling invaluable guides to archival sources on the Spanish borderlands, Bolton published a series of important works on this region, including *Spanish Exploration in the Southwest, 1542–1706* (1916), *The Spanish Borderlands: A Chronicle of Old Florida and the Southwest* (1921), *Rim of Christendom* (1936), and *Coronado* (1949). Also, as Turner had done, Bolton trained hundreds of graduate students, many of whom had an important impact on the field of Western history, helping to further scholarly interest in American Indian history, Hispanic history, and the Spanish borderlands as a region.

Meanwhile, as Bolton recorded the history of the Southwest, WALTER PRESCOTT WEBB produced a landmark work of Western regionalism, *The Great Plains* (1931). Webb argued that this harsh environment—arid, flat, and treeless—in large part determined the course of life there. Settlers had to adjust and conform to the demands of the environment, and this process of adjustment helped shape the Great Plains into a distinct region. The Great Plains, Webb suggested was not just another frontier to be settled and made a part of the nation. Instead, he argued that the region was definable—encompassing most of the land West of the Mississippi River—and it was different and always would be. While Turner's frontier was elusive, difficult to describe and define, there was no mistaking Webb's Great Plains for any other place.

Interestingly and ironically, in an important later work, *The Great Frontier* (1952), Webb viewed the West not as a region but as the final stage—the last frontier—of a four-century-long process of European expansion that ended around 1890. With the end of the boom, which had ensured a rising standard of living, the world faced the possibility of outstripping its resources and resorting to less democratic forms of government. While Turner had made the transition from frontier to region in his thinking about the West and the nation as a whole, Webb, it seemed, had made the transition from region to frontier. And then, five years after the publication of *The Great Frontier,* Webb wrote an influential essay for *Harper's Magazine,* "The American West: Perpetual Mirage" (1957), which once again emphasized the West as a region marked by its aridity.

While Webb was wrestling with the concepts of the West as frontier and region, Henry Nash Smith produced a tremendously perceptive work that emphasized the mythic construction of the West, *Virgin Land: The American West as Symbol and Myth* (1950). Smith was primarily interested in the West's place in American culture and its role in shaping national identity. Unlike Turner and Webb, who emphasized the effect of the West (whether frontier or region) on settlers, Smith chronicled the efforts of Americans in the nineteenth century to shape a mythic West that would meet their needs. The West, Smith explained, had been constructed through works of literature and popular culture. This was a powerful new analytical approach, so significant that it helped forge a new scholarly field: American studies. While Smith's exclusive focus on Euro-American culture (typical of his era and earlier ones) proved unsatisfactory for a later generation of scholars focusing on the West's racial and ethnic diversity, *Virgin Land* was a tremendously influential work.

At the time Smith was outlining the process by which Americans created an exceptional and mythic West, Earl Pomeroy focused squarely on the political realities of American Western history. In *The Territo-*

ries and the United States, 1861–1890 (1947), Pomeroy emphasized the theme of continuity between the national system of government and the newly established territorial governments of the West. The West's governmental systems, he contended, were no more democratic than those anywhere else in the country. Pomeroy was deemphasizing Western exceptionalism, which was an essential ingredient in the writings of Western regionalists and frontier theorists. He made the point more emphatically in an important essay in the *Mississippi Valley Historical Review,* "Toward a Reorientation of Western History: Continuity and Environment" (1955). Chiding both frontier and regional approaches, he suggested that it was time historians examined more carefully the impact of "'Eastern' institutions and ideas" on the West. Pomeroy took up his own challenge in his best-known study, *The Pacific Slope: A History of California, Oregon, Washington, Idaho, Utah, and Nevada* (1965). His book emphasized the urban character of the West and the development of Western institutions. The work was analytical, not romantic, and its analysis of political and economic developments in the West was extremely thorough and sophisticated.

From the 1960s to the mid-1980s, many Western historians feared that their field was undergoing a crisis. However, while courses in Western history seemed to be waning in popularity, scholars were laying the groundwork for a renaissance in the field that began in the mid-1980s and showed no signs of decline by the mid-1990s. Gerald Nash, in *The American West in the Twentieth Century* (1977), emphasized the importance of moving beyond the mythic Old West of the nineteenth century. Carl Abbott, in *The New Urban America: Growth and Politics in Sunbelt Cities* (1981), demonstrated the centrality of cities to the story of the West. William Goetzmann produced an important work on Western exploration, *Exploration and Empire: The Explorer and the Scientist in the Winning of the American West* (1966), and emphasized, in the tradition of Henry Nash Smith, the centrality of myth to the Western experience in *The West of the Imagination* (1986), as did Robert Athearn's posthumously published *Mythic West in Twentieth Century America* (1986).

The field of Western women's history also saw the publication of important works in this period, including Julie Roy Jeffrey's *Frontier Women: The Trans-Mississippi West, 1840–1880* (1979), John Mack Faragher's *Women and Men on the Overland Trail* (1979), Sandra Myres's *Westering Women and the Frontier Experience, 1800–1915* (1982), Glenda Riley's *Women and Indians on the Frontier, 1825–1915* (1984), and Anne Butler's *Daughters of Joy, Sisters of Mercy: Prostitutes in the American West, 1865–1890* (1985).

Important works of environmental history began to appear at the end of the 1970s and included Donald Worster's *Dust Bowl: The Southern Plains in the 1930s,* Richard White's *Land Use, Environment, and Social Change: The Shaping of Island County, Washington* (1980), and William Cronon's *Changes in the Land: Indians, Colonists, and the Ecology of New England* (1983). Even earlier, Roderick Nash's landmark work *Wilderness and the American Mind* (1967) demonstrated the importance of environmental history as an avenue for scholarly investigation.

Growing scholarly interest, beginning in the 1960s, in the West's many peoples of color—including African Americans, Asian Americans, Chicanos, and Native Americans—and in European ethnic groups in the West, produced a flood of literature that established race and ethnicity as organizing themes for the study of the American West. Building on these important developments in the history of the urban West, gender and race relations, and the environment, the new Western history (or Western revisionism), in the mid-1980s, began to deemphasize the frontier, with all its colorful, romantic, and triumphal images of Euro-American exploration and settlement. The revisionists, instead, stressed that the West was a distinct region. Their works emphasized the themes of Euro-American conquest and oppression—of peoples of color, women, and the environment.

Among the most important of these books of new Western history were Patricia Nelson Limerick's *Legacy of Conquest: The Unbroken Past of the American West* (1987), which was the most widely discussed of all the revisionist works; Donald Worster's *Rivers of Empire: Water, Aridity, and the Growth of the American West* (1985), the most influential scholarly work on the Western environment in decades; William Cronon's *Nature's Metropolis: Chicago and the Great West* (1991), a much-discussed work on the relationship between the rural West and the urban metropolis that governs much of it; Richard White's *"It's Your Misfortune and None of My Own": A New History of the American West* (1991), which served as a regionalist alternative to Billington's Turnerian text *Westward Expansion*; and William Robbins' *Colony and Empire: The Capitalist Transformation of the West* (1994), which used Marxist theory to develop a damning account of Western development. The impact of these key works, along with an impressive array of books and articles published after the mid-1980s on Western women, peoples of color, the laboring classes, the environment, and cities, made the West an important regional testing ground for the latest developments in academia. Western history, which, back in the 1960s and 1970s, seemed to have been relegated to basement status in academia, was, by the late 1980s and early 1990s, considered to be on the cutting edge. By the mid-1990s, Western history had become one of the most influential of the many fields that come under the broad umbrella of United States history.

Those looking for a fuller introduction to the field of American Western historiography are lucky to have at their disposal a range of valuable works. Michael Malone's *Historians of the American West* (1983) and Roger Nichols's *American Western and Frontier Issues* (1986) are both excellent introductions. An important collection edited by Patricia Nelson Limerick, Clyde Milner, and Charles Rankin, entitled *Trails: Toward a New Western History* (1991), includes a number of important historiographical overviews, especially of more recent writings. Richard Etulain has edited a superb collection of essays on key Western historians entitled *Writing Western History* (1991), and Gerald Nash has produced a sweeping overview of developments in the field during the last century, *Creating the West* (1991).

Given the richness of the Western legacy and the tremendous influence of Western themes on American thought, culture, and identity, it should come as no surprise that the West also has a rich and complex historiographic tradition. With the heightened emphasis, since the 1960s, on the diversity of Western peoples and environments, the West's historiographic legacy seems destined to become ever richer and more complex.

—*David M. Wrobel*

SEE ALSO: Arid-Lands Thesis; Frontier: Frontier Thesis; Borderlands Theory; West-as-Region School

SUGGESTED READING:

Bogue, Allan, G. "The Significance of the History of the American West: Postscripts and Prospects." *Western Historical Quarterly* 24 (1993): 45–68.

Cronon, William. "Revisiting the Vanishing Frontier: The Legacy of Frederick Jackson Turner." *Western Historical Quarterly* 18 (1987): 157–176.

Etulain, Richard W. "Prologue, A New Historiographical Frontier: The Twentieth-Century West." In *The Twentieth Century West: Historical Interpretations.* Edited by Gerald D. Nash and Richard W. Etulain. Albuquerque, N. Mex., 1989.

———, ed. *Writing Western History: Essays on Major Western Historians.* Albuquerque, N. Mex., 1991.

Gressley, Gene M. *Old West/New West: Quo Vadis?* Worland, Wyo., 1994.

Limerick, Patricia Nelson, Clyde Milner, and Charles Rankin, eds. *Trails: Toward a New Western History.* Lawrence, Kans., 1991.

Malone, Michael P., *Historians and the American West.* Lincoln, Nebr., 1983.

Nash, Gerald. *Creating the West: Historical Perspectives, 1890–1990.* Albuquerque, N. Mex., 1991.

———. "The Great Adventure: Western History, 1890–1990." *Western Historical Quarterly* 22 (1991): 5–18.

Nichols, Roger L. *American Frontier and Western Issues: A Historiographical Review.* Westport, Conn., 1986.

Nugent, Walter. "Western History, New and Not So New." *The Magazine of History* 9 (1994): 5–9.

Paul, Rodman W., and Michael P. Malone. "Tradition and Challenge in Western Historiography." *Western Historical Quarterly* 16 (1985): 27–53.

Ridge, Martin. "The American West: From Frontier to Region." *New Mexico Historical Review* 64 (1989): 125–151.

Thompson, Gerald. "Frontier West: Process or Place." *Journal of the Southwest* 29 (1987): 364–375.

Wunder, John R. *Historians of the American Frontier: A Bio-Bibliographical Sourcebook.* Westport, Conn., 1988.

HITCHCOCK, GILBERT MONELL

Nebraska newspaper publisher and politician Gilbert Monell Hitchcock (1859–1934) was born in Omaha. He studied in Germany and then returned to Omaha to found the *Evening Herald* in 1885. Four years later, he bought the city's *Morning Herald* and merged the two newspapers into the *World-Herald,* the largest newspaper and leading Democratic daily in the state. He was active in the Democratic party, and between 1903 and 1923, he served three terms in the U.S. House and two terms in the Senate. Before the United States's entry into World War I, Hitchcock campaigned to secure American neutrality by promoting legislation to prohibit the sale of arms to the warring nations. He was Senate minority leader from 1919 to 1920. In that capacity, he lost his struggle to secure ratification of the Treaty of Versailles.

—*Candace Floyd*

SUGGESTED READING:

Cherny, Robert W. *Populism, Progressivism, and the Transformation of Nebraska Politics, 1885–1915.* Lincoln, Nebr., 1981.

HOGG, JAMES STEPHEN (JIM)

Attorney general, governor of Texas, and reform leader James Stephen (Jim) Hogg (1851–1906) was born near Rusk, Texas, to Joseph Lewis and Lucanda McMath Hogg. Orphaned by the age of twelve, he worked on country newspapers, studied law, and, in 1874, married Sallie Stinson.

Hogg was county attorney and district judge in Wood County between 1878 and 1886. His reputation as a prosecutor gained him victory in the Democratic race for attorney general in 1886. In office, Hogg filed suits against insurance companies and railroads. With sentiment rising among Texas farmers for political and economic reform, he emerged as a leading candidate for governor. Guided by Senator John H. Reagan, he campaigned for a regulatory commission to supervise the state's railroads. In doing so, he gained the support of the Texas Farmers' Alliance. Hogg won the race and took office in January 1891.

Under Hogg's leadership, the Texas legislature enacted a railroad commission law in 1891. Hogg also secured other laws to regulate corporations and to segregate African Americans. Hogg saw his economic policies as a way to promote the Texas economy and lessen the influence of Eastern businesses in the state. He did not, however, endorse proposals to have a farmer on the railroad commission, and he opposed other schemes to assist cotton growers through government programs. Angry farmers wanted him to do more, and the new Populist party opposed him after 1891. Facing challengers from conservative Democrats and the Populists in the 1892 election, Hogg defeated both rivals in a bitter campaign.

Retiring in 1895, the rotund Hogg practiced corporate law and grew wealthy from personal oil holdings. He remained a leader of the reform wing of the Democrats. Hogg is often seen as the guiding spirit of Texas PROGRESSIVISM, but as such he had little quarrel with corporations. It was their non-Texan character that he found most disturbing. His political career reflected how regional interests shaped Western leaders' responses to the rise of industrialism during the late nineteenth century.

—*Lewis L. Gould*

SEE ALSO: Agrarianism; Populism

SUGGESTED READING:

Barr, Alwyn. *Reconstruction to Reform: Texas Politics, 1876–1906*. Austin, Tex., 1971.
Cotner, Robert C. *James Stephen Hogg*. Austin, Tex., 1959.

HOGS

From the beginning of American settlement, hogs were important farm animals. First imported to the New World by Spanish explorers, hogs became feral creatures. They ran wild in the forests and range lands and were harvested later by returning explorers or subsequent colonizers.

As population increased, most farmers and planters raised hogs, which continued to run wild in the forests. Some of the early hogs in Virginia are thought to be descendants of the eight hogs brought to Española by Christopher Columbus. Even when raised as part of farming operations, most hogs often lived on acorns, chestnuts, and other natural food before being rounded up and slaughtered locally or driven to markets. The razorback-type hogs were lean, long, and tough and were sometimes so wild that they had to be shot. Some farmers fed their hogs a little corn before butchering, but often the hogs received no supplementary feed.

While there were some herds of two thousand head or more in the South, most colonial farmers had only a few hogs to provide the family with meat for its own use and for sale. Pork was a prominent part of the American diet, especially on the western fringes of settlement and in the South. Large quantities of pork products were also shipped to the West Indies and Europe. Export figures show that about six million pounds of pork products were exported from the United States by 1790.

In the early nineteenth century, progressive farmers began selective breeding of hogs. They introduced purebred Hampshire and Berkshire boars from England and cross-bred them to native sows. The practice greatly improved the stock. The main American breeds were the Chester Whites, Poland China, and Duroc-Jersey hogs. The new breeds were stockier and heavier than native hogs and produced better bacon and hams and more fat in the form of lard. Virginia hams became famous early in the nation's history.

In 1840, Tennessee had more hogs than any other state, but Ohio, Indiana, and Illinois also had large numbers, which foretold the emerging corn-hog belt in the Midwest. Iowa and Illinois grew the most corn and were the nation's leading hog producers by 1900. When it was found that corn was more valuable as feed for hogs than as a primary farm product, both corn and hog production rose dramatically in the Midwest. Between 1850 and 1900, the number of hogs in the United States increased from 30.3 million to 62.8 million. The quality of hogs also continued to improve as a result of continued emphasis on breeding. In the 1870s and 1880s, swine-breeders associations were organized to help propagate the best breeds.

Farmers raised hogs as part of their general farming operations. By 1900, between 75 and 80 percent of the farmers in the Midwest raised hogs. They were an important producer of income on most farms and, by the 1920s, were responsible for about 10 percent of the value of the nation's agricultural production. Farmers often referred to hogs as "mortgage lifters." There were fewer hogs per farm in the South, and the quality of animals there was poor in comparison to hogs in the Midwest. Many hogs in the South lived on the open ranges and received little grain.

Hogs were susceptible to a number of diseases. The census of 1890 reported that 9.8 million hogs died from various diseases in 1889 alone. Cholera, first reported in Ohio in 1833, was one of the most devastating diseases. Although scientists in the Bureau of Animal Husbandry developed a serum for vaccination as early as 1907, it was not until about 1913 that the protective serum came into general use. Thereafter, losses from cholera dropped sharply. In the 1920s, swine erysipelas began to take its toll, either killing hogs or leaving them scrawny with skin lesions and swollen joints, which reduced their market value. Hogs also suffered from tuberculosis. Immunization, more sanitary conditions, and better balanced rations overcame most health problems in hogs by the mid-twentieth century.

The number of hogs remained fairly steady between 1900 and 1950, usually ranging from 50 to 60 million. Hog numbers were down drastically in the 1930s because of the federal government's program of restricted production. From 1950 onward, however, hog populations increased rapidly. In 1980, farmers marketed 100 million hogs. By that time, many fewer farmers raised hogs, and most production was concentrated in the hands of large producers who raised hundreds and even thousands of head in confinement. From farrowing to fattening, hogs were kept indoors in a clean, confined space. They were fed balanced rations, kept free of disease, and raised to the desired weight of about two hundred pounds. Hog raising had been transformed from a family farm operation to a pork industry, which was in the hands of about 188,000 producers by 1992. This was a drop from more than one million producers three decades earlier. By the late twentieth century, scientists had bred hogs with less fat in keeping with contemporary dietary trends. The large hog operations presented some environmental concerns by the 1980s. The amount of concentrated waste, when not restrained, ran into creeks, rivers, and lakes, as well as ground water, and polluted drinking-water supplies. To solve the problem, producers built holding basins to retain hog waste.

Hogs were not as important in the trans-Mississippi region as cattle or sheep. In 1900, eleven Western states had 1.5 million hogs, about half as many as found in Indiana alone. However, farmers in the eastern parts of South Dakota, Nebraska, Kansas, Oklahoma, and Texas raised a substantial number of hogs.

—*Gilbert C. Fite*

SUGGESTED READING:

Crosby, Aldred W. *Ecological Imperialism: The Biological Expansion of Europe, 900–1900*. Cambridge, Mass., 1986.

Towne, Charles Wayland, and Edward Norris Wentworth. *Pigs from Cave to Corn Belt*. Norman, Okla., 1950.

HOLLADAY, BEN

Transportation entrepreneur and financier Ben Holladay (1819–1887) was born in Carlisle County, Kentucky. As a young man, he moved to Weston, Missouri, where he had a variety of occupations: operating a general store, saloon, and hotel and serving as postmaster. He also engaged in trade with the Indians in Kansas. He became known as a boisterous, coarse, and crude man, fond of whiskey and gambling.

With the outbreak of the UNITED STATES–MEXICAN WAR in 1846, Holladay furnished and freighted supplies for STEPHEN WATTS KEARNY's Army of the West. At the end of the war, he purchased wagons and oxen from the government at bargain prices, and, in partnership with Theodore F. Warner of Weston, he took fifty wagon loads of goods to Salt Lake City in 1849. To ensure success, he shrewdly took along a letter of introduction from Colonel ALEXANDER WILLIAM DONIPHAN, a well-known friend of the Mormons. In 1850, Holladay and his partner bought a herd of oxen, drove them to California, and made a handsome profit.

His business affairs were closely intertwined with RUSSELL, MAJORS AND WADDELL, a large freighting company, for whom he bought large quantities of stock. When the firm transferred its interest into stagecoaching and established the Central Overland California and PIKE'S PEAK EXPRESS COMPANY, Holladay advanced money to the company and cashed its drafts. He later assumed a mortgage on the company's holdings and took over its stage properties in a bankruptcy auction in March 1862. He also obtained the unexpired mail contract and the Kansas charter under which it operated. He organized the Overland Stage Line, which operated the eastern section of the trans-Missouri stage line, formerly operated by Russell, Majors and Waddell under subcontract to the OVERLAND MAIL COMPANY.

Between 1862 and 1866, Holladay obtained eight mail contracts. He operated branch lines in Nebraska and Colorado. In his 1864 contract with the government, he was given the job of carrying mail eastward from Salt Lake City and on extensive new lines in Idaho, Montana, Oregon, and Washington. He used his mail contracts to subsidize his stagecoach passenger service. Operating five thousand miles of stagecoach lines, Holladay became known as the "Napoleon of the Plains."

Suffering financial reversals during the Indian uprising on the Plains in 1865 when his STAGECOACHES, way stations, and stock were attacked, he sold out the following year to WELLS, FARGO AND COMPANY at a profit.

Just as he transferred his profits from freighting into stagecoach operations, he invested his capital from stage and mail lines into the steamship business. As early as 1863, he organized the California, Oregon and Mexico Steamship Company. Capital was invested in the Northern Pacific Transportation Company, which operated vessels from Alaska to Mexico. In 1868, he plunged into a railroad fight in Oregon, became the chief owner of the Oregon Central Railroad Company, and sold his steamship interests to build 240 miles of track. In the panic of 1873, he suffered tremendous financial reverses. German bondholders who had invested in his railroad promotions took control of his company in 1876 and eliminated Holladay's influence; he retired from business.

Holladay was a self-made man who trusted no one. His business and political morals were deplorable: he lied to investors; he juggled his books; he bought influence; he resorted to unscrupulous tactics to undermine competitors. At the same time, he was a champion of the underdog and generously contributed to charities. He built a pretentious mansion for his family known as Ophir near White Plains, New York, but spent most of his time in Washington, D.C., where he lavishly and somewhat vulgarly entertained politicians and men of influence when Congress was in session. He traveled in a private coach trimmed with silver and outfitted with a food locker and silver decanters. Two of his daughters married titled Europeans. Holladay died in Portland, Oregon.

—*W. Turrentine Jackson*

SEE ALSO: Overland Freight

SUGGESTED READING:
Frederick, James Vincent. *Ben Holladay, the Stagecoach King.* Glendale, Calif., 1940.
Lucia, Ellis. *The Saga of Ben Holladay.* New York, 1959.
Settle, Raymond W., and Mary L. Settle. *War Drums and Wagon Wheels.* Lincoln, Nebr., 1966.

HOLLIDAY, JOHN HENRY ("DOC")

Dentist, gambler, and gunfighter "Doc" Holliday (1852–1887) was born in Georgia, the son of a well-to-do family. In 1862, the family moved to Valdosta, where Holliday's mother died four years later. Grief-stricken over her death and unhappy with his father's remarriage, Holliday became restless and distant.

In 1872, Holliday graduated from a dental college in Baltimore. Opening an office in Griffin, Georgia, and later in Atlanta, he suffered from such a severe cough that he began losing his patients. He discovered that he had contracted tuberculosis and was told that unless he moved to a more healthful climate he would die.

In 1873, Holliday arrived in Dallas, where he worked as a dentist, but gambling and traveling from town to town took up more of his time than dentistry. In DODGE CITY, KANSAS, Holliday befriended Wyatt Earp after supposedly saving Earp's life. By that time, Holliday had taken up with Kate Elder.

After killing a man in New Mexico, Holliday moved to Tombstone, Arizona. Sicker and more quarrelsome than ever, he was drinking heavily and became an embarrassment to Earp, especially after Holliday was implicated in a stage robbery and murder for which he was never tried.

On October 26, 1881, Holliday helped the EARP BROTHERS in the famous gunfight at O. K. Corral against the Clanton clan. Rumored to have been involved in two more killings, Holliday left Arizona in 1882 and moved to Glenwood Springs, Colorado, where he died five years later.

—*Richard A. Van Orman*

SEE ALSO: O. K. Corral, Gunfight at

SUGGESTED READING:
Jahns, Pat. *The Frontier World of Doc Holliday.* New York, 1957.
Myers, John. *Doc Holliday.* Boston, 1955.
Schoenberger, Dale T. *The Gunfighters.* Caldwell, Idaho, 1971

HOLLISTER, WILLIAM WELLS

Prominent California rancher William Wells Hollister (1818–1886) took up farming in his native Ohio after an aborted college career at Kenyon College. In 1851, Hollister bought several hundred cattle and drove them to California for sale at a good profit among the emigrants who were beginning to settle West Coast lands. Two years later, he drove five thousand sheep and several hundred head of cattle and horses across the same route. Once in California, he established a 60,000-acre ranch near present-day Monterey and, in 1869, formed a partnership with Thomas and Albert Dibblee. The partners acquired four large ranches, including 150,000 acres of the Rancho Lompac, which they sold when the partnership dissolved in 1874. In addition to his ranching and land interests, Hollister engaged in civic improvements, including, among other activities, his support of Santa Barbara College.

—*Kurt Edward Kemper*

HOLLOW HORN BEAR (SIOUX)

Chief of the Upper Brulé (Sicangu) Orphan Band (Wablenicha) of the Sioux Indians, Hollow Horn Bear (1850–1913) was the son of Iron Shell. Although some writers indicate that Hollow Horn Bear was the son of SPOTTED TAIL, he was actually a close friend, if not an adopted relative, of the more famous Brulé leader. Among Hollow Horn Bear's brothers and cousins were a younger Iron Shell and Kills-In-Sight. Through distinguished heritage and popular acceptance, Hollow Horn Bear rose to a rank recognized in federal records as "chief" in the Orphan Band, which took shape after Shoshones killed some men in a Brulé war party and their families gathered as a "band of orphans" to survive.

Hollow Horn Bear first entered public life when he joined a tribal soldiers' society *(akicitas)* at the age of sixteen. He participated in military confrontations between Brulés and Pawnees and emerged as a leader of attacks against non-Indians during RED CLOUD'S War.

During the 1870s, Hollow Horn Bear stood out among the majority of Brulés who with Spotted Tail advocated diplomatic accommodation as the alternative to war with the United States. Their focus on accommodation placed Hollow Horn Bear and Spotted Tail at odds with an opposing faction of Brulés led by CROW DOG and Dog Hawk. In 1879, both Hollow Horn Bear and Spotted Tail received silver presidential medallions for their efforts in diplomacy.

After Crow Dog killed Spotted Tail in 1881, Hollow Horn Bear, as captain of police for the Rosebud Agency, assumed responsibility for Crow Dog's arrest. Thereafter, he emerged as the most visible leader of Upper Brulés because, according to his friend Remington Schuyler, "Chief Hollow Horn Bear felt it necessary for survival that Indian people adapt to the white man's ways" setting "an example of regularly exhibiting vegetables and horses at the Cut Meat [Rosebud Farm District] and Agency [agricultural] fairs." He also served as a tribal spokesman during negotiations with General GEORGE CROOK on the 1889 Sioux Agreement that reduced tribal lands by nine million acres and at other times surfaced as an able diplomat. At the same time, Hollow Horn Bear and his family remained loyal to tribal tradition.

Hollow Horn Bear appeared at THEODORE ROOSEVELT's second inauguration and led an Indian contingent in the inaugural parade of Woodrow Wilson. Soon after the latter function in 1913, he fell ill with pneumonia and died in Washington, D.C.

Eastern observers were so captivated by the image presented by Hollow Horn Bear—an image of accommodation combined with traditionalism—that they preserved it in several ways. The handsome, headdressed profile of Hollow Horn Bear appeared on a five-dollar silver certificate, the reverse side of the buffalo nickel, and a fourteen-cent U.S. postage stamp issued in 1923. Head dress, long hair, presidential medallion, and business suit accurately represented the prominent Upper Brulé leader who favored diplomacy over war but openly refused to sacrifice the philosophies and practices of Native American tradition.

—*Herbert T. Hoover*

SEE ALSO: Sioux Wars

SUGGESTED READING:
"Hollow Horn Bear." *The Indian Sentinel* (1914): 8–9.
National Archives. Record Group 75, Rosebud Agency.

HOLLYWOOD

SEE: California; Film; Los Angeles; Motion-Picture Industry

HOME, WASHINGTON

Home, Washington, was founded in 1896 on Von Geldern Cove (Joe's Bay) on the southern shore of Puget Sound by a group of anarchists. Founders George Allen, Oliver Verity, and B. F. Odell were the last remaining members of a dying communal effort southeast of Tacoma. Using meager funds left from the venture, the three set out to establish a less structured community. They aimed to encourage individualism and a tolerance for varied life styles and espoused unpopular beliefs free from outside pressures.

The three men secured twenty-six acres along the shore of the narrow inlet and up the hillside. Ideally, members would take two acres, one near and one above the water. An early arrival, the well-to-do Martin Dadisman, financed further land purchases for sale to newcomers. During the next several years, more than two hundred settlers spread across the bay and into a neighboring valley. While home lots were privately held, the colony communally held the beach front, a meeting house known as Liberty Hall, and a succession of cooperative stores. Residents sought to limit government and laws even among themselves, but of necessity, the Mutual Home Association was created to handle the property.

Home attracted persons of diverse views, and their lives were intellectually stimulating despite geographical isolation and poverty. In newspapers, lectures, and casual conversation, residents addressed controversial aspects of political and economic reform, religion, spiritualism, privacy, violence, the emancipation of women, and sexuality. A succession of newspapers became forums for residents' expressions and their contact with the wider world. During its heyday, prominent radicals and thinkers—anarchist Emma Goldman, INDUSTRIAL WORKERS OF THE WORLD founder WILLIAM D. ("BIG BILL") HAYWOOD, future Communist leader William Z. Foster, and the popular philosopher and utopian Elbert Hubbard—visited Home.

Most colonists came from other states and some from Europe; many were Jewish. Free lovers, or couples living outside the formalities of state-sanctioned marriage, also came to Home. Children of all ages were schooled in free thought and expression along with basic subjects and cultural advantages.

Periodically, government officials and community leaders from nearby Tacoma attempted to disrupt and possibly destroy the community. The mailing of allegedly obscene publications prompted closure of the Home post office. When a self-proclaimed anarchist assassinated President William McKinley in 1901, Tacoma newspapers railed at the "nest of anarchists" living nearby, and a raiding party threatened to wipe out Home. Cool heads, coupled with transportation problems for the raiders, defeated the action. A more far-reaching conflict occurred a dozen years later when arrests for nude swimming prompted Home editor Jay Fox to write a column later judged disrespectful of the law and courts. Fox eventually served two months for violating an antisedition law. Internal dissension and conformist pressures during World War I, along with the departure of younger residents, altered Home's character. It gradually became a more conventional rural and vacation community with suburban characteristics.

—*Charles P. LeWarne*

SUGGESTED READING:
LeWarne, Charles Pierce. *Utopias on Puget Sound, 1885–1915.* Seattle and London, 1975.

HOMESTAKE MINE

When rich placer deposits of gold were discovered near Deadwood, South Dakota, in the late 1870s, the BLACK HILLS GOLD RUSH that followed brought into the area one of California's most aggressive mining operators, GEORGE HEARST. Hearst was interested in the rich Homestake lode found by local prospectors Moses and Fred Manuel, who had learned how to mine gold in California, Nevada, and Idaho. Having first discovered a quartz, or lead, vein flecked with gold near a spot they named, prosaically enough, Lead, they worked the rich find they named Homestake for a few months, made some money, bought two more claims, and then—as capital-poor prospector-miners often did—sold out at a handsome profit. They sold one claim to a developer; the two others (including the Homestake) went to a group of San Francisco entrepreneurs—Lloyd Tevis, James Haggin, and George Hearst.

In 1877, Hearst established himself in the town of Lead and quickly took control of a score of claims beside or near the original Homestake. Not untypically, many claims were overlapping, and Hearst hired the best lawyers money could buy to muscle out his competitors in court. Facing at one point some twenty lawsuits, Hearst ultimately won them all. Understanding perfectly the requirements of hard-rock mining, Hearst was careful to buy mill sites and waters rights as well as mineral rights, and he gobbled up every speck of land he could find. Amid charges of fraud and hollow death threats, Hearst open his first mill in 1879, a large operation containing eighty stamps that could extract 240 tons of ore—about $2,000 worth of gold—a day. As the endlessly rich veins of the Homestake were opened, Hearst added ever more machines, until, by 1900, the Homestake Mine was operating no fewer than one thousand stamps. All told, Hearst's company would spend more than $650 million to dig and mill the gold at Homestake, recovering some 90 percent of the precious metal from the pulverized dust his machines made of the ore. The colossal mine Hearst put together would eventually extract hundreds of millions of dollars in gold, making Hearst—who went on to become a U.S. senator from California and to found one of the country's great newspaper publishing dynasties—a very rich man indeed, even as it revealed just how high-stakes a game hard-rock mining had become by the end of the nineteenth century.

—*Patricia Hogan*

SEE ALSO: Gold Mining; Mining; Silver Mining

HOMESTEAD ACT OF 1862

The Homestead Act of 1862 provided for grants of land not exceeding 160 acres from the surveyed public domain to heads of families or individuals twenty-one years of age, regardless of gender. Applicants were required to sign affidavits certifying their intent to use the land for individual benefit and to settle on and cultivate it. To carry the claim to patent, the settler was required to reside on the homestead for five years, make modest improvements, and pay a nominal fee. Commutation—the purchase of title before the end of the residence period—was allowed after six months of residence at a cost of $1.25 per acre.

The filing affidavit further required the applicant to assert that he or she had never borne arms against the United States or aided its enemies, thereby discriminating against Southerners. The Homestead Act was in fact promoted by Northerners and Westerners as a reform measure. Its inclusion in the Republican party platform in 1860 was no doubt the handiwork of Horace Greeley, who served on the platform committee. It was one of several planks that promised to benefit the industrious and aspiring laborer. President Abraham Lincoln, who signed the bill into law on May 20, 1862, viewed it as an expression of his long-held belief that "labor is the superior of capital and deserves much higher consideration."

The Homestead Bill was an important factor in forging a political alliance between the Northeast and the West. When the bill was first proposed in the 1830s, abolitionists supported it as a vehicle for promoting settlement of Western territories in less than plantation-size units. Although New England industrialists originally worried that a homestead law would siphon away their supply of laborers, the heavy influx of European immigrants by mid-century served to alleviate their concerns. Additionally, industrialists understood that a prosperous West meant new markets and a source of raw materials. Conversely, the South opposed homesteading and succeeded in defeating the several homestead measures introduced in the 1850s.

The Homestead Act went into effect on January 1, 1863. Not all the unsurveyed, unsold, and unappropriated lands were eligible for entry; nearly 440 million acres had already been reserved for RAILROADS, the states, and Indian reservations. In 1867, the GENERAL LAND OFFICE estimated the land available for homesteading at just over 600 million acres. Much of that was mountainous, desert, or otherwise unsuited for agriculture. Additionally, for the entire area west of the one-hundredth meridian, parcels of 160 acres proved to be of insufficient size for economically feasible farming operations. To address this deficiency, Congress passed the TIMBER CULTURE ACT OF 1873, which allowed homesteaders to file on an additional 160 acres if they would plant 40 acres, later amended to 10, in trees. Four years later, Congress liberalized

the land laws even further with the DESERT LAND ACT OF 1877, which granted up to 640 acres for $1.25 per acre to individuals who would bring barren Western lands into productivity through IRRIGATION.

From 1863 to 1880, nearly 500,000 entries were filed under the Homestead Act for approximately 56 million acres. Slightly over half, or 257,385 entries, were carried to patent. While these are certainly significant totals, they nevertheless represent barely one-sixth of the total farms in those states and territories where homesteading occurred. The evidence remains indisputable that the vast majority of the emigrants to the West preferred to buy farm land that featured advantages of location or fertility. People who lacked the means to buy farms, and thus were prompted to look to homesteading, lacked the capital to make improvements and buy the machinery, animals, and other items necessary to begin a farm—another factor serving to dim somewhat the optimism of the act's sponsors and advocates. Nevertheless, activity continued at a steady pace. Nearly another million entries were filed during the 1880s and 1890s.

Filing activity under the Timber Culture Act and the Desert Land Act was much more modest in scope. Approximately 43.5 million acres were entered under the former; much less under the latter. In both cases, the proportion carried to patent was a mere 25 percent. The Desert Land Act was a special disappointment in that it was badly abused by speculators and cattle interests. After much debate and political maneuvering in the late 1880s and early 1890s, Congress passed a sweeping land reform bill, signed into law on March 3, 1991, which repealed the Timber Culture and Preemption acts, amended the Desert Land Act, and prohibited further commutation under the Homestead Act.

The Homestead Act can be judged on several levels. As symbol for the aspiring laborer or farmer, it operated on a personal level to project the promise of opportunity and the hope for new beginnings. It also enhanced the image of the American West in the popular mind as an area of optimism, enterprise, and growth. Demographically, the Homestead Act certainly did promote settlement of the West although not precisely in the manner foreseen by its advocates. Speculators, railroads, and other monied interests preceded the homesteader throughout much of the West and often gained control of the most desirable land through largesse, purchase, or fraudulent entry.

Politically and economically, the Homestead Act represented the democratization of public LAND POLICY—away from sale and toward free disposal—that began a decade earlier with preemption. This commitment continued well beyond the close of the frontier and into the first third of the twentieth century as the FEDERAL GOVERNMENT worked at finding the right combination of acreage and conditions—legislative and geographical—that would best serve the land needs of the bona fide settlers. In addition to the Timber Culture and Desert Land acts mentioned above, the Kinkaid Act of 1904, Forest Homestead Act of 1906, Dry Farm Homestead Act of 1909, and STOCK RAISING HOMESTEAD ACT OF 1916 were all enlarged homestead measures enacted by the government in order to fit the needs of would-be farmers in the semiarid West. None of them ever quite lived up to expectations. Only about 10 percent of available Western land actually went to homesteaders.

—Stanford J. Layton

SUGGESTED READING:

Gates, Paul W. *History of Public Land Law Development.* Washington, D.C., 1968.

Peffer, E. Louise. *The Closing of the Public Domain: Disposal and Reservation Policies, 1900–50.* Stanford, Calif., 1951.

Robbins, Roy M. *Our Landed Heritage: The Public Domain, 1776–1936.* Princeton, N.J., 1942.

HOMESTEADING

By 1860, the movement of Euro-American agricultural settlement into the trans-Mississippi West had reached a line from roughly St. Paul, Minnesota, to Fort Worth, Texas. Of the 1.5 million American farmers in 1850, about 120,000 lived west of the Mississippi, the majority of them in states along the river from Iowa to Texas. Farther west, there were pockets of farmers in New Mexico and California, many of whom were Hispanic. A few thousand farmers had trekked to Oregon in the 1840s, and in the late 1840s and 1850s, thousands of MORMONS began farming in Utah. Census takers reported 1,000 farmers in Utah and California and 1,200 in Oregon. On the eastern edge of the "unsettled" West, farmers had moved into eastern Kansas and eastern Texas. Some members of the Five Civilized Tribes in the Indian Territory of eastern Oklahoma also carried on successful crop and livestock production before 1860.

Overall, however, the West was still an untapped agricultural "empire" on the eve of the Civil War. But within two generations, nearly all of the land suitable for agriculture between the western edge of Missouri and Iowa and the Pacific Coast would be brought into cultivation. At the same time, most of the trans-Mississippi farmers still continued to till their lands in the two tiers of states adjacent to the Mississippi River,

Three generations of the Cannon family, homesteaders at the turn of the century, pose on Christmas Day in front of their dugout home. *Courtesy Western History Collections, University of Oklahoma Library.*

and what was more, farming in the older states had kept growing. In 1890, Iowa's 201,903 farms represented more than double the number of farms in Washington, Oregon, and California put together. The number of new farms established in Iowa during the 1880s alone—16,552—was more than the combined total of farms existing in 1890 in Montana, Wyoming, and Idaho, and it nearly equaled the number in Colorado. The pioneers may have vanished from the Midwest by the turn of the century, but farms continued to proliferate, chewing up unimproved lands, developing and draining prairie wetlands, and chopping up older farms into smaller units. Late nineteenth-century homesteading, then, was not merely a matter of an advancing Western frontier, but also one of doubling back to lands once considered less desirable, but still more appropriate to small-scale agriculture than the arid soils promoted with such skill by the RAILROADS farther West.

Historical background

Americans had long been ideologically committed to the idea of a landholding citizenry. They told themselves in their literature and public pronouncements that they sought to settle the West—that is, a succession of American Wests, including the trans-Appalachian Ohio Valley and the Old Northwest—not merely to acquire and exploit it. American land law reflected such goals. Three pieces of Civil War–era legislation—the MORRILL ACT OF 1862, creating land-grant COLLEGES AND UNIVERSITIES; the Pacific Railroad Act, creating RAILROAD LAND GRANTS; and the HOMESTEAD ACT OF 1862 embodied this ideological allegiance to a Jeffersonian

Homesteaders in western Kansas display their sod house and valued possessions. *Courtesy Western History Collections, University of Oklahoma Library.*

yeomanry. As always, farmers, expanding into what American policy-makers longed to believe was the fertile trans-Mississippi West, would remain the backbone of the nation. (In reality, of course, much of the land west of the Mississippi was arid or semiarid, fit only for a highly irrigated, centralized "hydraulic" culture.)

On May 27, 1862, Abraham Lincoln signed into law the Homestead Act, authorizing any citizen or immigrant who intended to become a citizen to select any surveyed but unclaimed parcel of public land up to 160 acres, settle it, improve it, and, by living on it five years, gain title to it. Alternatively, after residing on the land for six months, one could "preempt" the land by purchasing it for $1.25 an acre. Or a homesteader could exercise preemption to augment his original 160-acre claim—though few settlers could ante up the $50 for the minimum purchase of forty acres the government required. President Lincoln was himself a product of a former "West" and sentimentally attached to its myths of rugged pioneering and social mobility, myths, in part, that had helped elect him. With the country in the midst of the Civil War, he hoped that rapid settlement of the new West would strengthen what was left of the Union by creating an unbroken link between East and West. Familiar with the ways in which previous areas had been "settled" by speculators and squatters grabbing up land often illegally, Lincoln and others ensured that this time settlers traveled west with the official blessing of an American govern-

ment touting the pioneer homestead as the cultural glue of a civilization stretching across the entire continent.

It did not work exactly as they had imagined. Although the number of farms in the United States increased from some 2 million in 1860 to almost 6 million by 1900, fewer than 600,000 of those farms were homesteads, and those that were patented accounted only for 80 million of the 400 million acres added to America's total farm land. And even if all those who filed claims under the 1862 act had been genuine homesteaders, they would have brought into production less than one-sixth of all the new farms and hardly more than that of all the new acreage. But the patent holders were not all bone fide pioneers; a good number of the so-called homesteads fell into the relatively few hands of the West's big landholders and did not become farms until once again speculators sold them to settlers. Nothing could have been further from the intentions of the framers of the act; indeed, Lincoln and his Congress, by offering the bounty of free land to needy people, had hoped to defeat, not promote, an American land monopoly.

Thus despite the fact that the Homestead Act was formulated expressly to avert the greedy speculative abuses to which Western land grants had traditionally been subject, as always, the unscrupulous found loopholes in the law. To begin with, federal land agents were few and far between, making it virtually impossible to inspect claims and enforce the provisions of the act. The law specified that homesteaders must secure their claim by constructing a house at least twelve-by-twelve, with windows. Some speculators perfected their multiple claims by building such a house on wheels, so that it could be trundled from claim to claim. Others, noting that the language of the twelve-by-twelve provision failed to specify feet or inches, set doll houses, twelve-by-twelve inches in plan—complete with miniature windows—on each of their claims. Abuses like these were practiced by solitary speculators and by railroads and mining companies, which claimed and preempted land by means of "dummy entrymen" hired to file as if they were legitimate homesteaders. Taking advantage of cash sales and public auctions, speculators moved in early, cornered the choice plots of public lands, the most likely town sites, and the stretches along streams and roads to hold for high prices. By the time homesteaders arrived to stake out claims, they had the pick of the least desirable, the worst located tracts. If they had money, they could, of course, pay the speculator's asking price. Land-jobbers bought up tens of millions of such acres, later adding more millions from former Indian reservations and from the holdings of the various states—all of it beyond the reach of the Homestead Act and its official bounty to small farmers.

But the trouble with the law went deeper than simply the ease with which it could be abused by the unscrupulous. Few Americans had the money to take advantage of the opportunities offered by the ideologically driven windfall in land. Even if they could afford to transport their families and worldly possessions to the public domain where the government was giving away pieces of the West, they could not pay for the expensive machinery they needed to make a go of it and stick out the hard years ahead until their farm became self-supporting. A farmer needed barbed wire, barns, outbuildings; to break just the first 40 acres of a 160-acre homestead and put it into production cost around one thousand dollars. Not many of those who could afford to do so fully understood the new type of agriculture they needed to practice on the arid plains. A better law—one that had any hopes of fulfilling its promise—would have offered homesteaders credit as well as free land, would have provided instruction in the special kind of farming they had to undertake were they to succeed, would have set up at least minimum safeguards against fraud. Sans money, sans expertise, sans legal protection, two-thirds of all the homesteaders before 1890 failed at their venture into independent farming and individual freedom.

The bottom line was that the Homestead Act was simply not appropriate to the region the government wanted settled. Congress was caught in a dilemma when it came to federal LAND POLICY. Most Americans assumed that agriculture was the best use of Western land; it was a part of frontier metaphysics, part of the justification for acquiring Western land in the first place; and since at least Thomas Jefferson's time, it had been a basic tenant in American politics: the country was run not for those who continued to get so mysteriously rich but for the independent farmer. But in the arid West, the mechanics of the political dream would not work. The land, by and large, could not be turned easily into small farms—a lot of it was desert; some of it was covered with gigantic trees. But that was precisely the one thing that a Congress in league with big business did not want openly to admit. For without farmers pouring into the West for congressmen and senators to point toward, it would have been all that much clearer that most government action favored a few industrial and financial overlords. In the rapidly industrializing post–Civil War society, these men grew rich off an extractive economy that sent the majority of Westerners off to work in the mines or as migrant laborers for the lumbering industry and commercial agriculture. The government had an interest both in keeping up the myth of a Western Eden and in selling off the land it owned.

In truth, much of the available land out West after the Civil War was owned by the RAILROADS. In the twenty years after Appomattox, the U.S. government and its states and territories gave various railroads hundreds of millions of acres of public land in the hopes of attracting construction westward. These "checkerboard" parcels lining railroad tracks were not available under the Homestead Act, and the railroads used them not only to establish towns and supply depots but also to turn a profit in land sales. Often better land than homesteaders could buy from the government, these railroad land grants sold at a premium, especially since the railroads, unlike the government, also offered advice and training in the farming of such lands.

Becoming a major colonizer of the trans-Mississippi West, railroads expended considerable effort to attract settlers—and future customers—from the eastern United States and from Europe. They hired artists to illustrate pamphlets depicting a well-watered Eden and sent agents armed with such propaganda across the globe. Every Western railroad company had, in effect, its own immigration bureau and advertising agency, and their agents enticed millions of immigrant workers and European peasants to take up homesteading in the American West. Most were willing to pay the higher price for railroad land both because it was better acreage and because it came with other enticements such as special transportation rates to the homestake and company help in getting settled.

Solomon D. Butcher photographed the two-story sod home and family of Belgian-French homesteader Isadore Haumont in 1886 or 1887. Caption information placed the cost of the house at five hundred dollars. *Solomon D. Butcher Collection. Courtesy Nebraska State Historical Society.*

Western homesteaders

The trouble with the Homestead Act and the laws that followed aimed at "correcting" its mistakes (TIMBER CULTURE ACT OF 1873; DESERT LAND ACT OF 1877; TIMBER AND STONE ACT OF 1878; ENLARGED HOMESTEAD ACT OF 1909) was that Congress established a land system that, in reality, served the interests of capitalists and developers. That fact, combined with the amount of land enclosed by the railroads, the feeling that Western land laws in any case did not meet Western needs, and the knowledge that perhaps only 10 percent of the available Western land ultimately went to small homesteaders, has led some historians—not without reason—to belittle the importance of homestead legislation. But, in fact, between 1860 and 1920, the number of farms in the United States did increase by some 4.4 million, and even if the majority of those were not homesteads, during the same period, some 1.4 million homesteaders or their heirs received final patents, composing 32 percent of the increase in the number of farms. True, many quickly sold out either because they,

too, were speculating or because poverty and distress led them to fail. Nevertheless, the Homestead Act gave legions of poor Americans at least some access—inexpensive access—to Western land.

The most active homesteading areas in the nineteenth century were Kansas, Nebraska, and the Dakotas. There more the 430,000 settlers had filed claims by 1895. Between 1881 and 1885, a spectacular burst of settlement took place in the "Great Dakota Boom," when 67,000 settlers took up homesteads in the territory. After 1896 up to around 1920, Western homesteaders were also common in Colorado, New Mexico, and—especially with the OKLAHOMA LAND RUSH—in Oklahoma, as well as in North and South Dakota. Each of these states attracted at least 125,000 land entrants. When JAMES J. HILL began promoting the land in his High Plains railroad empire in Montana, nearly 200,000 settlers rush in, reaching peak numbers between 1906 and 1910; only the Dakotas had seen anything equivalent during the nineteenth century. After 1900, states on the plateau and in the Great Basin witnessed homesteaders moving into the cold desert of southern Oregon and Washington's interior. Although homesteading had begun in California in 1863, there most of all, the economic dynamics and political loopholes worked against the small farmer, and only 114,000 settlers filed homestead claims in the Golden State.

Those inhabiting the West's sod-buster Eden have frequently been described as egalitarian and hardworking people. Typically, a family would send the father or the older sons in advance to stake out a claim and build a house before the mother and other children followed. The prairie was a forbidding place, vast as a sea, flat, lonely, and forlorn, subject to extremes of weather—100° F in the summer to 40° F below zero in winter—periodically plagued by ravenous insects, its soil hard packed and reinforced by a massive tangle of roots that were resistant to the plow, mostly unforested, often unwatered—at least on the surface—and scoured by a wind as mournful as it was unrelenting. Yet it was from these very elements that the sod buster would build his family's life.

First, there was the sod itself. In the absence of timber, the hard, stubborn earth would provide shelter. Usually, the first sod structure a homesteader built was a somewhat elaborated hole in the ground called a "dugout." A rectangle was laid out on a rising slope of land or a knoll, and sod was excavated to a depth of about six feet. Next, using "bricks" cut from the tough sod, walls were raised to a height of two or three feet. The structure was roofed over with boards, straw—and more sod. The family would live there, raise its first subsistence crops, and then build a more substantial above-ground house, with real windows and doors, but, most likely, still constructed of sod bricks. Special plowshares were developed specifically for cutting strips of sod that could be chopped into the needed bricks, and SOD HOUSES—"soddies," they were called—became ubiquitous across the prairies. With walls as thick as three feet and well insulated, the soddies were nevertheless difficult to maintain. Roofs leaked constantly. Dirt and debris fell from the ceiling and walls. Mice, snakes, and insects, including plagues of lice and bedbugs thrived in the earthen walls and dirt floors. Yet, raised from the land, a soddy was cheap, sturdy, and essentially fireproof. And for most settlers, it was the first home they had ever owned.

Busting the sod into crop rows was backbreaking work and, until plows of tempered iron or steel were developed in the 1860s, sometimes impossible. For many homesteaders whose claims were distant from creeks and streams, there was the added task of digging a well. Since most settlers could not afford to hire a drilling rig, the work had to be done by hand, with pick and spade, sometimes to depths approaching three hundred feet. The dangers of working in such a hole included cave-ins, obviously, but also asphyxiation from such subterranean gases as methane and carbon monoxide. After all the work, of course, there was no guarantee that the well would reach water. Once a sod buster hit bedrock or shale without having tapped into the water table, he had to start all over, sinking a shaft elsewhere.

Once water was struck, it needed to be pumped to quench the thirst of livestock and to irrigate fields. The motive power for the pump was provided by the prairie wind. In 1854, David Halladay, a Connecticut toolshop tinkerer, invented a windmill with a vane that allowed it to pivot into the wind and that used centrifugal force to adjust the pitch of the mill blades so that the gusty, frequently violent winds would not tear them apart. Crankshafts transformed the rotary motion of WINDMILLS into the up-and-down action needed to operate pumps. Wind power could move hundreds of gallons of water a day.

As to the emotional desolation of prairie life, that may have been the most valuable natural resource of all. If the endless space and driving winds did not make a person insane, they reinforced the solidarity of the family as a bulwark against loneliness, despair, and danger. These conditions of the prairie also served to unite neighbor with distant neighbor, whereas, at least according to tradition, Westerners in the past had, for vocational reasons, shunned neighbors. In theory at least, a trapper wanted no competition; a prospector wanted his claim all to himself; an open-range cattleman needed space and more space, untrammeled by anyone, especially neighbors. In any case, sod busters treasured companionship and community, and if their

Immigrants from Sweden posed for the camera to record their settlement in Kansas. *Courtesy Kansas State Historical Society.*

claims were in the vicinity of a rough-and-ready cattle town, their influence frequently contributed to the conservative and Victorian values that helped to close the gambling dens, saloons, and houses of prostitution and create temperate, if sleepy, small towns.

Homesteading minorities

Homesteading laws, officially aimed at basing industrial expansion in the Northeast on the expansion of the family farm in the West, helped formulate an idealized husband and wife partnership in the family farm. The Department of Agriculture expressly described this ideal family partnership, one cemented by romantic love, in its 1862 Annual Report. From the beginning, it was clear that deviations—whether they came in the form of slavery, Mormon polygamy, or Native American communal farms—simply would not be tolerated. Slavery was abolished in the Civil War, Mormon polygamy outlawed in the West, and Native Americans reduced to reservations, which were steadily eroded as the Indians were encouraged to take up family farming and sell off their reservation lands to Euro-American farmers and ranchers. From 1862 to 1920, the family farm remained the national ideal, and the theory was that farm sons and daughters would begin as wage workers on neighboring farms, save their money, become tenants or renters, and eventually own their own small family farms. Most of them would marry, of course, and perpetuate the cycle, and eventually all America's ethnic groups would end up on family farms after putting in their time working for big industry in the East or commercial mining and agriculture in the West.

For a while after the Civil War, the government encouraged African Americans to take up homesteading. In 1866, Radical Republicans passed a special Southern Homestead Act that opened the remaining public domain in Alabama, Arkansas, Florida, Louisiana, and Mississippi to blacks and white Southern loyalists. These homesteads were to provide "cities of refuge" for former slaves, but the soil was poor, the land full of trees, and the local whites extremely hostile. The Freedman's Bureau, in the end, managed to settle only some four thousand African American homesteading families, three-fourths of them in Florida. A few hundred families settled in Alabama, others headed for Texas, but most of them stopped in Louisiana, where several thousand squatted on open land without filing claims. In 1876, Congress repealed the Southern Homestead Act as part of the compromise that ended Reconstruction and put Rutherford B. Hayes in the White House, and most of the South's public land went to big timber syndicates. Black families headed farther West into Oklahoma, Texas, Kansas, and Colorado and established hundreds of small, independent farm communities. Given the economic hardships of homesteading in general—heading West took money; farm equipment did too—many black families had to split work on the farm with wage work in nearby towns to survive. African American farm women generally looked after the homestead, while the men took day work in town. And not all blacks loved the notion of farming, even on land they owned. Many saw farm labor as an extension of slavery, especially as farms were lost and they became tenants. Increasingly, African Americans looked for opportunities in the burgeoning cities of an industrializing nation rather than on hardscrabble family farms in the trans-Mississippi West.

Under the territorial governments and new land policies established by the United States, Hispanic families, already settled in the West, found it increasingly difficult to retain the farm lands they already owned. After Anglo conquest in 1846, perhaps one hundred thousand Spanish-speaking people lived and worked on ranches and farms in the American Southwest. Most of them lived in villages, shared communal pastures, and farmed individual plots along the edges of their settlements. Just as the American legal system became the means by which Anglos dispossessed the big rancheros in California and New Mexico, the homestead laws help to disrupt the pattern of communal farming. Squatters moved in, set up farming, disputed earlier claims, and filed entrants; gradually the Hispanic poor, too, were deprived of their lands and went to work as migrants in the mines and on big commercial farms.

Some Native Americans, dispossessed of their hunting ranges and their communal gardens, took up homesteading. In 1869, twenty-five Santee Sioux families, determined to adopt the life style of white farmers as Indians had been long exhorted to do, occupied an unsettled area along the Big Sioux River in South Dakota. Joined by others, they established the Flandreau Sioux colony, and members entered individual holdings under the Homestead Act. Helped by friendly officials and missionaries, the Flandreaus were first required to surrender their claims on tribal assets. They fared well despite the usual pioneer problems: killing frosts, crop-eating grasshoppers, and a lack of livestock, farming equipment, and tools. Factions developed, taxes were burdensome, alcoholism increased, and whites tempted individuals to sell out, but the Indians continued to homestead. Despite an amendment to the Homestead Act in the early 1870s intended to make it easier for Indians to follow the example of the Flandreaus, few Native Americans could or would take advantage of the American laws, which required a turning away from their own culture and the loss of even more lands than had already gone into the public domain.

In at least one way, the Homestead Act of 1862 had been different from earlier land laws in that it explicitly allowed women as well as men to file for a homestead. Since the law assumed that farms would be worked by nuclear families, women who filed had to be single and over twenty-one years of age or the heads of households and either citizens or immigrants who had filed for citizenship. Over the next fifty years, Euro-American women moved onto Western lands in unprecedented numbers, filed their claims in their own names, and began improving their stake. Although the historical record is thin concerning women homesteaders, the information that is available indicates that independent women homesteaders were always a significant presence in the West, making up some 5 percent of all homesteaders in the early years and numbering almost 20 percent by 1900. Apparently, they were at least as successful as men in improving their claims and becoming owners.

For some women, homesteading provided the opportunity to live independently, to escape bad marriages, or even, occasionally, to live with another woman, but for most of them, family life remained the ideal, and they simply postponed marriage longer than their peers. A number of women homesteaders filed for land shortly before they got married as a way of doubling family landholdings. Others, once married, added their land to their husbands' claims, extending the family property. Most managed their own farms and hired men to do the field work. Sometimes, they traded domestic chores with male homesteaders in exchange for plowing or other heavy labor. A number of women homesteaders also worked as teachers, journalists, seamstresses, or at other "women's" jobs to support their farms. Some stayed on their holdings for years; others sold them off for money to open small businesses, buy an education, or send their children to school or set them up in families. Like their male counterparts, most of them failed to make good their claims, Forced out by bad weather, a lack of money, growing debts, collapsing crop prices, and excessive freight rates—all the troubles an industrializing nation threw the way of unmechanized farmers—women homesteaders moved on with their lives. Many, who found in homesteading a means to economic improvement and some upward mobility, did not count themselves failures at all, but instead treasured the experience of independence and of owning land in their own names.

—*Charles Phillips*

SEE ALSO: Booms; Exodusters; Working-Class Women

SUGGESTED READING:

Blodgett, Jan. *Land of Bright Promise: Advertising the Texas Panhandle and South Plains, 1870–1917.* Austin, Tex., 1988.

Cochrane, Willard W. *The Development of American Agriculture: A Historical Analysis.* Minneapolis, Minn., 1979.

Ebeling, Walter. *The Fruited Plain: The Story of American Agriculture.* Berkeley, Calif., 1979.

Emmons, David M. *Garden in the Grasslands: Boomer Literature of the Central Great Plains.* Lincoln, Nebr., 1971.

Fite, Gilbert C. *The Farmer's Frontier, 1865–1900.* New York, 1966.

Gates, Paul W. *History of Public Land Development.* Washington, D.C., 1968.

Jensen, Joan M. *With These Hands: Women Working on the Land.* Las Cruces, N. Mex., 1981.

Lindgren, H. Elaine. *Land in Her Own Name.* Fargo, N. Dak., 1991.

Luebke, Frederick C., ed. *Ethnicity on the Great Plains.* Lincoln, Nebr., 1980.

Nelson, Paula M. *Homesteaders and Town Builders in Western South Dakota, 1900–1917.* Iowa City, Iowa, 1986.

Opie, John. *The Law of the Land: Two Hundred Years of American Farmland Policy.* Lincoln, Nebr., 1987.

Paul, Rodman W. *The Far West and the Great Plains in Transition, 1859–1900.* New York, 1988.

Riley, Glenda. *The Female Frontier: A Comparative View of Women on the Prairie and the Plains.* Lawrence, Kans., 1988.

Schlebecker, John T. *Whereby We Thrive: A History of American Farming, 1607–1972.* Ames, Iowa, 1975.

Shannon, Fred A. *The Farmer's Last Frontier: Agriculture, 1860–1897.* New York, 1945.

Shover, John L. *First Majority, Last Minority: The Transforming of Rural Life in America.* DeKalb, Ill., 1976.

HONOLULU, HAWAII

According to legend, people who later would be known as Hawaiian natives first settled Honolulu, meaning "Protected Bay," in about 1100 A.D. The little fishing village on the southeastern corner of the island of Oahu, however, remained an outpost for several centuries. In 1792, the arrival of Captain William Brown, the first European to sail into Honolulu's harbor, signaled the beginning of the city's important role in Pacific trade.

The harbor's first wharf, put in service in 1825, was nothing more than an abandoned hulk towed into place and sunk. But some European seamen found that the Pacific Ocean's only deep-water harbor offered a place to resupply and repair ships used in the triangle trade of Chinese teas, Hawaiian sandalwood, and Pacific Northwest furs. Along with the seaman came merchants, settlers, missionaries, and drifters, who established a small community on the shores of the harbor. Hawaiian ruler Kamehameha, himself, moved to Honolulu in 1809.

Meanwhile, the economic base of Honolulu was about to change. When the sandalwood was all harvested and the furs of the Northwest exhausted, whaling ships, waiting out the winters of the Pacific's northwest waters, replaced the traders in the harbor. Whalers, in turn, disappeared from Honolulu when the trade collapsed in the 1860s. By this time, a number of Europeans and Americans, descendants of merchants and missionaries, had established homes and courted influence among the native rulers. Agricultural endeavors—long inhibited by the chiefs' reluctance to grant the clear land titles and long-term leases that could justify capital investment in land—received a boost with the Great Mahele of 1848 and with an 1850 law that permitted the importation of indentured laborers. Sugar first appeared on export manifests in 1857. When the United States issued the Reciprocity Treaty in 1875, which allowed the importation of Hawaiian sugar without duty, the transformation of HAWAII's economy from a maritime center to an agricultural kingdom ruled by Europeans and Americans was complete. Honolulu changed from a supply center to a sugar export center.

The new economy attracted thousands of Chinese, Japanese, Portuguese, Puerto Rican, Korean, Spanish, and Filipino sugar-plantation workers who not only expanded Honolulu's population but also eventually moved into Honolulu's ethnic neighborhoods and began their own businesses.

Into the twentieth century, American military forces established a strong presence at Pearl Harbor, just west of Honolulu. When the United States entered World War II, Honolulu became a major staging area for Pacific operations, a role it repeated in the Korean conflict in the early 1950s and again for the Vietnam War in the 1960s and 1970s. In peacetime, Honolulu remains an important base of U.S. military operations, and the military is second only to tourism in importance in Hawaii's economy.

Today, Honolulu functions as the state capital, the center of interisland services, the crossroads of trans-Pacific shipping, the focus of commercial and industrial enterprises, the heart of Hawaii's cultural and educational institutions, and the destination of hundreds of thousands of tourists. In 1990, Honolulu and its suburbs boasted a population of 836,231.

—*Patricia Hogan*

SUGGESTED READING:
Beechert, Edward D. *Honolulu: Crossroads of the Pacific.* Columbia, S.C., 1991.

HOOF-AND-MOUTH DISEASE

Along with TEXAS FEVER, hoof-and-mouth disease has periodically reached epidemic proportions in the American CATTLE INDUSTRY and has caused economic hardship to cattle growers. The highly contagious disease affects cattle and other cloven-footed animals and is caused by a filterable virus that is among the smallest of the viruses that cause disease in humans and animals. Cattle and swine are most susceptible to hoof-and-mouth disease, but sheep, bisons, goats, and antelope are also affected, as are such animals as llamas and buffaloes. Humans may contract a mild and generally nonfatal form of the disease as well.

Hoof-and-mouth disease has occurred in all parts of the world where cattle are raised. While periodic outbreaks occurred throughout the nineteenth century in the American West, the most devastating came in 1914, when livestock in twenty-two states were stricken. Traditionally, such outbreaks were contained through quarantine of affected regions and destruction of the infected stock.

During the 1950s, an effective vaccine against hoof-and-mouth disease was developed, and most animals are now routinely immunized. Although sporadic outbreaks are reported to this day, the last epidemic was in England in 1967, when almost one-half million animals either died from the disease or had to be destroyed.

—*Alan Axelrod*

SEE ALSO: Cattle Towns

SUGGESTED READING:
Dale, Edward E. *The Range Cattle Industry: Ranching on the Great Plains from 1865–1925.* Norman, Okla., 1960.

HOOKER, HENRY CLAY

Arizona cattleman and businessman Henry Clay Hooker (1828–1907) was born in Hinsdale, New Hampshire. He operated a hardware business in Placerville, California, in 1853. From 1866 to 1872, he worked as a cattle buyer for military contractors Hugh Hinds, William Hooper, and James Barney. In 1872, he started the Sierra Bonita Ranch, with a 160-acre homestead, to supply beef to nearby forts and reservations. Eventually, he expanded the ranch to eight hundred square miles, ten thousand cattle, a large herd of blooded stallions and brood mares, dairy cattle, and hogs. Later developed as a resort, Hooker's Hot Springs catered to the rich and well born of his day.

—*Harmon Mothershead*

HOOVER, HERBERT

President of the United States from 1929–1933, Herbert Hoover (1874–1964) was born in West Branch, IOWA, where he and his brother and sister were raised by Quaker parents. His father, a successful businessman, died when Herbert was six years old. His mother died three years later, and the child then lived with an uncle, Dr. John Minthorn, in Eugene, Oregon. Hoover entered Stanford University and graduated as a mining engineer. Thereafter, he became one of the world's leading mining engineers and accumulated an enormous estate.

Around the age of forty, Hoover gave up his mining career for public service. Based in London at the outbreak of World War I in 1914, he brilliantly aided the United States ambassador in directing the evacuation of more than one hundred thousand Americans from England to the States. Next, from London and Brussels, Hoover directed the feeding and clothing of hundreds of thousands of Belgian war victims. President Woodrow Wilson called him home to be his Food Administrator, a post that culminated in his return to Europe to oversee postwar relief.

After flirting with the idea of running for the Republican party's nomination for president, Hoover became secretary of commerce in the Harding-Coolidge administration. In his eight years as secretary, he directed a reorganization of the department and established new divisions to deal with radio broadcasting, commercial aviation, highway safety, and housing.

Viewed as the nation's foremost public figure in the 1920s, Hoover was handily elected president in 1928. His ineptness in dealing with Congress and, more seriously, the October 1929 stock-market crash mitigated the success of his policies.

Contrary to general impressions (then and subsequently), Hoover's efforts to stem the Great Depression were sophisticated and creditable. They included agricultural aid, public works, currency control, wage and price guidelines, deficit spending, relief to banks, and many exhortative antidepression policies directed at business, labor, and states, and philanthropic organizations. In foreign policy, he "forgave" European debts to the United States, a move that Secretary of State Henry L. Stimson viewed as a bold step. The Great Depression seemingly had to take its course, including a change of presidents. The Hoover presidency was a failed one, in no small part due to his own lack of skill at electoral politics and his "negative" political personality.

After his presidency, Hoover opposed Franklin D. Roosevelt's relief programs and attacked "radical" influences in the nation's capital. After World War II, he served as the head of federal commissions to eliminate waste in government and to examine government inefficiency.

—*Martin L. Fausold*

SUGGESTED READING:
Burner, David. *Herbert Hoover: A Public Life*. New York, 1979.
Fausold, Martin L. *The Presidency of Herbert Clark Hoover*. Lawrence, Kans., 1985.
Hoff-Wilson, Joan. *Herbert Hoover: Forgotten Progressive*. New York, 1975.

HOOVER, LOU HENRY

Lou Henry Hoover (1874–1944) was a club woman, physical-fitness advocate, Girl Scout leader, and wife of President Herbert Hoover. Born in Iowa, she moved, at about the age of ten, with her family to California. Her parents encouraged her interest in outdoor activities and intellectual pursuits. She attended Stanford University where she became the first woman in the United States to receive a B.A. degree in geology in 1898. While at Stanford she met Herbert Hoover, and the two were married in 1899. Over the next two decades, the couple traveled extensively due to his work as a mining engineer. When World War I broke out in Europe, the Hoovers lived in London, where he directed relief efforts for Belgians and she raised funds for the effort. The Hoovers moved back to the United States in 1917. When President Woodrow Wilson appointed Herbert Hoover head of the U.S. Food Administration, Lou Henry Hoover worked with him by organizing a Food Administration Women's Club and speaking on food conservation.

Lou Henry Hoover advocated traditional family roles, but she also believed women should participate in organizational life. She believed in the social and political equality of women, but she did not participate in women's suffrage activities and disagreed with the tactics used by some suffrage groups. Her major voluntary activities revolved around two groups: the National Amateur Athletic Foundation (NAAF) and the Girl Scouts of America (GSA). In 1923, NAAF appointed her vice-president, charged with the task of establishing a Women's Division to set policy for women's involvement in athletics. A number of debates surrounded women's participation in competitive sports, and the organization opposed women's involvement in the Olympics. The Girl Scouts of America also received significant support from Hoover. She served on the national board from 1917 to 1944 and was elected president twice.

Between 1929 and 1933, when Herbert Hoover was president, Lou Henry Hoover presided as First Lady of the White House and continued her voluntary activities. When she left the White House, she spent her time in Palo Alto, California, and New York.

—*Joanne L. Goodwin*

SUGGESTED READING:

Mayer, Dale C. "An Uncommon Woman: The Quiet Leadership Style of Lou Henry Hoover." *Presidential Studies Quarterly* 10 (1990): 685–698.

HOOVER DAM

Rising 726 feet above the bed of the Colorado River between Nevada and Arizona, Hoover Dam, at the time of its completion in 1936, was the largest, most massive structure of its kind in the world. Originally called Boulder Dam, but renamed for President HERBERT HOOVER in 1947, the structure was the first of a series of such dams and the initial step in a New Deal-spawned age of RECLAMATION. Donald Worster has described Hoover Dam as the cornerstone of the trans-Mississippi West's "hydraulic civilization," a mass society built in arid lands by human manipulation of the ecosystem. Constructed by HENRY J. KAISER and a conglomeration of six Western companies, Hoover Dam kicked off a building boom in the West and helped cement the marriage of private enterprise and federal financing that came to characterize the West's entire economy after World War II.

The dam provides flood control, hydroelectric power, irrigation, and drinking WATER to cities and towns in southern California. Courtesy of the Hoover Dam, Colorado River water has made the Imperial Valley one of the world's premiere farming areas and fed the massive growth of Los Angeles and San Diego, a growth unimaginable without such water. Both the

Hoover Dam. *Courtesy The Bettmann Archive.*

gleaming dam itself and Lake Mead, the dam's reservoir created by "impounded" river water, almost immediately became major Western tourists attractions. A leading symbol of twentieth-century technology and its "triumph" over nature, Hoover Dam rivals Egypt's pyramids in its ability to inspire visitors, which is partly the reason its completion introduced a new era of highrise dam building not only in America but across the globe. An engineering marvel that, as Worster claims, helped remake the face of the earth and turn the Colorado River into the life line of a booming Southwest, Hoover Dam also helped spawn a business culture that seemed bent on development at any cost, even ecological disasters and widespread degradation of the West's natural environment.

—*Candace Floyd*

SEE ALSO: Farming: Farming in the Imperial Valley and Salton Sea Region; Navajo Stock-Reduction Program

SUGGESTED READING:
Stevens, Joseph E. *Hoover Dam: An American Adventure.* Norman, Okla., 1988
Worster, Donald. *Under Western Skies: Nature and History in the American West.* New York, 1992.

HOPI INDIANS

SEE: Native American Peoples: Peoples of the Southwest

HOPKINS, MARK

One of the "Big Four" financiers of the CENTRAL PACIFIC RAILROAD, Mark Hopkins (1814–1878) was born in Richmond County, Virginia, and was raised in North Carolina. He moved to Kentucky with his brother Moses in 1843, and the pair set off for the California gold fields in 1851. Hopkins found the gold rush a profound disappointment and secured an alternative means of making his fortune. He started a grocery business in Placerville, California, in 1853 and became partners with COLLIS P. HUNTINGTON, a Sacramento merchant, two years later. The firm of Huntington and Hopkins rapidly became one of California's principal mercantile houses.

In 1861, the engineer THEODORE DEHONE JUDAH persuaded the partners to invest in his plan to build a transcontinental railroad. Hopkins and Huntington brought in two more merchants, AMASA LELAND STANFORD and CHARLES CROCKER, and the so-called Big Four bankrolled the Central Pacific Railroad. Despite

the partners' misgivings, which threatened to halt the progress of the line, it was completed in 1869 when it joined the westering UNION PACIFIC RAILROAD at PROMONTORY SUMMIT in Utah. Feeder lines soon spread throughout California.

The wealthy Hopkins became far wealthier. Remaining in Sacramento while his magnificent mansion on top of San Francisco's Nob Hill was under construction, Hopkins died in Yuma, Arizona, where he had gone as a health-seeker. His Nob Hill mansion, which was completed after his death, is now the site of the Mark Hopkins Hotel.

—*Alan Axelrod*

SEE ALSO: Railroads

SUGGESTED READING:
Lewis, Oscar. *The Big Four: The Story of Huntington, Stanford, Hopkins, and Crocker and the Building of the Central Pacific.* New York, 1938.

HORN, TOM

A cowboy, army packer, scout, detective, and assassin, Tom Horn (1860–1903) was born on a farm in Scotland County in northeastern Missouri. At the age of fourteen, he left home to escape his tyrannical father. Horn tried his hand at railroad construction before becoming an apprentice cowboy, trailing cattle from Texas to Dodge City. After prospecting in the Colorado gold rush and working as a railroad guard, he went first to New Mexico and then, at the end of 1879, to Arizona. There he worked as a stagecoach driver for the Overland Mail Company and then as a drover for the U.S. Army. During the winter of 1881 to 1882, Horn lived with a band of Coyotero Apaches. In the spring of 1882, he met AL SEIBER, the famed chief of scouts for the army in the Southwest. Sieber employed Horn as an army mule packer and gradually came to rely on him in the Army-Apache campaigns between 1882 and 1886.

In Horn's autobiography, he claims a much larger role in the conflicts between the army and the Apaches than he actually played. One of his glaring faults was that he continually tried to make his life bigger than it was. However, there is no denying that he was promoted to chief of scouts in November 1885. In that capacity, he was intimately involved in the pursuit and eventual surrender of GERONIMO in the spring of 1886. When the chief bolted with a few followers, Horn accompanied the army column sent south into Mexico to round up the errant warrior. Having located the

Tom Horn in the Lincoln County jail. *Courtesy American Heritage Center, University of Wyoming.*

as a ruthless hired killer of suspected cattle and horse thieves. However, the extent of his exploits is subject to question for he was a braggart and pathological liar. His braggadocio led to his confession to the July 19, 1901, murder of fourteen-year-old Willie Nickells, the son of a troublesome local rancher. The trial began on October 10, 1902, and a guilty verdict was rendered by the jury on October 24. Due to various legal maneuvers, including an appeal to the state supreme court and a request to the governor for clemency, the sentence was not carried out until November 20, 1903. Horn was hanged in the Cheyenne County jail.

—*Doyce B. Nunis, Jr.*

SEE ALSO: Apache Wars; United States Army, Scouts

SUGGESTED READING:

Carlson, Chip. *Tom Horn, "Killing men is my specialty . . ."* Cheyenne, Wyo., 1992.

Horn, Tom. *The Life of Tom Horn, Government Scout and Interpreter Written by Himself: A Vindication.* Edited by Doyce B. Nunis, Jr. Chicago, 1987.

Krakel, Dean. *The Saga of Tom Horn.* Norman, Okla., 1954.

LeFors, Joe. *Wyoming Peace Officer.* Laramie, Wyo., 1953.

Monaghan, Jay. *Last of the Badmen: The Legend of Tom Horn.* Indianapolis, Ind., and New York, 1946.

Nunis, Doyce B., Jr. *The Life of Tom Horn Revisited.* Los Angeles, 1992.

Paine, Laran. *Tom Horn: Man of the West.* Barre, Mass., 1963.

Apache leader, Lieutenant Charles B. Gatewood and Horn negotiated Geronimo's final surrender on August 24, 1886, thus ending Apache hostilities in the Southwest.

Horn then turned to several occupations: prospector, cowboy, and ranch foreman. In 1890, he became associated with the PINKERTON NATIONAL DETECTIVE AGENCY, and over the next four years, he took on a number of successful assignments for the agency; one resulted in his arrest on the charge of robbery. The first trial ended in a hung jury; the second one led to acquittal.

Bored with his Pinkerton job, Horn worked for the Wyoming Stock Growers' Association for a time and then became a private cattle detective in Wyoming in 1894. During the Spanish-American War, he served the army once again as a contract mule packer, rose in rank to chief packer, and participated in the Cuban theater. After leaving the army due to illness, he made his way back to Wyoming and resumed his work as a cattle detective until permanently employed by John C. Coble's Iron Mountain Ranch Company, headquartered at Bosler. He earned a fearsome reputation

HORRELL-HIGGINS FEUD

The Horrell-Higgins feud was the bloodiest range war in Texas; it pitted the six Horrell brothers against another Lampasas County cattle rancher, John Calhoun Pinckney ("Pink") Higgins. A deadly gunman throughout his life, Higgins regarded the Horrell brothers as cattle thieves. On March 19, 1873, four members of the state police, a widely loathed Reconstruction force, tried to arrest a brother-in-law of the Horrells in a Lampasas saloon. The Horrells killed three of the officers, and although Mart Horrell was wounded and later arrested, the Horrell faction broke him out of jail and moved the family to lawless Lincoln County, New Mexico. There the so-called Horrell War erupted, when the youngest brother, Ben, was slain in Lincoln. John Horrell had also been shot to death earlier in New Mexico for obscure reasons. The Horrells killed several locals in retribution and then fought their way back to Lampasas County.

"Pink" Higgins soon killed two Horrell cowboys in separate incidents for stealing his cattle and then gunned down Merritt Horrell in Lampasas on January 22, 1877. After several skirmishes and ambushes by both sides, a major battle erupted in Lampasas on June 14, 1877. Higgins then led a raid against the Horrell ranch, and the Horrells retaliated by bushwhacking a Higgins cowboy. At this point, the Texas Rangers intervened to negotiate a truce and begin legal proceedings. But the next year, Tom and Mart Horrell were arrested for robbery and murder in another county. On December 15, 1878, they were shot to death in their Meridian, Texas, jail cell by an angry mob. All charges were dismissed in Lampasas County, and "Pink" Higgins moved his ranching operation south of Spur, Texas, although twice more he became embroiled in fatal shootouts. The sole surviving Horrell brother, Sam, ranched peacefully near Lampasas for the remainder of his life.

—Bill O'Neal

SEE ALSO: Cattle Rustling

SUGGESTED READING:

Sinise, Jerry. *Pink Higgins: The Reluctant Gunfighter.* Quanah, Tex., 1974.
Sonnichsen, C. L. *I'll Die before I'll Run.* New York, 1951.

HORSES

The horse is unquestionably one of the most important animals, perhaps *the* most important animal, in the history of the American West. Its presence as a former native—returned in domesticated form to North America by Spanish colonists in New Mexico, Texas, Arizona, and California—became one of the shaping developments of Western history. The horse's initial appearance in the West in the sixteenth century helped make possible early European successes against the native tribes of the region. It went on to revolutionize the cultures of the Western Indians and made the horse-mounted Plains Indian an American icon the world over. Horses shrank vast Western distances and hauled riders and pulled loads that drew missionaries, explorers, fur traders, surveyors, homesteaders, and armies to protect them into every nook and cranny of Western mountains, deserts, and plains. Through their refinement among Spanish vaqueros, horse skills helped make possible the emergence of the American cowboy as yet another fixture of the West. In fact, it is impossible to imagine the West without the horse as a central actor.

The evolution of the horse is a uniquely American story. The horse is a quadruped mammal whose evolutionary roots were as authentically American as those of the pronghorn, or antelope, and more so than the bison, whose ancestors were Asian emigrants. Horses are, of course, an example of Darwinian natural selection, and they were used more than any other species in the nineteenth century by scholars—such as O. C. Marsh, first professor of paleontology in North America at Yale—to demonstrate the truth of evolution. Marsh had been stimulated by the discoveries of fossils in Nebraska and the Dakotas. In a famous lecture series in New York in 1876, Thomas Henry Huxley took Yale's Peabody Museum collection of horse fossils as the prime proof of evolution. Stimulated by Huxley, Marsh went on to assemble a chronology of the evolution of horses through the Eocene, Miocene, Pliocene, and Recent epochs and to show changes in hooves and molars from the three-toed, one-foot-tall *Hyracotherium* to the simplified single-hoof of modern *Equus*; he also pointed to the higher crowned teeth suitable for eating grasses on the spreading prairies of a warming climate. Browsing horses were mostly supplanted by grazing horses during the Miocene about eighteen million years ago. Three-toed horses continued to exist through the early Pliocene (about five million years ago) but were succeeded by *Equus,* the modern single-hoofed, grazing animals (horses, asses, and zebras) by the Pleistocene of the last two million years.

While the horse's primary evolutionary radiation took place in the Americas, various genera of horses migrated to the Old World several times over the past sixty million years. All became extinct, however, so that the existing horses over the entire world today represent the offspring of America's Pleistocene horses, which migrated to Eurasia across the Bering land bridge during the Ice Ages of the last two million years and spread across much of Asia, Europe, and into Africa.

William R. Leigh's *Leader's Downfall* depicts a method of capturing wild horses. *Courtesy National Cowboy Hall of Fame and Western Heritage Center.*

Westerners relied on horses for many enterprises. Nick Eggenhoffer's painting of a stagecoach depicts one of them. *Courtesy National Cowboy Hall of Fame and Western Heritage Center.*

Equus of the modern family *Equidae* emerged about 3.9 million years ago, and the domesticated horses that we know today *(Equus caballus)* are most closely related to Przewalskii's horse *(Equus przewalskii),* a nearly extinct species that still lives wild on the Asian steppes. Having spread to the Old World ten thousand years ago, the horse herds that remained in the Americas became extinct. The ecological niche that horses filled in the Americas, however, seems to have remained vacant, so that when the horse was returned in domesticated form to its original homeland, the animal underwent an extraordinary population explosion. From the center of dispersal in the American Southwest, by 1800, an estimated two million horses were running wild across the West.

The horses that were returned to the Americas in the sixteenth century were primarily Barb horses, a specialized horse bred to ride across arid north African deserts that much resembled parts of the American West. The knowledge of how to ride and care for horses was essential before the horse could play its transformative role in Indian history. In New Mexico, the Spanish missions had used Indians as herders since the early 1600s. And it was the PUEBLO REVOLT in 1680, when the Pueblo Indians rose up against Spanish rule and in the process seized the Spanish herds, that diffused horses to Indians across the West. Among groups like the Comanches, horses became symbols of wealth and status and objects of raiding and breeding to replenish the supply. Eventually, many tribes, like the Nez Percé, Flathead, and Cayuse Indians, were breed-ing specialized paints and spotted Appaloosas. And Plains Indians were evolving toward becoming stock pastoralists. But their dependence on horses also made Indians vulnerable to raids by other tribes and to attacks by the American military, which came to anticipate the kind of terrain needed to care for the large horse herds in the winter.

Distances between settlements in the early West and the success with which domestic Spanish horses went native made the horse important to the economies of the Spanish, French, and Anglo-American settlements in the West as well. In 1775, horses were being purchased in Sonora for import into the California settlements. Within six years, however, feral herds of horses and mules were reported as becoming numerous along the entire wilderness route between the two provinces. The California missions and presidios, which had few horses in the 1770s and 1780s, found themselves surrounded by horse herds as early as 1794. Beginning in 1806 in San Jose, and then in Santa Barbara in 1808 and 1814, in Monterey in 1812 and 1820, and generally throughout the California settlements in 1827, large numbers of horses in the surrounding countryside had to be slaughtered to protect pastures. It was reports of the incredible horse herds of California that drew American traders such as JOSEPH REDDEFORD WALKER to California in succeeding decades.

Texas and the neighboring Spanish provinces to the south also experienced a rapid build-up of wild horse populations through most of the eighteenth century. As one San Antonio, Texas, official put it in 1785:

"The number of mustangs in all these environs is so countless that if anyone were capable of taming them and caring for them, he could acquire a supply sufficient to furnish an army."

By the late nineteenth and early twentieth centuries, horses were largely being supplanted (but never entirely replaced) by automobiles across the West. Wild horses have remained a feature of the Western landscape, however, and as a Western icon are now protected by the Wild Horse and Burro Act of 1972. The Pryor Mountains National Wild Horse Refuge in Montana also serves to protect the West's wild horses. And the horse's central role in Western history remains fixed in the world's imagination through the work of Western artists such as FREDERIC REMINGTON and CHARLES MARION RUSSELL.

—Dan Flores

SEE ALSO: Cowboys; Mustang and Horse Trade; Native American Cultures: Warfare; Native American Peoples: Peoples of the Great Plains.

SUGGESTED READING:

Flores, Dan, ed. *Journal of an Indian Trader: Anthony Glass and the Texas Trading Frontier, 1790–1810*. College Station, Tex., 1985.

Kust, Matthew. *Man and Horse in History*. Alexandria, Va., 1983.

MacFadden, Bruce. *Fossil Horses, Systematics, Paleobiology, and Evolution of the Family Equidae*. New York, 1992.

Simpson, Gaylord. *Horses: The Story of the Horse in the Modern World and through Sixty Million Years of History*. New York, 1951.

HORSE THEFT AND HORSE THIEVES

Throughout the history of the West, horses were essential animals for ranchers, farmers, teamsters, stage lines, and travelers of every description. Animals of such widespread demand inevitably were stolen, sometimes by gangs operating on a regular basis, but more commonly by individual rustlers who only occasionally included horse theft among their nefarious activities. Indeed, horse theft had been a constant problem for colonial America, and the colonies prescribed harsh policies, which proved to be of little effect in curbing rustlers. By the nineteenth century, horse theft was an unfortunate but deeply established American tradition.

By far the most skillful and persistent horse thieves in the frontier West were the Native American tribes, who adopted the horse culture and who measured individual wealth in numbers of horses. Comanches were universally acknowledged as among the best horsemen, horse breeders, and horse stealers—the latter a highly

"George Ammong, the horse thief killed near Canon City, June 28, 1900." *Courtesy Denver Public Library, Western History Department.*

complimentary term among Native Americans of the West. Incessant Comanche raids in Texas and surrounding areas, especially Mexico, resulted in enormous herds of stolen horses. Texas ranches and farms were looted of horses, and one large hacienda in northern Mexico claimed to have lost hundreds of thousands of horses to Comanche raiders. Comanches customarily avoided the military posts of Texas but sometimes stole cavalry animals from the corrals of unfortified "forts." As late as 1872, Comanches, who had nominally settled on the Fort Sill Reservation, took at least 16,500 horses and mules out of Texas.

Within a few years of the opening of the Santa Fe Trail in 1821, there was a booming market in Santa Fe for horses and mules for trade. While many of the animals were legally purchased, many more were stolen by Ute Indians. Also involved in the traffic were MOUNTAIN MEN, many of whom increasingly turned to horse theft as the fur trade declined. Prominent among the horse-stealing mountain men was Thomas ("Peg-leg") Smith, who stole 300 horses in California and drove them to New Mexico; he then spent nearly a decade repeating this process, often selling his rustled animals at Bent's Fort. Soon rustlers regularly traversed the Horse-Thief Trail, which meandered by back routes from Salt Lake City through remote points in Utah, Arizona, and Texas to the border of Mexico. In the summer of 1860, residents of McLennan County, Texas, blamed Northern abolitionists for horse theft in their region rather than the Comanches.

After the Civil War, the Comanches and other horse Indians were conquered and confined to reservations, but horse theft was continued on a smaller scale by outlaws and occasional rustlers. The most notorious horse thief of the period was "Dutch Henry" Born, who, as a young buffalo hunter in 1869, lost his horses to Cheyennes. Appealing to the commander of Fort Lyon, Born was kicked off the post for disturbing the Indians. He retaliated by stealing stock from the fort and boasted that he intended to steal 100 Indian ponies. Finding the enterprise profitable, Born expanded his activities and operated for several years with perhaps as many as three hundred confederates throughout the Great Plains and as far west as Nevada. One band of rustlers would rendezvous with another and swap stolen herds to sell when they returned to their respective home neighborhoods. Briefly apprehended several times during the mid- and late 1870s, Born finally was sentenced to prison by Judge ISAAC CHARLES PARKER.

During the 1870s, Cap Brown apparently became the first horse thief to use the twisted ravines and scattered waterholes of Robbers Roost, and soon rustlers discovered the secluded grasslands of Brown's Park and the protected canyons of the Hole-in-the-Wall. These isolated hideouts became the principal stopovers of the Outlaw Trail, which stretched from northern Montana to El Paso. Cap Brown preferred to ride out alone, but as he collected horses, he usually gathered a few young cowboys to help him move his stolen herds. One youthful outlaw who began working with Brown in 1884 would become known as BUTCH CASSIDY. Other future members of Cassidy's Wild Bunch who ran horses along the Outlaw Trail included Harvey, Johnny, and Lonie Logan; Elzy Lay; Matt Warner; and eighteen-year-old Harry Longabaugh, who served seven months for horse theft in the county jail at Sundance, Wyoming, and thereafter was called the Sundance Kid.

One famous if short-lived band of horse thieves was headed by BILLY THE KID, who turned to rustling after the climactic battle of the LINCOLN COUNTY WAR in July 1878. Aiding the Kid were Charlie Bowdre, Henry Brown, John Middleton, Tom O'Folliard, Dave Rudabaugh, Doc Scurlock, and Fred Wait. After the gang moved a stolen herd from New Mexico to the Texas Panhandle, Brown elected to stay in Tascosa—where he soon was hired to track down horse thieves on the theory that it takes one to catch one. Other noted Western ruffians who at least sporadically engaged in horse rustling included Mysterious DAVE MATHER, Red Buck Waightman, Ned Christie, Jesse Evans, TIBURCIO VÁSQUEZ, and HENRY STARR. The Texas ranch of Jim, Frank, and John Manning near Canutillo was known as a haven for horse thieves.

In southern Kansas in the 1870s, a gang of horse and mule thieves apparently was organized by a stagecoach line to raid the stock of a rival line. A posse of 150 men descended upon the Caldwell area to engage in a mass roundup of rustlers, and WILLIAM L. BROOKS (known as "Buffalo Bill" or "Bully") was one of three outlaws taken from jail and hung by a midnight lynch mob. Throughout the nineteenth century and into the early decades of the twentieth century, horse rustlers frequently were lynched, and organizations began to spring up such as the Horse Thief Protection Society of Clinton, Iowa, and a Vigilance Committee in Clay County, Iowa, which distributed handbills reading: "Horse Thieves, Beware!" The great livestock associations of the post–Civil War West were formed by big ranchers primarily to control the theft of cattle; horse rustlers usually were given only secondary attention by these organizations. But in 1854, David McKee organized the Anti-Horse Thief Association of Clarke County, Missouri, and after an 1863 reorganization, membership grew to 1,100 chapters by 1912 (262 in Oklahoma alone). Horse thieves apprehended by the law faced a one-year minimum sentence in most Western states and territories, although Texas prescribed a five-year minimum in 1890, while Colorado, Nevada, and Wyoming had no minimum. The usual maximum sentence was ten years, but Texas imposed a fifteen-year maximum, and the maximum in Idaho, Montana, and Nevada was fourteen years. Because of inadequate jail space and the expense of maintaining prisoners, convicts usually were released after serving a fraction of their sentences. Of course, for men "on the rustle," the ultimate maximum sentence was an impromptu "prairie necktie party," from which there was no appeal.

—*Bill O'Neal*

SEE ALSO: Lynching; Mustang and Horse Trade; Vigilantism

SUGGESTED READING:

Fehrenbach, T. R. *Comanches.* New York, 1974.

Gard, Wayne. *Frontier Justice.* Norman, Okla., 1949.

Jordan, Philip D. *Frontier Law and Order.* Lincoln, Nebr., 1970.

Prassel, Frank Richard. *The Western Peace Officer.* Norman, Okla., 1972.

HORTON, ALONZO ERASTUS

Alonzo Erastus Horton. *Courtesy San Diego Historical Society.*

Town founder and "father" of "New San Diego," Alonzo Erastus Horton (1813–1909) was born in Connecticut and moved with his family to New York. At the age of twenty-one, he served briefly as constable of Oswego and ran a modest shipping business between that city and Canada. In 1836, he moved to Wisconsin, speculated in land, and founded the small town of Hortonville about twenty miles from Oshkosh. In 1851, he sold his holdings in Hortonville and headed for California, where he married, settled in San Francisco, and opened a successful store at Sixth and Market streets.

On April 15, 1867, Horton boarded the steamer *Pacific* and headed south in search of development possibilities in SAN DIEGO. Believing that San Diego's Old Town had little to offer, he purchased some land by the harbor instead. He acquired eight hundred acres for $265 and, with some additional purchases, put together Horton's Addition—an area that became known as "New Town" or "New San Diego." Horton offered incentives to businessmen, bankers, church groups, and residents to move to his land by the bay. His continuing work to promote settlement there and a fire in Old Town in 1872 allowed New Town to prosper. With proceeds from land sales, Horton completed a new wharf, a mansion on First Street, and the palatial Horton House, a one-hundred-room hotel that was the most elegant of the time. Horton's drive for civic development was so strong that he once traded San Francisco publisher HUBERT HOWE BANCROFT a city block in exchange for books to serve as the nucleus of a public library for the town.

San Diego's economy had its ups and downs during the period from 1870 to the early twentieth century, and each "bust" had its effect on Horton's holdings. Eventually, the Horton House was torn down to make room for the U. S. Grant Hotel, and Horton's fortune dwindled. Nevertheless, the founder of New San Diego retained his faith in his city and was gratified by each new development made there in his later years. He died in San Diego at the age of ninety-five.

—*Iris H. W. Engstrand*

SUGGESTED READING:

Engstrand, Iris H. W. *San Diego: California's Cornerstone.* Tulsa, Okla., 1980.

Heilbron, Robert F. "Horton's Purchase: The Real Story." *The Journal of San Diego History* 33 (Winter 1987): 63–71.

MacPhail, Elizabeth. *The Story of New San Diego and of Its Founder Alonzo E. Horton.* San Diego, 1969. Reprint. 1979.

HOTELS

Hotels were the centers of communities in the trans-Mississippi West. Besides offering travelers bed and board, they served as meeting places and hubs of social life, and they represented prosperity and permanency for the community.

The development of hotels—from the first dirty road ranches or stations (a combination of inn, store, stable, and saloon) and hastily built taverns to the grand hotels of St. Louis, Denver, and San Francisco—took only a short time. But in the decades of transition, from the 1840s to the 1870s, no Western institution improved as quickly as the hotel.

The earliest inns offered patrons community toothbrushes and horrid food. Often five to ten people, of both sexes, were packed in one room with sometimes three or more to a bed. But by the late 1870s, the West had some of the grandest hotels in the nation. Among the large and ornate houses were the Palace in San Francisco, the Windsor in Denver, and the Menger in San Antonio. Besides these urban hotels, the West also had a number of outstanding resorts; the Raymond in Pasadena, the Del Coronado in San Diego, and the Del Monte in Monterey were three of the best.

The hotel business was exciting, if often unpredictable. Hotel men were innovators who brought new ideas, construction techniques, and gadgets to the West. For some proprietors, business could be very good; for others, fires, the moving of railheads, or the opening of a new hotel by a competitor could mean financial disaster.

The success of many new Western towns depended on the success of their hotels. Hotels attracted atten-

The Merchants Hotel in Bismarck, Dakota Territory, 1876. *Courtesy State Historical Society of North Dakota.*

tion and people. To be successful, hotel owners had to treat guests well, serve good food, and remain on call twenty-four hours a day. Hotel owners were usually among the most popular community leaders. The Leland family of Vermont was a name well known in the hotel business.

There were a few African American hotel owners in the West, and hotels were among the few businesses that employed blacks. There were also several successful female hotel owners, often widows. Nellie Cashman, for example, operated a number of popular hotels in the West.

Advertising was important in attracting clientele. Most ads were banal and repetitious. A British traveler stated that nothing bothered him so much as looking for beautiful scenery and finding painted hotel ads on every commanding peak.

Among hotel employees, the most obnoxious were the hotel runners who went to train and stagecoach stations and docks and practically forced inexperienced travelers into their hotel buses. Not as boisterous as the runners but especially imperious were the room clerks. Waiters were the most talked about employees. A few dangerously flung dishes and silverware across the dining room; others served diners in grand style. Maids were criticized for waking guests up early in the morning, and it was difficult for hotel owners to employ maids for any length of time, for they often quit their jobs to marry.

No hotel captured the attention of the public more than the Palace in San Francisco. Opened in 1875 and called the "noblest hotel of the Western World," the Palace had 755 rooms, five elevators, and twenty-eight miles of water pipes. But because it was expensive to build and costly to run, it seldom turned a profit. The epitome of a great Western hotel, the Palace was destroyed by the 1906 earthquake and fire.

A hotel in Calloway, Nebraska. *Courtesy Nebraska State Historical Society.*

Although most of the nineteenth-century Western hotels no longer stand, those that remain are a reminder of a colorful and exciting era of the American West. Few institutions so captured that spirit, the aspirations, and the real flavor of the West as did the hotel.

—*Richard A. Van Orman*

SUGGESTED READING:

Lewis, Oscar, and Carroll D. Hall. *Bonanza Inn: America's First Luxury Hotel.* New York, 1939.

Pomeroy, Earl. *In Search of the Golden West: The Tourist in Western America.* New York, 1957.

Van Orman, Richard A. *A Room for the Night: Hotels of the Old West.* Bloomington, Ind., 1966.

HOUCHEN SETTLEMENT HOUSE

Affiliated with the Methodist Church, the Rose Gregory Houchen Settlement House provides educational and health services to the predominately Mexican residents of Segundo Barrio in El Paso, Texas. The settlement, staffed by Methodist women missionaries and lay volunteers, was founded in 1912. Its early curriculum followed the typical regimen established by Progressive-era settlements with an emphasis on vocational education, English, citizenship, cooking, and hygiene. The settlement also established a bilingual kindergarten and preschool with tuition based on a sliding scale. In keeping with its mission of "Christian Americanization," Houchen staff members scheduled a full array of Bible classes. Until the 1950s, an explicit goal of the project was the creation of a Protestant enclave within the barrio.

Health care, however, remains the most important contribution of the Houchen Settlement House. Methodist missionaries provided the first accessible, professional health care to barrio residents. In 1921, Freeman Clinic was established next door to the settlement, and in 1937, Newark Methodist Maternity Hospital opened its doors. Specializing in obstetrics and pediatrics, Newark relied on volunteer physicians, local staff, and nurses trained as missionaries. Patients paid for services on a sliding scale and on installment plans. From 1937 to 1976, more than twelve thousand babies were born at Newark hospital.

Houchen staff were missionaries, and they perceived themselves as harbingers of salvation. According to one document, "Our Church is called El Buen Pastor . . . , and that is what our church really is to the people—it is a Good Shepherd guiding our folks out of darkness and Catholocism [*sic*]." The women of Houchen held out unrealistic images of the "American dream" and glorified European cultures. Sometimes subtle, sometimes overt, the privileges attending race, class, culture, and color had painful consequences for their pupils. Relating the excitement of kindergarten graduation, one instructor included in her report a question asked by one of the young graduates. "We are all wearing white, white dress, slip, socks and Miss Fernandez, is it alright if our hair is black?" In other instances, former Houchen students remembered the settlement as a warm, supportive environment. "The only contact I had with Anglos was with Anglo teachers. Then I met Miss Rickford [a Houchen missionary] and I felt, Hey, she's human. She's great."

By the 1950s, Houchen Settlement became more ecumenical and more reflective of the population it served. The emphasis on conversion was dropped, and priests were even allowed to baptize hospitalized infants. Latina missionaries acted as cultural brokers and seemed more willing to listen to their clients. Indeed, during the 1950s, increasing numbers of local residents served as lay volunteers. For most Mexican women, Houchen was not a beacon of salvation, however, but a medical and social-service center. They consciously decided what resources they would use while ignoring the settlement's ideological premises. Health care and children's programs remained the most popular offerings. In 1986, the Methodist Church, citing rising insurance costs, closed Newark hospital. In the 1990s, staffed by social workers and volunteers, Houchen operated one of El Paso's largest nursery schools and continued a slate of educational programs, including karate and aerobics classes.

—*Vicki L. Ruiz*

SUGGESTED READING:

Ruiz, Vicki L. "Dead Ends or Gold Mines: Using Missionary Records in Mexican American Women's History." *Frontiers: A Journal of Women's Studies* 12 (1991): 33–56.

Sanchez, George J. "'Go after the Women': Americanization and the Mexican Immigrant Woman, 1915–1929." In *Unequal Sisters: A Multicultural Reader in U.S. Women's History.* Edited by Ellen Carol DuBois and Vicki L. Ruiz. New York, 1990.

HOUGH, EMERSON

An important environmental activist, Emerson Hough (1857–1923) was also a popular turn-of-the-century novelist. Born in Newton, Iowa, he was educated at the State University of Iowa (now the University of Iowa). After receiving his B.A. in 1880, Hough studied law and was admitted to the Iowa bar in 1881. He left Iowa for Whiteoaks, New Mexico, ostensibly to practice law there, but mainly to indulge his growing passion for hunting, fishing, and the wilderness generally. Hough began selling brief sketches and essays on hunting and fishing to various magazines and enjoyed sufficient success to prompt him to become a full-time writer. He worked briefly for newspapers in Des Moines, Iowa, and Sandusky, Ohio, before becoming head of the Chicago office of *Forest and Stream* magazine in 1889.

In the winter of 1894, Hough toured Yellowstone Park on skis in order to study game conditions. He found that the park's great bison herd had been all but destroyed by poachers, and he wrote a report to the government concerning the situation. Hough's eloquent document is credited with moving Congress to enact legislation on May 7, 1894, extending federal protection of the park's herds. From 1916 to 1918, Hough campaigned similarly for the protection of Yellowstone's elks, which were threatened by the encroachment of grazing herds of sheep.

Hough's first book-length work was *The Singing Mouse Stories* (1895), studies and meditations on the outdoor life. He also wrote popular nonfiction about the West, including *The Story of the Cowboy* (1897) and *The Story of the Outlaw* (1906). But he is best known for *The Covered Wagon* (1922) and *North of 36* (1923). The novels combined sentimental love stories with the rip-roaring adventures of rugged Western men, all set against an epically rendered backdrop of the majestic West. The works established the pattern not only for subsequent fiction about the West by other writers, but for the western film as well.

—*Alan Axelrod*

SEE ALSO: Film: The Western; Literature: The Western Novel

SUGGESTED READING:
Lyon, Thomas J., et al., eds. *A Literary History of the American West.* Fort Worth, Tex., 1987.

HOUSTON, SAM

First president of the Republic of Texas and later governor of the state of Texas, Sam Houston (1793–1863) was born in Rockbridge County, Virginia. He had little, if any, formal schooling. His family moved to Tennessee in 1806, and there Houston grew to adulthood. He saw military service during the War of 1812 as a lieutenant in the army commanded by ANDREW JACKSON. After the war, he returned to Tennessee, studied law, and became an attorney.

Sam Houston. *Courtesy Patrick H. Butler, III.*

Houston was elected to the United States Congress in 1823. Four years later, he became governor of Tennessee. In 1829, he married Eliza H. Allen; the marriage, however, came to a sudden end when Houston left his wife, resigned the governorship, and moved to the Indian Territory west of the Mississippi River to start a new life among the Cherokees. Houston took a Native American name, wore Indian dress, and became a tribal citizen. He also married a Native American woman according to the requirements of tribal custom. He lived among the Cherokees until 1832, when he left his Indian wife and migrated to Texas, then a Mexican province in political turmoil because of the increasing number of Anglo-Americans moving into the area.

Houston took an active role among those in Texas who wanted greater autonomy from the centralized political control of Mexico City. He signed the Texas Declaration of Independence as a delegate to the Convention of 1836. The members of that assembly, which served as the government of revolutionary Texas, selected Houston commanding general of the Texan army on March 4, 1836. He took formal command of his forces shortly after the fall of the Alamo. In a controversial reaction to the advance across Texas of Mexican troops led by General ANTONIO LÓPEZ DE SANTA ANNA, Houston turned his small army eastward and rapidly fled towards the Louisiana border in a retreat popularly known as the "Runaway Scrape." With Santa Anna in pursuit, Houston surprised the Mexican general by turning his troops and attacking unexpectedly at the Battle of San Jacinto on April 21, 1836. The Mexican army was routed, Santa Anna taken prisoner, and the independence of Texas made a reality.

Houston thereafter served as the first elected president of the Republic of Texas, a position to which he would be eventually reelected for a second nonconsecutive term in the 1840s. While serving as president, Houston remarried. He and his new wife, Margaret M. Lea, eventually had eight children together. Houston's term as president was not without opposition. He soon found a political rival in the person of MIRABEAU B. LAMAR. Factions formed around the two men as the rivalry between them determined much of the political history of the Lone Star Republic. Houston, a person of strong personality, often attracted controversy, in part due to his occasional heavy drinking. When Texas became a state in 1845, Houston was elected to the U.S. Senate. He refused to support blindly many of the Southern political causes of the 1850s. Instead, he embraced Unionism over Southern sectionalism. By the mid-1850s, he also embraced the Know-Nothing movement because of his strong commitment to preserving the Union.

Elected governor of Texas in 1859, he refused to cooperate with the state's secession convention, which met in early 1861, and he declined to take an oath of allegiance to the newly formed Confederate States of America. The state legislature, not wishing to impeach him out of respect for his previous accomplishments, thereupon simply declared the office of governor to be vacant. The lieutenant-governor, a Confederate supporter, assumed the office, and Houston reluctantly retired to his home in Huntsville after refusing an offer of federal troops from Lincoln to help him keep his office. It was a matter of personal honor to Houston not to raise an angry hand against his fellow Texans. His ejection from the governor's office embittered him and soured his few remaining years.

—*Light Townsend Cummins*

SEE ALSO: National Expansion: Texas and National Expansion; Texas Revolution

SUGGESTED READING:

Friend, Llerena. *Sam Houston: The Great Designer.* Austin, Tex., 1954.

Gregory, Jack, and Rennard Strickland. *Sam Houston with the Cherokees, 1829–1833.* Austin, Tex., 1967.

Houston, Sam. *Autobiography of Sam Houston.* Edited by Donald Day and Harry Herbert. Norman, Okla., 1954.

James, Marquis. *The Raven: A Biography of Sam Houston.* Indianapolis, Ind., 1929.

Williams, Amelia, and Eugene C. Barker, eds. *The Writings of Sam Houston, 1813–1863.* 8 vols. Austin, Tex., 1938–1943.

HOUSTON, TEXAS

A city of dreams, where fortunes have been made and lost overnight, Houston, TEXAS, was founded on August 26, 1836, by Augustus Chapman Allen and John Kirby Allen. As businessmen and financiers from New York, the Allens ventured to Texas and purchased the site for five thousand dollars in hopes of expanding their entrepreneurial activities.

The town was named for Sam Houston, a friend of the Allen brothers and the hero of San Jacinto, the decisive battle of the Texas Revolution, which transformed the Mexican state of Texas into the Republic of Texas, a sovereign and independent nation. The Allen brothers advertised the beginning of the enterprise in the *Telegraph* and *Texas Register*: "No place in Texas," they proclaimed, "possesses so many advantages for building, having pine, ash, cedar, and oak in inexhaustible quantities." On November 30, 1836, forty-nine members of the legislature of the Republic of Texas voted to make Houston the state capital, and it remained the seat of government until 1840.

Located on the west bank of Buffalo Bayou, Houston enjoys a temperate climate, abundant rain, a wealth of nearby forests, and excellent land. From the start, it was a center for political and commercial activities.

In its early days, manufacturing interests—metal foundries, brick works, sawmills, and textile and flour mills—established a strong economic base for the South Texas region. Although growth was interrupted during the CIVIL WAR, business activities increased steadily after the war. By the end of the 1870s, Harris County listed 64 manufacturing establishments and more than 164 commercial establishments. From medicine to jewelry, Houston merchants and manufacturers reached Boston, Baltimore, New Orleans, and Mobile.

Railroad development followed the same pattern as manufacturing. Paul Bremond, a local promoter, began the Houston and Texas Central Rail Road Company on January 1, 1853, to link the city of Houston with Austin. When the Civil War began, railroad expansion in Texas was temporarily halted. Expansion of transportation facilities resumed in 1869 and increased in 1876 when Thomas W. House, Abram Groesbeck, and others founded the Buffalo Ship Channel Company. Between the end of Reconstruction and the Great Depression of the 1930s, the transportation

Houston, Texas. *Courtesy Patrick H. Butler, III.*

network expanded to maturity. Roads, railroad lines, and the ship channel contributed to the development of trade and manufacturing.

On July 14, 1895, the *Houston Daily Post* described the city as "the first city of Texas and the pride of the Lone Star State." And the real economic boom was yet to come. On January 10, 1901, at a place known as Spindletop, near Beaumont, Allen W. Hamil discovered oil, an event that changed the character of Houston. Soon after the discovery, the giants of the American petroleum industry came to Houston and left an indelible mark on the social fabric, character, and environment. By 1930, eight refineries were operating in the Houston area. Humble Oil, Sinclair, Texas Company (Texaco), Gulf Oil Corporation, and others produced approximately 194,000 barrels of oil per day.

As a result, Houston's success in the twentieth century can be credited to the oil and chemical industry, the daring of the American business community, and the indomitable oil workers.

Development was especially strong during and after World War II. In 1940, Humble Oil and Refining Company (now known as Exxon Company, USA) provided the U.S. government with one billion gallons of aviation fuel. That refining achievement served as a catalyst for other industries to move in the area. Fortune 500 companies such as Monsanto, Dow, Shell, DuPont, Union Carbide, Celanese, Ethyl, Phillips, Amoco, and many others took advantage of the business climate.

The Bayou City's development leaped forward into the twentieth century primarily with the modernization of the ship channel, the continuing expansion of the Houston International Airport, and the establishment of the Manned Spacecraft Center by the National Aeronautic and Space Administration (NASA). In addition, the M. D. Anderson Foundation developed the Texas Medical Center, a large complex of hospitals and medical schools; in 1968, the center performed more heart transplant operations than any other facility in the world.

The growth and heterogeneity of the population of Houston point to a variety of demographic projections. In the late twentieth century, African Americans represented the largest minority, but in the twenty-first century, according to experts' predictions, Mexican Americans and Hispanics in general will become the largest minority. In addition, the influx of a significant number of Americans representing most of the other forty-nine states, Canadians, Europeans, Asians, Middle Easterners, and Africans has changed Houston to an important international center.

—*Fred L. Koestler*

SEE ALSO: Galveston, Texas; Medicine; Oil and Gas Industry

SUGGESTED READING:

McComb, David G. *Houston: A History*. Austin, Tex., 1981.
Sibley, Marilyn McAdams. *Port of Houston: A History*. Austin, Tex., 1968.

HOWARD, OLIVER OTIS

U.S. Army officer, known as the "Christian Soldier" or the "Praying General," Oliver Otis Howard (1830–1909) was born in Leeds, Maine, and graduated from Bowdoin College and the U.S. Military Academy, where he ranked fourth in the class of 1854.

When the Civil War broke out, Howard was considering the ministry. He joined the military, however, and earned a solid reputation as a corps commander during General WILLIAM TECUMSEH SHERMAN's Western campaigns, despite the loss of his right arm at Fair Oaks, Virginia, in 1862 and poor performances at Chancellorsville and Gettysburg. His connections with powerful Maine politicians, especially James G. Blaine, greatly helped in his rapid rise to major general of volunteers.

President Andrew Johnson selected Howard, known for his religiosity and humanitarian principles, to head the Bureau of Refugees, Freedmen, and Abandoned Lands (1865 to 1874), a government agency organized to assist African Americans in their transition from slavery to freedom. Lax administration of the agency marred Howard's reputation, and historians today debate whether the Freedmen's Bureau did as much as it could have to help the former slaves. To further the education of blacks, Howard helped establish Howard University and served as its president from 1869 to 1874. Later, he performed a similar service for underprivileged whites as one of the founders of Lincoln University in eastern Tennessee.

Howard's benevolence extended to Native Americans. In 1872, he arranged a peace treaty with COCHISE and the Chiricahua Apaches in southeastern Arizona, despite a public outcry and a chilly reception by department commander General GEORGE CROOK. His subsequent peacemaking efforts among Pacific Northwest tribes were less successful. After failing to prevent bloodshed between white settlers and the Nez Percé Indians, he aroused widespread criticism for a lackluster pursuit of CHIEF JOSEPH and his followers during their dramatic dash for the Canadian border. He eventually became embroiled in an acrimonious controversy with Colonel NELSON APPLETON MILES, who assumed the sole honor of having ended the Nez Percé War. Howard performed more creditably during the Bannock-Paiute and Sheepeater conflicts from 1878 to 1879.

Following his service as superintendent at West Point from 1880 to 1882, he returned to the West to command the Department of the Platte in Omaha. Promoted to major general in the regular army in 1886, he commanded the Department of the Pacific and, finally, the Military Division of the Atlantic. Howard was the army's second highest ranking officer when he retired in 1894 after forty-four years of service.

At his home in Burlington, Vermont, Howard devoted the remainder of his life to writing, lecturing, and Republican politics. In autobiographical books such as *Nez Percé Joseph* (1881), *My Life and Experiences among Our Hostile Indians* (1907), and *Famous Indian Chiefs I Have Known* (1908), he publicized the injustices being perpetrated against Western tribes and articulated his own philosophy toward native peoples. Like most advanced thinkers of his day, Howard believed that societies naturally progressed from barbarism to civilization and that savage races must give way to Anglo-Christian culture. Although he opposed extermination and blamed white settlers for instigating the Indian wars, he saw no alternative to the ultimate displacement of Indian tribes. Consequently, he stressed education as a strong tool for assimilating Indians into Anglo society. He remained a vocal spokesperson for humanitarian and philanthropic causes until his death at age seventy-eight.

—*Bruce J. Dinges*

SEE ALSO: Apache Wars; Pacific Northwest Indian Wars

SUGGESTED READING:
Carpenter, John A. *Sword and Olive Branch: Oliver Otis Howard.* Pittsburgh, Pa., 1964.
McFeely, William S. *Yankee Stepfather: General O. O. Howard and the Freedmen.* New Haven, Conn., 1968.
Utley, Robert M. "Oliver Otis Howard." *New Mexico Historical Review* 62 (January 1987): 55–63.

HUDSON'S BAY COMPANY

Founded in 1670 under a charter from King Charles, Hudson's Bay Company ruled over a vast area called by the English "Prince Rupert's Land" and stretching from the Hudson Bay to New Caledonia and north to the Arctic Ocean. Its arch rival in the British FUR TRADE, the North West Company, founded (after the collapse of France's New World) in 1783, operated out of Montreal west by lakes and portages up to and beyond the Rocky Mountains. Primarily business ventures, both struggled fiercely to control the Northwest fur trade, concerning themselves with imperial policy only as it affected their purses.

A London board of directors kept tight rein on Hudson's Bay and appointed a governor to see to the running of the outfit under careful instructions from the board's council. Interested in profit and carefully calculating costs, the board discussed at its annual meetings such mundane items as the price of salt beef and sausages, the number and weight and content of every bag on every canoe, the amount of tea and rum to be allotted daily for the Indian guides to consume, and the precise circumstances under which the board would suffer their lonely traders at isolated winter outposts to sleep with Indian women. The directors allowed their employees to explore the wilderness only when it helped rationalize their business, only when such explorations had the chance at least to yield new stands of beaver or to open new routes of portage.

Although the fierce competition between the two English giants spurred them on, it was actually the weakness of the American hold on the LOUISIANA PURCHASE territory that allowed Britain, through the monopolies, to control the far Northwest. By 1812, largely due the efforts of the North West Company explorers, the British interests had stretched their domination of the country west of the mountains well below the forty-ninth parallel with little but the Sioux standing in their way south. East of the Rockies, they held sway over the Missouri River above the Platte, and from posts in Wisconsin and Minnesota, they tapped the Missouri trade through the St. Peter's and Des Moines rivers just as far downstream as they cared to go. After profits rather than land, they ignored English treaties with the United States and turned a deaf ear to the diplomatic protests of the Americans. Although they were not shy in resorting to violence when necessary to protect their sphere of influence, they remained focused on fur and trade routes, which depended on a wilderness rich in wild animals and Indians who knew where to find them. To Hudson's Bay and the North West Company, white settlement was as much an anathema as it was to the Indians.

Although the taking of Fort ASTORIA in 1813 left the North West Company in control of virtually all the Rocky Mountain West as far south as it wanted to travel, decay and dissolution had set in during the course of the War of 1812. The renowned explorer DAVID THOMPSON, needed elsewhere, was called back to eastern Canada for good, and his replacements were conservative and, according to one company official, ridiculously inept. Profits fell, the Indians grew disenchanted with all white traders, and, for three years, hardly a brigade departed for the interior without running into hostility. The American wilderness, from the Cascades to the Missouri, claims scholar William Goetzmann, seemed one long Indian gauntlet.

In the spring of 1814, Donald McTavish came out of retirement in England to clean up the mess. But when the *H.M.S. Isaac Todd* arrived, not only was McTavish aboard, but also his mistress, a voluptuous blond barmaid from Portsmouth named Jane Barnes, the first white woman to reach the Columbia. The local Salish chief's son, although he already had four wives, offered the Indian version of a fortune for her hand; McTavish turned him down. Meanwhile, the until then pious Alexander Henry offered Jane his personal "protection," and she took up house with him in his modest quarters. An unhappy McTavish, who had—along with his entire crew—gotten drunk on rot-gut whiskey, dared Henry to row out to the *Isaac Todd* with him through the tempest that had set them to drinking in the first place. Henry accepted the challenge and drowned with the rest of them when the boat capsized on the Columbia bar. Having—in male eyes—destroyed one of the fur trade's few able men in the West, Barnes set sail on the *Isaac Todd* bound for the Far East, where she eventually married an East India Company official. Meanwhile, back on the Columbia, things grew

worse. Melancholic ships' doctors committed suicide; those men not in despair dissipated their time in high living; they all spent more effort on horse-racing contests with the Indians than on trade.

Not until DONALD MCKENZIE arrived at Fort George, as the British called Astoria, from Montreal in 1816 and took matters in hand did the company's fortunes revive. Formerly employed by JOHN JACOB ASTOR in the Pacific Fur Company, McKenzie had rushed to New York when things went bust on the coast to offer his services to the American millionaire once again, only to be rudely rebuffed by an angry Astor. The rejection proved to be short sighted, because McKenzie became one of the great captains of the Northwest fur trade. He made two changes in company policy. He decided a headquarters at Fort George, even at Spokane, was unnecessary for the inland trade. And, reasoning, as MANUEL LISA had, that the Indians' disdain for trapping limited them to only casual participation in the trade, he had the company itself organize brigades to go into the field and do the actual trapping. He realized, too, that the brigades could not depend on the rivers and canoes for supplying parties and bringing pelts to market; they would have to travel long distances in every direction overland. Only the American MOUNTAIN MEN on the Upper Missouri had tried it, and they were still bound, really, by the river.

This would then be the basic structure of the British trade when the two giants finally combined in the early 1820s, and company governor George Simpson, operating on instructions from London, established FORT VANCOUVER inland on the Columbia and launched the British scorched-earth policy of denuding the wilderness of beavers before the Americans could harvest them. They intended, as David Wishart points out, to create a "fur wilderness." Simpson appointed PETER SKENE OGDEN to head the Snake River brigades, a daring choice. Ogden had been born in Quebec in 1797, the son of an American loyalist who fled to Canada during the Revolution. At the age of seventeen, he went to work for the North West Company as a clerk. During the years of conflict between the now-merged companies, he had won a justly deserved reputation as the meanest and most ruthless of the Hudson's Bay's opponents. Once, he assaulted a Hudson's Bay official at his home post and left him for dead. At a captured post, Ogden threw twenty men, women, and children in prison, put them on starvation rations, and denied them sanitary facilities. Before the merger, he had been forced to flee the entire Northwest territory to keep free of the law, and after the merger, his name had been dropped from the employment rolls with a corporate sigh of relief. Now Simpson hired him back and gave him the Snake River. Hudson's Bay, says Goetzmann, had aimed its ultimate weapon at the Americans.

For all their ideological purposefulness and organizational cohesion, in the long run the British were at a distinct disadvantage in the struggle against the Americans over the fur-trading West. Their agents, products of a semifeudal monopoly interested only in profit, not settlement, never looked for wagon routes or good soil, or even the potential for development of mineral resources or lumbering except to support one of their faraway outposts. They looked only for beaver. By the time brigade leaders began reporting the incredibly fast rate at which the fur-bearing animals were disappearing and company officials realized the need for economic diversity, it was too late. No one had ever asked what happened when the fur was gone, if the Americans would keep coming, and why.

In the long run, the monopolies succeeded too well; in brilliantly accomplishing their commercial ends, they removed their reasons for being there in the first place. At the very moment that JEDEDIAH STRONG SMITH, a young American mountain man, was making mental notes for a report to American policy-makers in Washington on the ease of taking not merely wagons, but herds of livestock, through the South Pass of the Rockies to the Great Falls of the Columbia, he blandly informed the British agents that Americans would never migrate across the "impassable" sandy deserts, and they believed him. They were—institutionally—blind, and long before beaver hats went out of fashion in London, the British had lost their commercial empire in the West.

—*Charles Phillips*

SEE ALSO: Exploration: English Expeditions

SUGGESTED READING:
Cline, Gloria G. *Peter Skene Ogden and the Hudson's Bay Company.* Norman, Okla., 1974
Goetzmann, William H. *Exploration and Empire: The Explorer and the Scientist in the Winning of the American West.* New York, 1966.
Karamanski, Theodore. *Fur Trade and Exploration: Opening the Far Northwest, 1821–1852.* Norman, Okla., 1983
Wishart, David. *The Fur Trade of the American West, 1807–1840.* Lincoln, Nebr., 1979.

HUFFMAN, LATON ALTON (L. A.)

Photographer Laton Alton Huffman (1854–1931) produced thousands of photographs that record the evo-

lution of the early West, particularly southeastern Montana. Born near Castalia, Iowa, Huffman learned wet-collodion photographic skills from his father. In 1879, he moved to the Montana Territory, and while hunting and ranching, he became the post photographer at Fort Keogh (Miles City, Montana). By the turn-of-the-century, he had built a successful PHOTOGRAPHY business by featuring stereopticon cards and tinted prints of Great Plains natives, open-range cattle operations, the wonders of Yellowstone National Park, and railroad development.

L. A. Huffman's personal interests ranged from zoology to ethnology and geography. He periodically held local public office and was elected in 1892 to the Montana legislature. His career spanned the rapid evolution of photography from the wet-collodion process—executed with bulky, time-consuming apparatus—to gelatin dry film and the reliable box camera.

The major collection of Huffman's photographs is held by the Montana Historical Society in Helena. Less extensive but important collections are owned by the University of Michigan Museum of Art in Ann Arbor; the Graphic Arts Department of the Detroit Institute of Art; and the Amon Carter Museum in Fort Worth, Texas.

—*David A. Walter*

SUGGESTED READING:
Brown, Mark H., and W. R. Felton. *Before Barbed Wire: L. A. Huffman, Photographer on Horseback.* New York, 1956.
———. *The Frontier Years: L. A. Huffman, Photographer of the Plains.* New York, 1955.
———. "L. A. Huffman: Brady of the West." *Montana: The Magazine of Western History* 6:1 (Winter 1956): 29–37.

HUMBOLDT RIVER AND THE GREAT BASIN STREAMS

In addition to the Humboldt River, the principal streams of the Great Basin are the Owens, Carson, Truckee, and Walker rivers. Fed by meager run-off from the mountains in a very arid region, the streams are without drainage into the sea, and their waters are deposited in desert lakes and sinks. Forty-niners and others who traveled through the Great Basin called the Humboldt River the "Humbug River" because, shallow and muddy, it offered no relief from the parching desert. It seemed more a cruel hoax than a real river.

The most extensive of the Great Basin streams, the Humboldt is small, with a total watershed of no more than seventeen thousand square miles of north-central Nevada. Its origin is at an elevation of twelve thousand feet in the mountainous region of northeastern Nevada, and it empties into the Humboldt Sink at an elevation of thirty-nine hundred feet northeast of Reno. With a total run-off of nine hundred thousand acre-feet per year, the Humboldt does little to irrigate the surrounding land.

The last significant stream to be discovered by Western explorers, it was sited by trappers of the Hudson's Bay Company in 1828 and was named the Unknown River by PETER SKENE OGDEN. JOHN CHARLES FRÉMONT renamed it in honor of the German scientist and geographer Alexander von Humboldt. It became very familiar to those traveling by way of the Overland Trail and California Trail to the gold country of California, for it marked the safest route between the Great Salt Lake and the Sierra Nevada foothills below Lake Tahoe. The first emigrant wagon trains followed its course in 1841, and it effectively became an extension of the Overland Trail.

The Humboldt also became the route of expansion for MORMONS settling to the west of Salt Lake City. Mormon settlers established Carson City, Nevada, along its banks in 1851. They also developed the Overland Trail, paralleling the river, into a wagon road. By the 1860s, the CENTRAL PACIFIC RAILROAD tracks ran alongside the wagon road. The coming of the railroad increased settlement along the river.

Even before the wagon road and the railroad, the Humboldt River became known as the "highway of the West," because so many California-bound travelers followed it. Today, an interstate highway traverses its valley, and it remains a principal avenue through Nevada and into the Sierra Nevada region of California.

—*Alan Axelrod*

SEE ALSO: California Overland Trails

SUGGESTED READING:
McPhee, John. *Basin and Range*. New York, 1981.

HUME, JAMES B.

The first chief of detectives for WELLS, FARGO AND COMPANY, James B. Hume (1827–1894) was born in Stamford, New York, and lived in Indiana before setting off to the gold mines of California in 1850. Working in the gold fields for a decade, he became deputy tax collector, then city marshal, then chief of police in Placerville, California, a rough community often called "Hangtown." Hume cleaned up the town and moved on to become under-sheriff of El Dorado County, and in this position, rid the region of the notorious Hugh De Tell Gang. He was elected to one term as sheriff of the county in 1868.

Hume developed skills in detective work and interrogation, and after losing a second election for sheriff, he accepted a position with Wells Fargo to investigate a string of express robberies. Over a fourteen-year period, by Hume's accounts, the company lost $414,312.55 to robbers. Hume's work resulted in the apprehension of 206 road agents, or stagecoach robbers, twenty train robbers, and fourteen burglars in the same time period. He played a role in the 1883 capture, conviction, and imprisonment of the outlaw BLACK BART, who had eluded the authorities for eight years.

—*Patricia Hogan*

SUGGESTED READING:
Dillon, Richard. *Wells Fargo Detective: The Biography of James B. Hume*. New York, 1969.

HUMOR

In 1931, the American folk scholar Constance Rourke published her ground-breaking book *American Humor*, which she subtitled *A Study of the National Character*. It is a telling phrase, setting forth explicitly a cultural equation many of us take so much for granted that we have all but forgotten what it means. Much that we call the "American character" is defined in terms of humor. Take this a step further, and we realize that much of what we think of as typically American humor is distinctly Western. For all the hardships he endured—not just on the job, but in the absence of family and home—the cowboy liked to laugh. Typically, however, it was not the laughter of the buffoon. Western humor was—and is—a combination of self-mocking boast and understated dryness. In this, it takes into account the bigger-than-life dreams Americans have habitually wrapped around what they think of as the bigger-than-life West, and, simultaneously, it deflates them and puts them in perspective, even as it builds up the character and characters that lie behind those dreams. In the bunkhouse, around the campfire, over a rot-gut whiskey in a hole-in-the-wall bar, tall tales were swapped, some crude, some obscene, a good many of them very funny in the drawling vein that cowboy humorists such as Will Rogers later popularized.

Western humor, then, is closely related to the cowboy, America's outstanding contribution to world culture. Humor in the West was generally masculine, broad—even to the point of slapstick—and closely related to the everyday life of the working cowhand and his efforts to fight off the boredom of riding fence, treating calves for scours (diarrhea), or doctoring cattle inflicted with screw-work larva with a smelly mixture of chloroform and creosote usually carried in a bottle in an old boot top. Even that lowest of all cowboy chores, greasing windmills, could be a source of humor—like the waddy atop a windmill who hollers "Look out!" after having dropped a wrench. His helper, getting off the ground, asks "Why? You gonna throw another one?" Tall tales, stories about initiating a tenderfoot, and accounts of idiotic cowpoke behavior (both on the ranch and in town) are some of the major sources of cowboy humor. Like most tales told to relieve boredom, the typical cowboy yarn was spun slowly and developed incrementally.

C. L. Sonnichsen, in *The Laughing West,* claims that humor "offers escape from boredom on the one hand and from pressure and stress on the other." In fact, he says, "all humor, including Western humor, is based on human failure, at least on human deviation from the norm." Incongruity, the high and mighty being brought down low, or the impossible being stated with a straight face lay generally at the heart of Western humor.

In *Tall Tales from Texas Cow Camps,* Mody Boatright notes that plain understatement was one of the most useful tools of cowboy humor. Even in the tallest of tales, no old-time cowboy would claim that the ranch he worked for covered one billion acres of land (even if that could be a fact); he would simply say that "they used the state of Arizona for a cow pasture; that it took three days to ride from the yard's gate to the front galley; that the range reached so far that the sun never set between headquarters and the west line camp." The tall tale was often the very essence of humor—like the waddy who told of the time his horse bucked itself off the rim of the Grand Canyon in Arizona with him aboard. When the listeners asked, "What happened?" the cowpoke swore that he had jumped off the horse just before it hit bottom two thousand feet below. And Texas plainsmen and Indian fighter "Bigfoot" Wallace once saved himself from Indian attack by tying strings around his sleeves and leggins and filling his clothes up with hickory nuts he gathered from the ground around him. Indian arrows did not touch his hide during the attack, and he wound up with half a bushel of shelled hickory nuts inside his clothes.

Anecdotes, presented as truth, often served as the basis for Western humor. E. C. Abbott, in his account of trail driving, *We Pointed Them North,* tells of an experience that gave him his nickname. While exploring the upstairs of a hotel where "the girls" were, Abbot fell through a flimsy false wall onto the stage below, where a melodrama was being staged. He was not hurt, but figuring he had to be a part of the action since he was on stage, he straddled a chair backwards and "bucked" it all over the scene while hollering "Whoa, Blue!" To the end of his days, everyone called him "Blue." In another such anecdote, a self-righteous, pious-sounding cowboy, whose sincerity some doubted, became an example of the high laid low, of the deflation of hubris by the commonplace so typical of American humor in general: while the holier-than-thou cowboy rested his feet after dinner one day, one of "the boys" slipped a chunk of cactus into his empty boot, and when he put it on, the colorful language he bellowed proved the doubters right. The man was not the saint he pretended.

A good bit of Western humor arose out of such everyday events in the life of ordinary folks. Exaggeration, understatement, danger that fails truly to harm, outlandish activities, cowboy pranks, all of this the West found comic. There were other strains of humor in the West. Lumber and mining camps and towns gave rise to tall tales, legendary figures, and humorous stereotypes. California's sagebrush humorists, from GEORGE HORATIO DERBY to BRET HARTE to MARK TWAIN, developed comic tales of irreverent humor and satire, laced with myths, romantic settings, and local color, that typically juxtaposed innocent and unsophisticated ruggedness to cosmopolitan nastiness or intellectual pretension or social snobbery. There was the vulgar and slapstick rough and tumble of Western vaudeville, which comedians such as Eddie Foy so mastered. Much of Western humor, even much of cowboy humor, followed patterns initially established on what was once called the "frontier," the backwoods settlements where Anglo-American pioneers drawled lazy tales about country bumpkins who turned out to be quite wise, the hero-fools like DAVID (DAVEY) CROCKETT who made a career out of their feigned simplicity. Sagebrush realism, Western vaudeville, camptown satire, and cowboy humor all drank from the same frontier well, but it was the last of these that most came to associate with the American West, mainly because of one man. Nobody was better at cowboy humor, or more responsible for its wide dissemination than William Penn Adair Rogers.

Will Rogers was born on a ranch near Oologah, Cherokee Nation, Indian Territory (present-day Oklahoma), in 1879, the son of a mixed-blood and prominent Cherokee couple. He attended six schools, four in the Cherokee Nation, and emerged a literate and well-read man despite the theatrical reputation he later

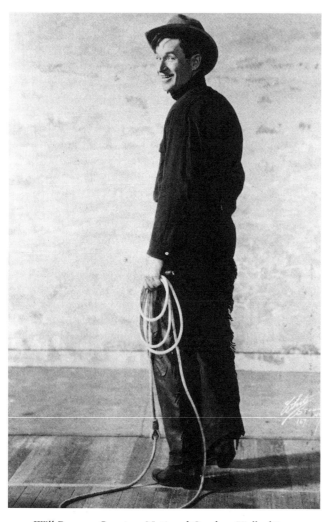

Will Rogers. *Courtesy National Cowboy Hall of Fame.*

developed for bad grammar and bad spelling. Working as a Texas cowhand, an Argentine Gaucho, a player in Texas Jacks's Wild West Show in South Africa, an act in Wirth Brothers Circus in Australia and New Zealand, Rogers perhaps inevitably came to vaudeville in the early 1900s. In the course of his travels, he had perfected riding, trick roping, and a Southwestern drawl that well displayed his trademark understated wit and made him the star attraction of the Ziegfield Follies after 1916. By then, his storytelling and his short pithy commentary had become the heart of the act, which took him in the 1920s to radio and motion pictures. There it was that the nation truly came to appreciate Rogers's dry wit. By the time of his death in an airplane crash in 1935, he was a beloved American figure and the cowboy style of humor a fixture of American life.

—John O. West, Alan Axelrod,
and Charles Phillips

SEE ALSO: Literature; Magazines and Newspapers

SUGGESTED READING:
Adams, Raymond F. *The Old-Time Cowhand.* Norman., Okla., 1952.
Boatright, Mody C. *Folk Laughter on the American Frontier.* New York, 1961.
———. *Talk Tales from Texas Cow Camps.* Reprint. Dallas, Tex., 1982.
Dedera, Don. *The Cactus Sandwich and Other Tall Tales of the Southwest.* Flagstaff, Ariz., 1986.
Erickson, Jon R. *Cowboys are Partly Human.* Perryton, Tex., 1983.
Kelton, Elmer. *The Good Old Boys.* Reprint. Fort Worth, Tex., 1985.
Patterson, Paul. *Pecos Tales.* Austin, Tex., 1967.
Roch, Joyce Gibson. *The Cowgirls.* Houston, Tex., 1978.
Rourke, Constance. *American Humor: A Study of National Character.* 1931. Reprint. Garden City, N.Y., 1953.
Sonnichsen, C. L. *The Laughing West.* Athens, Ohio, 1988.
West, John O. *Cowboy Folk Humor.* Little Rock, Ark., 1990.

HUNT, GEORGE WILEY PAUL

Born in Huntsville, Missouri, Arizona politician-to-be George Wiley Paul Hunt (1859–1934) left home in 1877 to take up prospecting in Colorado. Working his way southward on the railroad, Hunt took a job with the Old Dominion Commercial Company when he reached Globe, Arizona, in 1881. Less than a decade later, he was president of the company, which owned banks, general stores, and other real estate. In 1892, Hunt was elected to the territorial legislature; he served two terms in the lower house, one as its Speaker, and two in the senate. A consummate politician, Hunt worked closely with the business community while convincing voters he was just "plain folks," as his straightforward speech and his modest personal habits indicated. Running as a Democrat and a Progressive in 1910, Hunt became governor of Arizona. He won reelection in 1914 but lost in 1916 to a Republican before a recount reversed the election. He lost again in 1918, and became the U.S. minister to Siam until he regained his seat in the statehouse in 1922. There he remained until 1928, when he lost again, only to be elected for a seventh and final term in 1932. As governor, Hunt was a proponent of regulation for the railroads, a statewide highway program, prison reform, and other Progressive measures, although he fought hard against federal plans to build power dams on the Colorado River.

—Patricia Hogan

HUNT, WILSON PRICE

Fur trader Wilson Price Hunt (1783–1842) was born in Ashbury, New Jersey, the son of John P. Hunt and Margaret Guild. In 1804, Hunt moved to St. Louis and opened Hunt and Hankson, a mercantile partnership. Five years later, fur-trade magnate JOHN JACOB ASTOR sought Hunt's involvement in what became the Pacific Fur Company, a division of Astor's AMERICAN FUR COMPANY. Planning to extend his Western trade to the Pacific and establish a post (Fort ASTORIA) near the mouth of the Columbia River, Astor intended to capitalize the FUR TRADE in the Louisiana Territory, the Pacific Coast, and China.

Lacking real frontier experience, Hunt departed St. Louis in October 1810 in command of the overland expedition of the Astorians. After wintering near the Nodaway River, Hunt's group ascended the Missouri. Accompanied for a time by English naturalist JOHN BRADBURY and botanist Thomas Nuttall, the expedition was joined en route by three trappers, John Hoback, Jacob Reznor, and Edward Robinson, who guided the Astorians overland to the southern end of Jackson Hole via Union Pass. Finding the Snake River unnavigable near Jackson Hole, the expedition crossed Teton Pass to Henry's Fork, built canoes, and descended the Snake River to Twin Falls. From there, the Astorians traveled overland to the Columbia and reached Fort Astoria by February 1812.

The Pacific Fur Company became a casualty of the WAR OF 1812. A well-armed British contingent compelled Hunt to sell out in April 1814. He moved to St. Louis by 1817 and he returned to a merchant's life, dabbled in politics, became postmaster, and at times served as Astor's Western representative for the American Fur Company.

—*S. Matthew Despain and Fred R. Gowans*

SUGGESTED READING:

Brandon, William. "Wilson Price Hunt." In *The Mountain Men and the Fur Trade of the West.* Vol. 6. Edited by LeRoy R. Hafen. Glendale, Calif., 1968.

Irving, Washington. *Astoria: or Anecdotes of an Enterprise beyond the Rocky Mountains.* Edited by Edgeley W. Todd. Norman, Okla., 1964.

Ronda, James P. *Astoria and Empire.* Lincoln, Nebr., 1990.

HUNTING

The trans-Mississippi West provided bountiful and diversified wildlife to Native Americans and Europeans alike. In varying degrees, both peoples exploited this natural resource through subsistence, market, and sport hunting. And, in varying degrees, these hunting activities had an impact on the natural environment and peoples of the West.

Subsistence hunting—the individual harvesting of game animals for food and clothing—was practiced by Native Americans for generations before the European exploration. While small mammals and birds often were taken in snares or traps, larger game usually fell prey to bows and arrows or lances. Using still-hunting, stalking, and driving techniques, Indians harvested rabbits, wild turkeys, deer, antelope, ELKS, and BUFFALOES with these weapons. The harvest provided food, shelter, packaging, apparel, and adornment. Subsistence hunting did not greatly pressure wildlife populations; it allowed a natural equilibrium between man and his environment.

European influences, notably the introduction of HORSES and FIREARMS, altered the equation only marginally during the eighteenth and early nineteenth centuries. On the Great Plains, Indians moved from stalking and driving buffalo to chase hunting with horses, a technique that brought more animals within reach. But available guns actually provided less firepower than the bow, and they had little impact on game populations. Likewise, early European TRAPPERS, traders, and explorers, although armed with more accurate rifles, made little impression on wildlife numbers through subsistence hunting.

By the late 1830s, however, increasing European influence in the West brought change. Market hunting—the systematic harvesting and processing of selected wildlife species for economic or commercial purposes—moved from widespread beaver trapping to the killing of buffaloes for robes and tongues. By 1850, the robe trade, in which the Plains Indians were crucial participants with Anglo firms like the AMERICAN FUR COMPANY and Bent, Saint Vrain and Company, commanded a harvest of about one hundred thousand buffaloes a year. During the next two decades, the bison population drastically declined as the trade accounted for up to one-quarter million animal deaths annually.

After the Civil War, the impact of market hunting on Western big game increased as fresh meat became a focus of the harvest. Epitomized by WILLIAM F. ("BUFFALO BILL") CODY, market hunters armed with breech-loading and repeating rifles supplied quantities of meat to military posts, railroad construction crews, and hotel patrons in the West. Between 1865 and 1885, thousands of buffaloes, elks, deer, and antelope were harvested each year to feed laborers and epicureans alike. Combined with widespread, unregulated sport hunting in the 1880s and 1890s, market hunting dramatically reduced populations of deer, antelope, and elks across the Great Plains and the eastern slope of the Rockies.

The most destructive episode of market hunting was the "Great Buffalo Hunt," in which the populations of American bisons on the Great Plains fell from an estimated seven or eight million in 1870 to near extinction in little more than a decade. Through the efforts of hide dealers William C. Lobenstein and J. N. DuBois, as well as professional hunter J. Wright Mooar, experiments with tanning buffalo hides for serviceable leather proved successful in Europe and the United States in 1871. Orders for hides flooded Western dealers, creating a year-round occupation for scores, and then hundreds, of hunters, skinners, and freighters. By 1872, the "Great Buffalo Hunt" was in full swing on the plains of Nebraska, Kansas, and Colorado.

Professional buffalo hunters were not sportsmen, but businessmen pursuing profit. Rather than chase buffaloes from horseback, they employed a still-hunting method known as "shooting a stand." Stalking to within one hundred to four hundred yards of a herd, the hunter would shoot the herd leader in the lungs, causing much bleeding from the nostrils. Others in the herd, smelling the blood, tended to mill about in confusion rather than run. The hunter continued shooting at a measured pace until the herd scattered or all the animals were killed. Ensuring the maximum number of kills within the smallest area, the method greatly aided the skinning process that followed.

Using powerful breech-loading rifles, such as the Sharps and Remington single-shot models, the efficacy of this deliberate shooting technique was demonstrated across the plains. Hunting companies, which at a minimum consisted of one hunter, two skinners, and a teamster-cook, might harvest four thousand to five thousand hides in a five-month outing. While figures conflict among sources, it is likely that some 4.5 million buffaloes were killed by hide hunters on the Central and Southern Plains between 1872 and 1878. On the Northern Plains of the Montana and Dakota territories, the hunt began around 1878 and concluded in 1883 with perhaps another 2 million animals destroyed.

In concert with subsistence hunting and robe harvesting by Native Americans and increasing sport hunting among Anglos, the "Great Buffalo Hunt" reduced bison populations to perhaps fewer than three thousand by 1885. The impact of this near extermination was particularly severe on the Plains Indians, since it eliminated their principal source of subsistence and helped force them onto reservations as wards of the government. While the buffalo harvest cleared the way for an expanding range cattle industry, the destruction of a seemingly unlimited natural resource stained America's social, economic, and ecological record for generations.

Sport hunting—the harvesting of game birds and mammals "in fair chase" for recreation (as well as sustenance)—was an American tradition prior to the Civil War. Sport hunters in the West—such as JOHN JAMES AUDUBON, GEORGE CATLIN, GEORGE BIRD GRINNELL, William T. Hornaday, FREDERICK LAW OLMSTED, THEODORE ROOSEVELT, Ernest Thompson Seton, and FREDERICK JACKSON TURNER—were among the first to espouse the conservation of Western game species and habitat. They were particularly opposed to market hunters who depleted natural populations for profit.

Through organizations like the BOONE AND CROCKETT CLUB, founded in 1887 by Roosevelt and Grinnell, responsible sport hunters became the vanguard of wildlife conservation in the West. Their development and funding of wildlife-management policies at the state and federal levels during the early twentieth century ultimately returned depleted game species like deer, antelope, and elks to large and stable populations and ensured that the West remains a bastion of ethical hunting and principled conservation.

—*Richard C. Rattenbury*

SEE ALSO: Métis People; Native American Cultures: Ecology, Subsistence Patterns; Wildlife

SUGGESTED READING:

Baker, T. Lindsay. "Beaver to Buffalo Robes: Transition in the Fur Trade." *The Museum of the Fur Trade Quarterly* 23 (Spring 1987): 1–8; (Summer 1987): 4–13.

Dodge, Richard I. *Hunting Grounds of the Great West.* London, 1877.

Gard, Wayne. *The Great Buffalo Hunt.* New York, 1959.

Kimball, David, and Jim Kimball. *The Market Hunter.* Minneapolis, Minn., 1969.

Wilson, R. L. *Theodore Roosevelt: Outdoorsman.* New York, 1971.

HUNTINGTON, COLLIS P.

One of the "Big Four" financiers of the CENTRAL PACIFIC RAILROAD, Collis P. Huntington (1821–1900) was born in Harwinton, Connecticut. He had little formal schooling and set out to support himself as a traveling salesman in 1837. The gold rush of 1849 took him to California, where he quickly recognized that his fortune lay not in the gold fields but in supplying the needs of those who labored in them. He established a prosperous hardware business in Sacramento. In 1855, he entered into a partnership with MARK HOPKINS, another Sacramento merchant.

Collis P. Huntington. *Courtesy The Bettmann Archive.*

In 1861, the engineer Theodore Dehone Judah approached the partners to seek backing for a transcontinental railroad. Huntington was highly receptive to the idea. Together with two more merchants, Amasa Leland Stanford and Charles Crocker, they managed the construction of the Central Pacific, which joined the Union Pacific Railroad at Promontory Summit in Utah in 1869.

Huntington went on to develop the Southern Pacific Railroad, which eventually absorbed the Central Pacific and became the foundation of a southern transcontinental route. In 1869, he purchased the Chesapeake and Ohio Railway and extended its line to link with the Southern Pacific, thereby creating four thousand miles of track spanning Newport News, Virginia, and San Francisco.

In addition to his career as a builder of railroads, Huntington was a major force in the steamship industry. He invested in important Latin American and East Asian lines. He personally donated large sums of money to the Metropolitan Museum of Art in New York, and his nephew later founded and funded the Huntington Library, Art Collections, and Botanical Gardens in San Marino, just outside Los Angeles.

—*Alan Axelrod*

Suggested reading:

Lewis, Oscar. *The Big Four: The Story of Huntington, Stanford, Hopkins, and Crocker and the Building of the Central Pacific.* New York, 1938.

HUNTINGTON, HENRY EDWARDS

During the first two decades of the twentieth century, Henry Edwards Huntington (1850–1927), urban entrepreneur, railroad executive, and book and art collector, played a key role in the physical configuration, economic expansion, and cultural climate of southern California. His name remains prominent in the Los Angeles basin—Huntington Beach, the Huntington Hotel, and the Huntington Library—but his significance as the region's de facto regional planner is often overlooked.

Born in Oneonta, New York, Huntington was educated in public and private schools. At the age of seventeen, he went to work in a local hardware store. In 1871, his uncle, railway magnate Collis P. Huntington, employed the young man to manage a sawmill, and thus began their close, thirty-year business association. Huntington moved rapidly through a number of positions in his uncle's various railway enterprises and became a highly skilled railroad manager. When blocked by stockholders from following his deceased uncle as president of the Southern Pacific Railroad in 1900, Huntington used his experience and vast inheritance to create his own business empire in southern California.

Undoubtedly, Huntington's close ties to his uncle were instrumental in his business career, but they were also important in shaping his personal life. In 1873, he married Mary Alice Prentice, the sister of his uncle's adopted daughter, and the couple had four children. Divorced in 1906, he married his uncle's widow, Arabella Duval Huntington, in 1913.

Once in Los Angeles, Huntington invested large amounts of his personal fortune into three related businesses important for urban growth: street railways, real-estate development, and electric-power generation and distribution. With these three companies, Huntington dominated regional development. His street railways (the Los Angeles Railway and the Pacific Electric) held a near monopoly over the basin's public transportation; by 1910, Huntington trolley systems stretched over nearly thirteen hundred miles of southern California. His real-estate holdings, largely concentrated in the northeastern portion of Los Angeles County, made him one of the area's largest landowners. And by 1913, his Pacific Light and Power Company, besides providing electricity to his streetcars, supplied 20 percent of the power needs in the city of Los Angeles.

Because Huntington operated at a time when local planning commissions had little regulatory power, he acted, in effect, as the area's metropolitan planner. By building trolley lines where and when he wanted, he determined the physical layout of the area. Then, as a large-scale subdivider, he dictated the socio-economic mix of many suburbs.

Huntington further encouraged development in southern California through his involvement in local agriculture, industry, the hotel business, and many leading social and civic groups. To enrich and foster the region's intellectual and cultural life, he established the now famous HUNTINGTON LIBRARY, ART COLLECTIONS, AND BOTANICAL GARDENS in San Marino, a wealthy suburb northeast of downtown Los Angeles.

—*William B. Friedricks*

SUGGESTED READING:

Crump, Spencer. *Ride the Big Red Cars: How the Trolleys Helped Build Southern California.* Los Angeles, 1962.

Friedricks, William B. *Henry E. Huntington and the Creation of Southern California.* Columbus, Ohio, 1992.

Pomfret, John E. *The Henry E. Huntington Library and Art Gallery from Its Beginnings to 1969.* San Marino, Calif., 1969.

Post, Robert C. *Street Railways and the Growth of Los Angeles.* Glendale, Calif., 1989.

Thorpe, James. *Henry Edwards Huntington: A Biography.* Berkeley, Calif., 1994.

HUNTINGTON LIBRARY, ART COLLECTIONS, AND BOTANICAL GARDENS

Henry Edwards Huntington (1850–1927), nephew and long-time business associate of COLLIS P. HUNTINGTON (one of the founders of the Central Pacific Railroad), had built a great fortune through successful ventures in California real estate and transportation. In his later years, however, he devoted most of his time and much of his fortune to accumulating books, manuscripts, and works of art to document the story of British and American history and literature. He opened the Henry E. Huntington Library and Art Gallery on August 30, 1919. Given the nature of Huntington's career and his unshakable belief in the potential of southern California, it comes as no surprise that materials about California and the Far West occupied a prominent place in his burgeoning library.

Building upon the founder's impressive acquisitions, subsequent generations of librarians assembled an exceptional collection of materials documenting the exploration, settlement, and development of the transMississippi West in the nineteenth and twentieth centuries. Currently, the library's holdings incorporate original editions of most essential printed works about the region as well as several hundred manuscript collections on the California gold rush and the transcontinental migration, the critical role of transportation and of extractive industries such as mining in the region's evolution, the creation of the Mormon Zion in the West, and the history of California from the Spanish era through the 1990s. Similarly rich collections of visual images include significant bodies of work by Western photographers from Carleton Watkins to Edward Weston as well as artists working in other media such as GEORGE CATLIN and the gold-rush immigrant J. Goldsborough Bruff.

The research library attracted the attention of Western historians from its earliest years, when Max Farrand, the first director, induced FREDERICK JACKSON TURNER to accept a position as a senior research associate in 1927. Since then, hundreds of Western historians have relied upon the Huntington's great collections

Henry Edwards Huntington. *Courtesy The Bettmann Archive.*

to pursue their investigations, with the support and encouragement of other leaders in the field such as Robert Glass Cleland, RAY ALLEN BILLINGTON, and Martin Ridge, who have followed Turner as senior research associates.

—*Peter J. Blodgett*

SUGGESTED READING:
Pomfret, John E. *The Henry E. Huntington Library and Art Gallery from Its Beginnings to 1969.* San Marino, Calif., 1969.
Spurgeon, Selena A. *Henry Edwards Huntington: His Life and His Collection.* San Marino, Calif., 1992.
Thorpe, James. *Henry Edwards Huntington: A Biography.* Berkeley, Calif., 1994.
———, et al. *The Founding of the Henry E. Huntington Library and Art Gallery.* San Marino, Calif., 1969.

HUPA INDIANS

SEE: Native American Peoples: Peoples of California, Peoples of the Pacific Northwest

HUSKIES

SEE: Alaskan Huskies

HUTTON, MAY ARKWRIGHT

May Arkwright Hutton (1860–1915), suffragist, political activist, and philanthropist, was born in Ohio. During the 1883 gold rush, she immigrated to Wardner in the Idaho Territory where she operated a restaurant. In 1887, she married train engineer Levi W. (Al) Hutton.

The Huttons played starring roles in the infamous Coeur d'Alene Mining War of 1899, one of the most notorious incidents of labor violence in Western history. On April 29, union miners commandeered a Northern Pacific train and forced engineer Al Hutton at gunpoint to take them to Kellogg, where a dynamite explosion destroyed the Bunker Hill and Sullivan Company ore concentrator valued at $250,000. Governor FRANK STEUNENBERG declared martial law, and federal troops rounded up alleged unionists, including Al Hutton, and incarcerated them in makeshift jails known as "bull-pens." In response, May Arkwright Hutton wrote a probably libelous fictional account of the entire incident. Entitled *The Couer d'Alenes or a Tale of the Modern Inquisition* (1900), the book is a diatribe against mine owners and their political allies.

In 1901, the Huttons' own economic position changed radically, when their investment of $880 in the Hercules mining claim near Wallace made them partners in one of Idaho's richest strikes. The Huttons became millionaires. May Arkwright Hutton's imposing frame (well over two hundred pounds), her penchant for outrageous dress, and her colorful speech made her one of the Pacific Northwest's best-known women.

May Arkwright Hutton played a prominent role in the successful campaign for Idaho WOMEN'S SUFFRAGE in 1896. When the couple moved to Spokane, Washington, in 1906, she again enlisted in a state suffrage effort. She served as vice-president of the Washington Equal Suffrage Association and was instrumental in the success of the 1910 campaign for women's suffrage in Washington.

In 1912, Hutton was elected the first woman delegate to a national Democratic convention. Her statement that she wished to be referred to as "May Arkwright Hutton," not "Mrs. Hutton," attracted considerable attention from the press in Baltimore.

May Arkwright Hutton's philanthropic activities included work for the Spokane Florence Crittenton Home; she advocated jail reform, vocational education for women, the establishment of day-care facilities, and the women's peace movement. In 1985, she was inducted into the Washington State Hall of Fame.

—*Katherine G. Aiken*

SUGGESTED READING:
Horner, Patricia Voeller. "May Arkwright Hutton: Suffragist and Politician." In *Women in Pacific Northwest History: An Anthology.* Edited by Karen Blair. Seattle, Wash., 1988.
Montgomery, James. *Liberated Woman: A Life of May Arkwright Hutton.* Fairfield, Wash., 1985.
Schwantes, Carlos A. "The World of May Arkwright Hutton." In *The Pacific Northwest: An Interpretive History.* Lincoln, Nebr., 1989.

HYDE, ORSON

Mormon Leader Orson Hyde (1805–1878) was born in Connecticut and settled as an adult in Kirtland, Ohio. He was associated with SIDNEY RIGDON as a pastor in the Campbellite faith and then embraced Mormonism in October 1831. After serving several Mormon missions in the East, he joined Zion's Camp in 1833 and marched with other MORMONS to Missouri. There, he and Parley Pratt appealed to Governor David Dunkin to intercede on behalf of Mormons who were being persecuted by Missourians. Hyde was chosen as one of the original Twelve Apostles in 1835. After serving other local missions, he helped open the British mission. He returned with his wife Marinda and settled at the Mormon center in NAUVOO, ILLINOIS.

In April 1840, Hyde was sent to Palestine. Traveling alone by way of Turkey and Egypt, he dedicated that land for the gathering of the scattered descendants of Judah on October 24, 1841. After the death of JOSEPH SMITH, JR., and the expulsion of the Latter-day Saints from Nauvoo, Hyde joined the dispersed church members on the plains of Iowa. When church members moved to the Great Basin, he took charge of the church near the Missouri River. From 1847 to 1851, he published the *Frontier Guardian* at Kanesville, one of the first newspapers in the region.

After Hyde moved to Utah, church leaders gave him responsibility for founding a permanent settlement in Carson Valley in present-day Nevada in 1855. He returned to Salt Lake City within a year, however.

Around 1860, Hyde moved to Sanpete County where he lived for the rest of his life. He represented the region as an effective territorial legislator and was one of the primary movers who initiated the construction of the Manti Temple.

—Leo Lyman

SEE ALSO: Campbellites; Church of Jesus Christ of Latter-day Saints

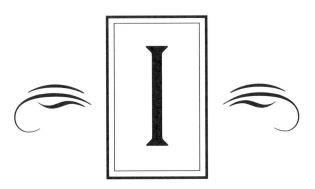

I.C.C.

SEE: Interstate Commerce Act of 1887

ICKES, HAROLD L.

Under the stewardship of Harold L. Ickes (1874–1952), secretary of the interior from 1933 to 1947, the face of the American West was transformed by RECLAMATION projects and massive hydroelectric dams. New national parks, monuments, wilderness areas, WILDLIFE refuges, and public-works projects of all sorts are part of his legacy.

Harold L. Ickes, in 1936. *Courtesy National Park Service.*

Ickes spent most of his life as an urban progressive in Chicago. As a young man, he had admired the natural-resource conservation programs of THEODORE ROOSEVELT and his Chief Forester GIFFORD PINCHOT. When Ickes was nearly sixty years old, President Franklin Roosevelt appointed him to the cabinet. Ickes entered public office determined to expand policies of wise use of resources and the protection of public lands, but the Department of the Interior he inherited had been rocked by years of scandal, and the country was in the midst of the Great Depression. During the New Deal period, Ickes worked to bring order to the OIL AND GAS INDUSTRY and to control the ravaging of the nation's timber, mineral, and grazing lands. As administrator of the Public Works Administration, he championed the construction of large public-works projects, particularly for the development of hydroelectric power and reclamation in the West. A believer in the value of regional planning for watersheds and resources, Ickes also advocated wilderness preservation and the creation of vast national parks delimited by ecological boundaries.

A man of enormous energy and personal integrity, Ickes trusted few others. Difficult, suspicious, and easily offended, he served Roosevelt with skill and dedication.

Throughout his tenure, Ickes urged Roosevelt to create a Department of Conservation by transferring the UNITED STATES FOREST SERVICE from the Department of Agriculture to the Department of the Interior. Although Ickes was able to create the new Fish and Wildlife Service, Roosevelt refused to support Ickes's departmental reorganization.

During World War II, Ickes administered the nation's petroleum reserves for defense and established policies for American access to oil fields in the Middle East. When Roosevelt died in 1945, Ickes remained uncomfortably in HARRY S TRUMAN's cabinet. Suspicious of private interests who wanted to develop the nation's protected lands and natural resources, he resigned in 1947, when Truman appointed an oilman as undersecretary of the navy. A liberal in civil rights, he was the first cabinet officer to integrate his departmental cafeteria. He arranged black soprano Marian Anderson's free public concert at the Lincoln Memorial and supported expanded rights for Native Americans.

A transitional figure between the conservation and environmental movements, Harold Ickes's vigilance left the nation richer than he found it.

—*Linda J. Lear*

SUGGESTED READING:

Lear, Linda J. *The Aggressive Progressive: The Early Career of Harold L. Ickes, 1874–1952*. New York, 1981.

Strong, Douglas. "Harold Ickes." In *Dreamers and Defenders*. Lincoln, Nebr., 1988.

Watkins, T. H. *Righteous Pilgrim: The Life and Times of Harold L. Ickes*. New York, 1990.

IDAHO

Idaho, the "Gem State," became the forty-fifth state in the Union in 1890. During the Civil War, Congress geographically carved Idaho out of the territories of Oregon and Washington. As originally organized and named in 1863, the territory surpassed Texas in size, but in 1869, Wyoming and Montana were created from its eastern side. What remained is a geographical entity whose boundaries resemble a side view of a rustic hand-carved church pew.

Idaho's southern boundary is more than three hundred miles long and follows the forty-second parallel, the line that separated American and English claims to the Rocky Mountains. After crossing the entire state from east to west, the SNAKE RIVER veers northward. At that point, the map-makers drew a line straight south to intersect the forty-second parallel and form the southwestern corner of the state. The Snake travels northward for approximately 200 miles through the spectacular Hells Canyon and then moves westward toward the Columbia. Where the Snake veers westward, a line was drawn north to Canada. Although national and international boundaries explain the creation of the state's northern, southern, and western borders, the eastern boundary is almost inexplicable. What exists is an 800-mile-long line that begins with an extension of the Utah border northward to the Con-

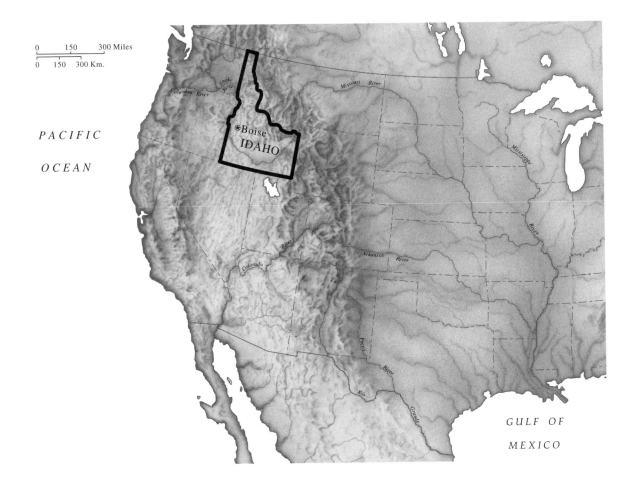

tinental Divide inside YELLOWSTONE NATIONAL PARK. The boundary follows the Continental Divide westward for nearly 200 miles and then moves northwest along the west side of the Bitterroot Range. One hundred miles from Canada, the line is drawn straight north. This narrow northernmost section sandwiched between Washington and Montana is the Idaho Panhandle.

Inside these borders are 83,557 square miles of land and more than one million people. Idaho ranks thirteenth among the states in land size but is fortieth in population.

Geographical features

Perhaps the single-most unifying geographical feature of Idaho is the roaring Snake River. Referred to as the "River of the Sagebrush Plain" by the Shoshones, the river has its source in the mountains of Yellowstone National Park. From the southern part of Yellowstone, it flows through the trappers' paradise of Jackson Hole and then west into Idaho. The river follows an inverted arc across the state to Oregon and then turns north through Hells Canyon—Idaho is to the east and Oregon and Washington are to the west. At Lewiston, it joins the Clearwater and swings west for 140 miles toward a confluence with the mighty Columbia River. In length, volume of water carried, and area drained, the Snake ranks sixth among the rivers of America. In more specific terms, it is 1,036 miles long and drains 109,000 square miles of country, an area larger than the entire state of Idaho. This gigantic stream drains the mountain run-off from all of Idaho except the Bear River valley in the southeastern corner of the state and the lake-dominated Panhandle. By the time the Snake reaches the Columbia, it has increased its volume from four to forty million acre-feet of water and has dropped more than 7,000 feet in elevation.

The Snake River was never viewed as a friendly stream by westward-moving pioneers. It was difficult to cross, and the canyons in many areas are so deep that water, although near, was inaccessible. The Snake flows through mountain gorges and lava beds and has a number of sizable waterfalls, including the spectacular Shoshone Falls, which at 212 feet is higher than Niagara Falls. The appropriately named Hells Canyon of the Snake River cuts a gorge deeper than any other in the United States. In some places, the canyon reaches a depth of 7,900 feet. It is also one of the more narrow canyons on the continent. In many parts of the canyon are green forests, but at other points are sheer walls splashed by the seasonal color of mountain shrubbery. When the Oregon-bound pioneers viewed the impassable canyon, they left the Snake and headed west across Oregon's Blue Mountains toward Willamette Valley.

Idaho's Snake River binds the state and provides irrigation and hydroelectric power for farms that line its banks. *Courtesy Idaho State Historical Society.*

To the extent that Idaho is tied together, it is the Snake River and its valley that provide cohesion. The state's five major cities are located on the Snake or its tributaries, and this one river system provides the irrigation water and hydroelectric power to ensure agricultural prosperity, domestic water supplies, and a degree of industrialization. Without the harnessing of the Snake's water, Idaho would still be a mountain and desert wilderness. The Snake is dammed at eleven places in Idaho alone, and most of its tributaries contain at least one major reservoir. The Boise River system has five dams, and several others have nearly as many. It is the diverted water that furnished the means of agricultural survival for the Euro-Americans who settled in the Snake River valley.

Idaho's mountainous terrain provides one explanation for the abundance of water. The average elevation of Idaho is more than 5,000 feet above sea level. Only four states are higher. Wildlife and minerals are found throughout the mountains, and these two resources led to European discovery, exploration, and organization of the area.

Central Idaho's mountains have yet to feel the full imprint of four-wheel-drive vehicles. The Sawtooth Mountains are distinct for beautiful high granite crags, wooded slopes, and well-watered miniature valleys and meadows. The White Clouds, Boulder Mountains, and Sawtooth Range all have many peaks above the 10,000-foot level, and these mountains are the habitat of numerous big-game animals.

The highest range in Idaho is the unique and mysterious Lost River Range, which runs in a northwestern-southeastern direction for 80 miles through central

Idaho. On each side of the range is a long, narrow valley with a sizable stream of water. In both cases, the Big and Little Lost rivers sink into lava beds southeast of the mountain range. The entire crest of the Lost River Range is in excess of 10,000 feet, except for a few passes. Idaho's three highest peaks, all higher than 12,000 feet, are found in this range, including Mount Borah, which at 12,662 feet is the highest point in Idaho. With a skyline so majestic and with the thick, green forests in contrast to the snowcapped peaks, the Lost River Range is a grand world of its own.

Agriculture

Agricultural products are the state's greatest source of wealth and attest to the success of IRRIGATION as a means to create productivity. The Snake River's state-wide valley system is where most of Idaho's farmers reside. Although Idaho potatoes have received considerable fame and publicity and a spot on license plates, Idaho has other noteworthy crops. Sugar beets, peas, and beans are grown throughout the southern part of

Although best known for its potatoes, Idaho also produces sugar beets, peas, beans, and wheat, corn, barley, and oats. *Courtesy Idaho State Historical Society.*

the state as well as in the Panhandle. Grains such as wheat, barley, corn, and oats all survive in Idaho's arid climate. Of course, the beef, dairy, and sheep industries operate throughout the state and are especially strong along the Snake River. In fact, beef and sheep ranchers use the vast public lands of Idaho for controlled grazing during the summer months. In the Snake River valley northwest of Boise and near Lewiston are numerous fruit orchards.

Mineral production

Idaho is the nation's leading silver-producing state, and Shoshone County in the Panhandle is the source of most of the silver. Many of the mines have been producing for nearly a century, and although miners have dug millions of dollars worth of silver out of them, tragic mine disasters and ecological devastation have created mixed emotions in Idaho's citizens. In part because of the type of ore found in northern Idaho, lead-silver or lead-silver-zinc ore is mined in the same operations. Idaho is the second leading lead producer in the nation. The silver-lead-zinc operations continue to bring some prosperity to northern Idaho.

Southeastern Idaho extracts considerable wealth from the mountains in the form of phosphate rock and its by-products, elemental phosphorous and vanadium. This industry has boomed since World War II, and the material is used mainly for the production of agricultural fertilizers. Idaho ranks second to Florida in phosphate production yet seemingly has unending reserves. In the phosphate trade-off between man and the mountains, however, the mountains are the losers. Much of the mining has been of the strip variety, and the small ranges of southeastern Idaho have felt the wrath of the bulldozer and "carryall." Severe air pollution has been a constant problem with the processing plants, and in some cases, the effect of pollution on adjacent properties has been disastrous.

In 1990, Idaho ranked thirty-sixth nationally in wealth provided by minerals. Periodically, mining engineers and modern prospectors seek to exploit the wild and primitive mountains of central Idaho. As more Idahoans redefine progress in noneconomic terms, it is likely that any new exploitation will adhere to strict environmentalist standards—a welcome development in preserving Idaho's heritage.

Lumber industry

If for no other reason than that trees can be replaced, the timber industry will probably continue to fare much better than mining. Currently, only four states produce more saw-timber than Idaho. The state was fortunate that massive exploitation of timber did not take place until a national conservation conscience

Main Street in Boise, Idaho, during a 1910 parade. *Courtesy Idaho State Historical Society.*

had developed. Of course, the mountains have aided in the preservation of a timber supply. In other areas of the United States, timber was cleared in order to till the land. That has rarely been the case in Idaho because most of the virgin stands are located in areas that are poorly suited to agriculture.

Multiple use has been the key management practice in Idaho's vast forests. During the Progressive period, Idahoans began thinking in terms of conservation and reforestation. While the state's timber industry is concerned chiefly with harvesting timber and perpetuating the supply, it also has had to cooperate with wildlife, recreation, and mining interests. Timber continues to provide the number one source of manufacturing income, and forest products are second only to AGRICULTURE in the entire state.

The FEDERAL GOVERNMENT owns 63.7 percent of all Idaho land. Only three other states—Alaska, Utah, and Nevada—have higher percentages of federal ownership. At times, contemporary Idahoans are irritated when they realize that Idaho is an economic colony of the federal government, with less than 40 percent of Idaho's land in private hands. Most of the nearly thirty-four million acres of federal property is national for-

est, but the BUREAU OF LAND MANAGEMENT, the Atomic Energy Commission, and the BUREAU OF INDIAN AFFAIRS control millions of acres.

Idaho's people

The bulging *L*-shaped state is largely uninhabited, and because of geography, Idaho is only now developing a statewide identity. Idaho has looked in three different directions for economic prosperity, media contact, and cultural compatibility, and there have been at least three Idahos: one in the Panhandle, one in the southeastern part of the state, and one in the southwest around Boise. The Panhandle is geographically isolated from the remainder of the state. With their mining and lumber orientation, the people of the Panhandle have looked to Spokane, Washington, as the center of their world.

Southeastern Idaho was almost completely settled by MORMONS moving north from Utah. The area from the Wyoming border westward to the Idaho Falls and south to the Utah line is an extension of the Mormon empire. It also reaches into the Magic Valley east of Twin Falls. Only Pocatello, a railroad, manufacturing, and university city, seems to break out of the cultural

In 1939, Dorothea Lange photographed the Unruf family on their farm in Boundary County, Idaho, for the Farm Security Administration. *Courtesy Idaho State Historical Society.*

pull of Salt Lake City, the Mecca of the Rocky Mountains. The CHURCH OF JESUS CHRIST OF LATTER-DAY SAINTS is the largest religious group in Idaho, and its adherents look to Salt Lake City for media, theological, economic, and, at times, political guidance.

For Boise, the state capital, it is a challenge to put together the elements of this divergent and divided state. While the rest of Idaho has grown very slowly, Boise is becoming a city of magnitude and force. Southwestern Idaho has maintained strong allegiances to the state capital.

Idaho's population reflects the mobility of the American people. The state imports more people from nearby states than it exports. More than thirty-two thousand residents of Utah were born in Idaho, but forty thousand Idahoans trace their birthplace to Utah. It is true that many Idahoans departed for the Promised Land of California at various times, but in the mid-1990s approximately 10 percent of Idaho's people were born in California. Idaho's lower taxes, spaciousness, and beautiful scenery make it an attractive oasis for urbanites. Slightly more than half of its residents were born in the "Gem State."

In Idaho, there were two major Indian groups, the Nez Percés in the north and the Shoshones in the south. In addition, Kootenai and Coeur d'Alene Indians lived around Idaho's Panhandle, and Northern Paiutes roamed through southwestern Idaho. Some Paiutes, called Bannocks, lived with the Shoshones in southeastern Idaho. Other Shoshone bands, Lemhis and Sheepeaters, lived in central Idaho and are important to Idaho's history. These culturally and linguistically divergent groups compose the historical and current Indians of Idaho.

Most of Idaho's seven thousand Indians reside on five reservations and in adjacent communities. Rarely, if ever, has the population of Native Americans in Idaho exceeded that number. In the 1990s, the Indian population composed less than 1 percent of the total population. While the Indians' imprint on Idaho was permanent and positive, eventually the new materialistic, exploitative Euro-American culture they confronted overwhelmed them.

Idaho was a gathering area for one special immigrant group, the Spanish Basques, who initially worked as herdsmen. Special immigration laws were passed to allow Basque herdsmen to migrate in order to maintain a needed labor supply. They quickly purchased land of their own or entered other occupations. Today, conscious of their heritage, second- and third-generation Idaho Basques have maintained a folk culture, which is exhibited at highly popular annual festivals.

Numerous Asian Americans also immigrated to Idaho. The CHINESE AMERICANS worked in the state's mines during the nineteenth century and influenced the development of Boise. Thousands of Chinese and Japanese were recruited to work on railroad construction. JAPANESE AMERICAN farmers migrated throughout the various high valleys and successfully tilled the land. The sugar-beet industry depended heavily on Japanese labor. Idaho's Minidoka County became home for a Japanese relocation center during World War II. Many young relatives of Idaho Japanese Americans came into the state to avoid the relocation camps. After the Vietnam War concluded, more than one thousand Southeast Asians found their way into Idaho.

The numbers of African Americans and Hispanic Americans in Idaho have remained small until recently. Black Americans were involved in trapping, settling, and railroad building and were enlisted in cavalry units in Idaho in the late nineteenth century. Hispanics are the state's largest minority, and as agricultural laborers, they have made a significant but often unappreciated impact. The food-processing industry, orchards, and row crops provide permanent employment for many of Idaho's Hispanic Americans.

Idaho's lack of ethnic diversity has led some individuals to view the state as "racially pure." Consequently, the Aryan Nations moved their headquarters into Idaho's Panhandle. Many Idahoans oppose the survivalists because they do not want their state viewed as a bastion of racism.

In its early days, political and labor radicalism flourished in Idaho. The Populist party received Idaho's first electoral votes in 1892, and the WESTERN FEDERATION OF MINERS (WFM) organized numerous strikes in Idaho mines. Violent confrontations occurred, and a former governor, FRANK STEUNENBERG, was murdered. In a celebrated case, union leaders were extradited to Idaho to stand trial for the murder. Clarence Darrow defended the WFM leaders, and WILLIAM E. BORAH led the prosecution. Although acquitted, the union leaders were discredited and thereafter sought more conventional political avenues to achieve their goals.

Idaho's political history is unique and somewhat paradoxical. The party affiliation of politicians is less important to Idahoans than staying in touch with the state and its interests. This is illustrated by the careers of numerous Idaho senators. William E. Borah, a Progressive Republican, served nearly six terms in the Senate. An international isolationist, he fought to keep the United States out of the League of Nations and other treaty commitments. He also doggedly pursued domestic Progressive reform measures that created a better life for his constituents. Democratic Senator FRANK CHURCH served four terms (1957 to 1981) in the midst of the Cold War. An opponent of the Vietnam War, he also was an avowed environmentalist who fought hard to defend mountains, streams, and lakes from exploitation.

Idaho is engulfed in a vigorous conservationist debate over wildlife, wilderness management, and WATER use. When the huge Mountain Home Reclamation Project was proposed in the late 1960s, conservationists touted the considerable damage to fish, wildlife, and especially, golden eagles and prairie falcons in their opposition to the project. Mountain sheep, ELKS, MOOSE, and steelheads—all are of concern to the educated environmentalist. Every proposed irrigation or hydroelectric project undergoes close scrutiny, and pork-barrel projects designed to bring prosperity to a locale rather than to provide an absolutely necessary dam may be a thing of the past. Rabid conservationists claim that the last two major projects on the Snake River system—the Dworshak on the North Fork of the Clearwater River and the Teton on the Teton River—were both based on pork-barrel politics rather than on agricultural or power needs. (The ill-fated Teton Dam broke on June 5, 1976, and flooded the entire valley.) Of course, other interest groups disagree vehemently, and thus the debate continues. Idaho's experience indicates that in this remote state, the battle among governmental bureaucracies, corporate interests, and environmentalists will be fought on more even terms than seemed possible before.

In many respects, Idaho is still a frontier, but one that decries the invasion of its privacy. Contemporary Idaho's most significant role in the future might be that of an example to the rest of the United States of how growth, exploitation, and use may be held in check. Important national conservation battles will be fought over Idaho wilderness, and every American has a vested interest in the outcome of these confrontations. The grave national issues—resource use, population growth, food production, industrialization, and energy consumption—are reflected in the mountains, streams, lakes, and people of Idaho.

Remote and isolated, Idaho has never been victimized by the mainstream onslaught of civilization. The rugged desert and mountain terrain made settlement, transportation, and communication difficult. After nearly two centuries of recorded history, it is clear that Idaho retains some simple individualistic, political characteristics and some complex cooperative economic tendencies. Obviously—and this fact compounds the issues, since most of Idaho is federally owned—there is still a great demand on the part of Idahoans for federal cooperation in the multiple use of land. The degree of use is the crux of the controversy.

—*F. Ross Peterson*

SEE ALSO: Farming; Japanese Internment; Lead Mining; Lumber Industry; Multiple-Use Doctrine; Populism, Progressivism; Reclamation; Sheep Ranching; Silver Mining

SUGGESTED READING:

Arrington, Leonard. *History of Idaho*. 2 vols. Moscow, Idaho, 1994.

Beal, Merrill D., and Merle W. Wells. *History of Idaho*. 3 vols. New York, 1959.

Peterson, F. Ross. *Idaho: A Bicentennial History*. New York, 1976.

Schwantes, Carlos A. *In Mountain Shadows: A History of Idaho*. Lincoln, Nebr., 1991.

Shallat, Todd. *Snake: The Plain and Its People*. Boise, Idaho, 1994.

ILFELD, CHARLES

The founder of the largest wholesale merchandise business in New Mexico, Charles Ilfeld (1847–1929) immigrated to New York from Hamburg, Germany, at the age of eighteen. He left for New Mexico almost immediately after landing and worked for Adolph Letcher in Taos as a clerk in a new company, A. Letcher and Company, formed to purchase grain for the surrounding military posts. When the company moved to Las Vegas, New Mexico, Ilfeld became a partner, and after his marriage to Adele Nordhaus in 1874, he bought out his partner and began to expand his wholesale operations.

In 1883, Ilfeld brought his wife's younger brother, Max Nordhaus, from Germany to serve as an apprentice, and four years later, Nordhaus and Ilfeld became partners. When the railroad came to New Mexico, Ilfeld and Nordhaus concentrated on sheep and wool, financed inventories of country stores, and extended them credit. The company assumed aspects of commercial banking—accepting deposits, paying interest, and introducing a check-writing system. Country stores established in El Monton de Alamos, Tecolate, La Junta, and Springer in the 1870s had disappointing financial returns, but by the 1890s, Ilfeld and Nordhaus controlled successful stores at Puerto de Luna, Liberty, and Tucumcari and directly invested in stores at

Fort Sumner, Pastura, and Corona. In the twentieth century, Ilfeld's warehouses and country stores blanketed New Mexico.

Throughout his career, Ilfeld, a Jewish American, enjoyed tremendous respect from the Anglo community and the Spanish dons of New Mexico. He served as postmaster in Tiptonville after 1876. He was a member of the board of regents of the Normal School in Las Vegas, and when his wife died, he gave the campus a building and auditorium in her name.

—*W. Turrentine Jackson*

SEE ALSO: Jewish Americans

SUGGESTED READING:

Parish, William J. *The Charles Ilfeld Company*. Cambridge, Mass., 1961.

———. "The German Jew and the Commercial Revolution in Territorial New Mexico, 1850–1900." *New Mexico Quarterly* 29 (1959): 307–332.

Tobias, Henry J. *A History of the Jews in New Mexico*. Albuquerque, N. Mex., 1900.

ILIFF, JOHN WESLEY

The first cattle king of the Northern Plains, John Wesley Iliff (1831–1878) was born in McLuney, Ohio. As a young man, he turned down his father's offer to buy him a farm and instead asked for money to go west. He moved to Kansas in 1857 and helped organize the Ohio City Town Company south of present-day Ottawa, Kansas. Not quite two years later, he joined gold-seekers and traveled to Cherry Creek (now Denver), Colorado. He took with him a stock of goods and engaged in business until 1861. He then used his profits to enter cattle ranching. His brand was the reversed *L. F.*

In 1868, he purchased a herd of cattle in New Mexico from CHARLES GOODNIGHT, who drove them to Iliff's ranch headquarters in northeastern Colorado. Iliff then took the herd to Cheyenne and sold the beef for five cents a pound. By then, he was buying land on which his cattle grazed. During the early 1870s, he made his home in Cheyenne, but in 1874, he moved back to Denver, where he died unexpectedly. At the time of his death, he owned more than one-half million acres of good grazing land stretching from Denver to Julesburg, Colorado. In Iliff's memory, his widow endowed the Methodist Iliff School of Theology at the University of Denver. Iliff, Colorado, is also named for him.

—*David Dary*

SEE ALSO: Cattle Industry

SUGGESTED READING:

Haley, J. Evetts, *Charles Goodnight: Cowman and Plainsman*. Boston, 1936.

Milligan, Edward W. "John Wesley Iliff." In *Brand Book*. Vol. 6. Edited by Denver Westerners. Denver, Colo., 1950.

IMMIGRANT GUIDEBOOKS

SEE: Emigrant Guidebooks

IMMIGRANTS AND IMMIGRATION

SEE: Alien Land Laws; Americanization Programs; Asiatic Exclusion League; *Bhagat Sing Thind, In Re*; Chinatowns; Chinese Americans; Chinese Exclusion; Chinese Wars; Compulsory School Law, Oregon (1922); Domestic Service; East Indians; Foreign Miners' Tax of 1850; Geary Act of 1892; Gentlemen's Agreement; German Americans; Immigration Law; Intermarriage; Irish Americans; Italian Americans; Japanese Americans; Japanese Internment; Jewish Americans; Language Schools; Mexican Immigration, 1900–1935; Mexican Settlement; Migrant Workers; Naturalization Law of 1790; *Ozawa v. United States*; Page Law of 1875; Picture Brides; Presbyterian Woman's Board of Home Missions; Protestant Home Missionary Programs; *Rodriquez, In Re*; Safety-Valve Theory; San Francisco: City of Immigrants; Woman's Home Missionary Society; *Wong Kim Ark v. United States*; *Yick Wo v. Hopkins*; Violence: Racial Violence

IMMIGRATION LAW

Immigration Law before 1900
  Lawrence B. de Graaf

Immigration Law after 1900
  Juan R. García

IMMIGRATION LAW BEFORE 1900

United States immigration laws restrict the people allowed to enter the country. In much of the nineteenth century, the United States did not have restrictive laws, and the development of the West was enhanced by immigrants from all over the world. The United States and especially its Western states and territories were interested in attracting people from other nations, not excluding them.

In welcoming foreigners, the West followed well-established traditions. Several colonies had used indentures, headrights, and advertisements to attract settlers. The U.S. Constitution was generous in allowing the foreign-born political rights; only the presidency was closed to individuals not born in the United States. The NORTHWEST ORDINANCE of 1785, which established a national land policy, put no restrictions of birth or citizenship on buyers of land, and the NATURALIZATION LAW OF 1790 allowed "free white" aliens to become citizens after residing in the United States for two years. Such openness to immigrants fit the emerging ideal of America as a haven for the oppressed of Europe.

The federal government honored this ideal by inaction. No immigration laws were passed until 1819 and then only to guarantee ship passengers healthy conditions. Regulation of immigrants was left up to the states on the Atlantic Coast. They inspected immigrants for illness and charged ships a tax on passengers to cover costs, but they made no effort to restrict whole groups or nationalities.

Most Western states used laws to attract immigrants and appointed agents to advertise their opportunities. By the 1860s and 1870s, thirty-three states and territories had such agencies, and several sent representatives to Europe. Private parties, especially railroad companies (which had land to sell), also promoted the West. Congress set up a Bureau of Immigration during the Civil War to advertise for immigrants and, in 1874, considered offering Mennonites from Russia their own tract of Western land.

The United States's earliest efforts to restrict immigration were aimed at the Chinese, who had arrived in California's gold rush and had encountered hostility. Chinese—and Mexicans and other Latin Americans—were discouraged from mining by the FOREIGN MINER'S TAX OF 1850, and cities tried to pass special taxes exclusively on them and their businesses, often on the grounds that they were aliens ineligible for citizenship. During the recession in the late 1860s, American citizens agitated for restrictions on Chinese employment and immigration. Chinese employment was covered in the California Constitution of 1879; attempts to restrict Chinese immigration were blocked by the Burlingame Treaty guaranteeing the Chinese the right to enter and leave the United States.

The earliest federal restriction on immigration was the PAGE LAW OF 1875, which barred Asian contract laborers and prostitutes. After the Burlingame Treaty was renegotiated, the United States passed the Chinese Exclusion Act (1882), which suspended the entry of Chinese laborers for ten years. This act was followed by stiffening regulations culminating in the Scott Act (1888), which forbade Chinese laborers from re-entering the United States; the GEARY ACT OF 1892, which extended the exclusion ten more years; and an Act of 1902, which made the ban indefinite except for merchants, students, and travelers.

By the 1880s, many Americans began to rethink the ideal of unlimited immigration. The federal government took charge of immigration in an 1882 act that also expanded the categories of people (for example, convicts and lunatics) who were barred from entry. The Foran Act of 1885 banned contract laborers. The 1892 Immigration Act further expanded the classes barred from immigrating to the United States and compelled shipping companies to take back people denied entry. These laws forecast more severe restriction to come in the early twentieth century.

Some immigrants still found the West wide open, particularly Mexicans. No laws were passed to restrict Mexicans; there were no border stations until 1894. If a passing West of limitless land no longer welcomed all foreigners, an emerging West of railroad building, mining companies, and agribusiness would resist laws to restrict some immigrants well into the twentieth century.

—*Lawrence B. de Graaf*

SEE ALSO: Chinese Exclusion

SUGGESTED READING:

Archdeacon, Thomas J. *Becoming American: An Ethnic History.* New York, 1983.

Corwin, Arthur F., ed. *Immigrants—and Immigrants: Perspectives on Mexican Labor Migration to the United States.* Westport, Conn., 1978.

Stephan Thernstrom, Ann Orlov, and Oscar Handlin, eds. *Harvard Encyclopedia of American Ethnic Groups.* Cambridge, Mass., 1980.

Higham, John. *Strangers in the Land: Patterns of American Nativism, 1860–1925.* 2d ed. New Brunswick, N.J., 1988.

Hing, Bill Ong. *Making and Remaking Asian America through Immigration Policy.* Palo Alto, Calif., 1993.

Jones, Maldwyn Allan. *American Immigration.* Chicago, 1960.

IMMIGRATION LAW AFTER 1900

The changing nature of immigration from Europe and the rapid changes created by modernization made Americans insecure and more open to the idea of excluding immigrants. The Immigration Acts of 1917, 1921, and 1924 were selective and exclusionary. Their intent was to restrict immigration from Asia and Southeastern Europe. The enactment of these laws brought an end to unrestricted immigration from Europe.

World War I magnified the social, political, economic, and ethnic divisions in American society. Further-more, the war heightened isolationist sentiments and intolerance toward anyone not considered "100 percent American." Demands for conformity, national unity, and homogeneity virtually swept from the American consciousness the old belief in unrestricted European immigration. This led to the passage of the Immigration Act of 1917.

The law began the United States's transition to a policy of immigration that was restrictive for Europeans. Selective in method, the law codified existing immigration laws, expanded the number of excluded classes, made immigration more a federal concern, and prohibited the recruitment of contract laborers. It increased the head tax from four dollars to eight dollars and imposed a literacy test on immigrants. Woodrow Wilson vetoed the law because of the literacy test. However, due to the extreme attitudes spawned by the war, Congress overrode his veto.

The Western states strongly supported the Act of 1917 because it continued a ban on immigration from China. The Asiatic Barred Zone proviso, which prohibited immigration of laborers from an expanded list of Asian countries, also garnered Western votes. The law and America's entry in World War I brought about a severe labor shortage in the Far West and Southwest. Fewer immigrants arrived from Europe, Asia, and Mexico, and the war siphoned workers into military or industrial jobs. Agricultural interests contended that unless restrictions were waived to permit the importation of Mexican workers, the war effort would be severely hampered. They appealed to the secretary of labor, who, under the 1917 act, had the authority to set aside any of the law's provisions if there was a shortage of labor. In 1917, he exempted Mexican workers from the literacy, head-tax, and contract-labor provisions of the law. The waivers continued until 1921. Exemptions were also extended to nonagricultural workers from 1918 to 1921 to meet labor needs in mining, railroads, and construction.

After World War I, immigrants became the scapegoats for many of the problems and frustrations that plagued the United States. Economic depression, unemployment, labor unrest, racial violence, bombings, and the Red Scare in 1919 further intensified xenophobia, intolerance, and isolationist sentiments. Because of these problems and the waning of the Americanization movement, restrictionists became convinced that the selective aspects of the Immigration Act of 1917 (the literacy test and head tax) were not sufficient to stem the flow from southeastern Europe. In effect, Congress abandoned the policy of selection for one of absolute restriction.

In 1921, Congress enacted the Emergency Quota Law, which established the principle of restriction based on nationality. The act placed a yearly ceiling on immigration from Europe by imposing a quota. Using the 1910 census as a base, quotas were set at 3 percent of each foreign-born population living in the United States. The yearly quota was set at 387,803. The temporary quota law favored immigrants from northwestern Europe, who were allowed a quota of 200,000. The law was extended twice by Congress until a more stringent immigration law was enacted.

The Johnson-Reed Act of 1924 reduced the yearly quota to 2 percent of each foreign group living in the United States and was based on the 1890 census. The law also reduced the total quota from 387,803 to 186,437. The law, for the first time, provided for consular inspection and the granting of visas at the source of immigration. It also made the immigrant responsible for proving his or her admissibility. Reflecting the widely accepted notion that immigration policy should be based on racial considerations, the new law was intentionally designed to reduce the proportion of immigrants admitted from eastern and southern Europe.

The Immigration Acts of 1921 and 1924 were supported by legislators from the Western states because the laws did not apply to immigrants from the Western Hemisphere. Western agribusiness, railroads, and other large employers welcomed the exemption because of their dependence on labor from Mexico. They also favored the anti-Asian provisions in these laws. The 1924 law reaffirmed the exclusion of the Chinese and prohibited immigration from Japan. The decision to exempt Mexicans, however, was not supported by all Westerners. During the congressional hearings, one of the more outspoken advocates of restricting immigration from Mexico was Representative John C. Box of Texas. Those who favored quotas on immigration from the Eastern Hemisphere contended that America had closed its front door to outsiders and left its back door open. However, efforts to exclude Mexicans failed.

The Quota Laws of 1921 and 1924 were unequivocal in their language. The enforcement machinery was efficient and located at the source of emigration. Penalties for violations were strict. Visas issued were counted at the source of immigration rather than at the American port after the immigrants had arrived. Funds for enforcement—including money for establishing the Border Patrol in 1924—were immediately appropriated by Congress. In 1929, the National Origins Act reduced the annual quota to 153,714 based on the "national origins" of the American population in 1920. As a result, the proportion of English immigrants was increased at the expense of other groups, especially those from southern and eastern Europe.

—*Juan R. García*

SUGGESTED READING:
Bernard, William S. "Immigration: History of U.S. Policy," In *Harvard Encyclopedia of American Ethnic Groups*. Edited by Stephan Thernstrom, Ann Orlov, and Oscar Handlin. Cambridge, Mass., 1980.
Calavita, Kitty. *U.S. Immigration Law and the Control of Labor, 1820–1924*. New York, 1984.
Higham, John. *Strangers in the Land: Patterns of American Nativism, 1860–1925*. 2d ed. New Brunswick, N.J., 1988.
Hutchinson, Edward P. *Legislative History of American Immigration Policy, 1798–1965*. Philadelphia, 1981.

IMPERIALISM

SEE: Gadsden Purchase; Manifest Destiny; Mexican Border Conflicts; Mexican Cession; Missions; National Expansion; Oregon Boundary Dispute; Spanish Settlement; Texas Revolution; United States–Mexican War

IMPERIAL VALLEY AND THE SALTON SEA

SEE: California; Farming: Farming in the Imperial Valley and the Salton Sea

INDIAN AFFAIRS, BUREAU OF

SEE: Bureau of Indian Affairs

INDIAN ART

SEE: Native American Basketry; Native American Beadwork; Native American Ledger Drawing; Native American Pottery, Southwestern; Native American Silverwork, Southwestern; Native American Weaving

INDIAN CAPTIVITY NARRATIVES

SEE: Literature: Indian Captivity Narratives

INDIAN LITERATURE

SEE: Literature: Native American Literature

INDIAN NEW DEAL

SEE: Federal Government; Navajo Stock-Reduction Program

INDIAN POLICY

SEE: Burke Act; Dawes Act; Grant's Peace Policy; United States Indian Policy

INDIAN POTTERY

SEE: Native American Pottery, Southwest

INDIAN RIGHTS ASSOCIATION

The Indian Rights Association, the most influential American group advocating Indian assimilation, emerged from a meeting of forty prominent Philadelphians on December 17, 1882. HERBERT THOMAS WELSH was the driving force behind the meeting and the central figure in the organization for its first fifty years. The purpose of the association was "to secure to the Indians of the United States the political and civil rights already guaranteed to them by treaty and statutes of the United States and such as their civilization and circumstances may justify."

The Indian Rights Association rapidly established itself as the most effective of the several organizations that arose in the East following the military conquest of the Western Indian tribes. From its beginning, the association had a full-time central staff engaged in fundraising, investigating, and lobbying. From 1884 to 1939, it maintained an agent in Washington, D.C. The quality of its investigations and the continuity of its staff gave unusual force to the association's lobbying efforts. Welsh and two other leaders, Matthew K. Sniffen (Welsh's successor as executive secretary) and Samuel M. Brosius (who served as agent in Washington from 1898 to 1933) gave a combined total of 138 years of service to the organization.

The Indian Rights Association achieved its greatest prominence in its first twenty years while Welsh was at the helm. By its fiftieth anniversary, the extent of its service to Indian peoples were apparent. Many tribes and especially the more progressive members could point to individual episodes in which the association had limited the exercise of white greed. The group's advocacy of assimilation, however, encouraged a federal policy that contributed to the divestment of two-thirds of tribal lands and the impoverishment of Indian communities. In its second half-century, the association became less visible but more committed to securing Indians rights through self-determination rather than through assimilation. The history of the Indian Rights Association, still in existence at the close of the twentieth century, revealed the mixed impact and varying degrees of influence of philanthropic reform on UNITED STATES INDIAN POLICY and on American Indians and their white neighbors.

—*Wilbert H. Ahern*

SUGGESTED READING:
Guide to the Microfilm Edition of the Papers of the Indian Rights Association, 1864–1973. Glen Rock, N.J., 1975.
Hagan, William T. *The Indians Rights Association: The Herbert Welsh Years, 1882–1904.* Tucson, Ariz., 1985.

INDIAN RUGS

SEE: Native American Weaving

INDIANS

SEE: Berdache; Black Hills Gold Rush; Black Legend; Bureau of Indian Affairs; Burke Act; Changing Woman; Cherokee Male and Female Seminaries; *Cherokee Nation* v. *Georgia;* Child Rearing: Native American Child Rearing; Corn Woman; Dawes Act; Federal Government; Fertility: Fertility among Native Americans; Film; Fur Trade; Gambling; Ghost Dance; Grant's Peace Policy; Hunting; Indian Rights Association; Indian Schools; Indian Shaker Church; Intermarriage: Marriages between Euro-Americans and Native Americans, Marriages between Spanish/Mexicans and Native Americans; Kachina Carving; Literature: Indian Captivity Narratives, Native American Literature; *Lone Wolf* v. *Hitchcock;* Medicine; Medicine Lodge Treaty of 1867; Métis People; Missions; Native American Basketry; Native American Beadwork; Native American Church; Native American Cultures; Native American Ledger Drawing; Native American Peoples; Native American Pottery, Southwestern; Native American Silverwork, Southwestern; Native American Weaving; Navajo Stock-Reduction Program; Noble-Savage Theory; Oklahoma; Oklahoma Land Rush; Polygamy: Polygamy among Native Americans; Scalping; Slavery and Indenture in the Spanish Southwest; Stereotypes: Stereotype of Native Americans; Trail of Tears; United States Army: Scouts; United States Indian Policy; Wild

West Shows: Indians in Wild West Shows; Women's National Indian Association; *Worcester v. Georgia*

INDIANS, CHRISTIAN

SEE: Missions; Native American Church

INDIAN SCHOOLS

Indian Schools off the Reservation
  Robert A. Trennert

Indian Schools on the Reservation
  Melissa A. Davis

INDIAN SCHOOLS OFF THE RESERVATION

The United States government assumed responsibility for educating Indian children during the late nineteenth century. Originally dedicated to "Americanizing" the native population, the most popular schools were located in or near urban communities off the reservation. Providing an industrial education and contact with mainstream society, these institutions forced Indian children to work and act like white Americans. Reaching a peak between 1890 and 1920, the schools frequently embittered both pupils and parents. During the 1920s, the effort to force assimilation drew severe criticism, and off-reservation boarding schools began to lose favor. Nevertheless, off-reservation education, although changed in curriculum and focus, survived on a limited scale into the late twentieth century.

Immediately after the Civil War, the federal government adopted a program of restricting the native population to reservations. The reservation system focused on "civilizing" the tribal population by forcing it to adopt Christianity, private property, written laws, and an agricultural economy. As part of that program, the Office of Indian Affairs established schools to replace the missionary schools already in existence. Reservation schools, although relatively inexpensive, did not satisfy government officials, who wanted the children removed from the tribal environment. Thus, while it seemed "manifest that barbarism can only be cured by education," officials preferred that children be removed from their parents. Although some church-run boarding schools already operated on that philosophy, a strong secular program did not develop until the 1880s.

Army officer RICHARD HENRY PRATT is regarded as the father of the nonreservation industrial schools, which quickly emerged as the most favored type of institution in a federal school system that also operated both day and boarding schools on the reserva-

tion. Pratt believed that Indians might benefit from direct contact with white society. He argued that they could best be civilized by transplanting them into an environment that would inspire them to work for a living, learn to speak English, and develop into productive citizens.

In 1878, Pratt enrolled several young Indian captives at Hampton Institute, a school for African Americans in Virginia. The seeming success of the experiment prompted Pratt to open a school exclusively for Indians in Carlisle, Pennsylvania. The Carlisle Indian School soon became famous as it went about "Americanizing" its students. The school used strict military-style discipline to "detribalize" Indian children of both sexes. They lived in dormitories, dressed in uniforms, spoke English, and worked—the boys at mechanical tasks and the girls at domestic chores. School routine usually required students to spend half of the day in class and the remainder at work, which also helped support the facility financially. Infractions of rules were severely punished. The school also developed an "outing system," which placed Indian children with local farm families to live and work. Although Indian parents theoretically surrendered their children on a voluntary basis, the government placed considerable pressure on the tribes to cooperate. Pratt expected graduates to merge directly into American society. By the mid-1880s, Carlisle housed more than five hundred Indian students.

The apparent success of Carlisle inspired the government to establish other nonreservation schools across the West. Between 1880 and 1900, some twenty-five off-reservation boarding schools were opened at locations such as Genoa, Nebraska (1884); Chilocco, Indian Territory (1884); Lawrence, Kansas (1884); Albuquerque, New Mexico (1886); Phoenix, Arizona (1891); and Riverside, California (1900). Following the Carlisle model, the Western schools also employed a two-tiered curriculum of vocational training and academic instruction. Even more than Carlisle, the Western institutions, some housing more than seven hundred students, emphasized manual labor and farming. The schools were fully dedicated to "civilizing" the pupil by obliterating every trace of traditional Indian culture. Because school authorities believed that Indians would enter mainstream life at the lowest level, academic training remained minimal. The equivalent of an eighth-grade education was all a student could hope to attain.

Between 1890 and 1920, off-reservation schools dominated the federal educational system for Indians. Eventually, the institutions began to restrict admission to pupils with some prior schooling. That policy eliminated the problem of having to deal with untutored

Top left: Photographer J. N. Choate recorded the arrival of young Sioux boys at the Carlisle Indian School in October 1879. *Courtesy National Archives.*

Bottom left: The military-style dress and discipline of the Carlisle Indian School was intended to "detribalize" its students. Photograph by J. N. Choate. *Courtesy National Archives.*

Top right: Students in their cadet uniforms at Forest Grove School, Oregon. *Courtesy National Archives.*

Middle right: At the Haskell Institute in Lawrence, Kansas, Indian girls learned shorthand in addition to domestic skills to prepare them for their emergence into American society. Photograph by Squires. *Courtesy National Archives.*

Bottom right: This 1900 image captured young Indian girls of the Phoenix Indian School reciting their prayers. *Courtesy National Archives.*

pupils taken directly from Indian camps. Nevertheless, most institutions enrolled youngsters ranging in age from seven to twenty-one.

By the mid-1890s, evidence began to appear that former students were not merging into white society. Despite heavy indoctrination, most pupils returned home, where their newly learned skills were nearly useless. After 1900, school officials focused more on preparing children to use their education at home, but few jobs existed on reservations, except with the Indian service. Finding themselves unemployable, many former students turned their back on the system.

Native students attending the off-reservation schools were significantly affected by the experience. The educational experience, which usually lasted from three to five years, brought tribal youths into sudden contact with the outside would. Many resented the experience and rebelled; others accepted the situation and achieved some success in Euro-American society. For many students, the initial de-Indianization process seemed brutal: they were stripped of their traditional clothing, forced to speak English and adhere to Victorian moral codes, and do manual labor. Violations of the rules resulted in whipping and even imprisonment. As a consequence, many students ran away and others refused to cooperate. Other students reacted more positively and learned vocational skills. They participated in the school's social life, which included athletic, religious, and academic activities. By the time they left school, many pupils had a good command of English. A few former students found employment in cities, although most eventually returned home. Because of their new ability to deal with outside society, some of the more successful students became "culture brokers" between the white and Indian culture. Many tribal leaders from the 1930s to the present were educated at off-reservations schools. But because the majority of students failed to use their education, the school program has been judged a failure. Nevertheless, the schools had their share of success stories, and many tribal elders look back upon their school years with fond memories.

Off-reservation schools began to lose favor by the third decade of the twentieth century. The schools seemed incapable of assimilating the Indian population and were costly to operate. Many campuses had deteriorated, resulting in learning, health, and sanitary problems. Frequently expressing dissatisfaction with the schools, many Indian parents preferred ones closer to home. In 1918, Carlisle, the most famous off-reservation school, closed. Soon thereafter, reformer John Collier began criticizing the government boarding schools for their inefficiency and failure to meet Indian needs. His criticism was supported by the 1928 Meriam Report, which detailed the failure of federal Indian policy. The report was particularly critical of the off-reservation schools because of their unhealthy and ethnocentric environment. The Meriam document strongly advocated expanding the system of community day schools, where children might remain in contact with their parents. The commitment to total assimilation also drew heated objections.

When Collier became U.S. Indian commissioner in 1933, he inaugurated a program of opening additional reservation day schools and providing a cross-cultural curriculum. During the 1930s, several off-reservation schools closed. Because of a lack of funds for the construction of new reservation facilities, however, many of the old schools remained open as Indian high schools. Much of the old assimilation curriculum—the strict discipline, uniforms, and English-only policy—was dropped, although vocational education continued to prevail.

After World War II and Collier's resignation in 1945, the surviving nonreservation schools received a new lease on life. During the 1950's termination program, which focused on ending the federal responsibility for Indian welfare and integrating Indians into American society, off-reservation schools regained popularity as locations where students might learn vocational skills. Indian students, many of them war veterans, flooded the schools under special instructional programs, which reflected the theory that a great percentage of the reservation population would relocate to urban areas.

Opposition by Indians ended the termination program. In its place appeared a new emphasis on self-determination. As a consequence, the popularity of the schools declined rapidly after 1960. Costly, run-down, and increasingly out of touch with native desires, the old boarding facilities were superseded by BUREAU OF INDIAN AFFAIRS and public day schools. A series of unfavorable public reports during the 1970s also contributed to the schools' demise. As a consequence, during the 1970s and 1980s, all the remaining off-reservation schools outside Alaska, except one, had closed.

During their heyday, off-reservation institutions instructed thousands of Indian children. They introduced students to the outside world, taught them "the white man's way," and provided them with leadership and economic skills. Because of the ethnocentric approach to education, however, they were frequently resented as symbols of colonialism and paternalism. Nevertheless, they played a significant role, for good or bad, in bringing Native Americans into the twentieth century.

—*Robert A. Trennert*

SEE ALSO: Literature: Native American Literature; United States Indian Policy: Civilization Programs; Reform Movement

SUGGESTED READING:

Coleman, Michael C. *American Indian Children at School, 1850–1930.* Jackson, Miss., 1993.

Pratt, Richard Henry. *Battlefield and Classroom: Four Decades with the American Indian, 1867–1904.* Edited by Robert M. Utley. New Haven, Conn., 1964.

Reyhner, Hohn, and Jeanne Eder. *A History of Indian Education.* Billings, Mont., 1989.

Szasz, Margaret Connell. *Education and the American Indian: The Road to Self-Determination since 1928.* Albuquerque, N. Mex., 1977.

Trennert, Robert A. *The Phoenix Indian School: Forced Assimilation in Arizona, 1891–1935.* Norman, Okla., 1988.

INDIAN SCHOOLS ON THE RESERVATION

The word *civilization* came into common use in English during the mid-1700s, about the time European settlers began to push west of the Appalachian Mountains into the Indian-occupied territory of the Ohio River valley. As Euro-American settlers encroached on more and more Indian land, confrontation led to conflict, and the infant United States deployed its military and other officials to accomplish two goals: first, they were to change the nomadic peoples native to the West from hunters into farmers; second, they were to instruct Indians already practicing traditional native agriculture how to farm on small tracts of tillable land. As early as 1794, the United States government had drafted policies on the education of Native Americans based on these goals—called "assimilation"—and aimed at "civilizing" the "savages."

With the Treaty with the Navajos in 1868, assimilation became the official goal of Indian education in the trans-Missouri West. The treaty called for the construction of the Defiance School on the Fort Defiance reservation and required attendance by all children between the ages of six and sixteen. Because Navajo parents needed their children to help establish households and tend sheep, they did not comply with the treaty's stipulations about attendance, and the government did not enforce them. The teachers employed at the school were inadequately trained to instruct the sporadic and inconsistent student body. Initially, that reservation school—and many like it—failed.

Although the BUREAU OF INDIAN AFFAIRS (BIA) began its own educational efforts in the 1870s, until 1897, it distributed ten thousand dollars annually to various religious groups to fund the work of missionaries who also sought to "educate" the Indians. During these years, the hope was that the missionaries might succeed where the government had failed, for after a decade of congressional spending following the founding of the Defiance School, no reservation-educated Native American could read or write English (or at least none would admit to being able to do so). But in the late nineteenth century, Commissioner of Indian Affairs E. A. Hayt suggested that tribal influences were primarily responsible for the government's failure to educate the Indians. From that premise grew the federal boarding school, which took children away from their parents' homes. Officials reasoned that if children were removed from their families for a minimum of eight years, they could become sufficiently "white" and would thus fit into society as needed.

The model for federal boarding schools, the Carlisle School in Pennsylvania, opened in 1879. By 1881, it had enrolled almost two hundred students, including the children of many Sioux leaders. It focused not on academic pursuits, but on industrial, vocational, and home-economic instruction. The students made clothing and other nontraditional items, which were shipped to the reservations for use by the Indians. The parents of the students vacillated between hope for complete assimilation of their children and despair over the separation of them from their tribes and their Native American heritage, but the boarding schools soon became a key part of government policy. In 1882, Congress began commissioning abandoned reservation posts as classroom buildings for the boarding schools. The boarding schools founded after 1890—when those teaching in them had to become certified in order to establish their qualification as educators—survive today. Many reservations have expanded the schools to include local day-school operations. Elementary-school children usually attend the day schools, while secondary-school students attend the boarding schools.

The extent to which boarding-school policy proved insensitive to the needs of Indian children can be seen in Oklahoma, formerly the Indian Territory and home to numerous "relocated" tribes. When Oklahoma became a state in 1907, the BIA took over responsibility for the Indian schools on the reservations. The agency deployed culturally insensitive social workers to Indian homes to determine the eligibility of prospective students. The presence of a sick family member, the lack of complete nutrition or essentials, and other indicators of extreme poverty were among the criteria agents used to determine whether a family's children should be sent away to school. In remote tribes, agents sometimes took first-graders from their homes and boarded them.

The criteria for the removals were evidence of a distant and disinterested perspective. Middle-class Euro-American social workers compared Indian households to their own, and nearly all Indian households appeared to them dysfunctional and inappropriate for child rearing. For decades, then, the majority of Indians continued to be ripped from their own culture and placed in schools or foster homes alien to Indian life, where they remained for the major part of their developmental years. The early and enduring separations further damaged the Indian family and Native American society. By the early decades of the twentieth century, some scholars estimate, nearly 35 percent of Indian children lived in non-Indian foster homes or government-run boarding schools. Instead of helping the Indians build a new world—a "civilized" world—the BIA's tendency to separate child and parent contributed to the decline of Indian self-sufficiency, which was one of the purported goals of government-sponsored Indian education, and it further destroyed traditional Indian culture, which few doubt was the true long-term goal.

In short, the government's policies concerning Indian education served the needs of the dominant Euro-

American culture rather than those of the Indians, and reservation schools became yet another mechanism for subjugating America's indigenous population, a linchpin in the ethnocide that eroded Indian culture and tradition and broke apart Indian families and institutions.

—*Melissa A. Davis*

SEE ALSO: United States Indian Policy: Civilization Programs, Reform Movement

SUGGESTED READING:
Coffer, William E. *Sleeping Giants.* Washington, D. C., 1979.
Hill, Edward E. *The Office of Indian Affairs, 1824–1880: Historical Sketches.* New York, 1974.

INDIAN SHAKER CHURCH

The Indian Shaker church combines traditional Native American and Christian religious beliefs and practices. It originated in the Puget Sound region of Washington in 1882. Its founder, John Slocum, a Salish Indian, reportedly died, received a vision, and came back to life. He told his followers to reject drinking, smoking, and gambling as well as traditional native healers. A year later, Slocum again became seriously ill. Mary, his wife, began to shake and used the power of the "spirit of God" to heal him. The church, which holds the belief in the Christian trinity, incorporates healing rituals as part of its services; it has no connection with the Shakers of the Midwest.

In 1892, the Indian Shaker church became an organized church and incorporated in 1910. The church is not monolithic. Some members believe they receive direct inspiration from God, while others prefer to use the Bible to a greater degree. Due to white opposition to native religious practices, the Indian Shakers structured their church after Protestant models, with a bishop, elders, and ministers. The Indian Shaker church spread north to British Columbia and south into northern California, and it continues to play an active part in the religious practices of many Native American people of the Pacific Northwest.

—*Annette Reed Crum*

SEE ALSO: Native American Culture: Spiritual Life

SUGGESTED READING:
Barnett, H. G. *Indian Shakers: A Messianic Cult of the Pacific Northwest.* Carbondale and Edwardsville, Ill., 1957.
Moss, Pamela T. "The Indian Shaker Church." In *Handbook of North American Indians: Northwest Coast.* Vol. 7. Edited by Wayne Suttles. Washington, D.C., 1990.

INDIAN SILVERWORK

SEE: Native American Silverwork, Southwestern

INDIAN TERRITORY

SEE: Oklahoma

INDIAN WARS

SEE: Apache Wars; Black Hawk's War; Central Plains Indian Wars; Fetterman Massacre; Grattan Massacre; Hancock's Campaign; Little Bighorn, Battle of; Mountain Meadows Massacre; Navajo Wars; Pacific Northwest Indian Wars; Pueblo Revolt; Sand Creek Massacre; Sioux Wars; Texas Frontier Indian Wars; Wounded Knee Massacre; Yuma Revolt

INDUSTRIAL ASSOCIATION OF SAN FRANCISCO

Launched by Atholl McCall of San Francisco's Chamber of Commerce on July 25, 1921, the Industrial Association of San Francisco (IASF) had one major goal: to rid San Francisco's business and industry of the closed shop, the policy that required all workers of a particular business to be union members. Composed of about one thousand member companies, including the biggest corporations in California, the IASF encouraged its members to refuse to sell materials to contractors who supported union-shop rules, thereby closing down operations that involved union members. Employing lockouts and capturing union apprentice programs, the Industrial Association of San Francisco broke the power of the building-trades unions in the city. By 1923, the IASF announced that 85 percent of San Francisco's workers were employed in open shops.

In place of the unions, the IASF offered workers a kind of welfare capitalism, supplying to workers benefits, such as insurance, that they had, in the past, received from their unions. The success of the IASF reflected the end of the unions' grip on San Francisco's economy and politics.

—*Patricia Hogan*

SEE ALSO: San Francisco Building Trades Council

SUGGESTED READING:
Kazin, Michael. *Barons of Labor: The San Francisco Building Trades and Union Power in the Progressive Era.* Urbana and Chicago, 1987.

INDUSTRIAL CHRISTIAN HOME FOR MORMON WOMEN

The Industrial Christian Home, an institution designed to provide a refuge for Mormon polygamous wives, was the brainchild of nineteenth-century Protestant women who believed that the Mormon marriage system of polygamy, in which church leaders took more than one wife, was an affront to the moral position of women. The guiding spirit behind the home was Nebraska Methodist ANGIE NEWMAN. In March 1886, she organized an interdenominational Industrial Christian Home Association, a group made up of Salt Lake City Protestant women, many of whom had been members of the local Ladies' Anti-Polygamy Society. Aware that they would find little support for their project in Utah, the members of the Home Association sent Newman to Washington, D.C., where she presented the plan to the U.S. Senate Committee on Education and Labor. Congress, already under pressure from EVANGELISTS across the nation to abolish polygamy, agreed to fund the project but insisted that it be placed under the direction of an all-male Board of Control.

The Industrial Christian Home Association opened its doors in temporary, rented quarters in December 1886. The home promised to provide not only refuge but also job training in typing, stenography, and silk-reeling for any woman who would leave her polygamous marriage. Mormon leaders, who defiantly opposed all congressional attempts to abolish polygamy, predicted that Mormon women would refuse to accept charity from their Protestant enemies, but during the first nine months of the home's operation, 154 women and children applied to enter the institution. Because the women of the Home Association and the men of the Board of Control fought over eligibility standards, the vast majority of the applicants were refused admission. Damaged by the all-too-public dispute between male and female sponsors, the home was further weakened when Miranda Boss, one of the thirty-three applicants who had been admitted to the home, charged the matron Ruth Wood with cruelty. Although Wood was exonerated by an investigation, relations between her and home residents remained tense. The grand program of vocational training never got off the ground, and home residents, who needed to make a living, ended up doing enormous amounts of domestic work, including laundry, sewing, and bread baking.

Meanwhile, the Home Association tried to solve its problems by going back to Congress to consolidate control over the institution and to request more funding. In 1888, Newman persuaded Congress to appropriate fifty thousand dollars to build a grand new building for the institution. The new Industrial Christian Home proudly opened its doors in 1889. It was no more successful than its predecessor in attracting residents, however, and the home project began to lose its congressional support after the Mormon church announced in 1890 that it would end the practice of polygamy.

The Industrial Christian Home closed in 1893, after having served a total of 150 women and children during its seven years of operation. Never effective at helping Mormon women, it stood as a monument to Protestant women's determination to abolish polygamy.

—*Peggy Pascoe*

SEE ALSO: Edmunds Act of 1882; Edmunds-Tucker Act of 1887; Mormons; Polygamy: Polygamy among Mormons

SUGGESTED READING:

Larson, Gustive. "An Industrial Home for Polygamous Wives." *Utah Historical Quarterly* 38 (Summer 1970): 263–275.

Pascoe, Peggy. *Relations of Rescue: The Search for Female Moral Authority in the American West, 1874–1939.* New York, 1990.

INDUSTRIAL WORKERS OF THE WORLD

Convinced that American workers needed to organize into large industrial unions, a number of American radicals met in Chicago in January 1905 to launch the Industrial Workers of the World, whom everybody was soon calling—for reasons that remain obscure—the "Wobblies." Among the IWW organizers were the WESTERN FEDERATION OF MINERS' WILLIAM D. ("BIG BILL") HAYWOOD, Socialist party leader Eugene V. Debs and party ideologue Daniel De Leon, and the seventy-five-year-old legendary coal-miner's champion MARY HARRIS ("MOTHER") JONES. All had been front-line troops in what Alan Trachtenburg has called the late nineteenth century's "American Civil War of Incorporation," during which a basically agrarian society in the American West was transformed by the introduction of government-sponsored railroads, large-scale extractive enterprises, and a relentless urbanization into a market economy's internal colony. The new patterns of development and employment fostered both conservatism among employers, their managers, and the merchants and shopkeepers who catered to them and radicalism among the vast army of the dispossessed and the transient produced by the social dislocations

Top: A San Diego, California, demonstration of the Industrial Workers of the World in 1913 included a speech by Emma Goldman. *Courtesy San Diego Historical Society.*

Bottom: Some IWW rallies turned into clashes between demonstrators and the authorities, as depicted in this image from San Diego. *Courtesy San Diego Historical Society.*

can West more so than else-where. Historian Robert L. Tyler suggested that the reason had to do with the "essential romanticism" of the Wobbly program, which could never reconcile practical business unionism with a commitment to social revolution. Eschewing politics for direct action, meaning sabotage, and conflating strikes with revolution itself, the Wobblies—Tyler implied—in their own way resembled the rugged individuals who were expanding and changing industry in the West and were tending toward oligopoly in the ownership of raw materials. In the "post-frontier" West, the big extractive industries of lumber, mining, and agriculture, having become less makeshift and transitory, suddenly needed a huge number of wage workers, whom they recruited mostly from hoboes and migrants. From 1909 until America entered the Great War in Europe in 1917, the IWW also threatened to become a real force among skilled and semiskilled, mostly immigrant labor east of the Mississippi and held a series of quick, well-publicized strikes—McKees Rocks, Pennsylvania (1909); Lawrence, Massachusetts (1912); Patterson, New Jersey (1913). But IWW influence fizzled when the unions established during these strikes proved short lived: although some three million joined the IWW over the years, the Wobblies ranked at most some 150,000 among their numbers at any one point. In short, strikes swelled IWW membership for a brief time; frightened local, state, and national governments; and provided Wobblies with raw materials for their revolutionary song book. But only in the Southwest, the Great Plains, the West Coast, and the Pacific Northwest—where "a frontier economy [was] in the throes of change," according to Tyler—did the Wobbly way of life truly catch on.

Wobbly culture

A stepchild of the Western Federation of Miners (WFM), the IWW was initially conceived as militant, class-conscious, and openly political industrial-union competition for the trade-union–oriented American Federation of Labor (AFL). American Labor Union's Father Thomas J. Hagerty wrote in the preamble to the IWW constitution: "The working class and the

of rapid industrialization. As "Big Bill" Haywood brought the thirty or so union leaders and radicals gathered in Chicago to order by pounding on a table with a piece of wood, he announced: "Fellow workers, this is the Continental Congress of the working class."

Spawned by the radicals' grand ambition to organize the entire working class of America, and after that, perhaps the world, the IWW took root in the Ameri-

employing class have nothing in common." Although the original and elaborate organizational plans called for creating thirteen industrial "departments" into which the whole of the working class could be organized, the blueprint never came to life. Instead, the majority of the Wobblies belonged to more or less autonomous industrial unions or were members at large. Once again, this development had much to do with the influence of Westerners, who, from the beginning, split with the leadership over questions of philosophy and tactics.

Western Wobblies were syndicalists, European-inspired anarchists who wanted to avoid obtuse socialist-style theorizing on the one hand and intricate negotiating with the class-enemy industrialists on the other and to keep dues low, the message simple, and the membership fluid. First, with the help of the doctrinaire Socialists, they deposed the WFM-installed secretary-president C. O. Sherman and abolished the office itself. The WFM, which had been the only functioning union within the IWW, withdrew from membership, and Haywood withdrew from the WFM to devote himself to the IWW. Next, they purged the ranks of the Socialists as well, including the likes of Daniel De Leon, who dismissed the Westerners as the "overalls brigade" and the "bummery." The Wobblies removed all mention of political action from their constitution, established a system of interchangeable memberships for those carrying the IWW's "red cards," declared that any member—laborer as well as Wobbly official—could be a full-time organizer ("an official whose headquarters became where he hung his hat"), and hit the streets to usher in the working-class millennium.

These Western anarchists, zealots free of middle-class social restraints, preached their gospel of "One Big Union" from corner soap boxes with the same religious fervor as the Christian evangelists they competed against for the souls of poor working men and women. For almost two decades, they sang irreverent songs, many of them written by union member Joe Hill and collected in their "Little Red Song Book," to the tunes of Salvation Army hymns, such as "In the Sweet Bye and Bye":

Long-haired preachers come out every night
Try to tell you what's wrong and what's right
But when asked how 'bout something to eat
They will answer with voices so sweet:

CHORUS
You will eat, bye and bye
In that glorious land above the sky;
Work and pray, live on hay,
You'll get pie in the sky when you die.

The Western Wobblies did more than turn phrases ("pie in the sky") that became part of the American language. They badgered law-enforcement officials; sometimes they fought pitched battles with local sheriffs, company "goons," and vigilantes. Hard-bitten, sometimes quite malicious, fanatics and idealists, they operated with a certain panache that guaranteed they would become the favorites of historians, folklorists, and novelists, while they drove the "establishment" as crazy as civil rights demonstrators and anti–Vietnam War protestors would in the 1960s by adopting many of their tactics.

Free speech

Under the banner of "solidarity," they marched into towns that had passed ordinances against radical assemblies and staged "free-speech" demonstrations as they waved their pamphlets decorated with cartoonish wooden shoes and black cats (symbols of sabotage) and urged workers to take direct action: destroy property; set forest fires; drive railroad spikes into trees to strip the teeth from the saws of lumber mills; throw tools into the moving parts of threshing machines. They pasted labels of a sunrise depicting a "cooperative commonwealth" wherever they could and swore like sailors (some may once have been sailors) at solid citizens as they delivered their diatribes against the "master class." As they flooded into towns, their arrivals announced well beforehand in their raucous rags named *Solidarity* (Chicago) and *Industrial Worker* (Pacific Northwest), they were tossed into jails en masse, where they continued their demonstrations with loudly announced hunger strikes and protests against harassment and mistreatment by the police. They pounded their bunks, rattled their cages, and shouted their curses in what appeared to everyone as a revolutionary exercise of something that was, in reality, a constitutionally guaranteed right: free speech. When they attracted enough members in an area—and it did not have to be many—they called for strikes. Should some mill owner meet their demand for an eight-hour workday (few ever did), they demanded clean bed linen three times a week. Unlike other unionists, the Wobblies were more interested in provoking a fight than in winning specific concessions.

They won the fierce loyalty of the army of hoboes and migrants who harvested wheat from Oklahoma to Canada, drove railroad spikes from Kansas to California, logged timber from Portland to Puget Sound, or mined silver, lead, and copper from Butte to Bisbee. Young, homeless, unattached, these wandering workers road the rails, in boxcars if they were lucky, suspended beneath the cars ten inches above the screeching rails if they were not. They drifted from Chicago to Minneapolis to Spokane to Seattle to Portland to San Francisco and back again; they saved travel money when they could; they stayed in skid-row flophouses and stood in Salvation Army soup lines; they worked for a season and moved on. And they went to hear such firebrands as Elizabeth Gurley Brown, "the Rebel Girl," who became one of the better-known Wobbly leaders and excelled in free-speech fights, which no doubt inspired her to found the American Civil Liberties Union years later. One who heard her was a young Western migrant named William Z. Foster, who later headed the American Communist party; another may well have been future U.S. Supreme Court Justice William O. Douglas, who was on the road in his youth. Many of the migrants were foreign-born, and there were enough of them to fill every jail in the trans-Mississippi West. Forty to sixty thousand showed up every winter in Chicago; Seattle learned to expect seven thousand and sometimes played host to thirteen thousand.

And fill every cell was exactly what the IWW planned to do. Almost all the twenty-six fights of the free-speech movement took place in California, Oregon, and Washington. The first victory, the one where the Wobblies learned what they were doing, came in Spokane during the winter of 1909 to 1910. Protesting the exploitative practices of local employment agencies, IWW speakers swept into the city, mounted soap boxes, and then clogged the courts and the jails by getting arrested. Not only did the confusion mount in Spokane's municipal halls, but so did the expense, until ultimately the city caved. Seen as wild-eyed radicals or rugged frontier individualists (depending on which side of the tracks the viewer stood), the Wobblies won another major success in San Diego in 1912. But in 1916, during the Wobblies campaign in Everett, Washington, local vigilantes struck back at the IWW and killed five Wobblies, although the campaign itself was successful, as were all the union's free-speech battles.

Class war

By then the reaction had begun to set in. Local organizing efforts on a hops ranch in Wheatland, California, in 1913 led to bloodshed and failure, with five dead, three of them Wobblies. Perhaps as a result of the escalation in the class war, on the Great Plains in 1915 and 1916, the Wobblies finally launched a real union—the eighteen-thousand-strong Agricultural Workers Organization (AWO), whose migrant harvesters were especially aggressive. In the Pacific Northwest, too, the IWW met with success in organizing a Lumber Workers Union, which in 1916 and 1917 would indeed help mitigate the more oppressive conditions in the squalid logger camps of the region. At the same time, however, IWW songwriter Joe Hill was found guilty of murdering two Salt Lake City policemen in a grocery-store robbery, and in 1915, he was executed by a Utah firing squad. Historians might continue to debate his guilt, and labor leaders might decry that Hill was framed, but the public's mind was made up. Over the course of little more than a decade, the Wobblies had forged a reputation for hard-nosed, grassroots radicalism, and people believed them capable of anything.

If any one thing sealed the fate of the Wobbly organization, it was probably the coming of World War I. As the Wilson administration and its propaganda wing, the Committee for Public Information, whipped up war hysteria, federal, local, and state governments—actively supported by an antiradical, antiforeign public—lashed out at immigrants, labor, and, in particular, the IWW. For all the Wobblies' revolutionary rhetoric and their reputation for VIOLENCE, they were ultimately more often the victims than the initiators of the killing. Their two major mistakes were organizing immigrants and calling for general strikes in a nation heading into war. For that they would be attacked by vigilantes, local policemen, and federal agents, who prosecuted them under any law they could find—espionage, sedition, even criminal conspiracy—or simply shot them down. New criminal syndicalism laws were passed by local governments making it illegal to belong to any organization "advocating crimes, sabotage, violence, or unlawful methods of terrorism" in order to bring about reform. Immigration agents used these and other laws to hold noncitizen, immigrant IWW members without benefit of bail or trial for rubber-stamp deportation hearings.

A 1917 copper miners' strike in Bisbee, Arizona, collapsed when company vigilantes rounded up twelve hundred strikers and deported them to the desert, where the strikers were left without transportation, food, or water. As arrests piled up, jury after jury handed down guilty verdicts, and judge after judge passed out stiff sentences against the Wobblies filling up Western jails; in 1918, the federal government swung into action with a drive that saw 105 IWW leaders arrested and tried for sedition in Chicago. The government won sixty-two convictions, among them one against "Big Bill" Haywood, who jumped bail and headed for Russia. During the so-called Centralia Massacre in 1919, Wobblies, who had been warned of an impending attack by the local American Legion on their headquarters in Centralia, Washington, armed themselves, defended the hall, and killed three legionnaires. In the mob violence that followed, a young veteran of World War I and IWW member named Wesley Everest was castrated and lynched. During a particularly violent copper strike in Butte, Montana, IWW organizer FRANK LITTLE was hung with a rope round his neck over a trestle, hauled back up, hung by a longer rope, then riddled with bullets from below. From 1920 to 1923, state governments in California, Kansas, Oregon, and Oklahoma arrested more than five thousand Wobblies under the criminal syndicalism laws.

By the late 1920s, caught up in the postwar hysteria over the potential for "Bolshevik-style" revolution in America, its leadership shattered, its members deported or languishing in prison, the One Big Union was broken. Although the Wobblies would linger on through the 1930s—and occasionally show evidence of regaining their former verve and dash—the IWW was, in fact, finished as a meaningful force in the LABOR MOVEMENT and in American politics. Never able, as Melvyn Dubofskey pointed out along with Tyler, to decide whether to concentrate on short-term goals or ultimate revolution, the Wobblies nevertheless left a legacy for later American radicals, one of adamantine egalitarianism and irreverent antiauthoritarianism, both in essence Western radical traditions.

—*Charles Phillips*

SEE ALSO: Arizona Mining Strikes; Vigilantism

SUGGESTED READING:

Brissenden, Paul. *The IWW: A Study of American Syndicalism.* New York, 1920.

Brody, David. *Workers in Industrial America: Essays on the 20th Century Struggle.* New York, 1980.

Clark, Norman H. *Mill Town: A Social History of Everett, Washington, from Its Earliest Beginnings on the Shore of Puget Sound to the Tragic and Infamous Event Known as the Everett Massacre.* Seattle, Wash., 1970.

Derickson, Alan. *Workers' Health, Workers' Democracy: The Western Miners Struggle, 1891–1925.* Cambridge, Mass., 1978.

Dubofskey, Melvyn. *We Shall Be All: A History of the Industrial Workers of the World.* 2d ed. Urbana, Ill., 1988.

Foner, Philip F. *History of the Labor Movement in the United States: The Industrial Workers of the World.* New York, 1965.

McClelland, John, Jr. *Wobbly War: The Centralia Story.* Tacoma, Wash., 1987.

Tyler, Robert L. *Rebels of the Woods: The I.W.W. in the Pacific Northwest.* Eugene, Oreg., 1967.

INDUSTRY AND INDUSTRIALIZATION

SEE: Agrarianism; Agriculture; Aircraft Industry; American System; Anaconda Mining Company; Arizona Mining Strikes; Banking; Bonanza Farming; Booms; Cable Act of 1922; Cattle Industry; Cattle Towns; China Trade; Coal Lands Act of 1922; Comstock Lode; Copper Kings, War of; Copper Mining; Cotton Farming; Crédit Mobilier of America; Cripple Creek Strikes; Dude Ranching; Dust Bowl; Emma Mine; Farming; Federal Government; Film; Financial Panics; Fishing Industry; Forest Management Act of 1897; Forest Reserve Act of 1891; Fruit and Vegetable Growing; Ghost Towns; Gold Mining; Greenback Party; Hawaiian Sugar Planters' Association; Hawaii Laborer's Association; Homestake Mine; Industrial Association of San Francisco; Industrial Workers of the World; Immigrants and Immigration; Interstate Commerce Act of 1887; Labor Movement; Lead Mining; Loggers; Lumber Industry; Mineral Lands Leasing Act of 1920; Mining; Mining Law of 1872; Motion-Picture Industry; Oil and Gas Industry; Overland Freight; Oxnard Agricultural Strike; Populism; Railroads; San Francisco Building Trades Council; Sheep and Sheep Ranching; Sherman Anti-Trust Act; Silver Mining; Socialism; Tariff Policy; Teapot Dome; Telegraph; Tourism; Union Labor Party, San Francisco; Urban West; Vigilantism; Violence; Western Federation of Miners; Whaling; Wheat Farming; Women in Wage Work; Working-Class Women

INGALLS, JOHN J.

Colorful Kansas politician John J. Ingalls (1833–1900) was born in Middleton, Massachusetts. He graduated from Williams College in 1855, studied law, and was admitted to the Massachusetts bar in 1857. The following year, he moved to the Kansas Territory to seek his fortune. There, he entered politics and played an important role in the Kansas constitutional convention and in the first state legislative session.

In 1873, at the age of thirty-nine, Ingalls was elected to the U.S. Senate as a Republican. He was reelected in 1879 and again in 1885. In 1891, he was defeated in his fourth bid for the Senate by the Populists. Although he spent many years in the Senate, Ingalls did not sponsor any significant legislation. He is remembered more for his oratorical and literary skills, which made him one of the more picturesque and striking figures in the nation.

—*Burton J. Williams*

SUGGESTED READING:

Williams, Burton J. *Senator John James Ingalls: Kansas' Iridescent Republican.* Lawrence, Kans., 1972.

INTERMARRIAGE

ANTIMISCEGENATION LAWS

A significant but often overlooked aspect of American racism, antimiscegenation laws were designed to ensure white supremacy by forbidding whites to marry members of other racial groups (the term *miscegenation*, first used in the 1860s, refers to a biological mixture of the races). Modeled on laws prohibiting whites from marrying African Americans that had been enacted in the American South during the colonial period, antimiscegenation laws were adopted by most Western states in the mid- to late nineteenth century. Before the Civil War, when slavery was the primary system of racial oppression in the United States, laws forbidding intermarriage were only a small part of the larger legal system of white supremacy, but with the end of slavery—and at just about the time they began to be adopted by Western states and territories—antimiscegenation laws took on new importance, becoming the "bottom line" of American racial SEGREGATION.

In the West, unlike the South (where the major target of the laws was African Americans), the laws applied to a wide variety of groups. Seventeen Western states (Arizona, California, Colorado, Idaho, Kansas, Montana, Nebraska, New Mexico, Nevada, North Dakota, Oklahoma, Oregon, South Dakota, Texas, Utah, Washington, and Wyoming) prohibited marriages between whites and African Americans. Ten states (Arizona, California, Idaho, Montana, Nebraska, Nevada, Oregon, South Dakota, Utah, and Wyoming) prohibited marriages between whites and Asian Americans, including Japanese, Chinese, and Koreans. Six states (Arizona, California, Nevada, South Dakota,

Utah, and Wyoming) prohibited marriages between whites and Filipinos. Five states (Arizona, Idaho, Nevada, Oregon, and Washington) prohibited marriages between whites and American Indians. In addition, Oregon prohibited marriages between whites and "Kanakas" (or native Hawaiians), and Arizona prohibited marriages between whites and Hindus.

The first Western antimiscegenation law was passed in Texas in 1837; the last, more than a hundred years later, in Utah in 1939. Although Kansas repealed its law in 1858 and New Mexico and Washington state repealed theirs after the Civil War, the vast majority of the laws remained in force well into the twentieth century. Antimiscegenation laws did not face significant legal challenge until 1948, when, in a decision known as *Perez* v. *Sharp,* the California Supreme Court declared its state law unconstitutional. After the *Perez* case, Western state legislatures gradually began to repeal the laws; in 1967, the remaining ones were declared unconstitutional by the U.S. Supreme Court in the case of *Loving* v. *Virginia.*

—*Peggy Pascoe*

SUGGESTED READING:
Martyn, Byron Curti. "Racism in the United States: A History of the Anti-Miscegenation Legislation and Litigation." Ph.D. diss., University of Southern California, 1979.
Osumi, Megumi Dick. "Asians and California's Anti-Miscegenation Laws." In *Asian and Pacific American Experiences: Women's Perspectives.* Edited by Nobuya Tsuchida. Minneapolis, Minn., 1982.
Pascoe, Peggy. "Race, Gender, and Intercultural Relations: The Case of Interracial Marriage." *Frontiers* 12:1 (1991): 5–18.

MARRIAGES BETWEEN SPANISH/MEXICANS AND NATIVE AMERICANS

Spanish women were in short supply in America during the early years of Spain's empire building. The Spanish had originally arrived in their "new world" armed with a long list of pejorative terms spawned by an established tradition of intolerance, which allowed them to distinguish Catholic ethnic stocks from Jews and Moors. This well-developed "class consciousness" of the conquistadors allowed them not only to distinguish among their own ranks, but to discern upper and lower classes among the Indians, and they took brides from among those Indians they deemed noble. At first, the church and Spanish law sanctified such unions, and the mixed children of these licit marriages were treated almost as the peers of "pure-blood" children. When more Spanish women arrived and married, the colonials created what they called "the castes" *(las castas)* to distinguish their children from the "mixed bloods."

The colonials designated freed Indians slaves and Indians who had deserted their tribes and who lived in colonial settlements *genizaros;* those of African and Spanish descent, *mulattos;* of mixed African, Indian, and European descent, *pardos* or *color quebrados;* of African and Indian descent, *zambos;* of American Indian and Spanish descent, *coyotes;* of Mexican Indian and Spanish descent, *mestizos.* To the *españoles,* the Spanish elite, these mixed-race categories were supposed to correspond to class divisions, and every person in Spanish America was supposed to belong to one of the racial castes. The nobility, the dons and doñas, had to be *españoles;* peasants were mestizos, *coyotes,* or mulattos. The nobles lived on estates provided by private land grants from the crown; peasants occupied much smaller farms, some of them private grants, but most of them shared communal lands, or *mercedes,* granted to peasants as a group; *genizaros,* the lowest class, had no land at all or, at best, took up residence along the Apache or Comanche raiding trails. In short, one's race was supposed to dictate one's place in colonial society. It did not always, of course, work that way in reality. Still the precedent for recognizing the special conditions of frontier sex had been established, and unlike in Puritan North America, the Spanish had incorporated intermarriage into their culture.

Intermarriage in many ways played a key role for the Spanish colonials who trekked north into present-day Texas, New Mexico, Arizona, and California in the wake of the Spanish missionaries and soldiers. The Spanish colonials were more than casually concerned with their racial ancestry, and their racial ancestry had much to do with mixed marriages. As a result especially of intermarriage with the Indians, people of pure Spanish descent were rare in the borderlands of New Mexico as they had been in the early empire. Since, for example, extraordinary service in Juan de Oñate's reconquest of the area in the late sixteenth century brought with it honor, land, and status, and since the Spanish colonials tended to equate honor, land, and status with being *español,* New Mexicans seemed to sprout the necessary Spanish ancestry as they came up in the world—one grew "whiter" as one acquired land, or married well, or earned fame and respect. Thus, the settlers and soldiers who returned to New Mexico after the Pueblo Revolt had been crushed in 1695 were generally of black, mulatto, or mestizo origin. Even the old, exiled New Mexican families who came back with them traced descent from the Mexican Indians who had originally traveled north with Oñate.

Likewise, the group Juan Bautista de Anza led from Sonora to settle and garrison San Francisco was mostly mestizo and mulatto. Of those who came to San Francisco and San Jose between 1776 and 1778, only one-third of the men and one-fourth of the women claimed to be *españoles,* and many of them were probably stretching the truth. In short, if a man was a don, he was Spanish, regardless of whom his father or mother had married. On the frontier, instead of race determining class, class determined race, and intermarriage with the natives, especially among those outside the Spanish elite, would continue to be a feature of Hispanic life in America.

—*Charles Phillips*

Suggested reading:

Gutierrez, Ramón. *When Jesus Came, the Corn Mothers Went Away: Power and Sexuality in New Mexico, 1500–1846.* Stanford, Calif., 1991.

Jennings, Francis. *The Founders of America: How Indians Discovered the Land, Pioneered in It, and Created Great Classical Civilizations; How They Were Plunged into a Dark Age by Invasion and Conquest; and How They Are Now Reviving.* New York, 1993.

MARRIAGES BETWEEN EURO-AMERICANS AND NATIVE AMERICANS

The greatest numbers of marriages between Euro-Americans and Native Americans occurred among the European or Euro-American fur trappers and Native American women of the American and Canadian West during the seventeenth through the nineteenth centuries. Such unions minimized violent conflict between whites and natives and secured the cooperation of native peoples as essential players in a fur-trade industry dominated by whites.

The motives for a marriage according to the custom of the country, or *à la façon du pays,* as such unions were called by the Europeans, were both social and economic. For Euro-American trappers isolated for months and years in the wilderness, there were few women of their cultural background to marry. At first believed by historians to be marriages of convenience, recent findings indicate that these unions of two different cultural groups lasted long after trappers retired from their trade, and despite cultural differences, many unions successfully weathered hostility from white society. In general, native tribes more readily accepted outsiders in their midst, since incorporating other Native Americans and Europeans through adoption and marriage was a long-standing custom.

More than companionship, however, the union of trappers and Indian women signaled the mutual exchange and dependency necessary for the effective operation of the fur-trading industry. Native wives hunted small animals; supplied "Indian" shoes or moccasins, snow shoes, canoes, and other equipment and preserved foods essential to trapping; served as diplomats and peacemakers between native populations and Europeans; and offered their native skill and know-how about the ways of the wilderness.

Native Americans, for their part, wanted the European goods that trappers exchanged for pelts. The mixed-blood "daughters of the country" produced by mixed marriages became valued as fur traders' wives for the next generation of trappers. Possessing the wilderness and trapping skills of their mothers' peoples, they also adapted successfully to the Christian ways and the white culture learned from their fathers. The presence of mixed-blood women within the trapper culture precipitated a change in attitude among fur-company officials. Where they had once sanctioned unions between European trappers and native women, by 1806, Canada's North West Company prohibited these marriages in favor of unions between whites and the mixed-blood offspring of Euro-American–Native American marriages. The company also imposed rules that made such unions more closely resemble the European concept of marriage. The native custom of the bride price was replaced with a dowry, and the company insisted on marriage contracts that emphasized the husband's financial obligations and recognized the woman's status as a legitimate wife.

By the beginning of the nineteenth century, marriages between Euro-American trappers and Native American women became less common, in part because of the arrival of Anglican missionaries who criticized the unions and in part because of the arrival of white women. As agrarian settlements replaced the fur-trapping wilderness, unions between native women and European men became less accepted among the dominant white society.

—Patricia Hogan

SEE ALSO: Fur Trade; Métis People; Mountain Men; Trappers

SUGGESTED READING:

Faragher, John Mack. "Custom of the Country: Cross-Cultural Marriage in the Far Western Fur Trade." In *Western Women: Their Lands, Their Lives.* Edited by Lillian Schissel, Vicki L. Ruiz, and Janice Monk. Albuquerque, N. Mex., 1988.

Van Kirk, Sylvia. "The Role of Native Women in the Creation of Fur Trade Society in Western Canada, 1670–1830." In *The Women's West.* Edited by Susan Armitage and Elizabeth Jameson. Norman, Okla., and London, 1987.

MARRIAGES BETWEEN EURO-AMERICANS AND SPANISH/MEXICANS

When fur trappers and Boston traders began trickling into Spanish California in the early decades of the nine-teenth century, they were bedazzled by the culture and society of the local *gente de razon*. Many historians have seen in the mountain men the harbingers of American imperialism, but as historian Richard White has pointed out, they were men first—single men living in an alien culture, men who needed women. And outside Native American women, Hispanic females were the only women in Spain's and Mexico's northern frontier regions. The Anglo-American trappers and traders could no more have prospered, nor even survived, among the Californios without the liaisons they formed with Mexican women than they had among the Indians of the prairies and the Great Plains without their "squaws." And just as the Indian women had been not merely sexual objects, but also mediators between cultures, the señoritas, too, eased the way for their men.

High-born Spanish and, later, Mexican wives provided American men with the family ties necessary to get ahead in a strongly patriarchal society and with the access they needed to land grants and trade connections. It is hardly surprising then that just as 40 percent of the mountain men had married Indian women in their first marriages, another 20 percent married Spanish, Mexican, or Mexican American women. Once they tied the knot, reasoned some ambitious American newcomers, all they need do was conveniently convert to Catholicism and become naturalized for the Mexican government to offer then land grants and for the Californios to begin calling them "dons."

"Don" Abel Stearns of Massachusetts, for example, married into the wealthy Bandini family and became in the process a large landowner and a ranchero. William G. Dana from Boston, uncle of author RICHARD HENRY DANA, arrived in Santa Barbara in 1826, converted to the Catholic church, and, after delaying his nuptials for two years (until he became naturalized), finally married the sixteen-year-old Josefa Carilla. General MARIANO GUADALUPE VALLEJO's daughter Rosalia married Jacob Reese, who learned Spanish, attended church ceremonies, and took up the rancho life. "While here [in San Gabriel]," an American visitor wrote home, "I met with a Yankee—Daniel A. Hill [from Santa Barbara] . . . who had been a resident in the country for many years, and who had become, in manner and appearance, a complete Californian."

Not all the well-married Americans "went native," not all the Americans who married Mexican women married so well, and not all the Americans in California approved of "mixed" marriages, well made or not. In fact, many of the Americans, especially as their numbers increased, expressed a certain scorn for Hispanic culture, a scorn colored by the peculiar racial moralizing and stereotyping common to frontier metaphysics.

After his arrival in California, Richard Henry Dana never deigned to visit his uncle, who called himself Don "Guillermo." In his autobiographical *Two Years before the Mast*, Dana noted with some disdain that many Americans were marrying "natives" and raising their children Catholic and Mexican. Yes, he admitted, some Mexicans of "pure Spanish blood" who ran the society were "even as fair" as the English, but they were "an idle, thriftless people" dependent on the laboring classes who "[went] down by regular shades" until they reached bottom with the "pure" Indians. Even if the gentry's laziness, which Dana called the "California fever," skipped the first generation, it "attacked" the second, for all Mexicans, he said, lacked the enterprise, industry, frugality, and sobriety that distinguished the Yankees in their midst.

Spanish and Mexican elites readily accepted the Anglos as suitors for their daughters, in part, because they too labored under frontier conditions in which appropriate husbands were not always abundantly at hand to fill the needs of the traditionally large families of the wealthy. And unlike the Anglo-Americans, the Spanish had a long tradition of intermarriage stretching back to the days of the conquistadors. Wealthy Spanish and Mexicans families, who considered themselves every bit as white and pure-blooded as the Anglos, were hardly conscious of breaking racial taboos when they gave their daughters' hands in marriage to up-and-coming young Americans.

Such marriages were by no means confined to the California coast. Since independence, Mexico had opened its borders to Americans. Beginning in the 1820s, traders, merchants, soldiers, and adventurers drifted into the Southwest borderlands. They arrived without wives or relatives and married into the territory's elite families. Here, too, marriages between Anglo traders and aristocratic Hispanic women became increasingly frequent occurrences. In San Antonio, for example, almost every mid-nineteenth-century upper-class family had at least one daughter married to an Anglo. Such marriages bridged the two cultures by making American trading partners, who had access to huge new markets in the United States, into sons-in-law and providing them with the freedom of movement enjoyed by Mexican citizens—a freedom that, given Mexico City's byzantine trade regulations and venal passport system, would otherwise have been denied to them.

The pattern was clear: prominent Hispanic families were the first group American traders sought out whenever they arrived in the borderlands, for it would be the ruling elite with whom they trafficked. In time, as trade relations developed, these contacts continued and, frequently, grew intimate. By the 1840s, for example, some sixty thousand Spanish-speaking settlers lived in New Mexico; the Anglos of New Mexico numbered somewhere between five hundred and twelve hundred, and many of them had married into the gentry. During the American conquest of the borderlands, first in the Texas Revolution, then in the United States–Mexican War, this foreign element among Tejano aristocrats and within the New Mexican ruling class helped smooth the transition to American rule. And later, in Tucson, Arizona, the large number of cross-cultural marriages kept relations between former Mexicans and the Americans amiable after the United States purchased the region in 1853.

By the time Americans began to arrive in the borderlands in large numbers after the Civil War, intermarriage had become quite common and not at all restricted to the local Spanish elite and the American entrepreneurs. The same dynamics held for intermarriages among the common folk as held for the elite. American males gained access to the local culture; Hispanic females, a means of assimilation into the region's new politically dominant culture. For many of the New Mexican women during this period, marriage to an Anglo meant a step up in social status. The American men, however modest their origins, tended to have more money to spend than their Hispanic counterparts, and they were usually better educated. The vast majority of the New Mexican women were illiterate, but those attracted to the Anglos tended also to be better educated, if only slightly, than their sisters. And in at least one respect, the poor among the New Mexican females had an advantage over upper-class Hispanic women: they were free to meet the American men on the streets and in the cantinas, whereas the carefully protected daughters of the Hispanic elite had to rely on introductions and arranged courtships. On the other hand, having come from more humble backgrounds, the women in these new cross-cultural marriages could easily be left destitute when their American husbands died or deserted them.

New tensions, in large measure absent from the older marriages between elite Hispanic females and ambitious Anglo males, plagued these humbler cross-cultural marriages. Both Anglo and Spanish cultures valued masculinity and emphasized male dominance. Upper-class Hispanic females were accustomed to an open double standard that demanded legal marriage and fidelity from women but allowed males to take mistresses and flaunt their sexual conquests. Since most of those conquests occurred among the lower classes, the double standard and folk customs sanctioned greater sexual freedom for poor women, a freedom that could prove threatening to American men after marriage.

In addition, the emphasis on the community—the village—and the family in Mexican life put Mexican wives under considerable strain, especially when married couples moved into sparsely populated regions and husbands left their wives alone for long periods of time. Interethnic marriages tended to crumble under such cultural differences, which in turn led to pressures for one—or both—of the partners to assimilate, at least partially, to their mate's culture. As in California, many among the Anglos looked down on Hispanic culture and Hispanic wives, thus frequently creating unbearable pressures for both partners. Not surprisingly, although most of the cross-cultural marriages endured until one partner died, some ended in divorce, and Hispanic women who married Anglos went through divorces more often than those who married within their communities. Not a few of the divorces came after the Anglo husband had simply deserted his Hispanic wife.

In short, intermarriage between Anglo males and Hispanic females—there were few marriages between Anglo females and Hispanic males—played a key role in the history of California and the Southwest. Such marriages introduced ambitious Americans into the Spanish and Mexican elite, eased the way for close trade relations, and helped introduce the growing American market into traditional Hispanic economies. They also provided Hispanics a door into the Anglo culture that was fast coming to dominate their lives, providing—for a while at least—a common ground between two historically different peoples.

—*Patricia Hogan and Charles Phillips*

SEE ALSO: Stereotypes: Stereotypes of Mexicans

SUGGESTED READING:

González, Deena J. "Spanish-Mexican Women on the Santa Fe Frontier: Patterns of Their Resistance and Accommodation, 1820–1880." Ph.d. diss., University of California, Berkeley, 1985.

Jensen, Joan M., and Darlis A. Miller. *New Mexico Women: Intercultural Perspectives.* Albuquerque, N. Mex., 1986.

Takaki, Ronald. *A Different Mirror: A History of Multicultural America.* Boston, 1993.

MARRIAGES BETWEEN ASIAN AMERICANS AND MEXICANS

Asian Mexican intermarriage was practiced in the early twentieth century by immigrants in the American West, although it was the dominant pattern only for those from India. Antimiscegenation laws prevented marriage across "racial" lines, but there was little objection to the marriages of Asian men with women of Mexican descent. When Chinese men came as prospectors for gold in the mid-nineteenth century, most left wives and children behind in China and did not marry again in the American West. Some Chinese Mexican families existed in Arizona and southern California (and more in Mexico). Japanese male immigrants who began arriving in the late nineteenth century could bring in "PIC-TURE BRIDES" until the 1920s, and most did so, although again some Japanese Mexican families appear. The two Asian communities where significant intermarriage with Mexicans occurred were the EAST INDIANS and the Filipinos.

East Indian men began arriving in America at the turn of the century and were barred from bringing their wives by new anti-Asian immigration laws. The East Indians found that they could obtain licenses to marry women of Mexican descent relatively easily, and 80 percent of their marriages in the American West before the 1950s were with such women (with a high of 93 percent in California's Imperial Valley). At the time of the Mexican Revolution, when Mexicans were just beginning to move in large numbers to the United States, cotton farmers from India's Punjab province met Mexican women picking in their fields in California's Imperial Valley. The marriages between Punjabis and Mexicans began in 1916 and continued well into the 1940s (in 1946, South Asians became eligible for U.S. citizenship and could sponsor family members from their homeland). The Filipino immigrants, also a heavily male group arriving in the 1920s and 1930s, looked to both Mexican and Anglo women for wives (despite a special 1933 law aimed at preventing their marriage with Anglo women).

Discriminatory laws helped determine marriage choices of Asians to a great extent, since the men were not free to choose among all women in the population. On the women's side, marriage to an Asian immigrant, particularly to a farmer, was often an economic step up, although it often meant estrangement from the Mexican American community. The largest biethnic community was that of the Punjabi Mexicans, and most of these five hundred or so biethnic couples lived in southern California. While the marriages between Filipinos and Mexicans were strongly based on a shared language and religion (Spanish and Catholicism), those between Punjabis and Mexicans brought together different languages and religions. The children, whose names showed their dual heritage (Maria Jesusita Singh, José Akbar Khan, Rudolfo Chand), were raised primarily as Spanish-speaking Catholics; very few learned Punjabi or much about East Indian culture. People outside the community called the men "Hindus" (from Hindustan or India, although most of the men were Sikhs or Muslims rather than Hindu) and the families "Mexican Hindus." The children grew up proudly claiming their "Hindu" ancestry. Despite little continuity of Punjabi culture in these families, the descendants are more likely to emphasize their Indian heritage—the one more unusual and distinctive in the American West and clearly marked by their surnames.

—*Karen Leonard*

SUGGESTED READING:

Leonard, Karen. "Intermarriage and Ethnicity: Punjabi Mexican Americans, Mexican Japanese, and Filipino Americas." *Explorations in Ethnic Studies* 16:2 (July 1993).

———. *Making Ethnic Choices: California's Punjabi Mexican Americans.* Philadelphia, 1992.

MARRIAGES BETWEEN ASIANS AMERICANS AND EURO-AMERICANS

The occurrence of marriage between Asian Americans and Euro-Americans happened only incidentally in the West in the nineteenth and early twentieth centuries. The few marriages that did take place usually involved Asian women, perhaps a Chinese prostitute hoping to leave her profession, and Euro-American men. On the other hand, Western states, fearing the nineteenth-century immigration of single Chinese, Japanese, Korean, and Filipino male immigrants, enacted anti-miscegeneration laws aimed at "protecting" white women from marrying Asian men.

JAPANESE AMERICANS, compared to other racial groups and other Asian American groups, outmarried (married individuals outside their ethnic group) at the highest rate. But, among the Issei (first) and Nisei (second) generations of Japanese Americans, the practice was discouraged by the Japanese as much as by whites, and the incidence of Japanese marrying outside their cultural group was rare. A study of Los Angeles County, for example, found that from 1924 to 1933, intermarriages constituted only 2 percent of all marriages involving Japanese Americans; by the years between 1948 and 1951, the figure was 12 percent. As the twentieth century progressed, the likelihood of intermarriage increased with succeeding generations of Japanese Americans born in the United States. The incidence of such marriages occurred more frequently in communities with low Japanese population densities.

World War II produced a number of marriages involving Japanese and non-Japanese. Many servicemen returned from overseas duty with Japanese war brides. In 1979 and 1980, about 43 percent of the Japanese Americans in the United States and Hawaii were in marriages involving a non-Japanese partner. After decades of American hostility toward Japanese Americans, their marriages to Euro-Americans in such numbers indicated the extent to which they had assimilated American culture.

—*Patricia Hogan and Charles Phillips*

SEE ALSO: Chinese Americans

SUGGESTED READING:

Kikumura, Akemi, and Harry H. L. Kitano. "Interracial Marriage: A Picture of the Japanese Americans." *Journal of Social Issues* 29 (1973): 67–81.

Spickard, Paul R. *Mixed Blood: Intermarriage and Ethnic Identity in Twentieth-Century America.* Madison, Wis., 1989.

INTERSTATE COMMERCE ACT OF 1887

In the 1880s, pressure grew from the reform elements of the Democratic party, Populists, the Farmers' Alliance, and other groups to regulate the structure of interstate commerce. Suspicion of monopolies, rebates, and other activities that favored big business interests and railroads at the expense of farmers and small-business interests grew rapidly during the decade as railroad barons tightened their control of the rail transportation network. After an 1886 Supreme Court ruling that forbade the states to regulate interstate commerce, the time for a national authority had clearly come.

Western politicians, led by Representative John H. Reagan of Texas, chairman of the House Committee on Commerce, introduced a bill to establish national regulation of the RAILROADS in 1887. The act provided for what was the second independent regulatory commission of the United States government. Initially the commission was made up of five members appointed by the president for six-year terms. Members of the commission could not be dismissed by the president. Eventually, membership was expanded to eleven individuals. Intended to prevent pooling, rebates, discrimination, and unequal rates for long- and short-haul service, the commission had investigatory powers over the railroads; its orders, however, did not have the force of a court decree, and the railroads were able to circumvent many of its decisions, while the Supreme Court reduced the commission's powers. In the early twentieth century, a series of reforms, beginning with the 1903 Elkins Act, expanded the commission's powers, and by 1948, all carriers of interstate commerce became subject to its powers.

The 1887 ICC Act did give additional strength to state efforts to regulate railroads, such as those under the auspices of JAMES STEPHEN HOGG of Texas. Reagan resigned his Senate seat to become chair of the Texas Railroad Commission, the local equivalent of the ICC.

—*Patrick H. Butler, III*

SUGGESTED READING:

Chandler, Alfred D. *The Railroads: The Nation's First Big Business*. New York, 1965.

Proctor, Ben H. *Not without Honor: The Life of John H. Reagan*. Austin, Tex., 1962.

IOWA

Iowa, the "Hawkeye State," lies directly West of the Mississippi River, which forms its entire eastern border. Located in the north-central United States, Iowa forms a bridge between the natural forest lands east of the river and the original grasslands of the Great Plains to the West. Iowa's 56,275 square miles of immensely fertile soil are bounded on the north by Minnesota, on the south by Missouri, on the east by Wisconsin and Illinois, and on the west by Nebraska and North Dakota. Iowa's population, which in 1970 fell just short of 3 million, had declined to 2,776,755 by 1990. Iowa's people are overwhelmingly of European descent and remarkably uniform in religion, social status, and economic position—mostly Protestant (Lutheran and Methodist), middle-class farmers and merchants.

But it was French Catholics who established Iowa's first settlement at Dubuque. The city still boasts a large Catholic minority, as do other of Iowa's larger urban areas. Before 1850, settlers in southern Iowa were likely to come from Kentucky and those to the north from Ohio, Indiana, Illinois, New England, and the Middle Atlantic states, but after that date, Iowa experienced a huge influx from Europe, mostly Germans, but also goodly numbers of British and Irish immigrants. In the last decades of the century, Scandinavians settled throughout the western and central portions of the state. By World War I, there were few foreign-born people in southern Iowa: an enclave of Croatians and Italians in the coal fields; some Dutch around Pella. Iowa's cities, on the other hand, especially those along the Mississippi, attracted a greater variety of immigrants.

Some ethnic and religious groups still thrive in Iowa. Czechs are prominent in Cedar Rapids; south of Iowa City and around Independence, the Amish hold to the old ways, occasionally coming into conflict with the state over health issues and education. The Amana Colonies, originally settled in 1855 by German utopians from Buffalo, New York, incorporated in 1932.

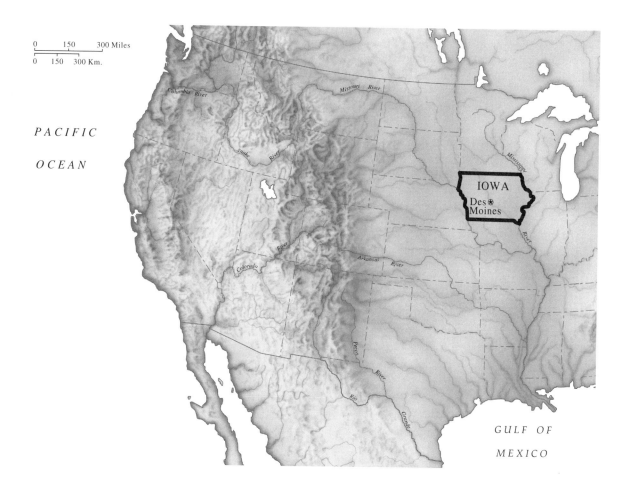

The Amanas modernized their economies while maintaining their beliefs. Some MORMONS crossing Iowa on their way to Utah in the 1840s settled in southern Iowa's Lamoni. President HERBERT HOOVER's Quaker ancestors settled near his home town of West Branch, ten miles east of Iowa City. African Americans, officially discouraged from taking up residence in the nineteenth century, composed Iowa's only significant number of emigrants during the twentieth century. They settled in the larger urban centers, especially in Des Moines and Waterloo. And in 1852, after having been "removed" by treaty to reservations in Kansas, the Fox (Mesquakie) Indians joined other members of the tribe who had never left the state, pooled money they had saved from their federal allotments, and purchased private title to eighty acres of river-bottom land in Tama County. There they managed to recreate their old tribal existence and to remain culturally independent of their neighbors and fellow landowners.

The first of Iowa's European settlers marveled at the region's rich soil, the beauty of its prairies, and its "salubrious" climate, which in truth is not all that salubrious, except for its long growing season. Deep in the interior of the continent, Iowa's winters are cold and dry, averaging about 14° F in the north and 22° F in the south, although temperatures of 50° below zero are not unheard of. Summers are warm and humid, with the temperature averaging 74° F and with frequent and intense spring and summer thunderstorms, fed by moist air from the Gulf of Mexico. Iowa receives four times as much rain in the summer as it does in the winter, averaging twenty-eight inches in the northwest, and thirty-five inches in the southeast.

Some Iowans live in cities. Des Moines is Iowa's political capital; Iowa City, its cultural mecca; Dubuque, Davenport, Cedar Rapids, and Sioux City, the major sites of the state's relatively skimpy industry. By and large, however, Iowa's population is as evenly distributed—in small towns and on farms—as its geography is uniform. The essential elements for Iowa's development were in place long before the first Indians hunted woolly mammoths on the prairie or the first Europeans crossed the Mississippi. The true forces shaping present-day Iowa had less to do with a rapidly expanding frontier or national politics than they did with the Pleistocene Age, when drifting glaciers left sheets of ice that bequeathed to Iowa 25 percent of the nation's grade-A topsoil.

Geography

The ice sheets started coming about 1.6 million years ago. The earliest sheets covered the northeastern portion of the state, where tributaries of the Mississippi River gouged deep cuts in the bedrock and left behind bluffs two hundred to three hundred feet above the river valley. The network of tributaries formed a scenic and hilly landscape. Underlying most of the state, however, was a somewhat later ice sheet, long eroded by some two hundred thousand years of running water and wind. The still later Illinoian sheet covered a small part of the state in the southeast and the east, and it diverted the Mississippi River, which created a valley along the river's current west front. Twenty thousand to twenty-five thousand years ago, the Wisconsin ice sheet moved south to about the present-day location of Des Moines. This Des Moines lobe began its final retreat around thirteen thousand to fourteen thousand years ago. Both the Illinois and the Wisconsin glaciers left massive deposits of windblown silt, or loess, carried by the ice into western Iowa from the Great Plains. Near the Missouri River valley on Iowa's western boundary, the loess piled eighty to a hundred feet high, producing the bluffs of present-day Council Bluffs as well as the highest point in the state, a northwestern hill 1,670 feet above sea level. Today, Des Moines lies amid broad, flat uplands, which together form a mildly sloping drift plain that covers the central and north-central parts of the state. Much to the chagrin of many Iowans, the state gets its popular image as a flat land from the Des Moines drift plain, when in fact the long-vanished lakes and swamps left by ancient ice produced a gentle and rolling, if uniform, landscape throughout most of the state. At any rate, the melting waters of the retreating glaciers deposited tremendous quantities of loess that constitute the basic ingredients of Iowa's soil.

Formed from that material under prairie vegetation, the thick, dark soils of Iowa, rich in organic matter, make up the twenty-six million (out of Iowa's thirty-six million) acres of today's grade-A farm land, the dirt of which New England poet Robert Frost once said: "It looks good enough to eat without putting it through vegetables." Such a soil perhaps begged for a future when 98 percent of Iowa's acreage would come under cultivation, the highest percentage of any state in the nation. "The rich land was here," wrote Iowa historian Joseph Wall, "only men and machines were needed to turn it into a garden."

Native inhabitants

For the Paleo-Indians, the nameless grasslands between the Mississippi and the Missouri rivers were hardly a garden. Ice sheets may well still have covered the ground around present-day Des Moines when these nomadic tribes first arrived in the middle land in search of mammoths and bisons. Hunting and gathering, they barely scratched out a subsistence because—then as now—the area was plagued by periodic drought. Even after the Indians took up farming around 800 A.D. in western Iowa, entire villages would occasionally vanish. To the east, along the Mississippi, those Native Americans whom archaeologists call "mound-builders" established their settlements beginning in about 300 A.D. Not long after Columbus arrived in the New World, however, these cultures disappeared, as did the big game on the grasslands. Afterwards, for the Indians of the woodlands and lakes to the east, the place had too few trees and too little water to be attractive; for those west of the Missouri, the Sioux tribes of the Great Plains, the grass was too high and too thin to entice the great herds of grazing buffaloes that sustained the Sioux way of life.

Then in the seventeenth century, the French began pushing Algonquian tribes such as the Winnebago, the Sac (Sauk), and the Fox out of their homelands around the Great Lakes and down the Wisconsin, Rock, and Illinois rivers into the Mississippi Valley and the lands lying to the west. The allied Sac and Fox tribes arrived in the area implacably bellicose, and they remained that way. In the century following, they undertook wars of extinction against the Illinois, the Iowa, the Missouri, the Peoria, and the Sioux tribes to the west. By the beginning of the eighteenth century, the Sac and the Fox held in undisputed possession all the territory north of the Missouri River and east of the Grand to the Mississippi. And this time, they meant to stay where they were. They became eager participants in Shawnee sachem TECUMSEH's transtribal Indian confederacy, and when Tecumseh fell in the WAR OF 1812, they remained staunch allies of the British. Despite American chicanery and bullying, they refused to give up their lands east of the Mississippi. Not until their great war chief was defeated and utterly humiliated during BLACK HAWK's WAR in 1832 did they reluctantly move west of the river completely, to their hunting grounds in Iowa and southern Wisconsin. There—under political pressure from their new U.S. government-certified tribal chief KEOKUK—they sold the rest of their lands to the whites. By treaty, most of them removed to Kansas, where they took up fighting the Comanches. A number of them hid out illegally in the Iowa hinterland and never left. With the Sac and Fox officially out of the way, the United States purchased the rest of Iowa from the Dakota Sioux in 1851.

Territorial period and early statehood

In 1673, French explorers LOUIS JOLIET and JACQUES MARQUETTE probably became the first Europeans to see Iowa, but the first European settler did not arrive until more than a century had passed. French Canadian JULIEN DUBUQUE got permission from the Fox to mine lead near present-day Dubuque in 1788, and the Spanish confirmed his title to the area in a 1796 land grant. After Dubuque died, the Fox ceremoniously buried him and then burned his home and took over the mines, which they controlled until Black Hawk's defeat in 1832. Meanwhile, French travelers of the woods and Indians explored and hunted in the area. The French and Indian heritage of the region would be reflected in Iowa place names: Des Moines, Le Mars, Ottumwa, Keokuk.

Iowa was part of the vast area included in the 1803 LOUISIANA PURCHASE, but it remained Sac and Fox territory even after the War of 1812, when the United States established a garrison on the Iowa side of the Mississippi at Fort Madison. After the purchase of eastern Iowa from the tribes in the 1830, settlers moved in to till the soil illegally before the area had been organized as a territory. The first public sale of land took place in Dubuque in 1838, the year the grasslands between two rivers officially became the Iowa Territory with a population of 22, 242 and a territorial capital in Iowa City. By 1840, more than one million acres had been sold, and more came on the market every year. Visiting Iowa in the 1850s, Ralph Waldo Emerson complained that all anyone ever talked about was quarter sections. Within thirty years, almost all the land had been sold or turned over as a land grant under the MORRILL ACT OF 1862. By 1890, the federal

Overland journeys began at Iowa's Council Bluffs on the Missouri River. An 1855 engraving shows covered wagons waiting for the ferry to cross the river. *Courtesy Library of Congress.*

government owned a mere five thousand acres of public land within the state.

Iowa became the twenty-ninth state in 1846. Six years earlier, there had been 43,112 Iowa settlers; four years later, there would be 192,214 Iowa citizens. In a decade, the population would triple: the 1860 census counted 674,913 Iowans. Some 38,000 of them were Germans; 28,000 Irish; 14,000 English and Scots; 5,600 Scandinavians; 2,600 Dutch; 2,500 Swedish; 2,400 French; and 1,609 African Americans. The phenomenal growth had to do, of course, with the fertile soil, but there was also the consideration that—compared to other states in the trans-Mississippi West—Iowa was relatively free of hostile Indians. No major battles between whites and Indians were ever fought in the state, and the only notable Indian "trouble" came with the 1857 Spirit Lake Massacre, in which a band of Sioux retaliated for the murder of their chief a year earlier. It was the last even remotely hostile Indian action in the state's history. Far more typical was the return of the Fox Indians to Tama County five years earlier. Instead of resisting the tribe's efforts to buy private title to lands in the area, eastern Iowans welcomed the Indians and the income their annuities would bring. Over the years, the Fox bought more land, until they held twenty-eight hundred acres in common by 1895, when responsibility for their well-being was transferred from the state to the Bureau of Indian Affairs, which could do little about the private property they had purchased.

One-third of Iowa's residents in 1860 were born in the state, one-third moved there from the Old Northwest, and only 8 percent of Iowa's population came from the South. It was hardly surprising then that Iowans flocked to the newly formed Republican party and fought resolutely for the Union during the Civil War. Iowa contributed an especially large number of troops to the Northern cause in proportion to its population, although no battles were fought on Iowa soil during the war. After the conflict, with the Indian threat completely gone and the railroad boom getting underway, Iowa's prairies were thrown open to massive waves of Easterners and Europeans, people who were eager to take advantage of the Civil War–spawned HOMESTEAD ACT OF 1862 and the rich soil of the grasslands. In the last half of the nineteenth century, Iowa became what it was to remain, a food basket to the world.

Economic and cultural life

Iowa lies at the heart of the Corn Belt; its crop income is second only to California; its livestock income, the highest in the country. Only Texas and Nebraska raise more cattle, and no state produces more HOGS. Iowa ranks high in every agriculture-related product one can imagine. In addition to corn, cattle, and hogs, Iowans grow soybeans, alfalfa, and other grains and raise dairy cows, sheep, and chickens. Mechanization, taking its toll among Iowa farmers, has cut their number in half since the late nineteenth and early twentieth centuries, down to about one hundred thousand. Most of them struggle hard—working seventy-hour weeks—to maintain a middle-class life style, a struggle periodically made even harder by unstable markets. Since at least the beginning of the century, technology and Iowa's fertile soil have led Iowa farmers frequently to produce surpluses, which, with equal frequency, depress farm prices. As a result, about one-quarter of Iowa's food production goes to international markets, netting in excess of $2 billion in sales per year and making Iowa's conservative farmers diehard free-traders.

No state has a higher standard of living in its rural areas than Iowa, and Iowans pour their hard-earned money into good roads and a first-class educational system. Iowa's first school opened in 1830, and since then, the state has consistently ranked in the upper half of all states in its support for education. The University of Iowa was founded in 1847, and the Iowa State University of Science and Technology, in 1858. In a state dotted with small towns and boasting only medium-sized cities, both institutions functioned as more than mere schools. The University of Iowa, for example, has long run a large medical complex in Iowa City and has always served as the center of much of the state's cultural life. There Grant Wood did most of his painting, and the Iowa Writers Workshop enjoys national esteem. Art museums of significance are found not only in Iowa City, but also in Des Moines and Davenport. Dubuque, Cedar Rapids, Fort Dodge, Sioux City, and even such small towns as Cherokee and Decorah have museums or art galleries of which Iowa, prickly about its "hick" imagine, is proud. West Branch houses the Herbert Hoover Presidential Library.

Some have criticized Iowa farmers for being careless stewards of the soil, and Iowa does indeed lose more topsoil through EROSION than any other state. However cosmopolitan they might be when discussing foreign sales to Russia or China, Iowa's farmers become crusty conservatives when their land use is questioned. Even under intense pressure from environmentalists in government and elsewhere, they have been slow to address Iowa's ecological problems, especially when the complaints include the heavy use of PESTICIDES by which Iowa farmers maintain their profits.

It has become customary for those writing about Iowa to point out that its reputation as the world's food basket is in many ways misleading. Certainly the following is true: many Iowans have left the land. Most

Iowans live lives far removed from farm chores, cash crops, grunting pigs, and lowing cows. Since World War II, Iowa has diversified its economic base to balance its overreliance on AGRICULTURE. Des Moines, for example, is industrially advanced with thriving insurance, banking, and printing enterprises. On the other hand, three-fourths of the state's population depend on either agriculture or industries closely related to agriculture, such as food processing, meat packing, or the manufacture of tractors and other farm equipment. In January 1982, once prosperous Dubuque posted the nation's highest unemployment rate, 23 percent, when the city's major employer, John Deere and Company, laid off half its work force. The following October, Dubuque's second largest employer, the Dubuque Packing Company, announced it was closing its doors. Cedar Falls and Davenport, too, are major producers of farm machinery, and Sioux City, with its famed stockyards, is clearly tied to Iowa agriculture as well.

In general, despite a few cities, a top-notch educational system, and some commitment to fine arts and culture, Iowa remains basically a state of farm communities and small towns dominated by a main-street culture—middle-class, middle-of-the-road, and Republican.

Politics

During territorial days, Iowa may have been briefly as Democratic as any agrarian, Jeffersonian frontier. But—although many Iowa farmers were quick to join the Grange, the Farmers' Holiday, and the Populist party during the massive downswings of post–Civil War industrialization in the trans-Mississippi West—Iowa's corn growers and hog farmers were never as radical as those in such cash grain states as Minnesota and the Dakotas. Since at least the Civil War, the majority of Iowans have been almost by nature Republicans. As their late nineteenth-century and very Republican U.S. Senator Johnathan P. Dolliver crowed at the height of his power: "When Iowa goes Democratic, Hell will go Methodist." A bastion of Protestant morality, Iowa became, in 1882, the second state (after Kansas) to enact statewide prohibition. Led by the WOMAN'S CHRISTIAN TEMPERANCE UNION's J. Ellen Foster, the Republicans adopted a "dry" plank after briefly losing their majority in 1877, when the Prohibition party drained off votes. Until the mid-twentieth century, Iowa remained free of Democratic "rum and Romanism."

Then, for a while in the 1960s and 1970s, it looked indeed as if Hell were going Methodist. Harold E. Hughes, an ex-truck driver, ex-alcoholic Democrat came to the governor's office in 1962 for the first of an unprecedented three terms, during which he abolished Iowa's ancient injunction against the sale of liquor by

the drink; eliminated capital punishment; established early-release farms for prison inmates; promoted modernization in the treatment of mental illness, law enforcement, and industrial development; and then ran for the U.S. Senate and won. In 1973, Hughes, disenchanted with the war in Vietnam, resigned to take up the lay ministry. In the U.S. Senate, two liberal Iowa Democrats, Dick Clark and John Culver together led the fight to cut federal funding for the seemingly endless war. Neither survived the coming of the neoconservative Republican New Right in the 1980s.

The thoughtful, low-key, utterly imperturbable Republican Robert Ray had followed the passionate, engaging, thoroughly candid Hughes into the state house. Four terms later, he was followed by the rigidly conservative Terry E. Branstad. By the late twentieth century, Iowa was safely back in the Republican fold where it had been for most of its history. Iowa's cities remained Democratic, but they were never sufficiently large to carry a state populated by essentially conservative, sober, and hard-working Protestant farmers who lived good, if sometimes anxious, lives deep in America's heartland.

—*Charles Phillips*

SEE ALSO: Colleges and Universities; Corn Growing; Farming

SUGGESTED READING:
Grant, J. Roger, and L. Edward Purcell, eds. *Years of Struggle: The Farm Diary of Elmer G. Powers, 1931–1936.* Ames, Iowa, 1976.
Gue, Benjamin F. *History of Iowa.* 4 vols. New York, 1903.
Ross, Earle D. *Iowa Agriculture.* Iowa City, Iowa, 1951.
Sage, Leland. *A History of Iowa.* Ames, Iowa, 1974. Reprint. 1987.
Schwieder, Dorothy. *Patterns and Perspectives in Iowa History.* Ames, Iowa, 1973.
Wall, Joseph Frazier. *Iowa: A Bicentennial History.* New York and Nashville, Tenn., 1978.

IOWA INDIANS

SEE: Native American Peoples: Peoples of the Great Plains

IRISH AMERICANS

From the end of the of the War of 1812 through 1844, one million Irish came to America. The Gaelic words they used to described themselves—*deorai* (exiles) or *dithreabhach* (homeless) or *dibeartach* (banished people)—made clear the fact that they did not want to

The mining industry drew numbers of Irish immigrants West to make their fortunes, hoping to be like James C. Flood, William O'Brien, James Fair, and John Mackay, who made their millions in the Comstock Mines. *Courtesy Bancroft Library.*

leave Ireland. They felt as if they had been driven from their home because of the brutal enclosures of tillable land by cattle-raising Protestant landlords in the late eighteenth century. Most of the Irish, however, did not exercise the "America option." Instead they became migrants at home, itinerant workers who left their cottages each spring to find jobs as field hands or construction workers and dragged themselves home in the fall with rent money sewn inside their clothes. While they were gone, their families planted potatoes. From planting to harvest, the family ate one meal a day—potatoes. They left the core, the "bones," raw in order to slow down their digestion and stave off hunger. By the 1840s, most of the Irish poor, which meant most of Ireland, existed on the one staple—potatoes. Then came the blight. When summer harvest time rolled round in 1845, the "crops looked splendid." Suddenly, as one Irish farmer recalled, "one fine morning in July there was a cry around that some blight had struck the potato stalks." That year, the Irish lost 40 percent of the potato harvest. And the blight came back year after year after year. Money that once went to rent was spent on food, and rents went unpaid; soon the food money, too, was gone. Before the Great Famine was over, one million Irish had died

of starvation or disease, and five hundred thousand more—mostly young, poor, and unskilled—had fled in a panic to America.

Those on board ship headed for America no longer saw the trip across the ocean as a banishment. They were escaping, not being chased out. They were looking for a fair living in a new country. Unhappily for the Irish, the search was not so simple as sailing into Boston Harbor or New York. They ran smack up against a hostile middle and upper class and an entrenched anti-Irish working class. They crammed together in urban tenements. The young men pouring out of the tenements into the streets of New York, Boston, Philadelphia, and Baltimore formed Irish street gangs like the Plug Uglies of Five Points and the Bowery B'houys. It was the luck of the Irish that they first came in such large numbers during decade of the 1840s, a decade in America marked by depression and war, beginning with the panic of 1837, closing with a divisive victory in the United States–Mexican War; it was the decade when Americans were first asking themselves what they were going to do with all these foreigners arriving on their shores. Most of America's anti-Irish stereotypes grew out of the middle decades of the nineteenth century when the immigrants were streaming into a economically depressed United States from a blighted and bleak Ireland.

Patricios

A few of them headed west; many joined the U.S. Army destined soon to invade Mexico; others traveled to California, especially after gold was discovered in 1848. The first to arrive on the West Coast adjusted quickly to the rancho way of life, which made them different from most of the other Irish in America who steadfastly refused to till the soil and clung to the cities, even after—later in the century—their priests began to promote homesteading. The Irish soldiers, too, were different, at first, from the Irish back in the cities of the East, who—like a large number of New Englanders and the working class—objected to expanding into Mexico basically at the behest of Southern slave holders and Texans.

The army General ZACHARY TAYLOR had hammered into a decidedly efficient fighting force on the Mexican border was remarkable in the U.S. military experience both because it was entirely made up of regulars and because many of the regulars, nearly 47 percent, were foreign-born: 24 percent of them were Irish. It was a brutal and nasty imperial war the Irish were being asked to fight, and a number deserted. The Mexicans cleverly appealed to the religious tastes of the Irish Catholics. They celebrated this or that saint's day almost every day across the Rio Grande in Matamoros. They held Masses, played music, and marched in processions. After giving royal treatment to two dragoons captured on the day of Taylor's arrival, the Mexicans returned them to the American camp where, flushed and aglow, the soldiers told stories of the comely women and congenial people across the river. Much discriminated against by the "real" Americans, many of the troops took the plunge, especially during the first few days, and the desertion rate mounted. When fourteen men swam the river in a single night, Taylor turned draconian. He ordered guards to shoot to kill deserters, and after a Frenchman and a Swiss were executed, the number of desertions declined.

Typical of the turncoats was Sergeant John Riley, a tough, good-looking Irishman, who had also deserted the British army in Canada to come to America and serve time as a drillmaster at West Point. A sergeant with the Fifth Infantry, Riley claimed later, with some irony, that he had been "seized with a desire to go to church." He swam the river one Sunday morning and never came back. It probably did not hurt that, after Mass, the Mexicans had offered him 320 acres of good Mexican land to stay. He soon had plenty of company, since, during the slack period at Matamoros, some two hundred men deserted, most of them—like Riley—foreign-born soldiers never made particularly welcome by American society. Many of them had joined the army, in fact, originally to escape the hostility they experienced in America. Now they were saying goodbye to all that. They were to form the nucleus of the San Patricio—or Saint Patrick's—Battalion, which turned out to be one of Mexico's finest fighting units.

At the end of the war, when General WINFIELD SCOTT's troops first assaulted Mexico City, they ran into the Saint Patrick's Battalion, commanded by Thomas Riley. The Patricios had continued to grow in number as the American volunteers and the regular army officers abused the foreign-born soldiers. Now they put up a fierce resistance, fighting until all their ammunition was gone, then fighting with clubbed muskets until there were only some eighty left alive to be taken prisoner. Some were pardoned; others, condemned. During the final assault against the National

Palace—the very Halls of Montezuma—on a small hillock near Chapultepec, thirty of the doomed men stood on mule carts, nooses around their necks, their manifest destiny being to die at the very instant the palace fell. All accounts have the men laughing and joking and aiming sharp-edged jibes at the brutal martinet Scott put in charge of the executions and who had planned their dramatic departure. They had seen the Americans through Irish eyes, and what they had seen during the Mexican War was something like imperial Britain reborn in the New World.

Westerners

The Patricios evidenced a trait that would become typical of Irish Americans. As David Emmons has pointed out: "English exploitation of Ireland and the Irish gave Irish-Americans a unique perspective on all exploiters, capitalists included." For Irish immigration

Irish immigrants moved West to take the backbreaking jobs in lumbering. *Courtesy Library of Congress.*

Irish workers built a substantial amount of the railroads that crisscrossed the West. *Courtesy National Archives.*

did not end with the lifting of the potato blight; the Irish remained, as they had been for decades, economically superfluous in Ireland, but—with the economy heating up in what was fast becoming one of the largest industrial nations in the world—the Irish were now economically indispensable in Boston or Butte, Chicago or San Francisco. Three-and-one-half-million more of them came between 1856—long after the blight was over—and 1921. They were part of the industrializing world's great floating proletariat, but they were different from the more swarthy-skinned immigrants who increasingly crowded into the landing stations beside them as the century wore on. Mostly southern Europeans, the others had not necessarily come to stay; their repatriation rates sometimes reached 80 percent. But Ireland had no more room for those who left in 1910 than it had in 1850, and only some 10 percent of the Irish ever returned to the homeland.

Most of them concentrated, as the Irish traditionally had, in the industrial towns and cities of the East and Midwest. But the Irish would go any place there was a job that promised a fair living, and the West offered some promise. Reasonably tolerant of an Irish Catholic work force and more fluid in its social arrangements, the West not only accommodated Irish communities but allowed them to flourish. Too social to homestead on an isolated prairie or too poor to file homestead claims, too proud to compete with the wretched former slaves in the South, all the Irish really knew how to do was dig and bend their backs, which left to them railroad jobs out West, dock work in SAN FRANCISCO, and hard-rock labor in the Western mining camps and towns. As the United States began rapidly to industrialize after the Civil War, the booming ex-

tractive industries in the West looked for just such a vagabond army of workers as the Irish might supply, and although they did not flock to the West precisely, they did come in sufficient numbers to make a life for themselves, and one quite different from that of the Irish in the East.

It was as miners, loggers, railroad workers, longshoremen, and industrial tradesmen of every ilk that the Irish took up life in the West. In 1860, there were 33,147 Irish in California, 1,266 in Oregon, and only 278 in Utah; by 1900, the total number of Irish in the West had inched up to 44,476. The vast majority of them lived in San Francisco, attracted there first by the gold rush, then by the urbanity of the place. Some struck it rich; a few worked their way into society. There, as they had in the East, they became Democrats; a Catholic, Democratic, urban machine soon held sway over the city's political life, so much so that Protestant vigilante groups, organized in theory to stop the town's rampant crime and corruption, were more truthfully determined to dislodge the city's Irish political bosses.

There were, however, other Irish enclaves in the West, most especially BUTTE, MONTANA. There, Thomas Edison had made a Gilded Age copper king out of an Irishman named MARCUS DALY by electrifying New York City; copper would prove the conductor of choice for electricity, and copper was precisely what Daly's Anaconda Mine produced. Daly hired primarily Irish workers; he gave the Irish laborers preferential treatment; he engaged their help in hiring for the mine, in staffing the Irish social and patriotic clubs, and in running the city. Butte became a company town; the huge Butte Miners' Union (BMU), the largest local in the WESTERN FEDERATION OF MINERS (WFM), became something of a company union that never called a single strike while Daly was alive; and the stable Butte working class, a check against the frequent labor unrest that flared elsewhere in mining towns. After Daly's death, as absentee owners disgorged the Irish from their entrenched positions at what was now called briefly Amalgamated Copper in favor of newer, cheaper, more transient labor, Butte, too, exploded into violence, becoming the scene of one of the more celebrated vigilante actions against the INDUSTRIAL WORKERS OF THE WORLD when IWW organizer FRANK LITTLE was brutally murdered.

Indeed, most mining towns were not so congenial to the Irish as Butte, nor were many mines so consistently productive as the Anaconda operation. And while it may be true that the Butte Irish were conservative and stable, many of the Irish throughout the rest of the West were not. Overwhelmingly working-class, many of them transients, the Irish played a role in the radical Western labor movement far out of proportion to their numbers, in part because—as Eric Foner points out—those Irish coming to America in the 1860s and 1870s "brought cultural and political traditions that merged in . . . expressions of . . . native American radicalism." Honed by the political instabilities that had come to seem inherent in Irish civil life, the Irish had perfected the tactics of civil disobedience, such as boycotts and hunger strikes, as well as those of terrorism, such as tossing bombs and committing assassinations, and they passed on these skills to the WFM and the IWW.

The boycott, Emmons says, is something of an Irish trademark, depending as it does on communal commitment and participation. In fact, close-knit Irish working-class communities, which allowed such groups as the Molly Maguires, for example, to thrive in the East, also characterized the Irish in the West. The less kind called it "clannishness" when the Irish, banded together by their political clubs and working-class organizations, took care of the Irish worker first, foremost, and often exclusively, just as the Irish political machines did in the big cities. Such clannishness had its uglier sides, as when Irish workers frequently led attacks against the Chinese on the West Coast. As more Irish Americans, particularly in the second generation, engaged in a class struggle that in many ways fit well their historical temperament, some tension developed between the Irish nationalists and the Irish American working-class heroes of the WFM, the IWW, and other radical groups.

With the coming of World War I, during which Ireland allied itself with Germany, both the nationalists and the radicals suffered equally from the hysteria among the general American public, one inflamed by a Protestant and Progressive administration intent on standardizing American life and breaking the power of society's "disruptive" elements. Like the German Americans, the Irish Americans became suspect because of the hyphen that had defined their ethnicity. Just how pugnacious the Irish in the West could be in the face of nativist backlash became clear when, after the war, San Francisco granted Irish republican leader Eamon de Valera the key to the city in 1919 while jeering down the pro-British American President Woodrow Wilson. In many ways, however, it was a hollow gesture. By then, the power of the old political clubs over the new generation of Irish Americans was decidedly on the wane, the Irish- and German-dominated radical parties had all but been destroyed, and the working class, to which the vast majority of the Irish in the West belonged, was everywhere in retreat. Having had an impact on the region that belied their relatively small numbers, the struggle for a fair living was now becoming one for Irish American identity itself.

—*Charles Phillips and Patricia Hogan*

SUGGESTED READING:

Ahearn, Robert. *Thomas Francis Meagher: Irish Revolutionary in the American West*. Boulder, Colo., 1949.

Bodnar, John. *The Transplanted: A History of Immigrants in Urban America*. Bloomington, Ind., 1985.

Brown, Ronald C. *Hard-Rock Miners: The Intermountain West, 1860–1920*. College Station, Tex., 1980.

Burchell, R. A. *The San Francisco Irish, 1848–1880*. Berkeley, Calif., 1980.

Emmons, David M. *The Butte Irish: Class and Ethnicity in an American Mining Town, 1875–1925*. Urbana, Ill., 1989.

Foner, Eric. *Free Soil, Free Labor, Free Men: The Ideology of the Republican Party before the Civil War*. New York, 1970.

Larkin, Emmet. *James Larkin: Irish Labor Leader, 1876–1947*. Cambridge, Mass., 1965.

Takaki, Ronald. *A Different Mirror: A History of Multicultural America*. Boston, 1993.

IRRIGATION

In prehistoric times, Indians in areas of the present-day American Southwest had irrigated their lands to support their subsistence crops. When the Spanish came to the region in the seventeenth century, they brought their own methods of irrigation for the pueblos, presidios, and missions they established. When BRIGHAM YOUNG, enticed to the West by what he read in the travel books of JOHN CHARLES FRÉMONT, took his fellow MORMONS on their long trek to Zion in the desert, the Latter-day Saints became ingenious irrigators. They built small dirt dams in local streams and diverted WATER to their dry but, as they were soon to discover, fertile fields. They used what they learned by the Great Salt Lake to spread irrigation to each of the new colonies they established, some in present-day Utah, others in neighboring states such as Arizona, Idaho, Wyoming, and California.

Other Americans began to imitate the Mormons' success in turning their desert into a garden. Non-Mormon colonies established irrigation works throughout the West. The first was in Anaheim, California, in 1857, but the most famous was the Union Colony of Greeley, Colorado. Established in 1870, it quickly garnered national attention and encouraged more settlers to try their hands at irrigation. Not only individual farmers, but groups of investors—most in the West, a few in the East—formed corporations and funded irrigation projects. The idea of irrigating the GREAT AMERICAN DESERT had become so popular that California passed the WRIGHT IRRIGATION ACT OF 1887, which authorized individuals to create irrigation "districts" and

Federal reclamation and irrigation projects transformed the American West, but individuals devised their own water systems to supply their small stakes. Here, the Martin brothers stand beside the first water works in Perry, Oklahoma Territory. *Courtesy National Archives.*

subsidized their efforts with taxes raised especially for purposes of irrigation. Sixteen other Western states soon followed, testing and improvising on the California statute.

From the 1840s, when the Mormons first began damming streams, over the course of the next three decades, irrigation spread throughout the arid and semiarid lands of the trans-Mississippi West. But irrigation was expensive when compared to dryland FARMING, which needed none of the up-front capital to build dams, aqueducts, and lateral ditches. Congress began encouraging irrigation when it passed the DESERT LAND ACT OF 1877, which offered 640 acres for a nominal fee to anyone willing to irrigate them, then followed with the CAREY ACT OF 1894, which promised one million acres to any state in the semiarid West willing to launch a RECLAMATION project. By 1894, when most of the irrigable lands—land that could be farmed without intensive capital investment—had been brought into production, only some 3.6 million acres of the vast Western dry lands had been irrigated.

But the dream of turning a desert into a garden would not die, and in the next century, powerful government agencies such as the BUREAU OF RECLAMATION and the UNITED STATES ARMY CORPS OF ENGINEERS developed irrigation projects the pharaohs of Egypt would

scarcely have dreamed of undertaking, projects that launched hugely profitable new Western enterprises even as they pitted states against states, cities against desert valleys, and farmers against suburbanites in a struggle for vast amounts of water where there was very little water to be had. As historian Donald Worster pointed out, the West's wild rivers were dammed nearly to death, its cities had become vampirelike drains on the region's entire ecology, and its governments found themselves trapped in the bitter water politics underlying a massive new hydraulic civilization that had come to dominate Western life in the late twentieth century.

—*Charles Phillips*

SEE ALSO: Agriculture; Climate; Hoover Dam

SUGGESTED READING:

El-Ashry, Mohamed T. and Diana C. Gibons, eds. *Water and Arid Lands of the Western United States.* Cambridge, Eng., 1988.

Reisner, Marc. *Cadillac Desert: The American West and Its Disappearing Water.* New York, 1986.

Worster, Donald. *Rivers of Empire: Water, Aridity, and the Growth of the American West.* New York, 1985.

———. *Under Western Skies: Nature and History in the American West.* New York, 1992.

IRVINE, WILLIAM C.

Born in Carlisle, Pennsylvania, rancher and Wyoming politician William C. Irvine (1852–1872) ventured to the West at the age of twenty to take a job with a ranching outfit on Blue Creek in Nebraska. Irvine was a quick study in the cattle business; he rose to the position of foreman and, four years later, left Nebraska to start his own ranch. On his Jay Y outfit, begun in 1876 along the North Platte River in Wyoming, his skill and good management doubled the size of a four-thousand-head herd in two years.

From his own spread, Irvine moved on to a series of associations with various ranching outfits and served as initial organizer and range manager of the Converse Cattle Company; general manager of the Ogallala Land

and Cattle Company; and general manager of the U Cross Ranch, near Buffalo, Wyoming.

Irvine held several positions as an officer in the Wyoming Stock Growers' Association. A prominent Republican, he spent two terms in Wyoming's legislature and four years as state treasurer. He also championed ventures in railroad construction and irrigation.

—*Patricia Hogan*

IRVINE RANCH, CALIFORNIA

Created by James Irvine in 1876 when he bought his partners' interests in a tract of land located between Los Angeles and San Diego, the Irvine Ranch developed from speculators' purchases of bits and pieces of land from three ranchos: the Santiago de Santa Ana, the San Joaquin, and the Lomas de Santa Ana. Irvine expanded his initial operations in sheep ranching to include cattle raising. Later, the ranch diversified into the production of beans, sugar beets, and walnuts. By the turn of the century, the ranch's primary crops were oranges and lemons.

The ranch remained mostly intact, encompassing 103,000 acres, well into the twentieth century. By the time Myford Irvine took over operations in 1949, the ranch's pastures gave way to the towns and streets of Orange County's urban development. Cattle operations were moved to Irvine holdings in Montana, and farming endeavors were transferred to the Imperial Valley. On January 20, 1961, the Irvine ranch deeded 1,000 acres for the construction of the University of California's Irvine campus.

—*Patricia Hogan*

IRVING, WASHINGTON

The American writer Washington Irving (1783–1859), was born in New York City. In 1815, he left the United States for extensive travels in England and Europe. Returning to the United States in May 1832, he was impressed with a brash, vibrant, and vigorous Jacksonian America. A former Federalist, he immediately embraced the Democratic party and America's expansionist vision, and for six years and in three influential books, he turned his literary attention to the American West.

In August 1832, Irving accepted the invitation of Henry Leavitt Ellsworth, U.S. Commissioner to the Indian Nations, to accompany him on a tour among the Southwest Indian tribes. The tour was Irving's remarkable introduction to the American West, and he meticulously filled five notebooks with valuable observations and descriptions of meetings with such figures as Auguste Pierre Chouteau, WILLIAM CLARK, SAM HOUSTON, Chief Black Hawk, William Campbell, and William Sublette. Although Irving would embellish Western reality with his romantic "filigree" (as he called it), he came to know the realities of Western life firsthand and described them with his usual graceful prose in *A Tour on the Prairies* (1835).

Irving's turn westward attracted the attention of his long-time friend, JOHN JACOB ASTOR, who urged him to write the history of Astor's ambitious fur-trading venture on the Columbia River. Working from the accounts of such Oregonnauts as Robert Stuart, GABRIEL FRANCHÈRE, WILSON PRICE HUNT, JOHN BRADBURY, Henry Marie Brackenridge, MERIWETHER LEWIS and William Clark, and Jonathan Thorn, Irving published *Astoria, or Anecdotes of an Enterprise beyond the Rocky Mountains* (1836). The romantic history remains a rich, often thrilling account of the Western FUR TRADE and is so accurate that for more than two decades pioneers used *Astoria* as a guidebook to the Rocky Mountains and the Oregon Trail.

While writing *Astoria,* Irving met U.S. Army Captain BENJAMIN LOUIS EULALIE DE BONNEVILLE, who had just returned from the Rocky Mountains. Irving purchased Bonneville's account of his mountain adventures and rewrote it as *The Adventures of Captain Bonneville, U.S.A.* (1837). A reliable account substantiated by other participants, *Bonneville* remains significant as a history of the early fur trade.

Although Irving made three important contributions to Western Americana, he was unable to envision the legend-making, mythic importance of the West to young America and its nascent literature. Furthermore, his artistic bent lay more with the quaint, the charming, and the picturesque than with the stark and often brutal Western landscape and experience.

—*Richard H. Cracroft*

SEE ALSO: Chouteau Family; Literature; Sublette Brothers

SUGGESTED READING:
Cracroft, Richard H. *Washington Irving: The Western Works.* Boise, Idaho, 1974.
Ellsworth, Henry Leavitt. *Washington Irving on the Prairie, or, a Narrative of a Tour of the Southwest in the Year 1832.* New York, 1937.
Irving, Pierre Munro. *The Life and Letters of Washington Irving.* 4 vols. New York, 1863.
Irving, Washington. *The Adventures of Captain Bonneville, U.S.A.* Edited by Edgeley W. Todd. Norman, Okla., 1986.

———. *Astoria, or Anecdotes of an Enterprize beyond the Rocky Mountains.* Edited by Richard Dilworth Rust. Boston, 1976. Reprint. Lincoln, Nebr., 1976.

———. *A Tour on the Prairies.* Edited by John Francis McDermott. Norman, Okla., 1956,

———. *The Western Journals of Washington Irving.* Edited by John Francis McDermott. Norman, Okla., 1944.

Williams, Stanley T. *The Life of Washington Irving.* 2 vols. New York, 1935.

ITALIAN AMERICANS

Italians participated in the earliest phases of European exploration of the American West. FRAY MARCOS DE NIZA's exaggerated accounts of his travels in the Southwest led to FRANCISCO VÁSQUEZ DE CORONADO's expedition from 1540 to 1542. In the 1690s, Henri de Tonti joined SIEUR DE LASALLE in exploring the Mississippi River basin. From 1681 to 1711, Father EUSEBIO FRANCISCO KINO explored and mapped the Southwest.

Fellow Jesuit Giuseppe Salvatierra established the Pious Fund to support mission operations in Baja California; the fund was used in the settlement of Alta California in 1769 along plans outlined by Viceroy Antonio Maria Bucareli. As early as 1786, Captain Alessandro Malaspina anchored off the California coast. In 1827, Paolo Emilio Botta, a ship's doctor, traveled to the California coast and then published an account that stimulated European interest in the Pacific slope, as had Father Francesco Clavigero's report published in Venice in 1789.

Italian contacts increased somewhat in the nineteenth century, but the number of Italian immigrants remained small in Western states, with the exception of California. Passage from Genoa to Los Angeles cost $120 in 1900, while tickets for steerage accommodations to New York cost only $28. Because of the high cost involved, most Italian settlers in the West were trans-migrants; that is, they negotiated the trip West in phases. They learned English and became acculturated as they sought employment to finance the next part of their journey. This extended period of adjustment resulted in more rapid assimilation.

After 1865, Italian settlers in Arizona were ministered to by the Sisters of Charity, a labor described by Sister BLANDINA SEGALE in her compelling autobiography, *At the End of the Santa Fe Trail.* Italians also worked as miners in Nevada and Colorado, where they were involved in labor disputes at Cripple Creek and Ludlow. By 1884, four rail lines spanned the West, and more than 9,000 Italians had helped lay the track and had worked on section gangs. Many more, attracted by the mineral wealth and land in Kansas,

Nebraska, and the Dakotas, rode the crowded railroad cars to scattered destinations. By 1910, about 2,000 Italians had settled in Arkansas, especially around Tontitown. An equal number worked largely as truck farmers in Wyoming. Italians worked in the mines and oil fields of Oklahoma and were scattered through the mines, oil fields, and orchards of Texas. Others were cowhands, such as CHARLES ANGELO SIRINGO, described as the first authentic cowboy to publish his autobiography. Religious conviction led 50 Italian converts to Utah in 1866. Among them was Susanna Cardone, whose silk worms launched silk production among the Mormons. Giuseppe Rosati, bishop of St. Louis, sent to Montana a handful of Jesuits including Gregory Gazzoli, Anthony Ravalli, and Gregory Mengarini, a skilled ethnographer. By 1910, there were approximately 6,600 Italians in Montana; many found work with the Anaconda Copper Mining Company.

In 1887, Joseph Cataldo established Gonzaga University in the Oregon Territory. In the 1880s, Italian settlers farmed, ran dairies, and worked in lumber camps in Oregon and Washington, thus continuing the tradition of industrious enterprise reflected by two early Italian settlers, Giovanni Dominis, who after his arrival in 1827, embarked upon a successful fur and salmon trade, and S. N. Arrigoni, a prosperous hotelier and Portland leader.

The first Italian settler in California was Juan (Giovanni) Bonifacio, who arrived in Monterey in 1822. The next year, Giovanni Battista Leandri became a shopkeeper in Los Angeles; he also served as a city official and was a part owner of Rancho San Pedro and a grantee of Rancho Los Coyotes. In the 1860s, Alessandro Repetto acquired a five-thousand-acre rancho east of Los Angeles. Between 1833 and 1835, Catalina Manzaneli de Munras was claimant to both Rancho Laguna Seca and Rancho San Francisquito in Monterey County.

The gold rush had attracted an international community to San Francisco, including half of the 6,000 Italians who lived in California in 1850. In 1858, several hundred of them purportedly trudged nine miles to present gifts to the first Italian woman to visit the mines. Once the immigrants were established, other women came as part of reunited families or as new brides. The old country family life—with its traditions and folkways—was thus sustained. Italian women also nurtured a cultural cohesiveness through their church and social organizations.

Italian settlers in California developed a thriving culture. Five newspapers served San Francisco's Italian community during and after the gold rush. Italians patronized nearly a dozen opera companies in San Fran-

Italian fishermen repairing their nets on a San Francisco wharf, about 1891. *Courtesy National Archives.*

cisco as early as 1854. Concerts across the state featured Adelina Patti, Luisa Tetrazzini, and Eliza Biscaccianti, the "American Thrush." Italians were also actively involved in California education. In 1851, Fathers John Nobili and Michael Accolti established Santa Clara College, and in 1858, Father Anthony Maraschi organized St. Ignatius College, later the University of San Francisco. In 1905, St. Francis Xavier Cabrini and her Missionary Sisters of the Sacred Heart founded a school and orphanage in Los Angeles.

Italians settled throughout California, including Andrea Sbarboro's fifteen-hundred-acre cooperative at Asti and the Italian-Swiss Agricultural Colony in Sonoma Valley, the site of Sbarboro's wine-making business. The Petri family in the San Joaquin Valley, the Mondavis in Napa Valley, Louis Martini in St. Helena, and Secondo Guasti's Italian Vineyard Company in Rancho Cucamonga to the south contributed significantly to California's leadership in wine production.

Noting that California's climate was similar to that of the Mediterranean region, botanists such as Dr. Francesco Francheschi experimented with more than 140 varieties of Mediterranean plants, and agriculturalists introduced broccoli, artichokes, bell peppers, and eggplant in the Central Valley and to the south. Extensive farming, canning, and distribution operations, such as the De Giorgio Corporation and Marco Fontana's Calpac, then developed.

Even the smallest Italian enterprises were ensured loans with a minimum of collateral at AMADEO PETER GIANNINI's Bank of Italy. By 1930, having become the Bank of America, the institution controlled more than 35 percent of California banking business.

By the 1920s, Italians represented the largest single segment, 11.4 percent, of California's foreign-born population. Following the passage of the National Origins Act of 1924, new arrivals were reduced to a handful—mainly Italians fleeing fascism and film specialists employed by the growing cinema industry. Nevertheless, by 1940, California led all Western states in first-generation Italians, with a population of 100,911. Missouri was a distant second with a first-generation Italian population of 13,168.

At the outbreak of World War II, thousands of Italians who had not yet become citizens were removed from Terminal Island and a narrow coastal area including San Francisco and Humboldt bays. The movements of all alien Italians, along with Germans and Japanese, were restricted; a curfew was imposed; and several dozen community leaders were interned at Fort Missoula, Montana, renamed Fort Bella Vista by the internees. Even after October 12, 1942, when Italians were withdrawn from the enemies list, 212 remained in camps located throughout the West. The postwar years brought a renewed influx of Italians, from war brides to entrepreneurs.

—*Gloria Ricci Lothrop*

SUGGESTED READING:

Fox, Stephen. *The Unknown Internment: An Oral History of the Relocation of Italian Americans during World War II.* Boston, 1990.

Gumina, Deanna Paoli. *The Italians of San Francisco 1850–1930.* New York, 1980.

Lothrop, Gloria Ricci. "The Italians of Los Angeles." *The Californians* 5 (1987): 28–43.

Rolle, Andrew F. *The Immigrant Upraised: Italian Adventurers and Colonists in an Expanding America.* Norman, Okla., 1968.

Segale, Sister Blandina. *At the End of the Santa Fe Trail.* Milwaukee, Wis., 1948.

INTERIOR, UNITED STATES DEPARTMENT OF

SEE: Antiquities Act of 1906; Ballinger-Pinchot Controversy; Bureau of Indian Affairs; Bureau of Land Management; General Land Office; Ickes, Harold L.; National Park Service; Powell, John Wesley; Roosevelt, Theodore; Taylor Grazing Act; Teapot Dome

IWW

SEE: Industrial Workers of the World

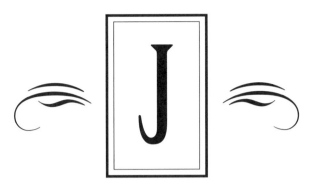

JACKRABBITS

Lepus townsendii (white-tailed jackrabbit), *Lepus alleni* (antelope jackrabbit), and *Lepus californicus* (black-tailed jackrabbit) are the three principal species of hares commonly called "jackrabbits." Both hares and rabbits are members of the *Leporidae* family, but hares are larger, longer-eared, and longer-legged. Unlike rabbits, the hares' young are born fully furred with their eyes open. White-tailed jackrabbits may weigh eight pounds with a body length of twenty-two inches and ears six inches long. Antelope jackrabbits are similar in length to their white-tailed relatives but may weigh thirteen pounds. Black-tailed jackrabbits may reach a length of twenty-one inches and a weight of seven pounds and have ears up to seven inches in length. Found from the Mississippi River to the Pacific Coast and from the Canadian border to Mexico, jackrabbits were a significant food source for Native Americans and early Euro-American settlers. White-tailed jackrabbits were even pursued by market hunters in the last decades of the nineteenth century and sold in some numbers.

Primarily nocturnal, these herbivores eat substantial quantities of herbaceous plants, grasses, and, when available, cultivated crops. It has been suggested that eleven jackrabbits may consume as much forage as one sheep eats in a day. They often damage alfalfa, grain, and melon fields and, during the winter, orchards. They are capable of escaping danger by running swiftly for long distances. Their vision, hearing, speed, and capacity for rapid starts allow them to avoid COYOTES, hawks, eagles, bobcats, and other predators. When the number of their predators decline, jackrabbit populations increase, and they become a problem for agriculture. That occurred from 1900 to 1950, and ranchers and farmers organized rabbit drives to reduce their numbers. Poison has also been used to limit their population.

—*Phillip Drennon Thomas*

SUGGESTED READING:
Bailey, Vernon. *Mammals of the Southwestern United States.* Washington, D.C., 1931.
Costello, David F. *The Desert World.* New York, 1972.

JACKSON, ANDREW

Frontier military commander and Indian fighter Andrew Jackson (1767–1845) became the first "Westerner" to be elected president of the United States. Born in the Waxhaw area, he was raised in the wilderness of this North Carolina–South Carolina border region. After serving in the Revolutionary War and squandering his modest inheritance, he studied law, gained admission to the North Carolina bar, and moved to Nashville, Tennessee, where, in 1791, he became attorney general for the Southwest Territory and, subsequently, circuit-riding solicitor in the area surrounding Nashville.

In 1791, Jackson married Rachel Donelson Robards; both he and Rachel believed that she and her first husband had been legally divorced. When that proved not to be the case, they remarried in 1794, but the incident dogged Jackson's private life and political career for many years.

Jackson served as a delegate to the Tennessee constitutional convention in 1796. After his election to Congress in 1796, he earned a reputation as a fierce opponent of the Washington administration's conciliatory stance toward Great Britain and the Indian tribes that had sided with the British during the Revolution. In 1797, Jackson was appointed to serve out the senatorial term of his political mentor, WILLIAM BLOUNT. Jackson's continual financial problems prompted him to leave the Senate in 1798. From 1798 to 1804, he served as a Tennessee superior court judge and then resigned to devote himself to recouping his fortune.

Commissioned major general of volunteers in the WAR OF 1812, Jackson defeated the pro-British "Red

Andrew Jackson. *Courtesy The Bettmann Archive.*

Stick" Creek Indians at the Battle of Horseshoe Bend on March 27, 1814. Federal authorities then appointed him to command the defense of New Orleans. Jackson devised a brilliant strategy and on January 8, 1815, soundly defeated the British. By the time the Battle of New Orleans was fought, however, the warring nations had signed a peace treaty (in Ghent, Belgium, on December 24), but the news failed to reach the commanders in the field.

Beginning in 1817, Jackson fought the Seminole Indians and pursued them into Spanish Florida during the spring of 1818. He was eager to interpret his mission as nothing less than the conquest of Spanish Florida, and he set about not only attacking Indians, but deposing Spanish authorities until passage of the ADAMS-ONIS TREATY of 1819, by which Spain formally ceded Florida to the United States.

Jackson resigned his army commission in 1821 to become provisional territorial governor of Florida. The following year, the Tennessee legislature nominated him for the presidency and then, in 1823, elected him to the U.S. Senate. In 1824, Jackson ran for president but lost the election to John Quincy Adams. During the Adams administration, Jackson worked to create the powerful popular movement that ensured his election in 1828. The movement became the nucleus of the Democratic party, which positioned Jackson as a critic of John Quincy Adams's support of a strong, centralized government at the expense of what was coming to be called "states' rights."

Jackson defeated Adams in his bid for a second term, but his inauguration was a bittersweet occasion, since it came after the death of his beloved wife. Jackson made sweeping changes in the government in order to make it more responsive to what he interpreted as the will of the people. One of his first actions was to introduce the principle of rotation in office, removing a number of long-term appointees from public office and instituting what his political foes called the "spoils system" in its stead. Another nod toward the common man was Jackson's program of internal improvements, especially in the West, where his administration authorized the construction of roads and canals.

Having been elected in part on a platform of states' rights, Jackson supported this principle only when it suited his program of general national expansion. When the Cherokee Indians of Georgia attacked that state's depredations against them by successfully pleading their case before the U.S. Supreme Court (in WORCESTER V. STATE OF GEORGIA), Jackson refused to enforce the court's decision and claimed that the federal government was powerless to intervene in the internal affairs of a state. Two years earlier, Jackson had signed the Indian Removal Bill, which authorized the removal of Eastern tribes to the Indian Territory, and Georgia's actions suited the president's program. Yet during the nullification crisis of 1832, Jackson demonstrated a firm commitment to the central government. When South Carolina declared the tariffs of 1828 and 1832 null and void and prohibited the collection of tariffs in South Carolina, Jackson responded with his Nullification Proclamation of December 10, 1832, announcing his intention to enforce the law—although also pledging a compromise tariff. South Carolina backed down, and the dissolution of the Union was postponed for almost three more decades.

Jackson vehemently opposed the Second Bank of the United States, a private corporation established in 1816 but operating under a federal charter. He charged that it not only failed to provide a stable currency but consistently favored the privileged few at the expense of the common man. When Congress passed a measure to recharter the bank, Jackson vetoed it, and the issue became important in the presidential election of 1832. After Jackson soundly defeated HENRY CLAY (a supporter of the bank), he waged war against the bank for the next four years. He offered no suitable alternative to the bank, however, and thus contributed to a highly unstable currency situation, especially in the South and West, where state-chartered banks freely engaged in the speculative issuance of paper currency. That situation stimulated a land boom, in which the sale of federal lands wiped out the national debt and even created a substantial surplus. Alarmed by the degree of speculation and the prevalence of paper currency, the Jackson administration issued the Specie Circular of 1836, which forbade the purchase of federal land or payment of federal debts in any currency except federally issued coins. This action created an instant demand for specie that triggered a tidal wave of bank failures—especially in the West and South—and brought on the panic of 1837.

Jackson was personally sympathetic to the American-organized TEXAS REVOLUTION against Mexico, yet he refused to take a decisive official stand in favor of Texas independence. He feared dividing the Democratic party over the expansion of slavery into a new territory (assuming the Republic of Texas were to be annexed to the United States), and despite his bellicose reputation, he did not relish the prospect of war with Mexico.

After his retirement to the Hermitage, Jackson, who was seriously ill, nevertheless remained a powerful force in the Democratic party. When he transferred his support from his successor, Martin Van Buren, to JAMES K. POLK, the latter not only captured the Democratic nomination, but became president in 1844.

Relatively little that characterized the Age of Jackson—the NATIONAL EXPANSION westward, the elevation of the common man, the displacement of the Native American—was due solely to his actions and policies as president. Yet Jackson was a powerful symbol and cultural icon: the embodiment of a Westerner or of what is popularly meant by the frontiersman.

—*Alan Axelrod*

SEE ALSO: Banking; Financial Panics; Native American Peoples: Peoples Removed from the East

SUGGESTED READING:
Davis, Burke. *Old Hickory: A Life of Andrew Jackson.* New York, 1977.
James, Marquis. *Andrew Jackson: Portrait of a President.* Indianapolis, Ind., and New York, 1937.
Meyers, Marvin. *The Jacksonian Persuasion.* New York, 1957.
Remini, Robert V. *Andrew Jackson and the Course of American Democracy, 1833–1845.* New York, 1984.
———. *Andrew Jackson and the Course of American Empire, 1767–1821.* New York, 1977.
———. *Andrew Jackson and the Course of American Freedom, 1822–1832.* New York, 1981.
Rogin, Michael. *Fathers and Children: Andrew Jackson and the Subjugation of the American Indian.* New York, 1975.
Schlesinger, Arthur M. *The Age of Jackson.* Boston, 1945.
Sellers, Charles. *Andrew Jackson: A Profile.* New York, 1971.
Van Deusen, Glyndon G. *The Jacksonian Era.* New York, 1959.

JACKSON, HELEN MARIA FISKE HUNT

Helen Maria Fiske Hunt Jackson (1830–1885) was an author and noted advocate of Indian reform. Born in Amherst, Massachusetts, she was the daughter of an Amherst College language professor. She married Edward Bissell Hunt, an army lieutenant, in 1852; the couple had two sons. In 1863, her husband died while experimenting on a prototype submarine. After the subsequent death of both sons, she began a professional writing career that continued for the rest of her life.

Using such pseudonyms as "No Name," "Rip Van Winkel," "Marah," and "Sax Holm," she wrote hundreds of poems, numerous travel articles, magazine and newspaper pieces, and books. Her letters and articles appeared in major New York and Boston newspapers, as well as the *Atlantic Monthly, Hearth and Home, Woman's Journal,* and *Scribner's Monthly Magazine.* Ralph Waldo Emerson once described her as the "greatest American woman poet," but she was convinced that her most important literary contributions were *A Century of Dishonor* and *Ramona,* both published under her own name. These books have been continually in print since originally published.

In the 1870s, several events—a trip to Colorado Springs for health reasons; her marriage to local banker and railroad promoter, William Sharpless Jackson; her visit to Boston for the seventieth birthday of Oliver Wendell Holmes; and her chance attendance at a lecture by Ponca Chief Standing Bear—changed the direction of her life. Jackson began writing articles and books on Indian-related issues, and these publications thrust her into the public eye as one of the foremost Indian policy reformers of the nineteenth century.

Moved by the tragic removal of the Ponca Indians, Jackson used her considerable literary and research skills to awaken the public to the mistreatment of all Indians. She criticized government policy in letters to the editors of major Boston and New York newspapers and was soon engaged in a controversial exchange of letters with CARL SCHURZ, secretary of the Department of the Interior.

A Century of Dishonor, published by Harper and Brothers in 1881, was a scathing indictment of the government's Indian policy. Displeased by the public's and Congress's response to the work, she wrote a protest novel, *Ramona,* hoping to "move people's heart" with the tragic story of the dispossession of California's Mission Indians. She gathered historical data while on assignment for *Century Magazine* and while working as a special Interior Department agent authorized to write a comprehensive report on the condition of the Mission Indians. That report, which included eleven specific recommendations, was published in 1883.

By that time, Jackson's Indian-related articles and books had helped shape the work of several reform organizations, including the WOMEN'S NATIONAL INDIAN ASSOCIATION (WNIA), the INDIAN RIGHTS ASSOCIATION (IRA), and the Lake Mohonk Conference of the Friends of the Indians. After her death, members of both the WNIA and the IRA carried on her work, and many of her recommendations were incorporated into a January 1891 bill for the Relief of the Mission Indians in the State of California. The resulting California Mission Indian Commission established or enlarged existing Indian reservations in the southern part of the state, reservations that continue to exist.

—*Valerie Sherer Mathes*

SEE ALSO: United States Indian Policy

SUGGESTED READING:
Banning, Evelyn I. *Helen Hunt Jackson.* New York, 1973.
Mathes, Valerie Sherer. *Helen Hunt Jackson and Her Indian Reform Legacy.* Austin, Tex., 1990.
May, Antoinette. *Helen Hunt Jackson: A Lonely Voice of Conscience.* San Francisco, 1987.
Odell, Ruth. *Helen Hunt Jackson.* New York, 1939.

JACKSON, HENRY MARTIN ("SCOOP")

A member of the U.S. House of Representatives from 1941 to 1953 and the U.S. Senate from 1953 to 1983, Henry Martin ("Scoop") Jackson (1912–1983), a Democrat, became one of the nation's most important post–World War II political figures. Born to immigrant Norwegian parents in Everett, Washington, a tough mill town, Jackson attended local schools and in 1935 earned a law degree from the University of Washington. Dissatisfied with the political corruption in his county, he ran for and was elected Snohomish County prosecutor in 1938. During his two-year tenure, he rid the county of gambling interests and won a celebrated murder trial, which propelled him in 1940 to his election to the first of six terms in Congress. In 1952, Jackson defeated incumbent Harry P. Cain to become a U.S. senator. As a member of the Armed Services Com-

mittee, he consistently took a tough stand against the Soviet Union and claimed that a missile gap existed between the United States and the Soviet Union. During the Vietnam War, he advocated expansion of the war. Tied to his fear of communist aggression was an interest in arms control and human rights. He reluctantly supported the 1963 Nuclear Test Ban Treaty, strongly criticized concessions made to the Soviet Union in SALT I by Richard Nixon in 1972, and forced President Jimmy Carter to withdraw SALT II from Senate consideration. Sometimes referred to as the "senator from Israel" because of his support of the Jewish nation, Jackson kept the Soviet Union from receiving most-favored-nation status until it relaxed Jewish emigration policies. An opponent of detente with the Soviet Union, he was an outspoken advocate of opening diplomatic relations with China in the 1970s. A liberal on most domestic issues, Jackson helped undermine red-baiting Senator Joseph McCarthy during the 1954 televised Army-McCarthy hearings. He created the Environmental Quality Act of 1969, an act that earned him the Sierra Club's JOHN MUIR Award. In 1972 and 1976, he unsuccessfully sought the Democratic presidential nomination.

—*Thomas M. Gaskin*

SUGGESTED READING:
Ognibene, Peter. J. *Scoop: The Life and Politics of Henry M. Jackson.* New York, 1975.
Prochnau, William W., and Richard W. Larsen. *A Certain Democrat: Senator Henry M. Jackson: A Political Biography.* Englewood Cliffs, N.J., 1972.

JACKSON, SHELDON

Presbyterian missionary Sheldon Jackson (1834–1909) was the oldest child of devoutly religious New York farmers. Educated at Union College and Princeton Theological Seminary, he was ordained in 1858 by the Presbytery of Albany, New York. Shortly thereafter he married Mary Voorhees; the couple had two daughters.

Jackson began his missionary career in 1858 in a Choctaw Indian school at Spencer in the Indian Territory. A year later, he moved to Minnesota and, for the next ten years, assumed a number of church organizational responsibilities, including his pastorate at Rochester, Minnesota, from 1864 to 1869.

By 1869, certain that his puny body could withstand the harsh demands of proselytizing in the Far West, Jackson accepted his church's appointment as superintendent for the Board of Domestic (National or Home Board) Missions of the Rocky Mountain Dis-

Even with the West's spreading railroad network, Jackson could not effectively administer such widespread responsibilities. His Home Board superiors were shaken in 1877 when they heard that their Denver-based superintendent had bolted to Wrangell, Alaska. Driven to spread Christianity to the far reaches of the Alaskan frontier, Jackson lobbied for congressional legislation to establish civilian government in the territory as a first measure of civilization. The district's 1884 Organic Act was in considerable measure his creation. In 1885, President Chester A. Arthur appointed him Alaska's general agent for education. By pestering Congress and taking annual trips aboard Revenue Marine cutters, he eventually stretched a church-state educational network all the way to the Arctic Slope. A vigorous partisan of the Friends of the Indians movement, Jackson infuriated frontiersmen and townsmen by insisting that Alaska remain dry, or free of liquor. His introduction of Siberian reindeer to assist Alaskan Eskimos remains controversial.

Ego-driven and at times vindictive, Jackson nonetheless ranks as one of the most influential Americans on the Alaskan frontier and as a tireless promoter of the socio-Christian values of late nineteenth-century Protestant America.

—*Ted C. Hinckley*

SEE ALSO: Protestants

SUGGESTED READING:
Hinckley, Ted C. *The Americanization of Alaska, 1867–1897*. Palo Alto, Calif., 1972.
Stewart, Robert Laird. *Sheldon Jackson, Pathfinder and Prospector of the Missionary Vanguard in the Rocky Mountains and Alaska*. New York, 1908.

Sheldon Jackson. *Courtesy Special Collections Division, University of Washington Libraries.*

trict. His enormous territory included Arizona, New Mexico, Colorado, Utah, Wyoming, and Montana. The manner in which the "Rocky Mountain superintendent" relentlessly drove himself reflected a reformer's zeal. In addition to publishing the *Rocky Mountain Presbyterian,* he mounted a marathon campaign to organize home missions. Riding on horses and mules, stagecoaches, and ox carts, he established churches, schools, and missions across eleven states and territories. At times, he established Presbyterian institutions justified neither by money nor by potential membership.

JACKSON, WILLIAM HENRY

William Henry Jackson (1843–1942) interpreted the American West through PHOTOGRAPHY and painting during a long, active life. A native of Keeseville, New York, Jackson left school at the age of fifteen to work as a colorist in New York and Vermont photography studios. In 1862, he enlisted in the Twelfth Vermont Volunteers but saw only guard-duty action during the Civil War. By 1868, after trekking to California and back, he settled in Omaha, Nebraska, where he opened his own photographic studio and began to document the settlement of the West.

From 1870 to 1878, Jackson served FERDINAND VANDEVEER HAYDEN's Geological Survey of the Territories as its official photographer and crisscrossed Wyoming, Utah, Montana, and Colorado. Using the

In the 1870s, William Henry Jackson accompanied Ferdinand Vandeveer Hayden's surveys of Wyoming, Utah, Montana, and Colorado. Top: Jackson photographed Hayden's party taking a noon meal in the Wyoming Territory in August 1870. *Courtesy National Archives.* Bottom: Jackson captured on film Hayden's pack train on the trail between the Yellowstone and East Fork rivers. *Courtesy National Archives.*

awkward wet-collodion process—and often packing his twenty-by-twenty-four inch view camera and dark tent to remote locations—he was the first to photograph the Mesa Verde cliff dwellings, the Grand Teton range, the Mount of the Holy Cross in Colorado, and landmarks along the Oregon Trail. His images of the Yellowstone land forms proved crucial to the congressional creation of the nation's first national park in 1872.

Jackson opened a commercial studio in 1879 in Denver, where he specialized in landscape photos and promotional images used by railroads. In 1898, he moved to Detroit, Michigan, and united his business with the Detroit Publishing Company. He returned each summer to photograph the West and spent winters in Detroit producing color prints. He retired in 1924, at the age of eighty-one, and moved to Washington, D.C., where he rekindled his childhood interest in painting.

Jackson became research secretary for the Oregon Trail Memorial Association in 1929 and executed dozens of water colors depicting the history of the route. In 1935, the ninety-two-year-old artist painted murals for the new Department of the Interior Building in Washington. His autobiography, *Time Exposure*, appeared in 1940.

Jackson's career spanned the evolution of photography, from the daguerreotype to trustworthy color film. For decades, much of the world knew the American West primarily through his images. His large-format black-and-white images of Western landscapes remain arresting works of art, as well as ethnological, geological, and geographical documents. He died at the age of ninety-nine in New York City—never having lost the capacity to be astonished by nature.

Major collections of Jackson's photographic and artistic work are held by seven repositories: the Bancroft Library at the University of California, Berkeley; the Colorado Historical Society in Denver; the U.S. Geological Survey Photographic Library in Denver; the National Anthropological Archives at the Smithsonian Institution in Washington, D.C.; the Art Museum at Princeton University in New Jersey; the International Museum of Photography at George Eastman House in Rochester, New York; and the AMON CARTER MUSEUM in Fort Worth, Texas.

—*David A. Walter*

SEE ALSO: Art: Surveys and Expeditions

SUGGESTED READING:
Hales, Peter B. *William Henry Jackson and the Transformation of the American Landscape.* Philadelphia, 1988.

Jackson, Clarence S. *Picture Maker of the Old West: William H. Jackson*. New York, 1947.

Jackson, William Henry. *Time Exposure: The Autobiography of William Henry Jackson*. New York, 1940.

JAILS AND PRISONS

Before the Civil War, jails in many Western towns were either primitive wooden stockades or one-room boxlike structures on the outskirts of town or nonexistent. Some towns regarded the construction of respectable-looking jails, together with a courthouse, as important tokens of civilization and essential symbols of LAW AND ORDER. However, after the Civil War, it was mainly the federal government that was responsible for introducing notions of Eastern penology to the West and financing the construction of institutions to carry out punishment.

By the early nineteenth century, the dominant penal philosophy was the so-called Auburn system, which isolated one man to one cell and imposed a rule of silence when convicts were together for such activities as dining and factory labor within the prison. The Auburn system was named for the New York state prison at Auburn, which featured an austere architectural style intended to promote solitude, order, and self-reflection. The Auburn system appealed to penologists and legislators alike. It allowed for productive industry among the inmates, yet it separated them from society, including the society within the prison itself. By promoting self-reflection, the system, it was believed, also encouraged repentance. The Auburn system influenced most of the major prisons built in the West through much of the late nineteenth century.

The first major federal prison built in the West was the Colorado territorial penitentiary built at Canon City beginning in 1868. It was followed by another large federally funded institution at Rawlins, Wyoming, in 1888. These prisons were built to conform to Auburn-system standards; they included many solitary cells, congregate dining facilities, and a congregate labor area. Even the planners of state-funded prisons characteristically looked to the East and, in particular, to the Auburn system for guidance. The Kansas State Penitentiary, opened in 1883, was essentially copied from the penitentiary at Joliet, Illinois, which had been built according to the Auburn idea.

The most demanding Auburn requirement, the one-man cell, destined the large Western prisons to premature overcrowding. By the 1890s, many Western jurisdictions compromised the Auburn pattern by placing more than one prisoner in a cell. In California, for example, white prisoners were incarcerated one to a cell, but African Americans or foreign-born prisoners were compelled to share their cells with several other inmates.

One Auburn concept most Western legislators embraced was the idea of prison labor. As early as 1839, Missouri initiated a program whereby prisoners were leased out as cheap workers. The system, which lasted four years, led to a rapid breakdown of security and a rash of escapes. The leasing of prisoners was ultimately abandoned. However, the idea that prisoners should work—at the very least to sustain themselves, but also, in some cases, to turn a profit for the state—persisted. Unincarcerated laborers, frequently put out of jobs, complained about the system of prison labor, however.

Until the Progressive era of the early twentieth century, Western prisons were, above all else, custodial institutions. Although rehabilitation—through reflection and repentance—was a prime objective of the Auburn system, it played a distinctly subsidiary role in Western prisons during the nineteenth century. Some scholars have suggested that rehabilitation played a minor role because the Western penal systems placed far less emphasis on reintegrating wrongdoers into society and because Western communities were marked by individualism rather than conformity—a condition reflected in penal philosophy.

—*Alan Axelrod*

SUGGESTED READING:

Axelrod, Alan, and Charles Phillips. *Cops, Crooks, and Criminologists: An International Biographical Dictionary of Law Enforcement*. New York, 1996.

Bookspan, Shelley. *A Germ of Goodness: The California State Prison System, 1851–1944*. Lincoln, Nebr., 1991.

Hollon, W. Eugene. *Frontier Violence: Another Look*. New York, 1974.

A crude wooden structure served as a jail in the Wyoming Territory in 1893. Photograph by Hart Merriam. *Courtesy National Archives.*

JAMES, EDWIN

Born in Weybridge, Vermont, botanist Edwin James (1797–1861) studied medicine with his brother and botany and geology with John Torrey and Amos Eaton after graduating from Middlebury College in 1816. In 1820, he received an appointment as surgeon, botanist, and geologist with an expedition commanded by Major STEPHEN HARRIMAN LONG to explore the region between the Mississippi River and the Rocky Mountains. After following the South Platte into Colorado, James departed from the main body of the expedition and made his way to the foothills of the Rocky Mountains. On July 14, 1820, he and two companions made the first ascent of Pikes Peak by Euro-Americans. The first botanist to explore the alpine flora of the Rocky Mountains and a careful observer of botanical specimens, James collected numerous plants during the fourteen-thousand-foot climb.

James wrote the report of the Long expedition, *An Account of an Expedition from Pittsburgh to the Rocky Mountains Performed in the Years 1819–1820* (two volumes and atlas, Philadelphia 1822–1823), which cast doubt about American settlement in the vast lands between the Mississippi River and the Rocky Mountains because of their aridity. The work helped characterize the region as the "GREAT AMERICAN DESERT."

After serving as an assistant surgeon in the U.S. Army from 1823 to 1836 and as a subagent for the Potawatomis, he spent the rest of his life farming in Rock Spring, Iowa. A determined abolitionist, he established a station for the Underground Railroad at his farm.

—*Phillip Drennon Thomas*

SEE ALSO: Exploration and Science

SUGGESTED READING:
Ewan, Joseph. *Rocky Mountain Naturalists.* Denver, Colo., 1950.

JAMES BROTHERS

Notorious Western train and bank robbers Alexander Franklin James (1843–1915) and his brother Jesse Woodson James (1847–1882) began their careers as Confederate GUERRILLAS. Both were born in Clay County, Missouri. After their father, a Baptist preacher, died in California where he had gone to mine gold, their mother, Zerelda, married two more times, the last to Reuben Samuel, a prosperous physician. Farm-

Frank and Jesse James. *Courtesy Denver Public Library, Western History Department.*

ers and slave owners, the family was sympathetic to the Southern cause during the CIVIL WAR.

Frank and Jesse both served in the infamous guerrilla band led by WILLIAM CLARKE QUANTRILL and WILLIAM C. ("BLOODY BILL") ANDERSON and were involved in some of the most atrocious raids and massacres on the Kansas-Missouri border.

Within months after the Civil War ended, the brothers, with some of their guerrilla compatriots, turned to outlawry. They committed their first crime on February 13, 1866, by robbing the bank in Liberty, Missouri. The James brothers allied themselves with the YOUNGER BROTHERS and, until Jesse was murdered, committed robberies in and around Missouri.

Jesse was the acknowledged leader of the gang. He could be charismatic when necessary and a cold-blooded killer when the occasion arose. One bandit who rode with him claimed that Jesse required each gang member to kill in order to keep the group together and to preserve secrecy.

In 1873, the gang added train robbery to its repertoire. By that time, attractive rewards had been posted, and the PINKERTON NATIONAL DETECTIVE AGENCY soon became involved in hunting down the gang. In January 1875, two men rumored to be Pinkerton agents bombed the home of the James brothers' mother and her family. During the incident nine-year-old Archie Samuel, a half brother to Frank and Jesse, was killed and their mother's arm was mutilated.

Because of the bombing, the persistent efforts of their friend, newspaperman John N. Edwards, and the 1876 publication of the first book about them and the Youngers, the James brothers came to be regarded by some as modern-day Robin Hoods, who robbed money-grubbing banks and railroads and gave the proceeds to the poor. The James gang scarcely deserved that canonization; its members, particularly Jesse, often killed wantonly and without mercy, and the gang did not donate the fruits of its efforts to the needy.

Both Jesse and Frank were married in 1874, fathered children, and lived with their families between robberies.

On September 7, 1876, the James-Younger gang rode into Northfield, Minnesota, intent on robbing the First National Bank. Employees of the bank resisted the attempt, however, and Northfield citizens, who quickly learned of the robbery, armed themselves and began shooting at the outlaws who were guarding the outside of the bank. The cashier and a bystander were killed, and the teller was wounded. Among the outlaws, two were killed in the street, and Cole and Bob Younger were wounded, the latter seriously.

The remaining gang members escaped and eluded the posses that sought them for two weeks but were finally surrounded in the town of Madelia where one gang member was killed and all three Younger brothers wounded. Jesse and Frank James escaped unharmed.

Just how many robberies credited to the James brothers were actually committed by them is not known, but after most were publicized, Jesse often wrote letters proclaiming the gang's innocence to local newspapers. Their friend Edwards granted Jesse considerable space in the *Kansas City Times*. Newspapers were Jesse's favorite reading matter, and he scoured them daily to catch items concerning his own activities.

Jesse James, at least, continued to commit robberies sporadically, but Frank attempted to settle down in Tennessee. Both moved often, however, when they feared capture was near. In 1881, Jesse, then living under the alias of Thomas Howard, moved to St. Joseph, Missouri, where he was shot and killed by newly recruited gang member Robert Ford on April 3, 1882. The thirty-four-year-old outlaw was buried in the yard of his mother's farm.

Frank surrendered to the governor of Missouri six months later. After much legal maneuvering, he was eventually acquitted of the charges brought against him. He moved from trivial job to trivial job and at one time was a partner in the James-Younger Wild West show. After he died in 1915, he was cremated in order to prevent an autopsy, a procedure he had feared. Also at his request, his ashes were kept in a bank vault until his wife died in 1944. Their remains were then jointly interred in a Kansas City cemetery.

—*Joseph W. Snell*

SEE ALSO: Northfield Raid; Social Banditry

SUGGESTED READING:
Horan, James D. *The Authentic Wild West: The Outlaws.* New York, 1976.
Settle, William A., Jr. *Jesse James Was His Name.* Columbia, Mo., 1966.

JAPANESE AMERICANS

Issei

Japanese immigration into the American West began in earnest after Chinese workers were barred from entering the United States by the Chinese Exclusion Act of 1882. Those Japanese coming to the country during the late nineteenth and early twentieth centuries were primarily laborers, many of whom went first to Hawaii before remigrating to the mainland.

Japanese laborers were drawn to work in the Hawaiian sugar industry, which, as part of the post–Civil War boom, was expanding rapidly, finding itself in need of ever more workers just as the native Hawaiian population fell into rapid decline, mainly from disease, and Chinese laborers—first imported by planters in 1852—were leaving the plantations for other work, to return home, or to head for California's "gold mountain." As early as 1865, Hawaii's foreign minister—himself a plantation owner—wrote to American businessmen in Japan seeking agricultural laborers to replace the Chinese. Three years later, on May 17, 1868, the *Scioto* set sail from Yokohama to Honolulu with 141 men, 6 women, and 2 children aboard, Japanese contract migrant workers called *Gannenmono Issei* (*Gannenmono*, or "first year people" because they left during the first year of Meiji rule; *Issei* from the Japanese linguistic character for generation number, in this case "one," meaning "first generation.")

These Gannenmono, including samurai, cooks, sake brewers, porters, printers, tailors, wood workers, a hairdresser, and a thirteen-year-old drunk called "Ichi the Viper," sailed for a month through harsh storms to take up hard labor on plantations where strict labor bosses imposed exacting regulations for ten hours of work a day. They arrived, many suffering from seasickness, only to be put to work stripping razorlike sugar-cane leaves, batching them in bundles, and hauling them off to mills—all under a blistering tropical sun. Fined if they were late or broke curfew, dunned of

In Hawaii, Japanese immigrant women at their sewing machines in a workroom at the University Club, Honolulu, 1919. *Courtesy Hawaii State Archives.*

their wages for losing tools, penalized with two days' extra work for every day they lost because they were sick or hung-over, the sun-burned Gannenmono raised their blistered hands in protest before the first month was out, and both planters and workers complained to the Hawaiian government. The planters wanted their money back for those workers who were sick and, in one case, for a man who died about the time he first stepped into a field of sugar cane. The workers were angry that the sugar-cane growers withheld half their monthly wage of four dollars and traded contracts among themselves as if the Japanese were slaves. The workers asked for pay on days lost to bad weather. Forty of them would leave before their three-year contracts expired; all but one of them signed a petition accusing Hawaii's growers of cruelty and dishonesty.

Almost exactly a year after the *Scioto* sailed out of Yokohama, the PACIFIC MAIL STEAMSHIP Company's *China* steamed into San Francisco Bay. On board that May 27, 1869, were a group of Japanese explorers— samurai, farmers, traders, and four women. Followers of Japan's feudal lord Matsudaira Katamori of Aizu Wakamatsu, they were fleeing the political upheaval that attended the collapse of the Tokugawa shogunate

and led to the Meiji restoration. They followed the Sacramento River to Placerville where they secured six hundred acres and established the Wakamatsu Tea and Silk Farm. They planted mulberry trees they had brought from Japan for silk farming and bamboo for food and furniture and tea seeds from whose growth they hoped to brew prosperity and happiness. But the American West was an arid land, and without water, their seedlings burned on the ground. The colony itself lasted less than two years, after which some of the Wakamatsu colonists went home to Japan; others drifted away to San Francisco and the coast; some stayed in place and tried to make a go of it.

From these beginnings sprang the first generation Japanese American community, the *Issei*. Many of those who followed were, like the Gannenmono in Hawaii, labor recruits and transients; others, like the Wakamatsu colonists, were settlers driven from their homeland and looking for the fabled Tenjiku, or "Faraway Place," where opportunities for a decent life abounded. A diverse lot, they first began to come in large numbers after 1886, when Hawaii and Japan signed a labor convention; migrant workers arrived in Honolulu, and student laborers sailed into San Francisco. Japanese immigrants discovered, as many Forty-niners had before them, that the West's dusty streets were not paved with gold, and their life was made difficult by labor recruiters, banks, and migration agents, who demanded extortionate fees, and by cruel labor conditions on the plantations of Hawaii or the cotton fields of Arizona and New Mexico or the orchards of California and the Pacific Coast.

Among the growing Japanese American community of San Francisco, which in 1890 numbered about three thousand, student laborers predominated, some of them young Christians who founded the Gospel Society. The more traditional among them were ministered to by Buddhist missionaries who established, in addition to temples, San Francisco's Young Men's Buddhist Association (YMBA) to rival the Methodist-spawned YMCA. They were the vanguard of a mass immigration that, according to the 1910 U.S. Census, would see within a decade 79,675 Japanese settle in Hawaii and 72,157 on the mainland, mostly in the Far West and the Southwest. Thirty-one percent, or 24,891, of the Japanese in Hawaii were women, but women made up only 12.6 percent, or 9,807, of those on the mainland.

The great gender gap among a group of marriage-age people meant that the Japanese women, most of whom were already married, had little contact with other women and suffered much torment, and even abuse, at the hands of Japanese men. Married women sometimes feared sexual harassment and, like Tsuru Yamauchi, insisted their husbands accompany them for even short trips outside the home. A few Japanese businessmen kidnapped women, imported them to work as prostitutes, and held them in slavery, but the numbers were small. A few Japanese women fled abusive husbands and took lovers from among the large bachelor population. After the 1908 GENTLEMAN'S AGREEMENT, whose intention was to stop the flow of Japanese immigration, Japanese men were allowed to import wives, most of whom came as PICTURE BRIDES. For example, while in 1910 there were only 13,970 married women in Hawaii and 5,581 on the mainland, by 1920 the number had all but doubled on the island (22,373) and had exploded in the American West to 22,193. The young wives and picture brides gave birth to the next generation, the *Nisei* ("second generation") and preserved and transmitted culture within the family, especially when it came to rearing children. They melded together the mix of tradition and innovation that came to characterize Japanese American culture, and they helped bridge the gap between the transient life of migrant workers and the settled society of immigrants by joining their men in the fields to produce two incomes for renting or buying land.

Japanese migrant workers faced a gamut of barriers to social mobility and advancement. As their numbers grew, so did racial discrimination, first in social attitudes, then in economic practice, and finally in political laws and statues. In Hawaii, workers were expected to be docile and obedient to their overbosses. On the mainland, they became increasingly subjected to hurled racial epithets and, more and more frequently, to physical attacks. Westerners discriminated against the Japanese in employment, forced them to live in segregated neighborhoods and to attend "Oriental schools," destroyed their homes and businesses in riots, and sometimes literally chased them out of town. A number of them returned to Japan, and Japanese immigration slowed considerably after the Gentleman's Agreement of 1908 and came to a virtual halt with the 1924 Johnson-Reed Act.

Although the Issei's own children, the Nisei, would come to characterize them as accommodating and conservative, even fatalistic and passive, many Issei mounted counterattacks against American racism and exploitation. As early as 1891, a Japanese worker named Mioshi argued that the contract-labor system was a form of slavery before the Hawaiian Supreme Court, and Ekiu Nishimura sued San Francisco's commissioner of immigration for denying her entry to the country and detaining her at the port; both lost their cases. Denied protection by the courts, some Issei took to the streets. In February 1903, five hundred Japanese joined two hundred Mexicans in Oxnard, California, to form the Japanese-Mexican Labor Association and, in March, to strike the sugar-beet industry. Despite the opposition of the American Federation of Labor (AFL), who denied the union a charter, the strike broke the contractors' monopoly on labor and forced a settlement within a month. In 1900 alone, Japanese workers staged some twenty strikes in Hawaii against plantation contractors, immigration companies, and their pet financial institution, the Keihin Bank. Workers joined the Japanese Reform Association, which in 1905 won concessions from the Japanese government, closed down the bank, and clipped the wings of emigration company agents.

The most significant of the Japanese protests took place in 1909, when seven thousand workers from all of Oahu's major plantations joined a four-month-long strike staged by the Higher Wage Association. From the time the Japanese workers walked off the job in May, planters—and some among Hawaii's Japanese community—condemned the strike as the work of agitators and loafers. Planters evicted strikers and their families, sometimes with as little as twenty-four hours' notice. By June, five thousand displaced Japanese were living in makeshift shelters in downtown Honolulu, the Higher Wage Association was branded as a criminal organization, and the area—according to an eyewitness—resembled a battlefield. Strike leaders were arrested and imprisoned for conspiracy, and two weeks before they were convicted, the association called off the strike. The strike itself had been in part a response to the exclusion policies embodied in the Gentlemen's Agreement. Clearly, the Issei no longer saw themselves as transients but as American settlers.

And just as the Issei began to see themselves as Americans, Western states began to pass ALIEN LAND LAWS, which forbade Japanese from leasing or owning land. California's 1913 law had the greatest impact, but the Issei circumvented the law by transferring property titles to their American-born children or by setting up dummy corporations, sometimes fronted by sympathetic whites, to hold title.

Nisei

In some measure, however, the younger generation was justified in seeing the Issei as conservative and fatalistic. Isolated from the American mainstream, the first generation of Japanese immigrants formed tight-knit communities and clung to the culture of their homeland, from arranging marriages in the traditional way to carrying on the ceremonies and festivals that emphasized the individual's connection to his ancestral past. They had built Japanese churches, both Buddhist and Christian, erected halls to serve as LANGUAGE SCHOOLS and as playhouses for Japanese dramas and samurai films, bonsai and *ikebana* exhibits, judo lessons, and poetry readings. The streets of each Little

Nisei students of Parkville, Missouri, take part in a flag-raising ceremony in 1942, while their white neighbors urged their internment during World War II. *Courtesy The Bettmann Archive.*

Tokyo were lined with shops that sold *miso* and tofu, rice and noodles, fresh fish and curative herbs. The Issei ran hotels and bath houses, restaurants and bars, gambling dens and dance halls. They operated trading companies and newspapers and owned farms and shops. Cut off by law not only from the society around them but from their homeland that once furnished them cultural sustenance and reinforcements from Japan, the Issei, by the mid-1920s, had determined, more or less, to keep to themselves.

The American-born Japanese, on the other hand, nearly all shared a common American past. Growing

The queen of Los Angeles's 1954 Nisei Week is seated on her throne surrounded by her ladies-in-waiting. *Courtesy The Bettmann Archive.*

up in rural settings, whether on Hawaiian sugar plantations or mainland family farms, they almost all spoke English as a first language, and therefore they were not limited as their parents had been in their dealings with whites. American citizens educated in both public schools and in private Japanese language schools, they—like Americans across the country in the 1920s and 1930s—were moving to cities in great numbers. With Japanese immigration all but cut off in the first two decades of the century, the second generation Nisei composed the large increases in the Japanese population, which by 1920 totaled 109,274 in Hawaii and 111,010 on the mainland, and by 1930, 139,631 and 126,948, respectively. In Little Tokyo, the ambitions of the Nisei, who had never known any other homeland, to share in the larger American world and to protest their exclusion from that world came into conflict with their parents' protective isolationism, which they saw as accommodation. Still bound together with the Issei as a single community, the Nisei had different hopes, experiences, values, and plans.

There were splits within the Nisei, one major division being that between those who were educated in the United States and the Kibei, who were sent as children to Japan for a part of their education and who, naturally enough, tended to be more Japanese in outlook. As they came of age in the 1930s, faced with the same lack of opportunity and discrimination visited on the Issei, many Nisei formed Japanese American Democratic Clubs in San Francisco, Oakland, and Los Angeles, called themselves "progressives," and worked to elect Democrats and outlaw racial discrimination. As a hedge against future exclusion, their parents had provided the Nisei with dual citizenship, registering them in Japan as nationals, but many in the second generation fought against this "twoness." They wanted to "lower the anchor" and fully identify with America. They hoped to educate the larger society about their educational and business achievements by disseminating information through local civic clubs, such as San Francisco's and Fresno's American Loyalty League (Seattle and Portland had similar clubs) and the national Japanese American Citizens League (JACL). At the founding convention in Seattle in 1930, the JACL exploded over whether to include a hyphen in the name between *Japanese* and *American,* or whether to drop all references to *Japanese,* deciding in the end to use *Japanese* as a subordinate adjective to modify *American.* The JACL, denouncing dual citizenship in 1936, focused on conservative and accommodationist strategies of enterprise and self-help and believed "patriotism" would be the key to American acceptance. "Deep in their hearts," however, said Ronald Takaki, "many Nisei did not want to be completely assimilated. . . .

They felt they were heirs to a complex combination of two cultures and that they should be allowed to embrace their 'twoness.'" Even while some formed clubs emphasizing their American-ness, members of the second generation also held "Nisei Week" in Little Tokyos celebrating their Japanese American heritage. Since, as Takaki says, *loyal* was the crucial word for the Nisei, it is tragically ironic that they ultimately achieved leadership of the community in the World War II internment camps.

For if Japanese exclusion was the defining moment for the Issei, the forced resettlement of those of Japanese descent living along the Pacific Coast during the war to concentration camps in the Western interior, where the racial rather than the political basis for their "twoness" became manifest, was the turning point in the lives of the Nisei. Grim as the camps were, the Nisei would, like their parents, survive, even thrive, and pass on their traditions to the third-generation *Sansei*, in an American West that had welcomed their labor but hardly tolerated their presence.

—*Charles Phillips and Patricia Hogan*

SEE ALSO: Asian American Churches; Chinese Exclusion; Hawaii Laborer's Association; Immigration Law; Oxnard Agricultural Strike

SUGGESTED READING:

Asian Women United of California, eds. *Making Waves: An Anthology of Writings about Asian American Women.* Boston, 1989.

Chan, Sucheng. *Asian Americans: An Interpretive History.* Boston, 1991.

Daniels, Roger. *The Politics of Prejudice.* Berkeley, Calif., 1962.

Hosokawa, Bill. *The Nisei: The Quiet Americans.* New York, 1969.

Ichioka, Yuji. *The Issei: The World of the First Generation Japanese Immigrants, 1885–1924.* New York, 1988.

Matsumoto, Valerie. *Farming the Home Place: A Japanese American Community in California, 1919–1982.* Ithaca, N.Y., 1993.

Okihiro, Gary. *Margins and Mainstream: Asian Americans in History and Culture,* Seattle, Wash., 1994.

Takaki, Ronald. *Pau Hana: Plantation Life and Labor in Hawaii, 1835–1920.* Honolulu, Hawaii, 1983.

———. *Strangers from a Different Shore : A History of Asian Americans.* Boston, 1989.

JAPANESE INTERNMENT

During World War II, the U.S. government placed approximately 110,000 Japanese aliens and Japanese American citizens into concentration camps. The in-

At the Heart Mountain center in Wyoming, barracks covered in tar paper housed ten thousand internees. *Courtesy National Archives.*

A Japanese family at the Granada Relocation Internment Center, Amache, Colorado, in their living quarters. Photograph by Tom Parker. *Courtesy Denver Public Library, Western History Department.*

ternment deprived people of their civil liberties and divided Japanese American families and communities.

After the Japanese attack on Pearl Harbor on December 7, 1941, many military officials expressed concern about Japanese Americans. Secretary of the Navy Frank Knox and several army and navy officers insisted that Japanese Americans in Hawaii had participated in the attack at Pearl Harbor, and they argued that Japanese Americans on the Pacific Coast would probably engage in sabotage. In support of the military's claims, West Coast newspapers published articles that emphasized the dangers of allowing Japanese immigrants and their children to remain in California, Washington, and Oregon. Strident voices within the military persuaded President Franklin D. Roosevelt to sanction the removal of all Japanese Americans from the Pacific Coast. On February 19, 1942, Roosevelt issued Executive Order 9066, which gave the military the power to designate "military areas" from which it could exclude "any and all persons."

Between March and June 1942, the army ordered all Japanese Americans in most of California, Oregon, and Washington to leave their homes and report to civil control stations—frequently Christian and Buddhist churches. Military authorities allowed the Japanese Americans to bring only as much luggage as they could carry. The army gave the residents of Terminal Island in Los Angeles Harbor less than three days to store or sell their personal possessions and arrange to rent homes, farms, and businesses; Japanese Americans in other areas had as much as ten days. Unscrupulous people took advantage of some Japanese Americans by buying furniture and automobiles for a fraction of their value. Other Japanese Americans stored their belongings in churches or community organization buildings, many of which were looted during the war.

Buses and trucks took Japanese Americans and their baggage from the churches to assembly centers. These temporary concentration camps were usually located at county fairgrounds and horse-racing tracks. In the summer and fall, Japanese Americans were shipped to more permanent relocation centers.

To administer the relocation centers, Roosevelt created the War Relocation Authority (WRA) in March 1942. The WRA operated ten camps: Manzanar and Tule Lake in the interior of California, Poston and Gila River in Arizona, Jerome and Rohwer in Arkansas, Granada (also known as Amache) in Colorado, Topaz in Utah, Minidoka in Idaho, and Heart Mountain in Wyoming.

Camp life strained family relationships. Most families lived in one-room apartments and were thus de-prived of privacy. Children often stayed away from the family dwelling and refused to eat with their parents. Parents complained that they could not discipline their children.

Women's experiences in the camps differed from those of men. Older women found themselves with more leisure time than they had had before the war. Working women received the same amount of pay as men, and the traditional patterns of arranged marriages disintegrated. For most women, as for most men, however, the internment itself was a traumatic experience.

The camp experience upset the social order within the community. Although at first the WRA deprived the older men of power within the community—a move that embittered many Japanese Americans—the traditional community leaders were later allowed to participate in camp "self-government." In December 1942, angry inmates at Manzanar attacked other prisoners whom they accused of collaborating with the WRA. Military police moved in to stop the riot and fired tear gas and bullets into the crowd. Two people died from gunshot wounds.

Many government actions exacerbated fear and despair within the camps. In 1943, for example, the WRA separated "loyal" from "disloyal" Japanese Americans and placed the "disloyals" in a segregation center at Tule Lake. In 1944, the army began drafting men from the camps, sparking a considerable resistance movement. Both the draft and the segregation of "disloyals" further split already divided families and communities.

Throughout World War II, U.S. courts upheld the legality of internment. In late 1944, however, the U.S. Supreme Court ruled that the government could not continue to impound people and exclude them from the Pacific Coast without proof of disloyalty. The army rescinded the exclusion order on January 1, 1945, and Japanese Americans were allowed to return to the coastal areas of California, Washington, and Oregon.

After internment, many Japanese Americans sought restitution from the federal government. In 1948, Congress passed the Evacuee Claims Act, which allowed Japanese Americans to receive monetary compensation. Claimants generally received one-tenth of the value of their losses. A redress movement resurfaced in the late 1960s and early 1970s and, over the course of two decades, achieved many of its goals. President Gerald Ford rescinded Executive Order 9066 in 1976 and issued a formal apology to Japanese Americans. Federal courts vacated opinions that had upheld the constitutionality of the internment. In 1988, Congress passed a bill issuing an apology and a payment of twenty thousand dollars to each survivor of the camps.

—Kevin Allen Leonard

SUGGESTED READING:

Daniels, Roger. *Concentration Camps USA: Japanese Americans and World War II.* Hinsdale, Ill., 1971.

Matsumoto, Valerie. *Farming the Home Place: A Japanese American Community in California, 1919–1982.* Ithaca, N.Y., 1993.

———. "Japanese American Women during World War II." *Frontiers* 8 (1984): 6–14.

Sone, Monica. *Nisei Daughter.* Seattle, Wash., 1979.

Weglyn, Michi. *Years of Infamy: The Untold Story of America's Concentration Camps.* New York, 1976.

JA RANCH, TEXAS

The JA Ranch was founded in 1877 under the terms of a five-year contract between John G. Adair, an Irish investment banker, and cattleman CHARLES GOODNIGHT. Having driven a small stock of cattle from Colorado into the Palo Duro Canyon region of the Texas Panhandle the previous year, Goodnight provided the foundation herd and ranching expertise in exchange for an annual salary and one-third of the assets. Adair, who financed additional purchases of land and cattle, received two-thirds of the assets plus 10-percent interest on his investment.

By 1881, Goodnight had secured nearly 100,000 acres including a number of strategic tracts that contained critical springs. When the profitable partnership was extended for another five years in 1882, land acquisition accelerated until the JA Ranch owned 650,000 acres outright and leased or otherwise grazed an equivalent amount of range. At the ranch's peak, JA cattle numbered one hundred thousand and included an outstanding herd of high-grade Herefords.

Adair's death in 1885 and depressed conditions in the CATTLE INDUSTRY and ranching brought an end to the partnership in 1887. The assets were partitioned, and Adair's widow, Cornelia Wadsworth Adair, retained ownership of the JA brand. Efficient managers, such as Richard Walsh, helped consolidate its range and improve the quality of its herds, water, and fences.

After Cornelia Adair's death in 1921, ownership of the nearly 400,000 acres of JA range passed to her heirs, who continue to operate the ranch.

—*B. Byron Price*

SUGGESTED READING:

Burton, Harley T. *A History of the JA Ranch.* Austin, Tex., 1928.

Haley, J. Evetts. *Charles Goodnight: Cowman and Plainsman.* Boston, 1936.

JAYHAWKERS

If the University of Kansas intended the name of its athletic teams to inspire fear, "the Jayhawks" certainly has historical precedent. The term comes from the CIVIL WAR–era, when border raiders crossed from Kansas into Missouri to plunder supposed Confederates and liberate their slaves. From a particular band called the "Jayhawkers," all such raiding became known as "jayhawking."

Economic depression in Kansas may have encouraged plundering, but jayhawking descended in a direct line from the famed JOHN BROWN, whose antislavery attacks in Kansas and then Virginia led to his capture and execution in 1859. Failing to rescue Brown, a zealous follower named James Montgomery returned to Kansas to resume raiding Missouri slave owners. Montgomery's associates included Charles R. ("Doc") Jennison, a brutal little man for whom the antislavery cause was hardly more than an excuse for indiscriminate pillaging. He organized the particularly notorious band of raiders that became known as the Jayhawkers.

At the outset of the Civil War, Jennison's Jayhawkers joined the Kansas Brigade, better known as Lane's Brigade, for JAMES HENRY LANE, the dominant Kansas politician of the time who raised it. Jennison's men pillaged Fort Scott, Kansas, for no known military reason, and then helped the brigade burn and loot its way to Osceola, Missouri. This achievement, plus Lane's advocacy for mounting "a great jayhawking expedition" through the Indian Country into Texas to attack Confederates and free and arm slaves there, led Lane himself to be called "the great Jayhawker."

Later in the Civil War, Jennison became colonel of a cavalry regiment that advertised for recruits as the "Independent Mounted Kansas Jayhawkers." John Brown, Jr., commanded fanatical abolitionists in one of its companies, while Marshall Cleveland, an exconvict jayhawker remembered for murdering and robbing his way through Missouri border towns, commanded another. The Independent Mounted Kansas Jayhawkers and other units under "Colonel" Jennison during the Civil War gained such a reputation for killing prisoners, mistaking Kansans for the enemy, and robbing private citizens including women and children, that Jennison faced a court-martial. Merely reprimanded, however, he resigned his commission and spent his remaining years among the gamblers in Leavenworth.

George Hoyt, one of Jennison's equally unscrupulous associates, headed a notorious jayhawker band called the "Red Legs" for the color of their leggings. Operating along the Missouri border, the Red Legs regularly showed up in Kansas towns with stolen stock and plunder to sell. But their propensity to assault Kansans as well as Missourians led to attempts by authorities in Kansas to suppress jayhawkers. Also, it became clear that jayhawking bands accomplished little more than inspiring retaliatory raids from Missouri's pro-Confederate "bushwhackers." These included the infamous sacker of Lawrence, Kansas, WILLIAM CLARKE QUANTRILL, once a jayhawker himself who changed sides. Jesse James and Cole Younger were among Missourians who became bushwhackers to avenge atrocities against their families by jayhawkers. It took a long time even after the Civil War for Kansans to end the indiscriminate banditry that became the legacy of both bushwhacking and jayhawking.

—*Gerald George*

SEE ALSO: Guerrillas; James Brothers; Younger Brothers

SUGGESTED READING:

Castel, Albert. *A Frontier State at War: Kansas, 1861–1865.* Ithaca, N.Y., 1958.
Richmond, Robert W. *Kansas, A Land of Contrasts.* St. Charles, Mo., 1989.

JEFFERSON, THOMAS

Author of the Declaration of Independence, governor of Virginia, minister to France, secretary of state, vice-president, president of the United States, president of the American Philosophical Society, and founder and architect of the University of Virginia, Thomas Jefferson (1743–1826) had a lifelong interest in the development of the American West. From the outset of the American Revolution, Jefferson viewed the vast Western lands beyond the Allegheny Mountains as a resource of freedom and democracy.

Jefferson was born in Albemarle County on the western fringes of settlement in the English colony of Virginia. As governor of Virginia (1779–1781) during the later years of the Revolution, Jefferson was aware of the need to maintain American military control over lands to the west. He played an important role in supporting the campaigns of George Rogers Clark to secure the Virginia frontier along the Ohio River to the Mississippi.

After the Revolution, as a member of the Congress of the Confederation in 1783 and 1784, Jefferson presented a plan for governing the Western territory. That plan became the basis of the Land Ordinance of 1785, which in turn became the foundation for the NORTH-WEST ORDINANCE of 1787, a law that established the basic principles of American territorial policy. Jefferson was secretary of state (1790–1793) when Kentucky became the first Western state to enter the Union in 1792.

Jefferson had his greatest impact—as president of the United States (1801-1809)—on NATIONAL EXPANSION westward. Alarmed by the anticipated transfer of Louisiana from a weak Spain to a powerful France and by the sudden closing of the port of New Orleans to American produce coming down the Mississippi River for export, Jefferson's administration began negotiations to purchase territory at the mouth of the Mississippi. Aided by circumstances in Napoleonic France, the American envoys—Robert R. Livingston and James Monroe—concluded the agreement for the LOUISIANA PURCHASE, signed in Paris on May 2, 1803. That extraordinary treaty not only met the immediate needs of trade down the Ohio and Mississippi rivers but also doubled the territory of the United States and destined the United States to expand westward across the continent. Jefferson saw the acquisition as "an empire for liberty."

Jefferson had a keen interest in the natural history of the undeveloped West. As vice-president of the United States (1797–1801), he had been enthralled by scientific information gathered by Andrew Ellicott in the newly opened Mississippi Territory. Even before the purchase of Louisiana was anticipated, Jefferson sought an appropriation from Congress to finance an

Thomas Jefferson. *Courtesy Library of Congress.*

expedition to explore the western reaches of North America from the Mississippi to the Pacific Ocean. Congress passed the necessary legislation in February 1803, more than two months before the Louisiana treaty was signed in Paris. Jefferson himself wrote the instructions for the expedition and named MERIWETHER LEWIS and WILLIAM CLARK to lead it. He was fascinated by information about the vast Western territory they traversed, the detailed reports they prepared, and the specimens of minerals and wildlife they brought back. The success of the LEWIS AND CLARK EXPEDITION (1804–1806) was the highlight of Jefferson's second term as president.

Jefferson saw two states west of the Mississippi River—Louisiana and Missouri—admitted into the Union before his death on the fiftieth anniversary of the adoption of the Declaration of Independence. The controversy over the admission of Missouri as a slave state alarmed Jefferson and darkened his vision of future expansion of the Union, but his interest in the West never faded.

Despite his love of the mountains and a lifelong interest in the West, Jefferson never traveled farther west than Warm Springs, Virginia, near the present-day boundary of West Virginia, where, at the age of seventy-five, he went to take the waters. For a traveler who had crossed the Alps into Italy, his lack of Western travel is surprising. In his *Notes on the State of Virginia,* published in 1785, Jefferson described the Ohio River as "the most beautiful river on earth," but he never saw it himself. Both George Washington and James Monroe far surpassed Jefferson in their first-hand knowledge of the West. Still, no early president had a more profound interest in the West or more impact on the Western expansion of the United States.

—*Noble E. Cunningham, Jr.*

SEE ALSO: Exploration and Science; Land Policy

SUGGESTED READING:
Cunningham, Noble E., Jr. *In Pursuit of Reason: The Life of Thomas Jefferson.* Baton Rouge, La., 1987.
Jackson, Donald. *Thomas Jefferson and the Stony Mountains: Exploring the West from Monticello.* Urbana, Ill., 1981.
Jefferson, Thomas. *Notes on the State of Virginia.* Edited by William Peden. Chapel Hill, N.C., 1955.
Peterson, Merrill D. *Thomas Jefferson and the New Nation: A Biography.* New York, 1970.

JEFFORDS, THOMAS J.

A stagecoach driver, Indian trader, and noted friend of the Chiricahua Apache chief COCHISE, Thomas J. Jeffords (1832-1914) was born in Chautauqua County, New York. He worked as a ship captain on the Great Lakes before moving to Taos, New Mexico, in 1859. There he drove stagecoaches, traded with Indians, and became mail superintendent on the stage line between Tucson and Mesilla. While he worked as mail superintendent, fourteen of his men were killed by Indians, and Jeffords believed that Cochise was their leader. Jeffords realized that his only recourse was to effect a deal with the enemy, although for years no white man had entered Cochise's camp and emerged alive.

Nevertheless, Jeffords boldly rode into Cochise's Dragoon Mountains retreat, dismounted, left his firearms on his horse's saddle, and approached the astonished chief. In a man-to-man talk in faltering Spanish with bits of Apache and English, the two men arranged an oral compact that permitted Jeffords's couriers safe transit through Apache country.

Jeffords subsequently met Cochise many times, and they became close friends. Jeffords arranged occasional meetings between Cochise and army officials and other whites; the most notable meeting was with General OLIVER OTIS HOWARD, who formally arranged peace with Cochise and persuaded him and his followers to move to a southeastern Arizona reservation, with Jeffords as agent. A good, though often controversial agent, Jeffords was forced to turn to other employment when Cochise died in 1874 and the reservation was disbanded.

Throughout his life, Jeffords made strong friendships and won widespread respect. He refused to his death to reveal where the Apaches had buried Cochise.

—*Dan L. Thrapp*

SUGGESTED READING:
Thrapp, Dan L. *Encyclopedia of Frontier Biography.* Glendale, Calif., and Spokane, Wash., 1988 and 1989.
Sweeney, Edwin R. *Cochise: Chiricahua Apache Chief.* Norman, Okla., 1991.

JENNINGS, WILLIAM

A leading Mormon businessman and mayor of Salt Lake City, William Jennings (1823–1886) was born in Yardley, England. He learned the butchering business from his father and migrated to the United States in 1847 to seek his fortune. He first lived in New York City and then migrated to Ohio and Missouri. There he met and married Jane Walker, a Mormon. Jennings joined the CHURCH OF JESUS CHRIST OF LATTER-DAY SAINTS after the young couple moved to Utah in 1852.

Jennings established a butchering business in Salt Lake City. Extremely successful, he then expanded his business into tanning, leather goods, and dry goods. By the early 1860s, he was Utah's leading merchant. He also was engaged in banking and brokerage and secured lucrative contracts to supply telegraph poles to the Overland Telegraph Line and grain to the OVERLAND MAIL COMPANY. Moreover, he worked with BRIGHAM YOUNG and other leading businessmen among the MORMONS to establish the Utah Central Railroad, the Utah Southern Railroad, and ZION'S CO-OPERATIVE MERCANTILE INSTITUTION.

Fully committed to Mormonism, Jennings embraced polygamy, taking a second wife, Priscilla Paul, in 1855.

In 1882, he was elected mayor of Salt Lake City, a position he held until 1885.

—*Newell G. Bringhurst*

SUGGESTED READING:

Alter, J. Cecil. *Utah: The Storied Domain*. Vol. 3. Chicago, 1932.

Arrington, Leonard J. *Great Basin Kingdom: Economic History of the Latter-day Saints*. Cambridge, Mass., 1958.

JEWISH AMERICANS

Jews first came to the American West in significant numbers during the years of the CALIFORNIA GOLD RUSH and immediately following. Part of a great wave of European migration between 1849 and 1870, Jewish émigrés from Bavaria, France, and central Europe joined the Germans, Poles, Irish and others in traveling to America; and like their middle-class German contemporaries, many headed to the West and set themselves up as merchants working in the retail and wholesale of food, clothing, tobacco, and hardware. The earliest Western Jews moved to San Francisco and Portland, in particular, where they established thriving and close-knit communities.

As a port of entry, San Francisco saw the arrival of many who would later become prominent—M. J. Brandenstein, Isaac and Joseph Magnin, ADOLPH SUTRO, and LEVI STRAUSS, to name a few—in the city's mercantile trade and in its politics. Others followed the gold, silver, and copper rushes into the mining camps of California and the interior, where they opened general-merchandise stores and other small businesses. Some of those traveling to the West's mining camps and towns were the sons-in-law, younger brothers, and nephews of already established merchants, many of whom had been brought from Europe by their more successful relatives to run branches of their businesses. As the minerals played out and the towns began to turn ghostly, Jewish merchants frequently returned to San

Ernst Kohlberg, a German Jew settled in El Paso in 1886. He established a cigar factory, founded a city railway service, and served on the city council. He appears here with his wife at Niagara Falls. *Courtesy El Paso Public Library.*

Francisco or moved to other burgeoning Western commercial centers and on occasion headed East.

The roll call is impressive: Michel Goldwater set up his family's business in Arizona. David May became a department-store magnate in Denver. Samuel H. and Theodore Auerbach set up their merchandise business in Salt Lake City. Nicholas Ransohoff opened his doors both in Salt Lake City and San Francisco. And Aaron Meier founded Meier and Frank in Portland. Any number of San Francisco merchants—the Zellerbachs, Aaron Fleishhacker, the Steinharts—first made a go of it in mining towns before returning to the Bay Area. By the turn of the century, some two decades after the mining economy had begun to decline, Jewish communities were established in such towns as Albuquerque, El Paso, Denver, Helena, Oakland, Sacramento, San Diego, San Jose, Salt Lake City, Stockton, Reno, and Victoria, British Columbia, as well as Portland and San Francisco.

The relative success of the Jewish immigrants, as a number of historians have recently pointed out, had much to do with the fluid social conditions of what, compared to much of the rest of the country at the time, was a rather cosmopolitan population, and to the fact that the West, in particular, with its thinly populated regions in need of settlement and business, valued some Jews for their talents and skills. Because, outside a few caustic comments made to researchers for Dunn and Bradstreet, anti-Semitism seemed relatively rare in the trans-Mississippi West, some historians have claimed that the large number of Asian and Mexican immigrants and Mexican Americans in the West served as a "racial lightning rod" for the Jews, much as African Americans did in the South. More recent scholars have dismissed the idea, pointing out that Jews did well even where there were no people of color, and that the Irish, for example, were frequently discriminated against even when there were large populations of Asians nearby. Instead, it seems that in Western minds, Jews were more closely associated with their fellow German immigrants, whose culture was viewed highly favorably, and they were perceived as filling a need in Western town building.

Jews were welcomed by their Western neighbors far more equitably than in the East; they formed a significant part of the Western electorate long before they did so in the East; and they were being accepted in elite circles in San Francisco, for example, when they were being excluded from New York society. Some Jews were the heads of German clubs and organizations whose doors would be barred to them in the fatherland, and the Western Masons had a Jewish membership far in excess of the Jewish percentage of the overall population. In the West, Jews were free not only to succeed in business by playing pioneer roles in founding Western towns, they were also elected to public office at every level. Five were members of the California supreme court, and Henry Lyons became chief justice in 1852. Jews were congressmen—Julius Kahn and his wife Florence Prag Kahn, for example, who represented San Francisco in Washington, D.C., for forty years. They were senators—Joseph Simon, Richard Nueberger, ERNEST GRUENING, and Solomon Hirsch. A number became governors—Edward Salomon of the Washington Territory, MOSES ALEXANDER of Idaho, Simon Bamberger of Utah, Arthur Seligman of New Mexico, Julius Meier of Oregon, and, again, Ernest Gruening of Alaska.

One historian has suggested that the very newness and contested nature of "Americanism" in the West after the Civil War created opportunities for immigrants ostracized in their homelands to define themselves as mainstream, middle class, and white. The construction of the Jewish identity in the West was part of the larger construction of Western identities, sometimes with odd consequences. Within the Western Jewish community, for example, which seemed to outsiders quite close-knit, there raged spectacular religious quarrels. In 1880, Rabbi Mayer May of Portland shot a member of his congregation in a dispute about school instruction, and the congregation paid the rabbi to leave town. In the early twentieth century, a new round of Jewish immigration hit the East Coast. German Jewish communities in Western cities, while they felt an obligation to the new and poor eastern Europeans arriving in New York, also resented and were ashamed of those they helped. The new arrivals sometimes seemed as ignorant and exotic to the German Jews as they did to other Americans. Western Jews had, in some measure, entered a contest among themselves over who was more American, and the religion they shared with East Europeans did not sustain a sense of shared community. Various Jewish enclaves in Portland and San Francisco became competitors divided by degrees of orthodoxy and different national origins. Many of these tensions would be resolved with the coming of communitywide organizations (such as B'nai Brith, originally a Jewish imitation of Masonry), which only underscored the Western Jews peculiar American orientation: they created voluntary organizations to establish a community identity.

Another scholar has pointed to a similar phenomenon among the Jews of Hollywood. Since the earliest days, when Jewish film-makers from New York had moved to Los Angeles to escape Thomas Edison's hated Trust and to take advantage of the West's cloud-free skies, the MOTION-PICTURE INDUSTRY had been something of a Jewish empire. Again the names tell the story: Louis B. Mayer, Samuel Goldwyn, Irving Thalberg, William Fox, Jesse Lasky, David O. Selznick, Harry Cohen, the Warner brothers, Carl Lammele, and Adolph Zukor. In the West, these innovative and talented businessmen, showmen, and artists created an industry that not only made them fabulously wealthy and caused southern California's entire economy to boom during the 1920s, but also found it in their purview to define the American dream itself with their immensely successful new medium. Some have argued that it is impossible to understand early Hollywood, the motion pictures it produced, and the industry itself—fascinated by success, scandal, and celebrity, but paying homage to marriage, and family, and honesty, while also insisting on happy endings—without considering the tensions within these men between their life in the American West and their origins in eastern Europe.

Not all Jews in the West in the late nineteenth and early twentieth centuries were successful businessmen, accomplished politicians, or powerful movie moguls. Many were average folk, going about their lives and practicing their religion in a new land that challenged and occasionally defeated them. A few tried farming; some established utopian communities and mostly failed; many others became workers and took up the cause of labor. Jews were certainly active in the West's rising labor movement, and they figured in its radical political organizations. Whether their actual numbers were as disproportionately high as some claimed became a matter of much debate.

In 1876, when Jewish migration began to drop off, there were around twenty thousand Jews in the American West, representing at that point perhaps 8 percent of America's Jews. A century later, when only some 2 or 3 percent of American Jews lived in the West, Los Angeles had the second highest Jewish population after New York, some six hundred thousand. By the early 1970s, too, San Francisco's Levi Strauss company had passed Chicago's Hart Schaffner and Marx on *Fortune*'s 500 list of the largest industrial companies. Nothing seemed so Western to America and to the world as the denim pants Levi Strauss had invented in gold-rush California to meet the needs of the Forty-niners. Despite their small numbers, Jews were important to the American West and its development.

—*Charles Phillips and Alan Axelrod*

Suggested reading:

Cohen, Naomi Weiner. *Encounter with Emancipation: The German Jews in the United States, 1830–1914*. Philadelphia, 1982.

Gabler, Neal. *An Empire of Their Own: How the Jews Invented Hollywood*. New York, 1988.

Glanz, Rudolf. *The Jews of California*. New York, 1960.

Rischin, Moses, and John Livingston, eds. *Jews of the American West*. Detroit, 1991.

Rochlin, Harriet, and Fred Rochlin. *Pioneer Jews: A New Life in the Far West*. Albany, N.Y., 1982.

Toll, William. *The Making of an Ethnic Middle Class: Portland's Jewry over Four Centuries*. Albany, N.Y., 1982.

JOHNSON, EDWIN CARL ("BIG ED")

Colorado politician Edwin Carl ("Big Ed") Johnson (1884–1970) was born in Scandia, Kansas. He homesteaded near Craig, Colorado, in 1910 and entered state politics as a Democrat in 1923. He served as a state representative from 1923 to 1931, as lieutenant-governor from 1931 to 1933, governor from 1933 to 1937 and from 1955 to 1957, and U.S. senator from 1937 to 1955. A spokesman for rural Coloradans and a tepid supporter of the New Deal, he fought for local control of federal relief programs in the 1930s and opposed the reelection of Franklin D. Roosevelt in 1940. As a senator, he strongly favored American non-involvement in world affairs before and after World War II. He is remembered for a short-lived attempt to use the Colorado National Guard to close the state's southern border to mostly Hispanic migrant workers in 1936.

—*Carl Abbott*

Suggested reading:

Lamm, Richard, and Duane A. Smith. *Pioneers and Politicians: Ten Colorado Governors in Profile*. Boulder, Colo., 1984.

JOHNSON, FRANK TENNEY

Painter Frank Tenney Johnson (1874–1939) was a native of Iowa and spent his childhood near Council Bluffs. At an early age, he became interested in Western history. Later deciding to pursue the study of art, he attended the Art Students League in New York City. He then traveled to Colorado, where he worked on a cattle ranch. Returning to New York City, he opened a studio and began contributing illustrations to various Western magazines and books—most often the novels of ZANE GREY. In 1920, a friend and fellow-artist, Clyde Forsythe, left New York to settle on the West Coast; Johnson and his wife soon followed.

For the next several years, Johnson and Forsythe shared a studio in Alhambra, California, where Johnson produced the nostalgic pictures of the West for which he is known today. The two artists eventually founded the Biltmore Art Gallery in Los Angeles, which handled the works of other Western painters such as CHARLES MARION RUSSELL and JOHN EDWARD BOREIN. With Borein and others, Johnson organized the Rancheros Visitadores, a group of California artists who met annually at Borein's studio in Santa Barbara.

Johnson won numerous awards for painting, including the Shaw Prize from the Salmagundi Club in 1923. He was elected an associate of the National Academy of Design in 1929 and a member in 1937, two years before his death. His work is represented in Western collections throughout the United States and abroad.

—*David C. Hunt*

See also: Art: Western Art

Suggested reading:
McCracken, Harold. *The Frank Tenney Johnson Book: Master Painter of the Old West.* New York, 1974.

JOHNSON, HIRAM WARREN

Hiram Warren Johnson (1866–1945), Progressive reformer, California governor, and U.S. senator, was born in Sacramento, attended the University of California at Berkeley, and then studied law in his father's office. After he and his brother Albert quarreled with their father over personal and political matters, the brothers moved to San Francisco in 1902. There Hiram worked with Francis Joseph Heney on the graft prosecution involving Abraham (Abe) Ruef, leader of the Union Labor Party and city boss. After Heney was seriously wounded during the trial, Hiram Johnson took control of the case and secured Ruef's conviction.

Running as a Republican, Johnson won the California governor's race in 1910. He promptly carried out his campaign promise to kick the Southern Pacific Railroad out of politics and went on to institute other Progressive reforms, including eight-hour workdays for women, employers' liability laws, and free textbooks for schoolchildren. He oversaw the passage of several amendments to the state constitution, including the regulation of public utilities and women's suffrage. These legislative reforms earned him a national reputation as a Progressive reformer and led to his nomination for vice-president by the Progressive, or Bull Moose, party in 1912. The Progressive party had split from the Republicans in the fall of 1911, when former president Theodore Roosevelt denounced the Republican presidential candidate Howard Taft. Roosevelt's Progressive platform called for a "new nationalism," with increased governmental regulation and welfare programs. Although Roosevelt led a stirring campaign, he and Johnson were defeated by Democratic candidate Woodrow Wilson.

In 1916, Johnson was elected to the U.S. Senate. Once in the Senate, he so strongly opposed international entanglements, including the United States's becoming involved in the League of Nations, that his domestic agenda was often pushed to the background. He did, however, lead the campaign for federal support of Boulder Dam (now Hoover Dam).

In 1920, Republican Warren G. Harding invited Johnson to be his running mate, but Johnson declined. Four years later, he sought the Republican nomination for president himself only to lose to Calvin Coolidge.

Meanwhile, Johnson served in the Senate from 1917 to 1945. Towards the end of his tenure, he strongly opposed President Franklin D. Roosevelt's New Deal and tried to tie the president's hands in matters involving the emerging threat of Germany and Japan in the pre–World War II period. Even when the tide of American opinion began to swing away from neutrality, Johnson announced that he would not vote for war even if 99 percent of the American people favored it. The bombing of Pearl Harbor changed his mind about voting for war, but Johnson continued his attempts to steer the United States away from international relations by voting against the creation of the United Nations.

Johnson died on August 6, 1945, the day that the United States dropped the atomic bomb on Hiroshima.

—*Candace Floyd*

See also: Progressivism

Suggested reading:
Olin, Spencer C., Jr. *California's Prodigal Sons: Hiram Johnson and the Progressives, 1911–1917.* Berkeley, Calif., 1968.
Weatherson, Michael A., and Hal Bochin. *Hiram Johnson: A Bio-Bibliography.* New York, 1988.

JOHNSON, LYNDON B.

Born August 27, 1908 in Gillespie County, Texas, Lyndon Baines Johnson became the thirty-sixth president of the United States. A product of the Texas Hill country, he grew up along the Pedernales River, the son and grandson of men who had served in the Texas state legislature. He graduated from Southwest Texas State Teachers College at San Marcos in three years. He married Claudia Taylor ("Ladybird") Johnson. The couple had two daughters, Lynda Byrd and Luci Baines.

In a career that included teaching school, working as a legislative assistant to Congressman Richard Kleberg, and directing the National Youth Administration for Texas from 1937 to 1939, Johnson also served six terms as the representative from the Tenth Congressional District in Texas. Johnson's career was often controversial. He supported minority rights in both the Hispanic and black communities. In Texas, he became associated with the leaders of the newly developing oil, aerospace, and construction industries, and his rise to power paralleled the growth of these industries in the 1940s and 1950s. In 1941, he failed in an bid for a seat in the U.S. Senate but won in another attempt in 1948 after a controversial Democratic primary that earned him the ironic nickname "land-slide Lyndon." As a member of Congress, both in the House and Senate, he supported the programs of the New Deal and created a consensus among the Senate Democrats during the 1950s that led to the successful defense of most of the New Deal programs and to the passage of the first two civil-rights bills in the twentieth century. His interest in space brought the Johnson Space Center to its site on the Texas Gulf Coast close to Houston.

After an unsuccessful bid for the Democratic presidential nomination, he was nominated as vice-president and was elected with John F. Kennedy in 1960. In 1963, Johnson succeeded to the presidency when Kennedy was assassinated in Dallas on November 22. The following year, Johnson was elected to the presidency in his own right and served one term. As president, his programs continued the reforms that had characterized his political career, as he used the same mix of negotiating talent and ruthless controls that he had used in the Senate. Much of his effort and attention was eventually drawn into the conflict over Vietnam, an issue that brought his presidency to an unsatisfactory end in 1968. Declining to stand for reelection, he returned to Johnson City, Texas, in 1969.

In the remaining years of his life, Johnson oversaw the development of his presidential library, wrote an account of his term in office, which was published as *Vantage Point* in 1971, and ran his ranch. Johnson died on January 22, 1973, just a week before the signing of the Paris accords, which led to the end of the Vietnam conflict that had bedeviled his presidency.

—*Patrick H. Butler, III*

SUGGESTED READING:
Caro, Robert A. *The Years of Lyndon Johnson: The Path to Power.* New York, 1982.
————. *The Years of Lyndon Johnson: Means of Ascent.* New York, 1990.
Dallek, Robert. *Lone Star Rising: Lyndon Johnson and His Times, 1908–1960.* New York, 1991.

JOHNSON, ROBERT UNDERWOOD

Editor and conservationist Robert Underwood Johnson (1853–1937) was a major voice in the preservation of the West's natural resources. Born in Washington, D.C., he came of age in Indiana and attended Earlham College, a Quaker school in Richmond, Indiana, from which he graduated in 1871. Two years later, at the age of twenty, Johnson obtained a position with

Scribner's Monthly in New York City. By 1881, he had risen to the post of associate editor of the journal, which had been retitled *Century Magazine,* under the leadership of Richard Watson Gilder. Following Gilder's death in 1909, Johnson succeeded him as editor and remained with the magazine until his resignation in 1913. In subsequent years, Johnson occupied his time with many causes and interests, ranging from the creation of international copyright standards for the protection of authors and publishers and the establishment of the American Academy of Arts and Letters to the formation of relief programs for Italy during World War I.

One cause of particular concern to both Johnson and *Century* was the conservation of America's natural resources. Like thousands of other Americans in the late nineteenth century, Johnson had become increasingly concerned about the unrestrained destruction of unspoiled forests and wild lands in the national rush to development. In 1889, Johnson visited California's Yosemite Valley in the company of the conservationist JOHN MUIR and was inspired to lend his support to the conservation movement. Capitalizing upon *Century*'s access to the homes of many reform-minded members of the upper-middle classes, Johnson assisted Muir's successful campaign to establish YOSEMITE NATIONAL PARK in 1890. Thereafter, Johnson supported many important conservation measures, including the creation in 1896 of the six-man Forestry Commission sponsored by the National Academy of Science to survey Western forests. He worked as well to close the gap between the utilitarian and preservationist wings of the conservation movement, as personified respectively by GIFFORD PINCHOT and John Muir. He enlisted in Muir's ultimately unsuccessful effort between 1905 and 1913 to defeat San Francisco's proposal to dam the Tuolumne River in Yosemite National Park to create a municipal reservoir at Hetch Hetchy.

Aptly described by Stephen Fox as "an eastern literary lover of wilderness," Johnson wrote with great feeling about the importance of preserving unspoiled nature for its inspirational and aesthetic qualities. He represented a wing of the nascent conservation movement that exerted a growing influence on the popular consciousness. Johnson and other well-bred and well-read Americans, especially in the East, successfully pressed a political agenda to place restraints on the use of America's undeveloped natural resources, especially in the West, despite the vehement opposition of many Westerners. From his perch at *Century* for more than thirty years, Johnson played an effective part in the unfolding crusade.

—*Peter J. Blodgett*

SEE ALSO: Hetch Hetchy Controversy

SUGGESTED READING:

Burke, W. J., et al., eds. "Johnson, Robert Underwood." In *American Authors and Their Books.* New York, 1972.

Fox, Stephen. *John Muir and His Legacy: The American Conservation Movement.* Boston, 1981.

Johnson, Robert Underwood. *Remembered Yesterdays.* New York, 1929.

JOHNSON COUNTY WAR

The Johnson County War (or Invasion) in 1892 was one of the more infamous and one of the last of the Western vigilante conflicts in the nineteenth century. The perpetrators of the incident were the owners of large cattle ranches, many of whom lived in Cheyenne, Wyoming, and left the day-to-day operations of their Wyoming ranches to managers. Most of the big ranchers were members of the Wyoming Stock Growers' Association, a private organization that had received quasi-governmental status through the control of roundups and the disposition of mavericks (unbranded calves).

The large cattle operations were fabulously successful until the mid-1880s, when a combination of speculation, overgrazing, and bad weather reduced profits. Sales of ranches through book count (an estimate of cattle made by multiplying the number of calves branded in a season by four or five to determine total herd size) promised speculators huge profits. Success depended on open range, ample water, and cheap labor.

Many large ranches, particularly in the Powder River Basin, suffered losses during the winter of 1886 to 1887, and some went out of business. Surviving outfits viewed with alarm the rising numbers of small ranchers, many of whom had been cowboys the big ranchers once employed in the halcyon days of the early 1880s. Large operators complained of increased incidents of rustling and accused many small operators.

The cattle barons had become accustomed to using state action for their own gain, but many complained that the courts, particularly in Johnson County, were refusing to convict cattle thieves. They hired former Johnson County Sheriff FRANK CANTON to put a stop to the rustling by any means necessary. Canton, who was later implicated in the murders of two small ranchers believed by the cattlemen to have been rustling, became a source of intimidation for the big ranchers against homesteaders in general. Still, the "problem" persisted, and the big operators planned a daring strike by a band of vigilantes they called "Regulators" and the people of Johnson County called "Invaders."

On April 5, 1892, a special train made up of six cars pulled out of the station at Cheyenne bound for Casper. Aboard were nineteen cattlemen, five stock detectives, twenty-two Texas gunmen and one Idaho gunman, two newspaper reporters, and four other observers. Leading the secret expedition were Frank Canton and cattleman Frank Wolcott. Many of the Wyoming participants had been prominent in state affairs; in fact, five had been delegates to the state constitutional convention three years before.

The Invaders disembarked at Casper and set out on horses for Buffalo, the county seat of Johnson County, some one hundred miles to the north. They carried with them a death list, containing the names of men they believed were rustlers or were sympathetic to rustling.

Forty-six miles short of their goal, the Invaders came upon two of the men on their list. Nate Champion and Nick Ray were staying in a cabin on the KC Ranch, near the present-day town of Kaycee. The Invaders surrounded the cabin. Ray was shot and killed, but Champion was able to stand off the fifty gunmen for almost twelve hours. The Invaders then set fire to the cabin and shot Champion dead when he ran from the burning building. During the stand-off, Buffalo editor Jack Flagg and his son happened by in a buggy. They escaped capture and got word to the citizens of Buffalo. The Invaders came within six miles of Buffalo but turned back when they were told the town had been warned. They took refuge in a barn at the TA Ranch, thirteen miles south of Buffalo.

Led by County Sheriff Red Angus, about two hundred Buffalo residents set out to intercept the invading force. On the morning of April 11, 1892, the Invaders found themselves surrounded. Before the invasion began, they had cut the telegraph lines and persuaded Acting Governor Amos Barber to ignore calls from Buffalo citizens for military intervention. But the Invaders were the ones needing army protection. They managed to send word to Barber, who immediately sent messages to Senators FRANCIS E. WARREN and JOSEPH MAULL CAREY, in Washington, D.C., both sympathetic to the Invaders. The story goes that the senators roused President Benjamin Harrison from bed to give an order to send troops. The cavalry, stationed at Fort McKinney near Buffalo, arrived in time to prevent further casualties.

Johnson County officials wanted the trial of the Invaders taken into U.S. Army custody to be held in Buffalo, but the federal troops had orders to escort their "prisoners" to Cheyenne. There, most of the Invaders waited in the comfort of the officers' quarters at Fort D. A. Russell, where they were held in loose arrest pending trial. Following nine months of delays, the case was dismissed because Johnson County could no longer afford the high costs of prosecution. In the 1892 general election, Dr. John Osborne, a Democrat, won the governorship largely because he and other Democratic party candidates blamed Republicans for the invasion. Although Republicans, indeed, predominated, the force was actually nonpartisan. Largely because of the fallout from the invasion, the state legislature deadlocked in choosing a U.S. senator and left the seat vacant for two years. The involvement of the Wyoming Stock Growers' Association in the incident was obvious, but there was no hard evidence that it officially sanctioned the invasion.

The inept invasion split the state politically for several years with most people taking the side of Johnson County against the wealthy few who supported the big ranchers. It left two generations of hard feelings, and traces of bitterness were said to remain a century later. In the immediate aftermath of the invasion, Cheyenne newspaperman Asa Mercer wrote an exposé, "Banditti of the Plains: The Crowning Infamy of the Ages," condemning the invasion. Author OWEN WISTER, a friend of the Invaders, canceled a vacation to the area in the summer of 1892, fearing involvement in the fallout.

The Johnson County War inspired numerous novels and plays, including Wister's own *Virginian,* the novel and film *Shane,* and, more recently, the movie *Heaven's Gate.* Champion and Ray became folk heroes, the subjects of folk songs and stories. Nate Champion's "diary," supposedly written during the course of the stand-off, was published, although some historians believe it was penned by Chicago newspaperman Sam Clover, who had accompanied the Invaders. Lines from the "diary" have been widely quoted as Champion's final defiant words: "It's not night yet. The house is all fired. Good-bye boys, if I never see you again."

—*Phil Roberts*

SEE ALSO: Cattle Rustling; Vigilantism; Violence

SUGGESTED READING:
Baber, D. F. *The Longest Rope.* Caldwell, Idaho, 1947.
Clay, John. *My Life on the Range.* Chicago, 1924.
Clover, S. T. *On Special Assignment.* Boston, 1930.
David, Robert. *Malcolm Campbell, Sheriff.* Casper, Wyo., 1931.
Frink, Maurice. *Cow Country Cavalcade.* Denver, 1954.
Mercer, A. S. *The Banditti of the Plains.* Reprint. Norman, Okla., 1954.
Smith, Helena Huntington. *War on Powder River.* Lincoln, Nebr., 1966.

JOLIET, LOUIS

French Canadian explorer and cartographer Louis Joliet (also spelled Jolliet, 1645–1700) was born probably at Beaupré near Quebec. Schooled by Jesuits, Joliet renounced the priesthood in favor of a life as an explorer. In 1669, he led an expedition in search of copper around Lake Superior and then from Lake Huron to Lake Erie.

The leaders of New France commissioned Joliet to lead a small expedition to explore the Mississippi River in search of a route to the Pacific. Accompanied by JACQUES MARQUETTE and five other voyageurs, the party set out from Michilimackinac (St. Ignace, Michigan) on May 17, 1673. Traveling first to Green Bay, the explorers went up the Fox River in central Wisconsin to the Wisconsin River and from there to the upper Mississippi. By July 1673, the expedition had reached the mouth of the Arkansas River on the Mississippi. From the Quapaw Indians living there, they determined that the Mississippi emptied into the Gulf of Mexico rather than the Pacific. They returned by way of the Mississippi to the Illinois River and from there to Green Bay. The expedition marked French claims to the Mississippi River system and was the first European expedition into the Mississippi Valley between the mouth of the Wisconsin and the mouth of the Arkansas.

Joliet continued to explore the boundaries of New France along Hudson Bay and Labrador. He was appointed royal cartographer of New France in 1697.

—*Patrick H. Butler, III*

SEE ALSO: Cartography; Exploration: French Expeditions

SUGGESTED READING:
Delanglez, Jean. *Life and Voyages of Louis Jolliett (1645–1700).* New York, 1948.

JONES, ANSON

The fourth president of the Republic of TEXAS and the "architect of annexation" of Texas to the United States, Anson Jones (1798–1858) was born in Seekonkville, Great Barrington, Massachusetts. Licensed to practice medicine in 1820 by the Oneida Medical Society in New York, he began his practice in Bainbridge, with little success. He moved to Philadelphia, where he attended Jefferson Medical College and graduated in 1827. When his medical practice failed to prosper, he moved to New Orleans and became a commission agent. Having heard that the new communities in Texas needed physicians, he moved to Brazoria in 1833.

Jones established a practice in Brazoria and became an immediate success. He entered public affairs by signing a petition that called for the Consultation (a convention to determine a course of action against the centralists in Mexico) in 1835. When war with Mexico came, Jones enlisted as a private and served in this rank as a surgeon during the San Jacinto campaign.

Following the organization of the Republic of Texas, Jones served in the Second Congress as chair of the committee on ways and means. President SAM HOUSTON then appointed him minister to the United States with instructions to withdraw Texas's offer to join the Union. Houston's successor, MIRABEAU B. LAMAR, recalled Jones, but when he returned home, he again was elected to the Texas Senate, where he became a leader of the anti-Lamar faction and served as president *pro tem* during the Fifth Congress.

Jones served as secretary of state during Houston's second term as president. He won election to the presidency of the Republic of Texas in September 1844. When the U.S. Senate rejected the treaty calling for Texas's annexation, the issue became important in the presidential campaign of 1844. JAMES K. POLK was elected on a platform calling for annexation. Faced with the certainty of annexation, Mexico also offered to recognize Texas's independence. Jones submitted the issue to the Texas Congress, whose members approved annexation.

Despite amassing significant personal wealth, Jones despaired when further political achievement was denied him and took his own life in Houston in 1858.

—*Archie P. McDonald*

SEE ALSO: National Expansion: Texas and National Expansion; Texas Revolution

SUGGESTED READING:

Gambrell, Herbert. *Anson Jones, The Last President of Texas.* Garden City, N.Y., 1948.

Jones, Anson. *Memoranda and Official Correspondence Relating to the Republic of Texas, Its History and Annexation, Including a Brief Autobiography of the Author.* Reprint edition. Chicago, 1966.

JONES, MARY HARRIS ("MOTHER")

Born in County Cork, Ireland, Mary Harris ("Mother") Jones (1830-1930), one of American labor's cherished heroines and a cofounder of the INDUSTRIAL WORKERS OF THE WORLD (IWW), traveled to America in 1835, when her father sent for his family. Schooled in Toronto, where her father worked, she taught for a while in a convent in Monroe, Michigan, before opening a dressmaking shop in Chicago and then moving to Memphis, Tennessee, to teach once again. There, in 1861, she married a staunch member of the Iron Molders Union named Jones but lost her husband and four small children when an epidemic of yellow fever ravaged the city in 1867. Bereaved, she served as a volunteer nurse in Memphis until the disease ran its course and then returned to Chicago and resumed dressmaking for the wealthy, whom she soon came to resent. When the GREAT CHICAGO FIRE of 1871 burned what little she had left, she sought comfort in a charred Knights of Labor hall and grew interested in the LABOR MOVEMENT.

As she increasingly identified with labor's struggle against low wages, long hours, and terrible working conditions, Jones grew more radical and begin participating in strikes, the first alongside Pittsburgh railway workers in the Great Railroad Strike of 1877. From 1880, certainly, her course was set. Without a fixed home, she moved from one industrial town to the next, depending on where conditions were bad or strikes were imminent. Sometime in the 1890s, she began organizing coal miners, who came to revere her as "the miner's angel"; building on her reputation as "Mother" Jones, she called them "her boys." She joined striking machinists against the SOUTHERN PACIFIC RAILROAD, gave firsthand support to the WESTERN FEDERATION OF MINERS, took up the cause of imprisoned Mexican revolutionaries in the Southwest, led a caravan of striking child laborers from the textile mills of Pennsylvania to President THEODORE ROOSEVELT's doorstep in Oyster Bay, New York, was convicted of conspiracy in West Virginia and pardoned by the governor, and witnessed the massacre of mine families in Ludlow, Colorado. In 1905, she was one of the founders of the IWW, the most radical union in American history, which carried on a virtual class war against industry, especially in the West, until it was dismantled by Woodrow Wilson's red-baiting, World War I administration.

Plain-spoken and disputatious, she rubbed some union leaders the wrong way, but she outraged more the mine owners and capitalists, who blamed her stirring speeches and charismatic presence for the trouble they experienced whenever she happened to be in town. Her own political views seemed to have evolved from an 1890's typical populism to true SOCIALISM. A founder of the Social Democratic party, she nevertheless denounced the anarchist rhetoric she heard at the Haymarket riots, refused to join the Ruskin colony in Tennessee in the 1890s, and disdained women's suffrage. "The plutocrats," she wrote in her autobiography, "have organized their women. They keep them busy with suffrage and prohibition and charity." By 1916, she found it possible to support Woodrow Wilson in his run for the presidency and championed the Democratic party as well. When she died in 1930, she quickly faded from mainstream history and official memory, although not from the annals of labor, which continued to celebrate an American original, who was also quite typical of some radical women from the working class—a militant union-man's wife, who could walk a picket line, rouse a crowd to action, tongue-lash a scab or an owner's goon to shame, and then insist that a women's true place was at home with her children.

—*Charles Phillips*

SEE ALSO: Ludlow Massacre; Working-Class Women

SUGGESTED READING:
Jones, Mary Harris. *Autobiography of Mother Jones.* New York, 1925.
Long, Priscilla. *Where the Sun Never Shines: A History of America's Bloody Coal Industry.* New York, 1989.
Steel, Edward M. *The Speeches and Writings of Mother Jones.* Pittsburgh, Pa., 1988.

JORDAN, DAVID STARR

Ichthyologist, teacher, and reformer who served as first president of Stanford University, David Starr Jordan (1851–1931) ranked as the most influential scientist and educator on the Pacific Coast at the turn of the century. His more than 640 books and articles ranged from popular essays on clean living, pacifism, and education to technical papers on systematic zoology.

Born near Gainesville, New York, Jordan entered Cornell University in 1869 as a scholarship student of broad interests including poetry, philosophy, and science—particularly systematic biology. Only three years later, he received the first master's degree in science granted by Cornell. In quick succession, he taught natural history at Lombard University in Galesburg, Illinois (from 1872 to 1873), served as principal of the Collegiate Institute in Appleton, Wisconsin (in 1874), and taught at Indianapolis High School (in 1875). By 1875, he had earned a medical degree from Indiana College and shortly afterward was appointed professor of biology at Butler University. After receiving his Ph.D. from Butler in 1878, he became professor of natural history at Indiana University and, in 1885, its president.

In 1891, Jordan became president of the newly created Leland Stanford Junior University, in what he considered "the wilds of California." Its wealthy founders, AMASA LELAND STANFORD and JANE ELIZA LATHROP STANFORD, gave Jordan full rein to develop the tuition-free, fully coeducational private university. He set a tone of experimentation, liberal educational policies, and youthful enthusiasm. During his tenure at Stanford (from 1891 to 1913), he balanced a broad and ambitious academic vision with the university's financial distress following Leland Stanford's death and intense public debate about coeducation, student discipline, and academic freedom.

Jordan was equally eminent in his specialty, ichthyology (the study of fish), which he had chosen after studying with Louis Agassiz for two summers (in 1872 and 1873). Jordan began by cataloguing fish of the Great Lakes and Mississippi Valley regions. After his move to California, he extended his studies of American and Mexican Pacific Coast fisheries to the whole Pacific Rim. He served on many government commissions, including the controversial investigation of the fur-seal industry of Alaska's Pribiloff Islands, and contributed to academic theories of dispersal, distribution, and specialization. He served as president of the California Academy of Sciences (from 1896 to 1904), president of the American Association for the Advancement of Science (from 1909 to 1910), and vice-president of the International Congress of Zoologists (in 1910) while he served as mentor to hundreds of young scientists. He was a founding member of the SIERRA CLUB and worked to establish Mount Rainier and Yosemite national parks and Big Basin State Park in California.

Jordan lent his name with flair and enthusiasm to a wide range of reform movements—from conservation to women's rights—but his leading role was as a pacifist. A member of the Anti-Imperialist League during the Spanish-American and Boer wars, he became director of the World Peace Foundation in 1910. Stepping down as Stanford's president in 1913 to devote all his time to the peace movement, Jordan accepted the new post of university chancellor. He incurred the wrath of Stanford's trustees by speaking out, until American intervention in 1917, against militarism and the European war. Largely retired from public affairs after World War I, he battled ill health until his death in 1931.

—*Roxanne L. Nilan*

SUGGESTED READING:
Elliott, Orrin Leslie. *Stanford University: The First Twenty-Five Years.* Stanford, Calif., 1937.
Evermann, Barton W. "David Starr Jordan, the Man." *Copeia* 4 (December 1930): 93–105.

Hayes, Alice. *A Bibliography of the Writings of David Starr Jordan.* Stanford, Calif., 1952.

Jordan, David Starr. *Days of a Man: Being Memories of a Naturalist, Teacher and Minor Prophet of Freedom.* Yonkers on Hudson, N.Y., 1922.

JOSEPH, CHIEF

SEE: Chief Joseph

JOSLYN ART MUSEUM

Built as a memorial to business and civic leader George A. Joslyn by his wife Sarah, the Joslyn Art Museum in Omaha, Nebraska, has served eastern Nebraska and western Iowa as a center for the fine arts since it opened to the public in 1931. The only Nebraska museum of its type, with an encyclopedic permanent collection, the museum houses works dating from antiquity to the present, although examples of European and American art of the nineteenth and twentieth centuries predominate.

Paintings, sculptures, and prints by artists of the American West constitute an important collection. Documenting the exploration and settlement of the trans-Mississippi West, these works relate primarily to the history of the Missouri River basin and the northern Great Plains. Of particular interest are paintings by GEORGE CATLIN, KARL (OR CARL) BODMER, and ALFRED JACOB MILLER, most of which the museum acquired in the 1960s through the generosity of the Northern Natural Gas Company of Omaha. These and other works by such artists as ALBERT BIERSTADT, SETH EASTMAN, CHARLES BIRD KING, and THOMAS MORAN form the basis for continuing exhibits, publications, and research in the Joslyn's Center for Western Studies, established in 1980 as a museum department devoted to Western art and scholarship.

The Joslyn Art Museum annually presents an average of five major exhibits organized from various parts of the permanent collection or obtained through national or international touring agencies. The museum also offers a wide range of public lectures, films, and classes for all ages. Performing arts programs appear regularly in the museum's twelve-hundred seat Witherspoon Concert Hall, the Storz Fountain Court, or out-of-doors during the summer months.

—*David C. Hunt*

SUGGESTED READING:

Joslyn Art Museum: Paintings and Sculpture from the European and American Collections. Omaha, Nebr., 1987.

Joslyn Art Museum, A Building History. Omaha, Nebr., 1994.

JOURNALISM

SEE: Magazines and Newspapers

JUANITA OF DOWNIEVILLE

Juanita of Downieville (ca. 1827–1851), also known as "Josefa," is famous for being the only woman hanged by a lynch mob in gold-rush California. Little is known about her life except that she was born in Mexico and lived in Downieville with a gambler named José. Some accounts state that she was a prostitute, but there is no clear evidence to support this assertion. After a raucous Fourth of July celebration, a drunken miner accidentally crashed through her door and then staggered off into the night. The next morning, when he returned to apologize, a quarrel ensued, and the miner evidently insulted Juanita, who then stabbed him to death. In short order, a kangaroo court assembled, took testimony, and sentenced Juanita to be hanged. As a crowd of two thousand men watched, she said that she would do the same thing again if she were similarly provoked. Then she coolly adjusted the noose about her neck, asked that her remains be properly treated, and awaited her fate.

News of Juanita's LYNCHING spread quickly. Most Californians condemned the act because it involved a woman, although some claimed that such lynchings tended to deter crime. Many mining camp mobs lynched victims during the gold rush, but Juanita was the only woman to be so treated. She became a symbol of racial oppression because, it is argued, if she had not been a Mexican, the mob probably would not have killed her.

—*Albert L. Hurtado*

SEE ALSO: Stereotypes: Stereotypes of Mexicans; Vigilantism; Violence

SUGGESTED READING:

Levy, Joann. *They Saw the Elephant: Women in the California Gold Rush.* Hamden, Conn., 1990.

Pitt, Leonard. *The Decline of the Californios: A Social History of the Spanish-Speaking Californians, 1846–1890.* Berkeley, Calif., 1970.

JUDAH, THEODORE DEHONE

The engineering mastermind behind the inception of the CENTRAL PACIFIC RAILROAD, Theodore Dehone Judah

(1826–1863) was born in Bridgeport, Connecticut, the son of an Episcopal clergyman. He was educated at the Rensselaer Polytechnic Institute and became a civil engineer specializing in the design and construction of RAILROADS. After working for five Eastern rail lines, including the spectacular Niagara Gorge Railroad, which he planned and constructed, Judah was summoned to California in 1854 by Colonel Charles Wilson, president of the Sacramento Valley Railroad. Wilson commissioned the engineer, not yet thirty years old, to survey a right-of-way from Sacramento to the rugged gold-mining town of Fulsom, twenty-two miles into the Sierra Nevada. After completing the task, Judah announced to his employers that it was possible to extend the right of way to the Pacific. Wilson and company were intrigued, but when the gold petered out at Fulsom, the rail line went no farther.

Based on his experience, however, Judah wrote and published a pamphlet entitled "A Practical Plan for Building the Pacific Railroad." He soon proved to be as effective a lobbyist as he was an engineer and made numerous trips to Washington, D.C., to promote the project. In 1860, while looking for a pass across the mountains in the region north of Lake Tahoe, he received a letter from a pharmacist and amateur surveyor named Daniel ("Doc") Strong. Strong had read Judah's pamphlet, which clicked with his own earlier observation of a relatively easy pass through the mountains to Dutch Flat, the mining town in which he lived. Strong personally led Judah through the pass, and the two retired to Strong's drugstore to draw up an agreement incorporating a Pacific railroad association.

Armed with an accurate survey laying out a workable passage to the Pacific, Judah recruited seven financial backers, among them the men who would constitute the "Big Four" of the transcontinental railroad: AMASA LELAND STANFORD, a wholesale grocer; CHARLES CROCKER, a dry goods merchant; and COLLIS P. HUNTINGTON and MARK HOPKINS, partners in a hardware business. Judah did not sell them the idea of a transcontinental railroad, but, rather, a line that would secure for them a trade monopoly in the mining camps of Nevada. It was only after rail was laid over the mountains that Judah proclaimed it to be the first link in what would become a transcontinental railroad.

He traveled back to Washington, where he successfully lobbied for passage of the Railway Act of 1862, authorizing the Central Pacific and Union Pacific railroads. Yet, even with authorization and basic funding in place, the project moved sluggishly. Judah's Big Four were inclined to halt construction of the Central Pacific at the Nevada line until more extensive settlement occurred to ensure profitability. In vain, Judah argued with them that the construction of the railroad would bring settlement. Disgusted, Judah set out once again for Washington, D.C., to find new backers. He chose the quickest route available at the time, by ship to the Isthmus of Panama, overland across it, and onto another ship bound for the East Coast. On the trip, Judah contracted yellow fever, a disease endemic to the Panamanian jungle, and died a week after arriving in New York. He was thirty-seven years old.

—*Alan Axelrod*

SEE ALSO: Transcontinental Railroad Surveys; Union Pacific Railroad

SUGGESTED READING:
Lewis, Oscar. *The Big Four*. New York, 1938.
Williams, John Hoyt. *A Great and Shining Road: The Epic Story of the Transcontinental Railroad*. New York, 1988.

JUDSON, EDWARD ZANE CARROLL

SEE: Buntline, Ned

JUH (APACHE)

A remarkable Chiricahua war leader, Juh (ca. 1825–1883) was born in Sonora or southern New Mexico. He was chief of the Nedhnis, or Southern Chiricahuas; GERONIMO was Juh's constant companion and subordinate. Because Juh had a speech defect, Geronimo sometimes spoke for him. His name, spelled variously, was pronounced "who."

In an 1855 engagement near Namiquipa, Chihuahua, Juh's brilliant leadership resulted in Apache victory. He may have participated in the July 15, 1862, Battle of Apache Pass. He staged the ambuscade on May 5, 1871, where Lieutenant Howard Cushing was killed.

In 1876, Juh and 207 followers fled to Sonora. Three years later, VICTORIO broke out of the San Carlos Reservation, and Juh's diversion allowed Victorio's band to escape from the New Mexico Black Range into Mexico. On October 27 and 28, 1879, Juh commanded a strong Apache force that held off an American attack in a ferocious moonlight action northeast of Janos, Chihuahua. He surrendered in 1881 but later escaped from the San Carlos Reservation and again blunted an army pursuit in a moonlight battle.

In April 1882, Juh led about sixty warriors in the most sensational Apache war victory on record: the extraction at gunpoint of Chief Loco and several hundred followers from San Carlos to the safety of Mexico through country coursed by searching troops. Juh refused to return to San Carlos following General GEORGE CROOK's daring 1883 penetration of the Sierra Madre.

Juh died in a fall from his horse into the Rio Casas Grandes, either while drunk or following a heart attack, according to his son, Ace Daklugie, an eyewitness and his only son to survive the APACHE WARS.

—*Dan L. Thrapp*

SUGGESTED READING:

Ball, Eve, with Nora Henn and Lynda A. Sanchez. *Indeh: An Apache Odyssey.* Norman, Okla., 1988.

Lummis, Charles F. *Dateline Fort Bowie: Charles F. Lummis Reports on an Apache War.* Edited by Dan L. Thrapp. Norman, Okla., 1979.

Thrapp, Dan L. *The Conquest of Apacheria.* Norman, Okla., 1967.

———. *Juh: An Incredible Indian.* El Paso, Tex., 1992.

JUNEAU, JOE

Joseph Juneau (1826–1899), the Alaska miner for whom the city of Juneau was named, was born near Quebec City, Canada. His family moved to Wisconsin while Juneau still was a child. There his uncle, Solomon Juneau, operated a fur-trading business and reputedly built the first cabin on the site of today's city of Milwaukee.

Juneau grew up in Wisconsin and apparently learned hunting and fishing skills rather than attending school, if, in fact, there was a school. In later years, it was said that he could neither read nor write English, but perhaps he was able to do so in French.

In about 1849, Juneau went to California to become a miner. Still later, he acquired land near the present-day city of Oakland where he raised horses for sale. He then undertook prospecting and mining once again and apparently visited most of the Western mining districts. In 1875, he reportedly went north to the Cassiar in British Columbia. He continued north and worked for a merchant in Wrangell, Alaska, in 1879, when Ed C. Hughes, the purser of the mail steamer *California,* recruited him to work for George E. Pilz, a German mining engineer at Silver Bay near Sitka, Alaska.

Juneau did some prospecting around Silver Bay and staked two lode claims for himself and for Pilz. Juneau had apparently worked earlier with Richard T. Harris, and on July 17, 1880, the two men signed a grubstake agreement with Pilz, an agreement that required them to prospect and locate mining claims and mill sites. They made two trips to Gastineau Channel and, during the latter voyage, discovered gold in and around what they named Silver Bow Basin near the head of Gold Creek.

In the summer and fall of 1880, Joe Juneau became one of the first settlers in the town that bears his name. He mined in Gold Creek Valley and sold several gold claims he had staked. He reputedly also supported the local economy by circulating his gold as fast as he mined it.

It appears that Juneau left for the Yukon in 1894 and certainly was in Circle City in 1895. He discovered some fairly rich ground in Birch Creek, a find that allowed him to spend the winter of 1896 to 1897 in San Francisco. He was back in Juneau in February 1987 and, late in the month, left for the Klondike gold fields in the Yukon Territory where a big rush had just begun. He doubtlessly attempted mining but apparently was not successful. In 1898, he was reported to be operating a restaurant in Dawson, and he died there

Joe Juneau. *Courtesy Alaska State Library.*

Juneau, Alaska, was the region's first boom town after Joe Juneau and Richard Harris discovered rich gold deposits in 1880. From the William W. Partridge Collection. *Courtesy Alaska State Library.*

the next year. Friends collected funds and moved his remains from Dawson to Evergreen Cemetery in Juneau.

—*Claus-M. Naske*

SEE ALSO: Alaska Gold Rush; Klondike Gold Rush

SUGGESTED READING:
De Armond, R.N. *The Founding of Juneau.* Juneau, Alaska, 1967.

JUNEAU, ALASKA

Located on the Alaskan panhandle, some 850 miles north of Seattle, Washington, Juneau sits on the Gastineau Channel. Sheltered from the Pacific Ocean by a barrier of islands, Juneau's coastal waters remain ice-free year round, and the town seldom accumulates more than twelve inches of snowfall. Juneau's location, topography, and climate, relative to other sites in the ALASKA, would have been ideal for settlement if only there had been an impetus.

Two hapless prospectors supplied a reason in 1850. Joe Juneau and Richard Harris, grubstaking when they felt like it for a German engineer, found gold—or rather had a rich vein pointed out to them by a chief of the Auks—on a stream flowing into the Gastineau Channel. They staked a claim and a town site of 160 acres. Soon prospectors poured into the region, and some became fabulously wealthy. Harris named the site Harrisburg, but miners angry with him called it Juneau. A boom town developed, partly to serve the gold mines across the channel on Douglas Island and the operations of the Alaska-Treadwell Gold Mining Company and its two thousand workers.

The influx of gold-seekers led the U.S. Congress to establish the beginnings of civil government in Alaska in 1884, and six years later, Juneau became the territorial capital. Although mining continued to feed Juneau's economy until 1944, as the twentieth century progressed, fishing, forestry, government activities, and tourism became more prominent. In 1970, Juneau merged with Douglas, becoming the largest city (8,050 square miles) in the United States.

—*Patricia Hogan*

SEE ALSO: Alaska Gold Rush

KACHINA CARVING

The Native American practice of carving Kachina dolls (*tithu*) probably began in response to a need to teach children about the Kachina part of a complex religious tradition. While Zunis also carve Kachinas for their children, Hopi Kachinas are probably the best known. The earliest Hopi Kachina dolls date from the early eighteenth century and were carved as flat pieces of wood with notches cut on each side to indicate the break between head and body. Once formed, the wood was covered with white clay (kaolin) and painted with detailed head and facial characteristics and strategically placed red lines that indicated which of the more than five hundred Kachina spirits was being portrayed. These flat dolls were given to very young girls and were hung on the walls of their homes. They provided a constant reminder of the Kachina cult. To the Hopi Indians, Kachinas are supernatural beings that help them in their everyday lives. Hopi men impersonate the Kachinas and perform dances to gain the assistance of these forces. The Kachina dolls are copies of the masked impersonators.

From 1870 to 1910, the form of carved Kachina dolls began to change. The early flat form was maintained in some examples, but in others the bodies also began to show a more lifelike realism. In particular, legs were carved so that they separated to the waist; hands placed in front of the body were carved or painted. The change in form coincides with a change in the function of Kachina dolls that occurred at the same time. Previously used to teach about and remember features of the Hopi Kachina cult, the dolls were now also items that could be sold to traders and outsiders for money.

With the sale of Kachina dolls in the twentieth century came a steady series of changes in their form. Through all the changes, however, Kachina dolls have maintained their religious association and the specific characteristics that the religion prescribes. The desire for steady sales and for increasing amounts of money, however, has caused many carvers to make the dolls lifelike copies of the Kachina dancers they represent.

The making of Kachina dolls in the twentieth century still follows the techniques and procedures used in the past although the tools, detail created with the tools, and certain materials have changed. To begin making a doll, a Hopi man (and in some cases, since 1970, a woman) searches the Arizona river courses for usable roots from cottonwood trees. The naturally rounded cottonwood roots are sawed into sections. Each section is then roughed-out with a saw or chisel. With the earliest Kachina dolls, the doll was then covered with the white kaolin clay and painted with mineral paints including iron oxide, copper oxide, and colored clay. Since 1900, however, carvers have refined the roughed-out dolls with improved carving knives, grinders, and sandpaper. Also after 1900, doll-makers used glue to attach created appendages. Arms, hands (some with fingernails shown), yucca whips, neck ruffs, moccasins, loin cloths, and dresses have become common on Kachina dolls since 1945. Each of these features has become more realistic as new paints and materials have become available.

Originally, Kachina dolls were carved in secret and presented to children as gifts from Kachina spirits and were never signed. The practice of signing Kachina dolls began in 1950 and has been widely used since then.

—*Jon T. Erickson*

SEE ALSO: Native American Cultures: Spiritual Life

SUGGESTED READING:

Colton, Harold S. *Hopi Kachina Dolls*. Albuquerque, N. Mex., 1959.

Erickson, Jon T. *Kachinas: An Evolving Hopi Art Form?* Phoenix, Ariz., 1977.

Wright, Barton. *Kachinas: A Hopi Artist's Documentary*. Flagstaff, Ariz., 1973.

KAISER, HENRY J.

A native of rural New York, Henry J. Kaiser (1882–1967) left school at the age of thirteen to help support his family. An energetic man who for most of his life worked eighteen to twenty hours a day, Kaiser was living in Washington State and working for a gravel and cement dealer by 1913. When a Canadian client, a road-building company, went out of business, Kaiser borrowed money to take over the company's project, and he turned a quick profit. From 1914 to 1926, he built dams in California, levees in Mississippi, and highways and bridges throughout the Pacific Northwest and along the West Coast. In 1926, he branched out to Cuba, where he constructed some two hundred miles of roads and highways around the island by 1930.

When the BUREAU OF RECLAMATION let bids for the construction of the massive Boulder Dam (now HOOVER DAM) as part of the New Deal's bold foray into public works, Kaiser regarded the chance to build the dam as a key to large-scale industrial development in the West and an opportunity for Westerners to declare economic independence from the East. He argued that Western contractors should combine their resources to take on what at that time was the world's largest construction venture, and he reasoned that, should they do so, they would pick up lucrative contracts sure to follow. Thus the Six Companies—a consortium of mostly little-known Western construction companies incorporated in 1931—won the contract and made some $10 million in profit from the $50 million paid out by the bureau. True to Kaiser's predictions, Boulder Dam launched the Six Companies (Bechtel and Kaiser and MacDonald and Kahn in San Francisco; Morrison Knudsen Corporation in Boise, Idaho; Utah Construction Company in Salt Lake City; and J. F. Shea and the Pacific Bridge Corporation of Portland, Oregon) on a path that would lead individual contractors to become multinational giants and that would mark the birth of the basic infrastructure of the modern American West. Working sometimes as a group, sometimes in smaller combinations, sometimes individually, but almost always with the Bureau of Reclamation, the Six Companies won contracts for building both the Bonneville and Coulee dams on the Columbia River and for numerous other projects. When they barely lost out in the bidding for California's Shasta Dam, Kaiser immediately came back with the lowest bid for cement for its construction, even though he did not own a cement plant. When he got the job, he built a mammoth cement plant at Permanente, California, and met the terms of the contract.

With the help of the New Deal's favored banker, AMADEO PETER GIANNINI, whose Bank of America had

Industrialist Henry J. Kaiser used federal funds to build the West's infrastructure and supplied the U.S. government with ships for World War II. An innovator in manufacturing technology, Kaiser pioneered medical-care coverage for his workers. *Courtesy The Bettmann Archive.*

backed Kaiser from the beginning, Kaiser guided the Six Companies in Washington, D.C. He became one of the more savvy business operators in the nation's capital and spent his long workdays assiduously cultivating New Deal officials. When World War II broke out, Kaiser saw yet another chance to promote what he called "higher industrialization"—that is, the use of the FEDERAL GOVERNMENT to spur Western development. Having made a fortune using the federal government to help him build the West's infrastructure, he now made a second one using the government to help him build the manufacturing industries that infrastructure made possible. At the beginning of the war, with an enormous $45 million line of credit from Giannini, Kaiser and his associates went into ship-building, first securing a contract to produce thirty ships for England, then supplying the United States. The government provided him with the capital he needed to build ships and hire workers and loaned him $150 million for a steel mill in Fontana, California. Using the new facility, the Pacific Coast's first completely integrated iron and steel plant, Kaiser developed prefabrication techniques that allowed him to turn out ships at an incredible rate in his seven new shipyards, six on the West Coast, one on the Atlantic. In less than four years, Kaiser built 1,490 ships; at his Richmond, California, shipyard, he produced a 10,500-ton Liberty ship in four days and fifteen hours; at the peak of production, his yards launched a new vessel every ten hours. By the end of the war, the federal government had sunk $5 billion into shipbuilding in California alone; employment in San Francisco's shipyards had expanded from four thousand to more than a quarter-million jobs; Kaiser's shipbuilding empire stretched from San Francisco Bay to the Columbia River; and the press was calling the rotund industrialist, cheerfully ensconced in his Oakland, California, headquarters, "Sir Launchalot."

Wartime pressures had allowed Kaiser and the government bureaucrats who worked with him to redefine the basic relationship between government and business in the American West. Government put up the capital for creating an industry; Kaiser (and other corporate leaders) provided the organization and the management—the "brains," Kaiser said—that made the new corporations successful. What had worked for him in concrete and steel, also worked in magnesium and, after the war, in aluminum. During the war, the New Deal Reconstruction Finance Corporation loaned him $20 million to finance Permanente Metals, which produced magnesium for bombs and planes, and after the war, the government sold him at bargain-basement rates its Columbia aluminum plants, which he used to launch his Kaiser Aluminum Company. He suffered perhaps his only major failure immediately after the war with an ill-advised venture into auto making. By the mid-1950s, however, he had spread his empire to Hawaii, where he constructed the Hawaiian Village resort center, which he sold to the Hilton hotel chain in 1961.

Fortune Magazine snipped that, having learned of the money to be made from federal contracts, Kaiser simply "backed a truck up to the mint," and some accused Kaiser (and Giannini) of being responsible for California's economic "colonizing" of other Western states. Kaiser's workers, however, loved him. During the war, he sent labor recruiters around the country, chartered trains to bring workers to the West, and paid them even before they went to work just to make sure they were available. He promised (and delivered) high wages, housing, and medical care. He pioneered comprehensive medical coverage for workers under the Permanente Foundation, later renamed the Kaiser Foundation, by producing the country's first health-maintenance organization, or HMO, which became a model for federal programs in the late twentieth century. In 1965, two years before his death, he became the first industrialist to receive organized labor's highest honor when the AFL–CIO bestowed on him its Murray-Green Award.

—*Charles Phillips*

Suggested reading:

Foster, Mark S. *Henry J. Kaiser: Builder in the Modern American West.* Austin, Tex., 1989.

Kotkin, Joel, and Paul Grabowicz. *California, Inc.* New York, 1982.

Lowitt, Richard. *The New Deal and the West.* Bloomington, Ind., 1984.

Nash, Gerald. *The American West Transformed: Impact of the Second World War.* Bloomington, Ind., 1985.

———. *World War II and the West: Reshaping the Economy.* Lincoln, Nebr. 1990.

Wiley, Peter, and Robert Gottlieb. *Empires in the Sun: The Rise of The New American West.* Reprint. Tucson, Ariz., 1985.

KALISPEL INDIANS

See: Native American Peoples: Peoples of the Pacific Northwest

KAMIAKIN (YAKIMA)

A war chief of the Yakima people, Kamiakin (ca. 1800–1877) was a leader during the Yakima War of 1855 to 1856 and the Coeur d'Alene War of 1858. Kamiakin's mother was a Yakima, but he was related through his father to the Nez Percés, Palouses, and Spokans. His varied ancestry gave him influence among the tribes of the Northwest. For many years, he used that influence to encourage the education of his people, and he advocated Yakima neutrality during the Cayuse War of 1847 to 1850. But the actions of Washington Territorial Governor Isaac Stevens following the Walla Walla Council of 1855 changed Kamiakin's views. Stevens had concluded a treaty with most of the tribes of the region, by which they agreed to cede tribal lands in exchange for reservations, schools, homes, livestock, and annuities. The treaty specified that the ceded lands would not be opened to white settlement for a period of two years. However, a mere twelve days after concluding the 1855 treaty, Stevens opened the lands.

Kamiakin attempted to engineer an alliance of the tribes to check white expansion. He counseled the avoidance of direct confrontation until the alliance was in place; however, his cousin Qualchin was one of six Indians who ambushed and killed five prospectors and, later, Andrew J. Bolon, the Indian agent who investi-

Kamiakin (Yakima) as portrayed by Private Gustavus Sohon in 1855. *Courtesy Washington State Historical Society.*

gated the incident. In response, army forces invaded Yakima territory, and war began.

The violence subsided after the building of Fort Walla Walla and Fort Simcoe and the replacement of aggressive militia forces with more disciplined regular army troops. However, in the spring of 1858, Kamiakin was among those who led an attack on an army column commanded by Major Edward Steptoe at Pine Creek. The army responded in force, and Kamiakin made the grave mistake of meeting the opposing forces on an open field in the Battle of Spokane early in September. This was precisely the kind of "conventional" battle at which the army excelled and the Indians characteristically fared poorly. Defeat there, coupled with defeat a few days later, at the Battle of Four Lakes, ended the Coeur d'Alene War and dispersed the Indians. Although badly wounded, Kamiakin fled to British Columbia, where he was given refuge by the Kootenais. He returned to the United States in 1861 and quietly lived the rest of his life on the Spokan Reservation. Kamiakin endured a final indignity in 1877 when, after his death, white souvenir hunters stole his head and put it on public display.

—*Alan Axelrod*

SEE ALSO: Pacific Northwest Indian Wars

SUGGESTED READING:
Axelrod, Alan. *Chronicle of the Indian Wars: From Colonial Times to Wounded Knee.* New York, 1993.
Lavender, David. *Land of Giants: The Drive to the Pacific Northwest, 1750–1950.* New York, 1956.

KANE, PAUL

Painter Paul Kane (1810-1871) immigrated with his parents from Ireland in 1818 to York (later Toronto), Canada, where he grew up and supported himself as a sign painter and portraitist. In 1836, he traveled to Detroit, Michigan, to meet fellow-artist James Bowman and accompany him on a tour of Europe. The trip was postponed, and Kane remained in the Detroit area before traveling south as far as Mobile, Alabama, where he opened a portrait studio. Sailing for Europe at last in 1841, he saw an exhibition of GEORGE CATLIN's paintings in London. Returning to Canada in 1845, he was determined to explore the American West for himself.

With the support of Sir George Simpson of the HUDSON'S BAY COMPANY, Kane journeyed westward via the company's network of overland trails and trading posts to Fort Vancouver, British Columbia, which he reached in December 1846. Back in Toronto in the fall of 1848 with a large collection of drawings and water colors, Kane set to work producing more than one hundred large paintings descriptive of his recent travels. Most of the paintings, sold first to a private collector, eventually were acquired by the Royal Ontario Museum in Toronto. Meanwhile, in London in 1858, Kane published *Wanderings of an Artist among the Indians of North America,* illustrated with reproductions of his Western paintings. He died in Toronto twelve years later, his reputation as a pioneering Canadian artist firmly established. His work was again published by Texas Press in 1971 as *Paul Kane's Frontier.*

In addition to the paintings at the Royal Ontario Museum, approximately two hundred of his Western field sketches and the original journal of his travels are preserved at the Stark Museum of Art in Orange, Texas.

—*David C. Hunt*

SEE ALSO: Art: Western Art

SUGGESTED READING:
Harper, J. Russell, ed. *Paul Kane's Frontier.* Austin, Tex., 1971.

KANE, THOMAS LEIPER

Defender of the MORMONS, lawyer, and soldier, Thomas Leiper Kane (1822–1883) was born in Philadelphia to a well-known and publicly active family. A tireless advocate of humanitarian causes, Kane joined the Free-Soilers while in his mid-twenties and participated in the Underground Railroad. During the Civil War, he raised a much-decorated regiment of volunteers and was brevetted a major general for bravery at the Battle of Gettysburg.

Kane is best remembered as a friend of the Mormons. First hearing of them early in 1846, he helped lay the groundwork in Washington, D.C., to enlist a battalion of Mormons to fight in the UNITED STATES–MEXICAN WAR. He then rushed to Iowa to gather data on the fleeing Latter-day Saints for a book he hoped would advance his own career. He fell desperately ill and became the Mormons' unwavering champion when they nursed him back to health.

Before leaving Iowa, he helped get the Mormon Battalion headed west. Later, he published statements defending the Mormon cause and steered the efforts leading to the creation of the Utah Territory in the COMPROMISE OF 1850 and to the appointment of BRIGHAM YOUNG as territorial governor. Kane's loyalty survived the public announcement of polygamy in 1852; he worked to quiet official agitation and co-authored articles explaining the church's position. In the events resulting in the UTAH EXPEDITION, he promoted Alfred Cumming, a proponent of states' rights, to succeed Young as governor, and when open conflict threatened, he hastened west. He first explained the moderating temper of the JAMES BUCHANAN administration to Young and then pushed on to Camp Scott where the U.S. Army was spending the winter. He supported Cumming's moderate position and set the stage for the successful mission of presidential peace commissioners Lasarus Powell and Ben McCulloch, but he also offended Colonel Albert Sidney Johnston and other hard-liners.

With the Mormons proceeding from one crisis to the next, Kane continued to advise them. At Young's invitation, he and his family spent the winter of 1872 to 1873 in southern Utah. Elizabeth Wood Kane collected the impressions that became her intimate and sympathetic *Twelve Mormon Homes Visited in Succession on a Journey through Utah to Arizona* (1874), while Kane and Young explored approaches to the Colorado River and discussed a far-flung Mormon expansion and a second place of gathering hinged on the port of Guaymas in Mexico. Kane headed east to initiate a drive for a Mexican land grant, and Young immediately dispatched a colony to Arizona. Neither effort enjoyed immediate success, but until his death, Kane continued to be both friend and adviser, earning a place of honor in Utah history and one of prominence in Western history.

—*Charles S. Peterson*

SEE ALSO: Church of Jesus Christ of Latter-day Saints; Polygamy: Polygamy among Mormons

SUGGESTED READING:

Cooley, Everett L. "Introduction." In *Twelve Mormon Homes Visited in Succession on a Journey through Utah to Arizona*. By Elizabeth Wood Kane. Salt Lake City, 1974.

Furniss, Norman F. *The Mormon Conflict, 1850–1859*. New Haven, Conn., 1960.

Winther, Oscar O. *The Private Papers of Thomas Leiper Kane, A Friend of the Mormons*. San Francisco, 1937.

Zobell, Albert, Jr. *Sentinel in the East, Biography of Thomas L. Kane*. Salt Lake City, 1965.

KANSAS

Kansas, known as the "Sunflower State," the "Jayhawk State," and the "Wheat State," entered the Union as the thirty-fourth state on January 29, 1861. Kansas lies at the center of the forty-eight contiguous states. Its area is 82,276 square miles, and its population in 1990 was 2,477,574. It rises from seven hundred feet to forty-one hundred feet, east to west. Topeka is the state capital.

Geographical features

Kansas has eleven physiographic provinces, representing several distinctive topographical and geological areas. The Flint Hills region is the last large area of native tall-grass prairie in the United States. The High Plains contain areas of broken country, sand hills, and chalk bluffs. The state is drained by streams that are a part of the Kansas-Missouri basin and the Arkansas River basin. While there are no natural lakes, more than twenty major reservoirs, created after World War II, provide flood control and WATER for agricultural and urban uses and recreation. Cheyenne Bottoms, a natural wetlands in Barton County, is a wildlife sanctuary vital to North American bird migrations.

Native American groups

Kansas was occupied by five groups of prehistoric peoples beginning about 10,000 B.C. They progressed through various levels of sophistication until they became the direct ancestors of tribes with familiar names: Kansas (for whom the state was named), Osage, Wichita, Pawnee, and Plains Apache.

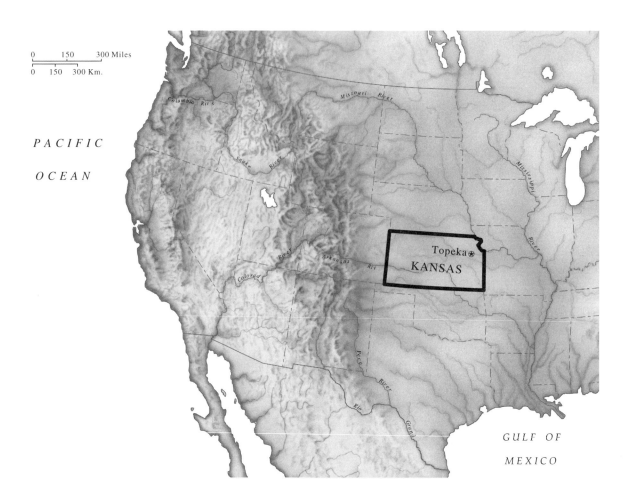

European and Anglo-American explorers who entered the Great Plains found the first four tribes in eastern and central Kansas. To the west were the Cuartelejo Apaches, a band composed of Plains Apaches and Pueblo Indians who had fled the Spanish Southwest in the late seventeenth and early eighteenth centuries. The Plains Apaches were driven from the area by the Comanches. With the Comanches in the west were the Arapahos, Kiowas, Kiowa Apaches, and Cheyennes, relative newcomers to the High Plains.

Exploration

The first European contact came in 1541 when a Spanish expedition led by FRANCISCO VÁSQUEZ DE CORONADO reached central Kansas. In search of the golden kingdom of Quivira, the Spanish found only Indian grass-hut villages. JUAN DE OÑATE and Pedro de Villazur led later Spanish expeditions, and Etienne de Bourgmont and Paul and Pierre Mallet explored for France. Neither the Spanish nor the French had any lasting impact on Kansas.

Most of present-day Kansas was ceded to the United States as part of the LOUISIANA PURCHASE. The LEWIS AND CLARK EXPEDITION from 1804 to 1806 touched the northeastern corner of Kansas. ZEBULON MONTGOMERY PIKE led an expedition in 1806 to obtain scientific data and foster friendly relations with the Indians. In 1819, STEPHEN HARRIMAN LONG commanded another expedition that met with Indians and gathered geographical and scientific information. Neither Pike nor Long was impressed by the Great Plains, and from Long's comments came the term GREAT AMERICAN DESERT. JOHN CHARLES FRÉMONT, the last of the military explorers, traversed the area five times before 1854.

Two great emigrant highways crossed Kansas. The Santa Fe Trail was the principal trade route to the Spanish Southwest, beginning in 1821, and the Oregon-California Trail was used by emigrants from the 1830s until the 1850s. Both roads had several branches.

The permanent American military presence began with the establishment of Fort Leavenworth in 1827. Fort Scott (1842) and Fort Riley (1852) followed. Federal legislation in 1825 and 1830 removed Indians from the East to lands in the West. Some 11,000 people moved to Kansas. Among the tribes relocated were the Potawatomi, Ottawa, Shawnee, Delaware, Wyandot, Iowa, Sac (Sauk) and Fox (Mesquakie), and Kickapoo Indians.

Christian missionaries, many of whom had worked with the tribes in the East, helped with relocation. The first Indian mission in Kansas, to the Osages in present-day Neosho County, was established in 1824 by Presbyterians and associated denominations. For five years, the mission served as school and church with limited success. The most extensive mission operation was established among the Shawnees by Methodists in 1830. It operated until 1862, and three of its structures still stand as national historic landmarks in Johnson County. Quakers and Roman Catholics also established MISSIONS, some of which existed for several years.

Territorial period

The KANSAS-NEBRASKA ACT opened the Kansas Territory to white settlement on May 30, 1854. The act repealed the MISSOURI COMPROMISE and provided for popular sovereignty, which allowed the settlers to decide by vote whether the territory should become a free or a slave state. Popular sovereignty led to violent disagreements between Free-Soilers and proslavery sympathizers.

The first settlers, most of whom came from Missouri, supported slavery. Abolitionists in New England, through organizations such as the New England Emigrant Aid Company, immediately recruited settlers to make Kansas free. Their first major settlement was Lawrence. Proslavery people established Leavenworth and Atchison, and a newspaper war of words began. There were very few slaves in Kansas, although free blacks were early residents.

Over the next four years, there were skirmishes between militia companies, arrests of Free-Soil leaders, isolated acts of murder and property destruction, and illegal voting. Three violent acts drew national attention to "Bleeding Kansas." On May 21, 1856, a proslavery posse sacked Lawrence, and three days later, JOHN BROWN and his followers killed five proslavery men in Franklin County. On May 19, 1858, five Free-Soil men were murdered by Missouri ruffians in Linn County. That incident, known as the Marais des Cygnes Massacre, was memorialized by the abolitionist poet John Greenleaf Whittier. Relatively few deaths can be attributed to political violence during the territorial period, but the conflict in Kansas magnified the nation's struggle over slavery.

Kansas's ten territorial governors represented both political viewpoints. The first, Andrew Reeder, had to flee the territory in disguise because of proslavery opposition. Free-Soilers, unhappy with the "Bogus Laws" of the official government at Lecompton, organized a separate government in Topeka.

A nineteenth-century illustration depicts the May 1858 proslavery attack on Free-Soilers at Marais de Cygnes. *Courtesy Library of Congress.*

Statehood

In 1859, Kansans approved the Wyandotte Constitution, the fourth attempt at a state constitution and the one under which Kansas was admitted to the Union. It remains the basis for state government.

During the CIVIL WAR, Kansans contributed twenty-three regiments and four artillery batteries to the Union. Included were three black and three Indian units. The only major engagement to take place in Kansas was the Battle of Mine Creek in 1864. During the battle, General STERLING PRICE and his Confederates, on a retreat from Kansas City, Missouri, were caught and defeated.

Extensive Confederate guerrilla activity took place in eastern Kansas, and Kansans replied with forays into Missouri. The culmination came with WILLIAM CLARKE QUANTRILL's devastating raid on Lawrence, Kansas, on August 21, 1863.

The political climate in Kansas was stormy during its first years as a state. CHARLES ROBINSON, the first governor, was opposed by JAMES HENRY LANE, one of the state's first U.S. senators. Both were Republicans but represented different party factions. After Robinson was impeached, and later acquitted, Lane attempted to control the governor's office until he died in 1866. Samuel Pomeroy, the other senator, ultimately was removed from office following a vote-buying scandal. Lane was succeeded by Edmund G. Ross, vilified in Kansas for voting to acquit President Andrew Johnson at his impeachment trial.

As the settlement line moved west, hostility between whites and Indians increased. The Plains tribes resented the intrusion of whites onto their land and the killing of BUFFALOES. They retaliated with depredations against the army and settlers. To combat the tribes, several new military posts were established. Two large treaty gatherings took place—on the Little Arkansas in 1865 and at Medicine Lodge Creek in 1867. However, the treaties were violated by both sides and accomplished little.

Hostile raids continued, and in 1868, Governor Samuel Crawford resigned his office to command the Nineteenth Kansas Cavalry, which participated in the winter campaign of 1868 and 1869. That campaign culminated in the Battle of the Washita in the Indian Territory. The last Indian-white conflict in Kansas took place in 1878 when Northern Cheyennes under LITTLE WOLF and DULL KNIFE fled their reservation, engaged the army in Scott County, and killed several settlers in Decatur County. The native tribes and most of the Eastern Indians were removed from Kansas by 1872. In the 1990s, remnants of the Potawatomi, Kickapoo, Iowa, and Sac and Fox tribes still occupied diminished reserves in Kansas.

Late nineteenth-century developments

Not all was conflict in the 1860s and 1870s. Hundreds of school districts were established, and several COLLEGES AND UNIVERSITIES, including the University of Kansas, Kansas State College of Agriculture, and the State Normal School, opened their doors. The line of settlement reached Wichita and Hays, and farm acreage increased tremendously.

Water transport was important during the early years, and most heavy shipments of goods came to towns along the Missouri River by steamboat. Stagecoach lines operated for several years on routes laid out by the firm of RUSSELL, MAJORS AND WADDELL and by the OVERLAND MAIL COMPANY. Both served traffic between the Missouri River and Denver. In 1860, Russell, Majors and Waddell, who first made money as army freighters, established the PONY EXPRESS. Eighteen months later, the Pony Express was supplanted by the transcontinental telegraph, and the firm was bankrupt.

Railroad construction progressed after the Civil War. The Union (Kansas) Pacific, following a central route from the Missouri River, reached the Colorado line in 1870; the Santa Fe Railroad, building southwest from Topeka, reached Colorado in 1872. They were followed by the Missouri Pacific and the Rock Island lines. The Missouri, Kansas and Texas was the first north-south line to reach the Indian Territory (1870), but at about the same time, two other roads reached the southern border. Branches of the major roads and many short lines were built between 1870 and 1910. During the settlement period, railroads promoted towns, recruited settlers, controlled millions of acres of land, and influenced Kansas politics.

The completion of the UNION PACIFIC RAILROAD into central Kansas opened a colorful period of Kansas history. Promoted by JOSEPH McCOY, Abilene became the first of the famed and often notorious cattle shipping points. Between 1867 and 1885, more than five million cattle from southern ranges were driven into Kansas. CATTLE TOWNS that followed Abilene as shipping points included Ellsworth, Newton, Wichita, Dodge City, Caldwell, Coffeyville, and Baxter Springs. The first herds followed the Chisholm Trail, and when Dodge City became the principal market in 1875, the drovers shifted to the Western Trail. The trail drives ended when Kansas farmers strung miles of BARBED WIRE, quarantine laws prevented the entry of Texas cattle, thought to be carriers of TEXAS FEVER, and the railroads reached Texas.

The end of the long drive did not end the Kansas CATTLE INDUSTRY. Attracting Eastern capital, large-scale ranching boomed until 1890 when FINANCIAL PANICS and severe weather brought ruinous losses. Cattle contin-

Dodge City, Kansas, one of the state's cattle towns, as it appeared in 1872. *Courtesy Kansas State Historical Society.*

ued to be brought to pasture in the Flint Hills, ranching was an important part of Kansas AGRICULTURE, and feed-lot operations handled more head each year than came over the trails.

Settlement greatly increased after 1870, and by 1890, the population of Kansas had reached nearly 1.5 million. Joining the American-born settlers were numbers of immigrants from Sweden, the British Isles, Germany, Russia, and eastern Europe. Two groups of Germans from Russia, Mennonites and Roman Catholics, came in the 1870s and settled primarily in south-central and west-central Kansas, respectively. The Mennonites brought from the Ukraine hard winter wheat, which flourished and started the state on its way to national leadership in the production of the crop. Smaller numbers of ethnic groups from Europe came also. Italians, many of whom engaged in COAL MINING, settled in southeastern Kansas. Mexicans came after 1900, mostly as railroad workers, and South Slavic people settled in Kansas City. Following the conflict in southeast Asia in the 1960s and 1970s, immigrants from that area arrived in Kansas, especially in the southwestern counties. Although the Kansas population is relatively homogeneous, many communities retain characteristics of an ethnic heritage.

From 1873 to 1878, black immigrants, known as EXODUSTERS, established four communities, notably Nicodemus in Graham County. Until 1881, poverty-stricken AFRICAN AMERICANS, believing Kansas offered more hope than the sharecropping South, came in great numbers and settled in both rural and urban areas of eastern Kansas.

Pioneers in eastern Kansas found timber, water, and agricultural conditions similar to what they had known previously. On the High Plains, this was not the case, and innovation was necessary. Houses were built of sod; WINDMILLS were used to bring water from deep wells; and the principal fuel was "chips"—the droppings of buffaloes or cattle. With wood in short supply, fence posts were cut from limestone where it was available. The rock was soft enough to cut with a hand saw but hardened quickly when exposed to the air.

Political life

The Republican party continued to dominate Kansas politics until 1882, when G. W. Glick, a Democrat, was elected governor. Throughout the 1880s, political unrest increased, due to low crop prices, high freight rates, oppressive mortgage interest, and monopolistic business practices. The protest reached fruition with the organization of the People's (Populist) party in 1890. Kansas elected a Populist congressman and several Populist state legislators. In 1891, Kansans sent a Populist to the U.S. Senate and in 1892 elected a Populist governor.

Kansas POPULISM included two forceful women leaders, MARY ELIZABETH LEASE and ANNIE LA PORTE DIGGS. Lease's oratory and Diggs's writing impressed voters and politicians. While the Populist party did not endure, it did lay the groundwork for major changes early in the twentieth century. Women broadened their roles in politics during this era as they could run for municipal office, and in several Kansas towns, women controlled the councils. Susanna Medora Salter of Argonia became the nation's first woman mayor in 1887.

Political and social arguments during the late nineteenth century centered on TEMPERANCE AND PROHIBITION. In 1880, Kansas became the first state to have constitutional prohibition. Repeal came in 1948, but liquor-by-the-drink was prohibited, except in private clubs, until 1986. CARRY AMELIA MOORE NATION called national attention to the issue in 1900 with her antisaloon crusade.

Twentieth-century Kansas

PROGRESSIVISM took over the Republican party after 1900 and provided strong leadership for a decade beginning in 1903. Progressive legislation included the regulation of railroads, public utilities, banks, and the sale of stocks and bonds. Inspection of meat-packing plants, child-labor laws, worker's compensation laws, the establishment of a juvenile-court system, and a primary election law were all products of the Progressive

Carry Nation, here escorted by a town marshal after destroying a tavern, began her crusade against saloons in Kansas. *Courtesy Kansas State Historical Society.*

the 1920s, farm fortunes fluctuated and then hit an unprecedented low in the 1930s when depression and blowing dust combined to make agriculture difficult.

Political and social thinking regressed in Kansas in the 1920s. Because of the recent war, "100 percent Americanism" was promoted, and a new Ku Klux Klan emerged. The Klan's activities led to an anti-Klan, Independent gubernatorial campaign by an outraged William Allen White. The Republican candidate won, but White made his point, and, as one writer put it, the Klan "was laughed out of Kansas."

When Herbert Hoover was elected president, his vice-president was Kansas Senator Charles Curtis, the first person of American Indian blood to hold the office.

Alfred M. Landon, a product of the Bull Moose era, capably led Kansas through four difficult years and was chosen by the Republicans as their presidential candidate in 1936. After his loss to President Franklin D. Roosevelt, he never again sought public office, but he remained a keen observer of world and national affairs until his death in 1987. In 1978, his daughter, Nancy Landon Kassebaum, became the first woman to be elected to the U.S. Senate in her own right.

The drought broke in 1939, and agricultural fortunes improved. Business generally began an upswing, and by 1940, because of the gathering storm in Europe, Kansas received government contracts for aviation production. Several Kansans were aviation pioneers—A. K. and E. J. Longren, Clyde Cessna, Walter Beech, Lloyd Stearman, and Glenn Martin. Wichita acquired the title of "Air Capital," ammunition plants opened in three Kansas towns, and Kansas City and Leavenworth had landing-craft factories.

Again, Forts Leavenworth and Riley were vital to the war effort, and sixteen army air bases and two naval air stations opened across Kansas, along with Camp Phillips near Salina. All European forces were led by Dwight D. Eisenhower of Abilene. More than 215,000 Kansans, both men and women, served on all fronts and in all branches of the service.

Sweeping change came after World War II, especially in mental-health care, highway construction, and

movement. When a constitutional amendment for WOMEN'S SUFFRAGE passed in 1912, Kansas became the eighth state to extend voting rights to women.

Kansas pioneered in public health during the early twentieth century under the leadership of Dr. Samuel Crumbine. Targeting unscreened windows, public drinking cups and towels, and misleading labels on foods and drugs as threats to the public health, Crumbine coined slogans like "Don't Spit on the Sidewalk." The phrase was so popular that Kansas brick manufacturers produced bricks with the slogan imprinted on them.

When war broke out in Europe in 1914, most Kansans wanted no part in the conflict and did not support President Woodrow Wilson's preparedness plans. However, when the United States entered the war, approximately eighty thousand Kansans went into the military. Camp Funston, a huge training area, was built at Fort Riley, and an aviation unit trained at Fort Leavenworth. Civilians participated enthusiastically in conservation and food-production efforts. "Win the War with Wheat" was the slogan in Kansas. Tilled acreage increased and farm production soared.

Kansas agriculture went through great changes even before the war. Increased irrigation, scientific advances pushed by the state agricultural college, crop rotation, improved dryland FARMING techniques, and mechanization all contributed to progress and prosperity. In

support for education. In the 1990s, Kansas had seven public universities, a technical institute, sixteen private colleges, eighteen community colleges, and a statewide system of vocational-technical schools.

Manufacturing surpassed agriculture as the major source of income for Kansas as early as 1953. The AIR-CRAFT INDUSTRY shifted its major production to commercial and private planes. Agribusiness became a partner of agriculture in the processing of farm products and the manufacture of farm-related goods. New crops such as soybeans and sorghum were important, but wheat remained the dominant money crop; Kansas produces on average 20 percent of the U.S. supply. As capital-intensive agricultural production increased, the number of farms and farmers decreased, and many family farms disappeared. Much of the future of Kansas agriculture depends on water and the recharging of the OGALLALA AQUIFER. Natural gas joined oil, gypsum, Portland cement, salt, and limestone as important mineral products. Coal mining declined steadily through the 1970s.

Since World War II, Kansas voted for Republicans for the presidency every year except 1964. Women became increasingly important politically. In addition to Senator Kassebaum, Kansas sent a woman to the House of Representatives, and increasing numbers of women were elected to the state legislature. Georgia Neese Clark Gray served as U.S. treasurer in the Truman administration. In 1990, Joan Finney, a Democrat, became the first woman governor.

Kansans have contributed to the literature of the West. Some were newspaper-editors-turned-fiction-writers, such as William Allen White and Edgar W. Howe. Kansas and the West provided the setting for novels by Paul Wellman, Margaret Hill McCarter, and Robert Day. William Inge used his native state as background for *Bus Stop* and *Picnic,* and John Ise dealt with his own family in the classic *Sod and Stubble.* Poets William Stafford, Kenneth Porter, and Bruce Cutler drew heavily on their experiences in Kansas and other Western states. Multitalented Gordon Parks portrayed his childhood in a small Kansas town in *The Learning Tree.* James C. Malin's historical work on Kansas and grasslands is unique. The foremost authority in the history and interpretation of American Indian music was Thurlow Lieurance, teacher and composer.

Kansas saw population shifts after 1960. Many small towns and rural counties declined, and the average age of their residents increased. Johnson County, which is a part of the greater Kansas City metropolitan area, grew from 62,000 in 1950 to 355,000 in 1990 and was projected to double by 2030. Eighty of the 105 Kansas counties, however, were predicted to lose population in the twenty-first century. In 1990, Wichita was the largest city, followed by Kansas City, Topeka, Overland Park, Lawrence, Salina, Hutchinson, Leavenworth, and Manhattan.

People have been trying to define, with difficulty, the Kansas character for 130 years. At times, Kansas has had an image problem, not helped by *The Wizard of Oz,* but Kansans have pride in their state. Kansas provided national leadership when it was needed in social, economic, and political areas. Carl Becker wrote that Kansas was a "state of mind, a religion, and a philosophy in one."

—*Robert W. Richmond*

SEE ALSO: Agrarianism; Cattle Trails and Trail Driving; Central Plains Indian Wars; Dust Bowl; Guerrillas; Homesteading; *Kansas* v. *Colorado;* Medicine Lodge Treaty of 1867; Sod Houses; Wheat Farming

SUGGESTED READING:
Barry, Louise. *The Beginning of the West: Annals of the Kansas Gateway to the American West, 1540–1854.* Topeka, Kans., 1972.
Bright, John D., ed. *Kansas: The First Century.* 2 vols. New York, 1956.
Clanton, O. Gene. *Kansas Populism: Ideas and Men.* Lawrence, Kans., 1969.
Davis, Kenneth S. *Kansas: A Bicentennial History.* New York, 1976.
LaForte, Robert S. *Leaders of Reform: Progressive Republicans in Kansas, 1900–1916.* Lawrence, Kans., 1974.
Miner, H. Craig. *West of Wichita: Settling the High Plains of Kansas, 1865–1890.* Lawrence, Kans., 1986.
Richmond, Robert W. *Kansas: A Land of Contrasts.* Arlington Heights, Ill., 1989.
———. *Kansas: A Pictorial History.* Lawrence, Kans., 1992.

KANSAS CITY, MISSOURI

The first settlers of what became Kansas City were French fur traders, who arrived in 1821. The site at the intersection of two navigable rivers, the MISSOURI RIVER and the Kansas River, had favorable possibilities in an age when river junctions appeared prime locations. However, the post established by the CHOUTEAU FAMILY failed to grow, and the settlements founded around it proved inconsequential. A predominantly transitory population had little interest in town building. In 1838, unscrupulous promoters incorporated the Town of Kansas, which included a prime river landing, but legal entanglements curtailed growth. By the 1850s, what came to be called "Kansas City" was a glorified frontier camp. Some progress followed the opening of Kansas for settlement under the KANSAS-NEBRASKA ACT of 1854. On the eve of the CIVIL WAR, Kansas City had 4,418 people and limited prospects of even advancing beyond the size of an agricultural village. But things soon changed.

During the war, Kansas City served as a military base for the Union and thus escaped the war's desolation. Meanwhile, the city's immediate neighbors were badly hurt by guerrilla fighting in Missouri. With the coming of peace, Kansas City competed with other towns—Leavenworth, Atchison, and St. Joseph—for the first permanent railroad bridge over the Missouri River. A general consensus held that the winner would become a regional metropolis. Kansas City's small, resourceful, and united business community—possibly by giving land as an inducement to the owners of the Hannibal and St. Joseph Railroad—gained the bridge. After it opened in 1869, Kansas City quickly moved forward and emerged as a major railroad and commercial center. In the 1880s, a large stockyard and the perfection of refrigerated freight cars encouraged Eastern interests to build meat-packing plants. Several wealthy leaders, especially from New England, arrived, bringing their social institutions with them and providing a cultural flavor absent in many other frontier communities.

By the 1890s, Kansas City's economy was based on transportation, commercial distribution, and agribusiness. This combination served the city well. In the twentieth century, the ushering in of a "Golden Age" of agriculture in Kansas further enhanced the city's future. The city became a financial center and gained a federal reserve bank. Through CITY PLANNING, Kansas City's physical appearance changed as well. It had been an ugly and crowded town until a "city-beautiful" movement led to the construction of a park and boulevard system. *Kansas City Star* owner WILLIAM ROCKHILL NELSON supported civic betterment projects and real-estate promoter Jesse C. Nichols developed the large upscale Country Club District.

The number of inhabitants reached 132,716 in 1890 and moved steadily higher to 399,746 in 1930. Kansas City never had a large immigrant element, but the rigidly segregated African American community accounted for 10 to 15 percent of the population from Reconstruction onward.

Kansas City politics were wild and woolly. A family Democratic organization headed by JAMES PENDERGAST started in the packing-house district in the 1880s. The faction gave aid to unfortunates and worked closely with gamblers. In 1910, James Pendergast's younger brother, THOMAS J. PENDERGAST, took charge. His "Goat" faction curried middle-class support and ruthlessly crushed opponents, notably the "Rabbits," to gain control of local Democratic politic and run the CITY GOVERNMENT.

In 1925, a change to the city charter allowed Tom Pendergast to take over Kansas City. Gangster enforcers and tens of thousands of illegal "ghost" voters kept the Pendergast machine in power. While Pendergast held no political office after voluntarily leaving the city council in 1915, everyone knew who ran "Tom's Town." Operating from modest headquarters at 1908 Main Street, Pendergast dominated all aspects, legal and illegal, of life in Kansas City. His Ready Mix Concrete Company provided cement for municipal projects. Companies that wanted to do business in Kansas City, right down to contracts for sidewalk repairs, made payments called "lugs" to the Pendergast machine.

Tom's Town was wide open, despite prohibition. Liquor establishments operated around the clock. Gambling and prostitution flourished. Underpaid African American musicians perfected a special brand of Kansas City jazz in after-hours clubs. Few people considered the cost in human and financial terms. Instead, boosters talked of an undefined "Kansas City Spirit" reminiscent of frontier days. The "House of Pendergast" did not collapse until Tom Pendergast went to the federal penitentiary for tax evasion in 1939. He left Kansas City $20 million in debt and its national reputation in tatters.

—*Lawrence H. Larsen*

SUGGESTED READING:

Brown, A. Theodore, and Lyle W. Dorsett. *K.C.: A History of Kansas City, Missouri.* Boulder, Colo., 1978.

Glaab, Charles N. *Kansas City and the Railroads: Community Policy in the Growth of a Regional Metropolis.* Madison, Wis., 1962.

Worley, William S. *J. C. Nichols and the Shaping of Kansas City: Innovation in Planned Residential Communities.* Columbia, Mo., 1990.

KANSAS INDIANS

SEE: Native American Peoples: Peoples of the Great Plains

KANSAS-NEBRASKA ACT

On May 30, 1854, after three months of bitter debate, Congress passed the Kansas-Nebraska Act, repealing the MISSOURI COMPROMISE of 1820 and throwing the decision of whether to allow slavery into the Western territories back to the territories themselves, whose settlers would exercise their "popular sovereignty" in

LIBERTY, THE FAIR MAID OF KANSAS—IN THE HANDS OF THE "BORDER RUFFIANS".

In a contemporary antislavery cartoon, Illinois Senator Stephen A. Douglas and President James Buchanan, popular sovereignty supporters, are characterized as no better than the "border ruffians" who terrorized Kansas in the late 1850s. *Courtesy Library of Congress.*

voting for or against slavery. The act was introduced by STEPHEN A. DOUGLAS of Illinois, whose motives have been seen variously as attempts to seek Southern support for the presidency, to enrich himself and his home state through the development of a transcontinental railroad, to ameliorate regional tension, and to force the pace of NATIONAL EXPANSION towards the Pacific.

In 1850, Congress had once again averted sectional disaster by delaying the national showdown over slavery, but the COMPROMISE OF 1850 proved to be a last, desperate act. More or less gutting the Missouri Compromise, which had held the country together for thirty years, the 1850 act set the stage on which the mere applications for statehood from KANSAS and NEBRASKA caused a major crisis. The Kansas-Nebraska Act spawned the Republican party and led the U.S. senator from MISSOURI, DAVID RICE ATCHISON, who had already broken with his respected fellow senator, THOMAS HART BENTON, over slavery, to swear that he would let the territory "sink in hell" before allowing it to be organized as a Free-Soil state. The Nebraskans, clearly, would opt for freedom, but in Kansas, the question of slavery was an open issue. Abolitionists in the North organized the Emigrant Aid Society and financed Free-Soil settlers in Kansas. New England authors such as William Cullen Bryant and John Greenleaf Whittier

mounted one of history's great propaganda campaigns, quickly joined by expansion-minded newspaperman Horace Greeley and other correspondents sent by Eastern papers to report on the Kansas-Missouri "situation."

Egged on by Atchison, thousands of proslavery Missourians, mainly from the tobacco- and hemp-growing western counties, flooded into Kansas to vote illegally and then returned to their farms. Overwhelming the Kansas settlers, the majority of whom were probably Free-Soilers, they elected a territorial legislature that immediately legalized slavery and won official recognition from the federal government for the Lecompton Draft Constitution. Free-Soilers poured in from Iowa to settle the land, formed their own legislature, set their capital up at Lawrence, and petitioned Congress for admission as a free state. Open warfare broke out along the Kansas-Missouri border as Atchison resigned his seat in the Senate, organized a posse of Missourians, and led a raid on Lawrence. In response to these "border ruffians," as Horace Greeley called them, a monomaniacal abolitionist named JOHN BROWN murdered proslavery settlers on the Pottawatomie Creek and mutilated their bodies. Ideologically motivated assassination had begun, and by the time the federal government could join with authorities in Kansas and Missouri to bring the guerrilla warfare in "Bleeding Kansas" more or less to an end in 1858, two hundred people were dead and $2 million worth of property had gone up in smoke.

An act designed to ameliorate tensions between North and South had instead exacerbated them. The question of how the nation should expand into the trans-Mississippi West was pulling it apart east of the river. The bitterness engendered by the Kansas-Nebraska Act continued not just through the CIVIL WAR, but, on the political front, lingered on for generations.

—*Patrick H. Butler, III*

SUGGESTED READING:

Freehling, William W. *The Road to Disunion: Secessionists at Bay, 1776–1854.* New York, 1990.

KANSAS PACIFIC RAILROAD

SEE: Union Pacific Railroad; Villard, Henry

KANSAS V. COLORADO

In May 1907, the justices of the United States Supreme Court announced their decision on the first suit involving an interstate conflict over river flow. The decision established the doctrine of equity in an attempt to resolve the issue.

Beginning in the 1890s, Kansans around Garden City nervously watched the yearly diminishment of the ARKANSAS RIVER flow, and they blamed Colorado irrigators to the west. Marshall Murdock, a powerful Wichita, Kansas, newspaper editor, also feared the effects of IRRIGATION both in western Kansas and in eastern Colorado on the Arkansas River. Murdock envisioned Wichita as an inland port if given some hefty help from the UNITED STATES ARMY CORPS OF ENGINEERS, but he saw his dream withering as canal companies in western Kansas, and especially the larger and more numerous systems in eastern Colorado, consumed the river flow before it reached Wichita. Consequently, Murdock used his enormous political clout to get the Kansas legislature to file suit against Colorado.

Kansas filed its opening briefs in May 1901, and the Colorado attorney general, Charles Post, quickly refuted any right of Kansas to bring suit. The Supreme Court justices announced their right to hear the case in April 1902 and, in March 1904, allowed the U.S. attorney general to intervene in the case to protect the interests of the newly created Reclamation Service. In May 1904, the court appointed a commissioner to oversee the testimony, and by the end of 1905, his stenographer had recorded more than 120 court exhibits and eighty-five hundred pages of testimony from more than three hundred witnesses. In October 1906, the attorneys made their respective positions clear. Kansans believed the riparian doctrine, which protected the quality and quantity of river flow, gave them the right to an undiminished river flow; Coloradans claimed the prior-appropriation doctrine, which protected beneficial uses of WATER in a "first-in-time, first-in-right" manner, allowed the state's citizens to use all of the water within its boundaries regardless of the effect on Kansans; and the United States attorney general made a case for congressional control of non-navigable rivers that crossed state lines.

In May 1907, the court announced its decision through an opinion written by Justice David Brewer, a former Kansan. He refused to favor either state's water code and instead formulated the doctrine of equity. Brewer had devised an accounting procedure to assess the relative gains each state had made in using the Arkansas River flow. In that manner, each state could maintain its own water doctrine, and the federal government could be prevented from asserting congressional control over the river. Brewer found the citizens from both states making economic advances throughout the valley and consequently ruled that Kansans had not made a case for restraining Coloradans' water uses.

Since 1907, the court has used equity as the governing principle for allocating stream flows from interstate rivers. Cases such as *Nebraska* v. *Wyoming* (1945) and *Colorado* v. *New Mexico* (1982 and 1984) reveal just how important the doctrine is in settling feuds between states over limited stream flows in the arid West.

—*James E. Sherow*

SEE ALSO: Bureau of Reclamation; California Doctrine (of Water Rights); Colorado Doctrine (of Water Rights); Reclamation

SUGGESTED READING:

Sherow, James E. "The Contest for the 'Nile of America': *Kansas* v. *Colorado*." *Great Plains Quarterly* 10 (1990): 48–61.

Wagner, Mark J. "The Parting of the Water—The Dispute between Colorado and Kansas over the Arkansas River." *Washburn Law Journal* 24 (1984): 99–120.

KAROK INDIANS

SEE: Native American Peoples: Peoples of California

KAWAIISU INDIANS

SEE: Native American Peoples: Peoples of the Great Basin

KAWEAH COOPERATIVE COMMONWEALTH

A utopian colony in California from 1885 to 1890, the Kaweah Cooperative Commonwealth reflected the desire of sixty-eight San Franciscan workingmen influenced by Laurence Gronlund's *Cooperative Commonwealth* (1884) to set up their own community based on socialist and cooperative ideas.

Led by a brilliant but erratic lawyer, Burnette Haskell, the group filed fifty-three claims for choice government land on the Kaweah River in the foothills of the Sierra Nevada east of Visalia in Tulare County. There they raised a tent city and at various times attracted anywhere from fifty to three hundred resident members. By 1888, the Kaweah Colony engaged enough attention to enroll nonresidents from as far away as Denver and New York City.

The colonists expected to become economically viable through the production of lumber, particularly redwood. To that end, they devoted a high proportion of their labor to the difficult task of building a road into the mountains. It was a four-year, monumental undertaking; long after the colony collapsed, the road remained the only access to the Giant Forest of the Sequoias.

Colony members were generally well read, skilled laborers, with a sprinkling of artists, musicians, and writers. Many lived in canvas houses but enjoyed a more permanent community center for meals and meetings. Most agreed that their lives held unusual intellectual and social rewards—outdoor concerts with the colony's orchestra, dances, picnics, and literary and scientific classes. Edward Bellamy's *Looking Backward* (1888) became an important ingredient in their thinking.

Despite their successes, however, internal bickering was frequent, and strong leadership never emerged. But the chief cause of Kaweah's demise came from external hostilities, especially from the United States government, which first withheld and then withdrew the cooperative's land from entry. In 1890, parts of the colony became SEQUOIA NATIONAL PARK, and the giant tree that colonists had christened the "Karl Marx" became known as the "General Sherman." No recompense was ever made to the colonists for their years of presumed ownership and improvements.

—*Robert V. Hine*

SUGGESTED READING:
Hine, Robert V. *California's Utopian Colonies*. Berkeley, Calif., 1983.

KEARNEY, DENIS

California labor agitator Denis Kearney (1847–1907) founded the WORKINGMEN'S PARTY OF CALIFORNIA, a political organization that effectively used the threat of violence to win concessions from San Francisco city leaders and paved the way for the 1882 federal ban on Chinese immigration. Born in Ireland, Kearney went to sea at the age of eleven as a cabin boy and later as a first mate on American ships. In 1868, he settled in San Francisco and a few years later bought a draying business. Becoming a U.S. citizen in 1876, Kearney educated himself through reading and attendance at a Lyceum of Self-Culture.

San Francisco erupted in anti-Chinese riots on July 23, 1877, during a protest meeting of the Workingmen's Party of the United States. Kearney took part in the pick-handle brigade organized by WILLIAM TELL COLEMAN to protect the interests of city businessmen. Suddenly, however, Kearney changed allegiance and formed the Workingmen's Party of California. While the party did not generally capture the support of union members, it did attract many unemployed citizens who blamed their lack of work on the presence of Chinese laborers. Kearney railed against capitalists, who imported Chinese to work at low wages, and against the established political parties. He became an expressive speaker, known for his flamboyant descriptions of capitalist oppression and for his rhetoric of hate. He often ended his speeches with the phrase, "The Chinese must go."

When Kearney dramatically stirred his followers to near violence in October 1877, Coleman formed a Committee of Public Safety to counter Kearney's mob. Kearney and other party leaders were arrested for using language "having a tendency to cause a breach of peace." Judge Robert Ferral dismissed the charges against them on a technicality. The San Francisco Board of Supervisors then enacted a gag law so strict that it severely limited freedom of speech. When Kearney violated the gag law, he was arrested again, on January 5, 1878. Many members of the Workingmen's Party of California, which had grown dramatically after the gag law was passed, then formed military companies throughout the city, while others prepared for the party's greatest fight: the passage of a new state constitution.

The party was the most important political force in San Francisco between 1877 and 1879 and was initially successful at the polls, especially in the election of Isaac S. Kalloch as mayor, eleven state senators and sixteen assemblymen, most of the state supreme court justices, and a large number of delegates to the state constitutional convention of 1878 to 1879. Once the party influenced the drafting of the new state constitution, it began to lose its hold on the city's workers, and its popularity waned. Kearney disappeared from the public scene in the early 1880s.

—*Candace Floyd*

SEE ALSO: Chinese Exclusion

SUGGESTED READING:

Kazin, Michael. *Barons of Labor.* Urbana, Ill., 1987.
Saxton, Alexander. *The Indispensable Enemy.* Berkeley, Calif., 1971.
Shumsky, Neil Larry. *The Evolution of Political Protest and the Workingmen's Party of California.* Columbus, Ohio, 1991.

KEARNS, THOMAS

Mining entrepreneur, newspaperman, and U.S. senator, Thomas Kearns (1862–1918) was born near Woodstock in Oxford County, Ontario, Canada, to Irish immigrant parents. At the age of about seven, Kearns moved with his parents to Nebraska. After leaving the farm, he worked in the Black Hills; Tombstone, Arizona; and Springville, Utah. In 1883, he moved to Park City, Utah, where he was engaged in mining as an employee and as an entrepreneur. A self-taught geologist, Kearns, along with several partners, acquired the Mayflower and Silver King mines and put together the Silver King Coalition Mines Company in 1907; Kearns served as president and general manager until his death.

During Utah's 1895 constitutional convention, Kearns championed the rights of working people and sponsored provisions to regulate the hours and conditions of work in underground mines. Elected to the United States Senate as a Republican in 1901—in part through the support of Lorenzo Snow, president of the CHURCH OF JESUS CHRIST OF LATTER-DAY SAINTS (LDS)—Kearns failed to obtain the support of Snow's successor, JOSEPH FIELDING SMITH, and was defeated by GEORGE SUTHERLAND in 1905. He had purchased the local newspaper, *Salt Lake Tribune*, in 1901, and in 1905, he used it to support the anti-Mormon American party, which held power in Salt Lake City until 1911. Thereafter, Kearns accommodated himself with Utah's Mormon majority.

A devout Catholic, Kearns helped build the Cathedral of the Madeleine and endow Kearns St. Ann's Orphanage and other charitable endeavors. On South Temple Street in Salt Lake City, he built the mansion that currently serves as the home for the governor of Utah.

—*Thomas G. Alexander*

SUGGESTED READING:

Larson, Kent Sheldon. "The Life of Thomas Kearns." M.A. thesis, University of Utah, 1964.
Warrum, Noble. *Utah since Statehood.* 4 vols. Chicago, 1919.

KEARNY, PHILIP

Philip Kearny (1814–1862) was the nephew of STEPHEN WATTS KEARNY (a hero of the UNITED STATES–MEXICAN WAR) and a distinguished soldier in his own right. Born in New York City and educated at Columbia College, Kearny was commissioned a second lieutenant in the First U.S. Dragoons. He served under his uncle during the disease-plagued but relatively peaceful expedition of 1834 into Pawnee and Comanche country. He also benefited from the training program Stephen Watts Kearny instituted at Fort Leavenworth, Kansas, which molded the First Dragoons into a crack unit. Philip Kearny received further instruction in cavalry tactics in France in 1839. He served the following year with the French army in Algeria and used his experience as the basis for a manual on cavalry tactics he wrote for the U.S. Army.

On his return to the United States, Kearny served Generals Alexander Macomb and WINFIELD SCOTT as aide-de-camp but resigned his commission in 1846. His retirement was short lived. With the outbreak of the United States–Mexican War, Kearny raised and equipped his own cavalry company, secured a captain's commission in December 1846, and began service with his company under Winfield Scott. Kearny performed gallantly on August 20, 1847, at the Battle of Churubusco in which he bravely led a charge into enemy lines. He lost an arm in the engagement but gained a brevet promotion to major and the praise of Scott, who called him "a perfect soldier" and "the bravest man I ever knew."

Kearny retired from service again in October 1851 but then joined the French Imperial Guard under Napoleon III. He won distinction at two major battles of the Italian War: Magenta (June 4, 1859) and Solferino (June 24, 1859). He was the first American to win the Cross of the Legion of Honor. At the beginning of the CIVIL WAR, he returned to the United States in 1861, became brigadier general of the New Jersey Volunteers, and served as a divisional commander in General Samuel P. Heintzelman's III Corps, Army of the Potomac. He fought in the Peninsular campaign (1862) and performed with his customary dash and distinction at Williamsburg (May 5) and at Fair Oaks (May 31).

At the Second Battle of Bull Run, on August 29 and 30, 1862, Kearny was instrumental in checking Thomas ("Stonewall") Jackson's pursuit at Chantilly. Kearny was cut down by a sniper while reconnoitering at Chantilly on September 1, 1862.

—*Alan Axelrod*

SUGGESTED READING:

De Peyster, J. Watts. *Personal and Military History of Philip Kearny, Major-General, United States Volunteers*. Elizabeth, N.J., 1870.

Kearny, Thomas. *General Philip Kearny: Battle Soldier of Five Wars*. New York, 1937.

KEARNY, STEPHEN WATTS

U.S. Army General Stephen Watts Kearny (1794–1848) played a pivotal role in the American conquest of New Mexico and California during the UNITED STATES–MEXICAN WAR. Born in Newark, New Jersey, Kearny began his thirty-five-year military career in the WAR OF 1812 where he exhibited gallantry in action and was later wounded and captured.

At the beginning of the United States–Mexican War in 1846, Colonel Kearny received orders to take possession of California and New Mexico. Leaving Fort Leavenworth, Kansas, in June 1846, Kearny's 1,600 troops, dubbed the "Army of the West," reached Santa Fe on August 18. New Mexico officials surrendered the capital without bloodshed. After establishing a civil government, Brigadier General Kearny (he had been promoted during his overland expedition) left Santa Fe on September 25 for California. A few days into the journey, Kearny received word that California had been conquered by Commodore ROBERT F. STOCKTON. Kearny returned 200 of his dragoons to Santa Fe to assist in the suppression of Indian raids. With only 120 men, Kearny continued the march to California.

On December 6, Kearny reached the village of San Pasqual, where he discovered that California remained unconquered. Californios (native-born Californians of Hispanic descent) under Andrés Pico attacked Kearny's column, and American casualties totaled one-third of his command. A few days later, sailors and marines from San Diego lifted the siege. Kearny then joined Stockton to march on Los Angeles. On January 8 and 9,

General Stephen Watts Kearny. *Courtesy Library of Congress.*

1847, Kearny and Stockton defeated the Californios at San Gabriel and La Mesa. These victories, combined with Lieutenant Colonel JOHN CHARLES FRÉMONT's victory over another Californio command on January 13, terminated Mexican armed resistance to the American takeover of California.

With the end of the war, Kearny and Frémont fought over who would lead the American occupation. After Frémont proclaimed himself the civil governor of California, Kearny arrested him and returned with him to Fort Leavenworth. Although the military court and President JAMES K. POLK supported Kearny in the dispute, he became the enemy of Missouri's U.S. Senator THOMAS HART BENTON, Frémont's father-in-law. In the spring of 1848, Kearny returned to active service. He spent three months in Mexico, first as military governor of Veracruz and later in a similar position in Mexico City. While in Mexico, he probably contracted yellow fever. Returning to the United States, Kearny received a brevet promotion to major general. He died on October 31, 1848, near St. Louis on the estate of Major Meriwether Lewis Clark.

—*Neil C. Mangum*

SUGGESTED READING:

Clarke, Dwight L. *Stephen Watts Kearny: Soldier of the West*. Norman, Okla., 1961.

Nevins, Allan. *Frémont: The West's Greatest Adventurer*. Vol. 1. New York, 1928.

KEARNY CODE

General Stephen Watts Kearny, commander of the Army of the West, ordered codification of laws for New Mexico after occupying Santa Fe in August 1846. Assisted by Private Willard P. Hall, Colonel ALEXANDER WILLIAM DONIPHAN worked quickly. These two lawyers were helped by Francis P. Blair, Jr., an army scout and lawyer in civilian life, and by another private, John T. Hughes. Doniphan gave major credit for the completed work to Hall.

Entitled "Laws of the Territory of New Mexico" and issued on September 22, 1846 (published October 7, in English and Spanish, 115 pages), the Kearny Code had origins in the organic law of the Missouri Territory; specific statutes of Missouri, Texas, and Mexico; and the code prepared for Louisiana in 1821 by Edward Livingston.

The code served its purpose very well as the basis for U.S. civil government in New Mexico. After the 1850 congressional organic act, provisions of the code were repeated, revised, and replaced over time, yet as New Mexico's state law librarian observed in 1943, "A surprising portion of the Kearny Code has survived, in reenacted form."

—*John Porter Bloom*

SUGGESTED READING:
Clarke, Dwight L. *Stephen Watts Kearny: Soldier of the West.* Norman, Okla., 1961.

KELLEY, HALL JACKSON

Hall Jackson Kelley (1790–1874) promoted the settlement of Oregon with great success during the 1830s and 1840s. Born in Northwood, New Hampshire, he was educated at Middlebury College. In his early life, he worked as a surveyor, teacher, and author of school textbooks. Interested in the lands of the Pacific Northwest, he advocated American migration to the region, which was jointly claimed by the United States and Great Britain. In speeches, pamphlets, circulars, and petitions, he promoted Oregon to New Englanders. In 1829, he established the American Society for Encouraging the Settlement of the Oregon Territory. Two years later, he published *A General Circular to All Persons of Good Character Who Wish to Emigrate to the Oregon Territory,* in which he claimed Oregon to be the most healthful location in the world. He proposed to form a joint-stock company of emigrants who would travel en masse to the territory and purchase land from

the Native Americans. He never received the federal backing he hoped for, but he himself traveled to the region in 1832.

By 1840, there were about five hundred American settlers in the Willamette Valley of Oregon. Three years later, a party of almost one thousand Americans traveled along the OREGON TRAIL, first pioneered by fur trappers and missionaries, from western Missouri, along the Kansas River and the Platte River, through Fort Laramie, to the Rockies. Crossing the mountains at South Pass, they then followed the SNAKE RIVER and the COLUMBIA RIVER to FORT VANCOUVER and proceeded south to the Willamette Valley region. Another twelve hundred settlers arrived in 1844.

Kelley's efforts to promote migration were in part responsible for the massive influx of settlers who migrated to the Oregon Country. While the question of a legal boundary between Great Britain's holdings and the United States was still unanswered, in 1843, many of the settlers formed the Provisional Government, an informal governmental structure that maintained law and order. In 1846, the British negotiated with the United States, and the two countries set the forty-ninth parallel between the Rocky Mountains and the Puget Sound as the boundary line. With the end of the OREGON BOUNDARY DISPUTE, the region became a territory of the United States on August 14, 1848, and Kelley continued to promote settlement of the region until the 1850s.

—*Candace Floyd*

SUGGESTED READING:
Clark, Malcolm, Jr. *Eden Seekers: The Settlement of Oregon, 1818–1862.* Boston, 1981.

KELLEY, OLIVER H.

The city-bred son of a tailor, Oliver H. Kelley (1826–1913), after westering to Minnesota in the mid-nineteenth century, became active in the Populist agrarian movement and a founder of the Order of the Patrons of Husbandry, better known as the Grange. A Minnesota Mason who arrived in St. Paul in June of 1849 from his native Boston via Illinois and Iowa, Kelley took to farming with an enthusiasm that belied his urban background. Only moderately successful as an agriculturalist, Kelley put his talent for promotion and journalism into farm-related political causes and wrote numerous columns on agriculture for papers both in and outside the state. In 1864, he secured a patronage job with the help of Minnesota's Governor Alexander Ramsey as a clerk for the federal commissioner of agriculture. On a government-sponsored tour of the South in 1866, Kelley first conceived of a national farmers' union modeled loosely on the Masons, believing that such an organization could bring to an end the sectional bitterness still simmering beneath the surface in the Reconstruction era by engaging all the nation's farm workers in a common cause. He promoted his idea among sympathetic friends working for the federal government. With six of them, Kelley established the Patrons of Husbandry on December 4, 1867, and for eleven years served as the order's secretary. The Grange spawned a slew of Granger laws and, ultimately, the agrarian movement called "POPULISM," a Western social phenomenon that over the course of the next few decades challenged the very idea of the market economy created by post–Civil War industrialization and thus shook the political foundations of the country.

—*Charles Phillips*

SEE ALSO: Agrarianism; Currency and Silver as Western Political Issues; Greenback Party

SUGGESTED READING:
Woods, Thomas A. *Knights of the Plow: Oliver H. Kelley and the Origins of the Grange in Republican Ideology.* Ames, Iowa, 1991.

KELLY, FANNY

Canadian-born Fanny Kelly (1845–1904) lived as a captive among the Oglala Sioux Indians for six months and produced a nineteenth-century best-seller entitled *Narrative of My Captivity among the Sioux Indians* from her experience. She had been headed for Idaho from Geneva, Kansas, with her husband, their adopted daughter, and several other families when the Sioux attacked the pioneers on July 12, 1864, as they traveled through the Wyoming Territory. Although her husband escaped, Kelly and her daughter Mary fell into the hands of the Indians. When Mary escaped at Fanny's urging, the Sioux tracked her down and killed her. Thereafter, Fanny Kelly made no other obvious or overt attempts to thwart the will of her captives, although she did manage twice to warn General ALFRED SULLY of impending Sioux treachery. Sully and his troops had been pursuing the band for two years after a series attacks in 1862. During peace conferences, the Indians asked Kelly to write out their messages to the general, and in these communications, she was able to warn him of the threat. Through wit and pluck, she earned the band's admiration and the jealousy of the chief's wife. The Sioux ultimately exchanged her for three horses and a load of food supplies.

Fanny Kelly's *Narrative of My Captivity among the Sioux Indians* featured illustrations of the initial Indian attack on her wagon train and an image of her terror at being held captive. *Courtesy Library of Congress.*

For a public fascinated by her ordeal—especially with whether she had been violated—Kelly wrote a captivity narrative that denied she had suffered any sexual abuse at the hands of the Indians, a denial common in many previous Indian captivity narratives. Putting aside the fact that early in what would become known as the Victorian Era, a married women could hardly admit publicly to sexual relations with a "savage," captive women were not often in danger of rape, since forced sex, in general, was seen among Indian tribes as deviant and unacceptable behavior. Despite the disappointments for the lascivious, Kelly's tale of harsh treatment and cruelty by her captors, leavened by her own growing understanding of the tribe, proved popular. A venerable genre of frontier literature, captivity narratives had become suspect by the mid-nineteenth century for the many melodramatic and outlandish tales they often contained after publishers realized how commercially successful those tales could be. In contrast, although no doubt Kelly's story boasted some misrepresentations, *My Captivity among the Sioux Indians* was viewed, both at the time and among more recent scholars, as a fairly sober-eyed account that revealed much of interest about Sioux life and its family structures and gender roles.

—*Kelly L. Lankford*

SEE ALSO: Literature: Indian Captivity Narratives

SUGGESTED READING:

Kelly, Fanny. *Narrative of My Captivity among the Sioux Indians.* Hartford, Conn., 1871.

Namias, June. *White Captives: Gender and Ethnicity on the American Frontier.* Chapel Hill, N.C., 1993.

Riley, Glenda. *Women and Indians on the Frontier, 1825–1915.* Albuquerque, N. Mex., 1984.

KENDRICK, JOHN BENJAMIN

John Benjamin Kendrick (1857–1933), cattle rancher, governor of Wyoming, and U.S. senator, was born near Jacksonville in Cherokee County, Texas. He drove a herd of Texas cattle to Wyoming in 1879, and for the next decade, the largely self-educated cowboy worked on ranches in the state. Following his marriage in 1891 to Eula Wulfjen, the daughter of a wealthy rancher, he successively became foreman, manager, and then owner of a large ranch. An officer in the state and national livestock organizations, he first entered politics at the age of fifty-three, when he served a term as Sheridan County's representative to the state legislature.

Kendrick was elected governor in 1914 but resigned midterm after his election to the U.S. Senate. A conservative Democrat, he was reelected to two more terms. His voting record was almost identical to that of his colleague Republican FRANCIS E. WARREN. Kendrick strongly supported RECLAMATION projects. His family home in Sheridan is now operated as a state historic site.

—*Phil Roberts*

SUGGESTED READING:

Carroll, Eugene T. "Wyoming's Senator John Benjamin Kendrick." *Annals of Wyoming* (Fall 1986).

Fley, Jo Ann. "John B. Kendrick's Career in the United States Senate." M.A. thesis, University of Wyoming, 1953.

KENEDY, MIFFLIN

Texas rancher and partner with RICHARD KING in the KING RANCH, Mifflin Kenedy (1818–1895) was born in Chester County, Pennsylvania, and was educated in local schools. In 1834, he sailed as a cabin boy to India. Returning to Pittsburgh, he worked as a clerk on a river steamboat along the Ohio and Mississippi rivers. He moved to Florida in 1842, and while a boat captain there, he met Richard King. In 1846, he worked with the U.S. Army to buy river boats for use in the United States–Mexican War and became a captain and master in the military. After the war, he was a trader in Mexico.

Settling in Hidalgo, Texas, he worked as a rancher and imported Merino sheep to Texas. He joined Richard King in a ranching and trading operation from 1860 to 1868. Kenedy then settled near Corpus Christi, Texas, as a rancher and trader on the Rio Grande. In 1869, he fenced his ranch with smooth wire—becoming one of the first ranchers to do so—spanning thirty-six miles along three sides. He sold his Corpus Christi operation in 1882 and started a new ranch in Cameron County. In 1876, he became engaged in railroad building.

—*Patrick H. Butler, III*

SUGGESTED READING:

Douglas, C. L. *Cattle Kings of Texas.* Fort Worth, Tex., 1968.

KENNEDY, KATE

A landmark reformer in education, Kate Kennedy (1827–1890) was born in Ireland. As a child, she studied in her spare time and educated five of her sisters at home. The disastrous potato famines of 1846 to 1847 forced the Kennedys to flee to the United States, where Kate began teaching. Drawn by opportunities in the West, the family moved to San Francisco in 1856, and Kate secured a job teaching at the Suisun School. Two years later, she was appointed principal of the North Cosmopolitan Grammar School but at a lower salary than received by her male counterparts. She launched a reform campaign demanding equal pay for equal work. The campaign gained so much public support that in 1874 the state legislature was forced to pass a bill setting state salaries without regard to sex. When Kennedy continued to speak on reform, from labor laws to the single-tax movement, of which she was an ardent supporter, her activities drew the censure of the school board. In 1887, she was transferred to a smaller school with lower pay. Kennedy sued the board, and the court found in her favor in 1890. The court's decision, which remains the legal basis for California's teacher-tenure law, held that teachers cannot be demoted or dismissed without evidence of professional misconduct or incompetency. She died three months later on March 18, 1890.

—*Kurt Edward Kemper*

KENT, WILLIAM

A social and political reformer and Progressive congressman from California, William Kent (1864–1928) was born in CHICAGO, ILLINOIS, and traveled as a child with his family to California's Marin County on the northern edge of San Francisco Bay. Graduated from the Hopkins School in 1883 and Yale University in 1887, he took up a conventional business career in Chicago. His career flourished as did his fortune, but his growing disgust at the political corruption and economic inequalities that he found endemic in late nineteenth-century Chicago drove him into urban politics. As the head of his own organization, the Municipal Voters League, he led anticorruption drives and served as an alderman from 1895 to 1897. He joined other reformers, such as Florence Kelley at Hull House, to campaign for government action to improve working conditions and recreational opportunities for the lower classes. In time, however, Kent's growing frustration with intractable urban problems led him to wind up his affairs in Chicago and move back to northern California.

Kent's personal commitment to social and political reform lured him into California's tumultuous political life soon after his arrival. In particular, he vigorously espoused tactics to ensure the protection and efficient use of natural resources. As in Chicago, he opposed the excessive power exercised by private corporations over the interests of the general populace. Believing that unchecked private exploitation of forests, watersheds, and mineral deposits would enrich the few at the expense of the many, he frequently proposed public management or even ownership of such resources just as he had fought for public ownership of utilities and transit systems in Chicago. He conducted successful campaigns to establish Muir Woods National Monument among the redwood groves on Marin County's Mount Tamalpais in 1908 and to defeat the planned diversion of water from Lake Tahoe into a series of privately owned irrigation projects in 1909. He followed these successes with a victorious campaign in 1910 for a congressional seat from Marin County.

During his three terms in Congress from 1911 to 1917, Kent achieved national stature as a fiercely dedicated and independent conservationist. His legislative efforts included the sponsorship of the 1916 act that created the NATIONAL PARK SERVICE as well as many proposals to restrict or regulate the use of grazing lands, mineral claims, and hydroelectric sites located in the public domain. Kent's disdain for party politics and for the many compromises required to shepherd bills through Congress, however, alienated many potential allies; the rejection of private enterprise, embodied in many of his bills, aroused overwhelming opposition among many Westerners. Kent's unswerving belief in the efficient and rational management of public lands even brought him into conflict, on occasion, with fellow conservationists such as JOHN MUIR. To free San Francisco from the baleful influence of a private water monopoly, for example, Kent supported the creation of a municipal reservoir inside YOSEMITE NATIONAL PARK by damming the Tuolumne River at Hetch Hetchy. As a sponsor of the 1913 Raker Act that finally authorized the dam, he helped bring that acrimonious dispute—the HETCH HETCHY CONTROVERSY—to an end.

Nominally a Progressive Republican, Kent had been elected to Congress for his second and third terms as an independent and had been a dedicated supporter of Woodrow Wilson, the Democratic presidential candidate in 1912. Again, with a lack of patience with political routines, Kent retired from Congress in 1917. He then accepted an appointment from the Wilson administration to the United States Tariff Commission on which he served until 1920. That year, he ran for the Republican nomination for a U.S. Senate seat for California and lost; the defeat marked the end of his involvement in electoral politics.

Kent remained active in conservation affairs for the rest of his life. He kept especially busy in the work of the Save-the-Redwoods League, which he had joined at its founding in 1918, and made a final donation of land to Muir Woods National Monument just before his death in 1928. During his lifetime, Kent's unrelenting advocacy of measures to institute rational management and use of the public domain involved him in bitter struggles over the proper ways to develop the West, while his unyielding sense of personal independence brought him into conflict with many other Progressives. In subsequent decades, however, Kent's vision helped shape the agenda of the conservation movement as it grew in strength and influence.

—*Peter J. Blodgett*

SEE ALSO: Progressivism

SUGGESTED READING:
Fox, Stephen. *John Muir and His Legacy: The American Conservation Movement.* Boston, 1981.

Hyde, Anne F. "William Kent: The Puzzle of Progressive Conservationists." In *California Progressivism Revisited.* Edited by William Deverell and Tom Sitton. Berkeley, Calif., 1994.

Nash, Roderick. *Wilderness and the American Mind.* 3d ed. New Haven, Conn., 1982.

KEOKUK (SAC AND FOX)

Born at Saukenak, the home of the Sac (Sauk) war chief Black Hawk located near present-day Rock Island, Illinois, Keokuk (ca. 1790–1848) was the son of a Sac warrior and a half-French mother. Despite hereditary injunctions among the Sac and Fox Indians against mixed-blood chiefs, Keokuk became a tribal leader owing to his considerable political skills and the backing of American officials, to whom he was fiercely loyal. Keokuk used his enchanting oratory and his manifest courage as a young man to gain recognition from the Sac and Fox council during the War of 1812. The two tribes' loose political structure and their emphasis on individual audacity provided the perfect opportunity for the ambitious Keokuk, who soon challenged the leadership of Black Hawk—an intrepid ally of the British—by heading a faction of Sac and Fox Indians wishing to accommodate the growing American demand that they remove themselves west of the Mississippi into their Iowa and Wisconsin hunting grounds and leave Illinois to white settlement. The rivalry ultimately culminated in BLACK HAWK'S WAR, which led to the older chief's capture, imprisonment, and public humiliation and to Keokuk's official installation under federal treaty as the civil chief of the Sac and Fox tribes. He began to fall from grace with the tribes when he made further cessions to the United States—cessions that led to the removal of many Sac and Fox Indians to reservation lands in Kansas. Late in his life, Keokuk proved to be intemperate, greedy, and autocratic, which created dissension and undermined the credibility of his leadership. After he died of dysentery following an alcoholic binge in 1848, his title passed to his son, Moses Keokuk, who like his father was an eloquent orator. Although Keokuk remained controversial among his own people, the United States recognized his many services by placing a bronze bust of him in the nation's Capitol building.

—*Charles Phillips*

SUGGESTED READING:
Hagan, William T. *The Sac and Fox Indians.* Norman, Okla., 1958.

KERN, EDWARD MEYER

Draftsman and water colorist Edward Meyer Kern (1823–1863) was employed as an artist with several Western surveys. He was born in Philadelphia and first exhibited there in 1841. In 1845, he accompanied explorer JOHN CHARLES FRÉMONT into the American Southwest and served in Frémont's California Battalion during the United States–Mexican War. With brothers Benjamin Kern, a medical officer, and Richard Hovendon Kern, who was also an artist, he joined Frémont's ill-fated expedition to the Colorado Rockies during the fall and winter of 1848 and 1849. During the trip, ten members of the party, including Benjamin Kern, died from sickness, exposure, and attacks by Ute Indians.

Richard and Edward Kern subsequently joined Lieutenant James H. Simpson of the U.S. Army CORPS OF TOPOGRAPHICAL ENGINEERS on a punitive campaign against the Navajos. Led by Colonel John M. Washington, military governor of New Mexico, the campaign took them through parts of Colorado, Utah, and Arizona, where they executed native portraits and drawings of ancient pueblo sites.

In June 1853, Edward Kern sailed with Captain Cadwalader Ringgold's exploratory expedition of the North Pacific and visited the Hawaiian Islands, Kamchatka, and Japan. Returning to San Francisco in 1855, he next accompanied Lieutenant John M. Brooke's survey of the sea lanes and coaling stations between California and China from 1857 to 1860. Kern was appointed captain of the topographical engineers in Missouri, again under Frémont, during the first months of the Civil War. When Frémont was relieved of his command, Kern returned to Philadelphia and spent his last days there as a drawing instructor.

Illustrations by Edward Kern appeared in a number of expeditionary reports published by the government in the 1850s. His original works are preserved at the Academy of Natural Sciences in Philadelphia, of which all three Kern brothers were members. His drawings and water colors are included in the collections of the Museum of Fine Arts in Boston, the Office of Naval Records in Washington, D.C.; the U.S. Naval Academy Museum in Annapolis, Maryland; the HUNTINGTON LIBRARY, ART COLLECTIONS, AND BOTANICAL GARDENS in San Marino, California; and the THOMAS GILCREASE INSTITUTE in Tulsa, Oklahoma.

—*David C. Hunt*

SEE ALSO: Art: Surveys and Expeditions

SUGGESTED READING:
Ewers, John C. *Artists of the Old West.* Enlarged ed. Garden City, N.Y., 1973.

Taft, Robert. *Artists and Illustrators of the Old West, 1850–1900*. Princeton, N.J., 1982.

Viola, Herman J. *Exploring the West*. Washington, D.C., 1987.

KERN, RICHARD HOVENDON

Western artist Richard Hovendon Kern (1821–1853) accompanied four major mapping and scientific expeditions to the West between 1848 and 1853. Published lithographs of some of his water colors and sketches gave Americans their first authentic views of native peoples and places in New Mexico, Arizona, Colorado, and Utah.

A trained draftsman who taught drawing at the Franklin Institute in his native Philadelphia, Kern first journeyed to the West at the age of twenty-seven as an artist on JOHN CHARLES FRÉMONT's fourth expedition. With a brother, Edward Kern, who had worked previously for Frémont, Richard survived a disaster in the Rockies that took ten lives, including that of another Kern brother, Benjamin. Rescued, Richard and Edward Kern made their way to Santa Fe, New Mexico. There, they joined Lieutenant James H. Simpson on the first official American reconnaissance of the Navajo country in 1849. The Kerns remained in New Mexico, and Richard found work that took him east to the Pecos River and south to Chihuahua. In the summer of 1851, Edward headed home, and Richard traveled across Arizona to California with another government exploring party, headed by Captain Lorenzo Sitgreaves.

Richard Kern returned to Philadelphia via Panama in early 1852. Recognized as an authority on the ethnology and topography of the Southwest, he won an appointment as artist on the thirty-eighth parallel railroad survey, led by John W. Gunnison. Kern's career ended in western Utah, where Indians killed him and Gunnison on October 26, 1853.

Kern was best known to his contemporaries through lithographs of his work that appeared in the published reports of Simpson, Sitgreaves, and Gunnison. His original sketches and water colors never appeared on exhibition during his lifetime. Most were presumed lost until they surfaced in the late 1950s and early 1960s, giving us a new appreciation of Kern the artist, rather than Kern the draftsman.

—*David J. Weber*

SEE ALSO: Art: Surveys and Expeditions

SUGGESTED READING:
Weber, David J. *Richard H. Kern: Expeditionary Artist in the Far Southwest, 1848–1853*. Albuquerque, N. Mex., 1985.

KERR, ROBERT SAMUEL

Robert Samuel Kerr (1896–1963), governor of Oklahoma and U.S. senator, was born in Ada, Indian Territory. He attended three Oklahoma colleges before becoming an artillery officer in World War I. After a brief legal practice in Ada, he entered the oil business with a series of companies that became Kerr-McGee.

Kerr won the Oklahoma governorship in his first race for elected office in 1942. He balanced the state's budget and paid off debts left from the Great Depression. Elected to the U.S. Senate in 1948, he championed the state's development through federal spending, particularly on water projects. He died while serving his third term.

—*Danney Goble*

SUGGESTED READING:
Morgan, Anne Hodges. *Robert S. Kerr: The Senate Years*. Norman, Okla., 1977.

KICKING BEAR (SIOUX)

A Minneconjou associate of CRAZY HORSE and participant in the Battles of the Rosebud, Little Bighorn,

Kicking Bear, an eloquent Sioux apostle of the Ghost Dance. *Courtesy Library of Congress.*

and Slim Buttes, Kicking Bear (ca. 1852–1904) garnered a considerable following among the Lakota as a
GHOST DANCE leader. He traveled from the Cheyenne
River Reservation to Nevada in 1890 to hear WOVOKA
and returned as one of the new religion's most ardent
adherents. His teaching skills earned him many followers and considerable notoriety. In October 1890,
SITTING BULL brought Kicking Bear to the Standing Rock
Reservation, but the government agent expelled him.
In late November, he and thousands of believers fled
to the Badlands "stronghold" after the arrival of troops
at Pine Ridge. Efforts to force their surrender failed
when word arrived of the December 29 massacre at
Wounded Knee. Along with SHORT BULL, another hold-
out, Kicking Bear did not surrender to General NELSON
APPLETON MILES until mid-January 1891 at the Pine
Ridge Agency. He was sent with other Ghost Dance
leaders to Fort Sheridan, near Chicago, Illinois, as a
military prisoner. WILLIAM F. ("BUFFALO BILL") CODY
persuaded the government to release Kicking Bear so
he could accompany his Wild West show on a European tour. Before his death, Kicking Bear returned to
teaching the Ghost Dance.

—*R. Eli Paul*

SEE ALSO: Little Bighorn, Battle of; Wounded Knee Massacre

SUGGESTED READING:
Jensen, Richard E., R. Eli Paul, and John E. Carter. *Eyewitness at Wounded Knee.* Lincoln, Nebr., 1991.

Kicking Bird urged his Kiowa tribesmen to make peace
with the U.S. government. *Courtesy National Archives.*

KICKING BIRD
(KIOWA)

A chief who signed treaties with the U.S. government
to establish reservations for Kiowas, Comanches, and
Kiowa-Apaches, Kicking Bird (ca. 1835–1875) was
three-quarters Kiowa and was descended from a Crow
captive, his paternal grandfather, who had been
adopted into the Kiowa tribe. His name (Tene-angpote)
actually means "Striking Eagle" or "Eagle Striking with
Talons."

A powerful proponent of peace and accommodation with whites, Kicking Bird signed the 1865 Little
Arkansas Treaty that first set aside a reservation for
the Kiowas and Comanches and the MEDICINE LODGE
TREATY OF 1867 that assigned the Kiowas, Comanches,
and Kiowa-Apaches a three-million-acre reservation
in the southwestern part of present-day Oklahoma.

Through his eloquence and forceful personality,
Kicking Bird faced down SATANTA, LONE WOLF, and

other war leaders and extended his influence over a
majority of the tribe. When his efforts to avert war
made him seem weak in the eyes of some tribesmen,
he led one hundred warriors on a raid into Texas and
fought a Sixth Cavalry patrol near present-day Seymour
in July 1870. He immediately regretted the action and
never again wavered in his efforts to promote peace.

With his cousin Stumbling Bear, Kicking Bird
calmed his angry warriors when Satanta, SATANK, and
BIG TREE were arrested at Fort Sill for their roles in the
1871 Warren Wagon Train Raid. Later, he returned
stolen mules and pleaded with authorities to release
the prisoners. In the 1930s, an elderly Kiowa told historian Wilbur Sturtevant Nye that "Kicking Bird must
have been appointed by God to lead his people during
these years, the most difficult ever faced by us."

During the summer of 1874, Kicking Bird resisted
pressure to join in the general outbreak of Comanches,
Cheyennes, and Arapahos. Following the Anadarko
Agency fight on August 22 and 23, he induced Big
Bow, Lone Wolf, and other Kiowas not living on the
reservation to surrender. Federal authorities recognized

Kicking Bird as principal chief and gave him the responsibility for selecting the prisoners to be sent to Florida.

He died suddenly on May 4, 1875, after drinking a cup of coffee at his lodge on Cedar Creek near Fort Sill. Nearing death, he stated: "I have taken the white man's road. I am not sorry for it. Tell my people to keep the good path. I am dying holding fast the white man's hand." Agency officials suspected that he had been poisoned, but many Kiowas attributed his death to witchcraft.

—*Bruce J. Dinges*

SEE ALSO: Central Plains Indian Wars

SUGGESTED READING:

Nye, Wilbur S. *Carbine and Lance: The Story of Old Fort Sill.* Norman, Okla., 1974.

———. *Plains Indian Raiders: The Final Phases of Warfare from the Arkansas to the Red River.* Norman, Okla., 1968.

KIMBALL, HEBER CHASE

Heber Chase Kimball (1801–1868), Mormon apostle and dedicated polygamist, was early Mormon history's most colorful leader after JOSEPH SMITH, JR., and BRIGHAM YOUNG. Born in Sheldon Town, Vermont, Kimball moved in 1811 with his family to West Bloomfield, New York, where he attended school briefly and became a potter and blacksmith. In 1820, he moved to nearby Mendon, New York, where he became a mason, married Vilate Murray, and met his lifelong friend Brigham Young.

His move to Mendon occurred during the Great Revival in western New York. Kimball joined the Baptist church in 1832. Later that year, he first heard Mormon missionaries preach, and he moved to Kirtland, Ohio, the headquarters of the new church officially known as the CHURCH OF JESUS CHRIST OF LATTER-DAY SAINTS.

Subsequently, Kimball participated in eight Mormon missions between 1832 and 1841, including two in England. These trips brought him the appellation "first Mormon in the Old World." In 1834, he participated in the Zion's Camp March from Ohio to Missouri. The march was an attempt to restore Missouri MORMONS to their lands in Jackson County—lands from which Missouri mobs had driven them. A year later, Kimball became a member of the First Quorum of Twelve Apostles, which generally governed church affairs. In 1838, he followed church headquarters to Missouri, and after the Mormons were driven out of

that state during the winter of 1838 to 1839, he helped create a new headquarters in NAUVOO, ILLINOIS.

Seven years later, the Mormons were driven from Illinois, and Kimball crossed the plains three times between 1846 and 1848 to Utah. In December 1847, he was named first counselor to Brigham Young, who succeeded Joseph Smith as president of the church.

Kimball married forty-three wives by whom he had sixty-five children and at least three hundred grandchildren. In Utah, he amassed land, cattle, and property and participated fully in the political, economic, social, and cultural development of the New Zion. He became chief justice of the unofficial state of Deseret in 1849, served in the territorial legislature from 1851 to 1858, and generally presided over all temple work, assisted in colonizing, and fostered economic independence. He died after being thrown from his wagon; his funeral was the largest ever held in the Utah Territory.

—*Stanley B. Kimball*

SUGGESTED READING:

Kimball, Stanley B. *Heber C. Kimball: Mormon Patriarch and Pioneer.* Urbana, Ill., 1988.

Whitney, Orson F. *Life of Heber C. Kimball.* Salt Lake City, 1888.

KIMBALL, J. GOLDEN

Mule skinner, hierarch, and folk hero, the irrepressible J. Golden Kimball (1853–1938) was a Mormon church leader from 1892 to 1938. Born in Salt Lake City, he was the son of BRIGHAM YOUNG's outspoken counselor, Heber Chase Kimball. He lived in Salt Lake City until his father's death in 1868 and then ranched in Bear Lake Valley until educator Karl G. Maesar, in 1881, awakened in him a latent sense for learning. Kimball then attended Brigham Young Academy, defused anti-Mormon hostility as a missionary, and, in 1892, was ordained to the Council of the Seventy. He fed delighted Mormon audiences with "bread and milk and cayenne pepper." He suffered chronic illness and healed others but, by his own admission, had faith sufficient barely to keep himself alive. He was an independent spirit, a splendid performer, a wit among sober preachers, and a beloved leader.

—*Charles S. Peterson*

SUGGESTED READING:

Cheney, Thomas E. *The Golden Legacy: A Folk History of J. Golden Kimball.* Salt Lake City, 1974.

Richards, Claude. *J. Golden Kimball: The Story, Sayings, and Sermons of a Unique Personality.* Salt Lake City, 1951.

KING, CHARLES

Army officer, novelist, and historian Charles King (1844–1933) served in the regular army and the Wisconsin National Guard. He rose to the grade of major general by his retirement in 1931. His seventy years of service and duty in five wars remains unmatched in American military annals.

King's enduring legacy, however, comes from his work as a novelist and historian. He wrote seventy-four books between 1880 and 1914, including the acclaimed *Campaigning with Crook* (1880), *The Colonel's Daughter* (1883), and *Laramie; or, The Queen of Bedlam* (1889). In such LITERATURE, he fashioned a sympathetic if romantic view of the army and its people. His portrait of life on the frontier was transformed into FILM as John Ford's trilogy *She Wore a Yellow Ribbon*, *Rio Grande*, and *Fort Apache*.

—*Paul L. Hedren*

SUGGESTED READING:
Russell, Don. *Campaigning with King: Charles King, Chronicler of the Old Army.* Edited by Paul L. Hedren. Lincoln, Nebr., and London, 1991.

KING, CHARLES BIRD

Although he never visited the West, Charles Bird King (1785–1862) is an important figure in Western art history because of the large number of American Indian portraits he painted between 1822 and 1842. Born in Newport, Rhode Island, King received his earliest artistic instruction there from Samuel King, who was not a relation. At the age of fifteen, King moved to New York, where he was apprenticed for five years to the portraitist and engraver Edward Savage. He moved to London in 1806 and studied at the Royal Academy under Benjamin West.

After returning to America in 1812, King practiced in several Eastern cities before establishing himself in 1819 in Washington, D.C., where his studio and gallery became an artistic center. He painted portraits of national leaders as well as landscape, genre, still-life, and literary and historical pictures.

In the winter of 1821 to 1822, King painted the first of more than 140 Indian portraits for Thomas L. McKenney, superintendent of the Bureau of Indian Affairs. McKenney brought leaders of potentially hostile Western tribes to Washington to impress them with American power and wealth. Sitting for a portrait destined for McKenney's "Archives of the American Indian" was an additional honor for the visiting Native Americans.

In 1858, the Indian portraits were moved to the Smithsonian Institution, where most were burned in 1865. Many, however, are preserved in copies, and all are reproduced as hand-colored lithographs in McKenney's *Indian Tribes of North America* (1837–1844), for which James Hall wrote biographical texts.

King's engaging personality, generosity, and high moral principles were admired by contemporaries. William Dunlap, however, thought that "nature [had] stinted him" in talent, and Henry Tuckerman characterized King's works as "not remarkable for artistic superiority, but often curious and valuable as likenesses, especially the Indian portraits." Since the 1970s, scholars have judged King as a painter of modest ambitions who failed to realize his full potential.

—*Joan Carpenter Troccoli*

SEE ALSO: Art: Western Art

SUGGESTED READING:
Cosentino, Andrew J. *The Paintings of Charles Bird King (1785–1862).* Washington, D.C., 1977.
Ewers, John C. "Charles Bird King, Painter of Indian Visitors to the Nation's Capital." *Annual Report of the Smithsonian Institution* (1953): 463–473.
McKenney, Thomas L., and James Hall. *The Indian Tribes of North America, with Biographical Sketches and Anecdotes of the Principal Chiefs.* Edited by Fredrick Webb Hodge. Edinburgh, 1933.
Viola, Herman J. *The Indian Legacy of Charles Bird King.* Washington, D.C., 1976.

KING, CLARENCE

Geologist Clarence King (1842-1901) was the head of the United States Geological Survey of the Fortieth Parallel (known as the "Fortieth Parallel Survey") and first director of the UNITED STATES GEOLOGICAL SURVEY.

Born in Newport, Rhode Island, King attended the Sheffield Scientific School at Yale University. He and his classmate James Terry Gardner headed west after graduation. They examined the mines at Virginia City, Nevada, and then went to California where they worked for the California Geological Survey. By the time this work ended, King had envisioned leading a geological survey from the Rocky Mountains to the Sierra Nevada following the approximate route of the Pacific Railroad. He got approval for his survey and was made its director under the supervision of the army chief of engineers. He and his team began field work in 1867. In 1880, the last of seven scientific publications encompassing their work and an atlas were published.

Clarence King. *Courtesy Library of Congress.*

The most publicized incident of King's survey was his exposure of the GREAT DIAMOND HOAX. In 1872, two miners claimed to have found diamonds in the remote northwestern corner of Colorado. After considerable detective work, King found the site, proved the claim to be a hoax, and exposed it to the public.

After serving nearly two years as the first director of the United States Geological Survey, into which the Fortieth Parallel Survey was merged, King resigned to try to make his fortune as a mining engineer. He was quite a *bon vivant*: chicken à la King is so named because he introduced the recipe to the chef at the Century Club in New York City.

—*Richard A. Bartlett*

SEE ALSO: Exploration and Science

SUGGESTED READING:
Bartlett, Richard A. *Great Surveys of the American West.* Norman, Okla., 1962.
Wilkins, Thurman. *Clarence King: A Biography.* New York, 1958. Reprint. Albuquerque, N. Mex., 1988.

KING, RICHARD

Founder of the KING RANCH in Texas, Richard King (1824–1885) was born in Orange County, New York. In 1835, he ran away from his apprenticeship to a jeweler and stowed away on a ship. Over the next six years, he worked his way up to river-boat pilot. He fought in the Seminole War, and during the United States–Mexican War, he transported supplies to ZACHARY TAYLOR's forces on the Rio Grande.

In 1852, King bought the Santa Gertrudis Spanish land grant in South Texas, half of which he sold in 1860 to MIFFLIN KENEDY, whom he had met in Florida. During the Civil War, Kenedy and King sold Confederate cotton in Mexico and established the base of their fortunes. After the war, the two men ended their partnership. King kept the Santa Gertrudis territory, which became the nucleus for the mammoth King Ranch.

—*Patrick H. Butler, III*

SUGGESTED READING:
Lea, Tom. *The King Ranch.* 2 vols. Boston, 1957.

KING, THOMAS STARR

Unitarian clergyman and public lecturer Thomas Starr King (1824–1864) was born in New York City and did not move to the Far West until the last four years of his life. Nevertheless, at the time of his death from diphtheria and pneumonia in San Francisco, he was so highly regarded by Californians that the state legislature and courts recessed in order for officials to join the thousands of people who attended his funeral.

His lack of formal education was a barrier to his advancement in New England's Unitarian circles, so the ambitious King was lured to San Francisco. Heading west with a reputation as a compelling preacher and public lecturer, he accepted a call to the pastorate of the First Unitarian Church of San Francisco in 1860.

Provincial San Franciscans tended to favor talent over formal credentials, but many also wanted Eastern-based "culture" to legitimate themselves. King's urbane rhetoric and theology, tinged with transcendentalism, instantly won him widespread popularity and powerful parishioners such as AMASA LELAND STANFORD and JESSIE ANN BENTON FRÉMONT. As a religious leader, he was a major figure in the institutional and cultural establishment of liberal Protestantism in the urban Far West.

He was equally effective as a political publicist. His years in California coincided with the Civil War, and his impassioned lectures extolling patriotism and the Union evoked broad support that fed the electoral victories of the state's Republican party. His work also helped raise more than $1.2 million over three years for the wartime work of the U.S. Sanitary Commission. In addition, his lecturing and letters to the *Boston Transcript* popularized the California landscape, foreshadowing the writings of conservationist JOHN MUIR. Two mountains have been named for King, one in YOSEMITE NATIONAL PARK and the other in the White Mountains of New Hampshire. In 1927, he was selected to be one of California's two representatives in Statuary Hall in Washington, D.C. The Unitarian seminary for the Western United States is also named for King.

—*Douglas Firth Anderson*

SUGGESTED READING:
Frankiel, Sandra Sizer. *California's Spiritual Frontiers: Religious Alternatives in Anglo-Protestantism, 1850–1910.* Berkeley, Calif., 1988.
Monzingo, Robert. *Thomas Starr King: Eminent Californian, Civil War Statesman, Unitarian Minister.* Pacific Grove, Calif., 1991.
Peterson, Richard. "Thomas Starr King in California, 1860–64: Forgotten Naturalist of the Civil War." *California History* 49 (1990): 12–21, 79–80.

KING RANCH

In 1805, the king of Spain granted Don José Lorenzo de la Garza and his two sons land that would become the King Ranch. Located forty-five miles southwest of Corpus Christi, Texas, along the banks of the Santa Gertrudis Creek, the land changed hands in the early 1850s to RICHARD KING and his first partner G. K. ("Legs") Lewis. After Lewis's death on April 14, 1855, King acquired full title to the property, which he shared in a partnership with MIFFLIN KENEDY between 1860 and 1868. During this time, the ranch adopted the running *W* as its brand.

With the death of King in 1885, Robert Justus Kleberg became manager of the ranch. He later married Alice, King's youngest daughter. Descendants of the Kings and the Klebergs continue today as stockholders in the ranch.

Over the years, ranch managers have engaged in cattle and horse breeding. The most famous result of this work was the Santa Gertrudis cow, a cross between Brahman and shorthorn cattle especially adapted to the South Texas climate.

During the twentieth century, the ranch expanded its interests by allying with Humble Oil and Refining. It also bred racehorses and included a timber operation. Ranch managers operated cattle businesses in Cuba, until the Cuban Revolution, and in Australia.

They also maintained substantial banking and mercantile interests in Kingsville, Texas.

Into the late twentieth century, the ranch operated its own archives and actively supported agricultural education at Texas A & I University in Kingsville and Texas A & M University in College Station. It also championed a variety of wildlife preservation projects.

—*Patrick H. Butler, III*

SUGGESTED READING:
Lea, Tom. *The King Ranch.* 2 vols. Boston, 1957.

KINGS CANYON NATIONAL PARK

SEE: Sequoia National Park

KINNEY, HENRY LAWRENCE

Entrepreneur and filibuster Henry Lawrence Kinney (1814–1862) was born in Wyoming Valley, Pennsylvania. A veteran of BLACK HAWK'S WAR and the Seminole Wars, he migrated to Illinois and then to South Texas, where he was engaged in land speculation and trade by 1840. He later dabbled in ranching, shipping, and meat packing and founded the town of Corpus Christi. Politically active, Kinney was elected to the senate of the Republic of Texas and later served four terms in the state legislature.

A quartermaster officer in the United States–Mexican War, the visionary merchant-adventurer mounted an unsuccessful filibustering expedition to Nicaragua in 1855. During the Civil War, Kinney, a Unionist, left Texas and was killed in Matamoros, Mexico, by an unknown assailant.

—*B. Byron Price*

SUGGESTED READING:
Brown, Charles H. *Agents of Manifest Destiny: The Lives and Times of the Filibusters.* Chapel Hill, N.C., 1980.
McCampbell, Coleman. *Saga of a Frontier Seaport.* New York, 1952.
Thrall, Homer S. *A Pictorial History of Texas.* 2d ed. St. Louis, Mo., 1879.

KINO, EUSEBIO FRANCISCO

Jesuit missionary and explorer Eusebio Francisco Kino (1644–1711) was born in Italy's Tyrol. He directed the establishment of Spanish missions among the Pima Indians in Pimeria Alta (present-day northern Sonora, Mexico, and southern Arizona) and in the process introduced the livestock culture that formed the basis of the CATTLE INDUSTRY of the American Southwest.

Although Kino was an Italian, he entered a German Jesuit order in 1665 and gained full admission to the Society of Jesus in 1669. He soon distinguished himself as a scholar specializing in mathematics, CARTOGRAPHY, and astronomy. In 1678, he decided to leave the world of scholarship for the hard life of a New World missionary. He left Genoa but did not arrive in Mexico until 1681. In 1683, Kino was commissioned royal cosmographer and attached to an expedition led by Admiral Isidro de Atondo y Antillon in an ill-fated attempt to colonize Baja California. The expedition did give Kino the opportunity to map the region accurately, and he was able to demonstrate that California was not an island, as had been believed.

After the Baja California enterprise, Kino began his extended mission to the Pima Indians in Pimeria Alta. Establishing a headquarters at Nuestra Senora de los Dolores in Sonora in 1687, he founded, in the greater Sonora region, twenty-four missions, including Guevavi (1691), the first of the Arizona missions; Tumacacori (1687), now a U.S. national monument; and the magnificent San Xavier del Bac (1700) near Tucson. In addition, Kino was an active and systematic explorer. He applied his skills as a cartographer to mapping the frontiers of New Spain, thereby promoting the northern advance of the Spanish colonial empire. Traveling twenty-five to seventy-five miles per day, he covered perhaps twenty thousand miles during his Southwestern career and mapped, in particular, the Altar, Sonora, Santa Cruz, and San Pedro rivers as well as the lower Gila River and the Colorado. His 1705 map served as the standard reference for the area for more than a century. Tireless and merciless with himself, he established the basis for twenty of today's Southwestern American cities.

Kino held his Pima charges in high regard and worked vigorously to establish missions and to diversify Pima agriculture. He introduced not only many varieties of livestock into the Southwest but also European grains, grapes, and pomegranates. He expanded the exploitation of the region's mineral wealth by establishing an efficient system of pack trains to transport ore. He also aided the Pimas in their continual warfare with marauding Apaches.

Kino was still traveling in 1711, when he died in the mission village of Santa Magdalena.

—*Alan Axelrod*

SEE ALSO: Missions: Early Franciscan and Jesuit Missions

SUGGESTED READING:
Bolton, Hubert E. *Rim of Christendom*. New York, 1936.
Kessel, John L. *Father Kino in Arizona*. Tempe, Ariz., 1966.
Rockwood, Francis Cummins. *With Father Kino on the Trail.* Tucson, Ariz., 1936.

KIOWA INDIANS

SEE: Native American Peoples: Peoples of the Great Plains

KLAMATH INDIANS

SEE: Native American Peoples: Peoples of the Pacific Northwest

KLIKITAT INDIANS

SEE: Native American Peoples: Peoples of the Pacific Northwest

KLONDIKE GOLD RUSH

Prospectors had first begun looking for gold in Canada's remote and rugged Yukon Territory around 1870, and after nearly thirty years, perhaps twenty-five hundred of them had been able to scratch out a million dollars worth of placer ore around Circle City in ALASKA and Forty Mile (forty miles from the area's main trading post) in Canada. Then in late summer of 1896, two men investigating a tributary of the YUKON RIVER made significant finds that launched one of the last and maybe the wildest of the nineteenth century's many gold rushes. Canadian Robert Henderson came across his more modest find in mid-August along one of the tributary's streams, which he dubbed "Gold Bottom Creek." Shortly afterward and ten miles away on Rabbit Creek, the San Francisco-born son of a Forty-niner, George Washington Carmack, and two Indian friends came upon a far richer find. Carmack, Skookum Jim, and Taglish Charlie scooped up enough dust to fill an empty shotgun shell, marked a nearby spruce tree to stake their claim, and headed off for the NORTH WEST MOUNTED POLICE post at Forty Mile to record their discovery. The Indians called the little tributary both groups had been traipsing the Thorn-Diuck, but tongues trained to enunciate European syllables had a

From 1897 to 1899, thousands of fortune-seekers jammed the White Pass trail leading to the Klondike gold fields. *Courtesy Special Collections Division, University of Washington Libraries.*

tough time with the Taglishes' guttural sounds, and when white prospectors tried to say the word it came out "Klondike."

From the moment Carmack walked into the Forty Mile claims' office, the news spread down the Yukon Valley. Within a fortnight, American and Canadian prospectors had staked dozens of five-hundred-foot claims along Rabbit Creek, which they rechristened Bonanza Creek, and spread out along a promising bank they dubbed, naturally, Eldorado Creek. The word reached the United States the following July 1897, when—after a winter of digging—several dozen miners brought their gold down the American West Coast. They caught small fur-trade steamers to the mouth of the Yukon on the Bering Sea, then grabbed ships plying the ocean and sailed south, and at last trundled into Seattle and San Francisco. As they debarked, local citizens—suffering through the long depression caused by the panic of 1893—were mesmerized by the riches the miners lugged ashore. The rush was on.

The best route to the Klondike lay back the way the miners had come: by ship to the Yukon delta, then by steamboat downriver to Dawson City, the boom town headquarters of the gold rush. But the few steamboats were small; the river filled with ice in winter and

became impassable; and ship fares to Alaska immediately inflated. In Seattle, for example, tickets jumped from two hundred to two thousand dollars almost overnight. Most people sailed only to Dyea and Skagway in lower Alaska, tent cities without amenities or natural harbors. There, the Klondikers headed on foot over the Alaskan coastal range, using the White Pass or the Chilkoot Pass through the mountains. On the other side, they built crude boats and sailed or paddled five hundred miles north to Dawson up a chain of lakes and rivers. The trek looked simple enough on a map, but the Chilkoot was subject to avalanches and riddled with glacial fissures, the White Pass's trails were steep and, in places, barely two feet wide, and Miles Canyon on the Yukon boasted raging white-water rapids. Ottawa's officials braced for the onslaught by beefing up Canada's Mounted Police at Fort Constantine and passing restrictions that called for each prospector to carry a half-year's supply of rations. Added to the already heavy burden of overpriced mining equipment, that meant shouldering eleven hundred pounds of goods into the wilderness, or paying for mules and their transport aboard ship, or at least hiring local Indians, who profited from portage fees and pilfered goods.

As the Klondikers poured into the Yukon in the winter of 1897 to 1898, so many pack animals died on the way that the travelers took to calling the Chilkoot "Dead Horse Pass"; abandoned gear clogged the trails as prospectors realized it would take thirty-five trips up the mountains just to bring in what Ottawa required; and the number of North West Mounted Police kept growing. Miles Canyon had claimed ten lives before the Mounties introduced stringent new safety measures and forced all women to make portage rather than run the rapids. Once the gold-seekers reached Dawson City, they discovered little gold but some very sobering truths: digging for gold through ten to fifty feet of permafrost was not the same as picking up placer nuggets from the stream beds of California; sphagnum moss, or muskeg, which covered the ground, produced, in spring, particularly rapacious mosquitoes; the Yukon was blanketed in twilight and dark for much of the year; and it was colder than they could ever have imagined.

By the time the rush was over in 1899, some three hundred members of the North West Mounted Police ranged the Yukon, urging those who had failed to bring proper rations—or who had abandoned food rather than equipment along the way—to go home. Perhaps one hundred thousand people had by then left the states headed for the Klondike; perhaps forty thousand of them actually reached Dawson. Exhausted and disenchanted, only half of them looked for gold, and only one in ten found any. A few hundred lucky people picked up enough gold to get rich. Food and equipment probably cost the whole crowd of Klondikers between $30 million and $60 million, while the Klondike's total gold yield in 1898 was somewhere around $10 million. Dawson became a rude and crowded metropolis for a year, from July 1898 to about July 1899. As the Klondikers lost heart and dragged themselves back to the United States or settled down in Alaska, the large corporations moved in and dredged up most of the gold, a grand total of about $300 mil-

Top: Alaska's hazardous Chilkoot Pass to the Klondike. *Courtesy Special Collections Division, University of Washington Libraries.*

Bottom: Dawson City, a raw mining town by any standards, made some semblance of propriety. The city forced its ladies of pleasure to locate their cribs across the Klondike River. *Courtesy Special Collections Division, University of Washington Libraries.*

lion. A few of the Klondikers later achieved some fame—Alexander Pantages became a movie magnate; Tex Rickard, a well-known fight promoter; Sid

Grauman, the owner of Hollywood's Chinese Theater; August Mack, the maker of a powerful line of trucks; and John Chaney (Jack) London, the chronicler of the Northwest wilderness—but most of them slipped back into the obscurity from which they sprang after having (to paraphrase a letter one of them wrote home) never worked harder, or bore more, and accomplished less in their lives.

—*Charles Phillips*

See also: Alaska Gold Rush; Gold Mining

Suggested reading:
Berton, Pierre. *The Klondike Fever.* New York, 1958. Reprint. 1985.
Coates, Ken S., and William R. Morrison. *The Land of the Midnight Sun: A History of the Yukon.* Edmonton, Alberta, 1988.
Marks, Paula Mitchell. *Precious Dust: The American Gold Rush Era, 1848–1900.* New York, 1994.
Murray, Keith. *Reindeer and Gold.* Bellingham, Wash., 1988.

KNOW-NOTHING PARTY

Growing out of the nativist anti-immigrant and anti–Roman Catholic sentiment in Northeastern cities during the 1840s, the Know-Nothing party was formed by members of the secret Order of the Star Spangled Banner, which had been organized by 1849 in New York City and spread to other centers. Although its official name was the American party, the group was called "Know-Nothing" because the response of members to questions from outsiders was "I know nothing." Growing rapidly in the early 1850s and providing a home for members of the foundering Whig party and conservatives uncomfortable with both proslavery Democrats and antislavery Republicans, the party did well in state and local elections. In response to the debate over the Kansas-Nebraska Act, the party held forty-three seats in the House of Representatives in 1855.

Although the group's membership was primarily in the East, the party had adherents in the West, where it won municipal elections in San Antonio and Galveston, Texas, in 1854. With the backing of Sam Houston, the party's nominee for the Texas governorship came within four thousand votes of winning in 1855. Yet the party began to decline after its national convention endorsed the Kansas-Nebraska Act in 1855. In 1856, when its national convention refused to call for a prohibition on the expansion of slavery, the antislavery delegates stormed out and merged with the Republicans. The remaining members, more concerned with support for the Union and nativist issues than with antislavery, ran former President Millard Fillmore as their candidate in the presidential campaign of 1856. Fillmore received 25 percent of the popular vote but carried only one state, Maryland. Failure to achieve legislation aimed against immigrants and Roman Catholics, combined with a split on slavery, led to the party's disappearance after the 1856 election. Yet, its issues remained important in American politics.

—*Patrick H. Butler, III*

Suggested reading:
Billington, Ray A. *The Protestant Crusade, 1800–1860.* Chicago, 1964.
Mandelbaum, Seymour J. *The Social Setting of Intolerance: The Know-Nothings, the Red Scare, and McCarthyism.* Chicago, 1964.

KOHRS, CONRAD

Cattleman Conrad Kohrs (1835–1920) became one of Montana's pioneer livestock magnates, even as he diversified his other economic investments. Born in Wewelsfleth, Holstein, Germany, Kohrs went to sea at the age of fourteen. In 1852, he landed at New York City and moved to Davenport, Iowa, in 1853. He worked on the Mississippi River as a flat-boater and then joined his brother as a retail butcher. Between 1857 and 1861, Kohrs mined on the West Coast and made and lost several fortunes. He reached Montana's Deer Lodge Valley in 1862 and immediately became a butcher in the gold-rush camp of Bannack. He followed the boom to Virginia City in 1863. There he established a very profitable butchering business and served in the vigilante eradication of William Henry Plummer and his gang of "Innocents."

In 1865, Kohrs returned to the Deer Lodge Valley and became a cattle raiser, purchaser, and supplier of gold-camp butcher shops across the territory. He purchased Johnny Grant's ranch in 1866 and embarked on an ambitious cattle-breeding program. Kohrs purchased thousands of additional acres in the valley and then brought the first shorthorn cattle to Montana in 1871. In 1882, he introduced the first purebred Herefords to the territory.

With his half-brother, John N. W. Bielenberg, Kohrs also pioneered open-range cattle methods along the Sun River. They experimented with hay cutting, winter feeding, and fenced-range operations—techniques that protected their cattle during the "Hard Winter of 1886–1887," which devastated the Montana livestock industry. Between 1890 and 1910, Kohrs annually

Conrad Kohrs. *Courtesy Montana Historical Society.*

shipped as many as nine thousand head to the Chicago market.

Kohrs also invested in mining ventures. He financed the construction of the thirteen-mile Rock Creek Ditch, which provided water for his hydraulic-mining operations at Pioneer. The significant profits he earned from his mines at Cable funded the expansion of his livestock holdings.

A staunch and active Republican, Kohrs maintained an interest in civic affairs and politics. He was elected a Deer Lodge County commissioner, serving from 1869 to 1872, and a member of the Montana Assembly in 1885, as well as a delegate to the 1889 constitutional convention.

Because of his fundamental, farsighted approach to livestock raising, his success brought him the title of "the cattle king of Montana." He exemplified the early Western entrepreneur who worked hard, provided a quality product to the public at a fair price, and thoughtfully expanded his operations. In an exceedingly risky business, Kohrs succeeded because he demanded quality on all levels.

—*David A. Walter*

Suggested reading:
"Conrad Kohrs." In A *History of Montana,* Vol. 3. Edited by Merrill G. Burlingame and K. Ross Toole. New York, 1957.

Gill, Larry. "From Butcher Boy to Beef King: The Gold Camp Days of Conrad Kohrs." *Montana: The Magazine of Western History* 8 (April 1958): 40–55.
Kohrs, Conrad. *Conrad Kohrs: An Autobiography.* Deer Lodge, Mont., 1977.

KRUTTSCHNITT, JULIUS

Chairman of the Southern Pacific Railroad, Julius Kruttschnitt (1854–1925) was born in New Orleans and educated at Washington and Lee University in Virginia. After teaching school for five years in Baltimore, he became a railroader in 1873. By 1901, he was a senior manager of the Southern Pacific in San Francisco when Edward Henry Harriman gained control of the vast enterprise. Eventually Kruttschnitt became chairman of the Southern Pacific. Quiet, dignified, patient, and courteous, he was a nationally respected spokesman for the railroad industry. He announced his resignation in April 1925 and died unexpectedly on June 15 the same year. At the moment of his interment, Southern Pacific trains across the system paused in their routes in tribute to Kruttschnitt.

—*Don L. Hofsommer*

Suggested reading:
"The Career of Julius Kruttschnitt." *Railway Age* 78 (June 1925): 1459–1462.
Hofsommer, Don L. *The Southern Pacific, 1901–1985.* College Station, Tex., 1986.

KU KLUX KLAN

Although the original Ku Klux Klan of the Reconstruction period of the 1860s and 1870s never developed a significant following in the West, the second manifestation of the secret order—The Knights of the Ku Klux Klan (Inc.)—succeeded in recruiting tens of thousands of Westerners during the 1920s. Founded in 1915, the second Klan restricted its membership to native-born white male Protestants and espoused a militant program that called for white supremacy, immigration restriction, strict enforcement of the law, and Protestant solidarity. A relatively small group during the first few years of its existence, the Klan launched, in 1920, a recruiting campaign that eventually increased its membership to more than three million, approximately 6 percent of whom resided west of the Rocky Mountains.

Klan recruiters first began soliciting members in the West in early 1921. Their efforts were particularly successful in California, where scores of klaverns (Klan chapters) soon flourished from Sacramento to San Diego. In late 1922, however, state officials acquired and released the names of the entire California Klan's membership, a setback that prevented the order from becoming a major influence in the "Golden State." The Klan developed a more enduring following in the state of Washington, where an emphasis on anti-Catholicism garnered thousands of recruits in Seattle, Spokane, Tacoma, and numerous smaller communities. The statewide rejection of a compulsory public school measure in 1924, however, signaled the Klan's incipient decline in Washington.

The Klan achieved its most striking success in the West in Oregon and Colorado. Establishing klaverns in almost every sizable community, including a fifteen-thousand-member chapter in Portland, the Oregon Klan rapidly evolved into a powerful political machine that elected a Klan-affiliated governor and secured passage of a law prohibiting parochial schools in 1922. Operating largely out of Denver, the Colorado Klan scored even greater electoral triumphs two years later, when two U.S. senators, a governor, and many other state and local officials associated with the Klan were elected. Yet, in both Colorado and Oregon, political success resulted in internal feuding that greatly reduced the secret order's appeal; by 1925, its membership was rife with dissent, and the second Klan was in severe and permanent decline in these two states.

The Klan possessed certain distinctive characteristics in the West. For the most part, members were nonviolent and were drawn from the socio-economic mainstream. Although certainly racist and religiously bigoted, the great majority of Klan members sincerely hoped to use the organization to improve their community and nation. The Klan also was a movement that was largely urban. In the West's more remote and rural regions—New Mexico, Arizona, Nevada, and Idaho, for example—the organization either failed to take root or never became a major factor in public affairs.

Since the second Klan's decline in the mid-1920s, no Klan group has developed a mass following in the West, although small pockets of Klansmen have occasionally appeared since the 1970s. Nevertheless, contemporary racial tensions, anti-immigrant sentiment, and the growth of other white-supremacist groups in the West indicate that the attitudes and impulses that once sustained the Klan remain viable.

—*Shawn Lay*

SEE ALSO: Compulsory School Law, Oregon (1922)

SUGGESTED READING:
Jackson, Kenneth T. *The Ku Klux Klan in the City, 1915–1930.* New York, 1967.
Lay, Shawn., ed. *The Invisible Empire in the West: Toward a New Historical Appraisal of the Ku Klux Klan of the 1920s.* Urbana, Ill., 1992.

KWAIKUT INDIANS

SEE: Native American Peoples: Peoples of the Pacific Northwest

KWALHIOGUA INDIANS

SEE: Native American Peoples: Peoples of the Pacific Northwest

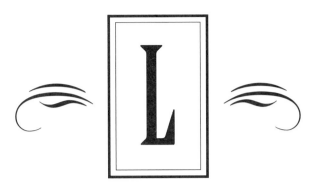

LABOR MOVEMENT

The working class in the West

Working life in the nineteenth-century trans-Mississippi West had a distinct regional character, different from that of the industrial centers of the East and the Old Northwest. As historian Carlos A. Schwantes has pointed out, that distinctiveness was determined by the "island" settlement of the region. The population was concentrated in business or agricultural enclaves based on a local economy (that is, on a specific industry or a particular crop or group of crops), and the whole region depended on extractive industries tied to natural resources, industries that were infamous for recurring boom-and-bust cycles and for seasonal employment. From the wheat fields to the oil fields, from the hard-rock mines to the lumber mills, from the cattle ranges to the canneries, an army of itinerant workers supplied the sweat and muscle that produced profits from the West's forests, plains, oceans, and mountains; they drilled the region's wells, dug its mines, loaded its ships, built its railroads, constructed its dams and canals, drove its cattle, and picked its fruit, vegetables, and grains. And, as Richard White has pointed out, although this army's wage labor was a keystone of Western economic development because the corporations that shaped and dominated the industrial landscape depended on their work, most people in the nineteenth-century West did not work for wages at all.

Family farms depended on household labor, not on wages; small merchants—saloonkeepers, general-store owners, livery operators—and most professionals were self-employed; and the majority of women received no wages for the work they did. Some people worked both in the wage-labor system and as self-employed or household laborers. Men frequently left the farm to work for a season in factories, mines, or mills or for large agribusinesses, and some miners spent at least part of the year trying to supplement their wages by working individual claims and leases. Single women might work as domestics, laundresses, seamstresses, and teachers; young women were sometimes pressed by families into agricultural labor. Married women, while their work usually remained tied to the home—to the feeding of families, caring for children, and the cleaning and running of households—occasionally combined domestic labor and wage work, particularly African American women, who worked mainly as domestic servants or laundry workers. In urban areas, fewer Hispanic women worked for wages, although in the Southwest, they often worked part-time as *vendadoras,* who sold prepared foods, handicrafts, and household wares in the marketplace. Profit making for women was, in general, centered around the home: some urban women took in boarders or turned their dining rooms into eateries, while most farm women and ranch wives produced butter and eggs for market and took up small domestic manufactures. The work was supplemental until the men fell ill or deserted their families, in which case the women frequently assumed full responsibility for the economic welfare of the family. Working-class wives tended vegetable gardens, kept chickens and sometimes a cow, made clothes, cleaned house, did the laundry, and, when they became widows or ex-wives, if they could not manage a rooming house or run a restaurant, sometimes took up PROSTITUTION or became dance-hall girls; they did not, however, typically work as laborers even if their lives consisted of hard labor.

White claims that within this larger work world, wage labor took on something of a privileged position in the West. While occasional labor might allow marginal households to survive, "the most vigorous sectors of the developing economy depended entirely on wage labor." Western business had to offer higher wages than Eastern employers in order to attract workers, and despite higher costs of living, Western wage workers earned higher real incomes than Eastern la-

The poor working conditions in Western mines drove many miners into the ranks of the United Mine Workers and other labor organizations. Miners in Trinidad, Colorado, armed for battle during the lead-mine strikes of 1914. *Courtesy The Bettmann Archive.*

borers. The work, however, was not steady, and the severe fluctuations of the Western business cycle, made more pronounced by the developing nature of the economy, periodically threw large numbers of men out of work. As a railroad was completed, a mine played out, a forest felled, or a harvest gathered, workingmen had to move on, some back to the family farm, but most to another town or another industry where there were jobs to be found. To be sure, some laborers enjoyed more stable employment. Every major urban center in the West had its printers, plumbers, painters, masons, carpenters, and other skilled workers. And then, too, there were the "operatives," the men and women who, although they were not skilled in the same way as these craftsman, nevertheless knew how to run the machines in sawmills, mines, canneries, and factories. But both the skilled and the semiskilled, although in many other respects no different from their counterparts in the East and the Old Northwest, suffered under the impact of the itinerant workers on the move throughout the West. If they arrived in too great a number in any given locale, the transients could depress local wages for operatives and skilled workers alike.

And few employers could resist the temptation to hire these outsiders as strikebreakers when their regular employees gave them trouble.

The BOOMS and busts and the seasonal employment of the West's economy not only forced the region's workers to become transients but also heightened their sense of dependency and fueled their resentments. One scholar has labeled them "casual" workers, and some may indeed have been casual about work, some perhaps simply hoboes and tramps, some social misfits and chronic alcoholics, but the truth of the matter was that, whereas a worker in Boston, Chicago, Detroit, or New York, upon losing a job, might trudge down the street in search of another, the loss of work in the West often forced a worker to head for another state or territory, to ride the rails to distant towns and cities known mostly by rumor. A dock worker in Seattle might wind up in eastern Washington, or California, or Nebraska, picking grapes or sacking wheat; in a year, a mine worker might move from Butte, Montana, to Bisbee, Arizona, from Coeur d'Alene, Idaho, to Juneau, Alaska. The frequent dislocations—which meant at least the temporary loss of close ties to family, friends, neighborhoods, and churches—created a kind of transient personality, a restlessness and rootlessness that saw men picking up and moving on at the least sign of trouble with a boss or coworkers or when too many new faces arrived in a locale or when rumors made the rounds that higher wages could be had elsewhere. In both the LUMBER INDUSTRY and in railroad construction, for example, the workers said that three crews were associated with any job, "one coming, one going, one on the job."

Because workingmen moved around so much, every large city had a district where wage workers congregated to hole up between jobs, an enclave of employment agencies, cheap hotels and flop houses, soup kitchens, saloons, and brothels, such as Skid Road in Seattle or Larimer Street in Denver. Like the MINING camps and towns in the Western mountains, like the logging camps and construction sites in the Pacific Northwest, like the ranches and orchards in California's Central Valley, the urban enclaves were male societies, and the cities and towns in which they sprang up remained predominately male long after sex ratios evened out elsewhere in the West. In 1900, Seattle had the highest percentage of men (64 percent) in its population among American cities with twenty-five thousand or more people, and Butte, Montana, ranked third at 60 percent, while the West as a whole had the greatest number of single-member households—10 percent—of any region in the country.

Not only was the Western working class mostly male and mobile, it was also ethnically diverse. Coming from a variety of nations, immigrants from common backgrounds frequently gravitated toward the same type of work. In the middle of the nineteenth century, the Chinese and the Irish worked in mines and railroad construction, Mexicans and Mexican Americans in citrus groves and the newly opened cotton fields. When the Japanese began to arrive in large numbers, many of them could be found working in sugar-beet fields and picking berries, while later European immigrants picked grapes, peas, and artichokes. Scandinavians were often attracted to logging, and newer Greek and Italian immigrants replaced the Chinese in railroad construction and maintenance. The Cornish frequently joined the Irish in working the hardrock mines. There was little that was static about the patterns of race and ethnicity in the West except that nonwhites were frequently limited to jobs that paid less and carried a lower status in any industry. In 1888, for example, four-fifths or so of all miners in Colorado were English-speaking, mostly Cornish and Irish, but cutbacks in wages and labor strife, early in the twentieth century, led many formerly stable, now disillusioned miners to leave the state. They were replaced by Italians, Austrians, Slavs, Serbs, Poles, Montenegrins, and Greeks. Although those picking cotton in California during the early days had been whites and blacks from Texas and the South, the ethnic mix in the cotton fields changed several times, with Hispanics and Filipinos predominating by the 1920s, who in turn were replaced by displaced farm families from Oklahoma, Arkansas, and Texas in the 1930s, and when these "Okies" and "Arkies" took up jobs in the booming shipyards and AIRCRAFT INDUSTRY of the 1940s, Mexicans and Mexican Americans came back to the cotton fields. Outside Texas and Oklahoma, there were relatively few African Americans—compared to the South and the North—laboring in Western industries before the middle of the twentieth century. At various times, Asians—Chinese, Japanese, and Filipino—were numerous in some industries, but far and away the largest minority group among the Western working class was Mexican and Mexican American, especially after the turmoil and social dislocations of the Mexican Revolution that began in 1910 and the completion of railroads north led thousands of Mexicans to head to the United States in search of better jobs.

At all times, racial and ethnic prejudice plagued the working class in the West. Despite the fact that some Mexican Americans had been Californians or Texans for generations, for example, they were almost always considered cheap and temporary "foreign" labor, and the early mining camps and towns were often strictly segregated between whites and nonwhites, meaning mostly Hispanics and Chinese. Moreover, in any period, those jobs dominated by nonwhites were denigrated, which led to the development of a dual-wage system. The top tier of jobs—managerial positions, skilled jobs, many semiskilled positions—went to white workers, while the bottom tier of arduous, unskilled, low-paying jobs went to the Chinese, the Mexicans, and the Filipinos, unless these were the only jobs available or new groups of European immigrants arrived on the scene, in which case the nonwhites were frequently cut out altogether. The dual-wage system had important consequences for the Western labor movement, for—like the high mobility of the Western working class—it tended to make Western workers harder to organize than their Eastern counterparts. Dividing workers on the basis of race and providing whites with certain advantages, the system gave white workers a powerful incentive to maintain racial barriers rather than look to class solidarity. Indeed, most white workers felt they had more in common with their white bosses than with their nonwhite coworkers, a belief reinforced by the free-labor ideology that had dominated the West since before the Civil War. The idea was that a man might start out working for wages, but by hard work and persistence, he could eventually come to own his own farm or business and employ others, who themselves were striving toward economic independence. The ideology required a belief in social mobility, and Americans had long identified the West with opportunity and with a second chance. The West was a place people could go and grow wealthy with the country. Thanks to highly touted examples such as MARCUS DALY—an Irish mine worker who came to own the Anaconda mine, rule over BUTTE, MONTANA, and run much of the state itself—the belief remained powerful throughout the nineteenth and twentieth centuries.

The labor movement in the West

Opportunities in the West, however, were never as great as the ideologues and popular writers claimed. Recent studies indicate that for at least a significant portion of the trans-Mississippi West, wealth was no more evenly distributed than in the East. Some remote regions had populations in which there were no great gaps between individuals, but that was because they were all poor, not prosperous. In thriving counties or urban areas, the gaps between rich and poor paralleled those in the rest of the country. As more immigrants entered the region, wealth tended to be concentrated at the top, just as elsewhere. Despite individual and frequently highly publicized exceptions, especially during gold-rush periods, most of those who began their lives in the working class ended their lives there as well. On the other hand, the experience of work in the West was often harsher than even in the hellish factories and sweatshops of the North and Northeast. All-male gangs worked as human machines doing heavy, dirty, dangerous work for interminably long periods in exchange for daily wages and not much else. Western workers gave up their health, their limbs, and frequently their lives to feed a growing economy, just as workers around the country in the nineteenth century did, and spent their days in mines and forests and fields that were as much chambers of horror as work places. The mines, with their airless underground shafts and tunnels, their killing extremes of temperature, their deadly gasses, their dangerous explosives, boasted perhaps the worst working conditions, and death rates among American miners were far higher than those suffered in the mining industry in Europe. The lumber industry, however, could sometimes rival the carnage in the mines. The mines destroyed a worker's general health, his lungs, his eyes, or his joints and sometimes crushed his body with cave-ins; the lumber mills took off his fingers, his hands, or his arms with saws or cut his body in two with snapped cables or crushed him under falling trees. At least miners and

loggers got higher wages than agricultural workers, who—if the work was not so immediately dangerous—suffered nonetheless from heat, squalor, and deprivation, given neither adequate food nor shelter, working under the hot sun all day and sleeping in straw-strewn hovels at night. The big farmers themselves used the wretched working conditions of their migrants to argue for admitting Chinese, Filipino, and Mexican immigrants, since no white worker, they said, except for real "tramps," would put up with such conditions.

The combination of seasonal employment, boom-and-bust cycles, unregulated and highhanded business practices, awful working conditions, massive worker mobility, constant racial tensions, and frequently dashed hopes made for a volatile labor movement, one filled with internal divisions and not a little VIOLENCE. The earliest labor-union organizing occurred in San Francisco and in the mining camps. From the gold-rush era on, San Francisco emerged as the strongest labor-union city in the West, while the first miners' union appeared in Virginia City, Nevada, in 1863, with other early miners' unions springing up in Butte, Montana (which became a traditional center of strong unions); Lead, South Dakota; Globe, Arizona; and Leadville and Aspen, Colorado. Skilled workers created the strongest unions in the West. They shared craft backgrounds, a dedication to worker independence, and a distrust and fear of racial minorities and the uses to which the owners might put them. They became devoted to bread-and-butter issues, tended to seek accommodations with their employers (especially when they shared ethnic ties with them), and promoted reforms aimed not so much at overthrowing capitalism as at increasing the power of organized workers as a check on corporate greed. They often enjoyed middle-class support, as the molders' and boilermakers' did in an early San Francisco strike in 1864. Frequently, they played to the nativist tendencies of the middle class as well, as did DENIS KEARNEY's anti-Chinese WORKINGMEN'S PARTY OF CALIFORNIA in the 1870s. The labor-inspired racial pograms of the late nineteenth century were only one manifestation of the fact that Western trade unions, preoccupied with job stability and protecting gains already made, never truly overcame the ethnic and racial divisions of the West's working class. So dedicated was the trade-union–oriented American Federation of Labor (AFL) to Chinese and Japanese exclusion, for example, that when Japanese and Mexican workers joined together in the successful OXNARD AGRICULTURAL STRIKE in 1903, AFL leader Samuel Gompers refused to recognize the union they formed until the Mexicans purged the Japanese from their ranks, which ultimately led to the dissolution of the union when the Hispanics refused to do so.

At the same time, the inordinate number of laborers employed in the West's extractive industries naturally led many workers to establish broad-based, more inclusive unions. In what Richard M. Brown, among others, has called the "West's Civil War of Incorporation," the tendency for big capital in the West to monopolize the economy forced even a divided working class to develop some class-conscious organizations. When the great national railroad strike of 1877, which itself enjoyed much middle-class support, spread into the West with a general strike in St. Louis and walkouts in Omaha and San Francisco, the working class got its first taste of industrywide organization, despite the fact that President Rutherford B. Hayes set a precedent by calling out the national guard and the U.S. Army to help the railroads' Pinkertons and local police forces put down the strike.

The broad-based Knights of Labor led men out on strike in the Southwest against railroads controlled by JAY GOULD in 1885 and 1886. Although the strike, after some initial success, ultimately failed when the railroad spurned a compromise and violence broke out in Parsons, Kansas, Fort Worth, Texas, and East St. Louis, Illinois, the Knights of Labor had proved itself a viable labor organization. In 1889, the Knights even broached the racial barrier by supporting the Las Gorras Blancas (the White Caps), a group of masked New Mexican working-class vigilantes who defended the territory's communal *campesinos* (Hispanic villagers), against capitalist intrusions by Anglo cattle ranchers and merchants. In what was both a racial and an ethnic struggle, Las Gorras Blancas attacked railroads, lumber operations, and Anglo businesses. The industrywide organizing of railway workers got an additional boost when socialist Eugene V. Debs founded, in 1893, the American Railway Union (ARU), which immediately launched another wave of railroad strikes lasting into 1894. The ARU's success against the Great Northern Railroad in 1893 emboldened labor's rank and file, and when GEORGE MORTIMER PULLMAN's workers went on strike in 1894, sixty thousand members of the ARU joined them. In the shadow of Chicago's world's fair—the Columbian Exposition—the federal government intervened and doomed the walkout. The U.S. courts issued injunctions against strike leaders for obstructing mail delivery, and President Grover Cleveland deployed federal troops. The blood bath that followed broke the back of the ARU, and that—along with the demise of the Knights of Labor—sent Western railway workers into the less radical railway brotherhoods in the twentieth century. These trade unions—both independent and affiliated with the AFL—of engineers, conductors, firemen, brakemen, and others would become powerful enough to force the eight-hour workday on railroad companies with the mere threat of a strike in 1916 and 1917.

Meanwhile, the brutal Pullman strike was only one among a number of violent outbursts (many of the most violent of them in the trans-Mississippi West) that had state and local officials, national politicians, businessmen, and newspaper and journal editorial writers worried about what seemed to them class warfare. The collapse of the ARU gave rise to the railroad "bummer," a former union member, now blacklisted by railroad companies, who roamed the West from job to job under various aliases, thus joining the growing army of transients in the Western working class. On the other hand, in the thinly populated Western states and territories, crisscrossed with rails, the huge number of railroad workers had a significant impact on the Western labor movement as a whole. Between 1890 and World War I, spokesmen and women for Western labor increasingly asserted that they had little in common with the "labor aristocrats" belonging to the cautious, craft-oriented AFL unions and the railway brotherhoods. The AFL's exclusionary policies, dividing workers on the basis not merely of skill and knowledge but of race, ethnicity, and job stability, had the effect of abandoning thousands of workers in the region's extractive industries to more radical organizations. Western workers, in turn, were drawn to those organizations that would have them, to militant industrial unions and to populist, anarchist, and socialist associations and political organizations, many of them influenced by the proud radical traditions of European labor that new immigrants, especially Germans, had brought with them beginning as early as 1848. As the violence escalated in the West and the middle class grew more troubled over radical labor's social revolutionary demands, establishment politicians and newspapers attempted to demonize the working class, much as they had Native Americans and African Americans, by characterizing working-class men not merely as swarthy, foreign-born, violence-prone anarchists but as subhuman aliens unworthy of common political rights. The transient tramps and bums of the Western work force were particularly vulnerable to such attacks.

The WESTERN FEDERATION OF MINERS (WFM) served as a rallying point for the West's industrial unionizing in the late nineteenth and early twentieth centuries. The union was formed in 1893 following a bitter dispute in Idaho's Coeur d'Alene mining district. The Coeur d'Alene strike had started in 1892 when the mine owners reduced wages. After the copper miners walked off the job, the owners vowed never to hire another union man and set to work breaking the local miners' union. In the course of doing so, they perfected tactics that owners would increasingly turn to over the next two decades whenever the unions had significant support in the local communities. First, they hired their own armed force. Then, knowing local officials were sympathetic to the strikers, they claimed that local authorities simply could not maintain law and order and began using their spies and provocateurs to create "incidents" if none developed on its own. They then appealed to the state's governor to send in the militia. If a governor balked, or if the militia refused to fire on the workingmen, or if state forces proved insufficient for breaking the strike, they asked the federal courts for marshals and the federal government for troops.

At first, the Coeur d'Alene strike was peaceful. Then, angry strikers, frustrated by the owners' truculence that was—in the workers' minds—dragging out the strike, by the constant harassment of the company's hired thugs, and by the federal injunctions the owners seemed able to get against them at will, took up arms and fought back. Gun battles broke out between strikers and strikebreakers as the workers assaulted the Frisco Mine on Canyon Creek and the Gem Mine on the Coeur d'Alene. The strikers burned the Frisco mill, captured all the guards and scabs, and then marched on the Bunker Hill and Sullivan mines. When they captured the company's ore concentrator, an expensive contraption costing one-half million dollars, they managed to force the owners' to dismiss all the scabs at the two mines. The fighting left six men dead and one or two dozen more hospitalized. The miners, for the moment, had won. But the sight of this rabble, flushed

with victory and in control of all the mining camps along the river, only made it easier for the Mine Owners' Protective Association to obtain a declaration of martial law. The governor sent in six companies of the Idaho national guard. Making wholesale arrests of union members and of local businessmen and lawyers who had supported the union, the national guard, reinforced by federal troops, rounded up six hundred men and herded them into hastily erected, crude stockades, or bullpens.

Although the Supreme Court overturned the convictions of those charged in the strike the following year, the owners had broken the local union. The strong-arm tactics had intimidated the merchants and lawyers who backed the strike and shared, for a time, jail cells with the workers, thus driving a wedge between the middle-class members of the mining camps—men and women who sold the miners goods, provided them with services, and sympathized with their customers—and the working class. Spawned by these troubles, the WFM functioned as a bridge between the old Knights of Labor, the idealistic and broad-based organization popular in the West throughout the 1880s, and the INDUSTRIAL WORKERS OF THE WORLD (IWW), the "one big union" that became perhaps the most famous of all labor unions in the region. In the long run, it would be the hard-rock miners of the WFM, spurred on by events in Colorado, who played the key role in organizing the IWW.

Among the many notorious incidents of violence in the working-class history of the American West, few reached the level of confrontation or lasted so long as the Colorado labor war of 1903 and 1904, with its dynamitings, deportations, and deaths that culminated in the CRIPPLE CREEK STRIKES. Although the strikes had run their course in 1904, the WFM stubbornly refused to call them off until 1907. Meantime, the union all but disappeared in the wake of Cripple Creek, while mine workers were required to hold employment cards issued by the Mine Owners' Association, which refused to issue cards to known union members. As the WFM fought for its very existence, its more militant members, in 1905, spearheaded the organization of the IWW in Chicago.

Members of the IWW, known as the "Wobblies," split with the WFM, which by then was dominated by

Much of the animosity of the miners at Ludlow, Colorado, was aimed at John D. Rockefeller, Jr., owner of the Colorado Fuel and Iron. *Courtesy The Bettmann Archive.*

the conservative local in Butte, Montana, where Irish workers, feeling much affinity with mine owner Marcus Daly, protected their own and never called a strike until after Daly's death. Former WFM leader WILLIAM D. ("BIG BILL") HAYWOOD stuck with the IWW, and during his tenure, the "one big union" found a happier home among the transient working class of the West than it did elsewhere in the country. Eschewing trade-union exclusiveness, the Wobblies emphasized the solidarity of all workers regardless of sex, national origin, or race. They kept their dues low, ignored political action, and refused to sign contracts with employers, whom they regarded as unredeemable class enemies. With an organi-

In December 1946, the American Federation of Labor led a general strike that tied up the city of Oakland, California. A mass meeting took place in downtown's Latham Square. *Courtesy The Bettmann Archive.*

zation and a philosophy perfectly pitched to migrant and transient workers, the IWW launched a free-speech movement that became a model for broad-based protest movements ever afterward. Although the establishment press quickly saddled the Wobblies with a reputation for violence, they were more often the victims than the perpetrators of such violence, despite their inflammatory and militant propaganda. Many of the violent events in Western working-class history occurred long before the IWW was organized, and the region's turbulent labor relations owed much more to the peculiar make-up of its working class—with its racial divisions and transiency—and the circumstances of its working life—with its brutal extractive industries run by ruthless men—than to one organization and its, in-truth, half-baked revolutionary philosophy. Developing a radical strain already present among Western workers, the Wobblies earned a prominent place in Western folklore, but of the four key traumatic events that Richard M. Brown claims undermined labor unionism in the West during the early twentieth century—the dynamiting of the *Los Angeles Times* building in 1910, the LUDLOW MASSACRE of 1914, the THOMAS JOSEPH MOONEY case of 1916, and the sedition case against "Big Bill" Haywood in 1918—only the last had any real connection to the IWW.

Unlike San Francisco, which had long been known for its militant labor tradition, Los Angeles—a bastion of the upper- and middle-class "Progressive" good-government movement—had become, by the late nineteenth century, an adamantine open-shop town, whose

antilabor sentiments found a spokesman in the powerful and aristocratic publisher of the *Los Angeles Times*, HARRISON GRAY OTIS. Brothers John J. and James B. McNamara, leaders of the AFL's Bridge and Structural Iron Workers Union, were among the union activists who challenged Los Angeles's prohibition against organized labor. When twenty people were killed in the dynamiting of the *Times* building on October 1, 1910, the McNamara brothers were arrested for setting the bomb. After claiming their innocence and winning the support of the labor movement nationwide, the brothers reversed their denials and admitted their guilt, thus discrediting the Western labor movement in general. In Ludlow, Colorado, after a long strike, beginning in 1913, against the Rockefeller-controlled Colorado Fuel and Iron Company, ten men and a young child were killed in a single day during an April 20, 1914, gun battle between the Colorado militia and United Mine Workers. A victorious militia, having overrun the workers' tent city, doused the canvas with kerosene and set it ablaze, suffocating two women and eleven children hiding among the tents. The "massacre" touched off a guerrilla war in the coal fields that left seventy-four dead in a matter of weeks before federal troops intervened. Although not a direct affront to labor's credibility like the bombing of the *Times* building, the Ludlow Massacre proved just as damaging in its own way since the carnage there revealed the horrid potential of class warfare. Widespread support for organized labor began to evaporate as several communities passed antilabor ordinances, the so-called criminal syndicalism laws that forbade membership in organizations calling for violence against society. A bombing of San Francisco's Preparedness Day Parade down Market Street on July 22, 1916, took ten lives and led to the arrest of two union activists and labor radicals, Tom Mooney and Warren Knox Billings. Unlike the McNamaras, the two maintained their innocence, but they were nevertheless convicted on the flimsiest of evidence. Billings was sentenced to life prison; Mooney, to death.

Although the Mooney case became a cause célèbre for Western labor and he was ultimately given a full pardon in 1939, the tide had clearly turned. Wobbly organizers in the small sawmill town of Everett, Washington, were challenged by gun-toting local patriots in November 1916, and twelve people, most of them IWW members, were killed. All over the West, union organizers were rounded up, tossed in jail, tried under any law available for espionage, sedition, or criminal conspiracy, and then deported or imprisoned. A series of ARIZONA MINING STRIKES ended in disaster at Bisbee, when the strikers were rounded up, carted off to the desert, and abandoned there by local vigilantes. After America entered World War I, Woodrow Wilson's administration, growing viciously anti-immigrant and antilabor, set out to destroy the IWW in particular. "Big Bill" Haywood, caught in a net of espionage indictments, was tried and convicted in Chicago, along with dozens of other IWW leaders, before he jumped bail and fled to Russia.

Labor's Western legacy

Organized labor around the country declined during the 1920s; the once powerful WFM, now the International Union of Mine, Mill, and Smelterworkers, lost its closed-shop agreements; big business bested the SAN FRANCISCO BUILDING TRADES COUNCIL and brought the open shop to the former bastion of unionism. The massive unemployment of the Great Depression revived workers' interest in unions and working-class collective action, and moribund organizations showed new signs of life. The Mine, Mill, and Smelterworkers regained the closed shop in the Rocky Mountains, and even the IWW, presumed dead, returned for a short time to the northern woods of Idaho and the Yakima Valley of Washington. As a result of New Deal legislation that favored collective bargaining, the ranks of organized labor boomed. Even in that stronghold of

the open shop, southern California, union membership tripled between 1933 and 1938, and the Screen Actors' Guild—led by the likes of Groucho Marx and Ronald Reagan—managed to win a closed-shop agreement from the Hollywood studios. As the growth continued, the old battle between trade and industrial unions broke out again, and when the craft-dominated AFL expelled industrial unionists in 1937, dissidents formed the Congress of Industrial Organizations (CIO) the next year. In the West, where industrial unionism had always been strong, the aggressive CIO adopted something of the old IWW's radical militancy and became powerful among loggers, miners, cannery workers, and longshoremen. As a result, turf wars between the AFL and the CIO were especially bitter on the Pacific Coast.

The most important of the New Deal labor strikes was launched by a CIO union, the International Longshoreman's Association, led by the charismatic Harry R. Bridges. Tying up ports from Seattle to San Diego for four months in 1934, Bridges and his longshoremen were denounced as communists by businessmen and frightened residents. In July, a battle between strikers and police in San Francisco led to a three-day general strike, and the longshoremen won not only most of their demands but gained supremacy over the West Coast docks. The Pacific Coast maritime strike only inflamed the ill will between the AFL and the CIO, and the former stepped up its war on all labor radicalism. Prominent among the AFL organizers was a fast-rising star in the Teamsters' Union, David Beck, who began by launching an organization drive among Seattle's laundry drivers and wound up becoming the union's national leader in 1952. By the mid-1930s, Beck was already the most powerful regional figure among the Teamsters and the dominant personality in Northwest labor. When Harry Bridges attempted to protect the flanks of his longshoremen by "marching inland" and organizing warehouse workers, Beck broke up the drive with a squad of club-swinging hired thugs. Often accused of connections to organized crime, Beck went to jail for income-tax evasion in the 1960s; Bridges came under constant attack as a suspected member of the Communist party; and the AFL and the CIO, in the long post–World War II wave of prosperity, worked out their differences after the latter had been decimated by purges of suspected communists or communist sympathizers during the McCarthy era. After merging in 1955, the AFL-CIO expelled the Teamsters' Union for racketeering.

The battle between conservative craft unions and the more radical industrial unions was not the only legacy of Western labor in the twentieth century. Racial tensions and the abuse of migrant workers continued to plague labor relations in the West as big agri-cultural interests took advantage of the open border between the United States and Mexico to exploit a growing number of Mexican immigrants who trav-eled north for the harvest and then returned to their families below the border. When Cesar Chávez launched a successful organizing drive among MIGRANT WORKERS in the 1960s, it was the Teamsters' Union, encouraged in no small measure by the growers them-selves, who ultimately rolled back many of the early and promising gains of Chávez's United Farm Work-ers. As all union membership fell off dramatically in the 1980s, the future began to look especially grim for the unskilled Mexican and Mexican American workers in the desert Southwest. Suffering in an ailing economy and a hostile political environment were not just the migrant farm workers but also manufacturing work-ers as well, who, since the 1960s, had been employed in the *maquiladora* (assembly plant) industrial parks along the Mexican border. As higher paying jobs in industries such as logging and mining began to disap-pear in a Western economy more and more geared to white-collar high-tech, tourism, and services industries, the Western middle class not only turned a deaf ear to traditional labor but also launched legislative attacks on the immigrant work force. If the 1930s reminded one of the heyday of the early IWW, the 1990s seemed perhaps to harken back to the exclusionary times of San Francisco's Workingmen's Party.

—*Charles Phillips*

SEE ALSO: Domestic Service; Foreign Miners' Tax of 1850; Financial Panics; Gorras Blancas, Las; Hawaii Laborer's Association; Industrial Association of San Francisco; Loggers; Pinkerton National Detective Agency; Socialism; Union Labor Party; Working-Class Women

SUGGESTED READING:

Brown, Richard M. *Strain of Violence: Historical Studies of American Violence and Vigilantism.* New York, 1975.

Brown, Ronald C. *Hard-Rock Miners: The Intermountain West, 1860–1920.* College Station, Tex., 1979.

Bykrit, James W. *Forging the Copper Collar: Arizona's Labor-Management War of 1901–1902.* Tucson, Ariz., 1982.

Daniel, Cletus E. *Bitter Harvest: A History of California Farmworkers, 1870–1941.* Ithaca, N.Y., 1981.

Friedheim, Robert L. *The Seattle General Strike.* Seattle, Wash., 1964.

Foster, James C., ed. *American Labor in the Southwest: The First One Hundred Years of 1901–1921.* Tucson, Ariz., 1982.

Gitelman, Howard M. *Legacy of the Ludlow Massacre: A Chapter in American Industrial Relations.* Philadelphia, 1988.

Kazin, Michael. *Barons of Labor: San Francisco Building Trades and Union Power in the Progressive Era.* Urbana, Ill., 1987.

Larson, Robert. "The White Caps of New Mexico: A Study in Ethnic Militancy in the Southwest." *Pacific Historical Quarterly* 44 (May 1974): 171–186.

Lingenfelter, Richard E. *The Hardrock Miners: A History of the Mining Labor Movement in the American West, 1860–1893.* Berkeley, Calif., 1974.

Lovin, Hugh T., ed. *Labor in the West.* Manhattan, Kans., 1986.

McGovern, George S., and Leonard F. Guttridge. *The Great Coalfield War.* Boston, 1972.

McWilliams, Carey. *Factories in the Field: The Story of Migratory Farm Labor in California.* Boston, 1939.

Nelson, Bruce. *Workers on the Waterfront: Seaman, Long-shoremen, and Unionism in the 1930s.* Urbana, Ill., 1988.

Ruiz, Vicki L. *Cannery Women, Cannery Lives: Mexican Women, Unionization, and the California Food Process-ing Industry, 1930–1950.* Albuquerque, N. Mex., 1987.

Saxton, Alexander. *Indespensible Enemy: Labor and the Anti-Chinese Movement in California.* Berkeley, Calif., 1971.

Schwantes, Carlos A., ed. *Bisbee: Urban Outpost on the Frontier.* Tucson, Ariz., 1992.

Schwantes, Carlos A. *Radical Heritage: Labor, Socialism, and Reform in Washington and British Columbia, 1885–1917.* Seattle, Wash., 1979.

Selvin, David F. *A Place in the Sun: A History of California Labor.* San Francisco, 1981.

Suggs, George G. *Colorado's War on Militant Unionism: James H. Peabody and the Western Federation of Min-ers.* Detroit, Mich., 1972.

Tyler, Robert L. *Rebels of the Woods: The I.W.W. in the Pacific Northwest.* Eugene, Oreg., 1967.

White, Richard. *"It's Your Misfortune and None of My Own": A New History of the American West.* Norman, Okla., 1991.

Wyman, Mark. *Hard-Rock Epic: Western Miners and the Industrial Revolution, 1860–1910.* Berkeley, Calif., 1979.

LA BREA TAR PITS

The Rancho La Brea tar pits are the world's richest known deposit of Ice Age fossils. Located seven miles west of downtown Los Angeles, California, the tar pits contain fossils that tell the story of the history of life in the Los Angeles Basin beginning about forty thousand years ago. Some of the tar pits are still active, and plants and animals continue to be preserved in them.

The tar pits formed because of a large reservoir of crude oil deep underground. Movement of the earth's crust resulted in the formation of faults and fissures through the rocks overlying the reservoir of oil. The cracks in the rock allowed the oil to seep upward and

A paleontologist displays a saber-tooth cat's pelvic bone excavated in 1985 from La Brea tar pits in Los Angeles. Courtesy *The Bettmann Archive.*

accumulate on the surface of the ground where portions of the liquid oil evaporated, leaving behind the sticky asphalt in which many forms of life were trapped and preserved.

More than 565 species of plants and animals—some living and some extinct—have been identified from the nearly two million fossils recovered from the La Brea tar pits. Many of the extant species no longer live in southern California, however, because the climate has become more desertlike since the last Ice Age. Plant fossils found in the pits include diatoms, pollen, seeds, leaves, and wood. Animal fossils include snails, clams, insects, spiders, fish, frogs, snakes, turtles, birds, and mammals. Some of the more spectacular extinct mammals whose fossils have been found in the tar pits include giant ground sloths, mammoths and mastodons, dire wolves, and saber-toothed cats. Just one human, known as La Brea Woman, has been found there. She is thought to have lived about nine thousand years ago.
—*Kenneth E. Campbell, Jr.*

SUGGESTED READING:
Harris, John M., and George T. Jefferson. *Rancho La Brea: Treasures of the Tar Pits.* Natural History Museum of Los Angeles County Science Series No. 31. Los Angeles, 1985.
Stock, Chester. *Rancho La Brea: A Record of Pleistocene Life in California.* Natural History Museum of Los Angeles County Science Series No. 37. Los Angeles, 1992.

LACEY, JOHN FLETCHER

Iowa congressman, author, and promoter of early conservation legislation, John Fletcher Lacey (1841–1913) was born in New Martinsville, West Virginia. He moved with his family to Oskaloosa, Iowa, in 1855. During the Civil War, he compiled an impressive battle record in the Union army, mustering out with the rank of brevet major in 1865. That year, he was admitted to the bar in Iowa and married Martha Newell. Over the next twenty-three years, he practiced law in Oskaloosa and launched his political career, serving one term in the Iowa legislature from 1870 to 1872. As a lawyer, state politician, and conservative Republican, he established a reputation for defending railroad interests and high protective tariffs. As a legal scholar, he compiled a widely used two-volume legal history of railroad decisions in U.S. courts, published under the title of *Lacey's Railway Digest.*

In 1888, Lacey was elected to the U.S. House of Representatives. Serving from 1889 to 1891 and from 1893 to 1907, he became interested in the conservation of natural, cultural, and human resources. To address concerns about miners' working conditions, he authored safety laws covering mines under federal jurisdiction, enacted in 1890 and 1902, and he was the first congressman to introduce legislation to create the Bureau of Mines within the Department of the Interior. As a long-time member of the House Indian Affairs Committee, he opposed attempts to cut appropriations for Indian schools, favored local schools over boarding schools, and supported citizenship for Indians.

In retrospect, Lacey wielded his most enduring influence in the House Public Lands Committee, which he chaired for twelve years. From this committee came the FOREST RESERVE ACT OF 1891, the Lacey Act of 1900 (which used the interstate commerce clause to bolster federal entry into wildlife conservation), and the Alaska Game Law of 1902. Lacey also sponsored legislation to establish game preserves in specific national parks and forests as well as bison breeding grounds in Yellowstone National Park and Oklahoma's Wichita Forest Reserve. After visiting pueblos and archaeological ruins in New Mexico, he introduced legislation to protect historic and prehistoric sites on public lands. Under the ANTIQUITIES ACT OF 1906, more than two hundred national monuments were established during Lacey's lifetime.

Although Lacey eschewed the term *progressive* (which contributed to his defeat in 1906), he nonetheless supported the MULTIPLE-USE DOCTRINE of forest reserves of his friend GIFFORD PINCHOT and worked to transfer the Bureau of Forestry from the Department of the Interior to the Department of Agriculture in 1905. After leaving office in 1907, he continued to lobby Congress as a representative of the League of American Sportsmen's Committee on Conservation. In that role, he promoted legislation to establish game preserves in national forests and to protect migratory birds. Lacey lived just long enough to see the fruits of his labor realized in 1913 with the passage of the Weeks-McLean Migratory Bird Game Act.

—*Rebecca Conard*

SUGGESTED READING:

Gallagher, Annette, C. H. M. "Citizen of the Nation: John Fletcher Lacey, Conservationist." *Annals of Iowa* 46 (1981): 9–22.

Iowa Park and Forestry Association. *Major John F. Lacey: Memorial Volume.* Cedar Rapids, Iowa, 1915.

LACEY ACT OF 1900

The Lacey Act of 1900 marks the first expression of federal policy on wildlife conservation. Authored by Representative JOHN FLETCHER LACEY, a Republican from Iowa, the act prohibited the interstate transportation of wild animals or birds killed in violation of state laws. Another provision of the act authorized the U.S. Department of Agriculture to prohibit the importation of birds or animals the secretary might declare injurious to the interests of agriculture or horticulture. The act also gave broad authority to the agriculture secretary to adopt measures for the preservation, distribution, introduction, and restoration of game birds and wild birds so long as federal measures did not infringe on state laws.

Introduced in January of 1900, Lacey's bill won support from the League of American Sportsmen, the Audubon societies, the New York Zoological Society, the Department of Agriculture, and several state fish and game associations. Opposing the bill was the Millinery Merchants' Association, which withdrew its opposition when Lacey accepted an amendment permitting milliners to use plumage from barnyard fowl. With the milliners appeased, the bill quickly passed the House and Senate, and President William McKinley signed it on May 25, 1900.

Constitutionally cloaked by the interstate commerce clause, the Lacey Act sanctioned the right of states to regulate the killing and shipping of game. Enforcement proved to be effective. After unlawfully shipped birds were confiscated in several large cities, the market for illegally obtained wildlife began to diminish. The Lacey Act also launched the practice of setting aside preserves as breeding grounds for birds.

—*Rebecca Conard*

SUGGESTED READING:

Environmental Law Institute, Council on Environmental Quality. *The Evolution of National Wildlife Law.* Washington, D.C., 1977.

Gallagher, Annette, C. H. M. "Citizen of the Nation: John Fletcher Lacey, Conservationist." *The Annals of Iowa* 46 (Summer 1981): 9–22.

LACLÈDE, PIERRE

A French fur trader and the founder of St. Louis, Pierre Laclède (1729–1778) was born in Bedous, France, and educated at the military academy in Toulouse. He moved to New Orleans in 1755 in search of his fortune. Becoming a partner in a trading house, Maxtent, Laclède and Company, Laclède entered into a relationship with the widowed Marie Thérèse Chouteau née Bourgeois and, in August 1763, took her teen-aged son, René Auguste Chouteau, on an fur-trading trip up the Mississippi River. Arriving in November at Ste. Genevieve, the only French settlement west of the Mississippi, Laclède found little storage there for the trading goods he had brought. Later that week, he crossed the river to Kaskasia (in present-day Illinois), where the local commander of Fort Chartres had offered him storage space. Seeing the need for a trading post in the area, Laclède and Chouteau went looking for a site on the west bank of the Mississippi, which they found sometime in December at the rocky bluff where today sits downtown St. Louis. Laclède marked a site on top of the bluff to ensure against flooding and then returned to New Orleans to hire workmen. In February, Laclède returned with thirty men, laid out the village, and named the place for a former French king, the canonized Louis IX. When word reached the French in Illinois that their territory now belonged to the British, courtesy of the 1763 Peace of Paris that ended the French and Indian War, about fifty families moved across the river to Laclède's new town. Laclède, who evidently possessed considerable skills of persuasion, had carved out a corner of the Missouri trade for himself and established such good relations with the local Indians that St. Louis did not even require a stockade. Then he got word from New Orleans that the French authorities, responding to complaints that Maxtent, Laclède and Company was attempting to create a monopoly, had cancelled his charter. Laclède bought out Maxtent, dissolved the company, and went into business with Chouteau, now his stepson, and with another young man who had married into the CHOUTEAU FAMILY, Sylvestre Labbadie. Having established a dynasty that would outlast several changes of sovereignty and that would remain prominent in the fur trade and local affairs long after Missouri became a state, Laclède died near the mouth of the Arkansas River, after falling ill on one of his numerous trips to New Orleans. He was buried on the shore of the river.

—*Charles Phillips*

LADD, EDWIN FREMONT

A chemist, teacher, and politician, Edwin Fremont Ladd (1859–1925) was born on a farm in Maine, graduated from the university there, and worked for the New York Agricultural Experiment Station in upstate before taking a position in 1890 at the North Dakota Agricultural College in Fargo teaching chemistry. Establishing an experimental station at the college, Ladd supervised the chemical testing that ultimately proved sugar beets could be suitably grown in North Dakota, thus laying the groundwork for a burgeoning new business. By the end of the decade, Ladd had made the college the home of the leading experiment station in the United States, one that discovered—among other things—the flour-making potential of lower grades of wheat and established screenings for stock feed, food, paint, and fertilizer. A crusader against adulteration of consumer goods, Ladd rode the issue into the United States Senate in 1920. Having won the endorsement of the progressive NONPARTISAN LEAGUE, Ladd allied himself with the likes of Robert M. La Follette and GEORGE W. NORRIS against vested interests and, for his troubles, was dropped from the Senate's Republican Steering Committee. In 1925, Ladd was killed in an automobile accident.

—*Charles Phillips*

LADIES' ANTI-POLYGAMY SOCIETY

The short-lived (1878 to 1884) but effective Ladies' Anti-Polygamy Society was organized in Salt Lake City,

Utah, as a pressure group to force the federal government to outlaw Mormon (CHURCH OF JESUS CHRIST OF LATTER-DAY SAINTS) polygamy, the practice whereby a man takes more than one wife at a time. The society's membership was composed primarily of former Mormon women and non-Mormon women and included nationally prominent members such as Jennie Anderson Froiseth and Cornelia Paddock, popular authors of best-selling antipolygamy exposés. Sarah A. Cooke, a disaffected Mormon, was head of the society.

Under Jennie Froiseth's editorship from 1880 to 1883, the society's newspaper, *Anti-Polygamy Standard*, promoted the crusade, carrying the standard, "Let every Man have his own Wife, and Let every Woman have her own Husband," a biblical verse from First Corinthians. The newspaper printed the personal accounts of "victims" of polygamy and articles by national sympathizers such as Harriet Beecher Stowe and Frances Willard. With their endorsements and those of the First Lady Lucy Hayes, the society mounted a successful national campaign in 1880—engaging the support of national women's organizations, memorializing Congress, initiating nationwide petition drives, and funding national lecturers.

Although the society met with strong opposition from Mormon women, its members insisted it did not want to "wage war against any party, sect, or person." Instead, they professed only a desire to persuade plural wives of the "lawless and degrading" influence of the system and to provide assistance to those who abandoned the practice. Successful in influencing public sentiment, the society was also instrumental in passage of the EDMUNDS ACT OF 1882, a measure designed to enforce an 1879 Supreme Court decision declaring polygamy unconstitutional. Although the MORMONS did not renounce polygamy until 1890, the Anti-Polygamy Society, which worked outside the channels of formal power, was a significant force in effecting notable political and legal reforms in Utah.

—*Carol Cornwall Madsen*

SEE ALSO: Polygamy: Polygamy among Mormons

SUGGESTED READING:

Dwyer, Robert Joseph. *The Gentile Comes to Utah: A Study in Religious and Social Conflict (1862–1890)*. Washington, D.C., 1941.

Whitney, Orson F. *History of Utah*. 4 vols. Salt Lake City, 1892–1898.

LAFLESCHE, SUSETTE

SEE: Tibbles, Susette LaFlesche

LA LLORONA

A ghost or *espantos* of Mexican folklore, La Llorona roams the countryside of Mexico and the American Southwest at night in search of her lost children. The wail of "the Weeper" can cause *susto* (mental anguish) among those who hear her, and should her crying be heard at one's front door, it signals sure death to an occupant of the household.

Thought to be a widow who drowned her children in a pond or a well so she would be free to remarry, La Llorona would probably kill other children if she found them at night, or she would cast an evil spell on whoever saw her. Some believe she is La Malinche, mistress of Spanish conqueror Hernan Cortés. She is believed to have drowned their illegitimate son rather than allow the Spaniard to take him to Spain.

Although no one has ever seen La Llorona, she began wandering throughout the Southwest two centuries ago. In the dark of night, her cries pierce the desert quiet.

—*Patricia Hogan*

SUGGESTED READING:

Campa, Arthur L. *Hispanic Culture in the Southwest.* Norman, Okla., 1979.

LA MALINCHE

The subject of countless folk traditions, interpretations, and damnations, La Malinche (1502–1527 or 1528) served Hernan Cortés as interpreter and strategist in his conquest of Mexico. For her role in the conquest of the Aztec people, La Malinche, for centuries, bore the label of traitor, although in recent times, she has been perceived by some as the first Mexican feminist.

Known as Doña Marina to the Spanish and Malintzin to the Aztec Indians of the sixteenth century, La Malinche—originally named Malinal—was the daughter of an Aztec chief in Coatzacoalcos, a pre-Columbian Mexican province. Of the privileged class, she received an education as a young girl. Upon the death of her father, her mother remarried and banished Malinal in an effort to gain her inheritance for the girl's half-brother, the product of the second marriage. Malinal was given to itinerant traders, who eventually sold her to the ruling *cacique,* or "chief," of the Tabasco province on the Yucatan coast. She thus became familiar with the Mayan dialects of

her adopted people, and of course, she spoke the language of the Aztecs.

When Cortés conquered the Tabasco province in 1519, he received from the *cacique* a customary gift of homage of twenty women, La Malinche among them, to serve the Spanish warriors as domestic laborers. The Spanish called her Marina, perhaps a confusion of Malinal, and addressed her as Doña, a title of respect. She quickly distinguished herself among the servants by her quick command of Castilian Spanish, her knowledge of the countryside, and her insight into native customs and traditions. She served the Spaniards as an interpreter and stood beside Cortés even in battle. She uncovered plots against the Spaniards and saved Cortés and his troops, on at least two occasions, from certain death. She became indispensable as an interpreter and advisor in his dealings with the conquered people and facilitated their conversion to Catholicism. With Doña Marina's assistance, Cortés nurtured allies among the Mayan people and accomplished the defeat of the Aztec empire and the demise of its ruler Montezuma.

Doña Marina became Cortés's mistress and bore him his first son. Even when Cortés's Spanish wife joined him in New Spain, he kept Doña Marina close at hand as an advisor and strategist.

What became of Doña Marina after Cortés's return to Spain is not known with certainty. Most likely, she died at the age of twenty-five during a smallpox epidemic that struck Mexico in 1527 and 1528.

For centuries following the Spanish conquest of Mexico, La Malinche was portrayed as a traitor to her people and as a detestable symbol of servile devotion to European invaders. More thoughtful historians of recent years, however, view La Malinche as an extraordinary woman whose intelligence, initiative, adaptability, and leadership enabled her to rise above the traditional place of women in both pre-Columbian culture and among the Spanish to become an important participant in monumental events of the sixteenth century. These historians point out that the regime of Montezuma was rife with internal problems and that its subjects, burdened by excessive taxes and victimized by the Aztecs' use of human sacrifice, were prone to rebellion anyway. Even without the Spanish *conquistadores,* the Aztec empire would have been destroyed. La Malinche, in fact, probably saved the lives of many native peoples by convincing Montezuma to relinquish his rule to the Spaniards.

La Malinche lives on in countless myths and legends. One claims that she is La Llorona, "the Weeper," who drowned her son rather than allow Cortés to take him to Spain. Her wailing, believers proclaim, can be heard in the night throughout the Southwest.

—*Patricia Hogan*

SUGGESTED READING:
Candelaria, Cordelia. "La Malinche, Feminist Prototype."
     Frontiers 5 (Summer 1980): 1–6.

LAMAR, MIRABEAU B.

Third president of the Republic of TEXAS, Mirabeau B. Lamar (1798–1859) was born near Louisville, Georgia, grew up at Fairfield, his father's plantation near Milledgeville, and was educated at local academies. After a brief career as a storekeeper, he became publisher of the Cahawba, Alabama, *Press,* in 1821. In 1823, he returned to Georgia to become secretary to Governor George M. Troup. He married Tabitha Jordan in 1826 and resigned his position to nurse his wife, who had tuberculosis. In 1828, he returned to the newspaper business as editor of the Columbus, Georgia, *Enquirer* and was elected to the state senate a year later. He withdrew from the race for a second term in 1830 after his wife's death. In 1832 and 1834, he was defeated in races for the U.S. Congress on a nullification platform. Selling his interest in the *Enquirer,* he followed his friend James B. Fanin to Texas in 1835.

Finding Texas in the midst of revolutionary turmoil, Lamar declared his support for independence, returned to Georgia to settle his affairs, and went back to Texas in time for the San Jacinto campaign. Enlisting as a private in the TEXAS REVOLUTION, he was given command of the cavalry at San Jacinto and distinguished himself on the field. Ten days later, he was named secretary of war under President DAVID GOUVENEUR BURNET and, within a month, had been appointed major general commanding the Texas Army. His troops, admirers of SAM HOUSTON, did not accept him, and he retired.

In September 1836, he was elected vice-president of the Republic of Texas, although he spent most of his time traveling, writing poetry, and studying Spanish, as well as founding the Philosophical Society of Texas, a scholarly society. With support of the anti-Houston faction, he ran for president of Texas, succeeding Sam Houston in 1838.

As president, Lamar advocated continuing independence from the United States and laid the foundations for higher education in Texas. He replaced Houston's conciliatory program towards the Indians with one of force. He drove the Cherokees to Arkansas in 1839 and fought the Comanches in 1840. After failing to sign a peace treaty with Mexico, he initiated an alliance with the Yucatan rebels in 1840. He also moved the capital city from Houston to the town of Waterloo on the frontier, which was renamed Austin. His administration eventually failed because it spent approximately four dollars for every one it took in taxes.

Lamar's great contribution to Texas was his plan to establish public education. In an act passed on January 26, 1839, lands were set aside to support public schools and two universities. The modern university system in Texas is still funded, in part, from this system.

Retiring in 1841 when he was succeeded by Houston, Lamar withdrew to his home in Richmond, Texas. After his daughter's death in 1843, he traveled to the East and eventually revived his interest in writing poetry. He actively supported annexation of Texas by the United States. During the UNITED STATES–MEXICAN WAR, he served with ZACHARY TAYLOR as a lieutenant colonel, fighting at Monterrey. After 1848, Lamar traveled extensively, remarried, and became an active supporter of secession to protect slavery. He served as United States minister to Nicaragua and Costa Rica from 1857 to 1859. Two months after his return to Richmond, Texas, he died of a heart attack on December 19, 1859.

—*Patrick H. Butler, III*

Mirabeau B. Lamar. *Courtesy Archives Division, Texas State Library.*

SUGGESTED READING:
Gambrell, Herbert Pickens. *Mirabeau Buonaparte Lamar: Troubador and Crusader.* Dallas, Tex., 1934.
Gulick, Charles, et al., eds. *Papers of Mirabeau Buonaparte Lamar.* 6 vols. Austin, Tex., 1921–1927.

LAMY, JEAN BAPTISTE

First bishop and archbishop of New Mexico, Jean Baptiste Lamy (1814–1888) was born in Lempdes, district of Puy-de-Dôme, France. His parents were prosperous and respected peasants. Bishop John B. Purcell recruited Lamy, after his ordination in 1838, for the American missions. He served in Ohio and Kentucky under Purcell and became an American citizen in 1847. Following the United States–Mexican War and the formal annexation of half of Mexico's northern territories by the United States in 1848, the American Catholic hierarchy sent a petition to Rome to ask that ecclesiastical administration of New Mexico be transferred to it from the bishopric of Durango. Pope Pius IX granted the request in 1850 and named Lamy vicar apostolic of a provisional diocese that included present-day New Mexico, Arizona, Colorado, and Utah. The diocese was made permanent in 1853; the archdiocese of Santa Fe was established in 1875.

In New Mexico, Lamy and his vicar general Joseph Machebeuf presided over a body of faithful that consisted of some fifty-seven thousand Hispanics. Most were poor and practiced "folk religion." The native clergy numbered only fifteen, six of whom were no longer active. Given the scarcity of priests, the Spanish religious heritage was preserved largely by a religious brotherhood commonly known as Los Hermanos Penitentes. Lamy and his successors would eventually come to view the religious rites of the PENITENTES as a problem, but troubles with the local clergymen began immediately; they refused to recognize Lamy as their ordinary. Lamy attempted to settle the question of ecclesiastical authority by traveling to Durango to be recognized as head of the New Mexico church by Bishop José Antonio Laureano de Zubiría.

The conflict between Lamy and local clergymen continued, however, and was especially marked between Lamy and Father ANTONIO JOSÉ MARTÍNEZ of Taos Parish. Martínez objected to Lamy's policy of vigorously collecting church tithes and his 1854 announcement that household heads who refused church levies were to be excluded from the sacraments. Other members of such families were to be charged triple fees for baptisms.

Lamy emerged victorious in his struggle against the native clergy; he then set out to reinvigorate the institutional church. He relied on French Christian Brothers, Kentucky Sisters of Loretto, and Ohio Sisters of Charity to found schools and hospitals. He saw to it that old churches were repaired and new churches and chapels were built and that the Jesuits, a group tolerant of the Penitentes, briefly established a school in Las Vegas before moving to Colorado to found Regis College. In 1867, Lamy reported that New Mexico had thirty-one missions and fifty-one active priests, most of whom were Europeans.

Despite these institutional contributions, historian Warren Beck has noted that not all of Lamy's accomplishments were positive. His most recent biographer, Paul Horgan, praised the archbishop but confirmed Beck's beliefs that Lamy never understood Hispanics and their manner of religious expression. As Howard Lamar observed, Lamy's struggle with Martínez and other local clergymen contributed to New Mexico's "politics of disunity." Finally, Lamy's placement of clerics in both public and parochial schools may have delayed the establishment of a "regular" public-school system in New Mexico.

Bishop Lamy, in the character of Father Latour, is the hero of WILLA CATHER's *Death Comes for the Archbishop*. The fictionalized history reinforced cultural stereotypes and portrayed Lamy as a son of light locked in conflict with the chief servant of the forces of darkness, Father Martínez.

—*Ralph H. Vigil*

SEE ALSO: Catholics

SUGGESTED READING:

Beck, Warren A. *New Mexico: A History of Four Centuries*. Norman, Okla., 1962.
Cather, Willa. *Death Comes for the Archbishop*. New York, 1927.
Francis, E. K. "Padre Martínez: A New Mexican Myth." *New Mexico Historical Review* 31 (1956): 265–289.
Horgan, Paul. *Lamy of Santa Fe: His Life and Times*. New York, 1975.
Lamar, Howard Roberts. *The Far Southwest, 1846–1912: A Territorial History*. New York, 1970.
Mares, E. A. *I Returned and Saw under the Sun*. Albuquerque, N. Mex., 1989.
Vigil, Ralph H. "Willa Cather and Historical Reality." *New Mexico Historical Review* 50 (1975): 123–138.

LAND GRANT ACT OF 1862

SEE: Morrill Act of 1862

LAND GRANT COLLEGES

SEE: Colleges and Universities

LAND OFFICE

SEE: General Land Office

LANDON, ALFRED MOSSMAN

Oilman and politician Alfred Mossman Landon (1887–1987) was born in Pennsylvania. After moving first to Ohio and then to KANSAS, he earned a law degree from the state university in 1908. He worked as a banker for a short time and then entered the oil business as an independent operator.

Landon became involved in politics in 1914, and this activity dominated the rest of his life. He served as governor of Kansas from 1933 to 1937 and was the Republican nominee for president in 1936. After his defeat, he assumed the role of elder statesman for the Republican party.

He was the father of Nancy Landon Kassebaum, senator from Kansas and the first woman to be elected to the U.S. Senate in her own right.

—*Joseph W. Snell*

SUGGESTED READING:
McCoy, Donald R. *Landon of Kansas.* Lincoln, Nebr., 1966.

LAND POLICY

Historical Overview
   Hal Rothman

Land Companies
   Charles Phillips

Land Ordinance of 1785
   Charles Phillips

Private Land Claims
   Charles Phillips

Land Law of 1851
   Patricia Hogan

HISTORICAL OVERVIEW

Land policy in the West has reflected the objectives of the governments that have had control of the region. Since the arrival of Spanish colonizers in New Mexico in 1598, a variety of regimes in the West developed policies that demonstrated the value system and predispositions of the culture implementing the decisions.

The limits of Spanish resources in northern New Spain dictated Spanish policy. The church and the state colonized together, and the mission and the presidio, a military installation, were the primary institutions of Spanish conquest. They often were locked in deep rivalry. On the upper Rio Grande in particular, where the sedentary Pueblo Indians were located, Spaniards simply added a mission, a priest, and a few soldiers to existing villages and sought to transform the lives of native peoples into something more acceptable in Spanish eyes.

The Spaniards sought to encourage the settlement and protection of their communities through the distribution of lands in their North American colonies. There were three ways for people to acquire land. The crown often gave community grants to groups of people, the most important way to create a landholding class. In these grants, each family had a residential grant and a plot of irrigated land, as well as the right to cut timber and graze animals on the *ejido,* the generally much larger area of common land that was part of the grant. The second system, the proprietary grant, gave land to an individual, who secured settlers, distributed land, and provided for irrigation works. In that scenario, the grant holder became the *patron* of the community. The crown used the third type of grant, the *sitio,* to reward military, political, and economic service. The grantee then functioned as the holder of a proprietary grant.

The three kinds of grants accomplished the goals of the Spanish. They maintained an elite, who, while wealthy in material terms, were not always that much better off than their peasants. The grants offered a means to create communities on the periphery of the Spanish world as a way to protect its core, and, in the best of times, generated wealth. A northern New Spain full of Spanish settlers was not an objective, and what resulted was a system that differentiated classes as much by land ownership as by parentage.

During the Mexican era in the Southwest, which lasted from 1821 to 1846, the Spanish forms of landholding continued. The Mexican authorities, even weaker than the Spanish who preceded them, gave many more grants in their brief tenure than the Spanish did in the preceding two hundred years. The Mexican government saw the settlement of landowners on the northern periphery as the only protection against encroachment from the growing republic to the north—the United States. Ironically, some of the Mexican grants worked against national objectives. MOSES AUSTIN, the father of Texas pioneer STEPHEN FULLER AUSTIN, as one of the EMPRESARIOS, received a proprietary grant, from the Mexican government in 1824. That grant was the first step on the way to the TEXAS REVOLUTION and the battle at the ALAMO.

When the American government consolidated its land acquisitions in the aftermath of the Civil War, the nation found itself in possession of vast areas of West-

Federal lawmakers intended to create a land policy designed to encourage the settlement of the West. In an image of Hollister, Idaho, buyers flock to a land office to make their purchases. *Courtesy Denver Public Library, Western History Department*

ern land, which many believed had great agricultural potential. In reality, much of the land was subhumid or arid, and little opportunity for unirrigated AGRICULTURE existed west of the one hundredth meridian. But Americans were committed to the idea of a landholding citizenry, and unlike the Spanish before them, they sought to settle the West, not merely colonize it. American law reflected such goals; the HOMESTEAD ACT OF 1862 gave settlers title to unclaimed but surveyed public domain land for five years residence, a filing fee, and the price of improvement. After six months residence and suitable improvement, homesteaders had the option to convert an entry to full title for the price of $1.25 an acre. In 1880, the Homestead Act was extended to unsurveyed land.

Along with two other pieces of legislation passed at almost the same time—the MORRILL ACT OF 1862, which created land-grant colleges, and the Pacific Railroad Act, which granted land to railroads as a subsidy for investing in transcontinental railroad construction—the Homestead Act reflected the predisposition of Americans for a classless, land-owning public. The new farmers, expanding into what was seen as fertile land, were to be the backbone of the nation, its producers and consumers.

But the reality of Western land made that impossible, and efforts to give Western agriculture a future embodied changes in law and policy. Acts such as the TIMBER CULTURE ACT OF 1873, the DESERT LAND ACT OF 1877, the TIMBER AND STONE ACT OF 1878, the Forest Lieu Act of 1897, the Kincaid Homestead Act of 1904, the Forest Homestead Act of 1906, and the ENLARGED HOMESTEAD ACT OF 1909 were all designed to alleviate

the burdens created for Western farmers by the lack of WATER and arability of much Western land.

Sadly, most of the legislation played into the hands of speculators, a fixture in American land transactions since before the Revolutionary War. The Timber Culture Act, which was supposed to help farmers acquire additional land by planting trees, was one example of how legislation could be circumvented. On the plains, timber would not grow, and the 40 acres of trees required in the initial bill to claim 160 acres was reduced to 10 acres of trees in 1878. Even that proved impossible, and instead of promoting settlement, the law was used to tie up land for ranchers. Cowboys filed claims on areas near rivers and streams to preserve water and the best grazing land from settlement. Although the commissioner of the GENERAL LAND OFFICE recommended repeal of the law as early as 1882, only in 1891 did Congress finally terminate this well-intended failure.

By the early twentieth century, most Americans recognized that HOMESTEADING held little opportunity. The best lands were long gone, and farming had lost its place in the American economy. The process of creating a large landholding class by giving away government land had been a failure. Some of the reasons were obvious: poor quality land and lack of water, capital, and appropriate technology. But an underlying process also contributed to the demise of homesteading. At the very moment free land became available to landless Americans and immigrants, land had ceased to be the measure of wealth in what was becoming an industrial economy. All of the policy strategies in the world could not change that.

—Hal Rothman

SEE ALSO: Farming; Northwest Ordinance; Public Lands Commission of 1879; Railroad Land Grants; Territorial Government; Territories and States

SUGGESTED READING:

Carstensen, Vernon, ed. *The Public Lands: Studies in the History of the Public Domain.* Madison, Wisc., 1968.

Gates, Paul Wallace. *History of Public Land Law Development.* Washington, D.C., 1968.

Johnson, Hildegard Binder. *Order upon the Land.* New York, 1976.

Hibbard, Benjamin H. *A History of Public Land Policies.* New York, 1941.

Opie, John. *The Law of the Land: 200 Years of American Farmland Policy.* Lincoln, Nebr., 1987.

Rohrbaugh, Malcolm J. *The Land Office Business: The Settlement and Administration of American Public Lands, 1789–1837.* New York, 1968.

Wyant, William K. *Westward in Eden.* Berkeley, Calif., 1982.

LAND COMPANIES

From the earliest days of English and Dutch encroachments on North America, land and trading companies provided the men and money that made settlement possible. They recruited settlers, transported them across the Atlantic, and subsidized the colonies they established. The London Company, the Plymouth Company, and the Dutch West Indies Company invested substantial sums trying to establish colonies that would produce minerals, furs, and other commodities to sell in the mother country. In addition, the companies acquired large tracts of lands as manors in hopes of receiving rental income from them. Over time, these companies failed to produce large returns for their investors from trade, but speculation in land itself proved more promising, and it became commonplace for governments to charter companies, grant them huge tracts of land and government powers, and send them off to settle land in the New World. As colonies were established and grew in the eighteenth century, investments in land to the west proffered at least the hope of profit and a rapid turnover of capital. New land companies sprang into existence, some of them—such as the Susquehanna Land Company—purely local affairs, others—such as the Transylvania Company—corporations that took investments both from the colonists and from English capitalists. The aggressive search for new fields of investment by such companies was a contributing factor in the advancing "frontier" between English colonies and the French-allied Indian tribes, who resisted having the land they owned bought and sold by others.

During the American Revolution, the speculative schemes of many of these companies collapsed as the frontier settlements were forced to retreat eastward, but in the peace that followed, proposals for the purchase of lands in the West again abounded, and such commercial enterprises as the Ohio Company (a New England–based operation named after an earlier Virginia-dominated land company) and the Scioto Company (an Ohio Company subsidiary) not only provided much of the political, economic, and social leadership in the newly "opened" lands, but also lobbied the Congress hard for the passage of the NORTHWEST ORDINANCE. Thus a Congress in need of money and an Ohio Company willing to provide it (in return for 1.5 million acres at greatly reduced prices) came to create the structure by which new territories—in effect, U.S. colonies—would be transformed into states and become equal partners in the body politic. As the original states, which, in centuries past, had laid claims to the land stretching west from their current borders, were forced to relinquish their claims, they either ceded these lands to the federal government or sold them to big land companies. American companies like Phelps and Gorham, Scottish-owned Pilteney and Associates, Dutch-controlled Holland Land Company, and the Ohio and Yazoo companies created a pattern of speculation and colonization of the West later adopted and expanded on by the land-grant RAILROADS.

Land speculation ran rampant. The companies invested millions of dollars in wildernesses far from any kind of transportation and unlikely to be turned into farms any time soon. Eventually, the companies—and various individuals—who had borrowed heavily to finance their investments could no longer carry their land holdings, at which point would come the inevitable crash as land companies were forced to liquidate their holdings and collapse into bankruptcy. The boom-and-bust cycles, in part established by land speculators and in part fed by them, came to dominate the economy of the West throughout its history. Land purchases, for example, reached their peak in the BOOMS immediately preceding 1819, 1837, and 1857, years witnessing major FINANCIAL PANICS followed by economic depressions. The difference between individual speculators and private land companies, however, was marked. The former bought up land, withheld it from settlement, and waited for the area to develop economically and to drive up the price of land before selling off at a profit; the latter initiated and directed immigration, lent settlers capital for land improvement, took livestock and crops for payment in lieu of cash, and tended to be understanding creditors when crops failed or disaster struck.

In the rapid industrial development of the trans-Mississippi West after the Civil War, railroad companies—which, like others before them, received generous land grants from the government and included among their investors European capitalists—became major land companies as well, often as concerned about the sale and the settlement of the land they held as they were about building the tracks and operating trains. As the railroads became the empire-building equivalents of the earlier land companies, such as the Holland Land Company and the Ohio Company, a new kind of land company began to appear in the West, one that developed its holdings through tenants, who had no equity in the land they worked. Whereas a land company like the MAXWELL LAND GRANT COMPANY, which built up its holdings with spurious land claims based on private Spanish and Mexican land grants, continued to operate much like the empire builders of the past, a company like the Kern County Land Company of California had no intention of selling its land, but regarded it instead as a permanent investment, not unlike the original colonizing British and Dutch merchant enterprises.

—*Charles Phillips*

LAND ORDINANCE OF 1785

The Land Ordinance of 1785 created a simple means for the acquisition and distribution of public lands in the West. Once Native Americans had vacated their lands, the federal government employed surveyors to mark the land off into large, six-mile squares, then subdivide them into sections, each one square mile. These sections were further divided into four others, each containing 160 acres. The government then sold these quarter sections at public auction—one tier of townships at a time. Surplus lands left after the auction could be purchased at the land offices established by the ordinance, with the minimum price initially set at two dollars per acre. Although that figure was later revised downward, it never fell below one dollar per acre. This, and subsequent legislation, pledged the use of revenues from public lands for the payment of government debts. The sale of public lands for the purpose of raising money was a feature of public-land policy from the start.

The pledge to use land revenues to pay debts strengthened the government's credit, but the lands did not became an important source of revenue until the mid-1830s, when sales boomed and land revenues constituted almost half the nation's income. By 1836, the public debt had been retired. Although any justification for keeping the price of public lands high had vanished as well, certain politicians—HENRY CLAY among them—wanted to continue to produce government surpluses that would be distributed to the states on the basis of their population, a plan much in favor by

the established states. Others, who saw the trans-Mississippi West as a place to maintain the country's native populations or who, for other reasons, wanted to discourage citizens from moving west, also argued for keeping the costs of public lands high. But a reform movement, headed by labor leader George Henry Evans and soon joined by the influential editor of the *New York Tribune,* Horace Greeley, got under way in the late 1830s and early 1840s. The reformers called for free land in the West to draw off surplus labor from the cities and improve labor's bargaining power with Eastern employers. Evans's SAFETY-VALVE THEORY, based on the AGRARIANISM of founding fathers Thomas Paine and THOMAS JEFFERSON, called for free land in small tracts for settlers, a limit to the amount of land one individual could own, and an exemption for the worker and his family from debt collection. The free-soil movement, adamantly opposed by slave-owning Southern planters and relentlessly promoted by Greeley, resulted in the emergence in 1848 of a Free-Soil party and ultimately in the passage, during the Civil War, of the HOMESTEAD ACT OF 1862. Meanwhile, within the context of the free-soil ideology, the Land Ordinance of 1785 became the basis for a land system in the West— a system whose premises remained unchallenged until the end of the nineteenth century.

Under the impact of the free-soil movement, land sales never became the important source of revenue they had been before 1836. Instead, Americans believed that Western land could best be put to use by placing it in private hands and ensuring its transformation into small farms that would form the foundation of the country's republican future. The United States would not be like Europe, a country of wealthy landlords and poor tenants, but a land of small, independent, individual property holders, whose efforts to "improve" their land would create the wealth by which the country, as a whole, would grow. Such widely dispersed land ownership, as Thomas Jefferson had always argued, would be the best safeguard against dangerous concentrations of power. In addition, the sale of public lands would be used to produce a basic public infrastructure for the West. Under the original land ordinance, one section in each township—Section Sixteen—was to provide income for public schools; in 1848, Congress added a second section, Section Thirty-six, as well. Although territories and states sometimes leased these sections and used the income to build and support schools, more often, they sold them off with congressional permission and then invested the proceeds in a permanent, interest-bearing school fund. Increasingly, Congress granted lands to the states in order to finance the building of canals, the dredging of rivers, and the construction of roads. In the process,

Congress passed hundreds of different land laws (some 375 of them before 1834), amending the original land ordinance to change the minimum price of land, for example, or first to offer credit and then to deny credit.

As the United States imposed the dictates laid out in the Land Ordinance of 1785, it created the checkerboard landscape that distinguishes much of the country from the air today. Nowhere else in the world would a stretch so large be so uniformly divided. The survey's very rigidity was meant to avoid the hopeless tangle of claims found back in Kentucky and Tennessee, and it also made the system itself infinitely reproducible. It seemed to presume growth, and the easily divided and combined squares of land, allowing for simple exchanges, produced a geometry ideal for speculation, for wheeling and dealing. In practice, the occupation of the trans-Appalachian and then the trans-Mississippi West was never as elegant as it was on paper.

Frequently, squatters moved in faster than surveyors, and individual speculators and land companies who bought up public lands for resale had a major impact on the price and easy availability of land. In Iowa, for example, in the mid-1850s, the distribution of land within the land system came to depend on speculation. In the decade between 1850 and 1860 somewhere between one-half and three-fourths of those buying farms got their land from speculators or from grants the federal government had turned over to the state. The farmers themselves sometimes became land speculators. By 1862, speculators held two-thirds of all private land in Iowa, and public lands had been reduced to a few small tracts set aside for education. In the end, nearly 90 percent of Iowa's farmers acquired at least part of their incredibly fertile farms from someone other than the federal government.

Under such circumstances, land originally available for a few dollars was often purchased and held under the "time-entry" system—by money advanced by land agents at 40 percent interest—and resold at considerably inflated prices. Not surprisingly, fights over land law became commonplace. At stake was more than the individual farmstead, since how the nation distributed its land basically defined American society and determined what version of that society it would reproduce west of the Mississippi.

—*Charles Phillips*

SEE ALSO: Northwest Ordinance

SUGGESTED READING:

Hibbard, Benjamin H. *A History of Public Land Policies.* New York, 1941.

Opie, John. *The Law of the Land: 200 Years of American Farmland Policy.* Lincoln, Nebr., 1987.

Rohrbaugh, Malcolm J. *The Land Office Business: The Settlement and Administration of American Public Lands.* New York, 1968.

Swierenga, Robert P. *Pioneers and Profits: Land Speculation on the Iowa Frontier.* Ames, Iowa, 1968.

PRIVATE LAND CLAIMS

In the course of acquiring the trans-Mississippi West through purchase and conquest, the United States found itself in control of a public domain that included private land grants from Great Britain, France, Spain, and Mexico and that created considerable confusion and legal problems with land titles—problems that, in many cases, involved extensive litigation lasting for decades and, in some cases, well into the twentieth century. In all, perhaps some thirty thousand private claims were filed as the United States added new Western territories to its domain, and the lands involved a total area the size of present-day Wisconsin. As late as the mid-twentieth century, disputes over land claims flared into violence, as they did when Reies Tijerina, unhappy with the court decision concerning his claims to land in New Mexico, launched a raid on the Tierra Amarilla Courthouse in 1967.

In the nineteenth century, the U.S. Congress, state legislatures, and the U.S. courts became deeply involved in sorting out these conflicting claims and concessions, which were critical to the future development of the trans-Mississippi West, particularly those private Spanish and Mexican land grants in Missouri, Louisiana, California, and New Mexico. Although there were problems with private claims as well in Mississippi and Florida, and some claims in Michigan, Illinois, Alabama, and Arkansas involved good farm land and desirable city plots, it was Western land claims that were most problematic. Settlers, traditionally accustomed to regarding "frontier" lands as "open" to squatting and preemption, not only set up homesteads on lands surrounding the big Spanish or Mexican grants but also frequently squatted on portions that the owners had failed to develop. Even when they understood that the lands, in some sense, belonged to others, they also knew that history was on their side and fully expected their holdings in these large and unused tracts would be confirmed by the government or the courts.

Adjudication of the conflicting land claims was made more difficult by the fact that the Spanish and Mexican governments who had made the grants had often been vague as to the nature of the grants, imprecise as to their extent, and lax in keeping records. In addition, squatting and preemption were hot political issues within the United States. Some portrayed the squatters as lawless vagabonds. Easterners and Southerners, especially before the Civil War, argued that squatters used property to which they had no legal title and subverted the civilized communities that U.S. land policy and laws had intended to create. If allowed to continue, they said, the American West would become a region of thinly scattered barbarians, living off the richest lands but unable to support republican institutions. Others, Westerners and Democrats especially, saw the squatters not as land pirates and barbarians, but as noble pioneers, capital-poor farmers who were securing the rapid development of the country and who, by using the land, would create the revenue needed to buy it. That not small homesteaders but large land speculators frequently benefited from this "theft" of private grants was ignored in a political atmosphere that characterized the battle as one of anarchy on the one side and economic development on the other. In Missouri and elsewhere, political factions coalesced around the land claims. Frequently, newly arrived lawyers took on established businessmen, each championing their own candidates for political office. In any case, until the land claims were ruled on, it was nearly impossible to open for settlement the lands immediately surrounding them unless the squatters moved in.

Congress, as it set about to pass judgments on the claims, created commissions to investigate the claims, gather information, report their findings, and make recommendations. In general, Congress seemed inclined to approve claims up to 640 acres, and later up to 2,000 acres, but looked with a jaundiced eye on larger claims. As political and financial leaders acquired interests in these claims, they hired some of the more famous lawyers of the time to defend them, while those defending the government's interest—claims-commissions members, district attorneys, Justice Department officials—were men with more mediocre legal reputations. Prominent Westerners such as Henry W. Halleck, a well-known general in the Civil War, JOHN CHARLES FRÉMONT, and Commodore ROBERT F. STOCKTON acquired claims and hired the likes of Daniel Webster and THOMAS HART BENTON to defend the claims in court. Even while serving in a Congress that established Western land policy, well-known legislators would appear before the Supreme Court on behalf of their wealthy private clients. And the higher courts tended to side with the high-profile, highly paid legal talent and almost routinely to confirm "borderline" claims the lower courts had rejected.

Before the Civil War, the land claims and the slavery issue often went hand in hand, since "free land" was a threat to plantations whose lands might be based on Spanish or Mexican grants. Many of Missouri's wealthy and influential early settlers, for example, depended on slave labor, and they objected bitterly when

the federal government split the Louisiana Purchase in two, creating the Territory of Orleans and the District of Louisiana and assigning administration of the latter to the Territory of Indiana, whose distant capital at Vincennes made it difficult for them to wield influence with the governor. Worried that Indiana's laws did not fully protect the institution of slavery and that they would be unable to press effectively their claims to land granted them by the former Spanish government, they called a convention in St. Louis to protest the location of the seat of government in Indiana. They couched their real worries in protests about new taxes, absent officials, endless delays, and unfair treatment. In 1805, Congress responded by renaming the district the Territory of Missouri and locating its capital at St. Louis. These men, who included among their ranks the CHOUTEAU FAMILY and Charles Gratiot, became known as the "little junto," or the "St. Louis junto," an established elite who were opposed by a younger group of mostly St. Louis lawyers in the attempt to have the federal government recognize Spanish land grants. The bitter feuds between these two groups over land titles dominated the politics of the early territorial government and led to a growing resentment among the "honest farmers" in Missouri against the St. Louis clique. Thomas Hart Benton fed that resentment to launch his career in the U.S. Senate, and it was no accident that he became the foremost spokesman for Western expansion and free land in the West and the sponsor of the temporary preemption acts of the 1830s and the permanent PREEMPTION ACT OF 1841, nor that ultimately he would resign his senate seat over Missouri's proslavery stand.

Just how much a stalking horse slavery happened to be when it came to a question of free land, however, became clear in California, where early on there was no question of squatters threatening the land holdings of slave-owning planters. In the Bay Area in the 1850s, disappointed gold-rushers squatted on the large but wholly undeveloped lands granted the local Californio elite by a weak Mexican government. The litigation, prolonged for decades, grew increasingly politicized, with the settlers' faction exercising considerable influence over the state legislature and the landed gentry controlling the unfriendly state and local courts. Local authorities sometimes sent posses out to dispossess large mobs of squatters, and the battle over land claims kept the state in a constant uproar for years, which ultimately led to attacks like those by HENRY GEORGE on the entire Anglo-American system of land laws and taxes. But California's land claims paled in their scandalousness compared to those in New Mexico, where the MAXWELL LAND GRANT COMPANY managed to turn one claim, which originally included fewer than

100,000 acres into a massive grant of nearly 2 million acres, one-fifth of the total land recognized by the courts as representing legitimate claims. By contrast, Texas, which indeed had potential problems from old Spanish and Mexican land grants, but in which public lands belonged mostly to the state and not the federal government, had less trouble and nowhere near the delays experienced by other states in confirming private land claims. There, however, as elsewhere, disputed land claims were used to dispossess the Hispanic elite and turn big landholdings over to a few powerful Anglo-Americans instead of the small freeholders in whose name the battles over such claims were usually fought.

—*Charles Phillips*

SEE ALSO: Claims Associations; Empresarios

SUGGESTED READING:

Carstensen, Vernon, ed. *The Public Lands: Studies in the History of the Public Domain.* Madison, Wis., 1968.

Gates, Paul Wallace. *History of Public Land Law Development.* Washington, D.C., 1968.

Robbins, Roy M. *Our Landed Heritage.* Princeton, N.J., 1942.

LAND LAW OF 1851

Passed by the U.S. Congress, the Land Law of 1851 required Californios—Mexican and Spanish residents of California under Mexican rule—to prove in U.S. courts valid titles to the lands they held prior to the United States's annexation of California in 1850.

The effect of the law was disastrous for owners of CALIFORNIA RANCHOS. Although the courts eventually accepted their claims for all but seven hundred thousand of the fourteen million acres in question, Californios spent years in court and hundreds of thousands of dollars in lawyers' fees. Most were forced to sell portions of their lands to finance their legal battles. Others incurred debts to money lenders, bankers, tax collectors, and squatters—debts they satisfied by selling land.

In the end, the ranchos of California were sold off to American immigrants from the East. Rancheros and the legions of Mexican vaqueros, sheepherders, and ranch workers they employed were forced into urban barrios of Los Angeles, Santa Barbara, and other cities. Subject to racial discrimination and violence, they became a distinctive minority in the second half of the nineteenth century.

—*Patricia Hogan*

SUGGESTED READING:

Pitt, Leonard. *The Decline of the Californios: A Social History of the Spanish-Speaking Californians, 1846–1890.* Berkeley, Calif., 1970.

LANE, FRANKLIN KNIGHT

California lawyer, newspaperman, and politician Franklin Knight Lane (1864–1921) was born on Prince Edward Island, Canada. When he was six years old, his family moved to California.

After several years of part-time study at the University of California, Lane passed the state bar exam, but before practicing law, he worked as the New York correspondent for the *San Francisco Chronicle.* He returned to California in 1894 and established a law practice. Drawn into politics through a campaign attacking civic corruption, he became San Francisco's city attorney in 1898.

In 1905, he was appointed to the Interstate Commerce Commission, where he made his name as a reformer. He believed that evils could be corrected by changes in the law and wrote many of the commission's important decisions.

In 1913, President Woodrow Wilson appointed Lane secretary of the interior. He displayed great zeal in carrying out his duties. He was a firsthand investigator who often traveled to Indian reservations, national parks, and reclamation sites.

Calling Indian reservations "orphan asylums," he attempted to "turn the Native American loose . . . individually," through education, not "in great masses" as some advocated.

Although Lane believed that the West's resources should be fully developed, he became a vigorous champion of the national parks and the NATIONAL PARK SERVICE.

Lane took great pride in his citizenship. He felt that Americans who boasted of raising the "largest pumpkin" or erecting the "highest dam" reflected not a "parochial-minded provincialism" but the "very essence of the highest creative quality." He held that every American was a "discoverer, . . . revealing to the world something it was not before aware of."

—*Ernest Morrison*

SUGGESTED READING:

Olson, Keith W. *Biography of a Progressive: Franklin K. Lane, 1864–1921.* Westport, Conn., 1979.

LANE, JAMES HENRY

James Henry Lane (1814–1866), soldier and politician, was born in Lawrenceburg, Indiana. Lane served on the city council of Lawrenceburg, Indiana; practiced law; was colonel of two volunteer regiments during the United States–Mexican War; was elected lieutenant-governor; and served one term in the U.S. House of Representatives.

An ambitious man, Lane moved to Kansas in April 1855 and was intent on being elected a U.S. senator when that territory became a state. Within weeks after his arrival, he cast his lot with the newly formed Free State Party, although he had been a lifelong Democrat. Because of his fiery speeches and oratorical ability, he soon became a leader of the party's fanatical faction.

Known as the "Grim Chieftain," he participated in several armed skirmishes between abolitionists and proslave advocates.

When Kansas was admitted to the Union in 1861, Lane was elected one of its first senators. During the CIVIL WAR, he was commissioned a brigadier general, while still holding his seat in the Senate. He raised five infantry regiments, one of which was composed of black soldiers, but did not serve with them.

After the war, he sided with President Andrew Johnson in the controversy over the Freedman's Bureau and civil rights. On a visit home in the spring of 1866, he learned that his support of Johnson had cost him the leadership position he had enjoyed in Kansas for many years. He became deranged, shot himself in the mouth, and died ten days later.

—*Joseph W. Snell*

SUGGESTED READING:
Stephenson, Wendell Holmes. *The Political Career of General James H. Lane.* Topeka, Kans., 1930.

LANE, JOSEPH

Soldier and politician Joseph Lane (1801–1881) was born in North Carolina. He first achieved national prominence in 1846 as a general in the United States–Mexican War. He was appointed the Oregon Territory's first governor in 1849 and also superintendent of Indian affairs—a role that won him popular support. He won election as one of Oregon's first two U.S. Senators and served from 1859 to 1861.

Openly sympathetic to the South, Lane ran as the vice-presidential candidate on the Southern Democratic ticket in 1860. His proslavery convictions lost him favor with the majority of Oregonians.

Lane withdrew from public life until, at the age of seventy-nine, he reemerged to run for the state senate and lost.

—*Shannon Applegate*

SUGGESTED READING:
Hendrickson, James E. *Joe Lane of Oregon.* New Haven, Conn., and London, 1967.

LANGUAGE SCHOOLS

Most common in communities of Japanese immigrants but also present among other immigrant groups, language schools sought to educate immigrant children in the traditions and language of their homelands. The schools supplemented the education children received in their community public schools. In the case of the Japanese, the first language schools appeared in Hawaii the 1890s, founded to serve the children of Japanese sugar-plantation laborers. By 1907, 120 schools served 4,966 pupils. Often, these schools received support from the sugar-plantation management as a means of keeping Japanese workers content. At the turn of the century, language schools had cropped up on the U.S. mainland, where, within two decades, the number of schools had grown to 80, and the number of students, to 2,442. The schools reached their peak popularity just before World War II. Language schools continued to operate well into the last decades of the twentieth century. Their students, at first Nisei (American-born children of Japanese immigrants), in later years were the Sansei (third-generation) and Yonsei (fourth generation) JAPANESE AMERICANS who were several generations removed from their ancestors' homeland.

Most schools operated after public schools released students on weekdays and on Saturday mornings. For some Nisei, the schools were a distasteful chore covering subjects from which the youngsters were far removed and taught in a language that seemed to erect a barrier between Japanese students and the world beyond their homes. For other reasons, attendance in the schools sometimes intensified generational conflicts within immigrant families. Among other students, however, the schools were a welcomed respite from the prejudice and discrimination they faced in public schools and an opportunity to interact with other Japanese American children of their own age and experiences.

Within white society, language schools were viewed quite critically. In the years before World War I, the schools were stereotyped as promoting "emperor worship" by Americans who charged that it was inappropriate for American-born children to spend so much time studying a "foreign" language and culture. In the antiforeign rhetoric following the war, the slogan "One Language Under One Flag" voiced opposition to the schools. In both Hawaii and on the mainland, legislators and local governments attempted to curtail or eliminate the operation of language schools. Beginning in 1918, Hawaiian lawmakers introduced bills restricting hours of operation, specifying qualifications for teachers, and levying special taxes on the schools. In 1921, California passed similar laws.

The restrictions on these schools provoked Japanese Americans to appeal to the U.S. courts. A case was brought before the territorial circuit court of Hawaii in 1922 on behalf of 16 schools. By the time the Supreme Court heard the case, 88 schools had signed on. They won; the court deemed all the attempts at regulation unconstitutional.

The battle over language schools raged, despite the fact that the schools were not much of a hindrance to Nisei Americanization. Numerous studies proved that the schools were not effective in teaching Japanese Americans the Japanese language. In a 1941 search for Nisei soldiers suitable for the intelligence service during World War II, for example, military authorities found that among the thirty-seven hundred enlisted Nisei tested, 90 percent of them did not know enough Japanese to be considered trainable. Only 4 percent possessed a proficiency in the language sufficient for intelligence work. In the end, language schools worked better as symbols of the hopes and dreams of immigrant parents—and determined nativist opposition—than as effective aids to Asian American CHILD REARING.

—*Patricia Hogan*

SUGGESTED READING:
Hawkins, John N. "Politics, Education, and Language Policy: The Case of Japanese Language Schools in Hawaii." *Amerasia Journal* 5 (1978): 39–56.
Morimoto, Toyotomi. "Language and Heritage Maintenance of Immigrants: Japanese Language Schools in California, 1903–1941." Ph.d. diss., University of California, Los Angeles, 1989.

LARKIN, THOMAS OLIVER

American consul to Mexican California and "confidential agent" for Secretary of State JAMES BUCHANAN, Thomas Oliver Larkin (1802–1858) settled in California in 1832. Larkin worked as a merchant in Monterey, carried on trade with Mexico and the Sandwich Islands, and was one of the town's most successful businessmen. He is credited with developing the Monterey colonial style of architecture. His own house, built between 1835 and 1837, was two stories and had adobe walls, redwood framing, broad verandahs on all sides, and a low hipped roof of shingles. The style, reminiscent of New England colonial houses, became popular among Californians over the coming years.

Unlike many other Americans who had settled in Mexican California, Larkin retained his U.S. citizenship. He did support, however, the 1836 revolution of Juan Bautista Alvarado to establish California's independence. In 1844, Larkin was named U.S. consul in

Mexican California, and two years later, Secretary of State James Buchanan named him a "confidential agent" with orders to secure the secession of California from Mexico and foil any plans the British might have to gain possession of California for themselves. While Larkin was undertaking peaceful negotiations, however, JOHN CHARLES FRÉMONT stirred up the Bear Flag Revolt in the Sacramento Valley, and war with Mexico began. Any hopes of peaceful cession of California were thus shattered.

In 1848, Larkin was a delegate to the California Constitutional Convention.

—*Candace Floyd*

SUGGESTED READING:
Caruso, A. Brooke. *The Mexican Spy Company: United States Covert Operations in Mexico, 1845–1848.* Jefferson, N.C., 1991.

LARPENTEUR, CHARLES

A native of France, Charles Larpenteur (1807–1872) spent forty years as a fur trader in the wilderness along the northern reaches of the Missouri River. As a young man, Larpenteur migrated to the United States with his family and settled in Maryland. As an adult, he moved to Missouri. By 1833, he was employed as a laborer for William Sublette and ROBERT CAMPBELL in their fur-trading business. Larpenteur's determination to become a fur trader was frustrated by his entry into the business just at the time of its decline.

Larpenteur worked for Sublette and Campbell until the two sold their enterprise to the rival AMERICAN FUR COMPANY. Larpenteur next served the larger concern for ten years as clerk and trader at FORT UNION on the Yellowstone River. From the mid-1840s into the 1860s, he worked ever harder to trap increasingly scarce furs. By 1864, he had settled at Fort Union handling supplies for the U.S. Army. He recorded the events of his career in *Forty Years a Fur Trader on the Upper Missouri: The Personal Narrative of Charles Larpenteur, 1833–1872.* The memoir, published in 1898, offered one of the best firsthand descriptions of the fur-trade business. After his stint as a trapper, he retired to farming in Iowa.

—*Patricia Hogan*

SEE ALSO: Fur Trade; Sublette Brothers; Trappers

SUGGESTED READING:
Larpenteur, Charles. *Forty Years a Fur Trader on the Upper Missouri: The Personal Narrative of Charles Larpenteur, 1833–1872.* Reprint. Chicago, 1933.

LA SALLE, SIEUR DE (CAVELIER, RENÉ ROBERT)

French explorer René Robert Cavalier (1643–1687), known by his family name of La Salle, was born in Rouen in Normandy and educated by the Jesuits. Stubborn and strong-willed, the twenty-three-year old La Salle set sail for Canada in 1666, after he had secured a land grant—a *seigneury*—there through family connections. Mastering both the Iroquois and the Algonquian languages, La Salle began exploring the Old Northwest in 1669, "discovering" for France both the Ohio and the Illinois river valleys before 1673. The next year, he returned home looking for financial backers and a kind word from his king and then sailed back to North America to build Fort Frontenac near present-day Kingston, Ontario. Jealousy at court and angry creditors forced his return to France again in 1677, but he turned the trip to his advantage by garnering a royal patent to explore and occupy the Mississippi River valley based on his assertions that the country lay close to Mexico and to a potential silver bonanza. The treasure proved chimerical, and La Salle set himself up in the Mississippi FUR TRADE, interests of which he sought to protect as he further explored the region in 1680 and struggled against business reversals and mounting debt. In April 1682, La Salle reached the Mississippi delta and named the entire valley Louisiana in honor of his king. On a final trip to France in 1683, La Salle recruited colonists for an expedition to settle regions west of the great river. On Matagorda Bay, he built Fort St. Louis in present-day Texas, where he spent two miserable years before heading to Illinois to resupply his outpost. La Salle's behavior, to the dismay of his half-starved and morally dejected men, grew increasingly unbalanced. Somewhere in eastern Texas, thinking him mad, they murdered him.

—*Charles Phillips*

LAS GORRAS BLANCAS

SEE: Gorras Blancas, Las

LAS VEGAS, NEVADA

For centuries, the Las Vegas Valley served primarily as an oasis for Paiute Indians who lived nearby. In the early 1830s, Mexican travelers, linked to caravans between New Mexico and Los Angeles, named the place Las Vegas, which is Spanish for "The Meadows." In 1855, Mormon settlers established a community as a way station for travelers along the "Mormon Corridor" between Utah and southern California, but within three years, internal dissension resulted in their abandoning the settlement. A series of proprietors operated the way station's ranch from 1865 until its sale in 1902 to former Montana copper magnate WILLIAM ANDREWS CLARK. His San Pedro, Los Angeles and Salt Lake Railroad needed the ranch and its water rights to support a division town and repair station. Clark's land company platted the community in 1905. By 1911, Las Vegas was an incorporated city of one thousand people and the seat of newly created Clark County. Native-born American families dominated the town's population until the 1940s, when defense plants encouraged the migration of more African Americans. The resort industry, which reinforced this trend, began attracting Hispanics and Asian Americans after 1970. By 1990, they composed about 20 percent of the metropolitan population.

For its first twenty-five years, the railhead town struggled as surrounding mines closed. Tourism began supplementing the town's railroad economy in 1931 when the construction of Boulder Dam (now HOOVER DAM) brought thousands of visitors each year. But development was still slow until World War II brought the town an army gunnery school and a giant magnesium factory. Defense became a more permanent industry when the gunnery school reopened in 1949 as an air force base. Then in 1950, part of its range became America's new continental nuclear test site.

Despite the legalization of table games in 1931, casino GAMBLING was not a major factor in Las Vegas's economy until the 1940s, when the soldiers and defense workers who thronged the frontier-theme clubs downtown demonstrated to locals that gambling could be the key to the city's future. Las Vegas's development as a resort city began in 1940 and 1941 when California hotel man Thomas Hull decided not to build his El Rancho Vegas Hotel downtown, where virtually all of the other casinos were, but south of town on the Los Angeles Highway. Hull's decision marked the beginning of the famed Las Vegas Strip, where spacious resort hotels had room for pools, showrooms, and parking lots. A succession of resorts followed, including the Hotel Last Frontier (1942) and Benjamin ("Bugsy") Siegel's Flamingo (1947). A variety of factors supported this development, including the growth of America's convention industry, jet travel, credit cards, disposable income, and leisure. By 1960, Las Vegas was in the vanguard of a new leisure culture being pioneered largely in the Southwest Sunbelt. A product of

America's postindustrial society, Las Vegas symbolized some of the oldest and newest trends in the American West.

—*Eugene P. Moehring*

SUGGESTED READING:
Findlay, John. *People of Chance: Gambling in American Society from Jamestown to Las Vegas.* New York, 1986.
Moehring, Eugene P. *Resort City in the Sunbelt: Las Vegas, 1930–1970.* Reno and Las Vegas, Nev., 1989.
Venturi, Robert. *Learning from Las Vegas: The Forgotten Symbolism of Architectural Form.* Cambridge, Mass., 1977.

LATHROP, AUSTIN E. ("CAP")

A private businessman who invested his profits in Alaska, Austin E. ("Cap") Lathrop (1865–1950) became an advocate of private development in Alaska and was probably the territory's first millionaire.

Born in Lapeer, Michigan, and raised in a farming family, "Cap" Lathrop left home as a teen-ager after one year of high school. In Seattle at the time of the great fire in 1889, he began a business clearing rubble, an enterprise he developed into a teamstering company. He went to the Cook Inlet region of Alaska in 1896 when there was a minor gold rush there. His profitable freighting business allowed him to add general construction to his activities. He married in 1901 (his wife died in 1910, and he never remarried) and moved to the new town of Cordova in 1907 where the Guggenheim Corporation was constructing a railroad to provide access to copper deposits. He served as mayor of Cordova and became an aggressive advocate for private development. He believed that emigrants to Alaska could develop the territory more rapidly without governmental bureaucracy than with government help. In 1911, he participated in and may have led a mob of three hundred men who dumped a shipload of imported coal into the bay at Cordova in protest over the government's refusal to open coal lands for investment and development. In the aftermath of the KLONDIKE GOLD RUSH, investors clashed with government Progressives who sought to manage economic development in the name of resource conservation and equality of opportunity. Lathrop put himself in the forefront of those urging a return to the unrestricted laissez-faire policies of the past.

Lathrop's businesses continued to prosper, and in the early 1920s, he acquired coal lands along the Alaska Railroad in the Nenana region north of Anchorage. He also secured the Alaska franchise for the Olympia

Brewing Company of Washington State and joined the company's board of directors.

Unlike many investors, Lathrop stayed in Alaska, rather than relocating elsewhere, and reinvested his earnings in Alaska enterprises. His businesses included movie theaters in Anchorage and Fairbanks, radio and later television stations, and eventually a newspaper, the *Fairbanks News-Miner.* In 1933, he became president of the First Bank of Cordova. During World War II, his companies provided experienced and reliable construction expertise for the unprecedented military build-up.

In the meantime, Lathrop formed a movie company, in 1923, for the filming of *The Cheechakos,* a successful full-length motion picture about the Klondike gold rush.

He became involved in politics in the 1920s and served as a territorial legislator for one term and later as a representative to the Republican National Committee. After World War II, he provided leadership and support for forces opposed to Alaska statehood. He believed Alaskans should further develop industry and commerce before undertaking the additional costs and taxation associated with governmental administration. After statehood was achieved in 1958, he continued to develop his enterprises, especially his coal business. He was killed at the age of eighty-five in a railroad accident while working at his mining properties.

—*Stephen Haycox*

SUGGESTED READING:
Gruening, Ernest. *The State of Alaska.* New York, 1954.
Webb, Melody. *The Last Frontier.* Albuquerque, N. Mex., 1984.

LATTER-DAY SAINTS

SEE: Church of Jesus Christ of Latter-day Saints; Mormons

LATTER-DAY SAINTS, REORGANIZED

SEE: Church of Jesus Christ of Latter-Day Saints, Reorganized

LAW AND ORDER

The structure of law enforcement in the nineteenth-century West was not much different from what it is

Clerical forces and deputy U.S. marshals posed for a photograph in the midst of a land rush in Perry, Oklahoma Territory, on October 12, 1893. *Courtesy National Archives.*

today. Each county had one elected sheriff, who was assisted by an under-sheriff and a number of deputies. The sheriff was responsible for enforcing the law in the unincorporated areas of the county, and he acted as court officer for the superior court. Counties were usually divided into townships. Each township generally had a justice of the peace, and each justice court had one or more constables whose duties were similar to those of the county sheriff. In addition to enforcing the law, these officials spent much of their time serving civil papers, acting as court bailiffs, executing judgments and attachments, and rounding up recalcitrant citizens to act as trial jurors.

Law enforcement in towns and cities was controlled by the city marshal or chief of police. A small town might have one city marshal and perhaps a night officer; a city like San Francisco employed five hundred policemen during the 1890s. In addition to preventing crime, a city marshal's duties often included catching stray dogs, collecting business-license fees, and repairing streets and bridges.

A few states employed state policemen, the most famous being the TEXAS RANGERS. They fought Indians, patrolled the Mexican border, suppressed civil unrest, and assisted local lawmen in tracking down criminals. The ARIZONA RANGERS (active from 1901 to 1909) and the New Mexico Mounted Police (active from 1905 to 1921) were modeled after the Texas

Rangers to suppress lawlessness and to help pave the way for those territories to achieve statehood.

States and territories also had FEDERAL MARSHALS AND DEPUTIES; some of the larger states had several. The U.S.

The discovery of gold in various regions of the West brought reckless men and spawned rough mining towns. Law and order was often slow to follow. Illustration by Frank Hoffman. *Courtesy National Cowboy Hall of Fame and Western Heritage Museum.*

Juan Nepomuceno Cortina, considered an outlaw by Anglo-Americans, was a folk hero to Spanish-speaking people. *Courtesy Archives Division, Texas State Library.*

Top: Sometimes settlers took the law into their own hands. Solomon D. Butcher photographed four Nebraskans, engaged in a range war, cutting fences on the Brighton Ranch in 1885. *Courtesy Nebraska State Historical Society.*

Bottom: The construction of a jail signaled a community's commitment to law and order. The first jails were often crude structures similar to the Larned County jail in Kansas in 1886. *Courtesy Kansas State Historical Society.*

marshal was the court officer for the federal district court and performed the same general duties for that court that the sheriff performed for the superior court. U.S. marshals and their deputies were also charged with enforcing federal laws related to bigamy, mail robbery, and selling liquor to Indians. Perhaps the most active federal lawman was the marshal of the Indian Territory, who had many deputies to police a vast area overrun by desperadoes and fugitives from justice. Among the least active was the U.S. marshal of California, who had few deputies and generally left enforcement of federal law to local officers.

Nineteenth-century Americans, especially in the West, expected justice to be quick and, if necessary, harsh. Nonetheless, the only capital offense in most states was murder; in some states, rape and train wrecking were also capital offenses. Condemned men were generally executed by hanging. The New Mexico Territory made train robbery a capital crime, but the hanging of Thomas ("Black Jack") Ketchum in 1901 appears to be the only time a man was legally executed for holding up a train. Contrary to myth, horse and cattle thieves were not sentenced to death but received prison terms instead.

With the advent of the California gold rush in 1848 and the opening of the first mining towns, law and order became a crucial issue. Large numbers of reckless young men left their homes and families and converged in the West. They were unencumbered by the settling influences of women and family and were well fortified with liquor, Bowie knives, and the newly invented six-shooter. Not surprisingly, VIOLENCE became commonplace. In one fifteen-month period from 1850 to 1851, there were 44 homicides in Los Angeles County, which then had a population of only a few thousand. There were 370 homicides in California during the first eight months of 1855, more than sixteen times California's modern rates when population is taken into account. Riches were everywhere, and luckless miners turned to theft and banditry, as did hundreds of disfranchised Hispanics. The fledgling criminal-justice system was unable to cope with the disorder, and vigilantes stepped in to fill the void. Once courts became established, however, VIGILANTISM did not vanish. It reappeared from time to time when the courts were seen as incompetent, corrupt, or too lenient. Vigilantes did not always hang their victims. A thief convicted by a vigilance committee might be sentenced to flogging or having one ear cropped to mark him as a criminal.

Racial strife, especially between Anglo-Americans and Hispanics, was a major component of violence in California as well as in Texas, Arizona, and New Mexico. Animosity was stirred up during the United States–Mexican War from 1846 to 1848 and existed in varying degrees throughout the territorial and early statehood periods. Hispanic outlawry flourished at times and included such noted figures as JOAQUIN MURRIETA, TIBURCIO VÁSQUEZ, and JUAN NEPOMUCENO CORTINA. Many such outlaws became folk heroes to the Spanish-speaking people. Ironically, the outstanding Hispanic peace officers, such as Phoenix lawman Henry Garfias and Los Angeles Sheriffs Tomas Sanchez and Martin Aguirre, have been ignored and forgotten by both cultures. The exploits of ELFEGO BACA in New Mexico, however, were widely celebrated.

California's experience with lawlessness during the 1850s served as the prototype for all subsequent Western territories, in which lax law enforcement, an unstable society, few women, and an overabundance of well-liquored and well-armed young men combined to increase the incidence of violent crime. Whether it was Dodge City, Tombstone, Deadwood, or one of many other CATTLE TOWNS or mining camps, each had its share of shootouts and knifings. In later years, Western myths tended to exaggerate the degree of violence, but not always: from 1872 to 1881, the tiny hamlet of Lincoln in the New Mexico Territory experienced 39 homicides, including several murders by "BILLY THE KID." With the exception of blood feuds, range wars, political strife, or unrest from the CIVIL WAR, however, few Western communities saw such ferocious bloodletting. Once traditional social systems were established with the introduction of families, churches, schools, and consistent law enforcement, crime and violence subsided in most Western communities.

—*John Boessenecker*

SEE ALSO: Cattle Rustling; Gunfighters; Horse Theft and Horse Thieves; Legal System; Mining: Mining Camps and Towns; Social Banditry; Territorial Government; Territorial Law and Courts

SUGGESTED READING:
Brown, Richard Maxwell. *No Duty to Retreat*. New York, 1991.
McGrath, Roger D. *Gunfighters, Highwaymen, and Vigilantes*. Berkeley, Calif., 1984.
Prassel, Frank Richard. *The Western Peace Officer*. Norman, Okla., 1972.

LAWYER (NEZ PERCÉ)

Lawyer (Aleiya, also called Hol-lol-sote-tote, 1796–1876) was a leader of the Nez Percés faction that signed two treaties with the government in 1855 and 1863 reducing tribal landholdings. Lawyer's family had always been friendly with whites. His father, Twisted Hair, was a Nez Percé chief, who welcomed MERIWETHER LEWIS and WILLIAM CLARK as they passed through his territory during their expedition. Lawyer's mother was a Flathead. Lawyer served as a guide and interpreter for explorers and missionaries and eventually became a chief of the Upper Nez Percés, who were based along the Clearwater River in Idaho.

Lawyer sided with fur traders JAMES (JIM) BRIDGER, Milton Sublette, and NATHANIEL JARVIS WYETH against the Gros Ventres at the Battle of Pierre's Hole in Wyoming in 1832. Six years later, he was working as a missionary interpreter and teacher, acquiring a command of the English language that earned him a reputation as a brilliant orator, not only among Indians, but among whites was well. Lawyer led the protreaty faction in the 1855 Walla Walla Council with Washington's Territorial Governor Isaac Stevens. Opposing a faction led by Chief Joseph (the Elder), Lawyer agreed to make vast cessions of Nez Percé lands. When the 1855 treaty was revised in 1863 to carve away even more Nez Percé territory, Lawyer agreed to the new terms as well, and thereby created a sharp division between his Upper Nez Percés and the Lower Nez Percés, led by Chief Joseph (the Elder).

Lawyer lived to see the government violate the provisions of the 1863 treaty, as white settlement encroached upon his tribe's greatly reduced lands. He traveled to Washington, D.C., in 1868 to protest the violations and also wrote a series of eloquent letters on the subject. The Upper Nez Percés removed him as principal chief in 1871 and replaced him with Jacob. Lawyer died one year before the outbreak of the Nez

Percé War between the U.S. Army and the Lower Nez Percés led by CHIEF JOSEPH (the Younger).

—*Alan Axelrod*

SEE ALSO: Pacific Northwest Indian Wars

SUGGESTED READING:
Brown, Mark H. *The Flight of the Nez Percé*. Lincoln, Nebr., 1967.

LEAD MINING

Lead mining in the American West predates the United States's acquisition of the area. Some reports suggest that the earliest mining in the region dates back to work done near Tucson, Arizona, in the 1650s, if not earlier, but there was little production of any consequence until the eighteenth century when the French discovered lead ore and began to open mines in the present-day states of Missouri and Wisconsin.

The chief French interest lay in southeastern Missouri. There in about 1720, miners opened Mine la Motte in present-day Madison County. From this beginning, mining spread here and there, but operations remained small and somewhat sporadic.

Reports of lead in Wisconsin came at least as early as 1658 when the French penetrated the region, but little work resulted until JULIEN DUBUQUE obtained permission from the Sac (Sauk) and Fox (Mesquakie) Indians to develop mines. Fox Indians did substantial mining in the years to come, but significant production did not occur until the 1820s and after. From 1820 to the 1870s, while the Missouri mines continued to operate, the focus of lead production shifted to Wisconsin, Illinois, and Iowa. Some writers have labeled the fifty-year era as the "Wisconsin Period" of American lead mining. The district flourished until mid-century when capital shortages, technological problems, and the California gold rush, which drew off huge numbers of miners, gradually pushed the region into decline.

Until the early 1870s, nearly all the lead produced in the United States had come from lead ores. But that changed dramatically when entrepreneurs first began to open the great silver-lead deposits of Nevada, Utah, and Colorado. Although prospectors had discovered some of these deposits earlier, they could not develop them because of a lack of transportation, technology, and capital. This changed at the end of the 1860s, particularly with the completion of the transcontinental railroad at Promontory Summit in Utah in 1869. The railroad, along with new capital investment and European mining technology, spurred the development of the West's silver-lead mines, first in Eureka, Nevada,

and then in Utah, where the EMMA MINE in Alta and the Horn Silver Mine in Frisco became important producers. Although the mines became the nation's principal lead producers during the 1870s, their heyday was short. They gave way to the enormous deposits opened at Leadville, Colorado, in the late 1870s. During the 1880s, the Leadville mines alone produced about one-third of the nation's silver-lead ore. But even that would not last. They in turn gave way to the Coeur d'Alene mines in Idaho during the 1890s.

—*James E. Fell, Jr.*

SEE ALSO: Silver Mining

SUGGESTED READING:
Fell, James E., Jr. *Ores to Metals: The Rocky Mountain Smelting Industry*. Lincoln, Nebr., 1980.
Ingalls, Walter Renton. *Lead and Zinc in the United States*. New York, 1908.

LEADVILLE, COLORADO

Located slightly more than ten thousand feet up in the Rocky Mountains, Leadville, Colorado, boasts of being the highest incorporated city in the United States. A MINING community still, Leadville once was among the most productive mining regions in the West. Beginning in 1860, extensive placer mining for gold took place in the nearby California Gulch, and in 1877, the discovery of major and immense silver beds made Leadville the silver capital of the nation. Billions of dollars in gold, silver, lead, zinc, copper, iron, magnesium, and other metals have been culled from the Leadville mines. During the SILVER-MINING boom years between 1878 and 1881, Leadville's population topped forty thousand souls, not a few of whom became millionaires. Perhaps most notably among them was HORACE AUSTIN WARNER TABOR, whose rags-to-riches story quickly became the stuff of Western folklore.

By 1880, Leadville was, according to one newspaper, home to four banks, three newspapers, ten dry-goods stores, four churches, and half a dozen schools, plus some 120 saloons and nineteen beer halls, 118 gambling dens, and thirty-five brothels. Its monthly payroll had reached eight hundred thousand dollars. Three railroads—the Denver and Rio Grande, the Santa Fe, and the Denver and South Park—ran through the town and competed fiercely with one another. Real-estate prices soared as thirty-one real-estate firms sold Chestnut Street lots they had bought for ten to forty dollars back in 1877 at prices ranging from five hundred to five thousand dollars. Thirty sawmills operated day and night to meet the demand for lumber, and even so, lumber remained so scarce that many of the recently wealthy had to make do with log cabins. The year before, in 1879, England's outrageously decadent poet, Oscar Wilde—on a lecture tour in the states—had put Leadville on the map by declaiming on the "Ethics of Art" to a crowd of hard-rock miners at the Tabor Opera House, a performance no doubt enjoyed by Tabor's wife Augustus if not by his mistress "Baby Doe," almost as famous locally as Wilde was throughout the world. "In the evening," Charles Francis Adams, Jr., wrote in his diary in 1886, "we saw Leadville by gaslight—an awful spectacle of low vice." And that was after the great boom, when Leadville's licentiousness had been at its peak.

Leadville attracted a vibrant and ethnically varied working class in the 1880s, and labor unrest became widespread as a result of a labor surplus that cut into real wages and of the brutal practices of mining magnates determined to exploit their rich veins of ore. Becoming one of the more unionized towns in the region, Leadville witnessed the rise not only of a miners' union but also of unions for barbers, bricklayers, printers, carpenters—even newsboys. Not that such union members were especially militant; most of them joined to protect themselves from price-cutting recent arrivals in their professions. The miners, however, did mount a major strike in June 1880, for higher pay—four dollars per day—and an eight-hour workday. The owners ignored them, and a public, at first indifferent, turned hostile when the threat of violence appeared. Isolated, there was little the miners could do as the strike was crushed and their union broken. Although the conflict was over, so too were the boom days.

Meanwhile, Leadville mine owners, hungry for immediate, ever-growing profits, practiced all the vote buying and political corruption common to mining towns throughout the mountain West. Ultimately, however, they fell victim to their own greed, when the silver deposits were quickly exhausted and the manipulation of mining stock forced others into bankruptcy. The final blows came with the repeal of the SHERMAN SILVER PURCHASE ACT OF 1890 three years later and a second violent strike in 1896 that hastened the slowdown in production already under way. In the late 1890s, Leadville bounced back briefly after James J. Brown struck gold and launched yet another boom. Once again, the town became known for its colorful citizenry and its extravagance, as Brown and his wife, the "Unsinkable" Molly Brown, constructed an elaborate castle out of solid ice, the Ice Palace, for Leadville's Crystal Carnival in 1895. Still, by the turn of the century, Leadville was ailing if not moribund. Three decades later, molybdenum mines in nearby Climax rejuvenated the region, although Leadville, in the New Deal 1930s, would never approach its glory days of

A Colorado militiaman guards a Leadville mine during an 1896 lockout of union miners. *Courtesy Denver Public Library, Western History Department.*

the late 1870s. In more recent years, artifacts from those days have attracted a growing number of tourists, who travel high into the Rockies to see the Augusta Tabor House, the Matchless Cabin where Baby Doe spent her last thirty years, and the elegant old Tabor Opera House.

—*Charles Phillips*

SUGGESTED READING:

Paul, Rodman W. *Mining Frontiers of the Far West, 1848–1880.* New York, 1963.

Reps, John W. *Cities of the American West: A History of Frontier Urban Planning.* Princeton, N.J., 1979.

Smith, Duane A. *Rocky Mountain Mining Camps: The Urban Frontier.* Bloomington, Ind., 1967

LEASE, MARY ELIZABETH CLYENS

Pennsylvania-born Mary Elizabeth Clyens Lease (1853–1933) was one of the most effective and best-known Populist orators in the People's party campaigns of the early 1890s. Her father and two of her brothers died serving the Union Army during the Civil War; partisan from an early age, she held the Democratic party responsible for their deaths. When she was sixteen years old, she taught school; resentful of lower pay for female teachers, she left Pennsylvania to teach at the Osage Mission in KANSAS. There she met Charles Lease, a local druggist; they were married early in 1873.

Mary Elizabeth Clyens Lease. *Courtesy Kansas State Historical Society.*

The couple homesteaded in Kingman County, Kansas, but grasshoppers forced them to relocate to Denison, Texas; in 1884, they moved to Wichita, Kansas. Supporting her four children by taking in laundry, Lease read law and was admitted to the bar. Instead of practicing law, she helped organize women's clubs, where her speaking abilities and ready wit attracted attention. Her public speeches to fringe political-party audiences dealt with Irish independence and women's rights.

She started campaigning in 1888 for Union Labor candidates and then worked for the Farmers' Alliance and the People's party in 1890. In an era when women could not vote, Lease was a major attraction. She spoke at more than 160 People's party rallies in 1890; her crowds were double the size of those of other speakers. Her listeners heard her advise farmers to "raise less corn and more hell!" She helped secure victories for Farmers' Alliance candidates for the Kansas legislature—victories that spelled defeat for three-term U.S. Senator JOHN J. INGALLS.

Lease campaigned nationally for the Populists in 1892. With their victory in Kansas, she became chair of the state Board of Charities. Opposed to fusion, the Populist strategy of combining forces with Democrats, she refused to support WILLIAM JENNINGS BRYAN, the party's candidate for president in 1896. She moved to New York City that year. Her subsequent career was anticlimactic.

—*Homer E. Socolofsky*

SEE ALSO: Populism

SUGGESTED READING:

Blumberg, Dorothy R. "Mary Elizabeth Lease, Populist Orator: A Profile." *Kansas History* 1 (Spring 1978): 2–15.
Clanton, O. Gene. "Intolerant Populist? The Disaffection of Mary Elizabeth Lease." *Kansas Historical Quarterly* 34 (Summer 1968): 189–200.

LEAVENWORTH, HENRY

Born in New Haven, Connecticut, Henry Leavenworth (1783–1834) served as an army officer from the War of 1812 until his death. In 1804, he studied law, became a member of the New York State bar, and started a practice in Delhi. He began his army career on April 25, 1812, when he became a captain in the Twenty-fifth Infantry. Promoted to major in the Ninth Infantry in August 1813, he served near the New York–Canada border. There he played a significant role in the July 1814 battles of Chippewa and Niagara or Lundy's Lane. A year later, the army decorated him for bravery in these engagements. His demonstrated skills in leadership helped him retain his rank during the 1815 demobilization.

On February 19, 1818, Leavenworth became a lieutenant colonel in the Fifth Infantry. The next year, he led troops from this regiment west to present-day Minneapolis where they began construction of Fort Snelling. After the 1821 army reduction, Leavenworth was transferred to Fort Atkinson, Nebraska, where he served with the Sixth Infantry. In 1823, he led nearly one thousand soldiers, fur traders, and Sioux Indians north along the Missouri River to punish the Arikara Indians in South Dakota for an attack on WILLIAM HENRY ASHLEY's employees. The campaign failed when the Indians escaped. In late 1824, he became colonel of the Third Infantry and supervised part of the building of Jefferson Barracks south of St. Louis. Three years later, he located and built Fort Leavenworth in eastern Kansas.

He died while leading the First Dragoons on the Southern Plains. His career represented those of many officers of the day, officers who trained small units, moved troops, built forts, and dealt with the Indians.

—*Roger L. Nichols*

SUGGESTED READING:

Hunt, Elvid. *History of Fort Leavenworth, 1827–1927.* Fort Leavenworth, Kans., 1979.

Robinson, Doane, ed. "Official Correspondence of the Leavenworth Expedition of 1823 into South Dakota for the Conquest of the Ree Indians." *South Dakota Historical Collections.* Vol. 1. Pierre, S. Dak., 1902.

LECOMPTON, KANSAS

Lecompton, Kansas, on the south bank of the Kansas River between Lawrence and Topeka, was founded in the spring of 1855 by proslavery advocates in the tumultuous debate following the passage of the KANSAS-NEBRASKA ACT. Intended to serve as the capital of proslavers in the territory, Lecompton had as early promoters the private secretary to the territorial governor, the chief justice of the United States District Court, and the territorial secretary. Named the capital of the territory by the first territorial legislature, Lecompton was the site of annual legislative sessions beginning in January 1857. In 1857, a constitutional convention drafted a proslavery document for admission to the Union, but it was not accepted by Congress.

Lecompton reached its peak population of about one thousand in 1857 and 1858. Hotels, churches, stores, and other business buildings were constructed, and the basement for what was intended to be the territorial capitol was dug. After free-state forces gained control of Kansas in 1858, Lecompton began to fade. The Santa Fe Railroad built through the town in 1872, and the town enjoyed a brief revival ten years later, although the construction of the territorial capitol never progressed beyond the first-floor walls. The basement sat empty until Lane University built a school on the south half of the foundation in 1882. In its new building, Lane University counted among its students Ida Stover and David Eisenhower. They married in 1885 and became the parents of Dwight D. Eisenhower, hero of World War II and president of the United States from 1953 to 1961.

In the late twentieth century, Lecompton was a town of about six hundred people and served mainly as a bedroom community for its larger neighbors, Topeka and Lawrence. The two-story building that housed the proslavery convention, and sometimes the legislature, still stood and was a state-owned historic site.

—*Joseph W. Snell*

LEE, JASON

Leader of the first American settlement in the Oregon Country, missionary Jason Lee (1803–1845) went to the Pacific Coast region to convert Native Americans to Christianity. Born in Stanstead, Canada, he studied at Wesleyan Academy in Wilbraham, Massachusetts. There Wilbur Fisk, president of the academy, asked Lee to head a Methodist mission to Flathead territory. Lee and NATHANIEL JARVIS WYETH arrived at FORT VANCOUVER on September 15, 1834, but, instead of traveling to Montana as had been planned, Lee and his group settled on the banks of the WILLAMETTE RIVER. The missionaries erected a mission house of hewn oak logs. To clear the land, they relied on native Hawaiian laborers provided by JOHN McLOUGHLIN of the HUDSON'S BAY COMPANY. Devoted to the spread of Methodism, Lee and his missionaries worked with the Chinook Indians of the Willamette Valley and the French Canadians.

In 1838, Lee returned to the East to secure financial backing for his work and to recruit settlers among New Englanders. He returned to the Willamette in 1840 with fifty-one settlers. Helping the Americans with capital and supplies, he strengthened his mission's influence, but his work was hampered by defections and the deaths of his recruits.

In 1843, Lee was dismissed by the mission board in New York because the Eastern office felt his mission was too secular and that his financial accounts were suspect. The board cleared him of any wrongdoing but did not offer him another post. He returned to Stanstead where he died. The Lee mission had been unsuccessful in converting Native Americans to Christianity, but when its work was publicized in the East, accounts of the Oregon Country attracted attention. Throughout the 1840s and 1850s, thousands of American settlers traveled along the OREGON TRAIL into the Willamette Valley.

—*Candace Floyd*

SEE ALSO: Missions: Nineteenth-Century Missions to the Indians; Protestants

SUGGESTED READING:

Brosnan, C. J. *Jason Lee: Prophet of the New Oregon.* New York, 1932.

Clark, Malcolm, Jr. *Eden Seekers: The Settlement of Oregon, 1818–1862.* Boston, 1981.

LEE, JOHN D.

Mormon pioneer, diarist, zealot, and scapegoat for the MOUNTAIN MEADOWS MASSACRE, John D. Lee (1812–

1877) joined the Mormon church in 1838. In the same year, he participated in the flight of the MORMONS from Missouri and helped found NAUVOO, ILLINOIS. An adopted son of BRIGHAM YOUNG and a member of the Council of Fifty, Lee was intimately involved in the exodus to Utah including the 1846 struggle across Iowa and a trip to Santa Fe to collect the payroll of the Mormon Battalion for its service in the UNITED STATES–MEXICAN WAR. In 1848, he led a wagon train west.

Lee located in Salt Lake Valley and became a man of some standing before moving to southern Utah in 1850. There he helped settled Parowan, Washington, and New Harmony. A polygamist, he ultimately married nineteen women.

In 1857, he was a primary figure in the Mountain Meadows Massacre in which Mormons, assisted by the Paiute Indians, killed more than one hundred emigrants from Arkansas and Missouri. Never popular, Lee increasingly bore the onus for the massacre as the Mormon community sought to play down its involvement. In 1870, he was excommunicated and forced to move, with wives Rachael and Emma, to Lee's Ferry at the confluence of the Colorado and Paria rivers. Federal marshals captured him at Panguitch in 1874. With Mormons still reluctant to testify, Lee's trial in 1874 ended in a hung jury. Two years later, several of his former colleagues testified against him. He was convicted and, in 1877, was executed at the site of the massacre. His journals remain classic sources on Mormon pioneering.

—*Charles S. Peterson*

SUGGESTED READING:
Brooks, Juanita. *John Doyle Lee: Zealot-Pioneer Builder-Scapegoat*. Glendale, Calif., 1972.
———. *The Mountain Meadows Massacre*. Palo Alto, Calif., 1950.
Kelly, Charles. *Journals of John D. Lee, 1846–1859*. Salt Lake City, 1984.

LEE, MARY PAIK

Author of an autobiography detailing the conditions of Asian pioneer women in the West, Mary Paik Lee (Kuang Sun Paik, 1900–   ) was born in Pyongyang, Korea. She immigrated with her family to Hawaii in 1905, when Japan declared Korea its protectorate. Her father, Paik Sin Koo, had studied for the Christian ministry, but after arriving in Hawaii, he worked on a sugar plantation. In 1906, he took his family to California, where they survived on his meager wages as a fruit picker and the income his wife, Song Kuang Do, who cooked for fellow farm workers.

There were merely a handful of Korean children growing up in California during the early decades of the twentieth century. Mary Paik Lee is the only one who has written her autobiography—the sole account available in English of an Asian pioneer woman in the American West. Published in 1990 as *Quiet Odyssey: A Pioneer Korean Woman in America* and covering the years from childhood to old age, the book portrays Lee's living conditions, which were quite similar to those faced by tens of thousands of Chinese, Japanese, Korean, Indian, and Filipino immigrants along the Pacific Coast in the decades before World War II. Regardless of their socio-economic status or educational level before arriving in the United States, many Asian immigrants could find work only as migrant farm workers, laundrymen, cooks, domestic servants, common laborers, tenant farmers, and operators of produce stands.

Mary Paik married Hung Man Lee in 1919. The couple earned a living as tenant farmers, produce sellers, and apartment managers. When she became an American citizen in 1960, she replaced her Korean given name, Kuang Sun, with the name Mary. In the late twentieth century, she lived in a retirement home in San Francisco.

—*Sucheng Chan*

SUGGESTED READING:
Choy, Bong-Youn. *Koreans in America*. Chicago, 1979.
Lee, Mary Paik. *Quiet Odyssey: A Pioneer Korean Woman in America*. Edited with an introduction by Sucheng Chan. Seattle, Wash., 1990.

LEFORS, JOE

Wyoming lawman Joe LeFors (1865–1940) was best known for trapping the hired killer TOM HORN. LeFors was born in Paris, Texas, grew up in western Oklahoma, and trailed a herd to northern Wyoming in 1885. He worked as a cowboy until 1895, when the Montana Livestock Association hired him as a livestock inspector to recover cattle stolen from Montana ranches.

From his headquarters at Newcastle, Wyoming, LeFors rounded up hundreds of rustled cattle and arrested the thieves. In the summer of 1897, the outlaws watched when LeFors, along with Johnson County Sheriff Al Sproal and fifty well-armed deputies, cleared out the stolen cattle from the notorious Hole-in-the-Wall country. Not a shot was fired. After train holdups at Wilcox station and near Tipton, Wyoming, LeFors began trailing BUTCH CASSIDY's "Wild Bunch" until the robbers finally escaped. In 1900, he traded badges to become a deputy U.S. marshal.

The murder of a young boy, Willie Nickell, brought a hired gun named Tom Horn under the marshal's suspicion. LeFors led Horn into claiming he was present when the youth was shot. In a sensational trial, Horn denied that he was the killer, but the jury accepted his "confession" and sent the gunman to the gallows. LeFors, already known as a fearless law officer, emerged a celebrity. Other cases involved arson, extortion, and conflicts between sheepherders and cattlemen. In later years, he reminisced about the sad contrast between modern criminals and the almost gentlemanly conduct of old-time train robbers.

—*John P. Wilson*

SUGGESTED READING:
LeFors, Joe. *Wyoming Peace Officer.* Laramie, Wyo., 1953.

LEGAL SYSTEM

The bulk of law in the West was like that in the East. Territories and states had legislatures, courts, and an executive; municipalities had justices of the peace, who had judicial and, often, administrative responsibilities. The substantive law that these institutions produced was very American, but in three significant ways, law in the West was distinctly different from that in the East. Spanish and Mexican law in place before American settlement or conquest influenced law in the West; aridity in the Rocky Mountain region influenced WATER law; and the existence of gold and silver forced lawmakers to confront land-use questions without federal guidance.

Congress first established a territorial system in 1787, the NORTHWEST ORDINANCE; by 1836, the general contours of the system had become firmly set in Washington, D.C. Territorial organic acts called for the establishment of the same basic structure that Americans possessed in their federal and state governments: a legislature, a hierarchical court system, and a governor. Justices of the peace were ground-level judicial officials who handled the bulk of minor cases on the local level. The president of the United States appointed the governors and justices of the territorial supreme courts. Politics generally governed decisions regarding territorial personnel. From the outset, the main business of territorial politics was the quest for statehood. The fact that all territorial legislation was subject to congressional review and that all political appointments were made in Washington, D.C., caused many territorial residents to push for statehood.

In general, competent jurists staffed the Western courts, whether territorial or state. Justice courts dispensed quality justice on the local level, and if not,

people could appeal to trial courts staffed by judges with legal backgrounds or training. In the territorial system, the justices of the territorial supreme courts also sat on the trial bench. Civil suits of significant value and felony cases were handled by trial-court judges, and cases could be appealed at the state or territorial supreme courts. An example of swift and sure due process in the Western courts was the case of George Tanner, who committed grand larceny on April 3, 1852. He was tried before the Yuba County, California, Court of Sessions, on April 14, 1852. The jury found Tanner guilty and recommended the death sentence. The judge sentenced Tanner, who then appealed to the district court, a trial court having appellate jurisdiction in felony cases. The district court affirmed the judgment on April 24, 1852. Tanner appealed to the California Supreme Court and lost. He filed for a rehearing on May 24, 1852. The petition was heard and overruled on July 16, 1852, and he was executed on July 23, 1852.

State constitutions maintained the structure of government—the legislative, judicial, and executive bodies—but altered the system of territorial trial courts. Appellate justices no longer sat as trial-court judges. States had separate trial courts to hear and decide civil and criminal matters. Justice courts remained the ground-level judicial institutions well into the twentieth century.

In terms of substantive law, the West was much like the East, with the exception of the Utah and New Mexico territories. English common law provided both the general rule of decision for courts and the guidepost for legislators. State codifications made law more available and rational and won general acceptance in the West, most notably in California and Montana.

The West was unique in several areas of law. The Spanish and Mexican heritage of the Southwest influenced land law due to Spanish and Mexican land grants. Problems of title in California resulted in federal legislation setting up a special land commission to hear and decide issues of ownership. The Hispanic heritage gave rise to the pueblo water-claim cases, popular with claimants and invented by their lawyers. The pueblo water right was a legal construct of argumentation used by lawyers representing Los Angeles against San Fernando. The doctrine held that any pueblo property constituted by Mexican authority was entitled to exclusive rights to water within its jurisdiction. The California Supreme Court, in confirming such a right to Los Angeles, gave the city the run-off of the entire five-hundred-square-mile watershed, guaranteeing its growth. The pueblo water doctrine gave rise to vested interests so powerful that Los Angeles was accorded such rights despite the fact that the doctrine was a historical fraud. The Spanish-Mexican heritage also gave rise to the concept of COMMUNITY PROPERTY. Marriage laws were first adopted in California and spread to the East over time.

The gold and silver rushes in the West put lawmakers to work sorting out issues related to titles, land use, and the resolution of disputes. Much of the gold and silver was grubbed from ground on public land. Miners working a piece of ground formed local mining districts out of which came rules for the possession, working, and transfer of interests in mineral lands. Territorial and state legislatures followed the contours of the local rules in writing statutes. Courts interpreted these mining district rules and state and territorial statutes with an eye to development within traditional concepts of land law. The first federal legislation on mining in 1866 only validated the work of local mining districts and legislatures. It was not until 1872 that Congress gave miners some rules to work with in their enterprise.

In the arid West, legislators and judges repudiated the English common law of waters—riparian rights—in favor of the doctrine of prior appropriation. The doctrine of riparian rights allows the owner of land abutting a waterway the right to use the water so long as the quality and quantity of water available to owners downstream were not diminished. The doctrine of prior appropriation, on the contrary, gave the first person to take water from a waterway the right to use as much water as taken as long as that water was applied to beneficial use. The prior appropriator did not have to be a landowner or the owner of the bank of the stream. The prior appropriation doctrine favored first-users of water and acknowledged that water was limited in quantity and seasonal in availability.

An important part of both water and mining law was the development of a Western concept of eminent domain—the taking of private property for a public use with just compensation paid to the property owner. The entity taking the property was usually a governmental agency involved in building a road or a bridge. In the West, legislators and delegates to constitutional conventions saw the need to put the right of eminent domain into the hands of mining and irrigation entrepreneurs. Lawmakers enabled mining and irrigation interests to cut water ditches across the lands of others in order to bring water to mines, farms, and ranches and declared such uses to be public uses. In its nineteenth-century context, this shifting of governmental functions into private hands was revolutionary.

—*Gordon Morris Bakken*

SEE ALSO: California Doctrine (of Water Rights); Colorado Doctrine (of Water Rights); Law and Order; Mining Law of 1872; Territorial Law and Courts

SUGGESTED READING:
Bakken, Gordon Morris. *Development of Law on the Rocky Mountain Frontier.* Westport, Conn., 1983.
Haywood, C. Robert. *Cowtown Lawyers.* Norman, Okla., 1988.
Hundley, Norris, Jr. *The Great Thirst.* Berkeley, Calif., 1992.
Pisani, Donald J. *To Reclaim a Divided West.* Albuquerque, N. Mex., 1992.
Reid, John Phillip. *Law for the Elephant.* San Marino, Calif., 1980.
Tyler, Daniel. *The Mythical Pueblo Rights Doctrine.* El Paso, Tex., 1990.

LEGEND OF PAUL BUNYAN

SEE: Paul Bunyan, legend of

LEGEND OF PECOS BILL

SEE: Pecos Bill, legend of

LEIDESDORFF, ALEXANDER

SEE: African Americans

LEIGH, WILLIAM ROBINSON

One of the more controversial and popularly acclaimed Western artists of the twentieth century, William Robinson Leigh (1866–1955) was born in West Virginia to embittered parents who had lost nearly everything in the Civil War. He suffered all his life from feelings of inferiority and hostility toward society. He achieved fame only in the final decade of his life. Trained in the draftsmanlike discipline of the Royal Academy in Munich, Germany, he was described more often than not as an illustrator rather than as an artist. Indeed, he made his living for many years providing illustrations for such magazines as *Scribner's* and *McClure's.*

Among his most famous works are *The Crucifixion of Christ* cyclorama at Einsiedeln, the African Hall backdrop paintings in the American Museum of Natural History, his Southwestern Indian scenes, a famous hunting scene entitled *A Close Call,* and a scene from his native state entitled *West Virginia Wood Chopper.*

Leigh lived long enough to see his strongly representational style of painting vindicated and to experience at last the acclaim he had desired. After World War II, as Americans reexamined their values in the face of the Nuclear Age, Leigh's work met with a new appreciation. Art critics praised him, and newspapers called him the "last of the great Russell-Remington-Leigh Triumvirate." Among his many awards were the Scroll Award from the New York Federation of Women's Clubs; Outstanding Painter of Outdoor Scenes and Wild Animal Life Award from the New York Natural History Club; the 1953 Benjamin West Clinedinist medal; and membership in the National Academy of Design and the Pi National Art fraternity.

He died at his studio in New York, where he was still painting at the age of eighty-eight and where, in the words of his wife, "he let his brush roam the windy plains."

—D. Duane Cummins

SEE ALSO: Art: Book and Magazine Illustration, Western Art

SUGGESTED READING:
Cummins, D. Duane. *William Robinson Leigh.* Norman, Okla., 1980.

LEON, PATRICIA DE

Born Patricia de la Garza in Soto La Marina, Mexico, to a wealthy frontier family, Patricia de Leon (1775–1849) was a prominent Tejana and wife of the Mexican Tejano empresario Martin de Leon. She and her husband, who was a native of Burgos, Nuevo Santander, are recognized as the cofounders of present-day Victoria, Texas. Patricia de Leon exemplifies the pioneering role performed by Hispano-Mexican women in the settlement of the Mexican Texas frontier in the 1820s.

De Leon and her husband lived in Gruillas during the first years of their marriage, but by 1805, the couple decided to move to Texas. They transported horses, cattle, goats, and mules to a location on the Arkansas River and later to present-day San Patricio on the east bank of the Nueces River. Within a few years, the de Leon family joined the revolt against Spain. The couple resettled in San Antonio de Bejar in order to cooperate fully with the town's patriot militia organized to fend off Spanish royalist troops sent to Texas in 1813 to restore control of the Spanish crown over the Texas frontier.

With Mexico's independence from Spain in 1821, Martin de Leon had a new opportunity to amass more land for his stock-raising business. The central government enacted a series of liberal colonization laws designed to boost the Texas economy. Martin de Leon soon petitioned local San Antonio officials to become an empresario, and in 1824, the de Leons led forty-one families, mostly of Mexican origin, to found the colony of Nuestra Senora de Guadalupe de Jesus Victoria on the Guadalupe River.

Patricia de Leon's status in the colony as the wife of an empresario improved with a substantial inheritance from her parents. For a time, the family enjoyed considerable material prosperity. With the death of her husband in 1833, de Leon's life took an unexpected direction. Her sons, who assisted in handling family business activities, along with her son-in-law, Placido Benavides, lent their support in 1836 to the cause of Texas independence. In the aftermath, Tejanos viewed the family as traitors, and Anglo-Americans treated them with contempt. One son, Fernando, was injured in a skirmish with Anglos. Another son, Agapito, was murdered by Anglos in 1836. As the anti-Mexican racial climate intensified in the following years, de Leon decided to abandon her home in Victoria and relocate to Louisiana with her daughter and son-in-law. When the family's fortunes did not improve, de Leon returned briefly to her hometown, Soto La Marina. In 1844, she moved for the final time to Victoria and spent the remainder of her life in the town she helped found. She never regained the material possessions she had amassed as the wife of a wealthy empresario.

—Gloria E. Miranda

SEE ALSO: Empresarios

SUGGESTED READING:
Hammett, A. B. J. *The Empresario: Don Martin de Leon.* Kerrsville, Tex., 1971.

LEOPOLD, ALDO

Recognized during his lifetime as the man who invented the applied science of wildlife management, Aldo Leopold (1887–1948) published his first textbook, *Game Management,* in 1933 and was the field's first professor at the University of Wisconsin. When he died fighting a neighbor's grass fire in his beloved Sand County, Wisconsin, he had an international reputation as a forester, wildlife manager, and wilderness advocate. But his book of seasonal musings on man's relationship with the land, published the year after his death as *A Sand County Almanac* (1949), marks Leopold as perhaps the most important conservationist of the twentieth century.

Born in Lawrenceville, New Jersey, in comfortable circumstances and educated at The Lawrenceville

School, Leopold was among the first graduates of the Yale School of Forestry in 1909. Sent by the UNITED STATES FOREST SERVICE to study wildlife management in the territories of New Mexico and Arizona, he was chiefly concerned with exterminating the predators of the deer herds and other game animals and thereby increasing their numbers. In 1919, he went to Gila National Forest to research soil erosion and watershed management. His enthusiasm for the roadless range and its unique properties led him to advocate its official designation as a wilderness area in 1924.

That year, he was sent to Wisconsin to work in the U.S. Forest Products Laboratory in Madison. Finding that work unfulfilling, he left the Forest Service. Between 1928 and 1930, he conducted game surveys in the north-central states for the Sporting Arms and Ammunition Manufacturer's Institute. The surveys were published in 1931, but Leopold was then an unemployed "consulting forester" with a wife and five children to support in a depressed economy. He used the time to complete *Game Management,* which explained wildlife problems in ecological terms for the first time. The book became the basic text in the field for the next forty years and won Leopold the chair of game management at the University of Wisconsin. He also consulted on state wildlife problems, worked for President Franklin D. Roosevelt's recovery programs, and lectured on wildlife and wilderness management. He was active in many professional and conservation organizations, and his attitude toward wildlife management and wilderness evolved over the years. Where once he had advocated the extermination of predators, he later recognized their importance in the habitat and regretted his earlier position. Symbolic of his mature views of wildlife management as a way to maintain diversity in the environment and wilderness as an area exhibiting a healthy biotic community, Leopold was a founder of the Wilderness Society in 1935. In his spare time, he and his family worked to restore barren land he had purchased in the "sand counties." It was in that setting that Leopold wrote the vignettes that appear in *A Sand County Almanac.*

In Leopold's view, conservation failed because people saw the land as a commodity they possessed rather than as a community to which they belonged. He believed that the future depended on a new attitude of respect and responsibility—an ecological conscience, which would make people aware that they belonged to a community composed of soil, water, plants, and animals. The adoption of a "land ethic," as he described it, would change humankind's role from conquerors to plain citizens of the land-community.

A Sand County Almanac became the "bible" of the contemporary environmental movement in the 1960s. It remains perhaps the best statement of attitudes necessary to achieve harmony with the land.

—*Linda J. Lear*

SUGGESTED READING:

Callicott, J. Baird, ed. *Companion to a Sand County Almanac.* Madison, Wis., 1987.

Flader, Susan. *Thinking Like a Mountain: Aldo Leopold and the Evolution of an Ecological Attitude toward Deer, Wolves, and Forests.* Columbia, Mo., 1974.

Meine, Curt. *Aldo Leopold: His Life and Work.* Madison, Wis., 1987.

LESLIE, NASHVILLE FRANKLIN (FRANK)

"Buckskin Frank" Leslie (1842–1925?) was a colorful frontiersman and a dangerous shootist who was given his sobriquet because of the fringed leather shirt he wore. Leslie claimed that he was born in Galveston, Texas, but he also claimed to have served as an army scout in Texas, the Indian Territory, and the Dakotas. He encouraged exaggerated rumors that he had killed fourteen men. The first confirmed information about

Nashville Franklin (Frank) Leslie. *Courtesy Arizona Historical Society.*

Leslie concerned his 1877 discharge as a scout in Arizona. He spent 1878 and 1879 as a bartender in San Francisco and then turned up in Tombstone the next year. He worked in the Cosmopolitan Hotel, tended bar at the Oriental Saloon, and prospected numerous mining claims.

Leslie consorted with May Killeen, was wounded in the 1880 shootout that proved fatal to Killeen's husband, and married the widow a week later. In 1882, Leslie pistol-whipped a man following a quarrel in the Oriental. Later in the year, another clash in the Oriental led to gunplay, which resulted in the death of "Billy the Kid" Claiborne. Over the next several years, Leslie worked as a rancher, occasionally scouted for the army against Apaches, and briefly rode as a mounted customs inspector. Leslie was divorced by his wife in 1887, but he took up with a woman named "Blonde Mollie" Williams from Tombstone's famous Bird Cage.

Williams moved in with Leslie at the small ranch he operated, but in 1889, he shot her to death following a drunken quarrel. Leslie also gunned down a witness, but he survived to offer testimony. Sentenced to life in Yuma Territorial Prison, Leslie was pardoned in 1896 and soon married Belle Sowell. Thereafter, it was rumored that he worked as a geologist's assistant in Mexico, as a prospector in Alaska, and in an Oakland poolroom. He is believed to have committed suicide in about 1925.

—*Bill O'Neal*

SEE ALSO: Gunfighters; Violence

SUGGESTED READING:

O'Neal, Bill. *Encyclopedia of Western Gunfighters*. Norman, Okla., 1979.

Traywick, Ben T. *Tombstone's "Buckskin Frank."* Tombstone, Ariz., 1985.

LEWIS, MERIWETHER

Famed explorer of the LEWIS AND CLARK EXPEDITION, Meriwether Lewis (1774–1809) was born in Ablemarle County, Virginia, near the home of THOMAS JEFFERSON. Lewis entered military service in the militia during the Whiskey Rebellion in 1794, joined the regular army, and quickly rose to a captain's rank. During those years, he met WILLIAM CLARK, with whom he became lifelong friends.

In 1801, Lewis became President Jefferson's private secretary, and the two began planning the Western exploration. As Lewis headed west in 1803 to meet Clark, the LOUISIANA PURCHASE was completed, and the transaction made the expedition all the more important.

After wintering in Illinois across from St. Louis, the Corps of Discovery set out up the Missouri River on May 14, 1804. Lewis and Clark initially commanded a force of about forty men, including regular army enlistees and French boatmen. The summer's trip, laborious but exhilarating, was marked by friendly relations with Indians except for one tense encounter with Teton Sioux. During the summer, one of the men died, apparently of a ruptured appendix. No other such losses occurred during the trip. By late fall, the explorers reached the Mandan and Hidatsa Indians living near present-day Bismarck, North Dakota, and settled in for the winter. In the spring of 1805, the corps, now numbering thirty-three people, including the Shoshone woman SACAGAWEA, continued up the Missouri. The explorers crossed the Rockies in late summer with the help of Sacagawea's people and found streams that carried them to the coast. Along the way, they met natives who had never seen white people, most notably Nez Percés, with whom they made friendly contact.

They spent the winter of 1805 to 1806 on the Oregon coast among Clatsop Indians and began their return trip in March 1806. The captains split the command in July on the crest of the Rockies. Lewis and a small detachment followed a short cut to the Missouri River and explored its northern tributaries, while Clark descended the Yellowstone River with the main party. On Lewis's excursion, the corps had its only deadly engagement with natives; Lewis and his men killed two Piegan Blackfoot Indians who were stealing horses and guns. Later, Lewis was accidentally shot in the hip by one of his men, but he mended quickly under Clark's care. The reunited corps reached St. Louis in September 1806.

Lewis was the nominal leader of the expedition, although Clark was given equal authority. Lewis served as the party's naturalist and astronomer and performed most of the scientific tasks. He is praised for his ecological descriptions and is credited with a host of natural history discoveries. As reward for his work, he was appointed governor of the Louisiana Territory in 1807. Jefferson also looked to him to write a report of the expedition, but it was barely begun when Lewis killed himself along the Natchez Trace in Tennessee in October 1809. Although some believe he was murdered, it is more likely that personal problems and professional difficulties drove him to suicide.

—*Gary Moulton*

SEE ALSO: Exploration: United States Expeditions

SUGGESTED READING:

Bakeless, John. *Lewis and Clark: Partners in Discovery*. New York, 1947.

Dillon, Richard. *Meriwether Lewis: A Biography.* 1965. Reprint. Santa Cruz, Calif., 1988.

Lavender, David. The *Way to the Western Sea: Lewis and Clark across the Continent.* New York, 1988.

Moulton, Gary E., ed. *Journals of the Lewis and Clark Expedition.* 12 vols. Lincoln, Nebr., 1983–.

LEWIS AND CLARK EXPEDITION

The Lewis and Clark Expedition was the first scientific expedition sponsored by the United States government. From May 1804 to September 1806, Meriwether Lewis, WILLIAM CLARK, and their Corps of Discovery became the first U.S. citizens to cross the North American continent, and only the second party of any nationality to do so north of Mexico. The geographical achievement, and the American claim of sovereignty in the Pacific Northwest, captured the popular imagination, but the principal sponsor, THOMAS JEFFERSON, intended the expedition to be much more than a romantic adventure. The president charged Lewis and Clark with a complex task. They were instructed to make a complete scientific survey of the regions along their route up the Missouri River, across the Rocky Mountains, and down the Columbia River to the Pacific and to determine the latitude and longitude of important sites. Jefferson asked them to de-scribe plant and animal life and the cultures of the native peoples they encountered. In addition, they were to evaluate the possibilities of the different areas for trade and agriculture and even try to establish peace with and among the native tribes they met.

Jefferson's interest in the trans-Mississippi West did not, as is sometimes implied, begin with the LOUISIANA PURCHASE. As early as 1783, while serving in Congress, he asked George Rogers Clark, the Revolutionary War hero and older brother of William Clark, if he would be interested in an expedition up the Missouri River. The expedition was to be sponsored by private funds and was intended to head off British attempts to secure a foothold in the West. The older Clark said no, but Jefferson continued to search for potential Western explorers. While serving as minister to France, he encouraged John Ledyard to undertake the mission. Ledyard had planned a one-man journey across Siberia followed by a trek across the North American continent beginning on the Pacific coast. The suspicious Russians frustrated Ledyard by deporting him, but Jefferson's hopes for a Western expedition did not die.

In the 1790s, while serving as secretary of state, Jefferson and friends belonging to the American Philosophical Society, the foremost association of American scientific men of the day, offered to sponsor first Dr. Moses Marshall, an American botanist, and then André Michaux, a French botanist, on an expedition up the Missouri River and across the Rockies to the

A woodcut illustrates Lewis and Clark's peaceful meeting with Indians. *Courtesy Library of Congress.*

Pacific. In both cases, Jefferson wanted the explorers to find the best and shortest route to the Pacific and to learn as much as possible about "the country though which it passes, its productions, inhabitants & other interesting circumstances." Neither expedition came about, however.

When Jefferson became president, he at last had the authority to put his long-desired expedition on an official basis. Jefferson selected the young army officer Meriwether Lewis as his personal secretary because of his knowledge of the "Western country." His selection may have been made with the intention of sending the young Virginian to the Pacific. There is no proof of this, but Lewis himself said that such an expedition had been a "darling project" of his for years.

Apparently, Alexander Mackenzie's publication of the account of his continental crossing in Canada from 1792 to 1793, the first north of Mexico, supplied the final catalyst for Jefferson's cherished expedition. Mackenzie's book, published in 1802, urged Britain to develop a transcontinental route. The book aroused Jefferson's fears of British preemption of the West. In any case, Jefferson and Lewis had made their plans and obtained necessary supplies, and Lewis was on his way over the Appalachians to Pittsburgh by the summer of 1803.

William Clark became Lewis's associate on the expedition because it was deemed necessary to have someone who could take over and carry out the mission if some disaster befell Lewis. Clark, four years older than Lewis, was an old army friend and was acquainted with Jefferson. It is possible that the president and Lewis had had Clark in mind for the purpose for some time, for in accepting the post Clark wrote to Lewis that "the enterprise &c. is Such as I have long anticipated." Lewis was perhaps the more intellectual of the two, although both were largely self-educated. Clark had perhaps more experience in wilderness travel and dealing with Indians. Lewis was the expedition's naturalist, and he wrote the first scientific descriptions of many Western plant and animal species. Clark, trained as a surveyor, was the map-maker; his maps were remarkably accurate considering that they were the first of so much of the route. Although Clark had been a captain during his previous army service, he received only a second lieutenant's commission for the expedition; it was a sore point with him, but he chose to continue, and the other expedition members were unaware of Clark's lower official status. The two were known to the party, and are known to history, as Captain Lewis and Captain Clark.

After leaving Pittsburgh in a specially constructed keelboat on August 31, 1803, Lewis sailed down the Ohio to pick up Clark at his home in Clarksville, Indi-

ana. As they journeyed down the Ohio and up the Mississippi to St. Louis, they began to pick up recruits for their party. The recruits were drawn from three principal sources: Anglo-American frontiersmen from the Ohio Valley, including the group later known as the "Nine Young Men from Kentucky"; French-speaking boatmen and traders from the "Illinois Country," which then included settled portions of Missouri; and regular U.S. Army enlisted men detailed for the expedition. The explorers spent the winter of 1803 to 1804 at Camp Dubois, or Camp Wood River, on the Illinois side of the Mississippi, waiting for the ice in the Missouri to melt and for the official transfer of Louisiana to the United States. The LOUISIANA PURCHASE had come after, not before, the planning of the expedition, contrary to popular impression, but the purchase and the transfer created more favorable conditions for the enterprise and made it more urgent as an assertion of sovereignty.

Their stay at Wood River also made it possible for Lewis and Clark to weed out some less desirable recruits. There they also introduced the explorers to military discipline; those lessons were hard for some of the independent backwoodsmen. By May 14, 1804, the party was ready to set out up the Missouri in the galleylike keelboat and two smaller boats, or pirogues. The first stage of the journey, on the lower Missouri, was through country relatively well known, at least to the French traders and trappers who had extracted its wealth in furs and established business relations with the Indians over the previous decades. The explorers had maps of the river from northeastern Nebraska to the Mandan villages in North Dakota—maps drawn in the previous decade by the trader John Evans, who had traveled under Spanish auspices. The explorers met with the Oto and Missouri Indian chiefs at the Council Bluff in eastern Nebraska and established official relations between these tribes and the United States for the first time.

A few incidents marred the early stages of the journey. The French boatman La Liberté and Private Moses Reed deserted in eastern Nebraska. Reed was apprehended, flogged, and dishonorably discharged, but he continued with the party until he could be sent back. Sergeant Charles Floyd died a little later, apparently from appendicitis, and was buried on a bluff overlooking the river in northwestern Iowa. A few weeks later, Private John Newman was arrested and tried for "mutinous expression." He too was punished and discharged but remained with the party until he could be sent back.

The party stayed a few days with the Arikaras in South Dakota. During their visit, the explorers participated in ceremonies to name chiefs (really a confirmation of the status quo), to give peace medals, and to establish a nominal sovereignty over the tribe. Taking an Arikara chief with them to make peace with the Mandans, they continued up river. At the Mandan and Hidatsa villages in North Dakota, they established Fort Mandan, their winter quarters from November 1804 to April 1805. There they met the Canadian trader Toussaint Charbonneau and his Shoshone wife SACAGAWEA and hired them to serve as interpreters and intermediaries with her people, who lived on the Continental Divide. The couple's son, JEAN BAPTISTE CHARBONNEAU, born in February 1805 at Fort Mandan, also became a member of the party.

Having sent back the keelboat loaded with excess party members, their journals to date, and some scientific specimens, the explorers continued up the river in the two pirogues and some dugout canoes in April 1805. After a month-long portage of the Great Falls of the Missouri, they passed the Three Forks of the Missouri and continued up the westernmost fork, which they named the Jefferson, to reach the Continental Divide in August. There they saw more mountains stretching out to the west and realized that the portage to the headwaters of the Columbia would not be as easy as they had hoped. Fortunately, they also met the Shoshones, Sacagawea's people, and obtained not only horses but a guide who could lead them across the tangled mountains to navigable waters heading to the Pacific.

The Shoshone guide, whom they called "Old Toby," took them on a tortuous trek across the Bitterroot Mountains, down the Bitterroot River in western Montana, and again across the Bitterroot Range at its widest part. Sergeant Patrick Gass described the region as "this horrible mountainous desert." As the first snows began to fall, the explorers survived on horse meat and condensed soup until they reached the country of the Nez Percés on the Clearwater River in western Idaho. They made canoes and, leaving their horses with the Nez Percés, continued once more by water down the Clearwater, the Snake, and the Columbia. Coming out of the mountains, they entered the barren Great Columbia Plain and then the thick rain forest near the coast. Clark's "Ocian in view! O! the Joy," written on November 7, 1805, was just a little premature, but a few days later they did indeed stand on the shore and watch the waves of the Pacific roll in.

The explorers spent the winter of 1805 to 1806 at Fort Clatsop—named for the nearest Indian tribe—in Oregon, south of the Columbia estuary. They subsisted largely on elk meat, which spoiled rapidly in the damp climate, and some roots and fish purchased from the Indians. Once they ate the meat of a beached whale. Lewis filled his journals with botanical, zoological, and

ethnological information, while Clark completed his detailed maps. The explorers hoped that some trading vessel would stop by during their stay, so that they could send some of their journals home by sea. None appeared, although there was abundant evidence that the local people had had extensive contacts with whites.

On March 23, 1806, the explorers began their return journey up the Columbia. They had delayed until then because they knew the interior country would be impassable from winter snows. They secured horses from tribes near the mouth of the Snake and continued overland to the Nez Percé country. Finding the Bitterroots still under several feet of snow, they stayed among the friendly Nez Percés for more than a month. Finally, some local guides enabled them to find the trail over the mountains despite the remaining snows.

Once over the Bitterroots, the explorers made a radical departure from their previous methods. Confident in their ability to survive, they split the party into two detachments in order to see more new territory. Traveling northeast across the Continental Divide to the Great Falls of the Missouri, Lewis intended to explore the Marias River. Clark went southeast to explore the Yellowstone. His trip was relatively uneventful, but Lewis's resulted in the only violent encounter with Indians of the entire expedition when he and three of his men had a skirmish with some young Blackfoot Indians who tried to steal their guns and horses. Traveling down the Missouri by canoe, Lewis encountered further misfortune when he was accidentally shot by one of his own men, the nearsighted Pierre Cruzatte, who mistook him for an elk.

The two parties reunited in North Dakota, revisited the Mandans, and persuaded the Mandan chief to accompany them to see the president. At the Mandan villages, they also left Sacagawea and Charbonneau. After visiting the Arikaras, the explorers raced downstream. On September 23, 1806, after being gone twenty-eight months, they reached St. Louis, where the citizens, who had long given them up for lost, gave them a noisy welcome.

Lewis reached Washington near the end of 1806 and turned the expedition journals over to Jefferson. The president intended for Lewis to write the history of the expedition, but he also appointed Lewis governor of Upper Louisiana (and Clark as superintendent of Indian Affairs for the territory). The appointment not only kept Lewis from working on the history but also led to personal disaster. The pressures and frustrations of office and a long-standing tendency to depression finally led Lewis to commit suicide in 1809 while on a trip to Washington. Clark then collaborated with Nicholas Biddle in producing an account of the great journey. Unfortunately, the scientific volume that was intended to accompany the narrative was never written. The scientific accomplishments of the Corps of Discovery were not fully appreciated until many years later.

Lewis and Clark had marked out a route to the Pacific, although it was not the one that would be followed by most travelers in the course of westward expansion. They had provided Americans, for the first time, with some idea of the extent and complexity of the Rocky Mountains and with the first notion of the geography of the Western continental interior. They had made the first scientific descriptions of many plant and animal species of the West—the prairie dog and the coyote, the ponderosa pine and Sitka spruce. They had produced the first accounts of three distinct types of Indian cultures: the village Indians of the Missouri; the people of the Rocky Mountain valleys; and the canoe Indians of the lower Columbia and the Northwest Coast. Considering their resources and time limitations, they had provided the world with a remarkably comprehensive view of regions previously little known or unknown to the white man.

—*Thomas William Dunlay*

SEE ALSO: Columbia River; Missouri River; Snake River

SUGGESTED READING:
Allen, John Logan. *Passage through the Garden: Lewis and Clark and the Image of the American Northwest.* Urbana, Ill., 1975.
Cutright, Paul R. *A History of the Lewis and Clark Journals.* Norman, Okla., 1976.
———. *Lewis and Clark, Pioneering Naturalists.* Urbana, Ill., 1969.
DeVoto, Bernard. *The Course of Empire.* Boston, 1952.
Jackson, Donald. *Thomas Jefferson and the Stony Mountains: Exploring the West from Monticello.* Urbana, Ill., 1981.
Lavender, David. *The Way to the Western Sea: Lewis and Clark across the Continent.* New York, 1988.
Moulton, Gary E., and Thomas W. Dunlay, eds. *Journals of the Lewis and Clark Expedition.* Lincoln, Nebr., 1983–.
Ronda, James P. *Lewis and Clark among the Indians.* Lincoln, Nebr., 1984.

LIGHT, THE (ASSINIBOIN)

The Light (Wi-jun-jon, ca. 1802–1833), renowned Assiniboin band leader, was born near the upper Missouri River. In 1831, he accompanied Major John F. A. Sanford to Washington, D.C. GEORGE CATLIN painted his portrait when the two met in St. Louis. Early in

1832, Wi-jun-jon returned to Fort Union where Catlin painted a dual portrait of him dressed in Indian clothing and in a general's uniform.

Following a dispute over his account of the trip East, another Indian killed Wi-jun-jon in 1833. The next year, federal agents sent his head, along with other Indian skulls, to a St. Louis doctor.

—*Thomas R. Wessel*

SUGGESTED READING:
Ewers, John C. *Indian Life on the Upper Missouri.* Norman, Okla., 1968.

LIGHTHORSE

A police force authorized by the Cherokee Indians in 1808, Lighthorse likely took its name for the mobility of its mounted patrolmen. The Cherokees of the Southeast had intermingled with Euro-Americans for two centuries before being forced westward in the 1830s. The Native Americans adopted some European cultural ways, including notions of personal property. The 1808 laws of the Cherokees, the first printed portions of their developing legal code, provided measures for safeguarding individual property, penalties for horse theft, and "regulating companies," consisting of two officers and four privates, to be paid from annuities received from the United States. Criminals apprehended by the Lighthorse were turned over to the tribal court for trial and punishment. When the Cherokees "removed" to Indian Territory, they transplanted their police force with them, and their institution of law enforcement was imitated by the other Civilized Tribes—Choctaw, Chickasaw, Creek, and Seminole—of the territory.

The tribal police of Indian Territory had a tough go of it. Lighthorse men were responsible for patrolling a fifty-thousand-square-mile area that became a haven for violators of United States criminal laws precisely because U.S. law enforcement had no jurisdiction within the territory. But the tribal enforcers had no power to restrain fugitives from other parts of the country. Nor did they have any jurisdiction over white criminals who violated the laws of the territory, including the 1834 Intercourse Act barring the introduction of alcohol in the territory. Only white courts could adjudicate non-Indian criminals. In addition, Indian courts had no power to prosecute Indians who committed crimes against whites or in the company of whites.

Lighthorse patrols faded from the Indian Territory for the two decades before the Civil War but were revived again at the war's conclusion and operated until the dissolution of tribal governments and Oklahoma's admission as a state in 1907.

—*Patricia Hogan*

SEE ALSO: Native American Peoples: Peoples Removed from the East

SUGGESTED READING:
Foreman, Carolyn Thomas. "The Light-Horse in the Indian Territory." *Chronicles of Oklahoma* (Spring 1956): 17–43.
Hagan, William T. *Indian Police and Judges: Experiments in Acculturation and Control.* New Haven, Conn., 1966.

LILIOUKALANI, QUEEN

The last Hawaiian ruler, Lilioukalani (1838–1917) was born the third of ten children of the high chief Kapaakea and chieftess Keohokalole. As was the custom of the royal family, the young Lydia, as she was called, was raised by her adopted parents, Abner and Konia Paki. Lydia became close to the couple's other adopted

Lilioukalani, about 1887. *Courtesy The Bettmann Archive.*

daughter, BERNICE PAUAHI BISHOP, while she received her education, command of the English language, and instruction in the Congregational church from missionaries at the Royal School.

At the age of twenty-four, Lilioukalani entered into an unhappy marriage with the son of a Boston sea captain, John Owen Dominis, who served as governor to the islands of Oahu and Maui. Lilioukalani herself became heir apparent to the Hawaiian throne, named to the post in 1877 by her brother, King David Kalakaua.

When her brother died in 1891, Lilioukalani ascended to the Hawaiian throne. She had the misfortune to reign at a time when American sugar-plantation owners were determined to maintain an island government favorable to their own economic prosperity. In 1887, they had forced Lilioukalani's brother to accept a new constitution that placed most of the power in the hands of the monarch's American cabinet. Even this cabinet, however, could not overcome the disastrous depression caused by the 1890 McKinley tariff, in which sugar growers lost their advantage in U.S. markets.

Queen Lilioukalani, called by some "strong and resolute," sought to restore royal power. She advanced a new constitution of her own in January 1893. The reaction of her American subjects was as swift as it was final. A Committee of Public Safety formed, secured the support of the U.S. minister and the might of the American navy, and then took possession of government buildings in Honolulu, overthrew the queen, established a provisional Republic of HAWAII, and appealed to the United States to annex the islands.

Before the annexation occurred in 1898, a counterrevolt struggled for ten days in January 1895 to restore Lilioukalani to the throne. The republic soundly defeated the queen's friends, and the queen was placed under arrest for eight months. Threatened with the execution of two hundred loyalist prisoners, she was forced to sign papers specifying her formal abdication and the end of the Hawaiian monarchy. She sat in the throne room of the Iolani Palace where she once ruled and faced the humiliation of a court martial. She could do no more than watch as the royal lands of her ancestors were arbitrarily taken from her.

Lilioukalani lived for another two decades in Honolulu on a pension of four thousand dollars and income from a sugar plantation she had managed to keep. State visitors made as much a point of paying her a respectful visit as they did the territorial governor. Through her autobiography, published in 1898, and the nostalgic songs she wrote, among them the haunting "Aloha Oe" ("Farewell to Thee"), Queen

Lilioukalani became for Hawaiians a cherished link to Hawaii's past glory.

—*Patricia Hogan*

SUGGESTED READING:

Kuykendall, Ralph S. *The Hawaiian Kingdom, 1874–1893.* Rutland, Vt., 1967.

Lilioukalani. *The Hawaiian Story by Hawaii's Queen.* 1898. Reprint. Rutland, Vt., 1964.

LILLIE, GORDON WILLIAM ("PAWNEE BILL")

Wild West showman Gordon William ("Pawnee Bill") Lillie (1860–1942) was born in Illinois. He developed an active imagination that was fired by dime novels and tales of adventure in the West. At thirteen, he moved with his family to Kansas, and while still a teenager, he struck out on his own. In later years, he told many tales of his adventures on the plains: he claimed to have killed a man in a gunfight in Wichita; he once helped lynch a cattle thief; at the age of eighteen, he was made "White Chief of the Pawnees"; and in 1884, he helped capture the notorious outlaw-marshal Henry Brown after the bank robbery in Medicine Lodge, Kansas. What seems more certain is that young Lillie lived on the Pawnee reservation in the Indian Territory, became fluent in the Pawnee language, and worked as an interpreter and teacher at the Pawnee Agency Indian school.

In 1883, WILLIAM F. ("BUFFALO BILL") CODY organized his first Wild West show and hired Lillie, known as "Pawnee Bill," as an interpreter for his Pawnee performers. The next year, "Pawnee Bill" toured again with "Buffalo Bill" Cody's show, which was hugely successful and played to audiences who had never seen cowboys, Indians, sharpshooters, or buffaloes. In 1888, "Pawnee Bill" organized his own Wild West show, which featured his wife, May, as a horseback sharpshooter. The show toured widely each year and, in 1894, performed in Europe. In 1909, "Pawnee Bill" merged with Buffalo Bill's financially troubled show. The partnership lasted until the 1913 season when Cody's creditors seized all the show's assets. "Pawnee Bill" left show business and returned to Oklahoma, where he had invested in land, oil, and livestock. He became a supporter of the Indian and worked to save the buffalo from extinction. He ranks with "Buffalo Bill" and William F. ("Doc") Carver as one of the greatest Western showmen and was instrumental in helping to create the myth of the romantic Wild West.

—*John Boessenecker*

SEE ALSO: Wild West Shows: Historical Overview

SUGGESTED READING:

Shirley, Glenn. *Pawnee Bill.* Albuquerque, N. Mex., 1958.

LINCOLN COUNTY WAR

Between February 18, 1878, and February 18, 1879, the Lincoln County War tore apart the little community of Lincoln, New Mexico, and left more than forty people dead. Everyone who survived lost something.

In the 1870s, most of Lincoln's citizens were farmers, and money was very scarce. Local businesses, including Lawrence G. Murphy and Company accepted crops as payment for purchases. Murphy and his partner, Emil Fritz, then sold the corn and beef to nearby Fort Stanton and the Mescalero Apache Indian Agency. By 1873, competition for federal contracts had driven prices so low that Murphy was heavily in debt. Fritz died, and James J. Dolan succeeded him in the partnership, later called J. J. Dolan and Company.

In 1876, a young Englishman, John H. Tunstall, arrived in Lincoln County. Looking for land and investment opportunities, he joined a local lawyer, Alexander A. McSween, in starting a store, a ranch, and even a bank. J. J. Dolan and Company saw Tunstall and McSween's ventures as an economic declaration of war. Two factions formed, one aligned with Tunstall and McSween, the other loyal to Murphy and Dolan.

Farmers, ranchers, and even outlaws were pitted against one another. Each side tried to grasp, legally, what Murphy never really had—a monopoly on government contracts and economic supremacy. Strong personalities and economic competition led to confrontations, then to murder, and finally to a collapse of law and order.

Early in February 1878, Sheriff William Brady attached McSween and Tunstall's store as part of a civil lawsuit. A sheriff's posse led by deputy Billy Mathews pursued Tunstall and shot him without warning.

McSween's supporters, styling themselves "the Regulators," began hunting down posse members. Both McSween's gunmen and Sheriff Brady, who was aided by Dolan and a band of hard-core outlaws called "the Boys," considered themselves lawmen. One Regulator, William H. Bonney, "the Kid," had recently arrived in Lincoln County.

On the morning of April 1, 1878, Bonney and other Regulators shot down Sheriff Brady and his deputy George Hindman on Lincoln's only street. Three days later, a shootout at Blazer's Mill cost the Regulators their leader, Richard Brewer, and left Andrew L. ("Buckshot") Roberts—a member of the posse that killed Tunstall—mortally wounded. That same day Lieutenant Colonel N. A. M. Dudley arrived as the new commander at Fort Stanton.

John N. Copeland, appointed interim sheriff, proved to be ineffective. Governor Samuel Axtell replaced him with George W. Peppin. Soldiers aided Sheriff Peppin until new orders prohibited the military from assisting civil authorities. Violence flared, and citizens fled the county. Two investigators from Washington drew different conclusions: Frank Warner Angel, an agent of the Department of Justice, blamed the anarchy on Murphy and Dolan, while Indian Inspector Ezra C. Watkins was disgusted with McSween.

Riding with his followers, McSween skirmished with Peppin's posses. Late on July 14, 1878, McSween led his private army back into Lincoln, where they "forted up" in his own house and other buildings. Then came the climax of the Lincoln County War, the "Five Days Battle."

The first three days saw McSween's forces and Peppin's men trade gunfire with few casualties. Pleas for help from an uninvolved citizen, Saturnino Baca, brought Lieutenant Colonel Dudley and his troopers into Lincoln on the fifth day. Dudley intimidated McSween's partisans into leaving all but the lawyer's own house, which caught fire. At dusk, William Bonney and five defenders dashed from the burning building and escaped. A second group delayed too long; McSween and four others, including posseman Robert Beckwith, died in "the Big Killing" while Dudley simply watched.

Sheriff Peppin holed up in Fort Stanton, and outlaws overran the county until mid-October, when the government lifted restrictions against army aid to civilian law officers. Frank Angel's report prompted Governor Axtell's removal and the appointment of Lew Wallace, a former general and budding novelist (he would become the best-selling author of *Ben Hur),* as the new governor.

On February 18, 1879, lawyer Huston Chapman was gunned down in Lincoln. Chapman's murder inspired Wallace to "clean up" Lincoln County. He persuaded Bonney to testify in the upcoming term of district court. The Kid complied but then found himself indicted for Sheriff Brady's murder. A military court of inquiry cleared Dudley of any misconduct during the Five Days Battle.

Lincoln settled down while Bonney slipped away and moved to Fort Sumner, New Mexico. By December 1880, the newspapers were calling him "Billy the Kid," a desperate outlaw. In the Lincoln County War, he played a minor role, but by mingling his later repu-

tation with episodes from the war, writers have forged an enduring legend of the American West.

—*John P. Wilson*

Suggested reading:

Nolan, Frederick W. *The Lincoln County War: A Documentary History.* Norman, Okla., 1992.

Utley, Robert M. *Billy the Kid: A Short and Violent Life.* Lincoln, Nebr., 1989.

———. *High Noon in Lincoln: Violence on the Western Frontier.* Albuquerque, N. Mex., 1987.

Wilson, John P. *Merchants, Guns, and Money: The Story of Lincoln County and Its Wars.* Santa Fe, N. Mex., 1987.

LINDSEY, BENJAMIN BARR

Judge and social reformer Benjamin Barr Lindsey (1869–1943) was born in Jackson, Tennessee, and moved to Denver, Colorado, with his family as a young man. At the age of sixteen, he was forced to leave school to earn a living for his mother and siblings after his father committed suicide. Working at menial jobs, he read law and was admitted to the state bar in 1894.

In 1901, Lindsey was appointed county judge and soon became the most renowned advocate of the juvenile-court movement in the United States. Writing and speaking widely on the subject, he believed in children's innate goodness and was convinced that they erred only in response to immoral stimuli or poverty. His efforts led to the establishment of the Juvenile and Family Court of Denver, over which he presided as judge. He also secured the passage of state laws that held parents and adults responsible for juvenile offenders and gave probate courts the power to protect children's moral, physical, and property interests.

Throughout his career, Lindsey was opposed by politicians and organized groups who disapproved of his outspoken liberalism. Opposition to him reached a climax in the 1920s when, as a vigorous advocate of the "sexual revolution," he endorsed contraception, compulsory sex education, and liberalized divorce laws. He became a target of the powerful Ku Klux Klan and, in 1927, lost a judicial reelection campaign after the Colorado Supreme Court invalidated all the votes in a pro-Lindsey Jewish precinct. In 1929, the Colorado Supreme Court disbarred him for rendering legal services during his years as a judge. Critics of the decision argued that his actions were neither immoral nor corrupt.

Lindsey moved to California in 1930 and was elected a judge of the Los Angeles Superior Court in 1934. He promoted numerous legal reforms, most significantly the Children's Court of Conciliation, which worked to save marriages and prevent divorce by providing dissatisfied couples with counseling. Lindsey presided over the Los Angeles Children's Court for Conciliation from its beginning until his death in Los Angeles in 1943.

—*Ruth M. Alexander*

SUGGESTED READING:

Larsen, Charles. *The Good Fight: The Life and Times of Ben B. Lindsey.* Chicago, 1972.

Lindsey, Ben B. *The Companionate Marriage.* New York, 1927.

———, and Wainwright Evans. *The Revolt of Modern Youth.* New York, 1925.

LISA, MANUEL

The first merchant-capitalist to venture north from St. Louis to the headwaters of the Missouri in search of furs and trade, Manuel Lisa (1772–1820) made a number of significant contributions to the development of the West and the nation. Born in New Orleans to Christobal de Lisa and Maria Ignacia Rodriguez of St. Augustine, Florida, Lisa early became a merchant and trader. Aggressive and ambitious, he had, by 1798, established his permanent home in ST. LOUIS, where his principal interest was exploiting the potential wealth of the upper Missouri country.

In 1807, with partners Pierre Menard and William Morrison, Lisa led the first trading and trapping expedition northward. Establishing Fort Raymond at the junction of the Yellowstone and Bighorn rivers, he began operations by sending out explorers, including JOHN COLTER, who found the wonders of what is now Yellowstone National Park. Leaving his crew in the mountains, Lisa returned to St. Louis in the spring of 1808. There he formed the St. Louis MISSOURI FUR COMPANY, a partnership including WILLIAM CLARK, Pierre Chouteau, Auguste Chouteau, Jr., Sylvestre Labbadie, Benjamin Wilkinson, Reuben Lewis, and ANDREW HENRY in addition to himself, Menard, and Morrison. With great expectations, the company sent an expedition upriver in the spring of 1809 only to meet with frustration. Hostile relations with the Blackfoot Indians and insurmountable problems of finance, transportation, and supply intimidated the conservative partners and stifled operations; the partners refused to invest further. Lisa engineered a reorganization of the company in 1812 by turning it into a limited partnership with himself, Labbadie, and Clark as the directors, but limited finances and the impending War of 1812 put him out of business in 1814.

Manuel Lisa, painted by an unknown artist. *Courtesy Missouri Historical Society.*

That year, William Clark named Manuel Lisa subagent for the tribes along the Missouri and charged him with maintaining peace. Performing the task quickly and well, he relieved St. Louis of its anxiety over a possible Indian attack. Lisa formed yet another Missouri Fur Company in 1819, and his partners—Joshua Pilcher, Andrew Woods, John Zenoni, Joseph Perkins, Thomas Hempstead, and Andrew Drips—represented the new and burgeoning American St. Louis. The second Missouri Fur Company failed too, for the same reasons as its predecessors, but Lisa was not there to see the ultimate end. Becoming ill upriver over the winter of 1819 to 1820, he returned to St. Louis, where he died.

In his incredibly active life, Manuel Lisa was the first in the American era to ascend the MISSOURI RIVER for purposes of trading and trapping, and his men were the first to cross the Continental Divide and winter in the Oregon Country. Lisa was the first to realize the benefits of leaving trappers in the mountains and supplying them from below, thus creating the prototypical mountain man. He opened the Missouri River to safe travel, and his care and concern for the various tribes with which he did business kept that water highway open. Just slightly ahead of his times, Lisa was unable to overcome the problems of finance endemic to the early FUR TRADE, but his activities earned him the title of first "King of the Missouri."

—*Richard E. Oglesby*

SEE ALSO: Chouteau Family; Mountain Men; Rendezvous; Trappers

SUGGESTED READING:
Oglesby, Richard E. *Manuel Lisa and the Opening of the Missouri Fur Trade.* Norman, Okla., 1963. Reprint. 1984.

LITERATURE

Covered here are genres and subgenres of literature of special historical significance to the trans-Mississippi West plus the major contributions of ethnic peoples to literature in the West. For "mainstream" literary works either set in the West or about the West, the reader should consult the various entries on individual works and authors. For the contributions specifically of women to literature in the West, see WOMEN WRITERS.

Travel Literature
   Charles Phillips

Indian Captivity Narratives
   Charles Phillips

Dime Novels
   Gary Topping

The Western Novel
   Gary Topping

Native American Literature
   Charles Phillips

Asian American Literature
   Stan Yogi

Mexican American Literature
   Charles Phillips

TRAVEL LITERATURE

Some of the more significant early writing concerning the trans-Mississippi American West appeared in the journals, reports and travelogues of explorers from ÁLVAR NÚÑEZ CABAZA DE VACA in the sixteenth century to the U.S. government-sponsored military and scientific surveys of the late nineteenth century. Not only did such writings serve the geopolitical purposes of the imperial powers encouraging the explorations,

they attracted a wide audience of readers and laid the groundwork for a tradition of literary works based on travel in the West. Especially the journals of Lewis and Clark inspired future works with some claim to literary standing. MERIWETHER LEWIS frequently went off by himself during the LEWIS AND CLARK EXPEDITION from 1804 to 1806 to meditate on the land he had entered with something of the historian's eye for the importance of detail and the dramatist's sense of moment and awe. From Lewis's journal descended such works of literary pretension as naturalist Thomas Nuttall's journals and writers WASHINGTON IRVING's and FRANCIS PARKMAN's travel books, not to mention the satirical version of such works produced by MARK TWAIN.

In many ways, Western travel literature was a American stepchild of the romantic movement or the cult of sensibility that sprang up in the late eighteenth and early nineteenth centuries, the former in Germany centered initially around the works of Johann Wolfgang von Goethe and the latter in England, with Laurence Sterne's seminal *Sentimental Journey in France and Italy.* Attracted to a romanticized wilderness that seemed especially attractive in a rapidly industrializing world whose burgeoning cities and countrysides ravaged by enclosures and mining were depressing and ugly places, the Europeans longed for a nature that was free and pure and fantasized about Jean Jacques Rousseau's noble savages who inhabited that natural world, men as yet uncorrupted by civilization and commerce. The American West seemed for such romantics just the Eden they were seeking. Thus Nuttall, one of the more accomplished scientists in the "virtuoso" period of American natural history, would write about the landscape he saw in the three trips he made to the West, in 1811, 1819, and 1834, as a "magnificent garden," while he denigrated the settlers he encountered at the fringes of civilization as bumpkins bound to ruin what they could not appreciate. In his *Journal of Travels into the Arkansas Territory, during the year 1819* (1821), the only one of his journals to survive, the British-born Nuttall recorded his delight in the flowers of the open prairie and dramatized himself as an enraptured and dedicated lover of nature. The work aped the literature of sensibility, fashionable in England during the 1790s. The note of Adam-like innocence, the joy of the sensitive poetic soul walking out into a beautiful and pristine natural world was part of a polished literary performance that would have made the snuff-sniffing, handkerchief-waving protagonist of *A Sentimental Journey* proud.

Washington Irving, having just returned from a Europe buzzing with the *strum und drang* (storm and stress) posturings of those who modeled their lives after the hero in Goethe's *Sorrows of Young Werther,* traveled for some time in 1832 through what would become Oklahoma. His description of the sunlight shining through the leaves of a grove of trees along the Arkansas River as like "the effect of sunshine among the stained windows and clustering columns of a Gothic cathedral" is pure European high romanticism, with its fascination for the Gothic and the natural. Irving continued with a passage worthy in sentiment of William Wordsworth: "Indeed there is a grandeur and solemnity in our spacious forests of the West, that awaken in me the same feeling I have experienced in those vast and venerable piles, and the sound of the wind sweeping through them, supplies occasionally the deep breathings of the organ." In such historical travel works as *Astoria* (1836) and *The Adventures of Captain Bonneville, U.S.A.* (1837), Irving helped establish the romantic image of the American West. Irving fixed for an American and European audience the notion of the mountain man as leading "a wild, Robin Hood kind of life" and fed the growing stereotype of Native Americans by describing the Osage Indians, for example, as having "fine Roman countenances" and looking in general "like so many noble bronze figures." The wilderness and its savage and part-savage heroes, ruggedly authentic men, were becoming, for the American romantics, the equivalent of Europe's brooding and ruined castles and vanished knight errants.

Popular historian and writer Francis Parkman was among those Easterners who produced works about the West in the tradition of European romanticism. Quite apart from his racist, military-minded, antinative frontier histories, in which historical figures play the role of white, Indian-killing heroes reminiscent on the one hand of JAMES FENIMORE COOPER, writing at about the same time, and on the other of THEODORE ROOSEVELT, whose work on the West came later, Parkman's *Oregon Trail* (1849) painted the West as a garden waiting to be occupied, and—particularly in his prefaces to later editions—introduced the romantic notion of a vanishing past: "Great changes are at hand in the region. Within a few years the traveller may pass in tolerable security through [the Indian's country]. Its danger and its charm will have disappeared altogether." In tones of high tragedy, Parkman began, in his literary travel book, the trend of viewing the West as a "withered" and "subdued" region alive in memory only—a trend that would flower three decades or so later in the powerful frontier thesis codified by FREDERICK JACKSON TURNER. Mark Twain, who made unmerciful fun of the likes of such romantics as Cooper and Parkman, also worked in the popular genre of travel literature. If in his *Roughing It* (1872), the West was not the vanishing land filled with noble

savages envisioned by the romantics, it was nevertheless a wild and woolly place, filled with odd and colorful characters worthy of memorializing, and Twain, too, for all his iconoclasm would earn a place in the tradition whose myths he challenged, but whose overriding vision—the possibility of escape from a constricting civilization, the consequent taming of a wild West—he also endorsed. It was, after all, Twain's Huck Finn, who, sick of the problems and dilemmas his relationship with the black slave Jim had created in the civilized world, decides to light out for the territories.

The West first portrayed in the aesthetically well-wrought travel works of such writers as Nuttall, Irving, Parkman, and Twain had an immense impact on the development of Western literature as a whole, in particular of the formulaic western, but also on subsequent mainstream literature and that of some Native American writers who were forced, in their own narratives, to come to terms with the vision of a vanishing culture, whose people—the writers themselves—were doomed by the steady progress of the "modern" world into a "primitive wilderness."

—*Charles Phillips*

SEE ALSO: Art; Exploration; Stereotypes

SUGGESTED READING:
Fielder, Leslie. *The Return of the Vanishing American.* New York, 1968.
Lyon, Thomas J. *A Literary History of the American West.* Fort Worth, Tex., 1987.
Smith, Henry Nash. *Virgin Land: The American West as Myth and Symbol.* Cambridge, Mass., 1950.

INDIAN CAPTIVITY NARRATIVES

Indian captivity narratives were a venerable tradition in Western literature by the time Euro-American settlers began pouring into the trans-Mississippi West around the middle of the nineteenth century—a tradition stretching back to the earliest days of the Spanish, French, and English conquests. ÁLVAR NÚÑEZ CABEZA DE VACA's *Relacíon,* for example, found a fascinated European audience as early as 1542, while Captain John Smith's fanciful account of his capture and salvation by Pocahantas in Virginia in 1607 captured the imagination of readers in both England and its colonies. By the eighteenth century, one of the great Euro-American pioneer fears was of being captured alive by Indians. The fear grew in part from Puritan demonizing of the Native Americans as savages and in part from the treatment some captives received at the hands of Native Americans. Indian captivity narratives, which exploited that fear to moral or titillating ends, preyed on the American psyche for some three centuries, developing from the essentially religious tracts of early Puritan New England into popular, mostly fictional "docudramas," not unlike the dime novels, by the late nineteenth century.

Captivity narratives, whose immense popularity was mostly an eighteenth-century phenomenon, went into decline after 1815, when responsibility for carrying on the intermittent war of conquest of native tribes passed from the hands of settlers to a U.S. Army trained for the purpose and the threat of capture by the Indians became relatively more remote in the West. Also, a new genre of romantic travel literature increasingly pictured the West as an Eden inhabited by noble, if vanishing, savages and edged out the captivity narratives even as guideposts to the ruling ideology and its thinking about the Indian "problem." Then, too, the rise of a scientific literature spawned by expeditions and academic study corrected, in some measure, the ignorance on which much in the Indian captivity narratives had been based. In the Far West, however, captivity tales continued to be written and were published; their circulation, though reduced, was still widespread; and they continued to function as anti-Indian propaganda that played to white fears based on stereotypes of Indian blood lust and licentiousness. Despite ample evidence that Native American tribes, many in the habit of adopting captives to replenish tribal populations depleted by war, treated prisoners as humanely as any other warring peoples, including the Euro-American pioneers; despite many examples of Euro-American captives coming to prefer Indian to Western culture; despite testimony after testimony from female captives that the Indians did not force their sexual attentions on defenseless women outside the heat of battle, the captivity narratives remained one of the major sources that led white Americans to believe in Indian depravity and "savagry" and fueled the cliché that, on the frontier, pioneers should save the last bullet in any fight against Indians for themselves, especially for the women among them.

The voyeuristic fascination among a relatively sexually repressed reading audience for Indian captivity narratives remained a factor in their sales, even as those published after the 1840s—the tale of OLIVE OATMAN in *Life among the Indians* (1857), Nelson Lee's *Three Years among the Comanches* (1859), FANNY KELLEY's *Narrative of My Captivity among the Sioux Indians* (1871)—grew more factual and less sensational. The appeal of the genre was still such that someone like E. D. Eastman, in a plagiarized and wildly inaccurate account called *Seven and Nine Years among the Comanche and Apache* (1874), which—among other things—described Aztec architecture in Texas, used a captivity narrative to help hawk his patent medicine, a "diuretic, a nervine, and gentle laxative" tonic he claimed to have discovered during his captivity. The deeply ingrained assumption of Indian licentiousness that lay behind the appeal of captivity narratives fueled much of the Indian stereotyping of Hollywood westerns as well, not the least being the brutal and disturbing portraits in some of John Ford's celebrated films, especially his cinematic masterwork, *The Searchers*. Later in the twentieth century, novels and films such as *A Man Called Horse* and *Little Big Man* used the gambit of Indian captivity to explore Indian life ways and demonstrate the inequities in Euro-American treatment of native peoples. In many ways, such works reflect a change in opinion among historians and scholars about captivity narratives. Whereas they were once dismissed as sensationalist tripe, captivity narratives are now valued by many scholars for their representations—and misrepresentations—of Indian life, family structure, gender roles, and the like, particularly for the details that can be gleaned from them of Native American society before white contact. One mark of this interest—and of the narratives' enduring interest—was the series edited by Wilcomb Washburn in the 1970s that put some 180 original Indian captivity texts back in print.

—*Charles Phillips*

SEE ALSO: Film; Stereotypes: Stereotypes of Native Americans

SUGGESTED READING:

Derounian-Stodola, Kathryn Zabelle, and James Arthur Levernier. *The Indian Captivity Narrative, 1550–1900*. New York, 1993.
Namias, June. *White Captives: Gender and Ethnicity on the American Frontier*. Chapel Hill, N.C., 1993.
Riley, Glenda. *Women and Indians on the Frontier, 1825–1915*. Albuquerque, N. Mex., 1984.

DIME NOVELS

Although dime novels were widely scorned in their day, and ours, for their improbable plots, bloodthirsty action, wooden dialogue, and overblown characters, they were widely read. They were America's first mass-market literature. Detectives, pirates, and other colorful characters found their way into dime novels, but it was the dime-novel western that most captured and shaped the American imagination.

Several developments in the mid-nineteenth century gave rise to the dime novel. One was the dramatic growth of a literate population that craved reading matter. Another was the invention of the steam-powered rotary printing press, which made mass publication possible. Finally, the imagination of the American public was fired by the West during the 1840s, with the opening of the Oregon Trail, the United States–Mexican War, the California gold rush, and publication of JOHN CHARLES FRÉMONT's colorfully written reports on his explorations.

Before the advent of dime novels, American writers had demonstrated the potential—both literary and sales—of stories about the West. During the 1820s, JAMES FENIMORE COOPER, for example, had built a lucrative literary reputation on his *Leather-Stocking Tales,* five novels recounting the frontier adventures of a character named Natty Bumppo. Although Cooper's novels were not without literary problems, he touched a responsive chord in the American mind by pointing to what he saw as the redemptive potential of the frontier, where an American character was being defined in terms of the hardy lives and pure virtues of those who lived close to nature. That experience would give Western civilization a new start by clearing away the false values and artificial society of the Old World.

The first dime novels were published in the 1850s by the New York firm of Beadle and Adams. While earlier popular literature had sold for as little as twenty-five cents, Beadle and Adams's publications sold for ten cents and eventually for as little as five cents. Printed on cheap newsprint and bound with paper covers, dime novels were marketed through the mail. Written for the lowest common literary denominator, dime novels represented something new on the American literary scene: inexpensive books enjoyable by everyone and available to anyone with access to a post office. They caused a literary revolution, whose effects have continued to the present.

Several types of heroes appeared in dime-novel westerns. Modeled on real characters such as DANIEL BOONE and DAVID (DAVEY) CROCKETT, one hero was the Appalachian backwoodsman who used his unique frontier skills to vanquish bloodthirsty Indians and save innocent heroines. The literary potential of the backwoodsman was limited in much the same way as Natty Bumppo's. While the backwoodsman represented the purer and more vital life of the frontier as opposed to the city, his lower-class origins made him ineligible for romantic matches with the genteel heroines—matches that would signal the development of a new American who embodied the best of both worlds. That union was accomplished when plainsmen such as WILLIAM F. ("BUFFALO BILL") CODY and CHRISTOPHER HOUSTON ("KIT") CARSON became models for dime-novel heroes in the 1870s. Both the real life Cody and Carson and their fictional counterparts functioned as well in the city as they did on the plains and were thus

endowed with enough sophistication to be proper love matches for Eastern women. A new American cultural type was emerging.

Outlaws were the heroes of many dime novels. In order to be acceptable to a civilized audience, their outlawry often was a reaction to a prior wrong done to them—a wrong that forced them outside the law to obtain justice. Many were Robin Hood–type figures who robbed from the rich to give to the poor and battled unjust laws and social institutions. During the late nineteenth century's Gilded Age when political, economic, and social corruption were rampant, such SOCIAL BANDITRY was appealing to readers outraged by the abandonment of democracy and virtue.

When the cowboy made his first literary appearance in dime novels, the authors seemed unable to free him enough from the drudgery of ranch work to develop his full potential as a romantic action hero. That development awaited writers such as OWEN WISTER and ZANE GREY after the turn of the twentieth century.

The immense success of the Beadle and Adams dime novels, some of which sold more than one hundred thousand copies, quickly attracted other publishers. Frank Tousey, George Munro, and the firm of Street and Smith enjoyed large profits from sales of dime novel during the 1860s and 1870s. Since dime novels adhered to a fairly inflexible formula of character, setting, and action, they were relatively easy to write and attracted numerous authors, some of whom wrote hundreds of titles. Among the most prominent were NED BUNTLINE, a New Yorker who turned the real life "Buffalo Bill" Cody into both a literary character and a theatrical star; Edward L. Wheeler, a flamboyant Philadelphian who dressed like some of his characters in a big Stetson hat and addressed people as "Pard"; and Edward S. Ellis, whose early dime novel, *Seth Jones, Or, The Captives of the Frontier,* sold six hundred thousand copies before it finally went out of print.

What happened to the dime-novel western? At least two developments during the 1920s and 1930s led to its death. One was steadily increasing postal rates that made mail-order marketing less and less profitable. Another was the development of western movies in which people could actually view their heroes performing their dramatic deeds on the screen—for the price of a dime novel.

In a larger sense, though, the dime novel never really died; it just transformed itself into other literary forms. Street and Smith, for example, began publishing their stories as pulp magazines (magazines printed on the same cheap newsprint paper as the dime novels). Such magazines as *Western Story* and *Ranch Romances* were selling twenty million copies per month during the 1920s and 1930s. Other publishers who had learned the lessons of the dime novel began publishing inexpensive paperback westerns by such authors as Zane Grey, MAX BRAND, and Louis L'Amour and reaped even greater financial rewards than Beadle and Adams had ever known. The dime novel thus continues to exert a vital influence on the popular literature of the American West.

—*Gary Topping*

SUGGESTED READING:

Ellis, Edward S. *Seth Jones, Or, The Captives of the Frontier*. New York, 1860.

Johannsen, Albert. *The House of Beadle and Adams*. Norman, Okla., 1950.

Jones, Daryl. *The Dime Novel Western*. Bowling Green, Ohio, 1978.

Smith, Henry Nash. *Virgin Land: The American West as Symbol and Myth*. Cambridge, Mass., 1950.

THE WESTERN NOVEL

The literature of the American West covers a wide spectrum—from highly original and complex works like Walter Van Tilburg Clark's *The Track of the Cat* to conventional action thrillers like most of the works of LUKE SHORT and Louis L'Amour. Best known are those works on the latter end of the spectrum, works written according to a fairly rigid formula in which such elements as setting, plot, and character are all very similar and thus predictable. Literary critics call these works "popular western novels" or simply "westerns." By far the largest number of fictional works about the West falls into this category. Westerns have had an immense influence on FILM, ART, and our images of Western history.

One of the elements in the western formula is the setting—the American West itself—a harsh and dramatic environment that tests human capabilities to the utmost and thus seems appropriate as a backdrop to plots that contain extremes of action and emotion. Another element is characters who dress and speak colorfully and who are motivated by rather simple forces, so they tend to be morally simplistic—either good or bad—and to react primarily to external pressures rather than internal conflicts. Finally, the plots feature violent confrontations between man and nature or man and man; they usually contain a love interest between hero and heroine; and they usually come to a happy resolution in which evil forces are defeated and hero and heroine are free to marry.

The heritage of the western can be traced from the ancient Greek heroes through medieval romances to the nineteenth-century romances of Sir Walter Scott and Robert Louis Stevenson. Even closer relatives include JAMES FENIMORE COOPER's *Leather-Stocking Tales*, the works of WASHINGTON IRVING, and local colorists such as BRET HARTE, who based entertaining stories on quaint local Western circumstances or folkways. The western novel arose in response to the social stresses of the Industrial Revolution of the late nineteenth century. Immigration, unequal distribution of wealth, and political corruption in Eastern urban areas caused Americans to look increasingly to the West, with its more primitive and apparently healthier social circumstances, for redemption. The western hero, with his manly competence, his untroubled morality, and his habit of direct, forceful action, became an important American model.

Although the western formula would later be refined and adapted to changing social circumstances, all of its basic elements are present in what is regarded as the first popular western, OWEN WISTER's *Virginian: A Horseman of the Plains* (1902). A Harvard graduate and friend of President THEODORE ROOSEVELT and the great novelist Henry James, Wister was a member of the Eastern aristocracy who, like many others of his class, had become disillusioned with the corruption and materialism of post–Civil War America. During several vacations to the West during the 1880s, he had discovered the cowboy and saw the literary potential of the cowboy's simple, hardy, competent way of life.

In *The Virginian*, the conflict between good and evil was represented by the anonymous Virginian's struggle with the villain Trampas. This struggle not only produced one of the more famous lines in western literature ("When you call me that, smile") but also introduced the "walkdown," in which two GUN-FIGHTERS advance toward one another to shoot it out on an empty street. Of perhaps even greater importance, however, was the hero's wooing and winning of Molly Wood, an Eastern schoolmarm. Previous writers had tried unsuccessfully to wed East and West through similar love matches, but Wister was the first to invest a hero with enough gentility to make the match convincing. Especially in his union with Molly, the Virginian combined the best of both regions and became a model for a new American culture rooted in authentic American experience and free from the corruptions of the Gilded Age.

Although *The Virginian* sold phenomenally well, Wister was less interested in making money than in exploring the literary potential of the West, so his great novel stands at the fork of the trail between the serious and popular western literary traditions. His most famous successor in the popular tradition was ZANE GREY, whose almost ninety books established and refined the popular western genre Wister had created.

Grey was a struggling New York City dentist who was trying, as a sideline, to build a literary career on stories of his ancestors' experiences on the Ohio River. During a trip to southern Utah and northern Arizona, he was impressed by the dramatic scenery and Mormon cowboys. Although his first efforts in the western genre brought only one modest success—*The Heritage of the Desert* (1910)—his persistence paid off, and in 1912, he published perhaps the most famous western of all, *Riders of the Purple Sage*. A story of revenge, the novel portrayed the black-clad gunman Lassiter who set out to destroy the lecherous and power-hungry Mormon leaders who had ruined his sister. In the process, he saved the Mormon girl Jane Withersteen and an Eastern weakling named Bern Venters. The book was full of vivid, if melodramatic, writing: Venters discovered that the Masked Rider, the terrible partner of rustler Oldring, was in fact a girl; he also found a passage under a waterfall into a hidden canyon where Oldring kept Withersteen's rustled cattle; and in the closing scene, Lassiter rolled an immense boulder that destroyed the pursuing Mormons, but sealed himself, Jane Withersteen, and little Fay Larkin in Surprise Valley forever.

Grey never repeated the gripping melodrama of his masterpiece, but in his great westerns of the 1920s, he expanded the formula to include a wide variety of character types, a Social Darwinist explanation for Western superiority in terms of the survival of the fittest, and contemporary social issues like the destruction of the Indian and the buffalo and the government's shameful neglect of World War I veterans. Few of his successors, however, borrowed more than his gripping action writing, his dramatic Western settings, and his vengeful gunfighters with their hard fists and fast guns.

One of Grey's most famous successors was a whirlwind of literary energy named Frederick Faust, whose best-known pen name was MAX BRAND. Brand's quick wit and broad reading won him acceptance into the University of California at Berkeley, but his wayward behavior—he once offered to take anyone's final examination in any course, passing grade guaranteed, for a fee—led to conflicts with the university president and kept him from graduating. Epic poetry on the ancient Greek model was Brand's great passion, but he found that its market was limited. In order to support his poetry writing, he turned to the immense market that writers such as Grey had created for the western.

Pulp magazines like *Western Story* and *Ranch Romances* largely replaced dime novels after World War I as the inexpensive medium for westerns, and Brand's career illustrates the success a hard-working writer could enjoy in that market. Brand could create stories and novels as fast as he could type, and marathon work sessions resulted in an immense output. On

Owen Wister. His novel, *The Virginian: A Horseman of the Plains*, contained all the elements of the popular western novel. *Courtesy American Heritage Center, University of Wyoming.*

more than one occasion, Western magazines contained nothing but Brand stories written under various pen names.

Brand was a better writer than Grey in several ways: his scenery descriptions were less tedious than Grey's, his dialogue was more realistic, and his plots were more tightly structured. But Brand had his faults as well, for his admiration for the Greek epic often carried over into his westerns with poor success. Brand held his western writing in contempt—his "Western junk," he once called it—and banged it out with minimal care. He sometimes borrowed his plots from ancient Greek dramatists including Sophocles, and his heroes often resembled Achilles or Hercules more than actual cowboys. Still, at the time of his death in Italy as a World War II correspondent, Brand had demonstrated the extent of the American public's appetite for well-written westerns and had established a record for literary production that may never be broken.

The enormous output of Grey and Brand brought the western formula to full development and created a vast audience willing to pay for its familiar features. As early as the late 1920s, while both were at the height of their careers, a younger writer named Ernest Haycox was making subtle changes in the formula—changes that would open up a new audience for the western and bring it closer to "serious" literature.

Haycox's earliest stories appeared in the pulp magazines, particularly *Western Story,* and were fully within the formula developed by Grey and Brand. He soon grew frustrated, however, with the limited pay and especially with the literary restrictions of the formula. Haycox was more interested in internal conflicts—characters who struggled with self-doubts and difficult moral alternatives—than with the purely external conflicts such as gunfights that characterized the formula. Accordingly, he began experimenting with what some critics have called the "Hamlet hero"—the doubt-ridden, indecisive hero based on Shakespeare's most famous character.

His experiments cost him his best outlet, for *Western Story* wanted him to stick to the established formula. But it was a fortunate loss; Haycox found he could sell his stories to better-paying pulps such as *Short Stories* and *Frontier.* Beginning in 1931, he even broke into the "slicks"— magazines like *Collier's* and *Saturday Evening Post* printed on expensive glossy paper instead of the cheap newsprint of the "pulps." The rates those magazines paid their authors were far beyond anything the pulps could offer, and Haycox was on his way to financial as well as literary success.

Haycox's contribution was to bring the western back to a position something like that occupied by *The Virginian,* with one foot in serious fiction and the other in the formula. While he continued to use cowboys, or at least frontiersmen, as heroes and to feature dramatic action and other formula elements, his introduction of difficult moral dilemmas, his probing of the psychological depths of his characters, and his introduction of historical depth into the background of his plots lifted his books into a more serious literary realm. This was especially true of his last novels, *Long Storm* (1946); *The Earthbreakers* (1952); *The Adventurers* (1955); and perhaps his best-known work, *Bugles in the Afternoon* (1944), one of the best novels ever written about the Custer massacre.

In spite of Haycox's innovations, the western experienced a crisis during World War II. Its three leading practitioners, Grey, Brand, and Haycox, all died either shortly before, during, or shortly after the war, and the markets for the western began to decline. Partly to cope with the crisis, a group of younger writers created the Western Writers of America in the early 1950s and began publishing *The Roundup* (more recently *The Roundup Quarterly)* in which they could exchange ideas on work habits, legal and marketing strategies, and literary craftsmanship. Assessing the effects of the group is not easy, but it seems certain that it has played a significant role both in promoting Western literature among the reading public and in easing younger writers into the profession.

One writer who did thrive during and after the war was Luke Short (Frederick D. Glidden). As a young man in the 1930s, Short admired Haycox's success and patterned his career after Haycox's. Probably because Haycox had blazed the trail for him, Short broke into the slicks at a very young age and with much less writing experience behind him than Haycox had when he sold his first story to *Collier's*. Industrious and talented, Short was making one thousand dollars a month by 1940 and soon began selling movies rights to his stories for as much as twenty-five thousand dollars. Although he lost interest in writing westerns during the 1950s, it was the beginning of the most lucrative phase of his career. Paperback publishers like Dell and Bantam were seeking reprint rights to westerns serialized in the slick magazines and were willing to pay established writers very handsome royalties.

Short's novels featured dramatic action and the conventional external conflicts of traditional westerns. The higher law theme, in which a moral man has to go outside the corrupt laws of a community to bring about justice, occurred repeatedly in his work. But he was an innovator as well, using strong heroines and treating minorities sympathetically. And—amazing for novels published during the Eisenhower era—Short introduced a sexual frankness, which, while not pornographic, featured extramarital relations and prostitution.

During the 1950s, Short was overshadowed by another name in Bantam's stable of western writers, Louis L'Amour. A handsome hobo who knocked about the world in his youth working as a roustabout, cowpuncher, prizefighter, and sailor, L'Amour led a restless, active life. He created a public image both virile and scholarly. His breadth of reading and immense personal library led to a close friendship with the scholar Daniel Boorstin, librarian of Congress.

L'Amour was proud of what he regarded as the factual accuracy in the historical background of his novels—a claim prominently featured in Bantam's advertising and one that evidently appealed to his audience. His readers were led to believe that this was the real West, even though presented in fictional form. But L'Amour never learned to integrate his history with his fiction, and some of his books contained awkward, undigested chunks of somewhat irrelevant history in footnotes or digressions.

The cultural values in L'Amour's novels were very conservative. Many of them were parts of a large saga featuring three families, the Sacketts, the Talons, and the Chantrys, each family representing various phases of conquering, settling, and molding the raw frontier into a civilized society. It is noteworthy that L'Amour considered this a family, rather than an individual, enterprise. His female characters, too, were representatives of a conservative tradition in which they were respected to the point of reverence by the males.

In addition to the family sagas, L'Amour's novels fell into two further groups: the individualistic, violent works about a single gunslinging, hard-fisted hero like *Shalako,* and the larger panoramic epics like *Bendigo Shafter,* sweeping romantic tales covering large quantities of time and space and contrasting dramatically with the short, lean action dramas of Luke Short or even L'Amour's own *Shalako.*

A more recent development was the role of the sex and VIOLENCE in westerns. Although the classic formula western always contained violence, it was restrained in descriptive detail. Sex was equally restrained, usually consisting of a developing love interest culminating in marriage. Both sex and violence began to be more graphic during the 1950s, and the process accelerated rapidly during the 1960s and 1970s, when permissive morals and the gore of Vietnam on the evening news invaded the American mind. Although L'Amour's conservative westerns sold phenomenally well during that period (in 1980, he celebrated the sale of one hundred million books since the beginning of his career), other writers began exploiting the grosser aspects of American taste. George G. Gilman's "Edge" series, for example, lingered fondly over bone-snapping, blood-spurting violent encounters that tested even the most strong-stomached of his readers. Similar series featured graphic sex, like Jove's "Longarm" series written by numerous authors under the pen name Tabor Evans, and Playboy Press's "Jake Logan" series.

One can only imagine the reactions of Wister, Grey, and Brand to such startling developments in the formula they had fashioned. But the new westerns reflected the social conditions and cultural values of their day just as the original westerns grew out of their own time. It is, if nothing else, eloquent testimony to the flexibility of the western formula.

—*Gary Topping*

SUGGESTED READING:

Erisman, Fred, and Richard W. Etulain. *Fifty Western Writers: A Bio-Bibliographical Sourcebook.* Westport, Conn., 1982.
Etulain, Richard W. "The Historical Development of the Western." In *The Popular Western* by Richard W. Etulain and Michael T. Marsden. Bowling Green, Ohio, 1974.
Grey, Zane. *The Heritage of the Desert.* New York, 1910.
———. *Riders of the Purple Sage.* New York, 1912.
Haycox, Ernest. *The Adventurers.* Boston, 1955.
———. *Bugles in the Afternoon.* Boston, 1944.
———. *The Earthbreakers.* Boston, 1952
———. *Long Storm.* Boston, 1946.
L'Amour, Louis. *Bendigo Shafter.* New York, 1979.
———. *Education of a Wandering Man.* New York, 1989.
———. *Shalako.* New York, 1962.
Topping, Gary. "The Western Novel." In *Critical Survey of Long Fiction.* Edited by Frank N. Magill. La Canada, Calif., 1983.
Wister, Owen. *The Virginian: A Horseman of the Plains.* New York, 1902.

NATIVE AMERICAN LITERATURE

Although the oral stories and songs of the various North American Indian tribes boasted formal structures, were highly organized and stylized, and enjoyed an extensive and cherished history, they were as different from one another as the tribes themselves had become over the millennia in which they had occupied separate regions of the continent. For all the tribes, however, the traditional "literature"—sometimes specific to special occasions or ceremonies, sometimes general explanations of the cosmos and tribal genesis, sometimes tales cautionary and instructive to daily life—played an integral role in their cultures. As anthropologists have long pointed out, the oral literatures of traditional tribal cultures were structurally similar and, at some level, shared a world view, not unlike the way in which the historical, fictional, and poetic productions of European and Euro-American culture shared common assumptions and understandings about the nature of the world and the people in it, regardless in which national language they happened to be written.

Rather than telling the story of individuals or expressing individual temperaments, a habit shared by most European and Euro-American literature, the Native Americans, in general, emphasized the unity of existence and the place of the community within that unity, a profoundly religious sensibility expressed, according to scholars Larry Evers and Paul Pavich, in four basic themes common to the oral literature of the Indians: the nature of the sacred, the appreciation of beauty, the special importance of particular places, and the centrality of community. "The individual," say Evers and Pavich, "is constantly reminded that he is part of the whole, not any more important than any creature around him." What Europeans and Euro-Americans often translated and defined inaccurately as "the Great Spirit" was the unifying concept of Native American oral tradition. "Wah'kon-tah," write Thomas E. Sanders and Walter W. Peek of that concept, "is the sum total of all things, the collective totality that always was—without beginning, without end. Neither a force nor a spirit, it is the inexplicable sharing-togetherness that makes all things, animate and inanimate, of equal value, equal importance, and equal consequence because they are all Wah'kon-tah simultaneously, their forms collectively creating the form of Wah'kon-tah which is, obviously, incapable of being anthropomorphized."

The old stories that came down from ancient times found a new shape in the late nineteenth and early twentieth centuries in personal narratives requested—and often recorded and heavily edited—by Euro-Americans. Some were simply drawn to native culture out of curiosity; a number of them were engaged in research and publishing; others were social reformers. Quite a few Native Americans contributed to the collecting of vast amounts of folklore and ceremonial literature, much of which was never published, and several Native Americans either wrote or dictated autobiographies that, in part, described the changes they had witnessed, often analyzed Indian-white relations, and frequently proposed ways to reach some accommodation between the two cultures. By the late nineteenth century as well, a transformation of native traditional materials and historical and political information into formal fiction had gotten under way, a process that would gain momentum between 1900 and 1940, then dwindle until the 1960s when Native American literature began to flourish.

Personal narratives and autobiographies dominated what Paula Gunn Allen calls "the long silence" that occurred between the mid-1930s and the late 1960s, a silence she attributes to the Great Depression, World War II, the growing influence of FREDERICK JACKSON TURNER's frontier thesis (with its emphasis on the "vanishing" native culture), and the "bland and blinding white cocoon of the 1950s, with its Red Scare, Cold War, and suburban fixations." As a result, autobiographies and folk tales, plus the works of a few Native American fiction writers, formed a native canon that would influence the new writing of the 1960s. Fed by two streams, the Native American oral tradition and Western fiction and its antecedents, Native American literature, according to Allen, used the traditional ceremonial texts much the way Euro-American literature used the Bible, as a referent—that is, as a major source of symbols, allusions, and philosophical assumptions about the world.

The publication of Native American writers began in 1854 with the appearance of JOHN RIDGE's melodramatic western, *The Life and Adventures of Joaquin Murieta*, a highly romantic tale, but one, nevertheless, critical of race prejudice among Anglo gold miners against the idealized, brave, sensitive, and revenge-hungry Murieta, a legendary social bandit not unlike some Anglo outlaws appearing in the dime novels of the day. Ridge's novel, which became a centerpiece of Mexican American folklore, was, however, followed by a "thundering silence," according to Allen, and it would be forty years before a Native American again published a work of fiction. Among those dictating or writing autobiographical texts, one the of the first in the West was SARAH WINNEMUCCA, a forthright Paiute who produced the *Life among the Paiutes: Their Wrongs and Claims* (1883), a candid, engaging account of her life and the role she played as an intermediary between those into whose world she was born, "a stone-age, hunter-gather people," says H. David Brumble, III, and the whites with whom the Paiutes first made contact in 1848, when Winnemucca was about four years old.

Omaha scholar Francis LaFlesche, with *The Middle Five: Indian Boys at School* (1900), and Santee Sioux physician CHARLES ALEXANDER EASTMAN, with—among many others—*Indian Boyhood* (1906) and *From the Deep Woods to Civilization* (1916), also used autobiography, a tool of the conqueror, to demonstrate their standing in the contemporary world and to record its continuity with the traditional. The title of LaFlesche's work hints at the broad influence the boarding-school system had on many early Native American writers, while Eastman—raised by grandparents while his father was in prison for joining the Minnesota Sioux uprising in 1862—was, like a number of early Indian writers, a survivor of the warfare between Anglo-American invaders and Native American peoples. Also like many other Indian writers, Eastman in his numerous works, all of them well edited by his wife, Eliza, freely crossed genre boundaries, moving from autobiography to historical writing to fiction.

The first Native American woman to publish a novel was MOURNING DOVE, a Okanogan whose white name was Cristal Quintaskit (or McLeod) Galler. Obsessed with the desire to write, she worked with folklorist Lucullus Virgil McWhorter to gather from relatives and friends traditional stories, which she typed out sitting on the ground outside her tent. She ultimately turned to fiction and produced in the same manner *Cogewea: The Half Blood* (1927). A deeply feminist if somewhat awkward work, a novel anchored in the popular Western genre, *Cogewea* interweaves traditional and modern themes and integrates strains of the ceremonial with an incisive protest against unreasoning prejudice to comment on the conflicting value systems of two cultures and to clarify the struggle for identity that characterizes much native writing in the twentieth century.

This essentially tragic cross-cultural theme, which inevitably featured a protagonist "caught between two worlds" and frequently drawn to alienation and self-destruction, in many ways reflected the effects of the Progressive vision of Native American culture propagated by the white boarding schools, especially the model for government-run education for Indian school children across the country—the Carlisle Indian School in Pennsylvania. The school's founder, RICHARD HENRY PRATT, held, as did most liberal opinion in the early twentieth century, that Indian culture, however attractive it might be, was doomed by the progress of the modern world and that the only hope for Native Americans was to abandon traditional tribal life and assimilate to white culture. Institutions like Pratt's, according to Allen, wished to produce "[c]hildren who . . . were profoundly alienated from their people and often became the primary proponents of Anglo-Christian values in their home communities after graduation." Writers such as Estelle Armstrong and Luther Standing Bear, both of whom attended school at Carlisle, captured the essence of what happened to natives under Euro-American rule and Progressive education.

Armstrong wrote short stories for the student paper, *The Red Wing*, while at Carlisle in the 1920s, only to vanish into obscurity afterward. In her brief, bitterly ironic tale, "The Return" (1925), which was anthologized by Allen, Armstrong scathingly depicts the abject humiliation of native peoples by white culture and education. Standing Bear, on the other hand, in *My People, the Sioux* (1928) provides a clear picture of life in the boarding-school system—a story that Allen finds "all the more chilling for its reasonable, accepting tone." Chief Standing Bear, a Lakota born in 1868 just as the great Sioux Reservation was being formed, came to admire and respect Richard Pratt, and his many books—precisely because of their "reasonable" acquiescence to what many have come to see as a kind of cultural genocide, a "deculturation" rather than acculturation—were reviewed in the *New York Times* and other major newspapers and journals. In 1933, Standing Bear wrote a letter to President Franklin D. Roosevelt in which he proposed a bill that would require all public schools to teach courses in Indian history, religion, philosophy, art, and culture.

The myth of the "vanishing Indian," as Brian Dippie has shown, had long been a dominant feature in white attitudes toward Native Americans; the Progressives—by institutionalizing the myth in Indian education—made it part of the Native American's own cultural baggage, a burden only reinforced by commercial publishers, who demanded that their writers work within the narrative conventions of European culture and produce works based on the conflict-crisis-resolution "plot" that stretched back to Aristotle's ideas about what constituted literature. In the 1930s, the dual impact of the education system and the publishing industry on Native American writers, who had to come to terms with a culture that claimed their society was outmoded in conflict-centered works, produced books that were in many ways structurally drawn to the "tragic" notion of a native world fast becoming extinct. In other words, the very act of writing in the forms of the dominant culture required that native writers focus on themes of dissolution, both cultural and individual.

BLACK ELK, a Lakota medicine man who lived through the Sioux Wars, suffered under the concentration of his people into camps during the reservation era, and came to tour Europe with Buffalo Bill's Wild West Show, narrated in his old age the story of his life to poet and writer John G. Neihardt. *Black Elk Speaks* (1932), as set down and edited by Neihardt, tells of the painful defeat of the Sioux, but Black Elk managed to break out of the confines of European narrative conventions in the section of the work entitled "The Great Vision," an assertion of the eventual triumph of the traditional spiritual powers in the modern world, and because of that, the book came to be praised not only as an aesthetically realized work of literature, but also as an interpretation of Native American spiritual thinking for a comparatively more secular, technology-dominated world. Two years later, John Joseph Mathews, a journalist and author from Indian Territory, Oklahoma, came out with *Sundown* (1934). Raised on the Osage Reservation, which was then awash with oil, Mathews received an education at Oxford University courtesy of his family's share of the income from oil leases. His novel focuses on the decline of the Osage people as a result of their wealth and the capitalists predators it attracted. Centered around the character Challenge Windzer, a "mixed-blood" like Mathews, whose Osage mother refuses to give up the traditional ways and whose mixed-blood father puts his faith in the federal government to protect the Osage people from the challenges posed by the influx of oil money, the book is a chronicle of betrayal and disillusionment. The conflict between Indian and white culture leads to community dissolution, loss of identity, and the suicide of Windzer's father. But Windzer himself is left with enough money to drink and drift, which, Allen claims, gives the novel a distinctly Native American structure, since rather than ending with the destruction of the protagonist, the book simply stops, leaving the reader with the clear impression that Windzer's story goes on and on.

More decidedly European in structure than either *Sundown* or *Black Elk Speaks* was D'Arcy McNickle's

Surrounded (1936), an autobiographical work squarely in the tradition of European naturalism. McNickle, the son of a Ojibwa-Cree-French mother and an Irish father, was adopted by the Confederated Salish and Kootenai tribes and was educated in mission and public schools and at the Universities of Montana, Oxford, and Grenoble. Cofounder of the National Congress of American Indians, he taught anthropology at the University of Saskatchewan and has been hailed by many as the most important Native American fiction writer before N. Scott Momaday. In many ways reminiscent of *Cogewea, The Surrounded* was set in the Pacific Northwest of 1935 and depicted the profound cultural and psychological discontinuities experienced by its mixed-blood protagonist, Archilde, in a bleak, if poignant account of the misery attendant to reservation life. No reader can deny that the book is pessimistic, although Euro-American scholars such as Thomas J. Lyons and Jon Tuska see the novel as a profound and intelligent work of art, redeemed by its "resolute affirmation of the Native American perspective . . . [its] recognition of a conflict that will not diminish soon, and its persevering sense of the honor and the rightness of the old ways. . . ." For the Native American Allen, however, *"The Surrounded* is a deeply depressing novel, satisfying readers who believe in the ultimate destruction of Native peoples and traditions however grieved they might be at our passing." McNickle's original novel, says Allen, was very different from the published version, a product of a publisher who was interested in profit and promulgating Euro-American cultural standards and who turned the work into the kind of "Dead Indian" story—like the film *Dances with Wolves*—that works well in an American society, Allen says, whose culture is based on such "Western myths" as the Crucified Lord and the Dying Warrior.

Depending on which viewpoint a reader adopts, *The Surrounded* can be seen as a work that foreshadows succeeding Indian fiction or the best expression of a dead-end tradition that has been superseded by the literary renaissance of Native American writing in the 1960s and 1970s. One product of that renaissance was McNickle's posthumously published *Wind from an Enemy Sky* (1978). Considered by many to be his finest work, the book is a vigorous and gripping drama about the Little Elk Indians seen entirely from a Native American view. Born in part in a tumultuous social and political period that saw a rekindling of interest in all things Indian, and perhaps—as Allen and others have said—a result of a recurring cycle deep in the nature of existence, the renaissance saw a remarkable creative outpouring of—in the West—such works as Leslie M. Silko's highly regarded *Ceremony* (1977)

and James Welch's sometimes controversial *Winter in the Blood* (1974), *Death of Jim Loney* (1979), and *Fools Crow* (1986).

Launching the renaissance was the Pulitzer Prize–winning *House Made of Dawn* (1968) by N. Scott Momaday, perhaps the most important Native American fiction writer of the twentieth century. Centered around Abel, a twentieth-century Indian who, plagued by the dislocation of modern urban life, longs to retreat to the mysticism of Indian culture, *House Made of Dawn* is a concentrated attempt to focus on the Indian as a human being, a complicated and sophisticated individual, rather than the "simple" Indian, or the "vanishing" Indian, or the "noble" Indian, or any other stereotype. Allen has hailed the work as "the first non-linear, non-chronological, ritual novel written by an American Indian," and Larry Evers has pointed out that the novel's movement from harmony to discord is common to the oral narratives of traditional Native American literature, as is the fact that the plot is "framed" by the necessary process of reconnecting with the land. Beginning with Momaday, says Allen, Native American writers were free again to use all aspects of the native narrative tradition in rendering their works of the imagination.

—*Charles Phillips*

SEE ALSO: Indian Schools; Native American Culture; Social Banditry; Stereotypes: Stereotypes of Native Americans

SUGGESTED READING:
Allen, Paula Gunn, ed. *Studies in American Indian Literature.* New York, 1983.
———. *Voice of the Turtle: American Indian Literature, 1900–1970.* New York, 1994.
Brumble, H. David, III. *American Indian Autobiography.* Berkeley, Calif., 1988.
Kroeber, Karl. *Traditional Literatures of the American Indian: Texts and Interpretations.* Lincoln, Nebr., 1981.
Krupat, Arnold. *The Voice in the Margin: Native American Literature and the Canon.* Berkeley, Calif., 1989.
Lyon, Thomas J., et al., eds. *A Literary History of the American West.* Fort Worth, Tex., 1987.
Swann, Brian, ed. *Smoothing the Ground: Essays on Native American Oral Literature.* Berkeley, Calif., 1983.
Velies, Alan R. *Four American Literary Masters: N. Scott Momaday, James Welch, Leslie Marmon Silko, and Gerald Vizenor.* Norman, Okla., 1982.
Wiget, Andrew. *Native American Literature.* Boston, 1985.

ASIAN AMERICAN LITERATURE

Asian American literature has been written mainly by authors who have lived in the Western United States, since the majority of Asian immigrants and their descendants settled in Hawaii and along the West Coast. The first one hundred years of Asian American literature in the West (from about 1850 to 1950) is distinguished by the efforts of Chinese, Japanese, and Filipino immigrants and the writing of second-generation JAPANESE AMERICANS.

Some of the earliest literary works by Asians in America were poems that were carved or written on the walls of what was formerly the Angel Island Immigration Station in San Francisco Bay. Composed by Chinese who were detained there, the poems record their hopes, frustration, and anger as they awaited, sometimes for months, either deportation from or entrance to the United States.

At the turn of the century, Chinese immigrants in San Francisco formed several literary societies, which sponsored writing competitions in various genres—classical poetry, prose, and political essays. At the same time, community newspapers like CHUNG SAI YAT PO published fiction, poetry, and popular Cantonese vernacular rhymes and satires. In 1911, the Tai Quong Company published *Jinshan ge ji,* an anthology of 808 immigrant-composed Chinese folk songs that dealt with immigrants' dreams of success in the United States, experiences with women and prostitutes, and the imagined lament of wives left behind in China. A second volume of 832 songs was published in 1915.

One of the first Asian American writers in English was Edith Eaton, the daughter of a Chinese mother and British father. Writing under the pseudonym Sui Sin Far, Eaton published numerous essays and short stories dealing with early Chinese immigrants; many of her works appear in her collection *Mrs. Spring Fragrance.* A pioneer crusader for acceptance of the Chinese during a time of intense anti-Chinese hostility, Eaton populated her stories with sympathetic Chinese characters to counter the widespread image of Chinese as subhuman.

As the Chinese immigrants did before them, Japanese immigrants, who began arriving in Hawaii and the Western United States after the 1882 Chinese Exclusion Act, established community newspapers that published literary works—mostly the Japanese poetic forms *haiku, tanka,* and *senryu.* Beginning in the late 1920s, Nisei (second-generation Japanese Americans) started writing poems, stories, and essays for the English-language sections of the community press. Up until America's entry into World War II, an increasingly sophisticated group of Nisei writers published literature in those papers, most notably *Kashu Mainichi* in Los Angeles and *The New World-Sun* in San Francisco. Young Nisei also produced small literary journals such as *Reimei* in Salt Lake City (published from 1931 to 1933) and *Leaves* (published circa 1935) in Los Angeles. Prewar Nisei literature reflects intergenerational tensions, reactions to racism, but also more generic concerns of adolescents and young adults.

The best-known Nisei writer of the prewar period was Toshio Mori, whose short stories appeared in national publications such as *New Directions in Poetry and Prose* and *Common Ground,* which also published works by authors such as Gertrude Stein and Langston Hughes. *Yokohama, California,* a collection of Mori's stories about the inhabitants of a fictional town situated across the bay from San Francisco, was slated for publication in 1942. The war, however, postponed the appearance of the book until 1949.

The wartime internment of the Japanese American population of the West Coast ended or dampened the literary aspirations of many Nisei. Despite their confinement, though, Japanese Americans in two of the Western internment camps published literature. In the camp in Tule Lake, California, the Japanese-language literary journal *Tessaku* appeared. The English-language *Tulean Dispatch Magazine* was also published. At the camp in Topaz, Utah, Nisei writers and artists produced *Trek,* the most sophisticated of the English-language camp publications.

Also during the war years, the Filipino American writer Carlos Bulosan was in the national spotlight. The author of numerous essays, stories, and books about Filipinos and Filipino Americans, Bulosan was best known for his autobiographical novel, *America Is in the Heart.* The novel chronicled the experiences of Filipino migrant workers who labored along the West Coast from Alaska to southern California in canneries, on farms, and in service industries. Significant Filipino immigration began after the 1924 Immigration Act, which halted Japanese immigration. Unlike the Chinese and Japanese, however, Filipinos were U.S. nationals because of America's annexation of the Philippines in 1898.

In the immediate postwar years, the Nisei short-story writer Hisaye Yamamoto gained national attention for her carefully crafted, powerful fiction depicting prewar Japanese American life. Several of her stories were noted by Martha Foley as the best American short stories of the years in which they were published.

—*Stan Yogi*

SEE ALSO: Chinese Americans; Japanese Internment

SUGGESTED READING:

Bulosan, Carlos. *America Is in the Heart: A Personal History.* New York, 1943. Introduction by Carey McWilliams. Seattle, 1973.

Hom, Marlon K., ed. and trans. *Songs of Gold Mountain: Cantonese Rhymes from San Francisco Chinatown.* Berkeley, Calif., 1987.

Kim, Elaine H. *Asian American Literature: An Introduction to the Writings and Their Social Context.* Philadelphia, 1982.

Lai, Him Mark, Genny Lim, and Judy Yung, eds. and trans. *Island: Poetry and History of Chinese Immigrants on Angel Island, 1910–1940.* San Francisco, 1980.

Mori, Toshio. *Yokohama, California.* Caldwell, Idaho, 1949. Reprint. Seattle, Wash., 1985.

Sui Sin Far. *Mrs. Spring Fragrance.* Chicago, 1912.

Sumida, Stephen H. *And the View from the Shore: Literary Traditions of Hawaii.* Seattle, Wash., 1991.

Yamamoto, Hisaye. *"Seventeen Syllables" and Other Stories.* Latham, N.Y., 1988.

MEXICAN AMERICAN LITERATURE

Writing in Spanish or English or a combination of both, Mexicans and, after the 1840s, their descendants in the United States produced a literature whose origins lay in the Spanish Southwest but that has continued, some scholars maintain, pretty much uninterrupted to the present day. In the Spanish colonial period before Mexican independence, the literature consisted primarily of historical writing, generally in the form of letters, diaries, memoirs, and even what might be called field reports. Most of this writing, when it was not private and meant for personal and family reminiscence, was aimed at an audience in the homeland, sometimes intended for a specialized audience of officials and courtiers, sometimes written for a more general educated readership. These works sought to describe Spanish explorations of the Southwest, the culture of the Native American inhabitants and the events attendant to their conquest, or the natural splendor of what was, for the writer, a new world. There was, for example, ÁLVAR NÚÑEZ CABEZA DE VACA's celebrated accounts of his explorations of the North American interior, but perhaps the most significant of these works was *Historia de la Nueva Mexico* (1610) by Gaspar Pérez de Villagrá, a poem in thirty-four cantos that described for the Spanish court the founding of New Mexico by JUAN DE OÑATE.

When early settlers from Mexico arrived in the northern reaches of Spain's New World empire, they brought with them some popular literary forms—the *pastorel* (shepherd's play), the *corrido* (ballad), the *cuento* (folk tale)—and, during the seventeenth, eighteenth, and nineteenth centuries, a folk literature grew up and thrived throughout the Southwest and California. Based on the Mexican equivalent to Spanish romances, CORRIDOS were, in their very structure, well suited for preserving and transmitting an oral tradition, and they were composed and sung throughout the region in present-day Arizona, California, southern Colorado, New Mexico, and Texas. Several of the *pastorelas,* among them the *Pastorela en dos actos* dating from about 1828, were staged at the missions in the region. Short narrative legends often centered around mysterious characters and miracles, *cuentos* not only played an important role in the folk literature of Spanish and Mexican times, but continue to be recounted in the Mexican American communities, especially the rural villages, of the Southwest. By the time of the Anglo conquest in the 1840s, the Spanish-speaking peoples of the Southwest had developed a literary tradition deeply rooted in popular folk genres inherited from Spain, one whose forms allowed them to pass the tradition along through the spoken word from generation to generation even as they modified the traditional stories and ballads and created new ones based on local heroes and events.

Most of the literature written by Mexican Americans between 1848 and the rise of what literary scholars and historians call the "Chicano literary renaissance" was published in local and regional newspapers. Some 380 of them, aimed at a Spanish-speaking readership, were published in the United States between 1848 and 1958. Within the pages of these periodicals, researchers Lupe Castillo and Hemino Rios have found a wealth of Mexican American literature. In 1959, José Antonio Villareal produced perhaps the most important work of the period, an autobiographical novel entitled *Pocho,* set in Santa Clara, California. The first Mexican American novel published by a major U.S. house, Doubleday, the work was a forerunner of the Chicano renaissance. The story of a Hispanic youth coming of age in a country whose dominant society held little place for him, *Pocho* captured the immigrants' sense of culture shock, the Mexican American experience in California, and the impact of alien social pressures on a young man, but it failed to achieve widespread recognition until the Chicano movement itself was well under way a decade later.

Emerging from the Chicano movement, the Mexican American literary renaissance of the 1960s was, like that movement, an attempt to establish an identity of their own by writers who explored their cultural roots and history in Mexico and who protested against the domination by an Anglo society that denied the worth of Mexicano culture and portrayed Mexicans and Mexican Americans in its literature, films, and advertising with offensive stereotypes, particularly those of the *bandito* and the lazy Mexican. Disillusioned and angered by such portraits, Chicano writers emphasized their Mexican Indian heritage, included Indian themes in their works, and named the journals where these works appeared *El Azteca, Bronce,* and *Aztlán,* words culled from pre-Columbian culture. Frequently using Aztec and Mayan figures and symbols, including the Aztec calendar stone, to decorate their books, poems, and articles, the writers both fed the Chicano movement and received sustenance from it. In the early days of the movement in the late 1960s, Chicano writers identified themselves almost exclusively with their Indian past, but as their self-esteem grew and they developed a greater sense of cultural continuity, the need to create an identity became less pronounced. In their novels and *corridos,* they developed themes centered around immigration and Mexican and Mexican American labor and explored prejudice, discrimination, and exploitation, as well as the pains of cultural oppression. Some wrote in English, others in Spanish, and some combined the two, and, in general, their works continued to show a marked preference for the autobiographical.

Perhaps the quest for identity was best illustrated in Roldolfo ("Corky") Gonzales's 1967 *Yo soy Joaquin,* while Raymond Barrio's *Plum Plum Pickers* (1965)—the story of a migrant couple trapped by an inherently exploitative system of agricultural employment—sounded the attack on the socio-economic injustices of American society. An interest in Chicano works had developed nationwide by the early 1970s, and several new anthologies included short stories, which became an important Chicano genre, as well as excerpts from longer works. In 1970, Richard Vásquez published a historical novel, *Chicano,* tracing the immigrant experience through three generations of a family, and the same year Tomás Rivera's *. . . y no se tragó la tierra* won the first Primero Quinto Sol, a prize that consistently recognized quality literature. Published in 1971, Rivera's novel—twelve narratives linked by a single theme focused on the plight of migrant workers as seen through the eyes of a child—set a new and high standard for a generation of Chicano writing. Rolando Hinjoso-Smith also won the prize for his picturesque *Estampas de valle y otras obras,* published in 1973. With Hinjoso-Smith's *Klail City y sus alrede-dores,* published three years later, Chicano literature began to receive international recognition.

Among the more notable Chicano writers and their best-known works were John Rechy, *City of Night* (1963), the earliest of six novels dealing with homosexual life in the big city; Oscar Zeta Acosta, *Autobiography of a Brown Buffalo* (1972), a study in machismo, sex, and drugs, and *Revolt of the Cockroach People* (1973); Miguel Méndez, *Pereginos de Aztlan* (1973), the unhappy story of undocumented immigrants in the Southwest; Ron Arias, *The Road to Tamasunchale* (1975), a social commentary; Nash Candelaria, *Memories of Alhambra* (1977), the first of four novels about the Rafa family's search for identity; Arturo Islas, *The Rain God* (1984) and *Migrant Souls* (1990), both semi-autobiographical; and Victor

Villaseñor, *Rain of Gold* (1990), a nonfictional account of the author's family and its difficult move to California from Mexico. Perhaps the best-known Mexican American writer was Ernesto Galarza, one of the first Chicano Ph.D.s, whose autobiographical account of his family's move from Mexico, *Barrio Boy* (1971), was followed by a number of important works centering around Mexican and Mexican American labor. The most controversial was a second-generation Chicano writer, Richard Rodríguez, born in San Francisco and raised in Sacramento, whose *Hunger of Memory: The Education of Richard Rodríguez* (1982) upset many Mexican Americans. According to Rodríguez, not only did most immigrants long to be accepted by American society without feeling they had betrayed their traditional Mexican culture, but they also were dominated by a nostalgia spawned by the American rejection of all things Mexican. What angered some even more, however, was the direct attack on bilingual education and affirmative action to which his argument—presented in clear, precise, and prize-winning prose—led him. The short story too produced a number of other outstanding Chicano masters: Francisco Jiménez, Sabine Ulibarrí, Estela Portillo Trambly, Rosaura Sánchez, Sergio Elizondo, and others. Especially notable among the more recent writers were the collections of Sandra Cisneros, *The House on Mango Street* (1983) and *Woman Hollering Creek and Other Stories* (1991).

The best of these works, like that of all literature, rose from their solid groundings in Mexican American culture to create a universal appeal, one that has led mainstream scholars and literary critics to recognize Mexican American writing, despite the relatively new arrival of much of it, as a vital part of American literature.

—*Charles Phillips*

SEE ALSO: Film: Minority Images in Westerns; Stereotypes: Stereotypes of Mexicans; Theater: Hispanic Theater

SUGGESTED READING:
Jiménez, Francisco, ed. *The Identification and Analysis of Chicano Literature.* New York, 1979.
Lomelí, Francisco A., and Donaldo W. Urioste. *Chicano Perspectives in Literature.* Albuquerque, N. Mex., 1976.
Sommers, Joseph, and Tomás Ybarra-Frausto, eds. *Modern Chicano Writers.* Englewood Cliffs, N.J., 1979.

LITHOGRAPHY

SEE: Art: Popular Prints and Commercial Art

LITTLE, FRANK

A militant labor organizer, Frank Little (1880–1917) was the son of a Cherokee mother and a Quaker father. Working in the numerous mines of the West, Little quickly saw the need for labor organization. In 1900, he joined the WESTERN FEDERATION OF MINERS, but when the WFM did not go as far as Little felt it should in securing miners' rights, he lead a breakaway faction of militants for the INDUSTRIAL WORKERS OF THE WORLD in 1907. Little soon became the IWW's most outspoken and dynamic figure, surpassing even the legendary WILLIAM D. ("BIG BILL") HAYWOOD. He immersed himself in the free-speech struggles in Washington, Montana, and California and helped organize loggers, miners, oil-field workers, and others throughout the West and Southwest.

In 1914, Little joined the IWW General Executive Board. As a member of the board, he became a militant, outspoken opponent of World War I and claimed that the war was a classic example of capitalists' gaining on the backs of the laborers. The issue divided labor leaders; Haywood argued that the IWW should ignore the war. In the meantime, Little persuaded the IWW to organize migrant farmers and helped found the Agricultural Workers Organization in 1915.

When Little continued his vigorous opposition to the war after America's entry into the conflict, he found himself on the fringe of an already radical organization; his positions made him an easy target for the social anxieties of his day. In August 1917, while in Butte, Montana, helping lead a miners' strike, he was beaten and lynched from the Milwaukee Railroad trestle.

—*Kurt Edward Kemper*

SEE ALSO: Labor Movement

SUGGESTED READING:
Chaplin, Ralph. *Wobbly: The Rough-and-Tumble Story of an American Radical.* New York, 1972.

LITTLE BIGHORN, BATTLE OF

On June 25 and 26, 1876, on the Little Bighorn River in southeastern Montana, Sioux and Cheyenne Indians under SITTING BULL, CRAZY HORSE, and other chiefs fought the Seventh U.S. Cavalry commanded by Lieutenant Colonel GEORGE ARMSTRONG CUSTER. With his regiment numbering about 600, Custer attacked the Indian village from two directions. Approximately 2,000 Indian warriors annihilated five companies under Custer's personal command and besieged the other seven companies for two days. A total of 263 soldiers lost their lives, while Indian casualties probably did not exceed 40 or 50 killed, with many more wounded.

The Battle of Little Bighorn, also known as "Custer's Last Stand," was the most significant event of the Great Sioux War of 1876. The war was waged by the U.S. government to compel the buffalo-hunting bands of the Sioux and Cheyenne tribes to give up the chase and settle on the Great Sioux Reservation (present-day South Dakota west of the Missouri River), where other bands already lived under the terms of the Treaty of 1868. The hunting bands, the government correctly charged, had raided friendly Indians and committed scattered depredations against white settlers in western Montana. However, the true cause of the war sprang from the discovery of gold in the Black Hills, part of the Great Sioux Reservation guaranteed the Indians by treaty. White miners had overrun the hills, but the Sioux refused to sell them. By forcing the hunting bands onto the reservation and destroying their independence, the government hoped to weaken their ability to obstruct the sale of the Black Hills.

The army organized an offensive from three directions against the hunting bands in the Yellowstone River Basin of Montana. General GEORGE CROOK advanced from the south; Colonel JOHN OLIVER GIBBON from the west; and General ALFRED HOWE TERRY from the east. Custer and the Seventh Cavalry rode with Terry. On June 22, Terry detached Custer and his regiment to march up the Rosebud Creek and seek out the Indians, thought to be in the Little Bighorn Valley. Terry would accompany Gibbon up the Yellowstone and Bighorn rivers and cut off the northward flight of the Indians as Custer struck from the south.

Custer located the Sioux village early on June 25. He intended to defer his attack until the next day, but Indians discovered him, and, fearing they would scatter, he advanced at once to attack. He divided the regiment into three battalions led by Captain Frederick W. Benteen, Major Marcus A. Reno, and himself. Benteen departed on a mission aimed at ensuring that no Indians camped in the Little Bighorn Valley above the main village. Custer and Reno approached the village itself.

Although Custer's plan remains speculative and controversial, apparently he intended to strike from two directions. He sent Reno to cross the Little Bighorn and charge the southern end of the encampment, while he turned north to hit the other end. Reno, however, was repulsed and driven from the valley. When he took up a defensive position on the high bluffs lining the east side of the river, the warriors were free to concentrate on Custer at the northern end of their village. They kept him out of the village and confined to rough country east of the river. Within an hour, they wiped out his entire command of 210 men. Joined by Benteen, Reno entrenched on his hilltop four miles to the south and held out until the next day, when the approach of Terry and Gibbon from the north caused the Indians to withdraw to the south.

For the Sioux and Cheyennes, the Battle of Little Bighorn was a great triumph. For the United States, it was a major military disaster. The death of Custer, a flamboyant popular hero, and his entire immediate command stunned the American people and led to greatly intensified military activity. By the spring of 1877, most of the Sioux and Cheyennes had surrendered and settled on the reservation. The government forced them to give up the Black Hills.

Controversy immediately surrounded the battle and has raged ever since. Custer, Reno, Benteen, Terry, and even President Ulysses S. Grant—all had their partisans and detractors. Whether a reckless fool or a victim of the failures of others, however, Custer won immortality, and the Battle of Little Bighorn became firmly embedded in the history and folklore of America. The spectacle of Custer and his little band of troopers dying on their Montana hilltop is one of the most vivid and enduring images in the popular imagination.

—*Robert M. Utley*

Little Crow. *Courtesy Library of Congress.*

SEE ALSO: Black Hills Gold Rush; Sioux Wars

SUGGESTED READING:
Gray, John S. *Centennial Campaign: The Sioux War of 1876.* Norman, Okla., 1988.
———. *Mitch Boyer and the Little Bighorn Reconstructed.* Lincoln, Nebr., 1991.
Hutton, Paul A., ed. *The Custer Reader.* Lincoln, Nebr., 1992.
Utley, Robert M. *Cavalier in Buckskin: George Armstrong Custer and the Western Military Frontier.* Norman, Okla., 1988.

LITTLE CROW (SIOUX)

The principal leader of the Minnesota Uprising of 1862, Little Crow (1810–1863) was the son and grandson of chiefs of the Kaposia band of Mdewakanton Santee Sioux. He assumed leadership of the band after his father died in 1834 and lived at the present-day site of St. Paul, Minnesota. Little Crow harbored no particular hatred of whites and, in fact, maintained cordial relations with them throughout most of his life. Not only did he invite the Reverend Thomas Williamson to live among his people in an effort to curb the use of liquor among them, he also signed the Treaty of Mendota in 1851, whereby he voluntarily ceded a vast tract of land in exchange for a reservation on the upper Minnesota River and an annuity. Little Crow cooperated with the U.S. Army in its campaign against the renegade Wahpekute Sioux Inkpaduta (leader of the attack against settlers at Spirit Lake, IOWA) in 1857, and he served as part of a Sioux delegation to Washington, D.C., the following year.

As was often the case in relations between Indians and whites, friction developed through a combination of escalating white settlement, escalating dependence on government supplies, and an escalating degree of inefficiency and corruption within the system in charge of making good on treaty promises and delivering supplies. During the summer of 1862, the local Indian agent, Major Thomas J. Galbraith—presumably awaiting his customary kickback—deliberately delayed distribution of food stored at the Yellow Medicine Agency's warehouse. With the people of the Kaposia band approaching starvation, a group of warriors attacked the warehouse on August 4. Military intervention forestalled a general uprising, but an August 15 meeting with local traders—among them Andrew Myrick—triggered a full-scale uprising. To their entreaties for food, Myrick responded that, if the Indians were hungry, they could eat grass.

Little Crow attempted to persuade his young warriors to maintain peace. He argued that they would "all die like rabbits when the hungry wolves hunt them in the Hard Moon." But after a group of braves forced the issue by killing five settlers, Little Crow assumed leadership of the uprising and persuaded other Santee chiefs to join him. On August 18, Myrick was slain, his mouth stuffed with grass, and on that day, too, Santee Sioux swept through white settlements in southern Minnesota and killed some four hundred settlers.

The uprising lasted through the rest of August and well into September before troops under General HENRY HASTINGS SIBLEY fought a decisive battle at Wood Lake on September 23. Many Sioux died, and many other surrendered. Subsequently tried for murder and rape, 303 Sioux warriors were sentenced to death—a number reduced, after presidential review, to 38. Little Crow, with two or three hundred others, fled to the Northwest. In May 1863, he sought refuge among the British at Fort Garry (Winnipeg, Manitoba) but was rebuffed. In June, he reentered Minnesota and conducted a horse-stealing raid. On July 3, while he was picking berries with his son near the town of Hutchinson, he was ambushed by white settlers, who killed him in order to collect a twenty-five-dollar bounty on Sioux scalps. Little Crow's sixteen-year-old son Wowinapa escaped but was later captured and sentenced to be hanged. The sentence was commuted to a prison term, and while in prison, Wowinapa converted to Christianity. Little Crow's body was thrown on a slaughterhouse dump, but the skull and scalp were recovered and placed on display by the Minnesota Historical Society, which eventually returned them to Sioux officials for proper burial.

—*Alan Axelrod*

SEE ALSO: Sioux Wars

SUGGESTED READING:
Anderson, Gary Clayton. *Little Crow.* St. Paul, Minn., 1986.
Axelrod, Alan. *Chronicle of the Indian Wars: From Colonial Times to Wounded Knee.* New York, 1992.

LITTLE RAVEN (ARAPAHO)

An Arapaho leader, Little Raven (?–1889) was the most prominent spokesman for the southern division of his tribe for more than a quarter century. The cigar-smoking Little Raven appeared as the principal representative of Southern Arapahos at the February 18,

1861, signing of the Treaty of Fort Wise, Colorado, through which he agreed to surrender land claims recognized in the Fort Laramie Treaty of 1851 and to encourage acculturation of his people on individual land assignments within the boundaries of a federally recognized reservation. Thereafter, he maintained a community for the main body of Southern Arapahos several miles south of Sand Creek in Colorado and led the band's escape from the Chivington Massacre on November 29, 1864. The following year, he and six other Arapaho spokesmen along with Cheyenne, Kiowa, and Comanche leaders met with the General John B. Sanborn and negotiated the 1866 Treaty of the Little Arkansas.

During the winter of 1869, Little Raven and nearly fifteen hundred of his followers surrendered at Fort Sill in Oklahoma, moved to Camp Supply, and accepted a sedentary existence under the kindly U.S. Agent Brinton Darlington. At the Darlington Agency, Little Raven turned his attention to agriculture, lived in a frame house, sent his children to the Carlisle Indian School, and in other ways assumed a posture of accommodation. In cooperation with federal employees, he and his followers remained separate from a "war

Little Raven. Photograph by William S. Soule, 1868–1874. *Courtesy National Archives.*

faction" of Southern Arapahos and Northern Arapahos who mingled with "SITTING BULL people" above the Platte River. Little Raven's legacy on the southern Great Plains was his commitment to peace.

—*Herbert T. Hoover*

SEE ALSO: Sand Creek Massacre

SUGGESTED READING:
National Archives. Record Group 75, Cheyenne-Arapaho Agency.
Trenholm, Virginia Cole. *The Arapahoes, Our People.* Norman, Okla., 1970.

LITTLE WOLF (NORTHERN CHEYENNE)

Little Wolf (1830?–1904), a So-taaeo-o, was a great Northern Cheyenne military leader, Old Man Chief, and Sweet Medicine Chief. He was born on the north central Great Plains and was originally named Two Trails, but Euro-Americans later called him Little Wolf. He first appears in the historical record in 1865 at the Upper Platte Bridge incident as chief of the Elkhorn Scrapers, a Cheyenne military society. After earning a reputation as a masterful military tactician, he was selected in 1864 by the Cheyenne Council of the Forty-four to serve as an Old Man Chief. Old Man Chiefs were living representatives of the Maheyuno—sacred persons at the semicardinal points in the Cheyenne universe. Although most Old Men Chiefs gave up their military positions after being chosen to serve on the Council of the Forty-four, Little Wolf retained his leadership of the Elkhorn Scrapers. The council also elected him caretaker of the chief's medicine bundle and Sweet Medicine Chief, the holiest and most politically prominent position in Cheyenne society. After 1864, Little Wolf presided over the Council of Forty-four and became one of the most powerful political, religious, and military leaders in nineteenth-century Cheyenne society.

Little Wolf's emergence as a political leader came at a critical juncture in Cheyenne history. His people faced a continual loss of lands and resources and a growing permanent Euro-American presence. The Cheyennes and their allies found themselves in a continual state of conflict with the United States. For two decades, Little Wolf worked as a diplomat, negotiator, military leader, and respected religious authority.

Although Little Wolf was not at the Little Bighorn battle in 1876, the U.S. military attacked Northern Cheyenne bands and forced their surrender in 1877 at Fort Robinson, Nebraska. That year, Little Wolf's band, along with MORNING STAR's (Dull Knife) people, was forced to join the Southern Cheyenne at Darlington Agency in the Indian Territory. There the Northern Cheyennes were ravaged by disease and confronted with a hostile environment. On September 9, 1878, Little Wolf, Morning Star, and other leaders lead 353 Northern Cheyennes north to their homeland. After eluding the U.S. military, Little Wolf's band wintered in the Black Hills region. He and his people eventually were discovered on March 25, 1879, by troops led by Lieutenant W. P. Clark of Fort Keogh. Little Wolf surrendered peacefully and was escorted to Fort Keogh.

Little Wolf's surrender marked a turning point in his political career. He no longer fought against the U.S. military but enlisted in 1879 as a military scout. Once again, his decision was motivated by his people's welfare. As long as they served as scouts, his people could remain in their homelands.

For three years, Little Wolf scouted for the U.S. military against the Dakotas before personal tragedy struck. In 1881, Little Wolf shot Starving Elk, and he was jailed and discharged from military service. In accordance with Cheyenne law, Little Wolf then attempted to relieve himself of his political and religious duties and banish himself from his people. Many Northern Cheyennes refused to accept his resignation and followed the chief into exile. He lived in the Rosebud Valley until his death.

—*Gregory R. Campbell*

SEE ALSO: United States Army: Scouts

SUGGESTED READING:
Grinnell, George Bird. *The Fighting Cheyennes.* Norman, Okla., 1977.
Hoig, Stan. *The Peace Chiefs of the Cheyennes.* Norman, Okla., 1980
Powell, Peter J. *People of the Sacred Mountain: A History of the Northern Cheyenne Chiefs and Warrior Societies, 1830–1879, with an Epilogue 1969–1974.* 2 vols. San Francisco, 1979.
———. *Sweet Medicine: The Continuing Role of the Sacred Arrows, the Sun Dance, and the Sacred Buffalo Hat in Northern Cheyenne History.* 2 vols. Norman, Okla., 1969.
Roberts, Gary L. "The Shame of Little Wolf." *Montana, The Magazine of Western History* 28 (3): 36-47.

LLANO DEL RIO

Llano del Rio was a utopian colony founded by JOB HARRIMAN. In the years immediately before World War I, newspaper baron HARRISON GRAY OTIS and his

Los Angeles Times fought against an array of Progressives and socialists who rode a high tide of national discontent against the excesses of American capitalism. In this conflict, the *Times* building was bombed and twenty men were killed. Three radical unionists were arrested and tried. Harriman, one of their lawyers and a socialist, was at the same time a prime candidate for mayor of Los Angeles. On December 1, 1911, two of the accused admitted their guilt, and four days later, in the run-off elections, the city rejected Harriman for office. Discouraged with politics, he planned a utopian experiment to demonstrate the possibilities of a socialist cooperative society run by and for the workers. The result was the Llano del Rio Colony.

The experiment in utopian SOCIALISM started in Antelope Valley (a branch of the Mojave Desert) and lasted from 1914 to 1918. The colony then moved to Newllano, Louisiana, where it continued for seventeen years. It went into receivership in 1935 and finally collapsed a few years later as a victim of the Great Depression, among other things.

At its height in California, the colony numbered between eight and nine hundred people. It was organized as a joint-stock company; the members purchased from a quarter to a half of their two thousand shares and worked out the rest at the colony at a guaranteed wage rate of four dollars per day. The building of adobe houses always lagged behind need, and many members lived in tents with floorboards. But community buildings rose—barns, workshops, a silo, and a central hotel with great stone fireplaces around which the members gathered for meals and assemblies.

The colony's chief problems were internal dissension that was exacerbated by weak screening of prospective members and a serious, unforeseeable shortage of water necessary to an agricultural community in the desert. Nevertheless, its four years in California were characterized by a wealth of intellectual opportunities in reading, discussions, and the arts, as well as by happy times, dancing, singing, and celebrating. Hard work on a difficult terrain was rewarded by hundreds of acres of alfalfa and fruit orchards, animal husbandry, crafts and industries, and the publication of socialist journals that reached a national audience.

—*Robert V. Hine*

SUGGESTED READING:

Conkin, Paul. *Two Paths to Utopia: The Hutterites and the Llano Colony.* Lincoln, Nebr., 1964.

Greenstein, Paul, Nigey Lennon, and Lionel Rolfe. *Bread and Hyacinths.* Los Angeles, 1992.

Hine, Robert V. *California's Utopian Colonies.* Berkeley, Calif., 1983.

LOG CABINS

The quintessential frontier dwelling, the log cabin was not only the practical structure of everything from living quarters to barns, it also became a symbol of frontier America. Although wooden structures appeared at the Jamestown settlement in Virginia and in New Amsterdam in what became New York, the first traditional log cabins appeared in the Delaware Valley of Pennsylvania around 1640. Constructed by Swedish immigrants, the structures were made of horizontal logs notched in the ends and filled with either mud or clay or both. From its first appearance in the mid-seventeenth century, the structure changed little over the next 250 years for one reason: its simplicity. A log cabin could easily be built by one man with an ax and knife and required no hardware or special skills.

Log cabins were usually only one room where all cooking, eating, and sleeping were done. Sometime during the eighteenth century, lofts appeared, separating the sleeping area from the rest of the cabin. Construction remained relatively simple. Logs were stacked horizontally with notched ends that formed a joint with intersecting logs. The joints and cracks between logs were filled with a mixture of any available pliable material, including straw, grass, mud, clay, and animal dung. Cabins were usually situated next to a stream or backed up to a hill, giving some natural defense against Indians, rustlers, or claim jumpers. Each cabin was equipped with an oversized fireplace, which provided heat and served as an oven, large enough to accommodate a spit of fresh game. Early versions had openings that served as windows, closed by heavy shutters, instead of glass. Later, a thick paper coated in either animal fat or some sort of wax was installed to allow for a translucent window. To increase storage space, attached lean-tos were built for farming implements or tack.

Due to the lack of large wood stands on the grasslands of the Great Plains and in deserts of the Southwest, few log cabins appeared in places like Kansas, Nebraska, South Dakota, Texas, Arizona, and southern California. However, in Colorado, Utah, Wyoming, Montana, Washington, and Oregon, and sections of northern California, the log cabin predominated. In the mountain passes of the Rocky Mountains, huge stands of ash, fir, beech, and maple offered a ready supply of logs of a uniform diameter.

The construction of log cabins began to wane in the early part of the twentieth century. Fewer people lived away from urban areas, prefabricated construction materials were more readily available, and wood stands were less common. However, the power of the frontier log-cabin mythology remains in the form of

The log cabin, an enduring symbol of the American frontier, required only the tools commonly used by settlers and was relatively easy to construct. In the construction of a cabin in Idaho, three men and a rope hauled logs into place. *Courtesy Idaho State Historical Society.*

summer cottages and do-it-yourself kits that are marketed towards the more "manly" set who wish to get back to their roots.

—*Kurt Edward Kemper*

SEE ALSO: Architecture

SUGGESTED READING:

Buley, R. C. *The Old Northwest: Pioneer Period, 1815–1840.* Indianapolis, Ind., 1950.
Weslager, C. A. *The Log Cabin in America: From Pioneer Days to the Present.* New Brunswick, N.J., 1969.

LOGGERS

Commercial lumbering in the West dates from the region's mining rush and railroad-building days. At that time, however, it was not considered an industry in and of itself. Because of America's belief that the highest use of Western land was for farming, lumbering was seen as a kind of handmaiden to the farming frontier—a temporary enterprise to be carried on until the agrarian empire took root. For this reason, in the 1860s and 1870s, the system of disposing of land did not provide for logging, and few laws were written to deal with it.

Over the course of two decades, the industry underpinned both the century's last Western mining regions and its new railroads. But in the process—with no laws to guide or constrain them—lumbermen destroyed millions of acres of virgin timberlands. When the federal government created legislation to curb fraud, loggers simply ignored it. Not until the early 1890s was the industry finally contained by the conservation movement.

In 1891, the United States Congress passed the General Revision Act, which created a massive forest-reserve (later national forest) system that put millions of acres of forest lands under federal lock and key essentially forever. At the same time, with lumbering capacity finally outstripping demand, many individuals, companies, mills, and pools finally went out of business. By 1900, with the industry in decline, large-scale consolidation drove out the last of the small operators and left the field in the hands of such giants as Weyerhaeuser and Southern Pacific.

While lumber barons lived in luxury from the earnings of their companies, their workers generally lived in poverty. Working twelve-hour days, for two dollars an hour, they were routinely crushed by falling trees and mutilated by snapped cables and mill blades. In company towns, where the cost of room, board, and tools was deducted from their wages, they recuperated in crowded bunkhouses, where liquor and weapons were prohibited, and ate in giant mess halls, where mealtime conversation was outlawed. The threat of unemployment kept loggers docile and servile.

Increasingly angered by their condition, many loggers joined the radical INDUSTRIAL WORKERS OF THE WORLD (IWW) shortly before World War I. Those years were filled with VIOLENCE and strikes. In the Red Scare years of 1918 and 1919, when Western states finally smashed the IWW, the workers' power was broken for good.

Despite years of unrest in the camps, the industry itself prospered from World War I, with its unprecedented demands for lumber, until the collapse of the great postwar construction boom in 1927. Not until after the Great Depression did health return to the lumber industry. By the 1940s, profits increased through the production of such new products as plywood. The lumber industry adopted sustained-yield methods of replanting as it harvested and entered a new era that lasted for years.

In recent times, confronted with controversies over wilderness areas, clear-cutting, old-growth forests, and endangered species, the industry has faced more than its share of challenges. For all this, though, lumbering still remains a vital part of the West's extractive economic life.

—*Michael McCarthy*

SEE ALSO: Labor Movement; Lumber Industry

SUGGESTED READING:

Robbins, Roy. *Our Landed Heritage.* Gloucester, Mass., 1960.

White, Richard. *"It's Your Misfortune and None of My Own": A New History of the American West.* Norman, Okla., 1991.

LOGGING

SEE: Lumber Industry

LONDON, JOHN GRIFFITH (JACK)

Author Jack London (1876–1916) was born in San Francisco. The best evidence indicates that he was the out-of-wedlock son of Flora Wellman of Masillon, Ohio, and Maine-born astrologer and self-styled "professor" William H. Chaney. After his mother's marriage to John London, a Pennsylvania farmer, in September 1876, the nine-month-old child was given the surname London.

Even before his first published story appeared in 1899, and for the seventeen years following, London led a restless, roving life, which provided the grist for his more than fifty books, many of them autobiographical. By the age of twenty-three, he had been a cannery worker, an oyster pirate on San Francisco Bay, an able seaman on a sealing schooner in the Bering Sea, a tramp with the Western detachment of Coxey's Army, a member of the Socialist Labor Party, and a gold-seeker in the Yukon.

Largely self-educated and, as he told his first book publisher in 1900, having "no mentor but myself," he thirsted for adventure. He served as war correspondent for Hearst newspapers in Manchuria during the Russo-Japanese War in 1904 and for *Collier's* during the Mexican Revolution in 1914. He wrote the finest

Loggers lived in poverty, crowded into bunkhouses supplied by lumber companies. For these accommodations, lumber barons deducted room and board from the loggers' two dollars per hour wage. *Courtesy Special Collections Division, University of Washington Libraries.*

John Griffith (Jack) London. *Editors' collection.*

His best-known and most beloved novels were, in some manner or other, autobiographical: *The Call of the Wild* (1903) and its companion story *White Fang* (1906), *The Sea Wolf* (1904), *Before Adam* (1907), *The Iron Heel* (1908), *Martin Eden* (1909), *John Barleycorn* (1913), *Valley of the Moon* (1913), and *The Star Rover* (1915).

Of London's short fiction, his "To Build a Fire" (1908) is perhaps his most celebrated and anthologized story; its memorable opening line ("Day had broken cold and gray, exceedingly cold and gray . . .") sets the stage for an almost painful evocation of the murderous cold of the subarctic Yukon region. Incredibly, the story was written during London's voyage to the South Seas and completed in Hawaii.

—*Dale L. Walker*

SUGGESTED READING:

Labor, Earle, Robert C. Leitz, and I. Milo Shepard. *The Letters of Jack London.* 3 vols. Palo Alto, Calif., 1988.

Walker, Dale L. *In a Far Country: Jack London's Tales of the West.* Ottawa, Ill., 1987.

LONE WOLF (KIOWA)

A Kiowa chief, Lone Wolf (Gui-pah-go, ca. 1820-1879) was one of the signers of the Little Arkansas Treaty that established a reservation for the Kiowas and Comanches on October 18, 1865. As head chief of the Kiowas following Dohausen's death in 1866, Lone Wolf "did not have enough force of character to restrain or command all his people," according to historian Wilbur Sturtevant Nye. Subsequently, the tribe split into a war party under his direction and a peace faction led by KICKING BIRD.

Along with SATANTA, Lone Wolf was a persistent thorn in the side of federal authorities. After the Washita fight, in December of 1868 Lieutenant Colonel GEORGE ARMSTRONG CUSTER seized the two men and threatened to hang them unless the Kiowas surrendered and remained peaceful. Lone Wolf was present at Fort Sill for the arrest in 1871 of Satanta, SATANK, and BIG TREE for leading the Warren Wagon Train Raid. He then accompanied an Indian delegation to Washington, D.C. As chief spokesman for the tribe in the councils of 1872, he refused to halt Kiowa raiding in Texas.

During the spring of 1874, Lone Wolf exacted revenge for the death of his son Tau-ankia, who was killed by soldiers while returning from a raid into Mexico. He participated in the June 27 attack on the Adobe Walls trading post and in the Lost Valley fight

of all the eyewitness accounts of the SAN FRANCISCO EARTHQUAKE of 1906; lectured on SOCIALISM at Yale; sailed his own yacht to Hawaii, Tahiti, the Marquesas and Solomons, Samoa, Fiji, and the New Hebrides from 1907 to 1909; and voyaged on a four-mastered barque around the Horn in 1912.

London was married twice and was the father of two daughters. In the last few years of his life, he built a ranch in the Valley of the Moon in Sonoma County, north of San Francisco, and engaged in experimental farming, pig raising, growing eucalyptus trees, and breeding horses. Following his return from the South Seas, his once robust health failed steadily, and his decline was exacerbated by bad diet and excessive drinking.

London died on November 22, 1916, two months before his fortieth birthday. The cause of his death, as with the circumstances of his birth, remains in dispute. Examining physicians stated the cause of death as uremic poisoning complicated by an self-administered overdose of painkilling drugs, including morphine.

During his seventeen-year writing career, London produced an astonishing body of work: 22 novels, 190 short stories, 7 nonfiction books, 4 published plays, and an estimated 400 miscellaneous works. From *The Son of the Wolf* (1900) to *The Turtles of Tasman* (1916), 43 books were published in his lifetime; another 10 were published after his death.

Lone Wolf. Photograph by William S. Soule, 1868–1874. *Courtesy National Archives.*

with Texas Rangers on July 12. Following the fight at the Anadarko Agency on August 22 and 23, Lone Wolf fled with other Kiowa war leaders to the Staked Plains. His warriors took part in the attack on Captain Wyllys Lyman's wagon train from September 9 to 12.

Lone Wolf surrendered on February 26, 1875, and was sent to prison in Florida. Upon his release, he returned to the Fort Sill Reservation in 1878 and died the following year of malaria. He was buried in an unmarked grave on the northern slope of Mount Scott. He was succeeded as chief by Mamay-day-te, who adopted the name Lone Wolf.

—*Bruce J. Dinges*

SUGGESTED READING:
Mayhall, Mildred P. *The Kiowas.* Norman, Okla., 1962.
Nye, Wilbur S. *Carbine and Lance: The Story of Old Fort Sill.* Norman, Okla., 1974.
———. *Plains Indian Raiders: The Final Phases of Warfare from the Arkansas to the Red River.* Norman, Okla., 1968.

LONE WOLF V. HITCHOCK

At the turn of the twentieth century, reformers and government officials who considered themselves "friends" of the Indians had been arguing for almost fifty years that individual ownership of land was the only salvation for Native Americans. Reformers agitated for a fee-simple title arrangement that they believed would protect Indian lands from the uncertainties of U.S. government treaty guarantees that could be—and often had been—ignored to free up large tracts of land for white settlement. Part of the same general thinking of Progressive reformers who had called for assimilation or "civilization" programs, fee-simple titles—which held an individual Indian responsible for selling or retaining an allotment—was yet another step in turning the Native American into a white U.S. citizens.

Many Indians who had been through similar arrangements before they were "removed" west of the Mississippi, however, knew that the only true protection individual Indians had came from their tribes and that Indians standing alone with private allotments were helpless when it came to pressing claims to land titles in white courts under white laws. Members of the Five Civilized Tribes argued as much to Congress and warned those among the other tribes about the consequences of the reformist wrinkle in Indian policy. But the officials in the BUREAU OF INDIAN AFFAIRS and the Congress reasoned that not only would individual Indians benefit from owning allotments, but also that after the allotments were made, much land would be left over for white settlement. And this, in turn, they argued, was a good thing because holding too much land under arrangements with the various tribes had only encouraged the Indians to continue their old, wild, roaming ways; less land, smaller holdings, would force the individual Indian to become more "civilized."

Beginning with the DAWES ACT of 1887, allotment formed the cornerstone of UNITED STATES INDIAN POLICY. In 1901, Chief Lone Wolf of the Kiowas, listening to the warnings of the Five Civilized Tribes and fearing the motives of those supporting fee-simple titles, decided to resist further usurpation of Indian tribal authority and, thus, Indian lands by challenging the allotment system in court. He argued that the MEDICINE LODGE TREATY OF 1867 had provided for tribal approval of all land cessions. In 1903, the U.S. Supreme Court settled the issue in *Lone Wolf* v. *Hitchcock* by ruling that the federal government had the power to abrogate the provisions of any Indian treaty. The ruling included the Medicine Lodge Treaty, thus clearing the way for the BURKE ACT three years later, which nullified the twenty-five-year trust provision of the Dawes Act and granted the secretary of the interior the power to issue fee-simple titles to all allotees "competent and capable of managing" their affairs. The temper of the decision in *Lone Wolf* v. *Hitchcock* can be measured by the court's language in asserting that "[i]t is to be presumed that in this matter the United States would be governed by such considerations of justice as would control a Christian people in their treatment of an ignorant and dependent race." The real truth behind the court's notion of Christian justice became clear when one Bureau of Indian Affairs official declared that he welcomed the *Lone Wolf* decision because it allowed the government to dispose of Indian lands without the consent of the Indians. If the government had been forced to wait for that consent, he said, it would have taken fifty years to eliminate the reservations. Now, he pointed out, the government had the power to allot Indian lands and sell "the balance" off in order to create "homes for white farmers."

—*Charles Phillips*

SUGGESTED READING:
Clark, Blue. *Lone Wolf v. Hitchcock: Treaty Rights and Indian Law at the End of the Nineteenth Century.* Lincoln, Nebr., 1995.
Hoxie, Frederick. *Final Promise: The Campaign to Assimilate the Indians, 1880–1920.* Lincoln, Nebr., 1984.

LONG, STEPHEN HARRIMAN

Born in Hopkinton, New Hampshire, Stephen Harriman Long (1784–1864) had a distinguished career as an engineer and explorer. After graduating from Dartmouth College in 1809, he was commissioned a second lieutenant in the UNITED STATES ARMY CORPS OF ENGINEERS in 1814. He taught mathematics at West Point for one year and then, in 1816, became one of the first six officers in the newly formed CORPS OF TOPOGRAPHICAL ENGINEERS with the rank of brevet major. From 1816 to 1823, Long participated in five government-sponsored exploring and mapping expeditions. Covering more than twenty-six thousand miles, he investigated and mapped locations for new fortifications, possible canals, river systems, portage sites, and the headwaters of the Mississippi, Canadian, and Arkansas rivers. He also collected information on the natural resources, Indian tribes, botany, topography, and geology of the areas through which he traveled.

In 1819, Long became commander of the scientific contingent of the Yellowstone Expedition after having proposed to President James Monroe that steamboats could be effectively used to explore the upper Missouri River. Although he supervised the construction of the steamboat, *Western Engineer,* the vessel was not adequate for the endeavor. Included in his scientific party were EDWIN JAMES, Thomas Say, TITIAN RAMSAY PEALE, and SAMUEL SEYMOUR. In the winter of 1819, when

Congress withdrew support for the exploration of the Missouri, Long and his detachment were ordered to explore the headwaters of the Platte, Arkansas, and Red rivers. In the early summer of 1820, after following the banks of the Platte River westward, they turned south and journeyed along the front range of the Rocky Mountains until they reached the headwaters of the Arkansas River but did not seek its source. They discovered Longs Peak but made no attempt to scale it, although some members of the expedition successfully climbed Pikes Peak, the first ascent of a fourteen-thousand-foot mountain by Euro-Americans in the United States. While on the upper reaches of the Arkansas River, the party divided into two groups. Long, James, and Peale found the Canadian River, but again they failed to follow the river to its source. In the report of the expedition prepared by Edwin James, Long, although always a powerful voice for Western exploration, advanced the idea of the "GREAT AMERICAN DESERT," with its corollary that the plains were not easily adaptable to agriculture and civilization. The results of Long's expedition were mixed. While it contributed to our knowledge of Western flora, fauna, and river systems, its failure to follow the Platte, Arkansas, and Canadian rivers to their sources limited its contributions to Western topography.

After spending eight years in military exploration, Long devoted the rest of his army career to civil engineering problems associated with the construction of railroads and bridges.

—*Phillip Drennon Thomas*

SEE ALSO: Art: Surveys and Expeditions; Exploration: United States Expeditions; Exploration and Science

SUGGESTED READING:
Nichols, Roger L., and Patrick L. Halley. *Stephen Long and American Frontier Exploration.* Newark, N.J., 1980.
Wood, Richard. *Stephen Harriman Long, 1784–1864, Army Engineer, Explorer, Inventor.* Glendale, Calif., 1966.

LONGHORNS

SEE: Cattle Breeds and Breeding; Cattle Industry

LONGLEY, WILLIAM PRESTON ("WILD BILL")

Born in Austin County, Texas, William Preston Longley (1851–1878) learned to shoot as a Texas farm boy,

William Preston Longley, in custody, flanked by peace officers, 1878. *Courtesy Western History Collections, University of Oklahoma.*

and he learned to hate blacks during the bitter atmosphere of Reconstruction. At the age of fifteen, he killed a black soldier, thus commencing a path of murder that so often was directed against African Americans that he became known as "the nigger killer," although the contentious "Wild Bill" Longley often shot it out with white men as well. From 1867 through 1876, he killed eleven men in a dozen shootouts in Texas, Oklahoma, Kansas, and Wyoming; and he was instrumental in the deaths of at least two other victims. Although he escaped custody several times and once was cut down after being lynched, Longley finally was apprehended and hanged in Giddings, Texas, just before his twenty-seventh birthday.

—Bill O'Neal

SEE ALSO: Gunfighters; Violence

SUGGESTED READING:
Bartholomew, Ed. *Wild Bill Longley: A Texas Hard-Case.* Houston, Tex., 1953.

LOOKING GLASS (NEZ PERCÉ)

With CHIEF JOSEPH (the Younger), Looking Glass (ca. 1823–1877) was a leader of the Nez Percé during their war against forces of the U.S. Army in 1877. Looking Glass inherited his name from his father, who passed on to him a mirror pendant he wore. The father sided with Chief Joseph (the Elder) in the Walla Walla Council of 1855 in refusing to sign a new treaty proposed by Washington's territorial governor Isaac Stevens. The treaty redrew the boundaries of Nez Percé lands and deprived many of them of their homes. Looking Glass (the Younger), leading the Asotin band, and Chief Joseph (the Younger), of the Wallowa band, likewise refused to sign a second treaty in 1863, which further reduced tribal lands. Nevertheless, for many years, both men counseled peace and hopes for a just resolution of the matter of tribal lands. Until white settlements actually encroached into the disputed land, peace prevailed. But on July 1, 1877, a combined force of militia and army regulars attacked Looking Glass's camp near the forks of the Clearwater Creek in Idaho.

About two weeks earlier, Chief Joseph had suffered a similar attack at White Bird Canyon, and the two

Looking Glass in 1877. *Courtesy National Archives.*

now joined forces to fight troops under General OLIVER OTIS HOWARD at the Battle of Clearwater on July 11. The fighting ignited a series of battles and skirmishes as the Nez Percés pressed toward the Canadian border. Looking Glass served as principal strategist during this period until Nez Percé forces suffered a defeat at Big Hole Valley on August 9. He continued, however, to advocate fighting without compromise, even after Chief Joseph counseled surrender. On October 5, during the final battle of the Nez Percé War, just south of the Canadian border in the Bear Paw Mountains, Looking Glass was struck in the face by a sniper's bullet and died.

—*Alan Axelrod*

SEE ALSO: Pacific Northwest Indian Wars

SUGGESTED READING:
Axelrod, Alan. *Chronicle of the Indian Wars: From Colonial Times to Wounded Knee.* New York, 1992.
Brown, Mark H. *The Flight of the Nez Percé.* Lincoln, Nebr., 1967.
Josephy, Alvin M., Jr. *The Nez Percé Indians and the Opening of the Northwest.* New Haven, Conn., 1965.

LOOKING-GLASS PRAIRIE

The wetland prairies of the Central Lowlands are residue of glaciers. Lakes and marshes were left as ice masses retreated. These areas acted as sponges and filters, helping to absorb rain, melting snow, and floods. Rivers and creeks formed a circulatory system, with run-off reaching them after delaying action by wetlands.

Early Euro-American settlers were struck by the appearance of the wetlands, where standing sheets of water reflected the sky and surrounding landscape as mirrors. These reflections led to the colloquial nickname "looking-glass prairie," in contrast to the tallgrass prairie, where the blowing wind caused them to resemble an ocean with a constant waving motion.

Euro-American settlers were impressed with the quantity and variety of waterfowl, fish, and other animals present on the wetland prairies, but they thought that land that could not be farmed was wasted. The wetland prairies, often called "swamps," "bogs," "sloughs," and "seeps" by settlers, were ditched, tiled, and otherwise drained. These actions altered the character of the wetland prairies so that they are now unrecognizable.

—*Loren N. Horton*

SEE ALSO: Prairie

SUGGESTED READING:
Madson, John. *Where the Sky Begins: Land of the Tallgrass Prairie.* Ames, Iowa, 1982. Reprint. 1995.
Thompson, Janette R. *Prairies, Forests, and Wetlands.* Iowa City, Iowa, 1992.

LOS ANGELES

Historical Overview
Charles Phillips

Industrial and Commercial Development
Leonard Pitt

"Car Culture"
Virginia Scharff

HISTORICAL OVERVIEW

Sprawling across about five hundred square miles of a broad coastal plain between the San Gabriel Mountains and the Pacific Ocean, Los Angeles has become the second largest city—in both population and metropolitan area—in the nation, after New York. "Grotesquely shaped," according to historian John D. Weaver, "like a charred scrap of paper," this semiarid metropolis is so dominated by the automobile that a universally recognized hallmark of its ARCHITECTURE is a dramatic (much about Los Angeles is dramatic) network of freeways. The shape and the highways reflect perhaps the most remarkable aspect of Los Angeles history, the fact that, for a century or more beginning in the 1870s, it just grew. A series of booms from the late nineteenth to the late twentieth centuries created a vortex of a city devouring all habitable space, then swirling farther into the desert. With its palm trees and swimming pools, its movie studios and aerospace labs, twentieth-century Los Angeles came to boast one of the more diverse economies on the planet and served as a model for younger Southwestern cities like Houston, Phoenix, and Denver, each of which soon had their own subdivisions, commercial strips, and shopping centers (not infrequently built by Los Angeles-based developers). Suburbs around the country—in Seattle, Cleveland, Long Island, Nashville—showed L.A. roots, and a new southern California life style— libertarian, mobile, affluent—had begun, by mid-century, to define "the good life" in America.

The city's history stretched back to August 2, 1769, when Captain Gaspar de Portolá, leading a Spanish expedition north from Mexico in search of mission sites, camped near a river he called Porciúncula to honor Nuestra Señora la Reyna de los Angeles de Porciúncula (Our Lady the Queen of the Angels of Porciúncula). The Spaniards traded gifts with a group of local Indians at nearby Yang-na and settled in for the night. As Father Juan Crespi was noting in his diary that the space between the trees on the river was a delightful place, with "all the requisites for a large settlement," the camp was rocked by three earthquakes. Portolá and his men left the next morning. Two years later, the Spanish established the Mission San Gabriel Arcángel nine miles north of Portolá's camp, but a decade would pass before Felipe de Neve, governor of Alta California, Spain's newest addition to its creaky world empire, persuaded forty-four Mexicans, most of them with Indian and African as well as Spanish ancestors, to colonize the fertile river basin Father Crespi had described. Poor and illiterate, the settlers set down on the west bank of today's Los Angeles River and laid claim to the land de Neve had promised them. In all likelihood, they called the place El Pueblo de la Reyna de Los Angeles (The Town of the Queen of the Angels) and commonly referred to it as El Pueblo.

El Pueblo emerged as one of the few California settlements occasionally to be called *cuidad* (city) in official Spanish records, although it was an isolated outpost that enjoyed infrequent contact with Mexico and almost none with the United States during its formative years. When Joseph Chapman, a pirate out of Boston, accompanied by African American privateer Thomas Fisher, landed near the town in 1818, the locals thought of Chapman not as a Yankee nor an American nor even a citizen of the United States, but as an Englishmen, and they called him "El Inglés" after he and Fisher settled down to become Angelenos. The town remained isolated and of little social and economic significance even after Mexico became independent of Spain. In a society centered around haciendas and whose economy was based on the autonomy and self-sufficiency of landholding rancheros and their Indian peons, it hardly mattered that El Pueblo was by far the largest town in Mexican California. The first outsider to arrive overland from the United States, mountain man JEDEDIAH STRONG SMITH in 1826, found the Los Angeles pueblo charming enough, despite some misunderstandings with the Mexican authorities. As Americans east of the Rocky Mountains began to hear of those charms—the people, they were told, were carefree, the climate incredibly salubrious—some came by land and by sea to settle or trade, mostly in tallow and hides. Not a few traders, "Bostons" the Angelenos sometimes called them, married into the local Californio elite, enough of them to cause RICHARD HENRY DANA—who looked in on the city in 1835—to disparage such intermarriage, as well as the "lazy" Angelenos in his *Two Years before the Mast* (1840).

By the 1840s, the Angelenos were heartily sick of the enterprising Americans, "the hordes of Yankee immigrants," California's governor PÍO DE JESUS PICO called them, who insisted on "cultivating farms, establishing vineyards, erecting mills, sawing up lumber, building workshops, and doing a thousand other things which seem natural to them, but which Californians neglect or despise." During the UNITED STATES–MEXICAN WAR, after U.S. forces under JOHN CHARLES FRÉMONT and Commodore ROBERT F. STOCKTON had occupied the city on August 13, 1846, without a shot being fired, it was Governor Pico's brother, Andrés, who led the only revolt against the Anglos, which was put down in January 1847, freeing the occupiers to celebrate the city's first American Independence Day on July 4, 1847. The transition from a Mexican pueblo to an American town would damn Los Angeles to being a backwater for half a century. A stable population of around 2,500, exclusive of the local Indians, in Mexican Los Angeles—the pueblo's 2,228 people in 1836 had increased only slightly to some 2,497 by 1844—would actually decline to 1,300 at the end of Mexican rule and reach only some 1,600 (895 men, 715 women) in 1850, when the place was, according to a disenchanted physician pioneer, a lawless, adobe cow town, where "gambling, drinking, and whoring are the only occupations."

A combination of factors—the discovery in 1848 of gold in northern California, the struggle over land between established Californios and Anglo newcomers kicked off by new legislation requiring validation of Mexican land titles to the huge California ranchos that had been the mainstay of Los Angeles pastoral economy, and floods and droughts in the 1860s—sapped the strength and livelihood of the native Angelenos. The expanding Sonora Town barrio filled with Mexican Americans, displaced rancheros and villagers from the outlying regions, and gold-rush immigrants from Mexico's Sonora province. A growing sense of Mexico as the "homeland," even among those who had been born in Los Angeles and who had never set foot south of the border, led many to leave the area and repatriate, although Spanish-speaking people would remain in the majority in Los Angeles until the 1870s. At first, the ranchero elite actually prospered in the wake of the gold rush, as hungry Forty-niners in San Francisco and Sacramento gorged on beef from southern California. The lure of the gold fields, however, depleted the lower classes and the surrounding farms villages and attracted a pass-through traffic of Mexican immigrants from Sonora. When the inevitable disappointments set in among the fortune-seekers, abetted by the Anglo miners' anti-Mexican violence and the foreign miners' tax passed by a miner-dominated state legislature, those returning from the gold fields found their rich ethnic fellow Angelenos in a losing battle against Anglo interlopers over the vast

Spanish and Mexican land grants. Unfamiliar with U.S. land laws and interest rates, the rancheros were dealt a devastating blow by a catastrophic drought from 1862 to 1865. This was followed by several years of declining cattle prices in one of the economic downswings with which Americans east of the Mexican Southwest had long been painfully familiar. High mortgages produced bankruptcies that helped hasten the end of the era of the ranchos and fed the growing power of the minority of "Americans" who had taken control of the city's government and its business life. As early as 1860, says Weaver, Los Angeles had banned bullfighting and formed a baseball club.

The forced breakup of the big ranchos provided a golden opportunity for growth: the diverse agriculture that sprang into existence created opportunities for a number of outlying communities, and all Los Angeles needed was the WATER to make them flourish in the semiarid southland and the means by which to string them together into a common market. In the 1870s and 1880s, the construction of transcontinental railroads provided the means to market, and the development of IRRIGATION projects produced some of the water. The railroads placed climate and scenery within the reach of settlers and tourists, and with the arrival of the Southern Pacific in 1876 and then the completion of the Santa Fe in 1885, Los Angeles shipped its oranges east and launched a massive advertising campaign to lure immigrants west. This new Eden took shape during a land boom in the 1880s, when railroads influenced the location of town sites and created the lines of the city's future sprawl.

As the countryside filled up, the "folks," mostly Anglo-Protestants from the Midwest, stimulated community growth. As interurban and street railways linked emerging towns to Los Angeles, the city learned to grow by swallowing up the countryside. Between 1859 and 1951, it annexed 121 towns, spreading the reign of Greater Los Angeles from 28.01 square miles to 453.5 square miles and making something new under the sun—suburbs—out of places like Pasadena, Long Beach, and Glendale. Its appetite for real estate would become insatiable; it transformed farm land and orchards into marketable properties; it placed beaches and mountains at the doorstep, so to speak, of the Angelenos; it offered detached bungalows in new housing developments as alternatives to the tenements in Los Angeles. Having learned to boom on agriculture, railroads, and climate, Los Angeles developed a taste for booming again and again, on oil and the automobile, on the MOTION-PICTURE INDUSTRY and the AIRCRAFT INDUSTRY, on public-works construction and government-funded big science, on TOURISM and computers. Every twenty years or so, the booms would

come, sustained always in some measure by the sale of real estate, which required the sacrifice of three thousand acres of farm land a day to the bulldozer. From 1940 on, with the construction of the Pasadena Freeway, in the words of Neil R. Pearce and Jerry Hagstrom, "Los Angeles pioneered" the superhighway, "annihilated the sidewalk, and slaughtered public transportation," its freeways alone eating up forty acres of farm land per mile. By the 1950s, because of this urban growth, Los Angeles had ceased to be the wealthiest agricultural county in the world, a boast it had made since 1910.

As Father Crespi's campsite was overrun by Anglo boosters determined to build a city in their own image, Los Angeles's style became imperial. Having no natural harbor did not persuade Angelenos to pick up and move to San Diego, where a perfectly good harbor beckoned, but to make one of their own by grabbing— Weaver says, "artfully gerrymandering"—land on the sea, creating a "shoestring strip" to connect the inland city with the two port towns—San Pedro and Wilmington— it "acquired" by consolidation in an epic 1909 struggle between the SOUTHERN PACIFIC RAILROAD and the Free Harbor League. Typically, work on the harbor itself had begun in 1899, long before the city had access to the sea, and the first municipal wharf opened in 1914, a few years after the Southern Pacific had won its fight against the harbor communities. When the Los Angeles River basin proved inadequate to meet the water needs of the burgeoning metropolis, WILLIAM MULHOLLAND—the city's chief water engineer—and others would take it from the Owens Valley 250 miles away. In doing so, they corrupted many of the city's prominent citizens and most of its government leaders through two syndicates of speculators and then outraged ranchers along the Owens River on the other side of the Sierra Nevada. The system Mulholland built supplied 80 percent of the city's water needs, but when it needed more, it did not hesitate to build the California Aqueduct to drain northern California or to dam the Colorado River and snatch water from other states.

The century of growth created a unique town, renowned for its strangeness. "Virtue has become virulent," wrote the *Smart Set* of Los Angeles in 1913, describing it as "an overgrown village" packed with "spiritualists, mediums, astrologists, phrenologists, palmists, and all other breeds of esoteric windjammers." Not a few of the newcomers were former *Smart Set* writers, or writers from its main rival, *The New Yorker,* who—along with such local colorists as toughguy writer Raymond Chandler—helped stereotype the city as a haven for the eccentric, the corrupt, and the dangerously unbalanced. Part of the image was justified. In the first decade of the twentieth century, parasol-toting prostitutes from the plush brothels of Pearl Morton and Cora Phillips plied the streets in open carriages much to the chagrin of the folks, who Weaver describes as the retired druggists, dentists, and wheat (and corn) farmers from the Midwest. They kept streaming into Los Angeles and earned the town the writers called "La-La Land" the sobriquet of "Iowa's West Coast." The folks also winced when the moviemakers began moving into Hollywood in the late teens and early twenties. A suburb eight miles northwest of the central city, Hollywood had been laid out in 1887 by Horace Wilcox, a Prohibitionist, who intended his town to be occupied by the sober, God-fearing folks themselves. The water ran low in 1910, and Los Angeles swallowed Hollywood up; the next year, the Blondeau Tavern at the intersection of Sunset Boulevard and Gower Street became the Hollywood's first motion-picture studio.

Hollywood not only brought permanent scandal—and thriving scandal sheets—to the city with its purveying of the glamorous and the highly sexed, it also joined the beach-and-auto society springing up to create a culture that bred materialism and hedonism, a fluid society impermanent and rootless and free, one aimed at a future with no past. The Los Angeles life style, like its urban sprawl, often came in for condemnation, but it had its attraction, and it was no accident that Los Angeles became overrun, in the 1940s, by refugees from Hitler's Europe such as Henrich and Thomas Mann, Arnold Schoenberg, Bertolt Brecht, Bruno Walter, Franz Werfel, and Alfred Nuemann. For if ever there had been a society more licentious, more open, and more fluid than Hollywood's, it had to be that of Berlin between the two world wars. In those years, Los Angeles earned yet another nickname: "The Fourth Weimar Republic." But in truth, the life style also attracted the folks, because it promised a better life for the masses—the possibility at least of owning a small single-family home with a patio and two cars, of personal liberty, of smooth roads, of good schools, of clear skies, of cheap entertainment, of relaxing in the sun.

The numbers tell the story of a century of growth, sometimes growth for its own sake. A population of 11,183 in 1880 had become 50,395 in 1890, 102,479 in 1900, 576,673 in 1920, 1,504,277 in 1940, 2,479,015 in 1960, 7,477,503 in 1980. Eccentrics, the FILM crowd , and the folks were not the only ones attracted to the growing metropolis. Much of the population was working class, "Hispanic," African American, and Asian. In fact, when the city celebrated its bicentenary in 1981, whites had once again become a minority, as they were when the city was incorporated on April 4, 1850. The 1990 census reported that Euro-Americans made up two-fifths of the population, Hispanics about two-fifths, blacks one-eighth, Asians and Pacific Islanders not much less than one-tenth. Some among these latter groups had been in Los Angeles all along, despite the fear and anger with which many white Angelenos reacted to the changing demography of the late twentieth century. At first the folks responded to the changes by moving into the San Fernando Valley, whose principal east-west artery, Ventura Boulevard, had been a dirt road in the 1920s. It became a seventeen-mile strip of specialty shops, ethnic restaurants, banks, medical buildings, shopping malls, real-estate offices, and automobile dealerships. In the 1980s and 1990s, the valley itself, once a sanctuary of middle-class white flight from downtown congestion and racial tension, began turning walnut orchards and truck gardens into housing complexes for blacks, Hispanics, and Asians working in new plants that ran the gamut from basic industry to high-tech computer companies.

Los Angeles paid for its spectacular growth with smog-filled air, polluted water, traffic grid lock, explosive ghettos, and city budgets teetering on the edge of bankruptcy. By the 1980s, there were years in which Los Angeles itself actually lost population as baby boomers left home and the city underwent racial and cultural conflicts. And in those years in which the population of the city did grow, the newcomers were Mexican nationals, Central and South Americans, Asian refugees, Yugolslavs, Koreans, and Filipinos. Their arrival produced a white backlash of legislation ranging from propositions to slash taxes and cut city services, especially to the poor, to attacks on nonwhite immigrant populations as illegal aliens. By the late twentieth century, Angelenos lived in enclaves, socially walled off from one another—some in fortress communities boasting million-dollar homes, others in ghettos and BARRIOS boasting high crime and crumbling houses, stores, factories, and families. As always, Angelinos went their own way—surfing, riding, skiing, yachting, hiking, golfing, playing tennis, shooting and shooting up, snorting, stabbing, stalking, gang banging, sometimes rioting—some pursuing happiness and fulfillment, some hunting connections and customers. Unabashedly hedonistic, Los Angeles had become a city at once envied, imitated, ridiculed, and reviled by a country rapidly coming not only to identify it with the good life of the American dream but also to associate it with the worst fears about the American future.

—*Charles Phillips*

SEE ALSO: California Gold Rush; City Government; City Planning; Colorado River Compact; Echo Park; Oil and Gas Industry; Owens Valley War; Spanish-Mexican Towns; Reclamation; Urban West

SUGGESTED READING:

Banham, Reyner. *Los Angeles: The Architecture of Four Ecologies.* Middlesex, Eng., 1971.

Bottles, Scott L. *Los Angeles and the Automobile: The Making of the Modern City.* Berkeley, Calif., 1987.

Davis, Mike. *City of Quartz: Excavating the Future in Los Angeles.* London, 1990.

Fishman, Robert. *Bourgeois Utopias: The Rise and Fall of Suburbia.* New York, 1987.

Fogelson, Robert M. *The Fragment Metropolis: Los Angeles, 1850–1939.* 1967. Reprint. Berkeley, Calif., 1993.

Griswold del Castillo, Richard. *The Los Angeles Barrio, 1850–1890: A Social History.* Berkeley, Calif., 1979.

McWilliams, Carey. *Southern California: An Island on the Land.* 1946. Reprint. Salt Lake City, 1993.

Pitt, Leonard. *The Decline of the Californios: A Social History of the Spanish-Speaking Californians, 1846–1890.* Berkeley, Calif., 1966.

Starr, Kevin. *Material Dreams: Southern California through the 1920s.* New York, 1990.

Weaver, John D. *Los Angeles: The Enormous Village.* Berkeley, Calif., 1980.

INDUSTRIAL AND COMMERCIAL DEVELOPMENT

The city of Los Angeles was born of deficient WATER and fuel, lacked a natural harbor, and was geographically isolated. By the late nineteenth century, however, the city had become a center of Western commerce and industry. Before the arrival of the railroads, the city's economy was based on vineyards and livestock raising—ventures that could develop without coal, rivers, or abundant labor. The completion of the SOUTHERN PACIFIC RAILROAD in 1876 connected the region with national markets, and the completion of the Santa Fe Railroad in 1885 ushered in one of America's greatest land booms. From 1886 to 1888, trains from the Midwest, sometimes as many as four a day, deposited 120,000 people in Los Angeles.

Next in importance to the railroads was the creation of a harbor out of a mud slough at San Pedro–Wilmington. The Los Angeles business community waged all-out political war to defeat the Southern Pacific's effort, beginning in 1890, to establish a port at Santa Monica. After a ten-year battle, known locally as the "Free Harbor Contest," Congress approved a subsidy for a breakwater and other improvements for a major port for Los Angeles. Harbor commerce evolved quickly, and by 1914, the city's traders took full advantage of the newly completed Panama Canal.

TOURISM became a leading industry in Los Angeles in the 1880s, as railroads and hotels fostered excursions to the area and local boosters capitalized on the year-round sunshine, clean beaches, snowcapped mountains, fragrant orange groves, romantic adobe

buildings, and, later, Hollywood glamour. By the 1890s, many affluent Easterners were abandoning their European itineraries in favor of trips to southern California.

By the turn of the century, the growing and marketing of oranges had made Los Angeles an agricultural powerhouse. From 1890 to 1940, local growers had as many as two hundred thousand acres under cultivation and shipped as many as fifty thousand refrigerated car loads to the East each year. The Southern California Fruit Growers Exchange (Sunkist Growers, Inc.), a marketing cooperative, orchestrated the industry's growth.

Employers relied on Chinese, Japanese, and Mexicans for railroad construction, agricultural work, and other manual labor but hired white, native-born workers for skilled craft work. Many craft workers had come to California in search of a more healthy climate and worked for low wages. In the 1880s, the local Merchants and Manufacturers Association mounted a fierce open-shop crusade to maintain the city's relatively low wage scale. The craft unions managed to withstand the onslaught and even gained ground between 1900 and 1910, but they received a mortal blow in 1911 when two labor officials, John B. and James McNamara, confessed to dynamiting the *Los Angeles Times* Building a year earlier. Not until the Great Depression, when the movie industry recognized the craft guilds and federal legislation granted unions the right of collective bargaining, did unions stage a comeback. Industrial unions associated with the Congress of Industrial Organizations (CIO) gained a foothold in southern California, making modest advances in the FILM, rubber, steel, auto, aircraft, food-processing, and garment industries.

The city's most powerful growth factor, after the railroads and the harbor, was the importation of water from the Owens River. Completed in 1913, the two-hundred-mile-long Los Angeles Aqueduct, designed by WILLIAM MULHOLLAND, also supplied cheap electrical power. The completion of the COLORADO RIVER STORAGE PROJECT in 1943 much affected the economy, too.

Oil drilling created additional economic activity, particularly in the 1920s, but even more important was the MOTION-PICTURE INDUSTRY, especially from 1914 to 1940. The clean and "smokeless" industry took advantage of the climate and scenery and produced huge payrolls that recycled back into the community. The movie industry attracted many tourists and newcomers and made Hollywood famous worldwide.

Economic development reached a new plateau between 1920 and 1945, when Los Angeles became the airplane capital of the world. The combination of mild climate and ample labor, venture capitalists, and trained engineers fostered a dynamic AIRCRAFT INDUSTRY. By the late 1930s, Los Angeles aircraft factories received significant government contracts. On the eve of World War II and afterward, government orders poured in, stimulating urban growth and providing a living for more than one-quarter of a million people throughout the metropolitan area.

—*Leonard Pitt*

SUGGESTED READING:

McWilliams, Cary. *Southern California Country: An Island on the Land.* New York, 1946.
Nelson, Howard J. *The Los Angeles Metropolis.* Dubuque, Iowa, 1983.

"CAR CULTURE"

Los Angeles, a vast urban center, is often considered to be the world's preeminent car-culture city. The term *car culture* refers to the transformation of American landscapes, patterns of habitation, and social relations by the popular adoption of the private automobile in the twentieth century. Car-culture cities typically display low-density development, segregation by function and race, suburban sprawl, and a proliferation of commercial zones. People who live in such cities tend to live beyond walking distance from the places they need to go everyday and depend on the automobile as their primary means of transportation. They tend to ignore the problems and prospects that widespread automobile use produces, including the increasing and sometimes incalculable daily time devoted to commuting. In such circumstances, people without access to automobiles are conspicuously disadvantaged.

Automobile use pervades the language people in car-culture cities use. "In the driver's seat," for example, means "in control." Also affected are decisions about familial economic resources; automobile purchases and associated loans compose the second largest investment of American families after housing. Car culture also brings about an increase in the power of the state over the lives of citizens through traffic regulations, licensing practices, and liability laws. The culture, as manifested in lovers' lanes, drag-racing, and drive-in restaurants and theaters, even extends its influence over the sexual and leisure practices of residents.

—*Virginia Scharff*

LOS ANGELES COUNTY MUSEUM OF NATURAL HISTORY

The official opening of the Los Angeles County Museum of History, Science and Art took place on November 6, 1913. The museum was part of a new cultural center in state-owned Exposition Park, just south of Los Angeles. The park was the brainchild of Judge William Miller Bowen, who used his considerable political influence to arrange a tripartite agreement among the state, city, and county governments to administer the park. The state of California leased the northwest corner of Exposition Park to Los Angeles County, which agreed to construct a museum on the site.

The brick Spanish Renaissance building housed the exhibits and collections in wings devoted to history, art, and science. Scientific specimens, historical artifacts, and art objects donated or loaned from various local institutions such as the Cooper Ornithological Club, the Southern California Academy of Sciences, the Historical Society of Southern California, and the Fine Arts League, soon filled it to capacity. Fossils from the LA BREA TAR PITS, where the museum had exclusive rights to excavate, took up most of the science wing.

After World War II, the uneasy coexistence of science and art under one roof led to a movement to create a separate museum for art. In 1964, the art collections moved to the Los Angeles County Museum of Art on Wilshire Boulevard. Despite the fact that the original museum still contained substantial and significant historical collections, the County Board of Supervisors decided to change its name to the Los Angeles County Museum of Natural History.

The institution is no longer a single museum but a network of museums with the original Exposition Park building serving as the flagship. In 1977, the first satellite, the George C. Page Museum of La Brea Discoveries, opened in Hancock Park. A decade later, the home of a silent-screen star WILLIAM S. HART became the institution's first history satellite. In 1993, the Burbank branch of the Natural History Museum, the only public museum in the San Fernando Valley, launched its exhibition program. The Peterson Automotive Museum, a new satellite dedicated to the interpretation of the impact of the automobile on Los Angeles opened in 1994.

—*Errol Wayne Stevens*

SUGGESTED READING:

Los Angeles County Museum. Museum Association *Quarterly* (50th Anniversary issue) 16 (Spring 1960).
"Sixty-Five and Still Growing." *Terra* 16 (Winter 1978).

LOST DUTCHMAN'S MINE

A legendary mine in the Superstition Mountains, near Mesa, Arizona, the Lost Dutchman's Mine was reportedly discovered in 1840 by a Mexican youth fleeing from his lover's father, a prosperous ranchero. The ranchero's Indian slaves found the young man hiding in a nest of gold nuggets and killed him. The slaves reported the mine to the ranchero, who immediately set about extracting its riches. Apache Indians then attacked the ranch and killed everyone there except for three Mexicans, who, after the massacre, continued to mine the gold. They showed their claim to the Dutchman Jacob Waltz, or Wolz, who killed them, hid their bodies, and took control of the mine. Waltz mined gold there for many years, shrewdly withholding the mine's location while bragging incessantly about his find. As he was dying, however, he gave a map showing the location of the mine to a friend. Although the friend and others searched for the mine for years, it was never found. Tales of fantastic riches continue to circulate despite the lack of evidence, over more than 150 years later, of the actual existence of the Lost Dutchman's Mine.

—*Candace Floyd*

SUGGESTED READING:

Fisher, Vardis, and Opal Laurel Holmes. *Gold Rushes and Mining Camps of the Early American West.* Caldwell, Idaho, 1979.

LOUISIANA PURCHASE

The agreement by which France transferred that part of its North American empire roughly defined by the Mississippi and Missouri River watersheds to the United States in 1803 for fifteen million dollars, the Louisiana Purchase was the final chapter in a centuries-long contest for sovereignty over an area of critical importance to the growth of the United States. THOMAS JEFFERSON set the tone when he wrote in 1802: "There is one single spot, the possessor of which is our natural and habitual enemy. . . . Every eye in the U.S. is now fixed on this affair of Louisiana."

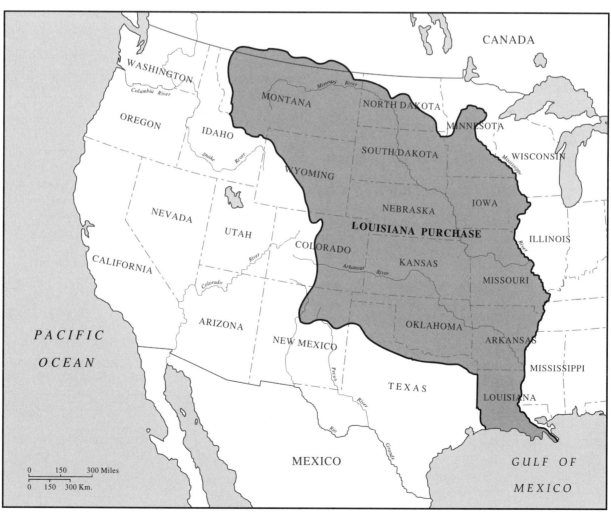

Louisiana Purchase, 1803

Although the region had been inhabited for thousands of years by an unknown number of Native American peoples, the European presence in the area designated as Louisiana dates from 1519 when Spanish sea captain Alonso Alvarez de Pineda sighted the mouth of the Mississippi River while exploring the Gulf Coast. In 1541, the Spaniard Hernando de Soto led a expedition of six hundred men along the lower Mississippi River in an unsuccessful search for fame and fortune. During the middle decades of the seventeenth century, French Jesuit missionaries came from the north to assert France's claim to the region. In 1682, the French explorer SIEUR DE LA SALLE descended to the mouth of the Mississippi River and claimed on behalf of King Louis IX all "the seas, harbors, ports, bays, adjacent straits, and all the nations, people, provinces, cities, towns, villages, mines, minerals, fisheries, streams and rivers comprised" of the vaguely defined area he named "Louisiana."

The territory's remoteness made Louisiana more a liability than an asset during the course of France's dominion. The French hold on the region was continually threatened by Anglo-Americans advancing down the Ohio River valley. Facing the loss of the region to the British as a result of defeat in the Seven Years' War, France ceded Louisiana to Spain in 1763. Spain's control of the territory soon was threatened when the independence of the thirteen colonies unleashed a flood of Americans into the Ohio and Mississippi river valleys. Friction with Spain was eased in 1795 by Pinckney's Treaty, which guaranteed Americans navigation rights on the Mississippi River and the right to deposit goods for export at New Orleans.

In 1801, rumors that Spain had transferred Louisiana back to France provoked near-panic in the United States. While Americans anticipated Spain's eventually losing its hold on Louisiana, the presence of France as a neighbor promised to block westward expansion indefinitely. Moreover, suspension of the right of deposit at New Orleans threatened to cut off a substantial portion of the nation's trade. Congressional War Hawks called for the territory to be taken by force, and President Jefferson dispatched Robert Livingston of New York and, later, James Monroe of Virginia to Paris to negotiate the purchase of New Orleans and Florida west of the Perdido River from France for no more than nine million dollars.

Meanwhile in the French sugar colony of Santo Domingo, the victorious uprising of an army of black slaves led by Toussaint L'ouverture dramatically changed Emperor Napoleon's colonial strategy. Faced with a rapidly deteriorating situation in the Western Hemisphere, Napoleon decided to unload *all* of Louisiana in order to consolidate his forces. On April 30, 1803, Livingston, Monroe, and French negotiator Barbe-Marbois initialed agreements transferring all of the Louisiana region to the United States in exchange for $11.25 million. In addition, the United States assumed $3.75 million in claims of its citizens against France. Significantly, Livingston and Monroe did not hesitate in agreeing to the purchase of the entire region, despite the fact that their instructions called only for acquiring New Orleans and West Florida. The two men knew that, because of the territorial ambitions of the United States and its citizens, this was an opportunity not to be missed.

Yet the deal did not clearly define Louisiana. The treaty stipulated the boundary as "the same extent . . . that it had when France possessed it" before 1763. French Minister Tallyrand, in what may have been an attempt to create future problems for the United States, remained purposely evasive about the region's limits. When Livingston and Monroe attempted to pin him down, Tallyrand replied "I can give you no direction. You have made a noble bargain for yourselves, and I suppose you will make the most of it."

Acquisition of Louisiana had enormous implications for the nation's development. Jefferson termed it an "empire for liberty," a domain designed to provide land "to the thousandth generation." The purchase represented a major increase in the constitutionally implied powers of the presidency and set the stage for future westward expansion. Negating the claims of Native Americans who inhabited the territory, the Louisiana Purchase also established a colonial hold over the region's fifty thousand French Creole inhabitants. New England Federalists, fearing that the region would tilt the balance of political power in the direction of Western and Southern states, opposed the acquisition.

Significantly, in January 1803 (three months before the deal was made), Jefferson had requested congressional funding for a cross-continental survey of the Louisiana territory and beyond. The LEWIS AND CLARK EXPEDITION from 1804 to 1806 produced the first scientific and economic knowledge of a land purchased literally sight-unseen by the United States. The Lewis and Clark Expedition became the basis of a U.S. claim extending the limits of the Louisiana territory as far west as the Columbia River region and as far south as West Florida and Texas. Spanish objections, first over the legality of France's sale of the territory and then over its boundaries, resulted in a dispute lasting until the signing of the ADAMS-ONIS (or Transcontinental) TREATY in 1819.

Out of the Louisiana Territory eventually emerged the states of Louisiana, ARKANSAS, IOWA, MISSOURI, NEBRASKA, NORTH DAKOTA, SOUTH DAKOTA, OKLAHOMA, and parts of KANSAS, MINNESOTA, COLORADO, MONTANA, and WYOMING. While the cost amounted to approximately three cents per acre, in the long run the United States paid a steep price in blood and treasure for the region. The question of whether or not to allow slavery in the new lands was a major bone of contention, necessitating the MISSOURI COMPROMISE of 1820 and its eventual repeal in the KANSAS-NEBRASKA ACT of 1854. In this respect, the Louisiana Purchase can be understood to be one of the long-term causes of the Civil War.

—*William Earl Weeks*

SEE ALSO: National Expansion: Nation Building and Early Expansion, Slavery and National Expansion

SUGGESTED READING:

Adams, Henry. *History of the United States of America during the Administrations of Jefferson and Madison.* Vols. 2 and 3. New York, 1889–1891.

DeConde, Alexander. *This Affair of Louisiana.* Baton Rouge, La., 1976.

Lyon, E. Wilson. *Louisiana in French Diplomacy, 1759–1804.* Norman, Okla., 1974.

Whitaker, Arthur P. *The Mississippi Question: A Study of Trade, Politics, and Diplomacy.* New York, 1934.

LOVING, OLIVER

Noted cattleman and pioneer Texas trail-driver Oliver Loving (1811 or 1812–1867) was born in Hopkins County, Kentucky. He settled in Texas in 1845 and a decade later was raising cattle in Palo Pinto County and trailing them to Shreveport and Alexandria, Louisiana. In partnership with John Durkee, he drove a herd north and east to Chicago, Illinois, in 1858. In 1860, he guided another herd north and west across the Indian Territory, up the Arkansas River, and into Denver, Colorado, to feed hungry miners.

During the Civil War, Loving supplied beef for the Confederacy. Following the conflict, he joined cattleman CHARLES GOODNIGHT in blazing a new route into Colorado. In 1866, the two men drove a herd west from near Fort Belknap, Texas, to Horsehead Crossing on the Pecos River, then north to Fort Sumner in the New Mexico Territory, and on to the South Platte River north of Denver. While only the latter third of this route was new, it became known as the "Goodnight-Loving Trail."

On a second drive in 1867, Loving was severely wounded on the Pecos River by Comanche Indians and died of complications at Fort Sumner. Goodnight transported Loving's body back to Texas, where it was interred at Weatherford. Although certainly not the first, Oliver Loving is considered by many as the "dean of the Texas trail-drivers."

—*Richard C. Rattenbury*

SEE ALSO: Cattle Industry; Cattle Trails and Trail Driving

SUGGESTED READING:

Haley, J. Evetts. *Charles Goodnight: Cowman and Plainsman.* Boston, 1936.

Kenner, Charles. "Origins of the 'Goodnight' Trail Reconsidered." *Southwestern Historical Quarterly* 77 (1973–1974): 390–394.

Meyercord, Madeline. "Oliver Loving, Pioneer Drover of Texas." *Southwestern Review* 21 (1936): 261–277.

LOWE, JOSEPH AND KATE

Joseph ("Rowdy Joe") Lowe (1845–1899) was born in New York and Katherine ("Rowdy Kate") Lowe (1851?–?) in Illinois. Joe served in the Civil War before entering the saloon business in Kansas. He met his common-law wife Kate in 1869. They separated in 1876.

Rowdy Joe Lowe. *Courtesy Kansas State Historical Society.*

"Rowdy Joe" was well known as a saloon man, brothel-keeper, and gambler. He stood trial in 1873 for the murder of his great rival Edward ("Red") Beard and was acquitted. He was unarmed when he was shot down in a Denver saloon on February 11, 1899.

—*Joseph G. Rosa*

SUGGESTED READING:
Miller, Nyle H., and Joseph W. Snell. *Why the West Was Wild.* Topeka, Kans., 1963.
Rosa, Joseph G., and Waldo E. Koop. *Rowdy Joe Lowe: Gambler with a Gun.* Norman, Okla., 1989.

LUDLOW MASSACRE

On April 20, 1914, in a United Mine Workers tent colony near Ludlow, Colorado, violence erupted after months of tension between striking coal miners, private mine guards, and units of the Colorado National Guard. By the end of the day, twelve children, two women, and ten men lay dead. In the day-long gun-battle, striking miners, many of whom were recent immigrants from southeastern Europe, fought the poorly paid state militiamen and gunmen hired by the Baldwin-Felts Detective Agency to protect company property during the strike. The women and children perished in a fire that swept through the colony in the early evening and suffocated them as they took shelter in a bunker beneath a family tent. For the next week, strikers ambushed guards and dynamited mining operations from Walsenberg to Trinidad. The strikers surrendered the field only when federal troops, sent by President Woodrow Wilson, arrived to provide neutral peacekeeping.

The Colorado coal fields, containing the nation's largest reserves of bituminous coal, had long been the location of struggles between mine owners and organized labor. In 1903, state militiamen commanded by Brigadier General John Chase broke the WESTERN FEDERATION OF MINERS' Cripple Creek strike, thus setting a precedent for what was to occur at Ludlow. The United Mine Workers, under the leadership of President Thomas L. Lewis, targeted the northern coal fields between Denver and Boulder for organization in 1907, and by July 1908, the UMW won its first major contract with seventeen small coal operators.

Italian miners and their families in an United Mine Workers' tent colony, April 1914, before the deadly confrontation between workers and guards. *Courtesy The Bettmann Archive.*

Top: Tent colony, Ludlow, Colorado. *Courtesy Colorado Historical Society.*

Right: A street scene in Trinidad, Colorado, one week after the Ludlow Massacre. *Courtesy The Bettmann Archive.*

Bottom right: In the aftermath of the conflict between coal miners and company guards, members of the Red Cross search the ruins of Ludlow's tent colony. *Courtesy Denver Public Library, Western History Department.*

In the southern fields, controlled politically and economically by larger companies like Victor-American and Colorado Fuel and Iron, UMW organizers John Lawson, Ed Doyle, and MARY HARRIS ("MOTHER") JONES faced greater obstacles. The ethnically diverse miners, speaking twenty-seven different languages, proved difficult to unify, and coal operators used their influence with county sheriffs and judges to intimidate immigrants with threats of imprisonment and deportation. Still, poor wages (estimated at $1.68 per day in 1912) and unsafe working conditions (464 Colorado miners died or suffered severe injury in 1913) provoked growing resentment within the coal camps. After leasing land for strikers to use in forming independent tent colonies, the UMW called the miners out of the company camps in September 1913. The strikers demanded union recognition, a 10 percent increase in tonnage rates, the eight-hour workday, pay for safety work, miner-elected checkweighmen, enforcement of existing mining laws, and free choices in shopping, boarding, and health care. The strikers suffered through a fierce winter and unremitting harassment by camp police and General Chase's National Guardsmen until the violence of April 20.

The Ludlow Massacre marked a turning point in industrial labor relations. Federal mediation and public pressure forced coal interests, led by Colorado Fuel and Iron Corporation, to offer an alternative model for resolving conflicts between labor and management. The Colorado Industrial Plan of 1915, designed by labor relations specialist W. Mackenzie King, was the first "employee representation" or company union plan of the era. It sought to provide workers with collective bargaining and grievance procedures within the company, rather than through the advocacy of an independent trade union like the United Mine Workers. Arguing that "the interests of Labor and Capital are mutual," King and John D. Rockefeller, Jr., owner of Colorado Fuel and Iron, offered workers a voice in company counsels, but without corresponding power. Concurrently, some of the worst abuses—payment in company scrip redeemable only at company stores; exorbitant payroll deductions for housing, utilities, and health care; and exploitative weighing practices—were suspended.

Having spent $4 million in the Colorado coal fields since 1910, the UMW, demoralized and nearly bankrupted by the costly strike, abandoned its organizing efforts. With another winter approaching and no union benefits available, dispirited strikers returned to the camps or drifted out of state. In October 1915, Colorado Fuel and Iron employees voted 2,253 to 483 in favor of the company's plan for employee representation.

Company unionism faced resistance from organized labor, which saw it as an attempt to destroy labor solidarity, and from miners, who chafed under the paternalistic restraints it placed upon their freedom of association. In the face of rising production and declining coal prices throughout the 1920s, coal companies began to roll back wages and benefits. Colorado coal miners continued their struggle and took part in major strikes in 1919, 1921, and 1927. Colorado Fuel and Iron maintained its employee representation plan until 1933. When new federal legislation like the National Industrial Recovery Act of 1933 shifted bargaining power in favor of independent unions, Colorado Fuel and Iron employees voted overwhelmingly to join the UMW and negotiate a contract.

—James Brooks

SEE ALSO: Labor Movement; Violence: Historical Overview

SUGGESTED READING:

Gitelman, H. H. *The Legacy of the Ludlow Massacre: A Chapter in American Industrial Relations.* Philadelphia, 1988.

Jones, Mother. *The Autobiography of Mother Jones.* Edited by Mary Field Parton with a forward by Clarence Darrow. Chicago, 1925. Reprint. 1977.

McGovern, George S., and Leonard F. Guttridge. *The Great Coalfield War.* Boston, 1972.

Papanikolas, Zeese. *Buried Unsung: Louis Tikas and the Ludlow Massacre.* Salt Lake City, 1982.

LUHAN, MABEL DODGE

An Eastern-born socialite who found her destiny in Taos, New Mexico, by dedicating her life to the formation of a vibrant artistic community there, Mabel Dodge Luhan (born Mabel Ganson, 1879–1962 in Buffalo, New York) was educated in girls' schools in Buffalo, New York, and Washington, D.C. She was married briefly to Karl Evans, who died in 1903. From their marriage came her only child, John Evans.

In 1904, she married Edwin Dodge, with whom she spent most of the next eight years in Europe. They separated following a move to New York in 1912 and were divorced in 1916. In the interim, Mabel Dodge became actively engaged in the intellectual and cultural life of the city. She promoted the 1913 "Armory Show," a watershed event in American art. She also became well known for her regular gatherings during which she entertained and was entertained by the city's cultural elite.

Following her divorce, she married Maurice Sterne, a photographer, in 1917. It was through Sterne that she discovered Taos. He, however, was not to be part of her life there, for their relationship deteriorated almost immediately following her move to Taos in 1918, and they were divorced in 1922. Fascinated with Taos and the spiritual richness of its Indian cultures, she built a home adjacent to the Taos Pueblo and threw herself into the life of her adopted community.

In 1923, she married Antonio Luhan, a Taos Indian. The marriage endured nearly forty years, until her death.

In the splendid isolation of Taos, Luhan craved the company of gifted and brilliant personalities. She actively pursued leading artists and writers and persuaded many of them to visit or take up residence in Taos. She maintained a close, if often stormy, relationship with the English novelist D. H. Lawrence. Others who were drawn to Taos at least partly through her efforts included writers WILLA CATHER, EDNA FERBER, Thornton Wilder, and Thomas Wolfe; poets Witter Bynner and

Robinson Jeffers; photographer Ansel Adams; painters GEORGIA O'KEEFFE and John Marin; and symphony conductor Leopold Stokowski.

In Taos, Luhan took up a variety of causes. She lobbied for a more enlightened Indian policy, promoted Indian art, and gave money to a local hospital. She also devoted herself to writing, producing a four-volume autobiography, a brief work on the artists of Taos, and two other books, *Lorenzo in Taos* and *Winter in Taos*.

Luhan's persona made her a frequent object of satire. She was generally spoofed in works of fiction by Myron Brinig, D. H. Lawrence, Carl Van Vechten, and others.

Luhan did much to enrich the already lively cultural mix of Taos in the 1920s and 1930s. Despite her philanthropy and contributions to the cultural life of Taos, she remained a foreign element to many of the natives. She died in 1962 and was buried in the Kit Carson Cemetery in Taos.

—*David L. Caffey*

SEE ALSO: Taos School of Artists

SUGGESTED READING:

Luhan, Mabel Dodge. *Edge of Taos Desert: Volume Four of Intimate Memories*. New York, 1937.

———. *Movers and Shakers: Volume Three of Intimate Memories*. New York, 1936.

Rudnick, Lois Palken. *Mabel Dodge Luhan: New Woman, New Worlds*. Albuquerque, N. Mex., 1984.

LUMBER INDUSTRY

Historical Overview
Thomas R. Cox

Logging Tools and Machinery
Thomas R. Cox

HISTORICAL OVERVIEW

The commercial manufacturing of lumber in the West, as distinct from subsistence-type production by settlers, dates from the early years of Euro-American settlement. It came especially early to the Pacific Coast. In 1827, the HUDSON'S BAY COMPANY erected a small sawmill on the Columbia River and dispatched its cut to Hawaii, CALIFORNIA, and South America. In the 1830s and 1840s, Isaac Graham and others operating around Monterey and San Francisco bays sawed planks, many of which they peddled to THOMAS OLIVER LARKIN who sold them in Hawaii and Latin America. Elsewhere, commercial lumbering generally began somewhat later, but the origins were usually equally modest.

The CALIFORNIA GOLD RUSH led to the first major trans-Mississippi lumbering operations. Sea captains en route from the East Coast sometimes brought cargoes of lumber to feed the demand in California. Among them was Asa Mead Simpson, who sold lumber from Maine at a profit and then erected a sawmill at North Bend, OREGON, to continue in his sales. Simpson soon added other mills along the Oregon, WASHINGTON, and California coasts, a fleet of sailing ships to haul his cut, tugboats to pull it out to sea, and shipyards in North Bend and in Hoquiam, Washington, to build the vessels he needed.

Others followed Simpson's lead, and numerous sawmills sprang up along the coast and glutted the California market. To survive, many of the larger mills began complementing sales in California with shipments to Hawaii, Latin America, China, Australia, and elsewhere. These maritime exporters, who came to be called "cargo mills," dominated on the West Coast until the 1880s. Then, completion of transcontinental rail connections to the Pacific Northwest, rail connections from Oregon to California, and various regional lines opened the way for a new set of competitors: railroad mills. Tapping inland stands not accessible to coastal cargo mills, the railroad mills sold much of their cut in interior markets. They also competed aggressively in the California market, vital to the cargo mills, and in the process gradually eclipsed them. Only Pope and Talbot and a few other cargo mills survived far into the twentieth century; most that did were located where they could sell in both maritime and rail markets.

Lumbering came more gradually to most other parts of the trans-Mississippi West. The opening of the Erie Canal and settlement of the Ohio Valley had stimulated lumber production in Michigan. As settlement pushed westward, so did lumber production. As the forests of Michigan were depleted, those of Wisconsin and then MINNESOTA came on line. By the 1890s, St. Paul and its hinterlands had become a major center of lumber manufacturing; the region's cut was distributed by rail and water routes to markets throughout the Midwest as well as on the East Coast.

Many lumbermen of the upper Great Lakes states had migrated there from earlier areas of lumber production—especially from Maine, New York, and Pennsylvania—but a number came from within the region. Unlike in most industries of the period, a high percentage of lumbering's leaders came from humble backgrounds, no doubt because they found it so easy to enter the industry, which required relatively little start-up capital, involved fairly simple technology and tools familiar to most people from a rural background, and drew upon a widely available (and thus difficult to monopolize) resource base.

Industrial growth

In the upper Great Lakes states during the late nineteenth century, lumbering operations took on a size and complexity hitherto unknown. Individual mills were larger, and the business combinations they formed were more complex than previously. Frederick K. Weyerhaeuser and many other giants of the industry emerged in the region at that time, and industrial associations that tried to regulate production and prices, and in other ways to stabilize the industry, appeared. However, efforts at combination were generally unsuccessful; lumbering remained much more fragmented than most American industries.

Looking to the day when they would have depleted the pineries of the Great Lakes states, many operators began acquiring timber and sawmills in the South and Far West during the 1880s. The Gulf South boomed first, and lumbering moved ever farther into its interior as RAILROADS opened new stands and provided improved access to Northern and Midwestern markets. Huge operations appeared, many erected by Northerners, but some—such as the operations of John Henry Kirby in eastern Texas—were the work of native Southerners. By the turn of the century, the South had become the nation's leading lumber-producing region.

While production was still rising in the Gulf South, some operators already foresaw the end of its untapped stands; interest in Western forests rose. The industry's movement into the Rocky Mountain states and Far West soon became a stampede that drove up the price of timberland, fostered fraudulent timber claims, and enriched many speculators. The drive to acquire Western timber gained added urgency because of the withdrawal from the public domain of large tracts of land into federal forest reserves under the FOREST RESERVE ACT OF 1891 and because of the widespread fear that the country would soon face a timber famine.

Established operators in the West were unable to stem this tide. The operations of the West's pioneer lumbermen had grown from modest beginnings through reinvestment of profits in sawmill expansion and improvement; in the acquisition of sailing ships, tugboats, and shipyards; and in strategically located lumberyards. Apparently assuming that timber would always be available from farmers clearing their land or from independent loggers cutting in public or private stands, early Western lumbermen had acquired limited stands of timber. In any case, the technology available during the early years confined logging to stands close to waterways. Under the circumstances, there seemed little reason to use scarce investment capital to tie up timberlands that might not be usable for years, if ever. Thus, plenty of timber was still available as those from other regions eyed the forests of the West during the late nineteenth and early twentieth centuries.

Frederick Weyerhaeuser was among the leaders in the industrial migration into the West. Weyerhaeuser had acquired substantial holdings in the South, and then in 1900, he and his associates purchased nine hundred thousand acres of prime Western timber from the Northern Pacific Railway Company. The Weyerhaeuser Timber Company, together with the rest of the family of companies under Weyerhaeuser's control, dwarfed all but a few of its competitors and in due course became a significant force for the adoption of responsible forest practices within the industry. However, the impact of Weyerhaeuser's operations was not always efficacious: the sawmills that the company erected in Longview (Washington), Klamath Falls (Oregon), and Lewiston (Idaho) during the 1920s were among the largest and most modern anywhere, but they added immensely to the surplus production plaguing the industry.

Cargo mills enjoyed a resurgence on the Pacific during the first three decades of the twentieth century as completion of the Panama Canal opened new maritime markets and a spurt of mining and railroad building led to the expansion of old ones. The Hammond Lumber Company and the Charles R. McCormick Lumber Company were key players in these developments.

In the pine country of the interior, the spread of the logging industry proceeded apace during the early twentieth century. Largely overlooked earlier because of geographical barriers and the small size of nearby markets, the pine forests represented America's last major lumbering frontier. Although distant and frigid ALASKA had huge stands, it did not offer the sort of opportunities that had beckoned lumbermen to one new area after another since colonial times. The sugar, ponderosa, and Western white pine of the far Western interior did, and new mills sprang up in place after place in northeastern California, east of the Cascades in Oregon and Washington, and in scattered locations in the Rocky Mountain states.

The Brooks-Scanlon and Shevlin-Hixon lumber companies from Minnesota came to Bend, Oregon, during the 1910s and quickly turned the tiny Deschutes River hamlet into a huge center for the production of pine lumber. In many other communities in the pine country, local leaders worked assiduously to attract major sawmills so that their towns might enjoy similar prosperity. Bend's sawmills cut their stands as if there were no tomorrow, but others in the pineries proceeded more cautiously by adopting selective-logging techniques, establishing tree farms, and implementing SUSTAINED-YIELD programs.

The stimulus to begin treating forests in this new manner came from government as well as from private sources. Huge portions of the interior pineries had been incorporated into national forests, and by the 1920s, the UNITED STATES FOREST SERVICE set strict guidelines for cutting timber tracts it put up for sale. Also, revisions in tax laws made it possible for lumber companies to defer most taxes on timber until the time of harvest, thus reducing the pressure to clear-cut land quickly and then abandon it to eliminate carrying costs. And the establishment of effective programs for the control of forest fires through state, federal, and private cooperation meant that trees on replanted tracts had a reasonable chance of surviving to harvestable size instead of going up in smoke while still young, thus destroying the investment in reforestation.

As a result of all these efforts, lumbering gradually ceased to be a frontier industry that extracted resources on a cut-and-run basis. It became instead a permanent enterprise supporting stable, lasting communities. The new approach demanded unprecedented cooperation between the public and private sectors, and while it first appeared as a major force in the interior pine country of the West, it was soon apparent wherever national and private forests stood in close proximity to one another.

Cooperation became especially close during the 1930s when industry leaders and government foresters combined to draw up a lumber code under the National Industrial Recovery Act. The code regulated prices, production, working conditions, forestry practices, and the like. The forestry-practices section of the code remained in force, voluntarily adopted by the industry, even after the NIRA was declared unconstitutional by the Supreme Court. It played a major role in advancing forest conservation.

Lumberjack to bindlestiff

Workers, as well as sawmill owners and their capital, migrated with the industry. People with the requisite skills were frequently not present in new areas of operation, and the populations were often too small to meet the demand for unskilled labor. French-Canadian and Maine LOGGERS had been common in the Great Lakes forests; they were augmented by a variety of immigrant and native workers. From this volatile, footloose mix sprang the larger-than-life image of the lumberjack, the irrepressible folk hero of the woods.

Other than those possessing special skills, few workers migrated with the industry when it moved into the Gulf South, for there was an ample supply of unskilled labor there. Still, the influx was sufficient to generate hostility from long-time residents of the piney woods. They felt their traditional life styles to be under siege

even as the sawmills brought new opportunities for employment and a higher standard of living. Their dissatisfaction contributed to scattered incidents of VIOLENCE and industrial sabotage.

Living and working conditions in the Southern woods and sawmill towns did little to alleviate discontent. John Henry Kirby and other industrial leaders long prevented unionization of their operations, and workers—tied to company store and company town—led an existence more akin to that of the impoverished tenant farmer than to the romanticized lumberjack of the Northern woods.

More workers migrated to the Far West than to the South. Few French Canadians made the leap to the Pacific Coast; instead, Scandinavians, who came into the area both from the Lake states and directly from Europe, became the most evident (if not necessarily most numerous group) in the Far West woods. Chinese and Japanese laborers sometimes worked in sawmills—especially running the lath-making machines, a dangerous job others tended to shun—but they were almost never employed in the woods. American Indians had done some logging during the very early years, but nearly all had disappeared from the industry before lumbering's big migration to the Far West began in the 1880s.

The working and living conditions of laborers in the lumber industry of the Far West deteriorated during the late nineteenth and early twentieth centuries. Workers turned first to the Knights of Labor and then to other labor organizations, including the radical INDUSTRIAL WORKERS OF THE WORLD, to try to win redress, but with little success. Other than leave an operation they found unacceptable, there was little else the impoverished and uneducated workers could do. Loggers were notorious for drifting from job to job with their bed roll in search of a better "show." Employers said they always had three crews: "one coming, one going, and one working." Often colluding with one another, unscrupulous camp bosses and operators of hiring halls added to the instability: camp bosses would fire workers for trumped-up reasons so that the hiring hall operator could supply a replacement and then kick back to the camp boss part of the commission he received for furnishing the new laborer.

Under such circumstances, and spurred on by growing antiunion and anti-immigrant sentiments, the status of woods workers plummeted in the public's eyes. Instead of being called a "lumberjack"—the Great Lakes region's term, with all of its positive connotations— a lumber worker was now called a *bindlestiff* (a working stiff who wandered from place to place with his "bindle," or bundle, on his back); it was a highly pejorative term akin to *tramp*. Not until the late 1920s, when automobiles began to bring an end to isolated logging camps, did married men begin to dominate in the woods; when they did, the social status of Western loggers began to recover at last. Improved working and living conditions, spurred by government pressure and belated union successes, also did much to change the quality and status of woods workers.

Technology, as well as men and capital, migrated from area to area with the industry, but conditions seldom precisely replicated those encountered earlier, thus making adaptation and invention constantly in demand. On the whole, change came faster in the mills than in the woods, so loggers were under unrelenting pressure to increase their output just to keep up with the ever-hungry saws. Widespread adoption, during the mid-nineteenth century, of circular saws for head rigs (the main saws that did the initial cuts on a log) sped production immensely. Their subsequent replacement by band saws—huge, toothed loops of

flexible steel driven by flywheels located above and below the log carriage—speeded production even more. The shift from water to steam power had similarly far-reaching effects. Steam-powered log carriages manipulated logs with unprecedented ease and speed, while rollers and conveyer belts hurried lumber on its way once it was sawn. Steam—and later electric—dry kilns replaced the slower yard drying of lumber, and first steam engines and then carriers powered by internal-combustion engines replaced muscle power, both human and animal, in moving lumber about the yards. By the early twentieth century, power equipment dominated nearly every operation of most larger sawmills.

From the 1880s, more and more loggers along the redwood coast and in the Douglas fir forests of western Oregon and western Washington adopted steam donkeys to pull logs to landings beside the railroads and steam engines to haul them from there to the saw-

In the 1880s, the labor-saving steam donkey, such as the one pictured here near Tacoma, Washington, hauled cut logs to landings beside railroads. *Courtesy National Archives.*

mills. Soon after, steam-powered equipment was also used to load logs on railroad cars and in laying of track as logging railroads were extended. Steam-driven equipment also played a major role in the forests of Minnesota, Texas, and elsewhere, although because the logs were smaller there, animal power long continued to be used too.

Railroads were used in the pineries of the Far West from the early years, but steam logging never loomed large there. When change came, it was more the result of the internal-combustion engine: tractors moved logs to landings, and trucks took them from there to the mills. In time, gasoline-powered chain saws also replaced crosscut saws in the felling of timber.

The larger companies were in the forefront of change in the woods, just as they were in the adoption of new sawmill technology, but many small operations functioning with considerably less than state-of-the-art equipment continued to exist. Small portable mills replaced the larger ones as the forests of the South were depleted, while on the tiny bar harbors of the Oregon Coast and the ports of California's redwood coast, small operations always dominated because only little vessels could reach them.

The ready availability of war surplus trucks following World War II made the logging of small, isolated stands practical. The "gyppo" loggers who owned these trucks sometimes worked on a piece basis for large companies. They also often sold their cut to small mills, thus giving the little operators a new lease on life, especially in the interior pine country of the Far West where stands were too small, thin, and isolated to attract the big companies.

Post–World War II developments

Since World War II, the lumber industry has been embroiled in a number of controversies. Japan's rapid industrial growth led to a considerable demand for building materials. Because few American mills were equipped to ship lumber that met Japanese standards and dimensions, a major export trade in logs developed, thus driving up the price of stumpage in the United States and making it difficult for some mills to obtain the logs needed to keep running. Jobs as well as logs were being exported, critics charged. In time, the government banned the exportation of logs from its lands, but sales from private stands and Washington State's government-owned lands continued, pushed stumpage prices ever higher, and forced many older mills to the wall.

Recreational use of forest lands grew rapidly during the postwar era too, and demands for forest preservation rose with it. Over the objections of various industry leaders, Redwood National Park was created in 1968; other tracts were reserved from cutting under the Wilderness Act of 1964. For its part, the United States Forest Service gave increasing attention to its recreational facilities and sought to provide a vehicle for balancing the complex demands on the national forests through the Multiple Use–Sustained Yield Act of 1960.

Controversies continued to swirl. When environmentalists turned to the Endangered Species Act during the 1980s in an attempt to protect the spotted owl by halting logging in the old-growth forests of the Pacific Northwest, the industry and those dependent upon it argued that they, not the owls, were in danger of extinction. And when devastating forest fires and pine bark-beetle epidemics swept through Western forests in the 1980s and 1990s, critics laid much of the blame at the feet of the Forest Service and the timber industry because of their forest-management practices over the preceding years.

In spite of popular perceptions and earlier fears of a timber famine, the acreage of forest land in the West during the late twentieth century was not greatly below what it had been before white settlement. The nature of the stands had changed, but vast forests remained, and the lumber industry continued to meet the demand for wood and fiber products. However, since the 1960s, lumbermen have found themselves increasingly on the defensive. In the West, only firms that owned the bulk of the stands on which they depended, such as Weyerhaeuser, were insulated against the pressures of the times. Georgia-Pacific transferred its main operations from the West back to Georgia, where it had originated, for opportunities there now seemed more attractive. Others struggled on as best they could.

—*Thomas R. Cox*

SEE ALSO: Booms; Fire; Forest Management Act of 1897; Forestry; Labor Movement; Multiple-Use Doctrine; Timber and Stone Act of 1878

SUGGESTED READING:

Clar, C. Raymond. *California Government and Forestry from Spanish Days to the Creation of the Department of Natural Resources in 1927*. Sacramento, Calif., 1959.

Coman, Edwin T., Jr., and Helen M. Gibbs. *Time, Tide and Timber: A Century of Pope & Talbot*. Stanford, Calif., 1949.

Cox, Thomas R. "Frontier Enterprise vs. the Modern Age: Fred Herrick and the Closing of the Lumberman's Frontier." *Pacific Northwest Quarterly* 81 (1993): 19–29.

———. *Mills and Markets: A History of the Pacific Coast Lumber Industry to 1900*. Seattle, Wash., 1974.

———. "Trade, Development, and Environmental Change: The Utilization of North America's Pacific Coast Forests to 1914." In *Global Deforestation and the Nineteenth Century World Economy.* Edited by Richard P. Tucker and J. F. Richards. Durham, N.C., 1983.

———, et al. *This Well-Wooded Land: Americans and Their Forests from Colonial Times to the Present.* Lincoln, Nebr., 1984.

Hidy, Ralph, Frank Ernest Hill, and Allen Nevins. *Timber and Men: The Weyerhaeuser Story.* New York, 1964.

Kohlmeyer, Fred C. "Northern Pine Lumbermen: A Study in Origins and Migrations." *Journal of Economic History* 16 (1956): 529–538.

Maxwell, Robert S. *Sawdust Empire: The Texas Lumber Industry, 1830–1940.* College Station, Tex., 1983.

Robbins, William G. *Lumberjacks and Legislators: Political Economy of the U.S. Lumber Industry, 1890–1941.* College Station, Tex., 1982.

Twining, Charles D. *Phil Weyerhaeuser: Lumberman.* Seattle, Wash., 1985.

Williams, Michael. *Americans and Their Forests: A Historical Geography.* Cambridge, Mass., 1989.

LOGGING TOOLS AND MACHINERY

To the forested regions of the trans-Mississippi West, lumbermen brought with them the tools and methods of their earlier seats of operation. The double-bitted ax, first widely used in Pennsylvania's forests, was the universal chopping tool; the peavey, developed in Maine, was used everywhere for manipulating logs by hand. In general, the methods used on the slopes of the Allegheny Plateau proved useful in mountainous areas of the West, while those used in Maine and the Great Lakes region came to dominate where the topography was more gentle.

Western lumbermen modified the techniques imported from the East, because conditions in the trans-Mississippi West never precisely replicated those encountered earlier. In New England and the Mid-Atlantic and Great Lakes regions, lumbermen felled timber and transported logs to streamside in the winter; log drives followed when the spring thaw brought high water ideal for floating the cut trees to downstream sawmills. In the West, however, log drives and the technology associated with them played a limited role; most streams were too fast and tortuous for driving. Similarly, along the Pacific Coast, winter brought rain and mud that bogged down attempts to fell trees and move logs to streamside. Summer, not winter, became the logging season, and a lumbermen developed a host of techniques for use in the summer season.

The size of trees in Pacific Coast forests also forced lumbermen to modify Eastern methods. Since colonial times, axes had been used to fell trees, which were then sawed into log lengths before moving them to the sawmills. The Far West's forests contained trees so large that felling them with axes was prohibitively slow.

Beginning in the 1870s, Western lumbermen used long, thin, flexible crosscut saws to fell the large trees, and output jumped. The development of the crosscut saws was made possible by the manufacture of tempered steel.

As the demand for lumber burgeoned along with the economic growth of post–Civil War years, sawmills grew ever larger. Sawmill operators responded to the increased demand by installing first circular and gang saws and then band saws to speed production. They increased the size and number of their mills and built ever more complex business combinations to finance and manage them. Struggling to keep up with the insatiable demand for timber, many lumbermen continuously invested in equipment and the adoption of new technology; others were unable or unwilling to do so. As a result, sawmill owners increasingly ran their own logging operations during the late nineteenth century and replaced independent operators who had dominated in many parts of the West.

Initially, lumbermen moved logs to waterways by muscle power and then floated them to mills. Both horses and oxen were used to pull logs. In Pacific Coast forests, lumbermen used carefully prepared skid roads, which had a series of small, notched logs set across them to keep logs pulled along them from miring in the mud. Grease applied to the notched crosslogs reduced friction. The skid roads were useful, however, only to lumbermen working no more than two miles from a waterway.

In interior forests, with their smaller pine trees, lumbermen used giant, paired wheels pulled by horses. The front end of one or more logs was raised from the ground and attached to the axle, which was so high that logs could clear rocks, underbrush, and other obstructions with relative ease. In time, tractors replaced horses, and devices with smaller wheels and arched axles (and subsequently *A*-frames) replaced the big wheels, but the basic principle remained the same.

Machine power gradually replaced muscle power in moving logs. The process began in 1881 with John Dolbeer's invention of the steam donkey, a steam engine attached to a capstan and mounted on a moveable platform. Heavy rope from the capstan was attached to a log, which was pulled in when the steam engine was engaged. Gradual improvements in design and the replacement of hemp by wire rope (steel cable) made it possible to log greater distances from waterways and to pull bigger loads. Steam logging spread rapidly in West Coast forests. It caused much environmental damage—destroying small trees, uprooting ground cover, and leaving prodigious quantities of debris to fuel forest fires (often set by sparks from the steam engines).

In time, high-lead techniques were developed in which logs were partially off the ground when pulled to loading areas; with friction thus reduced, logs moved with greater speed than ever. High-lead logging became widespread in Pacific Coast forests. Skyline logging, in which logs were hauled along cable systems completely above ground level, was another descendent of the techniques Dolbeer had pioneered.

Steam engines were important in other ways. They freed sawmill operators from dependence on water power, thus making it possible to build mills near previously unusable stands and to locate along railroads or in other places that would expedite sales. Logging railroads opened vast tracts beyond the reach of skid roads and the old water-based operations; steam tugs pulled huge rafts of logs to mills along the Columbia River, around Puget Sound, and elsewhere; and steam schooners replaced sailing vessels in carrying lumber from the numerous little ports along the northern California and Oregon coasts.

In the interior, the internal-combustion engine was more important than the steam engine. Instead of steam donkeys, tractors equipped with crawler tread brought power logging to the West's pine country. Tractor logging did more environmental damage than earlier methods, but it was faster and could be used on more rugged terrain. Logging railroads were used for some time in the pine region, but logging trucks began to appear in the 1920s; by the late 1940s, they were becoming dominant, not only in the pineries but in the redwood and Douglas fir regions as well.

The internal-combustion engine also revolutionized the felling of timber. In 1927, Andreas Stihl of Germany built the first practical, gasoline-powered chain saw. During World War II, the United States government released Stihl's patents, and American production of chain saws burgeoned. They caught on rapidly, especially after Joe Cox, a Portland logger, developed an improved saw chain. Machine power largely replaced muscle power in every basic aspect of logging.

The development of giant shearing devices to cut trees, the use of helicopters to transport logs, and many other innovations in the postwar era represent continued adaptation of technology in Western woods. However, many of the changes since the 1960s have been less motivated by the drive to reduce labor costs than by a need to reduce environmental damage and the waste of scarce resources. Technological change and adaptation continue, but the direction of much of the change is new.

—*Thomas R. Cox*

SUGGESTED READING:
Conway, Steve. *Logging Practices.* San Francisco, 1976.
Cox, Thomas R., et al. *This Well-Wooded Land: Americans and Their Forests from Colonial Times to the Present.* Lincoln, Nebr., 1985.
Lucia, Ellis. "A Lesson from Nature: Joe Cox and His Revolutionary Saw Chain." *Journal of Forest History* 24 (1981): 158–165.
Williams, Michael. *Americans and Their Forests: A Historical Geography.* Cambridge, Mass., 1989.

LUMBERJACKS

SEE: Loggers

LUMMIS, CHARLES FLETCHER

During the late nineteenth and early twentieth centuries, Charles Fletcher Lummis (1859–1928) was the most conspicuous writer and editor of books and articles on the culture of the American Far West and Southwest of his time. Born in Lynn, Massachusetts, the son of Henry Lummis, a classics professor, and Harriet Fowler Lummis, he attended Harvard University from 1877 to 1881, where he became a lifelong friend of THEODORE ROOSEVELT. While he received no degree, Harvard awarded him an honorary bachelor of arts degree in 1906.

Early in life, Lummis developed a strong interest in history, archaeology, and classical literature. In 1884 in Chillicothe, Ohio, he learned about the extensive archaeological sites in the American Southwest. He applied for and was offered a job as the city editor of the *Los Angeles Times.* However, instead of taking the train to California, Lummis chose to walk to Los Angeles from Chillicothe. Along the way, he sent letters ahead by mail to be published in the *Times;* those letters later appeared as a book, *A Tramp across the Continent.*

His "tramp" took him to southern Colorado and northern New Mexico. There Lummis became entranced by the region's landscape and people, and he experienced what amounted to a spiritual and aesthetic conversion to become a passionate "Southwesterner."

Over the next forty years, Lummis stood out as one of the most active proponents of "Southwest culture" who has ever lived. Subsidized generously by the Santa Fe Railroad and other southern California business interests, he became a promoter and a publisher of the region. He encouraged and supported artist Maynard Dixon, writer MARY HUNTER AUSTIN, photographer WILLIAM HENRY JACKSON, archaeologist ADOLPH FRANCIS ALPHONSE BANDELIER, and many others.

Lummis led efforts to reform U.S. Indian policy, to preserve and rebuild the California missions, and to collect historical and anthropological documents and artifacts. He campaigned vigorously to preserve the natural wonders of the region. In 1911, he founded the Southwest Museum in Highland Park, California. His photographs of the region rank among the best of that period.

During his most productive period, Lummis served as city editor of the *Los Angeles Times* (from 1885 to 1888); editor of *Land of Sunshine* (from 1893 to 1901) and *Out West* magazines (from 1901 to 1905); head librarian of the Los Angeles Public Library (from 1905 to 1910); and director and secretary of the Southwest Museum (from 1911 to 1915).

His major publications include: *Some Strange Corners of Our Country,* (1892; reprinted as *Mesa, Canyon, Pueblo* in 1925; and reprinted again with its original title in 1989); *A Tramp across the Continent* (1892); *The Land of Poco Tiempo* (1893); *The Spanish Pioneers* (1893); and *Flowers of Our Lost Romance* (1929).

During his later years and for several decades after his death, both scholars and the general public lost interest in Lummis's work; however, since 1970, he has received a broad new awareness and appreciation.

—*James Byrkit*

Suggested reading:

Bingham, Edwin R. *Charles F. Lummis: Editor of the Southwest.* San Marino, Calif., 1955.
Byrkit, James, ed. *Charles Lummis's Letters from the Southwest.* Tucson, Ariz., 1989.
Fiske, Turbese Lummis, and Keith Lummis, *Charles F. Lummis: The Man and His West.* Norman, Okla., 1972.
Gordon, Dudley. *Charles F. Lummis: Crusader in Corduroy.* Los Angeles, 1970.

LUX V. HAGGIN

Lux v. *Haggin* was a case heard by the California State Supreme Court in 1886. Henry Miller and Charles Lux had obtained lands along the Kern River. Below their land, James Haggin and Lloyd Tevis acquired lands and then diverted the entire river. Miller and Lux sued, contending that as riparian owners they had a right to have the river flow through their land undiminished. In April 1886, the California court ruled in favor of Miller and Lux. In writing the majority opinion, Justice E. W. McKinstry assumed that the riparian doctrine was law in California, at least on lands patented before 1866, but also ruled that under certain conditions the appropriation doctrine would prevail.

Riparian rights are primarily determined by the legal possession of land bordering the stream; appropriation rights are primarily determined by the priority of actually using WATER. The result was the creation of a legal hybrid, known subsequently as the "California Doctrine."

—*Kazuto Oshio*

See also: California Doctrine (of Water Rights); Water Politics

Suggested reading:

Dunbar, Robert G. *Forging New Rights in Western Waters.* Lincoln, Nebr., 1983.
Hundley, Norris, Jr. *The Great Thirst: Californians and Water, 1770s–1990s.* Berkeley, Calif., 1992.

LYNCHING

The term *lynch law* came into the language during the American Revolution with the activities of Colonel Charles Lynch and his associates in Virginia who responded to unsettled local conditions by taking the law into their own hands and punishing those they considered Tories and criminals. Some claim the term originated later, in 1780 in association with vigilante leader William Lynch of Pittsylvania County, Virginia, In either case, wherever similarly unsettled social conditions appeared in the rapidly expanding new nation—in the outpost settlements of the American West, for example—the summary justice of "lynching" sometimes became popular. Although some Western scholars are at pains to distinguish between vigilante groups and lynch mobs, it seems that both grew in similar soil: in remote settlements during raw periods or episodes, such as extended feuds, that attend the breakdown of LAW AND ORDER—during situations, in other words, where people believed a need existed for swift punishment for real or imagined or even anticipated criminal behavior in order to assert or reassert social control through the direct actions of lynch mobs or vigilantes.

In the nineteenth century, cattle rustlers, gamblers, horse thieves, and certain desperadoes—especially those of an ethnic minority—became targets of lynch mobs. Far more frequently than bringing swift justice to hardened outlaws, however, lynching was used to attack racial, ethnic, and minority groups whose presence angered or threatened those in the majority. Before the Civil War, Native Americans, Mexican Americans and Mexican immigrants, Asian immigrants, and sometimes Jews became targets in the West and Southwest as well as African American slaves in the plantation South, who were lynched for the slightest of infractions. In the trans-Mississippi West, mob violence was often the result of economic fears concerning wage competition, especially from the Chinese in the Far West, or later against labor-movement leaders, political radicals, and outspoken critics of America's entry into World War I—people who, like members of the INDUSTRIAL WORKERS OF THE WORLD, voiced ideas unpopular with the dominant white majority. Indeed, increasingly after 1880, vigilante groups and lynch mobs reflected white contempt for those felt to be of an inferior race and became a means for "true Americans" to reassert their superiority by confirming everyone's place in the social hierarchy. Thus, those participating in the lynchings frequently lived and worked together or at least knew one another socially, while those being lynched were more often outsiders unknown to the members of the lynch mob or social outcasts despised by them.

Although vigilante action did occur with some frequency in the West, and some lynchings—such as that of JUANITA OF DOWNIEVILLE in the gold fields of California—gained widespread notoriety, lynchings were much more characteristic of the Reconstruction and pre–civil-rights eras in the South. Standard Hollywood formula westerns may have depicted lynch mobs as commonplace, but they were not. Movies portrayed mobs that formed spontaneously to break into local jails in hopes of hanging usually wrongly accused prisoners only to be faced down and dispersed by a lone, brave lawman. By the 1890s, in both the West and the South, lynch mobs were not simply the outbreak of a revenge-hungry rabble seeking a spurious racial or economic justice nor the assertion of a superiority about which poor whites felt insecure; instead, such mobs were often encouraged—and sometimes led—by people prominent in the area's political and business circles. Lynching had clearly become a ritual of interracial social control and even a kind of recreation, rather than a punishment for crime, as evidenced by anti-Asian pogroms in the West where Chinese (and later Japa-

Jim Miller, Allen Burwell, and a man identified simply as West, the victims of lynching that took place in a barn in Ada, Oklahoma. *Courtesy Western History Collections, University of Oklahoma Library.*

nese) exclusion had become a popular political cause among the dominant majority. Indeed, some historians have treated the internment of Japanese Americans during World War II—though no internees were strung up by rope-wielding vigilantes—as an example of lynch-mob mentality at work among the Western middle class and among many officials within the federal government.

—*Charles Phillips*

SEE ALSO: Cattle Rustling; Horse Theft and Horse Thieves; Vigilantism; Violence: Racial Violence

SUGGESTED READING:

Axelrod, Alan, and Charles Phillips. *Cops, Crooks, and Criminologists: An International Biographical Dictionary of Law Enforcement.* New York, 1996.

Cutler, James E. *Lynch Law: An Investigation into the History of Lynching in the United States.* New York, 1969.

For Reference

Not to be taken from this room